CARLOS LACERDA, BRAZILIAN CRUSADER
VOLUME 2: THE YEARS 1960–1977

CARLOS LACERDA, BRAZILIAN CRUSADER
Volume 2: The Years 1960-1977

John W. F. Dulles

 University of Texas Press, Austin

First edition, 1996

Requests for permission to reproduce material from this work
should be sent to Permissions, University of Texas Press,
Box 7819, Austin, TX 78713-7819.

⊗ The paper used in this publication meets the minimum
requirements of American National Standard for Information
Sciences—Permanence of Paper for Printed Library Materials,
ANSI Z39.48-1984.

Library of Congress Cataloging-in-Publication Data
Dulles, John W. F.
    Carlos Lacerda, Brazilian crusader / by John W. F. Dulles.—
1st ed.
      p.   cm.
    Includes bibliographical references and index.
    Contents: v. I. The years 1914–1960
    v. II. The years 1960–1977
    ISBN 0-292-71125-5 (cloth) (vol. I)
    ISBN 0-292-71581-1 (cloth) (vol. II)
    1. Lacerda, Carlos. 2. Brazil—Politics and Government—
1930–1954. 3. Brazil—Politics and Government—1954–
1964. 4. Brazil—Politics and Government—1964–1985.
5. Journalists—Brazil—Biography. 6. Politicians—Brazil—
Biography. I. Title.
F2538.22.L3'85   1991
981.06'092—dc20
[B]   90-38782

Frontispiece: Governor Carlos Lacerda, 1964. (P.I.P. photo by Farabola)

Contents

In memory of
The Reverend Allen Macy Dulles

Preface

Support for research about the activities of Carlos Lacerda was provided by the Institute of Latin American Studies at the University of Texas at Austin from funds granted to the Institute by the Andrew W. Mellon Foundation.

Among the individuals to whom I am indebted are Cacilda M. Rêgo, who saw the typing through many revisions, Lamy Cunto, widow of Lacerda's friend Walter Cunto, Silvana Lucia Rios Safe de Matos, director of the Brazilian Senate Library, and Flavia Biraghi, director of *O Estado de S. Paulo*'s archives. Many factual errors in the manuscript were corrected by Pedro Ernesto Mariano de Azevedo, Newton Rodrigues, Sebastião Lacerda, and Ivan Hasslocher. More than anyone else, Daphne F. Rodger is responsible for good things that might be found in this and my earlier volume about Lacerda. The reference notes, indicating some of her many findings, especially helpful in the case of the personal side of Lacerda's life, fail to reveal the enormity of her contribution.

Carlos Lacerda was governor, presidential candidate, and outspoken oppositionist between 1960 and 1968, a period of drastic political changes in Brazil—more frequent than in any earlier or later eight-year period. In an effort to recapture the situations and events that he influenced and that influenced his career, attention has been given to the forces that clashed and to the views of newspapers that participated in the heated debates.

A conclusion, discussed at end of this study, is that Brazil would have benefited if Lacerda had achieved the presidency, but it is a conclusion not easily accepted by those who fail to separate the administrator from the sometimes irresponsible headline maker, who accused Planning Minister Roberto Campos of unpatriotic behavior and only late in life admitted that as president he would have chosen Campos to be his finance minister.

Another conclusion is that Lacerda did, indeed, cause significant political transformations of Brazil and that these transformations prevented him from reaching the presidency. However, the conclusion about Lacerda transforming Brazil is not based on his role of attacker of presidents in the years before Humberto Castello Branco assumed the highest office. President Jânio Quadros fell because his scheme to obtain extraordinary powers was ill-conceived; and President João Goulart was deposed by discipline-minded military officers, whose rage reached a peak following his settlement of a sailors' mutiny and his conduct at a meeting of sergeants and corporals. It is true that Lacerda wanted Castello Branco to take over after Goulart fell, but of greater importance was the surge of military and civilian opinion in favor of that idea.

Lacerda's opportunity to reach the presidency was killed by transformations of Brazil that marked Castello Branco's administration and that were directly attributable to Lacerda. When Congress was considering political reforms in July 1964, Lacerda's failure to give definite voting instructions to a group of *Lacerdista* congressmen apparently hurt him; but perhaps he hurt himself more with his tirade at that time against the president of his political party and the federal legislators belonging to it—a tirade that helped some of them, such as Senator Afonso Arinos de Melo Franco, garner votes to extend Castello's term by one year for the sole purpose of dealing a blow to Lacerda's ambition to be elected president in 1965. In a dramatic roll call Castello's term extension was adopted by a majority of a single (and questionable) vote.

After that, a letter from Lacerda to Castello resulted in the defeat of Castello's wish to have a direct presidential election in 1966. The letter produced a shakeup of Brazil of such magnitude that it would be hard to find another letter that was so effective in changing the country's destiny. It brought about the rejection, in March 1965, of the *mandato-tampão* arrangement for one-year governorships that would have avoided the crisis that developed from the direct gubernatorial elections in October of that year.

Because two governorships were won by men associated with pre-1964 regimes, Castello had to face the fury of hard liners, strong in the military. He sought, however, to avoid carrying out their wish that the executive decree a second institutional act (the first was decreed before he became president) of a radical nature, pleasing to critics of democratic and judicial procedures. He therefore proposed that Congress adopt more moderate measures that War Minister Costa e Silva and other military leaders agreed would be sufficient to end the crisis. But Lacerda, constant belittler of the legalistic ideas of Castello and Justice Minister Milton Campos, put the finishing touch on the burial of a direct presidential election when he denied to the administration the votes of *Lacerdistas* that it needed in Congress late that month. Lacerda considered Castello's proposals the "drivel" of a president who was not a revolutionary, and he described the proposals as "clownish little laws" that were insufficiently drastic. As Guanabara Vice Governor Raphael de Almeida Magalhães remarked later: "The only beneficiary of the failure of Congress to act was Costa e Silva. Lacerda hurt himself. Lacerda blocked Castello from acting on our side."

One can argue that Lacerda, who had alienated a small group close to Castello in the course of gaining mass support, might have been eliminated even if he had saved Brazil from Institutional Act Number Two, that did away with all the existing political parties and the direct presidential election of 1966. However, the elimination of Lacerda by the Castello group, which later proved unable to eliminate the candidacy of Costa e Silva, was no certainty. The wiser course of *Lacerdistas* late in October 1965 was to support the passage of the "clownish little laws" and preserve the possibility of a 1966 direct election victory by Lacerda, still a popular civilian. Lacerda had the support of the rank and file in his political party, along with that of many outside the party who disliked the government's austere economic policy. He was on good terms with the military, including hard liners.

Thanks to Institutional Act Number Two, Marshal Costa e Silva achieved the presidency in an indirect election by Congress in which he was the only candidate. After that, Lacerda acted in a manner that he hoped would persuade the Costa e Silva administration to accept him as an associate. When this hope came to naught, Lacerda resumed the role of oppositionist, the most vocal critic of military rule and United States influence in Brazil. But he became a crusader whose day had passed because, as public opinion polls revealed, he lost popular support by allying himself with politicians he had been describing as corrupt, such as former Presidents Juscelino Kubitschek and João Goulart. Oppositionist students, participating in 1968 in a movement more dynamic than Lacerda's Frente Ampla, indignantly rejected his offer of support. They shouted against him in the streets, and their leaders denounced what they called his opportunism and sham populism.

Deprived of his political rights by Costa e Silva's military regime late in 1968, Lacerda concentrated on traveling, writing, book publishing, and business. But, as newspaper director Ruy Mesquita has written, he grieved at his lack of an opportunity to play a role in preventing Brazil from continuing to be politically underdeveloped. Having demonstrated, as governor, that a civilian administration could be innovative and spectacularly successful while eliminating immoral practices, he endured the waste of his administrative abilities, just when they had reached their peak.

This ardent man, often ebullient, was often deeply depressed. Tragedy hung heavily upon him during his last visits to São Paulo, made in 1977, when his health was declining and when he contemplated, at the age of sixty-three, what he believed to be his failures as a politician, businessman, and family man. But the purpose of his weight reduction program, carried out until doctors forbade it in his last week, was not to slim his body for burial. His death was not caused by his business reverses and what he deemed to be his other failures, as is often maintained, nor by foul play by people who still considered him a threat to the military regime.

A fatal infection, undetected until it was too late for doctors to try to save his life, prevented his further pursuit of the cultural role that he had been planning in his last months with an enthusiasm that writer Luís Forjaz Trigueiros described as "almost miraculous." Friends, early in Lacerda's career, had noted how he could become "like a boy," thrilled to find a new world; and now new friends used the same expression when they reported on his "rediscovery" of himself as a "creator and publisher," following the warm reception of his book *A Casa do Meu Avô*. Reminded that he would, before long, recover his political rights, he declared, with vehemence, "Now I am a writer and publisher." He explained that his new course for finishing his life would serve as a consolation prize for someone unable to carry out what his entire training had prepared him to do. His concern about his heart murmur and, later, the words he expressed in his closing hours contribute to the conclusion that his dominant wish at the end was to live in order to make the most of his consolation prize. It was this side of Lacerda that I saw when we had our last meeting, to discuss illustrations for *Anarquistas e Comunistas no Brasil*, shortly before he died.

J.W.F.D.

CARLOS LACERDA, BRAZILIAN CRUSADER
VOLUME 2: THE YEARS 1960–1977

Sette Câmara, outgoing governor of Guanabara, delivering message at the inauguration of Governor Carlos Lacerda, December 5, 1960. Cardinal Jayme Câmara (wearing glasses) at far left. (Fernando Bueno photograph. Arquivo Walter Cunto)

Guanabara state legislator Raul Brunini and Lacerda, December 1960. (Copyright Agência O Globo)

Legislative majority leader Amaral Netto and Lacerda, December 1960. (Copyright Agência O Globo)

President Jânio Quadros and Lacerda at governors' meeting, Rio de Janeiro, June 1961. (*Manchete*)

Hélio Beltrão (left), Júlio de Mesquita Filho, and Lacerda. (Courtesy Lacerda family)

Lacerda warns São Paulo Governor Carvalho Pinto that Quadros plans a coup, August 1961. (Courtesy Lacerda family)

Lacerda's August 24, 1961, broadcast denouncing Quadros was followed by Quadros' resignation. (*O Cruzeiro*)

Seated (left to right): Lopo Coelho, Danillo Nunes, Raphael de Almeida Magalhães, Lacerda, Afonso Arinos Filho, and Aliomar Baleeiro. Brunini stands between Raphael and Lacerda. Wearing white, above Baleeiro, are Gladstone Chaves de Melo and (far right) Hélio Beltrão. (Arquivo Walter Cunto)

Leonel Brizola (left) embracing President João Goulart. (*Correio da Manhã*)

Lacerda speaks on television about the telephone shortage, April 1962. (Fernando Bueno photograph, Arquivo Walter Cunto)

Letícia and Carlos Lacerda on Brocoió Island with their first grandchild, Carlos Augusto. (Arquivo Walter Cunto)

Letícia, wearing her prize-winning hat, aboard the *Giulio Cesare*, November 1962. Between Carlos and Letícia are Antônio Carlos de Almeida Braga and his wife, Vivi. (Courtesy Lacerda family)

Lacerda with President Kennedy, who inscribed the picture for Carlos Augusto, March 1962. (Arquivo Walter Cunto)

Enaldo Cravo Peixoto (left) and Veiga Brito with Guanabara's application to the Inter-American Development Bank for a sewerage and water supply loan. (Courtesy Lacerda family)

Inspection of the Guandu Aqueduct project by Lacerda, Hugh Mattos, and Veiga Brito. (Courtesy Lacerda family)

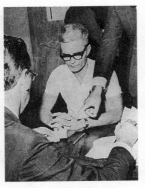

Colonel Francisco Américo Fontenelle. (*Manchete*)

Constantinos Doxiadis and Lacerda. (Courtesy Letícia Lacerda)

Lacerda and Veiga Brito. (Arquivo Walter Cunto)

Lacerda and Suzanne Labin at a school inauguration, August 1963. Alfredo C. Machado at far left. (Arquivo Walter Cunto)

Work on the Rebouças vehicle tunnel. (Fernando Bueno photograph, Arquivo Walter Cunto)

Maria Carlota de Macedo Soares, hand outstretched, directing Aterro do Flamengo work. Lacerda stands between her and Marcos Tamoyo (white shirt clearly visible). (Fernando Bueno photograph, Arquivo Walter Cunto)

Lacerda at a *favela*. (Fernando Bueno photograph, courtesy Magda Bueno de Almeida)

Lacerda addressing Braz de Pina *favelados*. (Courtesy Lacerda family)

End of the Favela do Pasmado. (Courtesy Lacerda family)

Lacerda inspecting. (Fernando Bueno photograph, courtesy Lacerda family)

Lacerda in the campaign plane, *Esperança*, with protective saint. (Arquivo Walter Cunto)

Lacerda sleeps on the plane while Roberto de Abreu Sodré gesticulates in front of Herbert Levy. (Fernando Bueno photograph, Arquivo Walter Cunto)

Campaigning in Mato Grosso. (Fernando Bueno photograph, Arquivo Walter Cunto)

Delivering a campaign speech in Goiás. (Courtesy Lacerda family)

Pernambuco Governor Miguel Arraes (left) and Admiral Cândido Aragão at the rally. (Copyright *Manchete*)

Rally of March 13, 1964. Goulart flanked by his wife and Osvaldo Pacheco. (Copyright Agência O Globo)

Former President Dutra (left) has received a visit from Armando Falcão (dark suit) and Lacerda early on March 19, 1964. (Courtesy Lacerda family)

Admiral Pedro Paulo Suzano with rejoicing sailors, Rio de Janeiro, March 27, 1964. (Copyright Agência O Globo)

Lacerda at the São Paulo home of Assis Chateaubriand (lower left), March 1964. (Courtesy Lacerda family)

President Goulart with sergeants, March 30, 1964. (Copyright *Manchete*)

Eduardo Gomes (left), Salvador Mandim, and Lacerda during the crisis of March 31–April 1, 1964. (Courtesy Lacerda family)

Magalhães Pinto.
(*O Estado de S. Paulo*)

Guanabara Palace during the crisis. Lacerda appears between General Mandim (in dark jacket) and Cláudio Lacerda. (Courtesy Lacerda family)

Before dawn on April 2, 1964, Chamber of Deputies President Ranieri Mazzilli (left) assumes the Brazilian presidency in the presence of Supreme Court President Ribeiro da Costa (center) and Senate President Moura Andrade. (Copyright *Manchete*)

Lacerda meets with governors early in April 1964. Between Governor Ademar de Barros (at left with dark tie) and Lacerda is the face of Congressman Jorge Curi. To the right of Lacerda are Governors Ildo Meneghetti (with glasses) and Fernando Correia da Costa (behind microphone). (Fernando Bueno photograph, courtesy Lacerda family)

Lacerda at the Brasília airport, accompanied by Jorge Curi (with suitcase) and Padre Antônio Godinho (in dark suit behind Curi). (Courtesy Lacerda family)

Lacerda with President Castello Branco (center). Presidential Press Secretary José Wamberto is next to Casa Militar Chief Ernesto Geisel (far right). (Courtesy Lacerda family)

Sandra Cavalcanti (left) listening to Padre Benedito Calasans. (*Manchete*)

Juracy Magalhães. (*Manchete*)

Roberto Campos. (*Manchete*)

Lacerda with his secretary of education, Carlos Flexa Ribeiro. (Courtesy Lacerda family)

Lacerda at his Praia do Flamengo apartment. (Arquivo Walter Cunto)

Maria Cristina Lacerda watches her father paint. (*Manchete*)

Standing: Lacerda's sons Sérgio (left) and Sebastião. Seated (from left): Vera Flexa Ribeiro Lacerda, wife of Sebastião; Letícia; Olga, Carlos' mother; Carlos holding Maria Isabel, daughter of Vera and Sebastião; and Maria Clara Mariani Lacerda, wife of Sérgio. On the floor: Ana Letícia Lacerda and Carlos Augusto Mariani Lacerda, children of Maria Clara and Sérgio. (Anonymous photographer, courtesy of Lamy Cunto and Sebastião Lacerda)

Sítio do Alecrim,
Lacerda's home in
Rocio, near Petrópolis.
(Courtesy Lamy Cunto)

Vila Aliança. (*O Cruzeiro*)

Inaugurating the Viaduto dos Marinheiros, February 25, 1965. Lacerda is between Public Works Secretary Enaldo Cravo Peixoto and Maria Cristina Lacerda. (J. R. Nonato photograph, courtesy Letícia Lacerda)

Opening a part of the Rebouças Tunnel, March 18, 1965. Lacerda is next to Public Works Minister Juarez Távora. Journalist Hélio Fernandes is at far right, next to young Hélio Fernandes Filho. (Courtesy Lacerda family)

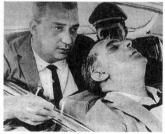

The Flexa Ribeiro campaign for the Guanabara governorship. Lacerda is between the candidate and Cravo Peixoto. September 26, 1965. (Courtesy Lacerda family)

While addressing a crowd, Lacerda fainted, September 30, 1965. Veiga Brito takes him to the Bangu Company hospital. (*Manchete*)

Congressman Oscar Passos. (*O Cruzeiro*)

Castello Branco (right) with federal congressional officers Aniz Badra (left), Adauto Cardoso (the tallest), and José Bonifácio Lafayette de Andrada. *(O Cruzeiro)*

Lacerda and former President Kubitschek, advocates of the oppositionist Frente Ampla, shake hands in Lisbon, November 19, 1966. (*Manchete*)

In Montevideo, Renato Archer (left) and Lacerda receive Goulart's support for the Frente Ampla. September 25, 1967. (*Manchete*)

Lacerda, with pipe, interviewing Shirley MacLaine in California, October 1968. (Courtesy Alfredo C. Machado)

Journalist Hermano Alves. (*O Cruzeiro*)

The Military Police in Rio crush a student-led demonstration, April 1968. (*O Cruzeiro*)

Priests protecting demonstrators from the Rio Military Police, April 1968. (*Manchete*)

Students with banners in Rio, June 26, 1968. (Kaoru photograph, Agência Jornal do Brasil)

Marshal Costa e Silva and his wife, Yolanda. (*Manchete*)

Student-led "March of 100,000" along Rio's Avenida Rio Branco, June 26, 1968. (Gonzales photograph, Agência Jornal do Brasil)

Demonstrators burn a police vehicle in São Paulo, October 1968. (*Manchete*)

Lacerda with Portugal's Antônio de Spínola, who found asylum in Brazil in 1975. (*Manchete*)

Lacerda at his Rocio home, 1977. (Courtesy Lacerda family)

Lacerda in Rocio with the *Jornal da Tarde* group that
interviewed him in March and April 1977, leading to the
posthumous publication of his *Depoimento*. From left to
right: Ruy Mesquita Filho, Letícia, Antônio Cunha,
Melchiades da Cunha Júnior, Ruy Portilho, Lacerda, Ayrton
Baffa, and Cláudio Lacerda. Lacerda's assistant, Tannay de
Farias, is at far right. (Courtesy Ruy Mesquita Filho, *Jornal
da Tarde*)

Lacerda autographing copies of his best-seller, *A Casa do
Meu Avô*, 1977. Luís Forjaz Trigueiros is behind Lacerda,
and near them is broadcaster Gilse Campos. Maria Helena
Trigueiros is at far right and next to her is Celso Mendonça.
(Courtesy Lamy Cunto)

I.

Governor during the Quadros Presidency (1961)

1. The New State (1960)

Guanabara was a peculiar state, fashioned out of the former Federal District in April 1960, when the capital of Brazil was moved inland from the city of Rio de Janeiro to Brasília. Writers called it a city-state because of its small size and the importance of the city of Rio. Rio, at the eastern end of the new state, occupied about one-quarter of its 1,200 square kilometers and housed about 85 percent of its 3,300,000 inhabitants.[1]

Carlos Lacerda, campaigning successfully for the governorship of Guanabara in 1960, described Rio as "devastated" by the misrule and corruption of past mayors, appointed by the federal authorities. Speaking to large audiences about the once proud city that had been overtaken industrially and demographically by dynamic São Paulo, he pointed out that it was beset with problems. It lacked adequate transportation, housing, sanitation, schooling, and telephone service, and faced shortages of water and electricity.

French researcher Marc de Lacharrière has written that in the fifteen years before 1960 not one step was taken to correct these problems, and he has called the city of that era the victim of governmental incapacity and "a lack of continuity of mayors, appointed and dismissed for political reasons and mostly corrupt." Former Brazilian Finance Minister Eugênio Gudin wrote late in 1960 of "the sordid political practices and swindling implanted on this poor city for over half a century."[2]

Neither sordid political practices nor corruption was unknown elsewhere. One can attribute the problems that faced Governor-elect Lacerda to the political clout of some of the great states in comparison with that of the tiny Federal District, the recent zeal for the costly construction of Brasília, and geography.

Guanabara's scenic geographical features, notable for massive peaks alongside the ocean front, provided little fresh water and no source of hydroelectric power and presented formidable obstacles to housing and traffic. These obstacles, according to geographer Lysia Maria

Cavalcanti Bernardes, had made expansion so difficult that the location of Rio would seem to have been unsuitable for the formation of a metropolis. But, as she also points out, the mountainous terrain and the large Bay of Guanabara were attractive to the Portuguese settlers of the sixteenth century, who considered the steep hills at the entrance to the bay appropriate places to set up forts for defense against Indians and the French.[3]

The town, which served for a while as an exporter of sugar, became at the start of the eighteenth century the colony's financial capital, a result of the discovery of gold on an unprecedented scale more than 200 kilometers to the north. While gold reached the port of Rio, aided by the opening in 1704 of a new road, the "Caminho Novo para as Minas," immigrants came from Europe to participate in the boom and slaves poured in from Africa. The boom helped Rio to grow with opulence and speed that historian Pedro Calmon says were unrivaled by any city in the colony. And although gold production declined in the latter half of the eighteenth century, it played a role in the decision that made Rio the colony's capital in 1763, thus initiating its two-century reign as Brazil's bureaucratic center.[4]

Following the arrival in 1808 of the Portuguese royal family and court, fleeing from Napoleon's armies, Rio became the capital of the Portuguese kingdom of Brazil and was the object of appropriate attentions, such as those given to streets and public buildings. As the capital of the independent Brazilian empire from 1822 until 1889 and as the principal port for the Brazilian southeast, it flourished. In return for imported manufactured goods, it exported a host of agricultural products, chiefly coffee, brought in from outlying provinces by new rail lines.

Financial austerity during the republican administration of President Manoel Ferraz de Campos Salles (1898–1902) made it possible for the succeeding administration to initiate a golden age for Rio, notable for new avenues and parks and attention to the city's health. In the early 1920s, the Castelo Hill, in the heart of the downtown area and the site of a bayside fort of the early settlers, was demolished to provide 200,000 square meters of space where the hill had existed and gain 600,000 square meters from the sea with fill. Further decongestion was achieved by the creation of Presidente Vargas Avenue in the early 1940s and the demolition in the 1950s of the Santo Antônio Hill, some of whose fill was still being used, shortly before Lacerda's election campaign, to extend land into the bay not far from the city's downtown area.[5] José Sette Câmara Filho, appointed governor of the new state for seven months preceding Lacerda's administration, sought to give life to the Superintendência de Urbanização e

Saneamento (SURSAN), created in 1957 to assist the city's development, and he spoke of the urgency of constructing an aqueduct of
more than 40 kilometers, much of it through rock, to bring 2½ million liters a day of Guandu River water to the city.[6]

Sette Câmara inaugurated a short stretch of an elevated avenue in
the downtown area. But what Rio traffic required most desperately
was a reform to make it unnecessary for vehicles to go through the
congested downtown area in order to move between the city's South
and North zones. Rio traffic promised to remain about the worst in
the world unless tunnels were driven through the Carioca mountain
range, which was in the middle of the city, west of the downtown
area, and which was the obstacle to a direct flow of vehicles between
the south and north.[7]

The South Zone had become populated with the spread of the
original town to the districts adjoining the beaches of Copacabana,
Ipanema, and Leblon and the shores of Rodrigo de Freitas Lagoon. It
was an area of apartment buildings, housing about 15 percent of the
residents of the new state. As the city's most privileged area, it enjoyed the greatest share of the sewer system of 1,029 kilometers,
much of it dating from the start of the century.[8] The South Zone
residents, many of them members of the middle and upper classes,
had been the most inclined to vote for Lacerda, whose principal political party, the UDN (União Democrática Nacional), was considered conservative.[9]

The North Zone, containing the rail lines, housed over 60 percent
of Guanabara's population. It had by far the largest share of the state's
industrial production, which was dominated by no single segment.
As of old, textile and clothing factories employed the most workers,
but chemical and pharmaceutical products had risen to the top in
economic importance. Rio's industrial workers also continued to find
employment in plants processing foods, bottling drinks, and making
electrical materials, construction equipment, furniture, paper products, and cigarettes.[10]

In contrast to Brazil's 5 percent annual increase in the gross domestic product between 1950 and 1960, the increase in Guanabara had
been only 4 percent annually.[11] São Paulo's metropolitan area gained
impetus with the birth there in the late 1950s of the country's automobile industry. Furthermore, the states of Minas Gerais and São
Paulo were taking steps that would assure them of large new steel
plants in the 1960s.

Contributing to Rio's below-average economic growth was the lack
of land served by utilities, such as sewers and telephones. Telephone
service did not exist outside the metropolitan area, and the service

there was poor. The 25,000 new phone lines installed between 1955 and 1960 failed to keep pace with needs brought about by population increase and left the number of applications for new instruments at around 200,000.[12]

Another drawback was the situation at Rio's crowded port, which continued, after the formation of the new state, to be under the federal government's authority. The port's labor unions, storage facilities, and handling equipment made it unattractive to use. Engulfed in the city and poorly served by roads and rail lines, it had been surpassed in 1954 by São Paulo's port city, Santos. Whereas in 1950–1951 Rio handled 36 percent of the value of Brazil's imports and 18 percent of the value of exports, these figures had declined to 30 percent and 12 percent by 1959–1960.[13]

Those who worked in Rio's business and industrial districts relied chiefly on a defective mass transit system made up of small, inefficient buses, trains moving on tracks used also for long distance goods traffic, and antiquated streetcars (*bondes*) whose movement on tracks created vehicle movement problems already complicated by congestion, insufficient parking space, and the disregard of parking and traffic regulations.

Subsidiaries of the Canadian-based Brazilian Traction, Light, and Power Company, with old concessions to provide streetcar, telephone, and electricity services, had fallen on hard times because of inflation and low utility rates. The supply of about 700,000 kilowatts of electric power by Rio-Light, one of the subsidiaries, was described by Lacerda and his engineers as "poorly disguised rationing." They foresaw serious deficits in energy in the five years following 1960 on account of the slow progress in completing new hydroelectric projects in Brazil and inadequate allotments from them for Guanabara.[14]

Both the North and South zones of Rio contained *favelas*, unsanitary squatter settlements mostly along hillsides and not far from places of work of the *favelados* who were employed. The fast-growing settlements, more than two hundred in number, provided shelter for around 400,000 persons in 1960, twice the Rio *favela* population in 1950. This 7 percent annual increase, more than double the 3.3 percent annual population increase of Guanabara as a whole, was partly due to immigration resulting from unfavorable economic conditions in rural areas of Brazil's east and northeast.[15] The 59 percent literacy rate for *favelados* (of five or more years of age) compared with 82 percent in the state and 92 percent in the South Zone's Copacabana district.[16]

In declaring that the children of the poor were not being educated, Lacerda pointed to Guanabara's primary school setup that had to refuse to admit 110,000 children in 1960 because of overcrowding.[17] Nor was anything being done to make housing available to the poor. Housing construction in the state, estimated at fourteen thousand dwelling units annually in the face of a demand for thirty thousand, was limited to units for high-income groups that could provide good returns to investors.[18]

Lacerda, who had spoken in the 1950s of the need to develop "green belts" of agricultural production for cities, could not be expected to ignore the rural part of the state. Much of it, like the metropolitan area, is hilly, some of it steeply so, for the state has three mountainous regions. Along the slopes facing south, most exposed to humidity from the sea and least exposed to the sun, bananas and chayote were raised, whereas the slopes facing north were more appropriate for oranges, papaya, and manioc.

These items, along with dairy products and other vegetables and fruits, were produced mostly on relatively small plots (less than 10 hectares) by workers who did not own the land and who, in some cases, were subsistence farmers. Many of them relied on burros for transport, lived in poor quarters, and gave no attention to the care of the soil. The incoming government of Lacerda found that "the Carioca farm worker received absolutely no encouragement and lacked effective help for increasing production." Geographer Nilo Bernardes wrote that the failure to consider soil erosion or to employ technical measures of cultivation was especially lamentable in an area so close to an important market.[19]

2. The Governor-elect (Late 1960)

Governor-elect Carlos Lacerda, who had offered to solve Guanabara's problems and give the city "the charm of its former days," was forty-six years old, handsome, energetic, intelligent, and imaginative. He was known for his brilliant debating skill and oratory, unequaled by any of his fellow-congressmen, and for the aggressive political columns he wrote for his newspaper, the *Tribuna da Imprensa.* His oratory and pen, unsparing in denouncements of corruption in government, had made him the foremost opponent of "the oligarchy," a term he used when referring to those who had ruled Brazil since 1930.

Many of Lacerda's followers were fanatical. Spellbound by his oratory and fascinated by his manner of presenting sensational revelations, they would leave whatever they were doing to be present where he spoke. They saw him as an independent and courageous knight, eager to battle superior political and economic groups on behalf of the public good and without regard for his personal safety or job security.

Veterans of his fan club reminded new members that he had never been deterred by physical attacks, ordered in the 1940s and 1950s by men whose crimes he had exposed, and that he had not hesitated to resign from the Rio city council and from prestigious positions on leading publications rather than be untrue to his beliefs.

Equally intense was the hostility he provoked in a substantial segment that included Communists and individuals loyal to the memory of President Getúlio Vargas, whose suicide in 1954 they blamed on Lacerda's attacks. They called his denouncements unfair and described him as inconsistent, unscrupulously ambitious, unstable, verging on insanity, and as possessing all the characteristics needed to become a dictator. Their votes might have prevented his election to the Guanabara governorship in October 1960 had they not been split among several anti-Lacerda candidates.

The crusader had achieved such fame for savage attacks that many questioned whether he had the qualities necessary to provide Guanabara with a constructive administration. Not a few thought he would be a disaster. But, during the recent election campaign, he had revealed an intimate knowledge of conditions in the new state. A Carioca by birth, he had spent most of his life in Rio and had studied its problems as a journalist, city councilman, and congressman.

Most of Lacerda's traits augured well for Guanabara. His honesty was matched by his determination to prevent the taint of corruption from soiling his administration. While campaigning he had chosen first-rate advisers to analyze the needs of the state, and he had listened to them, absorbing quickly their ideas. While directing his newspaper, he had shown the ability to build up an effective team, inspired and loyal. His enthusiasm for causes, demonstrated during the long hours he worked, was frequently infectious among fellow-workers, and, when it was not, he was likely to become exasperated.

Sensitive subordinates, feeling mistreated by Lacerda, have described him as an ungrateful and willful executive who trampled on them and their fellow-workers. Those who remained with him on the job found him always demanding, often difficult to work for, and occasionally explosive, but they could not deny that he administered with intelligent attention to details and a determination to get things done. They regarded the outbursts as the expressions of a talented but impatient leader, a restless genius, who was driven by a sense of mission and detested mediocrity. Learning how to work with him, they discovered that the answer lay not in submissiveness, which he found irritating, but in the presentation of useful ideas. And they came to find that Ruth Alverga, who had served long as Lacerda's secretary, was not beyond giving them warnings if she felt that they were trying to see him when he was not in an agreeable mood.[1]

Away from his work, whiskey in hand and relaxed in conversation, Lacerda was usually charming. As governor he could be expected to captivate distinguished visitors to Rio, surprising them with his interest in, and knowledge about, whatever made them remarkable—with the exception of sports. He might quote from foreign-language books that his visitors would hardly expect him to have heard of. A voracious and rapid reader with an extraordinary memory, he was attracted to the classics and to what was modern. He liked to discuss and explore. Detesting routine, he had abandoned formal education a few years after graduating from high school and educated himself, giving attention to literature, languages, philosophy, music, and art, and disregarding science and mathematics.

Carlos inherited his hunger for books from his father, Maurício de Lacerda, a willful prolabor journalist, orator, and congressman, famous for denouncing the oligarchy of the pre-1930 Old Republic. Maurício had separated long ago from his wife Olga; and therefore Carlos, during his adult years, had seen little of his father, who had died in 1959.

It has been said that the cordiality and courteous manners that Carlos often displayed were inherited from Olga, a gracious woman with dark, sad eyes and an enormous circle of friends. A longtime employee of the Rio municipal government (until her son, the governor-elect, demanded her retirement), she lived in Rio with her daughter Vera and son-in-law Odilon Lacerda Paiva when she was not in Vassouras, to the north of Rio, where she had a small house she loved. Mauricinho, the oldest of the three children of Olga and Maurício, has been called her favorite, perhaps because he was more like her and thus was calmer than Carlos or Vera. Mauricinho, who had received a degree in medicine, was known for his sarcastic wit.

The pretty Letícia Abruzzini, whom Carlos had married in 1938, suffered from a hearing problem that was not seriously noticeable but was aggravating to her. She tired much more easily than her robust, dynamic, demanding husband. Even when she was apart from the conversation she usually knew quite well what was going on, and, in her quiet and unassuming way, offered sensible advice.

Letícia did not look forward to the difficulties she felt Carlos' recent election would bring to family life, which had become increasingly disturbed by politics. Already, thanks to Carlos' aggressive journalism and politicking, threatening phone calls from Lacerda haters had become all too familiar to her and the three children: Maria

Cristina, nine years old, Sebastião, eighteen years old, and Sérgio, who became twenty-two late in 1960, shortly after succeeding Carlos as president of the *Tribuna da Imprensa.*

When Letícia, known as Ziloca, had married Carlos, he had been a fervent supporter of Communism. With equal zeal he had attacked it in the fifteen years before he became governor, and in 1948 he had been ardent in his conversion to Catholicism. He was intense about many things, including his hobbies, which ranged from gardening and cooking to writing stories and plays. Intense also in his feelings, he was often unable to hold back tears when he saw children suffering in poverty. He sometimes cried at the cinema and occasionally when moved by the Christmas spirit or by sentiments expressed in letters. He was generous to those who were fragile, but combative against those who were powerful.

Carlos was unrestrained. He would, a close friend of his explained, allow no one to put his ego in a birdcage or try to make him into something he was not. When called up for induction into military service in 1935, he chose to be a deserter. He has been likened to an exuberant boy who refuses to let himself be hemmed in by restrictions that limit freedom or expression. But the boyish exuberance was more in evidence in the adult, when he was in his prime, than during his formative years. Not infrequently the precocious youth had found the battle against conformity heartbreaking. On one occasion he had attempted suicide.

Carlos Lacerda could never be a subordinate. He was, rather, a leader, the center of attention, the frequent advocate of lines of action so bold as to appear preposterous, but which, it usually turned out, reflected keen political intuition. "You are in a canoe, attacking a cruiser," his brother Mauricinho warned him in 1953 when he decided to campaign against the leading pro-Vargas newspaper, *Última Hora.* He liked to be in that position.

Almost beyond belief was the so-called photographic memory of the book lover who would complete the reading of several volumes during a plane trip. Asked to give a press interview about the paper industry, Lacerda suggested that his friend, José Alberto Gueiros, prepare a report on the subject ahead of time. Gueiros, after carrying out considerable research and submitting ten pages, was disappointed because Lacerda merely leafed through them and then chatted with him about other things. With the arrival of the reporters, however, Lacerda gave a long interview in which he recited almost everything in the report, including the figures, and added appropriate comments. Another friend, José Cândido Moreira de Souza, was taken aback when Lacerda, meeting him quite by accident in an elevator, recited accurately and completely a poem that had been published by José Cândido's daughter some years back. "I gave Carlos a letter," says José Cândido's brother, José Luiz, "and he just looked at it and had a mental photograph of the page."[2]

Despite his memory, Lacerda did not follow the example of other great orators of the republic, such as Rui Barbosa and Otávio Mangabeira, in preparing ahead of time the wording of speeches. He loved guiding, and being guided by, the moods of audiences. With his superb voice he improvised in a way that appealed to a large range of listeners. Especially attractive to Lacerda were the challenges of arguing cases before hostile audiences. Not infrequently he won their applause. Such were his powers of persuasion that fellow-congressmen belonging to rival parties had sometimes avoided him lest they give him an opportunity to convert them to his views.[3]

Sensitive to the behavior of crowds, Lacerda was fascinated by speeches in Shakespeare's *Julius Caesar* (one of the many works he translated into Portuguese). As he was to reveal after he left the governorship, he was deeply moved by the oration given at the funeral of architect Le Corbusier by André Malraux, one of the men he most admired. Writer Antonio Carlos Villaça recalls the passion with which Lacerda read the oration to him in French late one night. Lacerda, as usual, put everything into what he was doing. He broke down in tears at the end of his reading.[4]

Night sessions of work or conversation with Lacerda were apt to last beyond 2:00 A.M. If, as has been said, he lost track of time, it can be added that his sleeping habits gave him no need to keep track of it. Four hours were enough for a good night of sleep; when he remained up all night, he recuperated fully during the next day by napping soundly for half an hour.

If Lacerda had traits that presented possible problems for his administration they lay in his manner of dealing with men of influence at the local and national level, regardless of whether or not they belonged to his own political party, the UDN. The frankness, fault finding, and failure to hide his disdain of what he considered stupid or malicious did not augur well for his relations with state legislators and others, such as press leaders, who exerted power in Guanabara. Besides, he was totally opposed to making deals or offering favors in return for the support of projects he favored. Distressing to men of influence, in the habit of placing friends and relatives in the municipal government, was Lacerda's decision to make no appointment for reasons other than merit.

Like his father, whose career might have been more successful with less defiance of national leaders, Carlos relied on support from the masses. He spoke out vigorously whenever he felt the people should share his indignation at positions taken by national leaders, and he could be expected to continue that practice no matter how important the goodwill of those leaders might be to his presidential ambition or to programs vital to Guanabara. Because he was always frank and open, was averse to deals, and never acted in an underhanded way, it is perhaps unfair to label him, as has been done, a man with a record of intrigue.

It might have been assumed that Lacerda's role of assailant of the top authorities would be altered as a result of the October 1960 elections, which would place former São Paulo Governor Jânio Quadros in the presidency early in 1961. Lacerda had fought tenaciously to have the UDN nominate Quadros, and then had joined him in the campaign against the two principal rivals of the UDN: the PSD (Partido Social Democrático) and the PTB (Partido Trabalhista Brasileiro). Furthermore, he professed a warm friendship for Quadros. But the career of Lacerda, who had called Quadros a sinister Hitler-like "'virtuoso' of felony" in 1955, was no exception to the practice that made political friendships fleeting.

From incidents during the recent campaign, Quadros received confirmation that Lacerda could be troublesome, and Lacerda received confirmation that Quadros behaved in an eccentric manner. For the time being, however, all was serene between Brazil's two leading spellbinders. The governor-elect, expecting to meet with the president-elect in Europe, directed Guanabara's finance secretary–designate to prepare a report for the meeting so that he could discuss the dire financial condition of Guanabara; and he called on War Minister Odílio Denys in Rio in order to be able to bring Quadros the marshal's word that the army would not look unfavorably on the new president's inauguration.[5]

3. Lacerda and Quadros Travel Abroad
(Late 1960, Early 1961)

As it turned out, Lacerda did not succeed in conferring with Quadros in Europe. The forty-three-year-old president-elect, in a twelve-week absence from Brazil that ended eleven days before his inauguration, searched for privacy in the company of his wife and mother, and opportunities to drink whiskey. His campaign to succeed Juscelino Kubitschek in the presidency had been an overwhelming success, but it had been an exhausting one during which the touchy Quadros had sometimes wanted to withdraw and had suffered, if we can believe a letter he wrote to Lacerda, "terrible psychological damage" caused by those who showed "indifference, selfishness, ambition, jealousy, and pure malice."[1]

Following an eye operation in London that kept him in a hospital for four days, the president-elect became irritated by the demands on his time and the inaccurate headlines stemming from casual words to reporters. Despite the plans of the British to have him received by the Queen and honored at a lunch attended by Prime Minister Harold Macmillan, he unexpectedly left London for Spain at the end of November.[2]

Until Quadros took a steamer for Brazil about six weeks later, he was so elusive that the *Correio da Manhã* described his "mysterious movements in Europe" as "arousing surprise and disappointment." The *Diário Carioca*, another prominent Rio daily, expressed regret that the president-elect failed to initiate discussions abroad that might bring capital and technical advantages to Brazil.[3]

Quadros disappointed newspaper reporters and countless Brazilians who had come to London and Paris to confer with him. And he surprised Brazilian embassies, which he kept uninformed, and foreign dignitaries, whom he avoided, in stark contrast to former Brazilian presidents-elect. He was wily, could use little lies to protect his privacy, and may not have been displeased to be called "history's most baffling president" by the Paris press and compared by it to Greta Garbo, famous for saying "I want to be alone."[4]

Among the many Brazilians in Paris, which Quadros had been expected to visit after London, was São Paulo Public Works Secretary José Vicente Faria Lima, dispatched to learn whom Quadros favored in the São Paulo mayorship contest and whether Marshal Odílio Denys would continue as war minister. After the Associated Press reported that the enigmatic Quadros had been seen "somewhere in Italy," Brigadeiro Faria Lima became one of the few Brazilians to have a word with him, but he returned to Brazil with no answers to his questions—only the news that Quadros, "concerning himself exclusively" with living conditions in Brazil, sent his best wishes to the Brazilian workers.[5]

Francisco Negrão de Lima, Brazil's ambassador to Portugal, belonged, like other ambassadors from his country, to the political group defeated by Quadros. On January 1 Negrão was temporarily absent from his Lisbon post when Alitalia Airlines telephoned Chargé d'Affaires Carlos dos Santos Veras to advise that the plane bringing Quadros, his wife, and mother would be two hours late. The news, the first to reach the embassy about the plan of the president-elect to come to Lisbon, resulted in the presence of embassy staff members and reporters at the airport. Their presence so annoyed Quadros that he spoke to Veras about punishing the airline. He was cold to the chargé and his wife, but, after helping himself to a generous supply of straight Scotch in their apartment, was less so than the women with him, who behaved in Lisbon as though they feared the president-elect was in danger of being poisoned. Quadros told Veras to see to it that the press did not mention him, an arrangement which was possible in Portugal at the time and which resulted in a curious situation because Quadros, making things awkward for the embassy, decided later in his Lisbon stay to give a press interview and appeared unhappy when nothing was published.

At the unfashionable Hotel Condestável, where the Quadros trio lodged, the president-elect liked to find an inconspicuous table in the bar, where he would sit with working papers and drink. He had been so aloof that it was a surprise to Veras and his wife to receive a telephone call from the president-elect inviting them to the Condestável. From the hotel, Quadros took them, with his wife and mother, to a nightclub whose girl performers held great attraction for him. In excellent spirits while consuming quite quickly most of a bottle of Scotch, he was pleased to be greeted by some of the dancing couples and remarked to Veras that, if he wished, he could be elected head of Portugal. After asking Veras if he knew the Brazilian constitution well, he asserted that the president of Brazil was the most powerful head of any democratic nation. "Like an emperor," he said. He added that during his first week as president he would have to make 473 appointments and wanted time in Lisbon to relax and study matters.[6]

The British press kept calling on Quadros to return to England lest he continue to disappoint Harold Macmillan and other authorities there. But Quadros remained in Lisbon. He did become a little less unbending: shortly before taking a steamer to Brazil he got together with Negrão de Lima, whom he had kept waiting for days.[7]

Lacerda, during a one-month trip around the world, was less regal and less elusive. He enjoyed meeting people and giving interviews to reporters. As he told the press before leaving, he expected, on the trip, to promote industry for the state and develop plans for a subway system. He also explained that he hoped to persuade the Japanese to install a thermoelectric plant to serve the new industrial zone he envisaged for the Santa Cruz area, along the coast in the west of the state, and he predicted that by 1965 Guanabara would be receiving nuclear power at a favorable cost.[8] Walter Cunto, who made the trip with Carlos and Carlos' son Sérgio, issued a constant stream of press releases to keep Brazilians advised of the activities of the governor-elect.

Cunto, a longtime *Tribuna da Imprensa* employee, was to become the press adviser of the incoming Guanabara administration.

On his way from Rio to Tokyo, Lacerda reached New York, and there he was questioned by reporters who wanted to know whether Quadros continued to admire the regime of Fidel Castro. Declining to speak for Quadros, Lacerda told of his own "disappointment in Cuba," but he would not agree, at least for the time being, that Cuba was a "Soviet satellite."[9]

The trip was filled with official dinners and conferences with businessmen. After spending eight days in Japan, proclaiming the virtues of a new Brazil inspired by free enterprise, and inspecting motor plants and temples, Lacerda went to Taiwan, where he and Sérgio were received by Chiang Kai-shek. Speaking to reporters about the violent transport strikes taking place in Rio, he called the agitation the work of Communists, strong in the outgoing government, and a result "of delirious currency emissions for building Brasília."[10]

The European tour began in Italy, where Lacerda invited Alfa-Romeo to manufacture motors in Brazil and pleased Rio taxi drivers by reporting that Fiat, in exchange for coffee, would make taxis available to them at low prices. In Paris Lacerda drove a train in a subway and told the French that he would not be bound by subway agreements reached with them in 1951 but would seek bids for subway cars for a system to be connected to Rio's suburban trains. His Paris hotel, the Lord Byron, was crowded with industrial representatives of countries that hoped for a visit, and he had to explain to businessmen from Germany, England, Holland, Switzerland, Poland, and Czechoslovakia that his time was too short to accomplish all he wanted. He examined subway and thermoelectric plant proposals brought to Paris by Germans.[11]

Among the papers that flowed to Lacerda from Brazil was a study of the Guanabara political situation by Fidélis Amaral Netto, scheduled to be government leader in the state's recently elected Constitutional Assembly. The report was brought by Mauricinho, Carlos' older brother, who later joined Carlos and a few others on an automobile trip through France and Spain to Portugal. Carlos observed that "one cannot be in Europe without going to Portugal"[12] and might have added that he disliked missing an opportunity to order *bacalhau* (codfish) *à la mode* at Lisbon's Restaurante Tavares.

The flight to Rio, made after Sérgio's return, brought Carlos and Cunto to Rio's Galeão Airport on December 1. So large was the crowd that Letícia, on hand to welcome her husband, was assigned police protection. Nine-year-old Maria Cristina made her way onto the plane and received a fatherly kiss.

4. Inauguration (December 5, 1960)

Politicians hoping for posts in the Quadros administration were left in doubt about the new cabinet until January 27, four days before the new federal administration took office. Lacerda, whose inauguration date was uncertain late in October, when he went to Japan, did not depart from Brazil before choosing his team, conferring frequently with it, and leaving assignments for it to carry out. Among its members were thirty-year-old Raphael de Almeida Magalhães (chief of the governor's office), Antônio Arlindo Laviola (secretary of transport and public works), Mario Lorenzo Fernandez (secretary of finance), Marcelo Garcia (secretary of health), Hélio Beltrão (secretary of interior), and José Arthur Rios (coordinator of social services).

Looking for a director of public safety, Lacerda turned first to General Ernesto Geisel and then to Colonel Golbery do Couto e Silva.[1] They shared Lacerda's dislike of Labor Party (PTB) leader João ("Jango") Goulart, who had been elected vice president in 1955 and again in 1960. After each declined the offer, Lacerda turned with success to another army officer, General Siseno Sarmento, who had been involved, like Lacerda, in the unsuccessful movement of 1955 to prevent the inauguration of President Kubitschek and Vice President Goulart.

Lacerda considered naming businessman José Cândido Moreira de Souza education secretary, but close adviser Raphael de Almeida Magalhães urged that this post go to educator Carlos Flexa Ribeiro, who had lost his race for the state Constitutional Assembly. Lacerda therefore put José Cândido in charge of the secretaryship of agriculture, industry, and commerce, which, according to organization charts being drawn up by Hélio Beltrão, was scheduled to become the secretaryship of economy when an administrative reorganization became effective. In planning the reorganization, Lacerda decided to create a new secretaryship to handle concessions granted to utilities, and hoped to put it in the hands of prominent UDN Congressman Olavo Bilac Pinto. Some thought was also given to the formation of a labor secretaryship, to be headed by Hélio Walcacer, who had participated long ago with Carlos in Communist activities and was now given the title of adviser for labor matters.[2]

For those elected in Guanabara, the Regional Electoral Tribunal ruled that the inaugurations would take place on December 5, and therefore at 1:00 P.M. that day the thirty-member Constitutional Assembly was installed in Tiradentes Palace. An hour later, while warships gave twenty-one-gun salutes and thousands of people waved white handkerchiefs, Lacerda entered Tiradentes Palace with his family. After taking the oath of office, he delivered a speech notable for its attack on Communism. "Communism," he said, "calls itself pacifist and only promotes war, speaks to the humble and only robs them, even of their right to think, speaks of self-determination and creates satellites, condemns colonialism and transforms once sovereign nations into colonies for . . . the triumph of the new totalitarian imperialism." "We declare," the new governor said, "that Guanabara will not tolerate Communism in its territory either in its open form of the past, which made use of assassinations and terrorism, or in its present form, which disguises itself as nationalist and populist, as anticolonialist and pacifist, in order to conspire against Brazil, leaving the country without allies or defined national objectives."

At Guanabara Palace, the seat of the governorship, a throng spent a part of the hot afternoon listening to a second speech by Lacerda, which reviewed the lamentable state of "essential services" for the people of the "abandoned" city. He announced the establishment of a foundation to raise funds for public schools. It would, he said, bear the name of Otávio Mangabeira, the anti-Vargas orator and UDN leader who had died on November 29.[3]

Roberto Marinho's popular afternoon newspaper *O Globo* praised the team selected by Lacerda and wrote that it "could never be mistaken for Goulart's gang of false labor leaders, still busy making off with what remains, if anything, of the social security funds." But the *Diário Carioca*, faithful to outgoing President Kubitschek and his party, the PSD, called the Lacerda team inexperienced, and bemoaned the "ever changing and uncontrollable temperament" of the "irascible" new governor. It described his dismissal of some of the municipal employees as niggardly and heartless.[4]

5. Governor Lacerda

Dismissals were occasioned by Lacerda's hostility to the custom that some municipal employees had of collecting paychecks without working. The new governor would have been pleased if he could also have dismissed about ninety nonworking members of the corps of over 120 state attorneys appointed in large part for political reasons during past governments. Foiled in this case by legislation about tenure, he took steps to upgrade future appointments by requiring applicants to compete in examinations (*concursos*).[1]

Political-minded chief executives, their eyes on the advantages to be gained by pleasing influential people, had for generations made use of their authority to appoint not only state attorneys but also the occupants of the highly remunerative notary public (*tabelião*) posts. In this area, too, Lacerda let *concursos* determine who were awarded positions. Thus a completely unknown clerk, who had been doing all the work for a notary, had the opportunity to compete against prominent candidates and was judged the winner by the commission of examiners appointed by the governor. Lacerda became so fond of *concursos* that he extended the practice to cover even those seeking to become streetsweepers.[2]

Lawyer Alcino Salazar, who was consulted by Lacerda early in the administration and later became the state attorney-general, points out that the same concern with merit guided Lacerda's appointments of judges and cites the case of a promotion to fill a vacancy on the state's top Justice Tribunal. The governor shocked men of influence by giving the promotion to a judge who had considered his chances hopeless because the governor's desk was covered with telegrams and letters from men of prestige recommending the two other candidates.[3]

"We were not elected," Lacerda declared on December 5, "to distribute jobs." Raphael de Almeida Magalhães, the right hand of the governor, has written that Lacerda would not arrange a job even to please his former school teacher. When Roberto de Abreu Sodré, UDN leader in São Paulo and a close friend of Lacerda's, asked that employment be found for a young man, Lacerda simply directed a subordinate to add the young man's name to a list of applicants who were scheduled to compete in a *concurso*.[4]

Lacerda, firm in demanding results from his team members, never asked any of them to employ anyone. Nor did he interfere in their negotiations with construction contractors. In the secretaryship of public works, which received many contractors' bids, he established a control center to make certain that the prices in bids made to all the secretaryships were not out of line. Contrary to custom, he rejected campaign contributions offered to his party by contractors.[5]

Seeking authorization of the legislature to increase the capital of the state bank in 1962, Lacerda was able to announce that the bank had not made a single loan on account of political pressure. Raphael de Almeida Magalhães' father Dario, who headed the bank for a while, asserts that Lacerda never asked him to have a loan made to anyone. Public Works Secretary Enaldo Cravo Peixoto, recovering from a heart attack, tried to obtain a loan from the bank in order to install an elevator in his apartment building because his doctor forbade him to continue using stairs to reach his fourth-floor dwelling. The bank advised that the loan would be against its regulations. Cravo Peixoto, who had to turn elsewhere, has observed that "it was a very rigid government" and that in other administrations he could probably have borrowed from the state bank.[6]

To make certain that state vehicles would be used only for official purposes, Lacerda established a daily transport bulletin for control and had yellow stripes painted on vehicles belonging to the state. José Roberto Rego Monteiro, who worked on the state budget, feels that the simple presence of Lacerda and the knowledge of how he did things kept the number of "unworthy acts" to a minimum.[7]

The war against illegal gambling in the form of the old *jogo do bicho* (animal numbers game) was described by Lacerda as being directed not against the small fry but against the game's top bankers, whose operations, he said, had been carried out in the past "with the connivance even of members of the police." Some of the bankers of the game were unpleasantly surprised when their contributions to the Otávio Mangabeira Foundation gave them no protection.[8]

Unable to resist the investigation of corruption, Lacerda was aboard the navy's *Barroso* in February 1961 when the navy, alerted by the Guanabara police, participated in an action that resulted in the capture of the contraband vessel *Aletes*; and he went on a torpedo destroyer to the smugglers' port at Angra dos Reis, used by the *Aletes* and other ships, during the Kubitschek administration, to unload cargoes and illegally export coffee. On television he explained his participation in the investigation as inspired by moral considerations and his resolve to eliminate contraband from Guanabara. In Brasília he gave Chamber of Deputies President Ranieri Mazzilli a report in which he accused two congressmen of "involvement in the national contraband network." The charge against Esmerino Arruda, which the Chamber voted to be unproven, brought a violent reaction in which the congressman from Ceará called Lacerda nothing more than an unscrupulous reporter whose egoism and evil made his downfall inevitable. But Lacerda kept encouraging the investigation and reported the findings in long letters to Clemente Mariani, the finance minister of Quadros.[9]

Hélio Mamede, who became urbanization director early in Lacerda's administration, points out that files were filled with unused plans for improving Guanabara and that, when Lacerda took over, "an explosion" took place with the decisions to put many of the plans into effect. "It was," he says, "an alive, switched-on government." Marcelo Garcia, who became chief of the governor's office after serving as secretary of health, stresses the importance of Lacerda's work in following through on the plans. Lacerda checked carefully to see that nothing was done imperfectly, and he reminded subordinates of details he might have discussed with them months earlier. In the case of construction projects, he was always inspecting. Needing little sleep, he would summon team members to go with him at odd hours. Hélio Mamede says that Lacerda, who had no timetable, would summon him at 10:00 P.M., 11:00 P.M., or 6:00 A.M. Cravo Peixoto has mentioned that Lacerda, after a flight from Europe that reached Rio early in the morning, set forth with him a few hours later on an inspection tour, during which the governor hurdled walls and climbed all over the place.[10] Lacerda, a fast walker, strode purposefully.

Military Police Major Carlos Osório da Silveira Neto, aide-de-camp and security officer, often accompanied Lacerda and was on the job so much that in two years, he says, he had dinner with his wife only on sixteen days. When Osório was in the car with Lacerda, the governor dictated so many memorandums, with orders to administrators, that the major installed a tape recorder in the car.[11]

Commentators have said that Lacerda used people, getting the most out of them. In many cases, like that of Osório, the team members enjoyed the experience, finding it stimulating. General Salvador Mandim, who came to occupy the secretaryship of public services, handling utilities, has remarked that Lacerda was the "toughest general I ever knew in my life, the most demanding, but also, in work relations, a best friend." According to Rego Monteiro, "Lacerda transmitted to all his assistants that élan of his. We would work all night. . . . My time in his government was a wonderful experience." Ruth Alverga reports that "everybody worked for the pleasure of it. I used to work until 9:00 or 10:00 P.M."[12]

Lacerda, on the Viaduto das Canoas one morning in the company of José Cândido Moreira de Souza, found the work stalled because a supplier had failed to furnish building material. He jumped into a dump truck at the site and, taking José Cândido with him, drove to the surprised supplier and saw to it that the truck was filled at once. Sandra Cavalcanti, after she became social services secretary, arrived one day with Lacerda and Major Osório at the site of a Vila Isabel district construction project begun in a previous administration. The contractor, explaining the delay, said that the contractors association, in determining who would bid for each project, had assigned him the Vila Isabel project, but, as it was a money loser, he was concentrating on other projects for which winning bids had come his way thanks to the collusive agreement of the association members. Lacerda told the contractor he was under arrest.[13]

The governor, who checked details and argued to bring about rapid accomplishments, wanted his cabinet members to know about the projects in all the departments. He therefore insisted that every member be present each Wednesday at Guanabara Palace for the cabinet meetings. A few at first complained that the weekly meetings were a waste of time. But, Lacerda said later, the result "was like having an orchestra led by a conductor. And so each instrument did not play all by itself." Broadcaster Raul Brunini, who was elected to the state Constitutional Assembly and joined the cabinet later, says the meetings, also attended sometimes by key legislators, allowed the government to act harmoniously after decisions had been reached. At the meetings, Lacerda called on the cabinet members to discuss what they were doing. Occasionally stimulating discussion by assuming the role of devil's advocate, he was critical of those who failed to express opinions. And he disliked having them present problems without recommending solutions. Often he offered his own recommendations with humility, and he would defer if the arguments against him were strong, as happened not infrequently when Mario Lorenzo Fernandez spoke about finances. In matters of politics, however, it was agreed by all that the opinions of Lacerda were final.[14]

Before assuming the governorship, Lacerda made plans to have the cabinet meet each Thursday in one suburb after another, preferably in a schoolhouse, where the people could bring up problems. The first such meeting, held in December 1960 in the Penha district, attracted four hundred people who spent two hours asking for street paving and better police protection. Soon these meetings came to be held monthly instead of weekly and were attended by only a few cabinet members; after about a year, they were discontinued.[15]

Lacerda delegated authority. This resulted in what Raphael de Almeida Magalhães considers a well-balanced division of the work load. Authority as well as responsibility was passed on to officials who, Lacerda maintained, previously had had neither. He was, he declared in a speech, merely inverting the administrative pyramid, whose apex had been "where the person farthest from the problem had been the only one with the authority to resolve it."[16]

Steps were taken to relieve the governor of the need of signing hundreds of documents each week. Finance Secretary Mario Lorenzo Fernandez, noting Lacerda's fondness of power but dislike of administrative routine, took the first step in this debureaucratization process by arranging that the signatures be limited to those of the administrators responsible for the rulings expressed in the documents.[17]

Lacerda was a longtime advocate of decentralization. He therefore worked with planner Hélio Beltrão to divide the state into twenty-one administrative regions, each to have an administrator to resolve local problems, such as those having to do with small public works, hospital personnel, and the maintenance of streets, school buildings, and hospital buildings. It was hoped that this arrangement, a part of the planned administrative reform, would set back demands of Lacerda's political opponents that Guanabara, like other states, be divided into municipalities, each with a mayor and city council. But the idea of having regional administrators, several of whom were appointed soon after Lacerda became governor, did not appeal to state legislators; they found people turning to the administrators, instead of themselves, to get local problems taken care of.[18]

Governor Lacerda, Enaldo Cravo Peixoto says, "was a very bad politician" because he did not handle legislators tactfully and "refused, absolutely, to take care of any political requests." When Amaral Netto pleaded with the governor to appoint the wife of legislator Samy Jorge to a social services position and thus secure the one vote needed for the passage of key legislation, the governor refused.

Another state legislator, eager to fulfill promises to voters in his district, arranged at Guanabara Palace to obtain an appointment with the governor. Hoping to please Lacerda, he advised that he favored the approval of the governor's accounts, being studied by the legislature; but Lacerda simply told him that if the accounts were in order he would do no one a favor by voting as he proposed whereas if he found them in error he would be a scoundrel to approve them. The legislator then asked for a couple of specific water and paving improvements in his district, leading Lacerda to declare that he was tired of talking with legislators who always ignored the momentous projects. Finally the legislator made three further requests. Lacerda replied that he was insulted by them and would do a greater favor than grant them: "I'm going to forget that you are capable of speaking of such things. Good day."[19]

When a superior court judge came to Guanabara Palace with two beauty pageant contestants whom he wanted to have photographed with the governor, Lacerda told him that he would give him time if he had government matters to discuss but not for being photographed with the two young women. Lacerda was equally uncordial when advised of an unexpected visit by a group of national UDN leaders, among them Governor Cid Sampaio and Congressmen Ernâni Sátiro and Rondon Pacheco. He ordered that they be told he had no time for them but that if they wanted to talk with him they could come to the palace at 6:30 the next morning and ride with him while he inspected construction works. Taken aback, they finally decided to follow the governor's suggestion despite the inconvenient hour.[20]

With his staff at Guanabara Palace, the governor was often critical. He rewrote documents he had ordered to be prepared, filling pages with rapidly written corrections. Poor expression or the use of inappropriate words could give him a fit, and it was sometimes difficult to predict what tone he wanted to use. Edgar Flexa Ribeiro, son of the education secretary and the most successful of the document writers, found that he might achieve a moderate final product by presenting a draft representing the furious side of Lacerda. "I asked you to prepare an answer and you give me a crisis," Lacerda once said to Edgar, who had been warned by Raphael de Almeida Magalhães that a brutal reply to a message from the legislature would complicate relations with the opposition during a budget dispute.[21]

Budgets, always important, had in the past been inventories of expenses, listed without any connection with projects being undertaken. Perhaps for that reason the 1,357-meter vehicle tunnel for traffic between the Catumbi and Laranjeiras districts remained unfinished after fourteen years. In any event, Lacerda wanted a different form of budget, and therefore Hélio Beltrão asked José Roberto Rego Monteiro to prepare a budget that would serve as a working plan, uniting for each sector all the pertinent items according to projects, and providing explanations of the administration's objectives. Rego Monteiro and his team of twenty-five young men gave Guanabara the first "program budget" adopted by a Brazilian state. It may have displeased some oppositionist legislators, accustomed to tradition and citing what they claimed to be the law, but it pleased the commission of state finance secretaries, working with veteran industrialist Valentim Bouças to standardize accounting and budgets. The commission, with the cooperation of the Guanabara team, produced what eventually became Federal Law 4,320 of March 17, 1964, requiring Guanabara-type "program budgets" for "the union, states, municipalities, and federal district."[22]

The budget for 1961, inherited by Lacerda, was not adequate for the staff he wanted and had so drastically reduced what was available for education, health, water, and transport that he described it as having been adopted "with hatred" by the unfriendly Municipal Chamber. To get pilot Wilson Lopes Machado on the staff, Lacerda telephoned the director of Panair and arranged for Machado to continue receiving his paychecks from the airline in return for little or no piloting. Machado attributes the traditionally small budget for the governor's staff to a past lack of interest in paychecks by men who accepted appointments to be in a position to make money in immoral ways.[23]

One can imagine Lacerda's displeasure to learn, after he became governor, that one of his cousins was telling builders that he could arrange to have the Lacerda administration modify the building code

if they would pay him a large sum, a part of which, he said untruth-
fully, was to go to Carlos' sister Vera. The cousin, who had been
among those who loitered in Guanabara Palace, was barred by Carlos
from returning there.[24]

For the sake of his family, Carlos decided not to reside in Guanabara
Palace. Feeling that the children of Vargas had not benefited from
palace life, he said to his niece Lygia, "Look at Vargas, who put his
children in the palace." Lygia, daughter of Carlos' sister Vera, had
found Carlos a "marvelous uncle" when she had been younger but,
with his election to the governorship, he was formal rather than
warm and assumed a watchdog role in the family. "Don't you know
us?" Vera felt compelled to ask him.[25] So careful was Carlos lest his
family embarrass him that he sometimes had family squabbles.

It was upsetting to Olga to be told by her son on the day he took
office that she had to relinquish her undemanding job in the municipal government. Not much later, when a job application was acted
upon favorably by Hélio Beltrão because it came to him apparently
recommended by Olga, Carlos was not tactful in cautioning his
mother, who had not been involved, and he ordered Beltrão to have
the appointment canceled both because, as he explained, his mother
would get no rest if it were felt that he favored applications made in
her name, and because the man she was said to have recommended
had arranged in 1948, on orders of Mayor Ângelo Mendes de Morais,
to have Lacerda brutally beaten up by thugs. Carlos annoyed his
family somewhat later when he went to open a branch of the state
bank and was told by the director of the ceremonies to expect a
pleasant surprise. The director proudly pulled aside a curtain, revealing a portrait of Olga, and declared her the patroness for the occasion.
Carlos was angry, provoking his outspoken sister Vera to ask, "Do
you think you are the only decent person in the family?"[26]

"The one thing I shall not give up," Olga said to Carlos, "is my
right to a box seat in the Municipal Theater," and Carlos saw to it that
this privilege was available to her. For Letícia the only advantages of
being the governor's wife consisted in participating with the family
at showings of movies at Guanabara Palace and spending weekends
with the family at the retreat house reserved for the governor on
Brocoió Island.[27] In other respects the new situation was trying.

Letícia played the role of the governor's wife in a patient way and
never put on airs.[28] She was pretty, had a captivating smile and good
intuition, and was held in affection by the governor's associates. She
had close friends among them and their wives, and liked to play cards
with them. If she sometimes seemed withdrawn, it was attributed to

her less than robust health and her hearing problem: the constant noise in one ear and a hypersensitivity to loud sounds. Because she suffered in this way, Carlos grieved.

Carlos, who liked to buy his wife dresses and was observant about clothes, kept his eye on what Letícia wore; before they went out, she might have to try on three or four outfits before he was satisfied.[29] He could seldom give information about whether he would be eating at home or not, or whether he would be bringing acquaintances to the apartment. Unexpectedly a crowd might arrive at a very late hour. Letícia, tired, might say she did not feel well and retire to bed.[30]

Among the close friends of Carlos and Letícia were Joaquim and Candinha da Silveira. Joaquim, who ran the vast Bangu Textile Company together with his brother Guilherme, had a splendid beach home in Cabo Frio, and there the Lacerdas, around the end of each year, spent a few days with the Silveiras and other friends, such as Roberto and Maria Abreu Sodré. Carlos had never learned to swim, but he loved steering boats and fishing. He also enjoyed, as Letícia did not, heated discussions, and these he could often find at the Silveiras'. Joaquim, deeply interested in Lacerda's career, liked to bring him together with leading politicians.

6. The Constitutional Assembly versus the Municipal Chamber (October 1960–August 1961)

Of the thirty members of the Guanabara Constitutional Assembly, elected on October 3, fourteen belonged to parties supporting Lacerda: nine seats were won by the UDN, two by the PTN (Partido Trabalhista Nacional), two by the PR (Partido Republicano), and one by the PDC (Partido Democrata Cristão). This left a majority in the hands of the opposition: the PTB held six seats, the PSD four, with two each in the hands of the PSB (Partido Socialista Brasileiro), PSP (Partido Social Progressista), and PRT (Partido Rural Trabalhista).

Therefore Lacerda, before going abroad on October 28, met at his Praia do Flamengo apartment with future *udenista constituintes* to discuss an alliance. The group abandoned the idea of having the UDN's erudite Aliomar Baleeiro become assembly president and agreed on the PSD's Lopo Coelho, who had occupied government posts under President Dutra and could provide two assembly votes besides his own and thus give the incoming administration a majority.[1] But it was a tenuous majority, especially as several UDN assemblymen were known to be quite independent. Problems therefore lay ahead for government leader Amaral Netto, a violently anti-Kubitschek journalist who had run for the assembly on the UDN ticket with enormous success.

The PTB, unable to get the election of Lacerda annulled for what it called fraud, urged its constitutional assemblymen to turn to the unions, factories, and *favelas* to gain popular backing for limiting his term to two years instead of the five stipulated by the San Tiago Dantas Law, adopted by the federal government in April 1960 to create the new state.[2] The Constitutional Assembly would have to handle this matter along with others, such as the possible division of the state into municipalities and the status of the six-thousand-man Military Police of the old Federal District. In October 1960, Kubitschek's justice minister, Armando Falcão, sought to "federalize" that troop, which, like the Rio fire brigade, was to continue receiving its pay from the federal government. Military Police officers wrote Lacerda a letter saying they would agree to nothing but "federalization." Lacerda took the position that Falcão's proposal was unconstitutional.[3]

While Temístocles Cavalcanti, a *udenista* elected to the assembly, worked on a draft of a constitution, a heated discussion arose about the future of the Rio Municipal Chamber, which had been elected in October 1958 to serve until January 1963. According to the San Tiago Dantas Law, the Municipal Chamber was to be the sole possessor of the legislative powers until the constitution was promulgated, and then its fifty municipal councilmen were to join the thirty constitutional assemblymen to form a new state legislature. Lacerda, opposed to this and other stipulations enacted by Congress, felt that the law was "a crazy thing" despite the talent of its author, Professor and PTB congressman Francisco San Tiago Dantas.[4]

The Municipal Chamber, living up to its reputation as "the gilded cage," interested only in "the gravy train," passed a law, just before the October 1960 election, which increased from 6 to 15 billion cruzeiros (from $30 to $75 million) the annual payroll for the ninety thousand employees of the state. The salary law would leave nothing for public services and threatened to bankrupt the state, and therefore on October 24 Sette Câmara vetoed much of it, thereby reducing the additional wage burden from 9 billion to around 4 billion cruzeiros. Even if the vetoes were upheld, Mario Lorenzo Fernandez wrote the traveling Lacerda, Guanabara would have a deficit in 1961.[5]

The vetoes were rejected by the Municipal Chamber on November 7. Lawyers Aliomar Baleeiro and Temístocles Cavalcanti then sought a court ruling to annul the rejection, and Amaral Netto called on the people to close ranks against the municipal councilmen, who, he declared, legislated on behalf of themselves. Auro de Moura Andrade (PSD, São Paulo), government leader in the Senate, said that if the new state could afford such a hefty wage increase, it probably did not need the 3 billion cruzeiros that the federal government had resolved to furnish it to help it get started.[6]

When the old Federal District had disappeared back in April 1960, Muncipal Council members Dulce Magalhães and Gladstone Chaves de Melo, associated with the PDC (Christian Democratic Party), had maintained that the change made the Municipal Council extinct. Gladstone, a professor of Portuguese and a favorite of Catholic leaders and voters, was elected in October to the Constitutional Assembly, where he continued to advocate that thesis.

Baleeiro drafted a Constitutional Act, to be adopted by the assemblymen, which would declare that the mandates of the municipal councilmen had expired on October 3 and that the assemblymen, elected on that day, were to have legislative powers. Oppositionists in the Constitutional Assembly, such as Roland Corbisier (PTB), Luís Gonzaga da Gama Filho (PSD), José Saldanha Coelho (PTB), and Waldemar Viana (PRT) maintained that the Constitutional Act was unconstitutional. School teacher Lígia Lessa Bastos, *udenista* municipal councilwoman elected to the Constitutional Assembly, shared this view and angered Amaral Netto by saying that the supporters of the Constitutional Act were "useful innocents" at the service of the Rio-Light Company.[7]

Supporters of the Constitutional Act, including the Brazilian Institute of Lawyers, called the San Tiago Dantas Law unconstitutional because, they said, it was improper interference by Congress. They denounced the "incredibly bad language" used in the "gilded cage" and broadcast to homes on the state's Rádio Roquete Pinto. Catholic writer Gustavo Corção called the "gilded cage" an "excrescence."[8]

Lawyers Heráclito Fontoura Sobral Pinto and Hariberto de Miranda Jordão agreed to defend the Municipal Chamber. But on December 15 the judge of the second district court in Rio issued an injunction, requested by assemblymen Raul Brunini (UDN) and Hugo Ramos Filho (PSD), upholding Sette Câmara's vetoes. The judge ruled that, in view of the state's limited economic strength, the Municipal Chamber had "abused" its power.[9]

Governor Lacerda, claiming that the injunction spelled the end of the Municipal Chamber, closed down Rádio Roquete Pinto and vowed that the councilmen would receive no more paychecks from the state. These developments, described by *O Globo* as "the first great victories of the Carioca people," led the *Diário Carioca* to write that Lacerda was an *enfant terrible* who enjoyed producing chaos.

After oppositionists, in a stormy session of the Constitutional Assembly, called for federal intervention to prevent a Lacerda dictatorship, Amaral Netto tried to explain that "what is bad is not the broadcasting but the expressions, that even prostitutes would not use, on a station legally established for recreational and cultural purposes." However, on December 27 the Municipal Chamber obtained an injunction that allowed Rádio Roquete Pinto to resume broadcasting.[10]

Two days later the Constitutional Assembly put the Constitutional Act to a vote. As neither Lígia Lessa Bastos nor presiding officer Lopo Coelho participated in the roll call, the result was sixteen votes in favor, the exact number needed for the "urgent" passage of a special measure. Twelve assemblymen voted against the majority. Within the Municipal Chamber, "the Lacerda gang" was assailed in violent speeches while a crowd, demonstrating outside, hurled insults and rotten eggs at the "gilded cage."[11]

In Brasília in January 1961, Rio municipal councilmen and their lawyers turned to Justice Minister Armando Falcão and the Supreme Court to have the Kubitschek government intervene in Guanabara to protect the Municipal Chamber. They were partially successful. Despite the arguments of Dario de Almeida Magalhães, Alcino Salazar, and UDN Congressman Adauto Lúcio Cardoso, Supreme Court Justice Ari Franco issued a temporary injunction against the Constitutional Act until the full Supreme Court, which was about to take a two-month vacation, reached a verdict. The Communist *Novos Rumos*, well pleased, explained that Lacerda's severe comments about the decision revealed that his government was fascist. In the Constitutional Assembly, Corbisier said that Lacerda's comments made him unworthy of heading the state, and he joined Saldanha Coelho in criticizing Lacerda for allowing the police to force Álvaro Moreyra, a seventy-two-year-old writer, to testify about his Communist connections and activities. Lacerda, who had benefited from Moreyra's friendship in his youth, called Corbisier a former fascist and explained that the police were merely trying to close an investigation of Moreyra that had been opened in 1957.[12]

In Brasília for the Quadros inauguration, Lacerda called on Supreme Court Minister Ari Franco and pleaded his case. But Franco remained unconvinced. Nor would he alter his position even though Quadros' prosecuting attorney asked that the injunction be set aside because the new government was withdrawing from the case, begun by the Kubitschek government, against Guanabara's Constitutional Act.[13]

In the Guanabara Constitutional Assembly in February and March the opposition presented over one thousand proposals. One would make the Municipal Council the legislature for the city and another would allow Municipal Council members to hold their seats until 1965. Still another would give the state legislature a staff of over a thousand, far in excess of the three hundred considered ideal by the assembly's constitutional commission.[14]

Thorny matters were handled on the night of March 16–17. The constitution writers ruled that the question of dividing Guanabara into municipalities should be determined by a plebiscite on April 21, 1963, and that, at least until then, municipal taxes were to go to the state. To protect the state finances, the assemblymen resolved that if the legislature should increase expenditures beyond those in the governor's budget, it would have to enact laws providing an equivalent increase of income. The governor was to serve for five years.

The Municipal Chamber was abolished by a 14-13 vote, with Lígia Lessa Bastos and Lopo Coelho again abstaining, and with the PTN's Paulo Alberto Monteiro de Barros, who had declared himself independent of the majority, voting against the Municipal Chamber. The Constitutional Assembly turned itself into the state legislature, to serve until replaced by a group of at least fifty members, who would be elected in October 1962.[15]

Municipal councilmen, meeting that night, called the majority of the assemblymen "prostitutes" and passed laws benefiting the city employees. Defaming Lacerda, they vowed to press their case in Brasília. In an official note, which Lopo Coelho ignored, they asked the assembly how it would handle the incorporation of municipal councilmen into the new legislature, and they advised that, since they would form the majority, they would choose new officers. The PTB foresaw the ejection of the councilmen from their "gilded cage," and therefore Assemblyman Lutero Vargas, head of the Carioca PTB and son of the late president, offered them the use of his party's office space.[16]

"Cidade Maravilhosa," now the official anthem of the state, was played by a Military Police band in Tiradentes Palace on March 27 during the ceremony promulgating the constitution. On the next day the new legislature voted to terminate payments for the councilmen, cut off utility services of the Municipal Chamber, and transfer to the new state government the thirty-six vehicles used by the councilmen. Orders by Lacerda ended the publication of the municipal *Diário Oficial* and again closed down Rádio Roquete Pinto. After police sealed off the Municipal Chamber, over six hundred members of the municipal council staff reported to work for the thirty-member legislature at Tiradentes Palace, thus adhering to a provision of the new constitution and defying a resolution of the Municipal Chamber.

Some of the municipal councilmen also appeared at Tiradentes Palace, but late in April a judge of the state's top Justice Tribunal issued an order against the incorporation of the Municipal Chamber into the legislature.[17]

With the promulgation of the constitution, Lacerda was able to present his plan, which Hélio Beltrão helped draw up, for reforming the state administration by giving it regional administrations, new secretaryships, and new state-run companies. This reform plan, like other projects of the governor, remained for so long without action by the legislature that Lacerda spoke on television late in July 1961 to complain that many legislators, concerned with personal grudges, held up work on which Guanabara's development depended. "I am not fighting the assembly," he said, "but I want to prevent it from becoming a new Municipal Chamber." The television speech criticized state legislator Afonso Arinos de Melo Franco Filho, the foreign minister's son who had been elected on the UDN ticket, and provoked a stormy legislative session.[18]

That the legislature might be reaching "the level of the old Municipal Chamber" was a fear expressed in July by the PSD's Hugo Ramos Filho following a move by "independent" Paulo Alberto Monteiro de Barros to impeach the governor. The impeachment proposal, which was eventually withdrawn, originally had the backing of Assemblyman Saldanha Coelho and Osny Duarte Pereira of the Guanabara Justice Tribunal. The judge was vexed at Lacerda's negative reaction to his decision that 182 girls, not 70, be admitted to the Institute of Education, a secondary school. Lacerda called Osny Duarte's ruling "a continuation of the Communist plan to set the executive against the judiciary in order to depose the government."[19]

The full Justice Tribunal, meeting late in July, ruled against Osny Duarte. Also, by a 29 to 2 vote (Duarte's being one of the two), it rejected the claims of the Municipal Council. Sobral Pinto, who had defended the Municipal Council before the state Justice Tribunal, took the case to the Supreme Court, but there in January 1962 lawyer Alcino Salazar won a verdict, by a 6 to 3 vote, that finally assured the demise of the "gilded cage."[20]

Lacerda and Sobral Pinto had been closely associated in the 1940s and early 1950s, with the lawyer representing the frequently sued journalist. Both were strong-willed and the break between them, formalized by a terse letter from Lacerda, had occurred in November 1955 after Sobral, supporter of Kubitschek, objected to Lacerda's vehement campaign against Kubitschek's inauguration. In June 1961, during the judicial battle about the Municipal Chamber, a son of Sobral committed suicide and Lacerda, attending the funeral, was moved to seek a reconciliation. At the end of the funeral, Lacerda asked his secretary to approach Sobral and say "the governor wants to take you home, pay you a brief visit, and leave you there; will you accept?" The lawyer accepted.[21]

7. The Water Crisis: "An Infernal Week" (March 1961)

A good example of Lacerda handling his executive post occurred early in March 1961 when large parts of Rio had no water because a torrent of rain inundated and paralyzed the five pump motors at the water treatment plant near the Guandu River, over 40 kilometers west of the city. This meant the cutoff of 450,000 liters a day, supplied through a leaky old distribution network by the so-called "first Guandu project."[1] Public Works Secretary Laviola and Water Department Director Homero Pedrosa went to the Guandu pump room to try to speed up the drying and cleaning of the pump motors.

The governor declared a state of public calamity, arranged emergency service by all the water trucks that were not broken down, and even managed to borrow water trucks from São Paulo, thanks to Governor Carlos Alberto de Carvalho Pinto.[2] Then he rushed to Brasília to confer with Jânio Quadros about the massive assistance he felt was owed the long-neglected city. Already the governor had explained to Industry and Commerce Minister Artur Bernardes Filho that the Cariocas, whose tax payments to the central government were exceeded only by those of the Paulistas, should be able to count on the Quadros administration to finance a thermoelectric plant and invest in a new steel enterprise, to be known as Companhia Siderúrgica da Guanabara (COSIGUA).[3]

Quadros, with whom Lacerda now spent four hours, agreed to provide an immediate credit of 424 million cruzeiros for handling the water emergency. And he spoke of making 4 billion cruzeiros ($17 million) available over two years to help build the "new Guandu" 43-kilometer underground aqueduct, more than $3^1/_2$ meters in diameter. Sette Câmara, before turning the governorship over to Lacerda, had earmarked for the start of the project 1.3 billion cruzeiros of the 3 billion committed by the Kubitschek administration to assist the new state.[4]

Lacerda told Quadros of his plan to create the Companhia Progresso do Estado da Guanabara (COPEG) to encourage and help finance firms interested in starting enterprises in the state, whereupon the president offered to have the federal government (a large Guanabara landowner) invest 900 million cruzeiros in COPEG in the form of real estate. Quadros also listened, not for the first time, to Lacerda's tale of his controversies with the Rio-Light group. The group had sued the state for not allowing adequate streetcar fares and was contesting the governor's charge that the equipment of a streetcar subsidiary, whose franchise recently reverted to the state, was in "inoperable" condition. The group, furthermore, was appealing to the courts to nullify the state's intervention into the affairs of the telephone company, Companhia Telefônica Brasileira (CTB). Lacerda discussed with Quadros a plan to form a new state telephone company in Guanabara. He told the press, after leaving the president, that in this way "no one will contribute to enrich Rio-Light but only to get telephones." Returning to Rio with satisfactory promises, he found students marching in protest to his administration, and the opposition press condemning his failure to provide water.[5]

The governor spent three days and two nights at the scene of the water problem, some of the time in a helicopter and more at the pump house and other installations. At the offices of the treatment plant on March 8 he was visited by a delegation of state legislators. Showing them the damaged motors, he ordered the engineers to solve the problem with no more delay. But an argument took place the next morning as to whether to try to use a motor that had been worked on in the shops of Rio-Light. Water Department engineers insisted that the motor's low voltage would result in burned coils if it were hooked up, whereas a navy engineer put the chance of failure at only 30 percent.

Disregarding the misgivings of the Guandu engineers and technicians, the governor ordered that the motor be used, with the happy result that water began to flow, after what Lacerda called "an infernal week." He told reporters, however, that he would not leave the scene until all the pumps were working normally.[6]

On March 10 Rio learned of the dismissal of Public Works Secretary Antônio Arlindo Laviola and Water Department Director Homero Pedrosa. Lacerda, who had already been critical of Laviola's work and plans,[7] now complained that these men had "deceived the government and the people" with a "false explanation." Maintaining that the problem had been "a technical failure and not the downpour of rain," he said: "Among other things, I found out that two of the pumps have not been working for a long time. It was all a farce." And he accused Laviola of having persuaded him to lie to the people when he gave assurances, early in the crisis, that all possible steps were being taken to remedy it.[8]

Laviola, in a letter relinquishing his post, told Lacerda that he had "great qualities and incorrigible defects," and compared him to

"Niagara Falls—a magnificent potential, wasting energy." He mentioned the chaotic condition in which he had found his "poor, despised secretaryship" and the "intrigue, treachery, and barbarousness" he had encountered. Journalists David Nasser and Danton Jobim wrote that he was unjustly dismissed.[9]

At Lacerda's request, air force Colonel Francisco Américo Fontenelle persuaded Brigadeiro Hélio Costa to become the new secretary of public works. Fontenelle, coordinator of transportation, also had a suggestion for the governor. Well impressed by work being done in transport by engineer Luiz Roberto Veiga de Brito, he recommended him for the newly vacant post of water department director even though Veiga Brito (as he was called) was unfamiliar with hydraulics.

The thirty-two-year-old Veiga Brito, unaware of Fontenelle's recommendation, was surprised to receive a phone call at night from the governor, whom he did not know personally, asking him to drive with him to Guandu. Veiga Brito had been miffed by the governor's depreciating remarks on television about engineers ("I prefer railroad switchmen," Lacerda had said); but he accepted and spent all night at the governor's side. Brought home at 6:00 A.M., he had no idea why he had been shown Guandu. Hoping to get some sleep, he was aroused an hour later by another phone call from Lacerda, who asked him to return to Guandu with him, this time by helicopter from Guanabara Palace. Veiga Brito, accepting again, began to wonder about the governor's mental condition.

When the helicopter was over the Bangu district, the young civil engineer was stunned to learn that he was to be the water department director. He said it would be presumptuous for him to follow Lacerda's order that he inform Hélio Costa that he was assuming the post; but Lacerda, knowing that Costa had accepted Fontenelle's suggestion, said: "Do as I say."

At the water department, Veiga Brito found resignation letters from all the engineers. Learning that their hostility had been aroused by Lacerda's public denouncements of their work, he offered to gain Lacerda's goodwill for them. With trepidation he called on the governor, who was preparing to give a television speech, and asked that it include words of appreciation for the engineers. But the governor, in his only reference to the situation in his speech, said: "As for the engineers who don't want to work but only request their last paychecks, these I shall give them."

Veiga Brito gained time. Two weeks later he arranged to take the governor on an inspection trip, and, after it was over, took him to the water department offices. "This is a trap," Lacerda said with a smile when he found that all the engineers had been assembled. "For me and for our work," Veiga Brito said, "it is fundamental that we have your opinion of the water department engineers." The governor was cordial, which was probably just as well in view of the new Guandu project that lay ahead. He said: "From what I have seen today, and from what I have been hearing about the difficulties, I appreciate that the engineers have made good use of the small resources put at their disposal."[10]

8. Salesman for Guanabara's Plan of Action (March–June 1961)

Vastly more satisfying to Lacerda than Laviola's performance was the work of Education Secretary Carlos Flexa Ribeiro. With the opening of schools in March 1961, it was no longer necessary to turn away 110,000 children, out of half a million, because of a lack of space. The prompt addition of fifty or sixty rooms to existing schoolhouses helped, but the key to Flexa Ribeiro's success was the increased use of the schoolhouses. While the children would attend school five days a week, as before, the schools would operate six days a week and, when possible, would receive three daily shifts of students instead of two.

In January 1961 Flexa Ribeiro went to the Constitutional Assembly to explain his plan to have the weekday holiday, formerly observed on Thursdays in accordance with French tradition, fall on different days for different school groups. Even oppositionist Gonzaga da Gama Filho, a former education secretary, was well impressed. The changes were so effective that it was possible to announce the availability of unfilled places in schools, and Flexa Ribeiro was able to turn to the enforcement of legislation making parents responsible if their children were not being educated.[1]

During the first months of the program, Lacerda and Flexa Ribeiro made a school out of the building that had housed Vargas' personal guardsmen near Guanabara Palace. Lacerda named the school after Anne Frank, the Jewish girl who had perished at the hands of the Nazis and whose diary, when published, so moved Lacerda that he painted an "Imaginary Portrait of Anne Frank." The choice of the name may have helped his relations with the Jews, many of whom had resented his articles, written in 1948, against Zionism and the creation of the nation of Israel. But later Lacerda called the honoring of Anne Frank at that particular place a "blunder" because it was in front of the German embassy.[2]

The lot of children was bettered also by pediatrician Marcelo Garcia, the longtime friend of Lacerda's who took over the secretaryship of health and found it almost entirely abandoned. During his campaign for the eradication of infantile paralysis, 93 percent of the state's children between the ages of six months and four years received the Sabin polio vaccine. The immunization program, organized in August 1961, was carried out with the help of volunteers. The armed forces supplied helicopters for reaching *favelas*. In January 1962, after 438,000 children had received the vaccine in a ten-day period, Garcia announced plans to immunize the 80,000 children who would be born in the state each year as well as the children in out-of-state municipalities that adjoined the state.

Russian-born Albert Sabin, who cooperated with the campaign, was taken to Guanabara Palace for a courtesy call on the governor. Lacerda, who enjoyed conversing with successful professionals, turned the fifteen-minute appointment into a two-hour session in which he discussed international politics. The governor's knowledge, courtesy, and sense of humor led the bacteriologist to remark later to Garcia that he had never met a man with so much intelligence and charm.[3]

It was hoped that Guanabara's high incidence of typhoid fever, attributed to pollution, would be reduced by the sewer construction program that was undertaken on an ambitious scale. The service fees for sewerage, like the users' fees for water, had remained constant in terms of cruzeiros since 1947 and therefore, on account of inflation, were practically nothing in 1961. Lacerda resolved to set realistic rates, which, as he pointed out in one of his fund-seeking letters to Industry and Commerce Minister Bernardes Filho, would serve as a basis for servicing the loans he was seeking.[4]

Loans and grants were uppermost on Lacerda's mind in 1961. He appealed everywhere, not overlooking the New York public relations firm of Joshua B. Powers, whom he had known in the Inter American Press Association. Powers, in reply to Lacerda's inquiries about money for slum clearance and schoolhouses, wrote that Brazil's credit was poor but that financially sound projects might attract loans from American insurance companies.[5]

Lacerda, seeking funds for hospital equipment and the proposed steel plant, negotiated with Germans. He appealed to the International Cooperation Administration of the United States for Point IV program money to advance education, water supply, sewerage, and low-cost housing (for inhabitants of *favelas* that could not be urbanized). The Inter-American Development Bank (IDB) was approached, and after Lacerda conferred in Rio with its president, Felipe Herrera, the *Tribuna da Imprensa* reported optimistically on what Guanabara could expect to receive to help the *favelados*, water supply, and the steel plant.[6]

Losing no opportunities to remind the Quadros administration of what it should do for the new state, Lacerda was likely to point out that money deposited by suffering Cariocas in the Caixa Econômica Federal was used to construct a hotel in Brasília and carry out other projects of no benefit to Guanabara. He argued that the Bank of Brazil and the National Economic Development Bank (BNDE) had over-looked the former Federal District. After COSIGUA President An-tônio Guedes Muniz recommended using the Santa Cruz area for both steel production and iron ore exportation, Lacerda sent Hélio Beltrão and Raphael de Almeida Magalhães to discuss these ideas, as well as power, with Mines and Energy Minister João Agripino, who, Lacerda has said, was a good congressman but knew absolutely nothing about mines and energy.[7]

Quadros, giving his first collective press interview in mid-April, promised federal financial assistance for Guanabara's power and *favela* problems. But by this time the impatient governor wanted more than promises from the president. On April 19, at the closing session of a convention of the Carioca UDN, he denounced the federal gov-ernment for "forgetting the Carioca people." Remarking that "the vision of the national executive must have become befogged by the solitude of Brasília," he declared that "the federal government has not complied with its commitments." He repeated his complaint the next day in a talk with Quadros at Laranjeiras Palace, the Rio abode and office of the nation's chief executive. The president promised to review the situation with the governor in the near future.[8]

In anticipation of this next meeting, Lacerda ordered his team to prepare documents for the presentation of Guanabara's "Plan of Ac-tion." On the part of the federal government, the plan called for port repairs and the alteration of rail lines contemplated in the subway system project. It also required federal assistance to help develop water, sewers, hospitals, education, COPEG, low-cost housing, and the collection and industrialization of garbage. Price tags, put on each item, called for a total of more than 10 billion cruzeiros ($40 million) from the federal government in four years. Besides, the BNDE was asked to supply money for a thermoelectric plant in Guanabara and the Funil power plant in Rio state. And the Quadros administration was asked to support Guanabara's application to the Inter-American Development Bank for $10 million to help with the *favela* problem.[9]

Quadros, receiving the stack of documents from Lacerda and Hélio Beltrão, said that final decisions would be reached at a conference he would hold in Rio in June with the governors of São Paulo, Guana-bara, and Rio states—the fourth of a series of regional meetings. To assist Guanabara with its presentations at the conference, to be called the Fourth Governors' Meeting, the president ordered Labor Minister Francisco Carlos de Castro Neves and BNDE President José Vicente de Faria Lima to establish task forces.[10]

The Quadros administration, also, was desperate for funds. It sent Walter Moreira Salles and Roberto Campos abroad to obtain foreign financial commitments and the postponement of due dates of past loans that could not be repaid. Finance Minister Clemente Mariani went to Washington, where, according to press reports, he received generous promises. Before he made his trip, he saw his daughter Maria Clara become the bride of Sérgio Lacerda, in a ceremony attended by three thousand, including cabinet ministers and the wife and mother of Quadros.[11]

While Lacerda's study groups prepared for the Fourth Governors' Meeting, the state Superintendência de Urbanização e Saneamento (SURSAN) announced that work was nearing completion on the 1,357-meter Catumbi-Laranjeiras vehicle tunnel and that over a billion cruzeiros would be needed for property expropriations to allow good traffic flow at both ends. Much more money would be required for the ambitious plan of engineer Marcos Tamoyo to construct a north-south roadway, some of it through rock beneath the statue of Christ on Corcovado Peak. One of this project's north-south tunnel sections was to connect the Rio Comprido district with the Cosme Velho district, a distance of 720 meters, and the other was to make the 2,040-meter connection between Cosme Velho and the Lagoa districts. Both connections would consist of parallel tunnels, with three-lane traffic in each, and therefore over 5,500 meters of tunnel evacuation would be necessary. This four-year plan to construct "the longest urban tunnel in the world" was described by the *Tribuna da Imprensa* in June 1961 as requiring 3.5 billion cruzeiros ($14 million), not including the cost of expropriating property for appropriate viaducts. The *Tribuna* wrote that with the completion of the work, invaluable for solving traffic congestion, residents in the south would be able to reach Maracanã Stadium "in three minutes." Lacerda said that bathers in the north would be able to reach Copacabana Beach speedily.[12]

None of the costs of vehicle tunnels, among them the proposed 220-meter Major Vaz Tunnel in Copacabana, were included in the program of assistance prepared for the Fourth Governors' Meeting. Nor were plans for more telephones or the costs of major hydroelectric plants scheduled for construction outside the state. Nevertheless, Lacerda and his cabinet came up with a book of projects requiring 22 billion cruzeiros in federal assistance as well as government support for applications to be made abroad for $87.8 million (22 billion cruzeiros). The largest items were for water, sewers, and an imported plant to industrialize garbage. In the case of water and sewers, the Inter-American Development Bank was to be asked to loan half the costs, with repayment guaranteed by the planned increases in users' fees.[13]

For the governors' meeting, held at the Foreign Ministry's Itamaraty Palace on June 29 and 30, the three participating states put up stands where descriptions of projects were accompanied by maps and pictures. Quadros, on his arrival, listened to Enaldo Cravo Peixoto, SURSAN's director of sewerage and sanitation, explain the propaganda at the Guanabara stand. After the president joined governors, cabinet ministers, and government bank presidents at the speakers' table, Lacerda opened the proceedings with a speech of welcome.

An early decision, made by Mines and Energy Minister João Agripino, was for the construction of a hydroelectric plant at Estreito, near the Furnas power project, to take care of Guanabara's future needs. More immediate power needs were to be covered by an authorization, approved by Quadros, for running a transmission line from São Paulo's Cubatão plant to Rio.

Although Quadros said the federal government lacked resources for taking care of all the projects of the three states, by the end of the two-day meeting the vast majority had been approved. "Guanabara," the *Tribuna* wrote, "will have the plants it needs for industrializing garbage and expanding its electricity system, and will be able to take care of its *favelas* and sewage; it can count on the endorsement of the central government for necessary financings and is going to have the indispensable monetary assistance that it requested for solving the problems it cannot solve alone." Lacerda told the Cariocas that 185 projects for Guanabara, about 95 percent of those submitted, had been approved, bringing the promised financial assistance to more than 16 billion cruzeiros ($60 million).[14]

Among the approved educational projects was one giving a television channel to Rádio Roquete Pinto. Lacerda, wanting to turn Roquete Pinto into a broadcaster of courses of instruction for seventy-five thousand listeners, had vetoed a bill of the Legislative Assembly to have the assembly debates broadcast on the radio station. In a victory for Amaral Netto, just before the governors' meeting, the assembly had failed to achieve the two-thirds majority vote for overriding the veto. But then federal Congressman Tenório Cavalcanti, popular in the Rio *favelas*, had announced that he would put his radio station in Rio state at the service of the opposition members in the Guanabara legislature.[15]

During an intermission of the Fourth Governors' Meeting, Quadros took Lacerda to Laranjeiras Palace, ordered a drink, and spoke, Lacerda tells us, more or less as follows: "Carlos, are you finding it possible to govern Guanabara? Are you able to get anything done with that Legislative Assembly?" Lacerda admitted that many of the assemblymen were unprepared for the work and put their local concerns ahead of the general interest, making things difficult. And he told the president that "they charge prices for their votes." "But," he added, "the fact of having a popular mandate, of being able to turn to the people, and the fear that the assemblymen have of a denouncement to the people, allow some containment of greediness."

Quadros observed, "[José de] Magalhães Pinto cannot govern Minas Gerais, and Juracy [Magalhães] cannot do so in Bahia, and Aluísio [Alves] cannot do so in Rio Grande do Norte." Then the president confided: "I have the impression that it is going to be very difficult to govern Brazil with this Congress." Lacerda pointed out that Quadros was popular. Besides, the governor said, the president could count on the backing of the army.

"You know," Jânio said, "when I had the marines disembark the other day in Recife, to break up a student strike, it brought a broad smile to the face of Navy Minister Sílvio Heck."[16]

9. Criticizing the President's Foreign Policy (April–August 1961)

Quadros had been president barely a week when it was reported that Brazil would follow a "new line" in international affairs, adopting an "independent foreign policy" that would mean renewing diplomatic relations with the Soviet Union and "officially recognizing the continental China of Mao Zedong." Quickly diplomatic relations were established with Hungary, Rumania, and Bulgaria. To please the Soviet Union, steps were taken to terminate relations with non-Communist diplomats who claimed to represent Lithuania, Latvia, and Estonia. Newspaper publisher João Ribeiro Dantas was sent on a mission to reach trade agreements with Eastern European countries.[1]

Adolf Berle, a man Vargas had liked to blame for his downfall in 1945, learned something about Brazil's foreign policy when he made a short trip to Brazil late in February 1961. The arrival of this special representative of President Kennedy coincided with the publication in the press of Khrushchev's cable thanking Quadros for a congratulatory message about a Russian achievement in space. The Brazilian people, Khrushchev said, "can count, like others in Latin America, on the backing of the U.S.S.R. in their aspiration to liberate themselves from foreign dependency."

Berle, speaking to Quadros in Brasília about Cuba and the situation in the Caribbean, urged that Brazil join the United States and other members of the Organization of American States in an inter-American action. Quadros made it clear that he would not support this idea. Berle concluded that the Brazilian president planned to use foreign policy to achieve the goodwill of the Brazilian Left, which was displeased with the administration's financial policy. It had been a frank but cordial discussion.[2] However, as soon as Berle returned to Washington, the Brazilian press pictured it as anything but friendly. News items from the presidential palace mentioned that Quadros had refused to shake Berle's hand when he saw him out of his office.

As the unsuccessful Bay of Pigs invasion of Cuba got underway in April, Quadros cited principles of self-determination and expressed his apprehension about the threat to Castro. Lacerda, on the other hand, welcomed the Cuban invasion "as the beginning of the liberty of a people betrayed by a revolutionary transformed into a tyrant." Fidel Castro, he said, threatened the peace and liberty of nations of the continent by "opening the gates of the Americas to Communist infiltration and an occupation by the vanguard of Russian imperialism." In Rio, politicians sympathetic to Castro helped organize a "pro-Cuba" rally in which students and workers participated.[3]

Lacerda, in a message sent to Recife in April for the UDN's Thirteenth National Convention, wrote that the Communists had turned to their arsenal of ideas for poisoning the world and come up with materialism, econometrics, and nationalism, calling them driving forces. He rejected the materialist philosophy for the UDN, which, he wrote, "is and should be a Christian party," and went on to say that it would be absurd to believe that "economics is the basis of everything." Calling nationalism "the most abused word of our times," Lacerda declared, "I am not a nationalist and do not think the UDN is, or I would not be in this party. . . . I consider nationalism, that is, the ideology that seeks to place the nation above everything, a totalitarian notion." Lacerda put Man ahead of the nation, and accused "modern nationalism" of responsibility for wars and conflicts. He backed legal action against the trusts, but said that to use an antitrust position as a pretext for doing away with free enterprise "condemns us to turning the state into our soul and master, and the nation into our idol."

Lacerda wrote that the UDN ought to assume "the duty" of fighting Communism. "Who else can carry it out? Is the problem of man's liberty and dignity a case only for the police?" The PSD, Lacerda wrote, was a conservative party and should oppose Communism; but, he contended, the PSD "does not know what it is conserving besides the privileges of its political clientele." And the PTB, he said, "is today the lodging place of the Communists."

"At the present moment," he told the UDN delegates, "what is called self-determination of Cuba is the right to impose tyranny under a bloody dictatorship and to shoot hundreds of people without any formal charges. . . . Shall we allow the fear of being called *entreguistas* or lackeys of Wall Street to paralyze our conscience to such an extent that we speak of 'American intervention' in Cuba when describing the landing of thousands of Cubans to liberate their land—many of them leaders of the revolution that Fidel Castro deformed?" An independent foreign policy, Lacerda wrote, should be one in which Brazil would tell the world "what the world would like to hear from Brazil, that is, that we are a nation that hates no nation and therefore we disapprove of the campaign of hatred against the United States unleashed by Russia."

"I do not doubt," Lacerda wrote before closing, "that the ideas I seek to outline will be distorted by the propaganda machine mounted in all the press by the Communists and their agents and by those whom Lenin called 'useful idiots.' "[4]

Lacerda did not attend the UDN convention, and it lacked the controversy he had stirred up in previous ones. The delegates, apparently not much moved by his written lecture, expressed their approval of the domestic and foreign policies of Quadros. They gave polite attention to the views of the party's recently formed Bossa-Nova wing of "center-leftists," sympathetic to reforms backed by nationalists; but the delegates chose, as party president and secretary-general, Congressmen Herbert Levy and Ernâni Sátiro, men who warned against "disguised Communism" in the Bossa-Nova program.[5]

Rio Grande do Norte Governor Aluísio Alves decided not to disturb the convention by giving voice to his list of complaints against his predecessor, Dinarte Mariz. And Bahia Governor Juracy Magalhães avoided controversy by withdrawing his plan to explain his reasons for supporting the senatorial candidacy of Kubitschek, to be decided in a special election about to be held in Goiás. Lacerda, who had strong views on the subject, had written outgoing UDN President Magalhães Pinto that he would leave the UDN if it supported the candidacy of Kubitschek, "the greatest enemy of my state of all time" and "a notoriously dishonest politician whose enrichment of himself and his friends is an affront to the nation."[6]

Lacerda's message to the UDN was praised by *O Globo* and *O Estado de S. Paulo* and by Cardinal Jayme de Barros Câmara, the archbishop of Rio. Dom Lourenço de Almeida Prado, influential in bringing Lacerda to Catholicism in 1948, sent the governor a note calling his declaration "the perfect word, the word that needs to be heard." Author Suzanne Labin wrote Lacerda from Paris to say she was "terribly worried" about the pro-Kremlin policy "being followed by your new president."[7]

According to the Communists' *Novos Rumos*, Lacerda's "ultra-reactionary manifesto" revealed once again his fondness of "foreign and domestic forces alien to the interests of the Brazilian people." PTB Congressman Sérgio Magalhães, supporter of pro-Cuba rallies, suggested that the Guanabara governor was working for a coup against Quadros. Therefore Lacerda sent a telegram to UDN Congressman Pedro Aleixo proposing that Sérgio Magalhães, who had almost won the Guanabara gubernatorial election of 1960, be put in an insane asylum. It was, Lacerda told Pedro Aleixo, inexcusable for Sérgio Magalhães to resort to lies to try to separate the governor from the president "at precisely the moment when it is most urgent for us to trust each other so that together we might handle the problems we received in this devastated land." But, he added, the Communists were interested only in intrigue.[8]

When the cultural attaché of the Cuban embassy, Narciso Mora Diaz, sought to exhibit a film about the Bay of Pigs invasion, he was told by journalist Ascendino Leite, head of the Guanabara Censorship Service, that it should first be viewed by the censorship office, a step required of all embassies wishing to show films. Mora went to Ascendino's office, not to make the film available but to insist on receiving explanations so that, he said, the matter could be handled by the highest authorities of Cuba and Brazil. After Ascendino called Mora an impertinent troublemaker and told him to get out, Mora said he would not leave before receiving the explanation he sought. He spoke of his diplomatic immunities and defied Ascendino to arrest him, whereupon Ascendino said he was under arrest and phoned the police. Colonel Carlos Ardovino Barbosa, head of civilian police, arrived and took Mora to the police department in a paddy wagon.

At Itamaraty (Brazil's foreign ministry), the Cuban chargé d'affaires demanded the recognition of Mora's diplomatic immunities; but Itamaraty Secretary-General Vasco Leitão da Cunha said those guarantees for foreign diplomats depended on their complying with Brazilian law. In the meantime Lacerda met with General Siseno Sarmento, Ascendino Leite, and a police representative, with the result that Mora learned he was not under arrest. Told that he was free to leave, Mora said he would await the Cuban chargé d'affaires. Finally he left with him.[9]

Lacerda charged Mora with trying to stir up divergences between the federal and state governments, and expressed the hope that the

Cuban chargé d'affaires, "an audacious troublemaker," would be transferred to Brasília. He refused to accept the resignation of Ascendino Leite.[10] Leitão da Cunha, however, was soon out of his lofty Itamaraty post. After he assisted Roberto Campos' negotiations in West Germany by repeating an earlier Quadros statement that João Dantas had no credentials to sign a protocol with East Germany, a furious Quadros told Afonso Arinos de Melo Franco to fire Leitão da Cunha. When the foreign minister demurred, Quadros told him that a politician must never put his heart above his mind.[11] Fortunately for Afonso Arinos' position, Leitão da Cunha resigned.

"Who said I should be president of Brazil?" Quadros asked Afonso Arinos during their talk. Speaking emotionally, he said that sometimes it is more difficult to stay in office than to leave office. The president was in the same pessimistic mood when he spoke with Raimundo Padilha, head of the congressional foreign relations commission. Padilha, opponent of Quadros' foreign policy, found the president nervous and not much interested in discussing foreign policy. "Some day," Quadros sorrowfully told him, "you may become president of the republic, in which case you should be a very sad man. The job should only be accepted if all the people get on their knees, pleading that you take it."[12]

Afonso Arinos, called to Congress in May to explain Brazil's pro-Cuba policy, delivered a defense that Lacerda declared "was understood perhaps by the president" but not by the foreign minister's "friends and companions, justifiably disturbed by a policy of double talk, subterfuges, and sophisms. We did not wait so many years to reach power in order to turn Brazil over to Russia on the pretext of not turning it over to the United States. I reject the thesis that foreign policy is the monopoly of one man." Quadros, speaking in São Paulo, replied that the constitution placed foreign policy in the president's hands and that he would pay no attention to those who might be surprised at his position, thinking the president would behave differently from the candidate.[13]

Justice Minister Oscar Pedroso Horta, denying that Lacerda and Quadros had broken relations, said that the governor had every right to disagree on foreign policy "details" and was exercising his right with his well-known "vehemence and brilliance." Lacerda thanked the justice minister for his "correct interpretation" and told him that the president's deplorable tactic of handling foreign policy for domestic reasons created "needless misgivings abroad."[14]

After United States Ambassador John Moors Cabot told reporters in July that Brazil's international commitments hardly allowed it to participate in a meeting of "uncommitted nations," Quadros answered indignantly in a speech in Rio. "Brazil," he asserted, "has an affirmative and independent international position and will not tolerate interference from anyone." Later in July, Quadros accepted Khrushchev's invitation to visit the Soviet Union and arranged for Goulart to head a mission to the People's Republic of China. Quadros' announcement on July 25 that Brazil would renew diplomatic relations with the Soviet Union prompted Luiz Carlos Prestes, head of the Brazilian Communist Party (PCB), to express the "applause of the Brazilian Communists."[15]

In two speeches on August 3, Lacerda condemned "Soviet infiltration." He called on the Americas to prevent the disappearance of "the very vestiges of liberty" by defending themselves from an aggression already on their soil. On August 17 he told reporters that he and Quadros had not broken, but he criticized the president for treating Russia better than he was treating Brazil's allies. The governor deplored what he said was the general feeling that "Russia is going to take over the world and we had better adhere to Russia. Younger people do not remember, but I remember, an exactly similar climate when Hitler appeared to be about to take over the world."[16]

Lacerda's dissatisfaction with Quadros was not the result of foreign policy alone. He was irked because Guanabara found it difficult to get the promised federal funds and because Quadros decided to transfer from Rio the headquarters of important government companies such as Petrobrás, the petroleum extraction monopoly, and Companhia Vale do Rio Doce, the iron ore exporter. The president, in Lacerda's opinion, "began to support our most ferocious adversaries in the state and to name, as federal authorities with jurisdiction in Guanabara, people who were openly hostile to me." Particularly annoying to Lacerda was his inability to have a long talk with the president about many matters.[17]

The UDN, apparently cast aside by Quadros, was becoming resentful. Minas Governor Magalhães Pinto, who had headed the party during the Quadros election campaign, gave his backing to the new foreign policy, but he found, nevertheless, that his voice carried little weight when federal appointments were made in his state.[18]

10. Lacerda's Break with Quadros
(August 18–23, 1961)

In Brasília on August 3 and 4, the Quadros administration received a visit from Douglas Dillon and other members of the United States delegation who were on their way to help launch the Alliance for Progress in Punta del Este, Uruguay. The delegates reacted favorably to the Quadros administration's ambitious half-a-billion-dollar emergency plan for Brazil's development. Later, in Punta del Este, the United States delegation let it be known that, under the Alliance program, Latin America could expect to receive $20 billion over a ten-year period.[1]

At Punta del Este, Hélio Beltrão persuaded the Inter-American Development Bank to send a team to Guanabara to study the state's water, sewage, and *favela* problems. The conference went smoothly except for the exchanges between Dillon and the bearded Che Guevara, the only uniformed member of the large Cuban delegation. The United States, in order not to betray "thousands of patriotic Cubans," refused to offer financial assistance to Cuba, whose regime, Dillon said, was controlled by the Soviet Union.[2] When Guevara criticized the United States, the Cuban was warmly applauded by Rio Grande do Sul Governor Leonel Brizola, a PTB leader chosen by Quadros to be special adviser on the Brazilian delegation.

Guevara, Cuban minister of industry and commerce, sought to bolster Cuban prestige by conferring with heads of state.[3] After his request for an audience with Quadros was passed on to Brasília by Clemente Mariani, head of the Brazilian delegation, Quadros agreed to meet him in Brasília. The meeting promised to intensify the controversy about Brazilian foreign policy. João Ribeiro Dantas, observing that Quadros "liked to move in mysterious ways and make the news," has explained that the Brazilian president wanted somehow to become the father of the readmittance of Cuba into the American family. Quadros also wished to secure for Brazil some Cuban commerce that no longer interested the United States, and hoped to straighten out the unpleasant situation at the Brazilian embassy in Havana, where 150 anti-Castro Cubans, including priests, had started a hunger strike to protest their failure to get authorization to leave Cuba.[4]

Guevara reached Brasília late at night on August 18. That was several hours after Lacerda arrived there in a small air force jet made available by the government. The arrangement for Lacerda to converse with the president had been worked out after Lacerda had told Quadros' wife Eloá that he had to see Jânio, whom he considered in the role of a father, about a "tremendously serious" personal problem.[5]

By the time Lacerda reached Alvorada Palace, the modernistic presidential residence, Quadros had already dined. He left off watching a movie in the basement to join the governor, who was served a meal on the second floor. What Lacerda had in mind, as he revealed to Quadros, was resigning the governorship. One reason he mentioned was his inability to give attention to the *Tribuna da Imprensa,* which had run up a debt of 20 million cruzeiros ($74,000) and was losing 2.5 million a month ($925 when the dollar was such that a monthly salary equal to $1,000 was considered adequate for the governor). Lacerda objected to his son Sérgio's having to make his start under such inauspicious circumstances. But he also spoke of other reasons for resigning, these connected with the way Quadros was running Brazil. "I told him," Lacerda has written, "that I was profoundly disillusioned. The promises of his government to the people of Guanabara were not being fulfilled and his government was following a different course from the one we promised the people, and therefore I felt I owed it to the people . . . to leave public life." Lacerda explained to Quadros that he considered himself "in a difficult moral situation" because he bore some responsibility for the president's election. "Up to now," he told Jânio, "you haven't told me anything about what you plan to do. And frankly I think you have done nothing except perhaps in the finance ministry. And there, from what I hear, you are retreating from the policy that you recommended at the outset, that is, the containment of inflation."

Lacerda alluded to conversations in which the president and Justice Minister Pedroso Horta had complained about Congress. During a discussion with Lacerda on August 15, Pedroso Horta had broached the possibility of Congress being sent on a paid vacation and had said that the support of some governors would be needed, starting with Lacerda, and that Carvalho Pinto, of São Paulo, was not yet ripe for these matters. Now Lacerda told Quadros that he had been deeply impressed by the president's remark to him in June, at Laranjeiras Palace, about the problem of governing "with this Congress." While Lacerda finished his Alvorada Palace meal, Quadros said that this was a subject he would be unable to discuss for thirty or forty-five days.[6]

The president said, "Let's see the movie." The governor, in the basement theater, was unable to concentrate on the cowboy film that Quadros substituted for a Jerry Lewis film. He repeated to Jânio that he was considering resigning and needed to converse with him about the federal administration. Therefore Quadros phoned Pedroso Horta and then told Lacerda that the justice minister was expecting him. The president, whose morning schedule included an early meeting with Che Guevara and then a trip to Vitória, Espírito Santo, urged Lacerda to go to Pedroso Horta's apartment. The unhappy governor was driven there in a palace car.[7]

The justice minister interrupted his after-dinner conversation with José Aparecido de Oliveira, presidential secretary, and PTB Congressman Francisco San Tiago Dantas, who had been named by Quadros to head the Brazilian delegation to the United Nations. He took Lacerda to a separate room, and, after hearing what he has called "a heart-rending story," tried to persuade the governor not to resign. He pledged the help of São Paulo friends for the *Tribuna* and promised Lacerda a long conversation with Quadros in Rio after the president went there from Vitória. The justice minister admitted that the administration's foreign policy was controversial but added that Lacerda's divergence with it did not worry the administration and asked why it upset Lacerda so much.

Lacerda spoke of his problems with the state legislature. Pedroso Horta and the president had been considering similar problems on the national scale, and therefore the justice minister asked for copies of Lacerda's articles, written in the *Tribuna da Imprensa* in the mid-1950's, urging the establishment of an emergency regime for decreeing reforms. Already Pedroso Horta, in the discussion on August 15, had requested copies of the articles and had also suggested that Lacerda sound out the aviation minister to see whether he would favor strengthening the executive branch in a movement that Pedroso Horta felt would appeal to the army and navy ministers. Lacerda, who had not followed the suggestion that he speak with the aviation minister, now told Pedroso Horta that he saw no reason to give him the *Tribuna* articles. The governor felt that conditions had changed since 1956.[8]

Before leaving Pedroso Horta's apartment, Lacerda mentioned that his suitcase was at Alvorada Palace. To save Lacerda the long walk between the palace and its gate, Pedroso Horta, after his visitor left, telephoned the palace and arranged to have the suitcase waiting for the governor at the gate. Somewhat later Pedroso Horta answered a phone call from the Hotel Nacional and heard the irate governor announce his resignation. "I was thrown out of the palace. They put my suitcase at the garden entrance gate and this is an insult to me personally and to the governor of Guanabara. They cover me with ridicule."

Pedroso Horta rushed to Lacerda's hotel room and tried to persuade the pajama-clad governor not to resign. He explained the misunderstanding about the suitcase and said that no arrangement had been made in the first place for Lacerda to spend the night at Alvorada Palace. Hours of talk and whiskey drinking followed. When the arguments became heated, pilot Wilson Lopes Machado, the governor's assistant who had accompanied him to Brasília, suggested that Lacerda not shout so loudly and withdrew discreetly to the adjoining room.[9]

Lacerda was threatening to tell the public that the president and

justice minister had antidemocratic intentions. According to Lacerda's notes, Pedroso Horta said, "Carlos, it seems to me you don't
understand all this very well. Jânio feels that it is impossible to govern with this Congress and plans a constitutional change for strengthening the executive in order to carry out some important reforms."
Lacerda said that, in the first place, he did not know what the reforms
were, and, in the second place, their enactment by Congress ought to
be possible, "especially by someone who won the election like Jânio
did and who . . . , as you have been telling me, has the support of the
armed forces." It was almost 5:00 A.M. when Lacerda, not much persuaded by the minister's words, thanked Pedroso Horta for his effort
and added, "I hope this political crisis won't harm our personal relations." Expressing the same hope, Pedroso Horta promised to keep
quiet about the affair of the governor's suitcase.[10]

At 7:00 A.M., an hour before returning to Rio in the air force plane,
Lacerda telephoned Congressman Adauto Lúcio Cardoso to say that
as soon as he reached Rio he would resign in order to be free to carry
out a full-scale political action that he could no longer avoid. He also
telephoned General Pedro Geraldo de Almeida, who, as head of the
presidential Casa Militar, advised Quadros on military matters. In a
reference to his resignation plan, Lacerda said to Pedro Geraldo: "Tell
the president I'm going to do what I said I was going to do." Quadros,
receiving the news at Planalto Palace just before meeting with Che
Guevara, told Pedro Geraldo that Lacerda had come to Brasília to
speak about the *Tribuna* indebtedness, not the sort of problem to be
taken to the president.[11]

Quadros spent half an hour with Guevara, making an appeal on
behalf of Catholics in Cuba and the refugees at the Brazilian embassy
in Havana. Then he escorted his uniformed visitor to the Green
Room, where he awarded him the highest order of the Brazilian decoration for foreigners, the Cruzeiro do Sul, in appreciation of Guevara's demonstrated desire for stronger ties between Brazil and Cuba.
Newspaper reporters and photographers were present, but Quadros
was the only important Brazilian official at the ceremony. Even Casa
Militar Chief Pedro Geraldo, usually on hand for such occasions, was
not called to the Green Room. Quadros, wishing a quick release of
the news about the decoration, dealt directly with presidential Press
Secretary Carlos Castello Branco, bypassing Francisco Quintanilha
Ribeiro, who, as head of the Casa Civil, was chief of staff in the
presidential office. The news disturbed the military ministers, who
noted that the decoration had been given "to an undesirable visitor"
without the usual prior approval of the appropriate council, but they
refrained from protesting publicly.[12]

While Pedroso Horta prepared notes about his talks with Lacerda, to be transmitted by wireless to the plane carrying Quadros to Vitória, UDN congressmen, led by Geraldo de Meneses Cortes, delegated Adauto Lúcio Cardoso to fly to Rio and try to persuade Lacerda not to resign.[13]

In Rio Lacerda replied to the decoration for Guevara by presenting the city's highest award for foreigners, symbolic keys to the city, to former Cuban Prime Minister Manoel Antonio de Varona and three other members of an anti-Castro group that was touring the continent. To reporters, who had been hastily summoned to Guanabara Palace, Lacerda refused to confirm or deny that he was leaving the governorship.

The Che Guevara decoration and the Quadros-Lacerda rift led to a flood of comments. Congressman Almino Afonso, speaking for the PTB, praised the president's search for markets in all countries of the world. Minas Governor Magalhães Pinto (UDN) reiterated his support of Quadros' policies and therefore received a message of thanks in which Quadros said that a purpose of his foreign policy was "to project our nation on the world stage."[14]

Última Hora, which had opposed the election of Quadros, supported his foreign policy, whereas the *Diário Carioca*, also critical of the UDN, wrote that Jânio had insulted and humiliated Brazil by decorating a simple *agent provocateur*. *O Globo* called Guevara the representative of a government that financed subversion in Brazil, and the fast-growing *Jornal do Brasil*, unhappy with Quadros and suspicious of his authoritarian tendencies, likewise condemned his foreign policy.

O Estado de S. Paulo, noting that Brazil seemed to be "on the eve of serious events," blamed the president for disregarding the UDN and wanting to wreck the whole political party system with the possible intention of using far-Left currents to help him establish a dictatorship. Minas state legislator Sinfronio Pacheco (PR), expressing the same fear, said that Quadros at any moment might follow the example of Fidel Castro.[15]

Lacerda met at his home with UDN leaders Adauto Lúcio Cardoso, Milton Campos, and José Eduardo Prado Kelly. He told them what he had learned in Brasília. But, he has written, they exhibited their "vocation for inertia." "They save themselves to make judgments about those who act. In those judgments, they are inflexible, demanding, and tough. However, they absolve all omissions, beginning with their own." When Lacerda got in touch with Aviation Minister Gabriel Grün Moss, he surprised the *brigadeiro* by telling him to be ready to participate in a coup. Grün Moss, incredulous, asked about the other military ministers. Lacerda, in indicating that perhaps the war and navy ministers did not really favor a coup, was giving an accurate description.[16]

The president, having completed his trip to Vitória, reached Rio's Laranjeiras Palace, and there, on the afternoon of August 19, he was urged by Pedro Geraldo to see Lacerda. Pedroso Horta made the same suggestion by phone from Brasília and found the president reluctant to take the initiative of inviting the angry governor to the palace. But Quadros yielded and received Lacerda there in the evening. Eloá Quadros and Letícia, having visited Petrópolis together, were at Laranjeiras Palace when their husbands had a friendly talk. Lacerda accepted an invitation for Letícia and himself to go on the presidential plane with Jânio and Eloá the next morning to Brasília, via São Paulo, and to spend the weekend with them. Quadros telephoned Pedroso Horta that all was well, and Lacerda, on leaving Laranjeiras Palace, told reporters that his reasons for resigning the governorship no longer existed.[17]

But that night Letícia told Carlos that he was making a mistake and that if what he had reported about Quadros was true, which she did not doubt, he would be in a weak position to denounce him after the proposed weekend of the families together. She refused to accompany him. Carlos, agreeing with Letícia, wrote a note that was delivered to the president at the airport the next morning just before his plane left Rio. It referred to the arrival in Rio that day of their son Sebastião from Germany and said that they did not want to disappoint him by not greeting him. "Letícia and I," the note read, "are sure that Eloá will excuse our absence. And you certainly will understand."[18] "Who is Sebastião?" the surprised president remarked on receiving the note.

Lacerda did more than greet his nineteen-year-old son. Speaking at a congress of the anti-Communist Inter-American Regional Organization of Workers (ORIT), he said he was prepared to leave his official position in order to struggle in the streets to defend the hopes of the Brazilian people. The ORIT representatives gave him a standing ovation when he declared that the working class of the Americas was firmly determined to prevent Communist aggression, whose chief allies, he said, were the opportunism of demagogues and the timidity of others. Labor Minister Castro Neves, representing Quadros, was given a difficult time by the ORIT representatives, some of whom shouted "*al paredón*" (Spanish for "to the wall").

That night, in a widely broadcast attack on Quadros' "suicidal" foreign policy, Lacerda said he was officially representing the people of his state for the last time. Pernambuco Governor Cid Sampaio (UDN) then sent an appeal to Lacerda to remain in office. But Lacerda replied that resignation would be the best solution, since he could count on support from neither the state legislature nor the federal government.

In the state legislature, where Roland Corbisier accused Lacerda of trying to stir up the armed forces against Quadros, the opposition called for a permanent session to deal with the crisis. But the majority, which had chosen jurist Temístocles Cavalcanti to act as leader, defeated the motion and asked Lopo Coelho to persuade Lacerda not to resign. Outside, on the steps of Tiradentes Palace, labor unions and the National Union of Students (UNE) held a large rally demanding Lacerda's resignation.

In the federal legislature, anti-Communist congressmen belonging to Parliamentary Democratic Action (Ação Democrática Parlamentar) clashed with the Parliamentary Nationalist Front (Frente Parlamentar Nacionalista), led by Bento Gonçalves Filho of Minas. The UDN's reform-minded Bossa-Nova wing joined the Frente in issuing a manifesto accusing the governor of Guanabara of attacking the government's foreign policy "precisely at the moment when Brazil affirms its defense of the principles of self-determination, the coexistence of regimes, and free commerce with the entire world."

On August 22 Lacerda went to São Paulo to give impetus to National Unity Week by delivering a speech that *O Estado de S. Paulo* hailed as one of the most important of recent times. Youthful hecklers kept shouting "Jânio yes, Yankees no!" as he made his main point: the Vargas government had surreptitiously encouraged Communists in order to have an excuse for imposing dictatorship in 1937. When an unfriendly listener shouted "*al paredón*," Lacerda compared his listener's conduct to that of the Nazis taking power in Germany. "Those who oppose me do not know how much I am defending them; if things continue as they are, perhaps we shall end up having this cordial discussion in the same jail cell." Labor Minister Castro Neves, more fortunate in his audience in São Paulo, was cheered by workers when he attacked Lacerda and defended the decoration for Guevara.[19]

While in São Paulo, Lacerda called on Governor Carvalho Pinto. Discussing the "grave matter" he had become acquainted with in Brasília, Lacerda urged Carvalho Pinto to invite Quadros to reveal his "great reform program" at a meeting of governors. The governors, Lacerda explained, could back the reforms and thus prevent any presidential pretext for closing Congress. But the São Paulo governor declined the suggestion, saying that neither Jânio nor Pedroso Horta had spoken to him about the matter. Lacerda, concluding that Carvalho Pinto was "timid" and "terribly remiss," lost his patience. These men, Lacerda told Carvalho Pinto, had not consulted him because "they think you will mull over the matter . . . and they are in a hurry." Quadros, Lacerda added, "told me you are a ruminant who takes six months to understand what he wants and then another six months to reach a decision." Carvalho Pinto, taken aback, said it would be impertinent for him to call a governors' meeting. Lacerda replied that, in view of the position taken by the UDN and by Carvalho Pinto, he had no choice but to denounce everything to the people on television. Back in Rio, Lacerda told the city's Historical and Geographical Institute that the Russians planned to install sixty-four cultural centers in Brazil and offer two thousand scholarships "for Brazilians who want to learn how to become fifth columnists."

In the meantime in Brasília Adauto Lúcio Cardoso defined the position of the UDN and its small ally, the PL (Partido Libertador), as one condemning Lacerda's "type of extreme protest." "Our warning and our program," he said, "is in opposition to anything in excess." He pointed out that Brazil's relations with "the old Communism of Khrushchev and Tito" and "the new Communism of Fidel Castro and Guevara" should be negotiated "with diplomatic courtesy." After UDN congressional leader Meneses Cortes, more pugnacious, objected to Adauto's speech and failure to consult him, Pedro Aleixo (UDN) and Nestor Duarte (PL) revealed that they had authorized the speech. The UDN argued that Adauto was simply reaffirming the party line adopted at the Recife convention. Magalhães Pinto, inclined to be cautious, said Lacerda was handling his foreign policy divergence with the government in a dangerous manner that would create intranquility. Governors, he said, should discuss such problems within governmental groups and not take them to the streets.[20]

Le Monde of Paris, citing the Guevara decoration and the visit Goulart was making to Red China, declared that the far-Left course of the Brazilian president was irreversible and saw the possibility of Brazil leading most of Latin America along the path chosen by Cuba. The *Diário Carioca*, worried about this possibility, wrote that all of Brazil was aroused by the foreign policy clash between Lacerda and Quadros.[21]

By this time, however, it had become known in political circles that Lacerda had a divergence more serious than foreign policy. And on the morning of August 24 the press told the public that the divergence, "of exceptional gravity," concerned the constitution.[22]

11. Quadros Resigns (August 25, 1961)

Late at night on August 24, seventh anniversary of the suicide of Vargas, Lacerda spoke from Guanabara Palace on radio and television networks to denounce Quadros for planning to close Congress. Writer Antonio Carlos Villaça calls the speech "the greatest, the most moving, and the strongest" of all the speeches he heard Lacerda give.[1]

Lacerda opened by saying that he had decided to yield to appeals that he remain in the governorship. Listing reasons that had made him want to resign, he brushed aside "reasons of a personal nature," calling them less important than his public duty. Problems with the state legislature, he said, were beginning to be cleared up. As for federal funds due Guanabara, he mentioned an appropriate decree, recently signed by Quadros, after the release had been held up for twenty-six days by "faulty, malevolent, unreliable, vagabondish, disorderly, incapable, and perverse" presidential advisers "who are sinking the Jânio Quadros government."

In a reference to a remaining reason, Lacerda called it "an insult to suppose that the president has not perceived the enormity of the error of his foreign policy." Denouncing the use of this policy for domestic purposes, the governor said that Pedroso Horta had described the Left as a possible source of support for an "institutional reform."

In the most sensational passages of the speech, Lacerda gave his version of conversations with the president and especially the justice minister to demonstrate that the government planned to push Congress aside in order to carry out reforms. Pedroso Horta, he said, had claimed to have Quadros' authorization to discuss such matters as Lacerda's old articles about an emergency regime and the advisability of Lacerda's sounding out one of the military ministers. "In recent days the justice minister has been giving his friends ten different versions, not one of them truthful, about his conversations with me." The governor, describing himself as shocked by those conversations, added that he had been struggling in his conscience "whether to reveal everything or resist alone in silence."

Lacerda declared that the deficiencies of Congress and the parties did not justify the "gimmick" of imposing the threat of leftist forces in order to get the democratic center "to submit to the personal power" of the president. The solution, he said, was for everyone to assist Quadros in every way possible so that he could govern "lawfully, legitimately, democratically." "For this it is essential that he no longer lose himself in the misdirections of a policy that is contrary to what the Brazilian people desire and struggle for." Lacerda promised to remain in the governorship so that the president not be left alone and so that "my country not leave the path that its founders delineated."[2]

Lacerda's accusation brought after-midnight life to the Chamber of Deputies. Word from Kubitschek encouraged those who wanted to convert the Chamber into an investigating commission. Over two hundred congressmen approved a resolution that Pedroso Horta appear quickly before the Chamber.[3]

At Alvorada Palace that night Quadros decided to resign. The purpose of the resignation was to force the military ministers to establish the emergency regime that Lacerda was denouncing. These ministers would intervene before turning Brazil over to Vice President Goulart, the corrupt associate of Communist labor leaders who was fulfilling his mission to Red China. Quadros, according to his own account of his thinking, expected the armed forces to establish a new, more authoritative regime, with himself or someone else at its head. That this could only be himself he had no doubt. "Brazil," he said, "needs three things: authority, capacity for work, and courage and rapidity in making decisions. Apart from myself there is no one, no one, who combines these three requisites." On his side also would be "the spontaneous clamor" of the people, making his return, as he put it, "inevitable."[4]

During his Cuba trip, Quadros had been fascinated by stories of how Fidel Castro had departed from the scene and then returned, "reclaimed by the people," apparently more popular than ever. Considering the effect of a "courageous" sacrifice and an appropriate farewell message, Quadros took comfort from the popular reaction to the steps that Vargas, under attack by Lacerda, had taken seven years earlier;[5] and he could consider the clamor for his own return, after his short-lived resignation, as a presidential candidate. He could also reflect that, with a weekend coming up, few congressmen would be in Brasília to receive the resignation; especially if it was not released until mid-afternoon on the 25th.

Shortly before 7:00 A.M. that morning, General Pedro Geraldo de Almeida became the first to learn of Quadros' decision to resign: "Seeing that I cannot carry out what I promised the people, I shall not remain one minute in the presidency. I was not born president." Pedro Geraldo, trying to dissuade him, told him that he had the support of 60 million Brazilians. Quadros admitted to having "the mentality of a school teacher" who could permit no breach of discipline.[6]

Later that morning, after the annual "Day of the Soldier" ceremonies, Quadros spoke in his office with the military ministers and Pedro Geraldo, Pedroso Horta, Quintanilha Ribeiro, and José

Aparecido de Oliveira. "I shall not," he said, "exercise the presidency with its authority undermined before the eyes of the world, nor shall I remain in office when there are questions about confidence, respect, and dignity, which are indispensable for the head of the state." After Quadros gave Pedroso Horta a short resignation message for Congress and a longer message for the Brazilian people, both to be released at 3:00 P.M., he explained to the military ministers that he could not govern "with this Congress." "Organize a military junta and run the country," he added.[7]

By 3:00 P.M., when his decision became known, Quadros was at São Paulo's Cumbica Air Base, where he had been flown with his wife and mother and baggage that included the presidential sash. Carvalho Pinto and his lunch guests, the governors of Minas, Paraná, and Goiás, and the labor minister, sped to the air base and heard Quadros describe the nation as "ungovernable."[8]

In Brasília, Senate Vice President Auro de Moura Andrade and Congressman José Maria Alkmin, both members of the PSD, sent taxis and buses to the airport to gather up lawmakers who were about to leave for the weekend. Thus about one hundred of them, in a joint session, learned of Quadros' messages. The longer one, addressed to the Brazilian people and bearing resemblances to Vargas' farewell message, told how Quadros had "worked indefatigably, day and night," but been "frustrated" in his "efforts to take the nation on the road of its true political and economic freedom." "I wanted," Quadros wrote, "a Brazil for the Brazilians, but in the case of this dream I faced corruption, lies, and cowardice, which subordinated the general interests to the appetites and ambitions of individual groups, including foreign ones. Therefore I find myself crushed. Terrible forces arose against me and plotted against me or maligned me, even on the pretext of collaborating. If I remain, it will not be possible to maintain confidence and tranquility." Quadros said he did not "lack the courage to resign," and added that he was returning to his work of lawyer and teacher. He paid a special tribute to the armed forces, "whose exemplary conduct, at every moment, I take this opportunity to proclaim."[9]

Moura Andrade told the lawmakers that the resignation was a unilateral "voluntary act, of which the National Congress should be apprised." As the vice president was abroad, Moura Andrade declared that Chamber of Deputies President Ranieri Mazzilli was acting president of Brazil; and in the Green Room of Planalto Palace, Mazzilli assumed his new post. This same Congress, as Quadros was aware, had recently cogitated for weeks before accepting the resignation of Congressman Mário Martins. Now it gave no heed to men like government congressional leader Nestor Duarte (PL) and Senate majority leader Filinto Müller (PSD), who were urging that Congress refuse to accept Quadros' resignation.[10]

At the Cumbica Air Base, Quadros was shocked to learn of the development in Brasília. "The congressmen did not even consult the justice commission!" he exclaimed. The military ministers, he knew, were determined not to allow Goulart to reach the presidency. But, while Goulart's presence in Red China may have been a reminder of old complaints about his Communist connections, his very absence from Brazil made it unnecessary for the military ministers to act quickly against the constitution.

Still at the Cumbica Air Base on the 26th, Quadros spoke with intimates. Asked about Lacerda, he said that instead of hating him, he pitied him. "He has done nothing constructive." Quadros spoke also about the inevitability of his own return to the presidency, the result of a spontaneous clamor. His return, he now conceded, might take more time than he had calculated; it might take three months.[11] Two days later he sailed for Europe on the *Uruguay Star* with his wife, mother, daughter, son-in-law, and new granddaughter. Before leaving he broadcast some last tearful words. Misquoting Vargas about his 1945 overthrow, Quadros said: "President Getúlio spoke well when he said: 'They send me away now, but I shall return.' Take note: the defeats have only been partial ones."[12]

The struggle over the fate of Goulart was so intense that Quadros' post-resignation declarations were given little attention.

12. Repression in Rio (August 26–31, 1961)

At Guanabara Palace on the afternoon of August 25, Lacerda was with José Cândido Moreira de Souza, his secretary of agriculture, industry, and commerce, when a brief phone call from Pedroso Horta advised him that the president had resigned and the governor should take measures necessary to maintain order in his state. Surprised and shocked, the governor told Pedroso Horta: "One doesn't do that to a nation."

Lacerda's first reaction to the news was to take the position that Brazil ought to demonstrate its maturity by adhering to the constitution. Phoning Juracy Magalhães, the governor of Bahia, he gave support to the inauguration of Goulart. After asking Raphael de Almeida Magalhães for a copy of the Brazilian constitution, he prepared a note for the press favorable to Goulart's claim to the presidency. "We would watch over him and combat him" if necessary, Lacerda explained later.[1]

But Lacerda did not release the note, for it became known quickly that the military ministers were advising Acting President Mazzilli of their veto against Goulart. Contemplating what might become of Brazil if dominated by the forces supporting Goulart, War Minister Denys proclaimed that "the situation obliges us to choose between democracy and Communism." Late that night, after the Guanabara government prevented a radio-television network in the state from broadcasting Pedroso Horta's reply to Lacerda's speech of the previous night, Lacerda used the network to declare that he was placing his trust "in the decision which, at this time, belongs to the organs responsible for the national security, the army, navy, and air force. It is not a time for politicians to speak."[2]

While few would agree that politicians should not speak, it was true that the situation seemed explosive. Afonso Arinos, resigning from the foreign ministry, forecast civil war unless Quadros were reinstalled.[3] Civil war, however, seemed more likely if the less austere João Goulart, known as "Jango," were denied his right to the presidency.

After declaring that Quadros' resignation was regrettable, Lacerda spent a sleepless night at the palace, keeping in touch with governors and other politicians and the military, and he followed the repression of disorders in Rio on a shortwave receiver that brought police reports. When journalists found him in the palace garden on the 26th, he told them he had nothing to say; as they insisted on learning his view about Goulart becoming president, he pointed out that he was simply "governor of Guanabara, not of Brasília."[4]

The war minister's hope that Congress would act against the vice president, as it had acted against Presidents Carlos Luz and João Café Filho in 1955, was not shared by Marshal Henrique Lott, who phoned Denys from Rio. Unable to persuade the war minister to change his mind, Lott issued a manifesto calling on all active forces in Brazil to protect the constitution.[5] For this, Lott was imprisoned in the rocky island fortress of Lage. For sharing his view, other military officers, including over thirty members of the air force, were also jailed.

Lacerda has admitted that his decision to cooperate with the military ministers was not a popular one.[6] Although the UDN governor of Alagoas, Luiz Cavalcanti, wired Lacerda that he agreed with him, many *udenistas* agreed with Aliomar Baleeiro when he said, "I do not think Goulart will be a good president, but it is the duty of all Brazilians to guarantee him the right to assume the post." Governor Magalhães Pinto worked for the inauguration of Goulart. Congressman Adauto Lúcio Cardoso asserted vehemently that the military ministers and Mazzilli, who forwarded their veto to Congress, were criminals, guilty of violating the constitution.[7]

According to Lacerda, "men like Abreu Sodré, president of the São Paulo state legislature, demanded the inauguration of João Goulart, wanting legality at any price," and "others, like Congressman Sérgio Magalhães, demanded the inauguration of Jango or civil war." Goiás Governor Mauro Borges Teixeira (PSD), in a long telegram to Lacerda, emphasized the need for a fight by the legalists if Goulart's inauguration were blocked by "the egoistic and obscurantist forces associated with the international trusts," which, he said, had been bleeding Brazil and had forced the resignation of Quadros.[8]

The boldest backing of "Jango," who had reached Paris from Hong Kong, was undertaken by his brother-in-law Leonel Brizola. He put his state, Rio Grande do Sul, on a war footing against the military ministers and blasted them in lengthy, explosive radio broadcasts that he called "The Voice of Legality." In support of Brizola, Fidel Castro issued a message that Mazzilli's justice minister, José Martins Rodrigues, considered "abusive foreign interference." Martins Rodrigues therefore asked Lacerda to prevent the release of Castro's message in Guanabara.

Lacerda's support of the military ministers was bitterly attacked by the opposition in the state assembly, which declared itself in permanent session. On August 28, oppositionist legislators Paulo Alberto Monteiro de Barros and Waldemar Viana reached such a state of hypertension that both had to be treated by the legislature's medical service; Paulo Alberto ended up in the Tiradentes Palace infirmary.[9]

In Brasília feelings were just as intense. Senator Aguinaldo Caiado de Castro suffered a stroke after giving a speech. Congressman Rui Ramos, leading a column of a dozen frenzied Gaúcho congressmen, advanced into the Chamber of Deputies with his arm extended and roared, "*Viva a Constituição! Viva a Legalidade! Viva a Democracia!*" Ramos cried out that War Minister Denys had sought to "massacre the governor of Rio Grande do Sul" and that if Mazzilli failed to jail Denys within forty-eight hours, he and other congressmen would either capture Denys or die in the attempt.[10]

Ramos' most important declaration was that General José Machado Lopes, commander of the Third Army in the south, had adhered "to Brizola and legality." This military break with Denys, and a march, later, by some Gaúcho soldiers into the neighboring state of Santa Catarina, made civil war a distinct possibility. Congress, which had showed its defiance of the military ministers by sending a warm message to the imprisoned Lott, sent a message to congratulate General Machado Lopes. Another congratulatory message, sent to the general from Havana in the name of Cuban workers, lamented the "vile aggression of Yankee imperialism and its agents."[11]

As soon as Lacerda gave the military ministers his support, the First Army, with headquarters in Rio, insisted on receiving the cooperation of the Guanabara Censorship Service and police for thwarting what it considered to be subversive activities. At the very outset of the crisis, soldiers were sent to protect the *Tribuna da Imprensa*, *O Globo*, and the American embassy from crowds shouting "Jânio yes! Lacerda no!" Subsequently the authorities had their hands full with labor leaders and student leaders planning strikes, pronouncements, and demonstrations against the military ministers and the "terrible forces" that had "driven Quadros from office."[12]

Leopoldina Railroad workers went on strike immediately after Quadros resigned and were supported on the 26th by a manifesto of Guanabara labor leaders who called for a general strike and deplored the "coup" against Brazil's independence by "reactionary forces and international monopolies." Hélio Walcacer, Lacerda's labor affairs adviser, asked the labor leaders to meet with the governor, but they declined with the explanation that the governor was "the intellectual mentor of the crisis." Lacerda, who called the Leopoldina strike illegal, maintained that the strike problem belonged to the federal government. At his suggestion, Mazzilli named José de Segadas Viana labor minister on August 28.[13]

A general strike in Guanabara did not materialize despite support from port workers, maritime workers, metalworkers, and textile workers. José de Segadas Viana, praising Walcacer for his help in bringing the Rio strike movement to an end within a few days, has written that most of the union leaders heeded a warning that the movement could result in "consequences that no one can foresee." The labor minister, as he has admitted, was assisted by strong-arm methods in which the Military Police of Guanabara cooperated with the army. After the arrest of a few labor leaders, including the president of the printers' union of Guanabara, and the invasion of labor unions by troops, the strike movement was dominated. Some of the unions moved their headquarters from Rio to Niterói.[14]

University students met and resolved to go on strike until legality was reestablished, "especially in Guanabara"; but the UNE building was taken over by the Military Police, leading student leaders to find asylum in the embassies of Uruguay and other countries. Directors of the Teachers' Union were arrested.[15]

According to Lacerda, it was Colonel Golbery do Couto e Silva, secretary-general of the National Security Council, who asked the Guanabara security secretary, General Siseno Sarmento, to install censorship in the state. Lacerda was agreeable, for he considered censorship "absolutely indispensable." To prevent the dissemination of reports that might "endanger public order," soldiers of the army and Military Police exercised "rigorous censorship" of broadcasting. They were just as rigorous in censoring the Rio press, starting with the invasion of the *Diário Carioca* and the *Diário de Notícias* on Saturday night, August 26, to prevent the publication of material that included Lott's manifesto. All the Rio dailies were assigned army officers to supervise the censorship of articles. On August 28 the Military Police seized the entire edition of the next morning's *Correio da Manhã* and arrested journalist João Batista de Paula of *Última Hora.* On the 29th the police seized an edition of the *Diário de Notícias* that contained an interview given by Goulart in Paris. By then so much news was being censored that on the 30th the *Jornal do Brasil* did not circulate and the *Diário de Notícias* appeared with large blank spaces throughout its pages.[16]

Guanabara distinguished itself among the states for the severity of its repression. Air force Colonel Francisco Américo Fontenelle, the state's coordinator of transport, has written that in view of the torrent of "subversive pamphlets, alarming rumors, and seditious incitements, in the streets and also by some newspapers and radio stations," he got in touch with military authorities in Rio in order to have "legal coverage of censorship, indispensable for maintaining order." "As the authorities acted slowly, we issued orders, in the name of the governor and often without his prior knowledge, to the state's civilian and military personnel for the censorship and the takeover of some newspapers and radio stations."[17]

Late on Monday afternoon, August 28, about two thousand people assembled around the bust of Getúlio Vargas in Cinelândia to hear a reading of Lott's manifesto and receive leaflets supporting Goulart that the police thought were being printed by *Última Hora.* Cecil Borer, of the political police, and army Colonel Carlos Ardovino Barbosa, head of the civilian police, took strong action. The hundreds of armed men brought to Cinelândia by Ardovino used their weapons and tear gas to disperse the stone-throwing crowd, leaving Cinelândia "a gas-filled desert" with its movie theaters and commerce closed down. Reports of thirty people wounded and sixty arrested on the 28th did not deter a new demonstration in Cinelândia the next evening "to show hostility to the civilian police." The demonstrators, singing the national anthem, again attacked with stones and sticks and even used firearms. But truckloads of soldiers put the protesters to flight.[18]

Using tear gas and machine guns on the 30th, and obeying orders of General Siseno Sarmento, the Military Police invaded and took over *A Noite,* the daily directed by Mário Martins. They seized its special edition, containing a report that General Machado Lopes had consulted his men before giving support to Brizola and Goulart.

The Brazilian Press Association (ABI) condemned "unconstitutional acts that gravely wound the national honor." On the same day, the 30th, the Guanabara Syndicate of Owners of Newspapers and Magazines sent a telegram to the Inter American Press Association declaring that it should expel Lacerda from membership. Congressman Antônio Chagas Freitas, head of the Syndicate, had already sent messages of protest to Lacerda and raised his voice in Brasília along with other congressmen. *Última Hora* director Paulo Silveira had telegraphed the Inter American Press Association, and so had the *Jornal do Brasil* and the *Correio da Manhã,* but censorship had prevented the transmission of these earlier cables.[19]

The courts supported the press, and on August 30, Raphael de Almeida Magalhães met with newspaper owners at their syndicate to bring them Lacerda's word that the censorship was at an end. Raphael telephoned the same information to Mário Martins, who also received assurances from Police Chief Hélio Tornaghi that a court order in favor of *A Noite* would be respected. The only trouble encountered by a Rio newspaper after the 30th was the result of an order by the war ministry to prevent *Última Hora* from distributing on the 31st an "extra" edition containing an interview by Sérgio Magalhães and an account of a meeting between Denys and General João de Segadas Viana, spokesman for a group of pro-Goulart generals. Policemen seized copies already on newsstands and told *Última Hora* to distribute no more. Then the Guanabara Syndicate of Owners of Newspapers and Magazines sent a second telegram to the Inter American Press Association, again demanding the expulsion of Lacerda from its ranks. *Jornal do Brasil* wrote that the seized edition of *Última Hora* contained accounts of pacification efforts and that it was therefore understandable why it was considered subversive by Lacerda, "faithful to his vocation of agitator and conspirator against the democratic institutions."[20]

The *Jornal do Brasil* wrote on August 31 that Governor Carvalho Pinto, although not a journalist, had preserved press freedom in São Paulo, thus revealing greater courage than Lacerda, who "was still a journalist until a few days ago." The *Correio da Manhã,* calling Lacerda a "Lawless King," pointed out that censorship was a crime when no state of siege had been enacted. Novelist Érico Veríssimo, in a well-publicized statement, condemned, "with the greatest indignation, the violent and arbitrary acts committed by the governor of

Guanabara," guilty of "criminally reviving the worst practices of the most barbarous totalitarian police."[21]

O Globo did not share the view of most of the Rio press. Although on the 30th its special edition had been seized, it wrote on the 31st: "We cannot agree with the effort to hurt a colleague, in his role of journalist, for acts he carries out in his position of governor." It surmised that the steps that Lacerda had to take "for the maintenance of security and order" were ones that "must cause displeasure to him, more than to anyone else."[22]

The newspaper fraternity was especially angry about the role played by longtime journalist Ascendino Leite, who had been editor-in-chief of the *Diário de Notícias* before heading the Guanabara Censorship Service. Ascendino has claimed that late in August 1961 he simply gave support to decisions of the chiefs of the armed services. But his former companions of the press accused him of using his journalistic ties with them to obtain information useful to military censors. In calling him a traitor, they pointed out that the invasion of the *Diário Carioca* on the night of August 26 had followed his phone call to a *Diário Carioca* colleague who, believing Ascendino to be still with the *Diário de Notícias*, had agreed to furnish a copy of Lott's manifesto.[23]

13. The Military Ministers Disappoint Lacerda (August 31, 1961)

As early as August 26 politicians discussed the possibility of settling the crisis by amending the constitution; one of the suggested amendments would have eliminated the vice president from the presidential succession. Congressman Eloy Dutra (PTB, Guanabara), blaming the political crises on "the personalities of leaders," spoke in favor of a parliamentary form of government, long advocated by Congressman Raul Pilla (PL, Rio Grande do Sul). Senator Afonso Arinos de Melo Franco also believed that such a system would prevent crises; he spoke about its merits when he happened to meet, at Rio's Santos Dumont Airport, Armed Forces Chief of Staff Osvaldo Cordeiro de Farias, who was supposed to go south and take command of the Third Army from General Machado Lopes. Cordeiro was enthusiastic about the idea and sent the recent foreign minister posthaste in a military plane to Brasília to work on it.[1]

In Brasília a commission of senators and congressmen, appointed on the 28th to consider the military veto of Goulart, concluded quickly that the veto should be rejected. Most of its members supported the suggestion of its *relator*, Antônio de Oliveira Brito, that

Congress consider giving Brazil a parliamentary form of government. This, it was hoped, would satisfy the military by limiting the powers of Goulart in the presidency. Telephone calls made from Brasília to Goulart in Paris were interpreted as indicating he would accept such a compromise.[2]

On the 29th the military ministers declared they would not accept Goulart even under a parliamentary form of government. The declaration pleased Lacerda, who appealed, in phone calls to congressmen, for a decision that would deny Goulart the presidency. But the sentiment for the compromise was growing in Brasília and elsewhere. Afonso Arinos helped it along on the 30th with a Senate speech in which he extolled its virtues, revealed Goulart's cooperative attitude, and denounced the situation in Rio. There, he explained later, Lacerda was trying to set up "his private dictatorship" because of his inability "to dominate the situation in Brasília."[3]

Afonso Arinos, in the opinion of Lacerda, ended their past friendship when he denied that his sensationally successful election to the Senate in 1958 had been achieved with Lacerda's assistance. After that, according to Lacerda, Afonso Arinos failed in the foreign ministry to use his prestige and intelligence to give dignity to Quadros' foreign policy and curb the "clownishness" of a president who provided an "intolerable climate" of mysterious affairs, cloak and dagger figures, spies, and trap doors, appropriate for "a silent movie comedy." "Worst of all," in the opinion of Lacerda, Afonso Arinos sought, during the August 1961 crisis, to assure his place as foreign minister in a Goulart cabinet by taking "to the terror-stricken Congress that formula of salvation," that "humbug parliamentary system."[4]

While Afonso Arinos worked in Brasília on August 30 for the parliamentary system, troops in Paraná prepared to defend the south against any march from the north, and a group of generals in Rio told General João de Segadas Viana, brother of the labor minister, that they disagreed with the latest veto by the military ministers. João de Segadas Viana, whose tenure as a four-star general put him at the top of the army hierarchy, sped to Brasília and brought Denys the news that these generals would support any solution adopted by Congress. Denys arranged for a meeting, before dawn on the 31st, at which João de Segadas Viana and some of the generals he represented conferred with the military ministers, the commander of the First Army, and Cordeiro de Farias. They all agreed to "back the sovereign decision of Congress." When Rui Ramos reported these events in Congress on the afternoon of the 31st, PSP leader Arnaldo Cerdeira exclaimed: "Were we not in a completely abnormal regime, it would be unthinkable for Congress to receive such important news from a congressman. Where is the president; where are his ministers?"[5]

Thus the crisis was over by the time governors assembled in Rio in answer to calls issued by Lacerda and Cid Sampaio. The military ministers, who met with eight of the governors at the war ministry late on August 31, examined the text of the proposed amendment to establish a parliamentary regime. Cid Sampaio, after the meeting, praised the patriotism of the military ministers and said the governors planned to work with Congress on choosing a prime minister. The governors were in a cheerful mood, except for Lacerda, who appeared sulky and refused to make a statement to the press. He did not attend a second governors' meeting held the next day in the Glória Hotel suite of Aluísio Alves.[6]

Lacerda felt betrayed by the military ministers, with whom he had cooperated so fully that a bill of impeachment against him was being drawn up in the state legislature. He particularly regretted that the military ministers had not consulted him before reaching their latest decision. He experienced, Raphael de Almeida Magalhães recalls, "the worst time of his life" and considered resigning. An early rumor that Lacerda would resign reached the legislative assembly late on August 30 and brought a suspension to the work on Saldanha Coelho's impeachment bill. On September 1, after it appeared that Goulart would reach the presidency, the press again reported that Lacerda wanted to resign. His friends, it also reported, were trying to convince him that he would do better to take a leave of absence and spend three months in Europe.[7]

A letter from Education Secretary Flexa Ribeiro, delivered to Lacerda on August 31, argued that he should not resign but should cease objecting to the solution that Congress was giving to the crisis. Flexa Ribeiro pictured the parliamentary compromise as leaving the president practically powerless, "a sort of eunuch of the republic," and said that, if the experiment did not work, it could be withdrawn peacefully. He urged Lacerda not to let himself be considered responsible for a military dictatorship and possible civil war, the alternatives to the parliamentary compromise, and said it would be difficult for Lacerda to defend himself against such charges if he resigned, "creating in our people the same climate of frustration that was created by the resignation of Jânio Quadros." Besides, he added, "as you know better than anyone, Brazilian political life has an unforeseeable dynamism, that is to say, situations change with enormous rapidity."[8]

Flexa Ribeiro pointed out that he had been unable to speak to the governor about his ideas because no cabinet meeting had been held for eight days. The governor, soon after receiving the letter, called a cabinet meeting—an unusual one because the discussion was about Lacerda's position on a national political issue. Aside from Flexa Ribeiro, the only person to raise his voice in favor of the inauguration of Goulart was José Carlos Barbosa Monteiro, substituting for absent Social Services Coordinator José Arthur Rios. Labor Affairs Adviser Walcacer denounced Goulart emotionally and exclaimed: "Carlos Lacerda, you must become the president!"[9]

The "parliamentary formula," which Lacerda considered "false and artificial," came up for a vote in Brasília on September 2. Most of the PTB supported their party leader, Almino Afonso, in trying to block the amendment. However, 19 PTB congressmen "defected"; they followed San Tiago Dantas and helped provide the two-thirds of the Chamber membership of 326 necessary for amending the constitution.[10] The measure was approved in the Chamber, 236-55, and in the Senate 48-6 (Kubitschek voting against it). According to the amendment, favored by many as a compromise to end the crisis, Congress might decide to call for a plebiscite, to let the people decide, in which case it was to take place nine months before the end of Goulart's term.

Goulart, who had come to Rio Grande do Sul from Montevideo, was prevented from flying to Brasília until September 5 because the military ministers found it necessary to take steps against a plot of rebellious air force officers to capture him after forcing his plane to land.[11] In the meantime in the Guanabara legislature he was praised by Afonso Arinos Filho, who had resigned as vice leader of the UDN bloc during Lacerda's attacks on his father's foreign policy. Sandra Cavalcanti, who replaced the senator's son as vice leader, disagreed with him. She said: "I consider João Goulart one of the worst figures to have appeared in the history of Brazilian politics."[12]

On September 2, after Senator Afonso Arinos was quoted as saying that Lacerda had decided to go abroad, the governor sent him a cutting telegram: "I am not thinking of traveling at this time . . . and at any rate not before looking for the last time at the face of morbid conceit which leads a certain type of person to treason and infamy." The senator, pleased with his role in helping to solve the crisis, wired the governor: "I made no reference to you, about whom I have not thought for a long time. Besides, trips would be useless for you because, while you are always inclined to run away, you can never get away from yourself and this is your punishment."[13]

Lacerda, speaking on radio and television on the night of September 3, said he would remain in office because the recent crisis no longer allowed him the right to think of resigning. In this, his first broadcast following Quadros' resignation, he defended the veto of Goulart by the military ministers and said their intentions had been deformed by "a tremendous propaganda offensive" that led public opinion to consider "formal aspects of legality" instead of "the defense of democracy and national security against the surreptitious offensive of international Communism." During the crisis, Lacerda explained, the state government had refrained from making pronouncements in order not to aggravate the situation. It had kept busy protecting streets and homes.

He told his listeners that "the days that lie ahead will be days of grievances and distrust, of insults and slanders against those who defend the constitution—not simply one of its articles—and who defend the nation rather than appearances." He warned the people against trickery and described Guanabara as strategically important for those who used confusion and Communism to try to conquer Brazil and, through Brazil, South America.[14]

14. Comments

The seven-month period that ended with the adoption of the parliamentary regime was a political setback for Lacerda. Quadros, while in the presidency, flirted with the PTB, made federal appointments in Guanabara that displeased the governor, and disappointed him in other ways. During the final days of the period it became clear that Goulart would become president, despite the efforts of Lacerda, and that the new federal administration would be in the hands of the governor's longtime foes.

It is true that Quadros failed in his dramatic move to achieve what Lacerda denounced, and that Lacerda added to his own fame of being a dangerous adversary. But the outcome of the quarrel was the result of a miscalculation by Quadros and did not mean that voters agreed with Lacerda about the "independent" foreign policy. Janistas, devoted to the latest "victim" of Lacerda and "the trusts," joined with Getulistas, Juscelinistas, and Janguistas in condemning the governor of Guanabara.[1]

Condemnation was not difficult when Lacerda supported the unpopular position of the military ministers following Quadros' resignation, and when he moved to suppress "subversion" in his state, thus alienating most of the press and giving impetus to anti-Lacerda charges of long standing.

In contrast to political developments that were unfavorable for Lacerda, his administration got off to a satisfactory start, with its accomplishments in education and with the introduction of new executive methods which, according to Congressman Laerte Vieira, "shook up archaic processes and found a substitute for the corrupt bureaucratic machine."[2] For the most part, however, it was simply an introductory period in which important projects remained dependent on funding, avidly sought within and outside the state.

The carefully drawn-up presentations of the projects were a positive sign for the future. So also was the ability, much needed in September 1961, of Raphael de Almeida Magalhães to deal with state legislators and federal authorities, and his determination to dedicate himself to improving the relations of the state executive with them.

The governor, although unlikely to modify his own tactless political ways, had become a more competent and assured administrator. César Seroa da Mota, of the public works secretaryship, maintains that Lacerda, in his first months in office, failed to see problems as engineers saw them, and that "the situation improved greatly when he decided to entrust himself to the engineers" of all departments, sharing with them his executive vision and providing dynamism with his demands. Lacerda, reviewing in 1965 the water crisis of March 1961, observed that the crisis was "perhaps providential" because "I learned many things from the bitterness and anguish of those days" and, after they passed, came to appreciate the dedication of the men who worked in the water department.[3]

Lacerda, at the outset, was less self-assured than he appeared. When he called on Dom Lourenço de Almeida Prado at the São Bento Monastery on the eve of his election, he said that the prospect of running the state "scares me very much." "I know," he added, "that I am impatient and rash." According to Raphael de Almeida Magalhães, Lacerda was "worried at the start, when he took over the government and faced the task of putting together a properly operating administration, not an easy thing." The governor, he says, "learned by doing" but suffered a great deal and wondered at times whether he had the patience and other attributes "to administer well."

"All this," Raphael recalls, "changed in 1961. He saw that he could be a good governor. This was very important."[4]

II.

Governor during the Parliamentary Experiment (1961-1963)

1. Repercussions of the Press Censorship (September–November 1961)

At a joint session of Congress on September 7, Goulart became president. In what was considered an appeal for an early plebiscite, he stressed that "we must now get a mandate from the people, faithful to the basic precept that all power emanates from them." After the ceremony the congressmen and senators of the PSD, the largest party, chose a prime minister satisfactory to Kubitschek and Goulart: Tancredo Neves, who had been defeated for the Minas governorship by Magalhães Pinto in 1960. Cabinet ministers, elected by Congress with the help of Goulart and other party leaders, included Foreign Minister San Tiago Dantas, War Minister João de Segadas Viana, Labor Minister André Franco Montoro, Justice Minister Tancredo Neves, Finance Minister Walter Moreira Salles, and Mines and Energy Minister Gabriel Passos. The choice of Passos (UDN, Minas Gerais), a foe of Tancredo Neves and Kubitschek, pleased Magalhães Pinto and the Parliamentary Nationalist Front. The *Tribuna da Imprensa*, displeased, called him a former pro-Nazi.[1]

O Estado de S. Paulo lamented the return to a state of affairs that had been defeated in the ballot boxes in 1960. The *Tribuna* correctly forecast the development of a movement by Goulart and his supporters to do away with the parliamentary system. It pictured the Communists as trying to use the movement to reach power and said that they saw but one obstacle: the political force of Lacerda. Therefore, it explained, the Communists were calling on students and workers to support the impeachment proposal, presented at the end of August by Saldanha Coelho, against the governor.[2]

The impeachment proposal said that Guanabara had become "a vast penitentiary," whose police beat up students and arbitrarily seized defenseless citizens. Aliomar Baleeiro, worried about the outcome, suggested that a good defensive move would be to have Guanabara adopt a parliamentary form of government at once instead of waiting until 1965, when, according to the new amendment to the federal constitution, all states were required to adopt the system. Lacerda rejected Baleeiro's suggestion.[3]

Speaking at the inauguration of the Vila Isabel administrative district on September 12, Lacerda proclaimed that "if they try to cancel my mandate, I shall defend it with bullets." It was better, he said, to die fighting than to live in a country dominated by Communists. "I'll only leave here dead or by the will of the people." He criticized the legislature for not passing laws and for giving him, instead, "nonsense like this impeachment."[4]

A legislative commission of five, named by Lopo Coelho to study impeachment, was made up of Sandra Cavalcanti (UDN), Roland Corbisier (PTB), Samy Jorge (PSD), Gladstone Chaves de Melo (PDC), and Paulo Alberto Monteiro de Barros (independent). Corbisier, like Paulo Alberto, was a strong proponent of impeachment. As *relator,* he called in labor leaders, students, Military Police officers, and newspaper directors, such as Mário Martins (*A Noite*), Manoel Francisco do Nascimento Brito (*Jornal do Brasil*), Paulo Silveira (*Última Hora*), Luís Alberto Bahia (*Correio da Manhã*), Antônio Chagas Freitas (*O Dia*), Antônio Cavalcanti (*Luta Democrática*), and João Ribeiro Dantas (*Diário de Notícias*).[5]

State legislator Afonso Arinos Filho, whose father had become the new government's ambassador to the United Nations, delivered a speech saying that Lacerda's prestige was in tatters and that it was better to leave him in that situation rather than take the chance of having impeachment turn him into a victim or martyr. The speech, with its reference to Lacerda's "attempt to overthrow the regime for his own political interests," annoyed Lacerda so much that he phoned the state legislator and spoke to him in a threatening way. Legislative Assembly President Lopo Coelho, advised by Afonso Arinos Filho of the phone call, sent a guard to protect the young man's home and took the matter up with the governor. Lacerda told him he had spoken in a manner that would, he hoped, assure a break in his relations with the legislator.

The *Jornal do Brasil,* commenting on this incident and Lacerda's rash vow to use bullets against Communists rather than conform to any impeachment ruling, wrote that the proponents of impeachment were playing the game of the governor, an agitator who screamed about Communist subversion to further his own interests. Calling him "the most inept and disastrous adversary of Communism ever to have appeared in Brazil," the *Jornal do Brasil* wrote that he only helped the PCB when he accused democratic leaders of being Communists, spoke of the press and army as having been infiltrated, and aroused suspicion about all the forces that could be effectively anti-Communist. He should, the *Jornal do Brasil* concluded, be forced to concentrate on administering the state even if this meant that the Cariocas would be sacrificing themselves for the peace of Brazil.[6]

These sentiments and the stand taken by Afonso Arinos Filho did not deter the advocates of impeachment, who saw in the process an opportunity to damage the reputation of the governor. Saldanha Coelho, Paulo Alberto Monteiro de Barros, and Roland Corbisier had the support of Lutero Vargas (PTB), José de Souza Marques (PTB), and Waldemar Viana (being wooed from the PRT by the growing PTB). They were criticized by *O Jornal*, leading newspaper of the chain of Francisco de Assis Chateaubriand, which wrote that "the names of legislators who head this effort to mock the will of the electorate" made it clear that impeachment was "the work of Communists and their accomplices."

The governor, in reply to a formal notice drawn up by Saldanha Coelho, argued that violations of the constitution had been made by those who had preached and carried out political strikes. Only "fools," he said, did not recognize the role of the Communists during the agitation. He was congratulated by the Pernambuco state legislature for his "serene, level-headed, and patriotic" handling of the crisis. São Paulo UDN regional directorships sent envoys to express their support.[7]

The popular Amaral Netto returned, early in October, to the majority leadership of the Guanabara legislature. There Raphael de Almeida Magalhães, described by Lacerda as "adroit as the devil," spent half his time reestablishing working arrangements that had deteriorated. He was helped by Raul Brunini, who read a letter from José de Segadas Viana absolving the governor from responsibility for labor union interventions.[8]

Testifying before the impeachment commission, João Ribeiro Dantas attributed censorship to the top military authorities but agreed that the governor may have been in connivance with them. Chagas Freitas argued that Lacerda should have resigned rather than let state officials carry out censorship. Mário Martins pointed out that the order for ending censorship on August 30 had been given by Lacerda and therefore it was clear that he had been responsible for establishing it.

The thirty-seven-page report of *relator* Corbisier said that all the witnesses to appear before the commission had put the blame for censorship and arrests on Lacerda. In a chapter on the life and personality of the governor, the report described Lacerda as an uneducated pamphleteer with little intelligence. Impeachment commission member Gladstone Chaves de Melo wrote a rather different report. It quoted a passage from a book, written years earlier by Corbisier, a former Green Shirt, that warned against the Communist danger. Lacerda, Gladstone wrote, had been guided by Corbisier's own words when he had acted against Communist agitators.

On October 20 impeachment failed to win approval of the commission because of the votes of Sandra Cavalcanti, Gladstone Chaves de Melo, and Samy Jorge. Samy Jorge, speaking of the need of "peace in our state," suggested it would be best to have the voters decide, in a plebiscite, whether or not to retain Lacerda. Three weeks later, in a plenary vote, impeachment was supported only by the five PTB legislators and Paulo Alberto Monteiro de Barros. Fifteen voted against impeachment. A blank vote was attributed to Afonso Arinos Filho, who had switched from the UDN to the PDC.[9]

In the meantime Guanabara Censorship Director Ascendino Leite ran into trouble with Police Chief Hélio Tornaghi and the Sindicato dos Jornalistas Profissionais do Rio. After Tornaghi gave a press interview denying responsibility for the press censorship, Ascendino assumed the responsibility for actions taken "in harmony with the decisions of the military commanders" and submitted his resignation to Tornaghi. Then Lacerda, accepting the resignation of Tornaghi but not that of Ascendino, stated that "the responsibility was mine although the decision to carry it out was not mine. I ended it as soon as possible. In carrying it out, we succeeded in avoiding what was going to happen."[10]

The resignation of Tornaghi was followed by the departures of Siseno Sarmento, the security secretary, and Lauro Alves Pinto, the director of the DOPS (Divisão de Ordem Política e Social), in conformity with a ruling of the new federal government that all armed forces officers in active service had to give up posts in state governments. Lacerda, after quarreling with the ruling, named former Labor Minister José de Segadas Viana security secretary and police chief with full powers to coordinate all the state's security forces, including the Military Police, the fire department, the Guarda Civil, and the traffic department.[11]

While Lacerda was in New York, defending himself before the Inter American Press Association, the Sindicato dos Jornalistas Profissionais do Rio expelled Ascendino Leite, a step that Ascendino called "totalitarian" and blamed on Communists, the *Correio da Manhã*, and the *Jornal do Brasil*. After Livraria Civilização Brasileira displayed posters in its bookstore calling Ascendino an "undesirable

person," Ascendino sued both the Livraria and the Sindicato, saying
that the former carried out "Soviet propaganda in Brazil" and the
latter sought to prevent him from practicing his profession. Citing
his exhaustion, he resigned from his censorship post, which, before
the August crisis, had been used chiefly to improve the moral standards of public shows. He reiterated his "political and personal support" of Lacerda.[12]

Lacerda, reaching New York's Idlewild Airport on October 14,
learned that *Última Hora*'s Paulo Silveira, in charges made against
him on the previous day, had told the Inter American Press Association that the governor and his Rio censorship had prevented the Association from receiving cables sent to it by *Última Hora* and other
Rio dailies.[13]

When Lacerda faced the Association's Freedom of the Press Committee, he heard its presiding officer, Jules Dubois of the *Chicago
Tribune*, present charges published in a harsh *Jornal do Brasil* editorial. Lacerda, speaking in English, explained that with Brazil on the
verge of civil war late in August, and with the government in Brasília
"practically isolated from the states," each governor had to take the
steps he considered necessary. He said that all the states suffered
press censorship for three or four days—a remark that was contradicted by Júlio de Mesquita Neto, who declared that São Paulo had
experienced no press censorship.

Lacerda expressed his disapproval of press censorship but argued
that he had had no alternative. The Communists, he maintained, had
filled the streets in a "campaign of agitation" during which several
newspapers, including his own, had been attacked. He spoke of Communist infiltration in the Rio press. Pointing out that some of the
dailies lacked top direction, he mentioned Chateaubriand, afflicted
by almost total paralysis since February 1960, and Paulo Bittencourt,
"also sick" and in Europe. In an attack on Luís Alberto Bahia, Lacerda said that among the newspapers that were "in the hands of
subordinates," *Correio da Manhã* was especially bad and known for
its "irresponsibility."[14]

The Freedom of the Press Committee, issuing its report on October 17, said: "There is no place in a responsible press for irresponsible
commentaries or reprehensible malice." The report concluded that
the appearance of press censorship in Brazil, "due to political episodes," could not be overlooked although it was of "short duration
and was not of a general nature."[15]

At the Waldorf Astoria Hotel the next day, during the closing session of the Seventeenth General Assembly of the Inter American

Press Association, Júlio de Mesquita Neto argued that Lacerda as a journalist had always defended freedom of the press and should not be judged for acts carried out as governor. Paulo Silveira said that Lacerda, in speaking to the Association about unrest in Brazil, had used the same words he had been using for a long time in Brazil— words that had made civil war there a distinct possibility.

The members of the Association unanimously approved a motion condemning the short-lived censorship in Brazil. The *Jornal do Brasil*, which had called Lacerda the "Huey Long of Latin America," denounced the Inter American Press Association for condemning the fact of censorship and not its author. Paulo Silveira, after returning to Brazil, wrote reports about the Association that provoked a reply from Jules Dubois, who denied Silveira's charge that he was "a well-known agent of the CIA." "If I were a CIA agent," Dubois wrote Silveira, "I would be serving loyally as an American citizen and not committing an act of treason as the Communists always do when they serve incessantly as spies of the Soviet Union, master of the most despicable and reprehensible tyranny in the world today." Dubois added that if Silveira had any doubt about the role of Communists as spies, he could refresh his poor memory by reading the "excellent and informative book *O Retrato*, written by your Brazilian colleague, Osvaldo Peralva."[16]

Lacerda, during his twelve days in the United States, addressed enthusiastic audiences of Cuban exiles. In New York, four thousand Cubans, including Manuel Antonio de Verona, filled the Yorkville Casino and a thousand more stood outside listening to loudspeakers that brought Lacerda's address, "The Four Lies about Cuba." Commenting on the "lies" (self-determination, nonintervention, neutrality, and independence), Lacerda asked whether one could speak of the "self-determination" of France, Holland, and Belgium when they suffered under German occupation. To rid the Cubans of dictatorship and Russian intervention, he urged the Organization of American States (OAS) to put aside inertia, cowardice, and sophistry. Recommending intervention in Cuba, he said Russia had already intervened. In Miami, where he spoke to Cuban refugees, Lacerda was heartily applauded when he predicted that "even if Communism advances in the world, Fidel Castro will fall in Cuba."[17]

Before returning to Brazil, Lacerda went to Washington to speak with Inter-American Development Bank President Herrera, to whom he had previously sent letters requesting assistance for Guanabara. Cleantho de Paiva Leite, the bank's Brazilian director, had been berated rudely by Lacerda in the past and would have nothing to do with him; fortunately for Guanabara, Cleantho recognized the importance of the water and sewer projects and was willing to support them if he could deal with someone else, such as Hélio Beltrão.[18]

Like Cleantho de Paiva Leite, Finance Minister Walter Moreira Salles had long been attacked by Lacerda, but he, too, was willing to help solve Guanabara's problems. Assurance of the cooperation of the new federal government, a stipulation of the Inter-American Development Bank, was secured for the new Guandu aqueduct project after Raphael de Almeida Magalhães and Marcelo Garcia spoke with Moreira Salles. The finance minister took Raphael to see Goulart and furnished the necessary letter. On October 22, an Inter-American Development Bank engineer, who had been in Brazil studying the Guandu project, gave it his blessing on condition that water rates in Guanabara be increased to assure repayment of the bank's loan to cover 50 percent of the project's cost.

The poor relations between Lacerda and Goulart, who enjoyed considerable power despite the parliamentary regime, did not prevent Guanabara's PSD senator, Gilberto Marinho, from getting promises from Tancredo Neves to do everything possible to achieve the release of funds promised by Quadros during the Fourth Governors' Meeting. The senator, a friend of Lacerda's, was assisted by Raphael de Almeida Magalhães and Lopo Coelho, who served as acting governor during Lacerda's absence.[19]

2. The Year Ends with a Prison Riot (December 1961)

Lacerda returned from the United States late in October to a situation which the *Tribuna,* citing a bankworkers' strike and a new water shortage, considered discouraging. The water shortage was caused this time by a break in an aqueduct near Nova Iguaçu and by the seizure of water, destined for Rio, by a town in Rio state that claimed the water. While the break underwent repair and Guanabara Attorney-General Eugênio Sigaud handled the problem of water rights, Veiga Brito and his engineers assigned 250 men to the work that would assure completion, before the year end, of the 7,800-meter Jacques-Acari aqueduct, begun in August.[1]

Lacerda transferred the water department to SURSAN, whose share of the budget made it more dynamic than the public works secretaryship, and he promoted Sewerage and Sanitation Director Enaldo Cravo Peixoto to head SURSAN, following the resignation of Djalma Landim. SURSAN had its hands full of projects, such as the creation of Flamengo Park and the demolition of the old Municipal Market in the crowded downtown district. The Catumbi-Laranjeiras tunnel, completed after fourteen years, was put in the hands of SURSAN and named Santa Bárbara, patron saint of the men who had constructed it, in order to honor the memory of twenty-three workers killed by a cave-in at the tunnel a year earlier.[2]

The prospect of the IDB loan, and perhaps explanations about water fees by Rego Monteiro, gave impetus to the administration's financial package, which was debated in the full assembly starting on November 1. To the disappointment of Saldanha Coelho, the administration received assistance from oppositionist Gerson Bergher, chairman of the finance commission; condemned by the PSB, Bergher left the party.[3]

The administration's bill, passed by the legislature in November 1961, contained wage increases for employees of the state government and provided realistic water and sewer fees; also it raised taxes. The most significant feature of the bill (Law 72) was the increase in the tax on sales (*vendas e consignações*), which supplied 75 percent of the state revenue. The former tax rate of 4 percent, less than the rates in the states of Rio de Janeiro, Minas, and São Paulo, was increased to 5 percent. Still awaiting action were the governor's messages about administrative reform, the state telephone company, and new capital for the state bank, and Lacerda therefore called for the legislature to hold a special session starting on February 1, 1962.[4]

The administration's first anniversary was observed by the inauguration of a new school and a ceremony to mark the conclusion of the Santa Bárbara Tunnel paving and roofing. The governor also opened modest headquarters for COPEG. While COPEG's president, businessman Guilherme Júlio Borghoff, corresponded with Joshua B. Powers about possible American investments in Guanabara, the governor kept the International Cooperation Administration of the United States apprised of the state's needs for assistance; and he took American embassy officials (and Peace Corps Director Sargent Shriver) to visit *favelas*.[5]

Those who criticized Lacerda for not fulfilling campaign pledges were told that the governor's team was busy looking for funds. They were kept informed of progress made by COSIGUA's president Brigadeiro Antônio Guedes Muniz, negotiating with firms in Europe in the hope of establishing a steel plant and iron ore exporting facilities in the Santa Cruz area. From Essen the *brigadeiro* advised Lacerda of his work on a protocol to specify the bases of a final contract to be signed only after receipt of the approval and guarantees of the governments of Brazil, Germany, France, and Belgium. Lacerda, speaking in Rio, said that "the Europeans are far ahead of the

Americans in understanding the need of the Carioca people to expand," and that, once the protocol was signed, the fate of the proposed port and steel plant would depend on the Brazilian government.[6]

After flying to Europe on December 15 to attend the signing of the protocol, Lacerda returned on the 23rd with the news that he had spoken to European companies about a garbage treatment plant and other needs of the state. Security Secretary José de Segadas Viana, at the airport to greet him, told reporters that the principal concern of the police department was the lack of men.[7] Nor was Segadas Viana's budget sufficient to provide for the proper handling of prisoners, as was demonstrated the next day when a riot broke out at the state prison on Frei Caneca Street.

The prison, with a capacity for 936 inmates, held 1,180. The lack of funds left 550 of them with nothing specific to do all day. Some smoked marijuana and others fabricated knives. The 150 prison guards could be divided into two categories: those eager to enforce rules, and those who were friendly to the prisoners and shared their dislike of prison Director Vitor Mehry. Feuding among prisoners had become worse with the recent arrival of two rival gang leaders known as Arubinha and Mineirinho (José Rosa de Miranda). Arubinha was said to have given the police information about Mineirinho.

Mineirinho, a veteran of prison escapes, was among the leaders who felt that it would be possible to get support for an insurrection during which they would make their getaway. It began with a protest against the poor food during a meal at 4:00 P.M. on Christmas eve. Prison Director Mehry, reaching the scene an hour later, found 700 prisoners, inmates of two of the four pavilions, refusing to eat and shouting "We want food." Mehry, promising to investigate the food question, was seized but managed to escape during a struggle in which one guard was killed with a knife. Prisoners took keys from guards and unlocked cells. Arubinha, his cell invaded, was tortured throughout the night and finally his throat was slashed. In the meantime Mehry phoned for the assistance of the Military Police, Army Police, and civilian police. During the three hours it took these reinforcements to arrive, Mehry tried to set off six tear gas bombs and found none of them would explode. The prisoners, some with revolvers, were in control. Many danced and sang songs insulting Mehry and the guards, while others set fire to one of the pavilions. The arrival of hundreds of police subdued the rioting; but, to the disappointment of Mehry and some of the troop commanders, they did not attack the rioters because Security Secretary Segadas Viana refused to give orders that might result in a slaughter.[8]

This was the situation when Lacerda arrived at 10:30 P.M. The governor, opposed to "general reprisals," verbally thrashed police who seemed to be about to use machine guns and throw grenades, and he told Mehry that he was suspending him from the directorship pending the outcome of an investigation. Then, at first alone and later with the prison chaplain beside him, he confronted 700 inmates in the prison's Meira Lima Patio. The prisoners, he said afterwards, were stamping, vaulting, and samba dancing around a large fire that was burning beds. Amazed to find the governor in their midst, they quieted down.[9]

"The governor of Guanabara," Lacerda told them, "is here to give you the tranquility that four or five prisoners are destroying. I am a man and not a coward. If you want to behave like cowards, I, the governor, shall go along with cowardice and get into the fight like a coward." "Those who have reasonable complaints," Lacerda also said, "will receive justice from the authorities; however, those who continue to use violence will, in return, be faced with the severity of the police. We are not afraid of those considered valiant because we are neither more nor less valiant than you. We are here to speak like men and reach understandings."[10]

Lacerda told the prisoners that he was going to set up an investigation to look into complaints. When asked for a change in the prison directorship and guards, he replied that "we do not do anything under threats." But he did reveal that he had provisionally dismissed the prison director and named in his place, also provisionally, Francisco Eduardo Monteiro, the director of the Lemos de Brito Penitentiary. These announcements brought shouts of approval.

"What is important," Lacerda said, "is that through punishment that the law establishes for all who break it, strength be found for improvement. And most assuredly that strength is not to be found when prison conditions are worse than those to which everyone, being a creature of God, has a right." Lacerda also said that "just as we, you and I, should never tolerate that a prisoner here raise his hand against a guard, we should never tolerate that a guard raise his hand against a prisoner." The prisoners applauded the governor and some of them promised to end the revolt and the aggression against guards.

When Lacerda went to the prison morgue to view the body of the guard killed with a knife, he was accompanied by guards who wished to carry out reprisals. One of them, calling himself "the leader of the guards," began giving a speech to the governor, but Lacerda cut him short by observing that the guards had no leader and that he, the governor, was present to speak for them.[11]

The calm that followed Lacerda's speech to the inmates came to an abrupt end after midnight, when police vigilance was weak. Inmates, fearing reprisals, took a guard as hostage. They started new fires and invaded the kitchen, barber shop, pharmacy, and carpenter shop in search of implements that could be used as weapons. Lacerda, ordering the police to continue showing restraint, went to the kitchen, where he found two prisoners; after he shouted at them they left. Then he confronted convicts who had seized the hostage and heard them describe their act as a measure of safety against retaliation. Lacerda, calling the act useless, argued that as long as the prisoners refrained from attacks, the police would not shoot. The guard was released after Lacerda declared that, if the threats continued, the police would act "whether or not you have a hostage."

But the situation deteriorated at 4:30 A.M. Prisoners decided to attack a gate en masse, in order to escape, while others distracted the authorities by starting fires throughout the jail and destroying the medical facilities, including the X-ray equipment. Segadas Viana authorized the use of gas bombs and told the police to scare prisoners by shooting into the air and to use their weapons seriously only if necessary for defense. After the prisoners shot and killed a soldier and wounded others, guards and members of the Military Police fired on mutinous prisoners, protecting the arrival of soldiers of Civilian Police Chief Carlos Ardovino Barbosa.

The prison rioters surrendered at 11:00 A.M., while the Military Police, aided by an air force helicopter, combed a nearby *favela*, from which weapons were believed to be reaching prisoners. The prison riot, according to reports, had resulted in thirty casualties, and the six deaths had included four prisoners, two of whom had been killed by fellow-inmates. Repairing the prison, Lacerda said, would require 200 million cruzeiros (half a million dollars).[12]

Lacerda ordered guards from the Lemos de Brito Penitentiary to replace those at the Frei Caneca Street prison because, he said, the latter were "very nervous" and might carry out reprisals. Then he participated in an investigation of food in the prison's kitchen and helped supervise the cleanup of cells and corridors carried out by prisoners.

In the director's office at 3:00 P.M. on Christmas, Lacerda met with Segadas Viana, state legislator Anésio Frota Aguiar, Penitentiary Director Monteiro, and Colonel Ardovino Barbosa. There he wrote out orders placing Monteiro in charge of the prison and naming an investigating commission, to consist of Monteiro and two lawyers.

Addressing a radio audience, Lacerda attributed the riot in large part to prison conditions inherited from the federal government, and he pointed out that the state had been waiting for over a year to receive funds promised for reequipping prisons. Calling the food at the Frei Caneca Street prison "bad, very bad," he said that the inmates had "a certain justification in their complaint, without this giving them a reason for the movement that was started."[13]

Dismissed Prison Director Mehry declared that a "premeditated attitude" of investigators and guards, unfriendly to him, was responsible for judgments about the inmates' food, which, he pointed out, was the same as that provided to employees of the prison and was prepared by prisoners because the budget lacked funds for paying cooks. He argued that casualties and destruction could have been greatly reduced by rapid action. He could not understand the three-hour delay in getting reinforcements to the prison nor the ensuing failure to give them orders to act. He put the blame on the governor and Segadas Viana, both of whom insisted that early action, before daylight, might have led to a slaughter.[14]

The investigators' report, completed in January, criticized Mehry, prison educational services, and the practice of guards of taking money from prisoners who wanted better cells and remunerative work. The report convinced Lacerda that the penitentiary and prison should be in the hands of professionally trained prison experts, and so Monteiro was replaced.[15]

A feud broke out between Security Secretary Segadas Viana and Colonel Ardovino, whose relations with Segadas Viana's girlfriend did not inspire friendship between the two men.[16] In March 1962 the colonel accused Segadas Viana of receiving 1.4 million cruzeiros a month in bribes from seven bankers of the illegal *jogo do bicho* gambling operation. Segadas Viana fired the colonel and was then dismissed himself. As the state legislature prepared to investigate charges of corruption in the highest echelons of the police department and the origins of the wealth of Segadas Viana, Saldanha Coelho remarked that the crisis had been inevitable ever since the Otávio Mangabeira Foundation had accepted contributions from bankers of the *bicho* game.[17]

Mineirinho, considered the chief instigator of the prison riot, ended up in the city's insane asylum. He knew it well and, for the third time in his career, escaped from it in April 1962. Apparently well armed and wealthy, he vowed that, before the police caught him again, he would kill a man he considered responsible for giving the police information about him. But he was shot to death by the police in May before he could achieve his vengeance.[18]

3. Charges against the Goulart Regime
(November 1961–May 1962)

Following the inauguration of President Goulart, Lacerda lost little time in attacking the new administration for favoring Communism. In November, after the council of ministers decided to renew diplomatic relations with the Soviet Union, he declared that "the government has just solved a problem for Russia and created one more for Brazil"—by granting "immunities to Russian agents in a nation that is unprepared civicly." Invited to attend the annual November 27 ceremony to honor the memory of those killed by Communists in 1935, Lacerda declined. In a letter to War Minister João de Segadas Viana, he wrote that "the rash and imprudent renewal of diplomatic relations, imposed by the Russian dictator as a condition for carrying out the dirty work of Judas in Brazil, is an outrage to the memory of the dead and the intelligence of the living." He asked the war minister whether the speech of Foreign Minister San Tiago Dantas would "commemorate the victims of Communism or the victory imposed by the Russian government" in exchange for trade relations.[1]

The Soviet Union, setting up embassy offices in Rio, appealed to Governor Lacerda on December 18 for a telephone. The governor's reply, written by Edgar Flexa Ribeiro in January, said that the warm reciprocity in "Brazilian-Soviet relations, to which your communication refers, in no way obligates the state of Guanabara." "We owe very little to the federal government, because we receive little or nothing from it. To Russia we owe much less." The Russians were told that the few available telephone lines were reserved for those who contributed to the well-being and progress of the people of Guanabara. "Positively we do not see how we can include the diplomatic representation of the Soviet Union in that criterion."[2]

Representatives of the Soviet Union, upon becoming established in Rio, were harassed by anti-Communists. Cardinal Jayme Câmara, Colonel Ardovino Barbosa, *O Globo*, and the Movimento Anti-Comunista (MAC) warned Cariocas that a Soviet Exposition, planned for May 1962, was "a Trojan Horse." On a Saturday evening, after the opening of the exposition in São Cristovão, Lacerda was told by an acquaintance of air force Major José Chaves Lameirão (participant in the 1956 anti-Kubitschek Jacareacanga rebellion) that the major had arranged to have a powerful time bomb placed in the exposition. The governor rushed to the scene and helped the police, already alerted, with the evacuation of people and the search for the bomb. After a Russian found the bomb, which experts said could have demolished the entire exposition, Police Chief Nilton Marques da Costa and

San Tiago Dantas bringing Russian bear to Brazil. (Edmondo Bigalti drawing in *O Estado de S. Paulo*, November 29, 1961)

the aviation ministry conducted investigations, which implicated an army major who had fled. During the investigations, three hand grenades were discovered in the vicinity of a motorboat that was scheduled to take Soviet diplomats for an outing on Rodrigo de Freitas Lagoon.[3]

Developments in organized labor led Lacerda to declare in December 1961 that the new Brazilian administration was turning the Confederação Nacional dos Trabalhadores na Indústria (CNTI) over to "the Communist *pelegos.*" The governor's declaration followed the most important event of the Brazilian republic's experiment with the parliamentary system: the biennial election of officers of the CNTI, the country's oldest and largest labor confederation. The anti-Communist leadership, which had dominated the CNTI since its organization, was defeated by the Communists and their allies by a vote of 29 to 23 federations—an outcome that Lacerda and the *Tribuna* correctly attributed to pressure exerted by Goulart and Gilberto Crockatt de Sá, the president's labor affairs adviser. It brought to the top of organized labor men such as Clodsmith Riani, friend of Goulart, Benedito Cerqueira, and Dante Pelacani. Lacerda, in a speech to businessmen, said that the Communist victory in "Latin America's largest labor organization" meant that "the Russian fifth column" would henceforth enjoy an annual income of 1.2 billion cruzeiros ($3 million) collected through the *imposto sindical* and other taxes.[4]

In January 1962, at the ceremonies installing the new CNTI

officers, President Goulart and Prime Minister Tancredo shared the spotlight with Francisco Julião, "leader of the peasant leagues" of the northeast. "Cuba, Cuba, Cuba," was the frenzied response to Goulart's heartily applauded speech about Brazil's "independent" foreign policy.

Following the CNTI election, Pelacani and other labor leaders organized strikes, mostly in São Paulo, to exert pressure on the lawmakers in Brasília to pass legislation to give workers each year a "13th month" of wages as a Christmas bonus and to restrict severely the remission abroad of company profits. When the "13th month" law was passed in April 1962 by the Chamber of Deputies, back from its summer vacation, the CNTI organized a victory celebration.[5] CNTI leaders made plans to join Communists and pro-Communists in other labor confederations to form what became known in June 1962 as the General Strike Command (CGG).

When the National Union of Students (UNE), cooperating with the strike movement of December 1961, asked Lacerda to turn Flamengo Park over to it, the governor had unkind words for its leaders, "almost always professional students," and for its activities. In January 1962 members of the MAC (Movimento Anti-Comunista) painted "House of Moscow Lackeys" on the UNE headquarters and wrecked installations inside. At a protest rally, which filled Cinelândia, students were joined by labor leaders, Piauí Governor Francisco Chagas Rodrigues (PTB), Congressman Sérgio Magalhães, state legislators Francisco Julião (Pernambuco) and Hércules Corrêa (Guanabara), and a representative of the Cuban embassy. The orators attacked Lacerda.

Lacerda, speaking on television, condemned the MAC and the "putrid" UNE and said he feared neither. The depredation, he said, was either a terrorist act by people fed up with UNE provocations or a Communist scheme "to agitate the country." He called the UNE "a Communist organization that openly preaches revolution" and "receives 300,000,000 cruzeiros a year from the education ministry."[6]

Novos Rumos called attention to a slogan, painted on a wall: "With Lacerda the MAC Will Win"; and it cited evidence to show the participation of Cuban exiles in the MAC. It found it significant that the terrorist activities of the MAC coincided with the approach of the meeting in Punta del Este, Uruguay, of foreign ministers of the American republics, who were to consider the expulsion of Cuba from the OAS and the adoption of economic sanctions against the Castro regime.

Lacerda wrote a statement to the foreign ministers to remind them that any comfort given to Castro would be "a contribution to those who plot with Russia to do to one of our countries what it did in

Cuba." Replying to an invitation to appear at a rally in Montevideo, he said his presence in Uruguay was unnecessary because a manifesto, calling on Brazil to be faithful to its commitments, had already been issued by four of its former foreign ministers: João Neves da Fontoura, Vicente Ráo, José Carlos de Macedo Soares, and Horácio Lafer.[7]

At Punta del Este, however, Foreign Minister San Tiago Dantas found juridical reasons for opposing the anti-Castro measures advocated by Secretary of State Dean Rusk. Brazil joined five other nations in abstaining, while fourteen provided the majority that expelled Cuba from the OAS. Back in Brazil early in February, San Tiago Dantas expressed regret at the expulsion and pleasure at the meeting's failure to enact sanctions against Cuba, "thanks to the invincible position of Brazil." Brazil's stand, he said, represented a victory for the Brazilian people, who were "showing their will."

Congress rejected a motion to censure San Tiago Dantas, whose stand was bringing him the applause of nationalists, Communists, and organized students and workers. When the PTB of Minas nominated him for reelection to Congress, CNTI President Clodsmith Riani presented a resolution extolling his performance at Punta del Este.[8]

4. Streetcars and Telephones (1960–1962)

In the 1950s the Rio-Light group, controlled by the Canadian-based Brazilian Traction, Light, and Power Company, fell on hard times. Rio-Light President Antônio Gallotti, writing to Lacerda in January 1961, explained that the deterioration of public services rendered by the group was the result of fixed tariffs and inflation that made "reasonable profits" impossible and therefore prevented new investment. The forty-five thousand Brazilian Traction shareholders, he pointed out, were receiving no dividends and found their shares quoted at the lowest prices ever. Gallotti also mentioned "ideological questions," demagoguery, and public protests against foreign concessionaires.[1]

In the case of the Rio-Light's streetcar (*bonde*) operation, the pre-Lacerda years were characterized by litigation, with the municipality claiming violation of clauses of the old concession agreement, and Rio-Light seeking indemnification for losses it said it suffered from inadequate tariffs. The streetcar concession in the South Zone, long held by Rio-Light subsidiary Companhia Ferro Carril do Jardim Botânico, expired on December 31, 1960. Despite the efforts of Raphael de Almeida Magalhães to persuade Gallotti to have Rio-Light continue the operation, the company refused and therefore the concession reverted to the state.[2]

Lacerda announced that the company was delivering "scrap iron" without even a repair shop, thus violating the clause that called for a service "in good condition" and able to function on its own. At the transfer ceremony, at the Largo do Machado streetcar station on Sunday, January 1, the governor refrained from signing a receipt. In reply to a speech there in which a Light Company representative spoke of the company's "desire to collaborate" with the state, Lacerda said the company's "desire" had consisted merely of relying on lawyers to work against the city, but that things would be different now that the city had a real government. He sent lawyers to Brasília to argue before the Supreme Court that the company should be forced to turn over what he felt was owed to the state. After the Supreme Court, in a unanimous decision in January 1961, rejected the arguments, Lacerda vowed to "continue struggling."[3]

The judiciary named a Junta Administrativa Provisória (JAP) to manage the South Zone streetcar service, which the state government was not yet organized to take over. In the meantime, the state sought to introduce a fleet of trolley buses (ônibus elétricos) to replace part of the streetcar system, whose tracks were in bad shape and whose operation often caused traffic congestion. The governor also worked to end the practice of having streetcars run the wrong way on one-way streets, a practice that had gained them the name of mata paulistas (because outsiders, unfamiliar with the unusual arrangement, would be run over by them). He spoke to Traffic Coordinator Fontenelle, who, on the pretext of needed repair work, tore up tracks where streetcars had been traveling against the flow of traffic.[4]

By the latter half of 1961, two hundred trolley buses, contracted for in 1957 with payment due in 1962, had reached the city's port facilities. The governor, who needed 75 million cruzeiros for installing the new system (including uprooting tracks and repaving streets), persuaded the legislature to act after he threatened to sell the buses. The first trolley bus line, using overhead cables of the streetcar system, was inaugurated in September 1962. Within one year all two hundred buses were in operation in the South Zone under the management of the state's new Companhia de Transportes Coletivos (CTC).[5]

Lacerda, at the inauguration of the CTC in December 1962, announced that the new company's functions included running the streetcars on Governor's Island and in the Campo Grande district, to the west. He also announced that the state was ready to negotiate with Rio-Light to take over the operation of streetcars in the North Zone. Rio-Light, whose concession there was due to expire at the end of 1970, lost 618 million cruzeiros on its streetcar operation in 1962 and was interested in bringing the concession to an early end.[6]

In the case of the telephone service, Lacerda inherited a law of the Municipal Council requiring the state to intervene in the affairs of Rio-Light's Companhia Telefônica Brasileira (CTB). Antônio Gallotti declared he would appeal to the courts. But Lacerda, asserting on December 9, 1960, that "the intervention is the law," said he would name a commission to execute it with "the fullest fiscalization" and "interference where necessary in all the operations, but not in the direction and execution of services." Two days later he spoke of using the intervention to reach an understanding with the CTB that would satisfy the needs of the Cariocas, and added that, if necessary, he would provide phones without the CTB.[7]

With help from the three-man intervention commission, Lacerda drew up a project that he hoped would be accepted by the CTB and the state assembly. It would create the Companhia Telefônica do Estado da Guanabara (COTEG), whose capitalization at the outset would be 51 percent in the hands of the state, with 49 percent of the shares going to the CTB in return for its assets. New phone users, paying in installments for new lines and instruments, would eventually become shareholders. Part of the income, to be augmented by a "reasonable tariff increase," would be used to redeem shares held by the CTB so that it would be totally expropriated in twelve years. The plan, described as being able to furnish 300,000 new phones in six years, was announced in April 1961 and submitted to the state assembly late in June. In August, when the assembly's justice commission started its study, Temístocles Cavalcanti said that a tariff increase for expanded service was unfair to the 230,000 current instrument holders, and added that it was difficult to act while the values of the company's capitalization and the CTB's assets were unknown. Frota Aguiar prepared a substitute project. Despite the special session, called for February 1962 to act on the telephone project and two others, none of the projects even came up for discussion in the full assembly. Brunini, blaming PTB leader Saldanha Coelho, told the assembly on March 1, 1962, that Lacerda expected to find a solution for the telephone problem that did not require legislation by the assembly.[8]

An old law, voted by the Municipal Council, was used by the Guanabara administration to justify direct negotiations with the CTB, regardless of the assembly. Lacerda and his team worked with Gallotti on an arrangement whereby the state would take over the CTB's Guanabara properties in return for debentures maturing in from six to eighteen years.[9]

In February 1962, while Lacerda made headway in these negotiations and while the Guanabara legislature procrastinated, Rio Grande do Sul Governor Brizola expropriated the Companhia Telefônica Nacional, a subsidiary of the International Telephone and Telegraph Corporation (IT&T). Brizola's state government deposited an indemnization check for only 20 million cruzeiros ($54,000) and then claimed that the expropriated foreign utility owed money to it. The act was embarrassing to Goulart, preparing for an official visit to Washington, and was described by Lacerda as "a mischievous prank," harmful to Brazil's credit abroad. It did nothing to promote passage by the Guanabara legislature of the COTEG telephone scheme. Roland Corbisier and Saldanha Coelho congratulated Brizola and announced that the PTB was offering, as a substitute to the COTEG scheme, a proposal to expropriate the CTB in Guanabara.[10]

In order that Goulart might visit the United States with as little embarrassment as possible, arrangements were made to have the Bank of Brazil extend a loan (pending court decisions) of 1.3 billion cruzeiros to IT&T. Also, consideration was given to the idea of "reducing areas of friction" by having the Brazilian government purchase foreign utilities. The idea opened up excellent possibilities for the CTB. Therefore Guanabara state officials, who had thought they could work out a deal with Gallotti by offering debentures to the CTB, found him dragging his feet. Lacerda, opposing federal government plans for outright purchase, argued that government funds should be used to provide more telephones rather than to pay foreign stockholders for worn out and obsolete equipment.[11]

Early in March the federal government authorized the National Economic Development Bank (BNDE) to purchase the shares of foreign telephone companies. Lacerda declared at once that Guanabara might quickly expropriate the CTB in the state, even before the conclusion of the property evaluation. He also vowed to carry out the expropriation if the federal government decided to pay for the indemnization of the expropriated Rio Grande do Sul telephone company.[12]

While Lacerda spent the last two weeks of March in Washington and New York, his intervention commission evaluated the CTB's Guanabara properties at 11 billion cruzeiros ($28 million), half the value claimed by the CTB. The federal government, displeased with reports that Guanabara might expropriate, let it be known that it might itself expropriate or have the BNDE purchase the property of the CTB. State Attorney-General Eugênio Sigaud went to court with a notification that such a purchase without the consent of the state would be illegal because it would disturb contractual arrangements and violate the state's autonomy.[13]

In Washington Lacerda picked up hints that the Goulart government might purchase the CTB, and he rushed back to Brazil after

Lopo Coelho and Raphael de Almeida Magalhães informed him that the purchase would be made. Calling Gallotti to the palace, he complained of his abandonment of negotiations with Guanabara and announced the state's expropriation of the company's properties in the state. Gallotti proposed suspending the meeting and then went to speak with Goulart. He returned with Goulart's instruction for the state not to proceed without consulting the federal government. Lacerda signed the expropriation decree and remarked that it was "incredible" that the president and governor found themselves dealing with each other through Rio-Light.[14]

Explaining the expropriation to the press, Lacerda objected to the use of money for the proposed purchase "when the important thing is to provide telephones to Rio." He said that the Brazilian constitution reserved to the states the handling of telephone concessions and service. Citing "public need and social interest" as the basis of the expropriation, he accused the CTB of failing to comply with its contract.

Commenting on Lacerda's dramatic step, Kubitschek's friend Augusto Frederico Schmidt suggested that it might have been taken to hurt Goulart's forthcoming mission to the United States, and Niles Bond, of the American embassy, said that the step worried him and his colleagues very much. Raul Brunini blamed it exclusively on the failure of the legislative assembly to resolve the problem. Congressman Tenório Cavalcanti said that "Lacerda has made up for many sins; now all that is lacking is his expropriation of the entire Light group."[15]

Seeking nullification of Lacerda's expropriation, Gallotti asked for federal intervention in the CTB of Guanabara,[16] and this was decreed by Tancredo Neves on April 1 on the grounds of "national security." General Jair Dantas Ribeiro was appointed *interventor* and authorized to use troops to assure compliance with the decree.

Lacerda told *Tribuna* reporters that the people and government of Guanabara were "appalled." The prime minister, he said, "was not ashamed to use a distinguished army figure to defend foreign interests represented here by his brother, Antônio de Almeida Neves, a director of the Light group." Asserting that the CTB's Toronto headquarters had "confirmed" the "clandestine" negotiations to sell the Light shares to the Brazilian government, Lacerda added: "I can recall no business deal as demoralizing for Brazil, nor any act of violence as shameful in the protection of unscrupulous interests. The prime minister has not allowed the president to appear in Washington for the defense of the interests of all the Brazilian people. He preferred to have the federal government appear as the perpetual defender of the

Light group, whose interests are stronger than the autonomy of the states and more powerful than the constitution."

"I wish," Lacerda also said, "publicly to congratulate Dr. Antônio Gallotti for the success of the first phase of his maneuver. This is the type of pressure to which Jânio Quadros may have alluded. But we are not going to resign from fulfilling our duties." Speaking a little later on television, Lacerda vowed not to comply with orders of the CTB. "For that to happen it will be necessary to have, besides an *interventor* in the company, an *interventor* in Guanabara Palace, but I can guarantee that he will not enter it without my leaving it, dead."[17]

While federal soldiers, armed with machine guns, guarded the doors of the CTB building in Rio, Magalhães Pinto asked Goulart to prevent the BNDE from buying the shares of the telephone company of Minas. He called the federal intervention of the CTB unconstitutional, whereupon the Goulart administration cited a wartime law (of December 1942) authorizing federal intervention in telephone services if required for national security purposes.

Guanabara, accusing the CTB of noncompliance with its contract, went to the courts on April 2 with its demand for expropriation in return for about 10 billion cruzeiros ($24 million). The governor used television to argue that Tancredo Neves was asking the Brazilian people to pay double this figure for obsolete equipment, in a move that would not provide a single new telephone. He also signed a decree increasing the CTB's telephone rates in order to assure its employees of a recently granted wage increase; but CTB *Interventor* Jair Dantas Ribeiro declared he did not recognize the authority of Lacerda to sign any decree about telephone rates.[18]

Goulart, who left for the United States on April 2, instructed the attorney-general of the republic, Evandro Lins e Silva, to request all organs of the government to hold off from debating or reaching decisions about the CTB intervention until he returned. During his absence, the courts denied Guanabara's request for an injunction against what Eugênio Sigaud called an unconstitutional federal intervention in a public service of a state. Sigaud had been maintaining that the "national security" argument was valid only during a state of siege, enacted by Congress.[19]

At the White House on April 4, Goulart suggested to President Kennedy that foreign public utilities in Brazil be "nationalized peacefully" by means of "just payments prescribed in the Brazilian constitution." The sellers, following the example set in Mexico, would reinvest 75 percent of the payments received in Brazilian undertakings considered useful by the Brazilian government. Kennedy expressed his interest and urged that the operation be carried out in a manner that would not give the appearance of confiscation. Such an appearance, he said, would reduce the flow of foreign private capital to Brazil and would make it difficult for the United States Congress to vote assistance programs for Latin America.

Speaking in New York a few days later, Goulart stated that "the Brazilian government intervened in the Light only to prevent the expropriation by the state government. We know that the expropriation in Guanabara caused apprehension in the United States. But I repeat what I said to the American Chamber of Commerce of Rio de Janeiro: Brazil wants foreign capital to remain in the country and to obtain a fair remuneration." In declarations to journalists at the United Nations, he pointed out that conversations had been started with American authorities for reaching a "friendly accord." One of the formulas for solving the problem, he said, would be the investment of the capital of public utilities in "other industries, more interesting to them and greatly needed by the country."[20]

Goulart's return to Brazil on April 11 was followed at once by Tancredo Neves' announcement of plans to place all of Brazil's telecommunications in the hands of the federal government. The prime minister said the CTB intervention could be interpreted as the first step for setting up this "national system."[21]

In June, as a result of the Kennedy-Goulart talk, the council of ministers created a commission to work out purchase terms with foreign utility companies. Furthermore, "unification" of the execution of all Alliance for Progress programs for Brazil was placed in the hands of the federal government with the establishment of COCAP (Comissão de Coordenação da Aliança Para o Progresso). Meanwhile in Washington congressmen cited the case of Brazil while discussing the Hickenlooper Amendment to cut off aid to countries that expropriated without fair compensation. (The amendment was passed by Congress in August.)

With Rio-Light looking forward to receiving fair compensation from the Brazilian government, and with the council of ministers prolonging federal intervention in the CTB, the Lacerda administration turned its attention to the formation of a state telephone company that would install instruments, by selling shares to their would-be owners, outside the area served by the CTB. The plan to form such a company was approved late in July 1962 by the legislature's economy commission, headed by retired General Danillo Nunes.[22] But formation of Companhia Estadual de Telefones da Guanabara (CETEL), like many of the plans of Lacerda, depended on the full legislature's approval of the administrative reform law, some of whose clauses, such as those establishing administrative regions, were not popular with the lawmakers.

5. A Chat with President Kennedy
(March 26, 1962)

Early in March, Joshua B. Powers and Antônio Carlos de Almeida Braga, a director of the state bank, urged Lacerda to accept an invitation to speak in New York on March 20 at the Overseas Press Club. "I feel that certain decisions favorable to COPEG may be taken in Washington at about that time," Powers wrote the governor.[1]

Already a state engineer had flown to Washington with a stack of documents for the Inter-American Development Bank (IDB) about sewers and the Guandu water project—a stack so high that photographs showed it to be taller than the governor's aide-de-camp, Carlos Osório. And on February 11, Raphael de Almeida Magalhães, SURSAN President Cravo Peixoto, and budget expert Rego Monteiro had gone to Washington to discuss the documents with the IDB and conclude details about loans. Cravo Peixoto and Rego Monteiro remained in Washington until March 28.[2]

The governor departed from Rio on March 16 with his son Sebastião and Almeida Braga. Before boarding the plane, Lacerda was asked to comment on a speech by Jânio Quadros, who was preparing to run for governor of São Paulo and had, in his speech, attributed his resignation to his helplessness in the face of attacks by Congress, Lacerda, some dangerous Communists, and powerful newspapers, and the activities of men such as Adolf Berle, Ambassador Cabot, and Treasury Secretary Dillon. Lacerda replied that if he could not sleep on the plane he would look at the speech although his interest was in the future, not the past.[3]

In New York Lacerda attended a performance of the Broadway hit "Come Blow Your Horn," and raved about it so much that Alfredo C. Machado, who was also in New York, agreed to buy the rights for presenting it in Brazil if Lacerda would translate it.[4] Thus the rights were bought by Machado, the witty book publisher whose good relations with foreign correspondents in Rio made him a useful associate of Lacerda's administration.

Speaking at the Overseas Press Club, Lacerda said that "what a country like Brazil wants is to be taken seriously, even if those responsible for it do not always conduct themselves in a manner that facilitates such an attitude." He forecast that nuclear power would give Latin America a "great leap forward," and proposed a Federation of the Americas as an appropriate response to the much discussed European federation. "With rare exceptions," he said, "the United States has relied too much on the power of money and not enough on the power of ideas."[5]

In Washington, Lacerda spoke at Georgetown University and worked with the lending agencies. For COHAB (Companhia de Habitação Popular), the state was seeking an IDB loan of $10 million to help with the construction of low-cost housing, to be occupied gradually by the residents of *favelas* that could not be urbanized. On behalf of COSIGUA, Lacerda explained to IDB President Felipe Herrera that even if Europeans furnished port equipment and locomotives, the cooperation of the IDB would be necessary for completing the first phase. COPEG, seeking investments (for an international airport hotel, fishing, cold storage, etc.), had applied to Washington's Agency for International Development for $5 million.

COPEG was trying to dispel the American business community's reluctance to invest in Brazil, caused in part by the unsettled status of the law project for drastically restricting the remission of profits abroad. Its job was not helped by reports published in the United States about Brazil's turn to the Left and its "precarious economic position," with large deficits, inflation, and wage increases. *Newsweek* predicted that the next victim of expropriation by Brizola would be the power plant of the American and Foreign Power Company in Pelotas, Rio Grande do Sul.[6]

On March 20, while Lacerda was in New York, the IDB announced its decision to assist the Guanabara water and sewer projects with three thirty-year loans to the state bank, totaling $35 million and bearing annual interest rates of between 2 3/4 and 4 percent. When Lacerda was in Washington for a signing ceremony, Cleantho de Paiva Leite, Brazil's member of the Bank's board, told Felipe Herrera, "I won't be present; I don't like Lacerda." Following the signing in Herrera's office, Cleantho was advised that Lacerda was coming to his office to see him. Cleantho made a quick disappearance.[7]

Robert W. Bialek, engaged by Powers to assist Lacerda and COPEG, worked with Kennedy adviser Richard Goodwin to set up Lacerda's appointment to visit the president on March 26. Lacerda, preparing for the visit, wrote a letter to hand to Kennedy, in which he argued that the pooling of resources to provide an "immediate massive" vocational training program for Brazilian youth was the best way to change "attitudes" in the country and prevent disappointing results in the elections of October 1962. He wrote that "reforms such as agrarian, tax, and free labor organization should be made simultaneously and not preliminarily to self help and cooperation from the

Alliance." Suggesting that "a sort of *credit risk insurance* be adopted to open the dam that now holds back the flow of private capital to Brazil," he added that "we must define and separate the concept and spirit of free enterprise from stagnation within the old formulas of public utilities corporations." Lastly, Lacerda described Guanabara, with its "deficit of ten thousand houses per annum and an accumulated ten-year deficit" as being the "biggest potential labor market in Brazil." "My state," Lacerda wrote, "is, and could be even more so, the showcase for Democratic progress in Brazil. It is the main center of the Communist effort. Powder may lie in the Northeast of Brazil but the wick is in Rio."[8]

Lacerda and Ambassador Roberto Campos found Kennedy in a rocking chair and in the company of Goodwin. After Goodwin jocularly introduced Lacerda as a politician who had driven presidents from office, Kennedy said he was not worried because "our political institutions are very stable."[9] The governor gave the American president a copy of *Estratégia da Paz*, the Portuguese-language edition of a Kennedy book for which Lacerda had written a preface. Kennedy, giving Lacerda a copy of his most recent book, *To Turn the Tide*, remarked that perhaps Lacerda would write a preface for a Portuguese translation of it, whereupon Lacerda said he would like, above all, to do a preface for *Profiles in Courage*, a book with lessons important to statesmen of all countries.

Kennedy, studying Lacerda's letter, was struck by the revelation that half of Brazil's population was under eighteen. "That reality," Lacerda said, "is a true challenge to us." Turning to Ambassador Campos, Kennedy explained that it was difficult to get Congress to go along with large-scale assistance, and that the United States could not solve all of Brazil's problems, but that, soon after the Quadros inauguration, the United States had made rather large credits available.

Kennedy called the Alliance for Progress a "thrust" but not "permanent assistance," and said that everyone, "here and there," should recognize the importance of the role of private initiative. As Goulart was about to make his trip to Washington, the American president asked Campos to keep him informed about the situation of foreign utilities in Brazil. From the ambassador's reply that everything was being taken care of, and that more complete information would be available when San Tiago Dantas returned from Geneva, Lacerda gathered that negotiations were making headway without (he has written) public disclosure.

Lacerda, discussing the technique of "self-help" for improving life in the *favelas*, cited the Favela do Vintém, "where we installed water and sewers with the voluntary participation of those who live there."

He acknowledged the presence in Rio of an American mission to study low-cost housing but said things moved too slowly. It was important, he said, to have evidence of Alliance for Progress accomplishments in housing before the October elections. Kennedy asked Goodwin to speed up steps being taken by Washington.

After an interruption for picture-taking, Kennedy kept the interview alive by expressing an interest in having the Alliance for Progress work become better known among the people in Rio. The governor repeated his suggestion about a program to finance vocational training for young people. "Today I can assert, without conceit, that the masses have more confidence in me than when I was elected. . . . If you wish, ask Sargent Shriver about our surprise visit to some *favelas* when he was in Rio for the Peace Corps. On the walls the Communists had written a series of insults to me, accusing me of being a lackey of the Americans, and making other such 'kind remarks.' However, as Shriver could see, the people of those *favelas* came cordially to embrace me and converse trustfully with me, which wasn't always the case before. This happened now for two reasons. First, because they feel we are not handling the *favelas* as though they are ghettos. . . . And, secondly, because we have given them schools. Imagine, Mr. President, the social and political effect, for the destiny of democracy, of an immediate program not only for children but for young people. . . . If, in Rio, we were to have results in a short period, I can't tell you what party will win, but I am certain that the Communists will be defeated."

Campos, reverting to the problem of the foreign utilities in Brazil, suggested the establishment of a fund for buying those companies. Lacerda, opposed to the idea, told Kennedy: "We don't need American money in order to put telephones in Rio." He mentioned the availability of "the money of those who use telephones and can thus become shareholders, carrying out nationalization naturally and increasing the capital democratically." "The financing of equipment," he said, "can be handled by private initiative, that is, by the manufacturers, competing for the business. . . . It is important for you to mitigate the anger of shareholders here, but that should not be done by impairing other initiatives for which we really lack capital in Brazil."

Campos explained that the governor was referring to the Light group, a Canadian company, and not the IT&T, an American company. Lacerda observed that "the Light group is an American-European organization, with headquarters in Toronto, Canada, in order to avoid paying taxes here in the United States." Kennedy smiled. "The IT&T group," Campos said, "is solely American and it is the object of negotiations." "And," Kennedy added, "it has shareholders scattered among all the American people." Campos then pointed out that the purchase of such utilities would be carried out with the guarantee that they would reinvest the proceeds in Brazil. Lacerda felt that the whole idea, which would be denounced by Communists, although for reasons other than his own, amounted to "a distortion" of the Alliance program and that the guilty parties were the Brazilian government and the utilities. But he restrained himself from getting into an argument with Campos in front of Kennedy. Changing the subject, he spoke of the need to give people "confidence in the principles we defend" and thus "contain the expansion of Communism." Before he and Campos left, Kennedy, at Lacerda's request, inscribed *To Turn the Tide*. Lacerda gave the book to his son Sebastião, who had not been present because Lacerda had been told by the Brazilian embassy that the visit should be limited to those who had been expected.[10]

When Lacerda reached Rio on the morning of March 30, he explained to reporters: "I had the pleasure of telling Kennedy that the Carioca people do not need one penny from the Alliance for telephones. It would be a crime to divert the Alliance resources to give money to the Light or other companies holding public service concessions."[11]

6. The Reconstruction of Guanabara Begins (1962)

In April 1962, soon after returning from the United States, Lacerda decided to name SURSAN Chief Cravo Peixoto head of transport and public works, a secretaryship whose shortage of funds was so great that when it needed a typewriter it had to ask SURSAN for one. About to enter Lacerda's office in answer to the governor's call, Cravo Peixoto spoke with his longtime friend Ruth Alverga, and she advised him not to take the post because SURSAN possessed "all the money." Lacerda, however, was agreeable to having Cravo Peixoto head SURSAN as well as the secretaryship. The press declared that the governor was eliminating past hostilities by making the state highway department and SURSAN subordinate to the secretaryship.[1]

The Inter-American Development Bank's loan, which would provide SURSAN with $35 million for water and sewers, was the largest loan the bank had ever made. IDB President Felipe Herrera, in Rio for a signing ceremony at Guanabara Palace, heard the governor express his gratitude to foreign and Brazilian authorities and to his "direct collaborators in this effort of almost ten months, foremost among them Raphael de Almeida Magalhães, with the always timely and wise advice of Hélio Beltrão." He suggested that the Alliance for

Progress follow the example of the Inter-American Development Bank, which had negotiated the new loan directly with Guanabara and had thus avoided that "the matter be delayed or weakened." He reiterated that Alliance for Progress assistance should not await the enactment of reforms and criticized those who maintained that nothing could be done without basic reforms. "Is it not revealing that those who speak most about certain reforms are precisely the ones who do not believe in them because they believe only in revolution?" Denouncing "slogans of agitation," he described "the leftist nationalism of today" as "the Communist version of the rightist nationalism of yesterday."[2]

The late 1961 increase in taxes and water and sewer fees led to protests, with *Última Hora* contending that Lacerda had "betrayed the Carioca people, crushing them with onerous taxes."[3] The legislature in May 1962 passed a bill to reduce some of the taxes, leading Amaral Netto, who was not a friend of the governor, to explain that only nine votes could be rounded up to oppose the bill because "the executive branch shows complete disinterest in matters handled in the legislature."

Lacerda, who vetoed the bill to reduce taxes, showed no lack of interest in the legislature when he addressed crowds. Blaming it for his inability to push forward with some of his plans, such as those related to the subway and telephones, he urged the people to give him a solid majority in the next legislature, to be made up of fifty-five members chosen in the elections of October 7, 1962.[4]

Lacerda complained about the failure of the federal government to act on his list of "fourteen unattended items," submitted to it by Public Works Minister Virgílio Távora. Salvador Mandim, the state's electric energy coordinator, forecast that delays by the BNDE would result in power rationing and discourage industry. Mandim, a retired general who had opposed the Kubitschek-Goulart inauguration in 1955, declared that the BNDE, with 32 billion cruzeiros to invest in projects, had allotted only 4 percent to Guanabara. *Última Hora,* in reply to such complaints, pointed out that in accordance with legislation that created Guanabara in 1960, the federal government in 1962 was furnishing 3.2 billion cruzeiros for the state's Military Police, 2 billion for its public safety department, 800 million for its fire department, and 440 million for the state justice system.[5]

The Inter-American Development Bank, limiting its assistance to Guanabara to the program for water and sewers, did not act on requests for a loan to help with the *favela* problem. However, the *favela* program benefited from 1 billion cruzeiros ($2,300,000), donated in June 1962 to the state-affiliated Fundação Leão XIII by the United

States Agency for International Development (USAID), using funds derived from wheat sales to Brazil. The agreement called for the "reaccommodation" of some *favelados*, the urbanization of the Vila Proletária da Penha *favela*, improvements in other *favelas*, and the construction of a medical clinic in Madureira (near several *favelas*); the state also agreed to contribute 3 percent of its tax revenue to the Fundação Leão XIII for use in dealing with the *favela* problem.[6]

The governor spoke of plans to build thousands of low-cost houses, with water, light, and sewers, at various places for the relocation of some of the *favelados*. Occupants of the new houses were to have bus service to work places and were to be encouraged to make additions to the small dwellings, which they would own. Their monthly payments over ten years were set at 12 percent of the ever-increasing minimum wage, an arrangement that was expected to keep the payments in line with inflation.

Land in Bangu was acquired on favorable terms from the Silveira family, of the Bangu textile firm, and there construction of the Vila Aliança proceeded. A lottery determined the occupants of the first houses. By the time Lacerda inaugurated the Vila Aliança on December 10, 1962, its 400 houses were occupied by families moved from the Bom Jesus *favela*. Lacerda announced that the Vila Aliança would soon have 2,250 houses and that construction was about to start on the Vila Esperança, scheduled to have 3,000 houses at nearby Senador Camará.

Much of the work of informing the USAID about the *favela* problem had been carried out by Social Services Coordinator José Arthur Rios, no advocate of the large-scale relocation of *favelados*. Professor Rios, well impressed by *favelados*, whom he encouraged to form self-help committees, believed that Raphael de Almeida Magalhães and Amaral Netto were eager to handle *favela*-related funds in a manner best suited for propaganda for the October 1962 elections. To Lacerda, whose aggressive notes indicated dissatisfaction with Rios, the social services coordinator sent a letter in February 1962 criticizing him for becoming "more and more inclined to consider the *favela* an urbanistic problem instead of a social one." "Your tendency," sociologist Rios wrote, "is to undertake work in the *favelas for* the *favelado* and not *with* the *favelado*, subordinating the *favela* work to a questionable administrative structure. Thus, using the same logic, you will end up evacuating *favelas* simply to take care of real estate interests." After offering to resign, Rios learned from the press and the governor's office in May 1962 that he had left his post at his own request.[7]

SURSAN, putting the finishing touches on the Santa Bárbara Tunnel, began work on two new tunnels for traffic. One, the 220-meter

Major Vaz Tunnel, between Tonelero and Pompeu Loureiro streets in Copacabana, was so short that it would not require ventilation. The other activity was the start on the "longest urban tunnel in the world" to connect the city's north with its south. Early in June 1962, after the National Highway Fund approved a 1,750,000,000-cruzeiro ($4-million) loan, jackhammers of the firm L. Quatroni, which had won the bid, started driving into the rock between Lagoa and Cosme Velho, the longer of the tunnel's two sections.[8]

SURSAN's demolition of the Municipal Market early in 1962 forced merchants to go to the São Cristovão and São Sebastião markets, thus alleviating the clogging of downtown traffic by trucks. Plans for the demolition had been successfully resisted for twenty years, and the merchants were in no hurry to leave. When it seemed that they might make trouble on the day set for the move, Cravo Peixoto got in touch with Colonel Ardovino Barbosa, who, at the time, still headed the civilian police. The colonel brought 150 armed soldiers to the vicinity and the move was carried out peacefully. During the ensuing demolition, a campaign by prominent Rio residents, including the American ambassador and Academy of Letters President Austregésilo de Athayde, was launched to preserve the Albamar Restaurant, operating in an old tower where the market had been. The appeal to Cravo Peixoto and Lacerda could not fail because Lacerda had had the same idea. The restaurant, a sort of monument, was saved by a decree that made its employees the owners. With the urbanization of the Praça XV de Novembro, where the old market had stood, the historic Praça XV fountain was moved to the Praça da Bandeira, which an architect was remodeling to make it a "triumphal entrance to the North Zone."[9]

SURSAN, prior to the Lacerda administration, had been carrying out plans, approved in 1958, for the future use of the Aterro do Flamengo—the landfill on the shoreline of the bay in the Flamengo district, a result of the demolition of the Santo Antônio Hill in downtown Rio. Early in 1961 Lacerda suggested to engineer Djalma Landim, then head of SURSAN, that he consult Maria Carlota de Macedo Soares ("Lota") about these plans. Lota, the fifty-year-old daughter of *Diário Carioca* founder José Eduardo de Macedo Soares, was the owner of the Samambaia *fazenda* in Petrópolis and had sold Lacerda the plot he used as his country place before he took to weekending on Brocoió Island and before his purchase, in 1962, of the Sítio do Rocio, near Petrópolis. Lota, a neighbor until the governor sold his Samambaia house, was admired by Lacerda for her intelligence, culture, frankness, and drive, and the creativity she showed in handling properties in Samambaia. She was described by the press as a chain-smoking friend of poets and artists, and a collector of paintings and objects of art.[10]

Lota, reviewing the plans for the landfill of over a million square meters, wrote the governor in February 1961 that changes should be made in them to prevent the area from becoming an amusement park and a four-lane traffic throughway connecting downtown Rio to Botafogo and Copacabana. "The area calls for special care to preserve the exceptional and lovely landscape, with its ocean breeze, and to transform a simple corridor for automobiles into an immense wooded area which before long will be a landmark of the city as famous as Sugar Loaf and the sidewalks of Copacabana." She wrote that, in order to take full advantage of its unique characteristics, it should not contain closed buildings for nightclubs and theaters, which could be constructed elsewhere.

Lota criticized SURSAN's project, already being carried out, to dig long passages beneath the vehicle avenues so that pedestrians could reach the park. She said they were impractical, deprived pedestrians of the view, and gave "the rather uncivilized idea that people are less important than machines." In addition to calling for passages above the roadways, she advocated that the roadways consist of two lanes instead of four, leaving space that could be used for gardens or grass if it were felt that four lanes would someday be needed. She called for a "traffic census" and argued that the new traffic tunnels, especially the Rio Comprido–Lagoa connection, would make oceanside traffic at the *aterro* much less necessary. She insisted that studies be undertaken to determine the exact form that the bay's beach would take.[11]

Lacerda liked Lota's ideas. Despite pressure for an amusement park, he favored large and attractive gardens, blended into an area suitable for rest and recreation. Final plans included a pond for model ships, a field for model planes, a train for children, and a puppet theater. When plans were developed for courts for tennis, volleyball, and basketball, and fields for soccer, Cravo Peixoto favored four soccer fields, but Lota insisted on ten and got her way. She argued that soccer was an integral part of recreation, especially in Brazil.

The studies advocated by Lota led to plans to extend the area and create an attractive beach, and therefore, after the National Engineering Laboratory of Lisbon sent beach experts to Rio, Cravo Peixoto arranged, early in 1962, to rent a Stern dredge, veteran of Panama Canal work, for the transfer of fill from the bottom of the bay. Famed landscape architect Roberto Burle Marx was placed in charge of landscaping the *aterro*. Others on the team for creating the park were Berta Leite, Eduardo Guinle, urbanist Afonso Eduardo Reidy, architects

Hélio Mamede, Jorge Machado Moreira, and Sérgio Bernardes, and botanist Luiz Egydio de Mello Filho.[12]

Lacerda appointed Lota to head the team. She was, according to John Dos Passos, a small woman who worked in black striped pants and drove her *aterro* team energetically. She argued passionately for her ideas and not infrequently won heated arguments with the governor. "Whenever she sought to resign," Lacerda said later, "she came in the morning to my place and told me: 'You stick with that rubbish of sewage, water, and whatever; you think you will be remembered for that? When they find that toilets work, they are not going to remember you. When someone has a child in school, never will it be remembered that the school was made by you. Water and schooling are normal things that all governments have the duty to provide. The one thing they will remember is that you made Flamengo Park.'" The governor, late in 1962, authorized an additional credit of 685 million cruzeiros for SURSAN's *aterro* work.[13]

The "rubbish" to which Lota referred was quite visible when she spoke. With 133 kilometers of sanitary sewers put in place in 1962, compared with 35 kilometers in 1961, the opposition in the legislature accused the governor of filling the streets with holes. So many schools were inaugurated (a new schoolroom every twenty-four hours) that journalists, to Lacerda's chagrin, no longer considered the inaugurations to be news. He proclaimed, late in 1962, that "just as this year has been the year of education, 1963 will be the year of health," and announced a campaign of vaccinations against diphtheria.[14]

Funds for health services in Guanabara were supplied by the state lottery, whose expenses (including the distribution of 70 percent of the revenue as lottery prizes) left 250 million cruzeiros annually; modest amounts were applied to school lunches and a home for domestic servants, leaving 200 million cruzeiros for projects of the health secretaryship. The only foreign assistance received in this field by Guanabara was a financing (at 3 percent annual interest) that Lacerda helped to conclude with Germany in 1962 to provide hospital equipment worth 8,200,000 marks.[15]

Hospital construction was not neglected by Marcelo Garcia, under whose administration the building of the Salgado Filho Hospital in the Méier district went forward. However, he concentrated heavily and effectively on preventive medicine, and it was his successor, who took over late in 1962, who favored the "big hospital" idea. Raimundo de Moura Brito, the new health secretary, had headed the state Hospital for Public Servants and was a *udenista* popular with the Carioca voters. Ambitious plans included a new building for the Souza Aguiar Hospital in Rio's central area and additions to the Miguel Couto Hospital in Leblon, the Moncorvo Filho Hospital in the central area, and the Getúlio Vargas Hospital in Penha.[16]

To sell bonds to raise money for public works appeared to be out of the question because the annual inflation rate in Guanabara was over 50 percent and because interest rates were limited to 12 percent per annum by the federal law against usury. During a discussion that Rego Monteiro had with Mario Lorenzo Fernandez, the finance secretary proposed the issuance of bonds whose 1 percent monthly interest payments would be calculated on face values that would be increased in direct proportion to the increase in the sales tax revenues (which went up as inflation lifted the prices of goods sold). The owners of the bonds (*títulos*) would be regarded as associates participating in the state's tax receipts and development. The scheme, approved by Lacerda, was presented to the legislature in August 1962, shortly before the August 31 deadline for the executive's submission of the 1963 budget—a budget that estimated a receipt of 4 billion cruzeiros from the sale of these *títulos progressivos*. Legislative approval in November was followed in 1963 by excellent sales of the *títulos*, because they were the only bonds in the country to provide protection against inflation.[17]

The second anniversary of Lacerda's inauguration was characterized by an optimism that was reflected in speeches broadcast during the following week by cabinet secretaries. By this time busloads of Cariocas, organized by state Press Secretary Walter Cunto, were making visits on Saturdays and Sundays to the works in progress. Originally scheduled to show and explain work underway on the Guandu aqueduct ("the undertaking of the century"), with a state engineer in each of about fifteen buses, the itinerary was expanded in December 1962 to include a series of stops, including those to show activities at the vehicle tunnels and viaducts, the Vila Aliança, the Aterro do Flamengo, canalization projects, the Praça da Bandeira, and the Maracanã Stadium, which was receiving substantial improvements. Many people used automobiles to accompany these *caravanas*. The so-called Guandu Girls helped Cunto and Ayrton Baffa handle the crowds, which were addressed, not infrequently, by Water Department Director Veiga Brito.

A new series of inaugurations—each opening a branch of the Banco do Estado da Guanabara—was begun in 1962. In the 1950s, when the bank was the Bank of the Municipality, it was a source of political favors and had a poor reputation. Becoming the bank of the state in

1960, it was a small institution with a capital of 100 million cruzeiros and seven branches. One branch was added in 1961, the year in which its good reputation was established. In 1962, the bank inaugurated six new branches, and the legislature authorized that its capital be increased to 1 billion cruzeiros.

Financier Antônio Carlos de Almeida Braga, whose wife was the older daughter of Lacerda's longtime friend José Nabuco, accepted Lacerda's invitation to take over the presidency of the bank from Dario de Almeida Magalhães after the lawyer rehabilitated it. The dynamic personality of "Braguinha," a sports enthusiast, expressed well the spirit of the state. The bank became known as the fastest-growing bank in Brazil. It was on its way to becoming one of the foremost in the country, and, Cunto and others have added, no small factor in financing state government projects.[18]

7. Political Crises, Strikes, and Riots
(June–July 1962)

The prospect of useful and tasteful public works aroused some interest among the Cariocas; in mid-1962, however, soaring prices and food shortages were foremost in their minds.

With Brazil's annual inflation rate approaching 40 percent in May, the Senate showed its low esteem of the Tancredo Neves council of ministers: by a 33-10 vote, it rejected the Mem de Sá Amendment, which would have set aside the requirement that cabinet members wishing to run for Congress in October leave their posts three months before the election. Senator Milton Campos called the rejection of the Mem de Sá Amendment "a conspiracy by the backers of the presidential system of government." Even before the rejection, which forced cabinet ministers to leave office, Goulart instructed PTB congressional leader Almino Afonso to suggest the names of men, acceptable to their party, for the formation of a new council of ministers.[1]

Lacerda, commenting on rumors that Lott might be chosen to succeed Tancredo Neves, called the marshal an honorable patriot. He likened his past "divergence" with him to a mere quarrel in a family that becomes united when necessary. But by June 8, when Lacerda left Rio for a three-day governors' meeting in Araxá, Minas Gerais, Goulart had made it clear that he favored San Tiago Dantas, and leaders of organized labor were preparing to exert pressure on behalf of the foreign minister. San Tiago Dantas had just explained to three thousand cheering workers in Rio that "policy is independent only if it finds backing in the popular interests." The "independent" foreign

policy, he had said, should be accompanied by a corresponding domestic policy: one that would control prices and foreign capital and
promote agrarian reform.[2]

The governors' meeting had been called by Magalhães Pinto with
the support of Goulart, who spoke with several governors before they
went to Araxá. The meeting was expected to recommend a way to get
more action out of the government, either by the delegation of legislative powers to the council of ministers or else by a return to the
presidential system. Rio Grande do Sul Governor Brizola, a backer of
the presidential system who was preparing to run for Congress from
Guanabara, sent his justice secretary, Professor Francisco Brochado
da Rocha, in his place. Brizola explained that he could not accept the
presence of Lacerda, "too deeply associated with everything that is
most harmful and that we have condemned."[3]

Lacerda, before leaving for Araxá, told reporters that he would work
for delegating more power to the council of ministers so that it could
handle serious problems, but he added that the delegation of power
should be controlled by Congress to avoid abuse. He said he had no
preference between the parliamentary and presidential systems. Upon
reaching Araxá, he immediately delivered an address against Communism. Most of the governors, like Goulart, contended that Brazil's
ills could be cured by the enactment of "basic reforms," but Lacerda
argued that "the first basic reform must be the fight against inflation." Without that reform, he insisted, "the other reforms will only
aggravate the crisis and result in chaos." The governors ended up
by condemning Communism and fascism, and recommending that a
plebiscite be held as soon as possible to decide whether Brazil should
return to the presidential system. Lacerda, leaving Araxá, said he
disagreed with holding an early plebiscite. "The parliamentary system has not yet been put into practice," he said.[4]

While Magalhães Pinto, supporter of an early plebiscite, advised
Goulart of what had transpired at the governors' meeting, the General Strike Command (CGG) sent busloads of workers to Brasília to
demand that Congress accept San Tiago Dantas as prime minister;
and it threatened a general strike on his behalf. The Pacto de Uni-
dade e Ação (PUA), dominated by Communists Osvaldo Pacheco and
Rafael Martinelli and strong among railroad, port, and maritime
workers, threatened to strike to have the recent 40 percent government employees' wage increase extended to workers in its unions.
Already most of the university students were on strike, called by the
UNE to force the government to grant their demand that one-third
of the members of the university directive boards be students. And
practically all of the sugar refinery workers were striking because a

promised wage increase was not paid by refiners, who claimed they needed a price increase.[5]

Thus sugar became scarce in the Rio area, like rice and beans, because of the pricing policy of the federal government's food supply and pricing agency, COFAP (Comissão Federal de Abastecimento e Preços). Merchants were required by COFAP to sell rice at prices below those they had to pay for it, set by the IRGA (Instituto Riograndense do Arroz).

Lacerda, delivering a speech marking an Alliance for Progress wheat fund donation of 150 million cruzeiros to help build five markets in the suburbs, said the new markets, good as they would be, would not solve the problem of providing food. So serious was the shortage that four thousand men from Guanabara and Rio state, in need of food, armed themselves with scythes and axes and invaded the Tinguá forest reserve in order to plant rice, beans, and corn. To save the forest reserve, whose springs supplied drinking water to Rio, state Attorney-General Eugênio Sigaud appealed to the Supreme Court, with the result that federal troops expelled the invaders.[6]

The governor, in a letter to Goulart, explained why the COFAP pricing policy would not allow retailers in Rio to sell rice. "There appears," he wrote, "to be a design to force upon the people an explosion of rage and desperation." He asked the state legislature for 100 million cruzeiros ($230,000) to get foodstuffs to Rio and immediately provided 20 million to the Military Police for acquiring rice and beans to be sold at cost to Cariocas (who formed long lines outside stores). The Military Police, besides trying to locate food, broke up student demonstrations in front of the Municipal Chamber. They maintained that the students' plan to enact plays demonstrating the reactionary character of the universities would cause traffic obstruction.[7]

Speaking on television on June 22 about the nomination of San Tiago Dantas, Lacerda called it inopportune "principally at a time when the nation is struggling against two powerful forces that want to destroy it: inflation and the fifth column." The foreign minister, replying on television on the 24th, called Lacerda and his supporters passé. Then Lacerda, again on television, asked: "When did we hear the word passé used to describe democrats? From the mouths of fascists, of course! Hitler and Mussolini and all their agents always considered us, the democrats, passé." In a reference to San Tiago Dantas' affiliation with the Green Shirt movement in the 1930s, the governor called him a fascist who had become converted "to a new type of fascism: Communism."

Lacerda also used the speech to describe the UNE strike as illegal and immoral and said its purpose was to stir up agitation throughout

Brazil at the very time when "legions of red *pelegos* prepare to coerce Congress." Lacerda put the blame for the "conspiracy" not on Luiz Carlos Prestes, "that public relations man of the Soviet Union," but on the Goulart government. He asserted that the president was leading the nation to despair, cutting off food supplies, in order to deliver a debilitated Brazil to Russia. "And who," he asked, "is the threat" to the plan? "We, the passé ones, who are working to repair the streets and put water in the faucets. We, who have so little time for politics."[8]

PSD congressmen, feeling that the prime ministership should be in the hands of the largest party, joined the UDN, PSP, PRP, and PRT in defeating the San Tiago Dantas nomination, 174-110. Then on July 2, Goulart, in an irritated mood, nominated Senate President Auro de Moura Andrade (PSD) after persuading him to sign an undated letter of resignation from the prime ministership. Moura Andrade won overwhelming support in Congress despite the opposition of the PTB and labor leaders, who threatened a general strike unless the politicians formed a council of ministers to their liking. On July 4, after Moura Andrade disagreed with Goulart and congressmen about cabinet names, the nation learned that Moura Andrade was stepping aside.[9]

Hours before Moura Andrade's withdrawal became known, labor leaders tested their strength by calling their general strike on behalf of a "democratic and nationalist council of ministers." It was considered a success in most of the states although authorities in São Paulo and Minas reported that only about 30 percent of the workers adhered there. Certainly it was a success in Guanabara despite Governor Lacerda's proclamation that political strikes were illegal and that the state government would protect those who defied the strike call and would, if necessary, use bullets against members of "the minority" who opposed "the peaceful, working majority." The governor's promise of protection led to arrests and clashes in which several dozen people were wounded.

Commerce and industry closed down in Rio, and the transport system of trains, buses, and ferries was completely stalled. With port facilities not functioning, incoming ships remained at sea; and few planes landed because airport services were paralyzed. The morning found all the banks closed; but Lacerda, during a trip downtown, offered the protection of the Radio Patrol to those wanting to work, and many banks opened in the afternoon.[10]

The sacking of stores in parts of Rio and especially in Rio de Janeiro state was a principal reason storekeepers kept their shops closed. With food shortages a serious problem in Rio state, a violent "hunger revolt" developed in Duque de Caxias, São João de Meriti, Nilópolis, and Nova Iguaçu. After the riots there were quelled by army troops, 42 people were reported killed and over 700 wounded. "The periphery of Guanabara," *Jornal do Brasil* wrote, "was transformed into a battlefield" in which a multitude, in a "generalized sacking operation, . . . left dead and wounded on a scale unknown in Brazil since 1935." Lacerda, giving a July 5 speech at the inauguration of improvements at the Praça da Bandeira, referred to "bands coming from Caxias and Nova Iguaçu, trained in guerrilla warfare by Cuban and Czechoslovak specialists." The police of Guanabara, he said, were "still being opposed by shots in several places."[11]

COFAP blamed the political crisis for the food shortage. Lacerda and Rio state Governor Celso Peçanha, critical of COFAP, were described by COFAP President Max do Rego Monteiro as "propagandists of the sharks" because, he said, they advocated either raising food prices or freeing them from price controls altogether.[12]

At midnight on July 5 the labor leaders yielded to an appeal, sent by Goulart to CNTI Interim President Pelacani, that they call off the general strike. The strike ended in Rio only after Lacerda agreed to release 17 labor leaders, arrested as "agitators." But the governor would not agree to withdraw charges that they were lawbreakers. And the Rio police continued to hold 22 persons accused of theft and other "disorderly acts." In Rio state, where 250 were arrested, the damages from the recent riots were estimated at between 2 and 3 billion cruzeiros.[13]

The tension continued with labor leaders set to mobilize a new general strike if political developments led them to consider it necessary. The Rio police, placed on "rigorous alert," went into action again on July 6 because of a renewed outbreak of disorders. With rumors of more sacking of stores, 2,500 stores remained closed. Lacerda, walking at his brisk pace through the downtown streets, called on storekeepers to ignore what he called a wave of alarming rumors.

While lunching at the Albamar Restaurant downtown, Lacerda was advised by Raul Brunini that depredations were being carried out in the Largo do São Francisco. Accompanied by Raphael de Almeida Magalhães, he went there at once and found, in his words, nothing more than "contagious panic." Then, in a radio broadcast, he appealed to banks and stores to open. He declared that Rio was not Caxias and quoted Franklin D. Roosevelt, saying that "the only thing we have to fear is fear itself." On the same day, during an inspection of construction at the Salgado Filho Hospital, he found hardly anyone on the job and therefore announced that if the contractors failed to meet their five-month deadline they would be blacklisted by the state.[14]

Less than a week later, truck drivers in Rio voted to strike after rejecting a proposed wage settlement handed down by the president of the Regional Labor Tribunal. Lacerda, prepared for this possibility, ordered the arrest of 43 members of the drivers' union, including its president, thus bringing on the threat of another general strike. Interim War Minister José Machado Lopes, who had supported Brizola during the August 1961 crisis, insisted that Lacerda release the strike leaders.

Lacerda went to see Machado Lopes, taking with him Lopo Coelho and Raphael de Almeida Magalhães, who had become secretary of the interior as well as chief of the governor's office. After the governor said he would have to resign if Machado Lopes remained determined to release the strike leaders, the general backed down. In an official note left with the general, Lacerda argued that the strikers, who had recently been striking illegally for political reasons, were now making a wage dispute the reason for a movement whose true purpose was to use "subversive action by organized minorities" to reduce the supply of food and stimulate "desperation among the orderly, working population of this state."[15]

Some of the bus drivers joined the truck drivers in what was supposed to become a "general transport strike." Lacerda took his message personally to every bus terminal in the city and backed his pledge of protection to nonstrikers with a force of 500 members of the Military Police. His government mobilized drivers to replace strikers, who retaliated by using paving blocks to try to disrupt traffic in front of Lacerda's apartment. Within a few days the state government was able to report that 90 percent of the buses were in operation. The lack of support for the truck drivers' strike brought it to an end in mid-July.[16]

The shortage of rice and beans continued serious, but was somewhat alleviated by the federal government. After the Bank of Brazil resolved to purchase rice and beans in the south, even if the operation caused it monetary loss, air force planes and army trucks brought tons of these commodities to Guanabara. While Goulart ordered punishment for speculators, a Senate investigating commission (CPI) opened hearings in Rio's Monroe Palace. Lacerda, in his testimony, blamed the shortages exclusively on the pricing policy of COFAP, which, he said, had forced producers to turn to markets other than Rio. He called the shipments received in air force planes and army trucks insufficient to meet the demand. And he revealed that the state legislature had agreed to his request for a 100-million-cruzeiro fund for the purchase of foodstuffs and had authorized the creation of a state company, the Companhia Central de Abastecimento (COCEA), to give attention to large-scale purchases, storage, and marketing. Asked about the sacking of stores in Caxias, he told the senators that it had been carefully prepared by agitators. COFAP President Max do Rego Monteiro told the CPI that he would not let producers impose higher prices, which would have serious social implications; he went to Goulart with a plan to expropriate the foreign meat packing plants, whose profits, he said, were considered excessive and intolerable by the public.[17]

The food shortages, riots, and killings, the *Tribuna da Imprensa* wrote, gave impetus to a "general feeling" in political circles that the parliamentary system was a failure. In the Senate, Argemiro Figueiredo (PTB, Paraíba) introduced a bill to suspend the parliamentary system, and in the Chamber of Deputies Oliveira Brito (PSD, Bahia) introduced legislation that would make it possible for the new Congress, to be elected in October, to do away with the system. Goulart had the republic's attorney-general, Evandro Lins e Silva, appeal to the Supreme Court to declare the parliamentary system amendment unconstitutional. According to Lacerda, the supporters of a plebiscite to decide the fate of the parliamentary system were simply presenting a hoax to divert the attention of the people from the lack of beans and rice.[18]

Late on July 8, one month after the Tancredo Neves council of ministers resigned, Goulart nominated Brizola's justice secretary, Brochado da Rocha, to be prime minister. The nominee was so little known that Lacerda guessed that 99.9 percent of the Brazilian people had been unfamiliar with his name. But he was accepted by Congress on July 10 because he belonged to the PSD and because the lawmakers, eager to start campaigning, wished to avoid being held responsible for prolonging the political crisis. He turned out to be a socialist professor who had helped expropriate the IT&T property in the south and whose views coincided with those of the UNE and far-Left labor leaders. He favored an early plebiscite and asked that his cabinet be delegated legislative powers to press forward in the fight for reforms and against international capitalism. Speaking at the time Congress approved his name, he argued that an urban reform was necessary to defeat "the large landowners of the cities" and that an agrarian reform would overthrow a structure that "prevents the masses from possessing the domain of a continent."[19]

The cabinet, which included Finance Minister Moreira Salles, Labor Minister Hermes Lima, and Mines and Energy Minister João Mangabeira, was approved by Congress on July 13. When it met a week later, it asked for legislative powers to allow it to arrange that students, still on strike, occupy one-third of the memberships of the university directive boards.[20]

8. Brochado da Rocha (July–September 1962)

Afonso Arinos, who became foreign minister again in mid-July 1962, writes that Brazil, during the Brochado da Rocha prime ministership, was so agitated that he could not give the necessary attention to international matters.

The CGG, warning against "the plundering of the nation by foreign trusts," was pleased with the new prime minister's views. It threatened to call a general strike if Congress would not yield to Brochado da Rocha's requests for an early plebiscite about the parliamentary system and for special powers to allow the cabinet to enact agrarian reform, nationalize the electric power and mining industries, create a federal police force, revise strike legislation, and control the foreign exchange market.[1]

Lacerda, speaking late in July in Tiradentes Palace at a UDN regional convention, supported the resistance of Congress to the wishes of Goulart and his new prime minister. Early in August, after the military ministers called for an early plebiscite, Lacerda prepared a video tape for a television speech in which he argued that if the form of government was "illegitimate," as Brochado da Rocha claimed, then Goulart's role as president was likewise illegitimate. In the speech, released late at night after being held up for four hours by censors, Lacerda said that Brochado's request for special powers was designed to establish a dictatorship and allow irresponsible UNE youths, parasites of the nation, to run the universities.[2]

A circular-letter from the prime minister invited Lacerda to Brasília for a meeting of the governors with Goulart and the cabinet. Lacerda, calling it a "meeting of candidates to be *interventores*," said he would not attend because he opposed exerting pressure on Congress. But because the food shortage continued serious, and because Magalhães Pinto said the meeting would not deal with the plebiscite, Lacerda changed his mind early in August. At the meeting he presented a program for combatting inflation by reducing government outlays. He advocated decentralization, giving states the control of appropriations for stimulating production, in order to "end congestion in a suffocating and inoperative administration."[3]

Congress, opposed to the delegation of its powers, maintained that reforms, including an agrarian reform, were already under study by the lawmakers. To show that it was reform-minded and able to act, it passed the more severe of the two principal versions of the long-discussed bill to limit profit remittances abroad. Early in September, after Goulart refused to veto three articles that especially irked foreign investors, Finance Minister Walter Moreira Salles resigned, his negotiations abroad undercut by the president. Lacerda remarked that Moreira Salles was "fed up" with the way Brazil was being "discredited" abroad.[4]

To get congressmen, busy campaigning, to consider the proposals of the prime minister, arrangements were made to fly them to Brasília for a "concentrated effort" between September 10 and 15. Brizola asserted that the people would "rise up" if Congress did not arrange for a plebiscite on October 7, date of the forthcoming elections, and he added that if the decision had been in his hands, "the present Congress would already be closed." Calling himself an enemy of capitalism, he announced that he would broadcast three times daily. He planned to use Rádio Mayrink Veiga, which he controlled, and a chain of radio stations.[5]

Lacerda, warning of a coup between September 10 and 15, gave frequent television speeches that were no longer held up by prior censorship because Adauto Lúcio Cardoso and other congressmen, interrogating Justice Minister Cândido de Oliveira Neto, received assurances that free speech would prevail. The September coup, Lacerda said, would be carried out by the men who really ran the government. These men, he explained, were not the ones whose names appeared in newspapers but were Goulart's "Communist advisers." He listed nine members of the "secret cabinet," among them presidential Press Secretary Raul Riff ("with his Stalin-like mustache"), Paraná University Professor Álvaro Vieira Pinto ("who preaches revolution by students allied with workers and peasants"), and Brizola adviser Cibilis Sousa Viana ("the sibylline mentor who gives a cosmic and universal vision to Brochado da Rocha's provincial mentality").[6]

Lacerda said the central government, refusing to function unless it received dictatorial powers, was on strike. When he compared Brochado da Rocha to an army-following wanton woman, the excitable prime minister exploded. He insisted on federal intervention in Guanabara. And while the council of ministers dealt with this new problem, Labor Minister Hermes Lima, on the nights of September 4 and 5, used television to accuse the Guanabara government of preparing a coup. Maintaining that it was impossible for the federal and Guanabara governments to live together, he said that energetic steps would have to be taken to preserve federative unity.

Lacerda, replying on television, declared that supporters of intervention would have to kill him to carry it out. He compared the situation to that in 1937, before Vargas established the Estado Novo.[7]

O Globo, in an editorial about the "strange" speeches of Hermes Lima, wrote that the central government, so zealous to control subversive expressions, was silent in the face of the pronouncements of Governor Brizola, "storming against the institutions, proclaiming the need to close Congress." In the state legislature, Brunini read the *O Globo* editorial aloud and said that federal intervention in Guanabara, threatened in the labor minister's words, was the only way the central government could find to defend the position of Brizola. PSD legislative leader Gonzaga da Gama said that although he had often attacked Lacerda, he would adhere to the "brave struggle" of the PSD against federal intervention, thus respecting the votes cast by the Cariocas.[8]

Mines and Energy Minister João Mangabeira argued that the constitution allowed federal intervention to be carried out for the maintenance of the "national integrity." But Foreign Minister Afonso Arinos, although on bad terms with Lacerda, rejected intervention and pointed out that personal slander of the prime minister was not a political crime. After War Minister Nelson de Melo opposed intervention, Brochado da Rocha threatened to resign. However, Afonso Arinos persuaded the prime minister to remain, with the understanding that a strong official note, condemning Lacerda, would be signed by the entire cabinet. Nelson de Melo signed in order to prevent the fall of the government.[9]

The official note, released on September 6, was broadcast every half hour by radio and television stations on orders of the justice minister. It said in part:

> In carrying out his subversive campaign against the National Government, which he slanderously accuses of preparing a coup, the governor of Guanabara builds up his position, hostile to federative harmony and to the respect that the nation's authorities owe each other. The existence of the Federation is incompatible with the continuation of such behavior. The Council of Ministers denounces publicly the attitude of the governor of Guanabara, who is jeopardizing public tranquility and the Nation's prestige abroad.

Magalhães Pinto, governor of Minas, agreed with the official note. After consulting Goulart, Brochado da Rocha, and Brizola, he declared that Lacerda was aggravating the crisis with his "disrespectful pronouncements, harming the authority of the prime minister."[10]

As soon as Lacerda learned of the official note, he joined vice gubernatorial candidate Lopo Coelho, who was addressing a television audience. In a reference to Brizola, Lacerda told the audience that it was true that one of the governors was carrying out a subversive campaign and proposing that Congress be closed. Repeating that he would leave Guanabara Palace only if he were killed, he expressed pleasure in knowing that the vice governor would be Lopo Coelho, an upright person.

At midnight, after meeting with his cabinet, Lacerda spoke again on television, this time to read a formal statement in which he said the note of the council of ministers was erroneously addressed because the government of Guanabara had been the defender of the state, Congress, and public peace, while patiently putting up with discriminatory acts, provocations, and noisy appeals which, in Guanabara, had advocated class warfare.

On the evening of September 7 a crowd of several thousand left an Independence Day celebration to gather in front of Guanabara Palace. There a committee of women delivered a document, reportedly signed by eighty thousand, expressing support for the governor's courageous and energetic struggle against Communist infiltration. Lacerda, addressing the crowd, said, "Those who have deprived us of beans and rice now also want to deprive us of liberty and honor."[11]

In Congress, a commission headed by Gustavo Capanema (PSD, Minas Gerais) studied Oliveira Brito's proposed amendment for giving the next Congress six months in which to reform the constitution. Party leaders had agreed in August to back the amendment, but on September 10 the agreement fell apart, with the PTB seeking a clause for holding a plebiscite on June 15, 1963, if the next Congress did not handle the matter before April 30.[12] Even this was unacceptable to the CGG, renamed the CGT (General Labor Command), and it threatened a general strike unless Congress arranged to have a plebiscite on October 7, 1962.

Lacerda said that the objective of the campaign for an early plebiscite was to disparage Congress and agitate Brazil, and he appealed to the armed forces to oppose it. "It seems," he said, "that the whole country has come to a halt to argue about a parliamentary system that is rotten and a presidential system that is worse." He described a plebiscite as "a false consultation about two regimes that never functioned in Brazil."[13]

In support of the view of Goulart and the labor leaders, a grave military warning from the south was issued by General Jair Dantas Ribeiro, recently named head of the Third Army. In his message, sent to the president, prime minister, and war minister, the general said that in view of the intransigence of Congress and the resulting demonstrations in the territory occupied by the Third Army, he was not in a position to assure the maintenance of order unless Congress agreed to a plebiscite on October 7, at the latest. War Minister Nelson de Melo, who felt the general was going too far, replied with a telegram in which he said that formulas were being discussed in Brasília. He also advised Jair that his message was conducive to indiscipline and should not have been sent. It was up to the war minister, Nelson de Melo said, to decide whether order could be maintained in the south, and he added that he believed Jair could maintain it. Brizola and Brochado da Rocha called Nelson de Melo a *golpista*.[14]

Brochado da Rocha, unable to persuade Congress to grant him special powers and arrange for a plebiscite on October 7, resigned on September 13. Congress, he said, consisted mostly of bankers, rich businessmen, owners of large landholdings, building contractors, and members of the old political oligarchy.[15]

The CGT at once declared a general strike, whose purpose, CNTI leader Pelacani said, was to influence the choice of a new prime minister and achieve economic and political objectives, such as radical basic reforms and a plebiscite on October 7. Guanabara transport was disrupted by the paralyzation of streetcars, train service, ferry service, and the distribution of petroleum products. Lacerda, ill with a severe cold and fever, issued orders for private vehicles to assist transportation and for the police to arrest agitators who interfered with those who wished to work. Cecil Borer, taking over the DOPS, arrested labor leaders. But, following an appeal from the labor ministry, the governor agreed to release about thirty of them, including Rafael Martinelli, head of the Federation of Railroad Workers.[16]

The Chamber of Deputies, unable to secure the two-thirds majority needed to enact the Oliveira Brito amendment, gave support to a law proposal of Gustavo Capanema for preventing administrative gaps by allowing a provisional prime minister, appointed by the president, to govern until dismissed by a congressional vote of no confidence. When the proposal went to the Senate, Benedito Valadares (PSD, Minas Gerais) introduced a modification stating that the parliamentary system should continue in force only if supported by a "referendum by the people" to be held on January 6, 1963.[17]

The Valadares modification, part of an ordinary law, was unconstitutional, as Congressman Bilac Pinto (UDN, Minas Gerais) pointed out, and was opposed in the lower house by the UDN, which argued that the plebiscite question should be resolved by the next Congress. But Valadares' proposal had plenty of support in the PTB and in the

PSD, which found it easier to deal with Goulart after the departure of Brochado da Rocha. It was accepted by the Chamber of Deputies by a 169-83 vote on September 15, the last day of the "concentrated effort." In the Senate the Capanema-Valadares bill even received a favorable vote from Afonso Arinos. The outgoing foreign minister said that he continued to favor the parliamentary system and recognized that the bill was unconstitutional, but that his vote was determined by his resolve to avoid civil war.[18]

The president, satisfied with the prospect of a plebiscite on January 6, named a provisional council of ministers, headed by socialist Professor Hermes Lima, ardent advocate of Brazil's independent foreign policy. The labor leaders brought an end to the general strike, with the explanation that Goulart had betrayed them. The president, they said, had given his blessing to their movement on behalf of a plebiscite on October 7 but had later made the political deal that led to the passage of the Capanema-Valadares bill. Goulart hastened to repair the damage by calling Pacheco, Pelacani, Hércules Corrêa, and Humberto de Melo Bastos to Granja do Torto, a government-owned farm used as a residence by the president in Brasília; there he discussed objectives of the labor movement, such as price controls and wage increases.[19]

Brochado da Rocha's sudden death, in Rio Grande do Sul on September 26, was attributed to Lacerda by *Última Hora*, whose headline said: "The Crow Gets One More Dead Body." *Novos Rumos* wrote that Brochado, like Vargas eight years earlier, was the victim of "the hatred and inhuman malice" of "the cold-blooded and vile Carlos Lacerda." Brizola declared that Brochado had been gentle and friendly until the "gruesome" governor of Guanabara, calling him a street peddler posing as a professor, had filled him with bitterness. "I am convinced that those insults contributed to the brain hemorrhage that struck him," Brizola told the press. Hermes Lima, in his *Memórias*, has written that Governor Lacerda's ridicule drove Brochado to despair and hastened his death. "Perhaps," Lacerda said later, "I denounced him too violently, because the poor man lacked the temperament for that sort of thing. Unable to resist, he ended up deeply shaken."[20]

With the appointment of Hermes Lima to succeed Brochado da Rocha, political commentators turned their attention to the campaigns for the elections on October 7. But the crisis of September was not forgotten by Lacerda, who published a letter to an officer of the Minas UDN condemning the role of Magalhães Pinto. "In a decisive moment, when military intervention against Guanabara was being prepared for purely political reasons, in Minas there was raised the

only voice in support of that crime. Once again we were betrayed by
the cunning and mediocrity of ambitious individuals who hide their
mediocrity with sonorous but hollow references to reforms they do
not define. . . . I hope that never again will a voice in Minas be raised
to support the conspiracies of the traitors of the Federation, the demagoguery of the corrupt, and the hoaxes of the incompetent. For it will
always be . . . a falsetto voice. Never a lofty and noble voice of the
people of Minas Gerais."

The Minas governor declared that he had not favored intervention
in Guanabara, and reiterated his conviction that Brazil needed reforms to bring about a harmonious development that would reach the
common people. He said he did not repent having defended Brochado,
a cordial and sincere person.[21]

9. The State Elections (October 7, 1962)

Two of Guanabara's three senate seats (the terms were for eight
years) were at stake in the 1962 elections. Lacerda decided to back
the reelection of helpful Gilberto Marinho of the PSD and persuade
Juracy Magalhães, governor of Bahia, to be the UDN candidate. Juracy, who attributed the invitation to the difficulties Lacerda was
having with *udenista* Afonso Arinos, elected senator by the Cariocas
in 1958, said he would consult his friends in Bahia. But he did agree
to join Lacerda, São Paulo Senator Benedito Calasans, and others in an
anti-Communist rally in Guanabara in July. At the rally, which attracted no more than two thousand, Lacerda announced the candidacy of Juracy.

The candidacy was launched more formally late in August with
Lacerda claiming that "only Juracy can break the Communist plot
against us" and Juracy promising to work in Brasília to preserve a
regime that was being threatened.[1] Thus Juracy participated in an
election campaign that was characterized in Guanabara by intense
radicalization.

As described by Congressman Eloy Dutra (PTB), opponent of Lopo
Coelho (PSD) for the vice governorship, the ideological split was between "the reactionary anti-Brazilian" forces, on the one hand, and,
on the other, the "nationalists," such as himself and Aurélio Viana,
the Socialist Party (PSB) candidate for the Senate. The PSD, feeling at
a disadvantage in the face of the "radicalization between the PTB and
the UDN," made an alliance with the UDN in support of Gilberto
Marinho, Juracy Magalhães, and Lopo Coelho, candidates supported
by Cardinal Jayme Câmara.[2]

Juracy, blaming Communists for the disorders at one of his rallies, told his audience that "Communism is the most terrible of ideologies because it prevents people from speaking, hearing, acting, and even thinking." Eloy Dutra, on the other hand, warned that Lacerda, "Brazil's fascist leader," was making use of a "profitable anti-Communism" in his drive to give the country a far-Right dictatorship. "Nationalist" candidate Brizola, running for Congress in Guanabara, said that Lacerda had turned Guanabara into "the center of the reaction," with the help of the rich, most of the press, and the United States ambassador. In the words of UDN legislator Mauro Magalhães, Brizola's expenditures for radio and television made his campaign "one of the most costly ever seen in Rio."[3]

Lacerdismo was identified not only with Lacerda's ideology, but also with his performance as governor. The governor, who used the inaugurations of public works to help his candidates, declared that the elections would allow the people to judge his administration. A group of "Friends of the State" filled newspaper pages with photographs entitled, "More Schoolrooms," "New Avenues," "Low Cost Houses," "Industrialization," and "The Second Guandu Aqueduct." Eloy Dutra spoke of "crazy" tax increases and police violence against workers. State legislature candidate Ib Teixeira, in his *Última Hora* column, said that Lacerda had promised to solve the water problem in six months and had failed. José Mauro, another *Última Hora* columnist, pointed out that Lacerda's predecessors had created the dynamic SURSAN and carried out much of the work on a traffic tunnel, a viaduct, and Flamengo Park, projects for which Lacerda took credit.[4]

Political scientist Ronald Schneider has written that "political campaigning in 1962 was affected more than usual by the influence of money and patronage. For the first time the resources of the federal government were overwhelmingly at the disposal of leftist, often ultranationalist, candidates favored by President Goulart. Business and industrial elements found it necessary to come up with large-scale financing of centrist and conservative candidates in these races." Ivan Hasslocher, member of a prominent Brazilian family and head of the anti-Communist Instituto Brasileiro de Ação Democrática (IBAD), organized Ação Democrática Popular (ADEP) to funnel money, whose sources were suspected to include foreign firms, into the campaigns of anti-Communists such as Amaral Netto. Eloy Dutra, on the black list of IBAD, has written that "as candidate for congressman and vice governor of Guanabara, I could not hide my alarm at the huge publicity machine put at the disposal of certain politicians and candidates." He described his own campaign as that of "the centavo against the dollar."[5]

Complaints of improper pressure were made on both sides. Eloy

Dutra arranged for Congress to set up a CPI to investigate IBAD. Brizola sought, without success, to have the Regional Electoral Tribunal act on his charge that Lacerda was using the Guanabara administrative machine to help the governor's favorite candidates. "Nationalists" claimed that Lacerda's government spent state funds for publicity on an unprecedented scale and suggested that it was assisted by the bankers of the illegal *bicho* gambling game.[6]

Lacerda declared that Petrobrás money financed more candidates than holes for finding oil, and he complained that the pension institutes had become election campaign centers. He pointed out that the *Diário Oficial* devoted an entire issue to listing twenty-six thousand government appointments made during the campaign. Lies about Lopo Coelho and Juracy Magalhães, he argued, were "supported and blown up by a broadcasting station purchased by an official purveyor of the federal government." In a video-taped recording for a Recife television station, Lacerda spoke of the splurging of money by pro-Soviet embassies that hoped to elect Miguel Arraes and spread Communism in Pernambuco and beyond.[7]

Each side accused the other of turning rallies into physical combats. The worst conflict was the one that took place after congressional candidate Amaral Netto, in the Caminhão da Liberdade (Liberty Truck), reached the square in front of the Pedro II Railroad Station. During the ensuing battle with clubs and stones, fourteen participants were wounded, among them Amaral Netto and Communist Hércules Corrêa, PTB candidate for reelection to the state legislature. Both were treated at the Souza Aguiar Hospital and showed up later in the legislative assembly with bandages on their heads.

Hércules Corrêa claimed that Amaral Netto was following the example of another "ruffian," Lacerda, who, he said, had pretended to be wounded during the 1954 shooting that killed Major Rubens Vaz. After Corrêa asserted that Amaral Netto had arrived at the recent rally with about forty armed men, *Novos Rumos* attributed the melee to an attempt by Lacerda's police and Amaral's "thugs" to murder Corrêa and savagely beat up on the followers of Brizola's Caminhão da Legalidade (Legality Truck) who had "booed *entreguista* Juracy Magalhães at the same place a few days earlier." Lacerda, speaking on television, said that Amaral Netto had done well to retaliate in the face of attack. "The time has come for us to respond to provocations. We shall not permit a minority to impose its will."[8]

A week later, at the closing rally of the UDN and its allies, Juracy Magalhães launched the candidacy of Lacerda for president. Amaral Netto, introduced by a legislative assembly candidate as the man who would succeed Lacerda as governor in 1965, appealed for a massive victory for Lopo Coelho. "We cannot," he said, "let Governor Lacerda be stabbed in the back by enemies who destroy at night the work he carries out by day. This election for vice governor is going to decide the destiny of our people."[9]

Not long after the counting of votes began at the Maracanã Stadium, it was clear that Eloy Dutra had won the vice governorship, defeating Lopo Coelho by a handsome margin, and had been easily reelected to Congress. Other candidates of the anti-Lacerda Aliança Social Trabalhista (PTB-PSB) also did well. Socialist Aurélio Viana gained first place in the Senate race and was followed by Gilberto Marinho (PSD-UDN), leaving Juracy Magalhães a loser. Brizola received more votes than had ever been cast in Brazil for a congressional candidate. His 290,000 votes were double the number given to Amaral Netto, who, in turn, had twice as many as his nearest rival, Chagas Freitas, who had left the PSP and joined the Frente Popular—an alliance of members of the PSD and PST (Partido Social Trabalhista) that included Communists.[10] Others who did well in the Guanabara congressional race were Sérgio Magalhães (PTB), Meneses Cortes (UDN), Juarez Távora (PDC), Marco Antônio Coelho (a Communist candidate of the Frente Popular), and Adauto Lúcio Cardoso (UDN). Of the 409 congressmen chosen by the nation, 119 belonged to the PSD, 104 to the PTB, and 97 to the UDN.[11]

The makeup of the legislative assembly that would be installed early in 1963 was not comforting for Lacerda. Of the 55 members, 14 belonged to the UDN (but 2 called themselves dissidents) and 12 belonged to the PTB. Ten other parties, including the PSD, won 39 seats, all of them with 3 or less, except for the Left-leaning PST, which won 4. The Goulart administration, in a move to provide allies for the Carioca PTB, distributed federal posts and Caixa Econômica loans as desired by the small parties.[12]

Eloy Dutra decided to accept the post of vice governor, thus opening the way for PTB alternate Roland Corbisier to be seated in Congress and making it unattractive for Lacerda to make long trips abroad or otherwise relinquish his post after the vice governor was sworn in.

Lacerda asserted that Kubitschek's support of Eloy Dutra had been influenced by his desire to make it difficult for Lacerda to leave the governorship and run for president against Kubitschek. He accused Kubitschek of "vilely betraying" the PSD's Lopo Coelho and added that "once more Kubitschek has demonstrated his hatred of Guanabara." Kubitschek replied that "the traitor to the PSD is Lopo Coelho, who in 1955 supported Juarez Távora," UDN presidential candidate opposing Kubitschek, "and who continues today to be supported by Lacerda."[13]

Novos Rumos hailed the defeat of the United States embassy, the IBAD, the top echelons of the Catholic Church, and the privileged minorities. Eloy Dutra, pleased with the defeat of the "reactionary," "anti-Brazilian," and "anti-reform" minded forces, called the electoral contest "purely ideological." Some of the victors, however, agreed with the explanation given by the *Jornal do Brasil*, which attributed the defeat of Lopo Coelho and Juracy Magalhães to the increase in taxes and water tariffs. *Última Hora* wrote that Lacerda had betrayed the people because, when political advisers had warned him against collecting higher taxes before the election, he had replied that the money was needed for public works and the taxes should be collected "at once."[14]

Losers pointed fingers at each other. Lacerda was blamed not only for tax increases but also for having chosen in Lopo Coelho a poor campaigner. Juracy Magalhães attributed his own defeat to Lacerda, who, he wrote, "began to radicalize positions and associate me directly with his name. . . . Many in the PTB, who in their hearts wanted to vote for me, abandoned me because I was described as a candidate of Carlos Lacerda." Sandra Cavalcanti was accused by *udenistas* of having spoken against the candidacy of Juracy. Amaral Netto charged that many, if not most, of the supposedly "apolitical" men, appointed to be regional administrators and to hold high posts in the finance and other secretaryships, had worked in favor of "adversaries." His assertion was considered an accusation against Raphael de Almeida Magalhães, described as the supervisor of the regional administrators. Raphael, like UDN congressional staff member Hugo Levy, has pointed out that by the time of the October 1962 elections, major accomplishments of the Lacerda administration were only just getting under way and were not yet visible.[15]

Lacerda, departing for Europe on October 10, called the Guanabara election results an "unfortunate accident," the result of lies and slanders. He added that the Communists had given special attention to winning in Guanabara and that he was pleased that the Paulistas had elected anti-Communist Ademar de Barros to the governorship over Jânio Quadros. According to Lacerda this victory and those of gubernatorial candidates Ildo Meneghetti in Rio Grande do Sul and João Cleofas in Pernambuco "compensated" for results in Guanabara. *O Globo*, likewise pleased with the news from Pernambuco, wrote that the victories of Virgílio Távora in Ceará and João Cleofas in Pernambuco "constitute new and indisputable evidence that the tendencies of the Brazilian people favor the preservation of spiritual values."

However, the lead of Cleofas gradually evaporated, and by the last week in October it became known that Miguel Arraes, favorite of the Left, had won the governorship of Pernambuco.[16]

10. A Pleasant Interlude
(October–November 1962)

Carlos, described as a "globe-trotter" by *Última Hora,* arrived by plane in Paris on October 11 with Letícia, eleven-year-old Maria Cristina, and the Wilson Machados. Prior to the three days in which he was an official guest of Paris, he showed the sights of the city to Maria Cristina, dined at well-known restaurants, such as Maxim's, and attended the theater. An attraction in Paris was the company of Geneviève Flusin, Catholic heroine of the French Resistance, who had helped Carlos when he had published the *Tribuna da Imprensa.* She loved Brazil and became a frequent guest there of the Lacerdas.[1]

The "eccentric pamphleteer" and "overthrower of presidents" whom reporters had expected to interview turned out to be a relaxed and charming gentleman who spoke, after careful thought, about the problems of Guanabara and the importance of European assistance for South America. He denied being a reactionary and used the term to describe members of the Brazilian oligarchy who "speak of agrarian reform and purchase more *fazendas* daily, who speak of fiscal reform but don't pay income taxes, and who speak of financial reforms but think only of increasing their deposits in Swiss banks." He said that cultural ties would be strengthened if France would send to Brazil prominent figures like Jean Monnet, father of the European Common Market, instead of "out-of-date" people like philosopher Jean-Paul Sartre.[2]

Early in the two-and-a-half-month European sojourn, Carlos reached an agreement for the French to supply equipment and technical assistance for the Rio Metrô, visualized as a partly underground rail system to be financed by French credits, the Brazilian National Railroad Network, and at least 5 of the 30 billion cruzeiros that the governor now expected to raise by selling Guanabara *títulos progressivos.* He wanted Metrô construction to start in January 1963 and felt that the chief obstacle was the lack of initiative of the Brazilian government. "France," Lacerda told reporters in Paris, "is even ignorant of the existence of a finance ministry in our country." In his Metrô negotiations, he was assisted by Enaldo Cravo Peixoto, who reached Paris after discussing Rio beaches with Portuguese engineers in Lisbon, and by state bank President Antônio Carlos de Almeida Braga.[3]

Braga, Wilson Machado, and COPEG President Borghoff were in

West Berlin with Lacerda late in October when he concluded the arrangements for the German financing of hospital equipment for Brazil. The governor, an official visitor to West Germany, inspected the Berlin Wall and told the city parliament that he would like to give the Cariocas a replica of a part of the wall as a reminder of the preciousness of freedom of movement.[4]

The three-day visit to Germany coincided with the Cuban missile crisis, and therefore, when Lacerda spent ninety minutes in East Berlin, he found a crowd at a pro-Cuba rally. Mingling with the participants, the Brazilian governor was out of place. Wearing a black overcoat, he displayed his red passport to several policemen and photographed children who begged for cigarettes and chocolates.[5]

A cable, sent by Lacerda from West Berlin to congratulate President Kennedy for his handling of the missile crisis, said that the "courageous" decision of the American president had been made on behalf of all who prized liberty and peace. In Brazil, on the other hand, Brizola rebuked his country's ambassador to the OAS, saying he had voted to support the United States against the orders of his government. Ambassador Roberto Campos did not escape criticism for having assumed the responsibility for that vote.[6]

The Lacerdas spent four days in London, where Carlos discussed "hemispheric defense of democracy" with Peruvian leader Victor Haya de la Torre, and then they went to Italy, to the delight of Letícia, whose father had been born there. After the Lacerdas, Bragas, and Wilson Machados had an audience with Pope John XXIII, Carlos described the Pope as a good-hearted, loquacious villager. He was, Carlos wrote in *O Estado de S. Paulo*, "a man of the earth who was in the heavens," whereas his predecessor, Pius XII, had been "a man from the heavens who was on the earth."[7]

Sérgio Lacerda, keeping his father posted on developments in Brazil, wrote that Goulart was turning to the governors to help him achieve a large vote against the parliamentary system in the January plebiscite, but that Ademar de Barros, extraordinarily independent, ridiculed governors who negotiated away their independence in return for promises of funds and other favors. With the cooperation of Ademar, Sérgio felt, the "political axis" of São Paulo, Guanabara, Ceará, and Rio Grande do Sul would become "the only curb" on the other force, made up of "Jango Goulart, Magalhães Pinto, Miguel Arraes and Company." Ceará Governor-elect Virgílio Távora, Sérgio wrote, "will be in the ambit of *your* UDN, a powerful ally for the next battle that you *must not lose:* the battle for the UDN presidency." Sérgio felt that the opportunity to defeat the wishes of Magalhães Pinto in the contest was excellent.

Sérgio called attention to the enormous emissions of paper money required for the "13th month" bonus. He also reported strong expressions of military discontent, such as the denouncement of Communism in government by General Emílio Maurell Filho, outgoing commander of the First Military Region, and a similar statement by Admiral Sílvio Heck, whose arrest (for his statement) was followed by the resolve of fourteen admirals to issue a manifesto. "Pressure," Sérgio told his father, "is slowly increasing, reminding one very much of the ides of 1955"[8] (which had resulted in a military coup).

Lacerda, after a few days of sightseeing in Sicily, returned to the Brazilian tempest in a leisurely fashion aboard the Italian liner *Giulio Cesare* with Letícia, Maria Cristina, and Antônio Carlos de Almeida Braga and his wife Sylvia ("Vivi"). "He whiled away his time," John Dos Passos writes, "preparing a volume of his speeches for publication, and translating a Broadway play, *Come Blow Your Horn*." (Lacerda's translation of Neil Simon's play, given the Brazilian title of *O Bem-Amado*, was produced in 1963 at Rio's Santa Rosa Theater and was a great success.)[9]

Reporters, coming aboard the *Giulio Cesare* when it docked at Rio's Praça Mauá on November 30, found that Lacerda had gained weight and was in excellent spirits. He told them that "the people in East Berlin are driven like cattle, are depressed, crushed, and without spirit," whereas, on the western side, "happy people smile, sing, dance, go to Mass, and work." Asked about the plebiscite, he said he had no interest in it. "What I want is beans, rice, meat, lights, water, telephones, transportation, sewers, etc., for the Carioca people." He praised the offer of Ademar de Barros to flood Rio with foodstuffs upon being inaugurated, and spoke of additional assistance promised by Ildo Meneghetti of Rio Grande do Sul. The obstacles, he said, were the COFAP, and a merchant marine that was being forced into bankruptcy by the privileges that strikes and demagoguery gained for sailors.[10]

Speaking on television on December 3, Lacerda admitted that he might run for president in 1965. Stating that he had reached no conclusion about the matter and that everything led him to wish not to be a candidate, he explained: "I am not a good politician and never shall be because I do not have the habit of hiding what I think."[11]

11. Administrative Reform (December 1962)

During December 1962 sailors went on strike, food shortages were evident in Rio, and COFAP threatened to take legal steps against bakeries and meat markets for not adhering to its price list.[1]

In the halls of the state assembly, *udenistas* tried to decide whether the president of the second legislature, to be installed in March 1963, should be Raul Brunini or retired General Danillo Nunes, a new-comer to the UDN who wanted the post and had received in October more votes for the legislature than any of his colleagues. *Petebistas*, now able to claim thirteen representatives in the coming legislature due to one switch of allegiance, spoke of putting the presidency in the hands of José Bonifácio Diniz de Andrada, who had headed the Municipal Council and fought against its extinction. But his selec-tion would violate the UDN-PTB agreement whereby the UDN, with fourteen of the fifty-five incoming legislators, was to have the presi-dency. *Udenistas* put Brunini, always faithful to Lacerda, in the presidency and made Danillo Nunes leader of the UDN bloc.[2]

The outgoing legislature, at its final meetings in December, pre-pared to act on hundreds of law proposals. For constitutional reasons, Sandra Cavalcanti explained, laws resulting from proposals modify-ing the state's administrative setup would have to be vetoed unless they were passed as amendments to the administrative reform proj-ect, submitted in June 1961 and known as Law Project 75. Therefore, when discussion of Law Project 75 began on December 11, 1962, op-positionist legislators converted their pet administrative reform law projects into proposed amendments, and in some cases Sandra was able to give assurances, to the proposers and to the opposition leader-ship, that amendments would not be vetoed by the governor. Sandra suggested to assembly President Lopo Coelho that a vote be held on Law Project 75 with inclusion of "all the better amendment propos-als." *Udenistas* as well as oppositionists proposed amendments.

During the flood of laws enacted on December 14 and 15, the last confusing days of the session, amendments to Law Project 75 were read aloud, with not much attention given to the reading and with the presiding officer saying "All who approve remain seated." Finally, Lopo Coelho, advised by Sandra, announced that "Project 75, as amended," was up for vote. Not much later, it was a surprise to oppositionist Gama Filho, entering the chamber, to be told that "Project 75 has just been voted."

Sandra was chosen to draw up the document to be presented to the governor. Named Law 263, it called for decentralized administra-tion and a complete reorganization of the cabinet, with the establish-ment of five new secretaryships and the modification and renaming of others. It authorized the executive to establish state companies, such as COHAB, CETEL, CEDAG (to handle water), and CELURB (to handle and industrialize garbage).[3]

Lacerda vetoed hundreds of laws approved by the assembly in its

Sandra Cavalcanti

Sandra Cavalcanti. (Courtesy of the artist, Cláudio Duarte)

December meetings. After he vetoed some of the clauses of Law 263, it was signed by him on December 24 and officially published. But even before Lacerda signed it, Eloy Dutra and other *petebistas* maintained that PTB leader Saldanha Coelho had made its passage possible in the assembly by entering into an agreement with the UDN leadership. Saldanha Coelho was accused of having been attracted to "advantages and benefits" provided to legislators who agreed to approve the administration's projects in return for a ride on the "gravy train."[4]

After the publication of Law 263, opposition legislators complained that the published law was not what they understood it would be, and they proposed that the governor call a special session to allow a new roll call to decide about the clauses "added after the voting" that authorized him to establish state companies that, they said, had not been approved by the assembly. Hércules Corrêa accused the administration of fraud, saying that the text sent to the governor differed from what was passed by the assembly on December 15.[5]

Sandra Cavalcanti, declaring that she was leaving the assembly with a clear conscience, pointed out that oppositionists, in the confusion that prevailed while so many amendments and laws were being voted, may not have been aware that the administrative reform law was creating the secretaryships of social services and public services and the water, telephone, and garbage industrialization companies. She remarked that, during the final vote, "some party leaders fortunately forgot to insist . . . on the suppression of various provisions" that subsequently gave rise to the controversy and without which the administration would be unable to create "organs of the greatest importance and necessity."

Oppositionist Paulo Alberto Monteiro de Barros, claiming that the problem lay in the differences between the final version and what he called Saldanha Coelho's agreement with the UDN, issued a note declaring "1. The PTB at no time agreed to vote for anything beyond that established in the accord between the party leaderships. 2. The final version, taken to the governor, did not have my approval because I was not aware of it."[6]

Lacerda told dissatisfied *petebistas* that the administrative reform law had been promulgated and published and could not be changed. He immediately filled some of the new cabinet secretaryships, appointing Sandra Cavalcanti secretary of social services and Lopo Coelho secretary without portfolio, a post involving political work. Colonel Gustavo Borges became secretary of public safety.

Lacerda asked Adauto Lúcio Cardoso to become secretary of justice, another of the new secretaryships. The congressman declined, but agreed to be Guanabara's "political coordinator" in Brasília, and therefore Lacerda named Alcino Salazar to the justice post. Salvador Mandim, the state's electric energy coordinator, became the first secretary of public works after Lacerda awakened the general at night, to give him the news, and then discussed until 7:00 A.M. what the job entailed. Raphael de Almeida Magalhães was appointed to the new secretaryship of government, in charge of administrative reorganization and the coordination of government plans and budgets.[7] Sérgio Lacerda, who took over Raphael's former post of chief of the governor's office, was no longer with the *Tribuna da Imprensa*, which had undergone two changes in ownership, one around the middle of 1962 and the other late that year.

The earlier change, transferring control of the money-losing *Tribuna* to the *Jornal do Brasil* and its successful director, Nascimento Brito, stemmed from an agreement reached late in 1961. During the subsequent negotiations, it was agreed that the purchase price of 10 million cruzeiros ($29,000), paid to Carlos Lacerda, would be regarded as payment for the literary rights to articles Lacerda had published in the *Tribuna*, such payments being exempt from income tax. According to the contract of May 15, 1962, the name or trademark,

Tribuna da Imprensa, which the new owners acquired the right to use, remained the property of Carlos Lacerda, with assurance of its ownership by Letícia in case Carlos died before she did. *Tribuna* stockholders received nothing.[8]

The "new *Tribuna,*" launched in the first half of July 1962, showed Nascimento Brito as president and Sérgio Lacerda as a director. The influx of new editors, such as Mário Faustino and Alberto Dines, left old hands depressed. They complained of little allotment of space for their writings and alleged that the new management sought to "delacerdize" the newspaper. Those who did not move out were taken in a group by Sérgio to Guanabara Palace to hear Carlos tell them that the new arrangements had been made necessary by a financial crisis at the *Tribuna* but that the new owners had promised not to "alter fundamentally the *Tribuna*'s line."[9]

The "new *Tribuna*" appeared on mornings instead of afternoons and was described to its readers in July 1962 as a "novel type of newspaper," one of "depth and analysis" that would avoid "fanatic or pamphleteering journalism." It featured articles by prominent figures such as Sérgio Magalhães (Lacerda's rival in the 1960 governorship race), Tristão de Atayde (Alceu Amoroso Lima), Antônio Callado, Lúcio Cardoso (brother of Adauto), and jurist Levi Carneiro. Carlos Castello Branco, who had taken up residence in Brasília starting with his role as press secretary of President Quadros, wrote a column that was first called "The *Tribuna* in Brasília," and appeared late in July as the "Coluna do Castello." Carlos Lacerda used the pen name Júlio Tavares for occasional articles in the *Tribuna,* and said in one of them that Kennedy's program for Brazil was doomed to remain untried "because the Brazilian government does not want the Alliance for Progress."[10]

Countess Maurina Pereira Carneiro, owner of *Jornal do Brasil,* was not pleased with the purchase of the *Tribuna* arranged by her son-in-law, Nascimento Brito. Therefore after Sérgio Lacerda learned, at a dinner party, that journalist Hélio Fernandes was interested in becoming the *Tribuna*'s owner, the governor's son got in touch with active young financier José Luís de Magalhães Lins, nephew of Magalhães Pinto and husband of the younger daughter of José and Maria do Carmo Nabuco. Magalhães Lins and lawyer Fernando Velloso completed the deal whereby the *Tribuna,* which was still losing money, passed into the hands of Hélio Fernandes in December 1962. Hélio Fernandes made no payment but took over the debts as well as the assets. Under his management, the *Tribuna* attacked the Goulart government fiercely, and Carlos Lacerda continued to provide it with articles.[11]

12. The Referendum (January 6, 1963)

The Goulart administration worked to have a massive vote cast against the parliamentary system in the plebiscite, or referendum, of January 6. "That campaign," Lacerda has observed, "was financed in large part by José Luís [de] Magalhães Lins, nephew of Magalhães Pinto, and other bankers to whom the presidency turned."[1]

Lacerda felt that he could not give his support to what he considered the "caricature" of a parliamentary system that was in effect; nor could he bring himself to vote against parliamentarism, because he opposed those who, "in the government, use the instruments of democracy to destroy democracy." Preparing to abstain from voting, he limited himself to denouncing the "orgy" of government-inspired publicity. The UDN's Milton Campos, on the other hand, vowed to vote against changing the political system. Having reported in the Senate that the Valadares amendment was unconstitutional, he said he could not support an illegal early return to presidentialism.[2]

Olavo Bilac Pinto, UDN congressional leader following the death of Meneses Cortes in a plane crash, agreed that the "referendum" law was unconstitutional. When he met with fellow-Mineiro Pedro Aleixo and UDN President Herbert Levy, it was decided that the UDN could hardly recommend abstention from voting while prominent *udenista* governors, such as Magalhães Pinto, appealed for a large vote against the parliamentary system. But the party's national directorship, in its directive to its local officers, did assert that no one could deny the unconstitutionality of the so-called referendum, and it did take issue with government authorities who maintained that the clause giving electors the "right to vote" in the referendum made voting obligatory. The directive also criticized "biased and heavily financed government propaganda" against a system that, it said, the government had not allowed to function.

In financing that propaganda, Amaral Netto argued, Goulart was resorting to blackmail. The popular Carioca congressman-elect explained that the president, "no supporter of private initiative," had sent Hugo Faria, chief of the presidential office, to collect funds in Rio from Standard Oil and Rio-Light and in São Paulo from other companies.[3]

Magalhães Pinto told reporters that he had spoken with Goulart and found him seriously concerned about organizing a new government capable of dealing with Brazil's needs. Goulart contributed to that impression by announcing that, with presidential powers restored, he would give Brazil a Three-Year Plan, prepared by economist Celso Furtado. The plan made good reading because it offered to

Celso Furtado concocting the Three-Year Plan. (Hilde Weber drawing in *O Estado de S. Paulo*, January 8, 1963)

reduce the rate of inflation from 52 percent in 1962 to 10 percent in 1965 while increasing Brazilian production 7 percent annually.

Lacerda, returning from his year-end holidays at the Cabo Frio home of Joaquim da Silveira, gave a speech at the Rio Yacht Club in which he suggested that the Three-Year Plan was a "lure," whose message was that if the parliamentary system were abandoned "rice will come raining down." The governor criticized the Plan for overemphasizing the role of the state. Furtado, he told his audience of industrialists, "confuses the enrichment of the people with the enrichment of the state and believes that the government creates wealth." "We want to plan to construct liberty and the authors of the Three-Year Plan want to plan to destroy it."[4]

Like Lacerda, Congressman Francisco Julião decided to abstain from voting in the plebiscite. The Peasant League leader called the plebiscite "one more farce for deceiving the humble," and said it would do nothing for the peasants. Going further than Lacerda, Julião called on his followers to abstain, thus infuriating most of his companions on the Left, who were determined to give Goulart full presidential powers. Sérgio Magalhães "guaranteed" that Julião was working with Lacerda in a plot to persuade the armed forces to overthrow the government. "Francisco Julião," he said, "has become an agent provocateur," seeking to "weaken the regime and turn the country over to the reactionaries and Carlos Lacerda." Julião indignantly denied the charges, and a move to expel him from the PSB was dropped.[5]

President Goulart, approached by Ademar de Barros, Kubitschek, Magalhães Pinto, and San Tiago Dantas. Quadros is at far right. (Hilde Weber drawing in *O Estado de S. Paulo*, March 8, 1963)

PSD President Ernâni do Amaral Peixoto, a congressman-elect from Rio state, disliked the referendum. But Kubitschek supported it, and the PSD asked everybody to vote. Goulart, on the eve of the referendum, declared that "if voting is always obligatory, it is more so now. . . . We are not going to choose persons, but vote for Brazil itself, which wants to hear the voice of its sons and daughters in order to choose, with liberty, the paths of its future." He compared the referendum to an expression of faith in the nation's destiny at a time when "the progressive forces . . . are being mobilized for the conquest of the great structural reforms and for giving support to the basic ideas of the Three-Year Plan."[6]

Of Brazil's total electorate of around 18.5 million, only about 11.5 million voted in the plebiscite. Of these, almost 9.5 million, or 77 percent, expressed preference for the presidential system. In Guanabara, where 73 percent favored presidentialism, the turnout of over 87 percent of the registered electorate was far ahead of that in any other state.[7]

Lacerda said, "I shall pay the legal fine that has been imposed on me for having deliberately refrained from voting in the so-called plebiscite." He called the fine "the price of liberty" and his failure to vote "a protest against corruption." Maintaining that "the power of money" had turned the plebiscite into a "totalitarian manifestation," he said that poor people had been threatened with the loss of their wages if they did not vote, and that Goulart's personal agents had forced businessmen to finance "untruthful and illegal propaganda."[8]

Prime Minister Hermes Lima and Justice Minister João Mangabeira argued that the proclamation of the result of the plebiscite automatically abolished the parliamentary system. Although Bilac Pinto could not accept this view, the UDN agreed not to block congressional action to amend the constitution to allow a return to presidentialism. The amendment easily received the required approval of two-thirds of the membership of both houses in two separate meetings of each house. With the second vote (259 to 8) in the Chamber of Deputies on January 22, the parliamentary system went out of existence.[9]

13. Comments

The very holding of the plebiscite, along with its outcome, was a victory for Goulart and for *udenistas,* such as Magalhães Pinto, who opposed Lacerda. Clearer evidence that the eighteen-month experiment with the parliamentary system was a period of political setbacks for Lacerda can be found in the outcome of the October 1962 elections in Guanabara, and in the power achieved by the Communist wing of organized labor.

Carlos was still in his canoe, fighting a cruiser.

On the other hand, no period during Lacerda's five-year term was as significant for his governorship as the one that expired on January 22, 1963. For one thing, it gave him the administrative structure, with its state companies, that he felt he required. Of even greater importance, his administration became assured of the receipt of most of the funds needed to revive the state, thanks to the tax and fee increases of November 1961, the scheme to sell *títulos progressivos,* the agreements with the IDB and USAID, a National Highway Fund loan, and the dynamism assumed by the state bank.

Promises had been made to the Cariocas in the earlier period. By the end of 1962 grandiose projects were physically under way.

III.

Governor and Presidential Candidate in 1963

1. "Killer of Beggars" (January–March 1963)

Reports that twelve bodies had been found in December 1962, in the area where the Guandu River flows into Sepetiba Bay, led to charges by *Última Hora* and Sérgio Magalhães in January that Lacerda, employing Nazi methods, had turned the police department's Service for the Repression of Begging (SRM) into an extermination squad. Security Secretary Gustavo Borges, summoned by the governor, said that *Última Hora* was as unreliable as ever and that the SRM merely sought to clean up the city by paying bus fares to beggars so that they would return to the villages from which they had come.[1]

On the night of January 17–18, SRM Assistant Chief José Mota and four SRM accomplices took six beggars onto a bridge and dumped them into the Guarda River, near the Guandu, after taking possession of what little of value could be found on them. Unfortunately for the murderers, they had been lax in administering the preliminary thrashing and revolver shots when handling beggar Olindina Alves Jupiaçu, and, although her body and face were injured, she swam to safety, keeping away for a while from the riverbanks where Mota's men stood ready to apply blows to the drowning, wounded beggars. Olindina's story, published in *Última Hora* on January 23, was a sensation.[2]

During the following days, a search of the Guarda River by police, firemen, and boatmen turned up several more bodies, and the security secretaryship took all SRM employees into custody in order that a state government investigation obtain as full a story as possible. Mota admitted that he and his accomplices, ordered by SRM Chief Alcino Pinto Nunes to follow the fortnightly custom of deporting demented beggars, had decided to resort to killing; and he confessed that the group drowned on January 17 had been his fourth group. He was accused of participating in the killing of fourteen beggars between October and January.[3]

Lacerda had the murderers locked up and he dismissed them from their jobs, along with SRM Chief Alcino, who the murderers said was innocent. The rapid dismissals violated the state Code for Employees and were illegal.[4]

The new state legislative assembly, preparing for the regular session to start in mid-March, adopted the resolution of *Última Hora's* Ib Teixeira, a new PTB legislator, to set up quickly a CPI to investigate beggar killings. The CPI came into existence on February 6, the day after the selection of Brunini (UDN) as the legislature's president, José Talarico (PTB) as first vice president, and Hércules Corrêa (PTB) as secretary. The PTB, thanks to a second switch in allegiance, had fourteen legislators, the same as the UDN; like the UDN, two of its members served on the CPI, which was headed by José Bonifácio Diniz de Andrada (PSD).[5]

The PTB members of the CPI maintained that Lacerda was responsible for the murders. After Nelson José Salim (without party affiliation) failed to persuade the Lacerda administration to move the assassins to a location "not under the influence of the state government," the CPI members went to the Military Police barracks to question the arrested men. They were denied admission by the officer of the day, and the denial was upheld by a judge, who cited the status of prisoners about to be tried.[6]

Novos Rumos wrote that Lacerda and his henchmen probably gloated at the paralyzation of the CPI, and it published the observations of an "amateur psychiatrist and longtime acquaintance of Lacerda" who attributed the governor's "secret satisfaction" with the beggar killings to a lifetime of frustrations.[7]

Speaking on television, Lacerda exhibited a photograph, taken in December 1962, showing Kubitschek standing between SRM Chief Alcino Pinto Nunes and confessed murderer José Mota. He said, "The police who kill vagrants are not my police; I inherited them." Irked a few days later by the "mass killing of beggars" stories in the foreign press, he asked foreign newsmen to be "more accurate" in their reporting.[8]

O Globo, also critical of the manner in which the governor and the state were being presented abroad, said that the state government, surprised as much as anyone by the crimes, had brought about an investigation notable for speed and efficiency. Marinho's daily condemned the "political exploitation" that led *Última Hora* to portray Lacerda as the author of the "Trips of Death" and originator of "the Final Solution" of "the beggar problem," reminiscent of Hitler's handling of "the Jewish problem."[9]

After Lacerda criticized press coverage of the affair, the *Jornal do Brasil* pointed out that newspaper denouncements were responsible for the discovery of the crimes. The *Diário de Notícias,* making the same point, praised *Última Hora's* investigative work and denied Lacerda's charge that the press had ignored steps he had taken, such as closing down the SRM. It wrote that Lacerda, who had called the last Vargas administration a "sea of mud," should understand the use of the expression by a part of the press in references to his own government.[10]

Carolina Maria de Jesus, an ex-*favelada* famous for her published diary describing the life of the destitute, told *Última Hora* on March 6 that Lacerda was a monster whose treatment of beggars was so loathsome that the death penalty was too good for him. This was just before Lacerda visited São Paulo, where students, preparing to receive him with signs reading "Paulistas Repudiate the Beggar Killer," spread the slogan "Beware, Beggars, Lacerda Is Coming."[11]

At Roberto de Abreu Sodré's home in São Paulo on March 8, Carolina Maria de Jesus entered the garden and was taken to the living room. There she asked Lacerda why he murdered beggars. Lacerda, reacting to what he considered her insults, told her that she could return to *Última Hora* and collect her check for providing the next day's headline. "You are a false *favelada;* I know who wrote your book," he said. Carolina, after being driven away in an *Última Hora* jeep, spoke to *Última Hora* reporters about the unhappy interview with Lacerda and said that in her next book, a novel, he would be the villain, "an evil, despotic ruler with the soul of a murderer." From the entire world, she added, she had been receiving letters asking why beggars were killed in Brazil.[12]

Lacerda, in a televised interview at the Sodrés' home, said he had inherited evil men in the police force because the federal government had relied on political criteria in making appointments. He pointed out that SRM detective José Mota had served in President Kubitschek's office and that SRM Chief Alcino Pinto Nunes had belonged to the personal guard of Vargas and had been the chauffeur of the wife of Gregório Fortunato, the guard who had ordered the assassination of Lacerda in 1954. Calling José Mota the principal culprit, Lacerda said that Mota had been receiving requests for favors from PTB politicians, written on stationery of the presidency of the republic. The governor, who had already declared that the only way to clean up the police was to eliminate officers associated with the PTB, showed his television audience a letter on presidential stationery addressed to "my dear friend Alcino" and signed on August 8, 1962, by PTB state legislator Rubens Macedo.[13]

Alcino Pinto Nunes, testifying before the CPI on March 14, confirmed that he had chauffeured Gregório Fortunato's wife and received promotions thanks to her influence; but he said his most recent post had been assigned by DOPS Chief Cecil Borer, whom he knew "only superficially." When José Mota was allowed to appear before the CPI he tried to implicate the DOPS chief in the murders.

The CPI, in a session notable for foul epithets hurled against Lacerda, adopted the recommendation of Hércules Corrêa (not a CPI member) that the governor be asked to dismiss Borer. Lacerda, in Curitiba for a regional UDN convention, told reporters that the CPI had no authority to make the request. His remark and his failure to reply in writing to questions submitted to him led the commission's PTB members to demand his impeachment; but CPI President José Bonifácio Diniz de Andrada, although displeased with Lacerda's disdain of the commission, concluded that the impeachment proposal had no legal basis.[14]

While the CPI held its meetings in March, the governor and his police officers faced a crime wave in the streets in which restless youths murdered three people, among them eighteen-year-old Odylo Costa, neto, whose father, a prominent journalist, had been a *Tribuna da Imprensa* director. Saldanha Coelho, maintaining that Lacerda had misgoverned for two years, cited the murder of Odylo along with the murders of beggars.

Lacerda, who had just observed his twenty-fifth wedding anniversary at a São Bento Monastery ceremony attended by important military officers, accepted the offer of the First Army to participate in a roundup of suspicious persons. On television he advised the Cariocas that the police would arrest those who had no identification cards and would shoot those who resisted arrest. José Carlos Oliveira wrote in the *Jornal do Brasil* that "the people asked for police in the streets, not a state of siege."[15]

Lacerda joined Gustavo Borges during some of the roundups, or "blitzes," and spent a part of the time following events from a helicopter. The first blitz yielded five hundred arrests and a subsequent one three hundred. Three young murderers were caught. One of them, the fifteen-year-old assassin of Odylo Costa, neto, explained that he had entered "a life of crime because the police of Lacerda did not find the murderer of my father," a taxi driver. The governor increased the pay of policemen and made arrangements to add 850 men to the force.[16]

2. The Pro-Cuba Congress (March 28–31, 1963)

Newsweek reported in March 1963 that many Americans regarded Cold Warrior Carlos Lacerda as the best friend of the United States in Brazil. It quoted the "fierily articulate anti-Communist" as saying:

"Brazil is headed for trouble with or without American aid, and the only unknown factor is the size of the U.S. losses. So I would say to my American friends, sit this one out. The problems we have go far beyond economic or technical solutions. These we must find ourselves." Lacerda's remarks, published while Finance Minister San Tiago Dantas was in Washington seeking $580 million for Brazil's Three-Year Plan, prompted *Última Hora* to call the governor a traitor.[1]

On March 23 Lacerda took a step that some members of the Goulart administration regarded as helpful to the Dantas Mission. He decreed that the four-day Continental Congress of Solidarity with Cuba, scheduled to begin on March 28 at the Brazilian Press Association (ABI), could not take place in Guanabara. Organizers of the so-called "Pro-Cuba Congress," whose supporters included Bertrand Russell, Lázaro Cárdenas, and Jânio Quadros, made a point of defying what they called the State Department's demand that Brazilian "hostility to the Congress" be one of the conditions for a successful Dantas Mission.[2]

Although the word "inopportune" was occasionally heard in presidential circles to describe the Pro-Cuba Congress, and although Foreign Minister Hermes Lima denied entry permits for Bertrand Russell and other distinguished foreigners, the government maintained that it could hardly "prohibit a peaceful political rally." The prohibition by Lacerda was eminently satisfactory for Goulart and he did not oppose it.[3]

Lacerda, in a broadcast on March 25, noted that the organizers of the Congress called it "an expression of the vanguard of the Latin American revolution." Citing clauses in the constitution and National Security Law of 1953, he said that it was illegal to prepare for strife, class struggle, and subversion, especially with the support of foreigners. His stand brought him messages of praise and condemnation and resulted in street demonstrations for and against the Pro-Cuba Congress. A group of Catholics organized a "Congress of Solidarity with Lacerda," and the anti-Communist Democratic Youth Front scolded UNE President Vinicius Brant for putting the UNE on the side of the Pro-Cuba Congress and "Red barbarism." Lacerda, replying to messages attacking his ruling, wrote Rio Metalworkers' Union President Benedito Cerqueira (a congressman) that he was a "de luxe Communist Party stooge," and he told Bahia student leader Sérgio Daudenzi: "Don't be stupid. Dedicate yourself to your studies, and think a little before sending silly messages."[4]

In the Chamber of Deputies Sérgio Magalhães maintained that Brazil could not continue with two presidents, Goulart and Lacerda, and therefore the lawmakers should vote for federal intervention in Guanabara. Congressman Max da Costa Santos, secretary of the Pro-Cuba Congress Organizing Commission, attributed Lacerda's step to the federal government's weakness and declared that Brazil, like Cuba, had decided to "proclaim its economic independence, . . . very probably in terms of 'independence or death.'" He and fellow-members of the Parliamentary Nationalist Front (FNP), supported by José Sarney and seven other congressmen of the UDN's Bossa-Nova, drew up a message that was taken to Goulart by a group that included Brizola and José Guimarães Neiva Moreira (PSB, Maranhão). Its forty-two signers, denouncing Guanabara's "climate of intolerance," said they planned to attend the Pro-Cuba Congress in Rio, and wanted guarantees that it would take place. Goulart, however, had a written opinion from Justice Minister João Mangabeira saying that Lacerda's edict was not illegal.[5]

A result of the FNP petition to Goulart was Lacerda's message to Chamber of Deputies President Mazzilli that the Guanabara authorities would respect the immunities of congressmen who might come to Guanabara, but would arrest others who sought to hold a Pro-Cuba Congress there. Lest attempts be made to hold the Congress at the UNE or the law school, their buildings were surrounded, along with that of the ABI, by troops of the Military Police. Over sixty Brazilian delegates were arrested in Guanabara, along with a Mexican who arrived at the Galeão Airport. In the state legislature, where the PTB bloc vowed to attend the Congress, Edna Lott said the governor had no authority to prevent foreigners with visas from entering Brazil.[6]

Like Minas Governor Magalhães Pinto, Rio state Governor Badger Silveira felt that the constitution protected the right of the pro-Cubans to assemble. The pro-Cubans, therefore, decided to hold the Congress at the Naval Construction Workers' Union building in the Niterói shipyards. With the Congress about to begin there, *Última Hora* and the *Jornal do Brasil* wrote that Lacerda was giving it national and international publicity. According to the *Jornal do Brasil*, the Congress would have been of little importance except for Lacerda's use of totalitarian methods to combat totalitarian ideas. But the conservative *O Jornal* said that Lacerda had done the right thing.[7]

The meetings in Niterói lasted from March 28 to March 30 and were attended by about five hundred delegates, a disappointing turnout. After the reading of messages of support from Fidel Castro, Khrushchev, Mao Zedong, and Zhou Enlai, the delegates drew up and adopted resolutions favorable to the "self-determination" of Cuba, "a Socialist Soviet Republic." The Pro-Cuba Congress ended as peacefully as it had begun and with fewer in attendance.[8]

After the Pro-Cuba Congress was over, Goulart said that he had been "completely opposed" to it and condemned extremism by the Left or Right. His handling of the matter was praised by *The New York Times*, whose editorial, "How To Help the Reds," argued that the "international Cuban solidarity conference" would have been a fiasco had not Lacerda made it "a Red triumph that will be exploited all over the world." Lacerda, in a letter to the *Times*, wrote: "It is sad to see a great newspaper falsely inform a great people about our effort and misjudge our intentions. . . . Your editorial gave substantial help to the Brazilian Reds."[9]

On the night of April 1 a crowd, following Catholic leaders, gathered in front of Guanabara Palace for a session of speeches in praise of Lacerda's prohibition of the Pro-Cuba Congress. One banner read: "Only Lacerda in '65 will hold back Communism in '66." The governor, addressing the demonstrators in a speech that was televised, called the gathering a show of "solidarity with Brazil" and warned that plans for fratricidal strife were being developed. He said that the president, a traitor to the regime, a perjurer, and a crook, should have been barred from office as the military ministers had wanted in 1961. "João Goulart, in asserting that he is neither to the Left nor to the Right, must consider the nation feeble-minded. He thinks all the people are idiots and will believe in the sudden centrist position of this man who has Communists as assistants, Communists as advisers, and a cabinet minister who returns from Cuba saying that the Cubans don't need elections because everyone there has a rifle." Goulart and Labor Minister Almino Afonso, Lacerda said, were preparing for federal intervention in Guanabara by stirring up agitation and strikes and placing the blame for them on the state government. The speech was so violently anti-Goulart and insulting in its language that the *Diário de Notícias*, which had supported Lacerda's ban against the Pro-Cuba Congress, called his behavior intemperate, uncivilized, paleolithic, and deserving of condemnation by everybody.[10]

A tape recording of the speech was taken by Brizola to Goulart. Men close to the indignant president, such as Casa Militar Chief Albino Silva and War Minister Amaury Kruel, came up with a plan to topple the governor. The move would begin with a mammoth anti-Lacerda rally at the Largo do Machado. The masses were to be incited to attack nearby Guanabara Palace, with the army intervening after the unarmed masses met resistance.

General Albino Silva was prepared to help Crockatt de Sá, Goulart's labor affairs adviser, persuade laborers to attend the rally. But on April 8 word came that Goulart had decided to postpone it. General Osvino Ferreira Alves, commander of the First Army, was refusing to guarantee army protection for the rally and was advising CGT leaders not to support it.[11]

Osvino, the "people's general" who enjoyed enormous influence in CGT and UNE circles, was on bad terms with anti-Communist Amaury Kruel. He said that Goulart, the "opponent of extremisms" who had called Pernambuco Governor Arraes "very dangerous," might work with Kruel to balance intervention in Guanabara by intervention in Pernambuco. The CGT, which accepted Osvino's argument, was unwilling to cooperate with Kruel, was suspicious of Goulart, and was violently opposed to the economic austerity that the government had promised Washington to adopt. Kruel, furious at Osvino, asked for dismissal of the First Army commander on the very day that Goulart "postponed" the rally; but Osvino, favorite of the powerful CGT, remained in his post.[12]

The administration limited its counteroffensive against Lacerda to televised speeches by Kruel, Brizola, and Hermes Lima. Hermes Lima argued that Lacerda was placing himself in a position where he could carry out a coup or become the false martyr of a federal intervention. Referring to the governor's use of "hoaxes, lies, slanders, and ridicule" to smear the president's authority, he exclaimed: "This must not happen again."[13]

3. Triumph in Curitiba (April 28, 1963)

During his televised interview at Sodré's home (following the departure of Carolina Maria de Jesus), Lacerda called Magalhães Pinto's presidential candidacy premature. Asked about his own candidacy, he replied that his ambition was to conclude an honorable administration as governor and then retire to write books, but that, if the UDN nominated him, he would, without pleasure, fulfill his duty like any soldier called up for military service.[1]

Lacerda, Brazil's most active presidential candidate, left Sodré's home the next day, March 9, to campaign for party support in Santa Catarina and Paraná. His eye was on the UDN's Fourteenth National Convention, to be held on April 26, 27, and 28 in Curitiba, Paraná. There the UDN would decide between Lacerda and reform-minded Magalhães Pinto by resolving whether or not it favored a constitutional amendment to facilitate a redistribution of land. Its other duty, the selection of a new party president, appeared to be a formality because of the widespread backing for Congressman Olavo Bilac Pinto, a former finance secretary of Governor Magalhães Pinto. Lacerda had declared for Bilac after receiving assurances that Magalhães, although a personal friend of Bilac's, was not enthusiastic about his becoming the party president. The scholarly congressman acted independently of the Minas governor.[2]

While Lacerda campaigned in Santa Catarina and Paraná, with UDN President Herbert Levy at his side, and later in Minas, cheering crowds greeted his message about the need for the Goulart government to reform itself instead of advocating reforms it did not understand. So eager was the city of Teófilo Otoni, Minas Gerais, to see Lacerda and launch his presidential candidacy that it chartered a plane to take him there from Belo Horizonte. He would, he declared to the enthusiastic Minas audiences, give up his weekends of rest on Brocoió Island in order to campaign against Communism and reveal the errors of Goulart.[3]

When the Carioca UDN met on April 7 to select thirty-four delegates to go to Curitiba, more appeals were made for Lacerda to run for president. In reply, he said that the time had come for the UDN—this time a "udenista UDN"—to occupy the presidency. Speaking of the Bossa-Nova, he said that people who were "eager to reach understandings with Communism" should find a place for themselves outside his party. Congressman Amaral Netto, who had been criticizing Lacerda's administration for ignoring requests of the UDN, promised not to create a party schism.[4]

Holy Week interrupted the campaign and allowed Lacerda to spend a few days away from crowds, in the rustic setting of a *fazenda* on the Paraná River. His fishing companions were his son Sebastião, his aide Carlos Osório, his assistant Wilson Machado, and Water Department Chief Veiga Brito. Veiga Brito, familiar with much of the Brazilian interior, was a close friend of the *fazenda*'s owner, Orlando Chesini Ometto, wealthy Paulista sugar producer. Before returning to Rio, they spent Easter Sunday at the *fazenda* of Abreu Sodré, who had become president of the São Paulo UDN and was scheduled to manage Lacerda's presidential campaign.[5]

The campaign was in full swing on April 18 when Sodré drove Lacerda to Itu, São Paulo, where the governor gave an address to commemorate the founding, ninety years earlier, of the old Republican Party. Lacerda compared the firm Republican leaders of 1873 with men in Brasília who showed no leadership, only fear of leftist propaganda. Patriotism, he said, had become fermented, turning into the curdled milk of nationalism, while socialism, once a movement of idealists, had turned into a servant of Communism. He denounced those who, talking about "basic reforms," sought merely to reform the constitution "in order not to have to comply with it," and who would "do away with private property under the pretext of curbing its abuses." Returning to Rio, Lacerda inaugurated the Major Vaz Tunnel with a speech praising the Cariocas for defeating, in a 874,137 to 49,707 vote, the scheme to divide Guanabara into municipalities.[6]

Then, on April 22, Lacerda released a "political bombshell." In a letter to Adauto Lúcio Cardoso, he advised that he would not attend the Curitiba convention, would participate no longer in UDN activity, and would retire from politics after completing his term in the governor's chair. In a telegram for Herbert Levy he said: "Consider me henceforth separated from your party."[7]

Explaining his reasons in his letter, Lacerda wrote of having learned from the press that the UDN congressional bloc was taking a position in favor of amending the constitution in order to enact agrarian reform. Agrarian reform, he argued, did not require the amendment, which would abolish the principal characteristic of private property and open the door for additional "reforms" desired by "personal power and Communism."

Lacerda rebuked the party for having ignored his message about foreign policy sent to the 1961 national convention—a message that could have been used for a collective warning to Quadros to prevent the president's resignation by making him see that he lacked the support to become a dictator. Since Quadros' resignation, Lacerda told Adauto, the UDN had worked with Congress to hand over to demanding dragons one maiden after another: parliamentarism, the plebiscite, presidentialism without fiscalization, and disregard for the constitution.

Lacerda, describing himself as "accustomed to give in and temporize much more than some people think," wrote that he was "perfectly agreeable to serve once more as the party's sacrificial lamb." He even thanked *udenista* congressmen who supported a constitutional amendment and thus freed him "from the possibility of becoming president." "Perhaps," he wrote, "even some close companions, such as you, thought the idea of being a presidential candidate would grip me so much that I would shun the defense of a principle that I consider fundamental." "I do not want," he added, "to be a candidate unless it is with a party that is worthy of that sacrifice."[8]

While Magalhães Pinto put the finishing touches on a pro-reform speech for Curitiba, Herbert Levy, Bilac Pinto, Ernâni Sátiro, Adauto Cardoso, Paulo Sarasate, Daniel Krieger, and Raul Brunini met with Lacerda at his apartment. Levy told the governor that reports about the UDN *bancada* were inaccurate. But Lacerda cited the well-known sentiment of Senate opposition leader João Agripino, who had declared that the UDN should be in the vanguard of the struggle for basic reforms and whose proposal to make private property subject to public convenience prompted Lacerda to remark that "not even the PTB has the nerve to propose such a subversive idea." The UDN, Lacerda said, was "playing the game of the Goulart government," which would use the precedent of a constitutional reform about land ownership to obtain one allowing the reelection of the president.[9]

Ademar de Barros remarked that "if the UDN loses Lacerda, it will lose a great deal." Abreu Sodré, rushing to Rio, told reporters that "the people are tired of resignations," and he added that Lacerda had too many responsibilities with the people to leave public life. But Lacerda, after a second conclave with UDN leaders at his apartment, told the Carioca delegates that he would not accompany them to Curitiba because he was not disposed to fight against old friends.[10]

More than three hundred voting delegates assembled in Curitiba, where they were greeted by hundreds of placards bearing Magalhães Pinto propaganda. The Bossa-Nova issued a manifesto, written by José Aparecido de Oliveira (Minas) and Clovis Ferro Costa (Pará), favorable to the independent foreign policy, the "democratization of education," the Three-Year Plan, banking reform, and a constitutional amendment to allow radical agrarian reform. It was signed by twenty-seven congressmen as well as Piauí Governor Petrônio Portela and Senator José Cândido Ferraz, also from Piauí. Half of Brazil's 75 million inhabitants, it said, "live in the most alarming misery" while, under the constitution, generation after generation "retain" vast areas "where, until now, no one has set foot."[11]

Lacerda, worried a month earlier about the economic power of Magalhães Pinto and the press contacts of adroit José Aparecido de Oliveira, had authorized Herculano Leal Carneiro, veteran of pro-Quadros and anti-Arraes political work, to carry the Lacerda message to the grassroots level in the north and northeast. Herculano had found Lacerda popular at that level and had, with the help of ADEP (Hasslocher) money, been able to give UDN delegates from that region a three-day stay in Rio, where they had discovered the constructive side of the candidate. However, not a few UDN leaders regarded Lacerda as an unpredictable politician they could not deal with, and felt that the party should take a strong position in favor of reforms. When Herculano reached Curitiba he found former companions of the Quadros campaign certain of the victory of their favorite, Magalhães Pinto. With the help of men supplied by Paraná Senator Adolfo de Oliveira Franco, *Lacerdistas* such as Herculano spent their first night in Curitiba replacing Magalhães Pinto posters with Lacerda posters.[12]

Hugo Levy, who had arrived in Curitiba a few days before the convention, found the pro-Lacerda preliminary work well done. Despite press reports that Lacerda would lose, and the advantage that Magalhães Pinto, already in Curitiba, was taking of Lacerda's absence, he telephoned Lacerda with an optimistic prediction. He was correct. Thirteen of the state delegations, a majority, declared themselves opposed to any constitutional amendment.[13] Most of the delegates favored Lacerda.

The resolutions adopted in Curitiba rejected extremes of the Right and Left, repudiated pressures on Congress, and gave support to agrarian reform, with the recommendation, however, that UDN congressmen oppose any constitutional amendment. The Bossa-Nova, defeated, was bitter. UDN leaders, worried lest the losers form a new party, succeeded in their somewhat difficult task of getting the delegates to accept José Sarney as a UDN vice president. Bilac Pinto agreed to serve as party president, although he had been hesitant a few days earlier when Lacerda had attacked UDN congressmen, threatening a serious party split.[14]

Magalhães Pinto, the loser, left the convention before the closing session and without delivering his speech. Upon reaching São Paulo, he told reporters that he had departed to avoid a schism. Had he remained in Curitiba, he said, he would have argued with Lacerda to try to prevent the UDN from adopting the suicidal position of combating reforms eagerly sought by the entire nation. Quoted as being vexed by the "knavery" of those who mistreated his propaganda posters, he went to confer with Jânio Quadros.[15]

Lacerda, reaching Curitiba's Afonso Pena Airport shortly after noon on April 28, participated in a procession of cars that made its way to a "fraternal lunch," served to 250. There he called for a show of respect for those whose views had not been adopted. He was attending a soccer game in the afternoon when his friend Luiz Carlos Mesquita, noting some crows flying into the field, told Lacerda: "They have come in honor of you." The joke was not appreciated.[16]

The convention's closing session of speeches, held that night at the Guaira Theater, was delayed because saboteurs disconnected the sound and radio transmission cables, cut off the lights, and set off a bomb in the darkness. This delay and the length of Lacerda's speech, interrupted eighty-five times by applause, kept the delegates in the theater well past midnight.[17]

Lacerda pointed out that much available land belonged to the federal, state, and municipal governments, and that he would have land available for distribution in Guanabara if branches of the federal government, in possession of 40 percent of the land there, would "return" it to his state. He urged the colonization of available land, as called for in a constitutional article not yet put into effect.

Arguing that agrarian reform required preparation, Lacerda said that if the manpower were not properly cared for, the land would not be properly cared for. Where, he asked, were the schools for agricultural workers, and what was being done by Agriculture Minister José Ermírio de Morais—a man he described as having "financed the election of the Communist governor of Pernambuco with profits derived from his aluminum monopoly in Brazil"? Lacerda called attention to the relatively large agriculture department budget in the United States, where, he pointed out, the production by one agricultural worker fed $4^1/_2$ people in Lincoln's day and 27 people currently. More and more, Lacerda said, advanced agricultural nations were finding that the agricultural problem was a problem of credits, machinery, electricity, roads, and schools for workers. He rejected as demagogic the "green belt" idea of "feeding millions of people by setting up vegetable gardens on skyscraper land."

Lacerda called SUPRA (the Brazilian government's Superintendency of Agrarian Reform) a corrupt and centralizing advocate of a false agrarian reform, headed by a former UNE president who had never studied but only taken courses in agitation, organized behind the Iron Curtain. Lenin, Lacerda observed, had introduced radical agrarian reform that had cost Russia 7 million dead of starvation before he had modified it.

Lacerda pleaded with his audience not to be imprisoned by the fear of being called reactionary. Was it reactionary, he asked, to construct schools and hospitals, to provide needed water and sewers, and to reduce infant mortality and infectious diseases? "Are we reactionaries because we pay teachers in our state more than they are paid anywhere else in Brazil? . . . Reactionaries because we do not steal and do not permit thievery? Reactionaries because we did not permit a congress of solidarity for a bloody dictator?"

Bilac Pinto, in the closing address, warned against dealing with agrarian reform, a complex matter, in an atmosphere dominated by pressures exerted in urban sectors. In many countries, he said, demagogic solutions to the problem had produced disastrous results. He described the Goulart government as infiltrated by Communists and called on the armed forces to bring peace to the Brazilian family by interrupting the "revolutionary process" that he said had been set in motion.[18]

The *Correio da Manhã* described the Curitiba Convention as a "brilliant personal victory" for Lacerda, resulting from "the magne-

Lacerda mounted on the UDN. (Claudius Ceccon drawing in *Brasil, Urgente,* May 5, 1963, reproduced in Paulo Cezar Loureiro Botas, *A Bênção de Abril*)

tism of his leadership" and from his popularity at the grassroots, or bases, of the party. But it called it "a Pyrrhic Victory" in a country desiring and needing the kind of agrarian reform that was blocked by the constitution. "Without the transformation of the great mass of our miserable proletariat, we cannot create the internal market that our industry needs." Afonso Arinos de Melo Franco was so discouraged by the outcome at Curitiba that he considered leaving the party.[19]

Lacerda owed his victory in part to trips that allowed him to address and mingle with people throughout Brazil. He enjoyed campaigning but was nervous about flights in small planes. A flight to Florianópolis, made by Lacerda in March in a five-passenger plane with Herbert Levy, Hugo Levy, and Wilson Machado, was particularly bad—a reminder of the frightening flight made to the Araxá governors' meeting in June 1962 by some of Lacerda's assistants.

Lacerda spoke to Abreu Sodré about the need of a plane suitable for his presidential campaign. As a result, Paraná coffee producer Oscar Hermínio Ferreira Filho made his DC-3 available, starting in June 1963. Its twenty-passenger-seat arrangement was altered to make room for a desk, tape recorders, and a sofa for the governor. Wilson Machado, known as "Foguinho" by Lacerda's friends, left his post in the governor's office to dedicate himself to the *Esperança,* the name given to the plane, and thus renew his profession of pilot.

Kubitschek, *Jornal do Brasil* wrote, would no longer be the only presidential candidate campaigning in a DC-3.[20]

4. The "Letter to the People" (July 6, 1963)

The Goulart administration's agrarian reform proposal would force landowners to rent their properties, for small payments, if they were considered to be holding them in an anti-economic or antisocial manner.[1] It also called for a constitutional amendment authorizing the government to pay for land expropriations with bonds offering 6 percent annual interest and face value adjustments (to reflect currency depreciation) of no more than 10 percent a year. The PSD, representative of many landowners, opposed compulsory rental of land and insisted that the face value of the bonds be adjustable to cover currency depreciation in full. In May 1963 the congressional commission studying the agrarian question came out against the government's proposal. Representatives of the PSD, UDN, and PSP opposed the bill; representatives of the PTB and PDC favored it.[2]

In other ways, also, May was disagreeable for Goulart. The Three-Year Plan, in its fourth month, was attacked by businessmen, consumers, and labor because the fight against inflation, led by Finance Minister San Tiago Dantas, produced a painful recession while inflation kept increasing. Organized labor was unhappy with War Minister Kruel and with San Tiago Dantas and his wage austerity program, and it broke with the president. Military men protested that their paychecks were inadequate. Brizola, critical of practically everything his brother-in-law was doing, met with representatives of labor and students to condemn the administration's decision to spend $135 million to acquire the Brazilian properties of the American and Foreign Power Company (AMFORP). On the issue of government purchases of foreign utilities, Brizola and Lacerda were on the same side; both called it scandalous to pay foreigners for what they said was "scrap iron."[3]

Under attack from all quarters, the president came to terms with Pacheco and other leaders of the CGT. He agreed with them that wage increases should not adhere to the arrangement worked out by San Tiago Dantas in Washington.[4] He abandoned the non-Communist overall labor organization he had sought to create as a replacement for the CGT. He decided to revamp his entire cabinet (thus dismissing Dantas and Kruel) and discard the Three-Year Plan. When the time came to make the first payment of $10 million to AMFORP, no payment was made. The CGT, allied again with Goulart in June, demanded radical agrarian reform, a break with the International Monetary Fund (IMF), the expropriation of foreign companies, and the promulgation of the law limiting the remission of profits abroad.[5]

After San Tiago Dantas assailed Brizola and Lacerda for opposing

Short circuit: Brizola of the "Negative Left" and, to the right, San Tiago Dantas of the "Positive Left." (Hilde Weber drawing in *O Estado de S. Paulo*, April 25, 1963)

the purchase of the AMFORP properties, Lacerda gave publicity to his letter to the former finance minister in which he called him a conceited opportunist, astute and insincere, who had blocked financial assistance for Guanabara and was serving Communism because of his belief that it would take over the world. The letter described San Tiago Dantas as a wealthy coward who had never believed in democracy, and called him the "Profumo" of foreign utilities—a reference to the British cabinet minister who fell from office following a sex scandal. San Tiago Dantas, returning the letter unanswered, told the press that it was "an abominable document, appropriate only for the hands of the one who had the time and scurrility to write it."[6]

Lacerda's attacks on the Goulart government constituted less of a problem for the president than some of the others he faced, but they contributed to a situation that the *Jornal do Brasil* deplored. The daily admitted that politicians might gain a bit of publicity with campaigns in which they called each other Communists or gorillas, just as "the spectacle of a cock fight, although savage and banned, always finds spectators."[7]

The *Jornal do Brasil* had company among newspapers when it criticized Lacerda's style. But Lacerda, stirring up controversies and using sensational language to denounce men in power, kept his name in the headlines and found opportunities to call the nation's attention to his work as an innovative and constructive governor. Describing himself as too frank and independent to be a good politician, he practiced the politics of antipolitics, as had been done a generation earlier by his father and more recently by Quadros. Lacerda's style helped place him at the forefront of the presidential hopefuls. A Marplan public opinion poll, published in June 1963, gave him a considerable lead over Kubitschek (40 percent against 26 percent) throughout Brazil.[8]

During a visit with the publisher of *O Estado de S. Paulo,* Lacerda said: "Dr. Júlio, I have disagreeable news for you, but I can count on your public spirit to understand. I am going to meet with Governor Ademar de Barros." "Really," Júlio de Mesquita Filho replied, "the country must have reached a very dismal and grave situation if a man such as you has to meet with a man such as Ademar de Barros."[9]

Lacerda lunched at Campos Elíseos Palace and found the São Paulo governor a pleasure to be with. Ademar was a kindred soul who had been assailing Communism in the Goulart administration in language as picturesque as Lacerda's and therefore was encountering problems with that administration. The two governors discussed with apprehension the plan of the Goulart administration to establish a federal police force,[10] and steps that the president and his advisers might take against their state governments. Lacerda gave Ademar a telephone voice scrambler, received from Gustavo Borges, so that unfriendly tappers would not understand phone conversations between the two governors.[11]

Following one of his meetings with Ademar, this one held secretly after midnight, Lacerda told São Paulo UDN legislator Nelson Pereira that Ademar was politically the best-informed Brazilian. "I do not doubt," Lacerda said, "that he has an informer even in my office."[12] Ademar kept abreast of plots developed by the presidential circle against Lacerda and himself. Without Lacerda's knowledge he would sometimes order his state police to give Lacerda protection in São Paulo. On one occasion, several hours after Ademar had sent police to protect Lacerda from an alleged plot, Lacerda was in an automobile in São Paulo, listening on the car radio to a speech by the presidentially ambitious Ademar. "If that man continues to talk," Lacerda remarked admiringly to a companion, "I'm going to end up voting for him."[13]

Lacerda, in São Paulo early in July 1963, autographed hundreds of copies of his books, among them *O Poder das Idéias* (speeches given in 1960, 1961, and 1962), *Reforma Agrária* (the speech given at the recent Curitiba convention), and *Xanam e Outras Histórias* (short stories). He visited the São Paulo Association to Help Retarded Children, and said, in reply to a question about the new justice minister,

Abelardo Jurema: "Ah! There we have a problem child." Lunching on July 6 with journalists at the home of local UDN leader Oscar Klabin Segall, he complained of malicious press distortions and blamed them principally on Communists. To prevent distortions of his video-taped "Letter to the People," scheduled to be broadcast by television stations that night, Lacerda released its text to the principal newspapers as *matéria paga* (paid-for material) for publication on Sunday, July 7. He justified this use of money of the Cariocas by citing the urgency of "alerting the people."[14]

The "Letter to the People" denounced what Lacerda called a conspiracy against the government of Guanabara by renegades, crooks, and incompetent people, Communists and their allies, "our enemies, enemies of the democratic regime," the sons of dictatorship and the fathers of putridity, those "who preach subversion and foster, actively and passively, the collapse of legitimate authority in Brazil." "They cannot forgive our work, honesty, and ability to solve problems that for years have defied administrators," and "they want to destroy confidence in the democratic regime" aroused by the example set by Guanabara. Describing Guanabara as under siege, he declared that the federal government was fighting against it with a zeal appropriate for a war against an enemy nation.

He referred to the refusal of authorities to release funds allotted to the state by the federal budget. Enemies of his administration, he said, were making it difficult for the state to raise 2 billion cruzeiros from the sale of property on Presidente Vargas Avenue, and were ruling that the states were not to deal directly with foreign lending agencies. He said that the Guanabara Tribunal de Contas, which refused to approve the governor's accounts, was playing politics and was irked at his refusal to grant sinecures to its favorites. He described the Goulart administration's plan for a federal police force as a plan to destroy "what still remains of the autonomy of the states and municipalities."

The "Letter" warned that the month of July would be decisive for the future of democracy because, after the first of August, when the second half of the presidential mandate would begin, the constitution provided a simple mechanism for replacing an ousted vice president who had assumed the presidency: the selection of a new president by Congress. According to the "Letter," the Communists and their allies appreciated that crises, starting in August, could be solved simply by the removal of Goulart and therefore would work with unusual vigor against Guanabara in July. And they planned, he said, to throw Congress against the army "at the very moment when the armed forces struggle legitimately and desperately to prevent Brazilian military careers from becoming condemnations to hunger for the children of the military."[15]

On Sunday, July 7, the politically neutral *Diário de Notícias* observed that although Brazilians wanted tranquility, "men like Lacerda and Brizola throw fuel onto the fire." It regretted that the governor's "political manifesto," containing nothing new, was released before the new federal cabinet had revealed its intentions and during a military crisis occasioned by War Minister Jair Dantas Ribeiro's arrest of eight army officers, including Military Club President Augusto Magessi, for "rebellious" conduct during a debate about military pay.[16]

Justice Minister Abelardo Jurema, called a "boob" in Lacerda's "Letter," issued a circular prohibiting television stations from rebroadcasting it, because, he said, it was "entirely illegal," stimulated military indiscipline, suggested a coup, and endangered the national security. Casa Civil Chief Darci Ribeiro, meeting with SUPRA Superintendent João Pinheiro Neto and *Última Hora*'s Samuel Wainer at the home of Foreign Minister Evandro Lins e Silva, prepared a televised reply to Lacerda—the first of a series in which Darci would be followed, on successive days, by Jurema, Mines and Energy Minister Oliveira Brito, and the government's legal adviser (*consultor geral*), Valdir Pires.[17]

Darci Ribeiro, in his broadcast of July 8, called Lacerda an obdurate conspirator who liked to present himself as a victim. "Why this refrain about August," Darci asked, "by the very one responsible for August 1954, the August of the suicide of Vargas, and the August of the resignation of Quadros, that almost led this nation to a social convulsion that might have lasted for years had not the orderly behavior of the defenders of legality, of responsible citizens, put a halt to the conspirator whose aim has been to upset the nation? This mischievous, frustrated governor seeks nothing less than to take the mandate from the president." Darci Ribeiro, contradicting some of Lacerda's statements, spoke of the hiring of Robert Bialek by COPEG and the use of *jogo do bicho* money; and he warned against businessmen "who finance television programs and the purchase of arms." He accused Lacerda of being associated with IBAD and of benefiting from 600 million cruzeiros spent on his personal publicity by the Guanabara government. Even before Darci Ribeiro had finished his speech, Lacerda phoned Rio from São Paulo with instructions that Alcino Salazar initiate, on the governor's behalf, lawsuits demanding that Darci Ribeiro prove these statements or pay 2 million cruzeiros for "moral damages."[18]

Jurema issued an order that prevented Amaral Netto from replying to Darci Ribeiro on television, and then, on July 10, gave his own televised denouncement of Lacerda, "violator of the National Security Law, Press Law, and Telecommunications Code." Valdir Pires, in the last of the series of four speeches, may have shown a spark of humor when he compared Lacerda, suing Darci Ribeiro for "moral damages," to Profumo case prostitute Christine Keeler, "were she to sue the London press for harming her unsullied reputation of a girl fulfilling her domestic duties."

The government's speeches, on time confiscated from regular television programs, were poorly received by the press. The *Jornal do Brasil,* dismayed by the "unenlightening" exchange of "aggressive epithets," accused Darci Ribeiro of a tactical error for dragging the discussion to the same level of name-calling used by the abler Lacerda. The *Diário de Notícias,* which found the speeches "interminable and monotonous," wrote that Darci Ribeiro, "a declared admirer of Cuba's Communist dictator," had succumbed to the hatred that Communists felt for Lacerda. The *Correio da Manhã* wrote that Darci Ribeiro had not proved his charge that the governor was conspiring. If a conspiracy existed, it said, the government should act; and if it did not exist it would do better to keep quiet than argue about Bialek, the *jogo do bicho,* and the Guanabara state lottery funds.

The press published a letter from Sobral Pinto to Darci Ribeiro in which Goulart and his advisers were accused of planning "to take this nation on the path of socialization, which, coming from the Muscovite steppes, has already dominated valorous Cuba and attempts to dechristianize Brazil." "To accuse Lacerda of threatening the national security is the very pinnacle of absurdity."[19]

Lacerda, continuing his campaign, went to Rio Grande do Sul. Hostile crowds, organized in Porto Alegre by Brizola's supporters, hurled a dead crow at the car of "Mister Lacerda" and threw garbage, stones, and dead vultures at the studio of Rádio Guaíba, where he spoke. They broke the windows of the building of the anti-Brizola *Correio do Povo* and set off three bombs at the office door of Pfizer do Brasil, a corporation said to have helped arrange for Lacerda's trip. In protest to Lacerda's presence, local stevedores, Petrobrás workers, and railroad workers went on strike.

After an anti-Lacerda rally in Porto Alegre's main square, a mob damaged streetcars and assaulted the offices of Agência Meridional (of Chateaubriand's Diários Associados). Brizola's brother Jesus, driving a car displaying a black flag of mourning, was hit by a brick thrown by a retired police officer, who was chased away by the mob.

In Rio, anti-Communist Danillo Nunes attributed the disorders in the south to Brizola's brother. Abreu Sodré, after returning with

Lacerda from Porto Alegre, blamed them on Communists incited by labor leader Roberto Morena, who, he said, had gone to Porto Alegre several days before Lacerda.[20]

5. Telephones and Traffic (1963-1964)

In January 1963, General Salvador Mandim set up the offices of the state secretaryship of public services as best he could with the few cruzeiros that Raphael de Almeida Magalhães said were available. The general was eager to get on with the organization of a state telephone company, imperative if rural areas were to be industrialized. The governor, equally eager, signed a decree on February 21 to create the Companhia Estadual de Telefones (CETEL), as authorized by the Administrative Reform Law.[1]

Telephone technicians unassociated with the Light group were not plentiful, but General Mandim found several from within the armed forces. After they developed the technical plans for a telephone service outside the CTB-controlled area, CETEL announced that the first sale of shares would be held at the Rio Branco Avenue office of the public services secretaryship on March 25.

The response was a line of about 2,400 share purchasers, described by *Última Hora* as "suckers." Each agreed to pay 110,000 cruzeiros (worth $135 at the time and clearly about to become worth less) for a CETEL share and the right to receive one of the twenty thousand instruments offered as part of a modern system scheduled to start operating in twenty-four months. At Guanabara Palace later in the day, Lacerda and retired General Lincoln Geolás Santos presided at a stockholders' meeting at which Lieutenant Colonel Gilberto Sampaio de Toledo was elected president of CETEL and General Santos technical director. Stockholders included Guanabara state, with 15 percent of the shares, the state bank, COSIGUA, and COPEG.[2]

The "suckers" received telephones at a lower cost than those who followed their example. CETEL spread all over the state. It used equipment made in Rio by Standard Electric, thus disappointing Juracy Magalhães, president of Ericsson do Brasil, who sought to sell Ericsson equipment, to be produced in São Paulo.

In the words of Lacerda, CETEL President Toledo was able to continue with his extraordinarily successful work because Brigadeiro Francisco Teixeira, the "sincere and honest Communist" who ran the office of the aviation ministry, phoned Toledo and said, "We have orders to take from the Guanabara government all military officers working for it. You, however, can stay because you are carrying out an excellent service installing telephones, essential for any regime;

and when we implant the type of government we want, we shall use the telephones you are installing."[3]

Still concerned about the deficient service in the crowded area not covered by CETEL, Lacerda wrote Goulart on May 22, 1963, to try to convince him that the solution lay in having the CTB accept the state government and telephone users as partners in an enterprise, which, with growth, would leave the CTB in a minority position. He furnished statistics to show that 56 percent of the CTB equipment, which the federal government in May was planning to purchase, was obsolete or worn out. In a reference to CTB's obligation to invest in Brazil the money received from the sale, Lacerda wrote that the result would be denationalization, the placing of Brazilian companies in foreign hands.[4]

The office of the president, which had not yet decided to miss making the July 1, 1963, payment to AMFORP, replied to Lacerda by publishing a note saying that "national security imperatives" required the prompt nationalization of foreign power and telecommunications properties and that the National Telecommunications Code obligated the administration to form a government company that would bring together the telephone operations in various states. Lacerda's charge about possible denationalization, resulting from the CTB's reinvestment of the purchase price, was dismissed with the explanation that the government would have the right to select the industries in which the reinvestment would be made.

Lacerda, writing to Goulart on June 3, objected to what he called the disrespectful tone of the note. As for the "obligation" stemming from the National Telecommunications Code, he pointed out that the code provided an "authorization," not a requirement, and covered "interstate" telephone service, leaving to the states, in accordance with the constitution, the handling of services within their borders.[5]

Lacerda and Mandim were still negotiating with the Light group about mass transportation. They suggested the replacement of streetcars by buses in the city's North Zone; but the Light company pointed out that its loss of 618 million cruzeiros on the concession in 1962 left it unable to make large new investments. At a meeting in Guanabara Palace late in May 1963, Lacerda told the Light that, in view of such losses, it should welcome paying the state 3 billion cruzeiros for an immediate recision of the concession, due to end in 1970. He said that if his suggestion was rejected, the state would be rigorous in the enforcement of all regulations and the collection of fines.[6]

On June 19 the Light agreed to the 3-billion-cruzeiro figure but proposed paying over a five-year period. The proposal also would require the state to forgive the company's 500-million-cruzeiro debt to the state bank and assume the labor law indemnification claims of its 7,250 streetcar workers.

This counterproposal left Lacerda pessimistic about reaching an agreement. But Mandim carried out a relentless campaign, stiffening penalties for infractions (such as the absence of a bell cord) and building up an imposing stack of fines payable. Thus he helped prod Light Company President Antônio Gallotti into accepting an agreement with the state. The state received, over a six-month period, 3 billion cruzeiros (worth $3.7 million in July and $2.3 million at the end of the period). But it was left with the 7,250 workers, most of whom would not be needed when several hundred CTC buses replaced streetcars. They were given jobs handling paperwork, whitewashing walls, and helping convert streetcar garages into bus garages. "They were distributed all over the place," Mandim has said.[7]

The trolley buses, an improvement over streetcars, were not giving the best possible service and therefore, in mid-1963, Mandim spoke to Lacerda about installing Mercedes Benz diesel buses. "I won't give any more money to the CTC," Lacerda said; "you people are rich; you have lots of property. Sell your streetcars and other things." Tracks turned out to be one of the most valuable of the disposable assets. Sold to the National Steel Company (Companhia Siderúrgica Nacional), the old tracks provided a billion cruzeiros toward the purchase of diesel buses.[8]

The asphalting of streets went forward at a rapid pace after Lacerda agreed with Enaldo Cravo Peixoto that the proposal of the Highway Department (DER) to build carefully prepared long-lasting foundations was too slow and costly. The increase in asphalting, from 500,000 square meters in 1961 to 1,000,000 square meters in 1964, was helped by the new, rapid process, later adopted throughout Brazil. It was also helped by the completion in 1962 of the state's chief asphalt plant, on Francisco Bicalho Avenue, and, to a lesser extent, by the building of another plant in Campo Grande to take care of rural roads.[9]

General Mandim started installing mercury vapor lighting in Rio's principal thoroughfares in January 1964. The idea occurred to him during the work he was doing on the governor's orders to install power and overhead lighting in *favelas*. Visiting the Padre Miguel *favela*, where he felt "a thousand lamp-posts would be needed," he found a solitary post installed earlier by a campaigning politician. The single post, lit by mercury vapor, gave good light, four times brighter than the dull, reddish incandescent lamps used on the streets throughout Rio. Each new post with good street lighting, he felt, was the equivalent of one policeman in ridding the streets of thieves.[10]

A further improvement resulted from Lacerda's demand for the removal of unauthorized billboards that in many cases obstructed beautiful views. After giving warnings to the owners of the unauthorized billboards, Mandim arranged for men to collect them in trucks. They were piled up in the Praça da Bandeira to be hauled away by their owners.[11]

The construction of viaducts and cloverleafs for vehicle traffic was among the foremost accomplishments of the public works secretaryship of Enaldo Cravo Peixoto. The lengthy tunnel excavation to connect the Lagoa and Rio Comprido districts would add more traffic to the already congested Ponte dos Marinheiros, at the western end of Presidente Vargas Avenue, and it was there that work was begun on the most ambitious cloverleaf, a group of four viaducts, to be called the Viaducts of the Armed Forces. Meanwhile, at the southern and northern ends of the Santa Bárbara Tunnel, the Engenheiro Noronha and Dr. Agra viaducts were completed. The Santa Bárbara was opened to traffic on July 30, 1963, during a day of ceremonies that included the inauguration of the twenty-fifth agency of the state bank (BEG).[12]

When Lacerda took visitors, such as Herbert Levy and Abreu Sodré in August 1963, to visit works in progress, he usually included a stop at the Morro da Mangueira Favela, where a program of paving, water, and sewage had been started. He seldom missed an opportunity to inspect the excavation, now under contract to the Servix Company, to give Rio its 5,500 meters of vehicle tunnels between the Lagoa and Rio Comprido districts. He had decided to name the world's "longest urban vehicle tunnel" after brothers André and Antônio Rebouças, black engineers whose railroad building plans, carried out in Paraná during the empire, had been a spectacular success in spite of the forebodings of French and British engineers.[13]

To give impetus to cleanliness in the streets, the state introduced new sweeping machines. It built, in Bangu, a garbage industrialization plant for producing fertilizers, and it imported American machines for cleaning sewers. The governor, acting to make Rio "the cleanest city in the world," posted large signs to warn ships that the fines for the pollution of water were very high.[14]

Colonel Fontenelle's campaign to straighten out the city's chaotic traffic situation went into high gear in 1964. He discouraged the unlawful parking of automobiles by having his men haul them away or, more frequently, take the air out of their tires. Diplomats, embittered by inconveniences caused by Fontenelle's campaign, complained to the Foreign Minister, but the governor, in a letter to the minister, pointed out that illegal parking, blocking throughways, contributed to traffic chaos, pedestrian insecurity, and an alarmingly high accident rate, harmful to everyone including foreign diplomats.[15]

Fontenelle, known as Colonel Fon Fon, was taken to court by angry Cariocas, one of whom asserted that "the emptying of tires of automobiles parked in forbidden places is the work of rascals and vagrants." But in mid-1964 a judge ruled that the traffic department was acting within the law. A few days later, Fontenelle gave the state legislature an order to keep two streets, near Tiradentes Palace, clear of the parked cars that had been interfering with bus traffic. When two legislators defied the order, Fon Fon himself, surrounded by applauding onlookers, emptied the tires of the two cars and issued orders for the cars to be hauled away.[16]

IBOPE pollsters found that Cariocas, by a 71 percent to 13 percent margin, felt the colonel's campaign improved traffic movement, and, by a 51 percent to 36 percent margin, wanted his measures to remain permanent rather than temporary. However, he was not popular with the legislators. In response to the governor's request for 200 million cruzeiros for the traffic department to use in the following year, 1965, the legislature voted a mere 15 million—not enough to cover the cost of the electronic traffic signals being imported. The governor and the colonel raised money by setting aside parking areas and charging fees for parking in them. This step, like the earlier emptying of tires, was attacked in the anti-Lacerda press. Oppositionist legislator Alfredo Tranjan (PST) introduced a bill early in April 1965 to prohibit the state from charging for parking.[17]

6. Administrating in the Face of Obstruction (1963–1964)

Fontenelle, before becoming famous for emptying tires, headed a team appointed by Lacerda to collect data considered useful in planning for the future of Guanabara. The governor wanted a master plan to prevent haphazard expansion. Alfredo C. Machado, publisher of Lacerda's books, exclaimed "There's your man!" after reading a *New Yorker* "Profile" about Constantinos Doxiadis, the Greek who had become known as the world's foremost city planner. Lacerda, who had already been shown the "Profile" by Lota Macedo Soares, was impressed by what he learned about Doxiadis. He made arrangements with the Greek to have men of Doxiadis Associates work with the governor's data collectors to produce a plan for Guanabara's development.[1]

In January 1964 Engineering Club President Hélio de Almeida asked for details about the "scandalous contract with a Greek firm." He said that Brazilian law stipulated that work being done for Guanabara by Doxiadis Associates should be done only by persons or firms certified by the Federal Council of Engineers and Architects. He called Lacerda's arrangement "illegal and unpatriotic" and "highly destructive of national technical and economic interests." The *Diário Carioca*, property of Danton Jobim, wrote that Brazil possessed world famous architects, such as Lúcio Costa, Oscar Niemeyer, and Roberto and Sérgio Bernardes. Only "an antinational administration, such as that of Lacerda . . . could threaten so terribly the social conquests of the Brazilians and our purest cultural values." Jobim's pro-Goulart daily suggested that a study of Hitler's youthful frustrations would lead to an understanding of why the "subliterate" and "anti-Semitic" Lacerda, frustrated in his youth, hated Brazilian culture, workers, and young people and was "capable of setting up concentration camps in Guanabara itself, the country's intellectual capital."[2]

A telegram from Lacerda to Hélio de Almeida accused the former transport minister of having sabotaged the state administration's subway plan by denying the cooperation of the Central do Brasil Railroad. Lacerda told Hélio de Almeida that, in commenting on the Doxiadis arrangement, he was meddling where he was not wanted and was making use of the Engineering Club for vile demagoguery and undisguised political objectives. Hélio de Almeida replied that Lacerda was the one responsible for the failure of the subway work to get started.[3]

Célio Borja, who was a state legislator at the time, points out that the collection of data about Guanabara was intensified and better organized after the Doxiadis Associates entered the picture. From the data, an ideal goal for the year 2000 was developed, and if the goal was beyond the funding possibilities, at least it indicated what direction public works should take. Lacerda, writing later about his friend "Dinos" Doxiadis, explained that the Greek believed that Rio could be prepared for the future only as a part of the metropolitan complex that included Niterói and other areas outside Guanabara.[4]

The Doxiadis report, later revealed to have cost U.S. $700,000, called attention to the "alarming proportions" reached by the problem of the fast-growing *favelas*. The governor, reporting to the legislature in August 1963, said that "from the social point of view the housing problem is the most important of the state. A million people, about 25 percent of the population, live in *favelas* or slum tenements. An equal number are in constant threat of eviction, with nowhere to go." In this budget message for 1964, the governor said the problem could not be solved without the help of private initiative, and therefore the state government hoped to create an active market for the construction of housing, needed by the middle class, and set an example by courageously presenting new formulas. The Fundação Leão

XIII would spend, he said, 500 million cruzeiros in 1964 urbaniz-
ing *favelas*, while the state's Popular Housing Company would spend
3.3 billion cruzeiros building low-cost houses.[5]

The Popular Housing Company (COHAB—Companhia de Habitação Popular) was established in March 1963 as one of the organs
reporting to Social Services Secretary Sandra Cavalcanti. Sandra succeeded in obtaining the resignation of COHAB's first president,
Romeu Loures, who became head of the organization that ran the
Maracanã Stadium. But the choice of Penha district regional administrator, Luiz Carlos Vital, to succeed Loures was a victory for
Raphael de Almeida Magalhães over Sandra.

Besides constructing low-cost houses at Cidade de Deus, Vila
Kennedy, Vila Aliança, and Vila Esperança, COHAB encouraged the
formation of associations of *favela* dwellers (Associações de Moradores). The associations picked leaders and organized work done by
favelados to make improvements. The education of the *favelados*,
especially about sanitation and the need to assume responsibilities,
was felt to be an important part of the program. Lacerda joined Sandra
Cavalcanti in attending meetings of the associations.[6]

Sandra Cavalcanti has described the Morro do Pasmado Favela, the
first of twenty selected for demolition, as being on a 50-degree incline
which *faveladas* (women) climbed several times daily with loads
frequently consisting of buckets of water carried on their heads. The
conditions, she writes, were "terribly unsanitary" and "extremely
dangerous," especially during torrential downpours. To purchase the
property, which was in the South Zone, from the owners of the land
and urbanize the small part that might have been urbanized was
beyond the state's resources. Sandra proposed moving the 1,100 families to the new housing units provided that the idea received a favorable vote of the association of Pasmado dwellers.

The association was dominated by the men, who favored remaining
in the *favela*. Although Lacerda had instructed Mandim to have CTC
bus lines give good service to the housing settlements, the men
pointed out that the *favela* was more conveniently located for their
work. Furthermore, the move was strongly opposed by the local electoral chieftains who controlled *favelado* votes.

Over fifty bus trips took women and children of the Pasmado Favela
to see houses being completed at Vila Kennedy and left the children
delighted with the shower baths and the women eager to move. But
the outcome recommended by Sandra was achieved only after she
gained the adherence of a group of influential *favelados*: the owners
of the little food and drink shops who extended credit. She arranged
that the new housing settlements would have corner stores, such as

had been vital to the lives of the *favelados*. After that, she and Lacerda have explained, the move was made because the women resolved to go, regardless of what the men might do. Under the direction of Sandra's office chief, Luís Pires Leal, the Pasmado Favela families were transferred during twenty-six days.[7]

Doctors at the Miguel Couto Hospital in Leblon said that people from the nearby Getúlio Vargas Favela came almost daily with cases of typhoid fever and diphtheria, not to mention children bitten by rats. Getúlio Vargas Favela families were given a choice of new locations and most chose Vila Kennedy. The president of the União dos Moradores da Favela Getúlio Vargas, who had been maintaining that he and his neighbors did not wish to move to Bangu, changed his mind; nevertheless, on the eve of the relocation, Justice Minister Abelardo Jurema appeared on the scene and declared that the relocation would not proceed.

The relocation was, in fact, proceeding on the next day, with the usual presence at the *favela* of curious passers-by and politicians giving speeches for and against, when Congressman Adão Pereira Nunes addressed the crowd and announced he would go and get a judicial order to stop the relocation. Lacerda instructed COHAB President Luiz Carlos Vital to disregard any such order and arrest the congressman if he brought one. Congressional immunities, Lacerda told Vital, did not apply to Nunes, since he had been elected in Rio state and was acting in Guanabara. After Adão Pereira Nunes returned with a judge, who brought the order, Vital let the judge discover, by chatting with *favelados*, that they were moving of their own free will. Nunes, although he lost the judge's support, started to incite the *favelados* against the move. He was therefore arrested by Vital and removed to a nearby police station.[8]

Many of those who were transferred from *favelas* complained of mosquitoes at their new residences, as well as the distance from workplaces and the downtown area. The *Diário Carioca* wrote in January 1964 that many families, moved "on orders of Governor Lacerda" from the Morro do Pasmado Favela to Vila Kennedy, were far from satisfied and found their new homes made of poor quality construction material. Raimundo Magalhães Júnior described the Bangu of the new houses as a remote, dreary place, away from the sea and the breezes that had pleased the *favelados* in the past. "Imagine the *favelado* now, in his cubicle of a living room in Bangu, without the Sugar Loaf and Botafogo Bay in view, far from his favorite club," moved by Sandra Cavalcanti "with an almost masculine truculence." Lacerda, referring in September 1965 to opposition politicians who had encouraged resistance to relocations, said that Sandra Cavalcanti had been "stoned under the 'protection' of federal troops furnished by Abelardo Jurema."

Última Hora, reporting about the "expulsion" of thirty-three families, in trucks, from the Brás de Pina Favela in December 1964, described an agitated scene in which the *favelados,* saying they did not want to move to Vila Aliança, were supported by twenty-four sympathetic priests. In the presence of social workers, police, Cardinal Jayme Câmara, and Luiz Carlos Vital, Lacerda had an angry exchange with Vicar José Saenz Artola, who had been campaigning against the forced transfers and was already regarded by the police as an "agitator."[9]

Lacerda hoped that job opportunities, conveniently accessible for the occupants of new low-cost housing, would develop in the Santa Cruz industrial zone. But steel plant construction was delayed by financing problems; and the governor's plan for a state-run iron ore export port in the area received no cooperation from large ore export companies, mining in Minas Gerais, who preferred to construct their private shiploading facilities, also in Sepetiba Bay. In reply to questions submitted in July 1963 by legislator Augusto Amaral Peixoto, the governor revealed that a 200-million-cruzeiro loan from the federal government to COSIGUA had been used, for the most part, to make payments for the property in Santa Cruz and an iron ore mine in Minas Gerais. He explained how power for COSIGUA would be furnished by CHEVAP (Companhia Hidroelétrica do Vale do Paraíba), partly from a thermoelectric plant to be built next to the steel plant.[10]

CHEVAP's hydroelectric plant construction in Rio state was going forward at too slow a pace to save Guanabara from the power shortage that Lacerda had forecast while running for governor. The Rio-Light Company, whose ability to furnish power depended on rainfall, was forced in April 1963 to resort to rationing, in the form of electricity cutoffs several hours each evening, in Guanabara and parts of Rio state. Lacerda blamed the federal government for holding back funds needed for the CHEVAP construction.

In May 1963 the governor announced that he had made arrangements for the importation from the United States of four gas turbine generators which would end the power shortage in September by furnishing 60,000 kw. According to the announcement, payments on the $7 million purchase price were not to begin until 1966, and the sellers, thanks to the governor's prestige, accepted the guarantee of the Guanabara state bank, instead of relying on the federal government or its banks. *Última Hora,* starting a new campaign against the governor, ran a headline: "The scandal of the generators wrecks the Guanabara treasury: a 5 billion cruzeiro purchase in the United States without competitive bidding." José Mauro's columns in *Última Hora* spoke of a shady deal involving Sérgio Lacerda, Robert Bialek, and Fernando Delamare, who headed COPEG after Guilherme Borghoff became the secretary of economy. Like *Última Hora*, the *Correio da Manhã* said that less expensive generators could be purchased in Europe. Sérgio Lacerda sued *Última Hora;* and Alcino Salazar pointed out that under exceptional circumstances the governor could purchase equipment without competitive bidding. Lacerda said: "They may jail me later, but those generators will be bought."[11]

In the state legislature Saldanha Coelho headed the campaign to prevent the purchase. The governor, inaugurating a state bank agency in June 1963, said that "if rationing continues after October, it will be exclusively due to the federal government, which through the well-known international thief Samuel Wainer [running *Última Hora*] is doing everything to prevent the purchase of the generators." He added that the U.S. Department of State was impeding the purchase in order to "save the faces of Brazilian political sharpies involved in the purchase of the utility concessionaires."[12]

Mines and Energy Minister Oliveira Brito, when he replied to Lacerda's "Letter to the People," denied that the federal government had obstructed the generator deal, and he told of the construction work at the Furnas hydroelectric plant in Minas that would prevent Rio from "collapsing." Reminding his listeners of arrangements made in 1960 to have the national treasury pay for Guanabara's workers in justice, police, and firefighting, he estimated that these payments in 1963 would reach almost 19 billion cruzeiros because of the 70 percent wage increase for public servants granted by Goulart in July 1963. A little later, the Goulart government stopped making the payments, thus violating the law that had created Guanabara. This refusal of the Bank of Brazil to honor a check drawn on it by Guanabara for the expenses led state Justice Secretary Alcino Salazar to start legal action to have the Bank of Brazil declared bankrupt. After that, the payments were renewed.[13]

In order to slap down charges that Guanabara had been especially favored by the Alliance for Progress and Inter-American Development Bank, Lacerda, addressing an American Chamber of Commerce meeting at the Rio Yacht Club, spoke of large credits made available to other states, such as $41 million for roads in Paraná, $38 million for water and sewers in São Paulo, $13 million for electric energy in Minas, $15 million for the city of Belém, $80 million for the northeast, and $57 million to remodel São Paulo's Sorocabana Railroad. Guanabara, he said, had received approval of about $25 million for water and $11 million for sewers; nothing had come from the request of $10 million for popular housing and *favela* urbanization submitted to Washington banks in May 1961 with the approval of the Quadros administration. Of the 2 billion cruzeiros granted Guanabara from the United States wheat money (Public Law 480), 1.4 billion, he said, had been received and was being spent on *favelas*, water, and health. He concluded by noting that the United States AID program had furnished Brazil with $709 million, of which "Guanabara has received nothing to this date."[14]

The 43-kilometer Guandu aqueduct, Guanabara's chief recipient of foreign aid, so fascinated Lacerda that when he learned of Suzanne Labin's plan to visit Rio in August 1963, he phoned Emil Farhat in São Paulo and exclaimed, "Come here! Suzanne Labin is coming and I am going to show her the Guandu aqueduct." Farhat, novelist and advertising executive, joined Lacerda at Guanabara Palace when the governor received the anti-Communist French authoress, whose latest book, *Il Est Moins Cinq*, had been praised and translated into Portuguese by Lacerda. She asked about the origin of Guanabara. The governor, leaving his seat, showed her a map on the wall and spoke for over an hour about the history and economy of the state. Then he took her to the Guandu excavation work, which included the creation of an underground chamber, the size of the main room of the Central do Brasil Railroad station, for a pump station to lift water 110 meters. After a long descent underground, Farhat reports, Labin had an "attack of enthusiasm" for the Guandu undertaking.[15]

Rumors of federal intervention in Guanabara preceded Suzanne Labin's visit to Brazil and were worriedly reported to Lacerda by lawyer Dario de Almeida Magalhães.[16] But in August 1963, during her visit, the idea was shelved, at least temporarily, by the Goulart people, who, instead, concentrated on a plan to transfer Guanabara's police, firemen, and penitentiary workers to the federal government. A clause giving these Guanabara employees, paid by the federal government, three months in which to decide to transfer was a part of Federal Law 4,242, of July 17, 1963, which increased the pay of federal employees. On the day before the law was promulgated, Lacerda went to the barracks of the Military Police to induct 700 new soldiers into the corporation, thus giving it a record membership of over 11,000.[17]

Because of the inconveniences of living in Brasília, where most of the transferred men were expected to go, the federal government offered extra pay. Therefore, of the approximately 17,000 members of Guanabara's police forces and firemen's brigades, about 90 percent said they wanted to transfer, although within the officer ranks of the Military Police only 50 percent requested transfer. Social Services

Secretary Sandra Cavalcanti pointed out that, as a result of political favors during previous administrations, 4,000 policemen, detectives, firemen, and guards resided in low-cost housing where rent was insignificant, and she gave those favoring federal employment thirty days to move out to make the housing available to impoverished invalids and widows, along with abandoned mothers with young children. Many firemen withdrew requests to transfer but then opted a second time after Lacerda vetoed the extra pay they wanted for risking their lives.

So popular was the option in the firemen's corps (the *bombeiros*), normally made up of 3,000 men, that only a few hundred chose to remain with the state, among them 20 members of the once famous 80-man musical band. The commander of firefighting urged industry and commerce to take extraordinary precautions against the outbreak of fires because, he said, they could no longer count on "the efficient help of the corporation in emergencies."[18]

Decree Law 52,694, written by Justice Minister Jurema and issued on October 15, 1963, ruled that the military organizations to be formed by those "returning" to the pre-1960 status of serving the central government would have commanders named by the president and would remain in Guanabara until moved to the federal capital. A federal commission, studying the problem of handling the 15,000 employees who opted for transfer, found that 3,500 could be taken care of by requests for men received from federal railroads and port authorities. Others, the commission decided, could be used in police contingents in Brasília.[19]

Lacerda, appealing to the Supreme Court in December 1963, maintained that the legislation about the options violated the law that created Guanabara. He stimulated a program to recruit volunteers for training courses to provide replacements. About 750 applications for voluntary police work, many from retired military men, were accepted late in December.

While alarming figures about transfers were reported in the Carioca press and in speeches by *udenistas* such as Congressman Raimundo Padilha, the reassignment of those who had opted to transfer proceeded at a snail's pace. Of the 2,700 firemen who had requested transfer, 300 were transferred in December 1963, leaving 2,400 impatient. As in the case of the firemen, only about 10 percent of the members of the police forces had actually been transferred by the first part of 1964. When the Parliamentary Nationalist Front's Max da Costa Santos demanded an explanation from Jurema, the justice minister spoke of Guanabara's needs during the 1964 Carnaval and promised a rapid solution thereafter.[20]

The *Diário de Notícias,* critical of Lacerda and the federal government for their feud, wrote in mid-December 1963 that "the option presented to the state employees in a manner to make acceptance difficult to refuse, cannot fail to entail serious consequences for the state administration." It suggested that the federal government, instead of gaining the victory it expected to achieve over Lacerda, would lose ground "on this generous Carioca soil, which has until now been so hospitable to it."

The publication of this editorial, "Malicious Option," coincided with the news of a large fire that broke out on Presidente Vargas Avenue and destroyed two buildings. One was a warehouse of the Guanabara Social Security Institute (IPEG). Lacerda, who witnessed the blaze, blamed the firemen's delay in arriving on the option scheme and said that, on account of the option, the state was short of ladder operators and hydrant technicians.[21]

7. The *Los Angeles Times* Interview (September 1963)

Late in August 1963 Lacerda turned to the sort of rustic relaxation he had enjoyed during Holy Week. The trip was made this time with Orlando Ometto, Veiga Brito, Wilson Machado, and the governor's aide, Tannay de Farias. The *Esperança* took them to a fishing lodge on Bananal Island, beside the Araguaia River, which separated Mato Grosso from Goiás. After privacy was disturbed by the arrival of a plane bringing more fishermen, Ometto arranged to have Lacerda's party flown in a small plane to ranch houses on one of his extensive landholdings. There, on the Araguaia River near the village of São Félix, Mato Grosso, Lacerda found the privacy he wanted.[1]

Soon after returning to Rio early in September, Lacerda went to Petrópolis to spend the last three weeks of the month resting on doctor's orders. He made infrequent trips to Rio to meet with his cabinet and attend selected public ceremonies.[2]

His "Petrópolis home," which he named the Estância do Alecrim, was in Rocio, a drive of fifteen minutes from Petrópolis. What Lacerda bought was a small country home, and from time to time he added to the building and improved the grounds, especially with plantings. He enjoyed cultivating plants, growing roses, and adding to his bird collection, and found time to make paintings and practice his culinary skills. He wrote of Rocio: "I adore its climate, the mountain that gives a restful change from the sea; each tree I plant is a celebration, each piece of land—in this soul of a rustic person—is a consolation."[3]

Lacerda was in Rocio when Brazil was stunned by the news of a sergeants' rebellion that broke out in Brasília at 2:00 A.M. on September 12. The uprising, by about six hundred men of the navy and air force, stemmed from the decision of the Supreme Court, handed down on September 11, that the constitution banned sergeants from participating in politics, thus making it impossible for Sergeant Antônio Garcia Filho, of the Parliamentary Nationalist Front, to hold the congressional seat to which he had been elected. Before daybreak on September 12, the rebelling sergeants, corporals, and enlisted men roved around in bunches, claiming control of the airport and the navy and justice buildings. They "arrested" a few dignitaries, including a Supreme Court justice. But they were disorganized and were handicapped in calling for uprisings elsewhere because anti-Communist infiltrators cut phone lines to the rest of Brazil. Army contingents, posted earlier in Brasília by War Minister Jair Dantas Ribeiro, subdued the rebels later in the morning in an action that left one marine and one civilian dead and two marines wounded.[4]

The uprising persuaded Goulart and Darci Ribeiro that steps should be taken to give the administration better relations with military men in the lower ranks.[5] It also persuaded the CGT to call a general strike in favor of a constitutional amendment to give political rights to sergeants. When Dante Pelacani and Clodsmith Riani told Goulart of the CGT's intention, the president averted a general strike by promising to strive quickly for the amendment. This he did, but Congress refused to give a priority position to the debate about the proposal.[6]

While arrested sergeants were flown to Rio to be tried, Brazil learned of the imminent arrival of Marshal Tito in Brasília for a state visit. Lacerda condemned the visit of the Yugoslav Communist leader and received over two thousand telegrams supporting his position. Thousands of the "faithful" acted on the suggestion of Cardinal Jayme Câmara that an "hour of atonement" be set aside to make amends for the visit.

Tito attended receptions in Brasília and visited the university there in the company of its *reitor* (president), Anísio Teixeira, and Miguel Arraes. But he saw little of Brazil beyond a visit to Goiânia. Although Magalhães Pinto uttered some words about hospitality being a characteristic of the Mineiros, the trip to Minas was canceled on the advice of Tito's security men. Before he flew to Chile, Tito received a Cruzeiro do Sul decoration from Goulart and distributed Yugoslav decorations to Darci Ribeiro, seven cabinet ministers, and others.[7]

Had there been any foundation to reports that Tito would travel incognito to São Paulo or stay in Rio at a hospital suite reserved for

Goulart,[8] he might have witnessed some of the strikes that were breaking out constantly. In São Paulo, Second Army Commander Peri Constant Bevilacqua issued a thunderous directive, warning his men against the "syndical evildoers," the CGT, and similar labor groups, whose support, he said, should be rejected lest the honor of the Brazilian soldier be defiled. For his directive the general was reprimanded by War Minister Jair Dantas Ribeiro and denounced by Governor Arraes, the Parliamentary Nationalist Front, the National Union of Students (UNE), and the Communists' *Novos Rumos*. Brizola, calling for more strikes, said that Bevilacqua was "at the service of imperialism."[9]

In Rio the streetcar workers struck on September 19 and returned to work a week later, by which time the Leopoldina Railroad workers had gone on strike. Students at Rio's Faculdade Nacional de Filosofia (National College of Philosophy) called a strike to protest the appointment of a new college director. A bankworkers' strike, very effective in Rio, got under way later in September.[10]

Under these circumstances Lacerda agreed to the suggestion of Alfredo C. Machado, his link to foreign correspondents, that the *Los Angeles Times* correspondent come from Rio to Rocio for an interview. The young correspondent, Julian Hartt, taped Lacerda's words on September 26, and they appeared in articles published in the *Los Angeles Times* on Sunday and Monday, September 29 and 30. The Sunday article pointed out that the governor, who "is saying nothing these days for domestic consumption," was directing his words "specifically to the American people, more than 1,000 of whom have written him in recent weeks." But the articles ("Governor Sees Goulart Fall, Urges U.S. to Withhold Aid Funds") were carried in part by the Associated Press and were quoted in Brazilian newspapers.[11]

In the articles Lacerda described the Brazilian government as in the hands of Communists and others who were determined to "stop the country," to stop transportation, to make work difficult, and to "degenerate the whole public economy and the whole public spirit. And the whole damned thing is done from the top down."

Lacerda pictured the "masses" as "nauseated, fed up with the artificial revolution, with this cabinet agitation and subversions." Speaking of the price-wage spiral, he said "the Communists know they will be answered 'yes' the day before they ask for an increase." Lacerda viewed agrarian reform as "untimely." "Social and political reform must come first, along with education of the peasants. It has been discovered that Brazilian farm labor is not even prepared—I would not say to run the land—but even to use it properly." Mentioning two Japanese workers, loaned to him to landscape his Rocio property,

Lacerda told Julian Hartt that they "do in one day what two Brazilians would do in twenty days."

The governor, in advising the United States to withhold further aid to Brazil, said that under the circumstances it would accomplish nothing and would be "like trying to sell roses in an opium den, or tranquilizers to people already gone amok." "Nonintervention is one thing but another thing is to ignore what is going on." The United States Department of State, Lacerda said, must learn "after all these years" that it makes a difference to know who is running Brazil.

Lacerda described the military as debating whether "it is better to tutor him [Goulart], to patronize him, to put him under control to the end of his mandate, or to choke him off right now." Indicating that Goulart would soon be toppled, he said: "I don't think this thing will go to the end of the year."[12]

The three military ministers considered Lacerda's remarks unpatriotic and perhaps even an invitation to the United States government to intervene in Brazilian affairs.[13] In a joint statement they praised Goulart's discernment and farsightedness and condemned extremist minorities of the Left and Right. In particular they condemned Lacerda, the "bad citizen" who was using conspiratorial techniques "learned when he was a leader of the Communist Youth." He was accused of presenting "our country like a subcolonial little republic" just when Finance Minister Carvalho Pinto was about to leave for financial discussions in Washington.[14]

The military ministers also condemned Ademar de Barros, who was touring his state, delivering speeches that blamed the government for continuous disorders that wrecked the economy. Remarking that he did "not quite believe" that elections would occur in 1965, he pointed out that "some people want to establish a socialist regime in Brazil."[15]

The statement of the military ministers was praised by the CGT. On the other hand, Lacerda issued a message calling the military ministers' statement a deplorable declaration in which they "seek pathetically to blame third parties for the disorder, impoverishment, and demoralization to which innocent people are being condemned." He promised soon to complete his rest and return to the fray with "redoubled vigor." Lacerda's message, read aloud in the state legislature by Nina Ribeiro (UDN), ran into opposition there. Gonzaga da Gama Filho (PSD) read a proclamation signed by twenty-five legislators, almost half the membership, condemning the governor's declarations to the *Los Angeles Times*. In Congress, PTB leader Bocaiuva Cunha called Lacerda's interview part of an "international plot" against Brazil.[16]

Catholic intellectual Gustavo Corção wrote that Lacerda was no less patriotic than a German who denounced the German government in the non-German press during Hitler's persecution of the Jews. Another well-known Catholic, Sobral Pinto, published an open letter in which he accused the military ministers of seeking, "in the most arrogant form," to force the political opposition to submit to the despotism of the president. Peri Bevilacqua, Sobral wrote, had dutifully told his subordinates no longer to tolerate disturbances to freedom to work, only to be reprimanded for his directive. Defending Lacerda against the charge of conspiring, the veteran lawyer told the ministers that they had "not the slightest notion, politically, juridically, or militarily, of what a conspiracy is. It is the opposite of positions that are open, clear and frank."[17]

The Rio press, in varying degrees, criticized Lacerda for making statements to an American audience. But it was inclined to agree with his assessment of the seriousness of the situation and criticized the military ministers for what the *Correio da Manhã* called a "violent" note complaining of conspiracy. How, the *Jornal do Brasil* asked the military ministers, could people work in peace if, "for the first time in Brazil's history, disorder is commanded from on top, is installed in the government?" *O Jornal* blamed the outbreak of illegal strikes on a government that was afraid of organized labor and therefore disregarded the decisions handed down by the labor courts. After Justice Minister Abelardo Jurema told the *Jornal do Brasil* that the war minister was "ready for the conspiratorial activities of the governor of Guanabara," the daily wrote that the "creator of crises is accusing the opposition of creating crises" and warned against the establishment of a dictatorship by the Goulart group.

The *Jornal do Brasil* felt, however, that Lacerda could not have chosen a worse time for breaking his silence. It wrote that his "political foolishness reveals the fragility of his electoral position" and added that "Lacerda forgets that the very votes he needs can be won by an eloquent silence and never by a repetition of theses that bind him to an image associated with the sort of political ideas that public opinion has repudiated."[18]

Polls taken by the Instituto Brasileiro de Pesquisas Eleitorais, just after Lacerda's exchange with the military ministers, seemed to contradict the *Jornal do Brasil*. They showed that, by speaking out, the governor was gaining support even in Rio, where voters usually preferred men like Brizola to men considered conservative. It was, of course, no surprise that in Copacabana, where Amaral Netto was the favorite gubernatorial candidate, Lacerda was shown to have twice the popularity of Kubitschek. What was surprising was the result of polling at the Central do Brasil Railroad station. The people polled there named Eloy Dutra and Sérgio Magalhães as their choices in the next governorship race, while at the same time favoring Lacerda over Kubitschek, radio broadcaster Alziro Zarur, Miguel Arraes, and Ademar de Barros for the presidency.[19]

8. The Attempt to Seize Lacerda (October 3, 1963)

After shots were fired at the Rocio house, Lacerda installed metal sheets for the windows.[1] Then, on October 1, he ended his period of rest. He sent Letícia to Rio, where he felt she would be safer, and drove to the Mesquitas' *fazenda* in Louveira, northwest of São Paulo city, to discuss the situation with Júlio de Mesquita Filho.

The veteran publisher was an admirer of Friedrich Nietzsche's *The Will to Power*, advocating the supremacy of those who are strong. In a serious mood he said:

> Dr. Carlos Lacerda, I want to speak frankly and hope you will not take offense, for I have a deep feeling of friendship for you and consider you the most able and best prepared to take over the presidency and accomplish great things. But at this stage of my life, I can tell you only this: my sons are ready to give their lives; and my newspaper and all that I have is at the disposal of Brazil. Nothing interests me more than seeing Brazil repaired, put on the right track, redeemed. I am risking everything, I won't say my life, which is worth little, but all that I value most, in order to bring about what is necessary for Brazil.
>
> I am convinced that the armed forces will end up by acting. You feel they won't do so, except perhaps too late and ineffectively. But I believe we can count only on them for action. I consider revolution indispensable. I fear that your position as presidential candidate, with every chance of winning, is leading you to temporize, to think that the crisis is one that allows a political solution. In this I cannot believe. Do not let your personal career, which is of the utmost importance for Brazil, stand in the way of your duty to Brazil—which is to assist immediate action, because further temporization is not possible.

"Do you think," Lacerda asked, "that the armed forces are really going to act?" "Without doubt," Mesquita answered, "and I only ask you not to put your candidacy above the revolution."[2]

Lacerda flew to Rio on October 3 in the company of Abreu Sodré and Mesquita's youngest son, Luiz Carlos ("Carlão"). By that time Ademar de Barros had replied to the military ministers, and the São Paulo railroad workers had gone on strike, along with the workers in the São Paulo departments of roads and highways and of water and sewerage. Congressman Tancredo Neves (PSD) observed that the government of São Paulo "has demonstrated absolute incapacity to handle the constant strikes that break out there."[3]

Goulart had gone to Rio's Laranjeiras Palace to handle the bankworkers' strike and take drastic action against "a conspiracy articulated by Carlos Lacerda and Ademar de Barros." Despite what he called the "intransigence" of the banking executives, the president was able to reopen the banks. Each bankworker received a 70 percent immediate pay increase together with a 10,000-cruzeiro monthly increase effective as of September 1963 (instead of March 1964, as ruled by the labor court), and also payments for the days of work lost while striking; future increases were promised.[4]

In dealing with "the conspiracy," the president was determined to dispel reports that "the federal government has lacked authority." With lawyers, cabinet ministers, congressmen, and members of his intimate circle he discussed ways to remove Lacerda from office. Whatever the plan, a strong show of military support for Goulart was to be given; and therefore, late on October 2, the military ministers ordered "rigorous alert" on the part of all troops in Brazil. Tanks from Vila Militar occupied the area around the war ministry building in Rio. Goulart, addressing the nation that night, said that agitators, false defenders of order, and agents of antinational interests were conspiring against Brazil and its emancipation, but that he had the support of most businessmen and of Brazilian workers, identified with the struggle to preserve the social conquests initiated by Getúlio Vargas.[5]

Laranjeiras Palace filled up with members of the president's circle on Thursday, October 3. Goulart and close advisers, pacing back and forth on the veranda, took a last look at their options. Labor leaders favored intervention or legal steps that would put Lacerda in prison. However, many advisers felt that Congress would oppose intervention in Guanabara and São Paulo, leaving Lacerda and Ademar stronger than ever; and legal consultants argued that Lacerda could be convicted of endangering the national security only if tried during a state of siege, which would modify constitutional clauses about individual guarantees that protected him. Finally, at the suggestion of War Minister Jair Dantas Ribeiro, the presidential group resolved to ask Congress to declare the nation in a state of siege. Brizola, consulted by Goulart, accepted the idea.[6]

The decision was festively commemorated with whiskey at La-ranjeiras Palace. For those favoring reforms, it was presented as part of a move to give the executive great authority, a sort of takeover of power by the reform-minded. CGT leaders were told that the state of siege request was a "pretext" for action against Lacerda and Ade-mar de Barros.[7]

The request was made to Congress at 8:15 A.M. on Friday, Octo-ber 4, after Goulart reached Brasília. Cabinet ministers Wilson Fadul and Osvaldo Lima Filho, who made the trip with Goulart from Rio, assured PTB congressional leader Luís Fernando Bocaiuva Cunha that the request would be accompanied by a troop movement to surround Lacerda and remove him from the governorship. According to Ju-rema, an armed takeover of Guanabara would occur immediately and government troops would act against Ademar if he supported Lacerda in opposing a state of siege. Jurema felt that without these immediate military steps against Lacerda and Ademar, "Congress, plainly, would not act favorably on the appeal of the president and his military min-isters." Bocaiuva Cunha, the leader of the PTB, felt the same way. In working hard for a while to get votes for the state of siege, he por-trayed it as a measure to complement the military action that was supposedly under way in Guanabara.[8]

During the festive discussions before dawn at Laranjeiras Palace on October 4, General Alfredo Pinheiro Soares Filho, commander of the army's paratroop division, was assigned the mission of having La-cerda seized at the time of his visit that morning, already announced, to inspect the Miguel Couto Hospital construction in Leblon. When the general, known as Pinheiro and nicknamed "Faz-Tudo" (He does everything), reached his barracks at 3:30 A.M., he had obviously been drinking. He spoke on the phone with the assistant head of the presi-dential Casa Militar, Colonel João Sarmento, and then explained the mission to his men. He said he had "coverage from the office of the war minister and from the First Army." But his chief of operations, Major Carlos Eugênio Rodrigues Lima Monção Soares, refused to cooperate with an operation that he felt was illegal and not likely to have been authorized by General Armando de Morais Âncora, who had succeeded Osvino Ferreira Alves as commander of the First Army.[9]

Earlier in the night, the major had gotten wind of what was afoot and expressed his fears in a phone call to his friend, Lieutenant Colo-nel Francisco Boaventura Cavalcanti Júnior, the artillery commander of the paratroopers, who was at home. Boaventura went to the head-quarters of the Paratroop Division, and there the paratroopers' chief of staff, Lieutenant Colonel Abelardo Mafra ordered him to take a group of fifty officers and sergeants, well armed with machine guns and grenades, to the Miguel Couto Hospital and capture Lacerda.

Boaventura, meeting with men at the barracks of his own unit, told them that he opposed the mission and might create problems that would delay it. In front of his men he phoned Mafra to say that he wanted written instructions. Therefore he was called back to head-quarters, where he found Mafra organizing an assault group with men from an engineering unit commanded by a captain who was new to his job.[10]

General Pinheiro, refusing to issue written orders, told Boaventura: "You want to be a good little boy and save yourself from responsibility, throwing it on me. The matter is one of trust." A little later Pinheiro met with his unit commanders and spoke of decisions reached at Laranjeiras Palace. Some of the commanders, like Boaventura, were surprised to learn that a state of siege was not yet in force; they had been advised otherwise by Mafra. Pinheiro ordered everyone to keep the mission against Lacerda secret lest the press "exploit" the story. Boaventura, who had dropped out of the venture, said he would pass the order of secrecy on to his men. However, he spoke by phone to a cousin, an assistant of Gustavo Borges, in order to have Lacerda alerted.[11]

The group that set forth under Mafra from Vila Militar consisted of about six officers and thirty soldiers. It understood from Mafra that Pinheiro had orders to cooperate with plans for an army intervention in Guanabara. While the group made its way along Niemeyer Avenue to the Miguel Couto Hospital in Leblon, one of the trucks broke down. The defective valves or spark plugs have been attributed to sabotage carried out by three young officers before the truck left Vila Militar.[12]

When the assault group finally reached the hospital, Mafra told the men to remain in the vehicles, which he stationed at street corners, and to attack the governor's car when it arrived. But the governor, who had started his tour at 6:00 A.M., had left the hospital and was visiting other sites in the company of Raimundo de Brito, Enaldo Cravo Peixoto, Carlos Flexa Ribeiro, and Sandra Cavalcanti. Mafra, after waiting in vain for Lacerda, used the telephone of the nearby Flamengo Regatta Club to make several calls and then took his group back to Vila Militar. The mission was called off.[13]

The governor and his party had a full schedule that included visits to a new school, the Rebouças Tunnel, Flamengo Park (where Lota Macedo Soares was waiting with her "Grupo do Aterro"), and the site to be used for building the state bank's headquarters at Nilo Peçanha and México streets. After these visits they went to see the new computer center of the finance secretaryship.

At the finance secretaryship, Security Secretary Gustavo Borges took the governor aside and told him that he had learned from DOPS Chief Cecil Borer that a paratroop group was roaming through the city with an order to capture Lacerda and kill him if he resisted. The information had come, Borer said, from a paratroop division officer who had refused to obey the order unless it were in writing.[14]

Lacerda gave the information to the members of his party and told them to return to their desks because the tour of inspection would not be continued. Except for his chauffeur, he went alone to Guanabara Palace because he felt the drive might be risky. He even forbade his aide-de-camp, Major Carlos Osório, to ride with him.

At the palace, with a revolver borrowed at the finance secretaryship, Lacerda awaited an attack. "May this at least serve," he wrote on a slip of paper, "to free Brazil from Communism, demagoguery, and corruption. I leave to my family a name that is clean and I hope a country that is free." He called for Professor Cláudio Soares, keeper of his agenda and former associate at the *Tribuna da Imprensa*, and gave him the paper. "Today," Lacerda wrote four years later, "this note might appear even ridiculous. Just as ridiculous as the sentence I wrote later and put in my desk drawer, taking it out only on the day I left the government. It was a message to God, who has a good memory, and to myself, who have a poor one: 'May God grant me a sudden death and may I be ever ready for it.'"[15]

9. The State of Siege Request (October 4–7, 1963)

In asking Congress for a state of siege, Goulart submitted documents from the justice and military ministers. According to the military ministers, strikes, occurring constantly, served as a pretext for political conspiracy; and governors, forgetting to administer, rebelled against democratic legality. "Nonconformist groups," they said, "preach violence and subversion as solutions of problems that afflict the working classes." Jurema criticized the "excessive political-ideological radicalization" of nonconformist minorities.[1]

President Goulart flew back to Rio and pleaded with Dante Pelacani and Rafael Martinelli for the support of organized labor. But these CGT chieftains found the other labor leaders alarmed lest the state of siege be used against constant strikes, mentioned in the military ministers' message to Congress. The CGT decided to call a general strike if the state of siege were enacted, and the Leopoldina Railroad workers, as a warning, struck for three hours on October 6.[2]

Miguel Arraes, worried that Goulart would move against him after deposing the governors of Guanabara and São Paulo, attacked the

state of siege idea. So did Magalhães Pinto, Communist leader Luiz
Carlos Prestes, San Tiago Dantas, socialist João Mangabeira, and Bahia
Governor Antônio Lomanto Júnior. While Sobral Pinto warned that
Goulart had called the work of Mao Zedong his ideal and might fol-
low his example, Augusto Frederico Schmidt asserted that Congress
should not put the nation in the hands of a man deserving no confi-
dence. A lonely pro-Goulart voice was that of Rio state Governor
Badger Silveira (PTB), who said the president had had no alternative.[3]

Lacerda, who was spending nights in Guanabara Palace, sent a message to the presiding officers of the houses of Congress to deny conspiring and point out that the military ministers had not presented
"one single shred of evidence" that he had done so. He stressed that
he had devoted himself to implementing his state's administrative
program, thus providing "true basic reform, which consists, essen-
tially, in governing." The state of siege, he warned, had been proposed
in a "crude form" not only to remove one or more governors but to
serve as "the instrument for the usurpation of power and implantation of tyranny."[4]

The press protested vigorously against a state of siege, which, *O
Globo* reported, would be accompanied by censorship of newspapers
and broadcasting stations. The conservative *O Jornal*, in a reference
to the implantation of the Vargas dictatorship, wrote "Remember
1937!"; the moderate *Jornal do Brasil* published a large "NO"; and
Novos Rumos wrote that the Communists wanted no state of siege,
but, rather, concrete anti-imperialist steps and an end of the government's "policy of conciliation." The National Union of Students,
in the hands of the Communists and the more radical Catholic leftist
Ação Popular, called a state of siege a measure against the people. It
demanded, instead, quick and effective steps against Lacerda and
Ademar de Barros.[5]

In Congress the PTB had little support. The Parliamentary Nationalist Front opposed the state of siege and so did the PSB, as announced
by Max da Costa Santos. While the PSD joined the UDN in opposing
Goulart's wishes, the PSD's Armando Falcão blamed the national
"anarchy" on Goulart. Brizola, after a day of silence, turned against
his brother-in-law's position. By that time, Jurema has written, the
army had disappointed those who had been expecting it to move
against Lacerda and Ademar de Barros.[6]

The final blow to the president was delivered by PTB leader Bocaiuva Cunha. After waiting in vain for the army's removal of Lacerda, he gave up seeking votes for the state of siege and, on Sunday,
October 6, called the government's request "reactionary, inopportune, and antilabor."[7]

The PTB and "Baby" Bocaiuva Cunha. (Hilde Weber drawing in *O Estado de S. Paulo*, October 11, 1963)

Although nothing had occurred to change the situation described on October 4 as requiring a state of siege, on October 7 the president advised Congress that "new circumstances" made it unnecessary. He mentioned his "natural aversion" to emergency measures, and announced that "making a withdrawal in order to side with the people, is not a humiliation." Jurema declared that Goulart's new position left him with greater popular support than ever for moving against Lacerda and Ademar "if they return to conspiracy."[8] But nothing could hide the humiliation suffered by the Goulart regime.

The president displayed the bitterness he felt toward leftists who had opposed his state of siege request. For their part, the leftists continued suspicious of Goulart. They announced that he was too "conciliatory" toward the Right and that they were separating themselves from him. The announcement was made by the Frente de Mobilização Popular, said to include Brizola, the CGT, the UNE, the Liga Feminina Nacionalista, and representatives of the Parliamentary Nationalist Front. Education Minister Paulo de Tarso Santos' resignation from the cabinet underscored the break between the Frente de Mobilização Popular and Goulart.[9]

The Frente de Mobilização Popular demanded that the president adopt a program of radical reforms to reconquer the goodwill he had lost. The president, however, was not in need of the advice. After withdrawing his state of siege request he told his cabinet that Brazil's ills were the result of an "outmoded social, economic, and political structure." He vowed, therefore, to concentrate on reforms, such as a "democratic agrarian reform," and a banking reform that would avoid banking strikes, "such as we have witnessed," and "distribute credit in a better way and not in accordance with the wishes of ego-istical private interests."[10]

10. The Attempt to Seize Goulart (October 1963)

Bocaiuva Cunha, influential member of the radical Grupo Compacto of the PTB, was replaced as his party's congressional leader by a more moderate *petebista* in a move that made it easier for the PSD to deal with the PTB. Kubitschek, assured of the PSD nomination for presi-dent and eager for the PTB's endorsement, welcomed good relations between the PTB and PSD. The two parties cooperated at once to debilitate the CPI that was to investigate General Pinheiro's move to seize Lacerda. CPI President Chrispim Bias Fortes (PSD, Minas) and CPI *relator* Murilo Costa Rego (PTB, Pernambuco) reported that there was nothing to investigate, a finding that pleased the CPI major-ity, the army, and government congressional leader Tancredo Neves (PSD, Minas). Padre Antônio Godinho (UDN, São Paulo) described the CPI as a "gift from heaven" for the PSD, hoping to receive a few favors from Goulart.[1]

At the army's internal investigation, General Pinheiro and Lieu-tenant Colonel Mafra said that the paratroop group, in going to the Miguel Couto Hospital, had been carrying out routine exercises, part of a training program. Lieutenant Colonel Boaventura, after present-ing testimony that contradicted the general, was dismissed from his command and transferred to Curitiba. Major Carlos Eugênio Rodri-gues Lima Monção Soares, who had also refused to participate in the paratroopers' action against Lacerda, was transferred to a frontier unit in Mato Grosso.[2]

Boaventura wrote the war minister to complain of being punished for trying to defend a governor's mandate against those who wished to deliver "a mortal blow to the democratic regime." After his letter was read by UDN leaders in the Senate and Chamber of Deputies, Boaven-tura was imprisoned for thirty days at a cavalry regiment in Rio. Soon the press published Boaventura's testimony at the army inquiry and letters from Lacerda praising Boaventura and Major Monção.

The governor told Monção that "on the night of infamy, thank God unsuccessful, you saved not only the life of the governor. You saved the honor of the army and therefore the honor of Brazil." He advised Boaventura that he hoped to pay him a call, upon his release, "with-out stirring up a new wave of provocations in the sea of mud." Almost fifty companions visited the imprisoned Boaventura before the war minister ordered the imprisonment of all army men who expressed support for the prisoner by visits or communications.[3]

While the UDN gained publicity from General Pinheiro's ill-conceived venture, the Goulart administration was given an opportunity to strike back thanks to an equally ill-conceived venture of Charles Borer—Cecil's brother—and two friends. These men, keeping a watch on Goulart's weekend farmhouse near Jacarepaguá in order to learn of his meetings with Communists, decided to kidnap the president in the company of a Communist visitor; therefore they made arrangements to install men and arms on the nearby property of Alberto Pereira da Silva, a wealthy Portuguese industrialist. Their plan to kidnap Goulart on the night when they believed he had received Francisco Julião was foiled by a brush fire that spread to the shed containing the weapons. A retired sergeant who helped put out the fire reported the arms cache to army men, who came and seized the weapons. Charles Borer, an employee of the Botafogo Soccer and Regatta Club, and Alberto Pereira da Silva went into hiding.[4]

General Paulo Torres, the army's director of arms and munitions, spoke to Pereira da Silva's wife after the war minister ordered him to investigate. He reported that the weapons, property of Guanabara state, had been conveyed to Pereira da Silva's *sítio* on October 5 in vehicles belonging to the state. Justice Minister Jurema told the press that the Guanabara police had "participated in the plot of storing arms on a Jacarepaguá property in order to liquidate Goulart's family in case a state of siege were declared." President Goulart, in a reference to the Miguel Couto Hospital affair, declared that Lacerda, "instead of continuing with this political exploitation of an imaginary attack, should explain the reasons why dozens of machine guns, with a capacity of 5,000 shots, were brought close to the house where I live with my family. He, Lacerda, thanks God for having escaped. And I? To whom should I give thanks? To Borer, perhaps?"[5]

General Paulo Torres' lack of sympathy for Goulart helped persuade Charles Borer and his Portuguese companion to leave off hiding after a few days. Smilingly they entered the Army Police barracks with their lawyer, Sobral Pinto. While held for questioning, they explained that the arms were necessary for defense against the seizure of lands by peasants who were being encouraged to grab land forcibly. They added that the arms might have been useful for a defensive operation in case of an attack on Lacerda. State Security Secretary Gustavo Borges testified that the weapons had been placed on Pereira da Silva's property for possible use against Communists who had a rural "agitation center" nearby.[6]

Lacerda, who had not been informed previously of the activities of Charles Borer and his friends, issued an official note referring to "invaders, poorly disguised as peasants, who have already tried improperly to occupy that area of the state, following examples carried out in other parts of Brazil." He had kind words for Pereira da Silva, who gave him a rare African bird. And he granted a merit promotion to DOPS officer Cecil Borer. The report of Paulo Torres found Lacerda and his government innocent and denied that Goulart had been threatened.[7]

Nor had Lacerda been threatened by paratroopers, according to the army investigators of the troop movement to the Miguel Couto Hospital. Their report said that the group, making its way to the Flamengo Regatta Club, had received no mission to seize the governor, and that the investigation provided no proof that General Pinheiro had asked his men to carry out the seizure. First Army Commander Armando de Morais Âncora simply criticized Pinheiro for having ordered a movement by members of his troop without the knowledge of superiors during a time when the First Army was on "alert."[8]

Late in November, at the ceremony in which Marcelo Garcia replaced Sérgio Lacerda as the governor's office chief, the governor remarked that "when army officers are punished for not having turned themselves into assassins and when authorities become protectors of bandits, it is necessary to assert clearly, regardless of the consequences: this country no longer has a government; it has a band of assailants that are devouring and betraying it every day."[9]

I I. Lacerda Declares Himself a Presidential Candidate (October–December 1963)

Cooperation between the president and the PSD lasted until the end of the year, when the president concluded that the PSD, opposed to his agrarian reform plans, would not give effective assistance to his program. During these last three months of 1963 the president punished the Communists for their failure to support his state of siege request, and, in doing so, subdued fears of the PSD, which had a horror of Communism. Crockatt de Sá, on the president's orders, offered favors to labor leaders in order to build, as a rival to the CGT, the reform-minded non-Communist União Sindical dos Trabalhadores (UST). Dante Pelacani, sticking with the CGT, was fired from his lofty labor ministry post of director-general of social welfare. When the president replaced Second Army Commander Peri Constant Bevilacqua, who had arrested labor leaders during the October general

Urgent connection: Kubitschek (with inflation) connecting the PSD and PTB to get his candidacy off the ground; Lacerda candidacy is aloft. (Edmondo Bigalti drawing in *O Estado de S. Paulo*, October 31, 1963)

strike in São Paulo, he chose anti-Communist Amaury Kruel, who, as war minister, had been a target of CGT attacks.[1] The Frente de Mobilização Popular and the CGT spent the three months issuing propaganda that described Goulart as antilabor. Brizola demanded an end of the president's "vacillation."

The good relations between the federal administration and the PSD of Minas coincided with the deterioration of the president's relations with Magalhães Pinto. The UDN governor of Minas complained that the federal administration reneged on a promise to furnish 15 billion cruzeiros to his state. When the president held a meeting with governors, he failed to invite Lacerda, Ademar de Barros, Miguel Arraes, and Magalhães Pinto, president of the council of governors.

The four snubbed governors were the governors most frequently considered to be seeking to succeed Goulart by winning the presidential election of 1965, a topic frequently discussed in the last three months of 1963. While Kubitschek was described by Carlos Castello Branco as fearful of defeat unless he could secure the backing of Goulart and the PTB, opponents of Goulart, such as Sobral Pinto and Congressmen Armando Falcão and Ernâni Sátiro, warned that Goulart was a *golpista* who wanted to call off the 1965 election.[2]

Lacerda, during a visit to São Paulo to open a branch of the Guanabara state bank, told newsmen on October 24 that he would run for president and that "my chief elector is Jango Goulart." The Cariocas' confidence in the Lacerda administration, he said, was reflected in the growth of deposits in the state bank, which had risen from 3 billion cruzeiros to 22 billion in thirty months. A new public opinion poll, based on inquiries at Rio railroad stations and bus stops, gave Lacerda 3,632 supporters in comparison with 2,201 for Kubitschek.[3]

In Rio multitudes chanted "Lacerda in '65" when the governor appeared at a bookstore to autograph copies of the third edition of his *O Poder das Idéias* and launch *Em Cima da Hora*, his translation of Suzanne Labin's *Il Est Moins Cinq*. Discussing his campaign with thirty congressmen during a tour of the Mangueira *favela*, he rejected the crow as a campaign symbol; he said he wanted a slogan derived "not from crows, duckbills, or guinea pigs, but from the Brazilian flag, because if Brazil is to progress it must have order." He suggested AEIOU: A for water (*água*) and agriculture, E for education and energy, I for industrialization, O for order, and U for urgency.[4]

A caravan of Paulistas, calling themselves the "Bandeirantes da Democracia," arrived in Rio, in hundreds of cars, with a Brazilian flag knitted by women. The governor, receiving the flag, the Paulistas, and a multitude of Cariocas in the rain in the garden of Guanabara Palace, described what he was doing for Rio after finding it "abandoned by the owners of Brazil, just as birds of prey abandon a decaying carcass." It was his duty, Lacerda said, to serve the nation one more time after leaving the governorship.

While the caravan returned to São Paulo, Júlio de Mesquita Filho spoke of the Lacerda candidacy to the Inter American Press Association in Miami, Florida. "If we should reach the point of having elections," he said, "Governor Lacerda will be elected by an unprecedented vote." Armindo Doutel de Andrade, the new PTB congressional leader, called Mesquita unpatriotic for giving the Miami interview, which, he said, suggested that the United States call off assistance because Brazil was ungovernable. But, Lacerda pointed out, if anyone was guilty on that score, it was the president, whose recent *Manchete* interview "declares that Brazil is on the brink of chaos." The president, in his interview, an appeal for reforms, had said that "the giddy inflationary process to which we are now submitted, will infallibly drag the country to bankruptcy, with a sinister social disaster of catastrophic proportions."[5]

Finance Minister Carvalho Pinto, displeased with the interview, resigned. The Frente de Mobilização Popular campaigned to have Brizola succeed Carvalho Pinto. But on December 20 Goulart pleased PSD President Amaral Peixoto by disappointing Brizola. He named the less controversial Nei Galvão, a former Bank of Brazil president.[6]

PULAR OU DERRUBAR

Brizola wondering whether to leap over or knock down the residency requirement barring him from the Guanabara governorship. (Hilde Weber drawing in *O Estado de S. Paulo,* November 13, 1963)

In mid-November Lacerda chose the closing session of the UDN municipal convention of Ilhéus, Bahia, as the occasion for formally announcing his presidential candidacy. There he responded to the pleas of eight orators, including Bahia UDN President Antônio Carlos Magalhães, by promising to take a combination of ideas and action to Planalto Palace. He said that "after having experienced so much of a worker party government, the time has come to have a working government. I do not know of a single problem in this country that cannot be solved by work and integrity."[7]

Ernâni Sátiro (UDN, Paraíba), congressional leader of the Lacerda candidacy, argued that the UDN national directorship should declare itself quickly in favor of the Carioca governor. "The Lacerda candidacy," he reported, "is alive in the cities and countryside."

But Magalhães Pinto, on announcing his own presidential candidacy on November 23, asserted that the UDN nominating convention should take place in April 1965. The Minas governor, who said he could count on the PR to nominate him if the UDN would not do so, received the backing of Jânio Quadros. The former president ignored an appeal by Lacerda, who had recently said, in a reference to 1959: "I did not have personal relations with Jânio Quadros when I learned, from Abreu Sodré, that Jânio wanted to talk with me about his presidential candidacy. I went at once to see him, and supported

him unconditionally. It would therefore be a demonstration of public spirit if he would do the same thing for me. I can be vehement in
my criticisms but, in contrast to what some people think, I never
place personalities above the public interest." Lacerda left the door
open for an understanding with Magalhães Pinto.[8] Instead of arguing
about a nominating convention date, he embarked on his presidential
campaign in the *Esperança*.

The *Esperança*, piloted by Wilson Machado, often carried about
twenty persons, among them Abreu Sodré, Hugo Levy, supply organizer Tannay de Farias, journalist Ayrton Baffa, and photographer
Fernando Bueno. Physician Jaime Rodrigues, feeling that the candidate should be accompanied by a doctor, persuaded Antonio Dias
Rebello Filho to reduce his workload at the Pedro Ernesto Hospital
and make the trips. Rebello was described by Lacerda as bringing
two wooden traveling cases with every medicine imaginable "from
snakebite remedy to blood for transfusions." He kept close to the
candidate. "If they shoot my doctor instead of me," Lacerda told him
playfully, "I'll have no doctor, and I won't know how to take care
of you!"[9]

Among those aboard the *Esperança* when it flew to Campo Grande,
Mato Grosso, on November 20, were Senator Paulino Lopes da Costa
(UDN, Mato Grosso), Congressman Afrânio de Oliveira (UDN, São
Paulo), and Guanabara Water Department Director Veiga Brito. The
group was joined by Orlando Ometto.[10]

At the Campo Grande airport, a resident of the city, Norma Se-
góvia, expressed a desire to make Lacerda a present of a figure of
Nossa Senhora das Graças, 50 centimeters tall, that she considered to
have miraculous powers, responsible for having saved one of her two
young sons from an airplane accident. The sons, the travelers were
told, prayed daily to the figure that Lacerda's life might be spared.
Lacerda accepted the gift from one of the boys with the understanding
that it would be installed, as it was, in the *Esperança* and remain
there as a protection throughout the campaign. It would, Lacerda
added, be taken to Alvorada Palace after the election.

Speaking to the press in Campo Grande about the stringent profit
remittance law that Goulart was considering promulgating, Lacerda
observed that many nations failed to develop because they lacked
foreign capital. In reply to the justice minister's resolve to cancel all
credits that Guanabara might receive from abroad, Lacerda pointed
out that those credits had been "approved by the federal government
through the finance minister."[11]

During the night in Campo Grande, shooting broke out between
Lacerda supporters and adversaries in front of the hotel where the

visitors were staying. Lacerda slept soundly throughout the fracas and attended Sunday church service the next morning. Then the party departed for Corumbá, on the Bolivian border, where General Siseno Sarmento was among the thousands who greeted the *Esperança*. Following lunch and the usual confabulations with local political leaders, the campaigners flew to Cuiabá, capital of the state that has more recently been divided into two Mato Grossos. In the company of Governor Fernando Correia da Costa, Lacerda spoke to students in a theater. He promised, if elected, to create a University of Mato Grosso to specialize in geological and agricultural studies. The students carried the candidate on their shoulders from the theater.[12]

Accompanied by Orlando Ometto, the campaigners flew to the area of the Xingu and Culuene rivers in the north of the state. They visited Indian tribes (leaving Dr. Rebello shocked by the deplorable physical condition of the Indians) and donated 500 kilograms of medicines to the Leonardo Villas Boas Post for aiding Indians. Lacerda received gifts from a tribal chief and, in return, donated the shirt he was wearing.

In a large, motor-driven aluminum canoe, loaned by the Villas Boas Mission, the party explored the Tuatuari River. Rebello, marveling at Lacerda's knowledge of the scientific names of plants, guessed that it stemmed from his familiarity with the works of his great-grandfather Joaquim Monteiro Caminhoá. A Toyota jeep, troubled by a poor battery, was driven by Lacerda at top speed over rough trails when he took Rebello, Baffa, and a few others through forests, inhabited by wild animals, on property recently bought by Ometto.

From northern Mato Grosso the *Esperança* took the party to Três Lagoas, on the Paraná River. Following a visit from there by car to the construction of a hydroelectric plant at Urubupungá Falls, the *Esperança* and its passengers returned to Rio, arriving in time to allow Lacerda to participate in the inauguration of public works that marked the completion of the third year of his administration. The plane was loaded with plants and birds for Rio's parks and Rocio. So many animals were brought for Rio's Jardim Zoológico that Rebello Filho likened the *Esperança* to Noah's Ark.[13]

12. Year-end Bedlam by Legislators (December 1963)

In October 1963, seven PTB Guanabara state legislators (including Sinval Sampaio and Edna Lott) told Justice Minister Jurema that they would vote for approval of Governor Lacerda's accounts for 1962 unless the federal government granted their requests in filling federal posts in the state. Jurema responded by arranging for the PTB of Guanabara to administer the port of Rio and some of the social security institutes. After he advised Goulart that he had built up a bloc of twenty-six anti-Lacerda legislators, the president got in touch with Lutero Vargas, who was serving as ambassador to Honduras, to make sure that Lutero would exert his influence to keep the Guanabara PTB in line.[1]

In an effort to keep the PSD in line, Juscelino Kubitschek participated in the battle. It was a critical battle for Lacerda because, according to the state constitution, a rejection of the governor's accounts by the legislature would open the way for the legislature, by an absolute majority vote, to find the governor liable to the penalty stipulated in the constitution: Lacerda would be unable, for five years, to hold any public office. Kubitschek, lunching in November with Jurema and PTB legislative leader Saldanha Coelho, promised to persuade PSD legislators Augusto Amaral Peixoto and Miécimo da Silva to vote against approval of the governor's accounts. Already two *pessedistas*, José Bonifácio Diniz de Andrada and Gonzaga da Gama Filho, were among the twenty-eight considered certain to vote against Lacerda. The group included these two of the PSD, fifteen of the PTB, four of the PST, two of the PR, one of the PTN, one of the PSB, two of the PSP, and one (Frota Aguiar) of the UDN. The vote of Amando da Fonseca, a *pessedista*, was reported to be uncertain.[2]

UDN legislator Célio Borja, in a speech that was surprisingly aggressive for so serious-minded a jurist, called Kubitschek and Goulart thieves who were determined to derail Lacerda's presidential candidacy. The speech was a commentary on the rejection of the accounts late in October by a 6-3 vote of the legislature's finance commission, which called attention, among other things, to what it maintained was improper accounting of funds collected by the state lottery and municipal theater. The PTB's Ib Teixeira, citing some of the many alleged irregularities listed in a long report by Accounts Tribunal Minister João Lyra Filho, asserted that the governor had used state money to influence elections in 1962.[3]

Última Hora, praising Ib Teixeira for tearing aside "the veil of corruption" practiced in Guanabara by Carlos and Sérgio Lacerda, wrote that Carlos made use of the propaganda methods of Joseph Goebbels. "Brazil," it said, "has its Hitler in Carlos and its Mussolini in Ademar." *Novos Rumos*, which frequently described Lacerda as becoming bald and having big hips, quoted Accounts Tribunal Minister João Lyra Filho to show that the governor was handling the accounts of the "mixed economy companies, recently created in profusion," in a manner that defied public control. "That is to say," *Novos*

PARA FÚHERER 65

O GORILÃO 63

Lacerda, the big gorilla, candidate for führer. (Claudius Ceccon drawing in *Brasil, Urgente,* March 7–13, 1964, reproduced in Paulo Cezar Loureiro Botas, *A Bênção de Abril*)

Rumos wrote, "Lacerda diverts, for his electoral campaign or for deposits abroad, money that he affirms is used by some of those companies—COPEG, COCEA, COHAB, etc.—and there is no legal way to control this. Without doubt a very clever maneuver of the swindler." *Novos Rumos* told its readers that it was regrettably unable to provide them with a personal interview with the governor because he resented "our observation that the hips of His Excellency grow larger each day."[4]

Following the finance commission's rejection of his accounts, Lacerda rebuked majority leader Danillo Nunes for having handled the matter too timidly. In a reorganization of the government's forces, Vitorino James (UDN) was named majority leader, with the vice leadership posts going to Joaquim Afonso Mac Dowell Leite de Castro and Nina Ribeiro, also *udenistas.* Danillo Nunes was allowed to remain as UDN leader with the understanding that he would leave it in 1964 to seek the governorship.[5]

Without a majority, the so-called majority leadership was unable to prevent the legislature from adopting, in place of the governor's budget, a budget drawn up by the PTB that would not recognize new taxes, such as an electric power tax, and would completely eliminate funds for what the opposition considered "organs not created by law, such as the regional administrations, CETEL, COSIGUA, and the secretaryship of social services."[6]

Lacerda vetoed everything about the budget that the legislature voted. His more than eight hundred vetoes eliminated large pay raises for the legislators. One of the vetoes wiped out a 600-million-cruzeiro subsidy for the Museum of Modern Art, a step that infuriated Museum devotee Niomar Moniz Bittencourt, who, as the second wife of Paulo Bittencourt, had taken control (contested in the courts) of the *Correio da Manhã* following Paulo's death in August 1963. While the *Correio da Manhã* attacked Lacerda viciously, the state of Guanabara tried unsuccessfully to get the daily to pay its back taxes and make payments it owed to the state bank.[7]

The governor instructed Justice Secretary Alcino Salazar to take legal action against the pay raises voted for the legislators. And he spoke on television to justify his vetoes. The legislature, he declared, was "intentionally and criminally" demolishing the work of the state government, which would have to abandon all projects on January 1, 1964, if the vetoes were overridden. After Lacerda called for the legislature to meet in a special year-end session, December 16–31, the twenty-eight oppositionists signed a document, drawn up by José Bonifácio and Alfredo Tranjan, which was presented to the criminal justice system and which accused the governor of libeling the legislature in his remarks on television.[8]

In the case of his budget vetoes, which needed a two-thirds majority to be overturned, the governor was narrowly saved, although *udenistas* Lígia Lessa Bastos and Paulo Areal joined *udenista* Frota Aguiar in voting with the opposition. However, in the case of the governor's accounts, which a simple majority could reject, the situation was menacing. Assembly President Brunini gained time on December 20: failing to include the matter in the order of the day, he sent the finance commission's decision back to the commission on the ground that a signature was missing. The commission, by a 5 to 4 vote on December 23, confirmed its rejection, but Brunini kept delaying a plenary vote, leading Saldanha Coelho to complain that "Brunini and the UDN bloc" were protecting the governor.[9]

At a PSD meeting a little later, it became obvious that Brunini would be able to count on the support of Amando da Fonseca, who proposed omitting the governor's accounts from agendas, and that two other *pessedistas,* Augusto Amaral Peixoto and Miécimo da Silva, apparently unmoved by Kubitschek's pleas, backed Fonseca in his decision. The opposition accused Fonseca and other "deserters" of having been influenced by favors, such as promotions they wished for employees of the state security secretaryship.

At the year-end session of the legislature, on the night of December 30–31, Fonseca introduced so many amendments to proposed resolutions that it appeared impossible to conclude the work before the end of the year. Communist Hércules Corrêa, failing to persuade Fonseca to withdraw his proposals, joined with Paulo Alberto Monteiro de Barros, Ib Teixeira, João Massena, Saldanha Coelho, and Sinval Palmeira (lawyer of Luiz Carlos Prestes) in a series of attacks on Lacerda, beginning with a pronouncement by Paulo Alberto. With the help of the pro-PTB gallery, and explosions of firecrackers in the chamber, the session became unruly. *Udenista* Edson Guimarães, a retired air force officer, waved a revolver, and *petebistas* Saldanha Coelho and Ib Teixeira set copies of the *Diário da Assembléia* on fire. While cups and bottles were hurled at Brunini, Amando da Fonseca stood at the side of the presiding officer to give him physical protection from Rubens Macedo (PTB), who also threatened Amaral Peixoto and Fonseca. José Talarico, who had been throwing copies of the *Diário da Assembléia* into the air, threatened to assault a guard when he saw him trying to expel one of his friends from the gallery.

After Brunini took advantage of the tumult to declare the legislature's year-end work finished, oppositionists claimed that the bedlam had been started chiefly by *udenistas* Nina Ribeiro and Edson Guimarães, eager to obtain the automatic approval of the governor's accounts that would follow the failure of the legislature to act before January 1. Gonzaga da Gama Filho and José Bonifácio undertook to have Amando da Fonseca expelled from the PSD. Lacerda, regarded as the beneficiary of the tumult, called it a "shameful spectacle."[10]

13. Year-end Bedlam by Students (December 1963)

Other year-end disorders accompanied graduation exercises at schools and universities. Anti-Communist students, such as those associated with the Frente da Juventude Democrática (FJD), flooded Lacerda with invitations to be the honored speaker (*paraninfo*) at graduation exercises; by early November he had already received forty-five invitations.[1] Among those he accepted were some that took him to Goiás, Minas, and São Paulo.

Lacerda agreed to be one of the three honored guests at the graduation exercises which twelve students of journalism planned to hold at 5:00 P.M. on December 30 in the auditorium of the Faculdade Nacional de Filosofia on Presidente Antônio Carlos Avenue in downtown Rio. The affair promised to provoke trouble not because of the anti-Lacerda sentiment of the thirteenth graduating journalism student, a young woman from Bolivia who worked at the Cuban embassy, but because a large majority of the two hundred graduating students of the college (*faculdade*), an organ of the Federal University of Brazil, adhered to the anti-Lacerda line of the UNE. They argued that it was improper for the journalism students to hold a separate ceremony at the college auditorium on a date later than that of the official ceremony, which had honored Professor Celso Cunha (*paraninfo*) and University of Brasília *Reitor* Anísio Teixeira (*patrono*).[2]

The graduating journalism students chose to honor Professors Eremildo Viana and Sobral Pinto along with Lacerda. Eremildo Viana had been driven from his post of director of the *faculdade* by a series of student strikes. Sobral Pinto, like the *Jornal do Brasil,* had denounced the strikes. Using stronger language than the respectable daily, he had described the Faculdade de Filosofia as becoming "Cubanized" and had added that Brazilian students, in serving Communists who wished to overturn Brazilian society, were encouraged principally by Goulart but also by the ministers of education, justice, and war.[3]

The students of the *faculdade* wrote insulting words on posters that announced that Lacerda, Sobral Pinto, and Eremildo Viana would participate in the ceremony of December 30. On December 27 the student directorship (*diretório acadêmico*) of the *faculdade,* representing most of the students, issued a note calling Sobral Pinto and Eremildo Viana "violators of the law," and "reactionary chief" Lacerda "the Number One enemy of the students." A sign on the college door forbade the entrance of the governor and bore a reference to his use of the police cavalry in Cinelândia during the disturbances following Quadros' resignation.[4]

Several hours before the graduation ceremony of the journalism students was to start, hundreds of anti-Lacerda students took over the building of the *faculdade.* They locked themselves inside, by means of a chain and large bolt on the main iron door; with help from port workers, they set a heavy safe against the other entrance.[5] Outside the building the honored guests mingled with a crowd, assembled in part at the call of Sobral Pinto. It included Augusto Frederico Schmidt (described by the UNE as a crook), "*malamadas*" (Lacerda-admiring women), and television broadcaster Flávio Cavalcanti, who took the lead in tearing down the posters that berated Lacerda, Sobral Pinto, and Eremildo Viana. Sobral, in touch with Faculdade Director José de Faria Góis and University *Reitor* Pedro Calmon, said the university authorities should not cooperate with "a band of Communist ruffians." The *reitor* asked the students to open the iron door, but the reply was a refusal expressed with insults to Calmon, Faria Góis, and Lacerda.[6]

Education Minister Júlio Sambaqui, fearing a conflict, turned to the army; and presently, on the orders of First Army Commander Morais Âncora, troops of the Army Police arrived. Sobral, hopeful that they would make it possible for the ceremony to take place, was

The gorilla is not to enter Rio's College of Philosophy. (Claudius Ceccon drawing in *Brasil, Urgente*, January 12–18, 1964, reproduced in Paulo Cezar Loureiro Botas, *A Bênção de Abril*)

disappointed. The soldiers, with orders to prevent a clash and protect university property, encircled the building, keeping the crowd away and leaving the students in control of it. Lacerda and Sobral, passing through the Army Police cordon, approached the building but could not enter. They argued uselessly with army officers and university officials. Finally Lacerda, who had been waiting for four hours for the ceremony to begin, made remarks about the "pusillanimity" of Pedro Calmon and drove off in a car that was stoned. Shouts of victory came from the windows of the building. A "hymn of triumph" was broadcast by Rádio Mayrink Veiga, the principal outlet of Brizola's propaganda in Rio.[7]

Having succeeded in their objective, the students in the building turned over the entrance keys to the Army Police, who gave them to the education minister. Pedro Calmon and Faria Góis, receiving the keys from the minister, announced that the *faculdade* would remain closed while auditors checked to see if the invaders had damaged anything. Air force soldiers guarded the building for a week, during which no damages were found, and on January 6 the *faculdade* was reopened.[8]

Following the reopening, the journalism students spoke to university authorities about a new date for their graduation exercises, and therefore the members of the anti-Lacerda student directorship (*diretório acadêmico*) of the Faculdade de Filosofia took over the building again. They rejected appeals to leave and were joined in the building by representatives of the students of most of the institutions of higher learning in Rio. The university board declared the *faculdade* closed again, although Faria Góis said the measure was fruitless because, when the college was reopened, the student directorship would "direct the students in the same manner" as it had in the past. Calmon, opposed to the use of troops to end the new student takeover, stated correctly that the students would leave "sooner or later."[9]

At the end of January the students' *diretório acadêmico* asserted that the students would "prevent, as often as necessary, the entry of Governor Carlos Lacerda in the college building." The university board, in a decision satisfactory to the *diretório acadêmico*, ruled that the journalism students were not to hold their graduation exercises in the auditorium of the college. But then Sobral Pinto, citing opinions previously given by college Director Faria Góis, went to the courts on behalf of the journalism students to get the latest decision of the university board set aside. An offer by Faria Góis to let the journalists' graduation take place as long as outsiders such as Lacerda did not participate failed to persuade the journalism students to abandon their court case.[10]

The disturbance of December 30 which had started the trouble, was the subject of statements and open letters. The Frente da Juventude Democrática called War Minister Jair Dantas Ribeiro guilty of "one more insulting slap at the constitution and legality," whereas Abelardo Jurema said the trouble at the *faculdade* was caused by Lacerda and Sobral Pinto. Sobral Pinto told First Army Commander Morais Âncora that the army's behavior marked "the end of law, public authority, and the armed forces as defined by the constitution." In one of his two open letters to Jurema, the lawyer called the justice minister a liar.[11]

Raimundo Magalhães Júnior, of the Brazilian Academy of Letters, wrote in the *Diário Carioca* that the December 30 disturbance was "a symptom of the radicalization of positions in our country. The young people are to the Left, some of them to the extreme Left." Lacerda, he wrote, was to the Right and was "not the journalist he was 33 years ago."

Arguing that Lacerda's journalism, "since he decided on a rapid political career," was no recommendation for his being chosen *paraninfo* of graduating journalism students, Magalhães Júnior wrote that Lacerda, inconsistent in his opinions, "is prolix, repetitive, and gives excessive emphasis to secondary arguments." The *Diário Carioca* columnist praised the decision of most of the philosophy college students not to allow Lacerda to deliver his personal propaganda, "in the style of Suzanne Labin." Advocating immunity against "the chronic disease of irrational anti-Communism," Magalhães Júnior wrote that "young people are always right. And if it were not so the world would be much worse. If Carlos Lacerda were eighteen years old today—and this I can assure you, because I knew him in other times—he would prefer to receive police beatings rather than choose a person like Carlos Lacerda (today's version) to be *paraninfo.* The sad truth is that some of the valiant and passionate young people who prevented the governor-*paraninfo* from entering the Faculdade de Filosofia may, in the future, renounce, like Carlos, their past role of leftist crusaders."[12]

14. Comments

Nineteen sixty-three was a satisfactory year for Lacerda.

The state legislature, it is true, was troublesome. But the governor, using appeals to the courts, his veto power, the flexibility provided by the state-controlled companies, and a defiant manner ("They may jail me later, but those generators will be bought"), usually had his way.

The governor also appealed to Cariocas over the head of the legislature, discussing his programs and presenting himself as the defender of the people against selfish interests. He was assisted by effective propaganda for his programs, some of it furnished by Walter Cunto's office, and by the low esteem felt for the legislature, fond of voting money for itself and its favorites. As demonstrated in the polls, the governor gained good marks even from Cariocas belonging to clienteles built up by leftist politicians. Legislators might object to the activities of Fontenelle, but the Cariocas supported what the governor's innovative traffic director was doing.

Lacerda's greatest success in 1963 occurred in Curitiba in April. The outcome was achieved because Lacerda, traveling throughout Brazil, appealed to the masses, impressing listeners with his personality—and interest in them—as much as with his message that the most needed reform was good governance and that would-be reformers of the constitution were playing the president's "Communist" game. The Curitiba decision against tampering with the constitution, described by the *Correio da Manhã* as an unexpected and clear-cut defeat of the UDN leaders, was a remarkable development because, by April 1963, it was considered politically expedient to blame Brazil's ills on an "outmoded structure" protected by the constitution;

the UDN was strongly tempted, more so than the PSD, to be in the vanguard of the struggle for basic reforms and thus bury its reputation for conservatism. However, Lacerda's work at the grassroots prevailed over the advice of Magalhães Pinto, João Agripino, and José Sarney, and made it virtually certain that he would be the party's presidential candidate when the time came for delegates to gather at a nominating convention.

Lacerda remarked in October 1963 that "Goulart is my chief elector." The remark, which Lacerda might have made about any president, contained ingredients of truth because, as Goulart admitted, the economic situation deteriorated during his administration, and because a majority of Brazilians was becoming impatient with constant strikes called by union and student leaders associated with the far Left. The inflation that the unfortunate president inherited might have been repaired by a long-term unpopular program; the only observable result of the four-month experiment with the Three-Year Plan was a recession.

As for the political situation, Goulart's 1962 alliance with the CGT made it difficult for him to convince the PSD, the PTB's natural ally, that he stood in the middle, between the far Left and far Right; and his effort to place himself in that position did more to alienate the now self-assured far Left than to obtain the congressional backing he needed if he were to achieve his goal of becoming a great reform president.

Goulart's only remaining option, unless he were to bow to declared foes of his goal, was a renewal of his alliance with the far Left. Rumors that it would take place disturbed military leaders late in 1963 and proved to be correct during the first days of 1964. The association of Goulart with participants of the Frente de Mobilização Popular could only benefit Lacerda, not because politicians were keen on becoming supporters of a man so independent, and not because they shared his extreme views about the Left and against modifying the constitution, but because the president's decision to abandon the PSD and work with the CGT polarized Brazil as 1964 got underway, leaving few followers for men in the middle, and because the Goulart-CGT realliance was regarded as the possible forerunner of a coup by a president who, having wished for a state of siege, might use the far Left and sergeants and sailors for purposes considered dangerous by politicians.

It may be true that Lacerda's "Letter to the People" contained nothing new and that his *Los Angeles Times* interview damaged Brazil's prestige among foreigners. It may also be true that he gave prominence to the Pro-Cuba Congress because he attacked it. But his aggressive warnings, issued while others avoided the charge of stirring up a harmful tempest, and while Kubitschek sought an understanding with Goulart, placed him at the forefront of a growing movement. This movement, in the tumultuous months ahead, saw itself as seeking to save democracy from the designs of Communist-dominated forces that had been made so powerful by Goulart that even the president could not restrain them.

The supporters and opponents of the movement would participate unrestrictedly in the traditional "political game," described by Sheldon Maram in his forthcoming article, "The Political Culture of Kubitschek's Brazil." It was a game, Maram writes, that was played with vehemence, in which "politicians found that it was necessary to get the crowds worked up about the evils of their opponents"— a game in which temperate speeches, according to Congressman José Bonifácio Lafayette de Andrada, did no more than send the crowds to the beaches.

IV.

Agitation and Upheaval
(January–April 1964)

1. Accusing Goulart of Favoring "Revolutionary War"
(January–February 1964)

Events that gave a new complexion to the political situation, beginning early in January 1964, confirmed the forebodings expressed during 1962 and 1963 by Lacerda.

The most important political event in January was the unruly biennial election of officers of the CNTI, chief component of the CGT. Following the advice of his closest advisers, Goulart at the last minute arranged for Communists to retain control of the CNTI. The delayed election was held in Rio on January 6, after the usual offers of bribes in the form of money and positions, made by the rival factions. The outcome was a disappointment to Crockatt de Sá, whose work on behalf of the anti-Communist UST, carried out in accordance with Goulart's earlier instructions, could have resulted in the defeat of the Communists.[1]

After the CNTI election, Goulart appointed Guanabara metalworker Benedito Cerqueira, a congressman and CGT leader, to replace Crockatt de Sá as his adviser on labor union affairs. Labor Minister Amauri Silva, satisfied with this change and the CNTI election results, spoke about expected support from the victors for the president's reform program.[2]

Goulart, as a start at reforming, signed and promulgated the ruling that strictly limited the remission of profits abroad, thus pleasing the Frente de Mobilização Popular and others who considered multinationals to be inimical to Brazil. During the signing ceremony, he attacked those who enjoyed special privileges and said that his accusers were the same men who had plotted against "fondly remembered Vargas" and, in 1961, against himself.[3]

At the presidential summer palace in Petrópolis in mid-January the president met with men who were trying to mobilize a broad front on behalf of reforms but who were often at odds with each other. Among the visitors to Petrópolis was the ailing San Tiago Dantas, whose program included legalization of the PCB (the Russian-line Brazilian Communist Party). Another was Brizola, who attacked San Tiago Dantas. Still another was Arraes, who agreed with the Frente de Mobilização Popular and Brizola when they told Goulart that he should act more boldly and go ahead with reforms that did not require congressional approval, such as the expropriation of the privately owned Capuava petroleum refinery and the expropriation of landholdings within 10 kilometers of federal highways, railroads, and water projects. After his talk with Goulart, the presidentially ambitious Arraes expressed the fear that Goulart planned to remain in office beyond his term.[4]

Luiz Carlos Prestes spoke publicly about his satisfaction with the advance that Communism was making in Brazil. Military leaders who had long been suspicious of Goulart agreed with Prestes about that progress and agreed with Arraes about Goulart's intention. Retired General Golbery do Couto e Silva, writing confidential reports for the Instituto de Pesquisas e Estudos Sociais (IPES—an anti-Communist businessmen's organization), concluded that Goulart would seek, by peaceful means or otherwise, to extend his term. Influential Army Chief of Staff Humberto Castello Branco, in a speech to graduating army officers, said that one had only to read the propaganda of the Communists to appreciate that they constituted a danger to the Brazilian institutions and were determined to "subvert the Brazilian armed forces."[5]

The Communists in the first three months of 1964 appeared to take every step imaginable to justify in the minds of the people the fears expressed by Castello Branco. In taking these steps, they were supported by men close to Goulart, such as the heads of the Casa Civil and Casa Militar, and by politicians who identified reforms with leftism and who saw the far Left as Brazil's wave of the future. Government men turned to the PCB and Ação Popular to bring about the formation of the Confederation of Workers in Agriculture (CONTAG), which was legally registered in January 1964 with a PCB member as president.

When the Communists' Latin American labor organization, CUTAL (Centro Unico de Trabajadores de América Latina), prepared to meet in Belo Horizonte late in January, with observers from Czechoslovakia, Hungary, and Rumania, Magalhães Pinto gave his approval and explained that the constitution guaranteed the right of the delegates to meet. But by this time anti-Communist propaganda was turning normally quiet citizens into active opponents of the "Red Peril." Mobs of Mineiros, stirred in part by Belo Horizonte's archbishop,

Uncle Sam extolling the Lacerda candidacy as a "gift from a friend."
(Claudius Ceccon drawing in *Brasil, Urgente,* February 2–8, 1964,
reproduced in Paulo Cezar Loureiro Botas, *A Bênção de Abril*)

demonstrated so aggressively against CUTAL that the meeting place
was transferred to Brasília. *Última Hora* wrote that CUTAL had been
faced with a "furious wave of McCarthyism."[6]

Strikes that broke out in Guanabara's public utilities in mid-
January were blamed by Salvador Mandim on the now all-powerful
CGT. A speech by Lacerda about the strikes was considered so slanderous by the Goulart government that Justice Minister Jurema, citing a request of the National Telecommunications Council, issued
an order suspending the activities of the Tupi television and radio
stations for twenty-four hours because they had broadcast the governor's speech. Congressman Ernâni Sátiro argued that the government, instead of punishing Tupi, should act against the speeches in
which Brizola, broadcasting daily on Rádio Mayrink Veiga, instructed
his listeners to form "Groups of Eleven Companions" to play combative roles in what Brizola described as the coming upheaval. Sátiro
accused Brizola of "openly preaching revolutionary war."[7]

UDN President Bilac Pinto spoke to journalists in Brasília on January 15 about the "revolutionary war" that he felt Goulart and Brizola
planned to unleash for the implantation of a Communist dictatorship. Lacerda used the same expression, "revolutionary war," on
February 17, when he released a "Manifesto to the Nation" decrying
the constant strikes and agitations, and calling them part of a scheme
to implant a totalitarian labor union–dominated regime. Warning

that the schemers had "revolutionary war" in mind, he declared that if the salvation of Brazil required his life, he would not hesitate to make the sacrifice.[8]

The Army Secret Service reported a plot to assassinate Lacerda during disturbances to be started by unfriendly workers and peasants in the northeastern state of Paraíba.[9] The candidate, carrying on with his far-flung campaign, was not deterred by such reports. Nor was he deterred by the expenses of the campaign, which frequently exceeded contributions, forcing members of the *Esperança* crew to wait as long as three months for their wages.[10]

Contributions would have been more abundant if the candidate had not refused to accept payments from firms, such as Guanabara contractors, whose motives, he felt, were suspect. Speaking with Abreu Sodré in his São Paulo home, he told him to reject a Lacerda campaign contribution offered by the owners of a petroleum refinery in Rio Grande do Sul, which, like other private petroleum refineries, was threatened by expropriation by the Goulart government. Lacerda, who adhered to his oft-expressed belief that the refineries should not be in private hands, explained to Sodré that the proposed contribution was not an "honest" one, because the refinery owners, seeking goodwill, had been making payments to *Última Hora*, "which has been attacking me." As one of the refinery owners phoned Sodré just when Lacerda was making these observations, Lacerda took the phone from Sodré and gave the refinery owner his views directly.[11]

During his visits to São Paulo, Lacerda was kept apprised of the work there of anti-Goulart conspirators, such as the group organized by prominent businessmen belonging to IPES and the group organized by openly conspiratorial General Olímpio Mourão Filho before Mourão's transfer in August 1963 to an infantry division in Minas Gerais. Civilian conspirators, among them the sons of Herbert Levy and of Júlio de Mesquita Filho, worked closely with a fast-growing group of young military officers. As Lacerda learned, when receiving visitors at the Hotel Jaraguá, they met frequently and prepared in detail how to act against the "revolutionary war" they feared. They developed a coded radio communication system to stay in touch with fellow conspirators in much of Brazil.[12]

Late in February 1964, at the home of Luiz Carlos Mesquita, Lacerda attended one of the meetings. Major Rubens Resstel and the other military conspirators went into a separate room for an hour to confer with a single civilian, Lacerda, whom they regarded as their civilian leader. The military officers told Lacerda that they were reaching the conclusion that defensive planning was not good enough. "Either we eat or we get eaten."[13]

In Rio Lacerda found Gustavo Borges also preparing. The security secretary was convinced that the pro-Kubitschek coup of 1955 had prevailed because of Lott's control of telecommunications, and therefore he set about developing a network of communications, walkie-talkies, and devices to intercept Goulart's phone calls.

Lacerda, Borges has said, refused to participate in the conspiratorial work. "He gave me a free hand but stayed out of it, telling me that this work of ours would never get us anywhere." In addition to his skepticism, he was, according to Borges, handicapped by his position, for he was constantly followed by the press and federal agents and felt it dangerous to play a role that would give substance to accusations and an excuse for intervention.[14] Not mentioned by Borges was Lacerda's reluctance to conspire or deal in any way that was not open.

2. The UDN Decides to Nominate Lacerda Quickly (February 1964)

In mid-January, when Lacerda was in Araraquara, São Paulo, to honor graduating pharmaceutical and dentistry students, he told reporters: "Give me the presidency and I shall make the necessary reforms. The job of the president is not to agitate. In Guanabara I carried out my little reforms even without a majority in the assembly. Democratic reform should begin with the expulsion of Communists from the government." Back in Rio, he inaugurated a school with a speech in which he declared that the education ministry, on the pretext of teaching reading, was carrying out "what Communists in China call brainwashing." "Hatred, frustration, envy, and revolt," he said, were being instilled among peasants, thanks to the reading primers distributed to them.[1] Among the sentences in *Viver É Lutar,* one of the primers to which Lacerda referred, were: "The Brazilian peasants continue to be expelled from the land," "A complete change in Brazil is necessary," "The people have a duty to fight for justice," and "There are many foreigners exploiting the people. How can one free Brazil from this situation?"[2]

Lacerda, on a flight in the *Esperança* in February to Uruguaiana, Rio Grande do Sul, was joined by Congressman Armando Falcão, whose support for Lacerda prompted PSD leaders to suggest his expulsion from their party. Those who saw Falcão as a running mate for Lacerda devised a refrain:

> The Crow and the Falcon
> This is the Salvation.[3]

CL '65: 5,000 handclaps for Carlos Lacerda, champion of democracy.

A sea of "Lacerda 65" placards, each bearing the picture of a sleek, black crow, greeted Lacerda when the plane landed at the Uruguaiana airport. Accompanied by a crowd of two thousand, in five hundred vehicles, he rode in an open car to the campaign headquarters, in whose window stood an enormous replica of a black crow. Upon reaching his hotel, he spoke to the press about Petrobrás, which had recently been described by engineer Glycon de Paiva as "the most important Communist bastion in America, after Cuba," a bank for financing subversion, and a "practical school of corruption." Lacerda, in telling Uruguaiana reporters that Petrobrás "ought to be producing petroleum instead of scandals," was referring to the large-scale corruption revealed in Petrobrás after its outgoing president, Albino Silva, called the petroleum monopoly a "rat's nest," crooked and in Communist hands.[4]

That evening a throng of five thousand, the most enthusiastic Lacerda had faced since declaring himself a presidential candidate, heard him speak about the need of reforms—but not "the reform that they desire, which is revolution." True agrarian reform, he said, should stimulate plantings and production, and should not imitate the Russian model, responsible for hunger. "What good is it to divide up the land to plant wheat if there is no wheat to plant?"

The candidate, in excellent spirits, went to a *churrasco* (outdoor barbecue party) given by rancher Trajano Silva. Rebello Filho cautioned him not to overeat, but Lacerda, pleased with the food, the colorful Gaúcho costumes, and the warm reception, told the doctor: "It is not every day that I come to Rio Grande do Sul." He remained at the party until 4:00 A.M.[5]

During the campaigning in January and February 1964, UDN leaders grappled with the problem created late in December when Lacerda, addressing *udenistas* in the Goiás legislative assembly chamber, made it clear that he was no longer satisfied to have the UDN remain silent about a nominating convention date. An early convention, he told the meeting, would place the UDN candidate in a good position to work out arrangements with generals to ensure that elections would take place.[6]

In mid-January, when it was reported that at least fourteen UDN state directorships favored an early convention to nominate Lacerda, Magalhães Pinto let it be known, through José Aparecido de Oliveira, that he would not attend an early convention. Then, on January 23, Lacerda explained his position in a letter to UDN President Bilac Pinto. After congratulating Bilac on his speeches attacking subversion and Communist influences in the government, Lacerda wrote that "a rapid decision" by the UDN about its candidate was required to "avoid confusion that would be harmful to the party and the nation, and intolerable for me." Lacerda stated that, despite his personal wish to close his political career, he was willing to be a presidential candidate because "most of my fellow party members believe that I can, with their help and that of the people in general, carry out something important and right for Brazil. . . . What would be unjust and unwise would be to wear me out and gain time at the expense of my losing my time."[7]

Bilac met in Rio with Lacerda and Magalhães Pinto but could do nothing to reconcile their views. Lacerda, the Minas governor said, was so radical that his nomination by the UDN might force opponents of his candidacy to carry out a coup. Writing to Bilac on February 6, Magalhães Pinto pointed out that Lacerda's support from state directorships was merely transitory because in 1964 most of the directorships would change hands. He added that he would not recognize the decision reached at an early nominating convention and that he had already agreed to support a party nominee to be chosen, as was "customary," during April of the election year, 1965.[8]

Among the state directorships that joined the Minas UDN in opposing an early convention were those of Ceará, whose Governor Virgílio Távora sided with Magalhães Pinto, and Maranhão, whose Congressman José Sarney, of the Bossa-Nova, was a member of the UDN national directorship. On the other hand, as Bilac announced in mid-February, seventeen state directorships favored an early convention.[9]

When the UDN national directorship met on January 20, the press was reporting that Magalhães Pinto planned to leave the UDN and form a new party, to be named the Partido Trabalhista Cristão, with

Brasil, Urgente describes Lacerda as saying on television: "Of course, we'll do something about infant mortality. We'll bring in foreign capital to enlarge our growing funeral industry." (Claudius Ceccon drawing in *Brasil, Urgente*, October 13–19, 1963, reproduced in Paulo Cezar Loureiro Botas, *A Bênção de Abril*)

the help of the Bossa-Nova *udenistas* and reform-minded members of other parties. The UDN national directors, as worried as they had been during the last day of the Curitiba convention, considered a possible compromise, the holding of a nominating convention in July or August 1964; but the Minas UDN rejected the compromise.

On February 25, after Magalhães Pinto assured Bilac that he had no plan to leave the UDN, the party's national directory met in Brasília, together with the UDN leaders of both houses of Congress. The decision to hold the nominating convention in São Paulo on April 11 and 12, 1964, would have been unanimous but for the vote of Rondon Pacheco of Minas. UDN Vice President José Sarney was absent.[10]

Although the outcome of the April convention was not in doubt, Lacerda continued campaigning in March. Crowds, stirred up by organized workers and students, were sometimes hostile, as in Salvador, Bahia, where he attended a governors' conference early in the month. When he found streets there filled with mobs bearing placards that insulted him, he insisted on being driven through those streets instead of following the advice of friends who urged the use of an indirect route. Students who had assisted Petrobrás workers in demonstrating against Lacerda provoked a riot at the ceremonies for opening the academic year at the University of Bahia. Perhaps not realizing that Lacerda had an appointment at a television station that would keep him away from the ceremonies, they gained support for the riot by announcing that the Guanabara governor would be present because the inaugural speech was to be given by Clemente Mariani, whose daughter Maria Clara had married Sérgio Lacerda. The ceremony had to be canceled before Mariani was able to address the gathering.[11]

From São Paulo, which he visited once a week, Lacerda was driven by legislator Nelson Pereira to Osasco on March 20 to meet factory workers. There the industrial director of the large Brown Boveri electrical equipment company told the candidate: "We are not able to receive you at this plant. We are worried about your safety. We have a Communist cell here." The candidate said to Pereira, "Let's go in!"

Lacerda, attempting to be friendly to workers during his tour of the plant, was greeted by silent hostility. Finally he climbed to the top of one of the machines, clapped his hands to get the attention of the 1,300 workers, and began a speech. One of the workers tried to drown out his voice by banging on metal, making loud noises.

Because Lacerda's speech attacked Communism and "false labor leaders," his friends worried about his boldness, especially in view of the absence of police protection. But after five minutes, members of the audience, captivated by his words, told the noise maker to stop banging. Before the governor finished speaking, it was clear that his ideas were being well received. The workers ended up carrying Lacerda on their shoulders.[12]

Returning to São Paulo city, the candidate hoped to spend hours discussing flowers with Germano Zimber, a native of Germany who had written what Lacerda has called "the first modern book about landscaping." But at the Zimber flower shop he learned of his friend's death from Zimber's widow. She gave him a catalogue illustrated with Zimber's paintings, chiefly of colorful meadow flowers, and sold him seedlings for Rocio.[13]

3. The Rally of March 13 (February–March 1964)

President Goulart, seeking demonstrations of support for reforms, especially a reform to allow bonds to pay for land expropriations, let it be known in mid-February that a mammoth rally would be held in Rio on March 13. He would, his followers revealed, expropriate the Capuava refinery on March 13, and, at the same time, sign the SUPRA decree to allow the expropriation of lands adjoining government highways, railroads, and dams (in return for the cash payments required by the constitution).[1]

The Frente de Mobilização Popular, which set out to make the March 13 rally a success, now included Arraes as well as Brizola, the CGT, the UNE, and the Parliamentary Nationalist Front. Officially it rebuked San Tiago Dantas for favoring "mere palliatives," but the declaration did not represent the Frente's unanimous opinion. It was suffering from dissensions, chiefly caused by Brizola, ever critical of the "peaceful path" ideas of Arraes and Luiz Carlos Prestes. Brizola clashed bitterly with the CGT when the CGT assumed the chief role in putting the March 13 rally together.[2]

Late in February Brizola went with his two "musketeers"—Congressmen Max da Costa Santos and José Guimarães Neiva Moreira—to Belo Horizonte to establish a local Frente de Mobilização Popular. The protection ordered by Magalhães Pinto could not save Goulart's brother-in-law from the wrath of Communist-fearing Mineiros. Women using their rosaries and reciting Ave Marias prevented Brizola from delivering his speech and joined the hostile crowd that chased him as he fled to the airport to return to Rio. Magalhães Pinto said the attack reflected the sort of radicalism the UDN should avoid, and Max da Costa Santos described Belo Horizonte as having "transformed itself into a national Dallas." But Ademar de Barros, his presidential candidacy already officially launched by the PSP, sent a warm message to the Mineiros, congratulating them for not permitting their "sacred soil" to be "stained" by Communist meetings. Following this message, former Goulart cabinet ministers Almino Afonso and Paulo de Tarso Santos joined UNE President José Serra at ceremonies installing a Frente de Mobilização Popular branch in São Paulo.[3]

Goulart and the CGT chose to hold the March 13 rally at Cristiano Otoni Square, which, being in front of the Central do Brasil Railroad station, was usually swarming with people returning home on late afternoons. Lacerda, remarking that the illegal Communist Party had chosen the square in order to have a crowd it could not otherwise muster, decreed on March 7 that Friday, March 13, would be a holiday for all Guanabara state employees. The decree might reduce the crowd, or, as Lacerda put it, spare the state's workers "from coercion and danger" (that might be serious if unions paralyzed train services) and would leave the square "to the promoters of disorder, whose directing agent is legislator Hércules Corrêa and whose official orator is the president of the republic." Lacerda pointed out that the square was one of the places where the local authorities, implementing a law dating from the Vargas days, had already prohibited rallies. "The army," he said in his message accompanying the decree, "is called on to guarantee, with arms for defending the nation, an illegal act promoted by the agents of a foreign power."[4]

The rally was a stunning success, in part because the CGT brought workers to the square from several states. A multitude, estimated at 150,000, heard hard-hitting speeches by labor leaders, UNE President José Serra, Pernambuco Governor Miguel Arraes, Sergipe Governor João de Seixas Dória, Rio state Governor Badger Silveira, Guanabara Vice Governor Eloy Dutra, Congressmen Sérgio Magalhães and Brizola, and President "Jango" Goulart. Lacerda, accused by the head of the Rio metalworkers' union of turning Guanabara into a police state, was hooted and booed throughout the rally. Placards read: "Reelection of Jango," "Lacerda Traitor to the Nation," "Legality for the PCB," "Gallows for the Gorillas," and "Out with the Yankees."[5]

Fernando Pedreira, in his *Tribuna da Imprensa* column, wrote:

> While the flames of the candles of [anti-Communist] Catholic women multiplied in the city's windows, television cameras gave the nation the picture of João Goulart, president of the republic and the PTB, between labor leader Osvaldo Pacheco and Professor Darci Ribeiro, preaching the expropriation of lands, the reform of the constitution, and the electoral eligibility of all Brazilians. In a way it can be said that the Central do Brasil rally confirmed all prognostications—the worst and the best—those of the adversaries of Goulart and those of his most fervent supporters. As a publicity promotion, as an affirmation of will and purpose, the rally was a success. Present to applaud the president were his brother-in-law Leonel Brizola, compact and uniformed formations of Petrobrás workers, unionized workers, common people rounded up by the electoral chieftains of the PTB and the pension institutes, members and enthusiastic followers of the various "leftist" organizations, starting with the ever less extinct PCB. Before that mass thus assembled, in the illumination of lights and torches, under a forest of placards, President Goulart said what his followers wanted to hear and what the nation feared.[6]

During the speechmaking, Brizola exhorted the president, whose name was always cheered, to "drop the policy of conciliation." He "guaranteed" that, if a plebiscite were held, the people would vote to "overthrow the present Congress and install a constitutional assembly with a view to creating a popular Congress, made up of laborers, peasants, sergeants, nationalist officers, and authentic men of the people." He saw in such an assembly the "only peaceful solution" for the "impasse."[7]

A thunderous acclaim of "Jan-go, Jan-go, Jan-go" greeted the president, who took his place on the platform with his attractive wife on one side and PCB Central Committee member Osvaldo Pacheco on the other. Goulart assailed the "so-called democrats" for whom "democracy is a thing of privileges, intolerance, hate, and the liquidation of Petrobrás—the democracy of national and international private monopolies, the democracy that took Getúlio Vargas to the extreme sacrifice." Calling the constitution antiquated, he said it legalized "an extinct social-economic structure, unjust and inhuman." The crowd reacted joyfully when the president told of having signed the SUPRA decree "with my thoughts turned to the tragedy of our Brazilian brother suffering in the interior." Prompted by Pacheco, he held up a paper and thrilled organized workers and students with the news that he had signed a decree whereby, "from today on, from this very moment on," all petroleum refineries "belong to the people." He also promised to establish rent ceilings, within a few hours, because rents were "exorbitant."[8]

Goulart was exhilarated by the rally. Looking forward to signing new decrees at future rallies, he flew to Brasília to call on Congress to amend the constitution. Among the purposes of the amendments, the president listed votes for illiterates, soldiers, and sergeants, the expropriation of properties without immediate cash payments, legalization of the PCB, and the delegation of legislative powers to the executive. His message also suggested that a way be found for holding plebiscites, in which everyone over eighteen could express opinions about "basic reforms."[9]

Congressman Max da Costa Santos said that the people, in a plebiscite, should decide whether or not to convoke an assembly to rewrite the constitution. On the other hand, Bilac Pinto expressed his amazement that the military ministers, present at the rally, had not arrested Brizola for having attacked the constitution they had sworn to defend. The PSD's Auro de Moura Andrade, presiding at the opening of Congress on March 16, appealed to all Brazilians to organize and raise their voices to defend the constitution.[10]

Lacerda, writing in the *Tribuna da Imprensa*, described Goulart's speech at the rally as "subversive and provocative, besides being stupid. The fear of losing control over shady deals and scandals of every sort has made him lose his head. That man no longer knows what he is doing. . . . Revolutionary war has been unleashed. Its ostensive chief is João Goulart until the Communists give it another chief." The *Jornal do Brasil* concluded that "Goulart, yesterday, chose his

Goulart contemplating a new constitution. (Hilde Weber drawing in
O Estado de S. Paulo, January 15, 1963)

option: he is going to try to remain in power," using demagogic words
and "promiscuous relations with open enemies of Congress and the
constitution."

O Jornal wrote that if the president would read the newspapers, he
would learn that the rally had provoked a feeling of "civic shame"
throughout Brazil. But, according to the *Diário Carioca*, the "participation of the masses" was meritorious, as were direct appeals to the
people, although regarded by conservatives as threats to Congress,
defender of their privileges. In addition to the *Diário Carioca* and
Última Hora, Goulart had the support of Congressman Tenório Cavalcanti's popular, but hardly intellectual, *Luta Democrática*. The
Correio da Manhã, whose editorial policy had become influenced by
financing from interested parties, dismissed as ridiculous all the talk
about a coup, a revolution, and civil war. "Nothing of this sort is
going to happen."[11]

On March 14, Lacerda appealed to the presidential candidates to
join forces at once "to defend the institutions, Congress, the constitution, and, above all, the national security." Noting that Ademar de
Barros had already taken such a position, Lacerda directed the appeal
to Kubitschek, whose 1955 alliance with Goulart and the PTB, he
wrote, had "created the monster that now wants to devour Brazil."[12]

Kubitschek replied that his prodemocracy credentials were the best and he needed no lessons in defending democracy. Lacerda, telling the former president to be less vague, submitted six questions for him to answer and thus open the way for holding "the first pro-Constitution and pro-Congress rally," to be addressed by Kubitschek, Ademar de Barros, and Lacerda. The questions called for Kubitschek's opinions about the legality sought by the PCB, the PCB's open activity "under the protection of the armed forces," a "totalitarian type" of plebiscite sought by Goulart, and the "illegal" decrees about rents and agrarian reform that bypassed Congress.

The former president said his replies would be contained in his acceptance speech, to be delivered at the PSD convention on March 21. While preparing the speech, he consulted public opinion polls conducted for him. They revealed that Brazilians were becoming ever more fearful of Communism, but that 70 percent of them favored reforms. One of the polls, carried out in Minas, showed that 68 percent of the respondents wanted agrarian reform, whereas they were split evenly on the question of whether the constitution should be modified to bring it about.

Kubitschek decided to go along with the position of PSD members who favored modifying the constitution provided that agrarian reform include provisions they considered reasonable, such as good protection against inflation for bonds used for expropriation payments. Goulart, opposed to the PSD ideas and irritated by PSD congressional leaders, was not cooperative with Kubitschek. Lacerda's reaction to Kubitschek's position was one of disappointment even before Kubitschek delivered his PSD acceptance speech, a vigorous appeal for reforms and a condemnation of "the atmosphere of irrational delirium unleashed by extremists of the Right and the Left."[13]

Lacerda, unsuccessful in his work on behalf of an alliance of presidential candidates, proposed, on March 17, an alliance of governors to thwart "the revolutionary war that has been unleashed by pressures exerted on the pretext of reforms." The proposal, made in letters to all the governors except Arraes, Badger Silveira, and Seixas Dória, warned that demagogic decrees, bypassing Congress, would lead to a "totalitarian plebiscite," whose "capricious questions" would omit the principal one of choosing between liberty and Communism. Some of the governors replied with expressions condemning pressures and attacks on Congress, but Goiás Governor Mauro Borges Teixeira told Lacerda that structural reforms were "really necessary."[14]

In São Paulo on March 16 Ademar de Barros used policemen disguised as students to prevent speechmaking by SUPRA Director João Pinheiro Neto and to start a riot at which Pinheiro, according to his own testimony, was almost killed by bombs and machine gun fire. On the same day in Juiz de Fora, Arraes was protected by a thousand of Magalhães Pinto's policemen at a rally of the Frente de Mobilização Popular. Magalhães Pinto, however, was becoming worried about "agitation used to perpetuate groups or people in power." He discussed a possible union for democracy with some of the governors, among them Miguel Arraes and Seixas Dória, who had orated on March 13. He found that Arraes, after recent conversations in Brasília, had come to fear that the leftists there regarded the mobilization for reforms as a means for carrying out a coup.[15]

Political and military circles were stirred on March 18 because former President Eurico Gaspar Dutra broke a silence of many years to declare that "respect for the constitution is the word of order of patriots." Lacerda, about to go to São Paulo by car early the next morning with Raphael de Almeida Magalhães, Hélio Beltrão, Armando Falcão, and Rebello Filho, followed the suggestion of Falcão to stop first at Dutra's residence in Rio to congratulate the marshal. On the way to Dutra's house, Rebello gave Lacerda a message from Mandim to warn that Casa Militar Chief Argemiro de Assis Brasil planned to carry out a pro-Goulart coup within twenty days and that Marine Corps Commander Cândido Aragão had chosen six men to "eliminate physically the governor of Guanabara." Lacerda called the rumor good news and put it on his list of matters to discuss with Ademar de Barros.[16]

Marshal Dutra spent the day receiving admiring visitors. Among the early ones was General Humberto Castello Branco,[17] and thus Lacerda and Raphael saw briefly, but did not meet, the Cold Warrior whom General Assis Brasil wanted to dismiss as army chief of staff in one more move to strengthen the presidential military apparatus.[18]

4. Lacerda Visits São Paulo and Minas (March 19-23, 1964)

One reason for Lacerda's trip to São Paulo was Ademar de Barros' invitation to attend an anti-Goulart rally. Lacerda, as he told Raphael de Almeida Magalhães, did not expect the rally, known as the March of the Family with God for Liberty, to amount to much. He was therefore surprised to find São Paulo in a state of frenzy. Hundreds of thousands of Paulistas, packed in the 3 kilometers between the Praça da República and the Praça da Sé, shouted anti-Communist slogans along with refrains such as "One, Two, Three; Jango in the Jail" (*Um, Dois, Três; Jango no Xadrez*). A Mass was held at the cathedral for the "salvation" of democracy.[1]

Lacerda told Abreu Sodré that he did not want his presence at the rally to be construed as an effort to garner votes. Hoping to attend it incognito, he removed his well-known spectacles; but, at the cathedral, a priest recognized him and shouted *"Governadooor!"* He returned to the hotel.[2]

That evening, after greeting Carioca women who had come to join the March, Lacerda attended a ceremony he had done much to bring about for ending the hostility between Júlio de Mesquita Filho and Assis Chateaubriand, creator of the Diários Associados newspaper chain. Chateaubriand, unable to use his limbs since his stroke, had expressed a few words faintly to indicate his agreement with Lacerda's proposal that supporters of democracy join forces.

The gathering at Chateaubriand's Casa Amarela (Yellow House) was a ceremony at which Lacerda—wearing cowboy clothes, like all the guests—was inducted into the Order of the Jagunços (Rough Riders of the Northeast), founded by Chateaubriand. When the host, dressed in his uniform of colonel of the Minas Military Police, met with Mesquita, he exclaimed, as well as he could, "Oh! Julinho!" Among the guests who applauded were Edmundo Monteiro, João Calmon, Raphael de Almeida Magalhães, Hélio Beltrão, Herbert Levy, Daniel Krieger, Armando Falcão, and São Paulo law Professors Waldemar Ferreira and Ernesto Leme. Chateaubriand's address, read by one of the guests, praised Maurício de Lacerda, Carlos Lacerda, and the Mesquitas.

São Paulo Education Secretary Carlos Rizzini, orator of the Order of the Jagunços, presented the Order's medal to Lacerda and asked everyone to support the Lacerda candidacy. Lacerda, in his reply, declared that Chateaubriand and Mesquita "are together again today for the love of liberty, in a lesson for politicians." He attacked understandings between "pseudo-Christians and Communists."[3]

The governors of São Paulo and Guanabara met the next day and discussed reports of plots for the "elimination" of the two of them. At a press conference Lacerda praised the Paulistas for starting "the resurrection of democracy," and Ademar thanked Lacerda for suggesting that they accept the invitation of the governor of Rio Grande do Sul to meet and develop plans for reestablishing tranquility.[4]

The governor of Minas, in the meantime, had decided to share with the public his misgivings about the Goulart administration. While Lacerda met with Ademar, Magalhães Pinto issued a manifesto to proclaim that the Brazilian people would not back individuals who, "presenting themselves as the proprietors of reforms, use the reform issue as a pretext for agitation with the object of allowing persons or groups to perpetuate themselves in power." Carlos Castello Branco,

Ademar de Barros and Carlos Lacerda. (Claudius Ceccon drawing in
Brasil, Urgente, January 26–February 1, 1964, reproduced in Paulo
Cezar Loureiro Botas, *A Bênção de Abril*)

writing in the *Jornal do Brasil,* said that leftists in the government
were becoming concerned lest the military be influenced by developments that included Marshal Dutra's statement, the Mesquita-
Chateaubriand reconciliation, the Lacerda-Ademar alliance, and the
manifesto of Magalhães Pinto.[5]

Carioca women who had participated in São Paulo's March of the
Family with God for Liberty began organizing for a similar concentration in Rio on April 2; many of them called on Marshal Dutra and
persuaded him to participate. It became evident, however, that their
enthusiasm for the São Paulo rally was not universally shared. São
Paulo student unions expelled from their ranks all students known
to have participated in the rally and resolved to bury effigies of Ademar de Barros and the state secretary of security. The left wing of the
Catholic Church expressed its "profound amazement" at the "exploitation of the faith" carried out by the March with God. This view
was shared by São Paulo Cardinal Carlos Carmelo de Vasconcelos
Mota, who conferred with Jurema and backed "the objectives of
Goulart." Ação Católica of São Paulo placed itself on the side of the
cardinal and of Ação Católica of Belo Horizonte.[6]

To develop support for Goulart and reforms, a new Frente Popular
was formed during discussions at which the CGT, the Parliamentary
Nationalist Front, and the UNE were joined by the CTI (Command
of Intellectual Workers), represented by journalist Álvaro Lins, book

publisher Ênio Silveira, and Brizola adviser Cibilis Sousa Viana. The discussions resulted in a program that was more radical than the one that San Tiago Dantas, dying of cancer, was seeking to put together to get congressional support. The aims of the Frente Popular, scheduled to be announced when Goulart revised his cabinet again, were reported to include expropriation of the pharmaceutical industry, large flour mills, meat packers, and powdered milk companies, and the "democratization of military regulations."[7]

That reforms were foremost in Goulart's mind was made clear when close associates of Kubitschek called on the president. Giving him the official news that "your friend Kubitschek has been nominated for president," they asked Goulart to announce his backing for that candidacy. Although such an announcement would have gone a long way to demolish rumors that the president hoped somehow to remain in office, Goulart simply told Kubitschek's friends that the people had no interest in elections, but only in reforms. Kubitschek's friends departed unhappily and with the conviction that if the president's interest in reforms were not demagogic he would not have opposed their wish to have full inflation protection for agrarian-reform bonds.[8]

Kubitschek maintained his own pro-reform image, continued cold toward Lacerda, and did not break with Goulart. It was to Magalhães Pinto that Lacerda turned to seek to bolster the anti-Goulart front. However, the two-hour meeting of the governors of Minas and Guanabara in Belo Horizonte on March 24 was unsatisfactory. It did nothing to dispel Lacerda's opinion that Magalhães Pinto, associated with Arraes, was acting in a "dubious" manner and "held the somewhat utopian idea that Jango would seek a conciliation and make him candidate for the succession."

"Up to now," Lacerda told Magalhães Pinto, "you have opposed going to the convention of your party because of political interest. Now you have to go for the sake of a greater interest." Magalhães Pinto refused to commit himself.

When a reporter, after the meeting, asked Lacerda whether he feared a split in the UDN, the Carioca governor replied that what worried him was "the division between the democrats at this time when the principal enemy, the Communist enemy, is so well entrenched. My appeal to Magalhães Pinto is to avoid that a man like him, with his responsibility as a former president of the UDN, . . . and, above all, as a man who embodies the virtues of moderation and the qualities of conciliation, give the idea, by his absence, that moderation and conciliation have disappeared from the UDN."

Magalhães Pinto, present when Lacerda spoke to the press, heard the Carioca governor describe their differences as more imaginary than real. "No one," Lacerda told the press, "is more aware than Magalhães of my fondness for him and my esteem for his qualities, which compensate for my defects."

On boarding the *Esperança*, Lacerda's first words were: "Magalhães is nuts."[9]

5. The Navy Mutiny and the Reactions (March 25-27, 1964)

In Rio on Wednesday, March 25, Lacerda informed Júlio de Mesquita Filho of his unsatisfactory meeting with Magalhães Pinto; and then he went to Rocio to relax during the last days of Holy Week.[1] Goulart at the same time went to relax in Rio Grande do Sul.

On the previous day Goulart had asked Navy Minister Sílvio Mota to rescind the ten-day prison sentences imposed on leaders of the Sailors' Association for having made pronouncements, against Mota's orders, at the Bank Workers' Union and on Rádio Mayrink Veiga, demanding better conditions for sailors and containing political observations.[2] Mota, described as "infantile" by the Sailors' Association, had refused to rescind his order. Some of the Association leaders, instead of reporting for imprisonment, organized a meeting which took place, with the help of the CGT, at the Guanabara Metalworkers' Union building late on March 25. Attended by about 1,500 sailors, together with representatives of Brizola and of the CGT, it became a tumultuous affair; the speeches demanded amnesty for the sergeants who had revolted in 1963, revisions of the nation's institutions and the navy's disciplinary regulations, and removal of the "subversive" navy minister. Goulart, before going south, asked Justice Minister Jurema to attend the meeting because, he said, the government did not want to lose the support of the "more than 20,000 sailors" who were "in revolution against the decisions of the minister." Jurema decided not to attend.[3]

On March 26, the navy minister sent a detachment of forty marines to arrest the rebels, but, after Marine Commander Cândido Aragão had a friendly chat with the rebels, the marine detachment joined the rebellion. From the president's office, where Darci Ribeiro conferred with labor leaders, orders were issued to avoid a conflict, and therefore army troops, sent to streets near the union building, took no action. Within the building, Sailors' Association President José Anselmo dos Santos vowed that the sailors would "resist until death." In their statement to the press, the rebels railed against "perverted minds," controlled by interests opposed to the people.[4]

Goulart returned from the south with Casa Militar Chief Assis Brasil at 1:00 A.M. on March 27, Good Friday. The sailors left the metalworker building in army trucks that afternoon only after CGT leaders Osvaldo Pacheco and Dante Pelacani, sent by the president to negotiate, agreed on amnesty for the rebelling sailors and the appointment of a new navy minister acceptable to the rebelling sailors and the CGT.[5] A delay in conveying the sailors in trucks to the army barracks at São Cristovão was ordered by Goulart at the request of Hércules Corrêa and Dante Pelacani to allow time for a conference they wished to have with the president to ensure that the army trucks would have a friendly and unarmed appearance.

Paulo Mário da Cunha Rodrigues, the frail, sixty-nine-year-old new navy minister, canceled Sílvio Mota's order for the arrest of Cândido Aragão and let Aragão return to the command of the marines. After Sailors' Association President José Anselmo spoke with Goulart and received confirmation of the CGT's promise of amnesty, Paulo Mário freed the rebel sailors.[6]

That evening the rebels celebrated Good Friday with a victory march in downtown Rio. Singing and shouting, they carried on their shoulders the two "people's admirals," Marine Commander Cândido Aragão and the new navy chief of staff, Pedro Paulo Suzano. Writing of the photographs of the Good Friday scenes that appeared on the front pages of the Saturday newspapers, Jurema says: "The repercussions were the worst possible."[7]

Sobral Pinto asserted that the Bolshevik Revolution had begun in Brazil in December 1963, when the Army Police had cooperated with the "insubordination of Communist students" at the Faculdade Nacional de Filosofia. Some newspapers recalled sailors' uprisings in Russia prior to the Bolshevik Revolution. The *Jornal do Brasil* lamented the blow to military discipline and warned that its demise would mean the rise of "political-military militias, extolled by Communists and Fidelistas."[8] *O Estado de S. Paulo,* reflecting on what air force officer Haroldo Veloso has called the "extreme Communist infiltration" among air force sergeants,[9] wrote that "we have no air force worthy of being called such," and it added that "what remains of the navy truly does not deserve to be described as a military corporation."[10] According to a CGT announcement, CGT-affiliated sailors had immobilized most of the fleet, and the cruiser *Barroso,* which could still function, was under the control of those same sailors.[11] Furious admirals issued manifestoes. The Military Club, expressing support for the admirals, condemned "union leaders at the service of Moscow."

Political analyst Wilson Figueiredo writes that the "disastrous decision to support a revolt of sailors seduced by labor union agents, destroying authority and discipline in the armed forces, . . . broke the morale of the government's supporters and shifted the mass of undecided individuals from one camp to the other." Army Chief of Staff Castello Branco, coordinator of an alliance of army officers to prevent a coup by Goulart, found that the settlement of the navy revolt had upset so many officers that a movement against Goulart seemed likely. Although it was probable that a majority in the army would support the movement and that the state troops of Minas and São Paulo, and many people in those states, would adhere, question marks remained, such as the position of Second Army Commander Amaury Kruel, Goulart's anti-Communist friend in São Paulo, and the situations in Guanabara, center of federal army strength, and Rio Grande do Sul. Castello favored enough delay to complete the anti-Goulart military organization; as he saw it, a problem was the prevention of some premature "barrack uprising" that might be rapidly crushed by well-armed federal troops.[12]

Retired Marshal Odílio Denys, meeting in Juiz de Fora on March 28 with Magalhães Pinto and Generals Mourão Filho and Carlos Luís Guedes, said it was time to act.[13] The Minas governor, returning to Belo Horizonte, phoned Herbert Levy and was told that most of the young São Paulo army officers were ready to topple the president.[14] With this news, Magalhães Pinto placed the Minas state police under the orders of Guedes, whose army headquarters were in Belo Horizonte, and prepared to issue a manifesto stressing the need of reforms but ending with the words "Minas will struggle with all the energy of its people for the restoration of constitutional order which in this hour has been dangerously compromised." Upon the release of the manifesto on March 30, General Mourão Filho dismissed it as insufficiently incisive, and the Goulart administration did not feel that it meant rebellion.[15]

The settlement of the sailors' mutiny was so serious a development that it brought Lacerda to Rio on March 27. Before being driven from Rocio by Hugo Levy, he made arrangements for Letícia and Cristina to stay with Joaquim and Candinha da Silveira at their Rio home. He would spend his days and nights at Guanabara Palace, relaxing at times by working on his Portuguese translation of the Broadway hit, *How to Succeed in Business without Really Trying.*[16]

Meeting with his cabinet, the governor named General Salvador Mandim commander of the palace defense. A defense against the tanks which Cândido Aragão might use would be difficult, if not impossible. But Mandim, a veteran of Brazil's participation in World

War II, set people to work, in the basement of the palace, making "Molotov cocktails" to be thrown at approaching enemy vehicles not only by defenders in the palace but also by neighbors from the windows of nearby buildings.

Mandim would, of course, be assisted by the large-scale plans that Security Secretary Gustavo Borges, foreseeing civil war, had spent months preparing, for they included defending Guanabara Palace. More recently, assistance was prepared by air force Colonel João Paulo Moreira Burnier, who had considered Lacerda a traitor to the Aragarças rebellion of 1959. Willing now to cooperate with the defense of Guanabara Palace, Burnier sent some dynamite there, and, at his home, constructed *gafanhotos* (grasshoppers), jeeps bearing rockets; the colonel also organized a defense group that met for training at the Anne Frank School near the palace. Dr. Rebello Filho, besides setting up an emergency medical service in the palace basement, went on a mission to get a supply of dynamite, as recommended by Fontenelle.[17]

Lacerda prepared a "Message to the Navy and the People," in which he described the navy as having been assassinated and its body shredded. The moral degradation of the government, he said, had facilitated Goulart's submission to the Communists, "who dominate that poor wretch, corrupted by covetousness and dishonor." He added that Goulart had "purchased, in three years, 550,000 hectares of land, four-and-a-half times the area of Guanabara state."

Congress, according to Lacerda's Message, had been reduced to reacting passively and tardily, while the armed forces were being dismantled. Asserting that "the hour is no longer one for manifestoes, interviews, petitions, or speeches," Lacerda closed by calling on everyone to resist and fight. "I shall fight to the end with all arms available."

When Mandim met with military conspirators, among them Golbery do Couto e Silva, they recommended that Lacerda remain silent until they had consolidated their work.[18]

Instead of releasing his unsensational Message to the Navy and the People, Lacerda decided to provoke immediate action because he continued to believe that anti-Goulart military would simply confabulate, during further dismantlement of the armed forces, and would do nothing—unless the Goulart people, going further than they had gone, resorted to some drastic measure, such as closing Congress, intervening in Guanabara, or arranging for Lacerda's assassination. Lacerda wanted to take some illegal step himself and in this way force Goulart to act against him and thus get a reaction on the part of the

anti-Goulart military. Using particularly violent language, he produced a proclamation on tape that declared, among other things, that
Guanabara was separating itself from the nation.

Raphael de Almeida Magalhães found Lacerda eager to have the
tape released at once. He worriedly told the governor that it would
simply give coverage to steps to be taken by Goulart. "I am willing to
pay, to make the sacrifice, in order to get them, the military, to act,"
Lacerda replied.

But the governor agreed to wait for forty-eight hours. He distributed
four tape recordings to four emissaries, and sent them to deliver the
recordings to friends in the Brazilian north and south as well as São
Paulo and Minas. Recipients were shocked by the violence of Lacerda's message, and considered it dangerous.[19]

6. Mourão Decides to March (March 31, 1964)

At Guanabara Palace on Sunday evening, March 29, General Mandim
found Lacerda and Letícia watching a movie with Hugo Levy and
Major Carlos Osório. Mandim reported that General Castello Branco
had advised that he could furnish no help for the defense of the
governor's palace and had recommended that Lacerda leave it. "I'm
not going to leave," Lacerda said. "A lesson in courage must be given
to these generals." For the benefit of Mandim, the governor added:
"I'm referring, of course, to those in active service."[1]

At a meeting the next morning with Mandim and Gustavo Borges,
Lacerda told Mandim to advise the generals that it was "impossible
to wait any longer." Borges, writing of a "climate" that he says had
become "intolerable" following the navy mutiny, mentions the turmoil among officers, principally captains and lieutenants, "unwilling
to put up with the situation anymore."[2]

In the Guanabara state assembly that day, March 30, legislators
exchanged insults. A resolution in support of the distraught admirals
was signed by twenty-eight legislators, among them retired Admiral
Augusto Amaral Peixoto (PSD), a Vargas admirer who regretted that
Getúlio was not alive to repudiate what Goulart was doing. "The case
of the navy," he said, "is simply one more step by the Communists
and the federal government people, who want to perpetuate themselves in power."[3]

Goulart and Casa Militar Chief Assis Brasil spent much of March 30
making sure that thousands of sergeants and corporals, from all
sections of the military and police, and from fire brigades, would
be present that night at the Automobile Club, where the president,

accompanied by his cabinet, was to address the Benevolent Association of Military Police Sergeants at a ceremony that the government
arranged to have widely broadcast. Congressional majority leader Tancredo Neves called on the president at his Copacabana apartment to
warn him against attending the ceremony, following so soon the controversial settlement of the sailors' mutiny. But Assis Brasil, speaking firmly, said there was nothing to worry about because Goulart
could count on military power such as no other Brazilian president
had possessed.[4]

Only about 1,500 sergeants and corporals went to the Automobile
Club—a disappointment considering the work done to provide transportation and attract Guanabara policemen and firemen who had opted
to serve the federal government. But friends and relatives helped fill
the auditorium. Thunderous ovations greeted Marine Commander
Cândido Aragão, Justice Minister Abelardo Jurema, "Sergeant-Con-
gressman" Antônio Garcia Filho, and Sailors' Association President
José Anselmo. The speeches were the exultant expressions of men
who were making it clear that their triumphant march could not be
slowed down. In the words of one of the speakers, the successful
struggle was against the "narrow-minded mentality of those who
make of military discipline an accursed whip to enslave the Brazilian
people."[5]

If the president wanted to provoke his opponents into testing their
strength against his strength he could not have done better. Throughout the nation television screens showed him surrounded by a sea of
sergeants and corporals, in uniform, chanting "Jan-go, Jan-go, Jan-go."
His words were those of the chief of invincible troops.

He would not, Goulart vowed, allow any disorder to be carried out
in the name of order. He explained that the national crisis had been
promoted by a privileged minority that feared to face the bright future, in which millions of Brazilians would become integrated into
the nation's economic, social, and political life. The minority groups,
he said, were led by "the eternal enemies of democracy." He added
that "in the crisis of 1961, these same hypocrites, who today show a
false zeal for the constitution, wanted to tear it up and bury it in the
cold grave of fascist dictatorship." "Who is trying to stir up trouble for
the president in the name of discipline?" "They are," he said, "the
same ones who in 1961, under the name of false discipline, arrested
dozens of officers and Brazilian sergeants."[6]

Sergeants, it was rumored, would attack Guanabara Palace after
their meeting. Lacerda, who had joined family members and friends
to watch a film again—this time a film about John F. Kennedy's

wartime experience—determined that his sons should carry out their palace defense work separated from one another to reduce the possibility that both be killed during an attack.[7]

The broadcast of the sergeants' meeting and its speeches defying military discipline guaranteed a military uprising. General Olímpio Mourão Filho, after hearing the broadcast in Juiz de Fora, decided to act at once; he would march the next morning with 2,500 men to overthrow a president who, he felt, was turning himself into the chief of a Communist government. Drawing up a manifesto to be issued later, Mourão spoke of Goulart's "support and stimulation" of "spurious organizations" that named and dismissed cabinet ministers and generals; he mentioned the work of demoralizing and humiliating the navy "in the most depraved and shameless outrage against its discipline and hierarchy."[8]

Mourão telephoned Belo Horizonte to get an infantry battalion from his subordinate, General Guedes, who had already assumed a position of rebellion against Goulart on March 30. Also before daybreak on March 31, Mourão sent messages about his marching plans to conspirators in São Paulo and Rio, and he phoned Armando Falcão. Falcão advised Lacerda and Castello Branco. Castello, in phone calls to General Guedes and José Luís de Magalhães Lins, nephew of the Minas governor, argued that it was too soon to start a military outbreak because the coordinating work had not been completed. Learning that he could not prevent the movement in Minas, Castello put at its disposal the apparatus in the army that he and his associates had been setting up throughout Brazil. "Mourão," he told his officers, "has acted ahead of time; we have the choice of supporting him or letting him be crushed."[9]

Lacerda, upon learning of Mourão's plan, met before daybreak with Gustavo Borges, police commanders, and Mandim. By that time protective bags of sand had been brought to the palace and loudspeakers set up for addressing crowds outside. Electric generators had been placed in the garden. Walkie-talkies were used to bring Polícia de Vigilância units to Guanabara Palace, reinforcing members of the Military Police already there, and to station Military Police platoons in the streets leading to the palace. Most of these Military Policemen, Gustavo Borges recalls, were new recruits, replacing soldiers who had opted to transfer to the federal government, and were "eager to participate in the fight against Communism."[10]

Volunteers swarmed to the palace. Some of them joined the contingent that Colonel Burnier, with the help of Colonel Osnelli Martinelli, had been training at the Anne Frank School, and were given the blue and white neckerchiefs of the contingent. But most of the arriving volunteers, as a group of thirty retired generals told Mandim, lacked weapons.[11]

An early arrival was Abreu Sodré, who flew from São Paulo with Colonel Rubens Resstel (in a plane loaned by Willys Overland Director Paulo Quartim Barbosa) after receiving the news about Mourão. On reaching Rio, Resstel and Sodré consulted officers of the Armed Forces Staff before Resstel returned to São Paulo with instructions for fellow-conspirators, who were eager to depose Second Army Commander Kruel if he would not adhere. Sodré, on joining Lacerda, told him of having learned that the tanks of Admiral Cândido Aragão's marines might attack Guanabara Palace.[12] It was a realistic and grim possibility.

Armando Daudt d'Oliveira gave Lacerda the news that Marshal Ângelo Mendes de Morais felt that resistance against Aragão's tanks would not last ten minutes and that the marshal was therefore inviting Lacerda to find safety in his residence, "the last place people will seek him." In response to this new evidence of the ability of the Goulart administration to unite the bitterest of old foes, Lacerda expressed his thanks but added that he would "only leave the palace dead."[13]

While Fontenelle took steps to have garbage trucks block the streets leading to the palace, Lacerda phoned Ademar de Barros to learn if he was adhering to Mourão's movement. Ademar simply cut off the connection. He felt that Lacerda was crazy to use the official phone. Lacerda, who was counting on Ademar's use of the scrambling device he had left with him, repeatedly phoned the São Paulo governor and finally heard his voice. Ademar, Lacerda learned, had forgotten about the device and could not find it. Speaking briefly, Ademar said the situation in São Paulo was difficult because "the man here has not decided yet."[14]

Amaury Kruel, to whom Ademar referred, was torn, throughout most of March 31, between his personal ties with Goulart and his disgust with Communist advances that shattered military discipline. During phone calls made by Goulart, which Gustavo Borges had taken steps to record, Kruel pleaded with the president to break with the people who surrounded him lest he "sink with them."[15]

The pro–Magalhães Pinto *Correio da Manhã* came out against Goulart, leading the surprised president to phone Samuel Wainer and remark that presidential adviser Jorge Serpa Filho had lost control of the newspaper. The *Correio*'s leading editorial, "Enough!," asked how far Goulart planned to go in abusing the patience of the nation and in "breaking up the armed forces by indiscipline, daily more uncontrollable." "Brazil has already suffered too much from the present government."[16]

7. Defending Guanabara Palace
(March 31–April 1, 1964)

Kubitschek and his advisers, after inviting Crockatt de Sá to handle labor matters for them in the election campaign, had been shocked on March 27 to be told by Crockatt that the plans of the Goulart group did not include a presidential election. Nonetheless Kubitschek rejected an offer of José Maria Alkmin to participate in the Minas movement against Goulart. Instead, he issued an appeal for peace, in which he emphasized the importance of military discipline. And, on March 31, he met with Goulart to warn that a bloody civil war might occur unless the president repudiated Communism and punished the sailors who had participated in the mutiny. But Goulart, pleased with the message he had given the nation at the Automobile Club, kept repeating to Kubitschek phrases he had used in addressing the sergeants. The president also revealed absolute confidence in the superiority of the military forces that supported him.[1]

Troops of the First Army, with headquarters in Rio, were marching north to crush the small force of Mourão, which had reached the Paraibuna River, on the Minas-Rio state border. In the meantime, in São Paulo, General Kruel held the last of his unsatisfactory phone conversations with Goulart and set to work arguing with subordinate generals who resisted his idea of breaking with the regime.[2]

In Rio that afternoon, CGT leaders met at the stevedores' federation building to declare a general strike. Policemen, sent by Gustavo Borges, threw tear gas bombs into the building and participated in a wild conflict, during which Osvaldo Pacheco, Rafael Martinelli, and other labor leaders were placed under arrest. Hércules Corrêa and retired air force Commander Humberto de Melo Bastos, claiming immunity from arrest, were released and appealed to Air Zone Commander Francisco Teixeira and marine Commander Cândido Aragão for troops. So many troops were sent that the episode resulted in a victory for the labor leaders and the escape of most of them, including Pacheco and Martinelli. Policemen described the outcome as a "tactical retreat" to keep sufficient men available for the defense of Guanabara Palace.[3]

Cariocas found commuting disrupted because railroad workers responded to the strike call. They also found that the banks were having difficulties in trying to accommodate long lines of depositors who wished to make withdrawals and convert cruzeiros into foreign currencies. Housewives with cash on hand on March 31 stocked up on foods. News was hard to come by, because the situation was unclear and because censors were placed by the government in the radio stations. Rádio Jornal do Brasil was kept off the air for one hour as punishment for broadcasting "alarming" reports from Minas.[4]

From Castello Branco's command post, after nightfall, Lacerda received a phone call from Marshal Ademar de Queiroz to suggest that he leave Guanabara Palace and not try to resist there. A little later, Castello called to tell the governor that martyrs were not what the cause needed. But Lacerda replied that he had consulted his wife and gotten in touch with Marshal Dutra and Brigadeiro Eduardo Gomes, and all of them disagreed with the advice of Castello.[5]

Much of the talk in Guanabara Palace was about Kruel. The position of the general remained unknown until 11:30 P.M., when he released a proclamation stating that the fight of the Second Army "will be against the Communists, and its objective will be to break the circle of Communism that presently compromises the authority of the government." Armando Falcão, who had been constantly using a Guanabara Palace telephone to get information about Kruel, was at last able to furnish the good news to Lacerda and the men with him in the movie projection room: Hélio Fernandes, Major Osório, and Pedro Ernesto Mariano de Azevedo, adviser to the governor and head of the UDN student sector. Then Lacerda went to address members of the Military Police guarding the palace. He told them that Kruel was on his way to Rio and victory was in sight.[6]

A phone call from Miami brought the voice of Jules Dubois of the *Chicago Tribune*. Lacerda discussed the situation and mentioned the invasion of Rádio Jornal do Brasil. After a comment by Dubois, Lacerda said: "We don't need anyone's help; the problem is ours."[7]

It was after 2:30 A.M. when the palace received a message from a navy officer advising that two marine battalions were on their way to Guanabara Palace, apparently the result of an order which he said he had overheard Jurema give to Cândido Aragão. Mandim, using a megaphone, instructed the people in the palace to lie on the floor. Outside, in a light rain, many stretched on the ground, weapons in hand. They expected to be killed by the superior weapons of the marines' tanks.[8]

The attack was not made; but the report of the threat spread through the city, bringing hundreds of new volunteers to the palace. Colonel Nemo Canabarro Lucas (a former Goulart supporter now opposed to "false Communist reforms") and Brigadeiro Eduardo Gomes reached the palace in time to participate in preparations for an attack following a second alarm, this one given at about 4:30 A.M.[9]

Again, no attack materialized, which is not to say that the danger was not real. Congressman José Guimarães Neiva Moreira was with the armed group of Colonel Dagoberto Rodrigues, director of mail and telegraph operations, when it resolved to join marines and surround Guanabara Palace, giving Lacerda "five minutes in which to surrender." The attack did not take place, according to Neiva Moreira, because Admiral Cândido Aragão, scheduled to command the movement of troops, undertook another mission and was replaced by Admiral Pedro Paulo Suzano, who took the troops directly to Laranjeiras Palace without knowing that the plan included attacking Guanabara Palace on the way. At Laranjeiras Palace someone sought the president's opinion, thus adhering to what some anti-*Lacerdistas* considered "a legalism inappropriate for the tumult of the moment." Word was received that the president forbade an attack on Guanabara Palace but felt that "the beast, Lacerda, is cornered and will surrender before daybreak."[10]

Jurema writes that the marines were eagerly awaiting an order to attack that never reached them, and he wonders why tanks were not set in motion to make the attack and generally play a more aggressive role. When Cândido Aragão learned of Goulart's opposition to an attack against Guanabara Palace, he told the navy minister and Pedro Paulo Suzano: "We are being betrayed."[11]

Neiva Moreira felt that "the fall of Guanabara Palace could have changed the direction of events"; but, as Goulart realized, the outcome of the struggle depended on developments in the army, such as those that occurred in rapid succession after Kruel's position became known.[12] The First Army's Sampaio Regiment, with orders to crush Mourão, joined Mourão and his men; and, in the northeast, the Fourth Army's commander came out against Goulart. Kruel, marching with his troops in the direction of Rio, was encouraged, like Mourão, by the adherence of units of the First Army.[13]

During the night Hugo Levy reported that phone lines to Guanabara Palace had been cut. But at least the line connecting the palace to Rádio Roquete Pinto remained in operation, as was evident when it brought, curiously, the voice of a friend of Alfredo Machado's and Lacerda's, phoning from New York. She said that she and others with her, including Argentine newspaper publisher Alberto Gainza Paz, had heard that Guanabara Palace was surrounded and Lacerda threatened. Lacerda told her what he knew and asked her to inform the United Press because, he said, no news or cables were leaving Brazil. The United Press told the world of the "encirclement of Guanabara Palace."[14]

The telephone to Rádio Roquete Pinto was used to deliver an appeal for Cariocas to come and close ranks around the governor. Censorship was lax at Rádio Roquete Pinto and the appeal went over the airwaves shortly before daybreak, bringing another wave of hundreds of volunteers, many of them youths wearing blue and white necker-chiefs.[15]

At sunrise Lacerda went into the street to express his thanks to each member of the Military Police and Polícia de Vigilância. To neighbors he apologized for having closed the street to traffic, where-upon one of them remarked that while Laranjeiras Palace was pro-tected by tanks, Guanabara Palace was protected by garbage trucks. Returning to the palace grounds, Lacerda participated in a ceremony at which the Brazilian flag was raised. "There we all were," Dr. Re-bello Filho writes, "with Lacerda in front, singing perhaps for the last time, the national anthem, all willing to die, if necessary, to prevent the fall of the last bastion of liberty, which Guanabara Palace had become."[16]

Following the applause of onlookers for the flag raising ceremony, Lacerda went inside and read to his followers an anti-Goulart mani-festo drawn up during the night by General Golbery do Couto e Silva and signed by "members of the high command," Generals Arthur da Costa e Silva, Castello Branco, and Décio Palmeiro de Escobar. Then Lacerda spoke on a telephone line connected to Belo Horizonte's Rá-dio Inconfidência and a few other radio stations—a connection that Raul Brunini, Walter Cunto, Cláudio Lacerda Paiva, Ayrton Baffa, and some military men managed to put together. Lacerda said: "My friends of Minas, my countrymen, help me, help the government of Guanabara, besieged but unconquered. . . . Brazil does not want Cain in the presidency. Cain, what have you done to your brothers? Your brothers who were going to be killed by your Communist accom-plices, your brothers who were robbed so that you could become the biggest landowner and thief of Brazil?"[17]

At this moment, a little before 10:00 A.M., some of the palace de-fenders, eating sandwiches supplied by neighbors, spied men they thought were marines in the distance on one of the streets. Lacerda seized a microphone connected to loudspeakers and shouted: "Gua-nabara Palace is being attacked at this moment by a band of despera-does. Marines, lay down your arms because you are being deceived by an unscrupulous officer. Aragão, coward, incestuous, leave your soldiers and come here to settle this dispute with me. I want to kill you with my revolver, Aragão, in a man-to-man combat." Richard Bourne, writing about Lacerda at the palace, says he was "leather-jacketed and armed to the teeth . . . in his element—histrionic, vola-tile, the schoolboy dramatics carried to extremes."[18]

Goulart had believed in Assis Brasil's assurances about his military strength; he was amazed as well as shocked by the news that reached him before sunrise on April 1, particularly by the news that the troops sent to crush Mourão had adhered to the rebellion, and that the coastal artillery in Rio had been seized by rebel forces. Before leaving for Brasília around 1:00 P.M. he said to Jurema: "Our military plan inexplicably failed. I can count only on the Third Army [in the far south] and that is not enough."[19]

Despite Goulart's departure, Rádio Nacional kept hammering out progovernment messages that were broadcast over PTB loudspeakers in Cinelândia. Messages called for lynching the anti-Goulart "gorillas" and helped persuade mobs to invade the Military Club with the result that two would-be invaders were killed by members of the Army Police. In clashes in the area one other person was killed and about twelve were wounded.[20]

Carioca television viewers, watching an episode of a film series on TV Rio, were surprised shortly after 4:00 P.M. when Lacerda and Sandra Cavalcanti appeared on the screen, thanks to arrangements made by state bank President Antônio Carlos de Almeida Braga. Speaking from Marcelo Garcia's office in Guanabara Palace, they called for calm and dismissed as untrue the information given in broadcasts by Goulart supporters. "At this moment," the governor said, "the justice minister is limiting his habitual slanders to those he is making at the cuspidor to which Rádio Mayrink Veiga has been transformed, bought by Petrobrás money for Leonel Brizola and the Communists. There the Communists dominate. . . . Therefore they do not shut up, but they are going to flee like rats in a few hours. . . . They are sewer rats who learned to speak on microphones."

Sandra Cavalcanti returned to the room and whispered to Lacerda. He smiled and announced: "Good news for everyone. The lying has ended. Rádio Mayrink Veiga has gone off the air."[21]

Following the applause by those around him, Lacerda went on with his speech. He called Roberto Morena "a sinister criminal," and attributed the choice of Wilson Fadul to be health minister to his association with the president in land deals. He professed no personal hatred for Goulart, and said that "regardless of everything they did to me, to this, my poor state, regardless of the persecution, I would have done nothing to break the rhythm of democratic life"—except that Goulart went too far, trying to destroy the navy and turn Brazil over to Communism.[22]

A Military Police officer rushed into the room and spoke to Sodré. Lacerda, receiving the message from Sodré, broke into tears and exclaimed: "God is good! Thank you, God, thank you very much!"[23]

Lacerda's tearful words, carried to the Cariocas on television, were inspired by the news of the arrival, in front of Guanabara Palace, of three tanks which had been guarding Laranjeiras Palace and whose men, led by Platoon Commander Freddie Pereira Perdigão, had decided to adhere to the revolution following Goulart's departure from Rio. The enormous crowd in front of Guanabara Palace joined the governor in hailing the adherence of the tanks. The people sang the national anthem and "Cidade Maravilhosa." Lacerda was effusively greeted by Captain Alcides Etchegoyen, who had arrived on the running board of an automobile—leading the press to report dramatically, but inaccurately, that the son or sons of illustrious General Alcides Etchegoyen, vehement opponent of Lott's 1955 pro-Kubitschek coup, had commanded tanks that had arrived to save the governor.[24]

The crowd was treated to a strange sight after Armando Daudt d'Oliveira, driving Marshal Mendes de Morais to call on former President Dutra, stopped at Guanabara Palace to have a word with Lacerda. The marshal, waiting in the car for Armando to finish his visit, saw Lacerda coming toward the car to speak with him. He left the car and, in front of the palace, the two old adversaries greeted each other to the applause of the multitude.

When Armando and Marshal Mendes de Morais resumed their drive to Dutra's residence, the marshal asked Armando whether Lacerda would be agreeable to having Dutra complete the presidential term with the fall of Goulart. Therefore Armando, after the visit with Dutra, returned to the palace, which was so crowded that he could speak alone with Lacerda only in a bathroom. Lacerda told him that it was too early to say anything, but that Dutra was a good man and a military man was needed.[25]

8. Comments

The outcome of the uprising against Goulart provided one more reason to regard Carlos Lacerda as the "overthrower of presidents."

It would be more accurate to say that Goulart did everything necessary to make sure that the revolt would break out and be a success. Army leaders, such as legalist Castello Branco, had to be provoked into going beyond their original plan of developing an alliance to defend the constitution. Presidential candidates and their supporters had to be convinced that Goulart and his group planned a coup to do away with the forthcoming presidential election. For the success of the movement against Goulart, it was important also that the press and its readers be filled with fears of a Communist takeover. The outcome of the navy mutiny was more effective than the anti-Goulart propaganda that conservatives, not surprisingly, had been carrying on for years. Wilson Figueiredo asserts that the mutiny settlement sent masses of people from one camp to the other.

It was not Goulart's espousal of reforms that Brazilians objected to. In identifying himself with agrarian reform (the most popular reform), Goulart presented a positive image. Politicians were aware of the prevailing pro-reform sentiment. Magalhães Pinto and Miguel Arraes clamored for reforms, and so did the UDN's Bossa-Nova. San Tiago Dantas, consulting political circles, worked out a program that hardly deserved the unfavorable comments made about it by the Frente de Mobilização Popular. The PSD, whose leaders wanted a Kubitschek-Goulart alliance, became reform-minded and Kubitschek himself extolled reforms.

Under these circumstances legislative negotiation might have been possible. Negotiation was important not only for political reasons but also because hearty approvals at street rallies, where workers were sometimes instructed how to react,[1] were not necessarily indicative of the merits of proposals. However, by March 1964 an impasse had developed. The PSD found it hard to understand why the Goulart group rejected full inflation protection for agrarian bonds unless the reform issue was being used for ulterior motives. After Miguel Arraes and Magalhães Pinto concluded that the presidential clique was using the reform issue as part of a plan to do away with the presidential election, Kubitschek felt impelled to declare that the nation would embrace a flag of reforms but not a reform of the flag. Then Goulart, who had attacked the constitution on March 13, remarked that the people were interested in reforms and not in elections.

Historian Michael L. Conniff, consulting polls taken in this period, has furnished data that make it clear that in 1963 and early 1964 the dislike of the Communist Party was expressed by margins considerably greater than those by which reforms were favored. Unfortunately for Goulart, the reform rally of March 13 was notable for pro-PCB placards. In a poll of voters taken in May 1964 to find out reasons for Goulart's overthrow, 34 percent said Goulart was giving Brazil to the Communists, 21 percent said he was going to close Congress and become a dictator, and 17 percent said he had undertaken popular measures that hurt foreign and national economic powers. (Corruption, which had been rife in the Goulart administration, was not mentioned.) Considering the anti-Goulart publicity following his fall, it is not surprising that, in this poll, the coup of March 31 was approved by 54 percent of those questioned and was condemned by only 20 percent.[2]

Goulart was poorly advised on how greatly the fear of the "Red Peril" affected the army and the public. Furthermore, he had nowhere to turn unless he were to retreat from his latest alliance with the CGT, plead with men he had denounced as reactionaries, desert and infuriate organized labor, and present what his political mentor, Vargas, might have called "a demonstration of pusillanimity."[3]

Goulart was in no mood for "a demonstration of pusillanimity." He was euphoric when he threw down the gauntlet, after the navy mutiny, by making sure of a wide radio-television coverage of the meeting at which sergeants and the president, accompanied by his cabinet, expressed their comments about military discipline. He appeared strong, confident that the cries of "Jango, Jango" at the Automobile Club were meaningful and that General Assis Brasil's assurances of military support were well founded.

Journalist Carlos Heitor Cony, explaining in April 1964 that a large part of the population supported Goulart's overthrow, wrote that Goulart was "weak" and "incompetent."[4] It was the word "weak" that had always struck a raw nerve in President Goulart. Important decisions, such as his rejection of a moderate speech prepared for his delivery at the sergeants' meeting, were the result of his determination not to be called weak. When, in June 1963, the president dismissed a strong cabinet that some people said was running Brazil, he explained to Congressman Maurício Goulart: "If I don't replace Kruel, all the people will tell me I have no power."[5] When he made up his mind on a show of military might and a state of siege to deal with the "Lacerda conspiracy" on October 4, 1963, he expressed his resolve to dispel reports that "the federal government no longer has authority."[6]

Momentary elation prompted a festive celebration at Laranjeiras Palace on October 4, 1963. Strong words from the president, cheered by his listeners, buoyed up the president's spirits and made it appear that he was, indeed, a strong president. No doubt in March 1964 it was exhilarating to contemplate the opportunity of having the government, in the person of Jurema, join with the "more than 20,000 sailors" who were "in revolution" against the navy minister. But the number was no more than 1,500. Fantasy, along with the desire to avoid being pusillanimous, played a role in decision making.

It was not easy to assess what Goulart's overthrow, in a setting of extreme emotion, would mean for Brazil. Preparations had been made to "save the constitution" from an illegal act by Goulart; but, as it turned out, it was the victors, lining up on the side of rebellious troops in Minas, who were the violators of the constitution. They found it a simple matter to justify the violation in the name of national security, and it remained to be seen whether one violation might lead to others, based on the same principle, perhaps even upsetting the normal political setting on which the Lacerda presidential candidacy depended. The trauma of 1964 bore resemblances to the trauma of 1954, when Lacerda, after the suicide of Vargas, had argued that the country, instead of holding elections in 1955, should go through a period—perhaps a harsh period—in which constitutional and electoral changes would be made to prevent a recurrence of the situation that had brought Brazil to calamity.

Lacerda flashed his wide smile frequently late on April 1, while Goulart, having ordered Lacerda's arrest,[7] flew from Brasília to Rio Grande do Sul. Most of the prominent victors were issuing proclamations and Lacerda was no exception. In a reform-minded television broadcast he said that the time had come to allow workers to elect their leaders, free of labor ministry pressure, and that "social reform must be carried out so that the demagogues won't say that we were opposing it when we were seeking to remove Communism." He also issued a proclamation to the people to say that "Russia has suffered its greatest setback."[8]

In a victorious mood and sitting on top of his desk, Lacerda chatted with his assistant, Edgar Flexa Ribeiro, and his budget director, José Roberto Rego Monteiro. Rego Monteiro, who was free of personal involvement in politics, surprised the others by remarking: "Neither of you knows the trouble that lies ahead, the tragedy that has happened to us." When Lacerda asked what he meant, the budget director pointed out that the governor had lost all the banners that he had been waving; he had become a horseman who had lost his spurs.[9]

The observation irritated Lacerda. But Raphael de Almeida Magalhães, speaking to the governor a little later, made the same point. He argued that the success of the revolution of March 31 made things difficult for Lacerda politically. "The reasons you had for being a strong factor have now disappeared."[10]

Would UDN leaders, often scolded by Lacerda and wary of his independence, continue to find need of the crusader who had led, in public debate, the campaigns against Communism and Goulart? Would they continue to regard as sacred the provisions of the constitution that mandated a presidential election in 1965?

Lacerda, Edgar Flexa Ribeiro maintains, knew in his heart that Rego Monteiro was right. In any event, Lacerda soon made it clear that he recognized problems that the new situation created for him. Always inclined to worry about plotting behind his back, we find him, after April 1, 1964, extremely alert to possible moves to derail his presidential candidacy.

V.

Defender of the Revolution
(April-June 1964)

1. Lacerda Decides to Support Castello Branco
(April 3, 1964)

In Rio, late on the afternoon of April 1, anti-Communists destructively invaded the UNE building and the offices of *Última Hora.* Samuel Wainer found asylum in the Chilean embassy while Eloy Dutra and fourteen other opponents of the coup went to the embassy of Uruguay.

General Arthur da Costa e Silva, who took over the war ministry with the explanation that he headed the army hierarchy, set to work to eradicate subversion and corruption. For the moment the eradication consisted of the arrest of many people considered to have cooperated with the Communist movement. Brizola, in the far south, was out of reach.

At Guanabara Palace, Lacerda spent the first hours of April 2 giving interviews for broadcasting stations and newspapers, domestic and foreign. At 5:00 A.M. he was driven to the Duque de Caxias petroleum refinery, where soldiers of Mourão, on their way to Rio, stopped to suppress pro-Goulart demonstrations. The tireless governor reviewed troops, offered a stadium in Rio for their encampment, and greeted Lieutenant Colonel Heitor Linhares, his former military aide.[1]

When Cariocas awoke on April 2 they learned that Congress at midnight had declared the presidency vacant (although Goulart was still in the country) and had named Chamber of Deputies President Ranieri Mazzilli to be interim president of Brazil. And they learned that Governors Miguel Arraes (Pernambuco) and Seixas Dória (Sergipe) had been deposed and arrested. Rio's March of the Family with God for Liberty, held downtown on the afternoon of April 2, was described by its organizers as nonpolitical, and therefore Lacerda decided not to participate. Letícia, however, attended the mammoth victory celebration and received a warm ovation. So did eighty-two-year-old Marshal Eurico Gaspar Dutra, the leading "conciliation candidate" in the election to be held by Congress to choose someone to complete the presidential mandate begun by Quadros in January 1961.

Arthur da Costa e Silva. (A. Lopes drawing in *Jornal da Tarde*, March 31, 1994)

God and the Brazilian soldier, praised at the March of the Family, were praised a little later by Lacerda when many of the celebrants went to Guanabara Palace. Addressing them, the governor described Marshal Dutra as "that guardian of democracy." He expressed his disapproval of the destruction at the UNE building and added that he hoped for a new UNE, to be created by "true students."[2]

While Cariocas celebrated, Costa e Silva assumed the leadership of what he called "the Revolutionary Command," consisting of himself and the new navy and aviation ministers. He dictated some cabinet choices to Mazzilli, including the appointment of a friend, University of São Paulo *Reitor* Luís Antônio da Gama e Silva, to be justice minister. He found Mazzilli so cooperative that he saw no reason why he should not remain interim president during the thirty days that were to elapse, according to the constitution, before Congress was to select a new president. The head of the Revolutionary Command hoped, during the thirty days, to carry out *Operação Limpeza* (Operation Cleanup).

Lacerda, on the other hand, felt that the moment was right for reaching a harmonious decision about the successor of Goulart and that in the thirty-day period divisions might arise, especially serious in the military. Retired General Danillo Nunes, UDN leader in the Guanabara legislature, conveyed Lacerda's idea to Costa e Silva.[3] Raphael de Almeida Magalhães submitted it to Army Chief of Staff Castello Branco. But Castello Branco, citing a legal opinion on his desk, pointed out that no new president could be chosen within thirty days. He asked that no consideration be given to his own name, which was being mentioned frequently, and suggested that a name be found at a meeting of civilian leaders of the revolution, governors and congressmen.[4] Lacerda, implementing a part of the suggestion, asked governors to come to Rio. It was a surprise to many that he included Mauro Borges Teixeira, the PSD governor of Goiás who had formerly been associated with Brizola's National Liberation Front; but by early March 1964 Mauro Borges had been ready to help depose Goulart, and he had cooperated with the movement of March 31–April 1.[5]

Lacerda at first favored Marshal Dutra for president and Juracy Magalhães for vice president. He called on Dutra and found the former president willing to accept. But the governor noted that Dutra was surrounded by the old crowd that had flourished when the PSD was on top.[6] Augusto Frederico Schmidt, the Kubitschek adviser who had known Castello Branco at the National War College, took the trouble to phone Lacerda from Europe to tell him that he had learned of the governor's support of Dutra. "You are a fool," he told Lacerda, "Dutra means the restoration of the old order. Castello Branco is a brilliant man. It is a miracle that at a critical moment there is a moral man, a patriot."[7]

Similar thoughts were expressed by others: members of the army and of business and women's groups, all of whom created a considerable ground swell for Castello. Lacerda also noted that Eduardo Gomes strongly opposed Dutra, and he reflected that Dutra's age was against him and that the revolution had not been fought to bring to power PSD politicians, such as Vitorino Freire, whom he had found at Dutra's residence.[8] Castello, ever since he had refused to adhere to the 1930 revolution, had built up a reputation of being a strict legalist, dedicated to upholding the constitution.

Lacerda expressed his inclination to support Castello at a meeting held on April 3 with Mauro Borges, Governor Nei Braga of Paraná, and José Monteiro de Castro, representative of Magalhães Pinto. Nei Braga and Mauro Borges, speaking as military men, praised the professional ability and "firmness of character" of Castello.[9]

On April 4, the day Goulart flew to Uruguay, *O Jornal* revealed Lacerda's pro-Castello position on its front page. *O Globo*, on the same day, published a first-page editorial calling for the selection of Castello Branco.

2. Lacerda Calls Costa e Silva a Usurper (April 4–5, 1964)

While governors traveled to Rio, the Military Police and the DOPS of Guanabara cooperated with Operação Limpeza. They were encouraged by Cardinal Jayme Câmara, an admirer of Operação Limpeza, who said: "To punish those who err is an act of mercy." Policemen raided the office of Hércules Corrêa and described it as a Communist cell full of propaganda and money furnished by the Soviet Union. They took over the CNTI and the pension institutes and arrested those of their officers who had not fled. In the case of the Transport Workers' Pension Institute, soldiers of the Military Police installed an army colonel as *interventor,* and he presided over an election in which new officers chose a new president of the institute: Hélio Walcacer, Lacerda's labor affairs adviser.

Among those arrested were nine members of a commercial mission from Beijing. According to Gustavo Borges, they were Communist spies, intent on using "a Chinese process" to "exterminate" Governor Lacerda and Generals Amaury Kruel and Castello Branco. After the Rio police announced that Artur Virgílio, PTB leader in the Senate, had received money from the Chinese Communist mission, Virgílio called the charge a sordid act of vengeance by Lacerda, "a man without guts who has a scoundrel as police chief." "If Lacerda gets away with this, he will pay with his life."

The *Correio da Manhã,* publishing editorials against terrorism and arrests, denounced the "fanaticism and intolerance of the *Lacerdistas*" and suggested that Lacerda himself may have been responsible for the assault on *Última Hora.* In the state assembly, members of the opposition praised the position of the *Correio da Manhã* during a heated session in which a PTB legislator used his fists to reply to a *udenista* who called Goulart corrupt.[1]

The governors, preparing to meet at Guanabara Palace on the evening of April 4, spent the day participating in political discussions and issuing declarations to the press about the revolution and usually about the need for the immediate selection of a new president. Lacerda warned that a "thirty-day hiatus" would favor "spurious concessions to congressional groups." The next president, he told the press, should be a military man able to prevent Kubitschek from becoming "a Brazilian Frondizi and robbing us of this revolution as he has robbed the country."

Lacerda had much to say. He denied having conspired ("My con-spiracies are carried out in public") and said that his big mistake had been "to let Jango take over the government" in 1961. In a reference to the UDN nominating convention, scheduled to be held in a week, Lacerda disclosed that he had written Bilac Pinto recommending postponement.

Answering questions of reporters, Lacerda said that cancellations of political rights would be proper where individuals had harmed the national security but should not be used for "personal vendettas or humiliation." "I am not in favor of imprisoning Communists just because they are Communists. I am not afraid of ideas. Our ideas are better than theirs. But I do favor jailing people who carried out subver-sive activities, who flouted the law and the constitution, threatening the national security."

Asked about the existence of a list of 126 journalists to be held for questioning, Lacerda said that those who were "simply journalists" would be set free. Declaring that the arrested members of the Chinese mission claimed to be newspaper correspondents of the New China Agency, he pointed out that their apartment had been found full of weapons "of every sort" as well as subversive propaganda and a large stack of dollars.

Lacerda confirmed the extinction of SUPRA and called its recent head, João Pinheiro Neto, the "biggest rat in Brazil." Asked to com-ment on the asylum granted to Eloy Dutra by Uruguay, Lacerda de-scribed the fallen vice governor as "not dangerous and therefore not deserving of imprisonment. If he wants to return home he can do so and I wish him well."[2]

Lacerda never forgot a remark of his father, made in 1930 after the overthrow of President Washington Luís: "Do not humiliate some-one who has fallen."[3] Immediately after the collapse of the Goulart regime, he sent a representative to the hospital where General Jair Dantas Ribeiro had undergone surgery, to extend "sincerest wishes" for the rapid recovery of Goulart's war minister. When the *Jornal do Brasil's* Nascimento Brito phoned him, asking for his help to prevent the imprisonment of journalist Luís Alberto Bahia, the governor did not let his bad relations with Bahia interfere with cooperation. He told General Siseno Sarmento, who was close to Costa e Silva, that Bahia was not important enough to arrest.[4]

Governor Nei Braga and Congressman-Colonel José Costa Caval-canti, both pro–Castello Branco, called on Costa e Silva and were joined by Juarez Távora. With disappointment they heard Costa e Silva declare emphatically that no thought should be given to plac-ing a military man in the presidency lest it foment divisions in the armed forces. The chief of the Revolutionary Command insisted that it was too soon to consider replacing Mazzilli and that all attention should be given to Operação Limpeza.[5]

The meeting that evening at Guanabara Palace was attended by Governors Lacerda, Ademar de Barros, Magalhães Pinto, Ildo Mene-ghetti, Nei Braga, Fernando Correia da Costa, and Mauro Borges. All favored an immediate election by Congress despite the thirty-day provision in the constitution. Magalhães Pinto, described by the *Correio da Manhã* as the "principal civilian leader" of the victorious movement, hoped for consideration if the choice were to be a civilian. However, most of the governors wished to turn to the military. Ademar de Barros, arguing in favor of a civilian, was told by colleagues that a civilian might become a puppet of the Revolutionary Command and that agreement on the name of a civilian would be difficult for the governors, as several of them were presidential candidates. "Jango," Ademar remarked later, "left such a devil of a mess that a military man was considered necessary." When the governors were asked to submit names, a few spoke only of Castello Branco, while others submitted more than one name with Castello Branco's always included.[6]

During the deliberation, the palace received a visit from General August César Moniz de Aragão, Democratic Crusade candidate for the Military Club presidency. Coming in his uniform from the barracks of Vila Militar and eager to impart the sentiment of army officers, he was greeted by Gustavo Borges and conducted to a large room filled with congressmen and other politicians. There he launched into a passionate speech in which he attacked the "subversive and corrupt governments of Getúlio Vargas, Juscelino Kubitschek, Jânio Quadros, and João Goulart." He called Castello Branco the choice of "the great majority, or quite possibly everyone," in the army.[7]

Lacerda, given a note by Lieutenant Colonel Heitor Linhares about the presence of Moniz de Aragão, suggested to the governors that the general be invited to join them and that, before receiving him, they agree unanimously on the name of Castello Branco, who was on each governor's list. Besides, Lacerda said, he had learned that Castello was the unanimous choice of the influential National War College group. The governors agreed on Castello, and then Lacerda escorted Moniz de Aragão into the room. After the general repeated pro-Castello sentiments he had expressed minutes earlier to the politicians, Lacerda told him: "You are trying to crash through an open door; everyone here favors the same solution."[8]

The governors resolved to present Castello's name to Costa e Silva and, after obtaining the agreement of the Revolutionary Command, speak with Castello and the party leaders. Before they went to the war ministry, some of them made declarations to the media. Nei Braga told reporters that the agreement on one name was a rare phenomenon in Brazilian politics.[9]

Television cameras recorded Lacerda's announcement of the governors' choice and their insistence on an election by Congress before the middle of the following week. The Carioca governor also criticized Kubitschek, saying that the former president, through spokesmen, was casting doubt on the eligibility of the army chief of staff. As the *Correio da Manhã* pointed out, the constitution ruled against the election of chiefs of staff of the armed services. But the situation was unclear, with former Justice Minister Vicente Ráo arguing that the constitutional restriction applied only to regular elections by the people. Anyway, this question and that of an early election by Congress were among the matters being considered by constitutional lawyer Carlos Medeiros Silva in the course of drafting articles for an "Ato Adicional," a set of emergency rules that Bilac Pinto and other congressmen hoped to have enacted by Congress.[10]

It was after 11:30 P.M. on April 4 when Siseno Sarmento escorted the governors, together with Congressmen Juarez Távora and Costa Cavalcanti, into a spacious office of the war ministry for the meeting with Costa e Silva. Lacerda, speaking on behalf of the governors, started to reveal their decision, but at the outset Costa e Silva interrupted to say that he should be addressed not as war minister but as commander in chief of the revolutionary forces.[11] Nor was Lacerda able to elaborate after explaining the governors' wish for an immediate election, with a military man as the candidate of the revolution. The commander in chief was quick to cut in with the assertion that a military candidate might disrupt the unity of the army's revolutionary forces. He stated that the election by Congress should not be held until Mazzilli had been in office thirty days and that during that time the nation should suffer penance and be purged of subversion and corruption. He added that the next administration should be spared this disagreeable work, and that Mazzilli was cooperating and doing what was requested of him.

Lacerda declared that the revolutionary ideals did not include having a puppet in the presidency. Besides, "Mazzilli and the PSD might wrap you up," Lacerda added, using the word *enrolar*. The general affirmed that no one was going to *enrolar* him. Lacerda suggested that he could use another word for a PSD maneuver if the commander in chief preferred, and he informed him of press reports that Mazzilli had named Israel Pinheiro, a Kubitschek man, to head the Casa Civil. "If Mazzilli appointed him," Costa e Silva retorted, "he is going to unappoint him."[12]

Costa e Silva was not cordial to Magalhães Pinto, who, Mauro Borges recalls, "spoke in a parochial voice, trying to carry on with thoughts Lacerda had originally sought to express." Costa e Silva, the Goiás governor has recorded, "referred to the separatist character of the movement started by the Minas governor and warned that he would not tolerate any whim in that sense." When Magalhães Pinto asked what had become of Seixas Dória, the commander in chief replied: "Seixas Dória is in prison," and in a loud voice he added that "many others will be put in prison." An inquiry by the Minas governor about the banking holiday brought a cutting remark from the commander in chief: "You, a banker, are just the right person to be asking about the banking situation."[13]

Magalhães Pinto decided that the meeting was fruitless and spoke of the need to return to his state. "Your return there," Costa e Silva said, "represents no danger to the armed forces, because my forces are much stronger than yours. . . . What we need to do is keep those forces united." After Mauro Borges, Ademar de Barros, and Nei Braga also mentioned the need to return to their states, Juarez Távora asked that Lacerda be heard. The Guanabara governor, who had been sullenly doodling, hotly defended his position. Costa e Silva then cited events during the first years of the republic to embellish his theme about the need of military unity.[14]

Lacerda accused the general of wanting to be a dictator. Defending his right to be heard without asking the general's permission, he exclaimed: "I don't know where you were in 1945. I don't know where you were in 1954. But I know where you were on November 11, 1955. You were at the side of General Lott!" Then, when Lacerda sought to emphasize a point by raising his hand and pointing his finger, Costa e Silva imitated the gesture and declared that he could summon stronger forces and arguments than the governor.[15]

But Távora did not agree with the arguments of the commander in chief. Banging the table for emphasis, Távora said: "I do not believe that in thirty days—or in sixty or ninety—the Military Command of the Revolution will be able to exterminate the germs of subversion and corruption from Brazil or even from its governmental machinery." Távora also felt that, with the passage of a month, the group commanding the revolution would lose the unity for easily arranging to have Congress elect a good president.[16] If governors of different political parties had been able to reach agreement, he did not see why the generals could not do so.

Costa e Silva smiled. "We are hearing the same idealistic and unwary *tenente* of 1930," he said.

"No, Costa e Silva," Távora answered, "it is not so. In 1930 we exercised restraint in not wanting to assume the government directly. We thought of putting the civilians in front and handling them from nearby. What an illusion, ours! Within a short time we were pushed back, . . . unable to do any of the things we had planned."[17]

As it was approaching 4:00 A.M. and most of the participants at the meeting were exhausted, Siseno Sarmento suggested that they adjourn and continue the discussion at a time to be set by Costa e Silva. While the men were leaving the room, Lacerda sought to have a word with Costa e Silva, but the commander in chief turned his back on the governor.[18]

Upon reaching his apartment, Lacerda discussed the situation with UDN colleagues. Among them was Bilac Pinto, who favored a military man in the presidency and had found the congressmen of their party wanting an immediate election.

During this discussion, which lasted until after sunrise, the distraught governor put his latest thoughts in a letter for Costa e Silva. He wrote that it was the general, not Lacerda, who had assumed a position that would divide the army—and the nation, "bringing disillusion and despair to millions of Brazilians." He accused the general of setting up a dictatorship and said, "I do not accept you as a dictator; I went to speak with a liberator, not a usurper." Lacerda also wrote that he would, on the following day, leave the governorship and public life. "I have the right to retire without being called a deserter. It is enough that I be called a loser."[19]

Lacerda summoned General Danillo Nunes to his apartment and told him that, if he did not deliver the letter to Costa e Silva, he would use television to denounce the war minister. At the war ministry, however, Nunes decided to take up the matter of the letter with Siseno Sarmento instead of waiting for Costa e Silva, who was presiding over a meeting of military commanders. After Sarmento and Nunes decided on a ministry wall safe as the best place for the letter until a "conciliation" could be arranged, Nunes was able to speak with a weary Costa e Silva and persuade him to call the governors soon to a new meeting.

Sarmento phoned friends of Lacerda to suggest that they try to have the governor withdraw his letter. Abreu Sodré and others, who gathered with Lacerda, argued that the letter had been a mistake. Juracy Magalhães, writing later, mentions "the terrible scene in the home of Carlos Lacerda, when he advised us—me, his son Sérgio, and some of his few friends—about the gist of the letter." Nei Braga and Costa

Cavalcanti rushed to the war ministry to obtain Sarmento's assurances that it would not be delivered.[20]

3. The Institutional Act (April 9, 1964)

On Sunday, April 5, while Sandra Cavalcanti led a pro-Castello rally, governors in Rio learned that Costa e Silva wished to meet with them that evening at 7:00 P.M. Lacerda decided to send Juracy Magalhães as his representative. Magalhães Pinto, also deciding not to attend, found a representative in PSD Congressman José Maria Alkmin, who had been appointed finance secretary in the Minas state cabinet late in March to give it an interparty complexion.

At the meeting, held again at the war ministry, Juracy explained that Lacerda felt it best to be absent, hoping in that way to contribute to the existence of an atmosphere less "brutal" than the one prevailing at the earlier meeting. The word *brutal* upset Costa e Silva because he thought it was used to describe himself.[1] Notwithstanding this unpromising start, the five governors, the two governors' representatives, and Costa Cavalcanti soon found that Costa e Silva had become more amiable. He said he had reached the conclusion that it would be best, after all, to select a new president quickly and decide on a military officer. After he asked for a suggestion about whom to select, Nei Braga presented Castello's name. The commander in chief praised the soldierly qualities of the army chief of staff. When his visitors prepared to leave, to go to Castello's residence, he cordially wished them a good night. The commander in chief, Mauro Borges noted at the close, wore an expression of sadness. Juracy, at the end of the meeting, received from Siseno Sarmento the letter that Lacerda had written Costa e Silva. Danillo Nunes, who was present, had no objection because Juracy was representing Lacerda. However, the UDN politician from Bahia never returned the letter to Lacerda.[2]

Castello, hearing the governors tell of their talk with Costa e Silva, agreed to be a candidate. The governors, pleased with Castello's decision, were making plans to get in touch with political party leaders, when Congressmen Bilac Pinto and Pedro Aleixo arrived at Castello's home with Carlos Medeiros Silva and his draft of an Ato Adicional for the consideration of Congress. It provided for a speedy presidential election in which no one would be ineligible, and it would allow the Revolutionary Command to suspend, for five years, the political rights of citizens considered to have played important roles in making the revolution necessary. The draft, read aloud by José Maria Alkmin, was approved by the men in Castello's home. Then Castello arranged to have a copy delivered at once to Costa e Silva.

Some clauses in the draft met resistance from congressmen; but PSD Congressman Ulysses Guimarães, as he told Mazzilli, Bilac Pinto, and Carlos Medeiros Silva, believed that passage might be arranged in six or eight days. Bilac argued that a tense military situation would not allow so much delay.[3]

Lacerda and Raphael de Almeida Magalhães felt it urgent that advice about the Ato be given by Francisco Campos, author of the authoritarian Constitution of 1937.[4] After military leaders agreed, Raphael and Costa e Silva phoned Campos and Bilac phoned Medeiros Silva, with the result that Campos studied the draft on April 8 and concluded that it might be issued outright by the Revolutionary Command instead of submitted to Congress. Phoning Raphael, Campos said: "The military are blind about reality. They talk about legality. They don't know what they have done. They think Goulart is still president!"[5]

At the request of Costa e Silva, Francisco Campos and Carlos Medeiros Silva set to work at the war ministry, in the company of Justice Minister Gama e Silva and some military leaders, to put finishing touches on the draft. One of the revisions stipulated that the suspension of political rights of individuals be for ten years, not five. Francisco Campos' chief contribution was a ringing prologue that proclaimed the responsibility of the victorious revolution itself, represented by the commanders of the three branches of the armed forces, to issue the Ato, now called the Ato Institucional. It asserted that the recently overthrown government had "deliberately sought to bolshevize the country."

Lacerda, asked by the press about the Ato, still unreleased, said that "with or without it, the revolution must fulfill its objectives: the cleanup of the country, the establishment of a stable and honest government, the preparation for democracy and the 1965 elections, and attention to fundamental problems, from the supply of foodstuffs to the definition of Brazil's position in the world." He included "free and prompt elections in all the labor unions," and warned that the achievement of the revolution's objectives might be blocked by "the vanity and ambition of some of the politicians."[6]

To help prepare the way for the immediate election of Castello Branco by Congress, Lacerda decided to speak with Mazzilli. He therefore got in touch with the Bangu Textile Company's Silveira brothers, Guilherme ("Silveirinha") and Joaquim, whose father, when serving as Dutra's finance minister, had been assisted by Mazzilli. Lacerda, recently a guest at the Rio home of younger brother Joaquim, was accompanied by the Silveira brothers and Abreu Sodré when he called on the interim president in Rio; he explained the need to preserve military unity and "save Brazil from a military dictatorship" by installing quickly in the presidency "the most prestigious" chief of the armed forces.[7]

Lacerda told Mazzilli about Costa e Silva's claim to be making the presidential appointments—along with the "unappointment" of Israel Pinheiro. "I took the liberty of telling the war minister, along with other things difficult to say, that we would not tolerate a disguised military dictatorship, with a civilian as a façade, and that you would not submit to that." Mazzilli cited his well-known ability to compromise but pointed out that he also had his dignity and would let no one undermine it. "Good," Lacerda said, and added: "It wasn't to put a PSD man in power that a revolution was made."

Mazzilli, according to Lacerda's account, said: "Carlos, I shall bow to your appeal. God grant that you won't repent having made it." The interim president told his family and friends that he could hardly wait to return to his Chamber of Deputies post.[8] For a man who had pledged himself to protect congressional immunities, the interim presidency was uncomfortable. Several congressmen, such as Neiva Moreira, Francisco Julião, and Fernando Santana, were reportedly under arrest, and others were in embassies. Habeas corpus petitions—312 submitted to the Guanabara Justice Tribunal and almost 200 to the Supreme Court—remained unattended while the country awaited the Ato Institucional.[9]

Finally, on the afternoon of April 9, the three military ministers signed the Ato at a ceremony at the war ministry. It stipulated that within two days Congress was to elect a president and vice president, and it established a period of sixty days in which the Revolutionary Command, and later the incoming president (in accordance with National Security Council recommendations), could cancel legislative mandates and suspend for ten years the political rights of individuals. Important for the incoming president were the provisions affecting congressional procedure. Legislative projects submitted by the president were to become law if not acted on within thirty days. Budgets submitted by the president were not to be increased by Congress. These provisions, together with one permitting presidentially sponsored constitutional amendments to be enacted by an absolute majority vote, were to expire, together with the Institutional Act, on January 31, 1966, when a new administration was to take office.

Lacerda spoke favorably of the Institutional Act, whereas Sobral Pinto, lawyer for the arrested mission from Red China, stated that the military ministers had not been delegated by the Brazilian people to act as they had and were shielded only by their weapons. The *Correio da Manhã,* agreeing with Sobral, said that the Ato made Congress "a mere consultative assembly of the Military Junta" and destroyed the constitution that the military and civilians had worked in March to defend. The *Jornal do Brasil,* however, saw the Ato as a necessary part of the movement to save the country from "disintegration by communization." It admitted that the Ato was a high price to pay and blamed the Goulart government, which, it said, had betrayed its mandate.[10]

With Costa e Silva insisting that Quadros was among those deserving punishment, the Revolutionary Command made it known quickly that it was suspending for ten years the political rights of Goulart, Quadros, and Luiz Carlos Prestes. On the next day, April 10, it issued a list of a hundred persons thus affected, including forty federal legislators, many belonging to the Parliamentary Nationalist Front, who lost their mandates along with their political rights. Among those listed were Congressmen Eloy Dutra, Bocaiuva Cunha, Leonel Brizola, Max da Costa Santos, Amauri Silva, Almino Afonso, Neiva Moreira, Abelardo Jurema, Francisco Julião, Benedito Cerqueira, Roland Corbisier, Sérgio Magalhães, José Aparecido de Oliveira, and Paulo de Tarso Santos. Others were Miguel Arraes, Darci Ribeiro, Raul Riff, Valdir Pires, João Pinheiro Neto, Hércules Corrêa, Roberto Morena, Clodsmith Riani, Rafael Martinelli, Dante Pelacani, Osvaldo Pacheco, Humberto de Melo Bastos, Samuel Wainer, Celso Furtado, Antônio Garcia Filho, Osvino Ferreira Alves, and Henrique Cordeiro Oest.[11]

The PTB, Hélio Fernandes wrote in the *Tribuna da Imprensa,* had lost by *cassações* (the suspension of political rights) its three leading candidates for the succession of Lacerda in the Guanabara governorship: Brizola, Sérgio Magalhães, and Eloy Dutra, leaving only Hélio de Almeida ("no one knows how he was overlooked"). Seeking to further Operação Limpeza, Hélio Fernandes recommended the *cassações* of Hélio de Almeida, San Tiago Dantas ("the Brazilian Pierre Laval"), Kubitschek, Afonso Arinos de Melo Franco, Tancredo Neves, Walter Moreira Salles, Rio state Governor Badger Silveira, and Pernambuco Senator José Emírio de Morais.[12]

4. Conversations with Castello Branco (April 1964)

On April 11 Congress elected Castello Branco president by a large vote and chose José Maria Alkmin as vice president over his fellow-*pessedista* Auro de Moura Andrade. The winners were scheduled to take office on April 15, which left the new president-elect little time to select his cabinet.

Humberto Castello Branco. (A. Lopes drawing in *Jornal da Tarde*, March 31, 1994)

Lacerda, according to Abreu Sodré, was so eager to see Castello Branco that he used "violent language against the future president" when it seemed that his wish would not be granted.[1] Finally Armando Falcão arranged for a meeting at the home of Juracy Magalhães.[2] Lacerda prepared for it by making a list of things he wanted Castello to agree to, among them the holding of the presidential election of 1965 as scheduled, and freedom for workers and students to run their unions. Sérgio Lacerda typed the list and therefore arrived at Juracy's home a little later than his father and Falcão.[3]

Castello, democracy-minded and eager to have the 1965 election take place on schedule, let Lacerda know that he had no quarrel with the items on his list.[4] He told Lacerda that he and his wife Argentina, who had died a year earlier, had voted for him in the elections that had made him city councilman, congressman, and governor. Now he listened with fascination while Lacerda, according to Falcão, gave a brilliant and comprehensive discourse about the country's problems.

"Mr. President," Lacerda said, "so many years of struggle have left me broken. I am physically worn out, emotionally exhausted, and financially in poor shape. Besides, I must take care of the health of my wife, who has a serious hearing problem—and I don't have the funds to take her to doctors abroad. All efforts here have failed." Juracy, seeking to praise Lacerda and the UDN, said: "See what kind of men we have in the party; Lacerda here has no money." Lacerda made it clear that he wished to be named to a mission abroad that would allow him to leave Brazil soon, and Castello said he would consider the matter.[5]

Lacerda had not met with Castello to seek to have people placed in cabinet posts, but he reminded the president-elect of the merits of Juracy Magalhães and Clemente Mariani. Castello, who had a team of army friends working on cabinet possibilities, remained silent.[6]

Before assuming the presidency, Castello invited Júlio de Mesquita Filho and Lacerda to his residence in Ipanema to hear his ideas about the cabinet. Because the short, stocky president-elect, descending stairs to enter the living room, was accompanied by a tall army officer, Lacerda saw him as "looking like a dwarf, rigidly holding himself in the military bearing of a marshal." Castello, extremely courteous, expressed his appreciation to Mesquita for the position taken by *O Estado de S. Paulo* and to Lacerda for having struggled so long "almost alone."[7]

When Castello mentioned Lacerda's secretary of health, Raimundo de Brito, as a possible minister of health and cabinet representative of Guanabara, Lacerda insisted that Raimundo de Brito not be considered "a minister representing Guanabara," and Castello was pleased to agree.[8]

Lacerda learned enough about Castello's ideas to be disappointed, more so than Mesquita, who did not share Lacerda's reservations about economists Roberto Campos and Otávio Gouveia de Bulhões.[9] What disappointed Mesquita was to find that Castello was not looking for suggestions, and thus he had no opportunity to offer the ones he had come from São Paulo to submit: industrialist Augusto Trajano de Azevedo Antunes to be finance minister and PL Congressman Raul Pila to be education minister.[10]

When Castello advised that he was going to ask Milton Campos to be justice minister, Lacerda warned that "Milton Campos is a man dominated by juridical scruples" who would be "an excellent minister for after a revolution, or to avoid a revolution. But for revolutionary work . . . he is going to create problems." Lacerda could not imagine Milton Campos working for the suspension of political rights or "removing legal obstacles so that the revolution could really be carried out." But Castello said that steps which went beyond legality did not appeal to him and that he wanted a jurist for rehabilitating legality.

Castello spoke also of appointing Juarez Távora minister of transport and Vasco Leitão da Cunha foreign minister. Lacerda, noting that Castello was advising about "consummated facts," remarked simply: "It is your cabinet."[11]

Speaking to Abreu Sodré a little later, Lacerda said he would not attend the inauguration of a government whose ministry was made up of "conservatives and *entreguistas.*" He named General Salvador Mandim and Sandra Cavalcanti to represent Guanabara at the inauguration and told them to advise the new president that Letícia was ill and that he was in need of a complete rest.[12] Mandim and Sandra, after flying to Brasília in the *Esperança,* heard a concise inauguration speech in which Castello spoke of his humility and need of support. Touching on foreign affairs, Castello declared that Brazil's allies would be the "democratic and free nations," and that the historic alliances with the great countries of the Americas would be preserved and strengthened. Turning to the domestic scene, he said: "Let us move ahead with assurance that the remedy for evil deeds by the extreme Left will not be the birth of a reactionary Right, but the reforms that have become necessary."[13]

Castello, later on April 15, phoned Lacerda to inquire about Letícia's health. The gesture, which deeply touched Carlos, was beneficial to a relationship that the new president valued. Castello hoped to be succeeded by a civilian, and he regarded the Guanabara governor, who had revealed administrative ability, as a logical choice.[14] Lacerda, on April 16, wired Castello to express "the applause of my family and my government" for the inauguration speech. "For a long time," Lacerda said, "the nation has been waiting to hear those words with the tone of dignity in which they were pronounced and with the just and humane spirit in which they were conceived." Lacerda mentioned the "personal reasons" that had prevented his trip to Brasília, and his plan to go abroad following "several years of extreme tension and unrelenting struggle."[15]

Lacerda, contemplating an absence from Brazil of as much as sixty days, submitted the appropriate request to the legislature, and it was approved by two-thirds of the members present. As Vice Governor Eloy Dutra had lost his political rights, Lacerda proposed that Raphael de Almeida Magalhães, the state's secretary of government, be elected vice governor by the legislature.[16]

At the ceremony that made João Luís Brito e Cunha the successor of Health Secretary Raimundo de Brito, Lacerda declared that more political purges were needed in Guanabara. He was determined, he said, to use the Institutional Act "to remove from public service and the judiciary and legislature all who do not have our confidence because we cannot leave to the armed forces alone this cleanup that is being carried out." He added that he would see to it that the Act was not used to carry out "political persecutions or satisfy personal ambitions." In another speech, he attacked the left wing of the Brazilian Catholic Church, mentioning Ação Católica and Archbishop Hélder Câmara. Speaking in his apartment to a group of young military officers, the governor gave the impression of considering himself the only person who had the answers to all of Brazil's problems. His conceit shocked the men, longtime admirers of the crusader against the Vargas regime.[17]

With Armando Falcão acting as intermediary, arrangements were made for Lacerda to lunch with Castello in Brasília on Sunday, April 19. In the presidential plane that Castello made available, Lacerda was accompanied by Guanabara Casa Civil Chief Marcelo Garcia, businessman José Luiz Moreira de Souza, Dr. Rebello, and aide-de-camp Carlos Osório.[18]

Foreign Minister Leitão da Cunha, also on the plane, sat next to the governor and told him that the president had spoken to him about a mission to take Lacerda abroad. He could, Leitão said, make Lacerda a member of a delegation that was going to Geneva for a conference on trade. He told Lacerda that he would not have to work at the conference, whereupon Lacerda became indignant and said he was not seeking a sinecure and that Leitão ought to know better than that.[19]

Lacerda, reaching Brasília for the first time in thirty-two months, was given a reception worthy of a head of a nation. Along with hundreds of citizens, who greeted the plane by waving white handkerchiefs and singing "Cidade Maravilhosa," were Casa Militar Chief Ernesto Geisel, Justice Minister Milton Campos as well as other cabinet ministers, and about thirty congressmen. The cars that took the visiting group to Alvorada Palace, the presidential residence, included the black Mercedes Benz formerly used by Assis Brasil. At the palace entrance the group was greeted by the president and his daughter.[20]

In the palace library, where Castello and Lacerda spoke alone for thirty minutes, Lacerda suggested that the president establish a ministry of information.[21] Castello's suggestion to Lacerda was that he explain the Brazilian revolution to governments and people abroad and give interviews. "All over the place," Castello said, "the revolution is being described as a fascist coup, as a coup by the Americans, and, above all, there is much distrust on account of stories about the military taking over and the military never leaving after taking over." Lacerda, who had recently made a "Face the Nation" video tape for release in New York to deny that the revolution was "a traditional

military coup," exclaimed "splendid" when he heard Castello's suggestion.[22] Thus he agreed to follow the footsteps of his father, who,
after the 1930 revolution, was sent to Uruguay to explain it.

During an interval at the Hotel Nacional, between this meeting
and the lunch at the palace, Lacerda told the press of his joy in seeing,
for the first time in years, a good man in the presidency. He confirmed
that he was still a presidential candidate. "Speaking without false
modesty, I expect to be living here in 1966."[23]

Following the lunch, Lacerda went to Congress to speak with UDN
senators and congressmen. Discussing *cassações* (suspensions of political rights and mandates), he suggested that the government arrange for the reexamination of some cases. He told of having been
asked by a Swiss television interviewer whether the victims of
cassações had the right of defense and of having replied that if the
Swiss were interested in "resolving our problems" they should collaborate by preventing the receipt in their banks of money "robbed
from Brazil."

Accompanied by Costa Cavalcanti, he went from Congress to pay
a courtesy call on General Costa e Silva, who was Castello's war
minister. He learned that when the general, punisher of corruption
and subversion, had spoken alone with Ademar de Barros on the night
the governors had found the commander in chief obdurate, he had
told Ademar that he would tolerate his remaining in the São Paulo
governorship only if he would abandon his presidential candidacy.[24]

Lacerda left the war minister's residence in an excellent mood.[25]
He looked forward to his trip abroad and to becoming the UDN's
presidential candidate after returning from it. Already, at a heated
meeting with Bilac Pinto at Guanabara Palace, he had rejected Bilac's
suggestion that he make an "unselfish and patriotic" gesture by stepping aside, because "a new process has begun in the country." "The
candidacy," Lacerda had declared, "is not mine. It was launched by
our companions, by the almost unanimous decision of the national
UDN."[26]

Kubitschek, Lacerda's chief opponent in the presidential race, was
beginning to be downgraded in the press and was in an insecure position, the result of the animosity of military victors who were establishing investigating commissions, some of them to look into the
former president's electoral deals with the Communist Party, as well
as the sources of his assets. Justice Minister Milton Campos, seeking
to explain "excesses" in "revolutionary purges," described them as a
reaction to "the first maneuvers of Kubitschek and the PTB" and a
result of the "intense desire of the revolutionary military leaders"
not to repeat the failure in 1954 to use an opportunity "to deal

effectively with Communism and corruption."[27] Lacerda, when talking with UDN congressmen in Brasília, said that Kubitschek, on the eve of the victory of the revolution, was still "proposing deals" with Jango Goulart. "Now Kubitschek has aged fifty years in five years."[28]

5. A New Vice Governor for Guanabara (April 21-25, 1964)

Lacerda was confident that his proposal to have the Guanabara legislature name Raphael de Almeida Magalhães vice governor would be good for the state. However, the state constitution provided for no such election, as Lígia Lessa Bastos (UDN) and oppositionists pointed out. It stipulated that if the governor and vice governor were out of the picture (as would be the case with Lacerda abroad and Eloy Dutra *cassado*), the state was to be run by the legislature's president and, if he were unavailable, by the presiding justice of the state's tribunal.[1]

Vitorino James, the legislature's president, did not like Lacerda's proposal and said no election was called for.[2] Quite a few of the oppositionist legislators who agreed with James said that, if there should be an election, they would vote for Danillo Nunes. Nunes, like Kubitschek, had been quoted as warning against "excesses" by the Revolutionary Command.[3]

Such warnings went unheeded. The Revolutionary Command, prior to Castello's inauguration, kept issuing lists of *cassações*. A list issued on April 14 included the names of six PTB Guanabara legislators, among them Paulo Alberto Monteiro de Barros, José Saldanha Coelho, Ib Teixeira, and José Gomes Talarico.[4] PTB spokesman Horácio Franco, a Danillo Nunes supporter, said that his party, under the circumstances, hesitated to express its opinions. The PSD, during the battle about finding a successor to Lacerda, displayed anxiety from time to time about rumors of new *cassações*.[5]

Oppositionist legislators were nervous on April 17 when Colonel Américo Fontenelle visited the state assembly and asserted that it would be in serious trouble unless it made Raphael vice governor. The colonel gave the impression of speaking for the Revolutionary Command, and therefore oppositionists in the legislature, along with Danillo Nunes and Vitorino James, reacted indignantly to the apparent pressure. After signatures were gathered to set up a CPI to investigate what lay behind Fontenelle's aggressive pronouncement, the colonel declared that he had simply expressed his own opinion about the desire of Lacerda.[6]

Mauro Magalhães, after consulting fellow-legislators, concluded that Raphael was far from their favorite and proposed to Lacerda that he settle on Célio Borja, saying that he would be a unanimous choice. But Lacerda was determined to turn the governorship over to Raphael before departing for Europe by plane late on the afternoon of Wednesday, April 22. It was rumored that he might cancel his trip if the legislature ignored his wish.

On April 22, when the legislature met to consider adopting a measure that would allow it to elect a vice governor that day, Lacerda used the telephone to have what Abreu Sodré describes as "terrible verbal altercations" with Vitorino James. Also, the governor announced that he had signed a decree creating a commission to carry out, during his absence, "summary investigations of assaults made in Guanabara against the national security."[7]

In the legislature, UDN leader Célio Borja argued that the lack of an elected vice governor might mean chaos and bring about federal intervention in the state assembly. But Augusto Amaral Peixoto (PSD), who said "Lacerda thinks he is dictator of Brazil," led an effective opposition, assisted by Gonzaga da Gama Filho (PSD), Jamil Haddad (PSB), Sinval Sampaio (PTB), Telêmaco Maia (PR), and Levi Neves (PSP). The opposition, supported by the UDN's Lígia Bastos, pointed out that the election was illegal and that the assembly's regulations required that Wednesdays be set aside for the work of its commissions. Mac Dowell Leite de Castro (UDN), head of the justice commission, was eager to reveal verbally his commission's report about the possibility of holding an election for vice governor, but the opposition demanded a normal handling of the report, including its publication. Enough signatures, twenty, were placed on a call for ending the morning session.[8]

The afternoon session was deplorable. During arguments about whether Gonzaga da Gama Filho had falsified a signature on the document ending the morning session and was, besides, guilty of corruption, Gama Filho disparaged the masculinity of his accuser, Everardo Magalhães Castro (PDC). Magalhães Castro gave him a bloody face with a blow struck while Gama Filho and Edson Guimarães were locked in a physical struggle.

As Lacerda demanded, Vitorino James called for an election for vice governor. He refused to let Lígia Bastos, Gama Filho, or Augusto Amaral Peixoto be heard, and therefore the opposition blocked the election by violence. Struggles to get control of the ballot box and the microphones ended in fistfights during which Telêmaco Maia took the ballot box out of the meeting place. The fighting became so serious that the police had to intervene.

Vitorino James, citing the riot, closed the session. He declared that he had explained to Lacerda that "pressure" ought not to be used in handling the matter. He also said that his own role in the affair, carried out against his wishes, had been to bypass the state and federal constitutions, the legislature's regulations, and the election law, and had placed him in a position that was not "compatible" with his running the state government. He was, he announced, taking a thirty-day leave for reasons of health.[9]

Therefore it was to Judge Vicente de Faria Coelho that Lacerda turned over the government. In the ceremony at Guanabara Palace, Lacerda said that the tumult at the assembly gave him the impression that "the revolution has not completed its cleanup work." He pointed out that the vice gubernatorial matter, set back by the minority's tactics, had yet to be handled. Vicente Coelho promised to do everything he could to help and told Lacerda to regain his health in order to return to run the state and later the nation.[10]

The next morning's headlines in the *Diário Carioca* and *Correio da Manhã* praised the legislative assembly for its victory on behalf of the constitution. The *Correio da Manhã* wrote enthusiastically that the candidacy of Raphael de Almeida Magalhães was "definitely buried."[11] But Célio Borja, with help from Raphael, Mauro Magalhães, and Mac Dowell Leite de Castro, was able to put together a progovernment bloc of twenty-six. Raphael was popular with the Cariocas and was supported, Mauro Magalhães recalls, by important figures outside the assembly who exerted influence on legislators. He listened sympathetically when legislators spoke of their needs and was in a position to promise appointments and other favors.[12]

On April 24, twenty-eight legislators, including the PSD's Miécimo da Silva, signed Célio Borja's call for a special session to elect a vice governor. In the election, on the afternoon of April 25, prolonged applause in the galleries greeted the twenty-eighth vote for Raphael, which gave him the victory. By the time the voting ended, he had forty-two votes.[13] The legislature's acting president, Amando da Fonseca (PSD), had been cooperative with the election and set a date, May 8, for Raphael to take office.[14]

After the election, Danillo Nunes declared that he could have beaten Raphael but at the cost of splitting the UDN, and the opposition revealed that it had appealed to Military Club President Augusto Magessi to run against Raphael but he had refused. Danton Jobim, writing in the *Diário Carioca*, explained the turmoil of April 22 as the only avenue open to men who had struggled for the independence of the legislature and against a flagrantly illegal act carried out to satisfy the "insolent" Lacerda.[15]

The PSD expelled Amando da Fonseca and Miécimo da Silva from its legislative assembly group. Under the leadership of Carioca PSD

President Augusto Amaral Peixoto, a so-called "strong opposition" bloc was formed of the eleven legislators who had refrained from voting for Raphael. It appealed to the courts to annul his election.[16]

Raphael, it was charged, had not been an eligible candidate, because he had not resigned from his state cabinet post. Lígia Bastos said that the Institutional Act's clause eliminating ineligibilities applied to candidates to federal executive posts, not state executive posts. Danton Jobim, however, guessed that a judge could be found who would support Lacerda by saying that "no incompatibilities exist in a revolutionary regime."

The Regional Electoral Tribunal was quick to call Raphael's election legitimate, but the Carioca PSD appealed to the Supreme Court. There the appeal was rejected, in an 8 to 2 decision, about a year after the election.[17]

6. The Orly Airport Interview
(Paris, April 23, 1964)

When Lacerda stopped at Guanabara Palace early in the evening of April 22 to transfer the governorship to Judge Vicente Coelho, he was on his way to Galeão Airport, where a crowd of 2,500 well-wishers was on hand. The Air France plane's departure was held up for almost two hours to allow him to board, with Letícia and Cristina, the Abreu Sodrés, and Joana Abreu Corrêa, a niece of Letícia's. He was, Abreu Sodré has written, "like a boy on a holiday" when he took his seat on the plane for the trip that was to take the party to Italy.[1]

Lacerda slept poorly during the transatlantic flight. Long before dawn, at a stop at the Lisbon Airport, he handled reporters' questions about Angola and Mozambique. Why, he asked, should Brazil favor self-rule for those Portuguese colonies, when they lacked political forces strong enough to demand self-rule and when neighboring countries, recently created, sought the independence of Angola and Mozambique in order to bring them into a system of imperialism led by Russia?[2]

In Madrid, where the plane landed at 5:00 A.M., Lacerda declared that he would be president of Brazil within two years. He praised Castello Branco, "the foremost intellectual among the generals and the foremost general among the intellectuals."[3]

Some of the questions of the Spanish reporters about the Brazilian revolution seemed so "indiscreet" to Abreu Sodré that he worried about what lay ahead on the trip. Meanwhile, in Paris, similar misgivings were felt by Brazilian journalist Newton Freitas, who had come from Algeria and found the Paris press pro-Goulart and unanimously determined to battle Lacerda, pictured by some Parisians as a "sombrero-wearing Mexican-type of general with cartridge-bearing straps on his chest." Abreu Sodré recommended that Lacerda be uncommunicative at the stop to be made in Paris. Lacerda agreed. He simply joked with reporters while he and his party made their way to the Orly Airport restaurant to gather with some of the Brazilians who were in Paris, such as Gilberto Amado, writer and former ambassador.[4]

The restaurant was invaded at 7:30 A.M. by a group of newspaper and television reporters, whose questions seemed to the Brazilians so insulting to their country that Lacerda, unable to remain silent, rebutted them. Shocked to hear talk of torture in Brazil, he denied it emphatically. He ended up in the airport press room, which adjoined the restaurant. There, under the lights of three television cameras, he faced a battery of radio and television microphones, forty reporters, and over twenty photographers. Four reporters in the front row opened with a barrage of questions about "the domination by generals," and the "fascist coup" unleashed "to protect North American interests, principally petroleum interests." Speaking in excellent French, Lacerda gave what Abreu Sodré has called "the most magnificent show of intelligence and courage I had ever seen."[5]

The questions about Brazil led Lacerda to say that some French correspondents, twisting facts completely, were either "imbeciles" or had "sold out." "I believe," he said, "that the French press also reported nothing correctly in the crisis of 1939, when a part of the press sold France to the Nazis. Today they are trying to sell it to the Communists, and they place Communist or pro-Communist correspondents in my country. . . . There's a person, a poor devil, a Brazilian who is a militant Communist and who is correspondent of *Le Monde*. . . . He sends false reports and therefore you ask me a question that would make no sense if you were in Brazil. The deposed government, the government of João Goulart, never made any reform. He bought 550,000 hectares of land for himself. That was the only reform that he really started."[6]

A reporter objected to Lacerda's attack against a newspaper that "is regarded as one of the most objective in France." "If you think it is objective to call the governor of Minas Gerais very rich simply because he is a banker, and you don't mention as very rich the Brazilian presidents who have numbered Swiss bank accounts, what is objective?" Lacerda shot back. He described the so-called objective reporting as "an insult to the intelligence of France, not to us, for we know the facts. You are the ones who don't know them."

But what, someone asked, were the plans the deposed president had

had for Brazil? "To make it a colony of Russia" was the answer. Asked whether the Brazilian revolution had been affected by "foreign pressure," Lacerda replied in the affirmative, citing "the pressure of some foreign newspapers." But, he added, "that did not impress us." What about "American support?" a reporter inquired, whereupon Lacerda said there was none, because "we don't have the Marshall Plan like you here, at least up to now."[7]

Asked if there had been bloodshed during the revolution, Lacerda got some laughs when he answered that "Brazilian revolutions are like wedding nights in France—no blood."[8] In reply to a question about "the witch hunt" in Brazil, the governor got more laughs by saying that the only witch he knew was Beuve-Mery, the director of *Le Monde,* but that he was a poor witch because he knew how to carry on witchcraft only on the pages of his newspaper. Speaking of the Communists in Brazil, Lacerda declared that they were "alive and well! We don't kill them!" He said that altogether 860 people had been "detained," but that only about 200 remained in prison. "Among them are nine Chinese, one of whom was an international spy."[9]

Asked about French-Brazilian relations, Lacerda spoke of a letter, "not very friendly," in which de Gaulle had written Goulart: "I accept your act of repentance." "It is not proper," Lacerda told the reporters, "for a French general to accept the repentance of the president of Brazil. I believe that France is not yet a monarchy . . . although at times it gives that impression." Asked what could be expected from de Gaulle's proposed visit to Brazil, Lacerda said: "Banquets and speeches." "But what else?" someone asked. "More speeches," he said, getting another laugh. He called actress Brigitte Bardot the best ambassador from France in recent years. Asked to comment on his reputation for overthrowing presidents, Lacerda said he did not overthrow presidents. "They fall like ripe fruit," he explained, and went on to say that "there is an overthrower of presidents more illustrious than I. He is the president of France, whom I respect, the illustrious General de Gaulle, who overthrew a president before I did."[10]

If Kubitschek should come to Europe, Lacerda said, "without doubt it will be to move to Switzerland." And what about Goulart, he was asked; would he be jailed if he returned to Brazil? "Probably, as a thief." "And if it were up to you to decide?" "I would send him to France and condemn him to read the correspondents of *Le Monde.*" Reporters laughed again.[11]

The French press reacted violently to Lacerda's interview. The best-selling *France Soir,* screaming that Lacerda had attacked France, explained that the governor, a man who "never forgives," had been miffed three months earlier because a French parliamentary mission

A LAGOSTA E NOSSA

"The lobster is ours," showing de Gaulle. (Hilde Weber drawing in
O Estado de S. Paulo, February 23, 1963)

had visited Brazil without calling on him. *Le Monde* called Lacerda
an ex-Communist supporter of a military dictatorship and said that
"General de Gaulle will be enchanted to know that his visit to Brazil
is going to be reduced to banquets and speeches, that he should not
behave as a king, and that Brigitte Bardot is the best ambassador from
our country." The leftist *Liberation* described Lacerda as "spitting in
the soup." But the conservative *Le Figaro* also attacked Lacerda, and
so did the right-wing *Aurore*, staunch supporter of the recent Brazilian revolution. Ireneu Guimarães, *Le Monde*'s correspondent in Brazil, denied that he had ever been a Communist.[12]

In Paris Gilberto Amado told French journalists that a proof of their
ignorance of Brazil was their failure to appreciate the brilliance of
Lacerda. Meanwhile in Rio, a group of pro-Lacerda students plastered
signs on the walls of the French embassy calling *Le Monde* even more
untruthful than *Última Hora*, and accusing France of wanting—as it
had wanted earlier—to make off with lobsters from Brazilian waters.

In the *Tribuna da Imprensa*, Hélio Fernandes wrote that de Gaulle
had entered into a "pact of common action" with President Goulart
to work for the reduction of the influence of the United States in
Latin America, and that the entire French press shared de Gaulle's
disappointment that the Brazilian revolution had terminated the

arrangement. Fernandes added that de Gaulle's anti-U.S. position had led him to approve the plan of President Goulart to carry out a coup on May 1 with Communist allies.[13]

The Orly Airport interview gave ammunition to Brazilians who felt that Lacerda was temperamentally unsuited to be president. Planning Minister Roberto Campos considered the interview "a disaster." General Golbery do Couto e Silva, who had been working closely with Castello Branco since February, found it "very aggressive."[14]

The interview also created difficulties for Itamaraty, the Brazilian foreign ministry, which was asked by French diplomats whether Lacerda had spoken as an official representative of Brazil. An angry de Gaulle advised the Brazilian government that he would decide whether to include Brazil on his Latin American tour only after Brazil "defined its position with respect to the interview."[15]

Lacerda had left for Europe so quickly after the official nature of his trip had been determined that there had not been time to furnish him with his diplomatic credentials. They would, he had been told, reach him in Milan, where he spent the first few days of his trip. The failure of the credentials to arrive in Milan, or in any of the cities he visited during his three-week stay in Italy, vexed him enormously. He told Abreu Sodré that the Brazilian government's failure to keep its word to him was a maneuver to liquidate him politically and destroy his presidential candidacy.[16]

Lacerda entered into an exchange of cables with Foreign Minister Leitão da Cunha that lasted beyond the Italian visit. Abreu Sodré, in charge of sending cables from Milan, Venice, and Florence, modified messages to make them less offensive; in this tactful work he was helped by Alfredo Machado and Antônio Carlos de Almeida Braga, who joined the group in Italy together with their wives. "Unfortunately," Abreu Sodré writes, when the travelers reached Rome on May 6, they stayed at a hotel that had a telex that Lacerda used himself, sending "expressions that became more violent each day." Sodré tried to explain to Lacerda, "whose patience was at an end," that the failure of the credentials to arrive had nothing to do with a conspiracy against him at home but was the result of de Gaulle's reaction to the Orly interview.[17]

Besides bombarding Leitão da Cunha with cables, Lacerda sent telegrams from Italy to Paris newspapers. Although he told *Le Figaro* that he had never "confused France and its people with certain troublemakers," the conservative daily remained displeased with the tone of the interview and with Lacerda's failure to modify his views about "imbeciles and people who sold out." "It is not my fault," Lacerda telegraphed *Le Monde*, "that Goulart is considered a reformer simply because he spoke of reforms, just as Hitler was called a pacifist because he spoke of peace." Lacerda's telegram to *France Soir* regretted that Paris press comments continued to be "untruthful."[18]

7. Sandra Cavalcanti's Peace Mission to Paris (May 1964)

While in Europe in the spring of 1964, Lacerda devoted so much time making arrangements for organizations abroad to participate in the observations of Rio's four hundredth anniversary in 1965 that Victor Bouças, the Guanabara secretary of tourism, came to feel that the governor's trip was undertaken chiefly for that purpose. While in Italy, Lacerda worked out preliminary arrangements for the participation of artistic and festival groups of Venice, industrialists of Milan, and performers of La Scala Theater. Plans were made to ship Italian paintings to Rio for exhibition.[1]

Lacerda enjoyed showing cultural and historic sights to his thirteen-year-old daughter Cristina. Sports enthusiast Almeida Braga, on the other hand, displayed no enthusiasm for visits to museums. Nevertheless, in Florence on the morning of April 30, Lacerda's fiftieth birthday, Almeida Braga joined the others in visiting an art gallery. Only Letícia, reportedly suffering from a cold, did not go along.[2]

As Maria Abreu Sodré was born on April 30, the dinner that night at the Excelsior Hotel was a joint celebration, at which Carlos gave her a silver snuff box he had bought that morning at the Ponte Vecchia; it displayed the head of Queen Victoria and was, he felt, appropriate for Maria, whom he liked to call Victorian. For Carlos, Alfredo Machado had a surprise: a painting that was revealed to the partying group with the removal of a large towel that had covered it. It was a portrait of Cristina that had been painted by the Italian artist Erico Bianco in Rio before the trip. A less welcome surprise awaited Lacerda on the following day: a May Day demonstration against him by Italians who opposed the revolution and military takeover in Brazil.[3]

In the Vatican on May 9, the travelers were received by the Pope, who accepted an invitation to send a delegation to Rio for the city's anniversary commemorations. According to Lacerda, the "most pleasant day" during the week in Rome was the one on which he felt he was able to correct the "confused" ideas held by students and Catholic teachers of the Pio Brasileiro School. He denied the "torture and imprisonment" of members of the Catholic clergy in Brazil.[4]

From Rome, Abreu Sodré flew to Paris, at Lacerda's request, to learn "the exact position" of the French government regarding Lacerda's mission. Lacerda, who flew with the others to Athens, chose to accept, at the Athens airport, the ride to his hotel offered by Constantinos Doxiadis instead of the one offered by Brazilian Ambassador Antônio Mendes Vianna. Nonetheless, Lacerda took second place to Alfredo Machado in alienating the Brazilian embassy. Machado, during the four-day stay in Athens, sent mischievous messages to the embassy declining to attend parties to which he had not been invited.[5]

A part of the stay in Athens was spent with Doxiadis, ideal guide to sights that particularly delighted Cristina, who had developed an interest in archaeology.[6]

While Lacerda brought his "telegraphic war" with Itamaraty to new heights of hostility, Abreu Sodré in Paris received Itamaraty's mission to fly to Athens to make sure that Lacerda would not go to Paris before receiving his credentials. Sodré, upon reaching Athens, was advised by Almeida Braga not to deliver the message lest it simply provoke Lacerda into going to Paris. Lacerda, as Braguinha predicted, resolved to go to Paris "with or without credentials" after he heard what Sodré had to tell him.[7]

The decision to go to Paris coincided with an announcement by Itamaraty confirming Lacerda's mission but explaining that it had become official only after his Orly Airport interview of April 23. Brazil's chargé d'affaires in Paris, Raul de Vicenzi, disliked Lacerda but was at the airport to receive him on May 18. No representative of France was on hand. The French press was avoided.[8]

The Communist L'Humanité deplored the presence of "the Brazilian fascist." To protest his presence, the French Communist Party organized a demonstration outside the Hotel Plaza Athenée, where the Lacerdas stayed. It attracted several thousand, mostly students, who shouted slogans written on the posters: "Lacerda assassin" and "Liberty for the Democrats." The noisy manifestation made a considerable impression on Joaquim and Candinha da Silveira, who had come to join the Lacerdas and who found Letícia ill and nervous. Candinha, also nervous, threw a glass of water from a hotel window on the demonstrators. Carlos calmly told her: "Don't do that, Candinha. I am quite accustomed to this sort of thing."[9]

Lacerda, explaining the Brazilian revolution a day or so later during a radio interview with an Associated Press reporter, said that his remarks about Paris press correspondents had been meant for only some of them, not all. He declared that de Gaulle's visit to Brazil would be welcome and important and explained that his earlier comment on the visit had been inspired by the poor planning for it made by prerevolutionary Brazil, "a Brazil that no longer exists." His remark about Brigitte Bardot, he said, had been intended to insult no one. Asked about what some Paris journalists called a "witch hunt" in Brazil, Lacerda admitted that imprisonments had perhaps been "exaggerated" in the "confusion" following the brief revolution, but he assured his audience that juridical order had been reestablished. "We had to suspend the rights of some congressmen in order to keep Congress open." "There is no press censorship," he added.

Speaking of his mission, Lacerda confirmed that he had received it from Castello Branco and announced that he would be received on May 25 by President Heinrich Luebke of West Germany and would be in London early in June as official guest of the British government.[10]

Lacerda's remarks to the Associated Press did not persuade de Gaulle to receive him. Therefore Lacerda, who had a letter of introduction to de Gaulle from Castello, handed it to de Gaulle Minister Louis Joxe during a small dinner. He told the French minister that he understood perfectly that de Gaulle would not receive him "because of the enormous intrigue" and went on to speak of his fondness for France, starting with his early education at a French school in Rio.[11]

In Brazil the press occasionally mentioned the possibility of Lacerda's heading the Brazilian delegation to the United Nations. From sources said to have been close to Guanabara Palace, Castello Branco heard that Lacerda was interested in leaving the governorship if he could become a roving ambassador. The president therefore consulted Sandra Cavalcanti, a longtime friend of the Castello Brancos and the author of a housing bank study being considered by Castello's team. She knew nothing about any wish of Lacerda to leave the governorship and attributed the report to Vice Governor Raphael de Almeida Magalhães, whom she did not like. "All people," she said to Castello, have their weaknesses. Yours was to name Roberto Campos minister. The weakness of Carlos Lacerda is Raphael."[12]

Castello asked Sandra to fly to Paris to learn firsthand what Lacerda had in mind. He also asked her to tell Lacerda that he opposed the suggestion of Senator João Agripino that his presidential term be extended for a year—an extension being given consideration by Congress in connection with a political reform that would allow congressional and presidential elections to coincide. In São Paulo, Júlio de Mesquita Filho had reached the conclusion that the extension of Castello's mandate would benefit Brazil, and he sent Oscar Klabin Segall to Paris with a letter to Lacerda to suggest that Lacerda head a movement in favor of the extension.

According to the press, Sandra flew to Europe to study popular housing there and clear up misunderstandings between Lacerda and Leitão da Cunha, arising from Lacerda's criticism of the Brazilian embassy in France. Sandra's trip, described by Abreu Sodré as "a peace mission," was a success. Strolling with the governor in the spring-time by the Seine, she informed him that Castello had authorized her to advise Lacerda of Castello's opposition to an extension of the presidential term. "He thinks you can feel tranquil and should protest, with help from our companions, against the extension," she told him. "For a moment," Lacerda said, "I thought your uncle [a reference to Castello, who was not her uncle] might have sent you here to get my support for the extension of his term."[13]

When Sandra asked Lacerda if he planned to return to the governorship, he answered that he would do so within a few weeks. "Why?" he asked. "What about your becoming a roving ambassador?" she asked in return. "I don't know who invented this," Lacerda said.

Lacerda was in a good mood. He appreciated the consideration of Castello in sending Sandra to ask about his plans and inform him of Castello's opposition to an extension of the presidential mandate. Sandra felt that it would be inappropriate to speak to him about Raphael, who, she believed, was plotting to step into the governorship by promoting an ambassadorial post for Lacerda.[14]

Back in Rio, after about two weeks in Europe, Sandra brought to the Guanabara legislature Lacerda's request for a thirty-day extension of his sixty-day leave. Invited to lunch with the president at Laranjeiras Palace, she reported on her visit with Lacerda. Castello, she found, was mostly interested in learning about the theatrical performances she had seen in Paris.[15]

8. Acclaim in Portugal (June 12-17, 1964)

In contrast to the French government, the governments of West Germany, Great Britain, and Portugal received Lacerda with honors and warmth. The governor, after his conference with President Luebke, spoke to the press about German assistance and investments that would make Brazil "a powerful Common Market ally." In West Berlin, he told Mayor Willy Brandt of his decision to construct in Rio a monument to the "Wall of Shame," thus contributing to Brazilian understanding of "the horrors of Communism."[1]

At the British Parliament Lacerda was in the Distinguished Visitors' Gallery during a debate in the House of Commons, and he was, after that, in Stratford-upon-Avon for an exposition marking the four hundredth anniversary of Shakespeare's birth. In talks in London with British cabinet ministers and bankers, and at a Chatham House meeting, he explained the Brazilian situation.[2]

Asked by reporters to comment on the suspension of Kubitschek's

Castello Branco with heads of Kubitschek and Quadros. Ademar de Barros looks from window. (APPE drawing in *O Cruzeiro*, July 4, 1964)

political rights, decreed by Castello Branco on June 8, Lacerda limited himself to remarks about the end of the PSD epoch in Brazilian politics and the start of a new era.[3] He had played no role in the decision about Kubitschek,[4] reached in the almost unanimous vote of the National Security Council (consisting mainly of the cabinet), but he may not have been surprised, in view of the aggressively anti-Kubitschek attitude of the "hard line" military, headed by Costa e Silva.

The greatest acclaim for Lacerda on foreign soil was that given by Portugal. Pictures and favorable accounts of his six days there filled the Lisbon press, and crowds received him as a hero. Guanabara Tourism Secretary Victor Bouças, who went to Lisbon two days ahead of Lacerda, calls the reception "fantastic, as though Lacerda were a visiting head of state." Walter and Lamy Cunto, who joined the Lacerda party in Lisbon, found the reception "simply stupendous" and concluded that Carlos was more deeply loved in Portugal than in Brazil. A loudspeaker announcement of his presence in a bull ring resulted in a great ovation.[5]

According to British author Richard Bourne, Lacerda "repaid" the compliments he received in the controlled Portuguese press by speaking in opposition to the desire of the United Nations to interfere with Portugal's administration of its overseas territories.[6] But if there was repayment, it may have been the other way around, for these opinions had long ago been formed and expressed by Lacerda.

Antônio Salazar, incredibly well informed about the views of prominent Brazilians,[7] was probably familiar with Lacerda's past pronouncements about Portugal and Salazar, such as those made in Congress in April 1959 and those published in the same month in the *Tribuna da Imprensa*, praising the "lucidity" of the Portuguese dictator.[8]

At Salazar's insistence, Lacerda remained with him for two hours on June 15, 1964. During a part of the time, Salazar defended his policy toward Portugal's colonies: "Some seek to compare the case of Portugal in Africa with the case of the independence of Brazil. But Brazil had a developed political formation when it became independent. It was the Brazilians who wanted independence. Not foreigners seeking to stir up civil war in order to replace Portuguese control with that of a more powerful outsider."[9]

Lacerda was "astounded" by Salazar's knowledge of Brazil. But Salazar confessed that he could not understand how a country "on the brink of an abyss, suddenly jumps across it." Lacerda, welcoming candid dialogue, told Salazar that he was handicapped in not having visited Brazil and in being "irremediably Cartesian." "You carry logic to the extreme. And Brazil is a Hegelian country. Brazil makes jumps. It is a country of theses, antitheses, and syntheses. Besides, if you will allow, I have something else to say. If liberty were a gland, Your Excellency would be without that gland. I hope I'm not offending you. What I want to say is that liberty for you is a secondary thing. What is important for you is security, unity, salvation, in short the preservation of the nation. . . . For Brazilians liberty is essential."[10]

Salazar, who said he found nothing offensive in Lacerda's remarks, joined the governor at a banquet a few hours later. During the banquet, given in Lacerda's honor, a group of girls presented a dress, typical of the province of Minho, to Cristina.[11]

Following the first official event of the visit to Portugal, a session during which President Américo Tomaz decorated and publicly embraced Lacerda, the schedule was a full one, with speeches, interviews, conferences with cabinet ministers, banquets, a trip to the Fátima shrine, and a session at the Lisbon Municipal Council.[12] Sometimes the official guest seemed to have too much to do. Forty-two writers, among them his friend Luís Forjaz Trigueiros, were kept waiting until 1:00 A.M. because Lacerda, following a banquet, unexpectedly made a recording at a television studio. And when Lacerda found the foreign minister among the writers, he closeted himself with him until 3:00 A.M. Only those who shared Lacerda's ability to stay up most of the night had the opportunity to chat and drink with him. He reached his hotel, the Ritz, at 6:00 A.M., bathed, and set forth on another schedule-filled day, starting with an interview at 8:00 A.M.[13]

Lacerda discussed the Flamengo Park beach at the Portuguese National Engineering Laboratory and made arrangements with the public works minister to have the laboratory study reports about pollution in Guanabara Bay. But Lacerda's chief activity on behalf of his state concerned Portugal's participation in Rio's Fourth Centennial commemorations. Portugal agreed to send a statue of João VI and to construct, for placement in Guanabara Bay, a replica of the caravel used by Pedro Alvares Cabral in discovering Brazil. Plans were made for a Portuguese pavilion to be set up in Rio and for Portuguese folkloric groups to perform in Guanabara and other states.[14] Victor Bouças, believing that the Guandu aqueduct was the foremost project of Lacerda's administration, presented the governor with an idea for a "monument made of water"—a jet of water to go 70 meters into the air from Rodrigo de Freitas Lagoon. Lacerda approved of the idea and therefore Bouças went to Lake Geneva to consult Swiss hydraulic engineers. Abreu Sodré went from Lisbon to Brazil, where he submitted a report to Leitão da Cunha about the accomplishments of Lacerda's mission in Europe.[15]

Before Lacerda left Lisbon for New York, he was again asked by reporters to comment on the *cassação* of Kubitschek. In reply, he called the question delicate. "If I express enthusiasm, I give the impression of being pleased with the elimination of an adversary. But this aspect of the matter does not please me." He said he had wanted to defeat Kubitschek in the ballot boxes and had felt confident that he would do so, because the "father of inflation could not benefit from the monster he created." On the other hand, Lacerda said, "if I comment unfavorably on the *cassação*, I give the impression of opposing an act that I consider an act of political courage, an act of civic vision. Therefore I avoid making a declaration about the problem created by Kubitschek, but I do believe that he himself understands that he cannot be the beneficiary of a system that was destroyed and at the same time continue to be the beneficiary of its destruction."[16]

9. Lacerda Cuts His Mission Short (July 1964)

United States journalists were far less friendly than the Portuguese. Lacerda found that out in Washington and New York after he and Letícia spent a day in Little Rock, Arkansas, consulting specialists about her hearing problems. In Washington on June 21, on a widely broadcast "Meet the Press" television program, Lacerda was kept on the defensive by questioners (Dan Kurzman, Peter Lisagor, Robert

MacNeil, and Tad Szulc) who appeared critical of a regime that had arrested thousands, and, without trials, suspended the political rights of men like Juscelino Kubitschek and Celso Furtado.

On the "Meet the Press" program, Lacerda said the number arrested was about 2,000, "of whom not more than 200 remain," whereupon Kurzman, of the *Washington Post,* revealed that Ademar de Barros had put the number arrested in his state alone at 3,500. In defending the *cassações* of 400 ("at the maximum") Lacerda argued that "we were in war, in a subversive war" and had to get rid of a thirty-four-year-old system of corruption, infiltrated by Communism. He called Kubitschek "a very smiling, nice, tropical version of Jimmie Walker," New York's lax former mayor, and lauded Castello Branco for having had the courage to "cancel his political rights." Pointing out that Castello had been faced with making a decision before the expiration of the sixty-day period allowed for *cassações* by the Institutional Act, Lacerda expressed the belief that a "fair judgment" would be granted to the *cassados* after the completion of investigations, still under way. He said that all he knew about Furtado was that he had sabotaged the Alliance for Progress program and, at the same time, had called it a failure.

After Peter Lisagor, of the *Chicago Daily News*, reminded Lacerda that despite his long role as an ardent, hard-hitting Brazilian oppositionist, he had never had his civil liberties suspended, Lacerda said: "No. They only tried to kill me several times. Nothing else." Commenting on another remark by Lisagor, Lacerda denied that President Johnson's rapid recognition of the new regime stirred up "latent anti-U.S. sentiment in Brazil." "On the contrary, I think it was a friendly gesture."[1]

At an American Brazilian Association banquet in New York two days later, Lacerda expressed his reaction to questions asked during the course of his mission. "So many people outside Brazil go around crying about the fate of men who robbed the Brazilian people that I am beginning to agree with those who think that many people here would prefer that Brazil be governed by persons of easy virtue, incompetent and dishonest. Is that really the sentiment of those who inform and guide North American public opinion about the so-called Latin American countries? The ignorance of some of them about my country, among them writers of books, is appalling."

Lacerda maintained that, if these writers wished, they could tell a great story of a Cold War battle "that we won without asking anyone's permission or receiving anyone's assistance." As the revolution had taken only forty-eight hours, leaving no time for "changes in the clichés and trite remarks about Brazil," Lacerda suggested that an understanding would have been easier to grasp if a large-scale civil war had occurred, with the bombardment of cities.[2]

Questions that had become familiar to him received his answers at the National Press Club in Washington on June 24 and at the Overseas Press Club in New York on June 25. He called Brasília "not a city but a problem" and described Furtado as having placed many Communists in high posts. Repeating that Castello had been courageous in suspending Kubitschek's political rights, he asked how a revolution could punish men who had carried out orders but overlook the commander who had issued the orders. He urged his listeners not to turn Kubitschek into a "myth."[3]

A new note was Lacerda's increased worry about political reform developments in Brazil. He admitted that in the past he had favored, for tactical reasons, an absolute majority requirement in presidential elections, but now he emphasized his opposition to the idea, which, he said, would not work where thirteen political parties existed and might put the final decision in the hands of Congress, which could ignore the wishes of the people.[4]

Brazil's new ambassador to the United States, Juracy Magalhães, was determined to help Lacerda's mission by setting up appointments for him in Washington. But soon after Lacerda went to the New York docks to greet Juracy on his arrival, their relations became cool. The first friction, of minor importance, occurred during a dinner at a small New York restaurant, also attended by Alfredo Machado and the Alfred A. Knopfs. Lacerda had the impression that Juracy was miffed because the Brazilian waiters, ignoring Juracy, expressed delight to be seeing Lacerda. After the diners found out that the waiters earned around $800 a month, mostly from tips, joke-loving Alfredo Machado remarked: "More than an ambassador." "And we people work," said a waiter, serving soup to Juracy. Juracy scolded the waiter for depreciating an ambassador's work, Machado assumed responsibility for Juracy's outburst, saying the waiter was not to blame, and the restaurant manager came over to find out what the fuss was about. "Nothing," Lacerda said. But he has described the atmosphere at the dinner as chilly. "The only warm thing was the food."[5]

Juracy and Carlos agreed that Carlos, following a speaking engagement in Akron, Ohio, on Saturday, June 27, would come that night from New York to Washington with Letícia. After resting at the embassy on Sunday, Carlos was to spend Monday with United States government officials. Juracy had his office arrange appointments with Walt W. Rostow and Thomas C. Mann, lunch with Congressman Armistead Selden and members of the House Latin American Affairs Committee, and visits with Secretary of State Dean Rusk,

Senator J. William Fulbright, and members of the Senate Foreign Relations Committee. The appointments were to be followed by a Brazilian embassy banquet, at which Carlos and Letícia would be the guests of honor.[6]

Juracy and Lavínia Magalhães waited in vain for the Lacerdas at the Washington airport late Saturday night. Although on the next morning Lacerda said he would arrive later on Sunday, Juracy's phone calls to New York's St. Regis Hotel on Sunday evening brought the news that Carlos would not go to Washington because he was tired and Letícia was suffering from a severe pain in the ear.

Juracy's phone calls were usually answered by Almeida Braga. Lacerda, primarily concerned with the seriousness with which the Brazilian Congress was considering a one-year extension of Castello's term, was exchanging cables and phone calls with Raphael de Almeida Magalhães.[7] In one of his cables, Lacerda said: "I consider this a betrayal of the Revolution. Under no circumstances am I willing to accept it. I shall not give up my candidacy." Another cable to Raphael objected to the proposed absolute majority requirement.[8]

Juracy, when he was able to get through to Lacerda, said that friends of Letícia could stay with her in New York on Monday and that cancellation of the appointments would put Brazil, its ambassador, and Lacerda in a bad light. But Lacerda, refusing to make the trip, maintained that Juracy himself was perfectly able to explain the revolution—provided it needed explaining in Washington, "the one place in the world where it is unnecessary to explain it."[9]

Among the men scheduled to receive Lacerda, only Congressman Selden expressed annoyance, and that was because he had persuaded other congressmen to forgo campaigning in their states in order to honor the governor at lunch. Juracy, seeking to smooth things over, invited Selden and his wife to be the guests of honor, in place of the Lacerdas, at the embassy banquet. "Carlos," Juracy told himself, "could assume the most unexpected attitudes" and was a difficult man to understand.[10]

A few days later, Juracy asked Júlio de Mesquita Neto, who had come from New York to Washington, if he knew why Lacerda had canceled his Washington trip. Mesquita Neto, calling himself "involuntarily" responsible, explained: "I brought Carlos a message from my father, telling him to return at once because President Castello Branco was coordinating Juracy Magalhães' candidacy for the presidency." Juracy felt that Castello would not act in such a way, especially without consulting him.[11]

Lacerda decided to return to Brazil on July 2, after learning that in Brasília the congressional special commission, in charge of studying political reforms, would be in session for eight days starting on June 30. Press reports at first attributed Lacerda's new travel plan and cancellation of Washington appointments to Letícia's health. But, before his departure on July 2, Lacerda told the press that Letícia had not been seriously ill and that the true reason for his failure to keep the Washington appointments was his "complete disagreement" with what he said was the support given by Ilmar Pena Marinho, Brazil's OAS representative, to positions of Chile and Mexico that were "identical" with the positions of Goulart and Cuba, with which Brazil had broken relations in May. If, Lacerda said, he had seen Assistant Secretary of State Mann, the press would afterwards have asked him questions about the delicate OAS matter, and he had no wish to say anything that might give rise to malicious interpretations that could hurt his relations with Castello Branco.[12]

10. Comments

During his last two days in New York, Lacerda devoted himself conscientiously to his mission, lunching with journalists and Latin American representatives to the United Nations, conferring with UN Secretary-General U Thant, and inviting Juana Castro Ruz, sister and opponent of the Cuban dictator, to visit Guanabara. "This valiant woman," he told the press, "should receive invitations from all the Latin American countries so that her message of liberty receive the maximum expression."[1]

During his mission, Lacerda's words had reached large audiences and left a positive image of the 1964 revolution in the minds of many who had been unfamiliar with Brazil. However, Abreu Sodré, in evaluating the mission, concluded that it was a failure.

As Lacerda's campaign manager, Sodré considered the mission an opportunity for Lacerda to strengthen his position with the military, by defending its role, while keeping away from the political scene, where critical remarks about the new regime might "damage his future" and his relations with Castello Branco. "Unfortunately, what was prepared as a positive step, became, during the mission . . . , a negative step. Such are the ways of politics and the temperaments of men."[2] Sodré's conclusion was reached after considering reactions to the Orly press interview, including de Gaulle's indignation, and the intemperate messages sent to Itamaraty by Lacerda, worried about a plot to derail his presidential candidacy.

While Castello Branco's advisers were inclined to point fingers at what they called the governor's instability, the president himself was careful to retain good relations with Lacerda. When he denied that his administration's interest in the absolute majority requirement was intended to hurt the traveling governor, he did so with the vehemence of a man who felt that the suggestion was impertinent.[3]

Castello was fascinated by men of intelligence, and, while he had long considered Lacerda one of his heroes because of the role he had played in combating shortcomings of previous regimes, he admired him also as one of the most intelligent men he had known.[4] Castello in April believed that Lacerda should be his successor, and he kept that possibility open. His minister of health, Raimundo de Brito, has written that Castello did not hide his preference for "Dr. Lacerda," but felt that, before making his choice known, he should weigh evidence carefully. "A cautious man, conscious of his responsibilities, he would not act emotionally." Navy Commander João Carlos Palhares dos Santos has explained that Castello's way of thinking was that of an infantry officer. "He thought slowly in deciding on the target and seemed to lack decisiveness, but, after he reached his decision, he was stubborn."[5]

When Lacerda resolved to return to Brazil, journalist Carlos Castello Branco was writing that the UDN would put up little resistance to the absolute majority requirement unless Lacerda fought against it "with the ardor he customarily gives to his campaigns."[6] Lacerda faced a period in which the fate of political reforms would be decided. It was also a period in which Castello Branco would gather evidence that would affect his decision as to how to deal with his feeling that Lacerda should be his successor.

VI.

Critic of Castello Branco's Team
(July-November 1964)

1. The Congressional Commission Favors Reform
(July 8, 1964)

Castello Branco wished to have Congress reach decisions about all the important reforms that had been discussed before he had assumed the presidency. As for political reform, he told Raphael de Almeida Magalhães, during Lacerda's absence, that he sincerely believed that no obstacle would prevent him and Lacerda from coming to an agreement.[1] He did not approve of a one-year extension of his mandate and made his position known to intimates in and out of Congress. Lacerda, on the day he arrived in Rio from New York, heard Abreu Sodré argue that if Castello's term were extended, it would be a consolidation of political reform and not a maneuver against the governor's presidential candidacy. Sodré told Lacerda to act calmly.[2]

When Lacerda lunched with Castello at Laranjeiras Palace on July 4, he received the president's congratulations for the way he had defended the Brazilian revolution and a request that he prepare a draft for a speech on foreign policy that the president was scheduled to give late in July.[3] Lacerda and Castello agreed that "absolute priority" should be given to combating inflation and making food available. Emerging from the meeting in a good mood and full of praise for the president, Lacerda told reporters that the Brazilian press was responsible for misgivings he had had and that the revolution "has not reached the press, which is full of little old women." He expressed his full support for the orientation of the Castello Branco government and added that "the PSD and PTB, and even the UDN, will not succeed in separating me from the president."

Speaking to the reporters about the suggested absolute majority requirement, Lacerda said that Castello had convinced him that the proposal "was not made intentionally against me." He attributed to Castello a "clearly defined doctrinal position that coincides with mine because we both understand that the proposal is intimately connected with the process of reforming our electoral system."[4]

Following the lunch, Raphael de Almeida Magalhães and Sandra

Cavalcanti found Lacerda sympathetic to the view that a *prorroga-ção* (mandate extension) for Castello was not a maneuver against his candidacy and might have some positive points. Considering the reform package as a whole, he agreed that it would be advantageous to have a new Congress decide a presidential contest if an absolute majority requirement forced the decision on Congress. Besides, he reacted favorably to the argument that inflation-fighting measures might make it difficult for a prorevolution candidate to win as early as 1965, before economic improvement had set in.[5]

Before flying to Brasília on July 8, to discuss food supply with Castello, Lacerda prepared a draft for the president's foreign policy speech in which he listed, among the revolution's objectives, a new election law to improve democracy. Although Lacerda said later that 98 percent of Castello's July 31 speech at Itamaraty was taken from this draft,[6] it would be more accurate to say that approximately 2 percent came from it. The draft was, in large part, an announcement of policies to be adopted at home, such as the election reform, a defense of private initiative, an agrarian reform emphasizing credits and large-scale production, the fight against inflation (to be helped by an inflow of capital), and the need to modify Goulart's "iniquitous and malign" limitation on the remittance of profits abroad. Lacerda's draft maintained that Portugal's colonies had demonstrated their desire to remain within the Portuguese Republic, which was urged to "accelerate the development of its overseas provinces" and perfect a mechanism whereby they could, if they wished, assume "autonomy within the Luso-Brazilian Community." The paper urged the United States to speed up the work of the Alliance for Progress, and said that Brazil would vote for sanctions against the Cuban government.[7]

Lacerda's discussion with Castello on July 8 was less important than his conversations in Congress. These confirmed his earlier suspicion that João Agripino's *prorrogação* proposal was, at least in part, a maneuver against his presidential candidacy, although not a maneuver by Castello.

Afonso Arinos de Melo Franco said later that the extension of Castello's mandate was supported primarily because it would block the "ambitions of Carlos." Asked who wanted to eliminate Lacerda, he replied: "Almost all of us. He was an extremely competent person, and to some extent a genius. Had he become installed in the revolutionary government, he would not have left; he would have remained as Mussolini did." The *prorrogação* proposal, written in Afonso Arinos' Brasília apartment by Afonso Arinos, Daniel Krieger, and João Agripino, was chiefly the work of Afonso Arinos but was given the signature of Agripino because the former foreign minister, associated with Brazil's "independent foreign policy," was held in disfavor by some of the "revolutionaries." Magalhães Pinto, rival of Lacerda for the UDN presidential nomination, came out in favor of the Agripino proposal. So did Ademar de Barros.[8]

Lacerda had no tolerance for political reform when he learned of the purpose of men like Afonso Arinos. In Brasília on July 8 he told the press that the advocates of Ulysses Guimarães' absolute majority proposal "want precisely to prevent my victory in the next elections." The idea of extending the mandates of the president and vice president, he said, was supported by "only one allegation: that the Revolution will become unpopular and that by 1966 it might become popular." But, he argued, "a revolution should not fear the judgment of the people. Its adversaries will be stronger in 1966 than in 1965 because by 1966 they will have time to reorganize and extend the rifts that will develop in the revolutionary movement." He called votes for illiterates a reactionary idea, "intended to retain the status quo," and "a humiliation for those who know how to read and write." "I do not believe that illiterates want to vote; what they want are schools."[9]

In Brasília Lacerda presented his arguments against *prorrogação* to congressmen and senators. He was still presenting them on the night of July 8, when the congressional special commission met and approved, without difficulty, the absolute majority requirement. With the help of influential PSD Senator Filinto Müller, *prorrogação* won the commission's approval by a 12 to 9 vote, leaving the UDN's Daniel Krieger, government leader in the Senate, ecstatic. Outside the commission meeting room, Krieger met Congressman Paulo Sarasate (UDN, Ceará) and exclaimed: "We have won the first round." Then, noticing that Sarasate was with Lacerda, the Gaúcho senator said: "Governor, the *prorrogação* is necessary and the postponement of the elections will not hurt your candidacy. You are our candidate. Keep calm. No one will take the presidency from you." Lacerda replied: "The future will reveal your error."[10]

After returning to Rio, Lacerda sent an irate telegram to Bilac Pinto asking for a UDN national convention "to decide on the presidential candidacy and pass judgment on the conduct of the party's representatives with respect to the proposed extension of mandates." He called the *prorrogação* an "act of cowardice" to benefit "only the opportunists and sinister adventurers who again enter into collusion to rob the people of the Revolution that liberated them." These enemies of the revolution, he wrote, had agreed to elect Castello Branco "due to their fear of tanks, and now want to extend his term due to their fear of the people." Calling it "our duty to explain to the people and their armed forces this infamous ruse," he vowed to start at once "preaching all over the country." "I see that the Revolution needs to be explained in Brazil, especially in Congress, much more than abroad."[11]

To those who worried about holding elections in 1965 lest the revolution be unpopular then, Lacerda replied at length on July 10, when he reassumed the governorship. In listing steps that he said would give the revolution popularity, he presented publicly for the first time a domestic program that constituted a criticism of what Castello Branco was trying to do. On this account, and because of observations about the economy that deserved respect, the speech should not have been called "insignificant" by Naldir Laranjeira Batista, PR leader in the state legislature.[12] Lacerda described himself as a "friend and collaborator" of Castello, which is not to say that the speech offered comfort to the president or lacked abrasiveness. The president was reminded that on April 1 he had "instructed" Lacerda to abandon Guanabara Palace and ignore a "duty" to resist the enemy and contribute to the victorious outcome. The president was described as surrounded by men who sought to make him a king and flattered him "with almost the same words they employed when praising Kubitschek and Goulart."

Lacerda's recommendations about the economy sprang from a conviction that production increases would be harmed by a directed economy with a planning ministry, "a scientific fiction," that issued a series of edicts, "magic formulas," based on statistics that were erroneous. He blamed Brazil's ills on the vanity of a group of presidential advisers who were blind to reality, lacked confidence in private initiative, and could not distinguish between purity and puritanism. He recommended that the government, instead of making the revolution unpopular, reopen the UNE, in a democratic form, and arrange for labor union elections without the "humiliating interference" of government representatives.

Lacerda argued that Castello's wish for an agrarian reform was causing the sort of panic that had impaired agricultural production in 1963 and should be replaced by a program of guaranteed minimum prices for producers, with incentives for the use of fertilizers, "practically unknown in Brazil." Asserting that "monetary correction for expropriation bonds puts beans on no one's plate," he suggested, instead, the elimination of taxes on foods of prime necessity. "Instead of votes for illiterates, let's speak of attracting capital and know-how." "Instead of postponing elections let's hasten the day when the poor will have more food, a matter that depends not on a miracle but on reviving the confidence of producers." He rejected the label of anti-reformist, given him by "many experts," and said that the reforms he opposed were "anti-economic, socialist but anti-social," whereas the reforms he favored were of the practical sort he had given the Cariocas in abundance and in record time.[13]

2. The Extension of Castello's Mandate
(July 16–22, 1964)

Castello Branco asked Daniel Krieger to cease working for *prorrogação*, but the result was Krieger's resignation as government leader in the Senate, a resignation that Castello refused to accept. Then, on July 13, three days before the first plenary session votes on the amendments, Castello addressed a letter to Krieger stating that Krieger's work for *prorrogação* was the "legitimate and exclusive" work of a legislator, not the work of the government's leader. Repeating his own opposition, Castello said in his letter that an extension would be a disturbing factor that would not help perfect the political institutions and could have unfavorable international repercussions. Also on July 13, Pedro Aleixo, government leader in the lower house, gave the lawmakers the president's "official word" against *prorrogação*.[1]

Krieger strove more zealously than ever for his objective. PSD President Amaral Peixoto, described as an enemy of the revolution by Lacerda, supplied what Krieger calls "priceless support." So did Osvaldo Cordeiro de Farias, Castello's minister for the coordination of regional agencies. The general, who had influence in Congress, felt that "to leave Castello with such a short mandate" was an "absurdity." Magalhães Pinto, drumming up support for *prorrogação*, predicted its passage by Congress despite "the superficial uproar provoked by the violent reaction of the governor of Guanabara."[2]

Lacerda, preparing to take his message to Belo Horizonte, received an unfriendly letter from Bilac Pinto saying that the governor's request for a UDN convention to pick a presidential candidate and judge the conduct of the party's representatives would be submitted to the directorship on July 22. Bilac urged Lacerda to be present so that he could hear the replies to his charges, which, Bilac wrote, were "based on sensational distortions of the facts." "Not even Your Excellency, with your brilliant talent, will be able to lead our party and capture its support by terrorist tactics."[3]

Lacerda, replying to Bilac by telegram, forecast a dictatorship in Brazil and announced his separation from the "owners" of the party, for whom he wished "a happy burial" because "they are already dead without knowing it." "You are presiding over the liquidation of the

UDN, which is not so serious. What is very serious is that all of you are liquidating what there was of democracy in Brazil."[4]

At the Belo Horizonte airport, Lacerda called Bilac Pinto's letter "incoherent" and added: "I do not have to contest the UDN leadership with anyone because I already have it." Upon being named honorary citizen of Belo Horizonte, he delivered an impassioned speech in which he proclaimed that it was time "to think less about amending the constitution and a little more about amending the amenders." He did not call the suspension of Kubitschek's rights a courageous step; instead, he told the Mineiros a grave error had been committed because no one should be punished without charges and the right of defense.[5]

On July 16 the press reported briefly on the contents of Castello's letter to Krieger. Abreu Sodré, returning that day with Lacerda to Rio from Belo Horizonte, criticized Bilac Pinto's failure to hold a UDN national directorship meeting that would have permitted the party's local sections to express their wishes before the roll calls in Congress. With the first roll calls scheduled to begin that evening, Hugo Levy phoned Lacerda from Brasília to say that he had lined up over a dozen UDN congressmen agreeable to vote against *prorrogação* provided Lacerda would give them direct instructions. Lacerda, however, simply replied that they should vote as their consciences dictated.[6]

The roll calls lasted until 5:00 A.M. the next morning. Ample majorities in both houses favored extending the franchise to the lower ranks of the military and adopting the absolute majority rule for presidential elections. Extension of the franchise to illiterates in municipal elections passed easily in the Senate and only just achieved the 205 necessary votes in the Chamber of Deputies.

At 3:30 A.M. senators began to vote on the João Agripino Amendment to extend Castello Branco's term to March 15, 1967, and to assure future coincidence of presidential and congressional elections by reducing the presidential term from five to four years. They adopted the proposal overwhelmingly, with all the UDN senators present (two were absent) voting in favor.

In the case of the lower house, Lacerda's condemnation of UDN conduct did nothing to weaken the sentiment that Afonso Arinos found to be a winner of votes for *prorrogação*. There the roll call was dramatic. At 4:40 A.M., when the last congressman's name had been called, the proposal had 203 votes, two short of the required absolute majority. Opponents shouted "Close the voting," but many opponents were absent and fervor for the proposal was strong. Although the president of Congress, Senator Auro de Moura Andrade, did not support the amendment, he called for time to allow missing congressmen to appear. Bedlam broke loose when a UDN congressman, Francelino Pedreira, changed his vote from "no" to "yes." After Moura Andrade said he was going to close the voting, Krieger argued that 204 was a majority because two seats, formerly occupied by men who had lost their political rights and mandates, had not been filled. The issue was settled when a PSD congressman announced that an absent UDN colleague was coming to the Chamber to cast a favorable vote; the latecomer was Luiz Bronzeado, who, in favoring the amendment, followed the example of most of the dozen-odd *udenistas* on whom Hugo Levy felt he could have counted if Lacerda had given the word. Moura Andrade then declared that the proposal had passed, 205-94, and that the second roll calls, necessary in the case of constitutional amendments, would take place during the following week. Of the 96 UDN congressmen, 61 had voted in favor of *prorrogação* and 14 had voted against it.[7]

The *Correio da Manhã*, although opposed to Lacerda, denounced the "opportunists" in Congress who had sought to gain favor with a group of generals by voting for "a military dictatorship that the entire nation repudiates." *O Estado de S. Paulo*, while hoping that the military chiefs would not allow *prorrogação* to weaken Lacerda's candidacy, agreed with War Minister Costa e Silva that the extension of Castello's mandate was indispensable for consolidating the movement that overthrew Goulart. The *Jornal do Brasil*, like *O Estado de S. Paulo*, favored both *prorrogação* and the economic policy of the new regime.[8]

Lacerda, on the evening of July 17, released an "official note" and quoted from it in a broadcast from Guanabara Palace. "To reach 204 votes," he said, "it was necessary to delay the voting for hours, awaken people in their homes, and bring them, practically under the stick, to Congress. Never, in the most tumultuous assemblies of aldermen, was there so disreputable a spectacle." "With the voting closed, never in all the parliaments of the world, including those in Brazil until early this morning, could anyone else vote. . . . The voting is illegal besides being immoral." He described Congress as a barnyard and said it was determined to demoralize the revolution and the president, "transforming him into a dictator, usurper, and king." He saw only a remote hope that Congress, meeting for the second roll calls, would repent. And if, he said, Congress "insists on this insanity, stupidity more than insanity, there remains to the people the right to struggle in public squares, to make demands in schools, factories, *fazendas*, cities, and the countryside, for the return of their right

Prorrogação; Lacerda '66 instead of '65. (APPE drawing in *O Cruzeiro,*
February 20, 1965)

that no one delegated to anyone—the right to choose the president."
As for himself, Lacerda said he would not yield to an impulse to play
the enemy's game of taking the road to disorder, but would continue
cooperating with Castello Branco despite the president's recent political error. This cooperation, he said, would consist of explaining to
Castello that unless the government's economic policy were changed
the people would never receive more food and "we shall have lied to
them when we told them that we made a revolution."[9]
    Especially grating to congressmen was Lacerda's use of the term
"barnyard" to describe Congress. Congressmen Mário Piva (PSD, Bahia)
and Cid Carvalho (PTB, Maranhão) said that Lacerda, in attacking
Congress, was following the example of Brizola. Congressman Carlos
de Brito Velho (PL, Rio Grande do Sul) read aloud a telegram he had
sent to Lacerda to accuse him of lying about Congress and having the
soul of a despot. Congressman Lírio Bertoli (PSD, Paraná) dismissed
Lacerda as neurasthenic.[10]
    When Lacerda lunched with the president at Laranjeiras Palace
on July 18, for another discussion about the supply of foods, Castello
showed the governor his letter of July 13 to Krieger. Lacerda, speaking to reporters later, expressed surprise that Krieger had neither
made the letter public nor been guided by it. He also said he was not
fighting the UDN. "It is the party leadership that has been fighting
against me."[11]
    Krieger made Castello's letter public on July 20, two days before

Congress was to vote on the amendments for a second time. Lacerda, on July 21, wrote one more letter to Bilac Pinto and sent Brunini to deliver it to him in Brasília. In the letter, more civil than his earlier messages, Lacerda said he was closing "this absurd correspondence" with a final appeal to common sense. He complained that he had been placed outside the UDN in an act that was treasonable or thoughtless, and described his position as defending the revolution from "our enemies" and the country from a military dictatorship. "We are," he wrote, "marching rapidly to an obscure and undefined Nasserism." With *prorrogação*, he predicted, elections would not take place even in 1966. "All that remains to be known is who the dictator will be, because certainly he will not be Castello Branco." Lacerda saw some slight hope, provided Castello would revise his government. "This government contains very little that is revolutionary."[12]

Pedro Aleixo warned that *prorrogação* would "wound the democratic regime." But UDN congressional leader Ernâni Sátiro, supporter of both Lacerda and Castello, said it would be enacted with the support of most of the *udenistas*. Sátiro, who had voted against *prorrogação* on July 17, was an able forecaster. On July 22 the João Agripino Amendment passed in the Senate, 46 to 6, and in the Chamber of Deputies, 238 to 94. The Ulysses Guimarães absolute majority requirement was even more successful, gaining victories of 42-3 and 294-38. On the other hand, the lower house, reversing its earlier position, rejected the partial enfranchisement of illiterates by a close vote.

O Estado de S. Paulo disagreed with Lacerda's oft-repeated assertion that *prorrogação* meant the end of direct elections for a long time. It assured its readers that the extension of Castello's mandate in no way diminished the probability that Lacerda would reach the presidency.[13]

3. Denouncing Castello's Team (July–August 1964)

There remained the problem of arranging to have gubernatorial elections coincide with the presidential and congressional elections of 1966. Mandates of eleven governors, including Lacerda's, would expire in 1965, and therefore one-year extensions by the state legislatures were being given consideration.

In the Guanabara legislature, where Jair Martins presented a proposal for extending Lacerda's mandate, the governor was having more trouble than usual. Unable to obtain a favorable vote on tax measures, such as a new electric energy tax and an increase in the sales tax from 5 to 5.5 percent, Lacerda promulgated the laws with the explanation that Article 4 of the Institutional Act, which turned presidential proposals into laws if Congress reached no decisions within thirty days, was applicable to the state government.[1]

Writing to Emílio Nina Ribeiro, the assembly's new majority leader, Lacerda declared emphatically that he would not serve beyond the period for which he had been elected and would then leave Brazil to the care of "the technical geniuses and drawing room political strategists." The letter, which Nina Ribeiro read aloud in the state assembly on July 30 at Lacerda's request, was the outpouring of a man who said he had been "wounded" and "betrayed" and was tired of being the sacrificial lamb, "first of the UDN and now of a Revolution that is being subdivided into lots."[2]

The letter became a sensation because, in the words of O Globo, "Up to now the Castello Branco government has not been attacked with so much rudeness and violence." In the letter, Lacerda wrote that the revolution had become old and wilted while the country suffered from unemployment and high prices and while the one great reform, the implantation of a competent and hardworking government, had yet to be carried out. He asserted that the revolution had no idea of what to do and that those who knew how to save it, such as himself, had been thrust aside because "the government of the Revolution is ashamed of the Revolution and daily seeks to be forgiven for the unorthodox origin of its mandate." Lacerda extended congratulations to Congressman Amaral Peixoto and others who had transformed the revolution "into a coup that fizzled."[3]

Ambassador Lincoln Gordon, in a cable to Washington, called Lacerda's outburst a "tantrum." Magalhães Pinto attributed it to personal frustration, whereas Congressman Francelino Pedreira (UDN, Minas), speaking in the Chamber of Deputies, maintained that Lacerda hoped, as an eventual presidential candidate, to win the support of forces defeated by the revolution.[4]

O Globo and the Jornal do Brasil, Rio's leading newspapers, condemned Lacerda and praised the work being started by the Castello Branco administration. That administration, according to the Jornal do Brasil, was indeed in command, was run by competent men, and needed no tutors, only more time. Lacerda, O Globo wrote, should appreciate more than anyone else how difficult it was for a new administration to show results in three-and-a-half months. The Diário de Notícias, defending Castello against those who criticized for the sake of criticizing, concluded that Lacerda's autocratic and illegal handling of tax increases served as a warning against having him in the presidency. State assemblyman Jamil Haddad (PSB), who had been leading the assault on Lacerda's "dictatorial" promulgation of

Lacerda attacking Castello (the castle). (Claudius Ceccon drawing in *Jornal do Brasil*, July 31, 1964)

new tax laws, ridiculed the idea that the increaser of sales taxes could put more beans on the plates of poor people. Haddad called Lacerda a "false popular leader," whose handling of the selection of a vice governor revealed the deceitfulness of his claim to be dedicated to the constitution and legal elections.[5]

In letters to the *Tribuna da Imprensa*, Lacerda denied breaking with Castello Branco and denounced Castello's government. He condemned what he called Roberto Campos' plans to have Brazil purchase the AMFORP properties and to allow the Hanna Mining Company to have a "private port" in Sepetiba Bay for loading its iron ore into vessels. The Castello administration, he said, respected San Tiago Dantas, took advice from Amaral Peixoto, and allowed Golbery do Couto e Silva to be guided by Luís Alberto Bahia, editorial writer of the *Jornal do Brasil*. Declaring that unemployment was more harmful than thievery, he predicted that the people would "return the power to the thieves—who at least provided employment." "It seems that we shall have to struggle all over again."[6]

Comfort for Lacerda was provided by *Jornal do Brasil* columnist Wilson Figueiredo, who wrote that the governor, supporter of the

UNE and free labor union elections, was doing well in the polls. "He is," Wilson Figueiredo wrote, "the holder of the biggest potential of popular backing" and was shaking off his "image as a reactionary." Comfort of a different sort was provided by Júlio de Mesquita Filho, who gave a television interview on July 28, in which he said that Lacerda, "the pure representative of the revolutionary spirit," was responsible for at least 65 percent of the effort that had made the movement of March 31 a success. Asked whether Magalhães Pinto had been the civilian head of that movement, Mesquita described the Minas governor as completely without idealism and so moved by ambition that he had openly supported Goulart.

What pleased Lacerda about *O Estado de S. Paulo* and Mesquita was their demand that Castello stop "vacillating" and cease giving attention to the PSD, the PTB, or the country's political groups, "made up of absolutely inefficient and negative individuals." Mesquita, proponent of the "irreversible revolution," called for a cabinet reform that would eliminate, among others, Justice Minister Milton Campos, "who has a horror of the word revolution." Although Mesquita disagreed with Lacerda about *prorrogação* and the government's economic team, Lacerda was so pleased with his interview that he sent him a long thank-you letter in which he repeated some of his views. It was one of six Lacerda letters criticizing the government to be published within seventy-two hours.[7]

Arguing that a federal cabinet reform was necessary, Lacerda belittled those in office. Speaking of Finance Minister Otávio Bulhões, he asked: "Do you think that a man who for sixty years was always a clerk can be a cabinet minister?"

Abreu Sodré felt that the federal administration might welcome the inclusion of Lacerda as education minister. "Brazilian youth," Abreu Sodré writes, "was so intoxicated by the ideas of the Left" that only a man of Lacerda's ability to communicate "could win that area." Like Gustavo Borges, the Paulista UDN leader believed that Lacerda, "besides gaining the young people for the Revolution, would be preparing himself for the electoral contest." Lacerda, Abreu Sodré also writes, was tired of the governorship and eager to "prepare himself for the next post."

Lacerda was enthusiastic about the idea of taking the place of Education Minister Flávio Suplici de Lacerda, whose conviction that students should stick to their studies annoyed politically inclined student leaders. To help bring about the change, Armando Falcão told the president that Lacerda, as minister, would not seek to eclipse the president, would not appear at Castello's side if such appearances might mean more acclaim for himself than for the president, and would avoid a repetition of the clashes that at times had separated him from the president. Castello, on August 12, told Falcão that he would be happy to receive Lacerda but had no desire to discuss his cabinet with him.

Lacerda, inaugurating a stretch of highway on Governor's Island, called Castello an honest and hardworking revolutionary. "But it is very difficult to carry out a revolutionary government without revolutionaries in it." Castello responded by denying publicly any intention of changing his cabinet. He also expressed a determination to stick to his economic policy, which had just been assaulted, with surprising vehemence, by Magalhães Pinto.[8]

Lacerda, lunching with Castello at Laranjeiras Palace on August 15, was again well impressed with the president. He found Castello sympathetic to criticisms of SUNAB, the price control organ, and the manner in which its superintendent, Arnaldo Taveira, ran it, leaving local authorities with no role beyond enforcing SUNAB decisions. Speaking later to reporters, Lacerda called the president "an excellent helmsman," only one degree off course. He expressed satisfaction at finding Castello still willing to help the Cariocas and unwilling to be moved by intriguers who wished to promote a break between the president and the governor.[9]

An intriguer, according to Lacerda's television broadcast on the night of August 18, was Castello's friend General Golbery do Couto e Silva, head of the SNI (Serviço Nacional de Informações). Lacerda accused Golbery's "Service of Misinformation" of spreading rumors in order to put the governor on bad terms with Castello and Admiral Sílvio Heck. He blamed it for the false report that Marcelo Garcia had gone to Europe as the bearer of a message from Lacerda to Kubitschek.[10]

Justice Minister Milton Campos was more correct than helpful to Lacerda when he pointed out that Article 4 of the Institutional Act, the basis of Lacerda's issuance of the new tax laws, did not apply to the states. Twenty-eight Guanabara state legislators, many belonging to the "Democratic Resistance" established by the small parties, agreed with the Justice Minister and signed a protest against Lacerda's handling of the new taxes; but Raphael de Almeida Magalhães, who was carrying out much of Lacerda's administrative work, included the tax increases in the 1965 budget submitted at the end of August.

While the tax matter awaited a decision of the Supreme Court, Lacerda said that, in applying the Institutional Act, he was testing the efficacy of the revolution. "If the Institutional Act has no application in the state that suffered the most from the regime that the Revolution overthrew, nothing more can be done in Guanabara"; he would have to leave "as a protest until this country gets a Revolution that is really worthwhile."[11]

4. The AMFORP Case (August–October 1964)

Célio Borja, UDN leader in the state legislature, was named secretary of government in July, while one of his predecessors in the secretaryship, Hélio Beltrão, was being described by the governor's office as a candidate for the election of 1965 to find a successor to Lacerda. The governor replaced Secretary of Tourism Victor Bouças with medical doctor Leopoldo de Castro Ferreira, an expert on Rio's history who had helped Lacerda plan for the city's Fourth Centennial. The change was unwelcome to journalists because Castro Ferreira ended Bouças' practice of paying journalists for publicity—a practice that had not pleased Lacerda.[1]

In other changes in Lacerda's team, the federal government played a role. Sandra Cavalcanti, while having tea with Castello in August, was invited to head the new National Housing Bank. Sandra had given the president a study on the subject, originally prepared for a future Lacerda presidency, only to see it considerably modified by lawyer José Luís Bulhões Pedreira before it was enacted into law. The new bank reported to Planning Minister Roberto Campos, who had received the impression from Raphael de Almeida Magalhães that Lacerda wanted to get rid of Sandra and that the appointment would therefore be regarded as a favor to Lacerda.[2] Luiz Carlos Vital succeeded Sandra as the Guanabara social services secretary.

The person whom Lacerda did want to replace was Economy Secretary Guilherme Borghoff. But, the governor told Almeida Braga, he did not feel like adding to his reputation of "being a good governor on account of having no friends because I dismiss them and fight them." "I don't want to dismiss Borghoff; I can't have another enemy. You have a good way. Speak with Borghoff and persuade him to quit." Braga, lunching with Borghoff, did not have to mention the matter, because the economy secretary was the first to bring up a problem; it was his problem of having to advise the governor that he wanted to leave his administration in order to accept the position of superintendent of SUNAB, offered by Castello Branco.[3] Lacerda, after learning of this development, wrote a letter to Borghoff in which he expressed his gratitude for the businessman's loyal collaboration, agreed to accept the sacrifice of his departure, and listed steps that he felt Borghoff should take to improve "that miserable organ, SUNAB."[4]

The state bank, being run by Almeida Braga, was praised by Lacerda during the ceremony at the installation of some of the electric generators that had been ordered by Lacerda from the United States during the Goulart administration. Lacerda also praised President Kennedy, whom he had cabled for help to get the generators. But the governor was critical of the American embassy, which, he said, had tried to kill the deal by cabling Washington that the generators would be unnecessary in view of the expected power output from the Furnas plant. Lacerda told his audience that the embassy's cable had been signed by the United States official who had "given the backing of the American embassy to the so-called Paulo Freire process of Communist infiltration in the Brazilian illiterate masses."[5]

More serious friction between the American embassy and Lacerda developed from the governor's campaign in opposition to the purchase by the Brazilian government of the electric utility properties of AMFORP. Before Lacerda spoke against the transaction in his television broadcast on August 18, the United States let it be known that its $50-million program loan, arranged during Ambassador Gordon's visit to Washington in June, depended on a Brazilian settlement with AMFORP.[6] Lacerda, in his television speech, accused Roberto Campos of reviving deals he had made as Goulart's ambassador in Washington. Speaking in São Paulo a few days later, he called the proposed arrangement "a hoax."[7]

A commission of representatives of four cabinet ministers, headed by Eletrobrás President Otávio Marcondes Ferraz, recommended execution of the 1963 purchase agreement subject to the approval of Congress and a new independent verification of the value of the assets to see if the price of $135 million, to be paid in installments, should be reduced. A previous requirement that 75 percent of the purchase price be invested in Brazil was to be replaced by the requirement that AMFORP make a series of loans totaling $100.25 million to Eletrobrás. The Marcondes Ferraz commission mentioned the acute energy supply problems that would arise from a prolonged impasse in the negotiations with the American utility, which operated in ten Brazilian states. Castello Branco's commission of the four most interested cabinet ministers—the commission that had selected the Marcondes Ferraz commission—spoke of the need "to reestablish Brazil's credit in international financial circles."[8]

After Brazil's National Security Council unanimously approved the recommendations of the commissions, Castello sent the findings to

Congress. There Roberto Campos, Marcondes Ferraz, and Mines and Energy Minister Mauro Thibau found a determined opponent in Senator João Agripino, who used the term "scrap iron" in referring to the AMFORP properties, as Lacerda had done in 1963. Now Lacerda maintained that the "high price" for the AMFORP properties was to be paid to keep the position of Roberto Campos "coherent" in the eyes of his "bosses," who included AMFORP.[9]

Eletrobrás President Marcondes Ferraz, upset at the failure of the UDN to defend him against "personal attacks" by *udenistas*, sent a letter to the UDN directorship to say that he was leaving the party to which he had belonged since its beginning. Lacerda, writing Marcondes Ferraz on August 31, said, "I cannot believe I have any blame in your decision." In the letter he accused Marcondes Ferraz of playing the "contradictory" role of supporting free enterprise and yet cooperating with a "pseudo-agreement" inherited from the Goulart government.[10]

Lacerda criticized the government's handling of the AMFORP matter in his correspondence with Ambassador Juracy Magalhães—a correspondence that followed Juracy's public denial of having any knowledge about Castello's wanting Juracy to be elected president in 1966. Lacerda informed the ambassador that Castello, by steering one degree off course, would miss his target, and that he had suggested to the president that better results for Brazil could be achieved if Juracy would renegotiate with AMFORP.

Juracy, in his reply, wrote: "In the same way that you canceled your trip to Washington, creating a difficult situation for me at the start of my mission, you fell into making the most unjust and unseemly attacks on our UDN companions and the Castello government." According to Juracy, Lacerda was not really sparing the president, because "when you attack his economic-financial policy and Golbery you are making his Herculean administrative task very difficult. Many think your ability to fight is your strength, but I repeat that it is your weak point. You become blind when you enter a campaign and commit the most terrible injustices."

Juracy was critical of Lacerda's "insinuations about the behavior of the American embassy and State Department" and description of the AMFORP arrangement as a hoax. "You know that the problem of the public utility concessions is a roadblock in the process of American aid to Brazil. Up here the law exists to be fulfilled. There is no point in discussing if Senator Hickenlooper was correct in defending the arrangement that prohibits United States aid to countries that expropriate American companies without just compensation. It is the law." "You know that the evaluation of the AMFORP properties is going to be carried out by a qualified company, a specialist, selected by both parties." "And why," Juracy asked Lacerda, "throw to the beasts an honest and competent man like Roberto Campos, in this game of words and insinuations?"[11]

A *New York Times* editorial described Lacerda as using demagoguery and showing "more intent in weakening the position of President Castello Branco to pave his own way to power than in helping Brazil out of its economic morass." It called the AMFORP arrangement a fair one and pointed out that the initial outlay was only $10 million, with the remainder of the $135 million payable over forty-five years. The *Times* emphasized Brazil's need of foreign investment, private and public, and wrote that this would be unlikely to materialize "if Mr. Lacerda is successful in whipping up Brazilian hostility to foreign interests." A *Times* news item quoted *udenista* legislator Danillo Nunes as defending the federal government against Lacerda's attack.[12]

Lacerda was campaigning in the northeast in mid-September when Castello submitted his message about AMFORP to Congress. In Salvador the campaigner declared that at least forty different legal solutions were available for avoiding the "unnecessary evil" proposed by the commissions appointed by Castello; and he said that the Rio Light Company had paid 5 billion cruzeiros to his state to free itself from the seven remaining years of its streetcar operation contract.[13]

Castello assured Magalhães Pinto that he would not mobilize progovernment congressional forces on behalf of a vote favorable to the AMFORP transaction, and the president expressed the same assurance publicly. Then the Minas governor, who had been supporting João Agripino's fight to kill or modify the transaction, explained on television that he believed that the Castello Branco government ought to comply with arrangements agreed upon before it took office.[14]

In Congress, where Herbert Levy at length found an opportunity to defend Marcondes Ferraz, projects submitted by Senators Agripino and José Ermírio de Morais were rejected by the commission studying the AMFORP case. Just before the congressional commission approved the administration's proposal, the PTB withdrew its members. It used the same tactic in plenary sessions, but on October 9 the attendance reached a quorum and the AMFORP purchase was approved by a vote of 187 to 91. Following a rapid confirmation by the Senate, the PTB announced that, despite its failure to defeat the proposal, it had shown by its obstruction that the government could count on an active opposition.[15]

5. De Gaulle Visits Brazil (October 13-16, 1964)

Lacerda, campaigning in the northeast, was seeking to have the UDN state directorships press the national directorship for an early nominating convention. In João Pessoa, where he was acclaimed by the largest street crowd of his campaign,[1] he told an audience at the University of Paraíba that Brazil needed more students of engineering and medicine. "In the last ten years, while the number of graduates in law and philosophy increased by 100 percent, the increase in medical graduates was only 11 percent."

To those who criticized the failure of the revolution to protect academic freedom, Lacerda spoke about Mário Schemberg, "our esteemed professor of theoretical physics who found time to be a Communist Party alderman in São Paulo and who, after losing his mandate, still found time every day to spend with other aldermen. Now aldermen may be versed in many disciplines but I certainly do not believe they are interested in discussing theoretical physics." He likened academic freedom to press freedom, which, he contended, was maintained on behalf of the reader, not the journalist. Asserting that academic freedom should be respected on condition that the professor respected students' liberty for learning, he criticized a course in economics he had taken in law school in the early 1930s because, he said, he had been taught "Marxism, nothing else." "Where was my freedom to learn? I was made to choose what my professor chose."[2]

Back in Rio late in September, Lacerda exchanged compliments with Senegal's President Léopold-Sédar Senghor, who was on an official visit to Brazil.[3] Charles de Gaulle, at the same time, began his "grand tour" of South America on the cruiser *Colbert*, with the purpose of promoting a "third position" closer to France than to the United States. Before setting out, the seventy-four-year-old French president had told Brazil's new ambassador in Paris, Antônio Mendes Vianna, that he wished to have as little contact as possible with Lacerda in Brazil, the last country on his itinerary.[4] The Brazilian authorities, making plans that eliminated Lacerda's presence from the receptions and ceremonies, arranged that de Gaulle would be met by Castello Branco at the Rio docks on October 13, and, after laying a wreath at the Monument to the Unknown Soldier, would be flown with his wife and party to Brasília. Following a visit to São Paulo, the French president was to give a farewell banquet on the *Colbert* in Guanabara Bay and spend a night in Laranjeiras Palace before flying to Paris on October 16.

Lacerda declared that as long as de Gaulle chose to ignore Guanabara, Guanabara would ignore de Gaulle. An official note about the

French president's plans, issued by the Guanabara government, stated that the failure to see Rio was equivalent to visiting France without seeing Paris.[5]

To coincide with de Gaulle's arrival, *Manchete* published an article, "The Great de Gaulle," by Lacerda. While calling de Gaulle "one of the greatest men of our times," it emphasized his defects and said that, like the Arch of Triumph, he was better seen from a distance. The article described his government as a sort of disguised dictatorship, a democracy with more than two thousand political prisoners, a republic in which lese majesty was a crime. It accused him of having seriously endangered the unity of free Europe and of being wrong and stupid with respect to Brazil, which, according to Lacerda, was regarded by de Gaulle as a sort of American colony that ought to be added as a reserve to the area dominated by what de Gaulle considered French luster. The de Gaulle visit, Lacerda wrote, had been prepared "in the worst possible manner," with no advance settlements of the conflicts between the two countries, many caused by businessmen with political connections. "If it had been up to me, the de Gaulle visit would be a great success, preceded by the felicitous solution of all the problems."

Lacerda admitted that de Gaulle's "erroneous concept of the Third World, a group of third-class nations dominated by France's brilliance," might serve a useful purpose if it would prevent the United States and the Soviet Union from reaching a Yalta-like accord to divide the world into two areas of influence. And he expressed the hope that the de Gaulle visit, with its banquets and speeches, would allow de Gaulle to get rid of misconceptions given him by intriguers. Comparing de Gaulle's visit with that of the president of Senegal, Lacerda wrote that the former, because of the way it was conceived, merely represented "the past, an illustrious past," whereas the latter was a truly historic event because it concerned the future.[6]

French journalists, arriving in Rio with de Gaulle, scuffled with Brazilian marines and were placed in a bus where they screamed: "*Brésil naziste! Brésil naziste!*" Front pages of the Brazilian press reported on "insults" hurled at Brazil in *L'Aurore, Le Figaro,* and *Paris Presse. Le Figaro,* commenting on Lacerda's absence from the official functions, likened him to a prima donna in a provincial theater who would allow no one to share the stage with him. *Paris Presse* wrote that Lacerda, in defense of United States interests, had incited the army to throw out Quadros and Goulart. And it reported that de Gaulle, on reaching Rio, would find it a city of corruption, "where girls sell themselves for the price of two packages of cigarettes." "Brazil, more than ever, is a sick giant."[7]

The Guanabara legislature passed a resolution making de Gaulle an honorary citizen of the state. Upon receiving the resolution on October 14, Lacerda agreed to sign it because, he said, the French president deserved the title. But he pointed out that it would be mailed to de Gaulle rather than presented to him. "I only regret that this means that Assemblyman Frota Aguiar will not have the opportunity to extend verbal greetings to the French president, as he seemed so much to want to do."[8]

Hélio Walcacer, attending a meeting in Louisville, Kentucky, reported that Lacerda's "decisive attitude in refusing to receive" de Gaulle caused "a great euphoria" in the United States.[9]

Lacerda had not refused to receive de Gaulle. But he had, in his *Manchete* article and elsewhere, made uncomplimentary remarks about him. In Brasília Adauto Lúcio Cardoso seized on what he called "the behavior of the Governor of Guanabara, notably in the case of de Gaulle's visit," as a reason why it would be inconvenient to hold a UDN nominating convention in the near future.[10]

6. The Break between Lacerda and *O Globo* (October 1964)

During de Gaulle's visit to Brazil, Lacerda delivered an address to a group of women in which he called the French president a "new Louis XIV." He renewed his attack on Castello Branco's "false technicians" and accused the United States of racial prejudice. In the course of criticizing the press, he told the women that *O Globo* had decided to oppose the Guanabara administration on account of the position he had assumed about Lage Park.[1]

Much of Lage Park, with its hundreds of thousands of square meters of forest in Rio's Jardim Botânico area, had been taken over from the estate of Henrique Lage by the Bank of Brazil years before. When the bank had put the property up for sale at an auction early in 1960, the successful bidder had been a firm whose principal shares were in the hands of Roberto Marinho and Arnon de Mello, former governor of Alagoas. A total of 552,000 square meters not far from Corcovado Peak, and including a splendid marble mansion, became the property of the real estate firm for about 300 million cruzeiros ($1.6 million), paid in part to Lage's widow and payable in part to the Bank of Brazil in the future. Although the National Historical and Artistic Patrimony Service had ruled earlier that the park had to remain a park, making it uninteresting for real estate developers, Marinho obtained a cancellation of the ruling from President

Kubitschek, giving the property an enormous value. Marinho drew up plans for dividing the park into building lots.

Lacerda, during his gubernatorial race, promised to conserve Lage Park, but Marinho, shortly before Lacerda's election, obtained from Public Works Secretary Ivo de Magalhães a permit to start work on his building lot project. Following the election, Lacerda reviewed the documents bearing on the permit and noted that all the opinions except that of Ivo de Magalhães had opposed the project.[2]

With Lacerda determined to obstruct the division of the park into building lots, Marinho suggested to him that a cemetery be set up in the park. Lacerda argued that it was ridiculous for O Globo's owner to transform such an important park into cemetery lots that could just as well be put in waste land. After Augusto Frederico Schmidt helped persuade Marinho to abandon the cemetery idea, Marinho asked Lacerda to assign someone to discuss with him his original plan, which he maintained would preserve woods on hillsides and protect the area's natural beauty. Lacerda named Lota de Macedo Soares. Unsympathetic to Marinho's plans, she remarked to Lacerda that if Marinho were to get his hands on the Bois de Boulogne in Paris, Hyde Park in London, or Central Park in New York, he would perhaps set to work there to make money by selling lots.[3]

Finally Lacerda proposed that Guanabara give Marinho some real estate it owned on President Vargas Avenue in exchange for Lage Park. It seemed that an agreement was reached when Lacerda, lunching at his home with Marinho, showed his guest the message he had prepared to deliver to the state legislature, asking for its approval of the exchange. But after Marinho discussed the proposal with lawyer Dario de Almeida Magalhães, he concluded that the exchange would be too unfavorable for him to accept.

Lacerda, preparing to expropriate the park, had Finance Secretary Mario Lorenzo Fernandez look into the evaluation used for the payment of taxes on it. He found that the annual tax payments were 735,000 cruzeiros ($415 in October 1964), for they continued to be the modest ones appropriate before Kubitschek's controversial ruling enormously increased the property's value. The governor saw no inconvenience in adhering to legislation that made expropriations possible with the payment of twenty times the amount paid annually in taxes. The state paid only 14,700,000 cruzeiros ($8,300) to expropriate the property; the real estate firm that lost Lage Park went to the courts.[4]

O Globo, in a front-page editorial on October 15, 1964, replied to Lacerda's remark to the women about the park expropriation being responsible for the newspaper's position. It said that it had usually agreed with Lacerda's political stands "until the advent of Castello Branco's government" and had collaborated with his administrative team, being especially impressed with Raphael de Almeida Magalhães, Marcelo Garcia, Hélio Beltrão, Flexa Ribeiro, Enaldo Cravo Peixoto, and Mario Lorenzo Fernandez.

Except for a complaint about Lacerda's letter of late July to Nina Ribeiro, *O Globo* had been restrained in criticizing the governor. But now, in mid-October, it assailed him for treating Castello's capable ministers as though they were ministers of Goulart and for making "preposterous" attacks that were violent, unjust, and dangerous. It claimed that Lacerda had expropriated Lage Park in order to strike back at Marinho for favoring Castello's team and in order to be able to declare that *O Globo* had turned against him because of the expropriation. This last accusation, *O Globo* wrote, relieved it of regarding its past support of Lacerda as a reason for remaining silent, as it had done in the face of Lacerda's recent "insults" to de Gaulle.

Pointing out that these insults were "true signs of mental insanity," it added that Lacerda's psychological problems could become "a serious danger to this nation—a nation that cannot put up with a repetition of the Jânio Quadros case." Even the governor's assistants, *O Globo* wrote, had advised that "his crises of depression have become more frequent, so that one can never tell whether he will fulfill his appointment schedule at Guanabara Palace or go to his country place in Rocio or to a friend's house in Bangu, all of which has been alarming his doctors, family, and close friends."[5]

Lacerda, replying quickly in a letter to *O Globo,* said that he did not like the "cruelty" with which the newspaper confused his state of health, which was good, with that of Letícia, a matter of concern. "When his financial interests are not at stake, Roberto Marinho is habitually more courteous." The governor accused *O Globo* of having called Goulart a statesman in 1963 and of having supported a return to the presidential system in exchange for a Caixa Econômica loan, authorized by Goulart. As for *O Globo*'s need to defend Castello Branco from Lacerda, the governor wrote that this was unnecessary "for the simple reason that the marshal does not own Lage Park." Lage Park, Lacerda wrote, was in greater need of defense than Castello. "The former is threatened by destruction. The latter is threatened only by the flattery of the owners of Brazil, for whom my presence is so inconvenient."[6]

Lacerda asked *O Globo* to publish his letter, "as required by law," on the same page on which its editorial had appeared, page 1. But *O*

Globo, three days later, published it on the twelfth page of an issue that contained another front-page editorial about Lacerda. In this, *O Globo* wrote that the idea of a cemetery had been accepted by Lacerda "with excitement, understandable in view of the gravity of the problem of burial in the city and the funereal nature of the governor." Calling Lacerda's comment about the Caixa Econômica loan "ridiculous," *O Globo* pointed out that everyone had favored the plebiscite. Lacerda himself, the editorial said, had turned to the Caixa Econômica for loans for his newspaper and his apartment purchase. According to *O Globo,* the encouragement given to Goulart in 1963, when he sought to separate himself from "agitators and subversives," was, at that time, a policy of the UDN, the party "which Lacerda now wants to force to swallow his candidacy at once."

Asserting that no one except the governor, "in an exhibition of bad taste," had mentioned Letícia's health, *O Globo* expressed its regret that she was unwell. "We regret also the depressions of the governor, which were not created in our imagination, but are verified by all who deal with him. Just last Thursday, after reading our editorial, he had a crisis and left for unknown parts, later revealed to be Bangu."

O Globo wrote that at one time it had believed that Lacerda's defects, "hatefulness, violent impulses, ingratitude, the desire to be justified," were compensated by qualities that gave him the ability to carry out an important role, but that derangements had overcome his positive side. It blamed his deplorable behavior on the discovery that his last banner, opposition to Goulart, had lost significance. It could see, it said, no further role for Lacerda in Brazilian politics; and it vowed to defend the nation against him. "Incidentally, he is in urgent need of someone who will defend him against himself."[7]

Lacerda's reply to this "long insult" was another letter to *O Globo* that reviewed the Lage Park case, including the "scandalous" arrangement to have the park no longer considered a part of the national patrimony—an arrangement that Lacerda said was obtained personally by Marinho from Kubitschek, thanks to the influence exerted by *O Globo.* The main point made by Lacerda was that it would no longer be possible, as Marinho was finding out, to exert effectively this sort of pressure to secure favors. Brazil was no longer "a large, abandoned Lage Park."

Lacerda announced in his letter that, in suing Marinho for the assault on his honor, he was simply trying to teach *O Globo*'s director that "his newspaper readers are not brokers of his business deals." "If I have quarreled and criticized," Lacerda concluded, "I have never done so for money."[8]

7. The UDN Sets a Convention Date (October 1964)

Magalhães Pinto explained on television that Brazil's political parties should be shut down and replaced by "really authentic and democratic parties that can arouse the enthusiasm of the young people, assist women, and protect, not exploit, the workers." After he said he would not turn to the UDN to launch his presidential candidacy, he reached an accord with the Minas PTB, which agreed to cooperate with his government.[1]

In the last week of September, Congressman Jorge Curi (UDN, Paraná) persuaded sixteen of the thirty members of the UDN national directorship to sign a request for an immediate convention. The request cited the petitions of "a large majority of the state directorships," which were sending in telegrams while Curi collected signatures. Although an early convention was opposed by many UDN congressmen, among them national directorship members Adauto Lúcio Cardoso, Paulo Sarasate, and Rui Santos (UDN secretary-general), UDN President Bilac Pinto appeared ready to call a directorship meeting to name a convention date and place.[2]

Bilac Pinto had his hands full with reform proposals being drawn up by Castello's team. In particular, he and many UDN congressmen from Minas and São Paulo, among them Herbert Levy, were upset with the agrarian reform proposal of the planning ministry. Bilac, who spent hours debating the question with Castello Branco, opposed a tax whose purpose was nonfiscal, being designed to bring about a "forced redistribution of property."[3]

When Bilac came to Rio on September 26 to discuss convention plans with Lacerda, the governor argued that an early convention was required to examine "unpostponable problems" such as agrarian reform. He showered praise on the UDN president for the "admirable coherence and tenacity" with which he combated "socialistic" agrarian reform ideas. Bilac returned to Brasília with plans for the UDN national directorship to meet within a few days.

Lacerda, ill with the grippe, wrote Bilac on September 29 to express his satisfaction with the party's intention to consult the party's grassroots. The government's proposed Land Statute, he wrote, would punish industrialized agriculture and transform Brazil into a nation of small land plots. "This plan pleases the Communists and a certain reactionary and anachronistic current in the United States that wants to keep Brazil in a position where it cannot compete in international markets or carry out the technological revolution." Like Lacerda, Herbert Levy warned against planners who lacked practical experience. It was inconceivable, Levy said, that the proposed tax on underused lands should be applied unless the government first carried out a complete census of all land properties.[4]

The UDN national directorship, after hearing Adauto Lúcio Cardoso attack Lacerda as dangerous, listened to Roberto Campos defend agrarian reform. The planning minister, with brilliance and wit, demonstrated that the administration's proposed Land Statute followed faithfully the directives appearing in past UDN programs. The father of the statute, he said, was not the SUPRA or João Pinheiro Neto of the Goulart administration but was the UDN. Campos impressed the *udenistas* but did not persuade Bilac Pinto to change his view.[5]

In mid-October, while the Castello administration revised its agrarian reform proposals in an effort to satisfy Bilac Pinto and others, Raphael de Almeida Magalhães received a phone call from the president saying that he wished to give public recognition to Lacerda, chief civilian leader of the March 31 revolution, and was considering naming him to head Brazil's delegation to the Organization of American States (OAS). Raphael, before exploring the matter with Lacerda, called the president back to say that it occurred to him that Lacerda would mistake Castello's motive and regard it as a way to get him out of Brazil just when he was trying to arrange to obtain the UDN nomination. If, Raphael added, Castello wished to proceed with his invitation, against Raphael's recommendation, could he make it for the United Nations instead of the OAS? Castello asked the vice governor to name someone who might sound out Lacerda. Raphael suggested Sandra Cavalcanti and Armando Falcão.[6]

When Falcão spoke to Lacerda about a UN appointment, the governor's first reaction was positive. "Come on," he exclaimed to Letícia and Cristina, "let's go to New York!" But Letícia dampened the governor's enthusiasm when she said, "It is obvious that the idea is to get you away so that they can harden the regime." Carlos replied: "Yes. I did think of that myself."[7]

Raphael, going to Lacerda's apartment at the governor's request, was not surprised to find Falcão there. Nor was he surprised to hear Lacerda say: "Do you know what Castello Branco is offering me? The headship of the Brazilian delegation to the UN. He wants to take me out of the country!" Raphael told the governor that he felt that the president's invitation was a sincere gesture to honor him and that a two-month absence from Brazil would not change anything. Lacerda disagreed. He told Falcão to inform the president that he felt honored but wanted time before replying.[8]

Minas UDN President Paulo Campos Guimarães announced that the Minas UDN opposed holding a party convention in 1964. Lacerda, fighting against further delay, held a press conference on

October 17, at which he said that the UDN was not in power and that a purpose of any political party was to achieve power. The principal ministries, he said, were in the hands of nonparty men with the exception of Roberto Campos, who "was going to join the PTB when the revolution came and made him a minister." The UDN, according to Lacerda, should prepare to take over the power by discussing projects that endangered democracy, such as the agrarian reform project, and by uniting behind a presidential candidate.[9]

Castello Branco, unhappy with the precipitation of the presidential campaign, called Lacerda to his second-floor office in Laranjeiras Palace on October 17 and told him that his vigorous voice was needed to defend Brazil in the UN but that it should be the voice of all Brazil, not that of a candidate. Lacerda observed that the UN was full of presidential candidates, including "my dear friend Adlai Stevenson." As Lacerda told the press when he left the president's office, his decision about the UN offer remained yet to be given Castello.[10]

Meeting in Guanabara Palace with his advisers, Lacerda surprised them by saying, "We are going to go all over Brazil to get the support of the grassroots of the UDN; otherwise its top people will discard my candidacy." Abreu Sodré protested that time was too short because the UDN directorship was about to set an early November date, but Lacerda replied that without the trip "there will be no elections because I shall not be a candidate." During the first part of the whirlwind campaign, made in the south between October 20 and 23, Abreu Sodré told reporters that, after listening to the views of delegates, he was convinced that Lacerda would receive 80 percent of their votes.[11]

The *Esperança* was still in the south when the UDN national directorship, meeting in Brasília, set November 7 and 8 as the convention dates. A committee of three, to decide on the location, adopted Herbert Levy's choice of São Paulo.[12]

Lacerda, upon returning to Rio from the south, learned of the government's "imminent" proposal to carry out political party and electoral reform. He asked Bilac to have the UDN take no position until after the convention.[13] In a long letter to Castello he wrote: "The simple formation of new parties, the result of rearranging the present ones, will not remove their defects and will probably cause some of them to lose qualities such as the UDN has acquired in the course of struggling and rendering services to the democratic regime." As for the talk of creating a new "party of the revolution," Lacerda asked why it would not be proper to turn to the party that had made the revolution before the army had done so.

In this letter, Lacerda criticized "our revolution" for "placing excessive hope in laws and very little in action." He also commented on a recent phone call from Castello about investigations of past corruption. Dismissals of wayward bureaucrats, Lacerda said, would do little good as long as lawsuits were judged by Supreme Court Justices Evandro Lins e Silva and Hermes Lima and their likes, and as long as "we are compelled to depend on the votes of enemies of the democratic regime for the approval of projects conceived as the prescriptions for public salvation."[14]

Lacerda, after meeting a group of convention delegates in Niterói, set forth on a 10,500-kilometer trip of one week to visit eighteen cities in the north and northeast.[15] During the trip, *Manchete* published his campaign message—an interview in which he said that as president he would apply the methods and ideas being used in Guanabara. It would, he asserted, be "antidemocratic" and cowardly not to allow the people to vote for this program, especially since eighteen of the twenty-two UDN state directorships had asked for a convention to select a candidate and sixteen of them had chosen him. "I am a candidate because I understood that the Revolution is to have either no program or else my program, which is not just mine but is our program, the program of the people. I did not invent anything. . . . I simply began to do something that has not been done for a long time in Brazil: govern. It is incredible how things happen when people begin to govern."[16]

Magalhães Pinto, during Lacerda's trip, told UDN directors that the planned convention and nomination of Lacerda would give the enemies of the revolution the perfect weapon for combating it.[17] Virgílio Távora, governor of Ceará, announced that he would not attend the convention, which he opposed, but would accept the "final decision of the party." In Rio Grande do Norte, where Governor Aluísio Alves carried on his feud with pro-Lacerda Senator Dinarte Mariz, the UDN state directorship was reported to be unenthusiastic about the convention. Amaral Netto, passed over by Lacerda for the Guanabara governorship, delivered a speech calling the convention "antirevolutionary." Rádio Nacional, the federal government's station, rebroadcast the entire speech.[18]

President Castello Branco, at a press conference on October 30, said that if the convention's consequence was a disturbance of the political arena, "the responsibility will be exclusively that of the party or parties that launch candidacies more than one year ahead of time. Let the parties and candidates keep out of the rough heat of the sun and the dampness of dusk of 1965–1966. The government will do everything possible to maintain and enlarge its political base, indispensable for its work of national reconstruction."

The president's "sun and dampness" expression, appropriate for his home state, Ceará, was called "rubbish" by Ernâni Sátiro, the pro-Lacerda UDN congressional leader; and Lacerda, during his travels, called it an ironic remark that Castello, a serious man, could not have made. In Bahia he asked: "Who says that we agitate against the government?" "No one owns the Revolution. Those who adhered to it at the last minute cannot teach me how to defend it. We were responsible for turbulence on behalf of the Revolution, mobilizing and enlightening the people, and bringing to Castello's attention the demands of the people."[19]

Lacerda concluded his trip on November 3 and 4 by visiting Belo Horizonte, Goiânia, and Brasília. In Belo Horizonte, where Congressman Oscar Dias Corrêa worked on his behalf, Lacerda expressed his gratitude for the decision of the Minas delegates to go to São Paulo. "The great advantage of launching a candidacy at this moment is to establish, in an irrevocable manner, the idea that elections must be held on the stipulated date. This statement is not an expression of distrust in the present government, whose honesty I acknowledge, but a recognition of the maneuvers of adversaries who are still in shock but not dead."[20]

In Brasília, Lacerda called on Castello Branco. According to accounts given by a part of the press, the president said he had no intention of interfering with the UDN convention, an internal affair of the party, and was so much attracted to Lacerda's candidacy that he might vote for him. The president's office was quick to issue an "official statement" denying the reports and reiterating that Castello felt that the immediate nomination of a presidential candidate might be a disturbing factor for the political organization of the revolution.[21]

The president phoned Magalhães Pinto to explain that, contrary to published reports, he had warned Lacerda of the risks of a two-year campaign, including the risk of overexposure of the candidate. Presidential candidate Ademar de Barros assured Castello that he would do his best to avoid an agitated campaign.[22]

On the eve of the UDN convention, the press was filled with comments about Lacerda and the UDN. The *Jornal do Brasil*, which considered the convention inconvenient for the revolution, wrote that the government, in giving insufficient attention to the presidential succession, had lost out to political parties which adhered to bygone customs; but, it added, the president could still regain the initiative. Both the *Diário de Notícias* and the *Correio da Manhã* wrote that "the party of eternal vigilance" was no longer vigilant, with the latter reminding its readers of the killings of beggars carried out by Lacerda's police and the "mass imprisonments" ordered by the governor.

Amaral Netto, vowing to lead a dissident wing at the convention, accused the party of becoming a Chinese secret society or a tribe of barbarians because it listened to only one voice.[23]

Lígia Lessa Bastos declared that Lacerda was temperamentally unfit to be president. But General Olímpio Mourão Filho, a member of the Superior Military Tribunal, was full of praise for the governor of Guanabara. The general, who had marched against Goulart despite the advice of Castello, was a critic of the president. "A Carlos Lacerda," he proclaimed, "is born only once in a century. If we thrust him aside now, we'll have to wait for another century."[24]

8. Nominated by the UDN (November 8, 1964)

On Saturday, November 7, while more than three hundred delegates checked in at the auditorium of the Gazeta Building in São Paulo, the Trem da Esperança brought journalists and several hundred Lacerda supporters in six railroad cars from Rio. The candidate, in the meantime, worked on his acceptance speech in his crowded suite at São Paulo's Danúbio Hotel.[1]

When Amaral Netto picked up his credentials at the Gazeta Building, he was greeted with jeers. He used the occasion to give a talk in which he said that the UDN, in nominating a presidential candidate so early, revealed its lack of confidence in the government. Denying that Lacerda's nomination would guarantee an election, he pointed out that elections were canceled in 1937 despite the campaigning of three candidates. He called the UDN undemocratic for listening to only one voice and added that if Congress approved electoral reforms, to be considered in March, "this convention will be without effect."[2]

At the opening session on Saturday afternoon, convention chairman Ernâni Sátiro called for a vote to decide whether or not to nominate a presidential candidate. Adauto Lúcio Cardoso reminded the audience of his previous opposition to the "inordinately" early convention but said he would adhere to the decision of the party. "Adauto," Amaral Netto remarked to those around him, "is prompting me to make critical remarks."[3]

When Amaral Netto arose, he was booed. Raising his voice above the clamor, he declared that he had often been jeered at by Brizola, Kubitschek, and Goulart. Without mentioning Lacerda's name, he said it was not right to criticize a minister of Castello Branco as one would criticize a minister of Goulart. "Perhaps in six or eight months you gentlemen will decide that my words, given at this convention, are correct." His fanatical detractors, he said, could save their jeers for the future, when he would again defend his right to defend his opinion. "If there is one thing I do not know, it is fear." Some delegates applauded while others shouted "Lacerda, Lacerda."

Herbert Levy called Amaral Netto a "brave and valiant companion" who had struggled in difficult situations, especially during the previous administration, when subversion had reached dangerous proportions. But, Levy added, "there is another who has been greater than all of us—an individual whose life hung by a thread. I speak of a companion of indomitable courage, one of those leaders who appear only now and then in history."[4]

The delegates resolved overwhelmingly to name a presidential candidate. Later, at a night session at the Arlequim Movie Theater, they saw a film about the accomplishments of the Guanabara government.

Lacerda, on Sunday, lunched with *O Estado de S. Paulo* directors at Júlio de Mesquita Filho's home and then went to his hotel suite, where he was advised by telephone of the result of the voting at the convention. Of the 373 delegates who had registered, 318 cast secret ballots, with 309 favoring Lacerda. After Bilac Pinto announced the result, paper streamers filled the auditorium and a large picture of the candidate appeared. The crowd shouted "Lacerda, Lacerda," and sang a Carnaval samba. The nominee, receiving congratulations at the Danúbio Hotel, called the outcome "a beauty"—a demonstration of UDN unity and strength.[5]

In a stirring oration at the evening session, Herbert Levy recalled the role of Eduardo Gomes in the 1922 *tenente* uprising and went on to say that the UDN's motto, "the price of liberty is eternal vigilance," had best been fulfilled by Carlos Lacerda. Sandra Cavalcanti maintained that the forthcoming campaign would be the "most beautiful page of democracy in the history of Brazil."

Lacerda's arrival was hailed by shouts and singing and the release of balloons, and was followed by speeches by Sátiro, Bilac Pinto, and Rui Santos. After Lacerda, holding flowers presented by a group of girls, reached the speakers' platform, São Paulo's Guarda Civil played the national anthem and "Cidade Maravilhosa." The singing was enthusiastic and an emotional atmosphere prevailed as the nominee began his long speech.[6]

Lacerda opened by mentioning the difficulties that he had been forced to overcome before "we could get this far: the malice, treachery, and hatred," the work of those "who do not want me in the presidency, and of others who never wanted a worthwhile revolution." Explaining that he had become accustomed to being the sacrificial lamb, he went on to quote a statement that asked: "Why should we accept this candidate for the presidency? All his political work . . . is that of an agitator, a revolutionary, a demolisher. In the press, in the tribune, in the government, he has been a devastating hurricane." The words, Lacerda revealed, had been written about the candidacy of Rui Barbosa in 1919.

In his own case, Lacerda said, it had been necessary to achieve the Guanabara governorship, after twenty years in the opposition, in order that "no one again can call me a destroyer." Denying that the constructive works and services developed by his state government had been largely "financed by the Americans," he pointed out that foreign financing amounted to less than 4 percent of the investment made by the Carioca people. Foreign and Brazilian government financing did not reach 7 percent. "Without denying or hiding the contribution of the Alliance for Progress and the Brazilian federal resources, it is necessary that the truth be known in order to have it understood that an honest and hardworking government, being the most simple, is the best answer to the problems of Brazil."

Lacerda, in his references to the Castello Branco government, kept calling it a "government of transition." It was, he said, characterized by honesty and a patriotic effort to carry out the objectives of the revolution while upholding not only the institutions but, "in an effort that many consider excessive," even members of the old oligarchy. "The Revolution," he warned, "should not support, or receive support from the oligarchy lest it be devoured by it—as happened to the 1930 revolution." He also warned that a return to dictatorship in Brazil was possible "if we do not use the arms of democracy with sufficient vigor."

"The greatest risk of the moment," the nominee said, was the cultivation of technocrats. Warning against planning carried out without statistics, he said that the 1960 census had not been published, due to "corruption and petty politics." And yet, he added, between 1960 and 1964 Brazil had been given three government plans, the new one being "the Plan of Economic Action, which is taking an entrance exam at the International Monetary Fund. All the plans were more or less prepared by more or less the same advisers."

Speaking of the confidence of the people in the government, Lacerda called it a confidence that depended on the confidence of the government in the people. He said that the revolution was in danger of losing that mutual confidence, and he promised, in the coming campaign, to work at building it up. Only false revolutionaries, he said, opposed agitation and campaigning, believing that the people would be saved by a series of law projects. He urged the government not to be fearful of true leaders, and not to give authority to advisers who did not deserve it.

According to Lacerda, the government ought to be guided by a policy of fair wages, not one that restricted wages without restricting profits and price increases. The speaker declared that "the people must not be starved in order to save the currency." He pictured the scarcity of foodstuffs as the factor that would be most responsible for separating the people from the government, and said that all the government bureaus for supplying food, about seventy in number, were monotonously repeating errors carried out for thirty years. "While agrarian reform deals with social justice in abstract terms of a merely romantic nature, the people will be unable to eat because the principal objective of the reform is not the supply of food."[7]

O Estado de S. Paulo praised Lacerda for his "courageous" warning against members of the presidential "entourage" who sought to separate Castello Branco from personalities who could link the president with the "revolutionary masses." The *Jornal do Brasil*, much less enthusiastic about Lacerda's speech, wrote that the presidency could not remain silent in the face of the disparagement of the Plan of Economic Action and the nominee's confusing claim to be both spokesman and critic of the revolution. The convention, it said, was a "festival of contradictions" because the UDN, participant in Castello's administration and backer of the extension of his mandate, had struck a blow against the revolution's survival by precipitating the problem of the succession and by nominating a candidate "who is clearly antigovernment and antirevolution." Columnist Carlos Castello Branco wrote on November 10: "The UDN of 1964 does not love Carlos Lacerda and is fearful of the paths he might follow if he is victorious. . . . It is coming to feel that a defeat does not offer it worse prospects than a victory with this candidate."

Amaral Netto declared that seventy convention delegates had absented themselves during the convention's balloting and that fifty-one of the ninety-six *udenista* congressmen had not voted for Lacerda. "Disunity in the party," he said, "is much greater than might be imagined." *Última Hora* pointed out that only two UDN governors (Lacerda and Correia da Costa) had attended the convention, whereas three (Aluísio Alves, Virgílio Távora, and Magalhães Pinto) had been absent, as had government congressional leader Pedro Aleixo. It wrote about schisms in the state delegations, preventing in every case a full representation. In Belo Horizonte, Senator Afonso Arinos de Melo Franco declared that he would not support Lacerda's candidacy.[8]

9. Comments

In the last six months of 1964, the two chief setbacks to Lacerda's presidential ambition were the extension of Castello Branco's mandate and the aversion to Lacerda's candidacy that came to be felt by the president's entourage and the president himself. Lacerda's aggressive attacks were responsible for both setbacks.

In the case of the mandate extension, which would have been defeated if a single one of the favorable votes had been unfavorable, it is impossible not to speculate what the outcome might have been without Lacerda's condemnation, just prior to the vote, of the behavior of the members of his own party in Congress. The UDN congressmen were wounded by Lacerda's belligerent accusations—described by Bilac Pinto as "terrorist tactics"—and almost all of them followed the lead of men alienated by Lacerda in the past, such as Afonso Arinos. Lacerda was right in concluding that *prorrogação* would not have been adopted except for the votes of those who did not wish to see him in the presidency.

President Castello Branco did everything he could to prevent an open break with Lacerda. But the president was known to regard attacks against members of his administration as attacks against himself. General Golbery do Couto e Silva, constantly attacked by Lacerda, could only conclude that Lacerda's purpose was to attack the president in an indirect manner.[1] Of greater importance, Castello Branco saw himself and his team as putting Brazil on the correct revolutionary path and wanted the administration's plans—especially about economic policy—to be carried out by his successor.

While the president welcomed discussion before policy decisions were reached, he was stubborn in adhering to the decisions once they were announced. It was no comfort to him to realize that Lacerda would spend two years stirring up the public against the path chosen by his government and was even declaring that the government lacked a revolutionary program.

The president clung to the hope that his successor would be a civilian. Juracy Magalhães and Bilac Pinto were possibilities that came to his mind. Lacerda entertained the fear that Castello Branco favored Roberto Campos, but the president, a realist, appreciated that his planning minister, like himself, would lose popularity while undertaking the steps that both felt were necessary for the country.[2]

Castello was eager to work with Congress on his wide range of reforms, and this meant dealing with PSD leaders. Lacerda's condemnation of this practice reflected his view of the political side of the revolution. This view was revealed also in his assault on the Supreme Court, begun in November 1964, and in his constant criticisms of Milton Campos, whom he regarded as a man who would not remove legal obstacles "so that the revolution could really be carried out."

This side of Lacerda gave encouragement to men who wished to throw aside legal obstacles, bury the PSD and PTB, and give Brazil what they called "a real revolution." Many of these men were in the military, where Lacerda had a large following, and they liked his denouncements of the constitutional path favored by the president and his justice minister, appointed precisely in order to have the institutions upheld.

Unfortunately for the legalist side of Lacerda, which proclaimed the sanctity of the institutions in the case of the presidential election, the men he stimulated when he attacked the government's political ways were men who felt that the "real revolution" did not include elections by the people. These men believed that past "popular choices" had invariably been disastrous. For them, the remaking of Brazil did not include upholding institutions that might allow the return of the electorally strong PSD-PTB-Communist combination that had favored politicians such as Kubitschek and Goulart.

In brief, Lacerda diminished his chances of achieving the presidency by bringing about the extension of Castello's mandate, removing himself from the president's list of successors, and attacking those who, like Milton Campos, clung to the hope that it would be possible to uphold the institutions.

VII.

From Criticizing Ministers to Defaming the President (November 1964–July 1965)

1. Guest of the *Reader's Digest* (November 1964)

In São Paulo on Monday morning, November 9, Lacerda boarded the Trem da Esperança. During the fourteen-hour trip to Rio, the train made eighteen stops so that the candidate could address crowds, usually from the back platform and occasionally in public squares alongside stations. The crowd at Queluz, the last stop in São Paulo state, heard from Lacerda, Abreu Sodré, Raul Brunini, and other politicians. As the train made its way through Rio state, larger and more enthusiastic crowds were on hand.[1]

Most of these larger crowds had to wait for at least two hours. The train's delay was caused in part by the report of a plot to blow it up when it passed through the Mantiqueira Tunnel. Colonel Gustavo Borges, coming from Rio, advised Lacerda that the police of the states of Guanabara and Rio de Janeiro had arrested conspirators, among them a geography teacher and a former military officer, who had planned to place dynamite in holes already prepared in the ground in the tunnel. As other members of the conspiracy were believed to be still at large, the question of continuing with the trip was discussed. An engineer volunteered to run a locomotive ahead of the Trem da Esperança to see if the way was clear. The test, which offered the possibility of the engineer's death, showed that the passage was safe, and the train resumed its trip.[2]

At Barra do Piraí and Japeri, reached after 9:00 P.M., the crowds greeted the candidate with fireworks. By this time Lacerda was making his speeches brief and promising to return. At Anchieta, just inside Guanabara, the *trem* remained at the station for only two minutes, a disappointment to residents in festive costumes, who had dancers ready to perform with samba music. The train reached Rio's Pedro II station at about 1:00 A.M. on November 10.[3]

At Laranjeiras Palace that evening, Lacerda handed Castello Branco a letter advising that the UDN, "in a memorable assembly," had

APPE

Lacerda with Castello Branco. (APPE drawing in *O Cruzeiro*,
December 24, 1966)

honored him with the nomination, and that he was leaving the decision about the UN appointment up to the president, who had said the
nomination might interfere with the appointment.[4]

After Gustavo Borges joined Lacerda, Castello questioned the security secretary about the plot to destroy the Trem da Esperança. Lacerda told palace reporters that, of all the attempts to kill him, this
had been "the most serious" because it had jeopardized the lives "of
at least five hundred people, including women and children." Asked
about his electioneering plans, he said that he was "freed" of having
to attend the UN and would be able to speak at year-end graduation
exercises following a trip to New York to address a *Reader's Digest*
lunch to mark the publication of Clarence W. Hall's article about
Brazil, "The Country That Saved Itself." When a reporter suggested
that the PSD, PTB, and other parties might find it difficult to agree
on an opponent, Lacerda remarked good humoredly that he was "in
the market," ready to discuss alliances. His interest in labor, he said,
might attract "sincere labor party people."[5]

Before leaving for New York, the governor gave Mauro Magalhães,
interim UDN legislative leader, a letter for the UDN national directorship, instructing it to register his presidential candidacy at once at
the Superior Electoral Tribunal. The letter warned against maneuvers
that might make use of new laws about political parties and elections
to cast doubt on the legality of the decision reached at the recent
convention.[6]

Investigators of the plot to destroy the Trem da Esperança pointed out that Brazilian terrorism was on the rise, encouraged by Brizola in Uruguay. To protect Lacerda, leaving for New York on November 11, one plane was made to appear ready to take off while Lacerda, to the surprise of reporters and well-wishers, left in another plane.[7]

At the *Reader's Digest* lunch, three hundred businessmen heard the magazine's Paul Thompson call Lacerda Brazil's next president and the man whose "voice of protest brought about the revolution against Communism and corruption." "It is," Thompson said, "a little difficult to find a United States figure who can be compared with Carlos Lacerda. He would, naturally, be a Republican. I think we would have to go back to Theodore Roosevelt. But we can say one thing: if Goldwater were like Carlos Lacerda . . . he would have come out victorious in the elections."[8]

Lacerda criticized the "over-simplified picture of Brazil, which looks like a mural by Diego Rivera." The Brazilian revolution, he told his *Reader's Digest* audience, had been "interpreted by the world press in a way conditioned by ideological prejudices." In truth, he said, it was a continuing process of a people progressing toward democracy, and he added that Brazilian oligarchies, using corruption that opened the way to Communism, "have survived through the years and have engulfed various revolutions precisely because the Brazilian Armed Forces refused to exercise dictatorial powers." What hurt, he said, was to hear "Brazilian democrats called rightists" and to hear the terms "reformists and progressives" applied to demagogues, totalitarians, and corrupt politicians.

He reproached the "experts and stern judges who decide the foreign financial policy" of the United States. Pointing out that they had made "notable mistakes in Latin America," he said they should not insist on "rigid financial conformity" by demanding the kind of fight against inflation that impoverished the low-income people and promoted "the decapitalization of our producers." In this speech and in a television interview the next evening, Lacerda advocated a higher coffee price to allow Brazil to pay for needed imports. And he blamed United States investments in Africa for a "sort of undeclared war against Brazilian coffee."[9]

In Washington, Lacerda called on Secretary Rusk and Assistant Secretary Mann. He also attended a lunch given by Ambassador Juracy Magalhães, who, the press reported, had recently sent a letter to Professor Charles Wagley about "a series of errors" in the professor's interpretation of the "Revolution of March 31."

In view of the speculation in Washington about Juracy's being a presidential possibility, Lacerda told reporters that he, the governor, was the only Brazilian presidential candidate in the United States. "My party," Juracy chimed in, "has chosen Governor Carlos Lacerda, and I shall naturally vote for him."[10]

On November 22, when Lacerda returned to Rio, Castello Branco wrote the governor a letter to say that it would not be proper to name the UDN presidential candidate to head the delegation to the UN General Assembly. In the place of Lacerda, described in the letter as "a great Brazilian and one of the foremost revolutionary leaders,"[11] the president selected Foreign Minister Leitão da Cunha.

2. Assailing the Supreme Court (November–December 1964)

In arguing that his tax increases of August were valid, Lacerda told the Supreme Court on November 5 that the Institutional Act, which turned presidential proposals into laws if not handled by Congress within thirty days, was derived from "the Revolutionary Constitutional Power" and that it, like the federal constitution, was binding on the states. He called the legislature's objection "an antirevolutionary act, born of the defiance, hatred, and frustration" felt by those who wished to destroy Brazil and "avenge, a thousandfold, their expelled partners in corruption and their banished accomplices in subversion."[1] Before leaving for his *Reader's Digest* lunch in New York, he told the court that a "legal revolution" was a "ridiculous" concept and expressed his contempt for "simple-minded fools" who lost themselves in "juridical mazes."[2]

Upon returning to Brazil, Lacerda officially notified the court that five of its eleven ministers (justices) should be disqualified from participating in the Guanabara case because they could not deal impartially with an Institutional Act that had been used to suspend the political rights of the presidents who had appointed them. In support of this complaint against Kubitschek appointees Vítor Nunes Leal, Antônio Gonçalves de Oliveira, and Antônio Martins Vilas Boas and Goulart appointees Hermes Lima and Evandro Lins e Silva, he presented documents signed by Senator Benedito Calasans and Congressmen Ernâni Sátiro, Antônio Godinho, and Antônio Gil Veloso.[3]

Lacerda's request for the disqualifications was rejected by Luís Gallotti, acting president of the court. The court's president, Álvaro Ribeiro da Costa, was reported in the *Correio da Manhã* and the *Jornal do Brasil* as saying that the governor's request was the act of a crazy person whose lack of stability and good sense had been revealed when he insulted de Gaulle. Ribeiro da Costa also criticized Lacerda for his "violent and lamentable" attacks against Goiás Governor

Mauro Borges Teixeira, whose right to continue in office, defended by Sobral Pinto and José Crispim Borges, had been unanimously upheld by the court.[4]

Lacerda sent a telegram to Ribeiro da Costa: "I have read in several Rio newspapers, one of which is reliable, serious declarations attributed to Your Excellency. In case of confirmation, I shall sue Your Excellency for insulting and slandering a public authority."[5]

The Supreme Court's support of Mauro Borges enraged military officers who associated the Goiás governor with subversion. Their spokesman, Congressman Costa Cavalcanti, declared that the ministers of the court did not understand what had happened in Brazil since March.[6]

Lacerda spoke of the "counterrevolutionary line" of the Supreme Court. Congressmen who had provided written opinions that had accompanied Lacerda's disqualification request read their opinions in the Chamber of Deputies. After Senator Krieger discussed the Guanabara case with Castello Branco, the president was reported to be considering increasing the Supreme Court membership from eleven to fifteen in order to "neutralize decisions of future cases of interest to the revolutionary government." Luís Gallotti said it was "fantastic" to describe the court as "making a counterrevolution."[7]

Lacerda asked Castello to have the attorney-general arrange for the court to consider the Guanabara tax case only after it had handled the thirty cases presented previously to it. But nothing came of Lacerda's request, and on November 30 the court ruled, by nine votes to none, that Article 4 of the Institutional Act was not meant to be extended to the states.[8] In a telegram to Castello, Lacerda advised that he was suing Ribeiro da Costa for slanderous statements and lamented that Castello had not responded to "the single piece of collaboration that I have requested of Your Excellency." "On the contrary," Lacerda wired, "the attorney-general has been submissive" to the wishes of *relator* Gonçalves de Oliveira about the timing of a decision in which the governor had been judged by five "personal enemies and political adversaries, an occurrence novel in any country in which justice exists."[9]

In a bitter television interview, Lacerda expressed his disappointment in Castello's disregard of "the only favor" he had ever asked of the revolutionary government. He told his listeners that Gonçalves de Oliveira had been the attorney-general who had prohibited him from broadcasting during Kubitschek's presidency. He would, he said, start writing immediately for the *Tribuna da Imprensa* because he could no longer be discreet about "the series of insane acts of Roberto Campos." Exclaiming that "things have now gone too far," he accused the government of restraining credit to such an extent that the Americans were gobbling up Brazilian industries, and he cited the Ricardo Jafet interests, which, he said, were falling under the control of an American group represented by Jorge Serpa Filho and Walter Moreira Salles. With money of Time-Life, he said, Roberto Marinho "controls an immense radio-TV chain." Blaming Roberto Campos for favoring the wish of the Hanna Mining Company to have a private "port" in Sepetiba Bay, he called on Castello to fire the planning minister, who "has become the prime minister of the failed revolution."

Returning to the subject of the Supreme Court, "protector of the Light Company," Lacerda informed his listeners that in Guanabara "we used the Institutional Act to dismiss two judges of the state Justice Tribunal." After calling the Supreme Court decision about the state taxes "an aberration unprecedented in justice since the Middle Ages or the times of the totalitarian regime," he vowed not to be deterred. "I shall continue to apply the Institutional Act in every way possible. And if they are dissatisfied they can intervene in Guanabara. I invite the chief justice to take command of the intervention."[10]

While inaugurating schools in Bangu, Lacerda exhorted the people to change "that factious Supreme Court, making it honorable like ourselves, creators of schools, sewer systems, and hospitals."

The congressional minority, represented by *petebistas* Doutel de Andrade and João Herculino, said that Lacerda's "insane" and "stupid" statements about the Supreme Court revealed his "complete incompatibility" with the democratic regime. The *Correio da Manhã* felt that the "mentally unstable" governor, hoping to install himself as a dictator, attacked the court in order to gain leadership among military hard liners. *Correio da Manhã* columnist Hermano Alves wrote that Lacerda, unlikely to win a direct election, was endeavoring to bring about a second institutional act and a "regime of exception" in which the military would put him at the helm.[11]

State Justice Secretary Alcino Salazar, who had been helping the federal government draw up the decree that led to federal intervention in Goiás, insisted, like Lacerda, that it was up to Congress, and not the Supreme Court, to decide whether to suspend the tax increases. While legislative leader Mauro Magalhães maintained that the court's decision could not be considered retroactive, the state speeded up collections by ruling that, after December 17, all unpaid taxes, fees, and debts would be subject to monetary corrections, based on living-cost increases. Finance Minister Mario Lorenzo Fernandez presented large taxpaying corporations with a study that compared Guanabara's taxes with those in adjoining states and that analyzed Guanabara's needs.[12]

If the state was to have fitting observance of its fourth centenary, it would need revenue, and therefore a tax bill, presented for vote in December, called for tax rates for just one year, 1965, to be 108 percent of what they had been a year earlier; this would set the sales tax at 5.4 percent, compared with the 5.5 percent that the Supreme Court had judged unconstitutional. So useful was the vote-getting work of the young government leader, Mauro Magalhães, that Raphael de Almeida Magalhães, in announcing the passage of the tax bill, observed that Guanabara "owes to Mauro Magalhães the observation of its fourth centenary."

Earlier in the year, Mauro Magalhães had been the unanimous choice of the fifteen UDN legislators to succeed government leader Nina Ribeiro, who had been able to count on only seven proadministration votes and had attacked fellow-*udenista* Mac Dowell Leite de Castro. After that, Mauro made it a point, when lining up proadministration votes, to gain the reputation of complying with promises, using for this purpose a knowledge of what was possible or what the administration planned to include in proposed legislation. Raphael de Almeida Magalhães was not always so careful and offers he made sometimes went unkept. (It can hardly be denied, however, that he had done his best in the famous case of the social services post for Samy Jorge's wife; he persuaded Walter Cunto to write a Lacerda-like signature on an appointment document—only to have the scheme collapse because Social Services Coordinator José Arthur Rios would not let her remain in the post.)

Working for the tax bill of late 1964, Mauro was indefatigable, joining legislators at their homes or in bars, gaining their confidence and that of their wives, and explaining to oppositionists that a government defeat would not mean a change of governor but only the replacement of himself, their friend, as government leader. Following the bill's passage, Mauro's promises about public works, such as street pavings, new health facilities, and new schools, were kept. But Lacerda vetoed pay increases, voted at the same time as the tax bill. He also vetoed a Museum of Modern Art appropriation, with the explanation that it would sizably reduce the 1.7-billion-cruzeiro budget item that the tourism department was setting aside for the Fourth Centenário.[13]

3. The Hanna Case (December 1964)

The Castello Branco administration, eager to stimulate exports from Brazil's immense iron ore reserves, found that it had inherited a thorny problem because of the export intentions of the Cleveland-based

Hanna Mining Company. Hanna, with iron ore properties in Minas Gerais, had been under attack in Brazil by nationalists, leftists, and the government-controlled Companhia Vale do Rio Doce (CVRD), which shipped iron ore from the port of Vitória, Espírito Santo. The dispute, like political campaigns, had been useful to some of the prominent Rio dailies. They had received payments from CVRD and Hanna.[1]

Those who objected to Hanna's wish to construct a private ore embarkation terminal in Sepetiba Bay were joined by COSIGUA, which Lacerda hoped would build a single ore export terminal. In September, while Lacerda and the *Tribuna da Imprensa* started a vicious campaign against Hanna, Roberto Campos, and Mines and Energy Minister Mauro Thibau, the problem of establishing regulations for all large-scale iron ore export projects was assigned by Castello Branco to an interministerial commission. Castello attended many of its meetings and contributed to its conclusions.[2]

Magalhães Pinto, in letters to Castello, objected to the private ore loading terminals desired in Sepetiba Bay by Hanna and ICOMINAS, a Brazilian company. Advocating a single port, under government control, he annoyed Castello by expressing the "certainty" that the president had no "proper understanding" of the matter. After Lacerda wrote the president on behalf of a single loading facility, to be constructed by COSIGUA in the Santa Cruz industrial zone, Hanna submitted studies to show that a great deal of dredging would be needed at the COSIGUA site. It mentioned "the difficult problems of coordinating ships and trains that inevitably and unfortunately occur in terminals with a large number of users."[3]

Castello, in a major speech on November 17, objected to a monopoly for CVRD and argued that the government had enough controls to protect CVRD in case competitors turned to unfair practices. In a reference to the attacks on some of his ministers, he spoke harshly about those who "seek to impede Brazil's development by beating the drums of *nacionalismo* and *entreguismo*. Through well-directed propaganda, a climate of real 'nationalistic' terror has been built up. People who do not adhere to the primer of the barkers of this propaganda are immediately crushed with the debasing label of treason."[4]

The speech did not dampen the campaign of the *Tribuna* and Lacerda. The *Tribuna* pointed out that Thibau and Roberto Campos, members of the interministerial commission, had received money from Hanna when they were associated with the Consultec consulting firm in 1960.[5] Thibau, whose work for Consultec had consisted of evaluating hydroelectric plants that Hanna planned to sell, was called a "Minister of Hanna" by Lacerda. When Lacerda wrote Castello about economic policy on November 28, he expressed surprise that Thibau and Roberto Campos had not disqualified themselves from making decisions affecting Hanna.[6]

Early in December, after congressmen set up a CPI to investigate iron ore and Hanna, Lacerda wrote in the *Tribuna* that Thibau and Roberto Campos would allow Hanna to "carry out the most shameful assault that our country has suffered IN ITS ENTIRE HISTORY." On television he called Campos and Thibau "traitors, liars, and cousins of Lucrezia Borgia." These two, along with Hanna executive Lucas Lopes and Hanna lawyer José Luís Bulhões Pedreira, were described as traitors also in *Tribuna* articles that often bore little relation to reality. "Consultec and Hanna," the *Tribuna* wrote, "seek to control the fleets of the nation and close down Petrobrás."[7]

Castello Branco on December 3 replied to Lacerda's letter of November 28 "despite the discourteous sentence in your follow-up letter of the 30th." The president admitted that the financial policy was unpopular, but wrote that he was "honestly convinced," after hearing from many men of merit, that Lacerda was wrong in charging that the policy was "leading the country to national and international disaster." Responding to complaints that the credit policy promoted the denationalization of Brazilian industry, Castello pointed out that the government was reducing its own expenditures to free resources for productive activities. It was also insisting that foreign loans be made available not only for indispensable imports but also for purchases of Brazilian equipment, and it was providing temporary help to companies needing it for adapting themselves "to the new climate of productivity and austerity."

Castello denied that the government was contributing to denationalizing the Jafet interests or any other. He wrote that he was unfamiliar with the radio and television deals of Roberto Marinho but had ordered an investigation of the matter, about which, "I see in the press today, you are proclaiming a great scandal."

A month earlier, Castello wrote, he had looked into the Consultec matter and learned that in the past Thibau had "limited himself to carrying out an evaluation, like any professional," and that Roberto Campos, when he was without government responsibility, had participated in a study of ore exports, "after ascertaining the government's intentions in that respect and after informing it of Hanna's intentions." Castello told Lacerda that his charge was "much more against me than against the two ministers. The information that comes to you is a lie. Morally and politically Thibau and Roberto Campos have conducted themselves irreproachably."

Castello pointed out that the work of the interministerial commission was presided over by the president of the republic, and that the governor's accusation was a direct attack on the commission. "Understand, Mr. Governor, that we, too, have the moral fiber and public spirit to deal with the national interests."

> I read yesterday, with grief, your article in the *Tribuna da Imprensa*, without understanding the reasons for it. . . . I am being attacked, aggressively and rudely, by Hélio Fernandes and the governor of Guanabara. The provocations are already innumerable. But I shall not be intimidated or lose my serenity or the dignity of my position. Absolutely I do not wish to enter into a polemic. I am ready, however, to make further clarification, should this be of interest to you.
>
> I express my profound sadness at losing the help of one of the most authentic and historic revolutionaries and, at the same time, acquiring an opponent. The initiative is yours.[8]

Castello did not provide the press with a copy of his letter. But Gabinete Civil Chief Luís Viana Filho disclosed that the president had defended Campos and Thibau in it. Newspapers speculated that the president had broken with Lacerda.[9]

Júlio de Mesquita Filho and Roberto de Abreu Sodré rushed from São Paulo to Rio in a private plane on December 4 to speak with Lacerda about his relations with the president. During their three-hour discussion at Guanabara Palace, Mesquita pleaded that Lacerda write Castello a letter that would mollify him. Lacerda replied: "That, Dr. Júlio, is very difficult. After all, we are all responsible for the Revolution. This is the same thing as my asking you to have *O Estado de S. Paulo* keep quiet. And maybe worse, because *O Estado de S. Paulo* can keep quiet but I cannot do so, for here I have a population that demands that I speak, witnessing, as I do, unemployment and a disillusioned citizenry." Finally, after Mesquita kept insisting, Lacerda agreed reluctantly. He said that if there was one person in Brazil who had the right to make such an appeal it was Dr. Júlio.[10]

Lacerda, typing the letter himself, wrote that his commentary of November 28 about economic policy had been "a serious and careful analysis of our divergence, which I never wished to be personal or a cause of danger to the Revolution." The governor, expressing concern about Castello's reported reaction of hurt and even revulsion, wrote: "That would be very serious for me, on account of the esteem I have shown for you and which I continue to hold. And even more for the Revolution and the country we both serve." To give Castello what he called proof of his sincerity, Lacerda, in his letter, placed in the president's hands the decisions about all matters Lacerda had discussed including the "political content of the government of the Revolution and the path of its economic policy."

> Accept these words as the manifestation of my friendship and confidence in your integrity. If this manifestation is what you did not have, you have it here. Your Excellency deserves this. And Brazil even more so.
> It would be unjust not to add that I owe these words to the good advice of those who are better than I am.[11]

Mesquita took the letter to Laranjeiras Palace and was with Castello when he read it. The president, well pleased, said he had never doubted the intentions of the governor, whose disinterestedness he said he recognized. He added that his opinion about Lacerda—an opinion he had not revised—was exactly that of the man who emerged from the letter. Mesquita, speaking later to journalists at the palace, expressed satisfaction at the outcome, made possible, he said, by Lacerda's letter and the understanding of Castello.[12]

Lacerda stopped writing for the *Tribuna*. The press, after mentioning a "truce," wondered on December 14 whether it had come to a quick end, because Lacerda did not appear in the state legislature when it received Castello and made him an honorary citizen of Guanabara. But on December 16 the president accompanied the governor on a tour of several hours to inspect public works in Guanabara.[13]

When Transport Minister Juarez Távora spoke on a radio-television program on December 8, he announced that private terminals built in Sepetiba Bay would become government property after thirty years and that companies using those terminals would have to finance the Central do Brasil Railroad for the purchase of locomotives and cars and for construction and rehabilitation of rail line. Pointing out that exporters who stole markets from CVRD would not be allowed to transport, he said Brazil did not fear Hanna, because Hanna was not greater than Brazil. The *Jornal do Brasil*, which was in the CVRD camp, accused Távora of committing a "crime against Brazil."[14]

Magalhães Pinto, also upset, addressed a nine-page letter to Castello and sent copies to the press. *O Estado de S. Paulo*, criticizing the statements of the Minas governor, said it would be absurd to be guided by his assertion that public opinion polls opposed Hanna. Asking whether banking reform and other complex technical matters should be decided by public opinion polls, it accused Magalhães Pinto of emulating Brizola and Darci Ribeiro in "a conscious and methodical exploitation of ultranationalist prejudices and grudges." It concluded that Castello was producing "a *general* solution for advancing the national interests."[15]

Castello listened to Armed Forces Chief of Staff Peri Constant Bevilacqua and Senator João Agripino object to the administration's iron ore policy ideas. Then, at Laranjeiras Palace on December 18, he held a meeting at which the National Security Council spent five hours examining the recommendations of the interministerial commission. After the meeting, the education minister told reporters that the views of the commission had been "totally victorious." Lacerda, addressing metalworkers in São Paulo, made a disparaging remark about Hanna and accused the government of preferring "half a revolution to one revolution and a half."[16]

On December 22 the government issued regulations that confirmed what Távora had told the public and that contained points not mentioned by him. One of them stipulated that Brazilian-controlled firms of exporters were to reinvest, in the states from which the ore was mined, 50 percent of the profits in excess of a 12 percent return on capital, whereas foreign-controlled firms were to reinvest all profits in excess of 12 percent. In addition, foreign-controlled firms were to invest, anywhere in Brazil, the 12 percent return for the first five years. Furthermore, foreign ore exporters with loading terminal authorizations had to offer at least 40 percent of their capital shares to Brazilian investors. *O Estado de S. Paulo* wrote that the obligations imposed on foreign companies were "really heavy," whereas *Última Hora* claimed that the new decree bestowed privileges on Hanna.[17]

Lacerda immediately issued a note to the press promising that, if he were elected president, he would revoke "the unconstitutional and illegal decree." Hanna, he said, had obtained a decree that would "promote the formation of a virtual monopoly." "I cannot refrain from protesting nor keep quiet about my desolation."[18] After Castello accepted the resignation of CVRD President Paulo de Lima Vieira, Lacerda wrote Lima Vieira to express his regret at the "temporary victory of Hanna." A few days later, Lacerda called the government's iron ore decision "a crime for which several Brazilian generations will have to pay."[19]

When Lacerda testified before the CPI in March 1965, he called it ridiculous to seek financing for three embarkation terminals in Sepetiba Bay, and he accused Hanna of opposing free competition. He also said that Hanna, a worldwide producer of iron ore, might be planning to abandon its Brazilian project after using the threat of its Brazilian exports to modify iron ore prices. According to Lacerda,

Ford had threatened to produce rubber in Brazil but had abandoned the project after the threat had obtained the price it wanted.[20]

The anti-Hanna *Correio da Manhã* maintained that Lacerda was inspired not by patriotism but by a desire to make up for his "past servility to foreign powers." It did not mention his hope for COSIGUA and the Santa Cruz industrial zone. In any event, Lacerda's positions appeared to be keeping him reasonably popular. A *Diário de Notícias* poll, said to have been conducted among 40,960 voters, showed that the governor, by far the best-known presidential candidate, was the favorite of 17,381. This gave him a comfortable lead over second-place Hélio de Almeida, whose count was 5,098. In the opinion of *O Globo*, however, a new candidate, probably a military figure, could be expected to be launched by important groups associated with the revolution. *O Globo* wrote that the principal military chiefs felt that Lacerda "does not belong to the revolution and is incompatible with it as a candidate."[21]

4. The Four Hundredth Year Begins (December 1964–March 1965)

For Rio in 1965, the last year of Lacerda's administration, plans were made for a series of celebrations to observe the city's fourth centenary. Helpful, no doubt, to the aim of presenting Rio at its best to Brazilians and the expected inflow of tourists was the agreement reached in December 1964 by Lacerda and Justice Minister Milton Campos whereby Guanabara was to make use of members of security and firefighting forces who had opted, during the Goulart regime, to transfer their services to the federal government.[1]

The governor, interested in promoting painting exhibitions and film and music festivals, was interested also in the presentation of first-class theatrical performances. Among those whom he and Municipal Theater President Murilo Miranda burdened with requests for foreign artists was Guilherme Figueiredo, Brazil's cultural attaché in Paris. In addition, Figueiredo helped organize a series of books about Rio to be published by Editôra Civilização Brasileira, among them Luís Martins' *Noturno da Lapa*. João Condé, collector of historical documents (the Arquivos Implacáveis), was asked by Lacerda to compile information about books describing the founding of Rio.[2]

To raise funds for the fourth centenary celebration, the governor did more than raise taxes. Late in December he presided over a ceremony to launch the sale of fourth centenary bonds, made unusually attractive because they provided coupons for admission to official events and served as lottery tickets.[3]

The four hundredth anniversary festivities were officially opened on the morning of December 31, 1964, at Fort São João in the Urca district. There Castello Branco, Lacerda, and other dignitaries gathered near an old tablet that commemorated the founding of the city, originally called São Sebastião do Rio de Janeiro. Following a twenty-one-gun salute by two cannons on the beach, the governor spoke of "this city that resisted invasions." He recalled that Rio had begun with two houses, one occupied by a judge and the other by a cobbler, "symbols of law and work," and described the city as "a victory of men over sea and rock." Calling on the president to inaugurate the ceremonies, he explained that they would occur all during the coming year and would "allow Rio de Janeiro to open its arms to its friends throughout the world."[4]

The ceremony at the fort was followed that day by a series of celebrations that lasted well beyond midnight. In the evening a mammoth parade made its way through the city, bringing from Presidente Vargas Avenue to the suburbs floats depicting scenes from four centuries in the life of the city. During the parade the governor read a "chronicle of Rio" on television, with references to Dom João VI and his son, "romantic cavalier of adventure and gallantry." As midnight approached, he closed his chronicle with an appeal to everyone to help "transform Brazil into a democracy."

At midnight the statue of Christ on the Corcovado Peak was illuminated—an act that the governor's office announced was carried out by the hand of the Pope in Rome. All the churches in Rio rang their bells and all the forts fired their guns. After planes gave the city a "shower of silver," the Cariocas received a new message from their governor, this one transmitted by video tape. He said that "the city we are transforming is a city reborn, a city rejuvenated." "At this moment there are festive celebrations in the streets. But I hope there are celebrations, even more festive, in the hearts of the Cariocas."

Samba dancers filled the streets, worshipers of the African cult of Iemanjá filled the candle-lit beaches, merrymakers filled the clubs, and the strains of "Cidade Maravilhosa" filled the air. Brigitte Bardot watched from her Copacabana Palace Hotel apartment, whereas Genevieve Page, in Rio to perform in *Le Martyre de St. Sébastien*, participated in the traditional New Year's ball at the hotel.[5]

Henri Doublier's new version of D'Annunzio-Debussy's *Le Martyre de St. Sébastien* was the first of a series of musical productions presented in 1965 at the Municipal Theater. The theater itself was given a costly refurbishing. By early February, when Rio was visited by the mayor of Miami and his group of forty-two officials and businessmen, the theater had regained its former interior splendor, together with improvements in acoustics, illumination, and air conditioning. At the same time, approximately a hundred workers renovated the João Caetano Theater.[6]

The Fourth Centennial's program of cultural events included painting exhibits, professional meetings, and performances by visiting singers, such as Connie Francis. Among the sporting activities were special soccer matches, swimming competitions, a deep sea fishing contest, and a yacht race from Buenos Aires to Rio.[7]

January 20, Saint Sebastian's Day, is considered the date on which the city was founded in 1565. The Mass held that day in 1965 at the Saint Sebastian Church followed the early morning firing of cannons and the pealing of church bells. After a heavy early afternoon rain interfered with the schedule, a colorful procession of military and religious groups left Praça XV for the Russel Garden, near the Glória Hotel, for the dedication in the garden of a granite statue of Saint Sebastian. Crowds, estimated at over 150,000, gathered alongside the 3-kilometer route of the marchers, some of whom carried on a litter an image of Saint Sebastian that had been brought to Brazil in the sixteenth century by Estácio de Sá. The multitude in the garden had to be content with a Mass that dedicated a plaster model of the new statue, it being reported that the rain had interfered with the transportation of the granite likeness of the saint. The governor concluded the day's ceremonies by delivering a speech from a stand in front of the National Library and reviewing there a march down Rio Branco Avenue of members of over forty Portuguese clubs, dressed in costume.[8]

Among the high points scheduled for the first months of the year was a night of "the music of old Rio," with participants parading, stopping at clubs, and concluding the observance with a "Dance of Remembrance." The Queen of the Fourth Centenary was crowned at the Maracanãzinho Arena on February 13 and was at Lacerda's side there on March 1 for the cutting of "the largest cake in the world." The 3-ton cake, lit with four hundred electric candles that the governor extinguished, was served to 24,000 people. In full swing at the time was a Carnaval that the *Jornal do Brasil* described as "the greatest in Rio's history, with an enthusiasm that exceeds all former records."[9]

Sightseeing on the water, considered a new form of sightseeing for Rio, was arranged for visitors during the centenary. One of the old Rio-Niterói ferries was turned into a "show boat" with restaurant, bar, and stage. A more modern launch, renamed the *Novo Rio* (New

Rio), was assigned to make daytime trips around Guanabara Bay. Gondolas, similar to those in Venice, were manufactured in Niterói for use on Rodrigo de Freitas Lagoon.[10]

5. Would-be Savior of Panair
(February–March 1965)

The decision to close down the thirty-three-year-old Panair do Brasil Airline stirred up so much emotion, Roberto Campos recalled, that it would have been difficult to carry it out without the "revered" Eduardo Gomes in the aviation ministry and impossible without the presidency in the hands of "a military man who could face the music." Panair do Brasil, the first Brazilian airline to fly abroad, had acquired the status of a "sacred cow." Its 4,600 employees included many placed in the company by politicians who had been under pressure to find jobs for supporters.[1]

Castello Branco and Roberto Campos, considering the heavy government subsidies going to airlines, concluded that Brazil could not afford two competing international carriers, Panair and VARIG, with the accompanying "inflation of training facilities" and diversification of equipment. Panair had gone downhill financially, especially after control of its stock had been acquired in 1961 by a group headed by Mário Wallace Simonsen and Celso da Rocha Miranda, and was 101 billion cruzeiros in debt early in 1965. Its passenger/kilometer transportation cost was the highest of any Brazilian airline and 50 percent above the average. The government, which hoped to eliminate airline subsidies in two years, had paid 38 billion cruzeiros ($25 million) to the country's domestic and international lines in 1964.[2]

Because Panair reported a loss of 39.3 billion cruzeiros in 1964, an aviation ministry study commission concluded that Panair could not be saved even if it were to receive the combined subsidies going to all the Brazilian airlines, and it also stated that Panair was flirting with danger by making flights not authorized by the directorship of civil aviation. Based on these and other findings, Brigadeiro Eduardo Gomes recommended the suspension of all Panair flights. Following Castello's approval of the recommendation in mid-February 1965, a court in Rio declared Panair in bankruptcy.[3]

At this point Lacerda set out to save Panair do Brasil. He would not save it for those who had controlled it, for he agreed with Herbert Levy when the congressman from São Paulo accused the company management of having been dishonest.[4] He would save it for the workers. After pledging support of the Guanabara State Bank (BEG) for the Rio-based Central Commission of Panair Employees and putting five of the state government's lawyers at the disposal of the Commission, he called on Aviation Minister Eduardo Gomes and presented a scheme whereby the majority stockholders of Panair would turn over the company assets to the employees as payment of the 29 billion cruzeiros owed them. These assets would be the basis of a "new Panair" which would assume none of the debts of the old company. The National Economic Development Bank (BNDE) and the Bank of Brazil would receive preferred shares in the new company as payment for what they were owed. The BEG would assume the responsibility of organizing the new company and putting it on a profitable basis "within a reasonable time." The plan envisioned the creation of a foundation to operate the company and to be in the hands of the employees, the BEG, the Bank of Brazil, and the BNDE.[5]

The Recife employees of Panair and their families telegraphed Lacerda to say that they and their colleagues "in all of Brazil and abroad" were deeply moved by his "brilliant initiative" and were convinced that Brazil's "greatest guardian of democracy" would be successful in the effort to restore Panair's "sovereignty over the South Atlantic." In Rio, Panair offices displayed photographs of the governor together with inscriptions such as "PANAIRIANOS HAVE FAITH IN HIM" and "ONE HOPE STILL REMAINS." The *Esperança*, stationed in front of a Panair hangar, was decorated with a Panair flag.[6]

Panair supporters filled the press with statements about the "asininity of the federal government," and the airline's employees made headlines with a one-day hunger strike in Curitiba and with plans in Rio to march on Laranjeiras Palace. The Central Commission of Panair Employees, thanking Lacerda on February 19 for his help, explained that its campaign had received such enormous support from the Brazilian people that it was "absolutely confident" of victory.[7]

While Lacerda's rescue plan was studied by the aviation ministry, employees of Panair, meeting daily in a company hangar, received encouraging messages from the governor. They announced that they would accept any decision that did not give Panair routes to VARIG, and, when it appeared doubtful that the president would accept Lacerda's scheme, they sent other suggestions in a letter to Castello: intervention by the federal government or the purchase of Panair by VASP, a São Paulo–based domestic airline. They begged the president to reconsider his "unilateral step," bearing in mind the fate of "5,000 families with more than 20,000 dependents" who were living "in agony."[8]

Eduardo Gomes wrote Lacerda on February 23 to explain that, according to the government's plans, 2,000 of Panair's 4,600 employees would be absorbed by VARIG, 300 by the Cruzeiro do Sul Airline, and

President Castello Branco. (APPE drawing in *O Cruzeiro*, January 23, 1965)

500 (radio operators) by the government's Air Transport Auxiliary Services (SATA). The *brigadeiro* reminded the governor that Panair had employed far too many workers, but he said that 1,400 of them had been on the job long enough to be retired with full benefits. In a reference to Lacerda's scheme to create a new company, or foundation, the *brigadeiro* listed difficulties related to the rights of different creditors, the need to get each of them and every stockholder to accept the proposal, and the illegality of capitalizing a company with more preferred shares than common shares.[9]

Lacerda, referring to this response, told the press on February 25 that the matter was not closed. At the invitation of the *brigadeiro*, he said, he was going to clear up points not understood by the ministry. He added that for the moment the most urgent matter was the status of dismissed workers and therefore Guanabara state would employ some of them, such as typists and radio technicians. In doing this, he said, the state would, for the first time in his governorship, dispense with its policy of awarding positions only to those who excelled in tests. Arguing that the closing of Panair was desired by no one, least of all the federal government, he claimed that his plan to establish a foundation was "the best step."[10]

Lacerda's role as would-be savior of Panair came to an end on

March 5 when Eduardo Gomes, in an official communication, reiterated that the federal government would not depart from its decision to close the airline. Later in the month, at the *brigadeiro's* request, João Agripino discussed the Panair case in the Senate. Accusing the Rocha Miranda–Simonsen group of draining Panair to benefit firms associated with the group, such as an insurance company, the senator defended the government's decision.[11]

Castello Branco, speaking in mid-March to a representative of Panair stewardesses who were encamped in front of Laranjeiras Palace, said that proposals to save Panair would not relieve the government of Panair's debts and therefore could not be accepted.[12] The stewardesses were furnished tents, blankets, and food by nearby residents and remained encamped for five days. Learning that Castello had gone to Brasília, they threatened on March 20 to continue their encampment in front of Planalto Palace. Instead, they reluctantly accepted the *brigadeiro's* plan for handling the Panair employees. This was after VARIG announced, on March 22, that the 2,000 it was absorbing would not be dismissed without just cause and would not lose the indemnification rights they had built up while working for Panair.[13]

6. The Gubernatorial Election Problem (February 1965)

A highlight of the social season of Rio's fourth centenary was the marriage on January 3 of the governor's music-loving son Sebastião to Vera Maria Flexa Ribeiro, daughter of the education secretary. The church wedding ceremony was performed by Father Antônio Godinho, with state bank President Almeida Braga and his pretty wife Vivi serving as the sponsors (*padrinhos*) of the bridegroom. Thirteen-year-old Cristina Lacerda, assisted by Sérgio's little children, served as bearer of the wedding rings. The governor, one society columnist noted, had put on weight. The distinguished crowd included only one member of the federal cabinet, Foreign Minister Leitão da Cunha. But Castello Branco was on hand, although his arrival did not reflect his usual punctual habits.[1]

Late in the month the governor went to Bahia with his wife and daughter for a ten-day vacation. Upon his return to Rio on February 4, reporters found him tanned and in good spirits and full of complaints. He could not, he said, understand why Magalhães Pinto had replaced Belo Horizonte Mayor Jorge Carone with Oswaldo Pieruccetti. The Minas governor, who claimed that Carone was dishonest, retorted that the "insolent" Lacerda, "filled with frustration and blind with ambition," did not understand the high ideals of the revolution and wished to be the revolution's "owner." He accused Lacerda of attempting to wound the honor of others, even if this meant defending corrupt people.[2]

More serious was Lacerda's denouncement of the deplorable economic and moral situation that he said he had found in Bahia. Asserting that the revolution had not reached that state, he blamed the chief of Castello's Gabinete Civil, Luís Viana Filho. With Bahia politics concentrated in Viana's hands, Lacerda said, everything there was done with an eye on the next gubernatorial election and in disregard of the people. He called the SUNAB representative in the state one of the most corrupt individuals he had ever heard of. "Luís Viana Filho has succeeded in sparing all the thieves of Bahia. At this high cost, the triumphal return of Juscelino Kubitschek is being prepared. And, thief for thief, Kubitschek is the best robber of them all."

Viana Filho, in a letter to Lacerda, accused him of knowing full well that his statements were slanderous, because he could not have heard such lies from the people he had seen during his vacation. He denied having had anything to do with appointing the SUNAB representative. "May God in His mercy forgive you for not having freed yourself from the miserable curse of defamation." Lacerda, after reading the letter, sent it back unanswered to Laranjeiras Palace. He told reporters that he awaited a call from the president, with whom, he said, his relations were "the very best," and that Viana's only interest was in becoming governor. "I don't have time for foolish disputes," Lacerda said the next morning in a reference to the letter, which had appeared in the press. Bahia's UDN leader, Congressman Antônio Carlos Magalhães, called Lacerda a frustrated fisherman who could not find divers in Bahia who would put fish in his basket to make him appear successful.[3]

In a letter written to Castello on February 6, Lacerda denounced the role of the federal government in fomenting intrigue and corruption in Bahia, and he complained of the "hatred and fury" of men who, he said, had been intriguing against his presidential candidacy "since the day you took office." Having heard that the president was trying to arrange to have gubernatorial elections coincide with presidential and congressional elections in 1966, Lacerda gave Castello his opinion about the problem.[4]

The problem affected eleven states, including Guanabara and Minas, where gubernatorial elections were scheduled to be held in October 1965. A one-year postponement of those elections would satisfy devotees of *coincidência* and was favored by military men and others who felt that 1965 was too early to hold direct elections that would be interpreted as rendering a verdict about a regime whose economic measures had not had a chance to provide beneficial results.

The postponements of direct elections in October 1965 opened possibilities of one-year extensions (*prorrogações*) of the mandates of incumbents or, on the other hand, *mandato-tampão* solutions, whereby the eleven states would be governed for a year by individuals selected by the state legislatures. Military leaders favored the latter because they objected to extending the mandates of governors they disliked, such as Aluísio Alves in Rio Grande do Norte. By the time Lacerda wrote to Castello, the president had made it clear that he objected to the work being done by Magalhães Pinto to get his own term extended, and Daniel Krieger, government leader in the Senate, was declaring that the administration favored the use of state legislatures to provide one-year *mandatos-tampões*.[5]

Lacerda wrote the president that the direct elections, scheduled for October 1965, should be held, regardless of the risk, provided that they were an "indispensable condition" for holding the direct presidential election in 1966; but he added that this was not the case because Castello had given clear assurances about 1966 "with the honor of your word." Lacerda expressed his opposition to the *mandato-tampão* and said that *prorrogação* would not affect him personally, because he would leave Guanabara in the good hands of Raphael de Almeida Magalhães upon the expiration of the term to which he had been elected.[6]

Following the delivery of the letter to Castello, the *Jornal do Brasil* quite naturally described it as favorable to the postponement of the 1965 direct elections. Lacerda, eager not to appear inconsistent when he insisted on direct elections in 1966,[7] and concerned lest reasons for indirect elections in 1965 might exist also in 1966, wrote the president again on February 9 and gave the press copies of his new letter. In it he said that intrigue now took the form of reporting that "the candidate for the presidential succession fears the judgment of the people and believes that postponement of the elections would be good." In lines that Castello underlined heavily, Lacerda wrote:

> If I have reason to appreciate the fear, which exists in your government, of the defeat of the Revolution in the partial elections of 1965, I have no doubt about our victory in the presidential election of 1966. Unless, that is, Your Excellency's government, on the pretext of national union, decides to act against me by means of a divisionist candidate.
>
> As for 1965, it seems to me foolhardy to replace elections by subterfuge. I am certain that Your Excellency will give the

nation reasons capable of convincing it that the elections are inconvenient without having the people think that the Revolution was made to end the right of the people to choose their government.

Lacerda, in his letter, claimed to have done nothing but support Castello from the moment he had taken his name to Costa e Silva and Interim President Mazzilli "in a manner even impertinent." He described himself to Castello as a man whose personal ambition was small and already well satisfied, and he added that he was not disturbed by insults. This remark may have surprised Castello if there was any truth to an article printed in *Realidade,* according to which the governor once confessed to the president: "I can't eat, or drink, or sleep when people speak badly of me." Castello, the article continued, told Lacerda that "when they speak badly of me, I eat and drink and sleep very well—especially when that speaking is done by you."[8]

The president, after receiving Lacerda's letter of February 9, told the press: "The Revolution that is restoring democracy in Brazil" should not fear elections; rather, it should guarantee them, as it was doing in the case of São Paulo's municipal election. He spoke also of the need to have *coincidência* in state elections and said he was still studying the two possibilities: *prorrogações* and *mandatos-tampões.*[9]

These remarks were answered by Lacerda in a strongly worded radio-television speech denouncing the suppression of direct gubernatorial elections in 1965. The revolution, he said, had been "embalmed" and was "received as a mummy in the drawing room of the group that seeks to seize it for personal designs." According to Lacerda, the arguments about the 1965 direct elections were being waged between those who opposed elections because they believed the government would be defeated and those who favored the elections despite the reverse they were expected to bring to the revolution. There must be, he declared, a very serious error when "a revolution fears the people and the people dislike the revolution." Speaking of Amaral Peixoto, Lacerda said that the PSD president's fear of an election in Rio state exceeded "his fear of a Revolution" that called him for consultations to Laranjeiras Palace. In a reference to Luís Viana Filho, Lacerda told his network audience: "It appears that the government detests the opinion of the revolutionaries, preferring to turn to those who purchased dollars on the eve of the Revolution to flee Brazil and who are mentors of the republic today."

Lacerda, who had asked Castello not to make use of subterfuges in explaining the cancellation of direct gubernatorial elections, told his radio-television audience that *coincidência* was a mere pretext—and an antidemocratic one because it reduced the number of elections. He said that if the government's real purpose was to continue in power it should have the courage to say so. The *mandato-tampão,* according to Lacerda, was an immoral arrangement whereby governors were chosen "because of their vices" by corrupt cliques that the revolution had spared. Expressing what he said was the sentiment of the people, Lacerda exclaimed: "We want elections. And if we don't have elections we shall have a revolution."[10]

Castello, addressing the Fourth Congress of State Assemblies, replied to Lacerda: "I am certain that the Revolution has no fear of elections and firmly wants them." He pictured the government as striving to achieve them, without subterfuge.[11]

Still, for the one-year interval (1965–1966), elections by state legislatures appeared to be the answer, although Justice Minister Milton Campos and government congressional leader Pedro Aleixo preferred adherence to the constitution by holding direct elections in October 1965 for full terms. The idea of Milton Campos and Pedro Aleixo was opposed by the military, influential senators such as Daniel Krieger and Filinto Müller, hard line Congressman-Colonel Costa Cavalcanti, and prominent governors, such as Magalhães Pinto, Paulo Guerra (Pernambuco), and Lomanto Júnior (Bahia).[12]

The *Jornal do Brasil* warned against "inopportune direct elections" and said that the government's inability to make up its mind was harmful to its most important objective: a gradualist anti-inflationary policy leading to development. *O Estado de S. Paulo* agreed with Lacerda that the government relied too much on enemies of the revolution, but it criticized his faith in the vision of the "electoral mass," which, it said, had elected "all the governments of Vargas and Goulart." Second Military Region Commander Carlos Luís Guedes pointed out that judgment by the people had sent Christ to his death and released Barabbas.[13]

7. Adopting Lacerda's Recommendation about Elections (March 1965)

Driven by his chauffeur Fabiano and accompanied by Armando Daudt d'Oliveira, Lacerda campaigned in Rio Grande do Sul late in February. After attending a Grape Festival in Caxias, he returned on February 23 to São Paulo, where he complained to Luiz Carlos Mesquita, Nelson Pereira, and Oscar Klabin Segall that a plot was afoot to isolate, and later eliminate, his "popular candidacy."[1]

The eyes of Brazil's political world at the moment were focused on the battle of the Castello Branco administration to win for Bilac Pinto

Castello campaigns for Bilac Pinto, causing Mazzilli to remark
tearfully: "Quite the contrary, he adores elections!" (APPE drawing
in *O Cruzeiro*, March 20, 1965)

the presidency of the Chamber of Deputies by defeating Mazzilli,
described by the *Jornal do Brasil* as a remnant of corrupt politics.
Lacerda declared in São Paulo that "the people—and I, too—are interested in other matters." However, the battle was worth watching
not only as a major test of Castello's strength but because UDN
President Bilac Pinto, if he became Câmara president, would have
responsibilities that lay beyond those to his party and its presidential
candidate; the Bloco de Ação Parlamentar, which was formed to elect
him in Congress, included men of many parties who backed Castello's ideas about the revolution.[2]

"The election of Bilac," Aliomar Baleeiro wrote later, "infuriated
Carlos, who wanted to extort from him a declaration of support for
his presidential candidacy." The victory made the Bloco de Ação
Parlamentar, known as the Bloco Parlamentar Revolucionário, a sort
of superparty of the revolution in the Câmara, with the power to place
its men on the congressional commissions. After its victory, Lacerda
praised Bilac, who responded by promising to remain faithful to the
UDN and its presidential candidate.[3]

Magalhães Pinto, advocate of political party reform, called the congressional vote one more demonstration of the fragility of Brazil's
old parties. The *Jornal do Brasil* wrote of the need to create a Party
of the Revolution and extinguish the "obsolete" parties of the past,[4]
and it reported that the government, with the support of "military

revolutionaries," planned to extinguish the old parties. As far as the major parties were concerned, the report was exaggerated, as was evident from the party reform ideas submitted by Milton Campos to the governors.[5]

When Lacerda discussed the matter with Castello at Laranjeiras Palace, the president repeated his promise not to allow another extension of his term and emphasized the need for political party reform. Lacerda, after leaving the president, was short with reporters, and presently the public learned that "difficulties in dialogue" had developed. Castello, however, was present at the dinner given in his honor by the Lacerdas at their Praia do Flamengo apartment on March 16. The evening, Bilac Pinto and Ernâni Sátiro declared later, was purely social and included no private chat between the governor and the president.[6]

A topic of dinner conversation was the return that day of Vice Governor Eloy Dutra from exile in Montevideo. Lacerda, earlier in the day, was about to have lunch at his apartment when he received the news that Eloy, upon reaching Rio, had been imprisoned by agents of the DOPS. Describing himself as "the jailer of no one," Lacerda sent for his assistant, Tannay de Farias, and went in Tannay's car to the Polícia Central, where Eloy was being held. He learned that the arrest order had come by phone and therefore demanded the immediate release of the prisoner. A little later, when the governor's official car reached the Polícia Central, Lacerda invited a surprised and grateful Eloy Dutra to join him in it, and the two former political antagonists were driven to the home of Eloy's parents. "I never thought you capable of doing something like this," the *cassado* remarked.

Five hours later, the Army Police arrested Eloy Dutra, with First Army Commander Otacílio Terra Ururaí explaining that requests for this step had come from the heads of several Military Police Investigations (IPMs) looking into corruption and subversion. Military Tribunal Judge Olímpio Mourão Filho asserted that Lacerda's release of Eloy Dutra had been illegal because a "preventive imprisonment" order for his arrest had been issued, but he added that Lacerda's act had been a noble one, revealing sensitivity.[7]

Within the next few days, Castello, Krieger, and others lined up support for a constitutional amendment calling for the election of governors to one-year terms by the legislatures of the eleven states in which the incumbents were serving their last year. Therefore on March 19 Lacerda wrote Castello to say that he understood that the president would, within hours, deliver a message to this effect.[8]

"The alleged reason for postponing the elections," Lacerda wrote, "is the inconvenience of submitting the Revolution to the judgment of the ballot boxes—the same reason that motivated the extension of the presidential mandate." And therefore, he pointed out, the revolution would be submitted to the judgment of men in the state assemblies who were controlled by its adversaries and who would "usurp the function that belongs to the people." Lacerda wrote that the Guanabara legislature, which had recently voted a billion cruzeiros for more than four hundred protégés, would select someone who would turn each state company over to a legislator and each secretaryship over to an electoral chieftain or agent of contractors.

Lacerda went on to say that "the failure to carry out state elections this year—inspired by the illusion of the 'coincidence of mandates,'" would be an error, damaging to the perfecting of democracy. He added that if the government were to declare officially that "elections are inconvenient," it should adopt *prorrogação.*

The president was upset by the letter, which he considered hypocritical.[9] After receiving it at Laranjeiras Palace, and marking it well in red pencil, he phoned Krieger to invite him for lunch at Alvorada Palace in Brasília on March 22. During the lunch Castello showed the letter to Krieger and said: "Concerned about his reputation, Lacerda prefers direct elections. Let's do what he wants. Will the change give you trouble?" The senator replied that the change, unwise "in the present emergency," would give him no difficulty because direct elections were "an aspiration" of most of the lawmakers.[10]

Castello sent for Governors Lacerda, Magalhães Pinto, and Nei Braga in order to make his decision known to them personally. Lacerda, returning to São Paulo from a trip to Curitiba, was flown to Brasília in the presidential plane with Abreu Sodré, Curi, and Godinho. He reached Planalto Palace on the evening of March 22 and was the first of the three governors to receive the news from Castello. Magalhães Pinto, considered to have lost the most from the new development, had gone to a resting place in Espírito Santo after the Minas legislature had extended his term, and was delayed in reaching Brasília.

Lacerda, following his meeting in the president's office, met until midnight at Bilac Pinto's Brasília apartment with politicians and a happy Milton Campos, supporter of direct elections. Then he spoke to reporters. "Today," he said, "I won the election of 1966."[11]

The president's decision, displeasing much of the military, came as a great surprise. "No one," Amaral Peixoto has written, "believed that elections would be direct in 1965." *O Globo,* startled, suggested that it would be better to hold elections in October 1966, when the revolution would benefit from its firm and courageous economic policy. It added: "Elections alone will not solve all our problems. If the antirevolutionaries win in October 1965, will democracy have won or lost in Brazil? The enemies of the Revolution and the legal minds of the government will call it a victory for democracy. But we have a better memory and cannot agree."

The *Jornal do Brasil* welcomed direct elections provided that steps were taken to remove "obsolete" electoral practices involving patronage and the use of money. It wrote that, despite such practices in São Paulo's mayorship election of March 21, the government had nothing to fear from the outcome, a victory for Brigadeiro José Vicente de Faria Lima (UDN). *O Estado de S. Paulo*, which had supported the candidacy of pro-Castello Paulo Egídio Martins, was disappointed in the election of Faria Lima, backed by "that famous demagogue Jânio Quadros," and felt that Justice Minister Milton Campos' democratic ideals were not realistic for a revolution.[12]

Within two weeks Congress passed a constitutional amendment that made the coincidence of gubernatorial elections effective in 1970 by stipulating that the eleven governors elected in October 1965 would serve for five years instead of four. The amendment also said that if the most-voted-for candidates did not receive absolute majorities, the contests would be settled by the state assemblies. In accordance with Castello's message to Congress, the amendment listed Minas among the states that were to hold direct elections in 1965. Magalhães Pinto, breaking brusquely with the Castello Branco administration, moved closer to Lacerda. Speaking on television, he said: "I am not, and never shall be, an instrument for liquidating Carlos Lacerda politically."[13]

Lacerda wrote that the few politicians who had played roles in the movement of March 31, 1964—men like Magalhães Pinto and himself—now found themselves "politely excluded from government deliberations." His article, appearing in the *Jornal do Brasil*, analyzed groups that he felt had taken over—public utilities, General Golbery's SNI, businessmen of IPES, Roberto Campos and his "propaganda machine," and American companies and their Brazilian representatives. He warned against the *entreguista* ideology that, he said, had prevailed, and regretted that so many of his countrymen lacked faith in the ability of Brazilians to solve the country's problems. He wrote about "people trained to disbelieve in Brazil."[14]

8. Enaldo Cravo Peixoto, Lacerda's Choice
(March–May 1965)

Early in 1965 Amaral Netto took steps to obtain the PL nomination for governor of Guanabara. That Lacerda was not enthusiastic about him had been evident as far back as December 1960 because, when the UDN *bancada* to the state *constituinte* had elected him its leader, an opposing vote had been cast by Brunini. But the relationship had not been a hostile one until late in 1964, when Lacerda had opposed the congressman's wish to become governor. Lacerda, considering Amaral Netto a better politician than student of administrative matters, told PL leader Raul Pilla that he would never turn over the state government to an "illiterate"—a remark that Amaral Netto attributed to his lack of a formal education—or to a compulsive gambler. The popular congressman, well known to be addicted to late-night gambling sessions, believed that Lacerda's opposition to his ambition was inspired by a determination to have the UDN nominate Raphael de Almeida Magalhães, described by Amaral Netto as "a young man completely lacking in character."[1]

Lacerda turned first not to Raphael but to his respected administration reformer, Hélio Beltrão. Soon, however, Lacerda had second thoughts about this candidacy. A speech by Beltrão and a statement by him in *Diário de Notícias* were regarded as critical of the governor. According to Lacerda, Beltrão appeared uninterested in carrying out a hard-hitting campaign, and made, on the contrary, speeches that were "tragic," and "not good enough to win votes even in Leblon." By the end of March, Beltrão's candidacy was dead and Raphael's candidacy was strong.[2]

In Laranjeiras Palace, Health Minister Raimundo de Brito announced his own candidacy, supported, he said, by many *udenistas* of Guanabara. Like Raimundo, Adauto Lúcio Cardoso was close to Castello and was a candidate. He was supported by much of the UDN congressional *bancada* and called on Lacerda late in March in the company of a pro-Adauto congressional group, whose spokesman was Aliomar Baleeiro. Lacerda, who was expected to veto Adauto's name, pointed out that Raphael, Danillo Nunes, and Sandra Cavalcanti were possibilities just as good as Adauto.[3]

As National Housing Bank president, Sandra Cavalcanti was dealing with building contractors who, her critics said, obtained excessive commissions, and was incurring the wrath of Roberto Campos, her superior. Some, including Lacerda, felt that she was interested in participating in the Guanabara gubernatorial race; and everyone knew that she did not want the nomination to go to Raphael. She told Lacerda, according to his account: "See here, Carlos, I have a message for you from Cardinal Câmara. Dom Jayme, who, as you know, is a good friend of yours, said it will be very difficult for the Church to recommend Raphael's candidacy because Raphael is not married. He is living with a young woman who has separated from her husband." In recalling the episode, Lacerda described the young woman, daughter of Paraná politician Bento Munhoz da Rocha, as a delight, but added that the situation described by Sandra was considered more serious than it would have seemed ten or twelve years later.[4]

"You would have," Lacerda said to Raphael, "the hostility of the Church, and our common enemies would turn your life, and especially that of the young woman, into an inferno." Raphael, Lacerda has written, preferred to spare the young woman, a noble decision that deprived the UDN of its strongest candidate, an amateur soccer star with a splendid television presence, "able to explain anything about Guanabara with as much knowledge as I could give, or more, because he lived with the problems daily."[5]

Raphael, who had urged Carlos not to provoke the federal government or demand state elections in 1965, was less certain than Carlos of victory that year and felt that if the UDN lost with himself as candidate it would be considered a serious setback for *Lacerdismo*, whereas it would be otherwise if Adauto, close to Castello, were the losing candidate.[6]

But Lacerda vetoed Adauto, and therefore Raphael suggested that the candidate be selected from among those who had worked in the state government. The name of Enaldo Cravo Peixoto came to the fore because of the state's spectacular achievements in public works, described in glowing terms in releases from Walter Cunto's office. Lacerda, meeting with twelve members of the state government, asked each to vote for two possible candidates. The *Tribuna da Imprensa* reported the following result:[7]

Raphael de Almeida Magalhães	12 (unanimous)
Enaldo Cravo Peixoto	6
Raimundo de Brito	2
Adauto Lúcio Cardoso	1
Carlos Flexa Ribeiro	1
Blank votes	2
	24

Lacerda, a presidential candidate whose base was Guanabara, needed a successor he could depend on. Of all the members of the state cabinet, none was more submissive to the governor than Enaldo Cravo Peixoto.[8]

The governor decided to speak at once with Enaldo, who was in the United States on a business trip. Learning on the phone that the public works secretary planned to leave in two days for Paris and then visit Doxiadis in Athens, Lacerda told him to change his plans, "because I have to see you." The governor wanted to make sure that Enaldo had recovered fully from a heart attack suffered late in 1963.[9]

Raphael accompanied Lacerda and Almeida Braga on the trip to New York on April 2, and therefore the post of acting governor was supposed to go to Danillo Nunes, who had been elected president of the state legislature on March 11 despite Lacerda's preference for the always dependable Brunini. In order not to become ineligible to run for governor, Danillo Nunes took a leave of absence from the legislature, and therefore state Justice Tribunal President Martinho Garcez Neto became acting governor.[10]

Enaldo Cravo Peixoto, after greeting Lacerda and his friends at Kennedy Airport, was taken by Lacerda to a hospital for a three-day checkup. Lacerda and Raphael were in the hospital waiting room when Enaldo came from the final examination, bearing an electrocardiogram, and exclaimed, "My heart is in great shape." "Then," Lacerda said, "you are the candidate."[11]

On April 12 Lacerda and Almeida Braga showed up unexpectedly in Lisbon for what turned out to be a four-day visit devoted to purchasing artefacts, with state bank funds, for Rio's new Museu da Imagem e do Som (Museum of Images and Sounds). "This museum," Lacerda told Lisbon reporters, "will provide historical documents, of a bibliographic and iconographic nature, for students of Rio life." João Condé recalls that Lacerda, whose custom of making abundant purchases contrasted to the style forced on him by circumstances in his youth, entered their Lisbon hotel and told Almeida Braga that he planned to buy an entire collection of Brazilian empire pictures that he had seen in an antiquarian shop; the shop owner, he explained, would sell the pictures only as one lot. Braga, whose state bank was about to inaugurate its costly headquarters building in Rio, said the bank could not afford to buy the entire collection. But Lacerda returned to the shop with Condé and bought all the pictures.[12]

Answering questions of Lisbon reporters, Lacerda said: "In Brazil, true large landholdings do not exist; what exist are tiny holdings (minifundios) and a lack of schools and conditions suitable for increased productivity by farm workers." Asked about a manifesto signed by Brazilian intellectuals opposed to Brazil's sending troops to the Dominican Republic, the governor dismissed it as of no importance. He said that Alceu Amoroso Lima, the first to sign, had much talent but "wishes to ignore Communism. This business of progressive Christians leaves me unconvinced, especially in the case of Amoroso Lima. In 1935 he recommended that Brazilian youth adhere to fascism." In reply, the Correio da Manhã reminded its readers that in 1935 Lacerda, an agitator, had been a follower of Luiz Carlos

Lacerda revealing the Enaldo Cravo Peixoto candidacy. "Don't applaud yet, there are more." (Claudius Ceccon drawing in *Jornal do Brasil*, April 23, 1965)

Prestes and had given publicity to Prestes' manifesto "calling for the Communist uprising."[13]

Upon returning to Rio, Lacerda presided over a cabinet meeting at which he revealed that Enaldo Cravo Peixoto would be the UDN candidate and learned that Education Secretary Flexa Ribeiro, Social Services Secretary Luiz Carlos Vital, and Justice Secretary Eugênio Sigaud objected to nominating a man who had no connection with the UDN and owed his career to being named director of sewer projects by Negrão de Lima. It was a long meeting, in which Flexa Ribeiro expressed his opinion emphatically and said he had belonged to the UDN since 1946. Following the meeting, Lacerda, Raphael, and Government Secretary Célio Borja made plans to persuade Danillo Nunes, Adauto Lúcio Cardoso, and Raimundo de Brito to withdraw.[14]

Danillo Nunes yielded to the pleas of Marcelo Garcia and Raphael when they visited him. Adauto, saying that his candidacy belonged to the UDN congressmen, refused to withdraw and told the governor, "Now, Carlos, you're going to learn what an insurmountable barrier is." Raimundo de Brito said he could count on thirty UDN regional convention delegates and proved difficult; but he agreed to cooperate during a two-hour meeting with Lacerda, Raphael, Armando Falcão, and Abreu Sodré.[15]

At Guanabara Palace on April 20, Lacerda told Enaldo, "In your campaign, do not accept money or collaboration from contractors;

I want a clean campaign." After Lacerda left, Marcelo Garcia told Enaldo that the governor was crazy to forbid a practice common throughout the world. Surrounded by reporters, Enaldo spoke of his pride at being chosen.[16]

Accompanied by Raphael, Lacerda called on Castello at Laranjeiras Palace to argue on behalf of Enaldo's candidacy. Then he told the palace reporters that he would ask the voters not to judge the revolution until 1966 but to decide in October 1965 whether they wanted the continuation of an administration that solved the state's problems. He expressed confidence in his ability to overcome the objections of *udenista* congressmen to Enaldo.[17] On April 22 he took Enaldo to the UDN regional directorship and saw to it that he joined the party.[18]

While Enaldo observed the missed opportunities that stemmed from Lacerda's ban against doing favors for politicians, his backers noted that Raimundo de Brito offered abundant favors. Raphael, in a phone call to Castello, said that Raimundo's use of the health ministry to garner support for his candidacy upset the governor, but the president promised to do no more than relay the message to Raimundo. Lacerda, who described Raimundo as "corrupting the UDN" and felt that Castello supported "that maneuver," became particularly distraught when told that General Golbery was encouraging Raimundo to continue as a candidate and that Roberto Campos wanted Lacerda's predecessor, Sette Câmara, to seek election to the governorship. Furious at what he felt was federal interference, he took a leave of absence from the governorship with the explanation that he did not want to be accused of coercion while the UDN made up its mind.[19]

In turning his post over to Raphael, Lacerda broadcast an emotional speech in which he suggested that Saint Sebastian was patron saint of both the governor and the state, "because here I pass my days receiving arrows coming from unknown places." He appealed to Adauto and Raimundo de Brito to withdraw and accused the latter of having broken his "formal pledge" to do so. Chiefly he argued that he had the right to be supported because of his leadership, "relied on to such a large extent and for such a long period." "I want to know if they recognize that leadership or if we are going to transform the UDN of Guanabara into the principal point of my defeat as a presidential candidate. . . . Either the UDN will emerge united from this episode—and united around its leader and not against him—or it will have to proclaim its rejection of my leadership."

The *Correio da Manhã*, persevering in its campaign against the governor, blamed "the tragic end" of the Carioca UDN on the megalomania and special talent of "the despot" for disparaging and alienating his own friends. The *Diário Carioca* described Lacerda as "decapitating" anyone in his administration who failed to place the state machine at the service of Enaldo Cravo Peixoto.[20]

During May it became clear that the situation had not been altered by Lacerda's oratorical appeal or by Raphael's talks with men who would attend the state convention. On May 8 Geraldo Ferraz, president of the Carioca UDN, reported that Enaldo, with seventy delegates, could be beaten by the seventy-five controlled by Adauto, Raimundo, and Amaral Netto. Congressmen Aliomar Baleeiro and Eurípides Cardoso de Menezes said that Enaldo, whom the governor wanted to "impose," lacked the UDN spirit and the independence from Lacerda that characterized Adauto and Raimundo. In the state legislature, where Enaldo was favored by a majority of the UDN bloc, Mauro Magalhães, Mac Dowell Leite de Castro, Cesário de Melo, and Raphael Carneiro da Rocha said that the party bloc in Brasília should not play the dominant role.[21]

Although Lacerda rejected a list of fifteen possible substitutes, "traditional *udenistas*," submitted by Adauto Cardoso and Aliomar Baleeiro, a compromise became the only means of avoiding a bitter convention battle. Lacerda himself, before leaving on May 28 for Rio Grande do Sul, finally opened the door to a compromise, because he delegated Edson Guimarães, vice president of the Carioca UDN, to negotiate the withdrawal of Raimundo, Adauto, and Enaldo Cravo Peixoto in favor of a traditional UDN man identified with his administration.[22]

9. The Niterói Convention of the UDN (April 1965)

After transferring the governorship to Raphael on April 23, Lacerda campaigned for a few days in São Paulo and then went to Belo Horizonte to join Magalhães Pinto in setting up "a joint action to restore the Revolution." During lunch the two governors discussed the UDN's fifteenth national convention, to be held in Niterói on April 29 and 30 to choose a party president to succeed Bilac Pinto.[1]

Arrangements to hold the convention had been made by Ernâni Sátiro against the advice of Castello Branco, who had suggested awaiting new legislation about parties. Sátiro, in the uncomfortable position of supporting both the president and Lacerda, was the *Lacerdista* candidate to head the UDN.[2]

To oppose Sátiro, Bahia Congressman Antônio Carlos Magalhães had launched a movement in favor of strongly pro-Castello Aliomar Baleeiro. Baleeiro, annoyed at Sátiro for excluding him from the commission studying the parliamentary system, was favored by his longtime friend Bilac Pinto and could expect some backing in Niterói from Ceará, Paraná, and Rio Grande do Sul, as well as Bahia. But his candidacy, regarded as anti-Lacerda, could not overcome the popularity enjoyed by Lacerda among the UDN's rank and file. Castello had said he would not get involved. Magalhães Pinto had declared for Sátiro early in April after Castello had put an end to *prorrogação* in Minas.[3]

Before his lunch with Lacerda, the Minas governor appeared on a radio-television program and confirmed his pro-Sátiro position. Most of his discourse was a condemnation of the "erroneous" policy of Castello, responsible, he said, for bankruptcies, inflation, and unemployment. Lacerda, after the lunch, told the press that he agreed with the analysis made by Magalhães Pinto and was in Belo Horizonte to confer with him just as he had done before Goulart's downfall. He said that the governors of Guanabara and Minas were being "stabbed in the back in a dark room" and had resolved to turn on the light "to see who is stabbing us."

Like Magalhães Pinto, Lacerda called for a meeting of the foremost makers of the 1964 revolution to discuss the course of the government and to decide about revising the cabinet, which, Lacerda said, "is no more revolutionary than that of Maria Theresa of Austria." "To deceive the people we do not need a general-president who transformed himself into a clever politician, of which we already have a large quantity."[4]

Before going to Niterói, Lacerda spent a day in Guanabara Palace, where he reassumed the governorship and told reporters of his unfavorable view of the Supreme Court, which had agreed unanimously with Sobral Pinto that Miguel Arraes should be released from prison.[5] He called the court's decision a demagogic act.[6]

Magalhães Pinto decided not to go to Niterói, because the UDN planned to adopt a motion praising Castello. The motion, presented on the first day of the convention by Rondon Pacheco and adopted by acclamation, reaffirmed support for the Lacerda candidacy and for the Castello presidency, "which has restored to the nation days of tranquility, order, and confidence in the destiny of democracy."[7]

The convention's second day was agitated. An admirer of Amaral Netto received jeers and applause when she read aloud an anti-Amaral letter from Lacerda and announced that she would support Amaral. Amaral belittled a party that would jeer a woman and was shouted down when he called Lacerda a "coward," "slanderer," and "Brazilian Hitler." Alberto Torres, president of the UDN of Rio state, appealed to him not to let the problems of Guanabara politics spoil a party-unifying convention in Rio state. Nevertheless Amaral, who had brought television cameras and microphones with him, threatened to interfere with Lacerda's speech.

A standing ovation greeted the arrival of the Carioca governor. When he made his way to the speakers' table he was loudly booed as he passed Amaral Netto and his group. All during Lacerda's speech— an appeal for party unity—the defiant, handsome Amaral Netto gave his own speech in a loud voice, defending his honor and calling Lacerda names; it was carried by his television cameras and microphones to listeners and television viewers outside the meeting hall. Although Lacerda's microphone was connected to the sound system in the hall, the hissing and booing of Lacerda by Amaral Netto's friends and family, and the simultaneous speech by Amaral Netto, made it difficult to hear the governor.

Lacerda said the outgoing party president would leave for his successor the "extraordinary unifying spectacle of the return en masse of the *udenistas* of Minas Gerais." Referring to his problems with the party in his own state, where he was still working for the nomination of Enaldo Cravo Peixoto, he declared: "Whoever wants to help my candidacy should help me maintain the Guanabara UDN united." He closed by saying that, despite the expectation of many, he was not going to attack Castello—"because what I desire is that the president remain in favor of us." But he promised to continue maintaining "objective opinions" about Castello's administration and to express them with the loyalty, severity, and faithfulness of a companion.

Following the simultaneous speeches by Lacerda and Amaral Netto, Bilac Pinto said that the penal law contained many clauses which Amaral Netto had violated and that he had refrained from arresting the congressman only because, as president of the Chamber of Deputies, he had the duty to uphold congressional immunities. But, Bilac added, "the author of the disturbances will not return here tonight. That I can guarantee."

After Bilac called for the election of the party's new officers, Sátiro won the presidency by a 221-60 vote over Baleeiro. The other officerships were not contested. Senator Adolfo de Oliveira Franco and Congressmen Godinho and Antônio Carlos Magalhães became vice presidents and Oscar Dias Corrêa secretary general. Sátiro promised to work for Lacerda's campaign and for the best of relations between the party and Castello.[8]

The *Jornal do Brasil* liked the "vitality" shown by the UDN in Niterói. It wrote that the convention represented the "reintegration of Lacerda into the structure of the Revolution," and it praised Senator João Agripino for having played a key role in convincing Lacerda that he was wrong in supposing that decisions made by Castello had the purpose of destroying his presidential candidacy.[9]

A more realistic appraisal was presented in Hilde Weber's *Estado de S. Paulo* cartoon, picturing the UDN as a perplexed girl, undecided between Castello Branco and Lacerda. Lacerda, commenting in *Manchete* on the UDN's motion to support both Castello and his own candidacy, said that the time had come "for Castello to support us and stop playing with the PSD because Brazil has long been fed up with clever gymnastics." In a reference to Raimundo de Brito, Lacerda said: "The president, who has not wanted cabinet ministers to be associated with candidacies, permits one of his ministers to become a candidate—a minister who gave me his word of honor not to create problems. Either the president is conniving with the maneuver, monstrous even to think about, or else he has no authority over the minister, although he considers himself attacked whenever one of his ministers is criticized."

In the article, Lacerda declared that if one thing could separate him from Castello it was the president's tendency "to put all of us—the Carioca governor and the corrupt and subversive—on the same level." Lacerda also said that he opposed granting amnesty to anyone punished by the Institutional Act. "Those people," he said, "do not repent. They seek the opportunity to return and carry out their crimes of the past."[10]

As for the government's economic program, Lacerda told reporters: "Magalhães Pinto is the one who is right." "In any other country of the world Roberto Campos would already have been fired."[11]

10. Criticizing the PAEG (May 17–18, 1965)

An effective fight against inflation required more suffering than was thought necessary by Lacerda or the Castello Branco administration—or, for that matter, many economists. Lacerda came out against the suffering. The Castello Branco administration said (and believed) that the suffering would produce, rather quickly, miraculous results: the inflation, despite the effects of eliminating distortions caused by unrealistic public utility tariffs, etc., was expected to fall from over 100 percent early in 1964 to 25 percent in 1965 and 10 percent in 1966, and yet the gross domestic product was expected to increase, at the same time, at a 6 percent annual rate.

These conclusions of the government, along with charts, policy decisions, and forecasts of production and demand of merchandise, were published in May 1965 in the planning ministry's *Programa de Ação Econômica do Govêrno, 1964–1966*, known as the PAEG.

Lacerda told the press on May 10 that he had read all 240 pages and found that "the plan has more holes in it than one of those shower heads in a boardinghouse." On the next day the president called the PAEG "a serious effort to formulate our economic policy."[1]

While preparing a study to show that the PAEG was a "disaster," the Carioca governor carried on long discussions with economists such as Dênio Nogueira, who had become the first president of the Central Bank of Brazil late in March 1965. He turned frequently to businessman José Luiz Moreira de Souza, under whose coordination a group of economists contributed ideas. Lacerda's final fifty-four-page study, worded by himself, included comments that the governor picked up from Eugênio Gudin and Antônio Dias Leite Júnior, a PAEG critic belonging to the government's Consultative Council for Planning (CONSPLAN).[2]

Wishing to have the study presented to Castello before it became public, Lacerda sent Marcelo Garcia to Brasília on May 18 with the document and a covering letter. In the letter, Lacerda cited the president's speech of May 12 that blamed prior administrations for the "virtual state of collapse" of statistical information, necessary for planning. "To the recognition of this truth," Lacerda wrote, it should be added that the government's so-called program was pure "rhetoric and is not being carried out because, among other reasons, it cannot be carried out."[3]

By this time Castello had apparently become convinced that Lacerda lacked some characteristics needed by statesmen. During a supper with Baleeiro at Alvorada Palace late in April, the president remarked that Lacerda had "positive qualities," but he agreed with Baleeiro that it "would be a national danger and even an international one to have Lacerda in the presidency." Castello, incidentally, had been letting subordinates know of his displeasure with the way the governor handled the press after calling on him. Lacerda, it seemed to the president, pressed very hard to get appointments and, regardless of the inconsequentiality of the conversations, followed them up by discussing national problems at length with reporters in a manner to suggest that the president sought out, and relied heavily on, the governor's advice.[4]

Castello, receiving Marcelo Garcia at Planalto Palace on May 18, turned quickly to Lacerda's letter and study. After a preliminary perusal, he said in a deeply serious tone, "I am going to read this with great attention. Then I shall communicate with your governor."

Setting the papers aside, the president discussed intelligent men he had known. "In all my life," he told Marcelo Garcia, "I became impressed with three men." One was Francisco San Tiago Dantas, who had died in September 1964 and who, the president said, could transform complex matters into simple ones. San Tiago Dantas, Castello added, "was knowledgeable about everything, including literature and scientific matters." Castello next named Roberto Campos, whom he described as a man of humanistic culture, with immense courage for carrying out unpopular missions. The third name was that of "your governor," who, Castello said, had a facility the other two lacked, a very effective way of writing and speaking. To illustrate his point, Castello picked up the papers he had just received and read sentences aloud.

"Why are you smiling?" the president asked Marcelo. Because, Marcelo replied, Castello was proving his point by reading accusations made against himself. Castello said: "Your governor is inclined to be overenthusiastic and get carried away."[5]

At Guanabara Palace that night, Lacerda made the fifty-four-page study public. Before television cameras, and in the presence of "especially invited representatives of the producing classes," Lacerda read his statements against "a government-run economy" directed by "one single group of technicians" that believed "economics to be an exact science." Commenting on the surplus of eggs projected by the PAEG and the projected deficit of eggs in Furtado's Three-Year Plan, he asked which of the two plans had most adulterated the figures or received the least cooperation from hens. "Global planning of the economy," he maintained, "is not compatible with a democratic society based on free enterprise."[6]

To show that the PAEG's goals were not being achieved, Lacerda argued that the gross national product had fallen in 1964 and in the first three months of 1965, that the same could be said about the inflow of foreign investments, and that the balance of payments deficit had increased (partly the result of the "erroneous" coffee policy). Denying that the PAEG was succeeding in its goal of helping the underprivileged sectors and areas, he said that the "increasing" unemployment in the northeast was creating a wish for the return of Miguel Arraes. As for "the progressive reduction of the inflationary process," described by Lacerda as the "easiest" and "most urgent" of PAEG's five goals, Lacerda pointed out that the cost of living had increased by 23 percent in the first four months of 1965.[7]

Lacerda argued that "gigantic" paper money emissions and the revenue from taxes, which he said had been increased, were going largely to the state-controlled companies, which accounted for over 50 percent of the economy and accounted for 77 percent of expenditures in the national budget. He said that the government should get out of areas appropriate for free enterprise and should apply its "restrictive, anti-inflationary" measures to state-controlled companies, instead of decapitalizing free enterprise in order to support them. "Let them combat inflation in the area of the government itself and give credits to the producers of wealth, the workers, technicians, and company owners."

For the private sector, Lacerda advocated "development regardless of inflation," and he added that control over credit expansion should be relaxed in case of the slightest sign of economic recession. He declared that prices should be determined by the free market, with bureaucratic controls curtailed, and he called for a wage policy that would restore to workers the purchasing power they had formerly enjoyed. Lastly, he called for a new cabinet, "able to galvanize the forces of production."[8]

11. Repercussions of Lacerda's Study (May 19–June 1, 1965)

Lacerda's brilliant study was particularly effective in its criticism of economic planning and statism, but it paid no attention to what the administration was doing to reduce the deficits of the government-controlled companies. It brought the governor messages of congratulation, leading O Estado de S. Paulo to observe that it was impossible to carry out "a wise economic-financial policy while adhering to the rules of a popularity contest." As O Estado also pointed out, Lacerda's study ignored the gravity of the situation inherited by Castello and recommended measures that would renew the inflationary spiral. The Diário Carioca, also critical of Lacerda's study, wrote that the PAEG did not represent rigid, totalitarian, global planning, and that the creator of new taxes and state companies was Lacerda.

The Jornal do Brasil, more sympathetic to Lacerda's study, agreed with his remarks about government company deficits and said the Brazilian people were justified in complaining about the poor economy after "an entire year" of financial restraint. O Globo and the Correio da Manhã were interested in assailing Lacerda's personality and seized on his call for a new cabinet to claim that he was similar to Hitler. O Globo, which called Lacerda's study a crazy quilt of resentments and complaints, was happy to regard it as marking the death of any possibility of the "petulant" advocate of demagogic, "Juscelinistic" measures being the presidential candidate of the revolution.[1]

Castello, in a speech in Florianópolis on May 21, pointed out that the government had been forced to adopt financial measures that caused sufferings "we would be immensely pleased to avoid." Unfortunately, he added, the abandonment of those measures, while perhaps providing immediate alleviation, would revive the ills that had been on the point of taking the nation to financial and social chaos.[2]

In Rio that evening Roberto Campos delivered a nationwide radio-television address in which he said that Lacerda, tired of administering Guanabara, was "fabricating catastrophes" which would allow him to appear as a hero and which did not allow the country the peace and confidence it needed. "Lacerda has been making these pronouncements for the last fifteen years and will continue to do so as long as the government is not his." The planning minister cited promises of new foreign investments, provided the investors were not deterred by uncertainty about future policy, and said that Lacerda had earlier pictured the "vast" receipt of foreign investments as ruining national industry. He denied that the government's program of coordinated action amounted to "total planning," and pointed out that Lacerda, accused of inertia during his first year as governor, had declared that "to govern is to plan."

Campos said that while Guanabara had increased tax rates, the federal government had not done so but had introduced a monetary correction to company accounts, thus eliminating taxes on unreal profits caused by inflation. In reply to the argument that statism caused inflation, Campos said that, quite the reverse, inflation caused statism because it destroyed private savings and decapitalized companies, and thus in the past the BNDE had been forced to turn to the government for funds for projects. He mentioned the numerous state companies created by the Guanabara government and said that the only state company created by the Castello government was the National Housing Bank, for stimulating private initiative. And he quoted statistics to show that Brazil's inflation rate was declining and that, contrary to Lacerda's assertion, the nation had had a favorable balance of payments of $70 million in 1964 and an increase in revenues from coffee.

"The governor," Campos said, "has already brought statesmen to desperation, and, it is said, one to suicide and another to resignation. As for me, a modest public servant with the thick skin of a person from Cuiabá, he wastes his time."[3]

Lacerda declared that he had received a kick instead of a reply to his fifty-four-page study. "I am being shot at by the propaganda machine set up by the owners of Brazil to prevent my election." He resented remarks made about himself by Campos and accused the planning minister, "creature of all governments," of hurling insults in the manner of Abelardo Jurema and Saldanha Coelho, "both more intelligent than the minister." He said he would try to reestablish the dialogue by writing another letter to Castello Branco.

Abreu Sodré accused the planning minister of resorting to the same slanders and lies that "the Brizolas used before March 31." Bilac Pinto, critical of Roberto Campos' policies, said the government's austere program should be modified. On the other hand, Governor Ademar de Barros praised the "courageous" economic policy of the Castello administration and quoted World Bank President George Woods as urging patience in the combat of inflation.[4]

Lacerda's new letter to the president, dated May 25 and consisting of only twenty-four pages, was largely a complaint about the behavior of Roberto Campos, whose speech, Lacerda insisted, was no substitute for the serious comments he had been expecting to receive, from the president, about his "impersonal" study. Lacerda expressed contempt for those who accused him of the suicide of Vargas and the resignation of Quadros; as for his attacks on the Kubitschek administration, he wrote that, if they were uncalled for, "why did Your Excellency suspend the political rights of that worthy president whose only error was to dismiss from the BNDE the great minister of the Revolution?" Commenting on Campos' remark that the governor of Guanabara was a political opportunist, Lacerda informed Castello: "Stupidity no longer irritates me but lying does. Of all the attacks, this one alone is unprecedented."

Lacerda maintained that Campos' speech showed that even he did not take seriously the program which he "made Your Excellency adopt," and he complained that Campos' rejection of the fifty-four-page study had been expressed with ironic airs and a haughty contempt for the governor and the public. He accused the revolution of losing the confidence of the people, a confidence that was needed to prevent the return of demagoguery and administrative disorder by the PTB and PSD. In Lacerda's opinion, confidence could be obtained and inflation gradually reduced if the private sector were to be provided with the means of increasing production.

Lacerda also wrote that the government of the revolution had already set up a "machine of propaganda and corruption of public opinion" that would soon eliminate criticism. "Your Excellency will hear only the chorus of adulation. But the country will explode in the midst of the firecrackers of flattery."[5]

Raul Brunini, calling on Castello in Brasília on May 25 to deliver the letter, was accompanied by Congressman Jorge Curi. Castello told his visitors that he would never take the initiative of breaking with the governor of Guanabara, whom, he said, he admired and considered, along with Magalhães Pinto, as having rendered "inestimable services to the Revolution." He expressed appreciation for what the governor had done to help place him in the presidency and remarked that his courage was largely responsible for preventing Brazil from reaching a condition "equal to or worse than" that of Castro's Cuba.

The president told Brunini and Curi that he was hurt by, rather than upset about, the latest episode. He conceded that the governor had a perfect right to criticize government policy, but said he could not accept the governor's effort to separate the president from policy carried out by his ministers, for whose acts he said he was responsible, just as the governor was responsible for what his state cabinet members carried out.

As for federal economic policy, Castello said: "I may go to glory or calamity, but I shall not change it." He revealed that he had authorized Roberto Campos to reply to personal attacks, and said he would rely on advisers to examine thoroughly the governor's study.

Brunini and Curi urged Castello to meet with Lacerda more frequently and for longer intervals. The president replied that he was always disposed to receive him and would give him all the time he needed when he received him on May 27. After Curi maintained that the infrequency of past contacts had favored intriguers who wanted to separate the president from the governor, Castello assured him that he was perfectly aware of the work of intriguers and was immune to it.[6]

Another politician who called on Castello that day was Magalhães Pinto. The Minas governor, charmed by the president, told reporters at Planalto Palace: "For the first time I was treated like a governor, a revolutionary, and a friend." He said he did not regard the extension of his mandate as essential but continued to feel that elections should not be held in 1965.[7]

Lacerda, accompanied by Bilac Pinto, spent almost three hours with Castello at Planalto Palace the next day and was equally charmed. "It was," he told the press, "a meeting that should be a great disappointment to our enemies and satisfy the many friends who want a perfect understanding in our area. We inoculated each other against intrigue."

> Our conversation is going to continue. The president is studying my proposals seriously, and the attention he gave to my exposition comforted me very much. Even if my proposals are not accepted, it was evident that the president is a man capable of receiving suggestions.[8]

As the president promised, a written reply to Lacerda's study was issued by the planning ministry's technicians. The paper, which contained some of the arguments already given by Roberto Campos, rejected "the appeal to economic irrationality" that "brought us to stagnation and hyperinflation." In discussing the increased revenue from taxes, it called attention to the beneficial effects of the severe measures taken to collect income tax payments from those who sought to avoid paying what they owed. Planning in a democratic economy, the paper contended, was merely an effort to coordinate monetary, fiscal, and wage policies, and "must not be confused with any coercion of free enterprise."[9]

Roberto Campos, defending the government's policy in Congress, spoke with optimism about how the private sector was beginning to recuperate. But the congressmen were unfriendly. An irritated Herbert Levy asserted that the private sector was being afflicted by credit restrictions and a "ruthless" fiscal policy. Like others from São Paulo, the *udenista* congressman called the coffee policy a disaster.[10]

Lacerda, who was campaigning in Rio Grande do Sul, declared that Roberto Campos was mentally retarded. He also said that the great mistake of the government was "to allow economists to express opinions about economic matters."[11]

12. Emergence of the Flexa Ribeiro Candidacy (Early June 1965)

Before Lacerda left for Rio Grande do Sul on May 28, the name of Education Secretary Carlos Flexa Ribeiro was being mentioned by Carioca UDN Secretary Pedro Paulo Pimentel as a possible gubernatorial candidate to break the stalemate in the party. The education secretary's name was on the list of fifteen "traditional *udenistas*" drawn up by Adauto Cardoso and Aliomar Baleeiro, and when Sandra Cavalcanti showed the list to Castello Branco, the president, an admirer of the education secretary's work, especially praised him.[1]

Raphael de Almeida Magalhães, working now to have Flexa Ribeiro selected, found Lacerda cold to the idea in the last half of May. In Lacerda's apartment, when Flexa was present, Raphael told the governor, "The UDN directors don't care for Enaldo; they like Flexa." Lacerda pointed out that as Flexa was Sebastião Lacerda's father-in-law, the selection would be an example of family favoritism.[2]

Like Raphael, Secretary Célio Borja promoted the Flexa candidacy. But the president and vice president of the UDN regional directorship, Geraldo Ferraz and Edson Guimarães, issued statements to demonstrate that they would not quickly abandon Enaldo, and

Baleeiro reported that many members of the UDN *bancada* in Brasília wanted to avoid nepotism. The *Tribuna da Imprensa*, writing energetically on behalf of Enaldo, published the findings of a survey that showed that all social classes in the state favored the public works secretary over other candidates of the UDN, as well as those being mentioned by the PTB and PSD. Hélio Fernandes' daily called the candidacy of Sebastião Lacerda's father-in-law a trap set for the governor—a formula that, even if accepted by him, emerged from an anti-Lacerda "conspiracy."[3]

The names of Traffic Director Fontenelle and Water Department Director Veiga Brito surfaced. Fontenelle, who was working with the Doxiadis team of city planners, took seriously the demonstrations and propaganda that suddenly appeared in his favor. Lacerda, however, discouraged the Fontenelle and Veiga Brito candidacies during telephone calls from the south; and, when he reached Rio on June 2, he told Fontenelle not to confuse prestige with popularity.[4]

At a Carioca UDN directorship meeting that day, Lacerda announced that Bilac Pinto, serving as mediator, had prevailed on the UDN congressional bloc to withdraw its support of Adauto Cardoso if Enaldo Cravo Peixoto would step aside. The governor, besides reading a letter in which Enaldo agreed to withdraw, authorized Célio Borja to persuade Raimundo de Brito to do the same. Lacerda, Brunini recalls, also appealed to the directors to pick anyone except the education secretary and then left the group, which, in his absence, reached no decision.[5]

The Carioca UDN directorship met again the next night, with Lacerda presiding, and settled the question. After Edson Guimarães said he had found Flexa Ribeiro favored by twenty-five of the thirty-two directors and by fifteen UDN state legislators, the education secretary was chosen by a 17-2 vote. Professors Raimundo Moniz de Aragão and Agnaldo Costa praised Adauto, who had become head of the Bloco Parlamentar Revolucionário, and said he was not withdrawing. A latecomer, Carlos Sampaio, said Raimundo de Brito also refused to withdraw.[6]

Statements that were bitter but nonetheless useful to Flexa were issued the next day by Raimundo and Adauto. Raimundo, liberating delegates committed to himself, spoke of the "imposition" of the Enaldo Cravo Peixoto candidacy, the "insistent pressure" for his own withdrawal, and the failure of the latest solution to permit a selection in a "free convention." Adauto denied plans to participate in a dissident movement but complained of Lacerda's veto of his candidacy, the early proposal of a candidate "unaffiliated with the party," and pressure on the regional UDN. Hélio Fernandes, in his *Tribuna* column, wrote that the "incredible" replacement of Enaldo Cravo Peixoto by Carlos Flexa Ribeiro was evidence of the confusion of Lacerda and would "add one more chapter to his possible memoirs that could be entitled 'Why I did not become president of the republic.'"[7]

Lacerda, commenting later on the selection of Flexa Ribeiro, said that a message from Adauto Cardoso, Bilac Pinto, and Raimundo de Brito informed him that it would be impossible to unite the party behind one candidate unless he would agree to Flexa's name. The purpose of this "maneuver," he added, was to have a candidate so closely connected to himself, by a family tie, that, in case of defeat, "the defeat would be attributed indisputably to me." Speaking on June 15 at the nominating convention, where Flexa received most of the votes of over a hundred delegates, Lacerda condemned talk in the congressional Bloco Parlamentar Revolucionário about having Castello's successor chosen by an indirect election.[8]

The *Jornal do Brasil* praised the choice of Flexa as preferable to Lacerda's "erroneous" and "personalistic" effort to impose a candidate. *O Globo* described the UDN as having come up with "a good name" but, like Adauto Cardoso and Raimundo de Brito, it charged that "pressure" had prevented a free debate in the convention about the candidates.[9]

13. *O Globo* and Time-Life; Lacerda and His Triplex (June–December 1965)

O Globo received a setback at the hands of Lacerda on June 7 when police of the DOPS grabbed a Cuban employee of Time-Life, Alberto Hernandez Catá, and interrogated him for four hours about his work for TV Globo. The Cuban explained that he and other Time-Life employees were helping TV Globo in accordance with contracts signed by the two companies; his specialty, he said, included administration and the organization of programs.[1]

Using information received from Catá, Lacerda wrote a letter to Castello, sent Justice Minister Milton Campos an official request that TV Globo be closed down, and used a television program to denounce TV Globo. Lacerda also made use of a report of a talk given by Time-Life President Weston C. Pullen, Jr., in October 1964 at a Hudson Institute conference on the development of Latin America. According to the report, a copy of which accompanied Lacerda's letter of June 9 to the president, Pullen had said that Time-Life planned to follow in other countries the formula worked out with TV Globo, and that the TV programming for Latin America, worked out jointly by companies north and south of the border, should interest the U.S.

government because it was an attempt by American groups to reach the people of South America. Lacerda cited these remarks in his official communication to the justice minister, dated June 15. When he communicated with Milton Campos again, a month later, he called his attention to an article in *Television Age*, of February 1, 1965, announcing the purchase of TV Paulista (of Pernambuco) by a group connected with Time-Life. He told Milton Campos that, "with the tacit approval of the authorities," approximately forty-five Brazilian radio and television stations had fallen under the "virtual control of a foreign group that finances Roberto Marinho."[2]

As far back as November 28, 1964, Lacerda had called Castello's attention to "the scandal." Soon after that, and with the help of lawyer Luiz Gonzaga do Nascimento e Silva, TV Globo and Time-Life replaced their "principal contract," a joint venture arrangement signed in 1962, with a new document. According to the new document, signed on January 15, 1965, TV Globo would use a building in Rio sold by it to Time-Life and would pay, as rental, an amount supposed to cover most of Time-Life's Brazilian expenses plus 45 percent of the profits of TV Globo. TV Globo had inaugurated broadcasts in April 1963.[3]

On June 19, 1965, Justice Minister Milton Campos let it be known that Lacerda's petition for closing TV Globo would be handled by the National Telecommunications Council (CONTEL). CONTEL, after some delay, managed to get a copy of the defunct "principal contract," but did not receive a copy of the rental contract until late in January 1966.

In the meantime, Marinho received loans from Time-Life that reached a total of over $4 million by the end of 1965. Competitors screamed. The campaign against TV Globo, begun in 1964 by Lacerda, found an effective leader in Congressman João Calmon, president of ABERT (the Brazilian Association of Radio and Television Broadcasters) and long associated with the Assis Chateaubriand publishing and broadcasting chain. In October 1965, 141 congressmen asked for the formation of a congressional investigating commission (CPI). The CPI questioned witnesses, among them Lacerda, Marinho, and the CONTEL president, and in August 1966 it concluded unanimously that the TV Globo–Time-Life contracts violated the constitution. But the commissions formed on the orders of Castello were not so certain that this was the case.[4]

Just as Roberto Marinho eventually prevailed, Lacerda prevailed in the case of a charge against him made by *O Globo* and others when he added a thirteenth floor at Praia do Flamengo 224, turning his duplex into a triplex. On June 8, the day after the DOPS seized and interrogated Time-Life's Alberto Hernandez Catá, *O Globo* wrote that it could not understand the involvement in "the triplex case" of Carlos Lacerda, "always so rigorous in condemning public men he opposes, assailing their errors, and even falsely accusing them of failings that exist only in his mean imagination."

O Globo pointed out that even if Lacerda had the legal right to build on the roof—a right that depended, in part, on the approval of the owners of the apartments on the other floors—he could not, under the law, construct a full-sized apartment but was required to have it set back from the building's front and limited to just a part of the roof. It suggested that the governor might be seeking, in this illegal way, to make a profit of 100 million cruzeiros ($54,000) by selling his eleventh-floor apartment.[5]

The governor's office told the press of documents that showed that Lacerda had received official permits along with the unanimous consent of the other apartment owners. But when it came to turning documents over to oppositionist legislators, who were trying to set up a CPI, the government's leader and vice leader, Mauro Magalhães and Raphael Carneiro da Rocha, repeatedly asked for time to organize the papers. When they finally furnished them, they omitted the only ones that mattered, the architectural drawings. They argued that technical details should not be made available to legislators who were spokesmen for "counterrevolutionaries" who might use the drawings to carry out an assault on the governor's life.[6]

After Mauro Magalhães declared that the drawings "are not going to fall into the hands of enemies," oppositionist Alfredo Tranjan went on television to denounce the governor. Tranjan, according to the *Diário Carioca*, revealed that "Carlos Lacerda is quite willing to act illegally in favor of his personal interests, in favor of his own luxurious living." *Última Hora* agreed.[7]

Late in June, Tranjan called *udenistas* Mauro Magalhães and Raphael Carneiro da Rocha "criminally responsible" and added that his principal purpose in setting up the CPI was to get the drawings. Mauro Magalhães, a construction industry professional, defended his position by maintaining that the matter had become political instead of technical. The CPI, finally set up in mid-July after the procrastinating UDN named its representatives, received all the papers except the ones it needed. Its *relator*, José Bonifácio Diniz de Andrada, concluded that Lacerda's construction was illegal and recommended that it be demolished.[8] This CPI, as was the one that examined TV Globo, was powerless to enforce its recommendation but served to stir up public opinion.

Hoping for another CPI to stir up antagonism toward Lacerda, Jorge

Serpa Filho said he would testify that he had been tortured by Lacerda's police on the night of July 8. Serpa, considered by many to
have been responsible for the financial scandal that had rocked the
Mannesmann do Brasil steel company during the Goulart regime,
was a favorite target of Lacerda, who declared on July 2, 1965, that he
had been part of a "gang" that had included Kubitschek and Negrão de
Lima. The Rio police were more interested in learning about Serpa's
connections with leading Brazilian figures, such as Walter Moreira
Salles, than details of the Mannesmann case when they forced him to
undress, hear their insults, and stand for hours, hands above his head,
while they questioned him.[9]

The *Jornal do Brasil* wrote that Lacerda, who was on a motor trip
from Brasília to Belém, should reveal publicly whether or not his
police behaved like the political police in totalitarian states. After
Colonel Gustavo Borges spoke on television to deny the use of torture, *O Globo* wrote that the "Nazi" colonel, speaking in the absence
of the principal figure, had failed in his explanation.[10]

14. Castello, "Angel" of a Red Light District
(July 2, 1965)

Early in June, while leaders of the PTB and PSD discussed possible
candidates for the gubernatorial elections, Congress complicated their
tasks by enacting Constitutional Amendment 14, inspired by those
who wanted to eliminate candidates they considered associated with
corruption and subversion. Besides stipulating that gubernatorial candidates were to have at least four years of voting residence in the
state where they sought office, the amendment left the elimination
of candidacies in the air because it declared that "a special law can
establish new ineligibilities."

In mid-June the PTB of Guanabara nominated Goulart's public
works minister, Hélio de Almeida, to run against Flexa Ribeiro. The
choice, recommended by Goulart, provoked a storm of protests from
hard liners. Colonel Gérson de Pina, head of the Military Police Investigation (IPM) looking into the affairs of the Institute of Advanced
Brazilian Studies (ISEB), took to interrogating Hélio de Almeida; he
held the former minister for long hours at military barracks and
threatened to imprison him. The Castello administration, gathering
ideas for the "special" ineligibilities law, drafted a clause that would
strike at Goulart's cabinet officers.[1]

Lacerda said he opposed vetoes against candidacies; he wanted, he
explained, to vanquish at the polls all who had failed with arms
"to defeat us." He did not, however, welcome the gubernatorial

candidacy of engineer Alim Pedro, a former Rio mayor who had been appointed by Castello to a post in the public works ministry. The Alim Pedro candidacy was launched by the Partido Democrata Cristão (PDC), which called Lacerda's government "totalitarian," and was backed by Public Works Minister Juarez Távora; the PST, MTR, and PRT issued a pro–Alim Pedro manifesto, nationalists in the PR exerted pressures on his behalf, and Eloy Dutra and Sérgio Magalhães came out in his favor. After the press reported that Quadros, another Alim Pedro backer, told Golbery that the only way to defeat Lacerda nationally was to have the opposition united in Guanabara, Alim Pedro made it clear that he wished to be the candidate of the united opposition but would withdraw if that was necessary to give the opposition a single candidate.[2]

This statement, Lacerda wrote Castello, revealed that Alim Pedro wished to "divide our electorate and unite the electorate of the adversary," a step that Lacerda said would be helped if the ineligibilities law eliminated Hélio de Almeida. The governor asked the president whether Távora would continue supporting a candidate launched to "destroy the Revolution in Guanabara."[3]

Opening the way for another clash between Lacerda and Castello, Colonel Gérson de Pina and Colonel Osnelli Martinelli, IPM heads, resigned from their investigative posts in a display of anger at the administration's refusal to allow them to arrest men suspected of corruption and subversion. Explaining their indignation in a written statement, Martinelli lamented what he called the government's protection of such men, in contrast to its poor treatment of revolutionary officers. Martinelli was therefore punished with thirty days of arrest and placed in Fort Copacabana. After Castello said he could "admit no further excesses by the hard liners," the Liga Democrática Radical (LIDER), of which Martinelli was president, issued a manifesto classifying Castello as "nothing more than a delegate of the Supreme Command of the Revolution" who could not act "contrary to revolutionary ideas, which are above those of the constitution itself."[4]

Lacerda, inaugurating the Blue and White Preprimary School on June 29, deplored "the situation" of one of those who, at Guanabara Palace on March 31, had worn blue and white neckerchiefs. Martinelli, he said, had defended the people and government of Guanabara, "while many who now avail themselves of the revolution were at their homes peacefully awaiting the victory in order to obtain positions they still undeservedly occupy."[5]

On the next day Lacerda autographed copies of his latest book, *Brazil between the Truth and the Lie,* a collection of his messages to Castello about the PAEG together with a letter of June 3 thanking

Herbert Levy for his support. The letter said: "Not even in the glory days of the Estado Novo was corruption so great as it is in the planning ministry, which pays for texts infiltrated into radio and television programs and the press after they are cooked up in the laboratories of corruption maintained in the minister's office."[6]

Lacerda had been accusing the government of wishing to sell the CTB telephone operations to an American group, and therefore, after Lacerda called on Castello at Laranjeiras Palace on July 1, reporters asked the governor if telephones had been discussed. "Ask the president," Lacerda retorted in a bad mood.[7]

On the next day the governor, accompanied by Gustavo Borges and Carlos Osório, made a much publicized call on Colonel Martinelli at Fort Copacabana. There he told Martinelli, Gérson de Pina, and others that he had informed Castello, during their "very gruff" conversation, of his intention to visit the imprisoned colonel. He had, he said, told the president that the ineligibilities law project was a "monstrosity" and that the correct way to handle the matter was to list all those who were "incompatible to the exercise of mandates" and make them ineligible to do so "for the rest of their lives." He pleased Gérson de Pina by asserting that Oliveira Brito, chairman of the congressional ineligibilities commission, should have his political rights "summarily" suspended. Appealing to Martinelli and Gérson de Pina to continue in active military service, he said that if they retired he would "abandon everything and go to the beach."[8]

Later in the day, the fiery governor gave a press interview at Guanabara Palace that went beyond what the president could put up with. In his most sensational statement, Lacerda said: "Marshal Castello Branco is an angel of Conde de Lage Street" (famed for its prostitutes). He added that the president had surrounded himself with grave diggers and that the behavior of his civilian ministers was worse than that of Goulart's ministers. Castello, he also said, was offering favors to congressmen to get them to vote for "idiotic laws."

Much of the press interview was devoted to rectifying what the governor called totally false reports made by the presidential palace press room about his July 1 session with the president. "I declared to Marshal Castello Branco that this cabinet's ministers do not work, and, when they do, they don't know how to work." Lacerda disclosed that he had also told the president that he had become so dissatisfied with the federal government that he was tempted to leave public life when his mandate ended on December 5 and was only prevented from doing so because he had found no one to take his place to continue with the revolution "that ended last year."[9]

The revolution, Lacerda declared to the press, was commanded by the Light Company and a group of businessmen who wanted to take over Guanabara in the person of Alim Pedro, "indicated by Jorge de Melo Flores, representative of the Rockefeller group." "What is going on in Brazil is a disgrace." The governor condemned the Caixa Econômica for planning to spend 60 billion cruzeiros to finance automobile purchases but refusing to loan 5 billion to Guanabara, where, he said, four public works were faced with paralyzation. He pointed out that Castello had alienated Magalhães Pinto, who had recently condemned the president for turning the revolution over to "spurious combinations." "I also informed the president that in my case it was useless to try to shove me aside because I am a presidential candidate."[10]

15. An Indirect Presidential Election? (July 1965)

Carlos Castello Branco, in his *Jornal do Brasil* column, wrote of three important factors in Lacerda's declarations: his definite break with the president, his support of Magalhães Pinto, and "the revelation of the visit to Colonel Osnelli Martinelli, expression and symbol of the hard line." Analyzing the movement to "depose" the president, the columnist noted that the governors of Minas and Guanabara were united, as they had been before Goulart fell, but that Governor Ademar de Barros was at Castello's side, as were the governors of the smaller states and the congressional majorities. "Marshal Castello Branco is not João Goulart and despite his difficulties with the military, there are indications that he has real strength in the armed forces, far different from that fantasy under the imaginary command of General Assis Brasil."[1]

O Estado de S. Paulo editorialized that if one were to put aside "excesses" expressed by Lacerda and discontented Admiral Sílvio Heck (new president of LIDER), it would be noted that their declarations faithfully depicted a state of unrest "that tends to become general, in a wave difficult to control." Magalhães Pinto warned that "the winds that have been growing stronger can turn themselves into a tempest."[2]

O Globo, after an editorial about Lacerda's "insanity," overcame, two days later, what it called its reluctance to mention his "vile" expression, "angel of that street." It offered the apologies of the Cariocas to the president and his government, insulted more rudely "than previous governments have ever been." Lacerda's "angel" remark was denounced in Congress and the state legislature and was cited by UDN Vice President Antônio Carlos Magalhães when he gave a radio-television speech in which he said that "the place for curing insanity is not Guanabara Palace." The Bahia congressman argued that *ude-nistas* should no longer feel committed to Lacerda's candidacy because he had violated the UDN convention's pledge to support the president. Castello, who said he would not reply to Lacerda, invited Antônio Carlos Magalhães to lunch, which was considered significant. Aliomar Baleeiro and Adauto Cardoso said that under no circumstances would Castello support Lacerda's candidacy.[3]

Lacerda's outburst stimulated a movement in favor of having the successor of Castello chosen by Congress. The movement, as described by Senator Krieger on July 2, was unorganized; but, Krieger added, it would gain a large acceptance, the ground being fertile for an idea that would avoid a series of problems. Bloco Parlamentar Revolucionário President Adauto Cardoso predicted on July 5 that the "crisis" would result in an indirect election for the next president. Following his prediction, the idea came to the fore in Brasília and much of the press. It gained a following that included Lacerda haters, advocates of a parliamentary system, supporters of a further extension for Castello, and PSD members of the Bloco Parlamentar Revolucionário, some of whom felt that the proposed change might improve the prospects of their party. Even before PSD President Amaral Peixoto spoke of his party's inclination to favor the parliamentary system, the *Jornal do Brasil* wrote of "the firm conviction in all responsible sectors that Congress will take over the election of the president."

O Estado de S. Paulo did not care for this idea of blocking Lacerda's path and called it "a goal of the PSD and PTB." But the movement, according to Carlos Castello Branco, reflected primarily the desire of the political directorship of the UDN to prevent Lacerda from reaching the presidency. It was Eurico Resende, UDN vice leader in the Senate, who prepared a project for a constitutional amendment to allow Congress to select the next president. UDN President Sátiro, who had refused to conclude that Lacerda's statements on July 2 represented a break with the government, dismissed the idea that the UDN leadership was opposed to Lacerda.[4]

Lacerdistas in Congress said they would ask Sátiro for a new convention so that the party bases could voice their feelings about the Lacerda candidacy, "opposed by parliamentary sectors of the UDN." This idea, which seemed likely to force the party to choose between Castello and Lacerda, did not appeal to Sátiro, and he called it inopportune.[5]

In mid-July Lacerda disclosed that he was authorizing Sátiro to set a date for a new convention. "I shall," the governor said, "win as many conventions as they want to hold, even if they hold one a week. However, I doubt if my enemies in Congress want the UDN to meet. What they really want is indirect presidential elections in exchange for extensions of their own mandates." He said he would answer the charges of Antônio Carlos Magalhães only when "he asks me for an audience in Planalto Palace." Alim Pedro's campaign, he said, was being coordinated by two Americans who had worked for the Goldwater presidential campaign and were doing political work in Brazil at the invitation of the Chase Manhattan Bank people.

Lacerda mentioned two matters that he found encouraging. One was a promise of assistance from the National Highway Fund for the Rebouças Tunnel. The other concerned conditions in the north, from which he had returned in the *Esperança II*, a DC-3 that Orlando Ometto had made available after the owner of *Esperança I* had sought favors that the governor had been unwilling to grant. Lacerda praised the Belém-Brasília highway and said that if he became president, but only if he became president, it would be asphalted. The people he met along the highway, he disclosed, were filled with optimism. "I have the impression that the north is marching ahead in a true burst of development."[6]

On July 17 Castello told Krieger to kill any move aimed at an indirect presidential election. Adauto, following a meeting with the president, concluded that an indirect election was improbable and told the press that Lacerda had "extraordinary qualities of national political leadership." "The governor has great prestige in Guanabara and still more in Minas, São Paulo, and Rio Grande do Sul, and generally among the common people of the entire country."[7]

Lacerda, speaking late in July at a Foreign Press Club lunch, called the president "a completely honest patriot, inexperienced in politics and power," and added: "I honestly think I am the best man to succeed Castello Branco." He also explained: "I won't stand by and let myself be trampled on. I act according to the situation. Sometimes I play roughly, sometimes mildly. I am applying new tactics. I'm trying to mobilize public opinion, thus neutralizing the actions of those who conspire against me."[8]

In Rio, the governor kept speaking at inaugurations, thus calling attention to achievements, such as homes for domestic servants and the "third stage" of the Guandu Aqueduct. When Miss Mato Grosso visited Rio, he presented her with books that included his own latest publication, *Uma rosa é uma rosa é uma rosa*, a collection of previously published articles, such as "The Great de Gaulle." The cover showed the author holding a bunch of roses.[9]

16. Comments: Lacerda's Mistake

When Lacerda attacked Castello Branco on July 2, he stated that of all the suggestions he had ever taken to the president, only one had been accepted, "and that after a long month of reflection": the adoption of daylight-saving time.[1] Had Lacerda been correct in making this statement, Brazil's history would have been different, perhaps very different, and perhaps more to Lacerda's liking.

Lacerda, persuading Castello Branco in March 1965 to favor direct gubernatorial elections in October, had one objective in mind, the scheduled direct presidential election of 1966. "Today I won the elections of 1966," he exclaimed after being notified by Castello that the 1965 gubernatorial elections would be direct.[2]

O Globo spoke more truthfully than it supposed when it asked: "If the antirevolutionaries win in October, will democracy have won or lost in Brazil?"[3] Election results in October 1965 might give the hard liners the ammunition they needed to defeat Castello's hope of turning the country over to his popularly elected successor.

There was merit in *coincidência,* making elections less frequent, and perhaps in the proposal to help achieve it by one-year governorship mandates that seemed hardly to call for direct elections. But Lacerda was always inclined to feel that the authorities in Brasília were "stabbing him in the back in a dark room."[4] He saw in the president's indirect election plan for 1965 a danger to a direct election in 1966.

Lacerda's reactions to his perceptions sometimes turned the perceptions into realities. In reacting as he did in July 1965 to the "maneuvers" of "the owners of Brazil," he irritated politicians so much that they did set about to change the rules to make the 1966 presidential election indirect. This, however, was no one-year mandate matter, and Castello, on July 17 and later, made it unmistakably clear to leaders of Congress and members of his administration that he would block any move in Congress that favored an indirect election for president in 1966. Amaral Peixoto, after Castello spoke, announced that the PSD opposed an indirect election in 1966.[5] The statements of Adauto Cardoso, following his visit with Castello, leave no doubt that the stubborn president had the support he needed to make his wish on this issue prevail in Congress. Which is not to say that Castello wanted Lacerda to win in 1966.

The presidential group and the anti-Lacerda politicians were given the opportunity, with the direct gubernatorial elections of 1965, to push Lacerda aside by contributing in Guanabara to the victory of the opposition over "his" candidate. He could, as Quadros reportedly told General Golbery, be eliminated from the national scene through a setback in October in Guanabara, the state which, in the words of Danillo Nunes, was to serve as "the base of Lacerda's future presidential campaign."[6] This was one trouble Lacerda brought on himself when he insisted on direct elections in 1965. For although Lacerda ingratiated himself with some of the hardest of the hard liners, reducing the likelihood of their interference in 1966 in case his candidacy were popular, he left himself open to being seen, from Guanabara's results in 1965, as a candidate who was unable to defeat the "antirevolutionaries."

The other trouble, a possible hard line revolt resulting from victories of the "antirevolutionaries" in 1965, was more serious for Castello and Brazil, and, if it occurred, would give fresh support to those who maintained that Lacerda had the greatest influence of anyone on the politics of Brazil during his time. For it was Lacerda, and Lacerda alone, who provoked Castello into asking Krieger to reverse the arrangement already set up to have indirect elections for one-year gubernatorial terms. The presidential decision, as Amaral Peixoto and others have noted, came as a surprise to everyone.[7]

It might be added that starting in March 1965, when the decision about the 1965 elections was made, the only choice politically open to Lacerda was to attack the Castello administration. The popularity of his cause, which would be badly hurt with an electoral defeat in the Guanabara contest, depended on an antigovernment position.

One can argue that Lacerda's political steps, including his insistence on the direct elections in 1965, made sense in case of a UDN victory that year in Guanabara. But it was a mistake to have as much confidence in that victory as Lacerda had in March.[8]

VIII.

The Elimination of Lacerda's UDN Candidacy (August–October 1965)

1. Lott's Candidacy (August 1965)

By a 210-115 vote at 4:00 A.M. on July 9 the Chamber of Deputies passed the Ineligibilities Law desired by the administration, and the Senate followed suit a few days later. The law managed to eliminate Hélio de Almeida's candidacy by voiding, until December 31, 1965, the candidacies of those who, without having had legislative mandates, had served as civilian cabinet ministers between January 23, 1963, and March 31, 1964. Hélio de Almeida proclaimed that Congress had approved a law that would "forever be a stain on the history of Brazil's political liberties."[1]

To find a substitute for Hélio de Almeida, the state PTB decided to hold a convention late in July. Marshal Henrique Lott, seventy years old, refused to be considered, making it likely that the party would turn, as Lutero Vargas wished, to Negrão de Lima, favorite of the PSD. But PTB leftists shared the anti-Negrão sentiment of socialist Aurélio Viana, who threatened to split the opposition by becoming the PSB gubernatorial candidate if the PTB nominated Negrão.[2]

Senator José Ermírio de Morais, seeking to wrest national control of the PTB from Lutero Vargas, launched the candidacy of Lott, who finally agreed to run if he were the unanimous choice of the PTB and PSB. Augusto Amaral Peixoto, president of the Guanabara PSD, called the sudden reemergence of Lott's candidacy a "desperate coup" by the PSB and the "ideological" wing of the PTB.[3]

During the PTB convention, which had to be extended because of unruliness, pro-Lott mobs invaded Tiradentes Palace and destroyed the ballot box after Negrão was felt to have received the most votes. Balloting was undertaken again three days later following the arrival of a protective navy contingent and the withdrawal, in Lott's favor, of one of the other favorites of the Left. While Lott's supporters, who had filled the galleries, jeered Lutero and Negrão, Lott was chosen over Negrão by a 64-60 vote.

The PSB quickly adhered to the PTB candidate, and so did the PDC and MTR after Alim Pedro withdrew. Lott was supported by the *Correio da Manhã* and by *Última Hora*, whose Danton Jobim called his candidacy "our great flag." The controversial marshal demanded the restitution of the political rights of those who had lost them, and was praised in a message of Kubitschek from Paris.[4]

Chateaubriand's *O Jornal* described Lott's backers as extremists interested in disturbing much-needed political peace. From Washington, Juracy Magalhães wrote Castello Branco that the selection of Negrão would have been no challenge to the revolution and therefore the Communists had taken advantage, once again, of the "senility of Lott."[5]

Lutero Vargas, despite this setback, overcame in Brasília on August 8 the challenge of José Ermírio de Morais for the PTB leadership. Pleased with what he called his victory over his party's "radicals," he expressed doubt that Lott's candidacy would survive a challenge based on the electoral residence requirement of the ineligibilities legislation. Lott, shortly before the PTB convention, had transferred his voting residence from Guanabara to Teresópolis, in Rio state, because at that time he wanted to avoid being nominated.[6]

While the hard liners' LIDER called Lott's nomination a victory for the forces of corruption and subversion, War Minister Costa e Silva declared: "The army repudiates the candidacies imposed by Communists and antirevolutionary forces." The other military ministers expressed similar sentiments in circulars to their troops, whereupon the president discouraged such military pronouncements and assured the military that Lott's candidacy would be voided by the Ineligibilities Law.[7]

Lott had alienated Tenório Cavalcanti (by ordering Tenório's house invaded in 1955) and the PSD, and was a satisfactory opposition candidate for Lacerda, who pronounced the candidacy "authentic and very good, although upsetting to the military." The candidacy, noisily supported by the far Left, had many opponents outside the military, was not a unifying one for the Carioca opposition, and was viewed with displeasure by the conservative men, who, according to Lacerda, were conspiring to eliminate him by handing a defeat to Flexa Ribeiro. The purpose of the conspiracy, Lacerda told the public, was to call off direct presidential elections with the argument that if the governor, after all he had done for his state, could not provide a victory there, no nonleftist could win a direct presidential election. "If Flexa does not win, there will be no presidential election in 1966," he declared.[8]

After the declaration appeared in the *Baltimore Sun*, Juracy

Magalhães wrote the governor to say he could not believe the reporting had been accurate. Lacerda cabled the ambassador that the *Sun* had distorted his statement. "What I said is that the Lott candidacy will be easily defeated and we must . . . not foster union among the adversaries as is being done by individuals whose only interest is to defeat me without considering the consequences." At a ceremony at the Rio Comprido–Lagoa Tunnel, Lacerda expressed his fear of "palace intrigue" and said that those who wished to void Lott's candidacy were not moved by a wish to defend the revolution or by the fear that Lott would be elected. "I want Lott on television making idiotic remarks, but I want him as he is, an honest, authentic expression of a political force. If that force is rotten let the people be the ones to say so." The governor also recommended that the people make the laws, and said that both the Institutional Act and the Ineligibilities Law were no good.[9]

O Globo pointed out that Lacerda, afraid of the stronger Negrão de Lima candidacy, defended the thesis that subversives could run for office. It argued that the government should eliminate subversive candidates and the UDN should eliminate the candidacy of Lacerda, "traitor to the Revolution and nation," lest it be responsible for "installing the cruelest and most vindictive of dictatorships." In the meantime, Lacerda and Negrão de Lima exchanged insults, with Negrão republishing, and reading on television, his vehement letter of June 1958, calling Lacerda a despicable thief, blackmailer, traitor, braggart, and buffoon, who lacked all moral fiber and was incapable of defending the honor of his own home.[10]

The nomination of Lott in Guanabara and Sebastião Paes de Almeida, Kubitschek's finance minister, in Minas rekindled the feeling that direct elections were a mistake. Carlos Castello Branco wrote on August 8 that "apprehensions about the electoral process are increasing in all areas," and Senator Krieger declared, two days later, that a reform of the regime with the suppression of the direct presidential election in 1966 had overwhelming military support and could be enacted without difficulty.[11]

During the discussions about reforming the regime, Congressman Gustavo Capanema argued that Brazil's long and bitter experience, marked by "episodes of civic immaturity," made the reform an "imperious necessity." *O Globo* blamed past "instability and inefficiency" on the use of "universal suffrage" to choose the chief executive. Calling an indirect presidential election "essential," it wrote that this reform could be achieved without turning to a parliamentary system. The *Jornal do Brasil*, on the other hand, advocated a direct presidential election, as the true democratic way, and criticized

The PTB advises the PSD: "They disqualified Lott." (APPE drawing in
O Cruzeiro, September 18, 1965)

those who, for "machiavellian personalistic" reasons, favored a different course.

Lacerda, in a warm letter to Magalhães Pinto, which appeared in
the press, said that the real reason the "conspirators" in the federal
administration "oppose my candidacy is because they do not want to
have the people voting." In his speeches, the governor complained
that Castello dedicated most of his time to political maneuvers, and
described the presidential palaces as beehives for distilling the honey
of capitulations, with the government seeking allies for promoting
continuismo. The political activities of Lott-supporting Communists,
he said, were being used by the government as a pretext for achieving
indirect elections. Adauto Cardoso replied that Lacerda's "vulgar expressions, insults, and disrespectful remarks have reached the point
where they make no impression."[12]

The congressional commission to study reform of the government
was starting its work late in August when decisions were handed
down by the Regional Electoral Tribunals of Guanabara and Minas.
Lott lost his case in a 6-0 decision, whereas the registration of Paes de
Almeida's candidacy in Minas was granted. The cases were appealed
to the Superior Electoral Tribunal, which, on September 6 and 7 ruled
against both candidacies in 4-2 decisions.[13]

On September 1, following the regional tribunal's unanimous ruling against Lott, Castello intervened again in favor of Lacerda's wish,
and his own, about 1966. In a widely reported statement to PSD

Senate leader Filinto Müller, he said he would in no way associate himself with a movement that favored reforming the executive power or the manner of choosing the chief executive. War Minister Costa e Silva spoke to Câmara President Bilac Pinto about the army's opposition to the parliamentary regime and lack of enthusiasm for the reforms from which Castello had separated himself. Bilac, majority leader Pedro Aleixo, and Justice Minister Milton Campos took positions that comforted UDN President Sátiro, violent opponent of any reform that would eliminate a direct presidential election in 1966.

Castello, speaking on September 3 to UDN congressional leader Adolfo de Oliveira, reemphasized his position. Filinto Müller, advocate of indirect elections (and another extension for Castello), expressed his disappointment. Afonso Arinos de Melo Franco, advocate of a parliamentary system, said that the commission studying institutional reform would have to "hibernate."[14]

2. *Lacerdismo* on the Rise (July–September 1965)

Late in July Lacerda began a new battle—this one to preserve the independence of the electric utility company CHEVAP (Companhia Hidroelétrica do Vale do Paraíba). CHEVAP had been formed in 1960 to construct the Funil hydroelectric plant in Rio state. A little later, at Lacerda's insistence and with $15 million of United States AID funds, it assumed the task of setting up a thermoelectric plant in Guanabara's Santa Cruz industrial area. CHEVAP's capital had been furnished almost entirely by the government-run Eletrobrás; among the minor shareholders were the Rio Light Company and the states of Guanabara, São Paulo, and Rio de Janeiro.[1]

Congress agreed in October 1964 with the government's proposal to end CHEVAP's independence, and therefore Eletrobrás prepared to incorporate CHEVAP into a former AMFORP property, the CBEE (Companhia Brasileira de Energia Elétrica). With CHEVAP's Funil work twenty months behind schedule and construction not even begun on the Santa Cruz plant, Mines and Energy Minister Mauro Thibau and Eletrobrás President Otávio Marcondes Ferraz argued that the fusion of CHEVAP into CBEE, which had excellent AMFORP technicians, would increase efficiency and be accompanied by a less costly power distribution arrangement. The plan would end the bickering among the members of the CHEVAP administrative team, where Guanabara was represented by Salvador Mandim. In the new setup, Guanabara, São Paulo, and Rio de Janeiro states would have voices on a consultive council but no longer in the administration.[2]

Lacerda pointed out that the plan for power distribution, to be handled by local concessionaires, would leave Guanabara at the mercy of the Light Company's monopoly. He arranged for Guanabara to go to the courts to block the fusion. Speaking to the press, he criticized the government's wish to eliminate the voices of those scheduled to receive CHEVAP power. *O Estado de S. Paulo* wrote that "nothing, absolutely nothing" could be found to "justify the delirium" used by Lacerda in his attacks on Thibau and Marcondes Ferraz and that his attacks on the Light Company resembled past campaigns of the Left carried out with "inflexible tenacity" against foreign collaboration.[3]

On August 14 Thibau sent a study to Lacerda, but Lacerda told the press that he was returning it to Thibau because its imbecility would not allow it a place in the state files. In a letter to Thibau, published in the press, he called the study insolent, inept, and full of grammatical errors. The letter rejected the ministry's statement that "to accuse the electric public utility of being a monopoly is evidence of a dismal ignorance of the industry because it cannot be handled in a different way." The statement, Lacerda wrote, was correct in the case of nongovernment utilities only in countries with governments that were feeble-minded or responsible for betrayals. After Lacerda learned that Castello Branco was indignant because the governor had returned the study, offending Thibau, he wrote in the *Tribuna da Imprensa* about the "untouchable ministers," saying that the president was responsible for them when they were criticized, but that when they conspired against elections and served antinational interests, Castello acted as though he had nothing to do with what went on.[4]

The *Tribuna* article appeared on August 26, after Lacerda, at a CHEVAP assembly meeting, cast the lone vote against the CBEE-CHEVAP fusion. The article assailed the "extortionary" electric power rate increases authorized by the government, and the government's "disgraceful business" of purchasing the AMFORP properties for what he said was "more than they are worth or was asked by the seller." The crime at the CHEVAP assembly meeting, he wrote, was simply a part of a greater crime: "usurpation of political power for use at the service of interests alien to democracy and the Brazilian people." Calling the substitution of CHEVAP officers by agents of federal politics "a very serious warning," Lacerda argued that the struggle to win the Guanabara election was not, as some might suppose, against Marshal Lott. "The struggle, unfortunately, is against another marshal. It is against Marshal Castello Branco," who, through the intervention of the Light Company, General Golbery, Jorge de Melo Flores, and the Walter Moreira Salles and Roberto Marinho groups, "seeks to divide us in order to defeat us. Anything goes—as in the days of João Goulart."[5]

The article, which pointed out that a brother-in-law of Castello Branco was the director of CHEVAP, filled two of the *Tribuna*'s pages and was called "interminable" and "bombastic" by the *Diário Carioca*. A few days after it appeared, Castello signed the decree that transferred the CHEVAP concessions to the federal government. "Little by little," Lacerda said, "we are going to see that the government of April 1, 1964, is more favorable to the Canadian Light group than to the Revolution."[6]

Dedicating a school on August 31, Lacerda said that Roberto Campos, in visiting Russia to seek funds that the United States failed to provide, was undermining international capital's confidence in Brazil. "I believe that the United States is not sending and will not send funds because subservience to public service concessionaires like the Light is not the way to attract foreign investments. Foreign investments are attracted by a courageous economic and social policy of affirmation of Brazil's ability to fulfill its own destiny."[7] He condemned "subservience" to an orthodox economic policy and "subservience" to an international prescription suitable for developed nations.

In a cool letter to Ambassador Gordon, Lacerda wrote that his position about public utilities did not affect his esteem and friendship for the United States. The letter expressed the governor's displeasure at the failure of the embassy program for the Fulbright Mission to include a reception by the state government. Jack Valenti, a member of the Mission, wrote a confidential report for President Johnson in which he described Lacerda as "a gifted, talented man with much charisma and demagogic charm, but unreliable and erratic." Valenti praised Castello for carrying out "unpalatable but necessary measures."[8]

The Castello administration's measures had succeeded in reducing the annual inflation rate in Guanabara from over 80 percent in mid-1964 to about 40 percent. But government workers were angry about the restrictiveness of the government's wage policy.[9] IBOPE, early in September, reported the following findings from polls conducted in Guanabara:[10]

Who wins the debate, Castello or Lacerda?

Lacerda	46%
Castello	14%
Don't Know	40%

Who better represents the objectives of the 1964 Revolution?

Castello   21%
Lacerda   44%
Don't Know   35%

About the contest of Lacerda against Roberto Campos?

Pro-Lacerda   56%
Pro-Campos   8%

Who has the greatest prestige in Guanabara?

Lacerda   45%
Kubitschek   32%
Goulart   5%
Castello   4%

If the presidential election were today, for whom would you vote?

Lacerda   49%
Carvalho Pinto   9%
(Less popular names follow.)

Carlos Castello Branco, commenting on the poll, noted that Lacerda had been able to "break down traditional resistances among Cariocas to his political career." Politicians in other states, he also wrote, agreed that Brazil was affected by *Lacerdismo* almost to the extent that it had been affected by *Janismo* in 1960. He concluded that Lacerda ought to be pleased with "the success of his tactical position of aggressively thrashing the federal government, which for a year and a half has faced the onus of unpopular decisions."[11]

After Finance Minister Bulhões said that foreign private investors wondered whether the next Brazilian administration would carry on with the economic-financial policy they welcomed, *O Globo* and *O Estado de S. Paulo* expanded on the theme, with *O Globo* writing that foreign investors feared that Lacerda was serious when he said that, as president, he would destroy the financial-economic accomplishments of the Castello government and reverse policies about iron ore and electric power. He had, it wrote, adopted "nationalism" as a campaign issue to attract those who had become political orphans with the expulsion of Brizola.[12]

What stung Lacerda was *O Estado de S. Paulo's* position and especially its statement that the governor was unable to judge economic policy with the necessary serenity and seriousness. It wrote that Finance Minister Bulhões' concern about foreign investments was due largely to Lacerda, who had made criticism of Castello's policy the theme of his presidential campaign, along with "impassioned accusations" against Hanna and the Light Company. Praising the "courageous policy" of Thibau and Marcondes Ferraz, it wrote that the Light Company was now in a position to go ahead after having been hindered by a "demagogic" rate policy of past governments—a rate policy "for which the governor of Guanabara appears to have a longing." Two days later *O Estado's* editorial was reproduced by the *Jornal do Brasil*.[13]

Lacerda's reply, published by *O Estado* on September 7, denied his lack of "serenity and seriousness" and said that the term "impassioned accusations" ought more fittingly to be applied to Roberto Campos' response to his own "objective suggestions." Lacerda pictured himself again as the "sacrificial lamb"—the one being blamed for the failure of foreign investments to materialize and for the "failure of the economic policy."[14]

3. "The Juracy Mission" (September 1965)

Reports that Juracy Magalhães was to play a leading role in the Castello Branco administration led to speculation that alarmed the *Lacerdistas*. On September 10, when the ambassador reached Rio for a week of discussions, the *Jornal do Brasil* proclaimed on page one that Juracy was Castello's candidate to be the next president and had been chosen to give the government a "more decisive" role in the "presidential succession." *O Globo* suggested that Juracy had been kept abroad to spare him from political erosion and was emerging as one of the most likely presidential candidates of the revolution. The *Diário de Notícias* announced that Juracy had agreed to seek the presidency. But Carlos Castello Branco wrote that the ambassador, while criticizing Lacerda's position in letters to the governor from Washington, remained faithful to the candidate chosen by his party, the UDN.[1]

In the exchange of letters to which the columnist referred, written in July and August, Lacerda complained of being "kicked" by Antônio Carlos Magalhães, prompting Juracy to reply that *udenistas* should not attack their candidate and their candidate should not attack the government. "I think," Juracy wrote, "that you are losing, if you have not already lost, the greatest opportunity of your life by your separation from the government. As governor you proved yourself able to construct and not just destroy. Now you have had the opportunity to

prove that you can furnish support and not just act as commander."
Juracy urged avoiding "that trap where we criticize each other in
public."[2]

Upon reaching Rio on September 10, Juracy told the press of his
regret that "some people are engaged in a conflict of mutual destruction." He expressed his "complete backing" for Castello's economic-
financial policy and said that if Lacerda should reach the presidency
he would find no alternative to it. *O Jornal,* in condemning positions
taken by Lacerda, cited the ambassador's "firm and authoritative"
words along with the opinion of German banker Herman Abs and
comments expressed by members of the Fulbright Mission.[3]

After a two-and-a-half-hour talk with Castello at Laranjeiras Palace
on September 11, Juracy told reporters that the rumors that "I'll be
a minister of this or that" were unfounded, and said he could not be
considered an agent to unify the revolutionary forces. Thus he denied
what Castello had in mind for him. He also denied being a presidential candidate,[4] although his name was among those Castello had in
mind when he considered the succession.

Juracy, displaying his benevolent smile and advocating harmony in
the revolutionary forces, set about interviewing political leaders, especially those in the UDN. To advance their ideas, they flocked to his
Rio house, which reportedly received as many as 150 visitors each
day between 7:30 A.M. and 10:30 P.M. One of them was Magalhães
Pinto, who was peeved at Castello because the president, in agreeing
to a meeting of the leaders of the March 1964 movement, had cleverly
killed the idea by leaving the Minas governor with the impossible
task of deciding whom to include. Now Magalhães Pinto asked Juracy
to arrange for two things he said he had been unable to get from
Castello: (1) a "union of the leaders of the March 31 movement" to
participate in government decisions, and (2) a program that would
give attention to "the aspirations of the people."[5]

Asked about a reform of the regime, Juracy told reporters that it was
a subject of his conversations and that neither he nor the president
cared for suggestions already made for a parliamentary system. It
turned out, as Carlos Castello Branco reported, that Juracy liked "the
formula of indirect election of the president, not by the present Congress but by the future Congress, whose members would be chosen by
an electorate informed ahead of time of the role they would be given."
It also became known that Juracy would replace Milton Campos as
justice minister after the October 1965 elections. Lacerda, often critical of Milton Campos' inclusion in the cabinet, regretted his imminent replacement. Cabinet changes, Lacerda wrote Magalhães Pinto,

were being planned in order to "remove those who oppose maneuvers for suppressing the direct vote."[6]

UDN President Sátiro was reported to have left Juracy's residence
in an angry mood, convinced that the "mission" had the objective of
blocking Lacerda and opening the way for Juracy to reach the presidency through some reform of the regime. After that, Juracy lost his
patience with the press. He said he had no mission, was conferring
on his own initiative, and would not carry out political coordination
work for his own benefit. Sátiro hastened to express his belief that
Juracy, a loyal companion, would not work against his party's candidate, but added that the ambassador had failed to provide a good
explanation of his recent political activity.[7]

According to *O Estado de S. Paulo,* the success of "the political
mission entrusted to Ambassador Juracy Magalhães by the president" depended on his ability to bring about a "reapproximation" of
Lacerda with the government. Although this task was impossible,
no one was more eager to inform Lacerda of Castello's virtues than
Juracy, who had remarked that in his thirty-four years of public life
he had never witnessed before, in any government, "the seriousness
with which the present one studies the solution of all the problems."
Lacerda, however, maintained that success in the ballot boxes in
October depended on criticizing the government, and that, without
that success, the whole system of direct elections would crumble.[8]

Asked by reporters whether he continued to support Lacerda's bid
for the presidency, Juracy replied that he did not answer questions
"having to do with uniting and disuniting; I prefer to converse about
philosophy, the philosophy of government, the philosophy of my
political action." He encountered delay in reaching Lacerda and had
to deny reports that Lacerda would not see him. They finally met at
Guanabara Palace on September 16. Following their talk, Juracy told
the press that Lacerda's administrative work was notable, and the
governor gave the departing ambassador some IBOPE poll results
favorable to Flexa Ribeiro.[9]

After Juracy left for the United States on September 18, Carlos
Castello Branco wrote about "the deadly outburst" with which Lacerda "struck at the Juracy Mission." The governor, in one of his
statements, said that if Flexa Ribeiro were elected, "the mission will
consist of convincing President Castello Branco of the need for direct
elections" and if Flexa should lose, "it will consist of trying to convince me of the need for indirect elections."[10]

On September 24, Castello cabled Juracy that his resignation as
ambassador had been accepted. "You leave your post when your prestige in the United States is at its peak and when the political situation

of my government is in great need of your services." It was felt that Juracy, as justice minister, would coordinate the work to bring about institutional changes, among them an increase in the number of Supreme Court justices, desired by Castello and opposed by Milton Campos. When an influential PSD congressman spoke of the possibility of Juracy's becoming "national unity" candidate for president, Juracy modestly observed that he did not consider the idea viable.[11]

4. "Brazil's Cleanest City" Becomes "The World's Cinema Capital" (September 1965)

During the last weeks of September, Rio's fourth centenary and the Lacerda administration's accomplishments were observed with a grand flourish. The intensified publicity campaign began on Saturday night, September 11, when the governor and his cabinet presented a marathon television program. September 15 saw the start of a two-week international film festival, the first in Rio's history. The busy tourism department, now headed by Enaldo Cravo Peixoto, ran advertisements calling attention to the offerings of the Novo Rio (New Rio), such as the opening of the Portuguese government's Fourth Centennial pavilion, soccer matches, boat trips in the bay, and "the festive inaugurations of innumerable public works." The state bank invited the public to exhibitions displayed in its new headquarters.[1]

The ten-hour television program that began at 10:00 P.M. on September 11 was described as "the longest ever presented by a head of government." During its opening hours, thousands filled the gardens of Guanabara Palace to observe at first hand the presentations made by the governor and his state secretaries; some visitors, such as hard liners Gérson de Pina and Osnelli Martinelli, remained until dawn. Marcos Tamoyo, the new secretary of public works, had the most to report.

The governor's final comments, given shortly before 8:00 A.M. on Sunday, found wide distribution on a phonograph record that served as election propaganda. "God gave me energy, physical stamina, and, who knows, even moral stamina. I thank God that in the period of five years I lacked none of these characteristics." Noting that it was almost time for him to turn the state over to his successor, Lacerda emphasized that he had served with probity. He explained that he had acquired his Petrópolis property by selling another property, and he attributed the money he still owed for his large Praia do Flamengo apartment to his having earned as governor less than he could have earned outside public service. Speaking of honesty in administration, he pointed out that he was "thoroughly familiar with the moral corruption they left me to clean up." "And now, on this eve of a decision by all the people, if they want elections in the coming year, let them vote correctly for a companion faithful to our achievements, our effort, and our work; and everyone, by now, knows who he is."[2]

By late September, the governor averaged seven inaugurations daily. When he dedicated the Escola Roma, said to have been the 180th school constructed during his administration, he was accompanied by the mayor of Rome, who was in Rio to attend the Roman Exposition, with its models of the Coliseum and the Capitoline sector, photographs, paintings, and reproductions of statues. The Benfica Viaduct for motor vehicles was publicized as the thirteenth viaduct completed since 1960. When keys were distributed for new dwellings for workers and domestic servants, the governor's office reported that COHAB would complete, by the end of the year, over 12,000 housing units. Most of those already built were in Vila Kennedy with 4,753, followed by Vila Aliança with 2,187, Cidade de Deus in Jacarepaguá with 1,656 (and 1,688 more scheduled before December 31), and Vila Esperança with 465. In addition, 1,193 residential units had been built in apartments for state employees.[3]

Cleanliness was the theme at the inauguration of the garbage treatment plant in the Irajá district on September 19. The governor recalled "the filthiness" of the city he had received in 1960, thanked the 6,500 street cleaners, and called Rio the "cleanest city in Brazil." He spoke of the new oversized collection trucks, fast-working mechanical sweepers, and dust removers, and attributed some of the improvement to decentralization. The system of administrative regions, he said, had ended the practice of exchanging favors for votes.[4]

Two of Rio's new parks were transferred to the people on Sunday, September 26. The 50,000-square-meter Ari Barroso Park, "the first public park installed in the suburbs," replaced a squalid Penha district *favela*, "refuge of vagrants." The Lacerda administration took pride in the park's lakes and waterfalls, within sight of picnic tables and sports fields, and in its wooded area, said to have been made up of 130 varieties of floral trees.[5]

The inauguration of the 552,000-square-meter Lage Park was a major political event, attended by thousands bearing Flexa Ribeiro placards. Lacerda, in his speech, reviewed the history of the park and his effort to make its lakes, grottos, and forest available to thousands of children "caged in apartments." "The park of the people," he disclosed, would become the site of university studies and cultural activities.

According to Lacerda, the firm of Roberto Marinho and Arnon de Mello had acquired the property illegally when the Bank of Brazil had accepted its bid "during a Carnaval week, suddenly, surreptitiously, and without giving public notice." He upbraided Kubitschek, who had reversed the ruling forbidding real estate development in the park, and Quadros and Goulart, who had upheld Kubitschek's decision; they had, he said, lacked the courage to defend the position of the Historical and Artistic Patrimony Service against Roberto Marinho. Lacerda quoted Marinho as having told him: "You are going to run for president, and don't forget that you will need the backing of *O Globo.*"[6]

Ceremonies marked the removal to Vila Kennedy of the last residents of the Esqueleto Favela, near Maracanã Stadium, and the opening of a COCEA warehouse for foodstuffs. They also marked the placing of the 43-meter light posts in Flamengo Park, the completion of the first phase of the CTC bus terminal, improvements in the zoo, the asphalting and new illumination of streets, the installation of fountains, the starting up of the ninth CETEL telephone center, and the opening of the new 4½-kilometer Avenida Brasil for alleviating traffic congestion. It would be difficult to say enough about the importance of the traffic viaducts, particularly those at the critical Ponte dos Marinheiros, where traffic from the north-south Rebouças Tunnel would converge with east-west traffic at the west end of Presidente Vargas Avenue. The Viaduto dos Fuzileiros, one of the four viaducts of the Marinheiros Cloverleaf, was inaugurated on September 30.

The end of the month also featured the inaugurations of hospital facilities, such as the three-floor annex of the Moncorvo Filho Hospital (still awaiting equipment from Germany) in the downtown area. The three-floor annex of the Miguel Couto Hospital in Leblon was presented to the people of the South Zone. When the governor, accompanied by Flexa Ribeiro and Health Secretary Brito e Cunha, inaugurated the new Souza Aguiar Hospital, facing the Praça da República, on September 29, a large crowd was on hand. The old, demolished Souza Aguiar Hospital, Lacerda said, was the image of the city he had received five years earlier, whereas the new facilities were the image of the New Rio. "We have given schools, hospitals, viaducts, water, sanitation. We have done everything we promised."[7]

Publicity-wise nothing could equal turning Rio into "the cinema capital of the world," with the opening, on September 15, of its First International Film Festival. Beginning several days before the opening, and continuing until the prize-awarding ceremony in the Maracanãzinho indoor arena on September 28, newspapers presented a steady stream of photographs of actresses taken on the beach or beside the Copacabana Palace Hotel pool. Twenty-two films were submitted by thirteen nations in a contest to be judged by experts from several countries. Copacabana's Rian Theater had been designated for the official presentation at nights of the films that had entered the contest, but the governor, after being advised of the Festival's program, said that public participation was desirable and ordered simultaneous showings at other theaters, especially in the suburbs.[8]

The grand opening, featuring an Italian movie, took place at Cinelândia's Palácio Theater. The crowd outside the theater applauded the governor and his smiling wife when they arrived with the mayor of Rome. The most fervent welcome went to Claudia Cardinale, star of the film to be shown. Ever since her arrival in August she had been the Cariocas' favorite visitor.

Cariocas could take pride in the talk about making the Rio film festival an annual affair, a matter that lay in the hands of the directors of the International Federation of Film Producers' Associations. But not everything went smoothly. Prominent stars, such as the Beatles, did not show up despite reports that had led the Cariocas to expect them. Others left early with expressions of disappointment. Yvette Mimieux declared, at the time of her early departure, that she had been led to believe that she would find herself in the company of first-rate performers, such as Sophia Loren; and she complained of being treated in Rio "as a mere starlet." Enaldo Cravo Peixoto complained that the Festival cost the state 550 million cruzeiros, whereas the budget had allowed a maximum of 350 million.[9]

Brazilian performers, directors, and producers, over one hundred of whom had received no credentials or invitations, began a rival "International Festival of the Beach" by erecting a screen on the beach in front of the Rian Theater and showing Brazilian films that had not been included in the official contest. On the official Festival's second "gala night," the noisy beach crowd booed the police in front of the Rian Theater and especially Colonel Fontenelle, trying to unravel a traffic tie-up. The dispute provoked by the Brazilian film people led the governor to demand a settlement by Cravo Peixoto and Raphael de Almeida Magalhães, who was defending the position of the aggrieved Brazilians. The Brazilian delegation to the Festival was increased from 70 to 133 members.[10]

The "Celebrities Ball," held on September 25 at the Copacabana Palace Hotel, lacked the enthusiasm of the traditional Carnaval balls; but the Golden Room, one of the three for which orchestras had been contracted, became animated when visiting cinema artists joined in the samba dancing. The final show, on September 28, was for the Cariocas, and they almost filled the 25,000-seat Maracanãzinho Arena. Before Claudia Cardinale handed out the prizes (an English Beatles film tied with a French film for first place), the crowd saw a lively show, "Rio of 400 Januaries."[11]

5. Gubernatorial Candidates and the Press in Guanabara (September 1965)

(A) The candidates against Flexa Ribeiro. Immediately after Lott's candidacy was invalidated by the Superior Electoral Tribunal, the PTB convention delegates chose, in an almost unanimous vote, sixty-four-year-old Ambassador Francisco Negrão de Lima. Negrão, a long-time friend of Castello Branco's, had served the Kubitschek administration as mayor of Rio de Janeiro (appointed) and then as foreign minister. The PSD quickly endorsed him and his running mate, *petebista* Congressman Rubens Berardo. So did the PSP, whose strongman Ademar de Barros called Lacerda "a national calamity." The small PST and PRT followed suit.[1]

Socialist Aurélio Viana, who called Negrão a reactionary, accepted the nomination of the PSB and PDC. But these parties had anti-Lacerda wings, led by state legislator Jamil Haddad (PSB) and Congressman Afonso Arinos Filho (PDC), which could be expected to give many votes to Negrão on October 3. Still, Viana's presence in the race was a pro-UDN factor. On the other hand, the presence of Amaral Netto, PL candidate, was considered damaging to the UDN.[2]

The UDN's best bet for depriving Negrão of votes lay in the devoted following of broadcaster Alziro Zarur, leader of the Legião da Boa Vontade (Legion of Goodwill). Perhaps 100,000 voters (out of an election total of 1,200,000) were at stake because, while they would turn to Negrão if Zarur were not in the race, they would not miss, if they could, the opportunity of voting for their beloved *Pai da Boa Vontade* (Father of Goodwill). Raphael de Almeida Magalhães assisted Zarur to enter the race on the PTN ticket and encouraged the wish of another broadcaster, humble, picturesque Antônio Luvizaro, also to become a candidate. Luvizaro, Raphael felt, might take as many as 30,000 votes from Negrão.[3]

Unfortunately for Lacerda and Flexa Ribeiro, the Castello administration decided to contest these candidacies. The government's prosecuting attorney at the Regional Electoral Tribunal (TRE) was Eduardo Bahout, closely connected with General Golbery, who was said to have saved him from losing his political rights on ethical grounds. In the case of Zarur, the office of Bahout was diligent. It found that, although Zarur had stepped out of the management of Rádio Mundial three months before election day in order to comply with the law in the case of broadcasting concessions, he had signed two Rádio Mundial checks shortly after stepping out.[4]

Raphael explained to Bahout that the checks had been signed because the broadcasting station had not at the time authorized anyone else to sign. Bahout told Raphael that he had to proceed against Zarur: "I am under orders."

The candidacies of both Zarur and Luvizaro were voided on technicalities. When the TRE, late in August, announced its decision against Zarur, by a 5 to 1 vote, an enormous Legião da Boa Vontade crowd, mostly women, was on hand. Many of the women broke down in tears. Zarur's running mate, Hélio Damasceno, remained in the race, now as gubernatorial candidate of the PTN, but lacked the personal following of Zarur.

Sandra Cavalcanti, who had told Castello that the key to defeating the opposition was to have it split, became upset with the government she was serving.[5]

(B) The pro-UDN press. From the outset the UDN could count on Antônio Chagas Freitas' anti-PTB *O Dia,*[6] whose crime stories for the poorly educated put its circulation at the top of Rio dailies.

The *Diário de Notícias,* still with a respectable circulation, was also an early supporter of Flexa Ribeiro. It wrote on September 12 that the voters should disregard politicians who maliciously tied the election to Lacerda's ambition, should overlook Lacerda's many personal and political defects, and should vote for Flexa Ribeiro in order to have a continuation of Lacerda's extraordinary achievements, the result of a dynamic government that was above party interests. These achievements, it wrote, included schooling for all children, the attack on the *favela* problem, and gigantic public works of enormous use to the urban and especially suburban populations. "Lacerda is transforming this city into what it ought to be."[7]

The *Jornal do Brasil,* which outsold the *Diário de Notícias,* had a hard time making up its mind and started out with praise for Negrão, Flexa, Viana, and Amaral Netto. Although it considered Negrão a proven administrator, it decided on September 26 that his supporters included the *revanchistas,* eager to get revenge against the revolution, and "old groups" that would demand "rake-offs" from Negrão. The election of Flexa, it wrote, would allow the "great public works" to go forward and would "consolidate the new spirit that inspires the state's public sector."[8]

The *Tribuna da Imprensa,* whose circulation was not large, was also slow to give clear guidance. Its procrastination resulted from its dislike of Flexa and Negrão, "two candidates who represent nothing."

Expressing admiration for Aurélio Viana on September 21, Hélio Fernandes wrote that Lacerda had "preferred the weakest" of possible UDN nominees. However, on September 29 the *Tribuna da Imprensa* concluded that votes for Flexa would have the merit of defeating the "subversive" Negrão, backed by "a billion cruzeiros from Walter Moreira Salles alone."[9]

O Jornal, whose collapse had reduced its circulation to around that of the *Tribuna,* disliked Lacerda's attacks on the federal government and felt, at the outset, that Negrão could not be accused of having understandings with the "Reds who took the Goulart government to the most brazen corruption." But it came to feel that it might be wrong about Negrão. When it made up its mind on September 28, it echoed the views of the *Jornal do Brasil* about the *revanchista* aims of the Negrão campaign. Praising Flexa Ribeiro's administrative experience, it wrote that Lacerda's style of government could be carried on only by someone who had served in it.[10]

(C) The pro-Negrão press. Of the serious dailies, the circulation of *O Globo* was at the forefront, in the neighborhood of that of *O Dia.* Analyzing the candidates on September 9, it wrote that it might be difficult to choose between the two leading ones, Negrão and Flexa, were it not that Flexa, as governor, would have to give coverage to Lacerda, supporting his presidential campaign and denouncements of Castello, and preventing public knowledge of the "outrageous, despotic, and improper acts" of the Lacerda administration. *O Globo* regretted that its candidate, Negrão, was critical of Castello's economic-financial policy, but added that he had been an excellent mayor.[11]

Última Hora, popular although outsold in the afternoon competition by *O Globo,* featured from the start the pleas of Danton Jobim for a unified opposition to defeat Lacerda. It repeated oft-made charges against the "malign" governor, and described the Aurélio Viana candidacy as a service useful to Lacerda.[12]

The *Correio da Manhã,* outsold for some time by the *Jornal do Brasil* and the *Diário de Notícias* in the morning competition, had close ties with Flexa Ribeiro, who had written for it. But, like *O Globo,* it hated Lacerda intensely. From the start of the campaign it called for unity in the opposition to achieve just one thing, the defeat of *Lacerdismo,* "which wants to perpetuate itself in the state and extend its tentacles to the rest of the country." It bemoaned the "wretched" PSB convention that nominated Aurélio Viana, "who never did anything for Guanabara and voted precipitously for the election of Castello Branco."[13]

The *Diário Carioca,* after the departure of Danton Jobim, was struggling with the help of Prudente de Moraes, neto, but was on its last legs. In support of Negrão, it filled its pages with sensational anti-Lacerda propaganda, such as PTB Senate leader Artur Virgílio's statement that the Lacerda government was, "without doubt, the most corrupt ever experienced in the state."[14]

Of all the pro-Negrão dailies, none attacked Flexa Ribeiro more bitterly than the *Diário Carioca.* The attacks were a feature of its column "Ponto contraponto," written by Lacerda's older brother, Maurício de Lacerda Filho (Mauricinho), and Isa Motta.

6. Ponto Contraponto (September 1965)

Mauricinho Lacerda, more easygoing than his brother or sister, was intelligent, cheerful, and sarcastic, and expressed himself well. He was a good medical doctor and had had his own clinic as well as medical employment with the state, dating from the 1930s. But his practice had been interrupted and hurt in the 1950s when he had helped Carlos run the *Tribuna da Imprensa.* After that he worked briefly at a clinic with Dr. Pedro Nava and then became a consultant to the Laboratório Lepetit. The consulting work lasted until the Dow Chemical Company bought Lepetit during the Lacerda governorship.[1]

It was after the sale of Lepetit that Carlos learned of Mauricinho's decision to separate from his wife Gilda. Such separations disturbed Carlos. Some thought him moralistic; others recalled that he had suffered more than Mauricinho or his sister Vera when their father Maurício had left their mother Olga. In any event, he was apt to try to play a role in preventing separations. On one occasion, when Letícia told Carlos not to agonize so much over the breakup of a marriage, he replied that he could not stand by and "see a family destroyed."[2]

To no avail Carlos argued with Mauricinho. Mauricinho, after separating from Gilda, made matters worse in Carlos' eyes because he went to live with Isa Motta, who had been the second wife of Samuel Wainer, founder of *Última Hora.* Isa Motta, for whom Mauricinho was passionate, had leftist ideas and some Communist friends. Carlos claimed that she was using Mauricinho. He exclaimed: "This has to do with the Communist Party!"[3]

Flexa Ribeiro's son Edgar put it strongly when he said that Mauricinho, in his "Ponto Contraponto" columns with Isa Motta, "was out to destroy Carlos Lacerda" by attacking everyone associated with the governor and the Flexa Ribeiro campaign. Mauricinho's son, Gabriel, a good friend of the Flexa Ribeiros, did not share the sentiments of the column, as he made clear in an emotional conversation with the UDN candidate.[4]

The columnists wrote that "the Flexa Ribeiro people throw bombs at the residences of responsible people and then declare cynically that it was done by the Communists." "In Guanabara everything evil that occurs is blamed on the Communists. It is a fascist technique." "Whoever is not for Flexa is labeled a Communist."[5]

Flexa Ribeiro was sometimes simply called "*o pior*" (the worst). More frequently he was called "Racist Ribeiro" (or "RR"), an epithet based on the charge, by Mauricinho and Isa Motta, that his Andrews School set quotas limiting the enrollment of Jews. In a reference to Carlos Lacerda, the columnists wrote that the people who condemned SURSAN when it was created by Mayor Negrão de Lima were the ones who "invented Ribeiro" and unjustly appropriated to themselves the public works of others.[6]

The "rats" of Guanabara Palace were described in the column as desperate, hysterical, and packing their bags for a future that would allow Edson Guimarães time to lie on a psychoanalyst's couch, Raphael time to play soccer on the beach, and Gustavo Borges time to make firecrackers—but they would be "without black heads, out of respect for the racism of Flexa Ribeiro." Fontenelle would end up in jail for continuing, from force of habit, to take air out of tires. Marcelo Garcia, "fare collector" on the "money train," would have to explain the financial accounts of the Flexa campaign, run by "venal" people. As for Danillo Nunes, the columnists wrote: "Ah, if repentance could kill."[7]

Mauricinho and Isa Motta called the "pitiful" Cinema Festival a good example of "the total failure of the much publicized Fourth Centennial." They called Aurélio Viana a dangerous false nationalist. Praise was bestowed on Amaral Netto and Juracy Magalhães; also Hélio de Almeida received praise after he gave "unconditional support" to Negrão de Lima.[8]

On October 2, the day before the election, the *Diário Carioca* announced that Isa Motta and Maurício de Lacerda Filho, after five months of "extraordinary success," were bringing their column to a close because they had completed their objective of demonstrating, "with brilliance and perspicacity," the reasons why certain candidates should never govern Guanabara. The two columnists "say good-bye with the refrain they made famous:

> Whoever votes for Flexa
> Will have 5 years of misfortune!"[9]

7. Negrão Forges Ahead (September 1965)

The IBOPE poll that Lacerda showed Juracy Magalhães on September 16 had been taken before Negrão de Lima's campaign was under way. It reported the following percentages: Flexa 41, Negrão 26, Amaral Netto 10, Aurélio Viana 5, and Hélio Damasceno 2. Things had been going well for Flexa, with the CAMDE (Women's Campaign for Democracy) backing him and with radios repeating the jingle *"Flexa vai ganhar"* (Flexa is going to win).[1]

Lacerda said later that it was otherwise after the adversary arrived on the scene. "And what an adversary! Negrão de Lima, a wretched character, indolent, . . . a politician I abhor, my personal enemy . . . , really one of the ablest political speakers of my time . . . , had the advantage of being very close to Juscelino and was a great friend of Marshal Castello Branco. . . . And he had with him Golbery and the others of the group."[2]

When Negrão accepted his nomination at a joint PTB-PSD-PSP convention on September 9, he said he was campaigning against the "insane acts" of Lacerda, responsible for hatred, slander, corruption, tyranny, intolerance, bigotry, capriciousness, despotism, fraud, and police terror. He denounced "crushing" increases in taxes and water and sewer rates, and stated that, despite this "gouging," the Lacerda administration had brought about a financial crisis, manifest in the chronic tardiness of paychecks to state employees. He added that although the governor had incurred debts abroad, SURSAN had failed to achieve the sanitation of "our abandoned suburbs by the canalization of their rivers." "And we see the dramatic social problem of the *favelas* submitted to violent solutions characterized by the use of the police."[3]

In his speeches, Negrão promised to "humanize" and urbanize the *favelas,* start a subway system, construct fifty thousand low-cost housing units and a bridge to Niterói, continue with transportation projects already started, and lower taxes. He would, he also promised, continue with the Perimetral roadway plan, "abandoned by Lacerda," to reduce to "a maximum of fifteen minutes" the time of driving from the city to Galeão Airport. Saying that he would give first priority to furnishing foodstuffs, "an area in which the present government has failed completely," he promised to establish a large center to make foodstuffs available at low cost. He called Colonel Fontenelle "excessively violent."[4]

Negrão condemned the federal government's "IMF-oriented" economic-financial policy, saying that it dealt ineffectively with inflation, increased unemployment, and restricted development. He felt that students should participate in "public life" and therefore rejected the policies of Education Minister Suplici de Lacerda. In advocating amnesty for all the *cassados*, Negrão said the judiciary alone should judge cases of subversion and corruption. Lacerda, on the other hand, spoke harshly about the *cassados*, calling them responsible for restricting popular rights in the past and for "condemning youth to become versed in a sinister monologue." "Now for the first time," Lacerda said, the *cassados* "know the bitterness of being out of power. For those who, for so long, prevented the people from voting, it is fair that some time be spent without the vote."[5]

When Negrão commented on the argument that a Flexa victory was necessary to assure direct elections in 1966, he described himself as the champion of democracy and direct elections and pictured Lacerda as responsible for abnormal conditions in Brazil. Negrão said that he could not believe the democratic sentiments of someone who disrespected the legislative power, opposed the Supreme Court, advocated coups, and ran a government that tortured defenseless prisoners. Quadros and Kubitschek expressed their support for Negrão, as did the families of congressmen who had lost their political rights.

Tenório Cavalcanti, who had lost his rights, received visits in his Caxias fortress from Negrão, Aurélio Viana, Ivete Vargas, and Lacerda, but played no important role in the campaign. However, after Negrão declared that the *cassação* of Tenório had been unjust, Tenório was reported to favor Negrão, a report that pleased the candidate's many followers.[6]

Negrão and his backers appealed to Aurélio Viana to withdraw. They were distraught to note that the socialist senator, who had spoken well of Lacerda before entering the race, never criticized the governor but devoted much of his oratory to calling Negrão a reactionary. Aurélio's rejection of the appeals led Negrão to label him a "turncoat," financed by Lacerda and the state bank. An indignant Aurélio retorted that Negrão was a liar, whose attack had stiffened his resolve to ignore all future appeals.[7]

Professor Alceu Amoroso Lima became a Negrão supporter and bewailed the schism created by Aurélio. Then Flexa Ribeiro called the Catholic intellectual a "totalitarian," who, in 1937, had maneuvered at the Federal District University to have leftist Professors Hermes Lima and Edgardo Castro Rebelo imprisoned so that he could replace them. The pro-Negrão press was quick to defend Amoroso Lima. Isa Motta and Mauricinho Lacerda called him a "pure idealist."[8]

Street fights between the supporters of Aurélio and Negrão marred the campaign, starting on September 13 with a clash in Cinelândia, where a participant threw a tear gas bomb. On the same night, when

Negrão entered the auditorium of TV Excelsior for an interview with broadcaster Flávio Cavalcanti, he was greeted by a tear gas bomb that sent the audience of 1,200 scurrying, some to the Miguel Couto Hospital. During a melee in front of the Central do Brasil Railroad station, a little later, Aurélio's microphone was snatched and his car damaged, prompting the socialist to accuse the PTB of turning the campaign into a "veritable street battle."[9]

The *Jornal do Brasil*, calling the campaign "degrading," complained of placards, written in bad taste, that defaced the streets, and wrote that loudspeakers, in vehicles that violated traffic laws, broadcast deafening speeches that were best not given. So scurrilous was one of Amaral Netto's personal attacks on Lacerda that the Regional Electoral Tribunal stepped in to cut the broadcast off the air.[10]

Not surprisingly, the opposition condemned Lacerda's "orgy" of ceremonies, arguing that they amounted to campaign propaganda paid for by the public. In the *Correio da Manhã*, Márcio Moreira Alves asked why no plaque was placed by the Guarda River, to commemorate killings of beggars, "the work of the Lacerda government," or ceremony arranged for the public to visit the wretched DOPS cell "reserved for the political enemies of the governor"?[11]

Thirty-two state legislators, a majority, asked the National Telecommunications Council (CONTEL) to reveal who had paid, and how much, for the "marathon" ten-hour radio-television program of September 11–12 that had interrupted the regular broadcasts of five television stations. Lacerda replied that the money had been provided by the lottery and state bank, whose businesses, he maintained, were immediately improved by the program. Former Mayor Ângelo Mendes de Morais could not see how the program would sell lottery tickets or bank shares and said the public's money could have equipped schools, "being inaugurated without furniture." Others spoke of the misuse of BEG depositors' funds and noted that state lottery money was supposed to be applied to specific purposes, not including campaign propaganda. Congressman Derville Allegretti (MTR, São Paulo) said the cost of the marathon broadcast was 180 million cruzeiros ($100,000); he called the performance an "abuse of economic power"—the sort of behavior that had nullified the candidacy of Paes de Almeida in Minas.[12]

O Globo, full of editorials about Lacerda's "abuse of political and economic power," was pleased that the PTB, PSD, and PSP went to the Regional Electoral Tribunal (TRE) to argue that Lacerda was using the state administrative machine and squandering "fantastic" amounts of state money on behalf of his candidate. They cited, as did Negrão and *O Globo*, an old Superior Electoral Tribunal ruling that prohibited "electoral propaganda carried out personally by" a governor, and cited a recent confirmation of the ruling by the TRE of Rio Grande do Norte. But on September 29 the Guanabara TRE ruled that the election law did not prohibit the governor's participation in the campaign. In the meantime the UDN went to the TRE to complain of slander by Negrão and Roberto Marinho, "whose newspaper carries on a vile and defamatory campaign."[13]

The *Correio da Manhã*'s "Dossier of Corruption," part of a series of anti-Lacerda articles, featured a "secret Guanabara Palace fund" for enriching the governor's close associates and family. The *Diário Carioca* published a photograph of a receipt for 630 cruzeiros (less than 50¢) to show that the governor's office had paid for two bottles of *cachaça*, said to have been a gift to employees at Lacerda's Rocio residence. The two bottles were first given publicity in the legislative assembly, where Alfredo Tranjan exhibited the receipt and exclaimed: "The New Rio of Carlos Lacerda is the New Rio [River] of Mud!"[14]

In the assembly, where Negrão had a majority, CPIs were investigating a businessman's charge of extortion by Geraldo Monnerat, adviser to the governor, and Lacerda's purchase of generators from the United States. When Flexa Ribeiro was called to testify at one of the CPIs, Lacerda declared: "For the first time an honest man will be interrogated by thieves, a serious man will be interrogated by clowns."

After the finance commission rejected, by a 7-2 vote, the governor's accounts for 1964, the opposition howled because the assembly's acting president, Edson Guimarães, followed the example of Brunini in 1963 in refusing to put the matter on the agenda for a plenary discussion and vote. The thirty-two oppositionist legislators signed a motion of "no confidence" in Guimarães. Lacerda said that if he were to agree to make a payment of 120 million cruzeiros ($64,000) for legislators' relatives and friends, named illegally to the already oversized assembly staff, he could get the accounts approved. "I assure you I'll not send money to thieves."[15]

The political world was stunned on September 18 by Lacerda's televised statement that he might, after all, send money to thieves. He declared sensationally that if none of the gubernatorial candidates received an absolute majority, forcing the legislature to choose the next governor, he was disposed to spend a billion cruzeiros on legislators to buy a victory for Flexa Ribeiro. Negrão called the "appalling" statement a crime and added that Lacerda "must be insane" to conceive of the assembly as so "criminally degraded." Senator Artur Virgílio, while admitting that other governors carried out corrupt acts in a hidden manner, demanded that the revolution punish Lacerda,

"that confessed briber," for deliberately, maliciously, and openly proposing to use the people's money to overturn the people's will.

The *Jornal do Brasil* felt that the governor's "unfortunate" statement was causing an even more unfortunate reaction because enraged legislators threatened, as a reprisal, to defeat the UDN candidate in the assembly even if he should have the lead in the popular
vote; and thus, the *Jornal do Brasil* wrote, they would allow Lacerda's
"personality and errors" to defeat the will of the people. Lacerda, on
September 22, repeated his controversial proposal and declared: "This
is the first time that a scandal is made out of a statement about buying
legislators' votes. The whole world knows about the purchase of
votes in the Carioca assembly. The only thing not known was that I
am willing to purchase them."[16]

The PTB campaign turned the inaugurations of public works into
reasons to vote for Negrão. As Marcelo Garcia has pointed out, the
petebistas associated the projects with the high cost of living. The
most popular slogan became "Viaducts do not fill stomachs." It was,
Dr. Rebello Filho has written, a slogan to be compared with the one
that helped defeat presidential candidate Eduardo Gomes in 1945 by
portraying him as uninterested in the *marmiteiros* (unskilled workers). At the Rebouças Tunnel, inaugurated on October 3 with band
music, people were given signs to display: "I went through the Rebouças Tunnel." Oppositionists altered the signs to read: "I went
through the Rebouças Tunnel, but I am voting for Negrão."[17]

8. A Discouraged Lacerda Quarrels with Flexa
(September 1965)

The polls, shortly after the middle of September, showed that Negrão
was ahead of Flexa, an ineffective campaigner. Flexa and others asked
Raphael de Almeida Magalhães to persuade Lacerda to play a more
active role, speaking at Flexa's side during rallies. The governor ac-
quiesced, but what followed strained the relations between the candidate and the governor.

The candidate became annoyed because, when they were at rallies
together, the governor would hardly allow him time to say anything.
On one such occasion, when Flexa was prepared to follow Lacerda
with a speech, the governor, to Flexa's surprise, turned to Father
Godinho and asked him to address the crowd.[1]

"There are," Lacerda said later, "people who are good at attracting
votes and others who are very bad at this. Raphael, for example,
would have been splendid. Flexa was very bad; he did not have an
attractive personality." Lacerda also felt that Flexa had so thoroughly

concentrated on problems of education that he "never took cognizance of any other problem of the state." After one broadcast of a TV Rio program, in which Flexa followed Raphael and Lacerda, the governor, angry at Flexa, went to Raphael's home and remarked: "I did my best to seem foolish but I couldn't equal Flexa. We are lost."[2]

The polls were starting to worry Lacerda when he spoke to Danillo Nunes, a popular speaker, and asked him to be Flexa's running mate. The position was still open because Chagas Freitas, of *O Dia*, had declined the offer of Flexa. Lacerda, in his conversation with Danillo, said: "Just you and I will talk at the rallies." The retired general, a vigorous anti-Communist and former DOPS director, accepted.[3]

About two weeks before the election, Lacerda called Flexa to his apartment to give him a grave warning. He told him he had already lost the election and this meant there would be no presidential election in 1966. Lacerda was thinking that his warning might persuade Flexa to withdraw; then perhaps voters would not go to the polls, or perhaps the UDN would turn to another candidate, one who lacked Flexa's ties to Lacerda, and Lacerda could keep apart from the election, saying that his government ought not to become involved.

Lacerda, in giving his warning, painted such a dismal picture of the situation that he wondered, during his almost sleepless night that followed, whether he had not been too pessimistic and hurt the cause by disheartening the candidate. So he spoke with him again the next day: "Don't take seriously what I said yesterday." Flexa, according to Lacerda, replied that he had not done so, for he considered Lacerda "completely mistaken" and the election already won. So complacent an attitude, Lacerda felt, meant that "the end had come."[4]

Lacerda's attacks on *udenista* congressmen and the Bloco Parlamentar Revolucionário were followed by Flexa's complaint that *udenistas* Adauto Cardoso, Aliomar Baleeiro, Eurípides Cardoso de Menezes, and Arnaldo Nogueira, all congressmen from Guanabara, refrained from participating in his campaign. However, Lacerda's friends in São Paulo, such as Abreu Sodré, Herbert Levy, and journalist Luiz Ernesto Kawall, came to help. Kawall interviewed politicians and furnished articles to the *Tribuna da Imprensa*. He and Sodré heard Lacerda excoriate Castello and declare, "We are lost."[5]

Throughout the city Lacerda had to contend with local politicians, resentful of treatment received and antagonized by the arrangement for administrative regions. The affluent South Zone, he told the press, was being "anesthetized by Roberto Marinho and the spokesmen of the group that took possession of the Revolution."[6]

If Lacerda had more trouble than in the past in attracting the votes of conservatives, it was because he had done nothing in recent pronouncements to mitigate fears that they had grown to have of him. In the words of Raphael de Almeida Magalhães, Carlos Lacerda, "always out of order," was so independent that the conservative interests, willing to make alliances with him when they wanted to defeat a common enemy, felt uncomfortable at the thought of Lacerda in the presidency. "It was," Raphael adds, "very difficult to finance the Flexa Ribeiro campaign because Lacerda was not trusted by business people."[7]

Among the less affluent, Lacerda had gained in popularity when he was the foremost critic of the government's economic policy. Now in Guanabara Negrão denounced the policy with equal vigor. Lacerda himself recognized that repeated blows to the pocketbook helped oppositionist Negrão more than the UDN; he complained, for example, of the damage done to Flexa's campaign by the 70 percent increase in railroad commuter fares, decreed by the federal government shortly before election day. To add to the economic discontent, the state's 120,000 employees found themselves, on election day, two months behind in receiving their paychecks, something that had not happened before in the new state. Money that Lacerda hoped to receive from the federal government for completing the Rebouças Tunnel did not materialize, and therefore the state had all it could do to prevent a sudden halt of work on the tunnel and other projects, such as the Guandu Aqueduct, which had been assisted by foreign credits. Raphael, finding that the state bank had been pushed to the limit, pleaded with Finance Minister Bulhões, but Bulhões said he had no cruzeiros.[8]

Some of the Flexa people felt that Lacerda was telling audiences that they should vote for the UDN candidate so that they could vote for Lacerda in 1966. Edgar, the candidate's son, told Lacerda that the message should be that people should vote for Flexa in order to be able to vote for president in 1966, even if their votes were against Lacerda. An irritated Lacerda responded: "So you belong to the group that opposes my becoming president!"

Edgar felt that the Communists ought to understand that if they wanted to try to defeat the revolution they should work for his father's election, which was likely to mean a continuation of electoral democracy, and they could vote against Lacerda in 1966. He found that they preferred to eliminate Lacerda in 1965.[9]

As election day approached, opponents of Negrão made an issue of the PTB-PSD candidate's alleged payment to the Communist Party (PCB) for its support. DOPS Director Cecil Borer claimed to have confirmation of payments by the PTB to the PCB, and Security Secretary Gustavo Borges spoke of a small sum that Negrão promised to

"Who are you for?" the PSB's Aurélio Viana asks the Communist Party, which has powerfully embraced, and points to, the PSD's Negrão de Lima. (APPE drawing in *O Cruzeiro,* October 16, 1965)

pay the PCB provided that operators of the *jôgo do bicho* would furnish the money. Hard line Colonel Ferdinando de Carvalho, head of the IPM investigating Communism in Brazil, felt he had evidence against Negrão that was serious enough to warrant a dramatic last-minute television revelation of the details. But before the colonel could go on the air, high authorities in the Castello government stepped in to prevent Ferdinando's IPM study from involving itself in current politics.[10]

The *Jornal do Brasil* published a "note to the press" by Giocondo Dias, described as the Communist Party stand-in for Luiz Carlos Prestes. Giocondo, according to the *Jornal do Brasil,* said that "it is not by chance that we choose Ambassador Negrão de Lima as our candidate. He represents an option between the *Lacerdista* police dictatorship and the restoration of liberties in Guanabara." The note called Lacerda "the people's worst enemy, responsible for the fascist coup of April 1," and went on to say that the opposition forces of Guanabara, "under the leadership of the glorious Communist Party," had united behind Negrão's candidacy, the first step for the return to democratic liberties, a general amnesty for the victims of "the fascist coup," legalization of the PCB, and liberty for the labor organizations, including the CGT.[11]

The campaign of the *Jornal do Brasil* to reveal a deal between Negrão and the PCB led the PTB-PSD candidate to sue Nascimento

Brito. Negrão said the *Jornal do Brasil* had made use of a false docu-
ment, just as Lacerda had done with the Brandi letter during the
presidential election of 1955. According to *Última Hora's* Danton
Jobim, the "new Brandi letters" represented a last-minute tactic of
the *Lacerdistas,* assisted by the appearance on the scene of former
DOPS Director Danillo Nunes. The *Correio da Manhã* and Alceu
Amoroso Lima attributed the latest "forgery" to the desperation of
Lacerda and his accomplices, "professional anti-Communists." *O
Globo* wrote that false manifestoes and hammer-and-sickle placards,
hoisted by Negrão's foes at his rallies, would not persuade Castello to
depart from his promise that the election victors would take office.[12]

It was hardly necessary for Negrão to make payments to get the
support of Communists, longtime Lacerda haters. Some Communists may have shared Aurélio Viana's qualms about Negrão; but,
during the last week of the campaign, many voters, including supporters of Aurélio, decided to forget about the minor candidates.[13]

Lacerda told the press that the Communists' support of Negrão de
Lima would lead to the cancellation of direct elections in 1966 and
was therefore "one more error by the leftists of Brazil."[14] The governor may have spoken rudely and unwisely to Edgar Flexa Ribeiro, but
his public pronouncements indicated that their ideas coincided.

9. Lacerda Collapses (September 30, 1965)

On the evening of September 28, thousands of umbrella carrying
"Women for Flexa Ribeiro" marched in the rain from the Glória Church
to the Largo do Machado to hear speeches by Sandra Cavalcanti, Education Secretary Maria Teresinha Saraiva, the UDN candidates, and the
governor. Lacerda, whose speech was carried by television, exclaimed:
"Either we win now or Brazil will have civil war." In response, pro-
Negrão newspapers published Amoroso Lima's contention that Lacerda's "threat" amounted to the "total negation of democracy."[1]

September 30 was the last day on which campaigning was permitted. In the morning Lacerda inaugurated the Moncorvo Filho Hospital annex with a speech in which he replied to charges published in
a Negrão propaganda release.[2] He explained once again about the
"cowardly killings" of beggars, and said that, like himself, Augusto
Amaral Peixoto had added a new floor to his apartment. He called
Fontenelle's traffic work a model admired in other states and blamed
the parking lot fees on the legislature's refusal to vote the funds for
installing and operating traffic signals. He had harsh words for the
legislature, which had been shown in August, in a study by Lígia
Lessa Bastos and Adalgisa Nery, to have employed a staff of 1,432

bureaucrats when only 463 were needed.[3] Most of the legislators, Lacerda said, could be bought. When medical students jeered him for attacking Negrão, the tired governor called them remnants from a stable that had existed where the Souza Aguiar Hospital now stood.[4]

Writing about the last days of the campaign, Dr. Rebello Filho notes that Lacerda "lacked the power of persuasion with which he was gifted." This appeared to be true at the inauguration of the final stage of the Guandu Aqueduct, held in the noon heat not far from Vila Kennedy. Coming from his long speech at the Moncorvo Hospital, the governor was a little late, and the audience of workers was sullen, giving no applause to his arrival or words. "They don't understand me," Lacerda remarked in an aside to engineer Veiga Brito.[5]

In a voice that had become hoarse from overuse, Lacerda was declaring that the people did not want the "enemies" of Guanabara to "return to power" when he fainted. A first aid unit was called and took him to the infirmary of the Bangu Textile Company, and there he was joined by his doctors, Jaime Rodrigues and Antonio Dias Rebello Filho, who had been summoned by Major Carlos Osório.

Lacerda told Rebello that the trouble was caused by "heat, exhaustion, and being fed up." The doctor, who attributed the collapse also to a lack of potassium, found the patient worn out. Electrocardiograms showed nothing abnormal. Admirers who phoned Guanabara Palace were told that the governor was in satisfactory condition, needed rest, and was receiving no visitors.[6]

That evening the pro-Flexa Caravan of Liberty paraded on Presidente Vargas Avenue and was greeted at the Praça da Bandeira by the fireworks and music that preceded the inauguration of the Viaduto dos Fuzileiros. At the inauguration, Danillo Nunes assailed "the corrupt and subversives," and Flexa Ribeiro called on the Cariocas to make Guanabara a "citadel in the defense of free elections for president in 1966." Raphael de Almeida Magalhães, addressing the crowd of tens of thousands, denounced the "insane battle by unscrupulous adversaries" that had "forced" the governor to be taken to the hospital. He read a message in which Lacerda asked the people of "my beloved city" to help him "keep democracy alive in Brazil" along with "the idea that a hardworking and honest government deserves the appreciation of the people."[7]

Meanwhile, along Rio Branco Avenue, tens of thousands of Negrão supporters marched in the Caravan of Victory parade that featured girls wearing yellow blouses bearing their candidate's name. A band played popular tunes for which the throng had words ridiculing Lacerda and denouncing his "triplex apartment" and the financial accounts he had submitted to the legislature. "Negrão is the solution," the people sang. In Cinelândia the candidate evoked the memory of Vargas and spoke emotionally of an election victory that would return peace to Guanabara.[8]

Later a heavy rain prevented the Flexa supporters from attending a closing rally, scheduled to take place at the Campo de São Cristovão.[9] It had less impact on Negrão supporters, many of whom braved the downpour to hear speeches, at the Jardim do Méier, by Edna Lott, Lutero and Ivete Vargas, Hélio de Almeida, Nelson Carneiro, Rubens Berardo, Artur Virgílio, and a representative of Jânio Quadros. Negrão lashed out against the "infamous torrent" of "slander" that described him as having made a deal with the Communist Party.[10]

Lacerda, who heard some of the final speechmaking on a radio, was told to continue resting. Among the well-wishers who were turned away on October 1 were groups from Vila Aliança and Vila Kennedy. Flowers from teachers were delivered to the invalid by his daughter-in-law, Vera Flexa Ribeiro Lacerda. The *Diário Carioca* wrote that he might have been upset by recent polls but was perfectly well and was simply trying to be dramatic. Bulletins from the governor's press office, the *Diário Carioca* added, contributed to the "pathetic fiction."[11]

The news that Kubitschek would reach Rio on October 4 brought Gustavo Borges to the infirmary on the 2nd. The governor and the colonel composed a note for the press saying that this "affront" should be answered by the president, "who believes that these elections are merely local affairs and will not affect the Revolution."[12]

Lacerda was still in the infirmary on October 3 and therefore voted in a special ballot box. Friends tried to cheer him. Writer Emil Farhat brought a poll showing Flexa in the lead. It contradicted other polls, considered more accurate, and Lacerda remarked, "I know we have lost." Rebello Filho spoke to his patient about the "veritable ecstasy of the people" with the inauguration of the Viaduto dos Fuzileiros and the opening of traffic through the unfinished Rebouças Tunnel.[13]

At 6:00 A.M. on October 4, before the election count began at Maracanã Stadium, Kubitschek arrived at Galeão Airport. He was greeted by a throng of five thousand that included Negrão de Lima. Admirers lifted him onto their shoulders. When he made his way to his Ipanema apartment, it was at the head of a parade of over a hundred cars. "Operation Return" was hailed by the Paris press, which called Kubitschek "the man of the day," but was considered unwise by much of the PSD, which feared the reaction of hard liners. Lawyer Sobral Pinto, a Negrão supporter, had been able to give the "green light" after consulting the government but had told Kubitschek that he personally felt the time was not right. On the afternoon of October 4, Sobral Pinto accompanied Kubitschek to the Army Police barracks, where the former president was forced to appear to answer questions put to him by the IPM investigating the ISEB. In the days that followed, Kubitschek had to spend much of his time in this way, interrogated by unfriendly army officers, some of whom were demanding his imprisonment.[14]

10. The Barracks React to Negrão's Victory (October 5, 1965)

An analysis of the election returns reported on the evening of October 4 demonstrated that Negrão would come out on top. Pro-Lacerda air force officers threatened to destroy the ballots, being counted quickly by six thousand fiscal agents. At the same time, most of the navy officers, many of them admirers of Lacerda, demanded intervention against the inauguration of Negrão.[1] Commanders of all the army units at Vila Militar met with First Army Commander Otacílio Terra Ururaí on the evening of October 4 to explain that the young officers were so upset that disturbances might occur. The barracks had just received copies of a manifesto, "The Revolution Is Irreversible," saying that the inauguration of Negrão would be "a premeditated, malevolent act, a defiance of the Revolution."[2]

The *Tribuna da Imprensa* wrote on October 4 that only a miracle would allow Negrão's inauguration. *O Estado de S. Paulo*, on the next day, concluded that neither the country nor the revolution had been prepared to hold an election and that the "glorious" movement of March 1964 was not understood by Castello Branco. The president, it wrote bitterly, was taking pleasure in the elections' repercussions abroad because "His Excellency is so much influenced by the opinions of those gentlemen who know nothing about Brazilian reality" and who "for months have been distilling their bile against the Revolution."[3]

The discontent of the military turned to furious condemnation of Castello Branco early on the afternoon of October 5 when it was learned that he insisted on the inauguration of the winners.[4] By then the victories of Negrão de Lima in Guanabara and Israel Pinheiro in Minas were certainties. In Guanabara Negrão appeared likely to receive a little more than 50 percent of the vote and Flexa around 40 percent.

The outcome, together with Kubitschek's arrival to a triumphant reception, was resented by an estimated 80 percent of the military officers in the Rio area.[5] Some officers took heart from statements by Costa e Silva about the need to prevent the return of those who had "for years and years harmed the nation." An inscription in large letters appeared on the pavement in front of the war ministry building: "They shall not return."[6]

So many officers favored direct action at once that Rio was full of rumors about the burning of ballot boxes, a coup, and a new institutional act. Aliomar Baleeiro has written of "panic in the banks" and "people stockpiling foodstuffs." Ten billion cruzeiros were reportedly withdrawn from the Guanabara State Bank (BEG).

It was said that Costa e Silva, popular with the hard line, would take over from Castello Branco, who was described as "too theoretical." Although it was not generally known, Magalhães Pinto was working hard for this change; when he called on the war minister, he told him to run the government "because Castello cannot continue."[7]

Lacerda, who moved on October 5 to the Bangu Textile Company house used by the Silveira family, received several visits from Costa e Silva's wife, Yolanda. She seemed to be full of conspiracy, criticized Castello, and gave the impression that her husband admired Lacerda. She pleaded with Lacerda to take the side of her husband against Castello. Lacerda was reluctant, but, during her last visit, finally agreed; and he promised to keep quiet about their talks. After she left, Guilherme da Silveira Filho told Lacerda that Castello would probably somehow learn of the governor's support of Yolanda's ideas. Lacerda made a remark that indicated he was not well impressed with the war minister as a person.[8]

Another visitor was Colonel Plínio Pitaluga, whose subordinates at the tank regiment at Vila Militar were ready to take direct action.[9] The colonel, dressed in his uniform, expressed his sympathy for the reverses suffered by the governor. He was, Lacerda noted with pleasure, eager to lead his men.[10]

After Pitaluga left, late on the afternoon of October 5, Lacerda asked Raphael de Almeida Magalhães and Congressmen Godinho and Curi to go to the colonel's barracks and convey the governor's thanks for the visit.[11] That night, when the governor's envoys went to Vila Militar, the unrest was so great in the barracks in the Rio area that Military Club President Augusto César Moniz de Aragão told his friend the president, who was at Laranjeiras Palace, that he had never seen the troops so agitated.[12] Castello conferred with the military ministers.

Vila Militar, Godinho recalls, seemed "ready for war," with six or eight regiments prepared to start things at midnight. Pitaluga's regiment had the tanks "all set to move" and his officers, wearing their uniforms, "filled the casino." Pitaluga himself, the visitors were told, was absent because of illness in his family.[13]

Lacerda's representatives talked with the officers and found that they associated Lacerda with the revolution and considered Castello Branco responsible for the revolution's losing direction. They blamed the president for the election result, which they felt doomed the revolution, and criticized his "dealings with undesirable congressional groups."[14]

Arguing that the revolution had to be saved at once, the officers asked the vice governor to remove the protection given to the Maracanã vote counters. When Raphael refused, saying that in the future he would not be proud of such behavior, the officers suggested the arrest of Negrão and again the vice governor objected. The third idea was to march on Rio to make demands and ask the chiefs "what happened to the Revolution?" This idea, Raphael said, was the least indefensible. He suggested that the men discuss it with Pitaluga, whom they trusted.[15]

When Pitaluga came to the barracks he persuaded his men to desist from precipitous action. According to the information that Lacerda received, Pitaluga and his officers had been set to move on Rio, but Pitaluga changed his mind because of "intervention from above."[16] They were to await a pronouncement that their hard line favorite, Costa e Silva, was expected to deliver very soon.

Lacerda lost his patience while speaking with another officer who visited him in Bangu. The governor exclaimed: "And you people, with all those tanks, are going to turn them into tanks for washing clothes, because you are going to swallow all of this and become responsible for a military dictatorship in Brazil."[17]

During the night, the military ministers issued orders for their troops in the area to be on the alert and maintain discipline. Furthermore, it was announced that Costa e Silva would go to Vila Militar the next day and give an important speech during a lunch held to observe the twenty-first anniversary of the arrival in Italy of the First Infantry Regiment. In an unusual request, the war minister asked that all the officers at Vila Militar, about 250, be present for the speech.[18] The officers had high hopes that the speech would at least contain a veto of the inaugurations of Negrão and Israel Pinheiro, particularly as a representative, sent by Costa e Silva to Vila Militar in the night, advised that the war minister agreed with the feelings of the young officers.[19]

On the morning of October 6 Costa e Silva and Castello Branco, both calm and apparently sure of themselves, went over the main points of the speech.[20] After it was delivered, a displeased Lacerda called it "a disappointment to the people." The general's listeners, too, were displeased, as was evident from the reception, that became colder the more he spoke.[21] "While we do not fear counterrevolutionaries, we are worried about the enthusiasm, the ardor of youth eager for more revolution. But I guarantee, my young subordinates, that we know where we are going. The present chiefs . . . are as revolutionary as the young revolutionaries. I guarantee that we are not returning to the past." Declaring that military unity made it unreasonable to worry about the antirevolutionary "dwarfs," Costa e Silva warned against intrigue designed to undermine that unity. He sought to demolish the idea that "the president is working to continue in office beyond his term." Giving the officers the president's word that this was a lie, Costa e Silva praised Castello Branco as "deserving of our credence and respect." And he defended the inauguration of the winners of the elections "so that we can demonstrate that men do not modify the regime and men are unable to undermine the Revolution."[22]

Castello, following the war minister's speech, worked with advisers on new regulations, including legislation to be enacted by Congress, to strengthen the government and calm the hard liners. The proposals considered on the afternoon of October 6 would reform the national security law and the judiciary, curtail the activities of the *cassados*, facilitate federal intervention in the states, and authorize the federal government to name the state security secretaries. A note to reporters, distributed by the president's office, advised that "it was decided to adopt rapidly various steps to strengthen revolutionary action." The *Jornal do Brasil*, pleased with the government's response to the crisis, wrote that Congress had the obligation to cooperate with that response.[23]

O Globo accused the defeated *Lacerdistas* of wanting to persuade the armed forces to act against the people. "Those defeated in Guanabara were the ones who wanted direct elections. And they got them as a reply to the insulting tirade of the governor, who accused the president of scheming against having direct elections."[24]

According to Carlos Castello Branco, the only civilian politician to benefit from the October 5 crisis in the barracks was Lacerda, regarded by many military officers as the interpreter of their views. However, as Raphael de Almeida Magalhães has pointed out, they were not going to support a direct presidential election unless they were convinced that Lacerda would win, and the state elections in Guanabara and Minas left them feeling that he could not. Furthermore, Father Godinho has observed, some of the hard line colonels did not want a civilian, and preferred Costa e Silva, thinking that he would be a weak president, one they could control.[25]

11. Lacerda "Returns" His Candidacy and "Vomits" Castello (October 7–11, 1965)

Lacerda, after leaving Bangu on October 6, had a talk with Flexa Ribeiro, who was preparing to send a congratulatory telegram to Negrão de Lima, victor by an absolute majority. Telling Flexa not to send the telegram, Lacerda explained that Negrão was not going to take office. The telegram was not sent.[1]

Flexa, who felt that antagonism to Lacerda was responsible for the election loss,[2] heard the governor say: "Although I think you have qualities for serving as governor, I want you to know that you were never my candidate." Flexa, upset, asked for an explanation, and Lacerda replied: "Because I know the reason why all those people forced your candidacy on us, and you alone did not understand. I knew you would be defeated and that, with your defeat, no more elections would be held in Brazil."[3]

On the afternoon of October 7, the governor met with his cabinet, which agreed unanimously that he should complete his term. Then he spent an hour with Magalhães Pinto. The Minas governor, on leaving Guanabara Palace, told reporters that he was now "unconditionally" at Lacerda's side. He added that he and Lacerda, "the civilian leaders of the 1964 movement," had suffered electoral setbacks because the revolution had mistreated the people. His discussion with Lacerda, he said, had dealt with the need for a new UDN convention "to seek solutions for the future policy of the country."[4]

Returning to Belo Horizonte, Magalhães Pinto telegraphed Lacerda to report that he was issuing a statement blaming the election results on Castello's "inhuman" policy that left people without employment, homes, or social justice, and constantly increased the costs of rent, electricity, transport, food, and medicines. The statement echoed the opinion of Herbert Levy, who had declared: "We should give Roberto Campos credit for the defeats."[5]

Following his chat with Magalhães Pinto, Lacerda appeared on a radio-television program to read a letter he had written to UDN President Sátiro. "I understand," the letter said, "that it is necessary for me to return to my party the presidential candidacy which it gave me." The letter explained that, with the people condemning the revolution, the party could garner no more than 41 percent of the vote in Guanabara, and it pointed out that the party could not continue to support, at the same time, his presidential candidacy and the government of Castello, opponent of that candidacy. "I think," Lacerda also wrote Sátiro, "I have the right to attend a national convention of the party to explain the reasons why I understand that my candidacy no longer makes sense. And to leave the party free to adopt, with the PSD and PTB and at the side of Castello Branco, the 'indirect election' and the destruction of the federation."[6]

Lacerda told his audience that Kubitschek was the "only national leader at the moment." He read from an interview given by Kubitschek in Europe, in which Kubitschek reportedly said he would soon be returning to the Brazilian presidency because his party, the PSD, "is strong in my country." "It is," Lacerda asserted, "the strongest because it is allied with the PTB, the Communist Party, and the president of the republic." Lacerda also said that Guanabara Palace, "where the reaction to the Goulart government started," would become, with Negrão's inauguration, "the site of the offensive in favor of the corrupt and subversives."

The *Diário Carioca* considered Lacerda's "violent monologue" a "subversive" appeal to the armed forces to overthrow Castello Branco. *The New York Times* wrote that the withdrawal of Lacerda's candidacy would doubtless be "a good thing for the future stability of Brazil" and suggested to its readers that the voters, by "soundly" defeating his "hand-picked" choice in Guanabara, had shown that they disliked Lacerda even more than they disliked the Castello government.[7]

Most of the Rio newspapers announced that Lacerda had resigned his candidacy. The São Paulo UDN, showing a better understanding of what the governor had in mind, telegraphed him that it would be "honored to ratify" the candidacy he had "returned"—a candidacy "more necessary than ever." It wired Sátiro asking for a national convention.[8]

Lacerda, displeased with the headlines about his withdrawal, held a press conference to explain: "I did not resign my candidacy. I submitted it to the party that proposed it. The party, the UDN, is the one to decide. . . . On December 5 I shall enter private life, earn my living, and if they need me they know where I live: Praia do Flamengo 224. If they need me I shall never fail the call. If they don't need me I shall give grateful thanks. But I did not resign anything. It is up to the UDN to give up my candidacy. I cannot give up something that was proposed by it, not by me."

Turning to what he called "that clownish series of little laws" which the president planned to send to Congress, he described the plan as "drivel," "tommyrot," and "one more subterfuge" by the president. Really, he said, the army ought to declare that it was resigned to the return of the corrupt and subversives. In a reference to one of the law proposals, Lacerda asked: "How can the president pick state secretaries if he does not know how to pick his own ministers? If his own government is rubbish?"

Speaking of the recent election, Lacerda stated that "Haroldo Poland, who represents foreign interests in Brazil, went all over the place raising money for the Negrão de Lima campaign, in the name of General Golbery." Castello, Lacerda told the reporters, had forbidden Colonel Ferdinando de Carvalho to reveal the information he had collected about "the money and vehicles" given by Negrão to the Communist Party "with the full knowledge of the government." He added that his patience to put up with traitors was reaching its end.

Lacerda spoke of Costa e Silva, now often mentioned as presidential candidate in an indirect election. He said that in the "disappointing" speech at Vila Militar, the general had promised the revolution would go forward, a promise he was violating by "betraying" the revolution in return for PSD support in an indirect election. Lacerda vowed never again to play a role in placing "an incompetent general" in the presidency, and predicted that Costa e Silva was in for a surprise because the president, a betrayer, would betray the war minister.

Lacerda derided General Osvaldo Cordeiro de Farias, who, he said, spent his time late in August 1961 sitting on a war ministry sofa, reading newspapers, when he was supposed to be marching south to deal with the Brizola movement. Contemplating "these men who threw away four revolutions in Brazil," Lacerda said: "I no longer have the patience to keep my mouth shut. Nor any reason to do so. The nation must prepare for suffering and know who caused the suffering."[9]

The *Jornal do Brasil* found Lacerda's "provocations" tiresome "relics of a bygone age" and warned that he was making a mistake in trying to separate the ardent younger military officers from the generals. But *O Estado de S. Paulo* wrote that it could not see how any authentic revolutionary could fail to support the governor. Agreeing with him that Castello was "solely responsible for the calamitous political situation," it blamed the president's "legalist obsession" for the decision to ask Congress to fortify the revolution. How, it asked, could Castello expect PSD leaders, such as Alkmin, Moura Andrade, and Filinto Müller, to support "laws of exception"? The PSD and PTB, it pointed out, had 70 percent of the votes in Congress.[10]

Castello, speaking in Porto Alegre, warned against "those who, under the pretext of defending the Revolution, want to crush liberty in the hope of benefiting from its disappearance." The warning was regarded by the press as a response to Lacerda's latest pronouncements, and therefore reporters asked Lacerda to comment. The governor replied: "If the president is ugly on the outside, he is, on the inside, a cause of horror." The governor added that he had "already vomited the president" and would not reply to him, "because I detest traitors."[11]

12. The UDN Favors a New Convention (October 21, 1965)

Lacerda was preparing, with the help of banker Antônio Carlos de Almeida Braga and others, to enter the business world. Participating at the same time in the state's administration, he set up new organizations designed to complete, without political interference, projects such as Flamengo Park and the Guandu Aqueduct.

The governor's appeal for a UDN convention was discussed on October 13 in Brasília, with the result that the party's national directorship was asked to settle the matter in a week. Congressman Manoel Taveira de Souza (UDN, Minas) said the idea made no sense because "we may be forty-eight hours away from a dictatorship."[1]

The Mineiro's words were prompted by Castello's proposals to Congress to fortify the revolution and by the whispers about the promulgation of a second institutional act if Congress rejected the proposals.[2] Despite the whispers, rejection seemed likely. The PTB, as Lutero Vargas made clear, was flatly opposed. Within the UDN *bancada* of approximately a hundred congressmen, the government's proposals were opposed by twenty-seven, including the *Lacerdistas*. The PSD worked to take teeth out of the measures, to the consternation of the hard line. The Bloco Parlamentar Revolucionário, afflicted by the bickering, declared itself officially dissolved.

Lacerda argued that the government's unpopular proposals were designed to establish an antirevolutionary dictatorship that might ally itself with the PSD. Magalhães Pinto called the proposals medicines but not cures. The *Correio da Manhã*, opposed to the proposals, wrote that the president should use the powers he already had to repress the "*golpista* offensive of Carlos Lacerda and his group of rebels."[3]

The Castello administration dropped its proposal for having the federal government name the state security secretaries. The proposals it submitted to Congress on October 13, after gaining approval of the military high command, would restrict the activities of the *cassados*, allow civilians to be tried for threatening the national security, bar the justice system from ruling on acts stemming from the Institutional Act, and allow federal intervention in the states "to prevent or repress serious disturbances."[4]

Cordeiro de Farias, minister for coordinating regional agencies, valiantly sought to persuade congressmen to vote for the proposals. At the same time he and Congressman Aniz Badra (PDC, São Paulo) worked for a constitutional amendment for an indirect election for the next president by Congress. Castello said that while it was important to settle the question of the 1966 presidential election, it was far more urgent to adopt the proposals submitted for strengthening the revolution.[5]

The military officers who considered Lacerda their spokesman explained to Raphael de Almeida Magalhães that they wished to suppress a direct presidential election in view of the unlikelihood of a Lacerda victory. Raphael then told the governor that if he were to make an alliance with Kubitschek it might save direct elections by assuring Lacerda's election. "The trouble with a Lacerda-Kubitschek alliance at that time," Raphael recalls, "did not come from Kubitschek, who was willing. But Lacerda, on good terms with part of the military organization, felt he had more to lose than gain from such an alliance."[6]

General Danillo Nunes, president of the Guanabara legislature, paid a call on Costa e Silva and then declared that the army was united behind the war minister. However, some hard line members of the Military Club, among them retired officers and a few young officers, decided to hold a meeting to endorse Lacerda's attacks on Castello. Prevented by Club officials from using the Club for this purpose, they met in Cinelândia, near the Club, and read proclamations. "If we deposed an unsatisfactory president," army captains declared, "let us depose a traitor." The angry officers were joined by *Lacerdistas*, members of LIDER, and anti-Castello women (CAMDE dissidents). A bust of Kubitschek was toppled. A few days later, admirers of Kubitschek replied with a meeting in Cinelândia at which a picture of Lacerda, together with garbage, was put in a coffin that bore a sign reading "Here lies the crow—the Hitler of Guanabara."[7]

Lacerda, in his apartment on the following evening, received a visit from Juracy Magalhães, who had become justice minister earlier in the day. Juracy said he was deeply hurt by the words the governor had used in referring to President Castello Branco, whereupon Lacerda said he was even more deeply hurt by acts against himself carried out by the president. Juracy criticized Lacerda for "radicalizing" election campaigns and said the habit had contributed to Flexa Ribeiro's defeat. Turning to the current Brazilian situation, he objected to a new UDN convention. He explored the possibility of an indirect presidential election and said that the PSD-PTB combination seemed unbeatable in a popular vote. Lacerda replied that the UDN candidate would be beaten by the PSD and PTB in an indirect election.[8]

At Senator Calasans' Brasília residence, Juracy expressed his views to pro-Lacerda congressmen. While making his case for an indirect presidential election, the new justice minister said Lacerda's candidacy had no future. Juracy was then accused of harboring "resentments" ever since 1959, when Lacerda had opposed his presidential aspirations.[9]

The feeling that the government had caused the recent UDN electoral setbacks was not limited to *Lacerdistas* and left the party badly split on the eve of the directorship meeting of October 21, held in Brasília to decide about a convention. João Agripino, speaking before the meeting, criticized Lacerda's request for a convention and said that if Lacerda felt he should resign his candidacy he should do so as a unilateral step.

During the meeting, Jorge Curi supported a convention and came close to exchanging blows with Antônio Carlos Magalhães. Some of the UDN directors, disgusted with the animosity shown by the two antagonists, threatened to walk out but were held back by others who wanted the meeting to end with a decision favorable to a convention. Like Agripino, José Sarney felt that a decision should not be reached until further study had been given to the tense political situation. Finally the directors, by a 14 to 12 vote, adopted the motion of Alcides Flores Soares Júnior, a Gaúcho, calling for a convention before November 30. Among those supporting Curi and Flores Soares were Godinho, Adolfo de Oliveira Neto, Oscar Dias Corrêa, Herbert Levy, and Senator Adolfo Franco. Opponents included Costa Cavalcanti, Raimundo Padilha, and Paulo Sarasate, along with Sarney and Agripino. Senator Krieger, opposed to a convention, abstained because of dissension among the Gaúchos.[10]

Juracy called the decision a mistake and said the convention would only "aggravate the difficulties." Irritated by a *Tribuna* headline, "Lacerda Defeats Castello," he explained that the twenty state sections had split evenly, ten for the convention and ten against.[11]

13. Institutional Act Number Two
(October 27, 1965)

With the Castello Branco administration studying a plan to increase the number of Supreme Court justices from eleven to sixteen, Chief Justice Álvaro Ribeiro da Costa gave a statement to the *Correio da Manhã* and *Folha de S. Paulo* calling the plan absurd and harmful.

The armed forces, he also said, had no right to express their opinion on the subject, "although, unfortunately, this has been happening, something never seen in truly civilized nations." He added that "the time has come for the armed forces to understand that in democratic regimes they do not exercise the role of mentors to the nation."[1]

Costa e Silva was filled with emotion when he replied in a speech given in the presence of Castello Branco and other dignitaries at a review of army maneuvers. He called the statement of the chief justice "without doubt the greatest injustice ever practiced against the Brazilian soldier." "We left the barracks at the call of the people. . . . And we shall return to them only when the people so determine." When Ribeiro da Costa prepared to answer the war minister, Juracy Magalhães appealed to the judiciary to end its "bitter dispute with the armed forces."[2]

The war minister's outburst had been wildly applauded by young army officers who heard it; but intimates of the president felt that he had gone too far, and Gabinete Militar Chief Ernesto Geisel even suggested to Castello that he dismiss Costa e Silva. The *Correio da Manhã* praised the chief justice and *O Estado de S. Paulo* praised the war minister. Lacerda, inaugurating a school in Copacabana on October 25, scolded those who now cheered Costa e Silva's remarks but who, he said, had heaped abuse on himself in the past for having made "identical accusations" against the chief justice. He called them cowards, influenced by the tanks controlled by the war ministry.[3]

Brazil's attention was drawn quickly from the quarrel to the political crisis: the administration's difficulty in obtaining, in the Chamber of Deputies, the absolute majority needed for passage of its proposals for fortifying the revolution. Juracy Magalhães and Cordeiro de Farias insisted that the administration was not bluffing when it threatened to promulgate a new institutional act if the chamber balked. Such threats, however, failed to move congressmen who agreed with Wilson Martins (UDN, Mato Grosso) on the need "to demonstrate a worthy attitude in opposition to those who humiliate us." If "laws of exception" were to be imposed, they said, let them be decreed by the executive, not by a self-respecting Congress.[4]

The new institutional act, Ato 2, was drafted at Juracy's request by Professor Nehemias Gueiros and was discussed for two days in meetings held by Castello with the military ministers, the justice minister, and Geisel. Castello, against the advice of Eduardo Gomes, Roberto Campos, and Bulhões, insisted on a clause making himself ineligible in the indirect presidential election called for by the Ato. When Pernambuco Governor Paulo Guerra told the president that his proposed clause would give "the command" to Costa e Silva, Castello explained that without the clause Lacerda would interpret the Ato "as though it were a maneuver of mine to continue."[5]

The draft of the new Ato was reported in the press to include a reform of the judiciary, a revival of the power to suspend the political rights of individuals, the extinction of all political parties, and the indirect presidential election. The very toughness of reported clauses was attractive to hard liners, and some of them therefore worked, for reasons unlike those of the nonradicals, to defeat the administration's requests to Congress.[6] Costa e Silva, as a member of the administration, called for a favorable vote on the requests, although their defeat promised an institutional act that would benefit his presidential ambition. But supporters of the war minister provided obstruction in the Chamber of Deputies.[7]

These obstructionists were aided by the *Lacerdistas* even though nothing in the "clownish series of little laws" would prevent a direct election or Lacerda's participation in it as the UDN's candidate. Lacerda's congressional backers dismissed as "professional politicians" all *udenistas* who planned to vote for the administration's projects. *O Estado de S. Paulo*, advocate of Lacerda's candidacy, called for a new institutional act in an editorial describing the nation as nauseated with "little amendments" and "little laws."[8]

Castello wished to avoid promulgating an institutional act. For the law proposals he could count on an absolute majority in the Senate. But in the Chamber of Deputies the administration appeared a little short of the necessary 205 votes. Rui Santos, able predictor of congressional roll calls, estimated that the administration might receive 199 votes.[9]

Jorge Curi, Lacerda's spokesman, announced with pleasure that the administration's proposals would fail because 30 UDN congressmen would oppose them. The split in the UDN, described in the *Jornal do Brasil* as "probably the most serious in its history," was attributed by UDN Congressman João Cleofas to Lacerda, "leader of the strongest UDN faction." The split meant that Juracy had to try to convince PSD congressmen. But PSD President Amaral Peixoto made it clear on October 25 that his party would not reach any agreement with the administration unless it could revise the proposals to its satisfaction. For one thing, many *pessedistas* felt they could hardly vote to abolish the immunities applicable to Kubitschek as a former president.[10]

The administration moved with unexpected swiftness on October 27. As Castello was disinclined to decree measures rejected by Congress, the administration's leaders prevented a vote by withdrawing senators and congressmen. Juracy telegraphed the news of a new institutional act to Magalhães Pinto but not to Lacerda. However, Sátiro alerted Lacerda; and Costa e Silva, in phone calls to the army commanders, asked them to notify the governors.[11]

Lacerda therefore gathered with Raphael de Almeida Magalhães and state cabinet members at Guanabara Palace to hear a radio broadcast of the proceedings in Brasília. He heard Castello open with remarks that emphasized the need for tranquility and denounced "agitators of various sorts and participants in the state of affairs that was put behind us, who insisted on taking advantage of constitutional guarantees." "Democracy," the president said, "supposes liberty but does not exclude responsibility or amount to a license to oppose the very political vocation of the nation."[12]

The new institutional act, scheduled to expire when Castello left office on March 15, 1967, was read by Luís Viana Filho. Besides increasing to sixteen the number of Supreme Court justices, it stipulated that the justice system was not to render judgments about steps of the federal government that were based on the institutional acts. The president was empowered again to suspend the political rights of individuals for ten years and could even force legislatures into recess. The clauses extinguishing all political parties and making the 1966 presidential election an indirect one by Congress killed the candidacy to which Lacerda had devoted years of effort.

Carlos Castello Branco wrote:

> What the governors of Minas and Guanabara preached has been carried out in large part by Ato Institutional No. 2. Both accused the government of not wanting to assume the responsibility of practicing revolutionary acts. This responsibility has been assumed. Both alleged that the corrupt and subversives, under the shadow of temporizations, were returning. Against these two classes there have been dictated steps of containment insisted on by the most radical groups. Magalhães Pinto preached the extinction of the parties. . . . And, finally, Lacerda became noteworthy in a certain stage of his life by advocating a regime of emergency of limited duration. We are now in it.[13]

Magalhães Pinto praised the "heroic measures" and joined Ademar de Barros and other governors in giving public support to the president. Armando Falcão, once considered a possible running mate of Lacerda, declared that the people of Brazil had for a long time silently been hoping for the new institutional act. In São Paulo the state UDN, about to go out of existence, met under the leadership of Abreu Sodré and issued a note applauding much of the new Ato but condemning an indirect presidential election and the extinction of the political parties.[14]

O Estado de S. Paulo shared the local UDN's reservations and added that, since the government had failed in its job (except in the economic and financial sectors), it might not know how to use its new powers. The *Jornal do Brasil* hoped that the powers would be used briefly to usher in an era of economic development and social well-being, and expressed surprise that Castello should "be prisoner of principles that are contrary to his and our democratic formation." The *Correio da Manhã*, attacking the Ato, quoted foreign newspapers and United States Senator Wayne Morse, whereas *O Jornal*, defending the Ato, wrote that Morse did not understand the Brazilian political situation.[15]

O Globo found "applause" for the Ato to be widespread. Eugênio Gudin's column in *O Globo* said the Ato should have a longer duration and chided the United States for ridiculously wanting to apply its own model everywhere. Former Justice Minister Vicente Ráo declared that it was absurd to speak about illegality and legality during a revolution. But Alceu Amoroso Lima described himself as "horrified" by the "anti-Brazilian character" of the new measure.[16]

Lacerda, making no comment, left Guanabara Palace and immersed himself in his new business affairs and in writing *O Duelo*, a film version of a story by Manuel Antônio Álvares de Azevedo, a nineteenth-century poet. By finishing the film adaptation in forty-eight hours, he surprised actor Agildo Ribeiro, who was to direct the production. Agildo, son of the well-known Communist Agildo Barata, told reporters that he found the governor filled with enthusiasm for new activities he was planning.[17]

Lacerda was asked by First Army Commander Otacílio Terra Ururaí to call on Costa e Silva on the morning of October 29 at the war minister's official Rio residence, Laguna Palace. Costa e Silva, upon receiving the governor, explained the reasons for the new Ato and asked whether Lacerda planned to make a declaration about it. Lacerda said that he planned to retire quickly from public life and therefore would make no pronouncement, but added that the Ato was, indeed, a grave matter. He told the war minister that, for the first time in the history of Brazil, the army—not the armed forces but only the army—was assuming the exclusive and full responsibility for what would happen and not happen to Brazil. "It was the same," Costa e Silva said, "with the proclamation of the republic." "No," Lacerda replied, "at the start of the republic there were the statesmen of the empire—and Rui Barbosa."[18]

Lacerda remained silent about his meeting with the war minister, and it was simply described as having been cordial. This led to rumors about Costa e Silva wanting a renewal of good relations between the outgoing governor and the government, and Lacerda was even quoted as admitting that he might collaborate. The *Jornal do Brasil* reported that neither Costa e Silva nor Lacerda had any comments on the speculation that Lacerda would become prime minister for planning in a Costa e Silva administration.[19]

14. Retiring from Public Office (November 4, 1965)

With a long weekend coming up, Lacerda and Letícia left on October 30 for the Cabo Frio retreat of Joaquim da Silveira.[1]

While they were there on November 2, a holiday, Juracy Magalhães learned at the First Army barracks of the determination of the hard line to prevent the inauguration of Negrão de Lima on December 5 and the inaugurations in January of the governors-elect of Minas and Mato Grosso. Generals Ururaí and Afonso de Albuquerque Lima and Colonel Ferdinando de Carvalho insisted that the justice minister call off the inaugurations. Ferdinando presented evidence that he said required the arrest and *cassação* of Negrão. First Army Chief of Staff Albuquerque Lima, leader of the hard line, believed that his group had been able to force Ato 2 on the government because of the overwhelming support given to him and Ururaí by the local army officers; and it was clear that the group felt itself very powerful.

Juracy reported at once to Castello about his meeting at the barracks. The president phoned the war minister, considered a friend of the Albuquerque Lima group, and told him about the need for an army setup (*dispositivo*) that would assure the inaugurations; the war minister therefore prepared to make command changes and transfer the officers with whom Juracy had spoken.[2]

Negrão followed the advice of Juracy, a veteran *tenente,* and spent each night at the home of a different person. Stories about efforts to kidnap him were plentiful, and therefore on November 3, when Lacerda announced he would leave office the next day, it was reported that the governor was resigning quickly to avoid being accused of responsibility for any move to prevent the inauguration of Negrão.[3]

In preparing to leave office, Lacerda considered problems that an incoming Negrão administration would create for men who had been doing good work in Guanabara Palace. For some of them, he believed, opportunities would become available in the businesses he was setting up. In the case of others, he adhered, with one exception, to his practice of not asking people to find positions for his friends. The exception occurred when he spoke to Veiga Brito about journalist Walter Cunto, whose loyalty, he explained, might have made him enemies among members of the press. Veiga Brito, now head of the Water Company that replaced the Water Department, agreed to take care of the matter; but, as it turned out, Cunto did not need the favor that had been sought by the governor on behalf of his longtime associate. Cunto was asked to head the Rio office of the *Jornal da Tarde*, about to be launched in São Paulo by Ruy Mesquita and others.[4]

On November 4 Lacerda signed his final decrees, the last of which gave a tract of land to the Vasco da Gama Regatta Club, "glorious participant in Rio sports." Then at noon, in the Guanabara Palace salon, he participated in the ceremony of transferring the executive branch of the state to the vice governor. The crowd, after singing "Cidade Maravilhosa," heard a short speech in which Lacerda read a notarized statement of his and Letícia's assets and debts. The former included the Rio apartment, the Rocio property, some Cabo Frio lots purchased nine months earlier, the *Tribuna da Imprensa* trademark, and a few equities. To the debts still owed on properties, Lacerda had added debts of 11,600,000 cruzeiros ($6,200 in September 1965), borrowed from two banks during his governorship. These loans, the statement said, had helped pay for trips made while he was in office.

Income from royalties had been considerable, with two book publishers furnishing about 20 million cruzeiros. Lacerda declared that this income, plus royalties from magazines and his monthly salary (which had increased from 200,000 cruzeiros in December 1960 to 1,940,000 in September 1965), had allowed him to support his family and maintain the apartment he had used as a substitute for the official residence. (In terms of dollars, the salary can be said to have gone from slightly less than $1,000 per month in December 1960 to a trifle more in September 1965.)

Lacerda turned the state over to "the loyal and honest hands of my faithful friend Raphael de Almeida Magalhães." The crowd outside the salon broke through a cordon, and Lacerda, hoisted on shoulders, was taken to the garden. He reviewed troops of the Military Police while the crowd sang the national anthem.[5]

O Estado de S. Paulo, explaining the simplicity of the ceremony, wrote that Lacerda took his leave, not in his role of a politician but in his role of an administrator, "the cold, efficient accomplisher of projects, for whom action comes ahead of everything else. Why use words if the facts speak for themselves?" It called his retirement "inevitably transitory" because, it said, in the Brazilian political "desert of values," it would be inconceivable that his talent not be utilized by those in power.[6]

15. Comments

Raphael de Almeida Magalhães, commenting on the failure of Congress to enact the government's proposals, has said: "The only beneficiary of the failure of Congress to act was Costa e Silva. Lacerda hurt himself. Lacerda blocked Castello from acting on our side. All the movement that Lacerda tried to conduct turned in favor of Costa e Silva. The radicals won."[1]

It is interesting to examine the role of Lacerda in the four events that eliminated his presidential candidacy. In the case of the first, the overthrow of Goulart, most of the credit goes to Goulart for defying military discipline. The second event, the extension of Castello's mandate, occurred after Lacerda failed to cooperate with work done among congressmen by Hugo Levy and because at least several federal legislators were moved only by antagonism to Lacerda. The third event was the holding of direct gubernatorial elections, which would not have happened except for Lacerda.

Lastly we come to October 1965, when Lacerda, with considerable influence in the military, encouraged the hard line. His reasoning, like that of O Estado de S. Paulo, was not that "laws of exception" were wrong but that they were not radical enough. And yet both he and O Estado must have known that the defeat of these law projects would mean Ato 2 and the end of the direct presidential election—an election that Lacerda believed to be of utmost importance for Brazil.

The UDN, João Cleofas told Castello, "is a company in which Carlos Lacerda has 60 percent of the shares."[2] Lacerda's influence within the party *bancada* of about one hundred congressmen was less than 60 percent. But it was not inconsiderable, as demonstrated when the party's directorship supported Lacerda's call for a new national convention. A handful of votes, needed to avoid Ato 2, was denied the government on account of a serious party split, attributed chiefly to Lacerda.

It can be argued that even without Ato 2, something might have prevented a direct presidential election a year later. However, that seems a weak reason for not testing the future. The outcome in Guanabara in October 1965 did not altogether rule out possibilities for Lacerda, a popular oppositionist acceptable to the hard line. After campaigning tirelessly in September for the need to preserve the direct presidential election, Lacerda might have accepted, for the same objective, the enactment of what he called "the clownish series of little laws." The top military leaders, including Costa e Silva, had agreed to accept them as a means of resolving the crisis created by the hard line.

IX.

Background for the Frente Ampla Crusade (November 1965–October 1966)

1. Status of Lacerda Administration Projects (November 1965–April 1966)

Raphael de Almeida Magalhães remained acting governor until early December 1965, when he and Legislative Assembly President Danillo Nunes resigned in order not to be the ones to transfer the government to Negrão de Lima.[1]

During this one-month period, the Castello Branco administration dealt with the First Army's opposition to Negrão's inauguration. It replaced Generals Ururaí and Albuquerque Lima, and arrested Colonels Francisco Boaventura Cavalcanti Júnior and Hélio Lemos. The Superior Military Tribunal failed to act on Colonel Ferdinando de Carvalho's petition for jailing the governor-elect, and therefore on December 5, with about two thousand security agents in attendance, Negrão was inaugurated. Kubitschek could not be present, for he had left Brazil on November 9, after First Army officers had threatened to jail him for "dishonestly handling income taxes, and other grave matters."[2]

Raphael, while serving as acting governor, was faced with the problem of unpaid wages of state employees. He persuaded Adauto Cardoso to support his appeal for federal assistance, and Castello at length authorized the release of 2 billion cruzeiros ($900,000). The finance ministry pointed out that the Lacerda administration, prior to the new payment, had received from the federal government 4 billion cruzeiros from the National Housing Bank, loans of 10 and 4 billion from the Bank of Brazil and Caixa Econômica Federal—and, from the national treasury, payments of 4 billion and loans of 9 billion.[3]

In the state legislature the anti-Lacerda forces were strong, with the Negrão people offering to make payments that Lacerda had refused and offering positions. By a 34 to 20 vote on November 29, it rejected Lacerda's accounts for 1964; and therefore its justice commission, in accordance with the laws about accounts, prepared to pronounce

Lacerda ineligible to run for public office for five years. During the plenary vote, *Lacerdista* Mauro Magalhães had noted that Negrão leader José Bonifácio Diniz de Andrada had sat by the booth and supervised the depositing of votes of his followers in a way that had not allowed them the possibility of voting against his wishes. Mauro therefore introduced a motion to annul the outcome, but it was greeted by jeers. He went at once to Guanabara Palace, where he found Eugênio Sigaud, and he persuaded the justice secretary to draw up a petition requesting the judiciary to rule on the voting. A temporary injunction was granted by the Guanabara Justice Tribunal, which was about to start its year-end recess, and this meant that no final judicial ruling was possible before January 1, on which date the accounts were considered approved because of no resolution.

The position of the anti-Lacerda legislators was weakened by Juracy Magalhães, who threatened to use the new institutional act to punish legislators who had tried to burden the state's precarious finances with unnecessary legislative staff members. In February 1966 Castello used Ato 2 to suspend the political rights of four Guanabara legislators who were considered corrupt: Amando da Fonseca, João Machado, Naldir Laranjeira Batista, and Gerson Bergher (Negrão's new legislative leader).[4]

Press reports in November made it clear that the great construction showpieces of the Lacerda administration would not be completed before Negrão took office. The Rebouças Tunnel could expect to handle limited traffic in February or March 1966, depending on the outcome of bids for illumination and ventilation, estimated to cost 16 billion cruzeiros ($7.2 million). The long awaited German hospital equipment was received before Negrão took office, but it was left to his administration to conclude construction work at the Souza Aguiar Hospital, to be financed by the state lottery. Popular housing, to which forty-two thousand *favelados* had been transferred in four years, found 3,500 units at the Cidade de Deus not quite finished.[5]

One of the last acts of the interim governor was to inaugurate a telephone connection that would allow CETEL users to dial directly into the CTB system. According to outgoing CETEL President Sampaio Toledo, the last four of the nine stations set up by CETEL (in Jacarepaguá, Santa Cruz, Paquetá, and Barra da Tijuca) were ready to operate. Colonel José Antônio Alencastro e Silva, who succeeded Sampaio Toledo, said that in the first half of 1966 it would install the last of the 14,300 telephones planned for the first stage of the state company's program.[6]

In December 1965, soon after Raphael left office, the CTB, owned by the Canada-based Brazilian Traction, Light, and Power Company,

The Guanabara legislature: "Appointments to jobs, etc., etc." (APPE drawing in *O Cruzeiro*, January 29, 1966)

was purchased by the Brazilian government's CONTEL. The national-ized company, operating with the improved rate structure established earlier for Brazilian Traction, agreed to pay a purchase price of $26.3 million, over twenty years, and assume the indebtedness of $70 mil-lion owed to Brazilian Traction by the CTB. CONTEL prepared to install 10,000 new instruments at once where waiting lists in Rio were the largest: the downtown business section and the residential areas of Copacabana, Leblon, and Gávea. CETEL President Alencas-tro e Silva said that the best way to handle the Guanabara telephone problem was to have a "fusion" of the CTB and CETEL, or a "unifica-tion" of their services.[7]

The work at Flamengo Park, according to Lota de Macedo Soares, could be completed in three years if funds were available. Lota, squab-bling publicly with Roberto Burle Marx because of modifications made without his prior knowledge, was now executive director of the Flamengo Park Foundation. The foundation had been set up by La-cerda to keep the park works administered by the team he had formed. However, in December the state legislature passed a law revoking Lacerda's decree and making Flamengo Park a state government–controlled company (*autarquia*). Lota said the "sole purpose" of the new law was to make jobs available for political purposes.[8]

For reasons similar to those inspiring the creation of the Flamengo Park Foundation, Lacerda on October 19, 1965, turned the state wa-ter department into CEDAG, the Guanabara State Water Company.

Luiz Roberto Veiga de Brito, president of the new company, explained that the state would own 51 percent of the capital, which would amount to 1 billion cruzeiros, and that the seven-man administrative board would include one representative of the employees and one representative of the opposition parties.[9]

Shortly before CEDAG was formed, a leading Guandu project contractor, Servix Engenharia, became insolvent. Aderbal de Miranda Pougi, the president of Servix, explained tearfully to Veiga Brito that payments by the state did not cover his company's costs and therefore he planned to sell his equipment. Veiga Brito devised a scheme to have the state water department itself carry out the final work and pay Servix for the use of its tools and equipment. After the state bank agreed to help, Veiga Brito met with the Servix creditors, about two hundred in number, because any one of them could have forced Servix into bankruptcy, disrupting the plan. The meeting was successful thanks in large part to the position taken by Hélio Gomide, an important supplier of Servix and an admirer of the enterprise of the Lacerda administration.[10]

Acting Governor Almeida Magalhães canceled a plan for testing the aqueduct because, he said, to do so would set back the revetment work. He predicted that the Guandu project would be finished on February 15, 1966. The Lameirão pump station, to raise water 107 meters, had been contracted to the Falharva Engenharia firm and was completed while Raphael was in office. Inaugurating it early in December, he threw a switch that operated one of the eight 4,500-horsepower motors.[11]

The Negrão de Lima government was quick to consult jurists to try to find a way to annul the election in November of the CEDAG administrative officers. But Veiga Brito, despite the ill will of the new state government, remained in the CEDAG presidency until January 21, 1966, when he became general director of the National Department of Public Works and Sanitation, and he was able to turn the CEDAG presidency over to his principal assistant, Antônio Augusto Lisboa de Miranda, young and stubborn. Veiga Brito hoped his own position in the federal government would allow him to obtain the money for completing Guandu.[12]

Late in December, before making this move, Veiga Brito warned that the Guandu project contractors would suspend work unless they were paid 2 billion cruzeiros they were owed. Guandu was not the only project in financial distress. Fernando Petrucci, president of the Association of Guanabara Public Works Contractors, revealed early in January that contractors were owed 22 billion cruzeiros ($10 million) for work carried out in November and December for the water company, the finance secretaryship, SURSAN, and SUSEME (the Superintendency of Medical Services).[13]

With suppliers unable to extend further credit, Negrão de Lima and Finance Secretary Márcio Alves (father of the journalist) conferred with Finance Minister Otávio Bulhões and Labor Minister Walter Peracchi Barcelos. Already the slowdown in Guanabara public works had cut thirty thousand from the payrolls, and the layoff of the remaining seventy thousand construction workers would have been a disaster. Following the meeting, Márcio Alves proposed to pay the contractors association 1.5 billion cruzeiros a week to liquidate the debt, and let payments on new indebtedness lag for four months. Some of the contractors responded by laying off more men, reducing construction further.[14]

Guandu project work was in suspense in mid-January, when Rio suffered from its worst torrents of rain in approximately eighty years. Floods and collapsing buildings killed about 190 people, left an estimated 20,000 homeless, and caused material damage reported at 50 billion cruzeiros. Castello quickly arranged for the Caixa Econômica to loan 5 billion cruzeiros to the state.[15]

One of the landslides in Jacarepaguá destroyed the principal pipeline of the old Guandu water system. As it would take at least a month to repair and clean the pipeline, CEDAG (the Water Company) was put to work again, now on a twenty-four-hour-a-day basis, to make a connection between the old aqueduct and the new one, thus partially restoring Rio's water supply within a week. "The new Guandu Aqueduct," Veiga Brito declared, "will begin operations under these dramatic circumstances."[16]

Veiga Brito, following his acceptance of the directorship of the National Department of Public Works and Sanitation, pleaded for federal funds for Guandu. His success in obtaining a 2-billion-cruzeiro loan in February assured completion of the project late in March, thereby raising Rio's available water supply from 1.2 billion liters daily to 2.4 billion.[17]

During March the suggestion of fraudulent contracts by CEDAG was made by journalist Luís Alberto Bahia, whose new position as head of Negrão's Casa Civil had been arranged, according to Lacerda and others, by General Golbery. Veiga Brito said he had nothing to fear and the offended Guandu team threatened to resign. But Bahia's proposal for a "high-level" investigation was dropped after the federal government warned against trying to develop scandals in connection with projects involving foreign financial assistance.[18]

The Guandu team held its own inauguration on March 31. It called the official ceremony, headed by Negrão on April 4, a mere "social

act." Negrão, in his address on April 4, made no reference to the Lacerda administration, but CEDAG President Antônio Miranda, speaking on the same occasion, said: "It would be unpardonable not to
remember that the construction of this monumental Guandu is the
result of Carlos Lacerda's dedication, enthusiasm, love, and courage,
along with that of Raphael de Almeida Magalhães."[19]

The plan of Lacerda to give Guanabara an industrial park in the
Santa Cruz area on Sepetiba Bay resulted in a park without much
industrial activity for the employment of workers in nearby housing
projects. "We succeeded," Lacerda said later, "in bringing the Central do Brasil Railroad line there and we also received the license to
build the port, but we did not manage to establish the steel plant,
COSIGUA. First, because our administration ended, and, secondly,
because, with all those conflicts, obviously the federal government
was opposed." In March 1966 the Negrão administration prepared
to revise the plans for COSIGUA, whereupon state legislator Cesário de Melo, originator of legislation creating the industrial park, denounced the proposed revision as sabotage by Negrão and economic
groups associated with Roberto Campos. Among the "saboteurs," he
listed the Hanna Mining Company, whose iron ore subsidiary in Brazil had recently become a minority shareholder in a new company
controlled by the Augusto Trajano de Azevedo Antunes industrial
group.[20]

Throughout November 1965, Security Secretary Gustavo Borges kept
insisting that former Guanabara policemen and firemen who had
transferred their services to the federal government should depart
from residences that he felt should be occupied by members of the
state Military Police. Like others in the state cabinet, he resigned several days before the Negrão de Lima administration took over. Fontenelle, one of the last to depart, set up a consulting firm, FONTEC, to
assist other Brazilian cities in dealing with traffic problems.[21]

Raphael, speaking on television on December 3, described the departing group as a team formed by Lacerda and inspired by the mys-
tique of work; it was, he said, made up of people who had "dedicated
the best of their intelligence, goodwill, and effort to the service of
a city." He estimated the state government's receipts for 1965 at
385 billion cruzeiros and expenses at 445 billion ($200 million). "The
government of the Revolution preferred not to help us in order to
help the incoming government."[22]

Negrão de Lima, soon after taking office, made the point that "Guanabara is no longer in continual conflict with the central government." "We can," he added, "maintain cordial relations that will permit a mutually beneficial collaboration."[23]

2. Businessman Carlos Lacerda
(October 1965–January 1966)

"I have no money," Lacerda said on the phone to Antônio Carlos de Almeida Braga early in October, during a conversation in which he persuaded the wealthy insurance executive and sports enthusiast to leave the presidency of the Banco do Estado da Guanabara. Quickly a lunch was arranged at Braga's home to discuss Lacerda's entry into the business world. Lacerda and his host were joined by lawyer Fernando Cícero da Franca Velloso, Sérgio Lacerda, and José Luís de Magalhães Lins. Magalhães Lins directed the Banco Nacional de Minas Gerais, in which Magalhães Pinto, his uncle, had a powerful influence; like Braga, Magalhães Lins had married a daughter of lawyer José Nabuco.[1]

A campaign was undertaken to find new capital to supplement that furnished by Braga and Magalhães Lins for Novo Rio Crédito Financiamento e Investimentos, a company established to make loans for durable goods purchases and other purposes. The campaign was so successful, Braga recalls, that "the goal was revised upward every night."[2]

Lacerda, in a press interview on November 5, spoke of the four companies with which he had become associated. The two new companies were Novo Rio, the investment company, and Editora Nova Fronteira, a book publishing firm named in honor of Kennedy's New Frontier. The existing companies, which felt that Lacerda's name would be helpful, were Lins Publicidade and Imobiliária Nova York. Lins Publicidade, of which Lacerda became president, had been founded four years earlier by its owner, Francisco Pimentel Lins, a first cousin of José Luís de Magalhães Lins. Imobiliária Nova York, the largest seller of real estate in Brazil, was owned by Mauro Magalhães and his brothers. The brothers provided Lacerda with 20 percent of their stock and made him president.[3]

Imobiliária Nova York founder José Sílvio Magalhães said at the company's Rio Branco Avenue office on November 5 that Lacerda would be like another member of the family and serve as a "sort of public relations director," making contacts and developing publicity. The real estate business, he added, was in the doldrums.

Taking off his jacket and rolling up his sleeves, Lacerda spoke from the desk in his new real estate office, decorated with framed photographs of Flamengo Park, John F. Kennedy, and a Statue of Liberty at the entrance of Vila Kennedy. He explained that the lack of political liberty made the practice of political journalism similar to taking a sunbath in the rain. "I hope to build up enough capital in four years to make myself independent. . . . Fortunately I have not had to start from scratch. But if it were necessary to sell combs and brushes on the streets, I would get more satisfaction than from seeking audiences with cabinet ministers."

Lacerda criticized the government. "Six months have passed without any regulatory decisions for the real estate laws. If we had them, it would be possible in one year to do more than can be done in ten years under present conditions. It is not enough to be concerned with housing people who have no money. It is necessary to think also of the problem of those who have some money and to adopt an aggressive policy involving new methods of large-scale production." Speaking of Novo Rio, which had set up an office at Rua do Carmo 27, Lacerda explained that the capitalization of 650 million cruzeiros ($300,000) had been raised in forty-eight hours, "which proves that Brazil is not a poor country. It is therefore unjust that the people be poor. The government should have the courage to stimulate private enterprise."[4]

Nova Fronteira was to be run by Sebastião Lacerda and Vicente Barreto (son-in-law of Catholic intellectual Gustavo Corção), but Barreto remained only a short time. Some of its capital came from friends like Braga and José Luís de Magalhães Lins, and 25 percent of it was furnished by Alfredo C. Machado, head of Distribuidora Record, which was to distribute Nova Fronteira's books. Lacerda, in his November 5 interview, said that the first three titles of the new firm, translations of foreign best sellers (including *Hotel* by Arthur Hailey), "have a guaranteed market." "We are arranging for an original work by Nelson Rodrigues." Reflecting on the change in his life, Lacerda told the reporter: "I feel the relief of a condemned person who is set free after serving a stiff sentence."[5]

Braga and Magalhães Lins accepted officership positions at Novo Rio. Mario Lorenzo Fernandez became vice president, Gustavo Borges became office manager, and Fernando Velloso served as adviser. Sérgio Lacerda and Tannay de Farias were active from the start. Mauricinho Lacerda, after breaking with Isa Motta, made his peace with Carlos and did some insurance work for Novo Rio, and his son Gabriel did some legal work. During the fourteen months that Gustavo Borges was with Novo Rio, Rubens Vaz Júnior assisted him.[6]

Before long Novo Rio spawned other companies, among them a securities distributing affiliate and Novo Rio Crédito Imobiliário, a real estate credit firm, with which Marcos Tamoyo, Carlos Eduardo Correia, and Epaminondas Moreira do Valle became associated. César

Seroa da Mota, who had worked for the Lacerda governorship, was persuaded by Tamoyo and Correia to construct houses for Novo Rio Crédito Imobiliário.[7]

Ruth Alverga, who had been Lacerda's secretary for fifteen years and was now studying law, did not receive the offer she would have liked. Instead, the first member of the Novo Rio secretarial staff was Maria Thereza Correia de Mello, sister of the wife of José Cândido Moreira de Souza. Recommended by Marcelo Garcia's secretary, she had been employed to assist the Lacerda presidential campaign and had worked briefly at Guanabara Palace. Devoted to Lacerda, she found him far less peaceful than Mario Lorenzo Fernandez and far less organized than Magalhães Lins. After she straightened out the papers on his desk at the Carmo Street office, he exclaimed: "This is not my desk. So organized. So mediocre. To be too organized is to be mediocre."[8]

Lacerda offered Raul Brunini a position at Novo Rio, but the broadcaster, a founder of Rádio Globo, learned that Roberto Marinho needed him at Rádio Globo and was willing to overlook his association with Lacerda. Brunini's work with Novo Rio was therefore limited to its initial stage, when it made successful appeals to the people to buy its *letras de câmbio* (sort of certificates of deposit). "Your prosperity," the newspaper advertisements said, "will construct the public wealth." Promising an "undisturbed return" on a "guaranteed investment," Novo Rio added: "Look who is responsible for the future of your investment. President Carlos Lacerda, Vice President José Luís de Magalhães Lins, Vice President Mario Lorenzo Fernandez, Superintendent Antônio Carlos de Almeida Braga, Director José Zobaran Filho."[9]

The capital of Novo Rio, after Lacerda's first business trip to São Paulo, was reported to have increased to a billion cruzeiros ($460,000). A little later, Orlando Ometto put up a large sum "for Carlos to administer."[10]

Even more than when he had been in public life, Carlos made personal purchases on a grand scale when he traveled. In São Paulo, after Luiz Ernesto Kawall acquainted him with Olinto Moura's shop of old books, he spent five hours stuffing boxes with books. He visited a Japanese fair and found so much to buy that he filled the car with artefacts and bamboo furniture. Notary public Carlos Alberto Aulicino was with him when he bought 70 kilograms of meat for Rocio, where he liked to cook when he gathered with friends. One day he came to São Paulo's Hotel Jaraguá with forty cages of birds for Rocio. A government police agent, protecting the national security by spying on Lacerda's movements in Rocio, secretly told the authorities early in December that the former governor was keeping his large collection of birds alive with "about seventeen sacks of feed each week."[11]

More worthy of the attention of the authorities was the goodwill Lacerda kept alive among humans. At Lage Park, where he received a rose of gold from 2,700 women, he delivered a bitter antigovernment speech. At the Eldorado Bookstore, he autographed copies of his books for people who waited in the street in long lines before gaining admittance. *O Poder das Idéias* and *Uma rosa é uma rosa é uma rosa,* containing speeches and articles, were much in demand; but the best seller was his latest literary accomplishment, a translation of Shakespeare's *Julius Caesar,* published, like the other titles, by Distribuidora Record. Besides translating the play, Lacerda made phonograph records of his favorite passages; these he sent, together with copies of the book, to prominent friends in Brazil and dignitaries in London.[12]

Responses to *Júlio César* were not always favorable. One Brazilian, in a scholarly letter to Lacerda, discussed poetic meter, listed translation errors, and suggested withdrawal of the book from the market. Another critic published what Lacerda called a "thrashing," and received in reply a thrashing from Lacerda, who condemned, in the *Tribuna da Imprensa,* the critic's "rage" and "the prevailing stupidity."[13]

Lacerda's autographing session at the Eldorado Bookstore on January 10 coincided with one of the downpours that contributed to the disaster that killed about 190 Cariocas. The disaster moved him to write Castello Branco pleading for massive resources to help the Cariocas. In the letter, which he distributed quickly to the press, he argued that Castello's government owed its existence in large measure to Guanabara, whose resistance had done so much for the March 1964 movement, "in decisive days quickly forgotten by Your Excellency." "With risks that I do not wish to emphasize, and with the suffering that economic and administrative sanctions imposed on them, the people here abbreviated the nation's agony, preparing it for the armed movement that took Your Excellency to the presidency. Up to now, all this has meant nothing to Your Excellency." Lacerda accused the president of having broken his promise to provide, on time and on the necessary scale, assistance for the "essential" Lacerda administration projects. And he listed "grave errors" of the Negrão administration: improper handling of the water problem, "brutal" steps against the state bank, failure to complete construction of the 3,500 houses in the Cidade de Deus, and "destruction of the Regional Administrations."[14]

In his Rua do Carmo office, Lacerda broke down in tears when he told Dr. Rebello Filho of the deaths of former Guanabara Palace employees, buried by a landslide during the downpours. He arranged for the family of one of them, a former driver of the governor, to receive a pension from the Novo Rio group, because it received nothing from the government. He decided to auction off some of the paintings he had made and thus raise money for those left without shelter.[15]

3. The PAREDE (November 1965–July 1966)

Following the extinction of the political parties, Justice Minister Juracy Magalhães and the president arranged for Brazil to have two parties, one to support the revolution and the other to oppose it. Ato Complementar No. 4, issued on November 20, required the formation, within forty-five days, of provisional parties, each with at least 120 congressmen and 20 senators. These minimums appeared to eliminate the possibility of a third party.

The so-called government party, known as the ARENA (Aliança Renovadora Nacional), had no trouble meeting the requirements, but the bitterness of local conflicts between old foes being brought into the same party made it necessary to extend the deadline to March 15, 1966. The oppositionist MDB (Movimento Democrático Brasileiro) had difficulty in reaching the minimums but received help from the local conflicts and from the government.[1]

Lacerdistas were in a quandary. Although Lacerda announced early in December that he would give no advice and told supporters, "You are adults and can do what you think best," it became evident that he had no desire to see them join the progovernment ARENA.[2] But the MDB attracted mainly members of the Lacerda-hating PTB and was not inclined to accept *Lacerdistas.*

Lacerda soon declared that both the ARENA and MDB were artificial and no good. He encouraged Raphael de Almeida Magalhães to try to form a third party, which, as Abreu Sodré saw it, had the purpose of "preserving Lacerda's pretension of being a presidential candidate." Brunini called the Ato Complementar a farce and contributed to Raphael's effort, as did Mauro Magalhães and Célio Borja.[3]

Lacerdistas were not alone in decrying the two-party system. Even before Ato Complementar No. 4 was issued, Ernâni Sátiro (UDN), Ernâni do Amaral Peixoto (PSD), and Juarez Távora (PDC) objected to the idea. After the Ato was promulgated, Ademar de Barros (PSP) pronounced against indirect elections and the two-party system.[4]

Castello Branco telephoned Carlos Flexa Ribeiro and asked him to serve as secretary general of the Carioca ARENA and help Adauto Lúcio Cardoso, who was to be president of the local ARENA but would be busy in Brasília. Flexa Ribeiro, deciding to accept Castello's appeal, called on Lacerda at the Novo Rio office. After Lacerda banged on the

The opposition party. (APPE drawing in *O Cruzeiro*, January 8, 1966)

table while expressing his displeasure, Flexa said he had never been subservient to him and added that he would help the ARENA and thus help the revolution.[5]

Flexa worked to have the local ARENA oppose Negrão de Lima, who joined no party but governed with the MDB legislative majority. The ARENA attracted *udenista* legislators Lígia Lessa Bastos, Geraldo Ferraz, Vitorino James, Francisco da Gama Lima Filho, Domingos D'Ângelo, Raimundo Barbosa de Carvalho Neto, Paulo Areal, Nina Ribeiro, and briefly, Edson Guimarães. Nina Ribeiro, hoping to be rewarded with the post of ARENA legislative leader, wrote Lacerda to give his reasons for supporting Castello; he added that he admired Lacerda and would be his follower "at the opportune moment." Lacerda returned the letter with a note describing it as full of "the shabby excuses of a career man."[6]

Raphael, whose contingent included nine Guanabara legislators, struggled against Flexa Ribeiro for leadership of the former Carioca UDN. He worked with Célio Borja and Brunini on a manifesto to be issued by their embryonic third party, the Partido da Renovação Democrática (PAREDE). The manifesto, released on January 27 with Lacerda's approval, called the two-party system a "Noah's ark without a flood, empty of contents," and attacked the "mockery of democracy." State assembly opposition leader Mauro Magalhães, the first of the assemblymen to sign, made plans to travel to gain adherents. Hélio Fernandes, another signer, turned the *Tribuna da Imprensa* into the PAREDE's propaganda organ.[7]

São Paulo *udenistas*, led by Abreu Sodré, took a dim view of their state's ARENA because its organization was in the hands of Arnaldo

Lacerda, holding the PAREDE, declines the UDN's invitation to join it
and the PSD in the ARENA. (APPE drawing in *O Cruzeiro*, February
26, 1966)

Cerdeira (PSP) and other longtime followers of Ademar de Barros.
Castello, however, convinced Abreu Sodré that the São Paulo UDN
should help the revolution by participating in the ARENA, thus following the example of São Paulo *udenista* Congressman Ernesto
Pereira Lopes.[8]

Abreu Sodré and Oscar Klabin Segall explained their decision to
Lacerda in Rio in what Sodré says was a "difficult" eight-hour meeting filled with "moments of great emotion." Sodré declined Lacerda's
invitation to join the PAREDE, whose Raphael de Almeida Magalhães, he has written, was not highly regarded by many former *udenistas.* The unsuccessful meeting was followed by an exchange of
"violent" letters.[9]

Early in February the PAREDE issued a second manifesto, said to
have been signed by over three thousand students, to denounce "the
imprisonment of PAREDE supporters." A third manifesto was issued
a few days later because the Castello administration, whose justice
minister was now Mem de Sá, promulgated Institutional Act Number Three, making gubernatorial elections indirect.[10]

In drafting its manifesto against the new Institutional Act, the
PAREDE held a meeting that was attended by Colonel Osnelli Martinelli; and therefore the *Tribuna* proclaimed that the hard line, enthusiastic about the PAREDE's position against corruption and subversion, had drawn close to the PAREDE and Lacerda. At the meeting,

in an office decorated by a large photograph of Lacerda, Célio Borja spoke of plans of other hard line military officers to join the PAREDE, and Raphael remarked that the new Ato revealed that the government's purpose was "to maintain in public life people who received no popular vote." Others at the meeting were Brunini, Mac Dowell Leite de Castro, Everardo Magalhães Castro, Cesário de Melo, Jair Martins, and several PAREDE women. Their manifesto concluded that the people were opposed to the political "farce" enacted by the "bewildered" Castello government.[11]

Institutional Act No. 3 was also attacked by the MDB, which called it dictatorial. Brunini then declared that the MDB people lacked the ethical standards needed for making their attack; he called them mere opportunists who had preached a different message during the Goulart administration, infiltrated, as they knew, by Communists.[12]

Lacerdistas were described in the press as sharing the hard line's enthusiasm for the presidential candidacy of Costa e Silva. It is true that the *Tribuna* gave the candidacy favorable coverage, and that Jorge Curi said that the reception to be given the general, on his return from abroad, would be a veritable popular convention. Raphael, on the other hand, cooperated with a movement, begun by João Agripino and Adauto Cardoso, to have the ARENA choose a candidate proposed by civilians and not a hard liner proposed by the military. They felt that Castello, who had reservations about the Costa e Silva candidacy, was paralyzed, unable to take a step that might be interpreted as splitting the military. Raphael, at the suggestion of Agripino and Adauto, took the step when he called on General Jurandir de Bizarria Mamede, the intellectual Vila Militar commander, and sought to persuade him to run for president. Mamede, liked by Castello, had already given the idea a cold reception, and he told Raphael that he had no interest in provoking disunity in the army. A letter from Raphael, saying that army unity was sometimes less important than the health of the nation, was likewise to no avail.[13]

Costa e Silva, returning from his trip abroad on February 17, was acclaimed by a crowd of 3,500, mostly members of the armed forces. Augmenting his overwhelming military support, he promised to "humanize" the revolution and thus attracted considerable sentiment among civilians tired of austerity. The ARENA's Magalhães Pinto, merciless in his attacks on Castello's economic policy, offered to coordinate the war minister's campaign to be elected president by Congress in October, but Castello refused to let Costa e Silva avail himself of the offer.[14]

Costa e Silva's respectable standing in Rio's entrepreneurial class was indicated in a presidential poll conducted by the *Boletim Cambial*:[15]

	Votes	Percentage
Carlos Lacerda	216	31.7
Costa e Silva	117	17.3
Roberto Campos	95	14.0
Nei Braga	60	8.9
Juracy Magalhães	54	8.0
Carvalho Pinto	29	4.3
Castello Branco	26	3.8
Magalhães Pinto	26	3.8
Jurandir Mamede	13	1.9
Ademar de Barros	10	1.5
Cordeiro de Farias	8	1.2
Blank votes	24	3.6

Lacerda, speaking to the press late in February, expressed the hope of maintaining "dignified personal relations" with Costa e Silva, but he observed that Brazil's problems could not be solved "by merely replacing one general in the presidency with another general." Aware of the antagonism of Generals Golbery and Ernesto Geisel to Costa e Silva's ambition, Lacerda once more stated that the war minister's candidacy would be "devoured" by "the maneuvers of Castello Branco."[16]

Early in March the PAREDE considered presenting a presidential candidate, "provided Marshal Castello Branco does not maneuver to block the party's registration." Célio Borja and Raul Brunini returned from a trip south with reports about the enthusiasm they found for a "truly authentic party." Mauro Magalhães called PAREDE the representative of "the struggle of the new generation." However, as he pointed out, most legislators wanted to affiliate with a registered party. They felt it important to do so in time to participate in the March elections for the officerships of the legislative bodies.[17]

While Adauto Cardoso, the ARENA's choice, won the Chamber of Deputies presidency, the Guanabara legislators discussed the state assembly officerships. Negrão de Lima and the Carioca MDB, whose twenty-six legislators were not quite an absolute majority, sent José Bonifácio Diniz de Andrada to negotiate with Flexa Ribeiro, whose ARENA was reported to have ten local legislators. José Bonifácio, Negrão's cabinet secretary without portfolio, offered the ARENA a few minor officerships in the legislature. Flexa, uninterested in cooperating with Negrão, rejected the offer.

The PAREDE announced that it would run its own slate if the ARENA slate, headed by Carvalho Neto, would not accept the

PAREDE's "Principles," which included the fight for democratic institutions and adherence to the Guanabara program-budget prepared by the Lacerda administration. With Raphael in attendance, the letter about the "Principles" was signed by eight PAREDE legislators: Mauro Magalhães, Brunini, Mac Dowell Leite de Castro, Célio Borja, Everardo Magalhães Castro, Cesário de Melo, Horácio Franco, and Carlos Sampaio.[18]

Carvalho Neto pleaded with the PAREDE to prevent an MDB victory by joining the ARENA's boycott designed to avoid a quorum. When the PAREDE refused, he declared that the PAREDE participants in the election would be denied entry into the ARENA. The PAREDE, saying scornfully that its members had no interest in joining the ARENA, participated in the election. The contest for assembly president gave twenty-seven votes to Augusto Amaral Peixoto (MDB), eight votes to Célio Borja (PAREDE), and two blank votes.[19]

The PAREDE next sought to become the leader of the opposition bloc, with Mac Dowell Leite de Castro arguing that the ARENA could not serve in that capacity because it included former PSD members close to Negrão. But the PAREDE failed to gather the eleven signatures needed to establish an opposition bloc, whereas Carvalho Neto, working with the assembly's new officers, gained for the ARENA recognition as "the only representative of the opposition." After that, the PAREDE and the ARENA devoted so much time to fighting each

Castello to Roberto Campos: "Bob, my friend, what does that boy Arthur mean about humanizing our government?" (APPE drawing in *O Cruzeiro*, March 4, 1967)

other that Governor Negrão de Lima was described as not having to worry about the opposition.[20]

The PAREDE appointed Salvador Mandim and Marcelo Garcia to organizing commissions and chose Eugênio Sigaud to draw up the party statutes. The application for the party's registration, presented to the Superior Electoral Tribunal (TSE) in mid-April, was signed by ten Guanabara legislators, because Edson Guimarães and Claudionor Machado joined the eight signers of the "Principles" letter. The ARENA's Carvalho Neto, asking the government to declare the PAREDE illegal, called it a "spurious" group with "subversive intentions" and cited Article 17 of Ato Complementar No. 4, which authorized the justice minister to close down electoral organizations which failed to comply with the Act's requirements. While the TSE studied the registration application, most of the PAREDE's Carioca legislators resolved to join the MDB in case of an unfavorable decision from the tribunal. The decision, handed down in May, was unfavorable.[21]

Raphael de Almeida Magalhães told the press that the PAREDE would work on behalf of a new constitution for Brazil—a matter to which Castello had already given attention, having named a commission to make a draft. PAREDE legislators, complaining that Raphael was taking positions and negotiating with politicians and military figures without consulting the PAREDE, announced that they recognized only one leader, Lacerda, and would take positions only after he returned from his European business trip and guided them.[22]

The ten PAREDE legislators had to wait until late in June, when Lacerda met with them for five hours at the home of his son Sérgio. Aware that they wished to campaign under the MDB banner, he made it clear that he had nothing to do with their decision and said he was sorry they had not split evenly between the ARENA and MDB in order to demonstrate that he had not indicated a path to follow. Of the ten, only Célio Borja chose the ARENA, and in doing so he explained that, while he opposed the Castello administration, he could not separate himself completely from the movement of March 31, 1964. In opting for the ARENA, he joined others who, like himself, had served in the Lacerda administration: Raphael de Almeida Magalhães, Salvador Mandim, Sandra Cavalcanti, and Carlos Flexa Ribeiro.[23]

Amaral Netto, who joined the MDB, remarked that "those who want votes should join the opposition to the federal government." However, the nine PAREDE legislators who were eager to follow this advice found early in July that the Carioca MDB would not accept them. They therefore appealed to the MDB's national directorship in Brasília, considered less hostile to *Lacerdismo*.[24]

On July 11 they received a favorable ruling from the MDB national directorship, thanks principally to the efforts of Vieira de Melo, Nelson Carneiro, Martins Rodrigues, Hamilton Nogueira, and former UDN leader Adolfo de Oliveira (Rio state). As a result of the ruling, the MDB's congressional leader and vice leader, Vieira de Melo (Bahia) and Nelson Carneiro (Guanabara), were denounced by the Carioca MDB. MDB Congressman Afonso Arinos Filho objected to the admittance of a bloc that might prefer to be guided by Lacerda than by the party. The Guanabara MDB took legal action against the ruling of its national directorship but lost the case, thanks in part to lawyer Raphael Carneiro da Rocha, a state legislator who had signed the original PAREDE manifesto.[25]

In São Paulo, *Lacerdistas* Antônio Godinho, Benedito Calasans, and Afrânio de Oliveira joined Abreu Sodré in the ARENA. However, in July, when Castello persuaded the ARENA to run Carvalho Pinto for the Senate seat that Calasans occupied, Godinho, Calasans, and Afrânio de Oliveira switched to the MDB.[26]

4. Traveling Columnist (March–June 1966)

Lacerda, the businessman, devoted himself to two of his predilections, traveling abroad and writing for the Brazilian press. Together with Braga and Magalhães Lins on March 15, he left Galeão Airport (where a crowd shouted "Viva Lacerda") to spend three weeks in Europe in search of Novo Rio investors and Nova Fronteira book titles.[1]

Kubitschek, in Paris, said he had "absolutely no intention" of seeing Lacerda. After they almost met accidentally in a hotel in Lisbon, where Kubitschek planned to head a real estate company, Lacerda supplied the Mesquita's *Jornal da Tarde* with a column criticizing Kubitschek for not having saved Brazil by joining the governor's anti-Goulart position in March 1964. Noting Kubitschek's popularity in Portugal, Lacerda wrote that the Brazilian government had transformed the former president into a victim and "sort of legend." Mediocre people, he said, made "idealists" out of those who lacked "even the slightest measure of greatness."[2]

Letícia wrote to Carlos in Paris from Rio's Hotel Leme Palace, where the Lacerdas had been living since late 1965 while alterations were made at the Praia do Flamengo apartment. "I miss you a great deal. At home it is easier to be without you. Hurry back." She was looking forward, she also wrote, to being in Honolulu, Japan, and Hong Kong on their forthcoming world tour.[3]

When Carlos and Letícia left Rio on April 17 for their two months of travel, they were accompanied by Joaquim and Candinha da Silveira. The invitation to visit Japan had been extended to Lacerda to show appreciation of his defense of Japanese immigration to Brazil; but, as Lacerda reported to the Brazilian press, Japan was doing so well that emigration was no longer required to find work for its youth. "In no other place but here," he wrote, "can one say that a conscientiously made visit is a traveling university."[4]

From the Orient, Carlos and Letícia went to the Middle East and Europe. Carlos received letters about business matters from his sons. Sérgio, also discussing politics, wrote that Abreu Sodré would become governor of São Paulo, having passed "with flying colors" the Castello government's "tests of submission" and "humiliation." Sérgio called Raphael's secret conversation with Quadros useful for the development, with Carlos, of "a common strategy for the return of civilians to public life." "I become more and more convinced that you, in choosing 'liberty,' have made the best selection for all of us."[5]

The Lacerdas were joined in Europe by Congressmen Curi and Godinho, and they returned to Rio with them on June 18, just in time to be with Olga on her seventy-fourth birthday. Thus they missed the performances in May of *Júlio César* at São Paulo's Municipal Theater. Critic Decio de Almeida Prado wrote that Lacerda's translation could be "easily grasped by the listener," but he called the production "cold and distant from the audience" and said the lack of dynamism might have resulted from the Brazilian actors' unfamiliarity with the classics.[6]

The trips abroad did not seem to interfere with the publication of Lacerda's newspaper articles, which appeared almost daily in the *Jornal da Tarde* and *Diário de Notícias* and infrequently in the *Jornal do Brasil*. The articles spoke not a little of mediocrity and stupidity ("the worst of evils"), predicted that civil war would result from the path chosen by the government, and were spiced with unkind remarks about the writer's favorite targets. The worst fault of Adauto Cardoso, he wrote, was not his well-known vanity, but was ignorance; and he added that Adauto might perform a generous act once in ten years, whereas Golbery, who had consciously become a neofascist, would never perform one. Juracy Magalhães was also called a neofascist, but, Lacerda wrote, "he does not know he is one."[7]

The longest article, written from Japan, decried "the transformation of Brazil into American economic territory" and called the Communist Party "the only one open to the new generation." Sérgio wrote his father that the *Jornal do Brasil*'s Nascimento Brito found the article "repetitive and too long," but that João Dantas would print it in the *Diário de Notícias* in three installments. Soon the article appeared there in nine installments.[8]

The readers of Lacerda's articles learned that President Quadros had chosen a correct foreign policy but had presented it in too sensational a manner and with the help of a foreign minister, Afonso Arinos de Melo Franco, who was "perpetually immature." When the Castello Branco government decided to furnish troops for the Inter-American Peace Force, sent to the Dominican Republic at the urging of the United States, Lacerda called the Brazilian step "the most stupid in the military and political history of the republic." Referring to still another foreign affairs "disgrace" for Brazil, Lacerda reported that only its "lack of government" could explain its failure to sell coffee, cotton, textiles, and industrial products to the Far East and Middle East.[9]

On the domestic front, Lacerda denounced the Castello administration for wishing to find a substitute that would do away with *estabilidade,* the Vargas ruling that provided tenure to all workers who had been with companies for at least ten years. He called Castello's proposal a threat to the workers, designed, like steps against the students, to provoke the chaos that could be cited as a reason for Castello to continue in office. Lacerda argued that *estabilidade,* a "guarantee" for the workers, should be "perfected, never suppressed." Upon learning that the rate of inflation was declining, Lacerda wrote that the change had been simply an automatic response to the downfall of the Goulart government. As for the Supreme Court, Lacerda seemed to have developed new ideas; he wrote that Institutional Act No. 2, which allowed the appointment of new justices, had "destroyed the judicial power." Noting also that the Ato had been used to suspend the political rights of four Guanabara legislators, he called it a "mockery."[10]

Lacerda's "On the Path to the Monarchy," written with sardonic humor in Lisbon, suggested that people entering the ARENA were "on the lookout, with greedy eyes, for the title of count." "Sr. Adauto Cardoso, for example, with his splendid white hair, would be a good count of Curvelo, Minas Gerais. Sr. Luís Viana Filho, a reedition of the Marquis of Bahia." Lacerda suggested that General Golbery do Couto e Silva, unable to be Prince Talleyrand, "might be content to be the new Baron Münchhausen." Castello, a possible monarch to be known as "Humberto the First and the Last," was described as delighted with the praise of Roberto Marinho, who could become "the Grand Master of the National Order of Flatterers."[11] Marinho did hold the title of Chancellor of the National Order of Merit, and for this "disgrace" Lacerda attacked Castello more than once. Late in

May Marinho resigned from the chancellor's post in a letter in which he told Castello that it had best not be held by anyone subject to slanderous accusations.[12]

Lacerda, calling himself a man who could have earned a living as a professional prophet about Brazil, prophesied "free of charge" that Brazil would stage Latin America's most serious and popular anti–United States movement, and that Castello would either continue as president beyond his term, or else fall, "deeply mortified," flat on his face. Support for General Costa e Silva, he wrote a little later, was strong because his election represented the only peaceful means the army had of ridding the government and itself of Castello. However, Lacerda criticized the general for announcing no program and maintained that the offer to "humanize" economic policy was meaningless. Writing about Colonel Álcio Costa e Silva, the war minister's son, Lacerda said: "With his father's candidacy emerging, he shows so little confidence in his government that he is leaving the army to dedicate himself to a career in a firm that has business dealings with the government."[13]

When he brought his series of articles to a close on July 4, Lacerda told his readers that he had been hurt more by the misunderstandings of his presentations than by the attacks and "betrayals" they had aroused. He explained that he had simply been providing, without bitterness, disinterested warnings and guidance, and had demonstrated that Brazilian youth was faced with choosing between the only two militant and true parties that existed: the Communist Party, on the one hand, and, on the other, the Party of the Americans, which had eliminated him because of his democratic and patriotic ideas, and which was now making sure that the next president would be "domesticated." If he continued writing his articles, he said, it would be easy for those who were handling things badly to blame him for the "coming crisis." But he made it clear that his "farewell to arms" was not prompted by any fear of being *cassado*. "I have already been *cassado;* if they would deprive me of my political rights they would be doing me a favor, and so they do not do it."[14]

5. Preparing an Alliance with Former Foes (August 1966)

Lacerda's friend Joaquim da Silveira was a friend of Kubitschek's and sought to bring about a Kubitschek-Lacerda alliance for promoting democracy and economic development in Brazil. In the first part of 1965, at an all-afternoon lunch in Paris with Juscelino and Sarah Kubitschek and former ambassador Hugo Gouthier, he found that the idea did not appeal to Gouthier, unfriendly to Lacerda, but pleased Juscelino. "If this conversation has positive consequences," Juscelino said, "I'll speak with Lacerda." The former president gave Joaquim permission to sound out the governor and said that if Lacerda seemed interested, Joaquim should ask Congressman Renato Archer (PSD, Maranhão) to look up Lacerda.[1]

Lacerda was not interested, as he made known to Joaquim in Rio. "You are," he told the textile executive, "going to end up being arrested, and if you are arrested I won't release you!" But a little later, at the Silveira house in Bangu, Joaquim found the governor, who was preparing to go to Pará, in a calmer mood and willing to consider the idea.

In the north in July 1965, Lacerda praised the Belém-Brasília highway in a public statement. This praise for a Kubitschek project led the hopeful Joaquim to believe that Lacerda was coming to view Kubitschek in a different light. When he next saw the governor, he said: "You have changed." As Lacerda did not object to Joaquim's proposal to report "the change" to Kubitschek, Joaquim suggested that Lacerda speak with Archer about an alliance with Kubitschek.[2]

Sandra Cavalcanti, Lacerda has written, was another who brought him a message from Kubitschek. The former president, speaking with Sandra in New York, told her that an understanding might be useful for saving the civilian power. Despite this message and the work of Joaquim da Silveira, Lacerda did not look up Kubitschek when both were in Europe in March and April 1966, a failure that he later called a mistake, "because, if we had met, the understanding would have been quicker and easier."[3]

During Lacerda's visit to Brasília, to testify on August 11, 1966, at the CPI investigating the TV Globo–Time-Life deal, several oppositionist congressmen, among them Hermógenes Príncipe de Oliveira (MDB, Bahia) and MDB leader Vieira de Melo, spoke to him about the merit of his reaching an understanding with Kubitschek. Back in Rio, he found that a scheme to bring Kubitschek, Goulart, and Lacerda together in a prodemocracy movement was being promoted by Artur de Lima Cavalcanti, a former PTB congressman from Pernambuco who had lost his political rights for activities considered leftist.[4]

Lima Cavalcanti first expressed his ideas in a letter to Sérgio Lacerda, whom he knew. Carlos Lacerda was cool to the scheme at the outset; but later he asked Hélio Fernandes to explore it with Raphael de Almeida Magalhães, who, Lacerda said with affectionate humor, was demonstrating his Machiavellian characteristics by dealing with *Juscelinistas*. As Raphael was busy preparing to run for Congress as an ARENA candidate in the elections of November 15, 1966, it was

Stranded Lacerda, with paddle, and an unenthusiastic MDB. (APPE drawing in *O Cruzeiro*, August 2, 1966)

Hélio Fernandes who implemented Lima Cavalcanti's idea by inviting representatives of Kubitschek, Goulart, and Lacerda for discussions at the Fernandes home. Sérgio Lacerda represented Carlos.[5]

Carlos Lacerda, in the meantime, published a letter which government people felt had the objective of making him the leading oppositionist. The letter, addressed to the *Jornal do Brasil*, made it evident that Lacerda would no longer abide by the appeal of Magalhães Pinto that Costa e Silva be spared from his attacks. Lacerda wrote that he had no interest in the election of "another general, manifestly and alarmingly unprepared to occupy the position of usurper of the Revolution." Costa e Silva was described as taking a training course "in kindergarten" to become a public figure, and as having approved the filthy mess being carried out by the government. His inauguration, Lacerda wrote, was "more of a threat than a promise."[6]

The preparatory meetings, arranged by Hélio Fernandes, were followed by formal ones in the luxurious home of industrialist Alberto Lee, more satisfactory for secrecy than that of Hélio Fernandes because cars could be parked within the surrounding walls. Lee was a cousin of the wife of Ênio Silveira, the leftist director of the Civilização Brasileira book publishing firm who had been visited by Lima Cavalcanti. The first such meeting, on the night of August 22–23, was attended by Carlos and Sérgio Lacerda, Lima Cavalcanti, Hélio Fernandes, Ênio Silveira, Brigadeiro Francisco Teixeira (leader of the air force during Goulart's presidency), and Wilson Fadul, who had been

Goulart's health minister. Subsequent meetings were held without Lima Cavalcanti, who had to leave for Pernambuco.[7]

Renato Archer, who had been a PSD opponent of Lacerda, was not at the first meeting at Lee's home. Although Lacerda had phoned him to say that he had a letter for him from Kubitschek, Archer had qualms about the proposed alliance and did not hurry to receive the letter. He finally yielded to Kubitschek's wishes after the former president's daughter Márcia and her husband transmitted her father's plea. A Kubitschek-Lacerda alliance, Archer concluded, would probably be useful to Kubitschek, long accused of corruption by Lacerda, and he felt that the aggressive Lacerda, considered to have good military connections, might do more than anyone to weaken the regime and speed up a return to democracy.[8]

Starting with the second meeting at Lee's home, on the night of August 24–25, Renato Archer was constantly in attendance. For a while his authorization from Kubitschek was simply to listen and report. Later he was so active that Ernâni do Amaral Peixoto has stated that it was Archer, not Lacerda or Kubitschek, who did the most to keep the movement alive. A man of intelligence and many connections, Archer lunched and dined with politicians whom he invited to join the movement.

At Lee's home, Archer was well impressed by Lacerda. So was Hélio Fernandes, who writes that, at the "nine meetings" there, "people who had been engaged in hostile conflicts never imagined that the meetings could have been so cordial. No one accused Lacerda of anything, and at no time did Lacerda have a word censuring anyone."[9]

In describing the "collective spirit" as "the best and most unselfish I have known," Hélio Fernandes confirms the observations of Sérgio Lacerda, who had leftist friends and helped organize meetings. Sérgio's wife, Maria Clara Mariani, had separated from Sérgio, to the regret of Carlos and Letícia, and Sérgio was living in a bachelor apartment. There he arranged for Carlos to meet with Communists and was pleased with the cordiality and respect shown for differing opinions. The meetings at Lee's house, he has said, were "wonderful." "My father acted with grace. He knew the sacrifice to himself. There was not the bravado of the UDN. My father had been utilized most of his life. He had been seen as the champion of the far Right, only to be left aside when the far Right took over. He was still so strong that he could gather former foes. My father went again to the main stream of his life." What was happening, according to Sérgio, was "really democratic." Cassette tapes of the discussions at Lee's house were taken to Kubitschek in Lisbon, sometimes by members of the former president's family.[10]

At the August 22–23 meeting it was decided to avoid setting up one of those *frente única* (united front) movements that often ended in the hands of Communists and were apt to be short-lived. The new movement, it was resolved, should stress the need of Brazilian development and "democratization." Lacerda, rejecting the term "redemocratization," said it suggested a return to the past, and he argued that Brazil had never enjoyed real democracy. Toward the end of the meeting, Lacerda asked whether it would be a good idea to issue a manifesto that, without attacking individuals, would denounce crimes committed by the government and submit suggestions for putting Brazil on the right track. After the idea was warmly accepted, the discussion about who should sign the manifesto was left unfinished because of the lateness of the hour.[11]

At the next meeting a majority rejected a suggestion that the manifesto be signed by one hundred prominent Brazilians. Instead, it was agreed that the signers, and leaders of the movement, should be former Presidents Kubitschek, Goulart, and Quadros, and former Governor Lacerda, whose presidential campaign had been canceled. The names of former President Dutra and former Governor Magalhães Pinto came up, but their involvement in Costa e Silva's presidential campaign made it unlikely that they would join the movement. The general feeling was that Quadros would likewise decline to participate, but Lacerda insisted on approaching him. Hélio Fernandes objected and called Quadros "a complete buffoon, without integrity, honor, or responsibility, whose participation in any undertaking will assure its becoming either ridiculous or a failure." He was overruled by those who argued that the movement should be as broad as possible.[12]

Lacerda, who planned to be in São Paulo after attending a wedding ceremony in Curitiba on September 1, got in touch with Quadros and learned that he was very interested in conferring with him. Arrangements were made for the two to meet at the home of a São Paulo industrialist at 8:00 A.M. But Quadros failed to appear. Instead, he informed the industrialist by phone that he found it necessary to testify on behalf of a friend's daughter who was separating from her husband. The former president, who had a history of inventing excuses for not keeping appointments, said he would be at the industrialist's home at 5:00 P.M.; and so Lacerda, canceling his afternoon schedule in Rio, returned to the industrialist's home for the new appointment. But at 5:00 P.M. Quadros telephoned again, this time to say that he had gone to his retreat in Guarujá, near Santos, and would be happy to see Lacerda there. Lacerda, declining this suggestion, concluded that those who had spoken of Quadros' probable reluctance had been right. Quadros, he and Hélio Fernandes have written, neglected his duty in order to please the government in the hope of regaining his political rights, perhaps through his friend General Golbery. In the words of Lacerda: "On a crucial question, he once more took refuge in flight; one could say that he renounced his leadership, just as he had renounced his presidency."[13]

During Lacerda's trip to Curitiba, *Visão* magazine came out with an article in which the former Carioca governor called on all democratic forces, whether progressive or conservative, to overcome their divergences and animosities and unite in a broad antigovernment union. Newsstand copies of *Visão* were quickly sold, perhaps because the article suggested the use of arms to overthrow the regime. "To oust a usurper," Lacerda wrote, "all arms are legitimate, including those used to bring the usurper to power. If a coup can be made to install a semi-dictator, why should not the same arms be used to install a government capable of quickly reestablishing direct elections, democratic guarantees, and inalienable human rights?"[14]

The article, which *Visão* explained was contrary to its own views, presented in a forceful manner the chief points that Lacerda had been proclaiming in his battle against Castello Branco. It dealt with "the reactionary, *entreguista* mentality" of the National War College's Sorbonne Group, whose orientation, "condemned even in the American military, infiltrated the so-called IPES, where notorious agents of private American interests arranged to have the power militarily occupied by individuals who opened the way for those agents."[15] Brazil, Lacerda wrote, was governed by the IMF and the CIA. Castello's administration was described as so "cringing, unpopular, and imbecilic" that it would lead to a Communist victory.[16]

According to the *Visão* article, Costa e Silva, instead of leading the army to overthrow Castello, betrayer of the revolution, had "purchased the right to impose his presidential candidacy on Castello, who detests it." But, Lacerda wrote, Costa e Silva might be even worse than Castello. He called Costa e Silva's "unknown" candidacy the offspring of the crisis of October 1965, "that is, a sleight of hand that is unjustifiable morally, politically, juridically, and historically."[17]

Asked in Curitiba to comment on his *Visão* article, Lacerda replied: "I have never said anything that had consequences on the following day. Generally they start by calling me wrong and then, a little too late, say I am right. This time I believe the routine is different. I have found no one capable of stating that my declarations are not completely true."[18]

Vieira de Melo declared that Lacerda's call for military action conflicted with the policy of the opposition. Military men issued a statement saying that the army would not allow Lacerda to go un-punished if he continued offending the president.

Carlos Castello Branco, in his daily *Jornal do Brasil* column, pointed out that no one in the MDB had dared combat the president as Lacerda was doing and that Lacerda had become the chief inter-preter of the opposition's sentiments. "He is winning," the columnist wrote, "the leadership which the oppositionists deny him today, just as his UDN companions denied it to him formerly." "The truth is, his interviews and declarations are having an increasing resonance in a political atmosphere saturated with pessimism and eager for an assertion of strength against the massive power of the dominant military."[19]

6. Reactions to the Frente Ampla Idea (August–September 1966)

During the first meeting at Lee's house, Lacerda was delegated to draw up the new movement's manifesto. At his Novo Rio office, he called for his son Sérgio and secretary Maria Thereza Correia de Mello and told them that what he was about to dictate was confidential. Sérgio showed no surprise at the dictation, but Maria Thereza was so shocked at the revelation of Lacerda's plan to associate with Kubi-tschek and Goulart that she found it difficult to take notes.[1]

Lacerda, about to spend a weekend in Rocio, took copies of the draft with him. He called it the manifesto of "a movement to be known as the Frente Ampla"—thus using the term Broad Front, invented by a part of the press when it started to mention rumors about what was afoot.[2]

At Rocio, Lacerda let his friends in on the contents of the draft. They were so absorbed reading copies when Antonio Dias Rebello Filho and his wife reached Rocio that the new arrivals went unno-ticed by everyone except Lacerda, who gave the doctor a copy. La-cerda, walking in the garden with Rebello, asked him for his reaction. The draft, Rebello said, repeated what Lacerda had been asserting about the need of civilian leaders to unite against a military dictator-ship; but, Rebello asked, "what fruits will this provide?" Lacerda compared it with the famous manifesto issued by Mineiros against the Vargas dictatorship in 1943. "It will provide fruits only many years from now."[3]

Walter and Lamy Cunto, at Rocio on Sunday morning, were with a group that heard Lacerda read the draft aloud. Like others, Walter Cunto was immensely surprised. He interrupted Lacerda's reading to say: "I don't think Brazil is ready for this." Letícia Lacerda agreed with Cunto and told Carlos: "It won't work; you are going to lose." Carlos turned away from Cunto and Letícia and went on with his reading, addressing the others, none of whom was critical. Joaquim and Candinha da Silveira were enthusiastic.[4]

Starting late in August, the Frente Ampla stirred up far more interest than the indirect elections for governors (won on September 3 by all twelve ARENA candidates including Abreu Sodré and Luís Viana Filho) or Costa e Silva's uncontested bid in the presidential race (to be settled by Congress on October 3). MDB leader Vieira de Melo defended the Frente Ampla but warned against an appeal to arms, whereas Hermógenes Príncipe, another defender, asserted that it was licit to use any means against a government of usurpation. Goulart supporter Armindo Doutel de Andrade, MDB vice leader in the lower house, praised the Frente. So did Congressman Osvaldo Lima Filho, vice president of the MDB.[5]

But most of the MDB leaders involved in the congressional elections of November 15 (which did arouse some interest) found little public support for the Frente and were, therefore, cold to it. An important opponent of associating with Lacerda was Oscar Passos, the MDB president. He warned that with Lacerda in it, the Frente might become an instrument for "those who broke with the present government not because of their love of democracy, but because of personal frustration." In another remark aimed at Lacerda, he said the front should not be so broad as to include men who, on the pretext of struggling for redemocratization, favored "objectives no less dictatorial than the present situation." Tancredo Neves, Carlos Murilo, and João Herculino, MDB congressmen from Minas, said that a union of oppositionists would be acceptable as long as Lacerda were excluded.[6]

Press reaction was overwhelmingly unfavorable. *O Estado de S. Paulo* could not countenance any union with Kubitschek and Goulart, and the *Jornal do Brasil* wrote that a consultation with political figures made it clear that the Frente Ampla was not viable. *O Globo* said the nation disliked the idea of the "folkloric front," a sack of cats, whose leaders lacked democratic identity cards. *Última Hora*'s Danton Jobim called the scheme a way for Lacerda to "unleash his coup," and the *Diário de Notícias* called it a "basket of crabs, discards of the Revolution and perpetrators of the subversion and corruption that so greatly harmed the country."[7]

Lacerda returned on September 6 to publishing daily newspaper columns, again using São Paulo's *Jornal da Tarde,* but, in Rio, substituting the *Tribuna da Imprensa* for the now hostile *Diário de Notícias.* He opened his new series by observing that, in the face of his recent silence, even Roberto Marinho had become bold ("although he never could become intelligent") and had supplied material for the investigation of irregularities attributed to the Guandu project. Lacerda vowed to carry out his patriotic duty of speeding the inevitable collapse of the Castello–Golbery–Roberto Campos–Haroldo Poland group and help prepare for the future. He apologized to Rio's "picturesque and lovable" Conde de Laje Street for having called Castello its angel.[8]

Like the *Correio da Manhã,* Lacerda's columns gave support to the movement of university students who clashed with police while demanding the reopening of the UNE and an end to the "dictatorship," to tuition payments for higher education, and to American "interference" in Brazilian education. After Education Minister Raimundo Moniz de Aragão blamed the students' manifestations on Communists, Lacerda scoffed at this explanation but wrote that if the government continued "abandoning the young people," the Communists would become the "heirs to their revolt." Instead of telling students to concentrate on their studies, as he had done in 1963, he reprimanded the government for taking that position and for not allowing the students "the right to participate in national reform."[9] Condemning elections that were not direct, he called the street disorders "a revolution by youth, the necessary revolution, the inevitable revolution." Justice Minister Carlos Medeiros Silva accused the Frente Ampla of stimulating the students to riot.[10]

In the meantime, MDB congressional vice leader Doutel de Andrade conversed about the Frente Ampla by telephone with Goulart, who was in Uruguay. He learned that Goulart was not opposed to a prodemocracy dialogue among all political forces but seemed disinclined to sign a manifesto with Lacerda and preferred that the various opposition forces sign separate manifestoes, "parallel and simultaneous." In Lacerda's opinion this idea was "a negation of the Frente Ampla, whose point of departure was the joint manifesto."[11] Brizola was consulted in Uruguay by an emissary, although at Lee's house someone had suggested that the inclusion of his name might make it difficult to have the manifesto published, because it was well known that he was working for guerrilla activities against the Brazilian government. Brizola said that the Frente Ampla would be ineffective, and objected to having the movement headed by Lacerda.[12]

Archer, after speaking with Kubitschek in Lisbon early in September, told the press that Kubitschek fully supported the Frente and a joint manifesto. The announcement hid from the public the problems Archer had with Kubitschek—problems that led Archer to observe later that it was difficult "to sell Lacerda's ideas to Kubitschek," and that Kubitschek "never really accepted that union with Carlos."

At the outset, Archer found it none too easy to be more persuasive than Sebastião Paes de Almeida, who was close to Costa e Silva intimate Mário Andreazza and who suggested to the exile that he might be able to return to Brazil and recover his political rights during the next administration if he would reject the Frente Ampla.

Kubitschek had so many objections to Lacerda's draft of a manifesto that, according to Archer, "practically every sentence had to be negotiated." The former president preferred "redemocratization" to "democratization," which, he said, implied that his own administration had not been democratic. After Edmundo Moniz, "representative of intellectuals," called on Kubitschek, the press reported Kubitschek's insistence that the manifesto leave no doubt that an armed coup was not contemplated. Kubitschek felt that the simple statement "We do not want to return to the past" would suffice without a long explanation, and he favored a clear, succinct program without many specific details.[13]

Ernâni do Amaral Peixoto, who did not like Lacerda, was asked by Kubitschek for a report about the reactions to the Frente Ampla in political circles. In speaking to the press, the former head of the PSD cited the unsuccessful effort of San Tiago Dantas to mold heterogeneous forces into a common front. The intent of Kubitschek and Lacerda to join forces, he said, did not mean that their followers, long bitter opponents, would view the union with favor. One woman, who had contributed generously to Kubitschek campaigns, was so upset at the Frente Ampla that she told Amaral Peixoto: "Your friend is not to come to my house again, because I won't receive him anymore."[14]

Lacerda, who had built much of his career on excoriating Vargas, Kubitschek, and Goulart, was in a more difficult position than Kubitschek. *Malamadas,* as his admiring women were called, were shocked; military supporters were horrified. Speaking to Raul Brunini and a few other close political friends, Lacerda predicted that the chief difficulty he would have would be with his former backers. He appealed to Brunini and others to convince these longtime admirers that Brazil's only possible salvation from twenty or thirty years of dictatorship lay in the united effort of "civilian leadership."[15]

On a trip to São Paulo, where anti-Getulista sentiment was strong among his friends, Lacerda was met with expressions of dismay. Nelson and Doris Pereira hated the idea of Lacerda trying to ally himself with Goulart and Kubitschek. Father Antônio Godinho, apprehensive about the reception to be given the Frente manifesto, heard Lacerda say it would be praised in the future. The *padre* remarked that what was important was the present.[16]

Speaking to the press in São Paulo on September 14, Lacerda

pointed out that longtime political opponents Winston Churchill and Clement Attlee had joined forces against the invasion of England. Castello, he added, had made use of former Goulart cabinet ministers. Writing in *Fatos & Fotos*, Lacerda said that the Frente was anything but subversive, because it was attempting to do away with the subversion in Brazil that Castello was carrying out by such acts as suspending political rights of Gaúcho state legislators in order to defeat the opposition there.[17]

Castello, speaking in Roraima on September 20, said the government understood "the real reasons why people of most diverse and antagonistic backgrounds unite in an effort to perturb or hinder" the work of creating "the bases to allow Brazil to become a rich and strong country." "Frustrated ambitions, vanished privileges, or political concepts that have been threatened by the national recuperation seek to join hands in a reconciliation which must be called spurious. . . . Those who have lost their memories or are blinded by ambitions are certainly forgetful that the people keep their eyes open and minds informed. And so no one is fooled, even when individuals change disguises and renounce ideas, judgments, and sentiments."[18]

Asked about the Frente Ampla at a Planalto Palace press conference on October 1, the president said he agreed completely with the *Diário de Notícias* and quoted it: "Inwardly nobody forgets or abjures what he has felt and said about another person. But outwardly one pretends— because each wants to make use of the possible strength or prestige of the other, the assistance that the other might bring to hidden purposes. In short, each believes he is fooling the others." "But," Castello added, "they do not fool the Revolution, the government or the ARENA, nor the people and the armed forces." Congressman Rui Santos, ARENA vice leader, declared that the people, with their good memories, could not forget that Goulart, branded a traitor by Lacerda, had tried to have Lacerda seized, or that Kubitschek, whose *cassação* on grounds of personal corruption had been sought by Lacerda, had tried in 1957 to void Lacerda's congressional mandate.[19]

Hard line air force Colonel João Paulo Moreira Burnier, who had led the Aragarças rebellion against Kubitschek in 1959, did not hide his hatred of the Frente Ampla. Colonel Gustavo Borges shared Burnier's sentiment but for the time being sought to avoid the impression that he was betraying Lacerda by "leaving a sinking ship." The hard line's disapproval was expressed publicly by Colonel Boaventura Cavalcanti, in what the *Jornal do Brasil* called "one more blow to the Frente Ampla," and was expressed privately, in a courteous letter to Lacerda, by Colonel Ferdinando de Carvalho. Ferdinando wrote that he shared Lacerda's apprehensions about the Castello administration but that neither Jango nor Juscelino had the moral qualifications to join Lacerda in a campaign to build up Brazil. Lacerda, the colonel wrote, should not "pull from the mud those who became bogged down in it as a result of their own errors," but should recognize that new leaders, authentic nationalists, were needed in the fight against the internationalistic and unpatriotic oligarchy that upheld the government.[20]

Miguel Arraes, detested by the hard line, wrote from Algeria to tell a friend that Lacerda was apparently making some progress in his thinking because his *Visão* article called American influence in Brazil excessive. But the former governor of Pernambuco saw the new front as nothing more than an effort by its members to obtain "the right to participate in the traditional political game." He wrote that the Frente Ampla, if victorious, might carry out "a political policy more liberal in some respects," although it had already demonstrated "very grave defects." He said he was obviously not involved in the front, "so full of contradictions," but added that it would be an error to combat it.[21]

7. The Frente Ampla in Retreat
(Late September–Mid-October 1966)

In the latter part of September the *Jornal do Brasil* described the Frente Ampla as "in retreat." Problems were created by the MDB's "repudiation" of the Frente and by Goulart's reluctance to sign its proposed manifesto, and especially by what Kubitschek called the government's "intimidation campaign."[1]

Vieira de Melo, a supporter of the Frente Ampla, consulted members of the opposition party. He found that most of them did not share his view, and therefore he announced, on September 21, that the MDB would keep apart from the Frente and that if its members associated themselves with it, they were doing so in their own names. The announcement was hailed by the São Paulo state MDB.[2]

A few days later, word was received that the government planned to act against the Frente Ampla, which it considered a "political CGT" and therefore "spurious." Justice Minister Medeiros Silva warned that Institutional Act No. 2 prohibited political statements by the *cassados* and that violations would result in investigations and punishments. After investigators denounced Kubitschek for having omitted mention of a Mercedes Benz automobile in his 1963 income tax declaration, MDB congressional candidate Hélio Fernandes wrote

Frente Ampla sign held by people hidden by Lacerda's coat. (APPE drawing in *O Cruzeiro*, September 25, 1966)

that the Castello government was threatening to confiscate the possessions of Kubitschek and Goulart if they signed the Frente Ampla manifesto.[3]

Kubitschek, boarding a plane in Paris for New York shortly after the October 3 election of Costa e Silva, said that new charges of "administrative corruption," presented against himself to the Supreme Court, were part of the campaign to prevent his signing the Frente Ampla manifesto. The campaign, he said, included steps against his supporters. "The so-called democratic government accuses me of illicit enrichment because I received, as an homage from the people of Brasília, a piece of land worth about two thousand dollars." From New York, author Josué Montello brought the news that Kubitschek would not sign.[4]

The press reported that the Frente Ampla seemed destined to failure, with Kubitschek and Goulart unable or unwilling to sign its manifesto. But Lacerda, in his columns, declared that even if his new activity should be his "last service to his country," he would fulfill his duty by keeping in touch with the absent "authentic leaderships," which, he said, had become enhanced, rather than weakened, by adversity. He stepped up his attacks. Calling Costa e Silva "untruthful" for asserting that Brazilians were free to speak as they wished, he wrote that he was prohibited from discussing politics on radio or television, and that students had learned recently that liberty to speak in the streets was limited. He described the armed forces as not prepared to run the government of a country as important and complex as Brazil. When Costa e Silva used the word "violent" to describe him, Lacerda called the accusation a droll one. Where, he asked, would Costa e Silva be "except for my alleged violence?"[5]

Lacerda wrote that Castello, like Costa e Silva, was given to being tearful, and had broken down in tears upon learning that Congress on October 3 had selected the "future Benefactor of the Fatherland." "Brazil does not have a president. It has a sulky child whose importance wanes with each passing day. This is the reason he cried." As for Castello's remark that the Frente Ampla consisted of people seeking to fool each other, Lacerda said that the remark appeared to describe the Castello–Costa e Silva game. "But no, it was the Frente Ampla, frank and open, that the president wanted to describe. And in so doing he only described himself. . . . The absolute lack of generosity, the sterility of imagination, the morbid distrust, the total disbelief in people, the refusal to recognize what is noble and honorable in each person—all this makes up that twisted and forbidding figure."[6]

On October 10 it was rumored that Castello would cancel the mandates of some congressmen who were handling Frente Ampla affairs for Goulart and Kubitschek. Chamber of Deputies President Adauto Cardoso declared more than once that there would be no *cassações*. He was therefore shocked on October 12 when Castello suspended the mandates and political rights of ten politicians, some of whom had been corresponding with Goulart and Kubitschek. Six, including Doutel de Andrade, César Prieto, and Sebastião Paes de Almeida, were congressmen.[7]

With most of the congressmen campaigning for the November 15 elections, Adauto took it upon himself to sign a note saying that only the Chamber could suspend congressional mandates and leaving it clear that the six congressmen were considered unaffected by Castello's action. He was supported by Senate President Auro de Moura Andrade. Five of the congressmen remained in the Chamber building and condemned the government, leading *O Estado de S. Paulo* to write that the "counter-Revolution" was working in "open defiance of the regime installed after the victory of March 31." On October 20 Castello used the authority granted by Ato 2 to declare Congress in recess until November 22. Army Police Commander Carlos de Meira Mattos directed the military operation that closed Congress.[8]

Lacerda denied that Adauto's defiance of Castello was motivated solely by a desire to attract votes in the coming congressional election, and wrote that Adauto wanted, "a little late, it is true, to be a great Brazilian."[9]

MDB congressmen, assuming that Costa e Silva would act democratically and never close Congress, accepted the suggestion of Costa
e Silva admirer Amaral Netto that Padre Godinho and Renato Archer
ask Lacerda to speak with General Afonso de Albuquerque Lima
about the possibility of having the military put Costa e Silva in the
presidency right away. Lacerda dined with Albuquerque Lima, thanks
to arrangements made by the general's sister Geli, wife of José Cândido Moreira de Souza. He learned from the general that an immediate takeover by Costa e Silva would be impossible; and he was warned
that his activities might cost him his political rights. With the renewal of *cassações*, Albuquerque Lima said, Lacerda should be careful. "I shall," Lacerda told the general, "do everything possible to save
Brazil, even in the face of the threat you mention."[10]

Lacerda did not expect to gain the understanding of the generals.
When he and Joaquim da Silveira addressed young officers, Lacerda
faulted the senior officers, calling them set in their ways and lacking
in imagination.[11] In a major effort to regain the support he had lost
among the younger members of the military, he published his "Letter
to a uniformed friend" in the *Tribuna da Imprensa* on October 21 and
22 and in the *Jornal da Tarde* on October 21, 24, and 25. In a postscript
to the first installment, he wrote: "If the second part of this letter is
not published, please understand that it contains no slander or incite-
ment to revolt but is merely an expression of truth and of an intimate,
deep-seated, and profound indignation."[12]

The "Letter" was a plea for the military to redeem themselves
by immediately installing Costa e Silva as president and instituting
a democratic government with the elections "that you promised to
defend," and an economic program that would stress development
and thus bring about social peace.[13] When the military had left the
barracks in 1964, Lacerda wrote, the people had felt certain that they
would not permit the implantation of a dictatorship. But he contended that, with "direct and free elections" eliminated and Congress
recently closed, the people had lost faith in the military, and that, if
the armed forces did not assume responsibility by acting as he suggested, the people would hate and fear them.[14]

Lacerda was careful to point out that his call for the immediate
inauguration of Costa e Silva was not made, as "idiots" were saying,
in order "to get close to" the new marshal. Maintaining that he had
no need to get close to anyone, he added that he continued to lack
confidence in Costa e Silva, "frivolous in his relationships, halluci-
nated, and unprepared." Hoping for an improvement in Costa e Silva,
which he said would surprise him, Lacerda wrote: "I believe that up
to now he has been very inferior, ambitious, and opportunistic." In

any event, he also wrote, the immediate inauguration of the president-elect would free Brazil from the dictator that the country did not want.[15]

Lacerda maintained that the military had gone along with steps that had fostered, not reduced, corruption and subversion. Subversion, he contended, was at a peak because "personal power is subversive." As for the national security, Lacerda quoted United States Defense Secretary Robert McNamara as saying that "without development there is no security."[16]

Lacerda claimed that Castello had given the people reasons to think well of Communism because "its enemies are so vile, vain, egotistical, incompetent, and brutal." He said that the only political parties functioning in Brazil were the military and the Communists, "whose cause in the eyes of the people you have helped by permitting the elimination of all democratic leaderships." Goulart was described as having followers and Juscelino as enjoying popularity, whereas Castello, Lacerda said, could count only on brute force.[17]

Noting that Negrão de Lima had been the first governor to back Castello for closing Congress, Lacerda told his "uniformed friend": "You know that you are the one responsible for that monstrous collusion." Only once before, he added, had Congress been closed to set up a dictatorship, and that had been under very different circumstances, with a popular leader, Vargas, at the helm, in an international setting that featured totalitarian tendencies.[18]

Lacerda vowed to let no threat prevent him from expressing his "loyal and fraternal" words. "What most torments me and obliges me to write these words is the irremediable separation you are allowing to develop between the unarmed nation and those who wear uniforms and bear arms." He would, he wrote, be pleased to lay down his life "if in that way I could prevent Brazil from becoming divided between two unequal forces: one small but armed and the other immense but intimidated or unbelieving." Such a sacrifice, he told his "uniformed friend," would be well worthwhile if it would bring about the recovery of "the conscience you are losing."[19]

8. Comments

Castello Branco was a man who appeared most at ease when confronted by crises. Speaking in a relaxed mood to American journalist Hal Hendrix about the events that had led him to close Congress temporarily, Castello blamed the "episode" on some "desperate counter-Revolutionaries" who lacked public support. The aim of his government for almost three years, he said, had been to establish the best possible conditions for the installation again of a normal government on March 15, 1967.[1] The president had asked Justice Minister Carlos Medeiros Silva to submit, for his consideration and that of Congress, a revision of the draft he had received of the new constitution that he hoped would be "an instrument of peace and order, destined to last for decades."[2] "As far as the economic situation is concerned," he told the American journalist, "we have established the basis for the beginning of development again on a realistic basis."[3]

Analysts in the White House reported to President Johnson that they were worried about the recent *cassações*, following the closing of Congress, and the *cassações* decreed a few months earlier to influence indirect gubernatorial elections. But they added: "Castello Branco seems determined to assume personally all the criticism being leveled against the Brazilian Government for anti-democratic actions so as to permit Costa e Silva to assume the Presidency on March 15, 1967, with a relatively cleansed governmental structure and one free of authoritarian overtones."[4]

There were reasons to believe that the painful and unpopular economic austerity would pay off and that, as Castello Branco predicted to Hal Hendrix, 1970 would be an excellent year economically for Brazil. In the political area, however, one drawback to the use of antidemocratic actions for setting up a structure free of authoritarian overtones lay in the legacy of the antidemocratic actions. The antidemocratic actions during the Castello Branco administration were numerous, as Lacerda reminded Brazil. But when he took the lead in establishing the Frente Ampla, as the only means he saw of preventing a continuation of such actions for years to come, not a few people paid less attention to his message than to his past. His new role, they said, could be attributed to presidential ambition.[5]

Quite another view was expressed in a letter to Lacerda from Mauricinho's son Gabriel, who told his uncle that his participation in the Frente Ampla was a mistake because it eliminated any possibility of his reaching the presidency via the military who were in power. Lacerda's daughter Cristina, in noting that her father was guided by principles, points out that he rejected the fruits to be derived from accommodation.[6]

Lacerda's role in the Frente Ampla was warmly welcomed by his children, who, Sérgio Lacerda later told the *Jornal do Brasil*, "were never attracted to his political party position because we never trusted the UDN." "The moment of our total adherence, and the most generous moment of his political life, was during the Frente Ampla, when he never hesitated, even for a minute, to sacrifice himself."[7]

Renato Archer has stated that Lacerda was motivated by the desire to survive politically when he sought to ally himself with his "enemies of the past," Juscelino and Jango, but that, as the crusade progressed, he became "a man totally devoted to reestablishing the democratic regime."[8] Essayist Fernando Pedreira agrees that one of Lacerda's original motivations was pragmatic. "He wanted to be president." But, Pedreira adds: "He also had a more basic reason, a result of the age he had reached. And this final phase, in a way, represented a more mature vision of reality. Different from the one that viewed *Getulismo* as totally sinful and *udenismo* as totally virtuous." Mentioning a more profound change, Pedreira maintains that Lacerda was no longer the earlier crusader whose desire to "purify the world" had led him in his youth to favor the Communist Party and later to advocate military coups "for the salvation of the country."

In the opinion of Pedreira, Lacerda's earlier successes had been so remarkable that he was now handicapped.[9] The orator's past speeches and journalism, powerfully defending former positions, made it very difficult for his old followers or for the followers of his old foes to grasp his message about the need for the new movement. But Lacerda's past is no reason for not judging the Frente Ampla idea on its own merits. Nor can reasons be found in Lacerda's fondness for leading crusades aggressively against superior forces, or in speculation about Lacerda's ambition. The Frente Ampla was a bold effort to prevent a long-lasting dictatorial rule.

X.

The Frente Ampla
(1966-1968)

1. The Frente Ampla Manifesto
(October 27, 1966)

An early plan for launching the Frente Ampla was to have its manifesto read in Tiradentes Palace by Guanabara legislator Raul Brunini while simultaneous readings occurred in local and federal legislative chambers. Following the crisis that ended with the forced recess of Congress, Vieira de Melo agreed to read the manifesto in Tiradentes Palace.[1]

If the document were to bear the names of former presidents whose political rights had been suspended, the government would have to take drastic action, and therefore it did its best to put the former presidents in a position where they had to worry about bringing harm to friends as well as themselves. On October 21 the government said it had "discovered" that Goulart and some of his friends, before the 1964 revolution, had illicitly taken over 1.5 million hectares of land in Mato Grosso with the "connivance" of that state's governor, João Ponce de Arruda, currently a congressman. On the next day the press reported that further *cassações* were contemplated. Goulart, reticent about joining Lacerda and disturbed by government acts against his emissaries, could be expected to refrain from signing the manifesto and to await a less perilous moment before issuing a note agreeing with its objectives.[2]

Kubitschek, in Salt Lake City on October 20, said he had reached no decision and cited the Brazilian government's "violent reaction" to the Frente. Nevertheless, it was believed that he and Lacerda would appear as the signers of the "very important document" that Vieira de Melo offered on October 25 to reveal to representatives of the national and international press if they would join him at 5:00 P.M. that day at Tiradentes Palace.[3]

Thirty-two journalists, on time for the appointment, had to wait for two hours before a weary Vieira de Melo appeared and spoke of events beyond his control that had forced him to ask them to return on the next day. Apparently the MDB leader was having trouble communicating with Kubitschek, in the west of the United States, and with Archer, campaigning in the interior of Maranhão.[4]

While the journalists waited the next afternoon at Tiradentes Palace, it was reported that Foreign Minister Juracy Magalhães had warned Vieira de Melo that the presidency would react energetically to provocation, and that Castello had indirectly warned relatives of Kubitschek that investigations might be intensified and his possessions confiscated. Kubitschek, finally reached by Vieira de Melo and Lacerda in Oregon at 9:00 P.M., expressed concern about the risks and asked the MDB leader to undertake consultations about an opportune time for the manifesto's release. The journalists at Tiradentes Palace were advised that they had been let down again, and Vieira de Melo prepared to leave for Bahia to renew his campaign for a senate seat.[5]

Lacerda resolved that night to divulge the manifesto himself the next morning, October 27, and therefore Alfredo Machado summoned international press correspondents, and Hélio Fernandes summoned Brazilian journalists, to the *Tribuna da Imprensa* reporters' room. Among the two hundred who gathered were nonjournalists, such as women who had broken with the CAMDE.[6]

Besides reading the manifesto, Lacerda explained that he was the solitary signer because "the Castello government in the last forty-eight hours" had "unleashed" threats, such as the confiscations of properties of third parties, new *cassações,* and the reopening of IPMs. In the course of answering questions, he told the journalists that Golbery was the Madame Bovary of the government and that the "semi-literate" Sorbonne Group should be condemned for basing its philosophy on the idea that the world was divided into two blocs. Maintaining that Eletrobrás President Marcondes Ferraz represented a foreign group, Lacerda said that every economic foreign group had a representative in Brazil, always a member of the Castello government. Juracy Magalhães' trip to drum up interest in a permanent Inter-American Peace Force was termed a disaster. As for Filinto Müller, Lacerda observed that if the senator had known German he would have been tried at Nuremberg.[7]

The manifesto that Lacerda read was more sober than his lively answers to questions. It opened by pointing out that "we represent currents of opinion that, taken together, are those of the majority of the people." Exile and ostracism, the manifesto said, "do not release us from being Brazilians or from the obligation of establishing the paths to follow."[8]

The "signers" of the manifesto were presented as having contributed, while in the government or the opposition, to a constant effort to perfect the democratic system to which the people had made a "painful ascent" until that conquest, abnegated by a few, had become something "denied to all the people." Besides demanding direct elections and guarantees of individual rights, the manifesto advocated political parties and institutions that "represent the interests of the people."[9]

The manifesto offered something to everyone. The workers, "expelled from the community as though they were pariahs" and oppressed by unemployment and the loss of purchasing power, were told of "our resolve to forge this union for the defense of their right to exist and aspire to better living conditions." The young people, "denied even the right to demonstrate," were informed of the manifesto writers' resolve to give them the opportunity to have influence so that "by participating, they might prepare themselves to take charge of what is theirs."[10]

In addressing the women, the manifesto recalled how, before the 1964 revolution, religious sentiments had been "exploited by those who today attack the Church, which the usurpers want to prevent from fulfilling the duty of protesting against injustices." The new alliance, the women were told, would seek to guarantee peace—a peace of free and confident people. The middle classes were described as crushed and businessmen as denied credit, while foreigners, granted their every wish, purchased companies that Brazilians were unable to maintain. Even the rich received sympathy in the manifesto, which said they had been promised greater riches but had found themselves threatened by new taxes imposed by a regime that "declared war on profits." The military, described as steeped in the democratic tradition, were offered active participation in economic development, in accordance with "the modern concept of national security." "Even that is not provided by the government, despite its being headed by a military man."[11]

The manifesto was filled with its signers' wishes for the good of Brazil and had much to say about economic matters. It called for the "intransigent defense of the prices of exports" and the acceptance of only those "foreign contributions" that were "really useful." In an equally acceptable statement, it declared that "economic policy must be unequivocally guided only by the national interest."[12]

In the minds of the Frente leaders, this policy meant rejecting both "shock" and "gradualistic" anti-inflation measures. Both types of measures, the manifesto said, sprang from the false notion that the supreme problem "is saving the currency." "If inflation is not wiped out by the policy of development, neither is it, nor will it be, wiped out by the policy of stagnation." The IMF was said to have given Brazil devitalization, bewilderment, unemployment, decadence, disorder, and despair, and the balancing of the federal budget was called a falsehood because its achievement was without "the indispensable increases in civilian and military pay." "The 'favorable' trade balance is merely the result of the 'lack' of imports caused by economic stagnation." The "obsession of 'first putting the house in order' financially leads to the economic destruction of the house."[13]

Turning to foreign affairs, the manifesto spoke of the need to adopt a policy that "expressly excludes Brazil's participation in any political-military bloc." To prevent Brazil from losing its national sovereignty, thus leading to a continental conflagration and the disruption of world peace, Brazil was advised to cease being a "technological satellite" and to update itself scientifically, "an essential part of the struggle for development."

In conclusion the manifesto called for a "popular union to liberate, democratize, modernize, and develop Brazil!"[14]

The president's office said that the manifesto would have no more repercussion than any of Lacerda's recent articles. According to a statement authorized by Castello, "the president once more disagrees with Carlos Lacerda but has no thought of suspending his rights no matter how much the former governor asks, and even implores, that such a step be taken." A presidential adviser pointed out that Castello, wishing to bequeath the best possible conditions for his successor, felt that the *cassação* of Lacerda would eliminate the possibility of his trying to draw close to the future government as a last chance to avoid ostracism.[15]

Some of the military, resenting Lacerda's replies to journalists' questions, did not share Castello's determination to spare Lacerda. These replies, Justice Minister Medeiros Silva told the press, were "much stronger than the manifesto."[16]

Kubitschek, in a cable to his friend Osvaldo Penido, expressed support for the Frente Ampla but said that the release of the manifesto should have awaited a better moment. *Juscelinistas* described the cable as prompted by the former president's desire to have nothing interfere with the inauguration of Costa e Silva, who, he hoped, would put Brazil back on the democratic path.[17]

While ARENA spokesmen described Lacerda as motivated by "frustration," MDB leaders issued pronouncements that were generally unfavorable and revealed the party's wish to remain the principal voice of the opposition. Lutero Vargas asserted that an opposition had already been established and the working class was in no need of a leader who had always been alien to the workers' cause and hostile to Getúlio's ideas. Antônio Balbino, the former Goulart cabinet minister who was an MDB senator from Bahia, joined Congressmen Tancredo Neves and Ernâni do Amaral Peixoto in condemning a Frente that they said could only confuse and disturb the MDB. While Congressman Franco Montoro, interim president of the MDB, stressed that his party had never participated, for a single moment, in the understandings that had brought about the Frente Ampla, Senator Juvenal Lino de Matos, president of the São Paulo MDB, reiterated his disapproval of a "national union" movement that sought to function apart from the political parties. But he conceded that the manifesto might contribute to a useful dialogue even if the MDB had reservations about its timing and some of its points. He asked: "Who, in his right mind, can oppose the desire of all the people for better days?"[18]

O Estado de S. Paulo agreed with the manifesto's position on direct elections and party reform, but opposed its stand about an "independent foreign policy" and economic matters. Lacerda, it also wrote, was mistaken in attributing any importance to the corrupt Kubitschek and Goulart, and was following the bad example of Castello, who allied himself with men "the Revolution should have rooted out."[19]

O Globo found passages in *O Poder das Idéias* in which Lacerda denounced "false public men" who "even sustain that inflation is useful for development," and who would weaken Brazil's alliance with the United States and thus encourage new oppressions by Russia. "The abandoned musketeer," it wrote, "has now lost all that remained to him and has not gained one centimeter of new ground."[20]

The *Jornal do Brasil* pointed out that the interruption of the democratic process had made a victim of Lacerda and was the chief reason for the Frente Ampla. It maintained that the cure for political resentments and frustrations was not repression and punishments, and it therefore suggested that the Castello administration give attention to "a debate that could oxygenize the heavy Brazilian atmosphere of this hour."[21]

But the atmosphere remained one of punishments, because Alcino Salazar, who had become chief prosecutor of the republic, presented documents to the Supreme Court on October 29 to show that Kubitschek and Goulart had enriched themselves illicitly and to request that they be deprived of properties. The *Correio da Manhã* wrote that the government had ludicrously waited two-and-a-half years before presenting its case and was turning now to the court as part of its propaganda and pressure to defeat, in the November 15 congressional elections, the supporters of the former presidents.[22]

2. Congressional Elections and the *Cassação* of Hélio Fernandes (November 1966)

Participating in the campaigning for the November 15 elections, Lacerda sometimes said that he would support the best candidates of the ARENA and MDB, the parties being indistinguishable. He predicted an MDB victory in Guanabara and generally favored the opposition party. At a rally for MDB congressional candidate Raul Brunini, he read a manifesto recommending the PAREDE men in the MDB and MDB senatorial candidate Mário Martins.[1]

In a *Tribuna* article, Lacerda called Mário Martins "a rare bird—an independent journalist" who had left the UDN, because of Adauto Cardoso's antagonism, and had refused a place in Lacerda's government, because of a wish to criticize independently. Lacerda disparaged Mário Martins' three opponents: journalist Danton Jobim (MDB), Congressman Benjamim Farah (MDB), and former Carioca UDN President Venâncio Igrejas (ARENA). He called Jobim a mercenary old journalist who had praised Vargas in the dictatorship's DIP, then joined Eduardo Gomes and Dutra in insulting Vargas, and now played the Castello-Golbery game while posing as an oppositionist. Farah was dismissed as an insignificant demagogue. Lacerda admitted having named Igrejas to the Guanabara Tribunal de Contas at the urging of the UDN ("the only personal favor I granted") and added that Igrejas, after that, had joined a group that "sinuously, surreptitiously, and hypocritically betrayed us."[2]

As for his own plans, Lacerda told the press on November 8 that his two goals after November 15 were the formation of a great political party and the launching of his own presidential candidacy for the contest of 1970. At a rally for state legislature candidate Geraldo Monnerat (ARENA), he said that the new party, which might be called the Party of the Popular Union, would include all social classes and would strive for "the restoration of the rights that have been denied all Brazilians under the pretext of combating Communism."[3]

Hélio Fernandes, described by the *Tribuna* as a favorite of the voters, found himself among a group of MDB congressional candidates whose registrations were said by the government to be worded defectively. As the Regional Electoral Tribunal supported this charge in the case of Hélio Fernandes and two others, they appealed to the Supreme Court. Early on the afternoon of November 10, Supreme Court Justice Elói Rocha issued a preliminary ruling that would assure the registrations of the candidacies of Hélio Fernandes and retired Army Marshal Estêvão Taurino de Resende. But a little later on the same day, Castello made it known that, after hearing from the

National Security Council, he was suspending the political rights of Hélio Fernandes and seventeen others throughout Brazil.[4]

That evening, at a rally of the PAREDE-MDB group, Lacerda, Raul Brunini, Mário Martins, Mauro Magalhães, Cesário de Melo, and others decried the *cassações* and praised Hélio Fernandes. Lacerda, after declaring that "Hélio Fernandes deserves the acclaim of all Brazilians because he has had the honor of being *cassado*," proposed that the "fascists" be relegated to a museum, "in this case the museum of the Zoological Garden."[5]

Boarding a plane that night for Paris, Lacerda said that Hélio Fernandes had been *cassado* "because his independent position was becoming annoying to the American groups that took control of Brazil." He explained that in Europe he would meet with Kubitschek "in order to bring about the union of the people against what is going on here." He promised to return later in the month, but only after the fifteenth, "because I'm not going to vote in the parliamentary elections."[6]

On November 11, Hélio Fernandes published a defiant article in which he spoke of his determination to continue denouncing treasonable and arbitrary acts "based only on the personal will of an insane and crazy dictator who has used the entire nation as an arena to satisfy his self-worship and autocratic and frenzied egocentrism." "I have been *cassado* by the great tribunal of the international trusts, whose judges-representatives in Brazil are Castello Branco, Roberto Campos, Walter Moreira Salles, and others. I was *cassado* by Hanna, the petroleum companies, the international monopolies." "The object was to prevent my election." He wrote that everything, including public opinion polls, demonstrated that he was going to receive a spectacular vote, "even the most-voted in Guanabara, repeating the resounding vote given to Carlos Lacerda on consecutive occasions."[7]

As a result of the *cassação*, the *Tribuna* began showing a new *diretor-responsável* (Guimarães Padilha) on its masthead, and the daily column of Hélio Fernandes began appearing under the name of João da Silva, a pseudonym used by Lacerda in 1956 and at other times. The *Tribuna* pointed out that the *Jornal do Commercio, O Estado de S. Paulo,* and the *Correio da Manhã* were critical of the *cassação,* and it quoted Inter American Press Association President Júlio de Mesquita Filho as saying that the *cassação* "cannot fail to represent a threat to all the country's press."[8]

O Globo, on the other hand, wrote that Castello had been reluctant to suspend Fernandes' political rights lest the step be construed as a threat to the press but had received information that Fernandes was corrupt. The *Tribuna*'s owner, it said, was a "journalistic black-mailer" who, among other things, had accepted payments from the government's Fábrica Nacional de Motores before March 31, 1964, in return for articles praising those who had then directed the Fábrica. Fernandes, in reply to what he called *O Globo*'s "sordid lies," published a letter to Roberto Marinho that said that Fernandes had refused to be moved by Marinho's "heart-rending appeals," made six months earlier, that the *Tribuna* spare him from the attacks of Lacerda and others. The letter described Marinho as "one of the most consummate and renowned rogues the country has ever known," a man so obsessed with piling up a fortune that he would stab anyone in the back.[9]

In the November 15 elections, the ARENA was victorious in most of Brazil, and the MDB victorious by large margins in the states of Guanabara and Rio de Janeiro, and narrowly in Rio Grande do Sul. The final results in the congressional races gave the ARENA 8,731,638 votes to the MDB's 4,195,470. Castello hailed the outcome, although some of the winning ARENA candidates had not hidden their dislike of the government and its party. The ARENA's Magalhães Pinto won the most votes for congressman from Minas after campaigning with speeches that assailed Castello's policies and demanded the extinction of the ARENA.[10]

In Guanabara the federal senate seat was won handily by Lacerda's choice, *Jornal do Brasil* columnist Mário Martins of the MDB; and the MDB won forty of the fifty-five state legislative seats (with Edna Lott in first place). Among the MDB winners of federal congressional seats from Guanabara were *O Dia*'s Antônio Chagas Freitas (far ahead of all candidates), Raul Brunini, twenty-four-year-old businessman Rubem Medina, Nelson Carneiro, Gonzaga da Gama Filho, Amaral Netto, and *Correio da Manhã* journalists Márcio Moreira Alves and Hermano Alves. Successful ARENA contestants for federal congressional seats from Guanabara included Raphael de Almeida Magalhães (top vote-getter of the ARENA), engineer Luís Roberto Veiga de Brito, Carlos Flexa Ribeiro, Lopo Coelho, and Adauto Cardoso.[11]

O Estado de S. Paulo attributed the triumph of the MDB in Guanabara not to MDB prestige but to the influence of Lacerda and other politicians. Similarly, it called Carvalho Pinto's overwhelming senate victory in São Paulo a personal achievement and not an ARENA victory. It tended to view the overall results as a defeat for the government, taking into consideration the blank and invalidated votes (35 percent in São Paulo) advocated by student protesters, and the "climate of force and fear" instituted by the federal administration.

According to the *Jornal do Brasil,* the elections' true victor had been Lacerda, at least in Guanabara, where candidates recommended by him had done well. But the progovernment *O Globo* called the November 15 outcome an expression of "overwhelming support for the Revolution" and a rejection of "old leaderships" represented by Lacerda, Kubitschek, and Goulart.[12]

Lacerda, replying early in December to questions of *O Cruzeiro* magazine, denied that the ARENA victory was an expression of support for the Castello administration, and asked: "How many ARENA candidates were elected by campaigning against the government?" Milton Campos in Minas, he said, had won his ARENA senate seat "precisely with his manifesto against the government." Lacerda mentioned the ARENA congressional victory of Magalhães Pinto, and, in Rio Grande do Norte, that of Aluísio Alves, "vetoed by Castello." He said that Carvalho Pinto's victory had nothing to do with the revolution or Castello. Discussing the victories of Cid Sampaio and João Cleofas ("both passed over by Nilo Coelho," the pro-Castello governor-elect of Pernambuco), Lacerda attributed them also to the contestants' past records. "In Guanabara," Lacerda added, "the victory of our candidates was independent of the labels of the ARENA or MDB and was the victory of the government that we administered."

Why, he was asked by *O Cruzeiro,* had he not been a candidate himself? He replied that he understood that he "could not knock at the doors of the ARENA, nor enter by the window of the MDB." He preferred, he said, to wait for the "culminating act of my public life, my understanding with Juscelino Kubitschek, as the point of departure for the complete revision of Brazil's political problem."[13]

3. The "Declaration of Lisbon" (November 19, 1966)

In Lisbon on November 12, Kubitschek received a phone call from Lacerda, who was passing through the Portuguese capital on his way to Paris. Arrangements were made for the two men to meet at 10:00 A.M. on November 19 at the Kubitscheks' large, sparsely furnished Lisbon apartment.[1]

Lacerda, at the appointed time, was received by Kubitschek's wife Sarah, to whom he delivered a gift, a recording of Chico Buarque de Hollanda's music—which he considered "the only happy thing to have happened in Brazil since March 31, 1964." After the sixty-five-year-old Kubitschek greeted Lacerda, the two men were soon discussing international events. "We were getting along so well,"

Kubitschek wrote the next day in a report for *Manchete* magazine, "that it was as though we had been meeting together every week."[2]

In the same report, Kubitschek wrote that Lacerda spoke of Castello's "malicious" offer of the UN post and described himself to Kubitschek as the victim of "treason," so that Kubitschek came to appreciate that "within him, just as acutely as within me, lay the germ of a profound disenchantment with what has happened in Brazil." "Our temperaments are completely different, just as a meadow of green differs from a volcano that spews forth lava. . . . I have sought . . . to proceed with forgiveness and tolerance. How were the two of us to understand each other, speaking such different languages?"[3]

Addressing Lacerda, Kubitschek argued that what Brazil most needed was peace, and he added that the next president ought to display some of the spirit shown by Abraham Lincoln after the Civil War. "We must preach peace and not resentments. This is the only language that can persuade me to overcome any divergence. Bringing together whatever support we might have, let us launch the great idea of National Pacification. The new president, who will take over, will then need only to increase what has been sown."[4]

Kubitschek, who found Lacerda enthusiastic, wrote further about the meeting: "Pardon requires more greatness than hate. . . . We would give the example. Two hours were enough for agreement on the central thesis of our efforts for the future: PEACE. Within that concept I shall find no obstacles to making alliances. It is a banner the nation needs. I know that misunderstanding will surround our camp. However, people will end up accepting the serious steps that I have not feared to take."[5]

A reporter wrote that Sarah Kubitschek, "the angel of the home," played the Chico Buarque de Hollanda record while "the thundering voice of Lacerda and the soft voice of Kubitschek" could be heard from another room. By 12:30 P.M. the apartment was full of journalists. Kubitschek and Lacerda, with broad grins, posed for photographers. The two longtime political foes, according to one report, were "up in the heavens together . . . , smiling, embracing, their faces like those of schoolboys."[6]

"After two-and-a-half years of exile," Kubitschek told the journalists, "I think of nothing else but to see Brazil pacified so it can march ahead, and that is also the thought of Carlos Lacerda and has been the theme of our conversation." Asked about Brazil's "present government," both men refused to comment. "We have turned the page," Lacerda said, "and are now concerned only with the future of Brazil."[7]

The Kubitscheks and Lacerda left to lunch with Hugo Gouthier,

Sebastião Paes de Almeida, Lucy Bloch, Congressman Hermógenes Príncipe de Oliveira, and the Kubitscheks' daughter Márcia and her husband, Baldomero Barbará Neto. During the lunch at the Tavares Restaurant, it became clear to each of the two Brazilian leaders that the other had many friends in Lisbon. Kubitschek's popularity was hardly surprising to Lacerda, who has said that the former president was one of the most delightful men he ever met. Pointing out that the great difficulty in attacking Kubitschek had been the man's attractiveness, Lacerda added: "He really was a man without hatreds. He had this quality, I might say almost to a fault. He was incapable of holding grudges."[8]

During the lunch it was agreed that Lacerda would draw up an appropriate joint declaration. Lacerda's draft, made at his hotel after lunch, was modified a bit when they met again at Kubitschek's apartment, because the former president was eager to delete aggressive expressions. However, before the task was completed to the full satisfaction of Kubitschek and Lacerda, Portuguese journalists and foreign correspondents invaded the apartment and took sheets of paper from the table as fast as Lacerda completed them. "We might have produced a better document," Kubitschek wrote *Manchete*'s Adolpho Bloch, "but it was impossible under those circumstances."[9]

The "Declaration of Lisbon" affirmed that a policy of peace and liberty was necessary for the renewal and acceleration of development, "without which the nation is condemned to live between submission and despair." It described the directives of the manifesto of the Frente Ampla as indispensable and recommended that urgent steps be taken to form a popular political party. All Brazilians, especially the young, were asked to organize in order to be able to work "without tutelage, without fear, and without discouragement."[10]

"When the journalists left," Kubitschek reported in his note to Bloch, "we were tired but happy. I remarked 'We have thrown the bomb. Now let's wait for the explosion.'" Perhaps to tempt Castello Branco to explode, Lacerda that night distributed a note to the press to point out that his meeting with Kubitschek had been a public one because not for a single moment had he behaved "in a secret manner" as Castello had done in April 1964, when (according to Lacerda) the general had sought out Kubitschek to get his support to reach the presidency.[11]

Although the Lisbon newspapers publicized the Kubitschek-Lacerda meeting, the Portuguese authorities, careful about relations with the Brazilian government, stepped in to prevent the publication in Portugal of the Declaration of Lisbon. However, Lisbon's *Diário de Notícias* published remarks made by Kubitschek and Lacerda at a joint interview before they left Lisbon on November 21—an interview at which Kubitschek expressed his belief that his meeting with Lacerda would figure in political chronicles as a demonstration of how "personal divergences" could be overcome on behalf of the struggle for democracy.[12]

Kubitschek left by plane for New York and Lacerda went by automobile to spend a day in Madrid. Before returning to Rio on November 23, Lacerda told the press in Spain that Brazil would soon have a "popular party" and that his pact with Kubitschek was made "to free the people from reactionary and antinational rule."[13]

In the meantime in Portugal, two of Lacerda's longtime associates raised their voices against the pact. Herbert Levy, passing through Lisbon, asserted that the 1964 revolution had been made to eradicate the influence of men like Kubitschek. Governor-elect Abreu Sodré, who was being honored by Portuguese officials, said he did not believe in "the union of heterogeneous forces." He added that "time has shown that nothing false holds up, and this alliance is spurious, false, and senseless."[14]

When Lacerda landed at Galeão Airport he further upset the military and disappointed old friends (as well as his new friend Kubitschek), because he told reporters that Goulart might sign the Pact of Lisbon. He also said he did not expect punishments by the government. "Kubitschek has already been punished and I have committed no crime."[15]

4. Repercussions of the Pact of Lisbon (Late November 1966)

"I returned to Rio," Lacerda recalled later, "under heavy bombardment from all sides, and the truth is that most of my political friends, most of the UDN, and most of the electorate, understood nothing."[1]

The MDB's José Maria Magalhães, a former Lacerda spokesman in Minas who had recently been elected to Congress, said the "Lisbon Pact" would have no repercussions, because its signers "lack political command." Opposition leader Vieira de Melo, who had lost his bid for a senate seat from Bahia, called the "pact" inopportune and senseless now that the elections were over. His MDB companions, he said, saw no place for the party planned by Lacerda and Kubitschek.[2]

The ARENA's José Costa Cavalcanti, who had been reelected congressman from Pernambuco and spoke for most of the military who backed Costa e Silva, said that Lacerda had completed his self-destruction and lost the support of the armed forces. Another military voice from Pernambuco, that of Fourth Army Commander Rafael de

Souza Aguiar, was raised to protest the Kubitschek-Lacerda alliance; the general observed that only politics had been able to make allies out of Hitler and Stalin.[3]

A group of army and air force officers, among them Gustavo Borges, met with Lacerda to tell him of their "disgust." Lieutenant Colonel Leo Etchegoyen, who had reportedly reached Guanabara Palace with his brother and tanks on April 1, 1964, broke relations with Lacerda. Hard line Colonel Osnelli Martinelli, in a public statement, said: "We could never imagine the Revolution uniting with the anti-Revolution. We do not accept it. Perhaps it is politically judicious but from the point of view of ideals it is injudicious."[4]

A pleasant surprise for Lacerda was the position of retired air force Colonel Fontenelle, who entered the Novo Rio office and shouted "Where is the book?" because he wanted to add his signature in what he thought was a book listing Frente Ampla adherents. Congressman-elect Luís Roberto Veiga de Brito, also understanding, wrote in the *Tribuna da Imprensa* that a careful, unbiased examination of the Kubitschek-Lacerda meeting would show that it opened a great opportunity for Costa e Silva to have the popular backing "necessary to carry out the great administration that I sincerely desire."[5]

An invitation for Costa e Silva to join the Lisbon Pact signers was made by Lacerda, who proposed to serve as "a liaison between Costa e Silva and the people." "If Dr. Kubitschek and I can reach an understanding," Lacerda asked, "why cannot we both reach an understanding with Costa e Silva?"[6]

Oscar Pedroso Horta, Quadros' justice minister and now an MDB congressman-elect, saw the Frente Ampla as a movement inspired by Lacerda's hope that Costa e Silva would "tolerate" his "political resurrection." He felt that Lacerda's participation in the Frente was simply the act of "a demagogue, thirsty and greedy for power."[7]

The *Jornal do Brasil* also emphasized what it called political ambition. The most melancholy aspect of the Lisbon alliance, it told its readers, was that the two politicians who fraternized, representatives of old leaderships, were "moved by the same craving for power" and were always eager "to conquer it at any price." "Nothing," the *Jornal do Brasil* wrote, "is more paradoxical at a time when the nation is clamoring for new leaderships and new political styles." Danton Jobim, writing in *Última Hora*, was likewise antagonistic to Lacerda, "whose step," he wrote, "was taken because he is not in power and sees the paths to power blocked." But Jobim praised the magnanimity of Kubitschek for joining, on Brazil's behalf, his "rancorous enemy," and said his signing the joint declaration "does not force him to accept Lacerda's methods." Jobim saw the wording of the Lisbon

The pact. Kubitschek with Lacerda. (Hilde Weber drawing in *O Estado de S. Paulo,* November 24, 1966)

declaration as inspired by the ideals of Kubitschek, not the sentiments of *Lacerdismo.* The *Correio da Manhã,* under the editorial direction of Osvaldo Peralva, argued that while personal interests might have inspired the Kubitschek-Lacerda alliance, this was unimportant, because if the people would organize, as the declaration recommended, "the demagogues who desire democratic leadership for hidden reasons will be easily expelled."[8]

O Estado de S. Paulo found it inconceivable that anyone blessed with Lacerda's exceptional qualities could find a way to join up with men such as Kubitschek and Goulart. It called the Frente manifesto and Lisbon Pact "products of a phase of Lacerda's life in which he permits passion to take the place of lucidity." Their only effect, *O Estado* wrote, was to oblige his longtime followers to assume an attitude of formal disagreement.[9]

O Globo, which Lacerda said "poisoned everything," carried out the most intense bombardment against the Lisbon Pact. Its campaign, including eight page-one editorials in eight consecutive issues, opened on November 21, 1966, with a page-one photograph of the corpse of Major Rubens Vaz, following his murder at Lacerda's side in 1954. The caption proclaimed that the major's "sacrifice is now defiled by a spurious alliance." The defiler, *O Globo* wrote, was the very one "who is alive thanks to the death of the young patriot."

Below another page-one photograph, this showing the smiling Lacerda and Kubitschek in Lisbon, a note said that their joy "appears to sneer at the martyrs who fell in the struggle against corruption and subversion. To our astounded readers we recommend the article 'O Cafajeste Máximo' [The Foremost Scoundrel], published on page 6"— a reprint of Lacerda's *Tribuna* article of June 15, 1957, about President Kubitschek.

O Globo wrote that the two "conspirators" of Lisbon, with knives between their teeth, had joined forces in their morbid ambition for power. Calling the alliance an act of "cynicism unequaled in the political history of Brazil," *O Globo* declared that each man, now smiling and prosperous, had made a fortune in politics. Lacerda was accused of acting as the agent of a *cassado*, thus violating stipulations of the Institutional Act. What authority, *O Globo* asked, would remain to a government that punished labor leaders Dante Pelacani and Clodsmith Riani for disregarding the stipulations and "spared Kubitschek's new partner?"[10]

The Vaz family was quick to publish two letters to Roberto Marinho in the *Tribuna*, and they were read to the state legislators by Mauro Magalhães (MDB). One was signed by Rubens Vaz Júnior, who had shared Gustavo Borges' reservations about the Frente Ampla but who now wrote: "If my father were alive he would be with me today at the side of the man who has the same meaning for you as the cross has for the devil." Vaz Júnior told Marinho that his vile and slanderous methods of enriching himself and carrying out personal vengeance against Lacerda classified him as a coward. "You are not a man, but a worm." In the other letter, Vaz's widow Lygia and her four children pointed out that Lacerda would explain to the people the reasons for his latest step, because "he has never deceived us in any way." The signers added that "our press law does not punish journalists like yourself who act like common criminals, bringing suffering to an entire family with the scurrilous exploitation of the corpse of a hero."[11]

O Globo's call for immediate action against Lacerda, signer of a political pact with a *cassado*, was echoed in some circles in Brasília. But the government limited itself to releasing, on November 22, statements by Agência Nacional and Foreign Minister Juracy Magalhães. Agência Nacional advised that Kubitschek and Goulart, while illicitly enriching themselves, had violated Law 3,502 of 1956. Therefore, the statement said, legal proceedings were being carried out against both. One of the cases, the public learned, sprang from the allegedly irregular manner in which a group that included Sarah Kubitschek and César Prates and his wife had acquired lakeside houses and land in Brasília.[12]

Juracy's statement to the press, published on November 23, contained his denial of Lacerda's charge that he had "contemptibly" told a reporter that if Hélio Fernandes obtained a Supreme Court decision favorable to his candidacy, Castello would suspend Hélio's political rights. Juracy also said that in the past, when Lacerda's newspaper had called him a liar, he had sought, without success, to obtain redress from the courts. Now he called Lacerda a liar for having denied, in Cláudio Mello e Sousa's chapter in *Os Idos de Março*, that he had sent Costa e Silva a letter early in April 1964 calling the general a dictator and announcing his retirement from the governorship. Juracy described "the terrible scene" in Lacerda's apartment at that time and added that since he had possession of Lacerda's letter to the general he would donate it to a public library so that future historians could see "the liar is not I." Furthermore, Juracy disparaged Lacerda's conduct at Juracy's home, also in April 1964, when Lacerda, "instead of discussing the serious problems" with Castello, "proposed my name for a cabinet post, without a previous word to me, and then, in a deplorable defense of personal interests, asked to be sent abroad on the trip that later gave rise to the famous Orly Airport episode."

Juracy wrote that nothing could be added to the public's opinion of Lacerda, "long and correctly viewed as an incurable cyclothymic, whose acts and words can be considered credible for no more than a few minutes." Castello's foreign minister concluded by saying that whereas Lacerda had won some great battles by using tremendously destructive power, Castello had defeated Lacerda "by the power of intelligence, without restricting Lacerda's movements or words, but simply by letting him become entangled in his own vilification and buried under his own demolishing rage."[13]

Because Juracy mentioned the presence of Sérgio Lacerda at some of the scenes he described, Sérgio sent a letter to the press to advise that the foreign minister had sought to involve a son while attacking the father, and thus had followed "the example of what his associate Roberto Marinho does each day." According to Sérgio, Juracy adhered to his old practice of omitting important details when he failed to mention that Castello, at Juracy's home in April 1964, had agreed to the request of the governor "to respect the election calendar of that time and the candidates already chosen or in the process of being chosen for the future direct presidential election." Lacerda, at that meeting, was described by Sérgio as having advocated the right of free association for students and workers, and as having reminded Castello of the importance of leaderships, including that of Kubitschek. Denying that his father had asked that anyone be given a

Carlos Lacerda. (APPE drawing in *EX-16* of November 1975, reproducing Lacerda's *O Cruzeiro* article of December 24, 1966)

cabinet post, Sérgio said that he had simply suggested that use be made of men like Juracy, "one more witness of the democratic promises assumed by Castello." As for Lacerda's letter to Costa e Silva, Sérgio wrote that no one would have imagined that Juracy, in his old age, would be keeping papers received in "confidence and privacy."[14]

O Globo, defending Juracy, called Lacerda completely crazy for having stated, before going to Lisbon, that the foreign minister sought to sell Brazil to other governments. In ridiculing the Frente Ampla, it wrote that if Gregório Fortunato, responsible for the assassination of Vaz, were alive, he would "certainly also be invited to join." It objected to Lacerda's "fraternal contacts" made in recent months with "the extreme Left"—groups that *O Globo* argued were following the "direct action" line of the Tricontinental Conference of Havana. "The moderately good translator of *Julius Caesar* carries in his belt the dagger of Brutus."

Reiterating that Lacerda should be punished quickly, *O Globo* pointed out that, with Costa e Silva taking office on the effective date of the new constitution, the incoming president would lack the arms provided by the institutional acts. "He will not be able to carry out a government of peace and constructive work. He will have a veritable inferno with Carlos Lacerda."[15]

Defending himself in his articles and speeches to graduating classes, Lacerda denied that his meeting with Kubitschek was intended to create an inferno for Costa e Silva, and he called General Souza Aguiar asinine for comparing the meeting with the Hitler-Stalin alliance.[16] He suggested that a clue to the move to suspend his political rights could be found in a *Newsweek* article that maintained that it was United States Military Attaché Vernon Walters who convinced Castello to conspire against Goulart and head the 1964 revolution and then encouraged him to head the Brazilian government. These charges, according to Lacerda, were not rumors but "affirmations known to millions of readers." Lacerda also wrote that Brazil's American bosses and their Brazilian agents were taking steps to control Costa e Silva and for this reason "our peace proposal is being received with hatred."

Costa e Silva's reaction to Lacerda's statements was to express the hope that "Lacerda, with the new government, will continue in the opposition but become less violent." He called the opposition a form of collaboration, and called Lacerda "a man of rare talents, very impetuous as an adversary, and a Brazilian who attracts attention."[17]

5. The Constitution, Press Law, and National Security Law (January–March 1967)

Castello Branco planned to bow out on March 15, 1967, after decreeing a replacement for the National Security Law of 1953, which he considered "inefficacious," and after giving Brazil a new constitution and press law, both to be voted by Congress. On December 7, he issued Institutional Act No. 4, authorizing Congress to discuss, vote, and promulgate the new constitution, between December 12 and January 24, and he promised that no congressman or senator would be *cassado* during the debate. The administration's draft of a constitution, completed in October 1966 by Justice Minister Medeiros Silva, was modified by the president, after consultations with jurists, cabinet ministers, and congressional leaders, including Vice President–elect Pedro Aleixo. Costa e Silva was consulted several times, and was kept advised after his departure on December 14 for a long trip abroad.[1]

Before and during the congressional study, the debates were heated, and Castello was forced to abandon his idea of giving the executive the power to declare a state of emergency to prevent constitutional violations when the institutions were gravely threatened. But the new document, adopted by Congress on January 21, did establish a strong central government. "Dictatorships," Castello argued, "could develop where constitutions were ineffective on account of a lack of authority."[2]

Castello, supported by Senator Krieger, insisted on modifying Medeiros Silva's draft in order to include clauses, drawn up by Afonso Arinos de Melo Franco, to provide full guarantees of individual rights. In Congress much controversy preceded the adoption of a clause to have presidential elections carried out by Congress and some state assembly representatives, a simplified version of Medeiros Silva's idea for an electoral college. Proposals to open the way for revising punishments decreed by the revolution were defeated by the government's congressional majority (181 votes to 120, and 195 votes to 127).

The search for petroleum and its extraction were declared government monopolies, but Congress defeated the Adolfo de Oliveira amendment to prevent private companies from participating in the industrialization of petroleum. The mining of ores by foreigners was not banned. And, as Castello wished, Congress defeated seven proposals that would have guaranteed that specific geographical regions receive definite percentages of the central government's receipts. The economic innovations—which, according to Luís Viana Filho, were "probably more radical than the political ones, but aroused little debate"—called for a balanced budget and prohibited the increase of government expenditures at the initiative of Congress.[3]

Lacerda wrote that "Papa Doc" Castello, "the comic opera little general," dominated by "psychopathic vanity," had decided to become the "mother of a constitution" after being informed that Napoleon had been the author of laws. He told São Paulo journalists that the government's draft was a neofascist document with some articles copied from Brazil's 1937 Constitution and others copied from "the constitutions of Gambia or Tanzania"—all "very satisfactory" for Standard Oil, "which paid Golbery to organize the SNI at the time of the IPES." In quips to Rio reporters, Lacerda described the new constitution as "whimsical, primitive, and stupid," a hideous monster, inferior to Getúlio Vargas' dictatorial law of 1937, and, like Castello, "even worse on the inside than on the outside." In the *Tribuna*, he called it "the constitution of renegades," and asked whether Castello cabinet ministers Juarez Távora and Eduardo Gomes, former advocates of limiting subsoil rights to Brazilians, now agreed to revoke regulations that "defend the subsoil against the interests of groups whose political decisions are made outside Brazil."[4]

Speaking to Paulistas about their plans for a "festival of humor," Lacerda said flippantly that if he were present he would supply a biography of Castello that would make "all Brazil die of laughter." In a reference to Castello's poor back condition, he added that "Castello Branco is a snake with a broken spine, and snakes with broken spines must have their heads smashed."[5]

In the case of Castello's proposed press law, not much was heard from Lacerda because he was out of Brazil during most of January. Even his voice would have been a minor one, so intense was the furious barrage carried out by the press and politicians. "You are going to pay the price," Justice Minister Medeiros Silva had warned Castello when the president had made it known that he would seek to have Congress enact the new law, designed, he said, to assure liberty of expression "without giving room for abuses that place in risk the principal interests of the nation and the honor and dignity of its citizens." The *Jornal da Tarde*, citing possible inspirations for the project, listed Hitler's Germany, Mussolini's Italy, Communist Russia, and the People's Republic of China.[6]

Even *O Globo* found faults with the proposal; and Governor Abreu Sodré, who felt the new constitution would definitely place Brazil among the world's democracies on March 15, expressed misgivings. Júlio de Mesquita Filho declared on television that Castello was a man from the backlands of the northeast who knew nothing about the law and was enslaving Brazil, whereupon Lacerda, leaving for the United States with his daughter on January 2, congratulated the São Paulo publisher for his "gesture of courage in a nation cowardly dominated by opportunism." Also before departing, Lacerda added his name to a list of writers, journalists, and politicians who signed an appeal for the public of São Paulo to attend a rally to "repudiate" the law project.[7]

During the debates in Congress, Castello agreed with government leader Raimundo Padilha and other lawmakers who described as "absurd" a clause that would make press directors and editors-in-chief responsible in the case of signed articles. The elimination of this clause and some further modifications to the draft left a version that allowed the press to feel that the nation, rising as a body, had won a victory over the original "totalitarian" spirit late in January.[8]

The victory was voiced again in mid-February when Castello promulgated the Press Law without using his veto power to remove any important change enacted by Congress. But it was a short-lived victory. On March 12 the *Diário Oficial* published the National Security Law, written by Castello and Medeiros Silva after discussions with General Jayme Portella de Mello, Costa e Silva's choice to head the Gabinete Militar. Among other things, the law forbade acts or propaganda, in political, economic, psychosocial, or military areas, that had the purpose of stimulating or arousing "opinions, emotions, positions, or behavior . . . in opposition to the attainment of the national objectives."[9]

In joining the outrage expressed by the press, Lacerda criticized an opening clause, written by Castello, that defined the national

Castello delivering New Year turkey to Costa e Silva. (APPE drawing in *O Cruzeiro,* December 31, 1966)

security as "the guarantee of the attainment of the national objectives against internal and external antagonisms." "Internal antagonism," Lacerda wrote in a *Tribuna* editorial, "is the very condition of the existence of a democratic regime," and he said it was guaranteed by the constitution to allow people to make choices. He depicted "those fascists" as wishing to say that "there are permanent untouchable national objectives," and added that the law left the objectives "undefined."[10]

The long list of punishable crimes included offending the honor or dignity of the president and certain other high officials, causing an unregistered political party to function, and giving publicity in any way to anything that would "jeopardize the name, authority, credit, or prestige of Brazil." The list, Lacerda told reporters, was broad enough to find reasons for punishing Castello, who "alarmed the people for three years with the announcements of price increases," and Juracy Magalhães, "who confirmed his *entreguismo* when he observed that what is good for the United States is good for Brazil."[11]

The traveling president-elect expressed, more than once, his approval of indirect presidential elections. In mid-January he announced his "complete accord" with the texts, not yet finalized, of the new constitution, Press Law, and National Security Law, and said he would maintain them unchanged during his administration. He pointed out that he had reminded Castello of the need for the new National Security Law.[12]

6. Politicians, Cool to the Frente,
Await the New President
(December 1966–March 1967)

After Raul Brunini and Mauro Magalhães studied the Medeiros draft of a constitution, they announced that its conditions for a new political party could be met. But on December 12, ARENA lawmakers took the lead in altering party requirements to make it improbable that Lacerda and Kubitschek could establish their party. The alteration, which was maintained in the final version of the constitution, stipulated that political parties should have the adherence of at least 10 percent of the electorate that had voted in the last congressional election, distributed throughout two-thirds of the states, with a minimum of 7 percent in each of those states, as well as the enrollment of 10 percent of the congressmen, in at least one-third of the states, and 10 percent of the senators.[1]

Lacerda told reporters: "You can be certain that we are going to form a third party regardless of the requirements." Calling the requirements "imbecilic," he said that his position represented the "undeniable demand of the absolute majority of public opinion" and that a third party was a national security necessity, the only means of preventing "a large part of the Brazilian people from becoming attracted to Communist leaderships that will turn to conspiracy."[2]

Kubitschek, Carlos Heitor Cony writes, became more determined than ever to take a strong stand against the Castello administration after the federal chief prosecutor, Alcino Salazar, accused the former president of having improperly enriched himself, and after a Federal District judge issued an order for his arrest because of "irregularities" in the acquisition of materials for building the Hospital Distrital de Brasília. Faced with reports that congressmen and senators resisted turning to a third party, Kubitschek sent a message to Lacerda to make "every possible effort" to bring about a union of political currents.[3]

"Every possible effort" suggested an alliance with Goulart and the PTB people, who had been taken by surprise by the Lisbon Pact and declared that the authors of the Pact lacked the support of the working classes. Goulart, who had to consider his anti-Lacerda following, wrote Wilson Fadul in December to say that if Lacerda wished to talk with him he should list in advance the matters to be discussed, after which he would advise whether Lacerda's list had his approval. Lacerda, refusing to accept the "position of postulant," called Goulart's proviso a "demonstration of precaution, dictated by old resentments."[4]

Writing to friends in January, Goulart showed his lack of interest in a third party and his wish to see a structure given to the Frente Ampla, which, he said, should be "the broadest possible"—so broad that it would include members of the ARENA, such as Carvalho Pinto and Magalhães Pinto. He was willing to have Lacerda participate in such a front provided that Lacerda was simply one of its leaders and not the only leader.[5]

In the United States early in January, Lacerda left his daughter Cristina at the home of an old friend, Harvard Professor Evon Z. Vogt. Arriving in Portugal on January 11 for a ten-day visit, he held discussions with Kubitschek, in the company of Sandra Cavalcanti, who impressed Kubitschek with her "brilliant intelligence." Outgoing Congressman Hermógenes Príncipe de Oliveira arrived from Rio with the news that the MDB favored the inauguration of Costa e Silva and planned to discuss redemocratization with him.[6]

Kubitschek and Lacerda took the position that the movement they were organizing would be what Costa e Silva would need to "pacify Brazil," especially if they could get the *Janguistas* to adhere. Adopting positions mentioned by Goulart in letters to friends, they declared that the Frente's "structurization" would go forward, whereas the launching of a new party was to wait at least until after the inauguration of Costa e Silva. Archer, in Brazil, explained the postponement by pointing out that, as long as Castello was in office, regulations for forming parties could be further altered and adherents to a third party could be punished.[7]

No information about the Kubitschek-Lacerda meetings, nor about a new manifesto signed by both men, was given in the Portuguese press. Costa e Silva, during his visit to Lisbon, had complained of Brazilian oppositionists carrying out politics in Portugal and had maintained that Brazil was giving support to Portugal's African policy.

Copies of the new Kubitschek-Lacerda manifesto were distributed at Galeão Airport when Lacerda reached Rio on January 21. It contained nothing novel beyond an expression that both men adopted for future use: "the new abolition" to free Brazilians from fear, disbelief, and despair. Reporters were told by Lacerda that the Frente Ampla would set up a structure, mainly two commissions, and would then "go to the streets" to attract members, especially among the working classes and students.[8]

Of greater interest was Lacerda's statement at the airport that the time had come for him to go to Montevideo to talk with Goulart. When a journalist remarked that Goulart was reported to be displeased with the Frente Ampla, Lacerda attributed the report to Golbery's SNI.

Two days after Lacerda's return to Brazil, the press carried excerpts from Kubitschek's letter to a military officer giving his version of his meeting with Castello in April 1964. Kubitschek, in this reaction to attacks on his honesty and honor, asserted that Castello had given him and other PSD leaders assurances that the direct presidential election and the Kubitschek candidacy would not be interfered with. In New York Kubitschek declared that the new Brazilian constitution and Press Law "completely kill democracy." Positions recently taken by the Brazilian Congress, he exclaimed, "are terrible, terrible," and would unleash a reaction in all sectors of Brazilian life, forcing modifications in the near future.[9]

Writing Lacerda from New York on January 28, Kubitschek said he had spoken with outgoing Congressman Ranieri Mazzilli, who would "collaborate enthusiastically" with their movement and would talk with Paulistas who ought to join it. Mazzilli, he also told Lacerda, disagreed only with the decision, reached recently in Lisbon, to await Costa e Silva's inauguration before launching the new party, and had presented convincing arguments against any delay.[10]

Almost as soon as a messenger brought him Kubitschek's letter, Lacerda announced that he would initiate the third party when he addressed university students in Curitiba on February 13. Nevertheless, the Curitiba speech was no more than a promise to launch "a national movement, similar to that of the abolitionists." However, in São Paulo on February 15, he declared his intention to start the third party when he spoke at São Paulo's Mackenzie University on March 9; and he said he would at that time disclose the names of the twelve members of the Frente's National Executive Commission.[11]

In the meantime, Renato Archer and Lacerda exerted enormous efforts in São Paulo and made no headway. Among the many Paulistas who rebuffed them were Senator Carvalho Pinto and Mayor José Vicente de Faria Lima.

Archer was no admirer of Quadros, who, while president, had drunk too much and acted improperly with Archer's secretary during a visit to Archer's home state, Maranhão. He believed that Quadros, like Goulart, had never seriously presented reform projects to Congress. But, after the Frente Ampla was launched, Archer had friendly talks with the enigmatic former president. A press report about one of the talks prompted Pedroso Horta to announce in Congress that Quadros would not join the Frente, whereupon Archer accused the former justice minister of treating Quadros as though he owned him and of having contributed to the famous resignation.

The truth was that Horta could not forgive Lacerda for episodes that had led to the resignation, and Quadros spoke to Archer, not infrequently, of having an "absolute horror" of Lacerda. But Lacerda, on February 15, 1967, told reporters that he would remain patient, being convinced that all of Brazil's former presidents would eventually enroll. On the next day, news was received from Montevideo that Goulart, cold to the third party idea, had no interest in seeing Lacerda.[12]

Brunini had a difficult time in Minas. Former *Lacerdistas* there followed the anti-Frente line of José Maria Magalhães, who said that if Lacerda's objective was the "redemocratization of Brazil" he should not form another opposition party but join the MDB, whose purpose was precisely the same. Only three *Juscelinista* politicians in Minas expressed support for the Frente; the great majority of those who had formed the Minas PSD felt it would be prudent to see what developed after Costa e Silva took office.[13]

From Rio Grande do Norte came the news that former Governor Aluísio Alves, involved in an internal ARENA struggle, was inclined to abandon third party plans at least until the views of Costa e Silva became known. Spokesmen of the Frente Ampla in Pernambuco reported that nothing could be expected before the new president's inauguration on March 15.[14]

Politicians might hesitate to take positions before the inauguration, but Kubitschek feared that after the inauguration this attitude would become so prevalent that the work then would be even more difficult and remain so for weeks or months. He and Lacerda therefore agreed in their correspondence on the need to form the Frente's executive commission quickly.

Lacerda, reportedly working on *estruturação,* told the public that it would allow the Frente to last a long time and help it take over the power within the next few years. But the only organizational accomplishment was the announcement that the Frente presidency would go to Josafá Marinho, a senator from Bahia who had helped organize the MDB. The choice, described in the press as a "neutral" one, might satisfy Goulart and *Janguistas* who ruled out Lacerda for the top post.[15]

The difficulty in obtaining firm pledges plagued the organizational work and made it impossible for Lacerda to fulfill his promise to list, before Costa e Silva's inauguration, the congressmen who adhered to the Frente. He did, however, give the names of six senators, who, he said, were expected to join Josafá Marinho: Adolfo de Oliveira Franco (Paraná), Sebastião Archer (Maranhão), Pedro Ludovico Teixeira (Goiás), Vicente Bezerra Neto (Mato Grosso), João Abraão Sobrinho (Goiás), and Artur Virgílio (Amazonas).

Early in March, Senator Aurélio Viana, the socialist from Guanabara, disclosed that he, too, had been invited to join the Frente Ampla. Instead of replying to the invitation, he delivered a public criticism of the Frente and said that no one knew who was going to join, "with so many invitations and so many refusals."[16]

Kubitschek, writing Lacerda a week before Costa e Silva's inauguration, concluded that "we shall still have to struggle for a while against incomprehension." But he revealed his characteristic optimism and wrote that their movement for peace, democracy, and development had great popular support. Agreeing with Lacerda's recommendation of a friendly attitude toward the incoming administration, Kubitschek expressed his conviction that the public's faith in Costa e Silva would be used by the new president to bring about a much-needed change of direction for Brazil. He added that his own offices in Lisbon and New York were always filled with Brazilians, and, without a single exception, they expressed enthusiasm for the incoming government.[17]

Lacerda had said in February that the new political party would for the time being be known as the Frente Ampla. But in response to his plan to launch it at the Mackenzie University on March 9, the students there declared on March 8 that, when they had invited him to speak, it had not been in order to hear about the Frente Ampla. Lacerda, attacking militarism in his address to the students, observed: "It is an unpropitious moment to discuss the Frente Ampla because everyone is awaiting the inauguration of Marshal Costa e Silva."[18] He did not list, as he had promised, the twelve members of the Frente's National Executive Commission.

Journalist Flávio Galvão, writing in *O Estado de S. Paulo*, analyzed the predicament of the Frente in São Paulo. He pointed out that Governor Abreu Sodré clearly intended to strengthen the ARENA and that ARENA Senator Carvalho Pinto, his leadership position assured by the November election results, had spurned the Frente. Turning to the São Paulo MDB, Galvão reported that former PTB leader Ivete Vargas, although visited by Lacerda, had refused to commit herself, and that the local MDB president, Senator Juvenal Lino de Matos, was so opposed to the idea of the Frente's becoming a third party that he proposed expelling from the MDB any of its members who participated in such a party, especially Renato Archer, one of the MDB national directors. "And," Galvão added, "there are MDB members who are unwilling under any circumstances to accept the present or future leadership of Carlos Lacerda."

Admitting that the two-party system was artificial, Galvão described the ARENA and MDB as having been ordained from above. But he argued that the Frente Ampla was guilty of the same error. "It stems from understandings reached at the top between political chiefs." A still more serious sin, he wrote, "is the unworkable attempt to bring opponents together. No one, whether or not a participant or supporter of the Revolution, can accept the idea of a party

directed and guided at the same time by Lacerda, Goulart, Kubitschek, Quadros, and Ademar de Barros. This is a fish very difficult to
sell even if touted by a salesman of the talent of the former Carioca
governor. And for this reason the Frente Ampla makes no progress
in São Paulo and appears to make no progress in the rest of the
country."[19]

7. A Post for Lacerda in the New Administration? (April–July 1967)

On March 15 Castello Branco became a former president. During the
four months that followed, ending with his death in a plane crash in
Ceará, he witnessed the peaceful functioning of the regime he had set
up. The period, without political shocks, was one in which economic
activity increased and inflation continued to decline. Only in foreign
policy was there a change, with the new president and his foreign
minister, Magalhães Pinto, determined to show more independence
from the United States.

For those advocating changes in domestic policy, President Costa e
Silva proved disappointing, and he was called indecisive. Hard liners,
who had been unhappy with Castello and had helped put the new
president in office, complained that the administration was insufficiently radical; occasionally they described it as inoperative.[1]

Costa e Silva also disappointed those who looked to him to grant
amnesty to the *cassados*, increase wages, restore direct presidential
elections, and modify the stern laws he had inherited. The first test
occurred with Hélio Fernandes' signed editorial of March 15 about
the "sinister" and "hideous" outgoing president. Lacerda and lawyer
Evaristo de Morais Filho argued that Fernandes had the right to sign
it because restrictions imposed on *cassados* had expired along with
the institutional acts on March 15; but the new justice minister, São
Paulo Professor Luís Antônio da Gama e Silva, pointed out that the
new constitution specified that punishments based on the institutional acts and decreed before March 15 remained in effect. The president's office, commenting on March 22 on the National Security and
Press laws, said that Costa e Silva would not consider any revision of
"revolutionary legislation"; and, on June 6, Costa e Silva himself announced that for at least four years no alterations would be made in
these laws bequeathed by Castello.[2]

The MDB, described by Carlos Castello Branco as "powerless
and without ability," could do nothing. Some of the aggressive new
emedebista congressmen, such as journalist Hermano Alves, were

dissatisfied with the reelection of Oscar Passos as MDB president and said that it would have been better to have turned to Josafá Marinho, Osvaldo Lima Filho, Mário Martins, Mário Covas, or Martins Rodrigues.[3]

Hermano Alves, at the suggestion of Renato Archer, consulted these men and past statements of Lacerda and Kubitschek in order to produce the draft of a Frente Ampla manifesto. Its publication in the press brought a thunderous article by Lacerda denouncing the "supposed" manifesto as a provocation resulting from intolerable audacity and frivolity. Separating himself from its "radical demands," such as "an entirely new constitution" and "full and immediate amnesty," Lacerda said that all the Frente had in mind at the moment were revisions of the constitution and laws, and "revisions by the judiciary of unjust punishments." He explained that he and Kubitschek were determined neither to approve nor combat Costa e Silva, but, rather, "help create a friendly atmosphere in which the new government can overcome the immense difficulties that it encountered."[4]

Creating a friendly atmosphere before March 15, Lacerda congratulated Álcio Costa e Silva for having separated from "the American group," General Electric, that Lacerda said had briefly employed him; and he criticized those who, he asserted, maliciously misinterpreted statements of the president-elect about Portugal and Africa. After March 15, Lacerda praised the speeches of the members of the new administration, and said that if anyone deserved to be invited to join the Frente Ampla it was Costa e Silva, whose foreign policy pronouncements "emphasized exactly" the points defended by the Frente.

Archer, less friendly to the incoming regime, declared that Costa e Silva and those around him were so incompetent that the regime would collapse, and he explained that the Frente Ampla planned a recess during the next several months in order to avoid being held responsible for the collapse. Lacerda, however, defended the intelligence and ability of the new president in João Alberto Leite Barbosa's *bc/semanal.* He wrote that Costa e Silva, unlike Castello, "does not feign culture or pretend to be what he is not. I consider him more cultured, in the sense of having experienced life, than Marshal Castello, whose humanistic culture is dubious at best."[5]

The *Jornal do Brasil* wrote late in March that the Costa e Silva government might ask Lacerda to become Brazil's ambassador to the United Nations and that the former governor was inclined to accept. The press continued to speculate on this possibility and reported that Magalhães Pinto had discussed it with Costa e Silva. In May, when Lacerda was in the United States giving lectures, he told the World

Wide Lecture Bureau that he could not accept the speaker's fees if he found himself serving Brazil in an official capacity in the United States, "a hypothetical thing that may or may not happen."[6]

When the brief war broke out between Israel and Arab states, early in June, Lacerda worked on a letter to Magalhães Pinto. By then it had been reported that "discreet soundings" by friends of Lacerda's and the administration were going so well that "the integration of Carlos Lacerda in the political setup of the government is expected within three or four months." Lacerda's letter, sent to the foreign minister on June 8, called the Mideast conflict the result of the resolve of some Arab dictators to wipe out Israel, and thus an aggression against the UN. He recommended that Brazil assume a clear position in favor of the people of Israel, who "have demonstrated their capacity to exist as a nation and their desire for peace." Politely Lacerda added that, in writing his letter, he had no desire to create difficulties for the government or perplexity for his friend Magalhães Pinto.[7]

Brazil's foreign minister did not follow Lacerda's recommendation. Nevertheless, the delivery of Lacerda's letter to the minister was followed by the statement of oppositionist Senator Antônio Balbino that Magalhães Pinto was interested in having Lacerda join the government in a maneuver of the administration to avoid the possible emergence of a third party. Guanabara legislator Mac Dowell Leite de Castro, hoping that Lacerda would receive an offer, said: "The talent, intelligence, and public spirit of Lacerda are indispensable to national development."[8]

In the *Tribuna* in mid-June, Lacerda lashed out against those who sought to force premature decisions on the Costa e Silva government and himself. Calling them intriguers who spread lies in the hope of maintaining the people divided, he wrote that his early appointment to the UN would have opened a flank of the new administration to attack by "the system whose domination was consolidated" by the Castello administration. He added, however, that time was passing and that the people could not wait indefinitely for a decision from men who had acted in the name of the people without their consent.[9]

In Rio Grande do Sul a month later, Lacerda made favorable remarks about Costa e Silva and refused, once again, to discuss politics. Soon it was reported that Costa e Silva had agreed on the possibility of his government's accepting "the collaboration of Carlos Lacerda, possibly in a diplomatic post abroad." Political commentators guessed that Lacerda's interest in joining the administration sprang from his growing conviction that his only hope of reaching the presidency in 1970 lay in winning an indirect election dominated by the ARENA.

Has Lacerda a love more attractive than outcasts Quadros, Goulart, and Kubitschek? (Hilde Weber drawing on page 49 of Weber, *O Brasil em Charges, 1950–1985*)

His long silence about political matters was said to have been a useful contribution to his "reapproximation with the government."[10]

Goulart supporters complained in April that both Lacerda and Kubitschek were closer to the government than to the opposition. They could, however, understand the caution of Kubitschek, who had returned to Brazil on April 9 and been reminded by Costa e Silva and Gama e Silva to be discreet. In May the government prepared to prosecute him for alleged corruption in his government, and he fell ill. He felt hurt at the failure of his old friend Negrão to help him.[11]

In the case of Lacerda, the "PTB sector" of the Frente Ampla was irate because of "vacillations" that it blamed on his "self-interest." True, he made statements now and then about plans to structure the Frente, but nothing ever came of them, and the public became used to hearing about postponements. Early in April, when he ceased publishing daily columns, he was being faulted for having failed to attend meetings of Frente leaders. When he returned to Brazil on May 16, after his month of lecturing in the United States, he said "spirits have been disarmed" and suggested that the time might have come to mobilize a third party. But, three days later, he rejected "for all time" the third party idea because it seemed likely to kill the Frente Ampla, which could, unlike a third party, have adherents belonging to the existing parties. He devoted attention to Rocio, particularly to raising pheasants there, and advised his son Sebastião of his plan to translate, for publication by Nova Fronteira, a book by Churchill and one about Machiavelli by Georges Mounin.[12]

Former PTB members, hoping to prevent what they called "the total failure" of the Frente, insisted at least on its long-promised structuring. In June, when nothing came of that, they turned to Kubitschek, but he was being threatened with "geographical confinement" if he violated the rules governing *cassados*.[13]

Early in July the Frente was pronounced either dead or close to death. Goulart supporters blamed Lacerda, who, they said, had been "using the Frente in order to become close to the Costa e Silva government." Oscar Passos blamed "irreconcilable contradictions of antagonistic forces and the lack of seriousness of the Frente's principal spokesmen, each concerned only with his own interests." *O Estado de S. Paulo*'s remark about the "collapse of the effort to set up the so-called Frente Ampla" was less surprising than the view of MDB congressional leader Martins Rodrigues, a Kubitschek friend who was scheduled to become a member of the Frente's directive commission. Agreeing that the Frente had collapsed, Martins Rodrigues blamed the situation on Kubitschek's inability to act and Lacerda's timidity. The Frente's loss of impact and substance, he said, had become so great that a completely meaningless meeting between Kubitschek and Quadros, in Guarujá on July 1, had been interpreted as a Frente Ampla development. Sadly the MDB congressional leader confessed that no way could be found to activate the Frente.[14]

8. "Rosas e Pedras do Meu Caminho" (April–July 1967)

Colonel Américo Fontenelle, one of the few military friends of Lacerda to embrace the Frente enthusiastically, died at about the same time that Martins Rodrigues spoke of the Frente's collapse. Lacerda was inconsolable. Outside Rio's São João Batista cemetery chapel, where Colonel Fon-Fon's body lay, Lacerda leaned against a wall and cried. He insisted on being left alone.[1]

At the time of the burial, attended by two thousand people, Lacerda reminded Veiga Brito that it had been Fontenelle who had brought them together when an engineer to handle water was needed. Recalling Fontenelle's participation in the "air force group of Gustavo Borges and Rubens Vaz" that had sought to protect Lacerda from gunfire in 1954, the former governor told Veiga Brito: "He was a leader. Fontenelle was one of the few people who combined the man of action with the formidable organizer. No one understood me as well as he, and I believe no one understood him as well as I. Fontenelle had every virtue. Few equaled him as a family man."

Sandra Cavalcanti remarked that the colonel, both prudent and senseless, courteous and rude, had been "unable to do only two things: flatter the powerful and forget the public good." Commander Wilson Machado said: "He died on the field of battle; he died for the Paulistas"—a reference to the difficulties encountered by Fontenelle in his recent effort to reform São Paulo's traffic. Paulistas' attacks on the colonel moved the grieving Lacerda to exclaim: "What a terrible thing for a man like him, who was honest, correct, and died poor, to have to hear in São Paulo a repetition of all the slanders they hurled at him here in Rio."[2]

Lacerda's reactions to his own setbacks were given in parts of his autobiographical recollections "The Roses and Stones of My Path," which appeared in twelve installments in *Manchete*, between April 15 and July 1.[3] He wrote that his "wrecked presidential dreams" left him feeling unhurt and "freed from a sinecure" and that "the injustice" he suffered left him "a bit scornful" of political ways and politicians. He described himself as "prepared and available but not impatient or overanxious," and left no doubt that he would like to be called. He wrote that whenever he learned of the creation of a new nation, he felt like printing a small announcement: "For hire for a few years, a person with experience at governing, with training in public life, sufficiently idealistic not to fall into a rut and realistic enough not to be deceived by doctrines."[4]

Lacerda called his series in *Manchete* "a sort of collective purgation"—not a diary or autobiography but "a recollection for the history of the formation of a conscience in Brazil in the last fifty years. People and scenes."[5] The readability was enhanced by references to the weaknesses and quirks of the public figures he knew. Enaldo Cravo Peixoto, SUNAB director in the Costa e Silva administration, was described as timid, and Hélio Beltrão, the new planning minister, was described as not specializing in assuming responsibilities.[6] Lacerda's recollections, hardly kind to Juracy Magalhães or Carvalho Pinto, were distinctly unkind to *O Globo*, Golbery do Couto e Silva, Jânio Quadros, Oscar Pedroso Horta, and Castello Branco.

Kubitschek was praised for his "cordial spontaneity." Defending the Frente Ampla, Lacerda wrote that if Costa e Silva could have supported Kubitschek's inauguration for the sake of democratic continuity, clearly the marshal, for the same reason, could have no objection to an understanding being reached by Brazil's democratic leaders, "designed to win the war against backwardness, ignorance, and poverty."[7]

Lacerda told of his conversion to Catholicism in 1948 and "the perplexity in which I must say I find myself today. My faith has not diminished. Only—how shall I say it—it seems to have hibernated." "To live a social life in a Christian way is very important. But who will help us live our personal lives in a Christian way? . . . Most of those who applaud the social and political position of the last encyclicals do not believe in God and believe in the Pope only to the extent that they feel he is confirming the tendency that each one has to believe in Utopia, instead of believing in what many find so difficult, and which is easier to believe: eternal life." The teaching of the popes, he said, was to mobilize Christians to live social and personal lives in a Christian way, but "is not, I think, necessarily designed to transform all religious people into economists, sociologists, and amateur reformers. . . . I do not propose to teach the Lord's Prayer to the vicar. What I propose is that the vicar not let us forget to use it."[8]

When Dom Lourenço de Almeida Prado, a key figure in Lacerda's conversion to Catholicism, read Lacerda's statements, he found satisfaction in what he called Lacerda's fidelity, "maintained during so many years and such short (and infrequent) contacts." He wrote from Rio's São Bento Monastery to tell Lacerda that he had done well to emphasize the spiritual mission as the specific task of the Church. The preoccupation with the social aspect, Dom Lourenço wrote, "expresses itself not only in the form of resolving the problem of social disparities, but, more seriously, of reducing human problems to a simple question of social conviviality, to a sociability without sinew, without fiber."[9]

The response of Congressman Oscar Pedroso Horta to Lacerda's articles dealt with politics and appeared in *Manchete*. The former justice minister, attributing Lacerda's anti-Quadros "insults" to the recent refusals of Quadros to receive him, gave his own version of the governor's role in the events of August 1961, including Lacerda's trip to Brasília on the 19th, after Lacerda, "tearful and in a state of extreme agitation," persuaded Eloá Quadros to arrange for him to see her husband.

Noting that Lacerda's autobiographical articles "extolled" Kubitschek and "revered" Getúlio Vargas and João Goulart, Pedroso Horta called these positions "the chemistry of the movement which is supposed to popularize Lacerda, give him political strength, in the hope that President Costa e Silva, also spared, will tolerate the political resurrection of the former governor. Lacerda wants to reach the UN as Brazil's representative. From the international platform he will dictate rules for the national life and the government will swallow them or suffer the abrasion of scandal beyond its borders."

Pedroso Horta wrote that Lacerda, a demagogue who aspired to the presidency "with the same burning desire with which lungs demand oxygen," would now agree with any position of Costa e Silva if such agreement would bring him closer to the presidential palace. The São Paulo lawyer and MDB congressman also told his readers that Lacerda found the memory of Vargas, whose public and private life he had defiled, to be like an iron curtain, separating him from the people and spoiling his dreams of wearing the presidential sash. Therefore, according to Pedroso Horta, Lacerda hoped that the rust of forgetfulness would make the curtain disappear. Observing that these comments applied also to Lacerda's relations with Goulart, Pedroso Horta expressed the certainty that Goulart would not make a pact with Lacerda. He added that Vargas' family and friends, and the Brazilian workers, would turn their backs on Goulart if he joined hands with Lacerda. Calling Kubitschek's association with Lacerda an error, Pedroso Horta warned that other *pessedistas* should not make the same mistake, because "Lacerda, once in power, will behead them, hang them, guillotine them, one by one, until the third generation, and will call their ashes and descendents unpardonably vile."[10]

Lacerda's reaction, given in a letter for publication in *Manchete,* was to express the hope of never receiving praise from a "repetitive liar" such as Pedroso Horta, a "doleful" example of "a species that is on its way to extinction."[11]

9. Hélio Fernandes and Lacerda Anger Military Leaders (July–August 1967)

Lacerda was relaxing at a *fazenda* near the Uruguayan border when he learned of the death of Castello Branco in a plane crash in Ceará on July 18. He told reporters that he was "truly shocked and sorry" although he had "differed politically with him." "Brazil has lost one of its greatest men," he said. Asked about the impact of Castello's death on the Costa e Silva administration, Lacerda replied that it would have none, "because Brazil is being governed by Costa e Silva, who needs no tutelage."[1]

In the meantime in Rio, Hélio Fernandes signed and published a *Tribuna da Imprensa* article that called Castello "cold, merciless, vindictive, ruthless, inhuman, calculating, easily offended, cruel, frustrated, without greatness, without nobleness, dry inside and outside, with a heart that was a true Sahara Desert." Asserting that "Castello in his long life never loved or was loved," Hélio Fernandes suggested words for the gravestone: "Here lies one who scorned humanity and ended up scorned by it."[2]

Military men were indignant and some of them felt like wrecking the *Tribuna.* Hélio Fernandes, writing on July 20 about the violent reaction, blamed it on the international trusts, which, he wrote, were taking advantage of what he had written "to have his head." Reminding his readers of his "monumental campaigns" against the trusts, he wrote: "I have paid and shall continue paying whatever it costs to have the right to tell the truth—or at least what I believe is the truth."[3]

Costa e Silva found Fernandes' article about Castello "profoundly repugnant," but hesitated to have the journalist arrested because the step might turn Fernandes into a "victim" and would be based on dubious legal grounds. The Press Law stipulated that only Castello's family could sue the journalist for his description of the late president, and implementation of the National Security Law required a judgment by the military justice system, which was likely to recognize that the case against Fernandes was weak.[4]

Nevertheless Justice Minister Gama e Silva quickly came to feel that the pressure for Fernandes' punishment was so strong in the army that resistance to it could result in a "violent" military crisis. Pressure was exerted by hard liners who had already prevailed on Costa e Silva to authorize the illegal seizure of copies of Márcio Moreira Alves' book, *Torturas e Torturados.* Now, according to Hélio Fernandes, the pressure was led by Military Club President Augusto César Moniz de Aragão, who, he said, was furious at Costa e Silva for not appointing him minister of the army (formerly called war minister) and who told the justice minister that, unless Fernandes was punished, no way could be found to restrain those wanting to carry out "personal retaliation."[5]

Costa e Silva, after hearing Gama e Silva's dire description of the situation, authorized the justice minister to sign, on July 20, a resolution ordering Hélio Fernandes to be confined on Fernando de Noronha Island, off the northeast coast. The resolution admitted that a lower court judge had allowed Fernandes, a *cassado,* to continue practicing his profession, but it argued, nevertheless, that the measures decreed by the previous administration, based on Institutional Act No. 2, remained in effect in accordance with Article 173 of the new constitution. In conclusion, the minister said that he was obliged to act against the journalist to "preserve political and social order." Fernandes, who had been held in Rio by the Federal Police "for his own protection," was turned over to the Army Police and flown to the island on the evening of July 21. The punishment, Abreu Sodré remarked, was altogether fitting.[6]

Lacerda was in Pelotas, Rio Grande do Sul, discussing the Frente Ampla with friends of Goulart, when he learned about the fate of

Hélio Fernandes. He called the "loutish" punishment politically stupid, immoral, and a disgrace for the nation—a declaration of war against democrats and a "challenge that I accept." He said that he could not understand the president's use of his power to vent his rage. "I hope that Costa e Silva or his advisers come to their senses and revoke this measure, which disfigures the concept of goodheartedness that the people have of the president."[7]

The "virulent tone" of Lacerda's declarations in Pelotas was seen as marking the end of any possibility of his "integration" into the Costa e Silva administration. Passing through Curitiba, Lacerda said that he had broken no truce with the administration because he had had no truce. He called the government's treatment of Hélio Fernandes a violation of the law, an imitation of practices of Hitler's regime, and "a threat against all of us."[8]

Upon returning to Rio, Lacerda resumed his work of a *Tribuna* columnist. His column of July 31 reflected his belief, expressed in the south, that Castello's death "brought an end" to polemics and resentment. In the *Tribuna* he used the word "inopportune" to describe Fernandes' article, and pointed out that, while in some respects the article was both severe and correct, it failed to mention that in Castello's life traces of charm and generosity could be found, such as his faithful and touching love for his late wife. "If Castello often used his authority badly, I believe he did so with sincerity of purpose."

Lacerda wrote that most of the military officers, while sharing the general feeling that Fernandes' article was inopportune, had had no intention of physically attacking its author or his newspaper, and that neither Costa e Silva nor Gama e Silva had originally planned to punish him. The confinement, he wrote, resulted from the pressure exerted by a group, not exclusively political, that was determined to force Costa e Silva to follow the orientation of his predecessor. Lacerda added that the banishment of Fernandes to the island was a greater threat to the president than to Fernandes.

Gama e Silva, denying this explanation by Lacerda, said he had resolved "spontaneously, without any pressure," to punish Fernandes.[9]

Together with two of Fernandes' lawyers and a congressman, Lacerda made arrangements to visit the journalist. Lawyer Evaristo de Morais Filho remained behind to be on the scene when a lower court judge, Evandro Gueiros Leite, rendered a decision about the legality of the confinement. The decision, released on August 9, was unfavorable to Fernandes. In it the judge observed that "if one does not recognize the validity of the institutional acts, to the extent that they were not revoked by the present constitution, the constitution itself is invalid" because an institutional act authorized Congress to create the constitution. The judge also ruled that the justice minister should determine the length of the confinement and select a location suitable for the *cassado* to work and live with his family. Evaristo de Morais Filho quickly submitted a habeas corpus petition to the Federal Court of Appeals.[10]

In Recife on August 7, Lacerda told reporters that Gama e Silva was not a man of his word, because "he promised" the trip to the island "would be made today" in an air force plane. The travelers reached their destination on August 8 and spent six hours there. Hélio Fernandes complained of eighteen days of isolation. Lacerda took photographs.[11]

Upon returning to Recife, Lacerda announced that "the confinement of Hélio Fernandes was a provocation, designed to force me to break definitely with the Costa e Silva government, and originated from economic groups that dominated the Castello Branco period and want to return to power." Calling Roberto Campos the apparent head of the groups, he explained: "They counted on my attacking Marshal Costa e Silva quickly, and, as I did not do so, they forced my hand with the Hélio Fernandes case. The serious thing is the attempt to compromise the Costa e Silva government, leading it to depend on the same forces that controlled the Castello Branco government." Lacerda insisted that the army's so-called demand for Hélio's punishment was a myth, and illustrated his point by calling attention to the good treatment being furnished the prisoner by men of the Fourth Army.[12]

The *Tribuna* published photographs taken by Lacerda, along with poignant correspondence between Hélio and his family. Hélio's wife Rosinha and Sandra Cavalcanti were at Lacerda's side in Rio when he told the press that "the president's heart appears to beat on only one side." Costa e Silva, he explained, cried at Castello's burial but showed no magnanimity toward the journalist, separated so long from his children and enduring an illegal punishment. He called the Hélio Fernandes case "a sort of civilian Dreyfus Case."[13]

Lacerda was with Guilherme da Silveira Filho at Orlando Ometto's Mato Grosso *fazenda* when Roberto Campos, replying to the former governor, said that Lacerda's "fanciful imagination" was responsible for the charge that members of the Castello administration exerted pressures on Costa e Silva. Campos and Castello's son Paulo were taking steps to sue Hélio Fernandes for his article of July 19. Juracy Magalhães, also preparing to sue Hélio Fernandes, let it be known that he had never, while foreign minister, "authorized the sterilization of Brazilian women to satisfy the demand of the North Americans and obtain Alliance for Progress assistance."[14]

After the Federal Court of Appeals, by a 6-5 verdict, upheld the

decision of Judge Evandro Gueiros Leite in support of the confinement of Hélio Fernandes, the journalist blamed incompetent jurists
for the decision, and Gama e Silva complied with the stipulations laid
down by Gueiros Leite. In mid-August, Pirassununga, São Paulo, was
indicated as the place where Hélio Fernandes would complete his
confinement; and on August 23 it was decreed that he should stay
there until sixty days had elapsed since his arrest on July 20.[15]

General Moniz de Aragão was pained to read in the press that the
good treatment given to Fernandes by military authorities in Pirassununga proved Lacerda's assertion, made on radio and television, that
the armed forces held nothing against the prisoner. Therefore in *O
Globo* on the Day of the Soldier, August 25, he published a rejoinder,
"Keep Away from the Armed Forces." Fernandes' "repugnant" article, the Military Club president explained, was one of many attempts
to incite the military to react violently, thus presenting a dilemma
to the government, which, if it chose in this case to act against indiscipline, would alienate officers. Such alienation, Moniz de Aragão
added, would delight individuals who, "in an effort to satisfy spurious ambitions, do not hesitate to beg subversively for alliances with
enemies."[16]

Thus began the general's exchange with Lacerda, who initiated in
the *Tribuna,* also on the Day of the Soldier, a series of five articles of
such acrimony that Admiral Sílvio Heck distributed a note to express
disgust at Lacerda's "bruising vulgarity" against the Costa e Silva administration. *O Estado de S. Paulo* explained that Lacerda's "radicalization"—initiating a campaign to strengthen the Frente Ampla—
was his only option following the collapse of a possible tie with the
government.[17]

Fernandes, Lacerda wrote, had interpreted the sentiment of millions of Brazilians, "those who threw paper from buildings and set off
fireworks on the day of Castello's death." He described Costa e Silva's
"cowardly" government as degrading Brazil. Turning on August 26 to
Moniz de Aragão's article, Lacerda explained that the general had
portrayed individuals as begging because he found it hard to think
clearly and had the custom of speaking down to subordinates. He
described him as having been hesitant and evasive before March 31,
1964, and as presently serving interests that "really are spurious."

What irritated the general, Lacerda wrote, was not Gama e Silva's
view of military men as irresponsible and uncontrollable, but the
revelation, "which I now make loudly and clearly, that the article of
Hélio Fernandes about the late Marshal Castello Branco is nothing
but a magnified repetition of the opinion of General Moniz de Aragão himself about the late Marshal Castello." In explaining this

statement, which could only have shocked Castello-admiring Moniz de Aragão, Lacerda recalled that when the general had appeared at the governors' meeting at Guanabara Palace on April 4, 1964, he had said that Castello, having defects like all men, "is proud and obstinate." In conclusion, Lacerda wrote that the admonition "Keep Away from the Armed Forces" was an admonition made by those who wanted to use the military "for their own appalling purposes."[18]

Lacerda's article was read in the Chamber of Deputies by Raul Brunini so that it would be included in the congressional record.[19]

Costa e Silva's wish to have Moniz de Aragão desist from his polemic with Lacerda was conveyed by Army Minister Aurélio de Lyra Tavares to Army Chief of Staff Orlando Geisel. Geisel relayed it to Moniz de Aragão, who occupied the post of director of army education. Nevertheless, Moniz de Aragão published, in *O Globo* on August 29, an article about Lacerda entitled "His Fate Is to Rot While Alive." It was his duty, the Military Club president wrote, to present clarifications to the public and his military comrades, because intrigues stemming from Lacerda's political ambition were detrimental to the nation.[20]

Besides "clarifying" his own role in March and April 1964, Moniz de Aragão wrote much about Lacerda, whose article, he said, was "the equivalent of an epileptic spasm, slobbering hatred, intrigue, and malice." He pictured Lacerda as abandoned by the friends he had disappointed, scorned by the enemies he flattered, and living alone with his immense ambition, which, together with his sordid principles and lack of emotional stability, had finished him. The general wrote: "In the solitude to which he condemned himself, this man, for whom popularity is as necessary as air, broods over his perished ambitions, agitates in malice, and, as mentioned by Sílvio Heck, threatens the nation with his instability. Lacerda says he has a horror of hatred, but he himself is hatred personified. Hatred caused by nothing but frustration." Quoting Pedroso Horta in his closing lines, General Moniz de Aragão wished many years of suffering for "this inhuman and brilliant individual who poisoned the existence of the best men, his contemporaries."[21]

As Moniz de Aragão had ignored the army minister's warning to discontinue his polemic with Lacerda, speculation about his arrest was rife. But a large part of the military, increasingly hostile to Lacerda, came to his defense. With Lyra Tavares' threat to make him director of army horses instead of army education, the general withdrew from the polemic. At the same time, Justice Minister Gama e Silva ruled against Lacerda's appearing on television.[22]

Moniz de Aragão continued to be attacked in Lacerda's articles and was the recipient of a letter from Hélio Fernandes. According to the letter, written in Pirassununga on August 30, the general, "strategist and moralist," had committed a tremendous error in making use of *O Globo*, "the country's most corrupt newspaper, owned by the greatest traitor of the national interest that Brazil has ever known." Asking what army the general sought to bar him from, Fernandes told of his own imprisonment for opposing Goulart's army of the "people's generals," while Moniz de Aragão had remained quiet and Roberto Marinho had frequented the presidential palace. But, Fernandes wrote, Moniz de Aragão was wasting his time if he sought to keep him away from the "true" Brazilian army, the "nationalistic" and democracy-supporting army. If, Fernandes wrote, the general would join him in his battles to save Brazil from the foreign trusts, such as the Hanna Mining Company and Standard Oil, he would declare the general a hero and even visit him on Fernando de Noronha Island, where he might end up as a result of defending the national interests.[23]

Lacerda, writing in *Fatos & Fotos* magazine, pointed out that "those who speak too much in the name of the military and accomplish so little"—and who "place themselves at the service of vested interests"—were not representative of the military majority. He wrote that the typical military man was "as good as you and me," carrying out, with poor pay, his daily tasks in a routine and hardly productive manner, and "sharing the shortcomings of a backward country." The life and training of military officers, Lacerda said, rarely allowed the formation of a general culture and left them isolated and inclined in peacetime to display a sort of insolence that disguised timidity. Their distrust of civilians, he added, did not prevent them from being deceived by civilian big shots, nor from accepting, when they entered politics, vices that they condemned when observing from a distance.[24]

10. The Meeting with Goulart (September 24–25, 1967)

Lacerda told his *Tribuna da Imprensa* readers that in the UN he would have argued that the money spent in Vietnam could liberate millions of people from misery, because "one year of war in Vietnam costs more than 20 years of total assistance of the United States for all of Latin America." He explained, however, that he could not agree to go to the UN to advocate the self-determination of peoples when "my own people do not have that right."

Returning to his role of assailant of Brazilian administrations, he denounced "immaturity" in the Costa e Silva government, the "perplexity" of Finance Minister Antônio Delfim Neto, the "ever increasing omissions" of Planning Minister Hélio Beltrão, and the activities of Education Minister Paulo de Tarso Dutra, who, he said, distributed public money to assure his own reelection to Congress.[1]

Amaral Netto was chosen by military and political supporters of the government to reply to Lacerda. The Carioca congressman, who had switched from the MDB to the ARENA, gave his Chamber of Deputies speech of August 31 in his own name with the explanation that Lacerda, no longer a bugaboo, had ceased to scare anyone, least of all the government, "which will never give him the satisfaction of a reply because he does not deserve one." He attributed Lacerda's antigovernment attacks to the decision of "a majority of the cabinet members" to deny him the UN appointment. Lacerda, he said, had revealed his dictatorial spirit as governor of Guanabara, was largely responsible for Kubitschek's losing his political rights, and placed himself at the side of democracy and the Frente Ampla only because no other doors were open to him.[2]

Amaral Netto's speech was delivered at a time when Lacerda and the *Tribuna* were announcing that the Frente Ampla was about to embark on an active "new phase," with the participation of the masses. The "official launching" of the Frente, according to Osvaldo Lima Filho, would take place in Belo Horizonte early in October at a rally that he predicted would be "the largest prodemocracy rally ever held in Brazil." To organize for the new phase, a meeting took place at Renato Archer's residence on September 4. There Kubitschek and Lacerda gathered with *arenistas* Salvador Mandim, Veiga Brito, and José Carlos Guerra, and *emedebistas* Archer, Martins Rodrigues, Osvaldo Lima Filho, Josafá Marinho, Mário Covas, Hermano Alves, Nestor Duarte, Barbosa Lima Sobrinho, Mauro Magalhães, and Renato Azeredo. Archer was named executive secretary, and Josafá Marinho president of the "coordination commission." An "official note" was issued calling on the people to be present at the Frente's forthcoming "mobilization."[3]

Governor Abreu Sodré spoke disparagingly about the "new look" of an organization that "appears in new clothes each day." In Brasília, ARENA President Daniel Krieger and government congressional leader Ernâni Sátiro affirmed that ARENA members should not belong to the Frente. When MDB congressional vice leader João Herculino suggested that his party might also prevent its members from joining the Frente, he could cite a report showing that 120 of the 133 *emedebista* congressmen opposed entering the Frente.[4]

With *O Globo* and São Paulo ARENA President Arnaldo Cerdeira urging less tolerance by the government, Justice Minister Gama e Silva ordered Federal Police Director Florismar Campelo to investigate Kubitschek's participation in the recent meeting at Archer's residence. Lacerda and Archer, demonstrating support for Kubitschek, were photographed outside the police headquarters, while Kubitschek, who had been applauded in the street, faced interrogators in the building. The former president refused to answer the questions, and, instead, distributed a statement saying that for three years he had put up with humiliations incompatible with the respect due a former head of state. He had, he said, tried to contribute to Brazilian harmony when he lectured abroad and cooperated with investigations at home. Disappointed now by the failure of the new administration to reestablish political and juridical order, he had resolved, he wrote, to take refuge in his legal right to answer none of the authorities' questions. "Silence is the only weapon of protest available to me at the moment."[5]

Kubitschek returned to the United States, but, before doing so, sent an emissary to Goulart with a pro-Frente appeal, to which Goulart responded affirmatively on condition that the Frente not become a party and that former *petebistas* follow the personal guidance of Kubitschek. Despite his appeal, Kubitschek felt that a Goulart-Lacerda meeting would be a bad mistake, at least at this time. While he worried about the response of the military to such a meeting, work on its behalf was carried out by José Gomes Talarico, a *cassado*, and Congresswoman Lígia Doutel de Andrade, wife of a *cassado*. Reports that Goulart might be agreeable led Senator Mário Martins to declare: "Political events of recent days, related to the Frente Ampla, have been the most significant for the nation since the events of March 1964."[6]

Lacerda, telling some PCB representatives of his plan to visit Goulart, found the Communists split between those who felt they could make temporary use of Lacerda and others who opposed cooperating with the Frente Ampla lest they benefit Lacerda. Warned by one of the Communists that his meeting with Goulart might provoke government repression, he replied: "You people want the progressive unpopularity of the Revolution to bring the working class into your hands, whereas I want to see if I can harmonize the Revolution with representatives of labor, such as João Goulart, precisely to prevent the victory of you people." His alliance with the Communists, Lacerda believed, was clearly understood by both sides to be temporary.[7]

In the second half of September, while plans for Lacerda's meeting with Goulart were discussed in Montevideo by Wilson Fadul and Edmundo Moniz, Goulart appeared hesitant. Then Archer, who had served in the Goulart administration, sent Talarico from Rio to Montevideo with a letter emphasizing that the meeting was important for Brazil. Several days later, a telegram from Talarico advised Lacerda and Archer that Goulart would receive them on Sunday afternoon, September 24.[8]

Lacerda, calling on Joaquim da Silveira on the 22nd, asked for his opinion and was told that the plan, a poor one, would result in a declaration of war against him by the *Lacerdistas* who had continued to support him. During the conversation, Lacerda placed a letter in the hands of his friend with the request that its content be disclosed in case anything happened to prevent him from "revealing the truth."

The letter, which Lacerda had typed in his library, explained that the purpose of the Montevideo meeting was to convince the workers that "we are not their enemies" and thus complete the Frente with the inclusion of "the most numerous sector, the workers, which Goulart does not represent alone—far from it—but represents more authentically than all the 'leaders' of the UDN, today lying in the rough lap of the military government." Lacerda wrote that his effort to unite a divided country justified "every sacrifice"; and he expressed his hope for "a competent civilian government, able to resist the forces of American economic groups and their Brazilian agents, who have condemned us to be dominated by them or the Communists. And we should not want either."[9]

At the invitation of Lacerda, a *Manchete* photographer flew with him and Archer to Montevideo. There they were joined by Ivo de Magalhães, the Goulart administration's mayor of Brasília; Ivo, who had been the Guanabara Public Works secretary before Lacerda became governor, had been accused by him of having cooperated with Roberto Marinho's Lage Park Project.

Goulart, with a friendly smile, greeted Lacerda, Archer, and Ivo de Magalhães at his apartment at 5:00 P.M. In order to be alone with Lacerda and Archer, he told Talarico, who had been at the apartment, to take João Vicente Goulart, his young son, to a soccer game, and told Ivo de Magalhães to remain at the door and let no one come in.

Goulart and Lacerda had much to say to each other, and their conversation was so cordial that it helped Archer conclude that Goulart was more spontaneous than Kubitschek and that it was easier to deal with Goulart about the Frente Ampla. Archer also concluded that Goulart, perfectly at ease and "very objective" in his observations, had matured and become a different person from the politician he had known in Brazil. During the first seven hours the three men were together, Goulart interrupted the conversation to introduce his two children, "condemned," he said, "to carry out their studies in a foreign language."

With the discovery that it was midnight, Lacerda accepted an invitation to share sandwiches with Jango and his wife, Maria Theresa, while Archer went out to eat at a *churrascaria* with about ten Brazilian political exiles and deal with their objections to a joint Goulart-Lacerda statement. During the meal, Archer phoned Brizola and promised to visit him in Atlántida, Uruguay, where he was confined. Brizola learned from Archer that the purpose of Lacerda's trip was to see Jango, and he therefore told Archer that he would not see Lacerda. A visit from Archer, he said, would be welcome.

Lacerda, according to his recollection, opened his conversation with Goulart by saying: "It would not be fitting for me to approach Juscelino and not approach you, although, really, the things that separated you and me were more serious. . . . I hurt you a great deal, but you also hurt me. I think, however, that you represent a current in Brazil, and what interests me is this: to make that current, through you, a part of a national understanding." When Goulart said the inclusion of Quadros was essential, Lacerda and Archer, who had not yet left, pointed out that their efforts had been thwarted by the reservations felt about Lacerda by Pedroso Horta, José Aparecido de Oliveira, and Quintanilha Ribeiro. Lacerda said he hoped Goulart would forgive him for bringing up the problem of Brizola, whereupon his host admitted that his brother-in-law was a problem, but added: "The problem, above all, is one for me."

Archer, explaining what had been done, was interrupted by Lacerda, eager to make it clear that he was not a presidential candidate and the Frente was not a vehicle to promote any such candidacy. Goulart graciously remarked that the positions being defended by Lacerda made him a desirable candidate. They agreed about foreign policy and Brazil's need to become a nuclear power; they agreed also that Brazil was being denationalized by foreign companies.

As for the Frente Ampla, Goulart disclosed that he had consulted eleven people, of whom only three had spoken favorably of the movement. The Aranha and Vargas families, he said, were opposed to his discussing it with Lacerda, and Lutero Vargas was vehement about the matter. Nevertheless Goulart expressed a willingness to support the Frente provided it did not become a nucleus for the formation of a new party or for the advancement of Lacerda's presidential candidacy.

Goulart remarked that the answer for 1970 might lie in a military candidacy, and he recalled that Vargas in 1945 had wisely turned to General Dutra and had explained then to the protesting Goulart that, with Dutra in office, "we shall be able to breathe, and withdraw, until we can go ahead." Lacerda said the UDN had erred in failing to recognize positive points about Vargas, and proceeded to examine current military presidential possibilities. He said that Albuquerque Lima, "an excellent name," had only three generalship stars, while Mário Andreazza was merely a colonel; and he guessed that Lyra Tavares was handicapped by the resistance against putting another minister of the army in the presidency.

Lacerda, who enjoyed reminiscing, asked Goulart why he had left Rio on April 1, 1964, when, as Lacerda put it, "the military people responsible for the Revolution considered Rio lost." Goulart said that a resistance on his part would have meant a useless sacrifice of lives.

Archer returned from the *churrascaria* with Amauri Silva, as Goulart had requested. Amauri, labor minister during Goulart's administration, sat down with Archer to compose a joint declaration, but they were handicapped by the continuing conversation of Lacerda and Goulart. As it was 7:30 A.M., Archer and Lacerda went to their hotel, where Lacerda typed a joint note so full of Goulart-like paragraphs about the workers and the social problem that it was abbreviated by Archer when he incorporated some of the contribution of Amauri Silva.

In its final form, the note expressed the understanding by Goulart and Lacerda of the frustrations of the people, especially the workers, and their hope that Brazil's resources would be used to help her own people and not foreign and domestic groups "that bleed and exploit" the work of the Brazilians. Goulart and Lacerda called for better wages, direct elections, and "fundamental reforms," and described the formation of a true Frente Ampla of the people as a "great task." They were not, they explained, entering into pacts or considering new parties or future presidential candidacies. "We have no personal ambitions, nor do we harbor hatred."

The note was signed by Goulart and Lacerda in time for a press conference held late on the morning of September 25. Lacerda, responding to reporters' aggressive observations about his past relations with Goulart, said that it was now clear that Jango was no Communist just as he, himself, was no agent of the American embassy. He added that the support of the people had formerly been divided between Goulart, Kubitschek, and himself. "Now we are united and have the support of all the people."

Lacerda and Archer lunched in a restaurant with Goulart, Amauri Silva, Ivo de Magalhães, Talarico, and others before their scheduled departure for Rio at 3:00 P.M.—a departure that left Archer no time to keep his date with Brizola.[10]

Even before the joint Goulart-Lacerda note was released, it became known that Brizola had condemned the meeting. After the lunch, one of the reporters handed Lacerda a copy of Brizola's statement, written in Atlántida and distributed in Montevideo by Neiva Moreira: "I am not surprised that Goulart has come to an understanding with Lacerda. It behooves me to wish him good luck in such fine company. It was on account of that same lack of fidelity to his principles that Goulart lost his authority as president—and ended up being deposed with incredible ease." Speaking of Lacerda, Brizola said: "For me he continues the same as always."

"The sacrifice of Vargas and his farewell letter," Brizola said, "cannot be so easily forgotten. It was Lacerda, as spearhead of the international groups, who brought Vargas to the despair imposed on my country. As governor of Guanabara, Lacerda was a destroyer of liberty, an executioner belonging to the police, a tyrant. He is now in the opposition simply because the military do not allow him to be president. And also because his friends abroad have found other and better representatives in Brazil."[11]

Lacerda, after reading the Brizola statement, handed it to Goulart, who remarked that an early result of their meeting was public knowledge, at last, of "this cross" he carried. He spoke of the harm brought to himself and his government by Brizola but repeated that it was a family matter, to be left for him to handle.[12]

In Brazil, Goulart representative Osvaldo Lima Filho accused Lacerda of having left for Uruguay precipitately, before Goulart had commented on a proposed agenda, submitted at Goulart's request. Another example of Lacerda's precipitation, he said, was his earlier association in Rio Grande do Sul with a "minority" wing of the MDB, thus alienating the local MDB majority and creating for Goulart "problems that continue unsolved."[13]

When Lacerda, tired but satisfied, reached Rio's Galeão Airport with Archer on the night of September 25, he said that Kubitschek should get together with exiled economist Celso Furtado in Paris and seek his collaboration in the preparation of a program of action for the Frente.[14]

Describing later the impression he had gained of Goulart, Lacerda said he was not a stupid person but had simple tastes and lacked "Vargas' Nietzschean craving for power." According to Lacerda, Goulart enjoyed power to the extent that it permitted him to help friends and annoy foes, but was uninterested in being a statesman. Goulart, he added, had been "absolutely unprepared" for the presidency he had unexpectedly occupied and was temperamentally disinclined to deal with the "millions of problems" of that office.[15]

During an interview given soon after returning from Montevideo, Lacerda described Goulart as uninterested in becoming president again but wanting a position of influence in labor. Lacerda also guessed that Kubitschek, beginning to feel the years and "adding dye to his hair," was "not much interested" in returning to the presidency, but, like Goulart, desired a position of influence. In an excellent mood, Lacerda expressed the belief that Costa e Silva would come around to accepting a direct presidential election; and he spoke of Carvalho Pinto and himself as the leading civilian candidates.[16]

11. The Storm (September–October 1967)

Gustavo Borges, feeling that Lacerda had given a "solemn promise" not to deal with Goulart, was dismayed to see newspaper pictures of the Montevideo handshake and broke with Lacerda. When Brigadeiro Eduardo Gomes, who lived in the same apartment building as Lacerda, found himself in the elevator with the former governor, he silently hugged a corner to avoid him.[1]

Lacerda, at a lunch with foreign press correspondents, admitted that the handshake was especially shocking to what remained of his feminine admirers and said it was more devastating to *Lacerdismo* than to *Janguismo,* but he maintained that the only alternative to the Frente Ampla's peaceful route to democracy was violence.[2] *O Globo* called this contention a "false premise" and pictured "the Hitler and Stalin who shook hands" as "preaching rebellion and civil war in case of the evident failure of the Frente Ampla." It depicted the "Mephistophelean" Montevideo declaration, with its disclaimer of all personal ambition, as "probably the most cynical document of Brazil's political history." In *Última Hora,* Danton Jobim wrote that it would be very difficult for the working masses to swallow the Montevideo declaration, and even more difficult for them to swallow the photograph of the two former enemies fraternizing.[3]

In São Paulo, the *Diário Popular* also expressed doubt that the workers would be influenced by the "demagogic and vulgar" expressions of Goulart and Lacerda. The *Folha de S. Paulo* apparently felt the same way, because it saw the "so-called Frente" as "an artificial composition of leaders without followers." It expressed the greatest contempt for Goulart, responsible for the chaos that had justified the military intervention of 1964, and said he was in no way to be compared with Kubitschek, who had contributed to Brazil's development and whose *cassação* was perhaps unfair, especially since investigations had not proved him guilty of serious sins.

O Estado de S. Paulo lamented the "unbelievable" and "incomprehensible" act of Lacerda, who, it wrote, had turned his back on his noble anti-Vargas and anti-Goulart campaigns of the past. Calling Lacerda the "ex-leader of Brazilian liberal democracy," it wrote that he had decided to join the confused antidemocracy group, known as leftist, and to adopt views used by the *caudilho* Goulart when the former president had tried to justify "outrages" that had led to his overthrow in 1964. In the eyes of the Mesquitas' gloomy daily, this new setback added to the peril of the political situation, already suffering from Costa e Silva's inept dealings with Congress as revealed in the vetoes with which he modified the congressional version of a worker accident law.

The *Correio da Manhã* congratulated Costa e Silva for not using police methods to crush the Frente Ampla but said he was making a mistake in leaving the anti-Frente work to the ARENA, part of a political party structure that gave the people no better representation than the old one that had allowed the rise of bosses such as Goulart and Lacerda. A truly representative system, it wrote, would reduce these *caudilhos* to their proper insignificance. The proadministration *O Jornal* asserted that Lacerda, having lost his head, supported people who had brought complete disorder to Brazil.[4]

The *Jornal do Brasil* called the Montevideo meeting a deal to obtain votes from a wealthy landowner, made by a man who had failed to receive a government post and who planned to demolish the constitutional process because it would not offer him, "on bended knees, the presidency for an indeterminate period." It also denounced the Frente Ampla's "irresponsible" and "incoherent" attack on the government's wage policy. "Much as we might wish it to be different, that policy is the result of a mathematical reality that is not altered by empty or asinine declarations aimed at the susceptibility of the ignorant" and made by the Frente's "well-remunerated spokesmen."[5]

In a letter to the *Jornal do Brasil*'s Nascimento Brito, Lacerda called the publisher incoherent and guilty of skepticism, of believing in no one, and of having an aristocratic contempt of the people that would lead him to accept despotism. Nascimento Brito, in a handwritten reply, said his skepticism was rational, and his position was coherent because he remained within his principles when he stated that nothing favorable for Brazil could result from Lacerda's "sudden revision of values, principally moral ones." He warned against a return to the past and rejected the conclusion that a popular insurrection would occur with a failure to follow the path Lacerda had chosen.[6]

In reply to Abreu Sodré's letter critical of his meeting with Goulart,

Lacerda wrote the governor that irreconcilable enmities did not exist—nor eternal friendships. After former *udenistas* of São Paulo sent a telegram to Sérgio Lacerda objecting to the Montevideo meeting, Abreu Sodré told *O Globo* that Lacerda was guilty of turning "to the symbol of everything condemnable in Brazilian history."[7]

Former President Dutra expressed his dislike of "the Montevideo Pact," and Jânio Quadros, in a letter that Pedroso Horta read in the Chamber of Deputies, reiterated that he had nothing to do with "that Frente Ampla—without a philosophy or program, a disturber of the reconquest of democracy." In the Senate, government leader Eurico Resende said the Lacerda-Goulart handshake had the virtue of encouraging the enactment of more regulations to govern the *cassados.* In the lower house, Breno da Silveira (MDB, Guanabara) pictured millions of MDB voters as stupefied and saddened to learn that Goulart had met with such a man as Lacerda, longtime insulter of Goulart and former scourge of the congressman and his friends.[8]

A fistfight seemed likely to break out after Congressman Amaral Netto denounced Lacerda's character and was called a traitor and stool pigeon by Brunini. Amaral Netto, crediting Brizola with coherence, asked how Goulart could face his children in the future when they would ask: "Papa, why did you make us shake hands with the man who insulted Mother?"

In the Gaúcho legislature, the president of the state MDB, Siegfried Heuser, declared that he remained opposed to the Frente; he was told by one of his followers that "not even Institutional Act No. 2, that closed down the PTB, harmed the labor sector as much as the Montevideo agreement." Guanabara legislator Nina Ribeiro, who had cooperated with the Lacerda gubernatorial administration, used the term "buffoonery" in referring to the Montevideo meeting and said that the Frente Ampla was nothing but an unpopular effort to return to an unhappy past.[9]

The ministry of the army reported a gratifying show of "military unity in favor of the government." Although commanders were apt to frown on meetings of hard line colonels, now they found them acceptable because they were held to express disapproval of the Frente Ampla. Admiral Sílvio Heck, after meeting with Costa e Silva, declared that Lacerda, seeking to revive his frustrated hopes of becoming president, had no military coverage and no friends among the revolutionaries. The hard line admiral called the Frente Ampla an illegal movement of millionaires and playboys who traveled to Europe, the United States, and Uruguay.[10]

As Amaral Netto suggested, Goulart was in for trouble and Brizola gained stature in labor circles. From Paris, Samuel Wainer wrote his longtime friend Goulart to say that he could not, even by silence, give support to the Montevideo meeting. In Rio, Congresswoman Ivete Vargas, niece of Getúlio, said that Goulart had taken "his most tragic political step," renouncing the ideal of the labor movement, throwing doubt on the authenticity of Getúlio's farewell message, and "disclaiming his paternal house." She called the Frente Ampla "a diversionary instrument at the service of American imperialism," but admitted that it included some good people, such as Barbosa Lima Sobrinho.[11]

Alzira Vargas do Amaral Peixoto also condemned the Montevideo declaration, prompting Jânio Quadros to congratulate the daughter of the "unforgettable President Getúlio Vargas" and observe that "posterity will not pardon treason to the dead." Congressman Osvaldo Lima Filho, replying to Ivete and Alzira, said that Getúlio would have supported the Frente Ampla, just as he had tried, in 1945, to safeguard the institutions by allying himself with Communists who had sought in 1935 to overthrow him. Ivete then issued a note expressing doubt about Lacerda's conversion to popular and nationalist causes. She said she had not broken with Goulart. "It is he who has broken with me."[12]

Completing the solidarity of the Vargas family, Getúlio's son Lutero issued a note on October 2 mentioning "the insurmountable barrier between the workers and some people who claim to lead the Frente Ampla," and expressing his inability to believe that a trip to Montevideo could redeem "the permanent assailant of the ideal consubstantiated in Getúlio's Farewell Letter." He told *O Globo* that Lacerda was the same man who had arranged to toss beggars into the Guarda River, carried out arrests and press censorship, taken extravagant trips abroad, joined commercial enterprises while he was governor, favored a "state of emergency," and tried to prevent the inaugurations of elected officials. Aurélio Viana, MDB leader in the Senate, praised the position of Lutero Vargas. The socialist senator, who had spoken well of Lacerda in 1965, placed the blame for the split in the opposition on the shoulders of Lacerda, "the bitterest assailant of the men who can most contribute to social peace."[13]

Goulart, in a message to Lutero, said that Lacerda's visit, on behalf of redemocratization, represented, in a way, a public act of repentance of past accusations, and he reminded Lutero that Getúlio had become reconciled with Vicente Ráo despite the Paulista lawyer's call for his assassination in 1932, and had written later, in his Farewell Message: "To hatred I reply with forgiveness." In a long letter to Osvaldo Lima Filho, Goulart argued that Getúlio had not hesitated to enter into alliances with bitter adversaries when necessary to preserve social conquests. Denying that the Montevideo meeting would be detrimental to the MDB, he pointed out that he had not supported a third party or any candidate, or entered into a pact. In phrases meant for workers who held out against the Frente Ampla, he argued that Brazil could be restored by a "union of all patriots in a *movimento amplo, without electoral positions, that is, a true frente ampla.*"[14]

Lutero replied that the one who had changed was not Lacerda, plotter of coups against democracy, but Goulart, "who allied himself with an enemy who mocks political justice." The popular Minas oppositionist, João Herculino, returned to Brasília from Rio Grande do Sul and reported that Gaúcho politics were under the influence of Brizola and the ideology of Getúlio Vargas. But Brizola was not alone in being mentioned to fill the vacancy in the *Getulista* sector of the PTB, brought about by the Vargas family denunciations of the Montevideo declaration. Quadros was reported to be playing a role, allying himself with the Vargas family and giving support to a new *frente cívica,* or *frente nacionalista,* whose formation was being sought by Ivete Vargas.

Martins Rodrigues, after a futile attempt to persuade Quadros to join the Frente Ampla, observed sadly: "My meeting with Jânio lasted for merely one whiskey."[15]

The *Correio da Manhã,* returning to the fray early in October, wrote of the positions taken by Quadros, the Vargas family, oppositionist leaders, and even hard line colonels against the "plot set up by Lacerda," and concluded that seldom had anything been so overwhelmingly repudiated as the Frente Ampla. The *Jornal do Brasil* said: "Until this country is made completely insensible by a process of collective amnesia, the reaction of the Brazilian people to dangerous collusions and spurious conspiracies, such as that of Montevideo, can only be one of the most complete and total repulsion."[16]

The *Jornal do Brasil*–Marplan poll of Cariocas showed that the "Kubitschek-Lacerda alliance" had been unpopular but that the "Goulart-Lacerda alliance" was even more unpopular. Twenty percent expressed approval of the latter, 19 percent were indifferent, 16 percent had no opinion, and 45 percent were opposed.[17] The breakdown by classes was as follows:

	Upper Class	Middle Class	Lower Class
Opposed	77%	51%	32%
In favor	3	20	24
Indifferent	10	19	21
No opinion	10	10	23

Asked for whom they would vote in a presidential contest, those polled revealed a change in sentiment in one year:

	October 1966	October 1967
Kubitschek	26%	32%
Lacerda	45	29
Costa e Silva	12	11
Goulart	4	6
Magalhães Pinto	3	5
Mário Andreazza	—	5

Only 10 percent felt that the Costa e Silva government was unsatisfactory.

A São Paulo city poll, conducted after the Montevideo meeting and used by Quadros in dealing with the Vargas family, stated that Quadros was favored by 21 percent of those consulted, compared with 10 percent in August. It showed that Kubitschek's support had increased from 11 percent to 12 percent and that Lacerda's had fallen from 7 percent to 5 percent. Friends of Quadros were quick to point out that in the city, the mainstay of Quadros' strength, Goulart was named by only 3 percent of those answering the question, "Who is Brazil's greatest living politician?"[18]

12. Preparing to Go to the Streets (October–December 1967)

Lacerda, visiting São Paulo, found Carvalho Pinto sympathetic to direct presidential elections and wage increases. The popular senator and some other ARENA leaders in Brasília said that these positions would gain mass support for the government party in its contest with the Frente Ampla. They decided to try to convince Costa e Silva.[1]

On October 5 Lacerda wrote to Júlio de Mesquita Filho of his wish to help this endeavor of the ARENA. He asked Mesquita to publish his letter, written without consulting other Frente members, announcing that if the men in power would adopt the reported program, he would consider his missions in the Frente and in public life to be finished. "I shall have nothing more to ask of anyone."[2]

Costa e Silva reiterated, in his talk with the ARENA people, his determination to limit the battle against the Frente to the political field. Congressman Raphael de Almeida Magalhães, who congratulated the president for finally deciding to mobilize and consult the ARENA, was a member of the party's commission to recommend positions it should take on questions such as presidential elections. The commission chairman, Carvalho Pinto, had already broken with Abreu Sodré on the election issue, and now he helped persuade the commission to deliver a unanimous opinion in favor of direct elections, thus rejecting a report by Raphael that leaned toward indirect elections. The finding of the Carvalho Pinto commission was doomed, however, by the position taken by the ARENA congressional leadership and Costa e Silva.

Liberal wage increases, the other chief demand of the Frente, were opposed by Labor Minister Jarbas Passarinho, who said: "The people would not forgive us for a weakness that could mean a return to inflationary chaos."[3]

In order to explore the possibility of mobilizing public opinion on behalf of the wage and election issues, approximately thirty Frente Ampla lawmakers, federal and local, met with Lacerda at Archer's Rio residence. Following the meeting, Frente spokesman Hermano Alves told the press of plans to stir up workers with the wage issue, and students with the issue of interference in Brazilian education by the United States assistance program. However, Lacerda and Frente Executive Secretary Archer announced that action in the streets would be postponed until January 1968. For the time being, Archer explained, the principal objective would be to overcome "resistances" in PTB circles.[4]

Instructions had been sent by Goulart for *petebistas* throughout Brazil to join the Frente and form centers of pro-Frente activity. In Rio Grande do Sul, where Mariano Heck and five other state legislators already favored the Frente, messages were received from Goulart inviting Gaúcho mayors, aldermen, and political friends to come to Montevideo; there he asked them to speed up the formation of Frente Ampla commissions all over the state. Some of the Rio Grande do Sul legislators, upon receiving pro-Frente letters from their constituents, abandoned their hostility to the Frente.[5]

Former Congressman Doutel de Andrade, after visiting Goulart and Brizola, told MDB leaders that Brizola, while not a Frente supporter, had no intention of opposing it. Although the Porto Alegre MDB leadership, devoted to Brizola, continued cold to the Frente, some of its members were seen as likely to assume, with a little more time, a neutral position—provided that the Frente, which they feared as a rival, would show no hostility to the state MDB.[6]

Where the MDB was weak, the Frente sometimes prospered. The Frente in Minas, which had experienced a slow start, was assisted by the limited appeal that the MDB held there for workers. The MDB vice leader of the state assembly, a legislator close to Tancredo Neves, spoke of the "collapse" of the Minas MDB and the "nascent" strength of the Frente, assisted by the federal government's obvious dislike of the Frente. Tancredo remarked: "The MDB is being outstripped by the Frente."[7]

Miguel Arraes, in exile in Algiers, declared that he was taking a neutral position and was not, as previously reported, opposed to the Frente Ampla. Kubitschek, upon returning from Europe on October 11, ended speculation about his abandoning the Frente Ampla in favor of another combination favored by Ernâni do Amaral Peixoto, the Vargas family, *Janistas,* and former PSD and PTB members. Kubitschek was even reported to be telling friends that he liked the presidential candidacy of Lacerda, who, he felt, could give the country an administration similar to his own. Goulart, in a letter to Lacerda, wrote that no attention should be given to rumors that he might desert the Frente. He agreed with Lacerda that the "economic crisis" would become more serious after the new year, and asked that the Frente give primary attention to the wage issue.[8]

Lacerda was in a good mood on October 19, when he spoke with reporters at Galeão Airport before leaving to lecture for five weeks at universities in the United States. He offered to bet with anyone that the 1970 presidential election would be direct. For the elucidation of American students, he said, he was taking a copy of the book in which Alcindo Guanabara asserted that President Campos Salles' defense of the currency around the turn of the century had paralyzed Brazilian development, for which reason Brazil continued to be chiefly a supplier of raw materials. Lacerda called Campos Salles "the precursor of the other Campos, the one maintained by Castello Branco."[9]

The lecture tour allowed Lacerda to criticize American expenditures of billions of dollars "to kill people" in Southeast Asia while failing to provide for Latin America a foreign aid program that attended to "the basic needs." He said that the Costa e Silva government was "directed by an oligarchy that helps neither Brazil nor the United States," and "retards" Brazil's economic development. After Students for a Democratic Society at Stanford University distributed anti-Lacerda leaflets, calling him "the Barry Goldwater of Brazil," he defended his support of the "military coup d'etat" of 1964 by arguing that "a poor country cannot long put up with disorder."[10]

Lacerda was in the United States when articles appeared in *Realidade* magazine, one of them co-authored by Quadros, disclosing that Quadros had resigned the presidency in order to participate in a coup. In a cable to friends in Brazil, Lacerda said: "I have just seen it confirmed that I prevented a dictatorship in 1961." The Brazilians, he added, now had "a clear confession" about a matter that caused "me to suffer so much injustice and incomprehension."[11]

While Lacerda was in the United States, Archbishop Hélder Câmara declared that he would not join the Frente Ampla because he felt he could best help the poor by continuing apart from "political parties." Lacerda had clashed with Dom Hélder in the past but was hoping for an expression of support for the Frente from the controversial archbishop, who was influential in the fast-growing progressive wing of the Brazilian Catholic Church. Hélder Câmara and Ação Católica Brasileira attacked injustices suffered by the poor. Like the Frente Ampla, they denounced the "starvation wage policy" of the Costa e Silva administration when it proposed in November that increases for government workers and the military, to start in 1968, be limited to 20 percent, approximately equal to the annual cost of living increase.[12]

Before Lacerda returned to Brazil, Goulart suggested that he visit Chile and use his powers of persuasion there on former Goulart cabinet ministers Almino Afonso and Paulo de Tarso Santos, whose hostility to the Goulart-Lacerda alliance was considered harmful to the Frente in PTB circles. But Lacerda dismissed the idea and reached Rio on November 23, in time to testify on behalf of Hélio Fernandes, who was being sued for slander by Roberto Campos. In his testimony, Lacerda pictured the "Hanna group" as wanting to control Brazilian mining policy in order to prevent Brazil from exporting ore, and he declared that the United States had arranged for Brazil to have high income taxes, thus retarding capital formation and weakening Brazilian companies.[13]

December was a month for addressing graduating classes, and Lacerda used the opportunities aggressively, bringing an end to what the *Jornal do Brasil* had called the Frente's "recess." After his speech in Rio on December 9 to the Colégio Santa Dorothéia graduating class, Hermano Alves observed: "Only now is Carlos Lacerda becoming a part of the Frente Ampla." In the speech, Lacerda drew applause when he declared defiantly that he feared no threats because he owed "nothing to those who rose to power at my expense" and who had earlier been "submissive when I alone was protesting." In addition to his usual bill of fare (the Vietnam War, Brazilian wage scales and economic development, and broken military promises about democracy) Lacerda denounced "army bayonets" for protecting corruption, and analyzed the position of the Catholic Church, which he said had come under pressure to avoid defending privileges.[14]

Before leaving Rio to speak at the Catholic University of Porto

Alegre, Lacerda told reporters that if the Church was straying from its chief mission, as some people claimed, the reason was the lack of freedom for other institutions. Making the same point to the press in Porto Alegre, he called the Church "the only institution that is still free to respond to the appeal of the masses."[15]

The speech to the graduating students in Porto Alegre had already been described by Lacerda as "extremely important" and as enjoying the "total approval" of Kubitschek and the "*Janguista* sectors." In it Lacerda replied to those who said he was violent by defining violence as taking over the nation and not knowing what to do with it. Again he accused the military of protecting corruption. And he promised to take, at long last, the Frente Ampla "to the streets." He explained the delay as caused by the refusal of the government to let him speak on television, and added that the first to take the Frente to the streets would be the students. "It will be like a new abolition campaign." Lacerda radiated confidence and sounded as though he were delivering an ultimatum. "No power in the world," he exclaimed, "will be able to prevail against youth."[16]

O Estado de S. Paulo, although agreeing with "the great tribune's" criticism of the regime, continued to lament his association with "men expelled by the Revolution." But nationalistic General Peri Bevilacqua, a Military Tribunal judge, liked Lacerda's appeal for amnesty and praised him for seeking to promote peace among Brazilians. Lacerda, on December 26, called Bevilacqua "an illustrious republican" during an address to Rio economics students that condemned the size of the federal deficit and the rate of inflation. He took credit for having warned the Castello administration against inflation's tragic results, and blamed the economic situation for contributing to the general anguish, melancholy, despondency, and hopelessness. He told his cheering audience of almost a thousand: "I am able to protest only because no one in this country, with laws or rifles, has the moral authority to suppress my word."[17]

Interior Minister Afonso de Albuquerque Lima, lunching with reporters, said that Lacerda's charge of corruption in the government had "no foundation," and that the government should act drastically against the Frente Ampla. He was so upset by Lacerda's reference to him as one of the generals who sought to succeed Costa e Silva that he wrote Lacerda to say that "no act on my part has indicated that I am competing with my dear friend Colonel Andreazza, or with you, yourself, or with anyone else in the dispute for an elective post. I hope you understand that not everyone is ambitious for power."[18]

The new life that Goulart and Lacerda were bringing to the Frente Ampla angered MDB President Oscar Passos. After the MDB state legislators in Paraná resolved unanimously to join the Frente and urged that the national party do the same, Carlos Castello Branco wrote that the Frente, with "mass adherence of MDB state director-ships," could become "the MDB plus Carlos Lacerda and minus Os-car Passos." Passos responded by declaring on December 7 that the Frente existed only in the press and that it was a "shameless lie" to say that any MDB directorships adhered to the Frente. Some *eme-debistas*, offended by the "shameless lie" remark, reported that only the MDB directorships of Acre (Passos' state) and Alagoas were unaf-fected by the Frente movement; but their state by state list of Frente advocates and "sympathizers" was a weak rebuttal to Passos and failed to show any mass adherence by MDB directorships.[19]

13. The Government, Nervous about Lacerda, Mobilizes Troops (January 1968)

Lacerda, after seeing the new year in with the Silveiras in Cabo Frio, busied himself with roses and vegetables in Rocio. In Petrópolis he opened a branch office of his Novo Rio investment firm and set up a market stall to sell products he had grown. He told reporters: "I have no television and do not listen to the radio or read the newspapers because I want to rest."[1]

In the meantime, the PCB gave support to the Frente Ampla, and, at its clandestine Sixth National Congress, condemned the MDB for behaving timidly. However, the Frente's hope of winning over the Brizola sector of *trabalhismo* was dealt a blow on January 10, when Goulart's brother-in-law announced that he found the Frente still in Lacerda's hands and therefore would no longer refrain from attacking it. In a letter written a little later to the *Jornal do Brasil*, he accused the Frente's leaders of advocating a return to a "senseless past," and said that Lacerda was entirely self-centered and had no political or moral significance.[2]

By mid-January, Lacerda was ready to crusade again, and he told reporters at his *sítio* that the military rulers were incompetent and unscrupulous. In Belo Horizonte on January 17 he criticized Mineiro politicians, especially Milton Campos and Vice President Pedro Aleixo, and advocated the return of Goulart to Brazil, "necessary for restoring the *trabalhista* idea."[3]

The speech welcoming Lacerda to Belo Horizonte was delivered by José Geraldo de Oliveira, a colonel in the Minas state troops who disliked the path being followed by the men in power. Inspired by the colonel's words, the *Jornal do Brasil* concluded that the only solution for the general dissatisfaction and the growing separation

The sweet peace of Petrópolis: Costa e Silva relaxes while Lacerda cultivates flowers. (APPE drawing in *O Cruzeiro*, February 17, 1968)

between the people and the military lay in the restoration of civilian leadership.[4]

In Congress, rife with rumors about cabinet changes, government leader Ernâni Sátiro blamed the opposition for the intranquility. Senator Krieger called the moment "a grave one" in which everybody should collaborate against the "subversive" Frente Ampla. The ARENA's Raphael de Almeida Magalhães felt the people's confidence could be restored if the government would embark on a program, and therefore he gathered with technicians to draw one up. Resigning as the government's congressional vice leader, he said he would not join the Frente Ampla, because it did not offer solutions. He denied that he had seen Lacerda or exchanged holiday gifts with him.[5]

Public discontent with the do-nothing government, and the prospect of a more vigorous Frente Ampla campaign, hardly made the situation as grave as it was described; however, military pronouncements appeared with a frequency that Carlos Castello Branco regarded as indicative of a crisis. The pronouncements blended backing for the government with evidence that the military was unable to refrain from reacting to accusations. When Costa e Silva attended a Military Club lunch on January 18, he heard Brigadeiro Antônio Guedes Muniz, former head of COSIGUA, call on him to act against "the brazenfaced lies" of those who "thirst for power and seek to demoralize the military."[6]

A couple of days later, the military sector associated with the president announced that he had to bring an end to the "unsustainable"

situation created by Lacerda, "advocate of the overthrow of the regime." Hard line Minister Albuquerque Lima and his group presented
the president with a written demand for an end to the government's
"excessive tolerance" toward Lacerda's political activities. Fourth
Army Commander Souza Aguiar agreed that the "democratic institutions" were threatened by men "full of intelligence and lacking common sense." He proclaimed that the army would fight without fear
and would prevail because the armed forces were "invincible," leading the *Jornal da Tarde* to warn that if Lacerda carried on with his
mistaken ideas and aggressive tactics, he would destroy both himself and the country's last hopes of avoiding an undisguised military
dictatorship.[7]

On January 26 troops were put on the alert throughout Brazil and
ordered to carry out maneuvers. The maneuvers, ordered by Costa e
Silva, displayed abundant weaponry and were interpreted as a show of
government strength on the eve of a speech that Lacerda was scheduled to give in São Paulo. Official sources called the maneuvers routine exercises and denied, with vehemence and irritation, that they
had any connection with Lacerda's speech. But the explanation was
received with disbelief. While 1,300 marines were dispatched from
Rio to Santos, the city of São Paulo was the scene of troop movements
by 18,000 soldiers, and air force planes swept through the skies. The
government ordered radio and television broadcasters to report nothing about Lacerda.[8]

Federal policemen, with instructions to obtain a text of Lacerda's
forthcoming speech, waited for over an hour at the Hotel Jaraguá
before Lacerda arrived in his Ford Galaxy, which contained parrots
and other birds he had procured for Rocio. He surrendered a copy of
the speech, to be given that night to the graduating economics students of the Álvares Penteado College. Then, in the company of Brunini, Mauro Magalhães, and several São Paulo politicians, he spoke to
reporters. "The principal objective of the Frente Ampla," he said, "is
to overthrow the regime and not the government; if the government
falls it will be the fault of those who form it."

While an air force helicopter hovered over the area, policemen at
the Municipal Theater relieved reporters of their tape recorders. Lacerda, always under police observation, was followed by an army jeep
when he made his way on foot to the theater. Outside the building a
crowd shouted: "Viva Lacerda!"[9]

"My words," Lacerda told the audience, "are not for the government, which is incapable of understanding." He was speaking, he
said, to express the feelings of the people. Citing passages from John
Kenneth Galbraith's *The Triumph*, a novel about a Latin American

Lacerda, with bird, embraces Padre Godinho in São Paulo, while secret
agents watch and a policeman grabs a bystander's tape recorder.
(Lourival Viegas drawing in *Jornal da Tarde*, July 4, 1972)

coup and United States diplomacy, Lacerda called Brazil humiliated,
degraded, ignorant, and heartsick. "An ambitious and undisciplined
military faction, with its cops, its sneers, and its fears, is making a
reality out of Galbraith's novel." He accused the men in power of
institutionalizing corruption in the course of combating the alleged
corruption of a few, and using their "television monopoly" to lie to

the people. They were protected, he said, by "the false constitution." Occasionally he strayed from the text he had given the police.[10]

During the speech, retired army General Waldomiro Meirelles Maia cried out from his place in the audience: "I shall not permit this fellow to continue talking." He kept on shouting while Lacerda tried to carry on with his address. Then, for a while, Lacerda and the heckler yelled at each other. An exasperated Lacerda accused the police force of not fulfilling its duty and vowed to evict the heckler himself. But the general finally agreed to leave at the urging of a friend, São Paulo legislator Américo Sugai. Before he left, he indignantly told the audience: "Lacerda is all wrong if he thinks a general who is president can be overthrown as easily as the others."[11]

On the following afternoon, Lacerda was accompanied by Brunini and Mauro Magalhães when Fabiano, his chauffeur, drove him to Rio. No longer followed by the federal police, he worked in the car on the translation he was making of *The Triumph* while music flowed from the Galaxy's tapedeck. "I think," he told Brunini, "that Galbraith was writing mainly to get things off his chest. What's important is that in his country he can say what he thinks and then become ambassador or hold some such public post."

Before they reached Rio, Lacerda decided to pay a surprise visit to his mother in Vassouras. He found the seventy-five-year-old Olga in splendid health and attributed it to the Vassouras climate. During their thirty minutes together, she hid the worry that reports from São Paulo had caused her. "Di Cavalcanti," she said, "was here this morning and liked Vassouras so much that he plans to buy a house here."[12]

Late in February, Carlos Castello Branco revealed in his column that Lacerda, shortly before his trip to São Paulo, had received a visit at his Rio apartment from United States Ambassador John W. Tuthill, and that more recently the two had met again in Rocio. The ambassador had been eager to defend positions his country was taking about the Vietnam War, the proliferation of nuclear weapons, and Brazilian exports of soluble coffee, and he wanted to reply to some of Lacerda's statements about the United States. At the first two-hour lunch meeting the two men had had a lively discussion, during which Lacerda had made references to Galbraith's book.[13]

Military men associated with the Costa e Silva government were furious with Tuthill for having conferred with "the advocate of the overthrow of the institutions." ARENA Senator Dinarte Mariz asked how the American government would react if the Brazilian ambassador in Washington were to become friendly with radicals like Rap Brown and Stokely Carmichael. Although the *Jornal do Brasil* felt that the government's sudden show of coldness toward Tuthill was not called for, *O Globo* assailed the ambassador's meetings with Lacerda in a page-one editorial. Between March and May, Tuthill made three efforts to speak with Costa e Silva and found he could not reach the president. Early in May, after American diplomats arranged for Tuthill to meet with Brazilian military officers, the ambassador explained that he had met Lacerda at the request of three American senators, interested in the views of all currents of opinion. He added that Ambassador Juracy Magalhães' conversations with oppositionist Goldwater had not been viewed as acts of hostility by the American government. But Tuthill continued to be spurned by Brazilian officials, reducing his usefulness.[14]

By the time that the Tuthill-Lacerda talks became public knowledge, politicians were discussing plans for "political pacification" offered first by Governor Luís Viana Filho and then by Governor Abreu Sodré to put an end to the political "crisis." The nebulous plans, for giving the MDB a feeling of participating in government policy making, had the stated purpose of preventing the MDB from joining the Frente Ampla. "Pacification," it was also felt, might prevent the current of discontent from getting too far out of hand, inviting dictatorship.[15]

In São Paulo, Viana had agreeable talks with Sodré and Mayor Faria Lima, whose turn to Sodré and the ARENA had weakened the MDB. Then he went to Brasília and got nowhere. Costa e Silva refused to provide a piece of the government cake to the MDB. MDB leaders like Martins Rodrigues considered Viana's ideas the equivalent of a "surrender by the opposition." Oscar Passos, the recipient of two written proposals from Viana, pointed out that they would grant none of the MDB's demands, such as amnesty and direct elections. As an oppositionist often accused of timidity, Passos had no desire to be associated with Viana's ideas, especially with an MDB leadership meeting coming up on April 17 where he would test again his claim to the party presidency and his contention that the MDB should keep apart from the Frente Ampla. His considerable support included the party's senators, with two or three exceptions, and, according to Ivete Vargas, forty congressmen belonging to the *bloco trabalhista*.[16]

The *Jornal do Brasil* wrote that pacification required a reform of the cabinet, whose members were fighting each other. Lacerda, in a speech given in Governador Valadares, Minas Gerais, in mid-March, said that true pacification had been proposed by the Frente Ampla and that if the Costa e Silva government did not enact reforms, "we shall have to carry them out tomorrow amidst the blood of the people, shed by rifle bullets."[17]

Raphael de Almeida Magalhães, who had formed an Independent

Bloc of about eighteen congressmen ("the Red Guard"), declared that
the government was unpopular everywhere. He repeated that Costa e
Silva should call on the people to back major projects, such as those
related to education and housing. Again dismissing the Frente Ampla, he now described it as interested only in direct elections to bring
Lacerda to power. He compared Lacerda to an unpredictable gust of
wind and added that the former governor might very well return to
the "Revolutionary family," abandoning Kubitschek and Goulart, if
direct elections were established.[18]

By this time, according to an update of the Marplan poll of Carioca
sentiment, Lacerda had lost a little more ground as a presidential
favorite:

	October 1966	October 1967	March 1968
Kubitschek	26%	32%	33%
Lacerda	45	29	27
Costa e Silva	12	11	10
Goulart	4	6	7

A majority felt that the leadership of the opposition should be in the
hands of the MDB, whereas 26 percent favored having the Frente
Ampla assume that leadership. Sixty-four percent opposed banning
the Frente (with only 13 percent expressing approval of such a step).[19]

14. The Frente, Finally, Participates in Street Rallies (Late March 1968)

The Frente Ampla's participation in an antigovernment street demonstration on March 23, in São Paulo's São Caetano industrial district, was hailed by its leaders as the start of a new phase. The *Tribuna
da Imprensa* wrote, not quite accurately, that the demonstration, "the
first public rally carried out by the Frente," was a success. The demonstration, to protest low wages, was organized by the MDB, which
had distributed 300,000 leaflets in São Paulo's suburbs in the preceding week and used loudspeakers starting at noon on Saturday, the day
of the rally. An enormous statue of the "Black Mother," which the
police had placed in a position to hide the speakers from the audience,
was moved away by local MDB directors and some of the workers.
But not much could be done to counter the effect of the suspension of
train and bus service, ordered by the authorities.

At the appointed hour of 7:30 P.M., only about 500 people were in
São Caetano's Praça do Estudante. With the arrival of the curious, and

latecomers uninterested in the early speeches, and with the attraction gained by a display of fireworks, the crowd grew to about 2,500 or 3,000, hardly the size of a major rally. Worst of all, the crowd was not pleased with the rally.[1]

The twenty-one speakers who preceded Lacerda were frequently booed, not because of their messages condemning Labor Minister Jarbas Passarinho, the Vietnam War, and the "American invasion of Amazônia," but because they took up so much time. Half a dozen state assemblymen were followed by prominent national orators, such as Mário Covas, Hermano Alves, and Josafá Marinho. Lígia Doutel de Andrade and Osvaldo Lima Filho brought messages from Goulart against "imperialism" and "the spoliation of the people."

Lacerda's speech—although occasionally evoking applause, particularly when he criticized Governor Abreu Sodré—was received coldly in almost its entirety. His appeal that the people remain for the closing speeches was ignored.

Lacerda told his listeners that his presence demonstrated that "the place of the Frente Ampla is the public square," and predicted that the São Caetano rally would be the start of a national movement. He called on his audience to assume command of "the struggle" and criticized the "masters of Brazil" for regarding their own gatherings as inspired by "pacification" while using the term "agitation" in speaking of rallies and meetings at which workers expressed their demands.[2]

Ignoring his own appeal, Lacerda left the scene after delivering his address. He was accompanied by the bishop of Santo André, Jorge Marcos de Oliveira, whom he had come to know but not respect in the 1950s when they had attended a course at the National War College. "Carlos," the bishop said as they left the São Caetano rally, "do you know that they are calling me a Communist here?" Lacerda concluded that Dom Jorge was much more afflicted by confusion than by Communism. What distressed him about Dom Jorge and practically all the bishops was not their political position but what he considered a lack of knowledge necessary for taking that position. It was easy, Lacerda thought, to denounce an unjust social order, but it was another thing to explain what social order should be set up. He felt that the bishops were unable to handle the question.[3]

Taking his campaign to the students, Lacerda spoke in Campinas on March 25 in an auditorium packed with three hundred of the thousand who sought admittance. He praised those who wore long hair and outlandish clothes as a sign of protest, and reminded them that student-poet Antônio de Castro Alves, active around 1870, had been the "long-haired abolitionist." Lacerda criticized the government for not undertaking a "revolution in education," and for "proudly" constructing one more hydroelectric plant while all the great nations were setting up nuclear plants.[4]

In Limeira, Lacerda purchased seedlings for Rocio, and, in Piracicaba, he received an honorary citizenship. Then he went to the state capital to address the legislative assembly on the evening of March 28, as requested by its MDB members. Assembly President Nelson Pereira, representing the ARENA majority, asked Lacerda not to attack Governor Abreu Sodré, who had raised no objection to the appearance of the guest speaker. "Carlos," Pereira said, "we are still *Lacerdistas* although you are not." Lacerda told Pereira that the remark made him feel that he was in a position similar to that of a conservative girl who had been caught in some immoral act for which she ought to be ashamed.[5]

The refusal of the legislative majority to allow the public to be present at Lacerda's talk was overcome by the MDB, whose assembly leader signed hundreds of "invitations" for distribution to all who came to the Palácio Nove de Julho. Thus about three hundred invited guests joined about sixty legislators, over half the total membership, to hear Lacerda discuss the economy. Sensationally he spoke of a "program that I know and can recommend, with absolute assurance, for ending the Brazilian inflation in twenty-four hours." The program, he said, would eliminate the budget deficit by postponing the completion of numerous public works projects and would devote so much attention to production that it would replace inflation as a topic of conversation. But, he added, the program was impossible without a competent, courageous government, able to count on the confidence of the people, bring about pacification by amnesty, and mobilize the national will as in wartime.[6]

While Lacerda delivered his lesson in economics, students in Rio met at the dilapidated Calabouço Restaurant with plans to carry out a march to protest the failure of the Guanabara state government to fulfill its promise to construct a satisfactory student eating place. Members of the state Military Police, sent to prevent the march, were jeered and hit by stones. They retaliated by using machine guns, killing a sixteen-year-old student, Edson Luís de Lima Souto, and wounding fifteen others. The killing led *O Estado de S. Paulo* to observe that "all other current political problems have been relegated to a secondary place."[7]

Lacerda commented on the killing in his speech at a vocational institute in Londrina, Paraná, on March 29. He called on all Brazilians to join the students in protesting the death of the youth who had "demanded the right to study, to have food, and to have opinions." Speaking of the plans of the students to march with flags of Brazil and the Vietcong, Lacerda asked, "What is bad about that?" He argued that "a flag does not kill anyone," and said that "the United States, which is at war with Vietnam, lets its students carry the Vietcong flag in front of the White House."

Brazilian youth, he said, was desperate and disillusioned and had been butchered when it sought to have Negrão de Lima fulfill his broken promise about a new restaurant. He called Negrão a worthless reactionary who had been elected by the opposition and then entered into an alliance with Costa e Silva, "who claims to have headed the Revolution."[8]

Frente Ampla people spoke of the possibility of a "monster" May Day rally to be held in Santos to denounce, again, the government's wage policy. In the meantime, on March 30, the Frente's "second public rally" took place in Maringá, in the north of Paraná, and attracted several thousand. It was notable for the lusty cheers that broke out whenever Lacerda, discussing alliances of former adversaries, mentioned the names of Vargas and Goulart. The Frente, Lacerda said, had no further need to explain its alliances, because its two public rally "tests," in São Caetano and Maringá, revealed that the public understood them. It would seek, he promised, the reactivation of the dialogue with youth and all the people, a dialogue interrupted by the post-Goulart regime, responsible for the slaughter of Edson Luís de Lima Souto.

Speaking at the rally and more informally at a barbecue in Maringá, Lacerda maintained that military officers were beginning to appreciate that their activities conflicted with public sentiment. He predicted, at the barbecue, that six more months of Frente campaigning would persuade a majority of the officers to favor direct presidential elections, amnesty, and a return to economic development. "They never have remained for long opposed to the people."[9]

15. The UNE Arouses the People and Repudiates the Frente (March–April 1968)

In Rio during the night of March 28–29, students brought the corpse of Edson Luís de Lima Souto to the Legislative Assembly, which was in session at Palácio Pedro Ernesto in Cinelândia. While the students won their argument to have an autopsy carried out at the Assembly, news of the killing was broadcast and Cinelândia became filled with people. They lined up to view the corpse and heard speeches by students who, during the rest of the night and part of the next day, heatedly condemned the Brazilian government and the Vietnam War.

On the afternoon and evening of March 29, tens of thousands

participated in the funeral procession to the São João Batista Cemetery, in Botafogo. After the burial, groups of young people scuffled with men in uniform. An air force vehicle was set on fire.[1]

Plans for a mass rally, to start in Cinelândia on the evening of April 1, were vetoed by Governor Negrão de Lima. Following his appeal to Justice Minister Gama e Silva for federal assistance, War Minister Lyra Tavares issued a note to warn army commanders against plans, made in several state capitals, for "public marches of clearly Communist orientation, taking advantage of the emotional state of the student class."[2]

The Guanabara Military Police, assisted by federal troops, succeeded in dominating Cinelândia on April 1, but only after clashes. Further skirmishes occurred as 4,000 civilians, many with clubs and stones, and some with revolvers, set forth from Cinelândia for Presidente Vargas Avenue; groups darted quickly from place to place and engaged in conflicts that left policemen wounded, a DOPS car overturned, another car burned, and an ambulance damaged. These activities, and others elsewhere in the city, led journalist Arthur José Poerner to call the rallies of April 1 "the greatest movement of protest yet carried out against the present regime." He noted the violent deaths that day in Rio of two civilians, one of them a student, and the wounding of 60 civilians and 39 policemen. Two hundred thirty-one people were arrested. Downtown shops were pillaged. *O Estado de S. Paulo,* shocked, wrote that the Communist domination of the student movement was much greater than had been imagined.[3]

Throughout Brazil the demonstrations to protest the killing of Edson Luís were mostly nonviolent. But in Goiânia the police killed one student and wounded two. In Fortaleza, students ravaged the installations of the United States Information Service and burned an American flag. In São Paulo, where the police maintained order, students orated, marched, and shouted against "the dictatorship," "imperialism," the 1964 revolution, and the MEC-USAID agreement for American assistance to Brazilian education. In front of the São Paulo Municipal Chamber, they booed city councilmen and cried: "Down with the Frente Ampla!"[4]

The student leaders were dedicated idealists with far-Left, antibourgeois sentiments, and rejected the Brazilian Communist Party (PCB) as unrevolutionary.[5] They rejected also the view of the Frente Ampla, which said, in a statement released in Curitiba, that it favored "victory" through the ballot boxes, and opposed adding to the agitation lest it cause the government to fall and be replaced by an "even more intolerable regime."[6]

Lacerda, flying from Paraná, reached Rio on the evening of April 1, when the worst of the disturbances began. He refused to speak to reporters and went to his apartment to learn more about the situation from state legislators and other politicians. As the press noted, he hesitated at first to make any declaration; but former PTB members wanted him to support the students, and Renato Archer reminded him that already, in Paraná, he had, on every possible occasion, condemned police action against the students.[7]

When Lacerda lunched with Kubitschek on April 2, he had a declaration to show the former president. Later in the day he authorized Archer to release it, and it was read in the Guanabara legislature by Salvador Mandim. In part it was a reply to General José Horácio da Cunha Garcia, who had bewailed the activities of a "horde of subversives" in Rio. Lacerda wrote that while probably a few agitators were at work, "agitation is, today, a widespread sentiment, brought on by insecurity, the lack of legitimate authority, and the criminal brutality of repression." Noting that the nation was "outraged by an orgy of violence," Lacerda maintained that violence had become the official doctrine and the army had become converted into a police force against "'the horde,' that is, the people."

According to Lacerda's declaration, Gabinete Militar Chief Jayme Portella de Mello was de facto president, eager to have arbitrary power and blood, the price of usurpation, "and so the students must die, silenced." Lacerda said the students' revolt was a just one, and called their nonconformity the sign of the rebirth of Brazil. "It is with those who are brave, not cowards, that the nation defends itself. If a few committed excesses, one must remember that they are struggling unarmed."[8]

Vladimir Palmeira, Rio's foremost student leader, asserted: "The students find no merit in the manifesto issued by Carlos Lacerda because he, once again, waited for the situation to become defined in order to decide which side to join." UNE President Luís Travassos and other UNE leaders issued a statement saying that Lacerda "continues to be a personalist politician who simply pursues personal objectives, without the slightest connection with the goals of the students and the people." The statement called on the students to act in a firm, united way, and "thus overthrow our enemies, just as the Vietnamese are defeating imperialism." They were told to condemn censorship, support workers on May 1, and denounce the Frente Ampla and the "sham populism with which it tries to hide its ruling class character and *golpista* tendency to take over the power."[9]

In Brasília, where the university president prohibited students from holding meetings on the campus, the Frente Ampla was attacked by Honestino Guimarães, president of the recently closed Federation of

University Students of Brasília. "Our struggle," he declared, "has no room for opportunists, and our program is the program of the UNE and not of the Frente Ampla." "We do not accept the Frente Ampla because it is not a mass movement. Our struggle is not against the dictatorship but is for overthrowing the entire structure, whereas the Frente Ampla is nothing more than a bourgeois movement of those who have satisfied their economic interests." He denied and denounced reports that Frente Ampla participants were at the front of the student demonstrations in Brasília. "Those reports were circulated, principally among congressmen, by members of the Frente Ampla itself."[10]

Lacerda's declaration was read on the phone by Justice Minister Gama e Silva to Costa e Silva, who was in Porto Alegre with Jayme Portella and other government figures. Gama e Silva also informed the president about plans for demonstrations on April 4, when church services would observe the seventh day following Edson Luís' death. Costa e Silva gave the justice minister carte blanche to deal with the situation.[11]

On April 4, according to the *Jornal do Brasil*, the students in Rio would have a splendid opportunity to "regain" public support by rejecting the influence of agents of agitation, responsible for the depredations of April 1. "Those depredations have nothing in common with the aspirations of the young people." The *Folha de S. Paulo* urged authentic student leaders to regain control from outside extremists.[12]

All over Brazil the authorities were ready on April 4. In Rio, 20,000 federal troops joined 10,000 members of the Military Police to keep order in the streets. During the parade that followed the Mass at the Candelária Church, zealous soldiers of the Military Police, some on horseback, used swords, billies, and tear gas. Over 500 people, among them women and children, were rounded up and taken to Fort Copacabana. After Rádio Jornal do Brasil reported excessive repression and the beating of a *Jornal do Brasil* photographer, the radio station was forced to go off the air. The *Diário de Notícias* wrote of widespread beatings by the "sadistic" Military Police, undeterred by Catholic priests, who sought to protect students, or by the army's example of respecting the people.[13]

In Belo Horizonte on April 4, schools and banks were closed, and in Brasília, university students were again prohibited from gathering in meetings. However, in São Paulo's Santo André district, a defiant rally took place that night. Originally organized by the MIA (Labor Movement against Starvation Wages), students sought to turn it into one of the nationwide demonstrations to observe the seventh day following the killing of Edson Luís. While some voices chanted "Strike!

Strike! Strike!," others were raised to condemn the dictatorship, the United States, imperialism, the Frente Ampla, Lacerda, Kubitschek, the ARENA, the MDB, and the Brazilian politicians in office. Someone made the mistake of shouting "Brazil is not Cuba" and was almost lynched. After several students and journalists were arrested, journalists asked Siseno Sarmento, commander of the Second Army, about the arrest of their comrades. "Those who have been arrested," he said, "are subversives."

On the next evening, April 5, São Paulo students organized, at the Praça da Sé, a "people's trial of the dictatorship"—a "trial" that attracted 6,000. During the march that followed, the students shouted: "Workers, yes; Frente Ampla, no!" They broke windows at the *O Estado de S. Paulo* building, damaged two vehicles (one belonging to the police), and burned an American flag amidst oratory against imperialism.[14]

Lacerda, reviewing the events of April 4, told the *Jornal do Brasil:* "Today Brazil is a country without law and order because the government itself instills insecurity." Asked about reports that he might be punished under the National Security Law, he said he gave no heed to the reports or the justice minister. "Prisons nowadays are the safest places," he said.[15]

In the Carioca press, Lacerda found himself under attack from the Left and the Right. *Última Hora,* defender of the students against police brutality, wrote that if Lacerda were governor he would be arresting and torturing the students, and if opposition politicians, "in this delicate hour," were to turn to "the crow, the specialist in confusion and disorder," it would be because they had "lost their minds." *O Jornal,* which felt that students and agitators were carrying out a plot hatched in Havana, wrote that Lacerda's manifesto of April 2 placed the Frente Ampla on the side of international terrorism. Following the events of April 4, it asserted that politicians who were disgruntled with the 1964 revolution were cooperating with the movement ordered by "Havana, Moscow, and Peking" because they felt that the moment was propitious for overthrowing the Costa e Silva government.

O Globo, supporter of the thesis that the turmoil had been the work of professional roughnecks who attracted few students, wrote that Lacerda's declaration of April 2 was the vilest demonstration of irresponsibility ever seen in Brazil. "The flower grower of Rocio appears in his true colors, seeking to throw young people against the army and bring about deaths to satisfy his morbid ambition." It published a study showing that Edson Luís had been killed by a ricocheting bullet and had not been fired at, and it praised the Catholic priests of

Cardinal Jayme Câmara for helping prevent outbreaks feared by the authorities on April 4—and thus behaving in a way that contrasted with "the preaching of violence by the Red deacon of Volta Redonda."[16]

The news that Lacerda was scheduled to address discontented sugar workers in Campos on April 5 worried the authorities of the state of Rio de Janeiro. The DOPS there made plans to arrest him if he spoke in public, and the commander of the state's Military Police ordered a battalion to occupy strategic positions in the city and repress any sign of agitation. The people who gathered at the Praça São Salvador in Campos, to hear Lacerda, were obviously hostile to the police, and tension was high until a phone call from Archer advised of the cancellation of Lacerda's trip. Archer explained that the civil aviation authorities, alleging poor weather conditions, prohibited the flight of the chartered plane in which Lacerda had planned to fly from Rio.[17]

16. The Justice Minister Bans the Frente Ampla
(April 5, 1968)

Disturbances during the student manifestations strengthened the position of hard liners who wanted a new institutional act or a state of siege. President Costa e Silva, having been told that agents of the Communist Party were at work in university circles, examined the situation when he met in Rio on April 5 with the military ministers, Justice Minister Gama e Silva, and Gabinete Militar Chief Jayme Portella. Gama e Silva's suggestion of a state of siege was supported by the navy and aviation ministers. But the president, backed by Army Minister Lyra Tavares, argued that effective steps could be taken without a state of siege, which would have unfavorable repercussions at home and abroad. He decided that the justice minister should tell the governors to act energetically and prohibit parades and rallies, and he instructed the military ministers to order troop commanders to assist state police forces if necessary.[1]

Several days earlier Gama e Silva received from Jayme Portella the president's request that he draw up a directive that would close down the Frente Ampla. The zealous justice minister needed only to turn to a draft he had written three weeks earlier. On April 5, after the president held his meeting in Rio, the directive was issued with the title of Portaria 177.[2]

The *portaria* pointed out that the Frente Ampla had not complied with requirements established for political parties and had no juridical standing. The Frente's "spurious objective," it said, was to obstruct "the continuity of the Revolutionary work," and the Frente's wish was to "reinstate in public life individuals banished by the

Justice Minister Gama e Silva blames the press for the crisis. (Orlando Mattos drawing in *Folha de S. Paulo,* April 7, 1968)

Revolution." For these reasons, the *portaria* banned all Frente Ampla meetings and activities. It instructed the Federal Police to collaborate with the state authorities in the arrest of violators of regulations governing *cassados,* seize all publications containing statements by persons prohibited from making them, and investigate cases where banned statements had already been made.[3]

The *Folha de S. Paulo* thought it was a strange time to close the Frente Ampla, which had been reviled by the students and had nothing to do with the problem. It published an article to show that Lacerda's tardy and disregarded stance, and the Frente's "total incompetence" in keeping abreast of developments, proved that the Frente had never been a real oppositionist force.

The *portaria,* the *Jornal do Brasil* wrote, was issued with the redundant pomp of an institutional act, but was really an unnecessary utterance by a government which, for thirteen months, had not used the instruments it possessed for repressing the activities of *cassados.* In the opinion of the *Jornal do Brasil,* the Frente Ampla had blossomed under circumstances that the press had interpreted as reflecting a slow relaxation of authoritarianism, and the surprising appearance of the *portaria* would not prevent the continued existence, under a new name or anonymously, of the Frente's arrangement of artificial alliances. *O Estado de S. Paulo* agreed that previously promulgated regulations made the *portaria* "useless" and called it nothing more than a revelation of "the complete bewilderment" of the authorities. It pointed out that the students had been denouncing Lacerda daily "in all their street demonstrations" and therefore he could not be held responsible for the crisis brought on by these demonstrations.

O Globo, on the other hand, wrote that "without the 'Frente Ampla'—subversion that was tolerated—the agitation we have seen would not have existed." It felt that the Costa e Silva administration had, quite understandably, sought at its outset to avoid unpopularity and act less harshly than its predecessor; but, *O Globo* added, it had chosen, unfortunately, to be conciliatory in the case of some "irreducible adversaries." In the opinion of *O Globo,* the justice minister's *portaria* was a purely tactical step and would amount to little unless accompanied by a new strategy that would closely identify the Costa e Silva administration with the revolution.[4]

Rumors about a hard line victory and the impending reactivation of Institutional Act No. 2 led Costa e Silva to deny emphatically that the government would turn to "measures of exception." His luncheon address to the Brazilian Press Association, delivered in Rio on April 7 to commemorate the ABI's sixtieth anniversary, was filled with assurances of his deep devotion to liberty and a free press. Speaking to reporters after the lunch, he declared that "the government has not considered, is not considering, and will not consider the promulgation of a new institutional act, despite unimpeachable evidence that extremist minorities have in readiness a vast plan for nationwide agitation to overthrow the government." "The nation," he also said, "is calm, and no reason exists to declare a state of siege."[5]

The reactions of ARENA congressmen to Portaria 177 were varied. Clovis Stenzel, admirer of a strong military government, disagreed with *O Estado de S. Paulo* and called the Frente Ampla the creator of the climate responsible for the student demonstrations. On the other hand, the ARENA's José Bonifácio Lafayette de Andrada, president of the Chamber of Deputies, said that the Frente, unlike Lacerda's oratory, constituted no danger at all, and he concluded that the *portaria* was inappropriate for a regime based on law. What vexed the ARENA congressmen was the failure of Costa e Silva to consult the party before authorizing the *portaria.* The prestige of government leaders such as Ernâni Sátiro was felt to have been badly damaged.[6]

The MDB's Gastone Righi advocated the adoption of a new name for the movement known as the Frente Ampla and said that if new *portarias* forced the exhaustion of a whole vocabulary of names, "we can finally give the movement still another name: the Revolution." Senator Josafá Marinho compared Gama e Silva to a monkey in an insane asylum and insisted that the *portaria* was unconstitutional. After MDB Congressmen Mário Piva and João Herculino threatened to seek a Supreme Court decision annulling the *portaria,* a more serious threat was issued by a congressional spokesman of the military. He said the government wanted to uphold the regime under which the country was operating, but whether this could be done depended on the future behavior of the opposition; and, he added, it was impossible to tell what would happen if the MDB supported the Frente Ampla against the regime. In the Senate, Aurélio Viana declared that his party, the MDB, had never had any connection with the Frente Ampla.[7]

Lacerda, in Rocio on April 6, was at first reluctant to give an interview to the reporters who called on him. But at length he seated himself in the station wagon of the *Jornal do Brasil* and wrote a statement about the *portaria.* Then he invited the reporters to his house for coffee and spoke of his pleasure at having received baby pheasants from a friend.

Lacerda's statement called the *portaria* "a confession and a tragic error." The so-called revolution, he wrote, "has at last revealed its true face: a little military dictatorship in the worst Latin American tradition." He complained that the regime, although confessing itself to be transitory, "prohibits any movement that aims at preparing the nation for the post-transition stage."

The statement ended with a plea to the people not to despair. Lacerda wrote that although some delay would result from the government's "dictatorial" act, "we shall not fail the people in achieving a revival of the democratic process. Has the Frente Ampla died? Long live the União Popular!"[8]

17. Comments on the Frente Ampla

On April 8 the *Tribuna da Imprensa* published an article by Lacerda that made no mention of the União Popular and gave the impression that he was retreating. "For the time being, I have become free of obligation. I have fulfilled my duty of warning those in positions of responsibility about the crime they are committing. . . . Greed for power, deceit, and incompetence prevail at the moment. So be it. Perhaps Brazil has to pass through this in order to cure itself permanently."[1]

Lacerda's *Tribuna* article and the news that he planned to leave for a long trip abroad prompted Fernando Pedreira to publish a sort of obituary of the Frente Ampla, whose demise, he wrote, could be explained by its "great timidity of ideas." Denying that the Frente had been subversive and the instigator of agitation for a change of regime, he argued that the sin of the Frente had been just the opposite "and for this reason it showed itself so weak and disoriented in the face of the student crisis, to the point of not resisting the ministerial slap." Pedreira, who favored the student demonstrations, "no matter how poor their ideas might seem," wrote that public opinion ought to be mobilized against the "antidemocratic" regime. Brazil's agitators, he said, were too few and were inspired by purposes that were petty as well as ideas that were timid. He ridiculed those who believed that a mere alliance of Lacerda, Kubitschek, and Goulart, "together with half a dozen politicians," could turn the country upside down. Denying that Kubitschek had ever been a leader, he wrote that "he might be seen at the Municipal Ball or in a fashionable restaurant, but neither the young people nor anyone else can expect to hear him express one word of orientation or leadership." Goulart, Pedreira wrote, had reached the presidency because of a resignation, and, in office, had taken his supporters and the nation into "the ditch." Discussing Lacerda, "who could have been something meaningful in the Frente Ampla," Pedreira expressed the hope that "he will return reinvigorated from the trip he is going to make."[2]

It is true that the Frente, demanding full-fledged democratic practices, was more moderate than students who favored elimination of the bourgeoisie. It is true also that the Frente Ampla's leading spokesman did not aggressively condemn the Costa e Silva administration until it became clear that it was antidemocratic. After that, Lacerda became aggressive again. Altogether, between October 1966 and March 1968 the Frente Ampla fulfilled, more than any other group, the mission that Pedreira's article recommended: the mobilization of public opinion against the military regime.

At the same time, Lacerda made appeals to the military. Even if the Frente Ampla had wanted to turn the country upside down, which it did not, support from at least a part of the military was essential at that time.

The student movement that eclipsed the Frente Ampla was influenced by the apparent success of radical student movements outside Brazil and was led by young orators, with much popular appeal, whose differences faded in the face of a common foe, the police. Their freshness and sincerity, their anticapitalist stance, and the battles of their many student followers in the streets took the banner from the

Frente Ampla, with its old politicians and its hope for a peaceful change from military rule. It was not the *portaria* of Gama e Silva that ended the movement begun by Lacerda in 1966. It was the new student risings, combined with increased urban terrorist activities, and Lacerda's fear that, under the tense circumstances that developed, renewed attacks on his part would do no more than make matters worse at a time when a collision seemed possible between extreme antigovernment radicals and extreme radicals among the men in power—a collision that would pave the way for a coup by the latter and shatter his dream of using persuasion and popular demand to bring about, within the administration, a move away from antidemocratic practices.

Lacerda liked to say that the manifesto of the Frente Ampla would come to be regarded in the same light as the Manifesto of the Mineiros, a call for democracy issued in October 1943 during a regime that lacked free expression, a Congress, and elections. The Mineiros' measured words, which even praised the Vargas dictatorship for achieving prosperity intelligently,[3] were devoted to the democratic theme and made their manifesto a noble voice raised in the wilderness of censorship.

The Frente Ampla manifesto, on the other hand, was a document for launching a campaign, altogether possible with a press that was free and an administration that was preparing to end the institutional acts and provide a new constitution. The manifesto of the Frente offered something for everyone, mentioning in turn the workers, the young people, the women, the Church, the middle classes, businessmen, and the military. For its lone signer, it was a springboard for action, the opening gun of a bombardment far more broad and controversial than the democratic theme proclaimed by ninety signers in October 1943.

The virtue of the bombardment was its principal objective: the elimination of injustices and the curbing of a minority rule that would, before long, turn Brazil into a land notable for police violence, torture, and the scrapping of any pretense of democratic ways. The less virtuous features of the bombardment are those usually associated with effective political campaigning.

Lacerda referred maliciously to the public figures he attacked and sometimes called them traitors. He contended that Castello Branco's ailing back made him a snake with a broken spine, "and snakes with broken spines must have their heads smashed."[4] He engaged in what Roberto Campos called "fanciful imagination" when he asserted that the confinement of Hélio Fernandes was a provocation designed by economic groups to bring about the Lacerda–Costa e Silva break, and when he stated that Hanna came to Brazil for the purpose of preventing Brazil from exporting ore.[5]

Like a true oppositionist campaigner, Lacerda assured his listeners that his program would do away with government deficits and eliminate inflation in twenty-four hours, while reducing unemployment and providing liberal wages and credit, higher profits, and less onerous taxes. He courted nationalism and anti-American sentiment and damned the IMF.

The Manifesto of the Mineiros proclaimed emphatically that it rejected a return to the pre-1930 past. The Frente Ampla, while disclaiming that it wanted a return to the pre-1964 past,[6] laid itself open to charges that the disclaimer was not true, especially with the signing of the so-called "Pacts" of Lisbon and Montevideo, which gave the broad front its character. As a matter of fact, a desire for such a return characterized sizable groups defeated in 1964, and the "Pacts" brought the Frente the cooperation of some of the groups, such as a sector of *trabalhismo*, that helped reactivate the Frente late in 1967.[7]

That the "Pacts" were not of greater help, and that they cost Lacerda so much popular support, disappointed him and led him to reflect later that the Frente Ampla was "premature."[8] He had the idea, revealed more clearly in the last year of his life, that no matter how injuriously he had spoken in the past, people would be willing, if he wished, to let bygones be bygones and come to regard cruel remarks as simply a part of a savage political process. But many followers of Goulart and Kubitschek could not forgive Lacerda for his past, just as most of his own followers could not dismiss convictions they had shared with him for many years. Were long-held views properly labeled when they were dismissed as "old resentments" and "personal divergences"?

Furthermore, it was not clear that the abandonment of the "old resentments" in favor of the new alliance was as urgent as the formation, during World War II, of the Churchill-Attlee alliance against the German invasion of England. Lacerda, who had predicted before that bloody insurrections would occur if he were not heeded, was now explaining that a rejection of the Frente Ampla's proposals would mean large-scale adherence to "Communist leaderships" and that a reactionary military dictatorship (of the "American party") would be followed by a leftist dictatorship (of "the Communist party"), from which "escape is possible only at the price of civil war." Nascimento Brito wrote Lacerda that he could not agree that the accord with Goulart was necessary "to avoid a popular insurrection."[9]

Critics of Lacerda, including those who saw him trying to secure *trabalhista* support for a presidential bid, found in that accord more reasons than ever to raise their voices. Already those voices, raised by politicians, military leaders, columnists, and editorial writers, had condemned one step after another that Lacerda had taken, and one argument after another that he had delivered, on behalf of the Frente. Frequently, also, the man portrayed by Thomas E. Skidmore as "the reckless orator" furnished ample justification for objections to his accusations.[10]

Sensationalism characterized the crusade that Lacerda carried on, primarily against the government's increasing authoritarianism. It played no small part in persuading Carlos Castello Branco to describe the crusade as led by the chief interpreter of the opposition's sentiments, an orator who provided "increasing resonance in a political atmosphere saturated with pessimism" and who spoke as though he were delivering an ultimatum to the military who ran Brazil.[11]

XI.

The Silencing of Lacerda as a Politician (1968)

1. Students Demonstrate while Lacerda Visits Europe (April–June 1968)

Renato Archer explained Lacerda's forthcoming absence, on a trip to Europe with Letícia, as a "tactical operation." But the PTB wing of the Frente Ampla accused Lacerda of having been devious all along and having exceeded the bounds of tolerance ever since the appearance of Gama e Silva's *portaria.* Spokesmen of the *trabalhistas* said that Lacerda, after his European trip, would feel free to wash his hands of commitments made in recent years and seek a reconciliation with his military friends.[1]

Lacerda, meeting in Rio with Mário Covas and Martins Rodrigues, sought to dispel these ideas. He pointed out that the situation required a "tactical retreat" because the "useless sacrifice" he would make by continuing his attacks would simply keep the members of the ruling military united. As reported in the Brazilian press on April 17, he told a correspondent, sent by *Le Figaro* from Paris to Rio, that "the best thing we can do is let the military clash among themselves" and finally resolve not to continue disappointing the people.

Pernambucanos Osvaldo Lima Filho and José Carlos Guerra, irked by Lacerda's decision not to attend "Democracy Week" observations in Recife, canceled the observations and called Lacerda a "deserter."[2]

Before boarding his plane on April 20, Lacerda spoke of his "revulsion" upon learning of a serious bomb explosion at *O Estado de S. Paulo.* Such acts of "terrorist vandalism," he said, impeded "a frank dialogue between the government and the people," necessary for solving the Brazilian crisis. Upon reaching Paris, he answered reporters' questions about the "desertion" charge by saying that it was made to get him to talk before he felt it opportune. He spoke of plans to observe his fifty-fourth birthday in Paris and travel in Italy. His reluctance to discuss the Brazilian political situation was in contrast to the remarks against the Brazilian government made in Italy and France by Dom Hélder Câmara, whose reaction to the assassination of Martin Luther King, Jr., was to express fear of being killed by "the forces that hold Brazilian development in check."[3]

In Rio, Kubitschek declared that his alliance with Lacerda was "unalterable." Goulart, in Montevideo, called for a continuation of the struggle, under the name of the Frente Ampla or some other name. His followers in Brazil spoke with fiery words about breaking out of the limits that they maintained had circumscribed the work of the Frente Ampla. To turn the old Frente into a "real mass movement," they planned, they said, to make alliances with militant far-leftist groups, such as Ação Popular (AP).[4]

Throughout May and June, it was the university students, not the remains of the Frente Ampla, that shook Brazil with demonstrations. Appreciating that the workers, in need of supporting their families, were limited in their ability to agitate, student leaders espoused causes of the workers along with their own demands.[5] Lacerda, who had the opportunity to witness extreme student unrest in France, published an article about students in the June issue of *Esquema* (a monthly of the economics college of the Federal University of Rio de Janeiro). It blamed student "anguish" and "rebellion" on the "masters of life" who had educated the young people "in violence" and made them "feel rejected." "Youth," he wrote, "must be educated with the humility of one who recognizes that the world we have made is unworthy of youth."[6]

As the São Paulo state government prepared to celebrate May Day with official speeches at the Praça da Sé, students passed out leaflets of the new Partido Operário Comunista (POC), a fusion of PCB dissidents and POLOP, a Trotskyite revolutionary group whose youthful members had helped AP oust the PCB from the UNE in 1967. When Governor Abreu Sodré reached the speakers' platform, boos and derisive epithets prevented him from delivering his speech. In the conflict that followed, with students and their allies wielding clubs against the authorities, the governor was wounded in the head and had to leave. The mob turned the platform into a source of wooden weapons and set fire to what remained. Then about 2,000 marchers, mostly students, made their way to the Praça da República, inflicting damage, as they went, to the properties of foreign banks, and shouting against the "dictatorship" and the "wage freeze." Sodré blamed the disorders on a tiny group of totalitarian extremists.[7]

Despite frequent shouts against the "dictator," 76 percent of 3,750 voters, polled by IBOPE in leading cities, said they liked Costa e Silva as a person. In the poll, paid for by the federal government, 32 percent awarded the administration good marks and 45 percent called it only

Lacerda leaving the Frente Ampla for National Union. (APPE drawing in *O Cruzeiro*, April 27, 1968)

average; 68 percent said that Brazil had made "less progress" than it should have made, but 64 percent replied in the affirmative when asked if they felt that things would improve. Lacerda's complaint about corruption in the government was apparently not shared, because only 2 percent called the administration corrupt (in contrast to 41 percent, 23 percent, 12 percent, and 11 percent, respectively, for the administrations of Goulart, Kubitschek, Quadros, and Castello Branco). Nor was much interest shown in Lacerda's objection to the political party setup: 36 percent expressed no opinion, 45 percent wanted a continuation of the two-party system, 17 percent wanted a return to the pre-1965 parties, and only 2 percent asked for the creation of new parties. Thirty-seven percent agreed that Brazil should lead an alliance of underdeveloped nations, whereas 48 percent checked the alternate proposal of having Brazil ally itself with strong powers that could provide it with economic assistance. Only 19 percent opposed having more foreign capital come to Brazil.[8]

When the government made plans to meet with businessmen to discuss turning university colleges into foundations, partly financed by private capital, university student leaders in Rio protested and demanded, instead, that the government increase considerably the education budget. Led by law student Vladimir Palmeira, president of the União Metropolitana dos Estudantes (UME), protesting students converged on the education ministry building on June 19 and asked for a dialogue with Education Minister Tarso Dutra. The response was a repression by the state police that left 10 persons wounded. Among the approximately 100 arrested students was AP activist Jean Marc von der Weid, leader of the chemistry students of the Federal University of Rio de Janeiro (known as the University of Brazil until March 1967). Later in the day, after further skirmishes in the streets, students issued a manifesto assailing the "dictatorship" and demanding more government funds for education, the release of Jean Marc, and abandonment of the idea of the foundations.[9]

On June 20, Carioca students met at the university administration building to start a march to demand, once again, an audience with the education minister, but they were subdued by the police as they left the building. By the end of the day, 480 university students were under arrest. On the next day, a mass of students moved on the American embassy, which was defended by the Military Police, whose shots wounded three young women. The students reacted violently and the clashes downtown, lasting for almost six hours, left one policeman and two civilians dead, 80 persons wounded, and 1,000 under arrest. Classes at the Federal University of Rio de Janeiro (UFRJ) were suspended.[10]

Commentators wrote that students in Latin America were influenced by the uprisings of students in Paris. Raimundo Moniz de Aragão, head of the UFRJ, called the student movement "a universal phenomenon." But the *Jornal do Brasil* blamed the unrest on the Costa e Silva government's practice of keeping apart from the people and their problems. That government, it wrote, had not known how to respond properly, after being received in a friendly way by a nation that had put hatreds and resentments aside, and after becoming the sole beneficiary of the acts of the Castello government, which had faced unpopularity out of a love for the highest interests of the nation.[11]

For June 26, the Rio students planned a mass demonstration "against police repression," that would start at Cinelândia and include workers, intellectuals, members of the clergy and the liberal professions, housewives, and artists. Many were angered by the reports of the ordeal of theatrical director Flávio Rangel, held incommunicado for seventy-two hours and shorn of his hair by the Federal Police. Teachers, shocked at the violence of recent days against students, decided to participate in the mass demonstration.[12]

The students promised that the march would be peaceful, and the authorities agreed to let it proceed. Attracting a crowd estimated at 80,000, it became known as "the march of the 100,000." Only five arrests were made. Vladimir Palmeira, conducted triumphantly by his colleagues to Cinelândia, delivered five speeches during the six hours in which the throng moved from Cinelândia, via Avenida Rio Branco, to Avenida Presidente Vargas. He asked the students to remain orderly and asked the authorities to protect the "national interests" and provide democratic liberties, improvements for workers, and freedom of expression for artists and writers. He called for the release of the jailed students, more government funds for education, and the reopening of the Calabouço Restaurant. Describing proposals of the government as mere blandishments, he invited Minister Tarso Dutra to debate with students, in July, the administration's plan for restructuring the educational system.[13]

In the days before this mass demonstration, students in other parts of Brazil were eager to show support for their Guanabara colleagues, despite Amaral Netto's assertion that Costa e Silva was determined not to put up with manifestations by students or allow them to bring on the chaos that students in France had provoked. University students in Curitiba went on strike and demonstrated in the streets. Four students in Ceará were wounded by police shots. In Brasília, where the police took over the university, students went to the floor of the Senate to complain of being expelled from the campus. At the University of São Paulo, students invaded the office of the university president and put him through an interrogation during which they demanded representation on the commission for restructuring the university. Paulista students invited the public to join them on June 24 for a demonstration to show support for the Rio students, victims of police repression.[14]

Governor Abreu Sodré spoke favorably about student demands, but Second Army Commander Manuel Rodrigues de Carvalho Lisboa came out against manifestations in his territory. In a reference to the conflicts in Rio, he said on June 23: "We shall combat subversion wherever it is, be it in the churches, the universities, or the factories." Paulistas, ignoring the commander's words, demonstrated on June 24. Some of them hurled stones and bricks, and fired gunshots, at the *O Estado de S. Paulo* building; they broke its windows, and set fire to the wooden fencework protecting reconstruction in the area damaged by the April explosion. An official car from Guanabara state was set on fire, and the building of the São Paulo education secretaryship was damaged. Police did not interfere.

Before dawn on June 26, Paulista militants of the Vanguarda Popular Revolucionária (VPR) damaged the Second Army headquarters, where a bomb, thrown in April, had already wounded two people. This time they sent a station wagon, containing 50 kilograms of dynamite, crashing into the headquarters, resulting in the death of an eighteen-year-old soldier, Mário Kozel Filho, and inflicting injuries on five others. The funeral of Kozel, attended by 5,000, was followed by the theft, by Paulista urban guerrillas, of 448 kilograms of dynamite from a warehouse.[15]

The urban guerrilla movements, especially successful in robbing banks in São Paulo, attracted young people along with veteran Communists, such as Carlos Marighella, who advocated terrorism and condemned the more peaceful line of the PCB.

Jânio Quadros, returning from a trip abroad in the latter part of June, predicted that a great popular movement would alter the political situation and force the government to grant a general amnesty. Describing himself as having become a man of the Left, he promised to speak out, thus fulfilling his duty, regardless of the cost. He condemned the less aggressive attitude of the other *cassados,* calling them "connivers."[16]

2. The Para-Sar Case (June–October 1968)

While Lacerda was in Europe, the air force ministry in Rio was the scene of some curious secret meetings, called for the purpose of murdering him and others considered objectionable by anti-Communist extremists. The meetings were called after it became clear that some members of Para-Sar, a group established to rescue victims of plane accidents, objected to having been ordered in April to pose as civilians and act roughly, using their arms if necessary, against people who gave support to student demonstrators.[1]

One of the objectors, Captain Sérgio Ribeiro Miranda de Carvalho, was called to the air force ministry in June and told by the ministry's *chefe de gabinete,* Brigadeiro João Paulo Moreira Burnier, that Para-Sar had been assigned a key role in a plan to install an anti-Communist regime—of the type in Spain and Portugal—by carrying out terrorist acts in Rio, for which Communists would be blamed; the acts included dynamiting the Ribeirão das Lages water reservoir, and, during rush hour, the gas works on Avenida Brasil, where the explosion would kill thousands of people.

Burnier spent several sessions trying to "indoctrinate" Captain Sérgio. He had Brigadeiro Hipólito da Costa at his side on June 12 when he told the captain that Costa e Silva dealt weakly with Communism and that most of the *brigadeiros* were old and decrepit. It was then that he extolled killing in peacetime as training for wartime and as a means of eliminating "bad Brazilians," such as Lacerda, Brigadeiro Francisco Teixeira, and General Olímpio Mourão Filho. He assured the captain that he would "categorically" deny everything he was saying if their conversation were to be revealed. And he asked Sérgio, who had flown rescue missions over forests, whether the "bad Brazilians," dropped from planes over the ocean, would die before or after hitting the water. In closing, Burnier ordered Sérgio to bring all forty-one military members of the Para-Sar to a meeting to be held on June 14.[2]

To the thirty-six who were able to attend the meeting, Para-Sar's Major Gil Lessa de Carvalho introduced Burnier, who, he said, would explain "the special missions to be executed by Para-Sar from this moment on." Burnier then told the men that the orders, to be delivered verbally, were to be fulfilled zealously and not mentioned afterwards. Speaking of Lacerda, he said: "That scalawag, who everyone thinks is my friend," should have been killed in 1963 if the army's paratroopers had acted resolutely and not "become lost in innocuous discussions about fulfilling an order." Burnier started to ask the men, beginning with four of his supporters, whether they were in agreement with the secret "special missions" which called for killings "to save Brazil" even though no civil war existed. The fifth person to be asked, Captain Sérgio, would not agree and vowed to inform Air Force Minister Márcio de Souza Mello.[3]

By his resolve to protest, the thirty-seven-year-old captain obstructed Burnier's plans. However, as he wrote Lacerda, he could expect to suffer for his obstinacy. He lost his job with Para-Sar and was cited for indiscipline. So, too, was medical Captain Rubens Marques dos Santos ("Doc"), who shared Sérgio's ideas of what Para-Sar should be, and who, like Sérgio, was a Para-Sar founder decorated for missions of mercy in the Amazon region.

The aviation minister proved to be difficult for Sérgio to see. But the captain was assisted by retired Brigadeiro Eduardo Gomes, who recommended that an investigation be carried out by the directorship of the section handling aviation routes, which had not been informed of what had been going on, although Para-Sar was organizationally supposed to be supervised by it. After Routes Director Itamar Rocha began his investigation, he was ordered by the air force minister to desist, but he ignored the order and gathered written testimonies from thirty-two Para-Sar men. Twenty-six sustained Sérgio's account of the June 14 meeting, whereas only six agreed with the version of Burnier, who denied everything. Sérgio and medical Captain Santos were among those who testified that Burnier had told the men: "Political figures like former Governor Carlos Lacerda should already have been killed."[4]

Brigadeiro Itamar Rocha reported his findings to the air force minister late in September and was immediately dismissed from his aviation routes post and sentenced to two days of house arrest. With information from his daughter-in-law, the *Correio da Manhã* alluded to the investigation of a plan to eliminate people "considered inconvenient." Journalist Pery Cotta's article of October 4 in the *Correio da Manhã* showed detailed knowledge of the investigation's findings and led to the improper jailing of Cotta because he refused to divulge his sources.[5]

Air Force Minister Souza Mello, who had disciplined Itamar Rocha, was supported by *O Globo*, which called him "a bulwark of the Revolution" and the victim of a campaign begun by extremists and divisionists. He was also supported by his friend Costa e Silva. But in this case, Carlos Castello Branco wrote, most of the military disagreed with the government.[6] They shared the view of Eduardo Gomes, who observed, somewhat later: "Captain Sérgio has the honor of having opposed the diabolic and vile plan of Brigadeiro João Paulo Burnier."[7]

3. Buildup for a Real Crisis (July–October 1968)

Lacerda returned by plane from Europe on July 2, accompanied by his wife and Antônio Carlos de Almeida Braga. He continued to avoid speaking out about Brazilian politics. In Rio he made use of the studio of his literary friend João Condé to display oil paintings he had made, some while abroad. Condé, who had persuaded Lacerda to put the paintings up for sale, told reporters that Lacerda had much talent, and he praised especially two recent canvases: a landscape painted in Florence and a seascape painted in Yugoslavia. "Carlos," he said, "applies a lot of yellow, a color not easy to handle."

After the showing, Lacerda motored with Condé in the northeast. In Bahia, where Lacerda and a friend occupied the front seats, Condé objected to the many cages of birds, acquired by Lacerda, that surrounded him in the back. He argued heatedly that Lacerda was inconsiderate, and finally, at a hotel in Feira de Santana, set many of Lacerda's birds free.[1]

Lacerda's failure to attack the government irritated Hélio Fernandes. But, as Lacerda explained to the *Jornal do Brasil,* the delicate political thread that held things together was so taut that a yank could upset the armed forces and "enormously endanger redemocratization."

He told the *Jornal do Brasil* that he would not rectify false newspaper stories about himself. However, the frequent speculation about his possible reconciliation with the men in power prompted him to address a letter, early in August, to João Alberto Leite Barbosa, director of *bc/semanal.* He wrote: "I am not seeking a reconciliation with the military officers at the cost of abandoning the understanding I reached with other national leaders." "My silence is based on patriotic reasons and not on mere political tactics. . . . Why should I renounce what I conscientiously did at a time when my action gave me every sort of unpleasantness and lack of understanding—an action that has now begun to show results? . . . I do not reject an understanding in any area whatsoever if it will help Brazil free itself from the present crisis."[2]

Unlike Lacerda, Jânio Quadros was talkative to reporters. "The

The "presidential succession," held by the government of the 1964
revolution, smells sweeter to Lacerda than the company of Kubitschek
and Goulart. (Edmondo Bigalti drawing in *O Estado de S. Paulo*,
July 10, 1968)

government," he told them on July 17, "is useless because it is nothing." It could, he added, become an unmasked dictatorship or turn to
democracy "with the reconstitution of the political and juridical values it has destroyed." Asked if he would agree to meet Lacerda, he
said that friends of his and of Lacerda's, mostly friends of Lacerda's,
had worked for such a meeting and that, while it was not something
he sought, he would, if friends made the arrangements, fulfill his duty
and exchange views with Lacerda. He explained that he had "always
refused" to see Lacerda, "especially when he was preaching the Frente
Ampla," an instrument for "the promotion of the personalism of that
politician."[3]

When it became known that the justice minister was preparing a
portaria to punish Quadros for his declarations, student leader José
Dirceu de Oliveira called the former president "a populist and demagogue." Dirceu, who was president of the officially extinct State Union
of Students (UEE) of São Paulo, said that repression by the government had been frequent during the Quadros administration.[4]

Gama e Silva's *portaria*, issued on July 29, condemned Quadros
to 120 days of "confinement" in Corumbá, on the Bolivian border.

Brizola applauded Quadros, and Goulart wrote Osvaldo Lima Filho that he admired Quadros for courageously taking a stand. Lima Filho and Mário Covas were part of an MDB commission that went to Corumbá in August, with a letter of praise from Oscar Passos. They heard Quadros extol Kubitschek, whom he likened to Vargas.[5]

When Osvaldo Lima Filho returned to Corumbá in September, Quadros complained that the MDB was acting too weakly in Congress and said it should blame the ARENA for the "institutional crisis." This time Lima Filho brought the internee a letter from Goulart proposing a new oppositionist front which was to be truly popular and avoid the sins of the Frente Ampla, described by Goulart as simply an arrangement set up by top political figures. While Lima Filho, back in Rio, met with *Janistas* and *trabalhistas* to try to form the new union, Ivete Vargas returned from Uruguay bringing blessings from Brizola, who said the new union should not follow the example of "well-known politicians" who had worked for a return to the past.[6]

Lacerda, commenting on reports that he, too, would make a visit to Corumbá, observed a bit maliciously that it was now possible to know where he could find Quadros. But he showed no interest in the trip, leading his friends to point out that neither statements by Lacerda, nor a call on Quadros by him, would promote his wish to see the Brazilian "crisis" resolved peacefully.[7]

Juscelinistas were pleased to read early in September that Lacerda, in a televised interview with William F. Buckley, Jr., in New York, had called the construction of Brasília praiseworthy, in stark contrast to his statements in the 1950s. But reports of the interview, which did not point out that it had been taped in October 1967, displeased the oppositionists, especially the *trabalhistas,* because of Lacerda's remarks in favor of a "rapid and successful" intervention in Cuba to overthrow the Castro regime. *Janguistas* proclaimed that Goulart continued faithful to his views opposing intervention and favoring the "self-determination of people." Lacerda asked the UPI to explain that the tape was an old one and his comment in it about Cuba had "nothing to do with the present situation."[8]

On September 14 Lacerda set forth on a three-week trip to cover, for *Realidade* magazine, the presidential campaign in the United States. The situation he left behind was explosive, because the charges being made by oppositionists about how hard line military radicals might act had the effect of stimulating hard liners to act in that way. Lacerda's prudence was not without merit.

The military accused the radical Left of seeking a crisis. According to the labor minister, Colonel Jarbas Passarinho, a strike for higher wages in July by workers in Osasco, São Paulo, was the work of "a

radical political minority interested in provoking a regime of exception." In September he spoke of a widespread subversive plan being
developed in labor unions. Hermano Alves wrote that Passarinho was
much more a colonel than a senator, and was initiating psychological
warfare. The *Correio da Manhã* accused Passarinho of seeking a pretext for a putsch.[9]

Early in July, the United States announced the discontinuance of its
program to aid Brazilian education. But Costa e Silva made it known,
to a delegation of students, that the Brazilian government would not
accede to their other demands, including the release of prisoners and
the reopening of the Calabouço Restaurant. Students in Rio complained of the food prices at the UFRJ, and, at the School of Medicine,
they invaded the kitchen and broke dishes.[10]

Street rallies in Rio were led by Vladimir Palmeira, who had an
enormous following. He denounced Brazil's "structure" and its rich
and powerful groups, owners of Cadillacs who maintained that they
lacked the money needed for educating the people. After he described
the *Jornal do Brasil* as "sold" to such groups, students demonstrated
against it. He was arrested early in August but was freed in mid-
September thanks to a Supreme Court decision. He went into hiding
because the authorities drew up a new arrest order.[11]

The strife between students and the authorities relegated to second
place the UNE schism, notable for Vladimir Palmeira's public accusations against UNE President Luís Travassos and the declarations
critical of Vladimir made by Jean Marc von der Weid, defender of
Travassos.

On August 30, members of the DOPS invaded the University of
Brasília in five station wagons with the purpose of arresting five students. Stones were hurled at the invaders and one of the DOPS wagons was set on fire. Federal Police, arriving to help the DOPS, participated in a conflict, characterized by gunshots and tear gas, that left
two students wounded. Honestino Guimarães, one of the five students wanted by the authorities, was captured and beaten so badly
that an arm was fractured.[12]

Márcio Moreira Alves, referring on September 2 to the invasion,
asked in Congress: "When will the army cease being the asylum of
torturers?" In his speech of September 3, he said that on Independence Day, September 7, the military leaders would ask their colleagues to parade at the side of the hangmen of the students. He called
on all parents to understand that the participation of their sons in the
parade "gives aid to the executioners who beat up and machine gun
the young people."[13]

Some of the ARENA lawmakers, including Milton Campos, signed a manifesto protesting against the invasion of the University of Brasília, while, in the lower house, more than two hundred congressmen signed a petition that set up a parliamentary investigating commission (CPI) to look into "all the violent acts carried out by the Military Police against the people." Senator Mário Martins declared: "Nazism is on the rise and the government is impotent." Congressman Hermano Alves wrote in the *Correio da Manhã* that the military were subversive when they used arms improperly to subjugate the people.[14]

Army officers gave backing to police contingents in Brasília, some of which were headed by their fellow officers. General Meira Mattos, inspector of police forces, said: "We have a revolutionary war on our hands and the repression of it cannot be timid."[15]

Especially upsetting to the military were the articles written by Congressman Hermano Alves and the views expressed by his colleague, Márcio Moreira Alves. Army Minister Lyra Tavares, in a message to Costa e Silva, wrote of the repulsion aroused in military circles by Moreira Alves' speeches, and said: "The curbing of such violences constitutes a move in the defense of the regime."[16]

Justice Minister Gama e Silva, learning that the navy and air force ministers supported this view, instructed the government's chief attorney to take the case of Moreira Alves to the Supreme Court on the ground that Article 151 of the 1967 Constitution called for the suspension of the political rights of persons who took advantage of individual and political rights to oppose "the democratic order." Prosecution, in the case of congressmen, depended on the permission of the Chamber of Deputies, and therefore, on October 8, Gama e Silva told the government congressional leaders of the step being taken by his ministry.[17]

ARENA President Daniel Krieger wrote Costa e Silva on October 10 to express his belief that it would be unconstitutional to punish Moreira Alves for his speeches in Congress. In reply, Costa e Silva advised that he would be guided by the Justice Minister's proposal. "I am," Costa e Silva wrote, "fulfilling my duty as Head of the Nation and Supreme Commander of the Armed Forces." Krieger, Jayme Portella decided, had become influenced by discontented congressmen, such as Raphael de Almeida Magalhães.[18]

Governor Abreu Sodré, warning that "the radicals of the Right are hysterical," participated in the organization of a Frente Democrática to oppose what some observers felt was a hard line move toward dictatorship. He stated that the "radicals of the Right" existed only in the periphery of the government and could be dominated by Costa e Silva. Colonel Costa Cavalcanti, minister of mines and energy, retorted: "No radical military group exists in the government."[19]

At the University of Brasília, the authorities ordered the renewal of classes on September 9, but the order was ignored by so many indignant students and professors that it was ineffective. Neither the CPI's inquiry about the invasion, nor an investigation headed by SNI Chief Emílio Garrastazu Médici on Costa e Silva's orders, satisfied people who favored punishments for those responsible for the invasion. MDB members of the CPI left the investigation because the ARENA members, who constituted a majority, refused to support a resolution calling on General Meira Mattos and the commander of the Eleventh Military Region to appear and answer questions.[20]

The CPI abandoned the investigation on September 27, leading Hermano Alves to write that the government that silenced the investigation was the same government that punished officers who objected to violence by Para-Sar. And, in a reference to the arrest of 100 Carioca students on October 9, he added: "Any student march provokes a brutal reaction." The government, Jayme Portella observed later, "acted energetically, preventing demonstrations, but the students associated with the subversive line continued defying the police," and, although "arrests were made, the principal leaders always escaped."[21]

In São Paulo, where the police were less repressive than in Rio, students of "the Right," associated with the Mackenzie University, became engaged in warfare against their longtime rivals, students of "the Left," associated with the Philosophy College of the University of São Paulo. Mackenzie students, determined to rout "the Left," threw eggs on October 2 at students who were putting up barricades on Maria Antônia Street, shared by both universities, in order to collect toll payments to help finance the forthcoming Thirtieth UNE Congress. In the combat that the egg throwing provoked, about 2,500 students participated on each side, some of them using bombs and firearms. The combat lasted until nightfall and was resumed for a while the next morning, when Mackenzie students pulled down banners at the Philosophy College and set fire to the building. Dozens of students were wounded, a secondary school student was killed, and the public was disgusted at what looked like gang warfare. UEE President José Dirceu, who fought at the side of UNE President Travassos, found that the Mackenzie students were assisted by armed nonstudents, such as members of the Anti-Communist Command (CCC— Comando de Caça aos Comunistas); and he concluded that the combat was "the worst setback" to the student movement. It was, he declared, "the signal for unleashing the repression." The São Paulo police, becoming more active, made over 100 arrests during student demonstrations on October 8.[22]

For the São Paulo police, the crowning event was the arrest on October 12 of 739 student leaders, from all over Brazil, who were assembled near the town of Ibiúna for the Thirtieth UNE Congress. Among those arrested were Luís Travassos, Vladimir Palmeira, José Dirceu, Franklin Martins, and Marco Antônio Ribas. Jean Marc von der Weid, who managed to escape a little later by giving a false name, has written that "the collapse of the Thirtieth Congress was a tremendous blow to the student movement." The arrests prevented the selection of a new UNE president to succeed the radical Travassos, whose candidate, Jean Marc (of AP), was in a close race against Dirceu, backed by Vladimir Palmeira.[23]

What, the *Correio da Manhã* asked, was conspiratory about the UNE Congress? *O Globo* replied that the students, at their Congress, had discussed a program for developing a violent uprising and had planned to choose a delegate to spend a year in Havana. As "the defender of the Brazilian family," *O Globo* deplored the activities of student "extremists," leftist priests, and "radical" congressmen such as Márcio Moreira Alves. It asserted that the government should display greater energy in resisting this "new onslaught by counter-revolutionary forces."[24]

News of the arrest of the UNE leaders coincided with the news of the assassination in São Paulo of U.S. Army Captain Charles Chandler, who had served in Vietnam and was studying at Mackenzie University. His "execution," ordered by the VPR and ALN terrorist groups in the name of "revolutionary justice," was carried out by fourteen machine gun shots in front of his wife and young son as he left his home. In the words of Thomas E. Skidmore, the killing made it "clear that Brazil's military government faced a serious guerrilla opponent."[25]

4. Observing U.S. Politics, and Falling in Love (October–November 1968)

Lacerda's assignment for *Realidade* was an article about the campaign in which Richard M. Nixon, Hubert H. Humphrey, and George C. Wallace were presidential candidates. On the three-week trip Lacerda was accompanied by Alfredo C. Machado, whose firm, Distribuidora Record, was handling the distribution of Nova Fronteira books.

Lacerda discussed conditions in the United States with the candidates and other prominent figures, some of whom were old friends, such as Nelson A. Rockefeller and John Dos Passos. At a party in

California, an actor introduced him to Shirley MacLaine, who had been a delegate to the Democratic Convention in Chicago and who emphasized, in her conversations with Lacerda, the importance of paying attention to the discontented young people.[1]

Lacerda's article, "An Empire Chooses Its President," appeared in the November issue of *Realidade* and was devoted in large part to the protests of young Americans. Trying to capture the unrest in what Arthur M. Schlesinger, Jr., called a tormented and unhappy land, Lacerda credited Robert Kennedy with understanding that the defiance of youth was not an ideology. It was, Lacerda wrote, a revolt against a system of values, based on hypocrisy and sham, that caused injustice and war. The article reported the views of leaders of the Yippies (Youth International Party) and the SDS (Students for a Democratic Society). *Realidade*'s readers were informed that SDS founder Mark Rudd saw racism and imperialism as forms of domination used by American capitalism, and that Yippie founder Jerry Rubin, a thirty-year-old student, considered the universities to be "structured to emasculate the students." The "extremely bright" Miss MacLaine was quoted as saying: "These young people are against anyone who might represent the continuation of things, or patching them up."[2]

Lacerda wrote of the courage of young men who avoided serving in Vietnam, and he argued that the protesters were "indignant at the rubbish of the world in which they are condemned to live without living, like being forced to fulfill a punishment in a penitentiary."[3]

In predicting that Nixon would win the election, Lacerda cited Dos Passos' belief that Humphrey was too closely associated with President Johnson at a time when the atmosphere in the United States was one of "disappointment and despair." Everyone, Lacerda wrote, agreed with Nelson Rockefeller's judgment that the handling of the principal problems had been characterized by a lack of leadership. In conclusion, Lacerda affirmed that if the United States were to survive its crisis, it would have to transform itself from a society based on competition to one inspired by cooperation, and would have to heed the young people, who put justice ahead of dividends to stockholders.[4]

Following the election, Lacerda returned to the United States on a briefer trip, this time with Letícia and her friend Regina Costard, to be with Candinha and Joaquim da Silveira, who celebrated their silver wedding anniversary in snow-covered New York. Lacerda was impressed with the willingness of Johnson and Humphrey to cooperate with President-elect Nixon. Writing for *Fatos & Fotos*, he called the arrangement a Frente Ampla type of understanding that was in contrast to Brazil's "prohibition of pacification." Johnson's White House meeting with Nixon, Lacerda wrote, turned defeat into victory and served as a sort of "consolation" following the "many errors" committed by Johnson, described in Lacerda's writings as a nonintellectual "Cowboy Caesar."[5]

The errors, according to the *Fatos & Fotos* article, included contempt for the press, no effort to win the support of the Kennedy people, and a practice of politics and cleverness that failed to make him a leader, loved by the people. In fairness to Johnson, Lacerda furnished statistics revealing the progress made in social programs, and praised the civil rights program. But he wrote at length about "the principal error" of the president, who had "aged terribly" in the White House: the continuation of mistaken policies for Vietnam and Latin America. In Latin America, Lacerda wrote, Johnson had repeated the Americans' "historical error" of assisting, exclusively, reactionary groups and groups whose exploitation of the people incurred public wrath against the United States. Lacerda believed that the United States, by placing economic interests at the forefront of its policy in South America, was committing a major crime against its own national security—far more serious than the occasional seduction of some young people by the pseudo-Marxism of Herbert Marcuse or by the anticultural positions of the guards of Mao Zedong.[6]

It was when Lacerda was in Los Angeles, on his *Realidade* assignment, that he and Shirley MacLaine fell in love. The mischievous Alfredo Machado, during the plane trip that took him and Lacerda from Los Angeles to Las Vegas, said to his companion: "Did you notice the large size of Shirley's wrists? If she hits you, it will be very hard." Furious, Lacerda refused to speak to Machado for the next two hours. During the rest of the trip, Shirley and Carlos phoned each other frequently, and, during the last leg of the trip, a flight from New York to Miami, Carlos spent his time writing letters to her. After Carlos' return to Rio, the phone calls from Shirley to his office were frequent.

So, too, were phone calls from Brazilian actress Maria Fernanda Correia Dias, with whom Carlos had shared an affair of the heart and mind starting in the 1950s. Carlos, *Paulista* acquaintances reported, had also shared a São Paulo hotel room with her (leaving a "Do Not Disturb" sign on the door for most of the two days), and had showered her with roses. Therefore, according to gossip, his chief extramarital love affair was with Maria Fernanda. Carlos, late in his life, admitted to infatuation and a great, close friendship with Maria Fernanda, but said the relationship went no further. In the case of Shirley, he confessed that the affair went beyond infatuation and friendship.

It being difficult to phone Carlos when he was traveling in Africa in

May 1969, Shirley addressed a cable to him at the office of the president of Senegal in Dakar: "Impossible to meet you in Paris, but will be in London middle of July. Much love." A report in the Rio press about Carlos having an affair with Shirley prompted Carlos to call the report a "ridiculous prank" and say: "This is proof that they are violating my correspondence."

Alfredo Machado met Shirley again when he attended a book fair in Dallas or Atlanta and found her autographing copies of a book of hers. She recognized Alfredo, the publisher who had accompanied Carlos to California and had subsequently answered some of the phone calls she had placed for Carlos, and she asked him whether Carlos had yet left his family. The inscription she wrote in a book for Alfredo helped him to play a joke, still later, when his firm received a prepublication copy of another of her books. Alfredo, who had learned that Carlos had been with Shirley in Italy and elsewhere, phoned Carlos and found him vexed to learn that Alfredo, and not he, had received a copy of Shirley's latest work. Alfredo arranged to have the prepublication copy inscribed, in an imitation of Shirley's handwriting: "To Alfredo with all my love, Shirley." After Alfredo sent the book to Carlos, Carlos phoned in an explosive mood. Alfredo admitted the joke and said something about the convenience of going around with Shirleys closer to their own age, such as Shirley Temple.

5. Congress Supports the Immunity of Moreira Alves (December 12, 1968)

In Brazil late in November 1968, Lacerda fell ill with a kidney ailment that persisted beyond the first week of December. Doctors' orders for a complete rest were regarded by political observers as giving him an excuse for resisting the pressure exerted on him to comment on the government's desire to punish Congressmen Márcio Moreira Alves and Hermano Alves.[1]

Lacerda's silence was accompanied by reports that he was improving his relations with several colonels who had broken with him. Although Colonel Francisco Boaventura Cavalcanti Júnior was never on close terms with Lacerda and did not like the Frente Ampla, he did feel that the army should take steps to retire from governing. He is cited by Márcio Moreira Alves as having been the spokesman of some military men to whom *Lacerdistas* turned at this time in an effort to provoke "a schism in the armed forces" that would permit Lacerda to be a presidential candidate. Carlos Castello Branco wrote that Costa e Silva himself wished to be succeeded by a civilian, and other columnists speculated that Lacerda might be able to effect a reconciliation between civilian groups and officers in the military who favored the selection of a civilian president in 1970. Commenting on the fresh reports about Lacerda, Planning Minister Hélio Beltrão remarked: "*Lacerdismo* is like malaria: it comes and goes."[2]

The nation's attention was focused on the congressional justice commission, deliberating whether or not to recommend that the Chamber of Deputies grant a *licença* to allow Moreira Alves to be judged by the Supreme Court. It was a strange case, considered long after Moreira Alves made remarks in Congress that had not been considered important enough to be quoted in the press and for which he could not be deprived of his congressional immunity, as the Supreme Court would be certain to rule. Krieger had told the president that the authors of newspaper articles were in a different category and that perhaps a case could be made against them, but that, of course, if they were congressmen it would be necessary to have the Chamber of Deputies waive their immunities. The government did turn to the courts to seek a judgment against Hermano Alves; however, it decided to put its prestige on the line, and test its control over the ARENA lawmakers, with the case of Moreira Alves' remarks in Congress. Justice Minister Gama e Silva, acting as he had before the confinement of Hélio Fernandes, was telling the president that the military leaders (informed of Moreira Alves' remarks by SNI Chief Garrastazu Médici) would accept neither delay nor any of the available compromise solutions, such as the adoption by Congress itself of a temporary suspension of Moreira Alves' mandate.[3]

The congressional justice commission was headed by Djalma Marinho, an *arenista* who had joined with Raphael de Almeida Magalhães in seeking to have the government adopt a program of reforms. Twenty of the commission's thirty-one members belonged to the ARENA. But, from the beginning, eight of the *arenistas* let it be known that they would join the eleven MDB members in opposing the *licença*. And Djalma Marinho agreed with ARENA President Krieger that the *licença* would be unconstitutional and therefore another way should be found to deal with Moreira Alves when Congress reconvened in March 1969.[4]

Costa e Silva was unsuccessful when he tried to dissuade Djalma Marinho and likeminded ARENA commission members. Therefore the government, late in November, revised the makeup of the commission by replacing eight of its voting members and one alternate, José Carlos Guerra. Geraldo Freire, who had become acting government leader because Ernâni Sátiro was ill, maintained that the ARENA members could not vote against the party line. His revision of the commission, bringing relief to military circles, shocked Krieger and

"Now?" asks the ARENA, about to behead Márcio Moreira Alves.
(Orlando Mattos drawing in *Folha de S. Paulo*, November 29, 1968)

aroused a storm. After two freshmen congressmen, Raphael de Almeida Magalhães and fellow-*arenista* Marcos Kertzmann, proposed a
protest consisting of wholesale departures from congressional commission posts, *arenista* Raimundo Bogéa resigned his place on the
finance commission to show support for "party companions denied
the liberty of reaching decisions dictated by their consciences." The
Jornal do Brasil called the recomposition of the justice commission a
disaster for the government because it would alienate public opinion.[5]

MDB members of the justice commission, among them Hermano
Alves and Martins Rodrigues, were discourteous to their new colleagues, such as Arnaldo Cerdeira; and they helped delay a vote by
inscribing ninety-four persons to give testimonies. The government
therefore had to call Congress into a special session, starting on December 2, leading Costa e Silva to denounce Congress' "interminable
sessions and demagoguery."

Conciliatory words of top authorities were accompanied by threats.
The army ministry announced on December 4 that Congress was
"sovereign in its decision," whereupon the MDB desisted in its "obstruction." But Lyra Tavares, a little later, explained that the army
was unwilling to accept attacks on its dignity. Costa e Silva declared
that he respected the democratic regime, leading *Última Hora* to

proclaim, in an enormous front-page headline, that the president promised not to promulgate an institutional act. However, when Costa e Silva spoke to ARENA congressmen, he gave them a warning: "We are strong and our reaction will be strong." It was a mistake, he told the congressmen, to provoke the regime, because the regime would not accept the defiance of irresponsible people who wanted to take Brazil to chaos.[6]

The chaos, much of the press felt, could be attributed to the inertia of Costa e Silva and the government. According to the *Jornal do Brasil*, they failed to impose discipline on military extremists, such as those who had wanted to misuse Para-Sar, and such discipline was necessary before discipline could be imposed on urban terrorists. In Rio, both the *Jornal do Brasil* and the *Correio da Manhã* were the victims of bombings destructive enough to damage also nearby buildings. "The government," the *Correio da Manhã* predicted, "will promise to investigate and punish, and will do neither." The *Jornal do Brasil* wrote that the strangest thing about the "daily" acts of terrorism was "the impunity of the guilty."

The government could take credit only for the jailing, in Minas Gerais, of a few priests who had been associated with Ação Popular and possessed far-leftist papers. Three French priests were expelled from Brazil, prompting the National Conference of Brazilian Bishops to object to "an affront to the entire Church." Press Association President Danton Jobim deplored, in *Última Hora*, the "stupidity" of the authorities, whereas First Army Commander Siseno Sarmento declared: "The priests are subversives."[7]

On December 10, the revamped justice commission voted, 19 to 12, in favor of the government. Djalma Marinho resigned as chairman in a moving speech that was applauded by congressmen and the large crowd of spectators. His resignation was followed by those of all the MDB members of the commission.[8]

The Moreira Alves case went at once to the full Chamber of Deputies, amidst rumors that the justice minister had a drastic *ato adicional*, for reforming the constitution, ready to be promulgated in case of a government defeat. MDB vice leader Bernardo Cabral declared: "It is better to have the Chamber closed than to have it function without honor." Monseigneur Alfredo de Arruda Câmara, an *arenista* justice commission member who had voted against the majority, said that granting the *licença* would discredit the parliament. Colonel Francisco Boaventura Cavalcanti Júnior, as government spies found out, spoke with *Lacerdistas* Raul Brunini and Jorge Curi and then informed MDB leaders Mário Covas and Renato Archer that a part of the armed forces opposed the *licença* and that the MDB should take

The congressional justice commission. (Orlando Mattos drawing in *Folha de S. Paulo*, December 12, 1968)

advantage of the government's weakness, with the knowledge that no military reaction would follow a government defeat.[9]

MDB leaders feared that the colonel was wrong. Renato Archer was among those who had worked to extend discussions during the regular session in the hope that Congress would go home without voting, allowing another solution to be found in a new climate in 1969. He was convinced that Congress, although not fond of Moreira Alves, would vote to reject the government's request, and he feared that Gama e Silva and military hard liners were looking for such an outcome as an excuse for a tough institutional act.

Carlos Castello Branco, calling attention to "the electoral strength of the government," guessed that the *licença* would be granted, despite ARENA defections, and thus "the constitutional structure will be maintained," saved from another *ato*, "at least in this episode." But, he added, whatever the outcome, the government had suffered a setback. "The speech of Djalma Marinho is the start of the organization of a dissidence that is headed by none other than the president of the ARENA."[10]

A confident Geraldo Freire could point to prognostications showing a government victory, 190 votes against 170. Even *Última Hora* predicted a government victory. Costa e Silva, who received conflicting estimates, called the ARENA congressmen to Planalto Palace on December 11, the day before the secret ballots would be cast. He argued that without political unity the nation would break up because "the tide that dashes against its shores is violent."[11]

However, at the appointed hour, 24 *arenistas* failed to appear in the Chamber, although they were in Brasília. Ninety-three *arenistas* joined 123 *emedebistas* to give 216 votes against the *licença*, whereas only 141 votes favored the government. Twelve blank votes were cast.

During the balloting, early in the afternoon, Djalma Marinho and Arruda Câmara were acclaimed in the galleries and on the floor. After the outcome was clear, the Chamber was the scene of a spirited celebration, during which the national anthem was sung and people shouted: "the Chamber against the dictatorship."

That night, Jayme Portella writes, Brasília's Hotel Nacional became a "veritable carnival of rejoicing."[12]

The *Correio da Manhã*, thrilled, wrote of a new "horizon of hope" and refused to worry about what might follow, because, it said, the moral and political victory was too great to permit rash acts by those who had been defeated. Like *Última Hora*, which called a cabinet reform inevitable, *O Estado de S. Paulo* and the *Jornal do Brasil* emphasized all the errors committed by the government in the case. *O Estado de S. Paulo* wrote that governing Brazil was unlike commanding an army division. The *Jornal do Brasil* called Moreira Alves' "irresponsible" remarks too inconsequential to be considered a serious affront to the armed forces, and could see no reason to rejoice or bewail the whole "wretched episode."

The *Folha de S. Paulo*, gaining circulation with its new offset printing and the innovative editing of Cláudio Abramo, had been arguing that a return to "democratic normality" was hindered by the government's "intransigence and inflexibility" in the Moreira Alves case. The growing São Paulo daily had observed that always, in federal and local legislatures, the executive would be able to find, if it wished, speakers it considered "deserving of *cassação*" on account of some of their remarks. After the Chamber of Deputies refused to bow to the executive, the *Folha de S. Paulo* wrote that the outcome, if received with the respect it merited, could prove to be a defeat of the crisis and a victory "for all—for the institutions, for the independence of the powers, and for the government itself."

In Rio, *O Jornal* and *O Globo* felt otherwise. The former, defender of the "loyal services" of the justice minister, wrote that on December 12 the Chamber of Deputies had given an "absurd" interpretation to congressional immunities, and it added that the ARENA "is now semi-dissolved, incoherent, unfaithful to its mission." *O Globo*, while devoting most of its editorial attention to its campaign against the progressive wing of the Catholic Church, had been filled with alarm by the December political crisis. It had been shocked at the thought that forty *arenista* congressmen might take the "perilous" step of helping the MDB defeat the government, and had put some of the blame on the "supreme command" for failing to be firm and clear about necessary "lines of action." *O Globo*, unlike the *Folha de S. Paulo*, insisted that the governmental institutions were "interdependent," and it wrote that it was therefore a "serious mistake" even to speak about "the sovereignty of Congress."[13]

6. Institutional Act Number Five
(December 13, 1968)

Costa e Silva learned of the Chamber of Deputies vote from the radio of a car that took him from the Galeão Air Base to Laranjeiras Palace. "They are," he said to Jayme Portella, "going to receive the response. You people are witnesses that I did everything I could to take care of the appeals that satisfaction be given to the armed forces."[1]

At Laranjeiras Palace, Costa e Silva conferred with Army Minister Lyra Tavares and Armed Forces Chief of Staff Orlando Geisel. Lyra Tavares, whose Rio office had been filled with generals eager to learn how the government would reply to the "affront by Congress," spoke of the army's "absolute inconformity" with the situation. The president told him that he would make his decision known the following morning at a meeting with the military ministers, Portella, the justice minister, and SNI Chief Garrastazu Médici. After the two generals left, the president relaxed with a crossword puzzle and classical music. He also reviewed his list of items for an institutional act, jotted while he had flown from Belo Horizonte to Rio, and added: "a recess for Congress and the local legislatures for an indefinite period." Among the other items were more *cassações*, the right of the federal government to take over state and municipal governments, the right to dismiss military and civilian personnel and retire judges, the right to declare a state of siege, and the suspension of habeas corpus.[2]

During the evening, while the president watched a Wild West movie, Portella had his hands full protecting the president's privacy and dealing with generals who felt the president was vacillating, among them Moniz de Aragão, Antônio Carlos Muricy, and First Army Commander Siseno Sarmento. He sent word for the police to keep a close watch on congressmen whom he described as "Communists," such as Hermano Alves and Márcio Moreira Alves, so that they could be arrested as soon as the president's decision became known.[3]

At the meeting held on the morning of Friday, December 13, the military ministers opted for an institutional act. Gama e Silva, a late arrival, started reading his drastic *ato adicional*, which called for the immediate dissolution of the Supreme Court and all legislatures, along with federal intervention in all the states. Garrastazu Médici and Lyra Tavares felt that the justice minister was going too far. Costa e Silva, also declining to accept the *ato adicional*, told Gama e Silva that what was required was an institutional act. Gama e Silva found, in his briefcase, a draft of such an act and read it aloud; and the president read the list of items he had already decided he wanted. After Gabinete Civil Chief Rondon Pacheco and Gama e Silva were chosen to draw up the final document, the meeting was joined by the planning and finance ministers, who said the institutional act would not affect the economy adversely. Portella arranged for a 5:00 P.M. meeting of the National Security Council, made up of the president, vice president, cabinet, military chiefs of staff, and the heads of the SNI, Gabinete Militar, and Gabinete Civil.[4]

Prior to the 5:00 P.M. meeting, the military ministers secretly advised subordinates of the decision and received enthusiastic responses. But Vice President Pedro Aleixo opposed the decision, and, at the 5:00 P.M. meeting, suggested that a state of siege would be sufficient. He was outvoted 23 to 1. At 10:30 P.M. the justice minister appeared on television and radio for a reading of Institutional Act Number Five, whose authors had been assisted by Education Minister Tarso Dutra. The public also heard Complementary Act Number 38, which placed Congress in recess.

Foreign Minister Magalhães Pinto declared that he had voted in favor of the new institutional act "in order to guarantee the Revolution that I made." Phone calls to the president soon brought the support of the governors of Minas, São Paulo, Paraíba, Guanabara, and Rio Grande do Sul. Governor Abreu Sodré described himself to Costa e Silva as an upholder of the revolutionary process, and told the press that Ato 5 opened "immense perspectives" for the "nationalist, democratic, and progressive revolution desired by all of us."[5]

In Brasília on the night of December 13, Mário Covas, Martins Rodrigues, and other MDB leaders asked José Bonifácio Lafayette de Andrada to call the Chamber of Deputies into an extraordinary session, but the *arenista* congressional president refused on the ground that such an act would be provocative. However, on December 14, *arenista* Senators Krieger and Gilberto Marinho, the latter president of the Senate, persuaded nineteen of their colleagues to join them in sending a telegram to Costa e Silva objecting to the new institutional act. Among the signers were Milton Campos, Carvalho Pinto, Eurico

Resende, Nei Braga, and Mem de Sá. Signer Rui Palmeira, vice president of the Senate and father of student Vladimir, died two days later.[6]

Vladimir Palmeira, José Dirceu, and others still held after the Ibiúna arrests should have been released, because on December 12 the Supreme Court ruled in their favor. However, military authorities, anticipating that "something important" would take place on the 13th, prevented compliance with the Supreme Court order until it was superseded by the new Ato's suspension of habeas corpus.[7]

On December 13, before Ato 5 was promulgated, authorities seized copies of Rio's *O Paiz* and São Paulo's *O Estado de S. Paulo* and *Jornal da Tarde*, along with newspapers in Goiás and Rio de Janeiro states. Brasília's *Correio Braziliense* appeared that morning with blank spaces in the place of some of its columns. Seizure of *O Estado*'s December 13 edition was based on its editorial "Institutions in Tatters," which blamed the increasing unrest on "the errors of the president." *O Paiz* was accused of being subversive.[8]

Following the Ato, severe censorship was inflicted on the press, radio, and television. Differing from the Rio dailies, the São Paulo newspapers provided, on December 14, news about arrests. The *Folha de S. Paulo* ran an editorial regretting the government's decision to interrupt the democratic process in order to deal with agitators, "solely interested in creating problems." It expressed the hope that Ato 5 would be used only against "radicalisms" and would be of brief duration, because recent progress, especially notable in the economic and financial sectors, could best continue in an atmosphere of order and peace. The *Jornal do Brasil* editorial column was occupied by a photograph, and large parts of its pages, starting with page one, contained classified advertisements instead of news. A weather report stated: "Very black. Suffocating temperature. Unbreathable air. The country is being swept by strong winds."

On Sunday, December 15, the *Correio da Manhã*'s headline said: "Rich Cat Dies of Heart Attack in Chicago." The *Jornal do Brasil*, like several Rio newspapers, did not appear that Sunday, and when it resumed publication it was no source of political news. The "Coluna do Castello" was banned.[9]

Carlos Castello Branco, author of the column, was jailed in Brasília, accused of participating in the events that led to the government's defeat in Congress. No such charge could be made against *O Jornal*'s promilitary columnist Maurício Caminha de Lacerda, son of Carlos' father and Aglaiss Caminha. Attacking those who "defy the Revolution in the name of slingshot little discussions," he wrote that Carlos Lacerda and Mário Martins, "practiced in the vile art of politics," were "obstinately myopic," unable to see things correctly.

On the night of December 13 and during the next days, more than two hundred arrests were made, sending journalists, students, politicians, lawyers, professors, artists, and a few churchmen to prison. Among them were writers Carlos Heitor Cony and Antônio Callado, poet Ferreira Gullar, lawyers Sobral Pinto and Celso Nascimento Filho, Guanabara legislators Ciro Kurts and Alberto Rajão, Congressmen José Carlos Guerra and Raphael de Almeida Magalhães, Senator Mário Martins, Professor Darci Ribeiro, publisher Ênio Silveira, playwright Oduvaldo Viana Filho, composer and actor Mário Lago, Catholic University of Rio Vice President Raul Mendonça, *Correio da Manhã* Editor-in-chief Osvaldo Peralva, *Diário de Notícias* political commentator Otacilio Lopes, *O Paiz* director Joel Silveira, *Tribuna da Imprensa* director Hélio Fernandes, and *Luta Democrática* director Tenório Cavalcanti. Tenório Cavalcanti, like a few of the other prisoners, was held only briefly.

Ambassador José Sette Câmara Filho, former governor of Guanabara, had become director of the *Jornal do Brasil* and was arrested in Rio; but his friend, Armored Division Commander Ramiro Tavares Gonçalves, quickly secured his release. Sobral Pinto, arrested in Goiânia and jailed in Brasília with Carlos Castello Branco, learned from his jailer that Ato 5 had the purpose of establishing *democracia à brasileira;* the stubborn lawyer retorted that he had heard of turkey being served *à brasileira* but that "democracy is universal, without adjectives."[10]

Krieger, on December 13, sought to save Raphael de Almeida Magalhães from arrest by insisting that the young congressman join him in Rio's Hotel OK, but Raphael declined and was arrested that night. The policemen assigned by Jayme Portella to watch the group of "Communist" congressmen were ineffective and succeeded in arresting only one of the group, David Lerer. Márcio Moreira Alves went abroad and Hermano Alves eventually did the same after finding asylum in the Algerian embassy.[11]

On the orders of First Army Commander Siseno Sarmento, Kubitschek and former Ambassador Hugo Gouthier were arrested. When Magalhães Pinto objected to these imprisonments, Jayme Portella told him that such things happen when feelings are intense. Portella also pointed out that Kubitschek, although a *cassado,* was an organizer of the Frente Ampla and had sought to persuade congressmen to vote against the government in the case of the Moreira Alves *licença.*[12]

Journalist Carlos Heitor Cony, like Hugo Gouthier and Sette Câmara, was a friend of Kubitschek's. At the São Cristovão barracks where he was imprisoned, he asked why so many troops were setting forth in the night. The answer was given by a young army officer who conducted him to a cell in which he found fellow-journalist Joel Silveira. The troops, the officer said, had "much work" to do. "What kind of work?" Cony asked. "We are going to shoot Juscelino and Lacerda," he was told.[13]

7. The Imprisonment of Lacerda
(December 14, 1968)

Lacerda, who continued under medical treatment at his Praia do Flamengo apartment, was with Dr. Rebello, Tannay de Farias, Letícia, and a nephew of Letícia's on the night of December 13, when it became known that Ato Institucional No. 5 was about to be announced. Before the Ato was disclosed to the public, he tried to phone Abreu Sodré to offer to fly to São Paulo to be at Abreu Sodré's side if the governor would put up resistance.[1]

Sodré was unwilling to speak with Lacerda because he suspected that the phones were tapped. Therefore the governor's secretary, Oscar Klabin Segall, went home and phoned Lacerda from there. By then, not much support could be found in the São Paulo state government for the current that wanted Sodré to resign and participate in a resistance effort. The failure of Costa e Silva to adopt Gama e Silva's *ato adicional*, which called for federal intervention in the states, made it even more certain that São Paulo would not resist.[2]

"What now?" Dr. Rebello asked Lacerda after the television brought them the text of Ato 5. "Now," Lacerda replied, "we'll have a dictatorship of the Left."[3]

Lacerda phoned Hélio Fernandes, who was about to leave his home and go to the *Tribuna* office to await arrest. When Lacerda asked, "Do you think I, too, shall be arrested?" the *Tribuna* director startled him with the news that he could expect to be *cassado*. "If you are not *cassado*," Fernandes said, "then I know nothing of what is happening in my country." Fernandes felt that Lacerda had no ability to analyze political situations, particularly at the time they were occurring. He added: "Since you are going to be *cassado*, you can expect little delay before they come to your residence to get you."[4]

Lacerda told Rebello that the government men were not so crude as to have him arrested. The doctor, disagreeing, insisted on spending the night with him. With the help of sleeping pills, Lacerda fell asleep at 4:00 A.M. and was still asleep when Rebello left for his hospital work at 6:00 A.M.[5]

At Laranjeiras Palace, three hours later, Jayme Portella received a phone call from the Guanabara secretary of security, General Luiz França de Oliveira, who said he had received orders from the First

Army to arrest several people, including Kubitschek, but none to arrest Lacerda. Portella told Luiz França to arrest Lacerda, on orders of the federal government, and have him locked up in Fort Santa Cruz. Portella sought to advise Lyra Tavares and First Army Commander Siseno Sarmento of the order he had given, but could reach neither.[6]

When Lacerda awoke, Dr. Jaime Rodrigues was at his bedside with the news that two policemen were downstairs with an arrest order. Tannay de Farias, who had summoned Rodrigues, also summoned Rebello, and the two doctors told the police that Lacerda was unwell. A police doctor therefore arrived to examine him, but Lacerda told the policemen that he would dress and go with them. He said later that he was thankful that the authorities, in arresting enemies of the regime, had not overlooked him. Members of the press sought to photograph the fallen politician as he left his apartment building under arrest, but state agents would allow no pictures.[7]

Rebello accompanied Lacerda and the policemen on the launch that took them to Fort Santa Cruz. In the heat, the walk up the many stone steps to the fort was difficult for the former governor, who had dressed in clothing inappropriate for the weather and was feeling the effects of his recent illness, the sleeping pills, and a diet for losing weight. He sweated profusely and both he and Rebello feared he would faint.[8]

The fort's officer of the day, surprised to find the former governor under arrest, phoned the First Army headquarters and then said that Lacerda could not be held at the fort because the arrest order had not come from the army. When the policemen decided to take their prisoner away and look for another place to leave him, Lacerda refused to become "a general's yo-yo." "I want to know where I am going. I refuse to spend my time moving around Guanabara Bay from one end to another."[9]

The policemen, after making use of the fort's old magnetoelectric telephone, were finally able to state that Lacerda was to be returned to the city and driven to the cavalry barracks of the Marshal Caetano de Farias Regiment of the Military Police on Frei Caneca Street. The arrangement was made by Guanabara Security Secretary Luiz França de Oliveira and Jayme Portella after Portella learned of the situation at Fort Santa Cruz.[10]

Later Portella advised Costa e Silva of the arrest of Lacerda and received his approval on the ground that "the author of the Frente Ampla and disuniter of the Revolution" should not be spared. When Portella at length spoke with Lyra Tavares, he learned that Siseno Sarmento was displeased with Lacerda's arrest and considered such decisions prerogatives of the First Army commander, not of Portella.

Portella told Lyra Tavares that Lacerda's arrest was carried out on orders of the president and that it was not up to Sarmento to tell the government who should be arrested. Also, Portella reminded the minister that Sarmento was a friend of Lacerda's and had been security secretary in his government.[11]

The gloomy old prison at the cavalry barracks on Frei Caneca Street had the reputation of being the best urban prison in Brazil despite its darkness and dirt. In a cell there, Lacerda found journalists Osvaldo Peralva and Hélio Fernandes and twenty-three-year-old lawyer Celso Nascimento Filho. The group was soon joined by Rogério Monteiro de Souza, who had returned from exile in Chile and worked recently with opposition politicians, and by fifty-six-year-old actor Mário Lago, who had been jailed in 1964, reportedly on Lacerda's orders, for holding Communist ideas. Mário Lago's arrest in December 1968 occurred in the middle of a theatrical performance and so, when he reached the cell, his face was covered with makeup. He and Lacerda had had their differences as far back as student days, but, Mário Lago recalls, Lacerda was the first in the prison cell to extend his hand to him. The actor, deciding they were all in the same boat, shook it.[12]

The group was moved to quarters that were larger (two bedrooms and a common room) but were noisy because of the sounds made by the boots of soldiers, active on the floor above. Mário Lago, the oldest of the five prisoners, became secretary of their committee and was successful when he requested newspapers, a two-hour sunbathing interval, and better food. Prison Commander Hélio Miranda Quaresma agreed to Lacerda's request that a message be sent to Sérgio Lacerda, in charge of the nearby Datamec Company, that resulted in the delivery of a large fan for combating the heat and mosquitoes. Colonel Quaresma was indebted to Lacerda for having vetoed, during his governorship, the suggestion of Gustavo Borges that he be dismissed from the Military Police because he had voted for Kubitschek.[13]

Military Police Major Carlos Osório da Silveira Neto, who had served as Governor Lacerda's aide-de-camp, visited the cell frequently and was asked by Lacerda to obtain a Christmas basket from the Lidador Store. He returned with pâté, caviar, and other delicacies. "If I can resist all this," Lacerda thought, "I shall be able to carry out my hunger strike."[14]

Recalling his hunger strike, Lacerda has stated that he felt compelled to protest against his imprisonment but recognized that "any violent protest would get nowhere. And so I resolved not to eat. But I was afraid I might be unable to carry it out. I had never done such a thing and had just been dieting." Deciding for the time being to keep his plan a secret, lest he fail or lest the others feel he was setting an example he wanted them to follow, he pretended to eat. "I had my reasons to protest against an act of the revolution, that I had helped bring about. They, while obviously revolted at being in prison, did not have the same reasons."

Drs. Rebello and Rodrigues, visiting the cell on December 15, learned confidentially of Lacerda's decision and failed to dissuade him. He kept drinking water, as they recommended, but experienced dizziness. They recommended rest, and he spent his time in bed. Urine tests, the doctors said during one of their visits, revealed excessive acetone and other abnormalities; and they warned that his tendency to diabetes made it likely that he would fall into a coma. By this time, Lacerda's doctors had obtained his permission to let the barracks' doctor and commander in on the secret.[15]

After Lacerda told the seventeen-year-old Cristina why he could not take the chocolate she brought, his family tried unsuccessfully to persuade him to change his mind. His brother Mauricinho, the most persuasive, pointed out that what Carlos was doing was receiving no attention. "Carlos," he said, "the newspapers are not mentioning this; the sun is marvelous and everyone is on the beach; no one is aware of what you are doing! And so you are going to die stupidly." Carlos was impressed but decided not to turn back on something he had started.[16]

Mário Lago, the only prisoner advised by Lacerda of his secret, noted that Lacerda was treated with admiration by the soldiers and officers, who never failed to call him governor. "But," Lago adds, "he did not take advantage of that to assume a position above my post of secretary." Lacerda, according to Lago, participated little in the heated discussions about the military government, but "spent most of his days in bed reading Montesquieu and was always reserved. Perhaps the company of Montesquieu was more inviting than ours."[17]

Hélio Fernandes, with whom Lacerda shared the smaller of the two bedrooms, pugnaciously got into more arguments with Lacerda than Lacerda liked. "He found nothing more interesting," Lacerda said later, "than to provoke a discussion with me about my responsibility for everything." Lacerda was told by Fernandes that he had "erred seriously in the episode about the extension of the mandate of President Castello Branco, the key to everything." "You did not perceive," Fernandes continued, "that Golbery do Couto e Silva is the one who hatched the episode. I told you several times and you did not want to believe it."

What especially irked Hélio Fernandes was what he considered Lacerda's abandonment of the struggle in order to devote himself to making money. Fernandes was upset to hear Lacerda speak of plans to go to Europe, perhaps to live there, after getting out of prison. Lacerda, finding that Fernandes' arguments tired him, was relieved when Mário Lago said: "Hélio, let's finish with this. This is no place for such discussions."[18]

The prisoners were summoned individually to reply to questions of investigators. "We have with us," an officer of the day told Lacerda on December 19, "a DOPS official who has come with a notary public to question you." In his weakened condition, the climb up an old stairway to the interrogation room was difficult for Lacerda, and he dreaded being queried. However, the questions, presented by DOPS *Delegado* Darcy Araújo, were written ones about the Frente Ampla that he found it simple to answer.[19]

In justifying understandings reached with former adversaries, Lacerda mentioned examples he had supplied in the past, such as Castello's talk with Kubitschek in 1964 "to get votes." He added: "Just last year Minister Mário Andreazza arranged to propose to ex-President João Goulart an accord about the indirect gubernatorial elections in states that included Rio Grande do Sul, in exchange for Goulart's indirect support of Andreazza's candidacy in the indirect presidential election."[20]

Asked whether the Communist Party had been represented at "the second Frente Ampla meeting" with Goulart in Uruguay, Lacerda denied having asked for ideological identity cards when discussing the Frente with anyone, and denounced the "obsession" of seeing Communists everywhere. He had, he emphasized, "less fear of Communists who are within the law than of anti-Communists who are outside the law." And he warned that the method being used to combat Communism "is the best way of assuring its victory in the near future."

After Lacerda completed his answers to the written questions, the *delegado* added another to be answered while they awaited the arrival of two army colonels belonging to the SNI: "Does your testimony, already given, express your reasons for opposing the orientation of the revolutionary government?" Replying that this was not the case, Lacerda said the 1964 revolutionary movement was justified by the need to preserve order—"but order with liberty"—and to assure direct and free elections, along with respect for the Christian formation of the Brazilian people. He complained that the army had become Brazil's single political party "and, what is more serious, a single party that is bitterly divided into currents with candidates." This single party, he said, had been able to shun the people by allying itself with the political oligarchies.[21]

After checking the accuracy of the report of his replies, Lacerda received a copy. He gave it to Mauricinho, with the request that he make mimeographed copies. On the copies an introductory paragraph said that Lacerda had been on a hunger strike since 2:30 P.M. on December 14, "the only protest open to him," and was in a "precarious state of health." When Mauricinho told Carlos that no newspaper would publish the document, Carlos replied: "You don't understand. I want you to deliver this to the Associated Press, United Press, and France Presse. Abroad the fact that the former governor of Guanabara is imprisoned and carrying out a hunger strike is still news."

The United Press, Lacerda recalled later, arranged for the publication abroad, with the result that Richard Nixon, whom Lacerda had met during the American presidential campaign, sent an inquiry to the American embassy asking about him.[22]

8. Lacerda, Freed, Loses His Political Rights (December 21 and 30, 1968)

On the morning after the interrogation, Lacerda's deteriorating physical condition alarmed Rebello. The doctor, wishing to bring the situation to the attention of the country's top authorities, decided to write a letter for his friend and patient, presidential aide-de-camp Ariel Chaves de Castro, to deliver to Costa e Silva.[1]

Prison Commander Quaresma, also alarmed about Lacerda, phoned nineteen-year-old Rubens Vaz Júnior (Rubinho). The young man's mother wished to try to convince Lacerda that he should remain alive, to continue the fight; but she was not permitted to enter the cell, and so it was Vaz Júnior who brought her plea and that of Colonel Quaresma that Lacerda call off his hunger strike.

Vaz Júnior had with him the draft of a letter, objecting to the government's treatment of Lacerda, which he felt should be distributed to Costa e Silva and military officers. He showed it to Hélio Fernandes, who said he liked it. At the firm established by Gustavo Borges, who had left Novo Rio, the letter was examined by Borges and Colonel Francisco Boaventura Cavalcanti Júnior. Although Borges, a sort of stand-in father for Vaz Júnior, had broken with Lacerda as a result of the Lacerda-Goulart declaration, he agreed to type Rubinho's letter.[2]

Rubinho Vaz's resolve to distribute his letter was not affected by the scolding he received from Brigadeiro João Paulo Moreira Burnier, opponent of any step that might help Lacerda. Rubinho dropped his idea only when Padre Godinho, Sandra Cavalcanti, and Cristina Lacerda spoke to him about the plan that Cristina had discussed with Hugo Levy and Congressmen Godinho and Jorge Curi for her to write to the president.[3]

Lacerda, in the meantime, wrote a message to express his appreciation for the understanding of his wife and children—"you who know how fond I am of life, this life you give me." Always, Lacerda wrote, "I have had this to say to the military: on the day you commit the crime of placing Brazil again under the domination of a group that is ambitious, antidemocratic, and, as you well know, inept, and as corrupt as possible, you will have to hear from me—or else kill me." He told his family that if he could no longer defend the people ("mothers and children like you") by words ("which are my weapon") or by action ("which is my vocation"), he would defend them as best he could, with the only thing he had left, his life. "If anything happens to me, may it be a curse forever on the thieves who rob the people of the vote and the assassins who kill liberty. And those who do not speak up. And those who accept things. And those who participate. In their place, may there arise the certainty that Brazil is not without someone who knows how to give up his life in order to provide an example."[4]

Cristina, advising her father of her plan to write to Costa e Silva, was told not to do so because it could cause her trouble later. She replied: "I'm not asking you to end the hunger strike and therefore you have no right to ask me not to write." After composing the letter at home, she showed it to Padre Godinho and Hugo Levy. Godinho suggested unsuccessfully that she write with more tact, because some expressions, unkind to the president, might not help secure her father's release. Hugo Levy did persuade her to tone down the final product in a couple of places.[5]

Her father, Cristina wrote the president, had been under arrest since 2:30 P.M. on December 14 "without any plausible explanation" and had been on a hunger strike during his entire imprisonment, "having no other means to protest against the violence of the act." Pointing out that his precarious state of health became worse by the minute, she said the president had "nontransferable" responsibility for her father's situation. "Yesterday," she wrote, "I read your statement that 'those who struggle and suffer have nothing to fear.' In that case, Mr. President, let me ask you whether you have struggled and suffered more than my father for the good of Brazil and for liberty; or have you forgotten that the result of my father's lifelong struggle was your becoming the president of Brazil. These are the words of protest of a daughter as part of her father's own protest."[6]

Costa e Silva's aide-de-camp, air force Major Ariel de Castro, found himself with three letters about Lacerda to deliver to the president: those of Cristina, Dr. Rebello, and Cardinal Jayme de Barros Câmara.

Rebello's letter, copies of which went to the heads of Brazil's medical associations, called attention to Lacerda's serious condition of "keto-acidosis, officially substantiated by the doctors at the place where he is held," a result of "almost 150 hours of fasting." Each passing hour, the doctor wrote, increased the likelihood of "the fatal denouement, which, I believe, is desired neither by Your Excellency nor any other person of Christian and humane upbringing." Thanks to journalist Ayrton Baffa's ability to outwit censors, Rebello's letter appeared in the *Jornal da Tarde,* which had already managed to mention, on December 19, a report from the doctor about Lacerda's hunger strike and poor health.[7]

The letters to Costa e Silva, all dated December 20, were in Ariel de Castro's hands that night, but the president, very tired, had left orders not to disturb him. Nevertheless, at 1:00 A.M. the major decided to awaken him. Costa e Silva, Ariel de Castro recalls, showed himself unfamiliar with Lacerda's hunger strike or even his imprisonment. After reading Cristina's letter, he remarked: "She is just as disrespectful as her father."[8]

The president's statement about his lack of familiarity with Lacerda's situation would have surprised Jayme Portella, who had received the president's approval for the arrest and had learned from the president on December 16, both during and after the graduation ceremonies at the Army Staff and Command School, that he wanted Lacerda to be held awhile longer. The president, told by Portella of the pleas of Siseno Sarmento and Albuquerque Lima on behalf of Lacerda's release, had described the pleas as "droll." Speaking to the graduating officers, he had lashed out against those who "wished to create divisions among you" and disparage the government by warning against "a nonexistent militarism," by blaming the military for Brazil's difficulties, by speaking of "generalized corruption," and by "demagogically exploiting" poverty.[9]

When the president, soon after 1:00 A.M. on December 21, finished reading the letters brought by Ariel de Castro, he decided to order Lacerda's release. Before leaving by helicopter that morning for a ceremony at the Military Academy, he told Portella to recommend that the Guanabara security secretary set Lacerda free and that the army minister arrange to release Kubitschek and other political prisoners held by the First Army.[10]

Police *Delegado* Agnaldo Amado, long despised by Lacerda, came to the cavalry regiment prison cell at about 6:00 P.M. with an order for Lacerda to be moved, for reasons of health, to his residence and held there under house arrest until he was well again, when he should go abroad. Flatly refusing to abide by the order, Lacerda declared he would not remain a prisoner in his home but would go to the streets "because my home is not a prison." The *delegado* said that if Lacerda did not go home he would be fed artificially. The authorities, Lacerda responded, might use a derrick or strong men to convey him to the Military Police Hospital, there to insert a tube in his mouth or give him injections, but afterwards he would renew his hunger strike.[11]

Friends of Lacerda's and members of his family had come to escort him home but had to wait while authorities conferred. Security Secretary Luiz França de Oliveira told Portella that Lacerda had refused to be freed because he objected to being under surveillance at his residence. Portella replied that Lacerda should be taken home in a police vehicle and left there without restriction but that his residence should be kept under watch because it would be interesting to know who would visit him.

At about 11:00 P.M., *Delegado* Agnaldo Amado advised Lacerda that a change in orders set him free. "Then," Lacerda said, "I am free to go out of my residence. And there will be nothing of that business of my going abroad. Because I'll go abroad when I feel like it." Colonel Quaresma, all smiles, asked Lacerda to ride from the cavalry regiment in his car. "I'll ride with you," Lacerda said, "only if you'll agree to have a whiskey at my home." The colonel agreed.[12]

Lacerda's apartment was filled with friends. When Dr. Jaime Rodrigues arrived, he found his patient, pale, thin, and exhausted, eating *empadas* of pastry and cheese, about which, Lacerda told Cristina, he had dreamed during his imprisonment. Rodrigues forbade more *empadas* and Lacerda obeyed his friend.[13]

During the following days Lacerda showed his concern for the men he had left behind, still prisoners of the state security secretary. He arranged to have Christmas foods sent to the cell and persuaded Dr. Rebello to treat Osvaldo Peralva, ill with a virus infection. Peralva had been unable to find a doctor willing to visit him in prison.[14]

The National Security Council, authorized by Institutional Act No. 5 to suspend the political rights of individuals for ten years, met on December 30 to review accusations against thirteen men, most of whom were considered to have contributed to the recent political crisis. The Council accepted the suggestions of Costa e Silva that the rights of Márcio Moreira Alves and Hermano Alves be suspended, and turned to the cases of nine other congressmen: Renato Archer, José Carlos Guerra, David Lerer, Gastone Righi, Henrique Henkin, Mateus Schmidt, Hélio Navarro, Maurílio Ferreira Lima, and José Lurtz Sabiá. Except for *arenista* Guerra, they belonged to the MDB. All became *cassados,* considered guilty of "agitating in the Chamber of Deputies and elsewhere, and inciting the students." After a judge, deemed to have been corrupt, was removed from the bench and shorn of his political rights, the Council resolved that Superior Military Tribunal Judge Peri Constant Bevilacqua, often sympathetic to defendants, should also be removed.

In the case of the last name, that of Carlos Lacerda, the accusations were made by Costa e Silva himself, who had been shown remarks by Lacerda that he considered disparaging of the military. He pointed out that the former governor had organized the Frente Ampla and been prominent in "actions for destroying the Revolution." Several Council members spoke in Lacerda's defense.

Foreign Minister Magalhães Pinto cited his long association with Lacerda and mentioned also their rivalry during a UDN internal dispute, and concluded that he would abstain because he did not feel that it would be ethical for him to vote to *cassar* the former governor. Costa e Silva, turning to Planning Minister Hélio Beltrão, said that he supposed that he, too, as an "old companion" of Lacerda, would abstain. But Beltrão surprised the president. He said that the political positions recently taken by Lacerda required that his political rights be suspended.

In Lacerda's defense, no one was as eloquent as Interior Minister Albuquerque Lima, brother-in-law of Lacerda's friend José Cândido Moreira de Souza. Hard liner Albuquerque Lima praised Lacerda's past revolutionary work, but a majority agreed that he should lose his political rights for ten years.[15]

Actions against people associated with Lacerda or the Frente Ampla were continued after Lacerda lost his political rights, and resulted in the *cassações* of politicians such as Senator Mário Martins, Congressmen Antônio Godinho, Jorge Curi, Raul Brunini, Mário Covas, José Martins Rodrigues, and Alcides Flores Soares Júnior, and Guanabara legislators Geraldo Monnerat, Mauro Magalhães, Salvador Mandim, and Mauro Verneck. Institutional Act No. 5 was used to punish Francisco Boaventura Cavalcanti Júnior, ending his military career, it being argued that the colonel had had ties with Lacerda.

In longhand notes to friends who were struck in this way, Lacerda praised them for their firm adherence to virtues and asserted that injustice only enhanced the victims while reducing the standing of those who acted unjustly.[16]

Early in 1969, President Costa e Silva signed a decree withdrawing Brazilian government decorations that had been received by Lacerda and deleting his name from the list of those who had been awarded the navy's Order of Merit. At the same time, three other *cassados,* Osvaldo Lima Filho, José Martins Rodrigues, and the imprisoned Renato Archer were removed from the Order of Merit list by the president because they had participated in the Frente Ampla.[17]

9. Note about the Regime after 1968

Institutional Act No. 5 was seen by Carlos Castello Branco, General Meira Mattos, and others as required by Costa e Silva to prevent his overthrow by hard liners. The president embraced its concepts vigorously, issuing a series of new institutional acts, supplementary acts, and decrees that closed five state legislatures, removed judges from the Supreme Court, and deprived so many congressmen of their political rights that the independent wing of the ARENA was crushed and the MDB lost two-fifths of its membership in the nonfunctioning Chamber of Deputies. Censorship was made more rigorous, investigating commissions were formed, and control over the state security forces was placed in the hands of the central government. Many university professors were dismissed.[1]

If Costa e Silva hoped to reopen Congress, he was prevented by military opinion; and if he hoped to promulgate a new constitution, being written by Pedro Aleixo, he was prevented by the stroke that incapacitated him late in August 1969 and soon caused his death.

Following Costa e Silva's physical collapse, the military leaders took steps that began the process that placed three four-star generals in the presidency between 1969 and 1985. Not until late in 1978 was Institutional Act No. 5 abolished and habeas corpus reinstituted. During the harsh military dictatorship, elections were held for Congress—which was allowed to function with an opposition that was crippled, sometimes by alterations in the rules of the political game. Guerrilla movements were subdued by killings; "enemies" of the regime were often arrested; sometimes they were tortured; sometimes, as prisoners, they simply disappeared; and occasionally they were reported as killing themselves. In the meantime, mammoth, debt-producing government projects were commenced and, for a while (until 1974), the economy prospered.

The climate changed drastically in 1979, when an amnesty law went into effect and new political parties replaced the two-party system. But none of the so-called "big three" of the Frente Ampla—Lacerda, Kubitschek, and Goulart—lived long enough to witness these changes or even the end of Ato 5 and the return of habeas corpus in 1978.

When amnesty came in 1979 to air force Captain Sérgio Ribeiro Miranda de Carvalho, denouncer of the Para-Sar plot, he rejected it with the remark that amnesty was suitable for those who had committed crimes, not those who had prevented them. Because he had publicly opposed Burnier's wishes in June 1968, he had suffered nothing but punishments, humiliations, and, under Ato 5, *cassação* and forced retirement. Only after his death in 1994 was he rewarded with promotion to the rank of *brigadeiro.*[2]

XII.

Epilogue
(1969-1977)

1. Africa and Portugal

Lacerda, fond of writing and traveling, kept the Mesquitas' newspapers, *O Estado de S. Paulo* and *Jornal da Tarde,* well supplied with articles between 1969 and 1976, the year before his death. As a special correspondent of those dailies, in May 1969 he crossed the Atlantic with the announced intention of spending two or three months visiting approximately thirty-three African nations.[1]

Lacerda was accompanied by engineer Marcos Tamoyo, a Novo Rio business associate, who became exhausted and ill during the strenuous trip and found Lacerda a traveler sturdier than himself. Books from Africa, sent by Lacerda, poured into the Nova Fronteira office so that the publishing firm might acquaint Brazilians with African literature. If the travelers planned their visits to London and Paris, in the second week of July, as an interlude before further study in Africa, the plan was altered with the news of the death of Júlio de Mesquita Filho on July 12. To be present at the Seventh Day Mass for his agnostic friend, Lacerda returned from Europe to Brazil, thus concluding his trip. He had, *O Estado* announced, been in "more than twenty African countries."[2]

While in Africa, Lacerda became an impassioned advocate of the cause of General Odumegwu Ojukwu, who had been carrying on a civil war in Nigeria since 1967 with the purpose of gaining independence for the oil-rich Eastern Province that called itself the Republic of Biafra. Lacerda's articles, most of which appeared after his return to Brazil, praised Biafra's 4 million "intellectually elite," Christian Ibos, striving "heroically" to avoid "absolute domination" by Arab-minded "neocolonial" Nigeria; and he assailed the help that he said was given Nigeria by Britain, defender of the Shell oil group and British Petroleum, and by the Soviet Union, "seeking to expand its imperialism." He reported that British, Algerian, and Egyptian pilots, using Russian planes, shot down unarmed Red Cross planes that tried to bring food to millions of starving, dying Ibos.[3]

Lacerda's newspaper crusade on behalf of Biafra's Ibos ended in

January 1970, with the defeat of Ojukwu, and was followed by a longer crusade for defending Portugal against the world and especially the Left. Lacerda pointed out in 1970 that Nigeria, killer of black Ibos, always used world forums to support the sanctions that were adopted against Portugal, "accused of oppressing blacks" in its African "territories." ("To call them colonies is nonsense. Should Hawaii and Alaska be called colonies?")

Most of the members of the United Nations, Lacerda wrote in 1971, adopted the slogan "Africa for the Africans" to condemn the whites in Africa ("a reverse of racism") and engaged in demagogy for electoral purposes and to satisfy self-esteem. He opposed the guerrilla independence movements in Portuguese Guinea, Angola, and Mozambique, and said they would be "inexpressive" but for military support from world powers that simply wanted to replace Portuguese control. Critical of Itamaraty's "stupid and suicidal indifference," he wrote that Brazil "must not throw Portugal to the beasts" on the pretext of trying to please other nations. "Brazil has an interest in the Portuguese presence in Africa, although not necessarily in its present form."[4]

For years Lacerda had advocated a Portuguese-speaking federation, made up of Brazil, Portugal, and the Portuguese territories, which was to have democracy in all its members and the development of "autonomy of action" in the "associated states" in Africa. On his African trip in 1969, he discussed the proposition in Dakar with Léopold-Sédar Senghor, president of Senegal, and with Amilcar Cabral, leader (before his assassination in 1973) of the insurrection for the independence of Portuguese Guinea. Senghor told Lacerda: "The nationalist leaders of Portuguese Guinea and Angola, whom I know, would be willing to have independence by negotiation and in steps" and would join the "confederation" of Portuguese-speaking nations. Amilcar Cabral, according to Lacerda, had no interest in exchanging "Portuguese domination for that of North America, Russia, or China. We prefer an alliance with Portugal and Brazil."[5]

A Portuguese exile, writing in Buenos Aires about the "ultrarightist" Lacerda, "new chief of the Portuguese fascist lobby in Brazil," said that Lacerda misrepresented Amilcar Cabral, supporter of nothing short of "unrestricted independence." Indeed, the insurrectionists demanded immediate and full independence—a step that Portugal's prime minister, Marcello Caetano, felt would doom the whites in the "overseas provinces." Lacerda, displeased with Caetano's inflexibility, wrote in 1971 that Portugal was winning its wars but should negotiate, perhaps with Léopold-Sédar Senghor's help, because of the wars' costs to Portugal, not the least of which was the departure of young men from the nation to avoid serving for four years in Africa.[6]

The wars took a dramatic turn in May 1973, when land-to-air missiles shot down Portuguese planes in Portuguese Guinea. "This missile warfare," Lacerda wrote, was financed from abroad and was intervention by nations like Russia and the United States, seeking to replace Portuguese influence. "Now," he warned Léopold-Sédar Senghor and the Ivory Coast's Félix Houphouet Baigny, "rival tribes have the instruments for fratricidal strife."[7]

This setback for Portugal was followed, in February 1974, by the appearance in Lisbon of a sensational book, *Portugal e o Futuro*, by Antônio de Spínola. Spínola had become assistant chief of staff of the Portuguese armed forces after serving as governor of Portuguese Guinea and trying, while there, to negotiate with the guerrillas against Caetano's wishes. His book, favoring a gradual evolution to a Portuguese-speaking federation, enunciated ideas so close to those of Lacerda that Lacerda, being interviewed on April 30, his sixtieth birthday, had to deny having had a hand in writing it: "It was written by Spínola, and very well written." A Brazilian edition, with a preface by Lacerda, was published by Nova Fronteira early in April, with Lacerda explaining that he was rushing it into publication to have it appear before Itamaraty and the African wars had an opportunity to destroy the yet to be formed federation. In one of his many articles extolling Spínola, Lacerda explained that the Lisbon edition had been banned after selling fifty thousand copies.[8]

Prime Minister Caetano rejected Spínola's ideas and dismissed both Spínola and Armed Forces Chief of Staff Francisco da Costa Gomes. But, on April 25, the dismissed generals participated in the coup of the Movement of the Armed Forces (MFA) that overthrew the Caetano regime and made Spínola interim president. A happy Lacerda reached Lisbon by phone and heard a journalist there exclaim: "Do you know what it is like, after forty-eight years of dictatorship, to publish an entire newspaper without censorship?" "It is generous," Lacerda told the *Jornal do Brasil*, "to call me the guru of the Portuguese revolution, but it is not the truth." He added that he had been pleased to provide some collaboration, but felt that it had "not been absolutely necessary."[9]

Lacerda explained that, with dictatorship ended in Portugal, guerrilla warfare in the territories was no longer justified. The guerrillas, he wrote, had no interest in democracy or friendship with Brazil and were an armed minority, trained by foreign nations, but not very significant. "Life in Mozambique and Angola is 90 percent normal."

"Nowhere in Spínola's book can one find the remotest intention of turning Portuguese Africa over to the guerrillas."[10]

In June 1974 Lacerda went to Portugal and was shocked by the mass movements of the Communists and their allies and by the strength of Communist sentiment in the armed forces. According to his recollections, he told Spínola: "The movement of April 25 was seized by the Communists. Your Excellency will remain in government three months at the most. Call elections now, legitimize your mandate in order to strengthen your power—or the Communists are going to overthrow you." Lacerda has also written that he told Costa Gomes: "You know, don't you, that the MFA is strongly infiltrated by the Communists," which prompted the armed forces chief of staff to reply: "Yes, but that infiltration has been going on a long time and now can be more easily detected."[11]

In Lisbon in July, Portuguese author Luís Forjaz Trigueiros received an unexpected visit from his longtime friend Lacerda, who had learned from João Condé that the Portuguese revolution had hurt Trigueiros financially. Lacerda told the author that Nova Fronteira was in urgent need of two works to be written by him and would make an advance payment, and he suggested that Trigueiros join him in working at Nova Fronteira. Lacerda gave Trigueiros two plane tickets to Rio and said goodbye during a sentimental scene that brought tears to Maria Helena Trigueiros and her husband and Lacerda. Trigueiros and Maria Helena went to Brazil later in 1974, and in April 1975 he joined Nova Fronteira.[12]

Spínola's dream of a federation was opposed by the MFA, which favored immediate independence for the African territories. So did the ever more vocal and active Portuguese Communist Party, headed by Alvaro Cunhal, an influential member of Spínola's cabinet. An attempted "silent majority" demonstration, authorized by the Spínola government, was thwarted by roadblocks and other steps by the Left. Spínola, unable to control the armed forces, resigned on September 29, 1974, and was succeeded in the presidency by General Costa Gomes.[13]

Lacerda, called a fascist in the Portuguese press, complained in January 1975, in an open letter to Costa Gomes, that the term fascist was being used in Portugal to describe all Portuguese who had not been in exile or prison during the Salazar-Caetano dictatorship. In the letter, Lacerda noted that no one had been able to object to the observation in Portugal of "the week honoring Carlos Marighella." He argued that a "band of lawbreakers" exercised a pro-Communist censorship, "more severe and much more malign" than anything previously imposed. No Portuguese newspaper would publish Lacerda's letter, but photocopies of the text in *O Estado de S. Paulo* were distributed clandestinely.[14]

In the Mesquitas' newspapers during the first months of 1975, Lacerda reached the peak of his campaign. He called Portuguese troops in Angola a traitorous Fifth Column, and said the Portuguese Socialists were stupid to believe the Communist Party (PCP) would spare them. He argued that the PCP-led union confederation, sole representative of the workers, was dictatorial; and he described the MFA as run by men who were obedient to the PCP, bent on using Portugal "to destroy the Atlantic Pact" and thus increase Brazil's vulnerability. After Hélder Câmara spoke on an official Portuguese television program, Lacerda wrote that the archbishop, a "totalitarian" demagogue, had "exceeded all limits" and become "practically a servant of a dictatorship" that was turning the defenseless Portuguese people over to a system "much worse" than anything that had gone before. "I think," Lacerda wrote, "it is time to organize, in Brazil, commissions to defend the Portuguese people."[15]

In Paris in March 1975, Lacerda learned about a plot to murder Spínola in Lisbon; he telephoned Ruy Mesquita, thus providing the *Jornal da Tarde* with what Lacerda called a journalistic "scoop" of international dimensions. Spínola, having heard that he and others were to be assassinated, participated in an attempted coup on March 11. Following its dismal failure, he went to Brazil; and the Portuguese revolution went full speed ahead with land occupations and the nationalization of banks, insurance companies, electricity, oil, and transport. Independence, already achieved by Portuguese Guinea (Guinea-Bissau), was recognized, in June and July 1975, for Mozambique and the Cape Verde Islands, and a date, November 11, 1975, was set for Angola to become independent.[16]

Lacerda, at first, called reports of the attempted Spinolist coup of March 11 "a Communist lie," invented to distort a "sinister" armed movement by the Communists, and he campaigned for a boycott of the Portuguese government by the Portuguese residents of Brazil. Warmly he welcomed Spínola and a host of other Portuguese exiles. He spent much money, as did Guilherme da Silveira, furnishing the exiles with food and hotel accommodations, and he found jobs for many. His secretary, Maria Thereza Correia de Mello, recalls that Nova Fronteira became "filled with Portuguese people."[17]

In his articles, Lacerda wrote that Spínola's defeat was only temporary and that the general would continue his fight on behalf of Portuguese democracy. But Spínola, citing the silence required of political exiles, remained uncommunicative. Eventually Lacerda came to feel that Spínola lacked the qualities needed to run Portugal. Commenting in 1977 on Spínola's book, he no longer maintained that it was well written or had been written by Spínola.[18]

In Angola, three groups were in conflict. A free election, Lacerda wrote, would result in a spectacular victory for the two non-Communist groups. But, he warned, the least popular group, the Movimento Popular de Liberação de Angola (MPLA), was supported by the Lisbon government and by armaments from Moscow and was carrying out assaults and massacres that would result in the existence, in the Portuguese-speaking world, of two Communist countries: Angola and Portugal. He denounced the "pragmatic realism" foreign policy of Brazilian President Ernesto Geisel, saying that Brazil was losing the opportunity of having, as its across-the-seas neighbor, a friendly democracy, a door that would allow Brazil to enter Africa. Brazil's "ostrich-like" policy, he wrote, was turning Angola into a "Communist trampoline for the leap to Brazil—the trampoline that was missing in 1964 but is now being prepared without anyone here paying any attention."[19]

In the Portuguese election of April 21, 1975, for a constitutional assembly, the Socialist Party did better than the other parties. But the government remained in the control of the MFA and the far Left. In July 1975, after the government sanctioned the far-Left takeover of a Socialist newspaper, Mário Soares and his Socialists and their allies broke with the government, claiming that the PCP was running the country. This led Lacerda to write that Soares, although guilty of serious past errors, had redeemed himself with his brave effort to liberate the people from their "sinister" rulers and participate in a conflict whose outcome "depends not on him but on a national and international union."[20]

On August 8, in an open letter to *Le Monde*'s correspondent in Brazil, Lacerda scolded the Paris daily for suddenly turning against Soares because of his party's rebellion against the "dictatorship of the Communist minority." He likewise berated the newspaper for trying to make a hero out of an "irresponsible demagogue," Salvador Allende—overthrown, Lacerda wrote, not by the CIA but by the Chilean people, "unwilling to put their country at the service" of those who were praised by *Le Monde*, "a model of journalistic bad faith and vileness."[21]

At the annual gathering of the Inter American Press Association, held in October 1975 in São Paulo, Júlio de Mesquita Neto introduced Lacerda as one of the greatest experts on the current situation in Portugal and reminded the audience that, at the meeting a year earlier, held in Caracas, the North American journalists had displayed a complete lack of understanding, whereas Lacerda, alone, had correctly warned of the dangers and had forecast "the present climate of disorder." Lacerda now expressed his belief that Angola, "one of the three richest countries of Black Africa," was coveted by the Soviet Union for a "Communist offensive against Latin America." Asked by a listener whether Cuba was playing a role in Angola, he answered that it was logical but admitted that he had no evidence. When another listener asked whether Portugal should remain in NATO, he expressed his opposition to this "insupportable paradox, attributable perhaps to Mr. Kissinger"—whose so-called policy of *détente* he had attacked earlier in his talk, saying that the United States opposed no one in the world except Rio Grande do Sul manufacturers of shoes, interested in exporting to the United States. A Miami journalist summed up Lacerda's views as "very pessimistic."[22]

Lacerda was correct in supposing that the MPLA would gain the upper hand in Angola, which became, on November 11, 1975, the last of the territories to obtain independence. But in Portugal the far Left, which had alienated much of the population, especially in the north, began to lose influence. So did the MFA, following the clash of November 25, 1975, in which the men of Colonel Antônio Ramalho Eanes prevailed over military officers of the Left. During the first half of 1976, the political parties, led by the Socialist Party, gained strength, a socialist constitution was promulgated, and Eanes was elected president of a democratic country. Before the year was out, Prime Minister Mário Soares' government decided to give the free-market economy a greater role, and Spínola was able to return to Portugal without being arrested.[23]

2. Attacks on *Distensão* by a Productive Columnist

In his letter of August 1975 to *Le Monde*'s correspondent, Lacerda rebuked the Paris daily for "denouncing our revolution as a *golpe* at the service of American imperialism."

The former leader of the Frente Ampla took *Le Monde* to task for "seeking to unseat the revolution and have Brazil undo what has been accomplished: almost twelve years of relative peace and uninterrupted progress." While expressing his own hatred of torture, he criticized *Le Monde* for concentrating on torture in Brazil. Condemnable violence, he wrote, had been the response to other acts of condemnable violence—horrible assassinations, kidnappings, and assaults—carried out by opponents of the regime. The successful response by

President Ernesto Geisel. (A. Lopes drawing in *Jornal da Tarde*, March 31, 1994)

the authorities, during a period of "revolutionary war," allowed Brazilians to work in peace, "contrary to the wish of *Le Monde.*"

It was during the mid-1970s that Lacerda showed more respect for Roberto Campos than he had shown while promoting the Frente Ampla. Asked, at the Bangu residence of the Guilherme da Silveira family, whom he would choose to be finance minister if he were president, Lacerda replied: "Roberto Campos. He knows everything I don't know about economics and I know everything he doesn't know about politics." On another occasion, Di Cavalcanti was amazed to learn the same thing from Lacerda: Roberto Campos, "serious and competent," was the man he would choose to be his finance minister.[1]

When President Ernesto Geisel (1974–1978) spoke of *distensão*—the return of Brazil to democracy—Lacerda pictured it as meaning "the return to what existed before March 31, 1964." His campaign against *distensão* was a feature of a series of weekly articles that began in the *Jornal do Brasil* in June 1975 after Armando Daudt d'Oliveira persuaded Nascimento Brito to let Lacerda write for the Rio daily.[2]

According to one of the articles, a rather sensational one published on June 30, the transformation of Brazil that followed the 1964 revolution still had a long way to go, and it was a mistake "to propose, in the name of reestablishing the 'rule of law,' that the country disarm itself and turn itself over to disorder and a form of collective suicide." Lacerda wrote on July 27 that the equivalent of *distensão* had wrecked Portugal and was about to wreck Italy, and, perhaps "with our help," Spain; and he warned that *distensão* seemed likely to cause the collapse of Brazil. For the benefit of "opportunists and political intriguers," he added that his record allowed no one to give him lessons in democracy.[3]

In mid-May 1975, Congressman João Cunha, a Paulista opponent of the military regime, spoke in the Chamber of Deputies to denounce Lacerda for "raving" against Geisel's goal of "a return to democracy." Dealing with the subject again, late in June, the MDB congressman declared that the only risk in returning to the past was the possibility of the return of people like Lacerda, responsible for past tragedies and emulators of Salazar, Franco, Nguyen van Thieu, Augusto Pinochet, Stalin, Hitler, and Mussolini.[4]

"The new crusade of Carlos Lacerda" was the theme of an article, "The Return of the Crow," that appeared on August 25, 1975, in *Movimento*, a prodemocracy weekly launched in the previous month in São Paulo by well-known writers. The article's author, Oscar Macedo, thrashed Lacerda for opposing *distensão*, for emphasizing the importance of the role of the armed forces, and for writing, in the *Jornal do Brasil*, that only the Communists would benefit from a failure of the military to receive better pay and greater prestige. Lacerda was described as a fat and balding writer whose "tiresome articles" about Portugal revealed his loss of skill with words. "He is fond of the tranquility of the old Portuguese estates, such as the one used by his Brazilian friend Antônio Carlos de Almeida Braga, prosperous owner of land in Portugal." Macedo wrote that Nova Fronteira had employed the son of the owner of a diamond mine in Angola. He repeated rumors (untrue) about Lacerda's "many economic interests in Portugal and its colonies."[5]

Luís Alberto Bahia, the *Jornal do Brasil* editor handling articles of opinion, threatened to resign because Lacerda was writing for the newspaper. President Geisel, also opposed to Lacerda's *Jornal do Brasil* series, sent word of his displeasure to Armando Daudt d'Oliveira, who took the position that only Nascimento Brito could bring the series to an end. The *Jornal do Brasil* executive had been abroad, and, when he returned, was told in Brasília of Geisel's view. This put him in an awkward position, because he was inclined to let Lacerda continue. Lacerda, however, learned of the situation from Armando and

A NOVA CRUZADA DE CARLOS <u>LACERDA</u>

A VOLTA DO CORVO

The return of the crow: the new crusade of Carlos Lacerda. (Cássio
Loredano drawing in *Movimento*, São Paulo, August 25, 1975, *O
Jornal*, Lisbon, and in *Caricaturas*, book published by Ed. O Globo,
1994)

told Nascimento Brito that travel plans made it necessary for him to
bring the series to an end. He did not mention having learned of
Geisel's view; but the *Folha de S. Paulo* reported, in mid-August
1975, that the discontinuance had been "ordered by Brasília."[6]

   A review of Lacerda's post-1968 articles, mostly in the Mesquitas'
dailies, does not confirm the statement in *Movimento* that his style
had become "insipid and obscure." Lacerda, often using the pseudonym Júlio Tavares, was an incisive reviewer of books and a lucid
raconteur, writing sometimes about people he had known, such as
José Bento Monteiro Lobato, Anna Amélia Queiroz Carneiro de Mendonça, the Mesquitas, and Constantinos Doxiadis. His fondness for
Greece, which he enjoyed visiting with family and friends, was evident. In 1971 he published an informative and sensitive "Guide" to
Ernest Renan's "Oration" about the Acropolis and a week later gave
his readers his translation of the "Oration."[7]

   On Greek islands and in the Aegean Sea in 1972, Lacerda participated in a symposium at which Doxiadis and other planners imparted
knowledge about the "occupation of land by mankind." He made
arrangements for Athanasios Hadjopoulos, of the Doxiadis group, to
furnish suggestions for developing a part of the coast opened up by
the new Rio-Santos highway, where one of the Lacerda–Novo Rio

companies acquired considerable property. Searching for ideas, Lacerda visited the Languedoc-Roussillon Mediterranean area in order to become acquainted with the steps that the French government, following a Doxiadis preliminary study, was carrying out to create new cities and beaches. In articles about the Brazilian equivalent of the French Mediterranean coast, he suggested that the authorities adopt measures to prevent "pillaging by land grabbers for mere profit." He advocated the preservation of forests and a regulation requiring the builders of hotels and houses to engage in horticultural activities or farming. Urging plenty of marinas, he wrote: "Imagine the Rio-Santos area with many hotels and few boats."[8]

Doxiadis died in 1975 at the age of sixty-two, after a struggle of almost three years with multiple sclerosis. Lacerda, who had not yet left the *Jornal do Brasil*, recalled, in the Rio daily, the work done for Rio planning by "Dinos." Bitterly he wrote about the "injustices which the Communists and their accomplices heaped upon this great man simply because they wished to attack my administration."[9]

In 1970 Lacerda asked Antonio Carlos Villaça, a writer at the *Correio da Manhã*, to look over the articles he had written and make selections to be published in two volumes. Villaça, whose *O Nariz do Morto* (1970) had been labeled "good and bad" in one of Lacerda's reviews, was paid a handsome fee and spent a year consulting thousands of articles, some quite old, in scrapbooks at the Pompeu Loureiro Street apartment, in the Copacabana district, where Lacerda moved from Praia do Flamengo in 1970. There Lacerda enjoyed discussing literature with Villaça, who sometimes shared meals with him as well as the companionship of Letícia, Padre Godinho, Jorge Curi, Regina Costard, Joaquim da Silveira, and Candinha Silveira (the owner of a boutique that Regina Costard helped run). Late at night, Carlos would sometimes read aloud to Villaça, stirring him with his splendid voice and deep emotion. After reading a description of Vargas from his well-marked copy of *O Nariz do Morto*, Carlos said: "He was a great man but not a statesman."

Villaça came to appreciate that Lacerda, unlike Vargas, was a "universal man," a perceptive literary critic, more in need of intellectual, than political, conversation. He found that Lacerda identified himself with André Malraux and Winston Churchill. Churchill, Lacerda told Villaça, was a manic-depressive, "like me."[10]

Lacerda teased Villaça for not dressing well and frequently joked with him—pretending, during a phone call, to be the Swedish ambassador advising Villaça that he had won a Nobel Prize. He took to calling the heavy author, a former novice at the São Bento Monastery, "Dom Abade" (Abbot). Together with Lacerda, Dom Abade joined

Padre Godinho, Severo Gomes, and others in 1970 for a few days in the Serra da Bocaina, in São Paulo state, at the *fazenda* of Gomes, industrialist and agriculture minister of Castello Branco. In 1971 the travel-loving Lacerda took Villaça and other friends (among them young businessman Marco Aurélio Moreira Leite and the fifteen-year-old son of Maria Fernanda Correia Dias) on a trip to Parati, reached by boat from Angra dos Reis.[11]

The collections of Lacerda's articles sold well under the titles of *O Cão Negro* (1971) and *Em Vez* (1975). Like the former, which contained the pieces about the Acropolis and a long report on Africa, the latter avoided Brazilian politics. Villaça, describing *Em Vez* in the *Jornal do Brasil,* said it was concerned with human matters, such as the "Civilization of the Kitchenette," a critique about society written in 1946.

Lacerda's personality and controversial career fascinated people—to such an extent that Luís Martins, reviewing *Em Vez,* devoted his piece to the author, whom he described as "practically an outlaw, a sort of angel and demon," the eloquent tribune, the whirlwind, the fearful pamphleteer, and firebrand, who, in relations with intimates, was calm, intelligent, considerate, and lyrical in dialogue.

People waited in long lines in Rio and São Paulo to obtain inscribed copies of *Em Vez.* Noting its sales success, Mara Bentes wrote in *Fatos & Fotos,* "Lacerda has not lost his public."[12]

Em Vez contains Lacerda's articles about psychoanalysis, published in *O Estado de S. Paulo* in 1973 after a São Paulo judge ruled that psychoanalysts could practice without having to graduate from medical school. Pointing out that thousands of well-to-do people—"or, rather, victims"—were undergoing analysis, he called the practice a pseudoscience. "The explosion of egoism that psychoanalysis gives its patients" and "the principle that self-satisfaction is the supreme objective of human life . . . do not seem to be the best ways of curing the ills of contemporary society." Lacerda described Freudians as nonethical pessimists who considered the world a pigsty and life mere rubbish and used psychoanalysis to separate people from everything that connected them with reality or restrained them, such as the family and other ties.[13]

Maintaining that most people were neurotic, Lacerda wrote that all the cases of self-cure or self-compensation by the soul were not given scientific notice because the soul was not a physical organ. He stated that some people learned to live with their neuroses, but he admitted that others needed help. "I have, I believe, saved several people from neuroses. I only failed when psychoanalysis alienated them."[14]

Before the arrival of the pseudoscience, Lacerda wrote, assistance was provided by family and friends, and even enemies were able to "renew the connection of the neurotic with reality, or evoke in him the sentiment of responsibility—necessary for reacquiring lost equilibrium." But, Lacerda added, the type of collaboration that he favored was discouraged by the analyst, who aroused in the patient so much justification for irresponsibility that the time had come to start talking about "the victims of the victims." The patients of the analysts, "when they do not destroy themselves, become Frankensteins. They destroy everything within reach, even those who love them the most." He felt that the pseudoscience was disrupting families and hurling children against their parents.

Replying to a question asked by the *Jornal do Brasil* on his sixtieth birthday, this one about his relations with his children, Lacerda said that one of the errors of psychoanalysis was its development of the feeling that parents were responsible for the errors of their children. "Parents should stop acting like people asking to be forgiven."[15]

3. Books

Editora Nova Fronteira got off to a good start with the publication of a translation of Arthur Hailey's *Hotel*, a title that Distribuidora Record let it have. A translation of William Peter Blatty's *The Exorcist*, an enormous sales success, put Nova Fronteira in a position to go ahead with a vast project advocated by Lacerda: the compilation of the *Novo Dicionário da Língua Portuguesa* by Aurélio Buarque de Holanda Ferreira and his team. The publishing firm eventually received a loan from the National Economic Development Bank to help complete the huge dictionary, and benefited a great deal from an arrangement, negotiated by Sebastião Lacerda, for the publication of translations of Agatha Christie's detective stories.[1]

The public's good reception of the dictionary, published in 1975, contributed to Nova Fronteira's decision to become its own book distributor, thus terminating the arrangement with Distribuidora Record. Lacerda, breaking the news to Alfredo C. Machado, was accompanied by his son Sérgio, for Sebastião had left Nova Fronteira. Machado was shocked and displeased about the change for handling the dictionary. His firm, which had been marketing it, had an agreement with Nova Fronteira for the distribution of 50,000 copies and by that time only 20,000 had been distributed. Sales of the dictionary, during Lacerda's lifetime, reached 250,000 copies.[2]

With Nova Fronteira doing well under the management of Roberto Riet Corrêa, Lacerda expanded his book publishing interests by taking control, late in 1975, of an esteemed Brazilian book publisher,

Editora Aguilar, under an agreement reached with its founder, José Aguilar, a Spaniard. Editora Aguilar, which published handsome hardback editions of Brazilian and other classics on thin paper, was renamed Nova Aguilar.[3]

Books about Júlio de Mesquita Filho and his brother Francisco, who had handled the financial and administrative side of *O Estado de S. Paulo*, were on the minds of the Mesquitas in June 1973 as they planned for the centennial of the historic daily, which had been organized in 1874 and first appeared, as *A Província de S. Paulo*, in January 1875. *O Estado* director José Maria Homem de Montes phoned Lacerda to say that Júlio de Mesquita Neto and Ruy Mesquita wanted him to write a biography of their father, Júlio de Mesquita Filho. Lacerda declined, with the explanation that the task was beyond his ability. But he returned the call half an hour later and, full of emotion, said he had changed his mind after Letícia, enthusiastic about the idea, had told him: "This will be your great work." The invitation, Lacerda told Montes, was "the greatest honor" of his life. "I think I'll make it a history of the republic."[4]

Lacerda explained to Montes that he could accomplish the "mission" if he could have research assistance from *O Estado* people to supplement research that could be carried out by Luiz Ernesto Kawall, who had run the São Paulo office of the *Tribuna da Imprensa* when Lacerda had published the Rio daily in the 1950s. Lacerda sought suggestions in letters he wrote to Mesquita Neto and others on July 26, 1973, and added that if the work produced any profit it should be used to "finance an educational center in the area I am going to develop in the São Paulo northern coast, along the Rio-Santos road." Proposing titles, such as *Julinho* and *O Capitão* (The Captain), Lacerda mentioned, optimistically, a publication date of December 1974 at the latest.[5]

Instead of having separate authors for separate books about Mesquita Filho ("Julinho") and Francisco Mesquita ("Chiquinho"), the Mesquita family decided to have Lacerda handle them together. Nevertheless, Lacerda opted for two volumes, one to consist of easy-to-read narrative and interpretation and the other to contain "references and documentation."[6]

During approximately one year, documents and information were assembled by Kawall and two *O Estado* employees, Armando Bordallo, the archive superintendent, and Luís Roberto Souza Queiroz, a reporter chosen by Montes. Lacerda kept them busy (especially Kawall) and found pleasure in carrying out interviews in Brazil and picking up information there and overseas.[7]

When the researchers delivered forty fat files to his Rocio country

house, where he was accumulating material for the two books, Lacerda showed signs of discouragement, wondering how, in a short
time, it would be possible to write the biographies of "two men who
played, passionately, decisive roles in Brazilian life for sixty years."
He had become fascinated with the Bucha (Burschenschaft), the São
Paulo Law School secret society to which most of the civilian political leaders of the pre-1930 republic had belonged. Information about
the Bucha was hard to come by, presenting a challenge. Luís Arrobas
Martins, a *bucheiro* who had served in the state government of Abreu
Sodré, was helpful, and *O Estado* reporter Luís Roberto Souza Queiroz, a former press secretary of Arrobas Martins, obtained material
about the secret society.[8]

Kawall, arranging the files that had been delivered to the Rocio
house, heard Lacerda remark that it would be best to write first about
the Bucha, and Lacerda said the same thing to Carlos Alberto Aulicino, a Paulista friend. But the Mesquitas were sparing no assistance
or expenses for the work about Julinho and Chiquinho, and Lacerda
completed a preface for it. Writing in *O Estado* early in 1975 about the
nine-and-a-half years of research that went into the second volume of
the multivolume biography of Winston Churchill begun by Randolph
Churchill, Lacerda sounded dejected: "Poor me, having to relate the
lives of the two Mesquitas as readably as possible without violating
truth or good taste, following intermittent and uncertain research of
less than a year and troubled by other tasks and uncertainties, condemned to do what I have not wanted to do because what I have
wanted is forbidden me."[9]

Lacerda sent the Mesquita family a "circular letter" dated December 29, 1975, a year after the scheduled publication, promising to find
a month without interruptions to complete the work late in March
1976. Explaining that it would be "a history of Brazil, especially São
Paulo, for over half a century," he told the Mesquitas that "one of the
greatest satisfactions" he was finding in the work was the opportunity to clear up "many misunderstandings about Brazil's contemporary history."[10]

The task, more formidable than some people realized, was not completed, because Lacerda had many distractions, among them the financial problems of Novo Rio, and because he died in May 1977.
Bordallo and Alfredo Mesquita (brother of Julinho and Chiquinho),
attributed Lacerda's failure to produce the book to the difficulty they
say he had in dealing with the opinions and racism of Julinho, who
had openly expressed his poor opinion of blacks. Kawall and Carlos
Alberto Aulicino felt that the Bucha was too great a diversion. José
Maria Homem de Montes concluded that Lacerda, in the mid-1970s,

did not have the temperament to carry out the type of work that was required.[11]

While consulting *O Estado*'s archive, Lacerda decided that historians had not properly handled the Copacabana Fort revolt of 1922 because they had relied on newspapers in Rio, "subject at the time to censorship." He was inclined to criticize published accounts of what had occurred, and, not surprisingly, found faults with Luís Viana Filho's volume about President Castello Branco. Occasionally, in conversation, he criticized narratives written by Hélio Silva, careful researcher of Brazilian historical events. In 1976 he exploded after reading Silva's account of the resignation of Quadros. In a letter to *Isto É* magazine, he called Silva an imposter and liar who published asininities in order to have revenge against Lacerda because Lacerda would not furnish information for "his profitable but stupid work of confounding and attacking Brazilian culture." "To take him seriously is to risk transforming the imparting of knowledge into an instrument of stupidity, falsehood, and bad faith." Hélio Silva, a former writer for Lacerda's *Tribuna da Imprensa,* published a reply expressing regret at being thrust into the huge legion of Lacerda's ex-friends and at finding, in Lacerda's "diatribe," confirmation of reports about the "decay" of the former governor, struck down by an early affliction of old age.[12]

The scathing style of Lacerda's "diatribe" about Hélio Silva was used also in his letter of May 18, 1976, to *O Estado de S. Paulo* to denounce it for publishing articles that criticized Brazilian book publishers and that attributed past "crises" between Brazil and France to Lacerda's Orly Airport interview of 1964. Lacerda directed his fury at *O Estado*'s "irresponsible" reporter for interviewing "a grafter" who "uttered nonsense" about book publishing. According to Lacerda, the behavior of *O Estado* and *Veja* magazine, which also published "lies" about the Orly interview, was turning liberty of the press into "an instrument of stupidity" and "a vehicle for turmoil." Journalist Alberto Dines wrote that Lacerda's "violent" letter was "perhaps the most brutal attack on Brazilian journalism to appear in recent times." "His long silence," Dines wrote, "has not cramped his style." "'Old Charlie' has returned, even if fleetingly, with his smoking pistols."[13]

In the letter that provoked these comments, Lacerda pointed out that Brazilian book publishers were being "devoured" by government competition and threatened by a move to force them "to publish national authors before those authors decide to write books that the public wants to read." Thus Lacerda began a new campaign. It was against the government's BNDE, which controlled Editora Nacional and the debt-ridden Livraria José Olympio Editora, and was also against the Câmara Brasileira do Livro (CBL) and the Sindicato Nacional dos

Escritores de Livros (SNEL), which proposed that at least 20 percent of titles of books published by each firm be by Brazilian authors. The figure was to be raised later to 30 percent; but for textbooks the figure was to be 10 percent.[14]

By March and April 1977, when Lacerda was leading this, his last campaign, Roberto Riet Corrêa had left Nova Fronteira, to become manager of the Difel book publishing company,[15] and Lacerda was devoting full time to Nova Fronteira and Nova Aguilar, assisted by the young poet Pedro Paulo Sena Madureira.

In articles and letters to the press, Lacerda wrote that the BNDE was supposed to stimulate private initiative, but was doing the opposite and had become one of South America's largest book publishers. He and the Livraria Francisco Alves, he said, had inquired about conditions for acquiring the BNDE's two publishing companies and been told that Editora Nacional, a leading publisher of textbooks, was not for sale "because it is in the black."[16]

The position of the CBL and SNEL about Brazilian authors was a result of a request by Education Minister Nei Braga that these associations of book publishers and writers submit suggestions for the "protection of the industry." They had therefore set up a task force and issued circulars inviting publishers to meetings. Lacerda maintained that the meetings had been held without the presence of representatives of important publishers. But Ênio Matheus Guazzelli, CBL president, pointed out that CBL and SNEL circulars had been sent to all publishers including Lacerda, and he stressed the need "to discover new and good Brazilian writers and works that reflect national thought."[17]

Lacerda maintained that "writers are not created by decrees," and said that the "demagogic" proposal would make sense "only if it obliges bookstores to buy national books published by us and obliges readers to buy those books from the stores." Over a thousand Brazilian authors, he said, translated books into Portuguese and were being forgotten by the CBL and SNEL.[18]

According to Lacerda, Distribuidora Record, publisher of Jorge Amado and Graciliano Ramos, was portrayed as "simply a publisher of foreign best sellers" and had been marked "for destruction" because it resisted the proposed regulation. As for himself, Lacerda explained that he had, "in the last thirteen years, published 372 titles of which 78 (over 20 percent) are by Brazilians." Discussing Nova Aguilar, he wrote that "our latest conquests are Gilberto Freyre, Adonias Filho, and Murilo Mendes" and spoke of republishing Castro Alves, José de Alencar, Cecília Meireles, Graça Aranha, Augusto Frederico Schmidt, Jorge de Lima, Machado de Assis, Ronald de Carvalho, José

Lins do Rego, and Joaquim Nabuco's three-volume *Um Estadista do Império.* "It is," he also said, "the Agatha Christies of this world who allow the publication of new authors with the attendant risks of failure."[19]

Lacerda criticized the "festive Left—described by Manuel Bandeira as 'the cabaret side of Communist life'"—for using intrigue to try to destroy publishers it had been unable to infiltrate. "To hear that bunch speak about defending culture is, really, a joke." It was leftist Ênio Silveira, of Editora Civilização Brasileira, who expressed the need of "maximum protection for Brazilian culture," according to Guazzelli, who denied press reports that attributed the statement to himself.[20]

Guazzelli, whose style was friendly, reprimanded the press for saying he was mad at Lacerda. But Lacerda pulled no punches. He asserted that Guazzelli "lies with a really impressive—not to say enviable—brazenness." He described him as cowardly and wrote that "the CBL, in the hands of Guazzelli, is becoming a case for the police." Furthermore, he accused "publicity-loving" Guazzelli of sparing the "unscrupulous textbook mafia" that induced teachers and students to purchase books in return for being allowed also to purchase summaries, prepared by the publishers and containing all the questions and answers appropriate for the classroom.[21]

Lacerda disclosed, on April 30, 1977, that the CBL had failed to achieve what it wanted, and he accused Guazzelli of continuing, nevertheless, to keep the issue alive. But, Lacerda pointed out in several of his declarations, the chief problem that should concern everyone was not the nationality of the authors but the low volume of book sales in Brazil, "a country of 120 million people in which publishing records, such as those set by the *Dicionário Aurélio* and *O Exorcista,* reached only 250,000 copies." In his final article, printed the day after he died, he wrote that any Brazilian author whose books would attract 5,000 buyers was assured of a publisher. What was important, he argued, was the continuation of "an industry that is just beginning to be born in Brazil." He predicted that "the forced publication of unsalable books" would result in its "destruction."[22]

One of the distractions that interfered with writing about the Mesquitas was a new book by Lacerda, *A Casa do Meu Avô* (My Grandfather's House). In December 1976, members of the Confraria dos Amigos do Livro (Fraternity of Book Lovers), organized by Lacerda, received their copies of a deluxe edition (1,500 copies printed), with photographs by the author's son Sebastião. In March 1977, the regular paperback edition appeared for an eager and appreciative public.[23]

In an article published in 1969, Lacerda had recalled boyhood days

spent with his grandfather, Supreme Court Justice Sebastião de Lacerda, at the house on the Paraíba River. The article had persuaded
Walter Cunto to urge Lacerda to write a book on the subject. Lacerda
decided to do this in 1975 after seeing his son's photographs of the
dilapidated old house and its surroundings. He typed the chapters at
Rocio, where an annex had been built for his library, and read them
aloud to Letícia and the guests who were so frequently there.[24]

As Lacerda explained during some prepublication remarks to the
press, the chapters formed "a series of reflections and sensations
about episodes and people." He argued that this was no time for *memórias*, because *memória* writing represented the end of a lifetime,
whereas, for him, much remained to be done. Calling attention to the
subtitle, "Thoughts, Words, and Works," he said it would be "the
theme" of a continuation, "a more extensive work," that would include his book about the Mesquitas—covering "almost fifty years of
Brazil, so little known, . . . so disfigured by factious and improvised
historians, by ideological passion, or by systematic ignorance."[25]

Lacerda achieved, with *A Casa do Meu Avô*, his highest acclaim as
an author. To Pedro Paulo Sena Madureira he expressed much pleasure to receive praise from Alceu Amoroso Lima, a man he had frequently attacked, and from Carlos Drummond de Andrade.

Although a review by Carlos Vogt in *Isto É* faulted the book for a
tone that "self-commiseration and vanity impose," Gilberto Freire
called Lacerda "one of the greatest modern writers of the Portuguese
language." Pianist Maria Lúcia Pinho was reminded of Brahms, and
Josué Montello (writing in the *Jornal do Brasil*) was reminded of "the
great Portuguese pages of Raul Brandão." In *O Estado de S. Paulo*,
Paulo Rónai called Lacerda an observer, visionary, and lyric poet, and
Aires da Mata Machado Filho proclaimed the book a "literary beauty."
Luiz Carlos Lisboa wrote, in the *Jornal da Tarde*, that it followed the
literary tradition of Machado de Assis and handled philosophical
meditation and psychological observation in the manner of G. K.
Chesterton. "The author is, today, the absolute master of the spoken
and written word."[26]

These critics shared painter Maria Helena Vieira da Silva's admiration for the way in which the author connected subjects that were
apparently far apart. (Lacerda even managed to include Cristina's
letter to Costa e Silva.) But the book is most memorable because of
the talent with which Lacerda recaptured incidents of his childhood
and the settings in which they took place, and formed word pictures
of family members and others, among them his nanny, Clara Freitas,
and "Aunt Colodina," the cook with enormous hips. Lines about the
melancholic grandfather, sharing moments with young Carlos, form

lasting impressions. "In return for the little he received from me, he gave me what remained to him to give. . . . As I pass the age at which he began to die, I fear the same thing is happening to me. But I have no one around me to give what I received." What Carlos had to give and wanted to give was "eagerness to live."

Carlos wrote that, in his own solitude, he had come to realize that his grandfather had kept his true feelings to himself. After referring to his grandfather's "minor weaknesses and puerile explosions of anger," Carlos observed that people tried to make themselves appear strong. "Today, when I realize how weak he really was, how stoically weak in his solitude, I love him more than in those days when he appeared like a thundering Jupiter. I love him more for his imperfections. . . . With the passage of time, we have become closer, perhaps I should say, more alike."

Letícia, reading the book, told Carlos that it was "very sad" and that people could take steps against solitude, whereupon Carlos turned and left the room. In May, after the death of Carlos, his nephew Cláudio wrote that the book "is sad from the first to last page. A book by a solitary and grief-stricken man."[27]

"Many people," Lacerda told a reporter in April, "think my book is sad. But the sadness is in the reader when he sees how much he has lost through lack of opportunity or of courage to establish relations with older people. This book is about two solitudes, the boy's and the grandfather's, and is not nearly as sad as Hemingway's *The Old Man and the Sea* because in my book the two solitudes are joined together."[28]

4. Unsuccessful Businessman

After the establishment of Novo Rio Crédito Financiamento e Investimentos in 1965, Antônio Carlos de Almeida Braga worked at his desk there for about a year, longer than co-founder José Luís de Magalhães Lins, and then left because of his insurance company's demands on his time. He had differences with Sérgio Lacerda and criticized him for bringing José Zobaran Filho to Novo Rio.[1]

When Braga took the lead in setting up Novo Rio, he said he would teach Carlos how to make money. He was correct in placing a high value on Lacerda's name, for this was before the Frente Ampla alienated many of the former governor's admirers. "A lot of people," Braga has said, "were so crazy about Lacerda that they wanted to invest." The size of Orlando Ometto's investment surprised Braga, because the sugar planter's simple dress and manner belied his vast wealth. Another surprise was the considerable interest shown by people who had not known Lacerda personally, such as Fernando Teixeira, the elderly Portuguese owner of Rio's Hotel Guanabara. Thrilled at being received by Lacerda, Teixeira went to his well-filled safe, took out more money than he had originally had in mind, and became a major investor. This development, together with an arrangement about the voting of shares, put into legal form by Fernando Velloso, gave Lacerda a controlling position he had not enjoyed earlier.[2]

Lacerda was the administrator who had supervised public works as governor. Looking at the plans for apartments whose construction was to be financed by Novo Rio Crédito Imobiliário, he asked ironically if maids were to be shrunk so they could squeeze into the servants' rooms. "We won't finance buildings with such tiny maids' rooms." He had a remarkable memory for the details of projects in which he was interested, and, upon returning from trips abroad, would ask what had been done about matters that employees often regarded as trivial.[3]

He could fly off the handle. After his nephew, lawyer Gabriel Lacerda, concluded that two unsatisfactory employees, fired by Lacerda, had indemnity rights that the labor court would uphold, a ranting Carlos maintained that the dismissed employees were "terrible people" and therefore should not have those rights. Unable to accept a reality that was not in accord with his wishes, he demanded that Gabriel take the case to court. The verdict was as Gabriel had forecast. Some of the other people whom Lacerda occasionally fired in a rage were useful employees. Following the advice of his secretary and admirer, Maria Thereza Correia de Mello, they stayed away from the boss for a while and found him acting later as though he had forgotten having said that they were fired and that he never wanted to see them again. Braga, who felt that employees should postpone discussions when Lacerda was in a bad mood, concluded that Lacerda's manner may have contributed to his being left with yes-men.[4]

While Lacerda detested day-to-day routine, he found pleasure in plunging into new undertakings. By July 1973, when the Empresa de Administração, Serviços e Empreendimentos (EASE) was set up as a "control center," fifteen companies were on its roster. Absent was Novo Rio Crédito Imobiliário, the firm that had financed the construction of hundreds of houses and apartments. Marcos Tamoyo bought it and constructed houses for the National Housing Bank. He changed its name to Grande Rio Crédito Imobiliário and took Epaminondas Moreira do Valle with him.[5]

Among the EASE top executives were Carlos and Sérgio Lacerda, Mario Lorenzo Fernandez, and Jorge Curi. Five of the fifteen companies on its roster dealt with financial matters. One of these was an insurance company managed by Mauricinho Lacerda, father of law-yer Gabriel, and another was a brokerage business. Still another, set up in 1971 and 1972 by Sérgio Lacerda, was the Banco Novo Rio de Investimentos, an investment bank that obtained a Crédit Suisse loan of Swiss francs and a connection with Lloyds Bank International. Fernando Rodrigues, a Pernambuco real estate investor, became an important partner in the investment bank, which had a capital valued at $8 million.

When the investment bank was set up, Carlos Lacerda separated from Imobiliária Nova York of Sílvio Magalhães and his brothers. By then the original Novo Rio company, Novo Rio Crédito Financia-mento e Investimentos, had a capital equivalent to $6.5 million and held a minority position (30 percent) in a flourishing consumer fi-nancing business, CICLO, dominated by a much larger banking group, the Grupo Financeiro Ipiranga, headed by Júlio C. Lutterbach.[6]

The EASE "special ventures" consisted of Editora Nova Fronteira, Heliomar Empreendimentos (with 14,000 acres on the São Paulo coast), the Hotel da Praia on a beach in the Angra dos Reis municipal-ity, and Transcontinental, to carry out mining activities. Nova Miller, listed as an EASE "service company," was a tourist agency that had taken over the agency established in São Paulo in 1904 by Charles Miller, an Englishman who introduced soccer to Brazil. Nova Miller directors were Carlos Lacerda, Carlos Alberto Aulicino of São Paulo, and Rio hotel owner Fernando Teixeira.[7]

The Datamec computer company, also listed as a "service com-pany," overshadowed the other companies on the EASE roster. It was not a large company when it was purchased in 1966 by Sérgio Lacerda from the business group that had long been headed by the wealthy Carvalhos (Lauro and his son José) and then been transferred to José Carvalho's cousins, José Cândido and José Luiz Moreira de Souza. Sérgio brought in friends, knowledgeable in computer science, and later installed, as Datamec president, Gilberto Marinho, who left the Senate presidency in 1971, a result of his electoral defeat in 1970. The company developed data processing capabilities for government min-istries and for consumer credit sales; especially important was the data processing for the Loteria Esportiva (Sporting Lottery) of the Caixa Econômica Federal. Employing over a thousand workers and capitalized at the equivalent of $5.5 million, Datamec became known as the largest data processing company in Latin America.[8]

Carlos Lacerda was described as the head of an empire whose assets grew from $30 million to almost $60 million between 1970 and 1973. "Now, Carlos," he was told while lunching with João Condé and José Alberto Gueiros, "you are a successful businessman, and wealthy."

"I would," he replied, "give it all up if only I could be an alderman." He said much the same thing to Armando Daudt d'Oliveira, who left Novo Rio in 1969. Speaking to O Estado de S. Paulo, he said: "I would give up all that I have and am doing if I could do what I was doing before: govern." In a reference to the power to get things done that went with a top governing post, he told Regina Costard: "Once it is tasted, it alone is attractive."

The business success allowed Lacerda to become the biggest spender ever known by Condé. Maria Olívia Vianna de Aguiar, who handled Novo Rio accounts, was sometimes urged by Novo Rio people not to show large, favorable balances when Carlos asked for figures, lest they encourage his spending. Sérgio Lacerda bought himself a splendid old coffee *fazenda* in Rio state.[9]

All went well while Brazil, under President Emílio Garrastazu Médici (October 1969–March 1974), enjoyed its "economic miracle." But a different story began around the latter part of 1973 after the Organization of Petroleum Exporting Countries (OPEC) brought about a 300 percent increase in the petroleum price. In Brazil (importing 80 percent of its petroleum needs) and elsewhere, interest rates and inflation soared and economic recession set in. The collapse in Brazil of the Banco Halles in June 1974 was followed by the collapse of other Brazilian financial groups—those that suffered from a government policy that gave no encouragement to the smaller, independent groups and looked for mergers to help the large conglomerates. The independents had to make payments on *letras de câmbio* that became due at a time when the public refused to purchase more of these financial instruments from them.[10]

Early in 1974 the Novo Rio investment bank succeeded in terminating its unfortunate relationship with Fernando Rodrigues; but the BOLSA Group, that took over the Rodrigues 50 percent interest, would only do so with the understanding that the Novo Rio Group, principally Novo Rio Crédito Financeiro e Investimentos, assume full responsibility for advances and investments, some of them illiquid, made by the investment bank during its previous life in association with Fernando Rodrigues. To keep the investment bank from failing, the Novo Rio Group had to contribute new capital. It did so by arranging to receive a foreign currency loan from Lloyds Bank International; this borrowing, like the original one in Swiss francs, became a heavy burden with the devaluation of Brazil's currency.[11]

In April 1974, while these changes were made in the investment bank, the Novo Rio Group suffered a serious blow: the collapse of the Grupo Financeiro Ipiranga, which had held a 70 percent interest with it in the active CICLO business of loans to consumers and others. The

Novo Rio Group, already in debt to the Central Bank, sought further assistance. The Central Bank, with plenty of similar requests, issued a regulation in April 1976 making such assistance dependent on steps to be taken by the applicants to sell off assets and reduce their debts.

In the meantime, Datamec found itself burdened by the high interest rates on its debt and needed more money so that it could handle the expanding Loteria Esportiva. In August 1975 it increased its capital in a move that gave the Caixa Econômica Federal the largest stake, 49 percent.[12]

The situation was discouraging for many who had invested in Novo Rio in the 1960s and become involved in the coastal land development in the early 1970s. By all means possible Sérgio Lacerda fought to ward off complete disaster. Carlos, remarking that he was not interested in being a gangster, could not bring himself to participate in the rough aspects of business that the situation required, and he did not approve of everything that Sérgio did. But Carlos and Sérgio were in agreement when they maintained that President Geisel's aversion to Carlos was reflected in unfriendly attitudes at the Central Bank and Caixa Econômica.

An arrangement was worked out whereby Carlos would retire from the Novo Rio financial enterprises and receive a monthly check from them; and, at a Novo Rio stockholders' meeting held on October 2, 1975, Carlos' resignation was accepted. In the difficult work of handling the afflicted companies, Sérgio was joined by lawyer Fernando Velloso and Sebastião Lacerda, whose relations with his father had been impaired by a rude, uncalled-for statement of Carlos' in *Manchete* about what he thought psychoanalysis was doing to the young man.[13]

Still, Carlos was involved in the outcome of the business negotiations because, according to Fernando Velloso, his resignation from Novo Rio did not relieve him from being, for five more years, personally liable for debts and actions taken. When Carlos wrote in November 1976 to Maria Thereza Correia de Mello, who had moved to the United States, he said: "If I settle a business problem, I expect I'll be much more tranquil and restrict my work to the publishing houses. The rest I'll leave to Sérgio and Sebastião. I'll travel and travel."[14]

During 1976 the Novo Rio Group sold the property on the São Paulo coast and some other real estate, including four floors of CICLO office space in Rio, and disposed of a controlling interest in the Nova Miller travel agency. The sales reduced the Novo Rio Group's debts by one-third.

Together with presenting this evidence of compliance with the Central Bank's April 1976 regulation, the Novo Rio Group told the

Central Bank that it hoped to obtain a little more cash by selling the Hotel da Praia (a Datamec property) and land in the Angra dos Reis area. The Group also promised to close ineffective agencies, reduce personnel still further, dispose of forty-two phone lines and twenty-three vehicles, and move out of downtown Rio office space, including that of the Novo Rio headquarters on Rua do Carmo. But in the early part of 1977 the response of the Central Bank was to demand liquidation of the remaining debt within four years (less than the maximum time stipulated in the April 1976 regulation), with charges to be made semiannually (for interest and currency devaluation) at the rate of 30 percent per year on the balances (the maximum charge allowed at that time by the regulation).[15]

After the Caixa Econômica Federal became the largest stockholder of Datamec, it pointed out that it was also Datamec's largest creditor and client, and it exerted pressure to take over the data processing company. In May 1977 the Caixa put its own men in all of Datamec's administrative posts, including the financial ones, leaving only two former administrators, who held technical positions.[16]

Tannay de Farias, who took care of Carlos' accounts, wrote him in March 1977 that he did not know where to find funds needed for Carlos' bank account and to handle payments that were due. These included the amortization of a loan made to cover repair work on the house of Carlos' grandfather, on the Paraíba River, that Carlos was turning over to Sebastião. Carlos, now far from wealthy, borrowed against royalties he would receive from *A Casa do Meu Avô*.[17]

5. Personal Relations (1973-1977)

Carlos Lacerda had a strong attachment to family life.[1] Full of devotion to his children, he was hurt by what he regarded as rebelliousness when they reacted to his dominating personality and sought to be persons on their own. Cristina, with many of her father's characteristics, loved him deeply but now and then quarreled with him. When she explained later why she had, as an adolescent, fled three times from home, she pointed out that he was a difficult man to argue with. In 1973 she went to live in London, where she met her future husband, Luiz Eduardo Simões Lopes, son of Luiz Simões Lopes, a long-time colleague of Vargas and an antagonist of Lacerda.[2]

Carlos, writing to Letícia from Zurich in December 1974, said: "For a certain time, there was still our daughter, but she also took the path she wanted and I only get demands from her in exchange for a smile or one of the interminable and insoluble misinterpretations to which she subjects us."

In a letter to Cristina in London, Carlos made it clear that he wanted, "with all the strength of which my heart is capable," a reconciliation with Sebastião, who had found a life of music and professional photography; but Carlos attributed the trouble between them to Sebastião's "falling into a trap." In the letter to Letícia, Carlos mentioned the subject, calling it "the problem of a son who judged himself neglected and abandoned as if nothing we did counted and all that counted was what we couldn't or wouldn't do."

The letter to Letícia was the letter of a man "alone in the midst of many people"—and of a wounded man "deprived of being for my grandchildren what my grandfather was for me, by a kind of furiously sadistic shrew—whose destructive sadism has the disguise of benevolent, dedicated motherhood."

Carlos wrote: "It is not the proximity of old age that beats me down, but a truncated life, life reduced to earning money and arguing about it, the last thing I thought I would do in my life so full of high purposes and (I still think) legitimately ambitious goals. In all of this, at this juncture I find myself orphaned of grandchildren, and placed in judgment at each step by my children—whose love is as harsh and demanding of me as it is weak and condescending in relation to themselves, a poor love, without duties or rituals, that judges itself free because it withers and wanes." "You think you are very much alone; imagine me." Carlos interpreted quarrels that sprang from desires of independence as manifestations of weakness in love.

As for his relations with Letícia, Carlos wrote: "In life today only one profound and serious reason exists for me to cling to life. It's you. I well understand that recent times could have altered that idea in your mind. Just like mine being altered by your rages, your affronts, sudden changes in mood and even verbal abuse, intentional indifference, etc. But I know you love me. And I know, even more, that I profoundly, existentially love you." Carlos admitted, however, that: "I even thought for some time (these recent times) that everything depended on leaving you independent, solidly independent, with your own income, your own life, so you wouldn't have to beg—as you have done erroneously and in vain with children and grandchildren."[3]

Carlos had, in the late 1960s and early 1970s, given serious consideration to separating from Letícia and had, for hours on end, discussed the possibility with Cristina. His late-in-life depression, according to his older son Sérgio, resulted from his inability to "let himself go" and divorce Letícia, as "he wanted." "He was not at ease with her, but he was not at ease when he was away, separated. There was nothing my mother could do about the situation."[4]

Depression sprang also from preoccupation with death—a preoccupation evident in his free verse poem "Approaching Death," written during a plane trip between Rome and Tehran in July 1975, with its line: "Death advises me it is on its way."[5]

The deaths of friends moved him deeply. He mourned, sobbing, the loss in 1974 of his doctor, Jaime Rodrigues, a close friend and understanding confidant, whom he respected.[6] When he learned in August 1976 that Kubitschek had been killed in an automobile accident, he went at once to the home of Kubitschek devotee Adolpho Bloch, publisher of *Manchete*. Filled with emotion, Lacerda spoke about the former president until, with his head resting on Bloch's shoulder, he broke down in tears.[7]

Carlos was shattered by the loss of his older brother, Mauricinho, in a Rio hospital less than a month later. The death of Mauricinho, sixty-five years old, was from cancer, which Carlos feared would kill him also, and it occurred early on the morning of the day on which Cristina married Luiz Eduardo Simões Lopes at a religious ceremony at the Rocio house. Carlos, Maria Abreu Sodré recalls, had "done everything" to give his daughter a beautiful ceremony, officiated by Dom Lourenço de Almeida Prado. An altar was covered with orchids, and white chrysanthemums were massed all along the veranda. The news from Rio, of course, had a very dampening effect.[8]

After Mauricinho's funeral, decorated with orchids from the wedding, Carlos had a warm embrace for Guilherme Romano, Mauricinho's doctor, although the doctor had been dismissed from a post by Carlos as governor.[9]

Mauricinho toward the end of his life had married the lively Dirce Azambuja and had become a warm companion of Carlos', who wrote to a friend in Texas: "In his last days he was so close to me that now I feel lonesome; he was just great." *A Casa do Meu Avô* was dedicated, with affection and praise, to Mauricinho. According to Sebastião and others, the death of Mauricinho left Carlos with little interest in life. "All I want to do is die," he said to Regina Costard after his brother's death. He became, Costard and Alfredo C. Machado feel, self-destructive. He drank too much—but always with friends, because, as he said to Antonio Carlos Villaça, "I detest solitude." At the same time, he tried to adhere to a rigorous weight reducing regimen recommended by Geraldo Medeiros, eminent São Paulo physician. The regime's thyroid medication produced nervousness.[10]

Late in 1976 Carlos had another of his quarrels with Sérgio about a business matter—a bitter quarrel, this time. After Letícia sided with her son, Carlos left home and moved into an apartment on Rio's Barão da Torre Street, near Praça General Osório. He tried to explain his problem while drinking brandy at a dinner with João Condé, Luís Forjaz Trigueiros, and Maria Helena Trigueiros: "Letícia was wonderful. She accompanied me all my life. Now that she is undergoing psychiatric therapy, she has started to argue with me." Never before, Condé reflected, had he heard Carlos criticize Letícia.[11]

Letícia was not advised of the Barão da Torre Street address, but Cristina eventually learned of it from Tannay de Farias, in whose name the apartment was rented, and she and her father talked about her pregnancy. He brought presents for his daughter, whom he had loved long and deeply, and walked with her along the beach.[12]

Lacerda, during this period, was repairing his relations with men he had alienated. Through João Condé, he got in touch with Alfredo C. Machado, with whom he had quarreled about the distribution of the *Dicionário Aurélio*, and he had a four-hour lunch with him. José Nabuco arranged for Lacerda to get together with Afonso Arinos de Melo Franco, whom Lacerda asked to write an interpretive book about the Brazilian republican era, to be published by Nova Fronteira. Luís Forjaz Trigueiros opened the way for reconciliations with several writers, including Jorge Amado, with whom Lacerda exchanged books, and Odylo Costa, filho. And Trigueiros brought, he has said, Josué Montello back to Nova Fronteira. Through Di Cavalcanti, Lacerda hoped to meet with Roberto Campos, who was agreeable but was in England, serving as ambassador. Nearer the end of his life, Lacerda established good relations with journalist Joel Silveira and former Ambassador João Batista Lusardo, although in neither case was there time for a meeting. Joel Silveira received, through journalist Cristina Gurjão, Lacerda's offer to supply wine and cheese for an evening together that did not materialize because Silveira went on a trip. Glauco Carneiro's book *Lusardo, O Último Caudilho*, being published by Nova Fronteira, made it possible for Lacerda to develop a friendship with Lusardo, whom Lacerda had called "the centaur of the pampas—one half horse, and the other half also." The new relationship was crowned with a letter to Lusardo in which Lacerda wrote that the Gaúcho's "personal bravery and strength of convictions" had inspired him in his youth, and that reconciliations, exemplified by the Lacerda meetings with Kubitschek and Goulart, were necessary for uniting Brazil.[13]

Lacerda did enjoy the companionship of younger men, such as Raphael de Almeida Magalhães in the early 1960s, businessman Marco Aurélio Moreira Leite in the early 1970s, and Nova Fronteira Superintendent Pedro Paulo Sena Madureira in 1977, but he did not engage in homosexual activities as was asserted late in his life by a few of his detractors.[14] While he was living on Barão da Torre Street, he became infatuated with Maria Cecília Azevedo Sodré, a young woman about Cristina's age who had a Vassouras background and a job at the Nova Fronteira office. When Lacerda went to the Caesar Park Hotel in São Paulo late in February 1977, he took her with him. Tannay de Farias, thanks to a Vassouras doctor, came to believe that Maria Cecília planned to blackmail Lacerda, perhaps using passionate letters from him. Although Lacerda refused at first to believe Tannay, he concluded, at the hotel in São Paulo, that Tannay was right. Maria Cecília left.[15]

In São Paulo at the Giovanni Bruno Restaurant, Lacerda talked with Luiz Roberto Veiga de Brito from 9:00 P.M. until 4:00 A.M. Deeply depressed, he asked the engineer not to quarrel with him: "I haven't time to make new friends and I want to keep the friends I have." Before the conversation ended, Lacerda spoke as though he had been unfairly abandoned by people. He also spoke of himself as a failure. With tears in his eyes, he said: "I have failed as a husband, as a father, and as a politician."[16]

At the home of the Abreu Sodrés, Carlos would relax on the sofa and talk until early morning with Maria Abreu Sodré. Maria Cecília had left the Caesar Park Hotel and he was dejected. Maria Abreu Sodré sensed his need for a home. "You have," she said, "a nice place in Petrópolis, with all your roses." But she was not asked, as on previous occasions, to help him pick out gifts to take to Letícia.[17]

Carlos was back in Rio on March 12, his wedding anniversary, and went that day to the funeral of Roberto Riet Corrêa, Nova Fronteira's former manager. There he met Letícia and they made their appearance together. He went home with her. But the relations between husband and wife were strained.[18]

Lacerda found happiness at Nova Fronteira and in the collaboration he received from Pedro Paulo Sena Madureira, who had submitted, at Lacerda's request, a five-year plan to make the publishing firm a strong cultural force. He told Pedro Paulo, whom he considered a genius, "Only you and I will carry out the plan." He expressed pleasure at this association with a member of the new generation, "a generation that has the worst possible image of me, known as a *golpista* who over-threw Vargas."

Pedro Paulo had no separate office and worked at a large table he shared with Lacerda. There in Rio, and also in Rocio, Lacerda would speak to Pedro Paulo, Luís Forjaz Trigueiros, and João Condé about the "rediscovery" of himself as a creator and about the course he had chosen for the last years of his life, a consolation prize, he said, for someone unable to carry out what his entire training had prepared him to do. When Pedro Paulo pointed out that he would, before long, regain his political rights, he said with vehemence: "Now I am a writer and publisher." Happy with the reception given to *A Casa do Meu Avô* and with his talented young friend at his side, he occasionally demonstrated the enthusiasm of a boy discovering the world. "This is almost a miracle," Luís Forjaz Trigueiros remarked.[19]

A powerful reminder of the political world from which he had been barred was offered when the *Jornal da Tarde* asked him to recall, for taping, his political career and thus contribute to a historical project it was planning. Lacerda refused, citing his condition of *cassado* and his lack of interest in politics, and he revealed bitterness at what he felt to have been injustices suffered by himself and Brazil, whereupon the *Jornal da Tarde*'s Ruy Mesquita likened Lacerda's attitude to that of a betrayed lover fearing to encounter the woman he loved in the arms of another. But Ruy's son prevailed by invoking the warm relations that had existed between the Mesquita and Lacerda families.

Starting on March 19, 1977, Lacerda spent thirty-four hours during four weekends in his Rocio library annex putting recollections and observations on tape and answering questions of *Jornal da Tarde* reporters (Antônio Cunha, Ayrton Baffa, Cláudio Lacerda Paiva, Ruy Mesquita Filho, Ruy Portilho, Antero Luiz, and Melchiades da Cunha Júnior, conceiver of the newspaper's historical project). The recordings, edited by Cláudio Lacerda Paiva, appeared in the *Jornal da Tarde* between May 27 and June 15, and as a book, *Depoimento*, published by Nova Fronteira the following year. Lacerda's talent at narrative and characterizations was embellished by an excellent sense of humor that depended on what was ridiculous about situations and people. The publication provided reading that was fascinating as well as edifying. Many individuals were put in their places by pointed, unflattering remarks; and some of them, such as Hélio Fernandes and Juracy Magalhães, and others familiar with history, wrote long letters to *O Estado de S. Paulo* and the *Jornal da Tarde* to provide versions of events that differed from those of Lacerda.

When the interviewers, at the last of the taping sessions, asked Lacerda what he considered his greatest achievements, he spoke of two: his participation in the overthrow of "one or two or two-and-a-half dictatorships" and the creation of a state government with a mentality of serving the people. Having already dismissed Milton Campos and Eduardo Gomes as lacking any vocation for power, Lacerda described himself as having been delighted with the opportunity to use power to be constructive. He admitted being melancholic when he reflected that he had spent his entire life preparing for something that had been denied him when his abilities reached their peak; but he denied being bitter about it. What he felt, he said, was grief because of the lack of men adequately prepared to run Brazil. As for himself, he pointed out that when he regained his political rights he would be sixty-five or sixty-six, not the right age for entering a political career. He was through with banking, which he said he hated, and spoke of his pleasure to be publishing books. Ruy Mesquita, in his Preface, found Lacerda "reconciled to the great love that betrayed him" but unhappy at not having done all he felt that he could have done to prevent Brazil from continuing to be politically underdeveloped.[20]

For two days, starting on March 30, Lacerda was again in São Paulo, this time to autograph copies of *A Casa do Meu Avô*. The autographing session, at night at the Skultura Galeria de Arte, attracted a throng and was followed on the next day by an interview at the Caesar Park Hotel in which Lacerda told *Folha de S. Paulo* reporter Regina Penteado of his fears that Brazil, a large country like India, might end up like India. It was, he said, very difficult for a country to progress if it did not make use of intelligence and imagination. "Universities that do not allow free debate are useless."[21]

Lacerda's São Paulo friends found that he had changed. He was tired, *O Estado de S. Paulo* wrote, and almost always appeared sad. A rare expression of pleasure was displayed at the home of his friend Zulmira Lunardelli, when a woman familiar with astrology and the occult forecast a great future for Cristina's son, who had just been born.

Carlos Alberto Aulicino, at whose São Paulo home Lacerda had supper, was shocked at the appearance of his guest, his face a yellow-green with dark splotches under the eyes. After Lacerda said he had been able to lose some weight, Aulicino suggested that he would do well to abandon the dieting program.

Alfredo Mesquita, with an appointment to discuss a Nova Fronteira book project at his São Paulo house with Lacerda, found him exhausted and depressed. Lacerda spoke in a barely audible voice and was not the ebullient, joking Carioca Alfredo had known. Alfredo had witnessed the bitter closing days of other ambitious men and thought to himself: "How unfortunate it is to have consuming ambition."[22]

A week later, Luiz Ernesto Kawall reached Rio with photographs of old São Paulo for the book Lacerda had discussed with Alfredo Mesquita. At Nova Fronteira, Kawall was greeted with unusual formality by Lacerda, who was pale and despondent and was making phone calls to set up dates in Rio with Carlos Castello Branco, who was in Brasília, and Emil Farhat, who was in São Paulo. Lacerda, in a bad mood, expressed anger at people and things. When Kawall delivered a message from Quadros, suggesting they meet during Lacerda's next visit to São Paulo, Lacerda said he never wanted to hear about Quadros again. "Everyone makes mistakes, Luiz Ernesto, but treason is unforgivable."[23]

The days were past, Joel Silveira says, when Lacerda could drink whiskey without being very adversely affected. He was not the quiet man described by Alfredo Mesquita when he and João Condé, both drunk, phoned Alfredo Machado to offer conflicting opinions about what Machado should buy, on his forthcoming trip to the United States, to provide Bermuda grass for the Rocio place. Very late one night, Carlos and a group of his friends inconsiderately dropped in on Cristina, with Carlos announcing they were there to see the baby. Cristina, still unwell after childbirth, lost her patience and told them all to get out.[24]

But Lacerda was a considerate host when he and Letícia received Carlos Castello Branco, the Trigueiros couple, and Leo Gilson Ribeiro at their Rio apartment for dinner. Anti-Communist journalist Leo Gilson Ribeiro, invited earlier in the day at the suggestion of Pedro Paulo Sena Madureira, wanted to tape an interview with Lacerda and was therefore asked by Lacerda to stay behind after the other guests left. It was a long interview because Lacerda, although obviously tired, kept talking until 3:30 A.M. According to the journalist, the printed version of the interview did not fully reveal "the tone of despondency, of melancholy."

Lacerda described the Brazilian people as indisciplined and as having "an enormous tendency to flatter." "I find Brazil, at the moment, perplexed and confused . . . , without voices capable of interpreting the real sentiments of a large part of the population." Speaking of himself, he told Leo Gilson Ribeiro that he would find it extremely difficult to be only a writer. "I would not have the perseverance, the patience—that patience that I demand of professional writers to sit down for a fixed number of hours each day and write. I can go *months* without the need to write and then suddenly have a violent need and am unable to sleep unless I write."

Kawall, reading the interview later in *Status* magazine, described it as concerned with "the crisis of books, the crisis of education, the institutional crisis, and the crisis of the national asininity." It was the last interview given by Carlos Lacerda.[25]

6. What Killed Lacerda (May 1977)

Lacerda invited his mother and other family members, along with friends and *O Estado de S. Paulo* photographer Fernando Bueno, to be in Rocio around lunchtime on Sunday, May 15, 1977, for the inauguration of a schoolhouse to be named for his grandfather Sebastião, on a parcel of land he was giving to the state of Rio de Janeiro. The guests arrived, but among them was no representative of the state. Official documents about the gift were incomplete and the inauguration was canceled—but only when it was too late to call off the get-together.

In Rocio, a disappointed Lacerda seemed tired and old as well as sad. Saying that he felt poorly, he took a nap after sandwiches had been eaten. It revived his spirits and he discussed publication plans, amused guests with anecdotes about Emperor Pedro II's family, and asked João Condé, the Trigueiros couple, and Edite Glasner to join him and Letícia that night in the Rio apartment for some special wine that he looked forward to serving and fish that he wanted to cook.[1]

It was during that Sunday night repast that Lacerda was stricken by what he told his guests was an oncoming cold. On Monday morning he had a high fever and advised Tannay de Farias, on the phone, that he would not be able to read the papers he was supposed to sign about the gift of Rocio land. "I don't know what's happening to me," he told his helper. He forced himself to go to his Nova Fronteira office only because of his friendship for Emil Farhat, who was coming from São Paulo to lunch there.[2]

From the lunch, attended also by Trigueiros and Pedro Paulo Sena Madureira, Lacerda left early for home. There he phoned for Dr. Rebello, but learned that the cardiologist had the grippe and could not make a visit. Letícia was out, and Lacerda, fearing he had heart trouble, got in touch with Regina Costard, who came to the apartment. He asked her to summon the Prontocor emergency service, "because I have a very high fever and severe pains in the chest"; but the doctors who came found nothing wrong with his heart. When Letícia returned home at 7:00 P.M. she concluded that Carlos' concern about his heart was nonsense. "The trouble is grippe and has nothing to do with the heart," Regina heard her say.[3]

With Carlos complaining of his fever and pains in his joints, Letícia phoned Rebello at 10:00 P.M. The sick doctor recommended that Carlos take an aspirin tablet and an aluminum hydroxide tablet and repeat the treatment every four hours if necessary. A little later in the night a cardiologist, called in by a member of Lacerda's family, took a look at Carlos and then phoned Rebello to say that he was recommending the same pill treatment that Rebello had recommended and that the invalid, suffering from a virus, was feverish. Rebello was also informed that although Lacerda had a heart murmur, he had good circulation, and that an electrocardiogram showed nothing abnormal.[4]

The high fever continued, and on Tuesday the recently summoned cardiologist recommended that medical tests be made. Lacerda, who had been trying to work at home with help from Pedro Paulo Sena Madureira, was in a bad mood when he phoned Rebello and called special attention to the heart murmur. Some while back Lacerda had told Rebello that a São Paulo doctor had found him with a "congenital" heart murmur (a surprise to Rebello, who had detected no murmur late in April 1976); but, Rebello writes, on May 10 Lacerda had advised him that a subsequent examination in São Paulo revealed the disappearance of the "congenital" murmur.

During a phone call on Wednesday, May 18, Lacerda let Rebello know that he wanted no more visits by the cardiologist who had been called in on Monday. Lacerda had decided to place himself under the care of Dr. Pedro Henrique de Paiva, an able doctor recommended by Pedro Paulo Sena Madureira. Pedro Henrique, thirty-five, had never liked Lacerda's politics, but had the virtue, in Lacerda's eyes, of having been a student of Dr. Jaime Rodrigues. Amazed at all the pills Lacerda had been taking, Pedro Henrique insisted, as Dr. Rebello had done, that the thyroid weight reducing medication be ended. He agreed that the invalid was suffering from a virus, and recommended, as his predecessor had done, laboratory tests.[5]

On Thursday afternoon, when Lacerda was experiencing acute dehydration, three doctors gathered at his bedside: Dr. Pedro Henrique de Paiva; orthopedics Professor Carlos Giesta, who had had success, on Wednesday, in alleviating pains in the invalid's joints; and Dr. Rebello, who was brought, weak and coughing, by Sena Madureira and Carlos' driver in Letícia's car. No signs of cardiac insufficiency were detected in Lacerda. However, the heart beats had become very rapid and the heart murmur had become intense.

The three doctors decided that Lacerda should go to a hospital, for two or three days, where tests could best be made and rehydration carried out. Lacerda agreed, somewhat reluctantly. When Sérgio advised Cristina of the decision, he pointed out that their father had a bad cold and was sweating a lot but was all right.[6]

At the Clínica São Vicente, which Carlos reached in an ambulance at 1:30 P.M. Friday, Sérgio told his father that tubes would put serum into a vein to "beef" him up; but Carlos replied, with a half smile, "This time I won't make it." Sérgio felt that Carlos was making one of his jokes and decided to return to his *fazenda*. Carlos' sister, Vera, believed at first that her nephew should remain in Rio, but he convinced her that she was making "too much of a fuss." "He is getting better," Sérgio said, "but imagines he has cancer, like Uncle Maurício."[7] From time to time Carlos had been indisposed by grippe and sweating, and the family had been given no reason to feel alarmed.

When Carlos phoned Cristina from the clinic, he told her he was there "only for some tests." He was worried that Cristina's infant,

Luís Felipe, might not be all right. Cristina, who was not very well herself, assured him that the baby was fine. "Get better," she said, "so that I can see you tomorrow, my birthday."[8]

In truth, Lacerda was beyond saving because of an acute infection of his heart lining caused by a common bacterium which, in this case, was staphylococcus aureus. Such organisms can produce heart lining lesions, resulting in a condition characterized by murmurs, fever, positive blood culture, enlarged spleen, chills, and fast heart beats, all of which Lacerda revealed, as documented by the physicians who attended him at the end.

Pathologist Artis Quadros DaSilva, who expressed these thoughts in Austin, Texas, in 1987, after carefully examining the results of the tests made in the São Vicente Clinic, agreed with Dr. Pedro Henrique de Paiva's post-mortem verdict that Lacerda was killed by infective endocarditis. DaSilva concluded that Lacerda, who died at 2:00 A.M. on Saturday, May 21, "first had acute bacterial endocarditis and that fragment(s) of the valvular vegetations became detached (embolism), and became lodged in a coronary artery, leading to the myocardial infarct (heart attack) and death." DaSilva added that common causes of bacterial infections of the heart valves have been abscesses, skin boils, and intravenous injections with contaminated needles, and that Lacerda, as a diabetic, "would be prone to infections anyhow."[9]

A possible remedy, mentioned by Dr. Virgil Lawlis, also of Austin, would have been massive intravenous injections of penicillin or some other appropriate antibiotic, a three- to six-weeks treatment, known in Lacerda's day to have a fifty-fifty chance of success. But the treatment should have been started no later than Lacerda's miserable Monday. He was beyond cure when doctors began suggesting that tests be made. Incidentally, positive determination that the illness is infective endocarditis requires a waiting period of forty-eight hours before the return of cultures from blood samples. Lacerda's medical problem was diagnosed too late.[10]

Rebello had returned to his bed at home on Thursday night with the feeling that the steps taken for Lacerda, including the planned hospitalization, would mean "winning the battle." For a while this seemed to be the case. Pedro Henrique phoned Rebello at 7:00 on Friday evening to say that the patient's temperature was way down, circulation was good despite the fast heartbeats, and carefully controlled hydration was progressing. Rebello was euphoric. Speaking on the phone, he told Trigueiros that Lacerda was "out of danger" and told Lamy Cunto that he had learned from Pedro Henrique that all was going very well.[11]

Lacerda's appearance in the clinic that evening was less reassuring.

Vera found him objecting, in a voice weak with dryness, to the dis-
comfort caused by the intravenous needles and tubes in his arm, for
the rehydration, and near his neck, for taking blood samples. She
found the bed extremely wet from perspiration. According to Lamy
Cunto, his fingernails were purple and his eyes like those of a fish. He
was, she says, arguing: "I have to go to work, I've got to go to Nova
Fronteira; finish with these tests at once." When Regina Costard saw
him, his lips and nails "completely purple," she told the "eight medical men" she found there that he appeared to be practically dead. She
was assured that the proper measures were being taken to control his
fever, and that "a very low blood pressure" was resting his heart. "Is
there no danger?" she asked. "No," was the reply.[12]

Only a small adjoining room was available for someone to spend
the night with him and this was occupied by Letícia. She was given a
sedative by doctors who assured her that her husband "is quite all
right tonight." Despite the sedative and her deafness in one ear, she
heard Carlos call out around 11:00 P.M. A male nurse, she noted, then
gave him an injection.[13]

Rebello, learning at 11:30 P.M. that Pedro Henrique had returned to
the hospital because of Lacerda's turn for the worse, advised making
an electrocardiogram, because, he has written, "it occurred to me
that Lacerda, diabetic, infected, dehydrated, and with a fast beating
heart, might have had a myocardial infarction." He, too, rushed to the
hospital, where Pedro Henrique explained that Lacerda, in a state of
shock, had suffered from acute pulmonary edema and hypotension.
The dying political figure, his skin covered with cold sweat, was
breathing rapidly and turning blue from a lack of oxygen in the blood.
Very agitated, he pleaded with Rebello: "Take those tubes out; those
men are killing me."

Pedro Henrique reported years later: "Lacerda knew that it was
hopeless—not at first, but afterwards he could tell, from what was
said, etc. He was in shock but he knew he was dying. Letícia was in
an adjoining room." "He died with extraordinary dignity." Soon after
it was over, Pedro Henrique told the press that the death had been
caused by an acute myocardial infarct and that Lacerda had been troubled by dehydration, fever, diabetes mellitus, and an enlarged liver.[14]

The *Jornal da Tarde* quoted Lacerda as saying "I want to live" while
complaining of tubes and needles stuck into his veins.[15] The words
express the sentiments he displayed during his last hours. Specifically, he wished to return to Nova Fronteira.

Setbacks had depressed Lacerda so keenly that it became customary to conclude that he had wanted to die. Therefore it is frequently
said that his death was caused by the failure of Novo Rio, by the loss

of his political rights, by the realization that when he regained his rights he could never again be the political figure he had once been, and even by his difficult marital relations. Others suggest that foul play occurred at the Clínica São Vicente, part of a plot that eliminated, at about the same time, the three leading figures of the Frente Ampla—Lacerda, Kubitschek, and Goulart, considered to have been "threats" to the military government. But the fate of Lacerda was determined by staphylococcus aureus, which acted regardless of the wishes of anybody.

7. Post-Mortem

Controversy about Carlos Lacerda, a feature of his life, followed his death immediately and still continues. *O Estado de S. Paulo*, calling attention on May 21, 1977, to the lack of news about his death in the Lisbon press, wrote that Portuguese government circles used the term *Salazarista* to describe him. Some of Brazil's officialdom took its cue from President Ernesto Geisel's press secretary, who said, on May 21, that no comment would come from the presidency.[1]

This was the attitude of Admiral Floriano Peixoto Faria Lima, who, about two years earlier, had been named by Ernesto Geisel to be governor of Rio de Janeiro state after it had absorbed Guanabara state. The governor declared that he was in Teresópolis to get some rest and would have nothing to say. In Rio's City Council, the MDB majority defeated an ARENA motion for a special session to pay tribute to the man who had rebuilt the city. The outcome, reached amidst heated and hate-filled speeches, was blamed on the fear of MDB councilmen of displeasing political strongman Antônio Chagas Freitas, the last governor of Guanabara. On the other hand, the federal legislative chambers and most of the state legislatures observed Lacerda's death, an exception being the legislature of Rio Grande do Sul, where the MDB bloc opposed any observance.[2]

After Dom Lourenço de Almeida Prado had administered extreme unction at the Clínica São Vicente, Cláudio Lacerda Paiva told mourners there of the family's decision that the burial take place that afternoon without the honors appropriate for a former governor. But tributes were much in evidence at the São João Batista Cemetery, where a crowd of about one thousand saw Lacerda laid to rest in the family plot. Among those present were the widows of Kubitschek and Goulart. Another was Rio Mayor Marcos Tamoyo, who decreed three days of mourning for the city and gave, a little later, Lacerda's name to a school in Jacarepaguá. Because Lacerda's former aide, Colonel Carlos Osório de Silveira Neto, headed Faria Lima's Casa Militar, one member of the state's executive group can be said to have been on hand at the burial.[3]

The crowd, concentrated in a small space to see the casket lowered into the grave, sang the national anthem and "Cidade Maravilhosa." Feelings ran high, as demonstrated by shouts—"They are burying Brazil with him," "Lacerda, president," and "Lacerda, democrat"—and by informal speeches—"His ideals will not die in our consciences"— greeted by applause. When Ernâni Sátiro, like many dignitaries, told the press of his admiration of Lacerda, someone yelled: "Why didn't you speak that way when he was *cassado?*" Roberto Médici, son of Geisel's predecessor in the presidency, called Lacerda "the great leader of my generation."[4]

Commenting later on the burial, Teotônio Vilela (ARENA, Alagoas) said in the Senate: "The cemetery is gradually turning itself into the only place where multitudes of all ages and social categories can still express their sentiments freely. . . . Protected by the sacred memory of the dead, inspired by hymns, tears, and applause, they escape from the fear of repression, believing that the imperial Roman guards, who today surround universities, will not discover the catacombs."[5]

Starting on Sunday, May 22, the press was filled with accounts of Lacerda's career, along with the praises and comments of people who had known him, leaving readers with the feeling that Brazil would not be the same without him. Quadros described Lacerda as "the most responsible for my resignation." Roberto Marinho, writing in *O Globo,* called attention to Lacerda's changes of positions, some of which, he said, "did not coincide with Brazil's interests." He concluded that Lacerda had been "his own cruelest adversary."

The *Jornal do Brasil,* in its editorial, wrote: "Lacerda was a champion on behalf of elections. But Lacerda is dead and continually we have fewer elections." This type of protest, evident earlier at Lacerda's funeral, was the theme of Alberto Dines' column in the *Folha de S. Paulo,* with its condemnation of a nation organized on the basis of a fear of words and with "a horror of the free spirit that was so well represented by Lacerda."

Protest was evident also in pronouncements made by individuals who attended religious services held in Lacerda's memory about a week later. At Rio's Candelária Church, where three thousand gathered on May 27, lawyer Sobral Pinto condemned "the Brazilian dictatorship, suppressor of highly talented men." Alceu Amoroso Lima, recalling that Lacerda had recently congratulated him for opposing the censorship, said: "Lacerda carried out innumerable acts of greatness, precisely at a time when the government is completely lacking in greatness." Congressman Nina Ribeiro declared: "The foremost political leader of all times has died." The absence of Governor Faria Lima provoked sarcastic remarks about how he was "still resting."

At the religious service in São Paulo, former *udenista* Onadir Marcondes suggested that the "irreparable injustice" inflicted on Lacerda merited prayers asking God's forgiveness. Padre Godinho, in his sermon, called for the construction of the future dreamed of by Lacerda.[6]

8. Conclusion

During the special sessions of the Senate and Chamber of Deputies held in June 1977, references were made to Lacerda, the governor. Senator Danton Jobim (MDB, Rio de Janeiro), who had castigated Lacerda in *Última Hora,* called his governorship "honest, constructive, and dynamic." Congressman Celio Borja recalled the water aqueduct, sewers, hospitals, housing, education, new buses, state bank, administrative decentralization, and some of the cultural steps, such as the renovation of the Municipal Theater and state university, and the encouragement given to artists.[1] Indeed, Lacerda had transformed the city, with the attention given by himself and his team also to traffic tunnels, viaducts, and cloverleafs, traffic regulations, parks and playgrounds, telephones, street lighting and asphalting, cleanliness, and antipollution measures.

Knowledge about such achievements may have influenced some of the Cariocas who were asked, in a 1992 IBOPE poll, whether their impression of Lacerda was good or bad. In the case of the 81 percent who had heard of Lacerda, the poll showed that women and the best-educated people were the least likely to condemn him. The uneducated were the most critical.[2]

Impression of Lacerda	Total Percent	Age Group			Sex	
		16–24	25–39	Over 40	M	F
Good	49	28	33	65	49	49
Bad	13	9	8	18	17	10
No opinion	38	63	59	17	34	41

	Education		
	Primary School or Less	Secondary School Attended or Completed	University Attended or Completed
Good	47	50	50
Bad	20	11	10
No opinion	33	40	40

To the extent that these figures, favorable to the memory of Lacerda, reflect judgments about his administration, they are significant, because it is to his performance as governor, rather than to his headline-creating sensationalism, that attention should be given in answering the question of whether he would have made a good president. Before he became governor, his savage attacks aroused misgivings and hid the intelligent listener, the able analyst of projects, and the leader who could inspire associates to form an honest, effective, hardworking team. Again, on the path that might have taken him to the presidency in a popular election, he aroused misgiving among the men in power, and this time it was fatal because, as it turned out, they, and not the masses, would determine the presidential succession.

The IBOPE poll referred to above was conducted before the revelations of corruption in government led to mass demonstrations and the resignation of President Fernando Collor de Mello, and reduced, months later, the reputations of Brazilian politicians in and out of the legislature. As shown by wide margins in polls, Brazilians concluded late in 1993 that Congress was "just as corrupt" as Collor and that Brazilian politics were "more corrupt than politics in other countries." With the civilian chief executives in Brasília displaying their inability to handle the country's problems, an overwhelming majority of Brazilians concluded that "the country needs a strong president."[3]

The country needed a new way of governing, exemplified by Governor Lacerda's manner of making appointments, reliance on *concursos* instead of satisfying influential people, rejection of contractors' offers of political contributions, and dislike of the use of favors to obtain legislative votes. It was necessary to have a chief executive who would alienate friends, if necessary, as journalist David Nasser wrote in 1960 (when he said Lacerda "never had any friends"). And it was necessary to have the task master whom Salvador Mandim described as the toughest he had ever served under. The painting of state vehicles, part of a control system set up to prevent their use for personal purposes, may not seem especially important. Perhaps the same can be said about the enforcement of traffic regulations, previously flouted, an authoritarian measure regarded with favor by the people if not by the legislature. What was important was that action was taken to impose discipline in the place of chaos. Congressman Laerte Vieira (MDB, Santa Catarina), fascinated by Lacerda's method of governing, declared that he had been an "unusual administrator," whose complete dedication, indomitable dynamism, capacity for work, sure command, vision, and foresight "shook up archaic processes" and found "a substitute for the corrupt bureaucratic machine," thus achieving a great work "that penetrated all sectors of public administration."

"Do you know what's missing in this Collorgate?" "A Carlos Lacerda." (Ziraldo drawing in *Folha de S. Paulo*, July 4, 1992)

David Nasser, in his 1960 article, wrote that he disliked Lacerda's way of fighting, thus presenting a view expressed later by Juracy Magalhães. Nevertheless, in 1960 Nasser recommended votes for Lacerda, calling him honest and intelligent and probably able to get things done. Nasser in 1961 disapproved of Lacerda's dismissal of Public Works Secretary Laviola. But he was not disappointed in the governor and wrote in October 1965 that the Cariocas appreciated the work of Transit Director Fontenelle and that Gustavo Borges had made progress in the war against crime in the city in spite of the "mutilation" of the police force by the federal option arrangement. Nasser added: "What the state administration accomplished in the other sectors has no equal in the history of this city."[4]

Hard liners contended that with civilians in control of politics, Brazil would be weakened by corruption and subversion. This is not to say that the military presidents did much to rid politics of the vices that Lacerda abhorred. Chagas Freitas became governor of Guanabara (1971–1975) after First Army Commander Adalberto Pereira dos Santos, Army Minister Orlando Geisel, and Governor Negrão de Lima persuaded President Médici to favor the selection. About Chagas Freitas' term, the *Dicionário Histórico-Biográfico Brasileiro* has this to say: "The utilization of state government funds opened enormous perspectives for the Chagas group to expand its electoral and parliamentary strength. During his term, Chagas raised patronage, an age-old practice of Brazilian politics, to a peak of efficiency, developing a system of exchanging votes for personal favors, granted by the government."[5]

Even assuming that military rule was effective in containing corruption and subversion, the basic solution lay not in forcing the civilians out of power in Brasília, but in the improvement of the conduct of civilian politics—an improvement demanded by Lacerda during his lifetime of attacks on what he called the oligarchy. The shakeup of archaic processes was needed on a national scale.

Governor Lacerda's war against corruption had not been restricted to the political machine of Rio, mentioned by Laerte Vieira. Like the Brazilian press after it became free of the censorship of the military regime, he had denounced corruption wherever he had found it. With the instincts of a journalist, he had taken a keen interest in the misdeeds of the *Aletes*–Angra dos Reis smuggling ring and had not hesitated to place some of the blame on congressmen.

It is easy to visualize conflicts between a President Lacerda and Congress. Lacerda maintained that Quadros, feeling himself faced with such a conflict, should have presented a program of clearly defined reforms and worked to enlist backing for it by governors and others. Lacerda, never hesitant in taking positions, would have presented such a program and sought support through persuasion. He was, Afonso Arinos de Melo Franco has said, a brilliant convincer. Hugo Levy tells of congressmen who had avoided congressional minority leader Lacerda lest he persuade them to revise their positions. The workers at an Osasco factory, unfriendly at first and reluctant to let Lacerda proceed with his talk against Communism during the Goulart regime, had been so persuaded by his words, courageously delivered after he had jumped up on one of the plant's machines, that they had enthusiastically carried him on their shoulders.[6]

To fortify his efforts in decision-making circles, President Lacerda would have made use of his renowned radio and television oratory, which, historian José Honório Rodrigues has written, was remarkable in having effects that were instantaneous.[7] Lacerda had aroused the entire nation in the past, when he had denounced corruption during the last Vargas administration, and when, as the country's most-voted-for congressman, he had defended his mandate against the maneuvers of President Kubitschek, Vice President Goulart, and their congressional followers, considered to be in control.

As for the crusade Lacerda undertook after the presidency eluded him, Flávio Galvão was justified in writing that the Frente Ampla, viewed with suspicion by much of the MDB and by groups filled with intense dislike for each other, was "a fish very difficult to sell even if touted by a salesman with the talent of the former Carioca governor."[8] Besides, even before Goulart joined him, irking *Brizolistas* and many of his own followers, Lacerda was banned from broadcasting on television.

Lacerda, probably the most gifted political orator in the history of the Brazilian republic, was an incomparable genius on television. Speaking from the presidency with the ardent voice that Fernando

Pedreira has described as fantastic,[9] and sometimes displaying charts, Lacerda would have stood a good chance of rousing the masses effectively enough to defeat the opponents of a crusade designed to bring about responsibility in government, innovations, and a course of action for the achievement of his and the people's ambition: Brazil a world power, morally as well as materially. The masses could get Congress to act, as became clear when they demanded the punishment of corrupt politicians after the press disclosed scandals in the era that followed military domination.

Lacerda would have faced strong pressures from those who might have suffered from the necessary changes in the mentality of Brasília. In spite of his tenacity and abilities, it would be guesswork to suggest that he would have succeeded, and especially to suggest that the transition would have come about smoothly or quickly. But it would have been a worthwhile experiment. Crusades by President Lacerda would have had the virtue of advancing the idea that the views of a well-informed public were important and that it was necessary to have the public play a decisive role in the regenerative movement. Had he been in the presidency, dependent on the support of a few, generals or civilians, he would have worked to free himself from the dependency by turning to the people. He was a born crusader. Like his equally honest and independent father, he relied on the masses.

A Lacerda presidency, if successful, would have revealed that a government in Brasília, directed by civilians, could achieve on a national scale the sort of innovations that spectacularly transformed both the city of Rio and the caliber of its government in the early 1960s. And even if only partially successful, the experiment would have pumped a healthy tonic into Brazilian public service.

Notes

I. Governor during the Quadros Presidency (1961)

1. The New State (1960)

1. Maria do Carmo Correia Galvão, "Aspectos da geografia agrária do sertão carioca," on pp. 171–185 of Associação dos Geógrafos Brasileiros, Secção Regional do Rio de Janeiro, *Aspectos da Geografia Carioca* (Rio de Janeiro: Conselho Nacional de Geografia, Instituto Brasileiro de Geografia e Estatística, 1962); see p. 171.

2. Carlos Lacerda, *O Poder das Idéias*, 3d ed. (Rio de Janeiro: Distribuidora Record, 1963), pp. 150–151. Marc de Lacharrière, *L'aménagement et l'équipement de l'état de Guanabara: Essai sur Rio de Janeiro* (Paris: R. Pichon et R. Durand-Auzias, 1967), pp. 22–23, 15. *O Globo*, December 9, 1960.

3. Lysia Maria Cavalcanti Bernardes, "Importância da posição como fator do desenvolvimento do Rio de Janeiro," on pp. 3–17 of Associação dos Geógrafos Brasileiros, Secção Regional do Rio de Janeiro, *Aspectos da Geografia Carioca*; see pp. 3–4.

4. Ibid., p. 9. Marc de Lacharrière, *L'aménagement et l'équipement de l'état de Guanabara*, p. 20. C. R. Boxer, *The Golden Age of Brazil, 1695–1750: Growing Pains of a Colonial Society* (paperback edition, Berkeley and Los Angeles: University of California Press, 1962), pp. 39, 321. Pedro Calmon, *História do Brasil*, vol. 3 (Livraria José Olympio Editôra, 1961), p. 1054. Rollie E. Poppino, *Brazil: The Land and People* (New York: Oxford University Press, 1968), pp. 103–104.

5. Brasil Gerson, *História das Ruas do Rio de Janeiro*, 3d ed. (Rio de Janeiro: Editora Souza, n.d.), pp. 182–191. Dioclécio de Paranhos Antunes, "Transformações do quadro urbano e evolução do Rio de Janeiro," on pp. 19–32 of Associação dos Geógrafos Brasileiros, *Aspectos da Geografia Carioca*; see pp. 26–31.

6. *Tribuna da Imprensa*, November 26–27, 1960. *Correio da Manhã*, December 4, 1960.

7. Marc de Lacharrière, *L'aménagement et l'équipement de l'état de Guanabara*, pp. 114–117.

8. Ibid., p. 40. Govêrno Carlos Lacerda, *Mensagem à Assembléia Legislativa: 5 Anos de Govêrno* (Rio de Janeiro: Govêrno do Estado da Guanabara, August 31, 1965), p. 105.

9. Pedro Pinchas Geiger, "Esboço da estrutura urbana da área metropolitana do Rio de Janeiro," on pp. 81–104 of Associação dos Geógrafos

Brasileiros, *Aspectos da Geografia Carioca;* see pp. 91–92. Gláucio Ary Dillon Soares, "As Bases Ideológicas do Lacerdismo," on pp. 49–70 of *Revista Civilização Brasileira* 1, no. 4 (September 1965); see p. 52.

10. Pedro Pinchas Geiger, "A metrópole do Rio de Janeiro e suas funções atuais," on pp. 65–79 of Associação dos Geógrafos Brasileiros, *Aspectos da Geografia Carioca;* see p. 72.

11. Comissão Executiva para o Desenvolvimento Urbano (CEDUG)–Doxiadis Associates, *Guanabara: A Plan for Urban Development,* Document Dox-Bra-A6, prepared for the State of Guanabara (Rio de Janeiro, November 20, 1965) (hereafter called CEDUG-Doxiadis), pp. 12, 66.

12. Ibid., pp. 171, 118–119, 113. Carlos Lacerda, *Nacionalismo de Verdade e de Mentira: A compra da Telefônica; e a falta de telefones* (printed at the Oficina Gráfica da Penitenciária Professor Lemos Brito, Rio de Janeiro, 1963), p. 7.

13. CEDUG-Doxiadis, pp. 171, 69.

14. Carlos Lacerda, "Energia: Salto sôbre o Futuro," speech at the convention of the Guanabara section of the Partido Libertador, June 22, 1960, published on pp. 190–202 of Carlos Lacerda, *O Poder das Idéias,* 3d ed.; see p. 195. Govêrno Carlos Lacerda, *Mensagem à Assembléia Legislativa: Programa de Govêrno para 1964* (Rio de Janeiro: Govêrno do Estado da Guanabara, August 30, 1963), section about electric energy.

15. CEDUG-Doxiadis, pp. 69, 136, 142, 170–171.

16. Lennys Elizabeth Jameson, "An Analysis of the *Favelas* of Rio de Janeiro, Brazil," (master's thesis, Graduate School of the University of Texas at Austin, May 1971). See pp. 38–39, 41–42, 56, 99.

17. Govêrno Carlos Lacerda, *Mensagem à Assembléia Legislativa: 5 Anos de Govêrno,* p. 35.

18. CEDUG-Doxiadis, p. 171.

19. Nilo Bernardes, "Notas sôbre a ocupação humana da montanha no estado da Guanabara," on pp. 187–210 of Associação dos Geógrafos Brasileiros, *Aspectos da Geografia Carioca.* Govêrno Carlos Lacerda, *Mensagem à Assembléia Legislativa: 5 Anos de Govêrno,* p. 82.

2. The Governor-elect (Late 1960)

1. Hélio Mamede, interview with Daphne F. Rodger (hereafter shown as DFR), Rio de Janeiro, August 9, 1985. Carioca: native of, or pertaining to, the city of Rio de Janeiro.

2. José Alberto Gueiros, interview with DFR, Rio de Janeiro, March 23, 1983. José Cândido Moreira de Souza, interview with DFR, Rio de Janeiro, August 27, 1986. José Luiz Moreira de Souza, interview, Rio de Janeiro, August 15, 1983.

3. Hugo Levy, interview with DFR, Rio de Janeiro, March 7, 1989.

4. Antonio Carlos Villaça, transcript of interview taped by the Sociedade dos Amigos de Carlos Lacerda, p. 5, and interview, Rio de Janeiro, March 16, 1991.

5. Carlos Lacerda, letter to Mario Lorenzo Fernandez, Rio de Janeiro,

October 28, 1960, in the Carlos Lacerda collection at the University of Brasília (hereafter shown as CCL). Mario Lorenzo Fernandez, letter to Carlos Lacerda, November 6, 1960, in CCL. Carlos Lacerda, *Depoimento* (Rio de Janeiro: Editora Nova Fronteira, 1978), pp. 241–242.

3. Lacerda and Quadros Travel Abroad (Late 1960, Early 1961)

1. Jânio Quadros, letter to Carlos Lacerda, Rio de Janeiro, March 24, 1960, in CCL.
2. *O Estado de S. Paulo*, December 2, 3, 1960.
3. *Correio da Manhã*, December 27, 1960. *Diário Carioca*, January 3, 1961.
4. Pedro Dantas [Prudente de Moraes, neto], "Os silêncios de Jânio," *O Estado de S. Paulo*, December 24, 1960.
5. *O Estado de S. Paulo*, December 13, 21, 1960.
6. Carlos dos Santos Veras, interviews, Austin, April 26, 27, 1963.
7. Ibid. *O Estado de S. Paulo*, December 30, 1960, January 5, 1961.
8. *Correio da Manhã*, October 22, 26, 27, 1960.
9. Ibid., October 30, 1960.
10. Carlos Lacerda, speech delivered at the foreign minister's luncheon, Tokyo, November 1, 1960, in CCL. *Tribuna da Imprensa*, November 4, 8, 10, 1960.
11. *Tribuna da Imprensa*, November 17, 18, 19–20, 25, 1960.
12. Ibid., November 18, 24, 25, 1960.

4. Inauguration (December 5, 1960)

1. Golbery do Couto e Silva, interview, Brasília, August 23, 1983.
2. Edgar Flexa Ribeiro, interview, Rio de Janeiro, July 8, 1983. *Tribuna da Imprensa*, November 4, 1960, January 23, 1961. *Correio da Manhã*, October 27, 1960. Sra. Hélio Walcacer, conversation, Rio de Janeiro, July 14, 1984.
3. *O Globo*, December 6, 1960.
4. Ibid., December 5, 1960. *Diário Carioca*, December 7, 6, 17, 1960.

5. Governor Lacerda

1. Marcelo Garcia, interview, Rio de Janeiro, August 18, 1983. Alcino Salazar, transcript of interview taped by the Sociedade dos Amigos de Carlos Lacerda, p. 7.
2. Hugo Levy, interview with DFR, Rio de Janeiro, March 7, 1989. Alcino Salazar, transcript of interview, pp. 5–6. Walter Cunto, transcript of interview taped by the Sociedade dos Amigos de Carlos Lacerda, p. 10.
3. Alcino Salazar, transcript of interview, pp. 5–7.
4. Carlos Lacerda quoted on p. 102 of Guita Grin Debert, *Ideologia e*

Populismo (São Paulo: T. A. Queiroz, Editor, 1979). Raphael de Almeida Magalhães, quoted on p. 32 of Marília Pacheco Fiorillo, "O Esperto Charme da Burguesia," *Status*, no. 142 (May 1986). Hugo Levy, interview, Rio de Janeiro, August 1, 1989.

5. Luiz Roberto Veiga de Brito, transcript of interview taped by the Sociedade dos Amigos de Carlos Lacerda, August 28, 1985, p. 27. Enaldo Cravo Peixoto, transcript of interview taped by the Sociedade dos Amigos de Carlos Lacerda, September 18, 1985, pp. 21–22, 8.

6. *O Globo,* February 10, 1962. Dario de Almeida Magalhães, interview, Rio de Janeiro, July 7, 1983. Cravo Peixoto, transcript of interview, p. 8.

7. Ayrton Baffa, quoted on p. 62 of Antonio Dias Rebello Filho, *Carlos Lacerda, Meu Amigo,* 2d ed. (Rio de Janeiro: Editora Record, 1981). José Roberto Rego Monteiro, interview with DFR, Rio de Janeiro, August 13, 1985.

8. *Tribuna da Imprensa,* June 14, July 11, June 26, 27, 1961. Carlos Lacerda, *Depoimento,* p. 226.

9. *Tribuna da Imprensa,* February 21, 22, April 12, 1961. Esmerino Arruda and others, *Resolução N° 62 de 1961* (ninety-two-page booklet defending Arruda, n.p., n.p., 1961); see pp. 3, 5, 29, 55. Carlos Lacerda, letters to Clemente Mariani, Rio de Janeiro, February 28, March 3, 1961, in CCL.

10. Hélio Mamede, interview with DFR, August 9, 1985. Marcelo Garcia, interview, August 18, 1983. Cravo Peixoto, transcript of interview, p. 10.

11. Carlos Osório da Silveira Neto, interview, Rio de Janeiro, August 7, 1989. Ruth Alverga, interview with DFR, Rio de Janeiro, August 15, 1985.

12. Salvador Gonçalves Mandim, transcript of interview taped by the Sociedade dos Amigos de Carlos Lacerda, p. 24. Rego Monteiro, interview with DFR, August 13, 1985. Ruth Alverga, interview with DFR, August 15, 1985.

13. José Cândido Moreira de Souza, interview with DFR, August 27, 1986. Carlos Lacerda, *Depoimento,* p. 225.

14. Carlos Lacerda, *Depoimento,* p. 236. Raul Brunini, taped interview with Letícia Lacerda, Vera Lacerda Paiva, Cláudio Lacerda Paiva, Lamy Cunto, and DFR, Rio de Janeiro, March 9, 1989, pp. 10–11 of transcript by DFR. Hélio Mamede, interview with DFR, August 9, 1985. Edgar Flexa Ribeiro, interview, Rio de Janeiro, July 8, 1983. Marcelo Garcia, interview, August 18, 1983.

15. Carlos Lacerda, letter to Raphael de Almeida Magalhães, October 22, 1960, in CCL. *Correio da Manhã,* December 16, 1960. Célio Borja, interview, Rio de Janeiro, August 14, 1989.

16. José Cândido Moreira de Souza, interview with DFR, August 27, 1986. Raphael de Almeida Magalhães, interview, Rio de Janeiro, August 17, 1983. Carlos Lacerda, *Depoimento,* p. 236. *Tribuna da Imprensa,* May 3, 1961.

17. Raphael de Almeida Magalhães, interview, Rio de Janeiro, August 9, 1989. Mario Lorenzo Fernandez, interview with DFR, Rio de Janeiro, August 9, 1985.

18. Secretaria do Governo do Estado da Guanabara, "Regiões Administrativas do Estado da Guanabara" (Rio de Janeiro, August 1964), showing locations, populations, and areas of the twenty-one regions, reproduced in Gastão Cruls, *Aparência do Rio de Janeiro,* 3d ed., Edição do IV Centenário

(Rio de Janeiro: Livraria José Olympio Editôra, 1965), pp. 964–965. CEDUG-Doxiadis, pp. 21, 142. *Tribuna da Imprensa*, January 13, 17, 27, May 3, July 10, 1961. Raphael de Almeida Magalhães, interview, August 9, 1989. Célio Borja, interview, August 14, 1989.

19. Cravo Peixoto, transcript of interview, p. 2. Fidélis Amaral Netto, interview, Brasília, February 20, 1991. Veiga de Brito, transcript of interview, pp. 26–27.

20. Armando Daudt d'Oliveira, interview, Rio de Janeiro, August 14, 1983. Raul Brunini, transcript of interview, March 9, 1989, p. 9.

21. Edgar Flexa Ribeiro, interviews, Rio de Janeiro, July 8, August 15, 1983.

22. Ibid. Sérgio Lacerda, interview, Rio de Janeiro, July 31, 1989. José Roberto Rego Monteiro, interviews, Rio de Janeiro, August 6, 1989, March 3, 1991, and interview with DFR, August 13, 1985. Hugo Levy, interview, August 1, 1989. Raphael de Almeida Magalhães, interview, August 9, 1989. Governo Federal, Law 4,320 of 1964.

23. *Tribuna da Imprensa*, January 17, 1961. Walter Cunto, transcript of interview, pp. 8–9. Wilson Lopes Machado, "Algumas Lembranças de um Amigo," Curitiba, October 1988, p. 6.

24. Carlos Lacerda, *Depoimento*, p. 226.

25. Lygia Paiva Derizans and Vera Lacerda Paiva, interview with DFR, Rio de Janeiro, August 25, 1985.

26. Ibid. Cláudio Lacerda Paiva and Raul Brunini remarks on transcript of tape of Brunini interview, March 9, 1989. Raphael de Almeida Magalhães, interview, August 9, 1989.

27. Vera Lacerda Paiva remark on p. 23 of transcript of tape of Brunini interview. Carlos Lacerda, *Depoimento*, p. 236.

28. Regina Costard, interview with DFR, Rio de Janeiro, September 9, 1986. Hélio Mamede, interview with DFR, Rio de Janeiro, August 9, 1985.

29. Letícia Lacerda, interview with DFR, Rio de Janeiro, January 5, 1988.

30. Regina Costard, interview with DFR, September 9, 1986.

6. The Constitutional Assembly versus the Municipal Chamber (October 1960–August 1961)

1. *Correio da Manhã*, October 23, 20, 25, 1960. Raphael de Almeida Magalhães, interview, Rio de Janeiro, August 17, 1983. *Udenista:* associated with the UDN.

2. *Correio da Manhã*, October 12, 21, 25, 1960. *Tribuna da Imprensa*, November 24, 1960. Marcílio Marques Moreira (ed.), *Perfis Parlamentares 21: San Tiago Dantas, Discursos Parlamentares* (Brasília: Câmara dos Deputados, 1983), p. 583.

3. Carlos Lacerda, *Depoimento*, p. 273. *Correio da Manhã*, October 19, 27, 1960.

4. *Correio da Manhã*, December 31, 1960. *O Globo*, December 13, 16, 1960. Moreira (ed.), *Perfis Parlamentares 21: San Tiago Dantas*, pp. 584, 586. Carlos Lacerda, *Depoimento*, p. 196.

5. *Tribuna da Imprensa*, November 22, 7, 1960. *Correio da Manhã*, October 15, 21, 25, 1960. Mario Lorenzo Fernandez, letter to Carlos Lacerda, Rio de Janeiro, November 6, 1960, in CCL.

6. *Tribuna da Imprensa*, November 5–6, 7, 8, 11, 14, 26–27, 1960. *Correio da Manhã*, October 18, 1960. *O Globo*, December 10, 1960.

7. Gladstone Chaves de Melo, interview, Rio de Janeiro, August 12, 1994. *Tribuna da Imprensa*, November 11, 17, 26–27, 1960.

8. *O Globo*, December 12, 13, 17, 1960.

9. *Correio da Manhã*, December 13, 17, 1960. *O Globo*, December 16, 1960.

10. *Diário Carioca*, December 17, 18, 1960. *Correio da Manhã*, December 17, 28, 1960. *O Globo*, December 16, 1960.

11. *Correio da Manhã*, December 28, 30, 31, 1960.

12. *Tribuna da Imprensa*, January 9, 19, February 1, 2, 1961. *Novos Rumos*, February 3–9, 10–16, 1961. *Diário de Notícias*, February 3, 1961. *A Gazeta*, February 6, 1961. Adelar Finatto, *Álvaro Moreyra*, 4th ed. (Porto Alegre: Tchê Editora, 1985), p. 101.

13. *Tribuna da Imprensa*, February 1, 2, 3, 8, 1961.

14. Ibid., January 5, February 10, 20, 23, March 7, 1961.

15. Ibid., March 17, 14, 1961. *Constituição do Estado da Guanabara, promulgada em 27 de março de 1961* (Rio de Janeiro: Editôra Aurora, 1961), Articles 4, 7, and Articles 1, 5, 6 of the Disposições Transitórias.

16. *Tribuna da Imprensa*, March 17, 18–19, 24, 28, 1961.

17. Ibid., March 28, 29, 30, April 7, 28, 1961.

18. Ibid., March 29, June 16–17, 1961. Hélio Beltrão, draft of "Mensagem No. 37" to the Legislative Assembly, June 16, 1961 (in the collection of Edgar Flexa Ribeiro). *Tribuna da Imprensa* and *O Estado de S. Paulo*, July 26, 1961.

19. *O Estado de S. Paulo*, July 21, 22, 1961. *Tribuna da Imprensa*, July 13, 14, 19, 20, 21, 25, 1961.

20. *Diário Carioca*, July 20, August 1, 1961. *Tribuna da Imprensa*, July 24, 26, August 1, 9, 1961. *O Globo*, August 2, 1961, January 20, 1962.

21. Antonio Carlos Villaça, interview with DFR, Rio de Janeiro, August 17, 1985.

7. The Water Crisis: "An Infernal Week" (March 1961)

1. *Tribuna da Imprensa*, March 6, 1961. CEDUG-Doxiadis, pp. 111–112.

2. *Tribuna da Imprensa*, March 6, 9, 1961.

3. Carlos Lacerda, letter to Artur Bernardes Filho, Rio de Janeiro, March 2, 1961, in CCL. Paulista: native of, or pertaining to, São Paulo.

4. *Tribuna da Imprensa*, March 8, 1961. *Diário Carioca*, March 9, 1961. *O Globo*, December 5, 1960. Luiz Augusto Rocha, "Água Potável: Um Desafio Permanente," *Revista SEAERJ, edição comemorativa dos 50 anos da Sociedade dos Engenheiros e Arquitetos do Estado do Rio de Janeiro* (1985), pp. 5–14; see pp. 8–11.

5. *O Globo*, December 9, 10, 12, 1960. *Tribuna da Imprensa*, January 2,

7–8, 27, March 8, 1961. Antônio Gallotti, letter to Carlos Lacerda, Rio de Janeiro, January 30, 1961, in CCL. Carlos Lacerda, *Nacionalismo de Verdade e de Mentira*, p. 7. Carlos Lacerda, telegram to Jânio Quadros, Rio de Janeiro, March 2, 1961, in CCL. Estado da Guanabara, *Abusos do Poder Econômico: Light versus Estado da Guanabara* (Rio de Janeiro: Juizado de Direito da 1ª Vara da Fazenda Pública, 1960), p. 1. *Diário Carioca*, March 9, 1961.

6. *Diário Carioca*, March 10, 1961. *O Globo*, March 9, 1961. *Tribuna da Imprensa*, March 8, 9, 10, 1961. Carlos Lacerda, *Depoimento*, pp. 230–231.

7. Lygia Gomide, interview with DFR, Rio de Janeiro, March 26, 1983. Marcelo Garcia, interview, August 18, 1983. *Tribuna da Imprensa*, March 13, 1961.

8. *Tribuna da Imprensa*, March 10, 1961. Luiz Roberto Veiga de Brito, transcript of interview taped by the Sociedade dos Amigos de Carlos Lacerda, August 28, 1985, p. 13.

9. Antônio Arlindo Laviola, letter to Carlos Lacerda, Rio de Janeiro, March 10, 1961, in CCL. Danton Jobim in *Diário Carioca*, March 12, 1961. David Nasser, "As grandes amizades (9): Meu amigo Carlos Lacerda," *Manchete*, no. 802 (September 2, 1967).

10. Carlos Lacerda quoted in Jair Silva and Ricardo André, *Água, afinal* (Teleplan phonograph record). Veiga de Brito, transcript of interview taped by the Sociedade dos Amigos de Carlos Lacerda, pp. 14, 10, 12–13, 6, 7, 8.

8. Salesman for Guanabara's Plan of Action (March–June 1961)

1. Carlos Flexa Ribeiro, interview, Rio de Janeiro, July 5, 1983. *Tribuna da Imprensa*, January 6, 1961. *O Globo*, January 12, 1962. Edgar Flexa Ribeiro, interview, July 8, 1983.

2. Carlos Lacerda, "Rosas e Pedras do Meu Caminho," Chapter 5 (*Manchete*, May 13, 1967), p. 24. Carlos Lacerda, *Depoimento*, pp. 403–404. Carlos Lacerda, "Ana Frank, Noiva da Eternidade" (school inauguration speech) in Carlos Lacerda, *O Poder das Idéias*, 3d ed., pp. 321–326. Otto H. Frank, letter to Carlos Lacerda, Basel, August 25, 1961, in CCL.

3. Marcelo Garcia, interview, August 18, 1983. Govêrno Carlos Lacerda, *Mensagem à Assembléia Legislativa: Programa de Govêrno para 1963* (Rio de Janeiro: Estado da Guanabara, August 31, 1962), section about health. *Tribuna da Imprensa*, June 26, 1961. *O Estado de S. Paulo*, August 29, 1961. *O Globo*, January 8, 9, 17, 18, 1962.

4. Govêrno Carlos Lacerda, *IV Reunião de Governadores* (Rio de Janeiro: Estado da Guanabara, June 29, 1961), p. S2/1. Govêrno Carlos Lacerda, *Mensagem à Assembléia Legislativa: Programa de Govêrno para 1965* (Rio de Janeiro: Estado da Guanabara, August 31, 1964), section about Tarifa de Água e Esgôto. Carlos Lacerda, letter to Artur Bernardes Filho, March 2, 1961.

5. Joshua B. Powers, letters to Carlos Lacerda, January 6, February 3, 1961, in CCL.

6. Carlos Lacerda, *Depoimento*, p. 404. *Tribuna da Imprensa*, June 9, April 15–16, 1961. *O Estado de S. Paulo*, August 18, 1961. Leonard J. Saccio (International Cooperation Administration), letter to Carlos Lacerda, Rio de Janeiro, January 6, 1961, in CCL. William D. Austin (International Cooperation Administration), letter to Carlos Lacerda, Washington, D.C., January 24, 1961, in CCL.

7. Carlos Lacerda, letter to Artur Bernardes Filho, March 2, 1961. *Tribuna da Imprensa*, March 15, April 18, 15–16, June 9, 1961. Carlos Lacerda, *Depoimento*, p. 240.

8. *Tribuna da Imprensa*, April 15–16, 20, 22–23, 1961.

9. Ibid., May 5, 6–7, 8, 10, 1961.

10. Ibid., May 9, 1961.

11. Ibid., May 9, April 7, 1961.

12. Ibid., June 22, 9, 1961. Ayrton Baffa, quoted on p. 62 of Antonio Dias Rebello Filho, *Carlos Lacerda, Meu Amigo. O Globo*, January 11, 1962. Govêrno Carlos Lacerda, *Mensagem à Assembléia Legislativa: 5 Anos de Govêrno* (Rio de Janeiro: Estado da Guanabara, August 31, 1965), p. 119. Alcino Salazar, transcript of interview taped by the Sociedade dos Amigos de Carlos Lacerda, p. 4.

13. Gastão Cruls, *Aparência do Rio de Janeiro*, p. 893. *Tribuna da Imprensa*, June 21, 1961. *O Globo*, February 10, 1962. Govêrno Carlos Lacerda, *IV Reunião de Governadores;* see especially the table at the beginning of the section Quadros-Resumo.

14. *Tribuna da Imprensa*, June 30, July 1–2, 1961.

15. Ibid., April 11, May 20–21, June 30, 29, 1961. Carlos Lacerda, letter to Jânio Quadros, Rio de Janeiro, February 17, 1961, in CCL.

16. Carlos Lacerda, *Depoimento*, pp. 241, 251.

9. Criticizing the President's Foreign Policy (April–August 1961)

1. *Tribuna da Imprensa*, February 7, 8, March 21, April 29–30, 1961. Vasco Leitão da Cunha, interview, Washington, D.C., June 24, 1966.

2. *O Estado de S. Paulo*, February 28, 1961. Adolf A. Berle, interview, Austin, March 8, 1963.

3. *Tribuna da Imprensa*, April 18, 19, 1961. *Novos Rumos*, April 28–May 4, 1961.

4. Octávio Soares Dulci, *A UDN e o anti-populismo no Brasil* (Belo Horizonte: Editora Universidade Federal de Minas Gerais, 1986), pp. 168–169. *O Globo*, April 29, 1961. *Entreguista:* a person wishing to turn Brazil's assets over to foreigners.

5. Maria Victoria de Mesquita Benevides, *A UDN e o Udenismo: Ambigüidades do Liberalismo Brasileiro (1945–1965)* (Rio de Janeiro: Editora Paz e Terra, 1981), p. 115. *Tribuna da Imprensa*, May 2, 1961.

6. *Tribuna da Imprensa*, May 2, June 5, 1961. Carlos Lacerda, letter to José de Magalhães Pinto, Rio de Janeiro, January 2, 1961, in CCL.

7. *O Estado de S. Paulo,* May 3, 1961. *Novos Rumos,* May 19–25, 1961. Lourenço de Almeida Prado, note to Carlos Lacerda, Rio de Janeiro, May 9, 1961, in CCL. Suzanne Labin, letter to Carlos Lacerda, Paris, May 18, 1961, in CCL.

8. Orlando Bomfim, Jr., "As Provocações do sr. Lacerda," *Novos Rumos,* May 19–25, 1961. *Tribuna da Imprensa,* April 19, May 12, 13–14, 1961.

9. *Tribuna da Imprensa,* May 16, 20–21, 23, June 7, 1961. Orlando Bomfim, Jr., "As Provocações do sr. Lacerda."

10. *Tribuna da Imprensa,* May 16, 23, 20–21, 1961.

11. Ibid., June 2, 1961. Afonso Arinos de Melo Franco, interview, Rio de Janeiro, December 15, 1967.

12. Melo Franco, interview, December 15, 1967. Raimundo Padilha, interview, Brasília, October 13, 1965.

13. *Tribuna da Imprensa,* May 16, 18, 19, 24, 1961.

14. Ibid., May 26, 29, 1961. Carlos Lacerda, telegram to Oscar Pedroso Horta, May 27, 1961, in CCL.

15. *Tribuna da Imprensa,* July 11, 20, 14, 26, August 3, 1961.

16. Ibid., August 4, 1961. *O Estado de S. Paulo,* August 18, 1961.

17. Carlos Lacerda, *O Poder das Idéias,* 3d ed., pp. 329–330. Carlos Lacerda, *Depoimento,* p. 245. Oscar Pedroso Horta, "As Rosas e as Pedras do Caminho de Lacerda," *Manchete,* no. 799 (August 12, 1967), pp. 32, 35.

18. *O Estado de S. Paulo,* August 22, 20, 19, 1961.

10. Lacerda's Break with Quadros (August 18–23, 1961)

1. *O Estado de S. Paulo,* August 4, 15, 18, 1961. *Tribuna da Imprensa,* August 3, 1961.

2. *O Globo,* August 17, 1961. *O Estado de S. Paulo,* August 18, 1961. Lesseps S. Morrison, *Latin American Mission* (New York: Simon and Schuster, 1965), pp. 91–92.

3. Morrison, *Latin American Mission,* p. 103.

4. João Ribeiro Dantas, interview, Rio de Janeiro, December 20, 1965. *O Estado de S. Paulo,* August 5, 1961.

5. Eloá Quadros, statement, August 26, 1961, as reported in *O Estado de S. Paulo,* August 27, 1961. Luiz Alberto Moniz Bandeira, *O 24 de Agôsto de Jânio Quadros* (Rio de Janeiro: Editora Brasiliense, 1979), p. 46. Oscar Pedroso Horta, "As Rosas e as Pedras do Caminho de Lacerda," *Manchete,* no. 799 (August 12, 1967), p. 34.

6. Pedro Geraldo de Almeida, interview, Rio de Janeiro, November 4, 1965. Oscar Pedroso Horta, "Pedroso Horta defende-se por canais de TV," *O Estado de S. Paulo,* August 26, 1961. Carlos Lacerda, "Rosas e Pedras do Meu Caminho," Chapter 11 (*Manchete,* June 24, 1967), p. 116. Carlos Lacerda, *Depoimento,* p. 249. Carlos Lacerda, "A Crise de Agôsto," in Carlos Lacerda, *O Poder das Idéias,* 3d ed., pp. 329–343; see pp. 332, 335.

7. Carlos Lacerda, *Depoimento,* pp. 249–250. Oscar Pedroso Horta, "As Rosas e as Pedras do Caminho de Lacerda," p. 34.

8. Oscar Pedroso Horta, "As Rosas e as Pedras do Caminho de Lacerda," pp. 33–34. Jânio Quadros and Afonso Arinos de Melo Franco, "O Porquê da Renúncia," *Realidade* 2, no. 20 (November 1967), p. 31. Carlos Lacerda, "Rosas e Pedras do Meu Caminho," Chapter 11, p. 116. Carlos Lacerda, *Depoimento,* p. 251. Carlos Lacerda, "A Crise de Agôsto," pp. 334–336. Carlos Lacerda, interview, Rio de Janeiro, October 11, 1967.

9. Pedroso Horta, "As Rosas e as Pedras do Caminho de Lacerda," p. 34. Pedro Geraldo de Almeida, interview, November 4, 1965. Carlos Lacerda, *Depoimento,* p. 253.

10. Carlos Lacerda, "A Crise de Agôsto," p. 336. Carlos Lacerda, *Depoimento,* p. 253. Pedroso Horta, "As Rosas e as Pedras do Caminho de Lacerda," p. 34.

11. *O Estado de S. Paulo,* August 20, 1961. Pedro Geraldo de Almeida, interview, November 4, 1965.

12. Pedro Geraldo de Almeida, interview, November 4, 1965. Gabriel Grün Moss, declaration in *Jornal do Brasil,* November 7, 1967.

13. Pedroso Horta, "As Rosas e as Pedras do Caminho de Lacerda," p. 34. *O Estado de S. Paulo,* August 20, 1961.

14. *O Estado de S. Paulo,* August 20, 22, 23, 1961. *O Globo,* August 21, 1961. *Novos Rumos,* August 25–31, 1961.

15. José Eduardo de Macedo Soares, "Humilhação e Vergonha," *Diário Carioca,* August 22, 1961. *O Globo,* August 19, 1961. *O Estado de S. Paulo,* August 20, 22, 1961.

16. Carlos Lacerda, *Depoimento,* p. 254. Carlos Lacerda, "Rosas e Pedras do Meu Caminho," Chapter 12, pp. 103–104.

17. Pedro Geraldo de Almeida, interview, November 4, 1965. Pedroso Horta, "As Rosas e as Pedras do Caminho de Lacerda," p. 34. *O Estado de S. Paulo,* August 20, 1961.

18. Carlos Lacerda, *Depoimento,* p. 257. Carlos Lacerda, interview, October 11, 1967. Pedro Geraldo de Almeida, interview, November 4, 1965. Carlos Lacerda, handwritten draft of note to Jânio Quadros, August 19, 1961, in CCL.

19. *O Globo,* August 21, 22, 12, 18, 25, 1961. *O Estado de S. Paulo,* August 22, 23, 24, 1961.

20. Carlos Lacerda, interview, October 11, 1967. Carlos Lacerda, *Depoimento,* pp. 255–256. Carlos Lacerda in *Jornal da Tarde,* October 7, 1966. Carlos Alberto de Carvalho Pinto, "Ex-senador refuta depoimento," *O Estado de S. Paulo,* August 10, 1977. *O Estado de S. Paulo,* August 25, 1961.

21. *Diário Carioca,* August 25, 23, 22, 1961.

22. *O Estado de S. Paulo,* August 25, 24, 1961.

11. Quadros Resigns (August 25, 1961)

1. Antonio Carlos Villaça, interview with DFR, August 17, 1985.

2. Carlos Lacerda, "A Crise de Agôsto," in Carlos Lacerda, *O Poder das*

Idéias, 3d ed., pp. 329–343. See pp. 329, 330, 339, 334, 335, 337–338, 340, 343.

3. *O Globo,* August 25, 1961.

4. Jânio Quadros and Afonso Arinos de Melo Franco, "O Porquê da Renúncia," *Realidade* 2, no. 20 (November 1967), pp. 29–34. Carlos Castello Branco, "O Dia Seguinte," *Realidade* 2, no. 20, pp. 38–40.

5. Prudente de Moraes, neto, interview, Rio de Janeiro, August 31, 1963. Carlos Castello Branco, "O Dia Seguinte."

6. Pedro Geraldo de Almeida, interview, November 4, 1965. *O Estado de S. Paulo,* August 26, 1961.

7. *O Globo,* August 25, 1961. *O Estado de S. Paulo,* August 26, 1961. Genival Rabelo, "O Inquérito," *PN (Política & Negócios),* Rio de Janeiro, October 7, 1961, p. 20. Mário Victor, *Cinco Anos que Abalaram o Brasil* (Rio de Janeiro: Editôra Civilização Brasileira, 1965), p. 309, with the testimony of Odílio Denys quoting Quadros about "this Congress" and "organize a junta."

8. José Bonifácio Coutinho Nogueira, interview, São Paulo, November 22, 1965. Nei Braga, interview, Rio de Janeiro, December 21, 1965.

9. *O Globo,* August 25, 1961.

10. Hermano Alves, "O candidato do direito," *Afinal,* November 12, 1985. *O Globo,* August 25, 1961. PL: Partido Libertador.

11. Carlos Castello Branco, "O Dia Seguinte." Newton Rodrigues, FAX message to JWFD, Rio de Janeiro, May 26, 1994.

12. *O Estado de S. Paulo,* August 27, 1961.

12. Repression in Rio (August 26–31, 1961)

1. José Cândido Moreira de Souza, interview with DFR, Rio de Janeiro, August 27, 1986. Raphael de Almeida Magalhães, interview, Rio de Janeiro, August 17, 1983. Carlos Lacerda, *Depoimento,* p. 267.

2. *O Estado de S. Paulo,* August 29, 26, 1961. Mário Victor, *Cinco Anos que Abalaram o Brasil,* pp. 337, 367–368.

3. *O Estado de S. Paulo,* August 26, 1961.

4. Ibid., August 29, 1961. *Diário Carioca,* August 27, 1961.

5. Nelson Werneck Sodré, *História Militar do Brasil* (Rio de Janeiro: Editôra Civilização Brasileira, 1965), p. 376. Mário Victor, *Cinco Anos,* pp. 333–334.

6. Carlos Lacerda, interview, Rio de Janeiro, October 11, 1967.

7. Luiz Cavalcanti, telegram to Carlos Lacerda, Maceió, August 27, 1961, in CCL. *Diário de Notícias,* August 30, 1961. *O Estado de S. Paulo,* August 26, 29, 1961.

8. Carlos Lacerda, "Rosas e Pedras do Meu Caminho," Chapter 12 (*Manchete,* July 1, 1967), p. 104. Mauro Borges Teixeira, telegram to Carlos Lacerda, Goiânia, August 29, 1961, in CCL.

9. Mário Victor, *Cinco Anos,* p. 374. *O Estado de S. Paulo,* August 26, 29, 1961.

10. *Diário de Notícias,* August 30, 1961. *O Estado de S. Paulo,* August 29,

1961. Gaúcho: native of, or pertaining to, the state of Rio Grande do Sul.
11. *O Estado de S. Paulo,* August 29, September 5, 1961. Mário Victor, *Cinco Anos,* p. 356. Menelio Rosado Administración Revolucionaria Nery Castineira Sección Sindical, telegram to José Machado Lopes, Havana, August 31, 1961, copy in CCL.
12. Raphael de Almeida Magalhães, interview, August 17, 1983. Mário Victor, *Cinco Anos,* p. 321.
13. *Diário Carioca,* August 29, 1961. Mário Victor, *Cinco Anos,* pp. 325, 322–323. José de Segadas Viana, letter to Carlos Lacerda, Rio de Janeiro, September 9, 1961, in CCL.
14. *Diário Carioca,* August 29, 28, 1961. *O Estado de S. Paulo,* August 27, September 1, 1961. Mário Victor, *Cinco Anos,* pp. 359, 372–373. José Martins Rodrigues, telegrams to Carlos Lacerda, Brasília, August 31, 1961, in CCL.
15. *Diário Carioca,* August 31, 29, 1961. Mário Victor, *Cinco Anos,* p. 372.
16. Carlos Lacerda, *Depoimento,* p. 289. Carlos Lacerda, "Rosas e Pedras do Meu Caminho," Chapter 12, p. 104. *Diário Carioca,* August 29, 1961. Mário Victor, *Cinco Anos,* pp. 368, 369, 371. Ascendino Leite, *As Coisas Feitas* (Rio de Janeiro: EdA Editora, 1980), p. 301. *Diário de Notícias,* August 30, 1961. *Jornal do Brasil,* August 31, September 26, 1961.
17. Mário Victor, *Cinco Anos,* p. 373. *O Estado de S. Paulo,* September 1, 1961.
18. *Diário Carioca,* August 29, 30, 1961.
19. Ibid., August 31, 1961. *O Estado de S. Paulo,* September 1, 1961. Mário Victor, *Cinco Anos,* pp. 368–375. Paulo Silveira, interview, Rio de Janeiro, July 22, 1984. Paulo Silveira, interview with DFR, Rio de Janeiro, January 30, 1983.
20. Raphael de Almeida Magalhães, interview, August 17, 1983. *Diário Carioca,* August 31, 1961. *Última Hora,* September 1, 1961. Mário Victor, *Cinco Anos,* p. 375. *Jornal do Brasil,* September 1, 1961.
21. Carlos Lacerda, "Rosas e Pedras do Meu Caminho," Chapter 12, p. 104. Mário Victor, *Cinco Anos,* pp. 369–370. Érico Veríssimo's protest, in Porto Alegre newspapers, reproduced in José Condé's column, "Escritores e Livros," a copy of which was sent to Lacerda on September 3, 1961, by the *Correio da Manhã,* with a note that he meditate on its words and "not fall still further in the opinion of educated and intelligent Brazilians who love their country," in CCL. *Jornal do Brasil,* August 31, 1961.
22. *O Globo,* August 31, 1961. *Diário Carioca,* September 1, 1961.
23. Mário Victor, *Cinco Anos,* pp. 380, 382. Ascendino Leite, *As Coisas Feitas,* pp. 301–303.

13. The Military Ministers Disappoint Lacerda (August 31, 1961)

1. *O Estado de S. Paulo,* August 27, 1961. Afonso Arinos de Melo Franco, interview, Brasília, October 14, 1965. Aspásia Camargo and Walder de Góes,

Meio século de combate: diálogo com Cordeiro de Farias (Rio de Janeiro: Editora Nova Fronteira, 1981), p. 530.

2. Afonso Arinos de Melo Franco, *Planalto: Memórias* (Rio de Janeiro: Livraria José Olympio Editôra, 1968), pp. 177–178.

3. Ibid., p. 178. *Diário de Notícias,* August 30, 1961. Raphael de Almeida Magalhães, interview, August 17, 1983. *Diário Carioca,* September 2, 1961.

4. Carlos Lacerda, miscellaneous typewritten sheets (numbered 16 and 17), in CCL.

5. *O Estado de S. Paulo,* September 1, 1961.

6. Telegrams exchanged between Carlos Lacerda and other governors, August 25–31, 1961, in CCL. *Tribuna da Imprensa,* September 1, 1961. *O Estado de S. Paulo,* September 2, 1961. *Diário Carioca,* September 1, 2, 1961.

7. Raphael de Almeida Magalhães, interview, August 17, 1983. *O Estado de S. Paulo,* August 31, September 2, October 15, 1961. *Jornal do Brasil,* September 1, 1961.

8. Carlos Flexa Ribeiro, letter to Carlos Lacerda, August 31, 1961, in CCL.

9. Edgar Flexa Ribeiro, interviews, Rio de Janeiro, August 15, 1983, August 19, 1989.

10. Carlos Lacerda, *Depoimento,* pp. 268–269. Almino Afonso, interview, Santiago, Chile, June 28, 1967.

11. Tancredo Neves, interview, Rio de Janeiro, October 7, 1965. Tancredo Neves described the plan, known as Operação Mosquito, as "more than a rumor."

12. Afonso Arinos de Melo Franco, *Planalto,* p. 101. *O Estado de S. Paulo,* September 2, 1961. *Tribuna da Imprensa,* September 2–3, 1961.

13. Carlos Lacerda, telegram to Afonso Arinos de Melo Franco, Rio de Janeiro, September 2, 1961, in CCL. Afonso Arinos de Melo Franco, telegram to Carlos Lacerda, Brasília, September 7, 1961, in CCL. Aspásia Camargo, Maria Tereza Lopes Teixeira, and Maria Clara Mariani, *O Intelectual e o Político: Encontros com Afonso Arinos* (Brasília: CPDOC and Dom Quixote Editora, 1983), pp. 201–202.

14. *O Estado de S. Paulo,* September 5, 1961.

14. Comments

1. Janistas, Getulistas, Juscelinistas, and Janguistas: supporters, respectively, of Jânio Quadros, Getúlio Vargas, Juscelino Kubitschek and João ("Jango") Goulart.

2. Laerte Vieira, speech in the Chamber of Deputies, *Diário do Congresso Nacional* 32, no. 71 (June 30, 1977), p. 5673.

3. César Seroa da Mota, transcript of interview taped by the Sociedade dos Amigos de Carlos Lacerda, pp. 13–14. Carlos Lacerda quoted in Jair Silva and Ricardo André, *Água, afinal* (Teleplan phonograph record).

4. Lourenço de Almeida Prado, interview, Rio de Janeiro, August 15, 1983. Raphael de Almeida Magalhães, interview, Rio de Janeiro, August 9, 1989.

II. Governor during the Parliamentary Experiment (1961–1963)

1. Repercussions of the Press Censorship (September–November 1961)

1. *Tribuna da Imprensa*, September 9–10, 1961.
2. *O Estado de S. Paulo*, September 8, 1961. *Tribuna da Imprensa*, September 8, 11, 1961.
3. *Novos Rumos*, September 1, 1961. Mário Victor, *Cinco Anos que Abalaram o Brasil*, p. 377. Raphael de Almeida Magalhães, interview, August 17, 1983.
4. *Tribuna da Imprensa*, September 13, 1961.
5. Ibid., October 19, September 26, 1961. The CPI's *relator* had the task of digging up the facts on the matter being investigated and then describing those facts, in a report, in a manner to enable the CPI to vote intelligently on the matter.
6. *Tribuna da Imprensa*, September 13, 14, 1961. *Jornal do Brasil*, September 13, 14, 1961.
7. *Tribuna da Imprensa*, September 20, 27, 23–24, October 3, 1961. *O Jornal*, September 13, 1961.
8. *Tribuna da Imprensa*, October 3, 1961. Carlos Lacerda, *Depoimento*, p. 222. Raphael de Almeida Magalhães, interview, August 17, 1983. Edgar Flexa Ribeiro, interview, August 15, 1983.
9. *Jornal do Brasil*, September 26, 1961. Mário Victor, *Cinco Anos*, p. 378. Gladstone Chaves de Melo, interview, Rio de Janeiro, August 12, 1994. *Tribuna da Imprensa*, October 19, 20, 21–22, November 11–12, September 26, October 7–8, 1961. The Green Shirts, active in the mid-1930s, opposed Communism.
10. *Tribuna da Imprensa*, September 19, 10, 1961.
11. Ibid., October 3, 6, 10, 24, 1961. João de Segadas Viana, letter to Carlos Lacerda, Brasília, September 19, 1961. Carlos Lacerda, letter to João de Segadas Viana (misaddressed to "General José Segadas Viana"), Rio de Janeiro, October [date not shown] 1961. Carlos Lacerda, telegram to Tancredo Neves, Rio de Janeiro, October 5, 1961. Tancredo Neves, letter to Carlos Lacerda, Brasília, October 10, 1961. (Letters and telegrams in CCL.)
12. *Tribuna da Imprensa*, October 21–22, 24, December 15, 1961.
13. *O Estado de S. Paulo*, October 15, 1961. Paulo Silveira, interview, Rio de Janeiro, July 22, 1984. Paulo Silveira, interview with DFR, Rio de Janeiro, January 30, 1983. Carlos Lacerda, cables to Raphael de Almeida Magalhães, New York, October 15, 17, 1961, in CCL. Mário Victor, *Cinco Anos*, pp. 372, 383–386.
14. *O Estado de S. Paulo*, October 15, 1961.
15. *Tribuna da Imprensa*, October 18, 1961.
16. Mário Victor, *Cinco Anos*, pp. 384–385. *Tribuna da Imprensa*, October 19, December 1, 1961. *Jornal do Brasil*, October 15, 19, 1961.

17. *Tribuna da Imprensa*, October 16, 23, 1961. Carlos Lacerda, *Las 4 Mentiras Sobre Cuba* (n.p., n.d., booklet containing speech delivered in New York, October 15, 1961), pp. 6, 10, 9 (numbering based on considering editor's note as p. 1).

18. Carlos Lacerda, cable to Raphael de Almeida Magalhães, New York, October 15, 1961. Rollin S. Atwood (Banco Interamericano de Desarrollo), letter to Carlos Lacerda, Washington, D.C., September 12, 1961, in CCL. Carlos Lacerda, *A Linha de Yenan e as Fôrças Armadas* (Rio de Janeiro: Tribuna da Imprensa, 1957), p. 51. Cleantho de Paiva Leite, interview, Rio de Janeiro, August 14, 1984.

19. Raphael de Almeida Magalhães, interview, August 17, 1983. Marcelo Garcia, interview, August 18, 1983. *Tribuna da Imprensa*, October 12, 14–15, 23, 1961. Carlos Lacerda, *Depoimento*, p. 274.

2. The Year Ends with a Prison Riot (December 1961)

1. *Tribuna da Imprensa*, October 25, 24, 31, 30, November 7, 1961, February 1, 1962. *O Estado de S. Paulo*, October 12, December 26, 1961.

2. Carlos Lacerda, *O Poder das Idéias*, 3d ed., p. 160 (1st ed., p. 122). Enaldo Cravo Peixoto, transcript of interview taped by the Sociedade dos Amigos de Carlos Lacerda, September 18, 1985, p. 2. *O Estado de S. Paulo*, October 12, 17, 1961. *Tribuna da Imprensa*, November 14, December 23–24, 1961.

3. *Tribuna da Imprensa*, October 23, 25, November 23, 1961.

4. *Tribuna da Imprensa*, December 12, 1961. *Diário Carioca*, July 4, 1961. *O Estado de S. Paulo*, November 29, 1961. "Objetivos fiscais," in *Mensagem à Assembléia Legislativa: Programa de Govêrno para 1963* (Rio de Janeiro: Estado da Guanabara, August 31, 1962). Governo do Estado da Guanabara, "A Nova Lei Tributária: Lei N⁰ 72—de 28 de Novembro de 1961" (copy furnished by Tannay de Farias).

5. Joshua B. Powers, letter to Carlos Lacerda, New York, November 6, 1961. Guilherme Júlio Borghoff, letters to Carlos Lacerda and Joshua B. Powers, Rio de Janeiro, December 5, 1961, and letter to Powers, Rio de Janeiro, December 29, 1961 (all in CCL). Guilherme Júlio Borghoff, *Lampejos* (Rio de Janeiro: Edição do Autor, 1984), pp. 23–29. Carlos Lacerda, correspondence with International Cooperation Administration, 1961, in CCL. *Tribuna da Imprensa*, November 10, 1961.

6. *Tribuna da Imprensa*, December 6, 12, 1961. Cables between Carlos Lacerda and Antônio Guedes Muniz, December 7, 11, 12, 13, 15, 1961, in CCL.

7. *Tribuna da Imprensa*, December 12, 16–17, 21, 26, 23–24, 1961.

8. Vitor Mehry and others in *Tribuna da Imprensa*, December 27, 1961. *O Estado de S. Paulo*, December 28, 26, 1961. *Tribuna da Imprensa*, December 26, 27, 1961.

9. Edgar Flexa Ribeiro, interview, August 15, 1983. Carlos Lacerda, *Depoimento*, p. 143. Lamy Cunto, interview, Rio de Janeiro, March 21, 1991.

10. *Tribuna da Imprensa*, December 26, 27, 1961. Carlos Lacerda, *Depoimento*, pp. 143–144. Carlos Lacerda, "Rosas e Pedras do Meu Caminho," Chapter 12 (*Manchete*, July 1, 1967), p. 108. *O Estado de S. Paulo*, December 26, 1961.

11. *O Estado de S. Paulo*, December 26, 1961. *Tribuna da Imprensa*, December 26, 1961. Carlos Lacerda, "A Revolta no Presídio," on pp. 313–314 of Carlos Lacerda, *O Poder das Idéias*, 1st ed. (Rio de Janeiro: Distribuidora Record Editôra, 1962); the speech is not in the third edition.

12. *O Estado de S. Paulo*, December 26, 28, 1961. *Tribuna da Imprensa*, December 26, 1961.

13. *Tribuna da Imprensa*, December 26, 27, 1961. Carlos Lacerda, decisions handwritten at the prison (no date shown), in possession of Edgar Flexa Ribeiro. *O Estado de S. Paulo*, December 26, 1961.

14. *Tribuna da Imprensa*, December 27, 26, 1961. *O Estado de S. Paulo*, December 28, 1961.

15. *O Globo*, February 1, 2, 1962. *Tribuna da Imprensa*, February 2, 9, 1962.

16. Edgar Flexa Ribeiro, interview, Rio de Janeiro, August 19, 1989. *Novos Rumos*, March 30–April 5, 1962.

17. *Tribuna da Imprensa*, March 22, 23, 24–25, 27, 28, 29, 1962. *Novos Rumos*, April 6–12, 1962.

18. *Tribuna da Imprensa*, April 24, 25, 26, 27, 28–29, 30, May 2, 1962.

3. Charges against the Goulart Regime (November 1961–May 1962)

1. *Tribuna da Imprensa*, November 24, 1961. Carlos Lacerda, letter to João de Segadas Viana, Rio de Janeiro, November 27, 1961, in CCL.

2. Handwritten draft (by Edgar Flexa Ribeiro) of letter from Carlos Lacerda to "Sr. Ministro," Rio de Janeiro, January 15, 1962 (in possession of Flexa Ribeiro).

3. *Novos Rumos*, May 25–31, 1962. *Tribuna da Imprensa*, May 21, 22, 23, 26–27, 29, June 1, 1962. *Jornal do Brasil*, June 14, 1962.

4. *Tribuna da Imprensa*, December 11, 13, 1961. *Pelego:* union boss at the service of the government. *Imposto sindical:* labor union tax.

5. *Tribuna da Imprensa*, December 12, 14, 16–17, 20, 22, 1961, April 25, 1962. The "13th month" law was passed by the Senate in June 1962 and signed by Goulart in July.

6. *Tribuna da Imprensa*, December 20, 1961. *Jornal do Brasil*, January 5, 1962 (quoting Governor Lacerda's Ofício 194/61). *Novos Rumos*, January 12–18, 1962. *O Globo*, January 9, 10, 11, 12, 19, 1962.

7. *Novos Rumos*, January 12–18, 1962. *O Globo*, January 22, 17, 1962 (the manifesto of the four former foreign ministers was supported by Raul Fernandes but not signed by him, as he was to be an adviser at the Punta del Este meeting).

8. *O Globo*, February 6, 1962. Vladimir Reisky de Dubnic, "Trends in Brazil's Foreign Policy," in Eric N. Baklanoff, ed., *New Perspectives of Brazil*

(Nashville: Vanderbilt University Press, 1966), p. 93. *Tribuna da Imprensa,* May 30, February 6, 9, 1962.

4. Streetcars and Telephones (1960–1962)

1. Antônio Gallotti, letter to Carlos Lacerda, Rio de Janeiro, January 30, 1961, in CCL.
2. Estado da Guanabara, *Abusos do Poder Econômico: Light versus Estado da Guanabara,* pp. 90–94. Raphael de Almeida Magalhães, interview with Byron R. M. Coelho, Rio de Janeiro, July 12, 1990.
3. Estado da Guanabara, *Abusos do Poder Econômico,* p. 50. *Tribuna da Imprensa,* January 2, 7–8, 27, 1961.
4. Raphael de Almeida Magalhães, interview with Byron R. M. Coelho, July 12, 1990. CEDUG-Doxiadis, p. 100. Hélio Mamede, interview with DFR, August 9, 1985. *Matar:* to kill.
5. Govêrno Carlos Lacerda, *Mensagem à Assembléia Legislativa: Programa de Govêrno para 1963* (Rio de Janeiro: Estado da Guanabara, August 31, 1962), section on Onibus Elétricos. Estado da Guanabara, *IV Reunião de Governadores,* p. F5/1. *Diário Carioca,* July 21, 1961. Gastão Cruls, *Aparência do Rio de Janeiro,* Edição do IV Centenário, p. 888. CEDUG-Doxiadis, pp. 100–105.
6. *O Estado de S. Paulo,* December 22, 1962, May 28, 1963.
7. *O Globo,* December 9, 10, 12, 1960.
8. *Tribuna da Imprensa,* April 28, June 7, 27, August 2, 1961. *O Globo,* March 2, 1962.
9. Govêrno Carlos Lacerda, *Mensagem à Assembléia Legislativa: Programa de Govêrno para 1963,* section on Telefones. Raphael de Almeida Magalhães, interview with Byron R. M. Coelho, July 12, 1990. João Goulart, "Nota do Presidente da República," on pp. 11–16 of Carlos Lacerda, *Nacionalismo de Verdade e de Mentira;* see p. 14.
10. *O Globo,* February 17, 20, 1962. Testimony of Roberto Campos before the Comissão Parlamentar de Inquérito destinada a examinar a situação das emprêsas concessionárias, June 20 and 26, 1963, reproduced on pp. 487–660 of Instituto Brasileiro de Relações Internacionais, "A Compra das Concessionárias de Energia Elétrica," Part II, *Revista Brasileira de Política Internacional* 8, nos. 31, 32 (September, December 1965), see p. 532. *Tribuna da Imprensa,* March 3–4, 1962.
11. "A Compra das Concessionárias de Energia Elétrica," Part II, pp. 489, 530, 563–564 (testimony of Roberto Campos). Carlos Lacerda, *Nacionalismo de Verdade e de Mentira,* pp. 6, 9, 22, 8, 7, 19. Raphael de Almeida Magalhães, interview with Byron R. M. Coelho, July 12, 1990.
12. *Tribuna da Imprensa,* March 31, 24–25, 3–4, 8, 1962.
13. Ibid., March 24–25, 22, 3–4, April 5, 1962.
14. Carlos Lacerda, "Frente Ampla: o que é, o que não é, para que serve," *Manchete,* September 30, 1967, p. 20.
15. *Tribuna da Imprensa,* March 31, April 1, 1962.

16. Roberto Campos, *A Lanterna na Popa: Memórias* (Rio de Janeiro: Topbooks, 1994), p. 823.

17. *Tribuna da Imprensa,* April 2, 3, 1962.

18. Ibid., April 3, 5, 6, 1962.

19. Ibid., April 9, 5, 7–8, 1962.

20. "A Compra das Concessionárias de Energia Elétrica," Part II, pp. 495–496. Ministério das Relações Exteriores, *Viagem do Presidente João Goulart aos Estados Unidos da América e ao México* (n.p.: Ministério das Relações Exteriores, Seção de Publicações, 1962), pp. 35, 166–167. *Tribuna da Imprensa,* April 7–8, 1962.

21. *Tribuna da Imprensa,* April 7–8, 11, 12, 1962.

22. Ibid., June 9–10, 14, 26, 1962. *O Estado de S. Paulo,* December 18, 1962. Salvador Mandim, transcript of interview taped by the Sociedade dos Amigos de Carlos Lacerda, pp. 1–3.

5. A Chat with President Kennedy (March 26, 1962)

1. Joshua B. Powers, letter to Carlos Lacerda, New York, March 1, 1962, in CCL.

2. Carlos Lacerda, *Depoimento,* p. 231. *O Globo,* February 10, 1962. José Roberto Rego Monteiro, interview with DFR, August 13, 1985. *Tribuna da Imprensa,* March 29, 1962.

3. *Tribuna da Imprensa,* March 17–18, 1962. Quadros' speech is given in Carlos Castilho Cabral, *Tempos de Jânio e Outros Tempos* (Rio de Janeiro: Editôra Civilização Brasileira, 1962), pp. 297–309.

4. Alfredo C. Machado, interview, Rio de Janeiro, August 8, 1989.

5. Carlos Lacerda, "Os Estados Unidos, a América Latina e o Mundo," in Carlos Lacerda, *O Poder das Idéias,* 3d ed., pp. 269–277; see pp. 274–277.

6. Correspondence of Robert W. Bialek, Guilherme Júlio Borghoff, and Carlos Lacerda, March, April 1962, in CCL. Quotations from *U.S. News and World Report,* the Chemical Bank of New York, and *Newsweek,* in *Tribuna da Imprensa,* March 27, 1962.

7. *Tribuna da Imprensa,* March 20, 1962. Govêrno Carlos Lacerda, *Mensagem à Assembléia Legislativa: 5 anos de govêrno* (August 31, 1965), p. 166. Cleantho de Paiva Leite, interview, Rio de Janeiro, August 14, 1984.

8. Joshua B. Powers, letter to Carlos Lacerda, March 1, 1962. Robert W. Bialek, letter to Carlos Lacerda, April 4, 1962, and letter to Richard Goodwin, New York, April 2, 1962, in CCL. Carlos Lacerda, letter to John F. Kennedy, Washington, D.C., March 26, 1962, in CCL. Portuguese version is in Carlos Lacerda, *Uma rosa é uma rosa é uma rosa* (Rio de Janeiro: Distribuidora Record, 1965), pp. 66–67.

9. Carlos Lacerda, *Uma rosa é uma rosa é uma rosa,* pp. 41–43. Roberto Campos, *A Lanterna na Popa,* pp. 817–819.

10. Lacerda, *Uma rosa é uma rosa é uma rosa,* pp. 44–61. See also Roberto Campos, *A Lanterna na Popa,* pp. 817–819.

11. *Tribuna da Imprensa,* March 30, 1962.

6. The Reconstruction of Guanabara Begins (1962)

1. Enaldo Cravo Peixoto, transcript of interview taped on September 18, 1985, by the Sociedade dos Amigos de Carlos Lacerda, pp. 2, 1. *Tribuna da Imprensa,* April 25, 1962.

2. Raphael de Almeida Magalhães, interview, August 9, 1989. *Tribuna da Imprensa,* May 5–6, 1962. Carlos Lacerda, "A Aliança Para o Progresso: Significado e Condições," in Carlos Lacerda, *O Poder das Idéias,* 3d ed., pp. 243–260; see pp. 243–247, 251.

3. *Última Hora,* September 21 (column of Ib Teixeira), October 19, 1962. The household water fee, unchanged between 1947 and October 1961, was more burdensome (as a percentage of the minimum wage) in 1947–1951 than the new fee, which was, nevertheless, a drastic increase from the fee in 1960, which had become almost meaningless due to inflation. See Govêrno Carlos Lacerda, *Mensagem à Assembléia Legislativa: 5 Anos de Govêrno* (Message of August 31, 1965), pp. 205–206, including statement by Mario Lorenzo Fernandez.

4. *Tribuna da Imprensa,* May 23, 26–27, 1962. *Jornal do Brasil,* June 30, 1962.

5. *O Globo,* January 5, March 1, 1962. Salvador Mandim, interview, Rio de Janeiro, August 16, 1984. *Última Hora,* September 27, 1962.

6. *Tribuna da Imprensa,* March 10–11, May 26–27, June 8, 1962. Anthony Leeds and Elizabeth Leeds, "Favelas e Comunidade Política: A Continuidade da Estrutura de Controle Social," in Leeds and Leeds, *A Sociologia do Brasil Urbano* (Rio de Janeiro: Zahar Editores, 1978), pp. 186–263; see pp. 216–217, 251–253. *Jornal do Brasil,* June 13, 1962. Victor Vincent Valla and Jorge Ricardo Gonçalves, "O Período Autoritário de Remoções: Destruindo a Autoconstrução para 'Ensinar' a Auto-ajuda, 1962–1973," starting on p. 85 of Victor Vincent Valla (ed.), *Educação e Favela: Política para as Favelas do Rio de Janeiro, 1940–1985* (Petrópolis: Editora Vozes, 1986); see p. 90. Armando de Abreu, p. 2 of transcript of interview taped by the Sociedade dos Amigos de Carlos Lacerda.

7. *Tribuna da Imprensa,* May 31, June 13, 1962. Raphael de Almeida Magalhães, interview with Byron R. M. Coelho, Rio de Janeiro, July 12, 1990. Luiz Carlos Vital, interview with Byron R. M. Coelho, Rio de Janeiro, September 1989. Célio Borja, interview, Rio de Janeiro, August 14, 1989. *O Estado de S. Paulo,* October 30, December 8, 11, 1962. Leeds and Leeds, *A Sociologia do Brasil Urbano,* pp. 212–213. José Arthur Rios, letters to Carlos Lacerda, Rio de Janeiro, February 22, 1962 (in CCL) and May 13, 1962 (in files of Rios). José Arthur Rios, interview, Rio de Janeiro, March 4, 1992, and letter to newspapers, Rio de Janeiro, May 19, 1962 (in files of Rios).

8. *Tribuna da Imprensa,* April 7–8, May 26–27, June 8, 1962. "Operações de Crédito," in Govêrno Carlos Lacerda, *Mensagem à Assembléia Legislativa: Programa de Govêrno para 1963* (Message of August 31, 1962).

9. Enaldo Cravo Peixoto, transcript of interview taped by the Sociedade dos Amigos de Carlos Lacerda, pp. 22–23, 14. *O Estado de S. Paulo,* March 1, 1964.

10. Maria Carlota de Macedo Soares, letter to Carlos Lacerda, Rio de Janeiro, February 20, 1961, in CCL. John Dos Passos, *Brazil on the Move* (Garden City: Doubleday & Company, 1963), pp. 170, 156. Hélio Mamede, interview with DFR, Rio de Janeiro, August 9, 1985. *Jornal do Brasil*, May 1, 1990, September 28, 1967. Lloyd Schwartz, "Annals of Poetry: Elizabeth Bishop and Brazil," on pp. 85–97 of *The New Yorker*, September 30, 1991.

11. Maria Carlota de Macedo Soares, letter to Carlos Lacerda, February 20, 1961.

12. Carlos Lacerda, in Antonio Carvalho Mendes, "Carlos Lacerda, também um criador," *Revista dos Criadores* 47, no. 570 (July 1977), pp. 69–76; see p. 72. Enaldo Cravo Peixoto, transcript of interview taped by the Sociedade dos Amigos de Carlos Lacerda, pp. 18, 5. Hélio Mamede, interview with DFR, August 9, 1985. Luiz Fernando Gomes, article in *Jornal do Brasil*, September 14, 1987. Celina Cortes article in *Jornal do Brasil*, November 25, 1984. Roberto Burle Marx, "Sem amor não se faz coisa alguma," *Jornal do Brasil*, August 4, 1989.

13. John Dos Passos, *Brazil on the Move*, p. 170. Hélio Mamede, interview with DFR, August 9, 1985. Carlos Lacerda, *Depoimento*, pp. 60–61. *O Estado de S. Paulo*, December 12, 1962.

14. "Esgôtos," in Govêrno Carlos Lacerda, *Mensagem à Assembléia Legislativa: Programa de Govêrno para 1964* (Message of August 30, 1963). *O Globo*, September 22, 26, 1962. *Jornal do Brasil*, September 2, 21, 1962. Walter Cunto, transcript of interview taped by the Sociedade dos Amigos de Carlos Lacerda, pp. 12–13. *O Estado de S. Paulo*, December 6, 1962.

15. "Loteria Estadual," in *Mensagem à Assembléia Legislativa: Programa de Govêrno para 1963*. *Tribuna da Imprensa*, December 1–2, 1962. Govêrno Carlos Lacerda, *Mensagem à Assembléia Legislativa: 5 Anos de Govêrno*, p. 166.

16. *Tribuna da Imprensa*, July 7–8, 1962. Edgar Flexa Ribeiro, interview, Rio de Janeiro, July 8, 1983. *O Estado de S. Paulo*, December 7, 1962. *Jornal do Brasil*, December 14, 1962. Govêrno Carlos Lacerda, *Mensagem à Assembléia Legislativa: 5 Anos de Govêrno*, pp. 8, 54–55.

17. Mário Henrique Simonsen, "Inflation and the Money and Capital Markets of Brazil," on pp. 133–161 of Howard S. Ellis (ed.), *The Economy of Brazil* (Berkeley and Los Angeles: University of California Press, 1969); see table, p. 136. José Roberto Rego Monteiro, interview, Rio de Janeiro, August 22, 1989. Mario Lorenzo Fernandez, interview, Rio de Janeiro, August 23, 1989. *Tribuna da Imprensa*, August 11–12, November 28, 1962. "Operações de crédito," in Govêrno Carlos Lacerda, *Mensagem à Assembléia Legislativa: Programa de Govêrno para 1963*. *Jornal do Brasil*, December 1, 1962. The *títulos* were formally called *títulos de renda progressiva*.

18. *O Estado de S. Paulo*, December 8, 1962. Governor's office, Assessoria de Imprensa, press release of December 20, 1962 (in the Walter Cunto Collection). Walter Cunto, transcript of interview taped by the Sociedade dos Amigos de Carlos Lacerda, pp. 11–12, 9. Veiga de Brito, transcript of interview taped by the Sociedade dos Amigos de Carlos Lacerda, pp. 21–22. *Tribuna da*

Imprensa, July 21–22, 1962. Govêrno Carlos Lacerda, *Mensagem à Assembléia Legislativa: 5 Anos de Govêrno,* pp. 187–190. David Nasser, "Os Grandes Amigos (9): Carlos Lacerda," *Manchete,* no. 802 (September 2, 1967). Antonio Dias Rebello Filho, *Carlos Lacerda, Meu Amigo,* p. 173. "Estimativas Gerais da Receita," in Govêrno Carlos Lacerda, *Mensagem à Assembléia Legislativa: Programa de Govêrno para 1964.*

7. Political Crises, Strikes, and Riots (June–July 1962)

1. *Tribuna da Imprensa,* July 6, May 31, 25, 1962. Tancredo Neves, interview, Rio de Janeiro, October 7, 1965.
2. *Tribuna da Imprensa,* June 8, 1962. *Novos Rumos,* June 8–14, 1962.
3. José de Magalhães Pinto, telegram to Carlos Lacerda, Belo Horizonte, April 14, 1962, in CCL. *Tribuna da Imprensa,* June 7, 9–10, 1962.
4. *Jornal do Brasil,* June 12, 1962. *Tribuna da Imprensa,* June 8, 9–10, 11, 1962.
5. *Tribuna da Imprensa,* June 12, 11, 2–3, 5, 8, July 3, 20, 25, 1962. *Jornal do Brasil,* June 17, 1962.
6. *Jornal do Brasil,* June 15, 1962. *Tribuna da Imprensa,* June 11, 27, 28, July 5, 1962. *O Globo,* July 3, 1962.
7. *Jornal do Brasil,* June 15, 1962. *Tribuna da Imprensa,* June 15, 16–17, 19, 1962.
8. *Tribuna da Imprensa,* June 23–24, 26, 1962.
9. Ibid., June 28, July 2, 5, 7–8, 1962. Thomas E. Skidmore, *Politics in Brazil: An Experiment in Democracy* (New York: Oxford University Press, 1967), p. 219. Auro de Moura Andrade entry in *Dicionário Histórico-Biográfico Brasileiro, 1930–1983* (Rio de Janeiro: Editora Forense-Universitária Ltda., 1984). *O Globo,* July 5, 1962.
10. *Tribuna da Imprensa,* July 6, 7–8, 1962.
11. *Jornal do Brasil* and *Tribuna da Imprensa,* July 6, 1962.
12. *O Globo,* July 5, 1962. *Jornal do Brasil,* July 4, 1962.
13. *Jornal do Brasil* and *Tribuna da Imprensa,* July 6, 1962. *O Globo,* July 7, 1962.
14. *Tribuna da Imprensa,* July 7–8, 1962. *Última Hora,* July 7, 1962. *O Globo,* July 7, 1962.
15. *Tribuna da Imprensa,* July 12, 1962. *Jornal do Brasil,* July 12, 1962. Carlos Lacerda, letter to José Machado Lopes, Rio de Janeiro, July 11, 1962, in CCL.
16. *O Globo,* July 10, 11, 12, 13, 14, 1962. *Tribuna da Imprensa,* July 12, 1962.
17. *Jornal do Brasil,* July 10, 1962. *O Globo,* July 13, 17, 1962. "Abastecimento" in Govêrno Carlos Lacerda, *Mensagem à Assembléia Legislativa: Programa de Govêrno para 1963. Tribuna da Imprensa,* July 24, 25, 1962.
18. *Tribuna da Imprensa,* July 6, 1962. *O Globo,* July 6, 7, 1962.
19. *Tribuna da Imprensa,* July 9, August 8, 1962. *O Globo,* July 10, 1962.
20. *O Globo,* July 13, 14, 20, 1962. *Tribuna da Imprensa,* July 20, 1962.

8. Brochado da Rocha (July–September 1962)

1. Afonso Arinos de Melo Franco, *Planalto: Memórias*, p. 236. Francisco Brochado da Rocha, *Mensagem ao Congresso Nacional Remetida pelo Presidente do Conselho de Ministros, Solicitando Delegação de Poderes para Legislar*, August 10, 1962 (Brasília: Departamento de Imprensa Nacional, 1962).

2. *Tribuna da Imprensa*, July 30, August 8, 1962.

3. Carlos Lacerda, letter to José de Magalhães Pinto, Rio de Janeiro, August 2, 1962, in the Walter Cunto Collection. *Tribuna da Imprensa*, July 30, August 3, 14, 1962. *O Estado de S. Paulo*, January 4, 1963. (*Interventores* would run states on behalf of the central government.)

4. *O Globo*, September 4, 7, 1962.

5. *Jornal do Brasil*, September 2, 1962.

6. *Tribuna da Imprensa*, August 11–12, 1962. *O Globo*, *Correio da Manhã*, and *Jornal do Brasil*, September 1, 1962.

7. *O Globo*, September 4, 5, 6, 1962. *Tribuna da Imprensa*, September 8, 1962.

8. Afonso Arinos de Melo Franco, *Planalto*, p. 235. *O Globo*, September 6 (editorial), 7, 1962.

9. Afonso Arinos de Melo Franco, *Planalto*, pp. 235–236. *Tribuna da Imprensa*, September 8, 1962.

10. *Jornal do Brasil* and *O Globo*, September 7, 1962. Hermes Lima, *Travessia: Memórias* (Rio de Janeiro: Livraria José Olympio Editora, 1974), p. 253.

11. *O Globo*, September 8, 1962.

12. Ibid., September 12, 13, 1962. *Tribuna da Imprensa*, September 10, 1962.

13. *Jornal do Brasil*, September 1, 4, 1962. *Última Hora*, September 15, 1962.

14. *O Globo*, September 14, 17, 1962. Mário Victor, *Cinco Anos que Abalaram o Brasil*, p. 442. *Jornal do Brasil*, September 15, 1962. *Golpista*: supporter of a coup.

15. *O Globo*, September 14, 1962. *Jornal do Brasil*, September 15, 1962.

16. *Jornal do Brasil*, September 12, 16, 20, 1962. *O Globo*, September 15, 1962. John Dos Passos, *Brazil on the Move*, p. 176.

17. *O Globo*, September 14, 1962. Gustavo Capanema, interview, Brasília, October 23, 1965. Jânio Quadros and Afonso Arinos de Melo Franco, *História do Povo Brasileiro* (São Paulo: J. Quadros Editôres Culturais, 1968), p. 259.

18. *O Globo*, September 19, 15, 1962. Mário Victor, *Cinco Anos*, p. 444. Afonso Arinos de Melo Franco, *Planalto*, pp. 239–240.

19. *O Globo*, September 17, 19, 1962.

20. *Última Hora*, September 27, 1962. *Novos Rumos*, September 27, 1962. Hermes Lima, *Travessia*, p. 253. Carlos Lacerda, *Depoimento*, p. 270.

21. *O Globo*, October 2, 3, 1962.

9. The State Elections (October 7, 1962)

1. Juracy Magalhães, *Minhas Memórias Provisórias* (Rio de Janeiro: Editora Civilização Brasileira, 1982), p. 161. *Jornal do Brasil*, July 10, 11,

September 2, 1962. *Novos Rumos,* July 13–19, 1962. *Brazil Herald,* August 29, 1962.

2. *Tribuna da Imprensa,* October 11, 1962. Gilberto Marinho in *Tribuna da Imprensa,* October 17, 1962. *O Globo,* October 5, 1962.

3. *O Globo,* September 25, 1962. *Última Hora,* September 19, 12, 4, 1962. Mauro Magalhães, *Carlos Lacerda: O Sonhador Pragmático* (Rio de Janeiro: Editora Civilização Brasileira, 1993), p. 232.

4. *O Globo,* September 28, October 5, 6, 4, 1962. *Última Hora,* September 19, 21, 20, 1962.

5. Ronald Schneider, "Election Analysis," in Charles Daugherty, James Rowe, and Ronald Schneider, *Brazil: Election Factbook, Number 2, September 1965* (Washington, D.C.: Institute for the Comparative Study of Political Systems, 1965), p. 66. Eloy Dutra, *IBAD: Sigla da Corrupção* (Rio de Janeiro: Editôra Civilização Brasileira, 1963), p. 41. Mauro Magalhães, *Carlos Lacerda: O Sonhador Pragmático,* p. 232. *Última Hora,* September 19, 1962.

6. *Última Hora,* September 19, 20, 1962. *O Globo,* September 28, 29, 1962.

7. *O Globo,* October 11, September 4, 1962. *O Estado de S. Paulo,* December 4, 1962. *Brazil Herald,* September 5, 1962.

8. *O Globo,* September 26, 22, 1962. *Novos Rumos,* September 23, 26, 1962.

9. *Jornal do Brasil* and *O Globo,* October 4, 1962.

10. Antônio de Chagas Freitas entry in *Dicionário Histórico-Biográfico Brasileiro, 1930–1983.*

11. Ronald Schneider, "Election Analysis," p. 67. PDC: Partido Democrata Cristão.

12. *Jornal do Brasil,* October 11, 1962. *O Estado de S. Paulo,* October 25, 27, 1962.

13. *O Estado de S. Paulo,* October 27, December 4, 1962. *Tribuna da Imprensa,* October 11, 1962. *Jornal do Brasil,* October 12, 1962.

14. *Novos Rumos,* October 12–18, 1962. *Tribuna da Imprensa,* October 11, 1962. *Jornal do Brasil,* October 12, 1962. *Última Hora,* October 19, 1962.

15. Raul Brunini, interview, Rio de Janeiro, August 1, 1989. Hugo Levy, interview, Rio de Janeiro, August 1, 1989. Edgar Flexa Ribeiro, interview, Rio de Janeiro, August 19, 1989. Juracy Magalhães, *Minhas Memórias Provisórias,* pp. 161–162. *Correio da Manhã,* October 18, 1962. *Última Hora,* October 19, 1962. Raphael de Almeida Magalhães, interview, August 9, 1989.

16. *O Globo,* October 11, 16, 1962. *Tribuna da Imprensa,* October 11, 19, 22, 23, 1962.

10. A Pleasant Interlude (October–November 1962)

1. *Última Hora,* October 19, 1962. *O Globo,* October 12, 13, 1962. Wilson Lopes Machado's scrapbooks (in his possession) provide photographs, a list of places visited (with dates), and other information about the Lacerdas' trip in Europe, October–November 1962. Regina Costard, interview with DFR, Rio de Janeiro, September 9, 1986.

2. Renato Bittencourt, "A Sobriedade de Lacerda," Paris, October 15, 1962, in *O Globo,* October 16. *O Globo,* October 13, 1962.

3. *O Globo,* October 12, 19, 1962. *Brazil Herald* and *Tribuna da Imprensa,* October 19, 1962. *Jornal do Brasil,* December 1, 1962. *O Estado de S. Paulo,* October 11, 1962.

4. *Jornal do Brasil,* December 1, 1962. *Brazil Herald,* October 19, 1962. *Tribuna da Imprensa,* November 30, 1962.

5. *Jornal do Brasil,* October 26, 1962. *Fatos & Fotos,* November 10, 1962.

6. *Brazil Herald,* October 26, 1962. *Tribuna da Imprensa,* October 26, December 1–2, 1962. Lesseps S. Morrison, *Latin American Mission* (New York: Simon and Schuster, 1965), pp. 250, 258.

7. *Brazil Herald,* November 4, 1962. *O Globo,* November 8, 1962. Carlos Lacerda in *O Estado de S. Paulo,* June 4, 1963.

8. Sérgio Lacerda, letter to Carlos Lacerda, Rio de Janeiro, November 13, 1962, in CCL.

9. John Dos Passos, *Brazil on the Move,* p. 178. *Brazil Herald,* May 8, 1963. *O Estado de S. Paulo,* April 20, 1963. Alfredo C. Machado, interview, August 8, 1989. Sérgio Lacerda, interview with DFR, Rio de Janeiro, February 1, 1983. *Bem-Amado:* well-loved.

10. *O Estado de S. Paulo* and *Jornal do Brasil,* December 1, 1962. *Tribuna da Imprensa,* December 1–2, 1962.

11. *O Estado de S. Paulo,* December 4, 1962.

11. Administrative Reform (December 1962)

1. *Jornal do Brasil,* December 22, 27, 13, 1962.

2. Ibid., December 19, 25, 27, 1962. *Correio da Manhã,* January 3, 1963. *Petebista:* associated with the PTB.

3. Hélio Beltrão, draft of "Mensagem No. 37" to the Legislative Assembly, June 16, 1961 (in the files of Edgar Flexa Ribeiro). "Sandra historia aprovação da Reforma e nega enxertos," *Correio da Manhã,* January 8, 1963. Sandra Cavalcanti, interview, Rio de Janeiro, February 23, 1991. Lei Nº 263 de 24 de dezembro de 1962, on pp. 70–92 of Estado da Guanabara, *Leis e Decretos do Estado da Guanabara;* see Articles 1–4, 155–173, 181.

4. *Correio da Manhã,* January 22, 1963. *O Estado de S. Paulo,* December 23, 1962.

5. *Jornal do Brasil,* December 28, 1962. *Correio da Manhã,* January 3, 1963.

6. *Jornal do Brasil,* December 28, 1962. "Sandra historia aprovação da Reforma e nega enxertos," *Correio da Manhã,* January 8, 1963. *Correio da Manhã,* January 23, 1963.

7. *Jornal do Brasil,* December 28, 25, 1962. *O Estado de S. Paulo,* January 3, 1963. Salvador Mandim, transcript of interview taped by the Sociedade dos Amigos de Carlos Lacerda, p. 2. *Jornal do Brasil,* January 4, 1963. Lei Nº 263 de 24 de dezembro de 1962.

8. Fernando Cícero da Franca Velloso, interviews, Rio de Janeiro, August 16, 1983, August 15, 1984. Thomas Leonardos, interview, Rio de Janeiro,

August 6, 1984. Hélio Fernandes, interviews, Rio de Janeiro, July 6, 1977, August 1, 1984.

9. *Tribuna da Imprensa*, March 10–11, 22, June 21, 22, July 10, 12, 1962. Stefan Baciu, *Lavradio, 98* (Rio de Janeiro: Editora Nova Fronteira, 1982), pp. 128–142. *Tribuna da Imprensa* entry in *Dicionário Histórico-Biográfico Brasileiro, 1930–1983*. Sérgio Lacerda, interview, Rio de Janeiro, August 17, 1988.

10. Stefan Baciu, *Lavradio, 98*, p. 135. *Tribuna da Imprensa*, July 10, 12, 25, 26, 28–29, 1962. Júlio Tavares (Carlos Lacerda) in *Tribuna da Imprensa*, August 8, 10, 1962.

11. Sérgio Lacerda, interview, August 17, 1988. Hélio Fernandes, interviews, July 6, 1977, August 1, 1984. Fernando Cícero da Franca Velloso, interview, August 16, 1983.

12. The Referendum (January 6, 1963)

1. Carlos Lacerda, *Depoimento*, p. 269.

2. *O Estado de S. Paulo*, January 9, 3, 1963, December 4, 1962.

3. Ibid., December 7, 12, 13, 14, 1962. *O Globo*, September 19, 1962.

4. *Análise e Perspectiva Econômica* (APEC, fortnightly economic letter, Rio de Janeiro, APEC Editôra), June 27, 1963. *O Estado de S. Paulo*, January 4, 1963. *Brazil Herald*, January 5, 1963.

5. *Jornal do Brasil*, January 1, 3, 4, 8, 1963. *Correio da Manhã*, January 4, 1963. Francisco Julião entry in *Dicionário Histórico-Biográfico Brasileiro, 1930–1983*.

6. *O Estado de S. Paulo*, December 27, 1962, January 4, 6, 1963.

7. Charles Daugherty, James Rowe, and Ronald Schneider, *Brazil: Election Factbook, Number 2*, p. 81.

8. *O Estado de S. Paulo*, January 9, 1963.

9. Ibid., December 30, 1962, January 10, 23, 1963.

III. Governor and Presidential Candidate in 1963

1. "Killer of Beggars" (January–March 1963)

1. *Última Hora*, January 21, 1963. Carlos Lacerda, *Depoimento*, pp. 226–228.

2. *Última Hora*, January 23, 25, 1963. *O Globo*, February 15, 1963. *Jornal do Brasil*, March 13, 1963.

3. *Jornal do Brasil*, February 6, 9, 1963. *O Estado de S. Paulo* and *O Jornal*, February 7, 1963.

4. *O Estado de S. Paulo*, February 7, 1963. Carlos Lacerda, *Depoimento*, pp. 226–228.

5. *O Estado de S. Paulo*, February 6, 7, 13, 1963. *Correio da Manhã*, February 12, 1963.

6. *O Estado de S. Paulo* and *Correio da Manhã*, February 13, 1963. *Novos Rumos*, February 15–21, 1963. *O Globo*, February 15, 1963.

7. *Novos Rumos*, February 15–21, 1963. *Novos Rumos*, February 8–14, 1963 (column by Pedro Severino).

8. *Brazil Herald*, February 13, 16, 1963. *O Estado de S. Paulo*, February 13, 1963.

9. *O Globo*, editorial, February 2, 1963. *Última Hora*, January 21, 23, February 16, 1963.

10. *Jornal do Brasil*, March 12, 1963. *Diário de Notícias*, editorial, February 2, 1963.

11. *Última Hora*, March 7, 8, 1963. About Carolina Maria de Jesus, see Preface of Translator, David St. Clair, to Carolina Maria de Jesus, *Child of the Dark* (New York: E. P. Dutton & Co., 1962), her first book, which appeared in Brazil as *Quarto de Despejo* (São Paulo: Livraria Francisco Alves, 1960).

12. *O Globo*, March 9, 1963. *Última Hora*, March 11, 1963.

13. *O Estado de S. Paulo*, March 9, 1963. *Brazil Herald*, February 16, 1963.

14. *O Estado de S. Paulo*, March 9, 23, 1963. *Última Hora*, March 10, 11, 12, 14, 22, 23, 1963.

15. *Última Hora*, March 14, 15, 1963. *Jornal do Brasil*, March 14, 1963. *O Estado de S. Paulo*, March 13, 16, 1963.

16. *O Estado de S. Paulo*, March 17, 19, 21, 26, 1963. *Jornal do Brasil*, March 19, 1963.

2. The Pro-Cuba Congress (March 28–31, 1963)

1. Dwight Martin and Milan J. Kubic, "Brazil's Goulart: Power for the Sake of What?" *Newsweek*, March 11, 1963. *Jornal do Brasil*, March 25, 1963. *Última Hora*, March 12, 25, 1963.

2. *Jornal do Brasil*, March 27 (editorial), 24, 1963. *O Estado de S. Paulo*, March 27, 1963. "Congresso Continental de Solidariedade a Cuba," suplemento especial, *Novos Rumos*, March 22–28, 1963.

3. *Última Hora*, March 19, 1963. *Jornal do Brasil*, March 26, 27 (including Carlos Castello Branco, "Coluna do Castello"), 1963. *O Estado de S. Paulo*, April 4, 1963.

4. *Jornal do Brasil*, March 26, 1963. *New York Times*, March 27, 1963. *O Estado de S. Paulo*, March 26, 29, 31, 1963. *Brazil Herald*, April 4, 1963.

5. *Jornal do Brasil*, March 26, 1963. *O Estado de S. Paulo*, March 27, 28, 1963. *Diário de Notícias*, April 3, 1963.

6. *O Estado de S. Paulo*, March 28, 1963. *Jornal do Brasil*, March 29, 1963. *New York Times*, March 27, 28, 1963. *Última Hora*, March 27, 1963.

7. *O Estado de S. Paulo*, April 4, 1963. *Jornal do Brasil*, March 27, 1963. *New York Times*, March 28, 1963.

8. *New York Times*, March 28, 29, 1963. *O Estado de S. Paulo*, March 29, 31, 1963.

9. *Jornal do Brasil*, March 31, 1963. *New York Times*, editorial, April 2, 1963. Carlos Lacerda, letter to *New York Times*, published April 11, 1963.

10. *Jornal do Brasil* and *O Estado de S. Paulo*, April 2, 1963. *Diário de Notícias*, editorial, April 5, 1963.

11. Francisco Teixeira, interview, Rio de Janeiro, November 28, 1967. Osvino Ferreira Alves entry in *Dicionário Histórico-Biográfico Brasileiro, 1930–1983*. *O Estado de S. Paulo*, April 5, 1963.

12. Francisco Teixeira, interview, November 28, 1967. Adirson de Barros, *Ascensão e Queda de Miguel Arraes* (Rio de Janeiro: Editôra Equador, 1965), p. 97. *O Estado de S. Paulo*, April 9, 1963.

13. *Diário de Notícias, O Estado de S. Paulo*, and *Última Hora*, April 5, 1963.

3. Triumph in Curitiba (April 28, 1963)

1. *O Estado de S. Paulo*, March 9, 1963.

2. Ibid., February 12, 14, March 1, 2, 23, 1963.

3. Ibid., March 22, 23, 24, 1963.

4. Ibid., March 2, 24, April 9, 1963.

5. Ibid., April 16, 1963. Carlos Lacerda, memorandum to Wilson Lopes Machado, Rio de Janeiro, April 9, 1963, in Wilson Machado's scrapbooks. *Jornal do Brasil*, April 11, 16, 1963. Veiga de Brito, transcript of interview taped by the Sociedade dos Amigos de Carlos Lacerda, p. 29.

6. *O Estado de S. Paulo*, April 19, 23, 1963.

7. *Brazil Herald*, April 26, 1963. Carlos Lacerda, letter to Adauto Lúcio Cardoso, Rio de Janeiro, April 22, 1963, in CCL. Carlos Lacerda, draft of telegram to Herbert Levy, Rio de Janeiro, n.d., in possession of Edgar Flexa Ribeiro.

8. Carlos Lacerda, letter to Adauto Lúcio Cardoso, April 22, 1963. A mention of the "maidens" (*donzelas*) was also made in Lacerda's speech at the inauguration of the Major Vaz Tunnel.

9. *O Estado de S. Paulo*, April 24, 25, 18, 1963. *Correio da Manhã*, April 26, 27, 1963. *Brazil Herald*, April 26, 1963.

10. *O Estado de S. Paulo*, April 26, 1963. Paul Vanorden Shaw, "UDN and 'This Incredible Lacerda,'" *Brazil Herald*, May 3, 1963.

11. *O Estado de S. Paulo*, April 27, 28, 1963. José Sarney entry in *Dicionário Histórico-Biográfico Brasileiro, 1930–1983*.

12. Herculano Leal Carneiro, typewritten memorandum for JWFD, Rio de Janeiro, April 20, 1989, and interview, Rio de Janeiro, August 6, 1989.

13. Hugo Levy, interview, Rio de Janeiro, March 2, 1991. Otávio Soares Dulci, *A UDN e o Anti-populismo no Brasil*, p. 188.

14. *Brazil Herald*, April 30, 1963. *O Estado de S. Paulo*, April 30, 1963. Otávio Dulci, *A UDN e o Anti-populismo no Brasil*, pp. 188–189. Carlos Castello Branco, *Introdução à Revolução de 1964*, vol. 1, *Agonia do Poder Civil* (Rio de Janeiro: Editora Artenova, 1975), p. 168. Daniel Krieger, *Desde as Missões: Saudades, Lutas, Esperanças* (Rio de Janeiro: Livraria José Olympio Editora, 1976), p. 163.

15. *O Estado de S. Paulo*, April 28, 1963.

16. Ibid. Flávio Galvão, interview, São Paulo, August 2, 1983. Affonso Romano de Sant'Anna has written ("A história alegre da república," *Jornal do*

Brasil, October 24, 1984) that "the UDN was a party without prospects because it contained crows, university graduates (*bacharéis*), and a lack of a sense of humor."

17. *O Estado de S. Paulo,* April 30, 1963.

18. Ibid. Carlos Lacerda, *Reforma Agrária: Liberdade e Propriedade* (Rio de Janeiro: Distribuidora Record, 1963), pp. 14, 19, 15, 16–17, 21, 24–25. Maria Victoria de Mesquita Benevides, *A UDN e o Udenismo: Ambigüidades do Liberalismo Brasileiro (1945–1965),* p. 124.

19. *Correio da Manhã,* April 30, 1963. Afonso Arinos de Melo Franco, *A Escalada: Memórias* (Rio de Janeiro: Livraria José Olympio Editôra, 1965), p. 81.

20. Wilson Lopes Machado, "Algumas Lembranças de um Amigo," pp. 9–11, and letter to JWFD, Curitiba, March 9, 1990. *Jornal do Brasil,* July 10, December 25, 1963. *Correio da Manhã,* June 13, 1963. *O Globo,* June 27, 1963.

4. The "Letter to the People" (July 6, 1963)

1. Darci Ribeiro, interview, Montevideo, November 13, 1967.

2. *O Estado de S. Paulo,* May 11, 12, 1963.

3. Ibid., May 24, 28, 31, June 4, 1963. Instituto Brasileiro de Relações Internacionais, "A Compra das Concessionárias de Energia Elétrica," Parts I and II, *Revista Brasileira de Política Internacional* 8, nos. 30, 31, 32 (June, September, December 1965).

4. Luís Tenório de Lima, interview, São Paulo, November 21, 1968.

5. Instituto Brasileiro de Relações Internacionais, "A Compra das Concessionárias de Energia Elétrica," Part I, *Revista Brasileira de Política Internacional* 8, no. 30 (June 1965), pp. 275–280. *O Estado de S. Paulo,* June 5, 1963.

6. *Correio da Manhã,* June 21, 1963.

7. "Roupa Suja" (editorial), *Jornal do Brasil,* June 30, 1963.

8. *Brazil Herald,* June 25, 1963.

9. Carlos Lacerda, *Depoimento,* p. 275.

10. Nelson Pereira, interview, São Paulo, August 4, 1983.

11. Carlos Lacerda, *Depoimento,* p. 275.

12. Nelson Pereira, interview, August 4, 1983.

13. Antonio Dias Rebello Filho, *Carlos Lacerda, Meu Amigo,* pp. 113–114.

14. *O Globo,* July 6, 1963. *Correio da Manhã, O Estado de S. Paulo,* and *Diário de Notícias,* July 7, 1963. *Brazil Herald,* July 9, 1963. Cláudio Lacerda, *Carlos Lacerda: 10 Anos Depois* (Rio de Janeiro: Editora Nova Fronteira, 1987), p. 35.

15. Cláudio Lacerda, *Carlos Lacerda: 10 Anos Depois,* pp. 32–34. *Brazil Herald,* July 9, 1963. *O Estado de S. Paulo,* July 7, 1963. *New York Times,* July 8, 1963. A typewritten draft of the "Letter to the People," with handwritten changes by Lacerda, is in CCL.

16. *Diário de Notícias,* July 7, 1963. *Brazil Herald,* July 9, 1963. *Correio da Manhã* and *Jornal do Brasil,* July 6, 1963.

17. *O Globo* and *Jornal do Brasil,* July 9, 1963.

18. *O Estado de S. Paulo* and *Correio da Manhã*, July 9, 1963. *Jornal do Brasil*, July 10, 11, 1963.

19. *O Estado de S. Paulo*, July 10, 12, 1963. *Diário de Notícias*, July 11, 10, 13, 1963. *Jornal do Brasil*, July 9 (including column by Pedro Müller), 10, 1963. *Correio da Manhã*, July 9, 1963.

20. *O Estado de S. Paulo*, July 21, 23, 24, 25, 1963. *O Globo*, July 22, 1963. *Última Hora*, July 22, 23, 1963. *Correio da Manhã*, July 23, 1963. *Jornal do Brasil*, July 23, 1963.

5. Telephones and Traffic (1963–1964)

1. Salvador Mandim, transcript of interview taped by the Sociedade dos Amigos de Carlos Lacerda, pp. 3–4. *O Estado de S. Paulo*, February 22, 1963.

2. Carlos Lacerda, *Depoimento*, p. 278. *O Estado de S. Paulo*, March 21, 26, 1963. Mandim, transcript of interview, p. 4.

3. Mandim, transcript of interview, pp. 4–5. Edgar Flexa Ribeiro, interview, July 8, 1983. Carlos Lacerda in *Jornal da Tarde*, September 23, 1966. Carlos Lacerda, *Depoimento*, p. 278.

4. Carlos Lacerda, *Nacionalismo de Verdade e de Mentira*, pp. 7–8, 9, 10. Carlos Lacerda, letter to the President of the Republic, Rio de Janeiro, May 22 (shown as May 23), 1963, in CCL.

5. Carlos Lacerda, *Nacionalismo de Verdade e de Mentira*, pp. 11–16, 25–26.

6. *O Estado de S. Paulo*, June 20, May 28, 1963.

7. Ibid., June 20, 1963. Mandim, transcript of interview, pp. 13–14, 17, including remarks by Armando de Abreu during the Mandim interview.

8. *O Estado de S. Paulo*, June 20, 1963. Mandim, transcript of interview, p. 18, including remarks by Armando de Abreu.

9. Enaldo Cravo Peixoto, transcript of interview taped by the Sociedade dos Amigos de Carlos Lacerda, pp. 13–24. Govêrno Carlos Lacerda, *Mensagem à Assembléia Legislativa: 5 Anos de Govêrno*, pp. 131–133. Elazar David Levy, "Rio: Cidade Asfaltada," *Revista de Engenharia do Estado da Guanabara, Orgão da Secretaria de Obras Públicas*, Rio de Janeiro, vol. 31, no. 1 (January–March 1965), pp. 33–40. *O Estado de S. Paulo*, May 25, November 6, 1963.

10. *O Estado de S. Paulo*, January 18, 1964. Mandim, transcript of interview, p. 6.

11. Mandim, transcript of interview, pp. 6–7.

12. Raul Marques de Azevedo, "Viadutos da Ponte dos Marinheiros," *Revista de Engenharia do Estado da Guanabara* 30, nos. 1, 2 (January, June 1963), pp. 15–23. Fernando Nascimento Silva, "Vias, Viadutos e Túneis," *Revista de Engenharia do Estado da Guanabara* 31, no. 1, pp. 23–32. Ayrton Baffa, in Antonio Dias Rebello Filho, *Carlos Lacerda, Meu Amigo*, p. 62. *O Estado de S. Paulo*, July 31, March 17, July 28, 30, 31, June 19, 16, 1963. Enaldo Cravo Peixoto, transcript of interview, p. 15. Walter Cunto, transcript of interview, p. 9.

13. *O Estado de S. Paulo*, August 9, 1, 4, 16, 1963. *Diário de Notícias*, October 2, 1964. Emil Farhat, interview with DFR, São Paulo, March 11, 1983.

14. Cravo Peixoto, transcript of interview, p. 24. Governor's office, Assessoria de Imprensa release of July 23, 1964 (in the Walter Cunto Collection). Sandra Cavalcanti, interview, February 23, 1991.

15. Carlos Lacerda, *Depoimento*, p. 236. Carlos Lacerda, letter to Vasco Leitão da Cunha, August 17, 1964, in CCL.

16. *Diário Carioca*, June 17, 1964. *Jornal do Brasil*, June 26, 1964. Governor's office, Assessoria de Imprensa, releases of July 6, 7, 1964 (in the Walter Cunto Collection).

17. Governor's office, Assessoria de Imprensa release of July 7, 1964. Carlos Lacerda, speech at Moncorvo Filho Hospital Annex, copy in Governor's office, Assessoria de Imprensa release of September 30, 1965 (in the Walter Cunto Collection). *Correio da Manhã*, April 3, 1965.

6. Administrating in the Face of Obstruction (1963–1964)

1. Célio Borja, interview, Rio de Janeiro, August 14, 1989. Hélio Mamede, interview with DFR, Rio de Janeiro, August 9, 1985. Philip Deane (pseudonym of Gerassimos Gigantes), *Constantinos Doxiadis, Master Builder for Free Men* (Dobbs Ferry, N.Y.: Oceana Publications, 1965), p. 55. Carlos Lacerda, articles about Doxiadis in *Jornal da Tarde*, December 16, 1966, *O Estado de S. Paulo*, July 16, 1972, and *Jornal do Brasil*, July 28, 1975.

2. *Diário Carioca*, January 15, 1964. "O inimigo da cultura," editorial, *Diário Carioca*, January 16, 1964.

3. *Diário Carioca*, January 18, 1964. Carlos Lacerda, handwritten draft of telegram to Hélio de Almeida, Rio de Janeiro, in CCL.

4. Célio Borja, interview, August 14, 1989. José Roberto Rego Monteiro, interview, August 6, 1989. Carlos Lacerda, "Constantinos Apostolos Doxiadis," *O Estado de S. Paulo*, July 16, 1975. CEDUG-Doxiadis, pp. 177, 297.

5. Carlos Lacerda in *Jornal do Brasil*, July 28, 1975. CEDUG-Doxiadis, p. 111. Govêrno Carlos Lacerda, *Mensagem à Assembléia Legislativa: Programa de Govêrno para 1964*, section about Habitação.

6. Mauro Magalhães, *Carlos Lacerda*, p. 235. *O Estado de S. Paulo*, March 12, 1963. Victor Vincent Valla and Jorge Ricardo Gonçalves, "O Período Autoritário de Remoções: Destruindo a Autoconstrução para 'Ensinar' a Auto-Ajuda, 1962–1973," in Victor Vincent Valla (ed.), *Educação e Favela: Política para as Favelas do Rio de Janeiro, 1940–1985*, pp. 90–91. Armando de Abreu, transcript of interview taped by the Sociedade dos Amigos de Carlos Lacerda, pp. 2–4. John Dos Passos, *Brazil on the Move*, p. 171.

7. Salvador Mandim, transcript of interview taped by the Sociedade dos Amigos de Carlos Lacerda, p. 16. Richard Bourne, *Political Leaders of Latin America* (New York: Alfred A. Knopf, 1970), p. 238. Carlos Lacerda, *Depoimento*, p. 233. Sandra Cavalcanti, *Rio: Viver ou Morer* (Rio de Janeiro: Editora Expressão e Cultura, 1978), pp. 26–41.

8. Carlos Lacerda, speech at the Miguel Couto Hospital Annex, copy in Governor's office, Assessoria de Imprensa release of September 28, 1965 (in the Walter Cunto Collection). Célio Borja, interview, August 14, 1989. Governor's office, Assessoria de Imprensa release of March 19, 1964 (in the Walter Cunto Collection). Luiz Carlos Vital, interview with Byron R. M. Coelho, Rio de Janeiro, October 1989.

9. Célio Borja, interview, August 14, 1989. *Diário Carioca*, January 3, 1964. R. Magalhães Júnior, "A Miséria Escondida aos Turistas," *Diário Carioca*, January 5, 1964. Carlos Lacerda, speech at the Miguel Couto Hospital Annex, copy in Governor's office, Assessoria de Imprensa release of September 28, 1965. *Última Hora*, December 24, 1964. Maria Alayde Albite Ulrich, "Carlos Lacerda e a UDN," dissertação de mestrado (Porto Alegre: Pontifícia Universidade Católica do Rio Grande do Sul, 1984), pp. 410–411.

10. Carlos Lacerda, *Depoimento*, p. 233. Carlos Lacerda, replies to Augusto Amaral Peixoto, in Governor's office, Assessoria de Imprensa release of August 1, 1963 (in the Walter Cunto Collection).

11. *O Estado de S. Paulo*, April 11, 14, 24, May 1, June 2, 6, 1963. *Brazil Herald*, May 30, 1963. José Mauro, columns in *Última Hora*, June 3, 7, 1963. *Correio da Manhã*, June 6, 8, 12, 13, 1963.

12. *Jornal do Brasil*, July 5, 1963. *Correio da Manhã*, June 12, 1963. *O Estado de S. Paulo*, June 12, 1963.

13. *O Estado de S. Paulo*, July 12, 13, 1963. Mauro Magalhães, *Carlos Lacerda*, pp. 46, 137, 180, 191–192.

14. *Brazil Herald*, June 27, 1963.

15. *O Estado de S. Paulo*, July 5, August 6, 1963. João Condé, interview with DFR, Rio de Janeiro, March 23, 1983. Emil Farhat, interview with DFR, São Paulo, March 11, 1983. Emil Farhat in *O Estado de S. Paulo*, May 22, 1977. Suzanne Labin, *Em Cima da Hora;* preface and translation by Carlos Lacerda (Rio de Janeiro: Distribuidora Record, 1963).

16. João Condé, interview with DFR, March 23, 1983. David Nasser, "As grandes amizades (9): Meu Amigo Carlos Lacerda," *Manchete*, no. 802 (September 2, 1967).

17. Governo Federal, Law 4,242 of July 17, 1963, Clause 46. *O Estado de S. Paulo*, July 17, 1963.

18. *Diário de Notícias*, December 18, 19, 1963. *O Estado de S. Paulo*, December 18, 19, 20, 1963, January 5, 1964.

19. *O Estado de S. Paulo*, September 20, December 19, 18, 1963, February 5, 15, 1964. *Diário de Notícias*, December 19, 1963.

20. *O Estado de S. Paulo*, December 19, 20, 28, 1963, January 4, February 5, 15, 1964.

21. *Diário de Notícias*, December 19, 1963.

7. The *Los Angeles Times* Interview (September 1963)

1. *O Globo*, August 27, September 2, 1963. Luís Roberto Veiga de Brito, transcript of interview taped by the Sociedade dos Amigos de Carlos Lacerda,

pp. 29–31. Antonio Dias Rebello Filho, *Carlos Lacerda, Meu Amigo*, p. 100. Tannay de Farias, letter to JWFD, Rio de Janeiro, June 28, 1991.

2. *O Estado de S. Paulo*, September 14, 1963. *Brazil Herald*, October 2, 1963.

3. Carlos Lacerda, "Rosas e Pedras do Meu Caminho," Chapter 7 (*Manchete*, May 27, 1967), p. 36.

4. *O Estado de S. Paulo*, September 13, 1963.

5. Darci Ribeiro, interview, Montevideo, November 13, 1967.

6. *O Estado de S. Paulo*, September 15, 17, 18, 1963. *O Globo*, October 3, 1963.

7. *O Estado de S. Paulo*, September 17, 18, 21, 22, 14, October 5, 1963.

8. Ibid., September 22, 21, 1963.

9. Ibid., September 28, 1963. George W. Bemis, *From Crisis to Revolution: Monthly Case Studies* (Los Angeles: School of Public Administration, University of Southern California, 1964), p. 138. Mário Victor, *Cinco Anos que Abalaram o Brasil*, pp. 452–453. José Stacchini, *Março 64: Mobilização da Audácia* (São Paulo: Companhia Editôra Nacional, 1965), p. 62. *Novos Rumos*, October 4–10, 1963.

10. *O Estado de S. Paulo*, September 20, 21, 27, 18, 26, 1963. *Los Angeles Times*, September 29, 1963.

11. Alfredo C. Machado, interview, Rio de Janeiro, August 8, 1989. Carlos Lacerda, *Depoimento*, p. 270. *Los Angeles Times*, September 29, 1963.

12. *Los Angeles Times*, September 29, 1963. Cláudio Lacerda, *Carlos Lacerda: 10 Anos Depois*, pp. 35–39. See also excerpts from Lacerda interview with Julian Hartt reported in AP cable from Los Angeles, given in *Brazil Herald*, October 1, 1963.

13. Abelardo Jurema, *Sexta-Feira, 13: Os Últimos Dias do Govêrno João Goulart*, 2d ed. (Rio de Janeiro: Edições O Cruzeiro, 1964), p. 123.

14. "Nota dos Ministros," *O Estado de S. Paulo*, October 1, 1963.

15. *Brazil Herald*, October 1, 1963. Ademar de Barros, interview, São Paulo, December 1, 1965. *O Estado de S. Paulo*, October 1, 1963. *Correio da Manhã*, October 1, 1963.

16. *O Estado de S. Paulo*, October 2, 1963. *Última Hora*, October 2, 1963.

17. Gustavo Corção, "A Nota dos Ministros Militares," *Diário de Notícias*, October 2, 1963. *O Estado de S. Paulo*, October 2, 1963.

18. *Correio da Manhã*, October 1, 1963. *O Jornal*, October 1, 2, 4, 1963. *Jornal do Brasil*, October 1, 2, 3, 1963.

19. *O Estado de S. Paulo*, October 3, 1963.

8. The Attempt to Seize Lacerda (October 3, 1963)

1. Maria Cristina Lacerda Simões Lopes, interview, Petrópolis, August 3, 1983.

2. Carlos Lacerda in *O Estado de S. Paulo*, January 4, 1975. Carlos Lacerda, *Depoimento*, p. 63. Carlos Lacerda, "Rosas e Pedras do Meu Caminho," Chapter 7, p. 36.

3. *O Estado de S. Paulo*, October 4, 2, 1963. *O Globo*, October 5, 1963.

4. *O Estado de S. Paulo*, October 1, 1963. João Goulart, "Discurso do Presidente Goulart na reunião do ministério," *O Estado de S. Paulo*, October 10, 1963. *Jornal do Brasil*, October 4, 1963.

5. João Goulart, "Discurso do Presidente Goulart na reunião do ministério." *O Estado de S. Paulo*, October 3, 4, 5, 1963. *Jornal do Brasil*, October 3, 1963.

6. Abelardo Jurema, *Sexta-Feira, 13*, pp. 131–132, 126–127. Gilberto Crockatt de Sá, interview, Rio de Janeiro, December 12, 1968. *O Estado de S. Paulo*, October 1, 3, 1963. Edicio Gomes de Matos, "Com o sítio na mão, Ministros militares enquadram Lacerda," *Jornal do Brasil*, October 6, 1963. Luís Tenório de Lima, interview, São Paulo, November 21, 1968. *Jornal do Brasil*, October 4, 1963.

7. Gilberto Crockatt de Sá, interview, December 12, 1968. Carlos Lacerda, *Depoimento*, p. 272. Luís Fernando Bocaiuva Cunha, interview, Rio de Janeiro, December 5, 1968. Luís Tenório de Lima, interview, November 21, 1968.

8. Jurema, *Sexta-Feira, 13*, pp. 128–129. Luís Fernando Bocaiuva Cunha, interview, December 5, 1968.

9. *O Estado de S. Paulo*, October 5, 1963. Testimony of Francisco Boaventura Cavalcanti Júnior, pp. 246–250 of Carlos Castello Branco, *Introdução à Revolução de 1964*, vol. 2, *A Queda de João Goulart* (Rio de Janeiro: Editora Artenova, 1975); see pp. 247, 249–250. Carlos Lacerda, *Depoimento*, p. 272. Flávio Galvão, "Um novo general (História do atentado de 1963)," *O Estado de S. Paulo*, August 15, 1976. Mauro Magalhães, *Carlos Lacerda*, p. 153.

10. Testimony of Francisco Boaventura Cavalcanti Júnior, pp. 246–247 of Carlos Castello Branco, *Introdução à Revolução de 1964*, vol. 2. "Levy Denuncia à Câmara o Atentado contra Lacerda," *O Estado de S. Paulo*, October 8, 1963. Mauro Magalhães, *Carlos Lacerda*, pp. 153–154.

11. Testimony of Francisco Boaventura Cavalcanti Júnior, pp. 249–250 of Carlos Castello Branco, *Introdução à Revolução de 1964*, vol. 2. Padre Antônio Godinho, testimony given to the Parliamentary Commission of Investigation (CPI), as reported in *Diário de Notícias*, October 31, 1963.

12. Sandra Cavalcanti, interview, Rio de Janeiro, October 21, 1966. "Levy Denuncia à Câmara o Atentado contra Lacerda," *O Estado de S. Paulo*, October 8, 1963. Carlos Lacerda, "Rosas e Pedras do Meu Caminho," Chapter 7, p. 35. Padre Antônio Godinho, testimony given to the Parliamentary Commission (CPI), as reported in *Diário de Notícias*, October 31, 1963.

13. "Levy Denuncia à Câmara o Atentado contra Lacerda," *O Estado de S. Paulo*, October 8, 1963. Carlos Lacerda, typewritten notes based on information in the *Tribuna da Imprensa*, October 5–6, 1963, in CCL. Carlos Lacerda, "Rosas e Pedras do Meu Caminho," Chapter 7, p. 33.

14. Carlos Lacerda, "Rosas e Pedras do Meu Caminho," Chapter 7, pp. 33, 35. Sandra Cavalcanti, interview, October 21, 1966. *O Estado de S. Paulo*, October 5, 1963.

15. Carlos Lacerda, "Rosas e Pedras do Meu Caminho," Chapter 7, p. 35. See Guilherme J. Borghoff, *Lampejos*, pp. 75–76, for the version of Borghoff,

who, as the secretary of economy, had been scheduled to accompany Lacerda on a visit to a plant financed by COPEG.

9. The State of Siege Request (October 4–7, 1963)

1. Mário Victor, *Cinco Anos que Abalaram o Brasil*, p. 458.
2. Dante Pelacani, interview, São Paulo, November 24, 1968. *O Estado de S. Paulo*, October 6, 1963. *O Globo*, October 5, 1963. *Jornal do Brasil*, October 6, 1963.
3. Carlos Lacerda, *Depoimento*, p. 270. *Jornal do Brasil*, October 5, 6, 1963. *O Estado de S. Paulo*, October 5, 6, 1963. Abelardo Jurema, *Sexta-Feira, 13*, p. 130.
4. *Jornal do Brasil*, October 6, 1963. *O Globo*, October 7, 1963. *O Estado de S. Paulo*, October 6, 8, 1963. *New York Times*, October 8, 1963.
5. *O Globo*, October 6, 1963. *O Jornal*, October 5, 1963. *Jornal do Brasil*, October 5, 6, 1963. *Novos Rumos*, October 7, 1963.
6. *Jornal do Brasil*, October 6, 5, 1963. *O Globo*, October 5, 7, 1963. Abelardo Jurema, *Sexta-Feira, 13*, p. 129.
7. Luís Fernando Bocaiuva Cunha, interview, Rio de Janeiro, November 21, 1968. George W. Bemis, *From Crisis to Revolution: Monthly Case Studies*, p. 150. *O Globo*, October 6, 7, 1963.
8. *O Estado de S. Paulo*, October 8, 9, 1963. *Jornal do Brasil*, October 8, 1963.
9. Jurema, *Sexta-Feira, 13*, p. 133. *Jornal do Brasil*, October 11, 1963. *O Estado de S. Paulo*, October 15, 1963.
10. *O Estado de S. Paulo*, October 10, 1963.

10. The Attempt to Seize Goulart (October 1963)

1. *Jornal do Brasil*, October 13, 1963. *O Estado de S. Paulo*, October 13, 16, November 1, 7, 1963. Carlos Castello Branco, *Introdução à Revolução de 1964*, vol. 2, pp. 107–108.
2. *O Estado de S. Paulo*, October 11, 12, November 22, 20, 1963. Carlos Castello Branco, *Introdução à Revolução de 1964*, vol. 2, p. 250.
3. Carlos Castello Branco, *Introdução à Revolução de 1964*, vol. 2, pp. 245, 131. *O Estado de S. Paulo*, November 23, 24, 28, 26, 29, 1963.
4. Charles Borer, interview, Rio de Janeiro, October 6, 1967. *Jornal do Brasil*, October 12, 13, 1963.
5. *Jornal do Brasil*, October 12, 13, 1963. *O Estado de S. Paulo*, November 28, 1963.
6. Charles Borer, interview, October 6, 1967. *Jornal do Brasil*, October 15, 1963. *O Estado de S. Paulo*, October 16, 1963.
7. Charles Borer, interview, October 6, 1967. *Jornal do Brasil*, October 15, 12, 17, 19, 1963. *O Estado de S. Paulo*, November 7, 30, 1963.
8. *Jornal do Brasil*, October 26, 1963.
9. *Correio da Manhã*, November 27, 1963.

11. Lacerda Declares Himself a Presidential Candidate (October–December 1963)

1. Carlos Castello Branco, *Introdução à Revolução de 1964*, vol. 2, pp. 157, 151, 145, 108–109. Clodsmith Riani, interview, Juiz de Fora, November 2, 1968. *Jornal do Commercio*, Rio de Janeiro, December 24, 1963. *O Estado de S. Paulo*, October 15, December 25, 1963. Abelardo Jurema, *Sexta-Feira, 13*, p. 137. Olavo Previati, interview, Rio de Janeiro, December 18, 1968.

2. *O Estado de S. Paulo*, October 22, 15, November 21, 22, 1963. Carlos Castello Branco, *Introdução à Revolução de 1964*, vol. 2, pp. 96, 108. *Jornal do Brasil*, November 5, 1963.

3. *O Estado de S. Paulo*, October 25, 1963.

4. *O Globo*, October 29, 1963. *O Estado de S. Paulo*, November 10, 1963. *Brazil Herald*, November 12, 1963.

5. *O Estado de S. Paulo*, November 16, 19, 21, 22, 1963. João Goulart, interview, *Manchete* (November 1963), reproduced in Carlos Castello Branco, *Introdução à Revolução de 1964*, vol. 2, pp. 234–245; see p. 244.

6. Carlos Castello Branco, *Introdução à Revolução de 1964*, vol. 2, pp. 150, 151.

7. *O Estado de S. Paulo*, November 19, 1963.

8. Ibid., November 24, 22, December 3, 1963. Carlos Castello Branco, *Introdução à Revolução de 1964*, vol. 2, pp. 131, 126–127.

9. Antonio Dias Rebello Filho, *Carlos Lacerda, Meu Amigo*, pp. 72–73. Carlos Lacerda, *Depoimento*, p. 94.

10. *O Estado de S. Paulo*, December 1, 1963. Luiz Roberto Veiga de Brito, transcript of interview taped by the Sociedade dos Amigos de Carlos Lacerda, pp. 29–30.

11. *O Estado de S. Paulo*, December 14, 1, 1963. Rebello Filho, *Carlos Lacerda, Meu Amigo*, p. 81.

12. Rebello Filho, *Carlos Lacerda, Meu Amigo*, pp. 82, 90, 91. *O Estado de S. Paulo*, December 3, 1963.

13. Rebello Filho, *Carlos Lacerda, Meu Amigo*, pp. 93–97, 100. *O Estado de S. Paulo*, December 3, 4, 5, 1963. Luiz Roberto Veiga de Brito, transcript of interview, pp. 29–31.

12. Year-end Bedlam by Legislators (December 1963)

1. *Jornal do Brasil*, October 19, November 2, 1963. *O Estado de S. Paulo*, November 2, 1, 1963.

2. *Jornal do Brasil*, November 7, 1963. *Constituição do Estado da Guanabara, promulgada em 27 de Março de 1961* (Rio de Janeiro: Gráfica Editôra Aurora, 1961), Section III, Article 31.

3. *Jornal do Brasil*, November 1, October 31, 1963. *Última Hora*, October 31, 1963. *Diário de Notícias*, December 25, 1963. *Novos Rumos*, November 15–21, 1963. João Lyra Filho, *Finanças da Guanabara, 1962* (Rio de Janeiro:

Gráfica Record Editôra, 1963). See also João Lyra Filho, *Orçamento da Guanabara, 1962* (Rio de Janeiro: Irmãos Pongetti Editôres, 1962).

4. *Última Hora*, November 1, 7, 1963. *Novos Rumos*, November 15–21, 1963, and comments, in a late 1963 number, on Lacerda's physical appearance.

5. *Jornal do Brasil*, November 1, 2, 1963.

6. Ibid., November 6, 1963.

7. *Diário de Notícias*, December 5, 1963. *O Estado de S. Paulo*, December 12, 13, 14, 31, 1963. R. Magalhães Júnior, "O mais espantoso dos vetos," *Diário Carioca*, January 10, 1964. Jefferson de Andrade (with collaboration of Joel Silveira), *Um Jornal Assassinado: A Última Batalha do Correio da Manhã* (Rio de Janeiro: José Olympio Editora, 1991), pp. 53–54, 62. José Roberto Rego Monteiro, interview, March 3, 1991. Sandra Cavalcanti, interview, Rio de Janeiro, February 23, 1991.

8. *Diário de Notícias*, December 5, 12, 14, 18, 1963. *O Estado de S. Paulo*, December 12, 13, 19, 1963. *Diário Carioca*, January 3, 1964.

9. *O Estado de S. Paulo*, December 31, 1963. *Diário de Notícias*, December 21, 24, 25, 1963.

10. *Diário Carioca*, January 1, 3, 1964. *O Estado de S. Paulo*, January 1, 1964.

13. Year-end Bedlam by Students (December 1963)

1. *O Estado de S. Paulo*, November 9, 1963.

2. Nota do Diretório Acadêmico, December 27, 1963, in statement of Heráclito F. Sobral Pinto, *O Estado de S. Paulo*, January 8, 1964. *Novos Rumos*, January 3–9, 1964. *O Estado de S. Paulo*, January 1, 10, 1964.

3. *Novos Rumos*, January 3–9, 1964. "Estudantes e mandarins," editorial, *Jornal do Brasil*, November 5, 1963. Heráclito Sobral Pinto, testimony at CPI investigating the UNE, as given in *Jornal do Brasil*, October 25, 1963.

4. *O Estado de S. Paulo*, January 8, 1964. *Novos Rumos*, January 3–9, 1964.

5. *Diário de Notícias*, December 31, 1963. *Novos Rumos*, January 3–9, 1964.

6. *Novos Rumos*, January 3–9, 1964. *O Estado de S. Paulo*, December 31, 1963, January 1, 5, 1964. Letter of Professor Sobral Pinto to First Army commander, *O Estado de S. Paulo*, January 1, 1964.

7. Statements of First Army Commander Armando de Morais Âncora and Education Minister Júlio Sambaqui, *O Estado de S. Paulo*, January 4, 1964. *Novos Rumos*, January 3–9, 1964. *O Estado de S. Paulo*, December 31, 1963, January 1, 8, 1964.

8. *O Estado de S. Paulo*, January 4, 7, 1964. "Nota do I Exército," *O Estado de S. Paulo*, January 4, 1964.

9. *O Estado de S. Paulo*, January 8, 9, 11, 12, 1964.

10. Ibid., February 1, 2, 5, 8, 1964.

11. Ibid., January 4, 1964. "Sobral Pinto acusa Jurema de distorcer fatos," *O Estado de S. Paulo*, January 5, 1964. Letter of Professor Sobral Pinto to First Army commander, *O Estado de S. Paulo*, January 1, 1964.

12. R. Magalhães Júnior, "Lacerda e os Estudantes," *Diário Carioca*, January 4, 1964.

IV. Agitation and Upheaval (January–April 1964)

1. Accusing Goulart of Favoring "Revolutionary War" (January–February 1964)

1. Gilberto Crockatt de Sá, interviews, Rio de Janeiro, October 9, 11, 1967, December 12, 17, 1968. *O Estado de S. Paulo*, January 7, 11, 12, 1964. Anver Bilate, "O CGT, Império da Corrupção," *O Cruzeiro*, May 16, 1964.

2. *O Estado de S. Paulo*, January 7, 1964.

3. *Diário Carioca*, January 18, 1964. Mário Victor, *Cinco Anos que Abalaram o Brasil*, p. 466. *Última Hora*, January 18, 1964.

4. *Última Hora*, January 15–22, 1964. *O Estado de S. Paulo*, January 16, 18, 19, 26, February 2, 4, 5, 1964. Mário Victor, *Cinco Anos*, pp. 463–464. Adirson de Barros, *Ascensão e Queda de Miguel Arraes*, pp. 118–119.

5. *O Estado de S. Paulo*, January 16, February 6, 1964. Instituto de Pesquisas e Estudos Sociais (IPES) confidential intelligence report of February 17, 1964. Humberto Castello Branco, "A EsAO na Atualidade Militar," February 1964, in File L2 of Castello Branco papers, CPDOC.

6. *O Estado de S. Paulo*, January 21, 24, 1964. American Embassy, Rio de Janeiro, "Labor: Revision of Directory of Labor Organizations in Brazil" (sixty-eight-page mimeographed report, September 25, 1968), p. 44. Oscar Dias Corrêa and family, interview, Brasília, October 18, 1965. *Última Hora*, São Paulo, January 25, 1964.

7. *O Estado de S. Paulo*, January 16, 23, 14, 1964. *Brazil Herald*, January 23, 1964. Leonel Brizola, "Organização dos 'Grupos de Onze Companheiros' ou 'Comandos Nacionalistas,'" Rio de Janeiro, November 29, 1963 (eleven-page brochure). Leonel Brizola, interview, Atlántida, Uruguay, November 14, 1967.

8. Otávio Soares Dulci, *A UDN e o anti-populismo no Brasil*, p. 203. Olavo Bilac Pinto, *Guerra Revolucionária* (Rio de Janeiro: Editôra Forense, 1964), p. 49. "Lacerda lança manifesto," *Diário Carioca*, January 18, 1964.

9. *O Estado de S. Paulo*, February 1, 1964.

10. Antonio Dias Rebello Filho, *Carlos Lacerda, Meu Amigo*, p. 80.

11. Ibid.

12. Carlos Alberto Aulicino, interview, São Paulo, August 2, 1983. Luiz Werneck, Flávio Galvão, Roberto Brandini, Heber Perillo Fleury, and Luiz Maciel Júnior, interview, São Paulo, November 24, 1965. Eldino Brancante, interviews, São Paulo, November 23, 24, 1965. Olímpio Mourão Filho, interview, Rio de Janeiro, October 9, 1965.

13. Rubens Resstel and Flávio Galvão, interview, São Paulo, August 4, 1983.

14. Gustavo Borges, "Operação Salame," Part I, *O Cruzeiro*, May 30, 1964, p. 12. Gustavo Borges, interview, Rio de Janeiro, August 14, 1983.

2. The UDN Decides to Nominate Lacerda Quickly (February 1964)

1. *O Estado de S. Paulo*, January 14, 15, 1964.
2. Movimento de Educação de Base, *Viver É Lutar: 2.° Livro de Leitura Para Adultos* (n.p.: MEB, October 1963), pp. 56, 32, 54, 52.
3. *O Estado de S. Paulo*, February 22, 25, 1964, November 14, 1963. Armando Falcão, interview, Rio de Janeiro, August 26, 1983.

O Corvo e Falcão
Eis a Salvação

4. *O Estado de S. Paulo*, February 25, 28, 1964. Glycon de Paiva, "Petrobrás como Banco da Subversão Nacional e Escola Prática de Corrupção," *Jornal do Brasil*, February 16, 1964. Carlos Castello Branco, *Introdução à Revolução de 1964*, vol. 2, *A Queda de João Goulart* (Rio de Janeiro: Editora Artenova, 1975), p. 173.
5. *O Estado de S. Paulo*, February 25, March 8, 1964. Rebello Filho, *Carlos Lacerda, Meu Amigo*, p. 104.
6. *O Estado de S. Paulo*, December 24, 1963.
7. Ibid., January 17, 1964. Carlos Lacerda, letter to Olavo Bilac Pinto, Rio de Janeiro, January 23, 1964, in CCL.
8. *O Estado de S. Paulo*, January 28, February 7, 1964.
9. Ibid., February 20, 14, 15, 1964. *Diário Carioca*, January 18, 1964. *Última Hora*, February 17, 1964.
10. *O Estado de S. Paulo*, February 20, 21, 26, 27, 1964.
11. Rebello Filho, *Carlos Lacerda, Meu Amigo*, pp. 107–109. *O Estado de S. Paulo*, March 3, 4, 1964.
12. Nelson Pereira, interview, São Paulo, August 4, 1983. *O Estado de S. Paulo*, March 21, 1964.
13. Rebello Filho, *Carlos Lacerda, Meu Amigo*, pp. 108–109. Carlos Lacerda and Germano Zimber, *Quaresmas do Brasil* (Rio de Janeiro: Editora Nova Fronteira, 1971), introductory text by Carlos Lacerda. Carlos Lacerda in *Jornal da Tarde*, March 17, 1966.

3. The Rally of March 13 (February–March 1964)

1. *O Estado de S. Paulo*, February 18, 28, 29, March 6, 1964.
2. Ibid., February 18, 1964. Luiz Tenório de Lima, interview, São Paulo, November 21, 1968. Dante Pelacani, interview, São Paulo, November 24, 1968.
3. Oscar Dias Corrêa and family, interview, Brasília, October 18, 1965. *Última Hora*, February 28, March 2, 1964. *Última Hora* (São Paulo), February 26, 1964. *O Estado de S. Paulo*, February 27, 29, 1964.
4. *O Estado de S. Paulo*, March 8, 1964.
5. Clarence W. Hall, "The Country That Saved Itself," *Reader's Digest*,

November 1964, p. 146. Hélio Silva, *1964: Golpe ou Contragolpe?* (Rio de Janeiro: Editora Civilização Brasileira, 1975), p. 324.

6. Fernando Pedreira, "Diário de Brasília" column, *Tribuna da Imprensa,* March 14, 1964.

7. *Correio da Manhã, Tribuna da Imprensa,* and *O Estado de S. Paulo,* March 14, 1964. Mário Victor, *Cinco Anos que Abalaram o Brasil,* p. 475.

8. *O Estado de S. Paulo,* March 14, 1964. Hélio Silva, *1964: Golpe ou Contragolpe?,* pp. 457–466.

9. *Correio da Manhã,* March 17, 1964. Carlos Castello Branco, *Introdução à Revolução de 1964,* vol. 2, p. 199. George W. Bemis, *From Crisis to Revolution: Monthly Case Studies,* pp. 227–229.

10. *Tribuna da Imprensa,* March 20, 14, 1964. Mário Victor, *Cinco Anos,* p. 482.

11. Hélio Silva, *1964: Golpe ou Contragolpe?,* p. 325. Araújo Netto, "A Paisagem," in Alberto Dines et al., *Os Idos de Março e a Queda em Abril,* 2d ed. (Rio de Janeiro: José Alvaro Editor, 1964), p. 61. André de Séguin des Hons, "Os Diários do Rio de Janeiro, 1945–1982," (master's thesis, Universidade Federal do Rio de Janeiro, November 1982), p. 110. Coleção Memória do Brasil, *História Política do Brasil: Revolução de 64* (Rio de Janeiro: Editora Rio, n.d.), pp. 214, 211 (quoting newspapers).

12. *O Estado de S. Paulo,* March 15, 1964.

13. Carlos Heitor Cony, *JK: Memorial do Exílio* (Rio de Janeiro: Bloch Editores, 1982), pp. 58–59. Carlos Castello Branco, *Introdução à Revolução de 1964,* vol. 2, pp. 193, 202. *O Estado de S. Paulo,* March 18, 20, 22, 1964. *Tribuna da Imprensa,* March 18, 20, 23, 1964. Ernâni do Amaral Peixoto and Filinto Müller, interviews, Brasília, October 15, 1965. Carlos Lacerda, interview, Rio de Janeiro, October 11, 1967.

14. Carlos Lacerda, draft of letter to Plínio Coelho, Rio de Janeiro, March 1964, in CCL. *Tribuna da Imprensa* and *O Estado de S. Paulo,* March 19, 1964. Nei Braga, Aurélio Corrêa do Carmo, Mauro Borges Teixeira, letters to Carlos Lacerda, Curitiba, Belém, Goiânia, March 23, 25, 1964, in CCL.

15. Ademar de Barros, interview, São Paulo, December 1, 1965. *Correio da Manhã,* March 18, 1964. *Última Hora* (São Paulo), March 18, 1964. *O Estado de S. Paulo,* March 17, 19, 1964. *Tribuna da Imprensa,* March 21, 1964. Carlos Castello Branco, *Introdução à Revolução de 1964,* vol. 2, pp. 201, 203.

16. *O Estado de S. Paulo,* March 19, 1964. Rebello Filho, *Carlos Lacerda, Meu Amigo,* pp. 111–112.

17. Raphael de Almeida Magalhães, interview, Rio de Janeiro, August 9, 1989.

18. *O Estado de S. Paulo,* February 19, 25, 1964.

4. Lacerda Visits São Paulo and Minas (March 19–23, 1964)

1. Carlos Lacerda, telegram to Ademar de Barros, Rio de Janeiro, March 16, 1964, and telegram, Ademar de Barros to Carlos Lacerda, São Paulo, March 17, 1964, in CCL. Raphael de Almeida Magalhães, interview, Rio de Janeiro, August 9, 1989. Mário Victor, *Cinco Anos Que Abalaram o Brasil,* p. 487.

2. Antonio Dias Rebello Filho, *Carlos Lacerda, Meu Amigo*, p. 112.

3. *O Estado de S. Paulo*, March 20, 1964. Pedro Aguinaldo Fulgêncio, letter to Fernando Goldgaber, Belo Horizonte, April 25, 1985. Napoleão de Carvalho, letter to Fernando Goldgaber, São Paulo, May 12, 1985. Carlos Lacerda, *Depoimento*, p. 276.

4. Rebello Filho, *Carlos Lacerda, Meu Amigo*, pp. 112–113. *O Estado de S. Paulo*, March 21, 1964.

5. *Tribuna da Imprensa*, March 21, 1964. Carlos Castello Branco, *Introdução à Revolução de 1964*, vol. 2, p. 208 (entry for March 22, 1964).

6. *Tribuna da Imprensa*, March 23, 1964. Mário Victor, *Cinco Anos*, p. 487. Wilson Figueiredo, "A Margem Esquerda," in Alberto Dines et al., *Os Idos de Março*, pp. 213–216. *O Estado de S. Paulo*, March 25, 21, 1964.

7. *Tribuna da Imprensa*, March 23, 14, 28–29, 1964. Wilson Figueiredo, "A Margem Esquerda," pp. 213–216. Marcílio Marques Moreira (ed.), *Perfis Parlamentares 21: San Tiago Dantas*, pp. 62–66. "As Frentes Populares e o Brasil," *Jornal do Brasil*, March 29, 1964.

8. Ernâni do Amaral Peixoto, interview, Brasília, October 15, 1965.

9. Carlos Lacerda, *Depoimento*, p. 275. Hélio Fernandes column, "Fatos & Rumores: Em Primeira Mão," *Tribuna da Imprensa*, March 25, 1964. *O Estado de S. Paulo*, March 25, 1964. Rebello Filho, *Carlos Lacerda, Meu Amigo*, p. 118.

5. The Navy Mutiny and the Reactions (March 25–27, 1964)

1. *Tribuna da Imprensa*, March 26–27, 1964. *O Estado de S. Paulo*, March 27, 1964.

2. *Tribuna da Imprensa* and *O Estado de S. Paulo*, March 25, 1964. Mário Victor, *Cinco Anos que Abalaram o Brasil*, p. 494.

3. *Correio da Manhã* and *O Estado de S. Paulo*, March 26, 1964. Abelardo Jurema, *Sexta-Feira, 13*, pp. 152–155.

4. *O Estado de S. Paulo*, March 27, 1964. Araújo Netto, "A Paisagem," in Alberto Dines et al., *Os Idos de Março*, p. 54.

5. Dante Pelacani, interview, São Paulo, November 24, 1968.

6. *Tribuna da Imprensa*, March 28–29, 1964.

7. Jurema, *Sexta-Feira, 13*, p. 162.

8. *Tribuna da Imprensa*, March 31, 1964. *Jornal do Brasil*, quoted in Mário Victor, *Cinco Anos*, p. 502.

9. Haroldo Veloso, interviews, Marietta, Georgia, January 6–7, 1966.

10. *O Estado de S. Paulo*, March 29, 1964.

11. Wilson Figueiredo, "A Margem Esquerda," in Alberto Dines et al., *Os Idos de Março*, p. 235.

12. Ibid., p. 303. Antônio Carlos Muricy, *Os Motivos da Revolução Democrática Brasileira: Palestras Pronunciadas na Televisão Canal 2 nos Dias 19 e 25 de Maio de 1964* (Recife: Imprensa Oficial, n.d.), pp. 36–37. Siseno Sarmento, interview, São Paulo, November 21, 1967.

13. José Stacchini, *Março 64: Mobilização da Audácia*, p. 64.

14. Herbert Levy, interview, Brasília, October 20, 1965.

15. Olympio Mourão Filho, *Memórias: A Verdade de um Revolucionário* (Porto Alegre: L&PM Editores, 1978), p. 307, footnote 1. Carlos Castello Branco, "Da Conspiração à Revolução," in Alberto Dines et al., *Os Idos de Março*, p. 298. Carlos Luís Guedes, *Tinha que ser Minas* (Rio de Janeiro: Nova Fronteira, 1979), pp. 197–198.

16. Carlos Lacerda, *Depoimento*, p. 282. Hugo Levy, interview, Rio de Janeiro, March 2, 1991. Oscar Klabin Segall, interview, São Paulo, March 8, 1991. Alfredo C. Machado, interview, Rio de Janeiro, July 7, 1983. Claudio Mello e Sousa, "O Vizinho do Presidente," in Dines et al., *Os Idos de Março*, pp. 178–179.

17. Salvador Mandim, transcript of interview taped by the Sociedade dos Amigos de Carlos Lacerda, p. 24. Gustavo Borges, "Operação Salame," Part I, *O Cruzeiro*, May 30, 1964. João Paulo Burnier entry in *Dicionário Histórico-Biográfico Brasileiro, 1930–1983*. Carlos Lacerda, *Depoimento*, p. 191. Antonio Dias Rebello Filho, *Carlos Lacerda, Meu Amigo*, pp. 122–124. Claudio Mello e Sousa, "O Vizinho do Presidente," p. 181.

18. Carlos Lacerda, "A Marinha e ao Povo," in Rebello Filho, *Carlos Lacerda, Meu Amigo*, pp. 153–156.

19. Raphael de Almeida Magalhães, interview, Rio de Janeiro, August 9, 1989. Hugo Levy, interview, Rio de Janeiro, August 13, 1989. Oscar Klabin Segall, interview, March 8, 1991. Nelson and Doris Pereira, interview, São Paulo, August 4, 1983.

6. Mourão Decides to March (March 31, 1964)

1. Antonio Dias Rebello Filho, *Carlos Lacerda, Meu Amigo*, pp. 119–120.

2. Gustavo Borges, "Operação Salame," Part I, *O Cruzeiro*, May 30, 1964, p. 16.

3. *Tribuna da Imprensa*, March 31, 1964.

4. Abelardo Jurema, *Sexta-Feira, 13*, pp. 168–171.

5. Ibid., pp. 168–175. Mário Victor, *Cinco Anos que Abalaram o Brasil*, p. 506.

6. *Correio da Manhã*, March 31, 1964. Jurema, *Sexta-Feira, 13*, p. 174. Mário Victor, *Cinco Anos*, pp. 507–508.

7. Claudio Mello e Sousa, "O Vizinho do Presidente," in Alberto Dines et al., *Os Idos de Março*, pp. 174–175.

8. Olympio Mourão Filho, *Memórias: A Verdade de um Revolucionário*, pp. 308–309. *O Jornal*, April 1, 1964.

9. Pedro Gomes, "Minas: Do Diálogo ao 'Front,'" in Alberto Dines et al., *Os Idos de Março*, pp. 104–106. Olímpio Mourão Filho, interview, Rio de Janeiro, October 9, 1965. Armando Falcão, interview, Rio de Janeiro, November 30, 1966. Guedes, *Tinha que ser Minas*, pp. 195–213. Hernani D'Aguiar, *A Revolução por Dentro* (Rio de Janeiro: Editora Artenova, 1976), p. 146. José Stacchini, *Março 64: Mobilização da Audácia*, p. 75. Vernon Walters, interview, Rio de Janeiro, December 9, 1966.

10. Rebello Filho, *Carlos Lacerda, Meu Amigo*, pp. 121–122. Gustavo Borges, "Operação Salame," Part I, *O Cruzeiro*, May 30, 1964, p. 16, Part II, *O Cruzeiro*, June 6, 1964, p. 118. Claudio Mello e Sousa, "O Vizinho do Presidente," p. 174.

11. Rebello Filho, *Carlos Lacerda, Meu Amigo*, p. 124. Claudio Mello e Sousa, "O Vizinho do Presidente," p. 175.

12. Roberto de Abreu Sodré, interview, São Paulo, August 3, 1983. Rubens Resstel and Flávio Galvão, interview, São Paulo, August 4, 1983.

13. Armando Daudt d'Oliveira, interviews, Rio de Janeiro, August 10, 14, 1983.

14. Ibid. Carlos Lacerda, *Depoimento*, p. 283.

15. Gustavo Borges, interview, Rio de Janeiro, August 14, 1983. Amaury Kruel, interview, São Paulo, November 16, 1965.

16. Araújo Netto, "A Paisagem," in Dines et al., *Os Idos de Março*, p. 61. *Correio da Manhã*, March 31, 1964.

7. Defending Guanabara Palace (March 31–April 1, 1964)

1. Gilberto Crockatt de Sá, interview, Rio de Janeiro, December 17, 1968. *O Jornal* and *O Estado de S. Paulo*, April 1, 1964. Juscelino Kubitschek entry in *Dicionário Histórico-Biográfico Brasileiro, 1930–1983*.

2. Amaury Kruel, interviews, São Paulo, November 16, 1965, Guanabara, October 21, 1967.

3. Gustavo Borges, "Operação Salame," Part II, *O Cruzeiro*, June 6, 1964, p. 118. *O Jornal*, April 1, 1964.

4. *O Jornal*, April 1, 2, 1964.

5. Carlos Lacerda, interview, Rio de Janeiro, October 11, 1967. Carlos Lacerda, *Depoimento*, pp. 285–286.

6. Claudio Mello e Sousa, "O Vizinho do Presidente," in Alberto Dines et al., *Os Idos de Março*, pp. 179–181. Hélio Silva, *1964: Golpe ou Contragolpe?*, p. 387. Pedro Ernesto Mariano de Azevedo, FAX message to JWFD, Rio de Janeiro, April 25, 1994.

7. Claudio Mello e Sousa, "O Vizinho do Presidente," pp. 179–181.

8. Cândido Aragão entry in *Dicionário Histórico-Biográfico Brasileiro, 1930–1983*. Armando de Abreu in transcript of Salvador Mandim tape for the Sociedade dos Amigos de Carlos Lacerda, p. 26.

9. *Tribuna da Imprensa*, April 2, 1964. Nemo Canabarro Lucas entry in *Dicionário Histórico-Biográfico Brasileiro, 1930–1983*. Antonio Dias Rebello Filho, *Carlos Lacerda, Meu Amigo*, p. 125.

10. Neiva Moreira, *O pilão da madrugada: Um depoimento a José Louzeiro* (Rio de Janeiro: Editora Terceiro Mundo, 1989), pp. 172–175.

11. Abelardo Jurema, *Sexta-Feira, 13*, pp. 188–189. Cândido Aragão entry in *Dicionário Histórico-Biográfico Brasileiro, 1930–1983*.

12. Neiva Moreira, *O pilão da madrugada*, p. 177. Sérgio Lacerda, interview, Rio de Janeiro, August 17, 1988.

13. Amaury Kruel, interview, October 21, 1967.

14. Claudio Mello e Sousa, "O Vizinho do Presidente," p. 179. Carlos Lacerda, *Depoimento*, p. 284.

15. *Tribuna da Imprensa*, April 2, 1964.

16. Ibid. *O Jornal*, April 2, 1964. Rebello Filho, *Carlos Lacerda, Meu Amigo*, p. 125.

17. Luís Viana Filho, *O Governo Castelo Branco* (Rio de Janeiro: Livraria José Olympio Editôra, 1975), pp. 26–27. *Tribuna da Imprensa*, April 2, 1964. Carlos Lacerda, *Depoimento*, p. 284. Claudio Mello e Sousa, "O Vizinho do Presidente," p. 183.

18. Pedro Ernesto Mariano de Azevedo, FAX message to JWFD, Rio de Janeiro, April 25, 1994. Claudio Mello e Sousa, "O Vizinho do Presidente," pp. 182–183. Richard Bourne, *Political Leaders of Latin America* (New York: Alfred A. Knopf, 1970), p. 212.

19. Abelardo Jurema, *Sexta-Feira, 13*, pp. 194, 202. Gustavo Borges, "Operação Salame," Part III, *O Cruzeiro*, June 20, 1964. *O Estado de S. Paulo*, April 2, 1964. Abelardo Jurema, interview, Rio de Janeiro, July 27, 1976.

20. *O Jornal*, April 2, 1964. Gustavo Borges, "Operação Salame," Part III, *O Cruzeiro*, June 20, 1964, p. 12. *Tribuna da Imprensa*, April 2, 1964.

21. *O Jornal*, April 2, 1964. Claudio Mello e Sousa, "O Vizinho do Presidente," pp. 184–186.

22. *O Jornal*, April 2, 1964. Claudio Mello e Sousa, "O Vizinho do Presidente," pp. 184–186.

23. Ibid.

24. *O Jornal*, April 2, 1964. Claudio Mello e Sousa, "O Vizinho do Presidente," pp. 184–186. Rebello Filho, *Carlos Lacerda, Meu Amigo*, pp. 126–127. Hernani D'Aguiar, *A Revolução por Dentro*, pp. 162–163. See Carlos Lacerda, *Depoimento*, p. 288.

25. Armando Daudt d'Oliveira, interview, Rio de Janeiro, August 10, 1983.

8. Comments

1. Gilberto Crockatt de Sá, interview, Rio de Janeiro, October 11, 1967.

2. Summaries of polls consulted in 1987 by Michael L. Conniff.

3. F. Zenha Machado, *Os Últimos Dias do Govêrno de Vargas* (Rio de Janeiro: Editôra Lux Ltda., 1955), pp. 81–82.

4. Carlos Heitor Cony, "Da arte de falar mal: O mêdo e a responsabilidade," *Correio da Manhã*, April 11, 1964.

5. Maurício Goulart, interview, São José do Rio Prêto, November 12, 1968.

6. *O Estado de S. Paulo*, October 10, 1963.

7. "A Crise Vista de Brasília," *O Cruzeiro–Extra*, April 10, 1964, pp. 56–57.

8. *O Jornal*, April 2, 1964.

9. Edgar Flexa Ribeiro, interview, Rio de Janeiro, August 19, 1989. José Roberto Rego Monteiro, interview with DFR, Rio de Janeiro, August 13, 1985.

10. Raphael de Almeida Magalhães, interview, Rio de Janeiro, August 9, 1989.

V. Defender of the Revolution (April–June 1964)

I. Lacerda Decides to Support Castello Branco (April 3, 1964)

1. *Tribuna da Imprensa,* April 3, 1964.
2. Ibid. Governor's office, Assessoria de Imprensa release of April 2, 1964 (in the Walter Cunto Collection).
3. *Tribuna da Imprensa* and *O Jornal,* April 3, 1964.
4. Raphael de Almeida Magalhães, interview, Rio de Janeiro, November 19, 1975.
5. Ibid. Mauro Borges entry in *Dicionário Histórico-Biográfico Brasileiro, 1930–1983.*
6. Raphael de Almeida Magalhães, interview, November 19, 1975. Carlos Lacerda, *Depoimento,* p. 294.
7. Raphael de Almeida Magalhães, interview, November 19, 1975.
8. Carlos Lacerda, interview, Rio de Janeiro, October 11, 1967.
9. *O Jornal,* April 4, 1964. Mauro Borges, *O Golpe em Goiás: História de uma Grande Traição* (Rio de Janeiro: Editôra Civilização Brasileira, 1965), p. 111.

2. Lacerda Calls Costa e Silva a Usurper (April 4–5, 1964)

1. *Correio da Manhã,* April 3, 4, 1964. *O Jornal,* April 4, 5, 1964.
2. *Diário Carioca,* April 5, 1964. *O Estado de S. Paulo,* dateline Rio de Janeiro, April 4, 1964. *Jornal do Brasil,* April 5, 1964. Carlos Lacerda, letter to Olavo Bilac Pinto, Rio de Janeiro, April 4, 1964, in CCL. *O Jornal,* April 4, 5, 1964. Governor's Office, Assessoria de Imprensa, release dated April 4, 1964 (in the Walter Cunto Collection). Arturo Frondizi was president of Argentina, 1958–1962.
3. Carlos Lacerda, "Rosas e Pedras do Meu Caminho," Chapter 5 (*Manchete,* May 13, 1967), p. 28.
4. Memorandum to Marcelo Garcia, Office of the Governor of Guanabara, April 3, 1964, in CCL. Carlos Lacerda, "Rosas e Pedras do Meu Caminho," Chapter 12 (*Manchete,* July 1, 1967), p. 104. Carlos Lacerda in *Jornal da Tarde,* November 3, 1966.
5. José Costa Cavalcanti, "Depoimento do Ministro Costa Cavalcanti sobre a Escolha do Presidente Castello Branco para a Presidência da República" (transcript of tape), October 22, 1976, received by JWFD from Paulo V. Castello Branco, pp. 5–7.
6. *Correio da Manhã,* April 4, 1964. Mauro Borges, *O Golpe em Goiás,* p. 110. Ademar de Barros, interview, São Paulo, December 1, 1965. Carlos Lacerda, *Depoimento,* p. 294. José de Magalhães Pinto, interview, Brasília, October 23, 1975. Carlos Lacerda, interview, Rio de Janeiro, September 23, 1975.

7. Augusto César Moniz de Aragão, "O depoimento do General Moniz de Aragão," *O Globo*, March 30, 1975. See also Augusto César Moniz de Aragão, "O seu castigo é decompor-se vivo," *O Globo*, August 29, 1967, and "Um Momento Decisivo," in *Revista do Clube Militar*, March–April 1977.

8. Carlos Lacerda, *Depoimento*, p. 294. *O Jornal*, April 5, 1964.

9. *O Jornal*, April 5, 1964.

10. Ibid. *Correio da Manhã*, April 5, 1964. See also "Terrorismo, Não," *Correio da Manhã*, April 3, 1964. Olavo Bilac Pinto, interview, Brasília, October 21, 1975. Auro de Moura Andrade, interview, São Paulo, November 6, 1975. Carlos Medeiros Silva, interview, Rio de Janeiro, November 12, 1975. Brazilian Constitution of 1946, Article 139, Clause I, Section c; see *Constituições do Brasil* (São Paulo: Saraiva, 1963).

11. Mauro Borges, *O Golpe em Goiás*, p. 112.

12. Carlos Lacerda, interviews, Rio de Janeiro, October 11, 1967, September 23, 1975. Carlos Lacerda, *Depoimento*, p. 293. José Costa Cavalcanti, "Depoimento do Ministro Costa Cavalcanti," p. 10.

13. Mauro Borges, *O Golpe em Goiás*, pp. 112–113. Carlos Lacerda, interview, September 23, 1975. Carlos Lacerda, *Depoimento*, p. 296. Murilo Melo Filho, "O Dia em que Lacerda Renunciou," *Manchete*, November 7, 1981.

14. José Costa Cavalcanti, "Depoimento do Ministro Costa Cavalcanti," pp. 10–11. Mauro Borges, *O Golpe em Goiás*, pp. 113–114.

15. Nei Braga, interview, Brasília, October 23, 1975. Carlos Lacerda, interview, September 23, 1975. Carlos Lacerda, *Depoimento*, p. 297. José Costa Cavalcanti, "Depoimento do Ministro Costa Cavalcanti," p. 11.

16. Juarez Távora, "Esclarecimentos prestados pelo Marechal Juarez Távora à margem da escolha do Marechal Castello Branco para a Presidência da República em abril de 1964," typewritten manuscript, Rio de Janeiro, October 12, 1966, prepared for JWFD; full text given in Leoncio Basbaum, *História Sincera da República*, vol. 4 (São Paulo: Editora Fulgor, 1968), pp. 135–137. Juarez Távora, *Missão Cumprida: Relatório sôbre Atividades do extinto Ministério de Viação e Obras Públicas, no Triênio Abril 1964–Março 1967* (Rio de Janeiro: Seção Gráfica do D.N.E.F., 1969), pp. 15–16.

17. Mauro Borges, *O Golpe em Goiás*, pp. 114–115.

18. Ibid. Costa Cavalcanti, "Depoimento do Ministro Costa Cavalcanti," pp. 11–12.

19. Ibid. *Tribuna da Imprensa*, April 4–5, 1964. Nei Braga, interview, October 23, 1975. Carlos Lacerda, letter to Artur da Costa e Silva, Rio de Janeiro, April 5, 1964, in Juracy Magalhães, *Minhas Memórias Provisórias*, facsimile between pp. 172–173; text on pp. 303–304.

20. Danillo Nunes, interview, Rio de Janeiro, March 10, 1992, letters to JWFD, Rio de Janeiro, April 7, May 19, 1992, and letter to Floriano Peixoto Faria Lima, n.p., n.d. Siseno Sarmento, interview, São Paulo, November 21, 1967. Costa Cavalcanti, "Depoimento do Ministro Costa Cavalcanti," pp. 12–13. Roberto de Abreu Sodré, letter to Luiz Viana Filho, São Paulo, September 28, 1971, in Luiz Viana Filho, compiler, *Castello Branco: Testemunhos*

de uma época (Brasília: Editora Universidade de Brasília, 1986), pp. 83–105; see p. 87. Juracy Magalhães, "Juracy acha que Lacerda é ciclotímico," *Jornal do Brasil*, November 24, 1966. Murilo Melo Filho, "O Dia em que Lacerda Renunciou." Antonio Dias Rebello Filho, letter to Murilo Melo Filho, in *O Estado de S. Paulo*, November 19, 1981. Carlos Lacerda, interview, September 23, 1975.

3. The Institutional Act (April 9, 1964)

1. José Costa Cavalcanti, "Depoimento do Ministro Costa Cavalcanti sobre a escolha do Presidente Castello Branco para a Presidência da República," October 22, 1976, p. 19.
2. Mauro Borges, *O Golpe em Goiás*, pp. 115–116. Danillo Nunes, letter to JWFD, Rio de Janeiro, May 19, 1992.
3. "Como o General Castelo deu o sim," *Jornal do Brasil*, April 7, 1964. Carlos Medeiros Silva, interviews, Rio de Janeiro, November 12, December 18, 1975. Luís Viana Filho, *O Governo Castelo Branco*, p. 56.
4. Raphael de Almeida Magalhães, interview, Rio de Janeiro, November 19, 1975.
5. Carlos Medeiros Silva, interview, November 12, 1975. Francisco Campos, interview, Rio de Janeiro, December 14, 1965. Raphael de Almeida Magalhães, interview, November 19, 1975.
6. *Tribuna da Imprensa*, April 7, 8, 1964.
7. Roberto de Abreu Sodré, interview, São Paulo, August 3, 1983. Carlos Lacerda, *Depoimento*, pp. 292–293. Roberto de Abreu Sodré in Luiz Viana Filho, compiler, *Castello Branco: Testemunhos de uma época*, p. 88.
8. Carlos Lacerda, *Depoimento*, p. 293. *Tribuna da Imprensa*, April 9, 1964.
9. *Tribuna da Imprensa*, April 8, 1964.
10. Ibid., April 10, 1964. *Correio da Manhã*, April 10, 11, 1964. *Jornal do Brasil*, April 10, 1964.
11. *Correio da Manhã*, April 11, 1964.
12. *Tribuna da Imprensa*, April 11–12, 17, 1964.

4. Conversations with Castello Branco (April 1964)

1. Roberto de Abreu Sodré, letter to Luiz Viana Filho, September 28, 1971; see p. 88 of Luiz Viana Filho, compiler, *Castello Branco: Testemunhos de uma época*.
2. Armando Falcão, quoted in Luís Viana Filho, *O Governo Castelo Branco*, p. 63.
3. Sérgio Lacerda, letter to *Jornal do Brasil*, published November 24, 1966. Sérgio Lacerda, interview, Rio de Janeiro, August 17, 1988. Armando Falcão, *Tudo a Declarar* (Rio de Janeiro: Editora Nova Fronteira, 1989), p. 285.
4. Sérgio Lacerda, letter to *Jornal do Brasil*, published November 24, 1966. Sérgio Lacerda, interview, August 17, 1988.

5. Falcão, *Tudo a Declarar*, p. 285. Falcão, quoted in Luís Viana Filho, *O Governo Castelo Branco*, pp. 63–64. Carlos Lacerda, *Depoimento*, p. 310. Carlos Lacerda, interview, Rio de Janeiro, September 23, 1975.

6. Sérgio Lacerda, letter to *Jornal do Brasil*, published November 24, 1966. Luís Viana Filho, *O Governo Castelo Branco*, pp. 63–64.

7. Carlos Lacerda, interview, September 23, 1975. Carlos Lacerda, *Depoimento*, p. 299.

8. Carlos Lacerda, *Depoimento*, pp. 300–301.

9. Ibid.

10. Falcão, *Tudo a Declarar*, pp. 279–280.

11. Carlos Lacerda, *Depoimento*, pp. 300, 302. Carlos Lacerda, interview, September 23, 1975. Raphael de Almeida Magalhães, interview, Rio de Janeiro, November 19, 1975. Luís Viana Filho, *O Governo Castelo Branco*, pp. 64–65.

12. Abreu Sodré, in Luiz Viana Filho, compiler, *Castello Branco: Testemunhos de uma época*, p. 88. *Tribuna da Imprensa*, April 16, 17, 1964.

13. Humberto de Alencar Castello Branco, *Discursos, 1964* (n.p.: Secretaria de Imprensa, n.d.), pp. 12–15.

14. Abreu Sodré in Luiz Viana Filho, compiler, *Castello Branco: Testemunhos de uma época*, p. 89. Vasco Leitão da Cunha, interview, Rio de Janeiro, November 23, 1974. Artur S. Moura, interview, Rio de Janeiro, December 11, 1974. Raimundo de Moura Brito, interview, Rio de Janeiro, December 22, 1974. José Jerônimo Moscardo de Souza, interview, Brasília, October 23, 1975. Ruy Mesquita, interview, São Paulo, November 6, 1975.

15. *Tribuna da Imprensa*, April 17, 1964.

16. Ibid., April 15, 18–19, 1964.

17. Ibid., April 18–19, 1964. *Diário Carioca*, April 23, 1964 (referring to Lacerda's televised speech of April 18, 1964). Sérgio Mário Pasquali, interview, Brasília, February 15, 1992.

18. Abreu Sodré, in Luiz Viana Filho, compiler, *Castello Branco: Testemunhos de uma época*, p. 89. *Tribuna da Imprensa*, April 20, 1964. José Luiz Moreira de Souza, interview, Rio de Janeiro, August 15, 1983.

19. Carlos Lacerda, *Depoimento*, p. 310. Carlos Lacerda in *Jornal da Tarde*, March 3, 1966.

20. *Tribuna da Imprensa*, April 20, 1964. José Luiz Moreira de Souza, interview, August 15, 1983. *O Estado de S. Paulo*, April 21, 1964.

21. Marcelo Garcia, interview, Rio de Janeiro, August 18, 1983.

22. Carlos Lacerda, *Depoimento*, p. 310. *O Globo*, April 13, 1964.

23. *O Estado de S. Paulo*, April 21, 1964. *Tribuna da Imprensa*, April 20, 1964.

24. Ibid.

25. *Tribuna da Imprensa*, April 20, 1964.

26. Carlos Lacerda, *Depoimento*, pp. 303–304.

27. Lincoln Gordon, cable to Department of State, Rio de Janeiro, April 20, 1964 (copy in Lyndon Baines Johnson Library, Austin, Texas), describing conversation with Milton Campos.

28. *Tribuna da Imprensa*, April 20, 1964.

5. A New Vice Governor for Guanabara (April 21–25, 1964)

1. *Diário Carioca*, April 26–27, 1964. *Constituição do Estado da Guanabara promulgada em 27 de março de 1961*, Article 27, paragraph 4.

2. Raphael de Almeida Magalhães, interview, Rio de Janeiro, August 9, 1989. Célio Borja, interview, Rio de Janeiro, August 14, 1989. Abreu Sodré, in Luiz Viana Filho, compiler, *Castello Branco: Testemunhos de uma época*, p. 90.

3. *Correio da Manhã*, April 17, 10, 1964. *Diário Carioca*, April 11, 1964.

4. Edmar Morel, *O Golpe Começou em Washington* (Rio de Janeiro: Editôra Civilização Brasileira, 1965), pp. 253–254.

5. *Correio da Manhã*, April 17, 1964. *Diário Carioca*, April 23, 1964. *O Estado de S. Paulo*, April 26, 1964.

6. *Correio da Manhã*, April 18, 19, 21, 1964.

7. Mauro Magalhães, *Carlos Lacerda*, p. 302. Abreu Sodré, in Luiz Viana Filho, compiler, *Castello Branco: Testemunhos de uma época*, pp. 89–90. *Diário Carioca*, April 22, 1964. *Tribuna da Imprensa*, April 23, 1964.

8. *Diário Carioca*, April 23, 1964. *Correio da Manhã*, April 22, 23, 1964. *O Estado de S. Paulo*, April 23, 1964.

9. *Diário Carioca*, *O Estado de S. Paulo*, and *Correio da Manhã*, April 23, 1964.

10. *Diário Carioca*, April 23, 1964.

11. Ibid. *Correio da Manhã*, April 23, 1964.

12. Célio Borja, interview, August 14, 1989. Mauro Magalhães, *Carlos Lacerda*, pp. 302–304.

13. *Correio da Manhã*, April 25, 26, 1964. *O Estado de S. Paulo*, April 25, 1964.

14. Hugo Levy, interview, Rio de Janeiro, August 1, 1989. *Correio da Manhã*, April 26, 1964.

15. *Diário Carioca*, April 26–27, 1964. *O Estado de S. Paulo*, April 26, 1964.

16. *Correio da Manhã*, April 25, 26, May 20, 1964. *Tribuna da Imprensa*, April 28, 1964.

17. Raphael de Almeida Magalhães, interview, August 9, 1989. *Correio da Manhã*, April 26, 1964. Danton Jobim in *Diário Carioca*, April 26–27, 1964. *Tribuna da Imprensa*, April 28, 1964. *Jornal do Brasil*, April 20, 1965.

6. The Orly Airport Interview (Paris, April 23, 1964)

1. *O Estado de S. Paulo*, April 23, 1964. Abreu Sodré in Luiz Viana Filho, compiler, *Castello Branco: Testemunhos de uma época*, p. 90.

2. Carlos Lacerda, *Depoimento*, p. 311. *O Estado de S. Paulo*, April 24, 1964.

3. *O Estado de S. Paulo*, April 24, 1964.

4. Abreu Sodré in Luiz Viana Filho, compiler, *Castello Branco: Testemunhos de uma época*, pp. 91–92. Newton Freitas in *O Estado de S. Paulo*, April 29, 1964.

5. Abreu Sodré in Luiz Viana Filho, compiler, *Castello Branco: Testemunhos de uma época*, pp. 91–92. Newton Freitas in *O Estado de S. Paulo*, April 29, 1964.

6. Carlos Lacerda, "A Entrevista de Orly," in Carlos Lacerda, *Palavras e Ação* (Rio de Janeiro: Distribuidora Record, 1965), pp. 134–139; see pp. 134–135.

7. Ibid., pp. 135–137. *O Estado de S. Paulo*, April 24, 1964.

8. Carlos Lacerda, *Depoimento*, pp. 311–312. Roberto de Abreu Sodré, interview, August 3, 1983. Golbery do Couto e Silva, interview, Brasília, August 23, 1983.

9. Carlos Lacerda, *Palavras e Ação*, p. 135. *O Estado de S. Paulo*, April 24, 1964.

10. Carlos Lacerda, *Palavras e Ação*, pp. 136–137. *O Estado de S. Paulo*, April 24, 1964.

11. *O Estado de S. Paulo*, April 24, 1964. Carlos Lacerda, *Palavras e Ação*, p. 139.

12. *O Estado de S. Paulo*, April 24, 25, 1964. *Correio da Manhã*, April 26, 1964.

13. *O Estado de S. Paulo*, April 29, 1964. *Correio da Manhã*, May 1, 1964. *Tribuna da Imprensa*, April 27, 1964.

14. Abreu Sodré, in Luiz Viana Filho, compiler, *Castello Branco: Testemunhos de uma época*, p. 94. Roberto Campos and Golbery do Couto e Silva, interviews, Brasília, August 23, 1983.

15. *O Estado de S. Paulo*, April 28, 30, 1964.

16. Abreu Sodré, in Luiz Viana Filho, compiler, *Castello Branco: Testemunhos de uma época*, p. 92.

17. Ibid. Antônio Carlos de Almeida Braga, interview, New York, September 2, 1988.

18. *O Estado de S. Paulo*, April 30, May 1, 1964.

7. Sandra Cavalcanti's Peace Mission to Paris (May 1964)

1. Victor Coelho Bouças, interview, Rio de Janeiro, August 2, 1984. *O Estado de S. Paulo*, May 1, 8, 12, 1964.

2. Maria Abreu Sodré, interview, São Paulo, July 21, 1983. *O Estado de S. Paulo*, May 1, 1964.

3. Maria Abreu Sodré, interview, July 21, 1983. Maria Cristina Lacerda Simões Lopes, interview, Petrópolis, August 13, 1983. Alfredo C. Machado, interview, Rio de Janeiro, July 7, 1983. Antônio Carlos de Almeida Braga, interview, New York, September 2, 1988.

4. *O Estado de S. Paulo*, May 10, 14, 1964.

5. Roberto de Abreu Sodré, in Luiz Viana Filho, compiler, *Castello Branco: Testemunhos de uma época*, p. 93. Antônio Carlos de Almeida Braga, interview, September 2, 1988.

6. *O Estado de S. Paulo*, May 19, 1964. Maria Cristina Lacerda Simões Lopes, interview with DFR, Rio de Janeiro, January 4, 1988.

7. Abreu Sodré, in Luiz Viana Filho, compiler, *Castello Branco: Testemunhos de uma época*, p. 93. Almeida Braga, interview, September 2, 1988.

8. *O Estado de S. Paulo*, May 17, 19, 1964. Abreu Sodré, in Luiz Viana Filho, compiler, *Castello Branco: Testemunhos de uma época*, p. 93.

9. *O Estado de S. Paulo*, May 20, 22, 1964. Joaquim Guilherme da Silveira,

interview, Rio de Janeiro, August 9, 1983. Maria Cristina Lacerda Simões Lopes, interview with DFR, Rio de Janeiro, August 26, 1986.

10. Carlos Lacerda, "Entrevista na Rádio Europa," in Carlos Lacerda, *Palavras e Ação*, pp. 140–150; see pp. 142, 141, 143–144, 148. *O Estado de S. Paulo*, May 23, 1964.

11. Carlos Lacerda, *Depoimento*, p. 313.

12. *O Estado de S. Paulo*, May 17, 1964. Sandra Cavalcanti, interview, Rio de Janeiro, November 18, 1975.

13. Sandra Cavalcanti, interview, November 18, 1975. Oscar Klabin Segall, interview, São Paulo, March 8, 1991. *O Estado de S. Paulo*, May 21, 1964. *Correio da Manhã*, May 22, 1964. Abreu Sodré, in Luiz Viana Filho, compiler, *Castello Branco: Testemunhos de uma época*, p. 93.

14. Sandra Cavalcanti, interview, November 18, 1975.

15. Ibid. *O Estado de S. Paulo*, June 2, 9, 1964. *Correio da Manhã*, June 7, 1964. *Jornal do Brasil*, June 16, 1964.

8. Acclaim in Portugal (June 12–17, 1964)

1. *O Estado de S. Paulo*, May 26, 27, 1964.

2. Ibid., June 5, 6, 7, 9, 10, 1964.

3. Ibid., June 11, 1964.

4. Raphael de Almeida Magalhães, interview, Rio de Janeiro, March 21, 1991. Sérgio Lacerda, letter published in *O Estado de S. Paulo*, May 4, 1978.

5. Victor Coelho Bouças, interview, Rio de Janeiro, August 2, 1984. Lamy Cunto, interview, Rio de Janeiro, August 12, 1989. Roberto de Abreu Sodré in *Jornal do Brasil*, June 19, 1964. *O Estado de S. Paulo*, June 14, 1964.

6. Richard Bourne, *Political Leaders of Latin America*, p. 234.

7. Carlos Lacerda, *Depoimento*, p. 316.

8. *Tribuna da Imprensa*, April 28, 29, 1959.

9. Carlos Lacerda, *Depoimento*, pp. 315–316. Carlos Lacerda, in *Jornal da Tarde*, May 12, 20, 1966, and in *O Estado de S. Paulo*, May 20, 1973, January 12, 1975.

10. Ibid.

11. *O Estado de S. Paulo*, June 16, 1964.

12. Ibid., June 12, 13, 14, 16, 1964.

13. Luís Forjaz Trigueiros, interview with DFR, Lisbon, June 27, 1984.

14. *O Estado de S. Paulo*, June 13, 14, 16, 1964.

15. Victor Coelho Bouças, interview, August 2, 1984. *Jornal do Brasil*, June 17, 1964. *O Estado de S. Paulo*, June 19, 1964.

16. *Jornal do Brasil* and *O Estado de S. Paulo*, June 18, 1964.

9. Lacerda Cuts His Mission Short (July 1964)

1. *O Estado de S. Paulo*, June 20, 22, 1964. *Jornal do Brasil*, June 23, 1964. National Broadcasting Company, *Meet the Press*, vol. 8, no. 21, June 21, 1964 (Washington, D.C.: Merkle Press, 1964).

2. Carlos Lacerda, "Um Brasileiro Fala aos Americanos," in Carlos Lacerda, *Palavras e Ação*, pp. 151–156.
3. *O Estado de S. Paulo*, June 25, 26, 1964.
4. Ibid., June 26, 1964. *Jornal do Brasil*, June 30, 1964.
5. *Jornal do Brasil* and *O Estado de S. Paulo*, June 24, 1964. Carlos Lacerda, *Depoimento*, pp. 317–318. Carlos Lacerda, interviews, Tucson, Ariz.,
February 17, 18, 1976.
6. Carlos Lacerda, *Depoimento*, p. 319. *O Estado de S. Paulo*, June 27, 28,
1964. *Jornal do Brasil*, June 30, 1964. Juracy Magalhães, "Juracy esclarece depoimento de Lacerda," *O Estado de S. Paulo*, July 20, 1977.
7. Juracy Magalhães, "Juracy esclarece depoimento de Lacerda." Antônio
Carlos de Almeida Braga, interview, New York, September 2, 1988.
8. Carlos Lacerda, *Depoimento*, p. 319. *Jornal do Brasil*, June 26, 28, 1964.
9. Juracy Magalhães, "Juracy esclarece depoimento de Lacerda." Carlos
Lacerda, *Depoimento*, p. 319.
10. Juracy Magalhães, *Minhas Memórias Provisórias*, pp. 179–180.
11. Ibid., p. 180.
12. *Jornal do Brasil*, June 30, 1964. *O Estado de S. Paulo*, June 27, 30, July 2,
1964.

10. Comments

1. *O Estado de S. Paulo*, July 2, 3, 1964.
2. Roberto de Abreu Sodré, in Luiz Viana Filho, compiler, *Castello Branco:
Testemunhos de uma época*, pp. 90–91.
3. *Jornal do Brasil*, June 28, 1964.
4. José Jerônimo Moscardo de Souza, interview, Brasília, October 23, 1975.
Severo Gomes, interview, Rio de Janeiro, July 25, 1977.
5. Raimundo de Moura Brito, "O homem que perdeu a chance," pp. 4–5 of
recollections about Castello Branco, written for Luiz Viana Filho, in files of
Paulo V. Castello Branco. João Carlos Palhares dos Santos, interview, Rio de
Janeiro, November 22, 1975.
6. Carlos Castello Branco, *Os Militares no Poder*, vol. 1, *Castelo Branco*
(Rio de Janeiro: Editora Nova Fronteira, 1977), p. 86 (item for June 28, 1964).

VI. Critic of Castello Branco's Team (July–November 1964)

1. The Congressional Commission Favors Reform (July 8, 1964)

1. *O Estado de S. Paulo*, July 2, 1964.
2. Ibid., July 4, 1964. Roberto de Abreu Sodré, interview, São Paulo, August 3, 1983.
3. Carlos Lacerda in *Jornal da Tarde*, March 3, 1966.
4. *O Estado de S. Paulo*, July 5, 1964.

5. Raphael de Almeida Magalhães, interview, Rio de Janeiro, August 17, 1983. Sandra Cavalcanti, interview, Rio de Janeiro, November 18, 1975.

6. Carlos Lacerda, *Depoimento*, p. 391. Carlos Lacerda in *Jornal da Tarde*, March 3, 1966.

7. Carlos Lacerda, "Sobre Política Exterior," item 21 in File N4 of the Humberto Castello Branco papers, consulted at the home of Paulo V. Castello Branco.

8. Aspásia Camargo, Maria Tereza Lopes Teixeira, and Maria Clara Mariani, *O Intelectual e o Político: Encontros com Afonso Arinos*, p. 201. Afonso Arinos de Melo Franco, interview, Rio de Janeiro, July 29, 1984. *O Estado de S. Paulo*, July 9, 1964. Ernâni Sátiro, interview, Rio de Janeiro, December 17, 1975. *Correio da Manhã*, July 12, 1964.

9. *O Estado de S. Paulo*, July 9, 1964.

10. Ibid. Daniel Krieger, *Desde as Missões*, p. 183.

11. Governor's office, Assessoria de Imprensa release of July 9, 1964 (in the Walter Cunto Collection). Cláudio Lacerda, *Carlos Lacerda: 10 Anos Depois*, pp. 67–69. *O Estado de S. Paulo*, July 10, 1964.

12. *Correio da Manhã*, July 12, 1964.

13. Governor's office, Assessoria de Imprensa release of July 10, 1964 (in the Walter Cunto Collection). Cláudio Lacerda, *Carlos Lacerda: 10 Anos Depois*, pp. 70–75.

2. The Extension of Castello's Mandate (July 16–22, 1964)

1. Daniel Krieger, *Desde as Missões*, pp. 181–182. *O Estado de S. Paulo*, July 14, 1964.

2. Krieger, *Desde as Missões*, pp. 187, 188. Aspásia Camargo and Walder de Góes, *Meio Século de Combate: diálogo com Cordeiro de Farias*, p. 615. *O Estado de S. Paulo*, July 14, 1964.

3. Krieger, *Desde as Missões*, pp. 183–185. *O Estado de S. Paulo* and *O Globo*, July 16, 1964.

4. Cláudio Lacerda, *Carlos Lacerda: 10 Anos Depois*, pp. 82–83.

5. *O Estado de S. Paulo*, July 15, 16, 17, 1964. Governor's office, Assessoria de Imprensa, release of July 16, 1964 (in the Walter Cunto Collection).

6. *Correio da Manhã*, July 16, 1964. Governor's office, Assessoria de Imprensa, release of July 16, 1964. *O Estado de S. Paulo*, July 17, 1964. Hugo Levy, interviews, Rio de Janeiro, August 1, 1989, March 2, 1991.

7. *O Estado de S. Paulo*, July 17, 18, 1964. Hugo Levy, interviews, August 1, 1989, March 2, 1991. Auro de Moura Andrade, *Um Congresso Contra o Arbítrio* (Rio de Janeiro: Editora Nova Fronteira, 1985), pp. 317–319.

8. *Correio da Manhã* and *O Estado de S. Paulo*, July 17, 1964. *Jornal do Brasil* entry in *Dicionário Histórico-Biográfico Brasileiro, 1930–1983*.

9. Carlos Lacerda, "Prorrogação em vez de Eleição: Escamoteação," in Carlos Lacerda, *Palavras e Ação*, pp. 102–107. *O Estado de S. Paulo*, July 18, 1964. Cláudio Lacerda, *Carlos Lacerda: 10 Anos Depois*, p. 90.

10. *O Globo*, July 21, 1964.

11. *Jornal do Brasil* and *O Estado de S. Paulo*, July 19, 1964.

12. *O Estado de S. Paulo*, July 21, 1964. Daniel Krieger, *Desde as Missões*, pp. 185–187.

13. *O Estado de S. Paulo*, July 18, 21, 23, 22, 1964.

3. Denouncing Castello's Team (July–August 1964)

1. Carlos Lacerda, letter to Emílio Nina Ribeiro, in *Jornal do Brasil, Tribuna da Imprensa,* and *O Estado de S. Paulo*, July 31, 1964. *Diário de Notícias*, August 2, 5, 1964. *Correio da Manhã*, July 19, 23, 24, 1964.

2. Carlos Lacerda, letter to Emílio Nina Ribeiro, July 31, 1964.

3. Ibid. *O Globo*, August 1, 1964.

4. American Embassy, Rio de Janeiro, cable to Washington, D.C., July 23, 1964, in National Security Files, Country File, Brazil, Lyndon Baines Johnson Library, Austin. *Jornal do Brasil*, August 2, 1964.

5. *O Globo*, August 1, 1964. *Jornal do Brasil*, July 31, August 1, 1964. *Diário de Notícias*, August 8, 15, 19, 1964.

6. *Tribuna da Imprensa*, July 31, August 1–2, 1964.

7. Wilson Figueiredo in *Jornal do Brasil*, printed in English in *Brazil Herald*, July 28, 1964. *Brazil Herald*, July 23, August 4, 1964. Júlio de Mesquita Filho, "A Revolução: depoimento de um jornalista," *O Estado de S. Paulo*, July 29, 1964. "A propalada reforma ministerial," editorial, *O Estado de S. Paulo*, July 30, 1964. Carlos Lacerda, letter to Júlio de Mesquita Filho, A Ilha, Petrópolis, July 31, 1964, published in *O Estado de S. Paulo*, August 2, 1964.

8. Luiz Viana Filho, *O Governo Castelo Branco*, pp. 115, 114, 122. Roberto de Abreu Sodré, letter to Luiz Viana Filho, São Paulo, September 28, 1971, pp. 15–16 (given in Luiz Viana Filho, compiler, *Castello Branco, Testemunhos de uma época*, pp. 95–96). Gustavo Borges, interview, Rio de Janeiro, August 14, 1983. *Diário de Notícias*, August 9, 1964. *Tribuna da Imprensa*, August 11, 1964. *O Estado de S. Paulo*, August 11, 12, 14, 15, 1964.

9. *O Estado de S. Paulo*, August 16, 1964.

10. Ibid., August 19, 1964.

11. *Diário de Notícias*, August 19, 1964. *O Estado de S. Paulo*, August 18, September 2, 1964. Raphael de Almeida Magalhães, interview, Rio de Janeiro, March 21, 1991. *Última Hora*, September 5, 1964.

4. The AMFORP Case (August–October 1964)

1. Governor's office, Assessoria de Imprensa, releases of July 6, 8, 9, 17, 1964 (in the Walter Cunto Collection). Leopoldo de Castro Ferreira, interview, Rio de Janeiro, August 23, 1989.

2. Sandra Cavalcanti, interview, Rio de Janeiro, November 18, 1975. *O Estado de S. Paulo*, June 20, July 24, August 22, 1964. Ministério do Planejamento

e Coordenação Econômica, *O Programa de Ação e as Reformas de Base*, 2 vols. (n.p.: Escritório do Planejamento, December 1965), 2:13–49. Roberto Campos, interview, Brasília, February 19, 1991.

3. Antônio Carlos de Almeida Braga, interview, New York, September 2, 1988.

4. Guilherme J. Borghoff, *Lampejos*, pp. 69–70, 189–191.

5. *O Estado de S. Paulo*, August 27, 1964.

6. Department of State, Washington, D.C., cables to American Embassy, Rio de Janeiro, June 19, August 7, 1964, National Security Files, Country File, Brazil, Lyndon Baines Johnson Library, Austin.

7. *O Estado de S. Paulo*, August 9, 1964. *Tribuna da Imprensa*, August 22–23, 1964.

8. *O Estado de S. Paulo*, September 9, 1964. *Revista Brasileira de Política Internacional* (of the Instituto Brasileiro de Relações Internacionais) 8, no. 30 (June 1965), pp. 216–238, 287–289.

9. *O Estado de S. Paulo*, August 22, September 5, 13, 15, 16, 17, 1964.

10. Ibid., September 2, 1964. Carlos Lacerda, letter to Otávio Marcondes Ferraz, Rio de Janeiro, August 31, 1964, in CCL.

11. Carlos Lacerda, letter to Juracy Magalhães, Rio de Janeiro, August 18, 1964, and Juracy Magalhães, letter to Carlos Lacerda, Washington, D.C., August 30, 1964, both in Juracy Magalhães, "Juracy esclarece depoimento de Lacerda," *O Estado de S. Paulo*, July 20, 1977. Juracy Magalhães quoted in *Tribuna da Imprensa*, August 15–16, 1964 (column of Hélio Fernandes).

12. *New York Times*, September 2, 3, 1964.

13. *O Estado de S. Paulo*, September 17, 1964.

14. Ibid., September 18, 20, 1964.

15. Ibid., September 17, 22, 24, 26, October 1, 6, 7, 8, 1964. *Diário de Notícias*, October 1, 2, 1964.

5. De Gaulle Visits Brazil (October 13–16, 1964)

1. *O Estado de S. Paulo*, September 18, 20, 1964. Antonio Dias Rebello Filho, *Carlos Lacerda, Meu Amigo*, pp. 91–93. Carlos Lacerda, "Rosas e Pedras do Meu Caminho," Chapter 9 (*Manchete*, June 10, 1967), p. 111.

2. Carlos Lacerda, "A Reforma Universitária," in Carlos Lacerda, *Palavras e Ação*, pp. 79–92; see pp. 83, 89–90.

3. *O Estado de S. Paulo*, September 20, 29, 1964. Carlos Lacerda, "Senghor, o Africano," in Carlos Lacerda, *Palavras e Ação*, pp. 170–177.

4. Antônio Mendes Vianna, letter to Humberto Castello Branco, Rome, September 14, 1964, File 02 (p. 48) in the Castello Branco documents made available by Paulo Castello Branco.

5. *Tribuna da Imprensa*, October 12, 1964. *O Estado de S. Paulo*, October 13, 14, 1964.

6. Carlos Lacerda, "De Gaulle o Grande," *Manchete*, October 17, 1964, reproduced in Carlos Lacerda, *Uma rosa é uma rosa é uma rosa*, pp. 103–112.

7. *Jornal do Brasil*, October 13, 14, 1964. *O Estado de S. Paulo*, October 13, 14, 1964.

8. *Tribuna da Imprensa*, October 15, 1964. *O Estado de S. Paulo*, October 18, 1964.

9. *Tribuna da Imprensa*, October 17–18, 1964.

10. *O Estado de S. Paulo*, October 15, 1964.

6. The Break between Lacerda and *O Globo* (October 1964)

1. *O Globo*, October 14, 15, 1964.

2. Carlos Lacerda, "Roberto Marinho: Al Capone da Imprensa," *EX-16*, November 1975, pp. 23–25, reprinted from *O Cruzeiro*, December 24, 1966; see pp. 23, 25. Edgar Flexa Ribeiro, interviews, Rio de Janeiro, July 8, 1983, August 19, 1989. Carlos Lacerda, speech at Lage Park, Governor's office, Assessoria de Imprensa release of September 26, 1965 (in the Walter Cunto Collection). Carlos Lacerda, letter to Director of *O Globo*, Rio de Janeiro, October 16, 1964, in CCL, published in *O Globo*, October 19, 1964. "A Verdade contra a Perfídia," *O Globo*, October 19, 1964. Roberto Marinho entry in *Dicionário Histórico-Biográfico Brasileiro, 1930–1983*. Carlos Osório da Silveira Neto, interview, Rio de Janeiro, August 7, 1989. See also Roberto Marinho, "Resposta a Lacerda," *Jornal da Tarde*, April 12, 1966.

3. Carlos Lacerda, "Roberto Marinho: Al Capone da Imprensa." "A Verdade contra a Perfídia," *O Globo*, October 19, 1964.

4. Carlos Lacerda, "Roberto Marinho: Al Capone da Imprensa." Mario Lorenzo Fernandez, interview, Rio de Janeiro, March 17, 1991. Carlos Lacerda, speech at Lage Park. Roberto Marinho, "Resposta a Lacerda."

5. "Uma Revisão Melancólica," *O Globo*, October 15, 1964.

6. Carlos Lacerda, letter to Director of *O Globo*, October 16, 1964.

7. "A Verdade contra a Perfídia," *O Globo*, October 19, 1964.

8. Carlos Lacerda, letter to Director of *O Globo*, Rio de Janeiro, October 19, 1964 (copy received from Walter Cunto).

7. The UDN Sets a Convention Date (October 1964)

1. *O Estado de S. Paulo*, September 20, 29, 1964.

2. Ibid., September 25, October 15, 1964. *Diário de Notícias*, September 24, 1964.

3. *O Estado de S. Paulo*, October 2, 4, 1964. *Jornal do Brasil*, October 1, 2, 1964. Olavo Bilac Pinto, interview, Brasília, October 21, 1975. Luís Viana Filho, *O Governo Castelo Branco*, pp. 278–284.

4. *O Estado de S. Paulo*, September 27, 30, October 4, 1964.

5. Fernando Pedreira column in *Tribuna da Imprensa*, October 15, 1964.

6. Raphael de Almeida Magalhães, interview, Rio de Janeiro, December 21, 1977.

7. Maria Cristina Lacerda Simões Lopes, interview with DFR, Rio de Janeiro, March 24, 1983.

8. Raphael de Almeida Magalhães, interview, December 21, 1977.

9. *O Estado de S. Paulo*, October 17, 1964. Carlos Lacerda, "A Finalidade de um Partido Político," in Carlos Lacerda, *Palavras e Ação*, pp. 93–96.

10. *Tribuna da Imprensa*, October 19, 1964. Carlos Lacerda, interview, Rio de Janeiro, September 23, 1975. Carlos Lacerda, *Depoimento*, pp. 323–324. Aliomar Baleeiro, "Recordações do Presidente H. Castelo Branco" (typewritten manuscript, n.d., in possession of JWFD), p. 17. *Tribuna da Imprensa*, October 19, 20, 1964.

11. Antonio Dias Rebello Filho, *Carlos Lacerda, Meu Amigo*, p. 186. *Tribuna da Imprensa*, October 24–25, 1964.

12. *O Estado de S. Paulo*, October 22, 1964.

13. Ibid., October 25, 1964.

14. Carlos Lacerda, letter to Humberto Castello Branco, Rio de Janeiro, October 26, 1964, in File N4 (item 2) of the Castello Branco papers at the CPDOC.

15. *O Estado de S. Paulo*, October 25, 27, 1964. Rebello Filho, *Carlos Lacerda, Meu Amigo*, pp. 164–165.

16. *O Estado de S. Paulo*, October 28, 30, 1964.

17. Ibid., October 29, November 1, 1964.

18. Ibid., October 30, November 1, 1964.

19. Humberto de Alencar Castello Branco, *Entrevistas, 1964–1965* (n.p.: Secretaria de Imprensa, 1966), p. 33. *Jornal do Brasil*, November 1, 1964. *Diário de Notícias*, November 4, 1964. *O Estado de S. Paulo*, November 3, 1964.

20. *O Estado de S. Paulo*, October 30, 31, November 4, 1964.

21. Ibid., November 5, 1964. *Diário de Notícias*, November 6, 1964.

22. *Jornal do Brasil*, November 7, 5, 1964.

23. Ibid., November 7, 8, 1964. *Correio da Manhã*, November 6, 1964. *Diário de Notícias*, November 4, 5, 1964.

24. *Diário de Notícias*, November 4, 1964. *O Estado de S. Paulo*, November 6, 1964.

8. Nominated by the UDN (November 8, 1964)

1. *O Estado de S. Paulo*, November 6, 8, 1964. Antonio Dias Rebello Filho, *Carlos Lacerda, Meu Amigo*, pp. 191–192.

2. *O Estado de S. Paulo*, November 8, 1964.

3. Ibid.

4. Ibid.

5. Ibid., November 8, 10, 1964.

6. Ibid., November 10, 1964.

7. Carlos Lacerda, "O Que Penso e o Que Farei," in Carlos Lacerda, *Palavras e Ação*, pp. 13–35.

8. *O Estado de S. Paulo*, November 10, 1964. *Jornal do Brasil*, November 10, 8, 1964. Carlos Castello Branco, *Os Militares no Poder*, vol. 1, p. 154 (entry for November 10, 1964). *Última Hora*, November 9, 1964.

9. Comments

1. Golbery do Couto e Silva, interview, Brasília, August 23, 1983.
2. Roberto Campos, "O Grande Desencontro" (typewritten chapter of "Memórias"), pp. 20–21.

VII. From Criticizing Ministers to Defaming the President (November 1964–July 1965)

1. Guest of the *Reader's Digest* (November 1964)

1. *O Estado de S. Paulo*, November 10, 11, 1964.
2. Ibid. Antonio Dias Rebello Filho, *Carlos Lacerda, Meu Amigo*, p. 193.
3. *O Estado de S. Paulo*, November 10, 1964.
4. Ibid., November 11, 1964. Carlos Lacerda, letter to Humberto Castello Branco, Rio de Janeiro, November 9, 1964, in File N4 (item 5), Castello Branco papers, CPDOC.
5. *O Estado de S. Paulo*, November 11, 1964. *Tribuna da Imprensa*, October 19, 20, 1964.
6. *Jornal do Brasil*, November 12, 13, 15, 1964. *Última Hora*, November 13, 1964.
7. *O Estado de S. Paulo*, November 13, 12, 1964.
8. Ibid., November 13, 14, 1964. Paul Thompson's remarks have been translated from the version in *O Estado de S. Paulo*, November 14, 1964.
9. *O Estado de S. Paulo*, November 14, 15, 1964. Carlos Lacerda, "Brazil's Problems Today: An Address at a Luncheon Given by the Reader's Digest to Honor Brazil at the St. Regis Hotel, New York City, November 13, 1964," typewritten text received by DFR from the Lacerda family.
10. *O Estado de S. Paulo*, November 14, 18, 19, 20, 1964.
11. Humberto Castello Branco, letter to Carlos Lacerda, Brasília, November 22, 1964, in File N4 (item 5), Castello Branco papers, CPDOC.

2. Assailing the Supreme Court (November–December 1964)

1. Carlos Lacerda, Ofício GGG nº 1,048, to Antônio Gonçalves de Oliveira, Rio de Janeiro, November 5, 1964, in CCL.
2. *Última Hora*, November 10, 1964. *Jornal do Brasil*, November 15, 1964.
3. *Tribuna da Imprensa*, November 27, 28–29, 1964.

4. Ibid., November 28–29, 1964. *O Estado de S. Paulo*, November 28, 1964.

5. *Tribuna da Imprensa*, November 28–29, 1964.

6. *O Estado de S. Paulo*, November 24, 25, 1964.

7. Ibid., December 1, 1964. *Tribuna da Imprensa*, November 30, 29, 1964.

8. Carlos Lacerda, press interview in *Correio da Manhã*, December 1, 1964. *O Estado de S. Paulo*, December 1, 1964.

9. Carlos Lacerda, telegram to Humberto Castello Branco, Rio de Janeiro, November 30, 1964, in File N4 of the Castello Branco papers at the CPDOC.

10. Carlos Lacerda, press interview, *Correio da Manhã*, December 1, 1964. *Tribuna da Imprensa* and *O Estado de S. Paulo*, December 1, 1964.

11. *Tribuna da Imprensa*, December 2, 1964. *Correio da Manhã*, December 1, 2, 1964. Hermano Alves, "Nacionalista de Ocasião," *Correio da Manhã*, December 2, 1964.

12. *Tribuna da Imprensa*, December 1, 2, 1964. Governor's office, press release of December 3, 1964 (in the Walter Cunto Collection). Célio Borja, interview, Rio de Janeiro, August 14, 1989.

13. *Tribuna da Imprensa*, December 1, 2, 1964. Govêrno Carlos Lacerda, *Mensagem à Assembléia Legislativa: 5 Anos de Govêrno*, p. 197. *Brazil Herald*, December 11, 1964. Mauro Magalhães, *Carlos Lacerda*, pp. 27–30, and interview, Rio de Janeiro, March 9, 1992. Governor's office, press releases of December 9, 12, 1964 (in the Walter Cunto Collection).

3. The Hanna Case (December 1964)

1. The role of CVRD in the newspaper publicity against Hanna is mentioned by Lucas Lopes, quoting Gabriel Passos, in the testimony of Lopes, March 17, 1965, at the CPI examining the iron ore business and Hanna in Brazil. See p. 79 of Câmara dos Deputados, *Projeto de Resolução No. 171, de 1966* (Brasília: *Diário do Congresso Nacional*, Seção I, Suplemento ao No. 54, May 13, 1967).

2. Mauro Thibau, interview, Rio de Janeiro, June 6, 1972.

3. José de Magalhães Pinto, letters to Humberto Castello Branco, October 16, 29, 1964, in File N3 (items 1, 3), Castello Branco papers, CPDOC. Luís Viana Filho, *O Governo Castelo Branco*, p. 165. Carlos Lacerda, letter to Humberto Castello Branco, September 29, 1964, in File N4 (item 1), Castello Branco papers, CPDOC. Testimony of Lucas Lopes, March 17, 1965, in Câmara dos Deputados, *Projeto de Resolução No. 171, de 1966*, pp. 78–87. Cia. de Mineração Novalimense, statement, October 22, 1964, in *Diário de Notícias*, October 23, 1964.

4. Humberto de Alencar Castello Branco, *Discursos, 1964*, pp. 189–193.

5. Hedyl Rodrigues Valle, "Documento Número 1 para a CPI Hanna-Consultec," *Tribuna da Imprensa*, November 19, 1964. *Tribuna da Imprensa*, November 20, 23, 1964.

6. Carlos Lacerda, letter to Humberto Castello Branco, Rio de Janeiro, November 28, 1964, in File N4 (item 7), Castello Branco papers, CPDOC.

7. Carlos Lacerda, "Em defesa da Revolução," *Tribuna da Imprensa*,

December 2, 1964, and "A Revolução ou a Hanna," *Tribuna da Imprensa*, December 3, 1964. *Brazil Herald*, December 5, 1964. *Tribuna da Imprensa*, November 30, 23, 1964.

8. Humberto Castello Branco, letter to Carlos Lacerda, December 3, 1964, in File N4 (item 8), Castello Branco papers, CPDOC.

9. *O Estado de S. Paulo*, December 5, 1964.

10. Ibid., December 6, 1964. Carlos Lacerda, *Depoimento*, p. 328.

11. Carlos Lacerda, *Depoimento*, pp. 328–329. Carlos Lacerda, letter to Humberto Castello Branco, Rio de Janeiro, December 4, 1964, in File N4 (item 10), Castello Branco papers, CPDOC; the letter appears also in *O Estado de S. Paulo*, December 6, 1964.

12. *O Estado de S. Paulo*, December 6, 1964.

13. *Brazil Herald*, December 15, 16, 17, 1964.

14. *O Estado de S. Paulo*, December 9, 1964. "Privilégio da Hanna," editorial, *Jornal do Brasil*, December 10, 1964.

15. José de Magalhães Pinto, letter to Humberto Castello Branco, Belo Horizonte, December 15, 1964, File N3 of the Castello Branco papers at the CPDOC; the letter appeared in *Jornal do Brasil*, December 17, 1964. "Demagogia em Tôrno da Exportação de Minérios," editorial, *O Estado de S. Paulo*, [December 1964].

16. *Tribuna da Imprensa*, December 16, 1964. Peri Bevilacqua, "Hanna É Altamente Lesiva ao Legítimo Interêsse Nacional," *Tribuna da Imprensa*, November 22, 1967. *O Estado de S. Paulo*, December 18, 19, 1964. João Agripino, testimony, February 12, 1965, at the CPI examining Hanna in Brazil, Câmara dos Deputados, *Projeto de Resolução No. 171, de 1966*, pp. 24–31. *O Estado de S. Paulo*, December 19, 1964. *Brazil Herald*, December 10, 1964.

17. Clauses 5 and 6 of Complementary Instructions of Governo Federal, Decree 55,282 of December 22, 1964. *O Estado de S. Paulo*, January 1, 1965. *Última Hora*, January 15, 1965.

18. *Tribuna da Imprensa*, December 24–25, 1964. "Minérios: Protestos de Lacerda," *O Estado de S. Paulo*, December 15, 1964.

19. *Folha da Manhã*, January 4, 1965 (dateline Rio de Janeiro, December 30, 1964). *Tribuna da Imprensa*, December 31, 1964. *Brazil Herald*, January 1–2, 1965.

20. Câmara dos Deputados, *Projeto de Resolução No. 171, de 1966*, pp. 42–43.

21. *Correio da Manhã*, December 5, 1964. *Brazil Herald*, December 25–26, 1964, January 6, 1965.

4. The Four Hundredth Year Begins (December 1964–March 1965)

1. "TERMO de Convênio," between the Justice Ministry and the Guanabara government, December 9, 1964, in CCL.

2. Guilherme Figueiredo, interview, Rio de Janeiro, July 24, 1984. João Condé, interview with DFR, Rio de Janeiro, March 23, 1983.

3. *Brazil Herald*, December 23, 1964.

4. *O Estado de S. Paulo*, January 1, 1965.

5. Ibid., January 1, 3, 1965.

6. Eurico Nogueira França, *A temporada musical no ano do IV Centenário* (n.p.: Conselho Nacional de Cultura, Ministério da Educação e Cultura, 1966), pp. 5–6. *O Estado de S. Paulo*, February 3, 5, 1965.

7. *O Estado de S. Paulo*, January 16, February 2, 1965. *Brazil Herald*, January 13, 1965.

8. *O Estado de S. Paulo*, January 20, 21, 1965. *Jornal do Brasil*, January 20, 1965.

9. *O Estado de S. Paulo*, February 2, 6, 21, 1965. *Jornal do Brasil*, February 28, 1965. *Brazil Herald*, January 13, 1965.

10. *O Estado de S. Paulo*, February 5, 1965.

5. Would-be Savior of Panair (February–March 1965)

1. Roberto Campos, interview, Rio de Janeiro, December 23, 1974. Artur S. Moura, interview, Rio de Janeiro, December 11, 1974.

2. *O Estado de S. Paulo*, February 20, 24, 26, 1965. *Jornal do Brasil*, February 16, 1965.

3. *Jornal do Brasil*, February 16, 1965. *O Estado de S. Paulo*, February 13, 16, 1965.

4. *O Estado de S. Paulo*, February 19, 20, April 13, 1965.

5. Ibid., February 16, 17, 18, 19, 26, 1965. *Jornal do Brasil*, February 16, 17, 18, 1965.

6. (Panair do Brasil) Funcionários baseados Recife e Famílias, telegram to Carlos Lacerda, Recife, February 17, 1965, in CCL. *O Estado de S. Paulo*, February 16, 17, 1965. *Jornal do Brasil*, February 17, 1965.

7. *O Estado de S. Paulo*, February 21, 17, 1965. Comissão Central dos Funcionários da Panair do Brasil, letter to Carlos Lacerda, Rio de Janeiro, February 19, 1965, in CCL.

8. *O Estado de S. Paulo*, February 21, 24, March 18, 1965.

9. Eduardo Gomes, letter to Carlos Lacerda, February 23, 1965, in CCL.

10. *O Estado de S. Paulo* and *Jornal do Brasil*, February 26, 1965.

11. *O Estado de S. Paulo*, March 6, 19, 1965.

12. Ibid., March 18, 1965.

13. Ibid., March 21, 23, 1965.

6. The Gubernatorial Election Problem (February 1965)

1. Lourenço de Almeida Prado, interview, Rio de Janeiro, August 15, 1983. Wedding invitation, in CCL. *O Estado de S. Paulo* and *Tribuna da Imprensa*, January 5, 1965.

2. *Jornal do Brasil*, February 4, 5, 6, 1965.

3. *Jornal do Brasil* and *O Estado de S. Paulo*, February 5, 6, 7, 1965.

4. Carlos Lacerda, letter to Humberto Castello Branco, Rio de Janeiro, February 6, 1965, in File N4 (item 11), Castello Branco papers, CPDOC.

5. Daniel Krieger, *Desde as Missões*, pp. 191–192. Raphael de Almeida Magalhães, interview, Rio de Janeiro, November 19, 1975. *O Estado de S. Paulo*, February 4, 6, 12, 1965. Carlos Castello Branco, *Os Militares no Poder*, vol. 1, p. 193 (entry for February 11, 1965). *Jornal do Brasil*, February 9, 1965.

6. Carlos Lacerda, letter to Humberto Castello Branco, February 6, 1965.

7. Wilson Figueiredo and Carlos Castello Branco in *Jornal do Brasil*, February 9, 1965. Hugo Levy, interview, Rio de Janeiro, March 2, 1991.

8. Carlos Lacerda letter to Humberto Castello Branco, Rio de Janeiro, February 9, 1965, in File N4, Castello Branco papers, CPDOC. Luiz Fernando Mercadante, "Este É o Humberto," *Realidade*, June 1966.

9. *O Estado de S. Paulo*, February 12, 1965.

10. Ibid., February 13, 1965. Carlos Lacerda, interview, Rio de Janeiro, September 23, 1975.

11. *O Estado de S. Paulo*, February 14, 1965.

12. *Jornal do Brasil*, February 3, 10, 11, March 21, 1965. Daniel Krieger, *Desde as Missões*, pp. 191–192.

13. *Jornal do Brasil*, editorials, February 3, 11, March 9, 1965. *O Estado de S. Paulo*, editorial, February 14, 1965. *Jornal do Brasil*, January 20, 1965.

7. Adopting Lacerda's Recommendation about Elections (March 1965)

1. Armando Daudt d'Oliveira, interview, Rio de Janeiro, August 10, 1983. *O Estado de S. Paulo*, February 24, 1965.

2. *Jornal do Brasil*, editorial, February 4, 1965. Carlos Castello Branco, *Os Militares no Poder*, vol. 1, p. 203 (entry for February 25, 1965). *O Estado de S. Paulo*, February 24, 1965.

3. Aliomar Baleeiro, "Recordações do Presidente H. Castelo Branco" (typewritten), p. 20, reproduced in Luiz Viana Filho, compiler, *Castello Branco: Testemunhos de uma época;* see p. 15. *O Estado de S. Paulo*, February 26, 27, 1965.

4. *Jornal do Brasil* (editorial) and *O Estado de S. Paulo*, March 7, 1965.

5. *Jornal do Brasil*, March 6, 7, 1965.

6. *O Estado de S. Paulo*, March 9, 12, 17, 18, 1965.

7. Ibid., March 17, 1965. *Jornal do Brasil*, March 16, 17, 18, 20, 1965. *Jornal do Commercio*, Rio de Janeiro, March 17, 1965. *Correio da Manhã*, April 14, 1965. Carlos Lacerda, *Depoimento*, pp. 359–360.

8. Daniel Krieger, *Desde as Missões*, pp. 191–192. Carlos Lacerda, letter to Humberto Castello Branco, Rio de Janeiro, March 19, 1965, in File N4 of Castello Branco papers, CPDOC.

9. Luís Viana Filho, *O Governo Castelo Branco*, 3d ed. (Rio de Janeiro: Livraria José Olympio Editora, 1976), p. 294.

10. Daniel Krieger, *Desde as Missões*, pp. 191–192.

11. *O Estado de S. Paulo* and *Jornal do Brasil*, March 23, 1965.

12. *Jornal do Brasil*, March 21, 1965. Aspásia Camargo, Lucia Hippolito, Maria Celina Soares D'Araújo, and Dora Rocha Flaksman, *Artes da Política: Diálogo com Amaral Peixoto* (Rio de Janeiro: Nova Fronteira, CPDOC, Universidade Federal Fluminense, 1986), p. 481. *O Globo*, editorial, March 24, 1965. *Jornal do Brasil*, editorial, March 23, 1965. *O Estado de S. Paulo*, editorials, March 23, 24, 25, 1965.

13. *O Estado de S. Paulo*, April 9, 7, 1965. *Tribuna da Imprensa*, March 30, 1965. *Correio da Manhã*, April 6, 1965. Carlos Castello Branco in *Jornal do Brasil*, April 2, 4, 1965.

14. Carlos Lacerda, "A Revolução precisa ouvir e fazer," *Jornal do Brasil* (Caderno Especial), March 28, 1965.

8. Enaldo Cravo Peixoto, Lacerda's Choice (March–May 1965)

1. *O Estado de S. Paulo*, March 31, 1965. Sandra Cavalcanti, interview, Rio de Janeiro, February 23, 1991. Fidélis Amaral Netto, interview, Brasília, February 20, 1991. José Carlos Bardawil, "Amaral Netto: Você compraria um carro usado deste homem?," *Status*, October 1984. Carlos Lacerda, *Depoimento*, p. 337.

2. Carlos Flexa Ribeiro, interview, Rio de Janeiro, July 5, 1983. Raul Brunini, interview, Rio de Janeiro, August 12, 1983. Carlos Lacerda, *Depoimento*, pp. 346–348. *Jornal do Brasil*, March 31, 1965.

3. *Jornal do Brasil*, March 31, 1965.

4. *O Estado de S. Paulo*, March 23, 1965. Roberto Campos, interview, Brasília, February 19, 1991. Carlos Lacerda, *Depoimento*, pp. 344–345.

5. Carlos Lacerda, *Depoimento*, p. 345. *Correio da Manhã*, April 14, 1965.

6. Raphael de Almeida Magalhães, interview, Rio de Janeiro, August 9, 1989.

7. Carlos Lacerda, speech reported in *O Estado de S. Paulo*, April 24, 1965. *Tribuna da Imprensa*, June 2, 1965.

8. Danillo Nunes, letter to JWFD, August 29, 1992. Carlos Flexa Ribeiro, interview, July 5, 1983.

9. Enaldo Cravo Peixoto, transcript of interview taped by the Sociedade dos Amigos de Carlos Lacerda, p. 2. Enaldo Cravo Peixoto, letter to Carlos Lacerda, Rio de Janeiro, December 14, 1963, in CCL.

10. Danillo Nunes, interview, Rio de Janeiro, March 10, 1992. *O Estado de S. Paulo*, April 2, 3, 1965. *Jornal do Brasil*, April 3, 1965.

11. Carlos Lacerda, *Depoimento*, p. 346. Carlos Flexa Ribeiro, interview, July 5, 1983. Enaldo Cravo Peixoto in *O Estado de S. Paulo*, April 21, 1965. Antônio Carlos de Almeida Braga, interview, New York, September 2, 1988.

12. *O Estado de S. Paulo*, April 11, 16, 1965. João Condé, interview with DFR, Rio de Janeiro, March 23, 1983.

13. *Jornal do Brasil*, *O Estado de S. Paulo*, and *Correio da Manhã*, April 13, 1965.

14. *O Estado de S. Paulo*, April 21, 1965. *Jornal do Brasil*, April 20, 21, 1965.

15. Danillo Nunes, interview, March 10, 1992. *Jornal do Brasil*, April 21, 1965. *O Estado de S. Paulo*, April 21, 22, 1965.

16. Enaldo Cravo Peixoto, transcript of interview taped by the Sociedade dos Amigos de Carlos Lacerda, p. 8. *O Estado de S. Paulo*, April 21, 1965.

17. *O Estado de S. Paulo*, April 22, 1965.

18. Ibid. *Correio da Manhã*, April 22, 1965. *Jornal do Brasil*, April 23, 1965.

19. Enaldo Cravo Peixoto, transcript of interview taped by the Sociedade dos Amigos de Carlos Lacerda, p. 2. Cláudio Lacerda Paiva, interview, Rio de Janeiro, December 16, 1977. Raphael de Almeida Magalhães, interview, Rio de Janeiro, August 9, 1989. Carlos Lacerda, *Depoimento*, p. 345. *Jornal do Brasil*, April 24, 1965.

20. *Jornal do Brasil* and *O Estado de S. Paulo*, April 24, 1965. *Correio da Manhã*, editorial, April 24, 1965. *Diário Carioca*, May 6, 1965.

21. *O Estado de S. Paulo*, April 22, 1965. *Jornal do Brasil*, April 28, May 9, 13, 1965. Raul Brunini, interview, August 12, 1983. Marcelo Garcia, interview, Rio de Janeiro, August 18, 1983. Carlos Flexa Ribeiro, interview, July 5, 1983. *Tribuna da Imprensa*, May 29–30, 1965.

22. *Tribuna da Imprensa*, May 28, 29–30, 31, June 1, 4, 1965.

9. The Niterói Convention of the UDN (April 1965)

1. *O Estado de S. Paulo*, April 23, 24, 25, 1965.

2. Ernâni Sátiro, interview, Rio de Janeiro, December 17, 1975.

3. Antônio Carlos Magalhães, interview, Rio de Janeiro, August 11, 1977. Aliomar Baleeiro, "Recordações do Presidente H. Castelo Branco," p. 20, reproduced on pp. 15–16 of Luiz Viana Filho, compiler, *Castello Branco: Testemunhos de uma época*. Carlos Castello Branco in *Jornal do Brasil*, April 7, 1965. *Jornal do Brasil*, April 4, 11, 1965. *Correio da Manhã*, April 3, 1965.

4. *O Estado de S. Paulo*, April 28, 29, 1965.

5. *Correio da Manhã*, April 30, 1965.

6. *O Estado de S. Paulo*, April 24, 1965.

7. Ibid., April 28, 30, May 1, 1965.

8. *Jornal do Brasil*, *O Estado de S. Paulo*, and *Correio da Manhã*, May 1, 1965.

9. *Jornal do Brasil*, editorial, May 1, 1965.

10. *O Estado de S. Paulo*, May 7, 1965. "Lacerda contrário à anistia. Em entrevista concedida à revista *Manchete*," *O Estado de S. Paulo*, May 12, 1965.

11. *O Estado de S. Paulo*, May 11, 1965.

10. Criticizing the PAEG (May 17–18, 1965)

1. Ministério do Planejamento e Coordenação Econômica, *Programa de Ação Econômica do Govêrno, 1964–1966 (Síntese), Incluindo a Versão Revista do Programa de Investimentos para 1965* (n.p.: Documentos EPEA, May 1965), pp. 35, 17, 23. *O Estado de S. Paulo*, May 11, 12, 1965.

2. Dênio Nogueira, interview, Rio de Janeiro, December 20, 1977. Marcelo Garcia, interview, Rio de Janeiro, August 18, 1983. Antônio Dias Leite Júnior entry in *Dicionário Histórico-Biográfico Brasileiro, 1930–1983*.

3. Carlos Lacerda, letter to Humberto Castello Branco, Rio de Janeiro, May 17, 1965, in File N4 of the Castello Branco papers at the CPDOC. See also Cláudio Lacerda, *Carlos Lacerda: 10 Anos Depois*, p. 102.

4. Aliomar Baleeiro, "Recordações do Presidente H. Castelo Branco," p. 21, reproduced on p. 16 of Luiz Viana Filho, compiler, *Castello Branco: Testemunhos de uma época*. Júlio Pessoa, interview, Rio de Janeiro, November 21, 1975.

5. *Jornal do Brasil*, May 18, 19, 1965. Marcelo Garcia, interview, Rio de Janeiro, August 18, 1983.

6. *O Estado de S. Paulo*, May 18, 19, 1965. Economic study attached to Lacerda's letter of May 17, 1965, to Castello Branco, in File N4 of the Castello Branco papers at the CPDOC; see pp. 1–2, 11, 18. See also Cláudio Lacerda, *Carlos Lacerda: 10 Anos Depois*, pp. 104, 105, 108, 112.

7. Economic study attached to Lacerda's letter of May 17, 1965, to Castello Branco, pp. 27, 12, 31, 28. See also Cláudio Lacerda, *Carlos Lacerda: 10 Anos Depois*, pp. 117, 109, 119, 118, 120.

8. Economic study attached to Lacerda's letter of May 17, 1965, to Castello Branco, pp. 32, 43, 49–54. See also Cláudio Lacerda, *Carlos Lacerda: 10 Anos Depois*, pp. 119, 125, 128–131.

11. Repercussions of Lacerda's Study (May 19–June 1, 1965)

1. *O Estado de S. Paulo*, editorials, May 20, 23, 1965. *Jornal do Brasil* and *O Globo*, editorials, May 20, 1965. *Diário Carioca* and *Correio da Manhã*, editorials, May 21, 1965.

2. Humberto Castello Branco, *Discursos, 1965* (n.p.: Secretaria de Imprensa, n.d.), p. 221. See also *O Estado de S. Paulo*, May 22, 1965, and *Diário Carioca*, editorial, May 23, 1965.

3. *Correio da Manhã* and *Jornal do Brasil*, May 22, 1965. *O Estado de S. Paulo*, May 22, 23, 1965.

4. *O Estado de S. Paulo*, May 23, 25, 20, 1965. *Jornal do Brasil*, May 23, 28, 1965.

5. Carlos Lacerda, letter to Humberto Castello Branco, May 25, 1965, in File N4 (item 18), Castello Branco papers, CPDOC.

6. *O Estado de S. Paulo*, May 27, 1965. Carlos Castello Branco in *Jornal do Brasil*, May 27, 1965. Raul Brunini, interview, Rio de Janeiro, August 12, 1983.

7. Carlos Castello Branco in *Jornal do Brasil*, May 27, 1965.

8. *Jornal do Brasil* and *O Estado de S. Paulo*, May 28, 1965.

9. "Resposta do Ministério do Planejamento" (undated), in File N4 (item 17), Castello Branco papers, CPDOC.

10. *Jornal do Brasil*, June 2, 1965.

11. Ibid., May 29, June 2, 1965.

12. Emergence of the Flexa Ribeiro Candidacy
(Early June 1965)

1. Carlos Flexa Ribeiro, interview, Rio de Janeiro, July 5, 1983. Edgar Flexa Ribeiro, interview, Rio de Janeiro, August 19, 1989. Sandra Cavalcanti, interview, Rio de Janeiro, November 18, 1975.

2. *Jornal do Brasil*, June 1, 1965. Raphael de Almeida Magalhães, interview, Rio de Janeiro, August 9, 1989. Carlos Flexa Ribeiro, interview, July 5, 1983.

3. *Jornal do Brasil*, June 1, 2, May 30, 1965. *Tribuna da Imprensa*, May 31, June 1, 2, 1965.

4. *Jornal do Brasil*, June 2, 1965. Hélio Mamede, interview with DFR, Rio de Janeiro, August 9, 1965.

5. *Tribuna da Imprensa*, June 3, 1965. Raul Brunini, interview, Rio de Janeiro, August 12, 1983.

6. *Jornal do Brasil*, *Tribuna da Imprensa*, and *O Estado de S. Paulo*, June 4, 1965.

7. *Tribuna da Imprensa*, June 5–6, 1965. Hélio Fernandes in *Tribuna da Imprensa*, June 7, 1965.

8. Carlos Lacerda, *Depoimento*, p. 347. *Jornal do Brasil*, June 15, 16, 1965.

9. *Jornal do Brasil*, editorial, June 5, 1965. *O Globo*, editorial, June 10, 1965.

13. *O Globo* and Time-Life; Lacerda and His Triplex
(June–December 1965)

1. Câmara dos Deputados, *Projeto de Resolução No. 190 de 1966: Aprova as conclusões da Comissão Parlamentar de Inquérito para apurar os fatos relacionados com a organização Rádio e TV e Jornal "O Globo" e as empresas estrangeiras dirigentes das revistas "Time" e "Life" (da CPI criada pela Resolução No. 185, de 1966)* (Brasília: *Diário do Congresso Nacional*, June 7, 1967), p. 70 (testimony of Carlos Lacerda, August 11, 1966), pp. 25–26 (testimony of Roberto Marinho, April 20, 1966). Daniel Herz, *A história secreta da Rede Globo* (Porto Alegre: Tchê Editora, 1987), p. 135.

2. *Jornal do Brasil*, June 22, 1965. Câmara dos Deputados, *Projeto de Resolução No. 190*, pp. 70–71 (testimony of Carlos Lacerda), pp. 39–40 (statement by João Calmon during testimony of Roberto Marinho), p. 71 (testimony of Carlos Lacerda). Herz, *A história secreta*, pp. 136–137, 133–134.

3. Câmara dos Deputados, *Projeto de Resolução No. 190*, pp. 36, 39 (testimony of Roberto Marinho). Herz, *A história secreta*, pp. 128–129.

4. Câmara dos Deputados, *Projeto de Resolução No. 190*, p. 72 (testimony of Carlos Lacerda), p. 37 (statement by João Calmon during testimony of Roberto Marinho), p. 30 (testimony of Roberto Marinho). Herz, *A história secreta*, pp. 157, 240–241, 146–147, 183. Carlos Medeiros Silva, interview, Rio de Janeiro, August 9, 1977.

5. *O Globo*, editorial, June 8, 1965.

6. *Jornal do Brasil,* June 10, 1965. Mauro Magalhães, interview, Rio de Janeiro, March 9, 1992. *Tribuna da Imprensa,* June 26–27, 1965.

7. *Diário Carioca,* June 26, 27 (editorial), 1965. *Última Hora,* September 9, 1965.

8. *Diário Carioca,* June 29, 1965. *O Globo,* July 16, August 6, 1965.

9. *Diário Carioca,* July 14, 8 (editorial), 10, 1965. *O Globo,* July 3, 5, 1965.

10. *Jornal do Brasil,* editorial, July 11, 1965, reprinted in *O Globo,* July 12, 1965. *O Globo,* July 14, 1965.

14. Castello, "Angel" of a Red Light District (July 2, 1965)

1. Constitutional Amendment 14 of June 3, 1965, on pp. 812–815 of Floriano de Aguiar Dias, *Constituições do Brasil* (Rio de Janeiro: Editora Liber Juris, 1975).

2. *Jornal do Brasil,* June 18, 23, 25, 1965. *Tribuna da Imprensa,* June 21, 25, May 28, 1965. Alim Pedro entry in *Dicionário Histórico-Biográfico Brasileiro, 1930–1983.*

3. Carlos Lacerda, letter to Humberto Castello Branco, Rio de Janeiro, June 26, 1965, in File N4 (item 19), Castello Branco papers, CPDOC.

4. *Tribuna da Imprensa,* June 21, 22, 1965. *Jornal do Brasil,* June 21, 22, 23, 1965. *Diário Carioca,* June 24, 1965.

5. *O Estado de S. Paulo,* June 30, 1965.

6. Ibid., July 1, 1965. Carlos Lacerda, *Brasil entre a Verdade e a Mentira* (Rio de Janeiro: Bloch Editôres, 1965), p. 99.

7. *O Estado de S. Paulo,* July 2, 1965. Aliomar Baleeiro, "Recordações do Presidente H. Castelo Branco," p. 25, reproduced in Luiz Viana Filho, compiler, *Castello Branco: Testemunhos de uma época,* p. 18.

8. *Jornal do Brasil,* July 3, 1965. *Tribuna da Imprensa,* July 3–4, 1965.

9. *O Estado de S. Paulo* and *Jornal do Brasil,* July 3, 1965. *Tribuna da Imprensa,* July 3–4, 1965.

10. Ibid. *Jornal do Brasil,* June 27, 1965.

15. An Indirect Presidential Election? (July 1965)

1. Carlos Castello Branco, *Os Militares no Poder,* vol. 1, p. 275 (entry for July 4, 1965).

2. *O Estado de S. Paulo,* editorial, July 4, 1965. *Jornal do Brasil,* July 6, 1965. *Diário Carioca,* June 30, 1965.

3. *O Globo,* editorials, July 5, 7, 1965. *Diário Carioca,* July 6, 1965. *O Globo,* July 6, 8, 1965. *Correio da Manhã,* July 4, 1965. *Jornal do Brasil,* July 11, 1965.

4. *O Globo,* July 3, 1965. *Jornal do Brasil,* July 6, 13, 25, 4, 1965. *O Estado de S. Paulo,* July 9, 13, 14, 15 (editorial), 21, 4, 1965. Carlos Castello Branco in *Jornal do Brasil,* July 23, 1965.

5. *Jornal do Brasil,* July 7, 1965. *O Estado de S. Paulo,* July 7, 17, 9, 1965.

6. Antonio Dias Rebello Filho, *Carlos Lacerda, Meu Amigo,* p. 202. *Brazil Herald* and *O Estado de S. Paulo,* July 15, 1965. *Jornal do Brasil,* July 15, 16, 1965.

7. *O Estado de S. Paulo,* July 20, 23, 1965. *Jornal do Brasil,* July 18, 20, 1965.

8. *Brazil Herald,* July 24, 1965.

9. *O Estado de S. Paulo,* July 27, 28, 1965. Carlos Lacerda, *Uma rosa é uma rosa é uma rosa.*

16. Comments: Lacerda's Mistake

1. *O Estado de S. Paulo,* July 3, 1965.

2. Ibid., March 23, 1965.

3. *O Globo,* March 24, 1965.

4. *O Estado de S. Paulo,* April 29, 1965.

5. *Jornal do Brasil,* July 18, 23, 1965. *O Globo,* July 21, 1965.

6. *Tribuna da Imprensa,* May 28, 1965. Danillo Nunes, letter to JWFD, Rio de Janeiro, August 29, 1992.

7. Aspásia Camargo et al., *Artes da Política,* p. 481.

8. Raphael de Almeida Magalhães, interview, Rio de Janeiro, August 9, 1989.

VIII. The Elimination of Lacerda's UDN Candidacy (August–October 1965)

1. Lott's Candidacy (August 1965)

1. *O Globo,* July 9, 1965. *Jornal do Brasil,* June 23, July 10, 1965.

2. *O Estado de S. Paulo,* July 30, 31, 1965. *Diário Carioca,* July 15, 17, 1965.

3. *Tribuna da Imprensa,* July 31–August 1, 1965. *Jornal do Brasil,* July 30, 31, 1965.

4. *Jornal do Brasil,* August 1, 3, 4, 19, 1965. *Tribuna da Imprensa,* August 5, 6, 1965. *Correio da Manhã,* editorial, September 7, 1965. Danton Jobim in *Última Hora,* September 1, 1965. *Tribuna da Imprensa,* August 11, 1965. *Jornal do Brasil,* August 19, 1965.

5. *O Jornal,* editorial, September 7, 1965. Juracy Magalhães, letter to Humberto Castello Branco, Washington, D.C., August 10, 1965, in File O2 (items 14v and 15), Castello Branco papers (consulted at the home of Paulo V. Castello Branco).

6. *Tribuna da Imprensa,* August 5, 9, 1965. *O Globo,* August 9, 1965. *Jornal do Brasil,* August 5, 12 (editorial), 1965.

7. *Tribuna da Imprensa* and *Jornal do Brasil,* August 9, 1965.

8. *Jornal do Brasil,* August 19, 5, 4, 1965.

9. Juracy Magalhães, letters to Carlos Lacerda, Washington, D.C., August 5, 13, 1965, in CCL. Carlos Lacerda, cable to Juracy Magalhães, Rio de Janeiro, August 12, 1965, in CCL. *Tribuna da Imprensa,* August 7–8, 1965.

10. *O Globo,* editorials, August 9, 10, 13, 26, 1965. *O Globo,* August 9, 1965.

11. Carlos Castello Branco, *Os Militares no Poder,* vol. 1, pp. 294, 296 (entry for August 8, 1965). *Jornal do Brasil,* August 11, 1965.

12. *Jornal do Brasil,* August 27, 25, and editorials, July 20, August 14, 15, 1965. *O Globo,* editorials, August 12, 22, 26, 1965. Carlos Lacerda, letter to José Magalhães Pinto, September 1, 1965, in CCL.

13. *Jornal do Brasil,* August 25, 27, September 7, 8, 1965.

14. *Jornal do Brasil,* September 1, 2, 1965. *O Estado de S. Paulo,* September 2, 3, 4, 1965. Carlos Castello Branco, *Os Militares no Poder,* vol. 1, pp. 308–309 (entries for September 1, 2, 3, 1965). *O Globo,* September 3, 1965.

2. *Lacerdismo* on the Rise (July–September 1965)

1. *O Globo,* August 27, 20 (editorial), 1965. *Jornal do Brasil,* July 29, 1965.

2. Carlos Lacerda, "Um Crime contra o Brasil," *Tribuna da Imprensa,* August 26, 1965. *O Estado de S. Paulo,* September 1, 2 (editorial), 1965. *Jornal do Brasil,* July 29, 1965. *O Globo,* editorials, August 23, 27, 20, 1965.

3. Carlos Lacerda, letter to Mauro Thibau, Rio de Janeiro, August 18, 1965, in *O Globo,* August 20, 1965. *O Estado de S. Paulo,* July 27, 29 (editorial), 1965. *O Globo,* editorial, August 20, 1965. Roberto Marinho, letter to Manuel Francisco do Nascimento Brito, in *Jornal do Brasil,* September 4, 1965, and in *O Globo,* September 6, 1965.

4. *Jornal do Brasil,* August 18, 1965. Carlos Lacerda, letter to Mauro Thibau, August 18, 1965. Carlos Lacerda, "Um Crime contra o Brasil."

5. *Jornal do Brasil,* August 21, 1965. Carlos Lacerda, "Um Crime contra o Brasil."

6. *Diário Carioca,* editorial, August 27, 1965. *Jornal do Brasil,* August 31, 1965. *Brazil Herald,* September 1, 1965.

7. *O Estado de S. Paulo,* September 1, 1965.

8. Carlos Lacerda, letter to Lincoln Gordon, Rio de Janeiro, August 4, 1965, in CCL. Jack Valenti, "Report to the President: Fulbright Mission to Brazil," August 10, 1965, Confidential File CO 1-2 (1966), CO-37, Lyndon Baines Johnson Library, Austin.

9. *Jornal do Brasil,* August 5, July 31, 1965. *Tribuna da Imprensa,* August 12, 1965.

10. Carlos Castello Branco in *Jornal do Brasil,* September 4, 1965.

11. Ibid.

12. *O Estado de S. Paulo,* editorial, September 2, 1965. *O Globo,* editorial, September 3, 1965.

13. *O Estado de S. Paulo,* editorial, September 2, 1965. *Jornal do Brasil,* September 4, 1965.

14. Carlos Lacerda, letter in *O Estado de S. Paulo,* September 7, 1965.

3. "The Juracy Mission" (September 1965)

1. *Jornal do Brasil*, September 9, 10, 1965. *O Globo*, September 10, 1965. *Diário de Notícias*, September 11, 1965. Carlos Castello Branco in *Jornal do Brasil*, September 10, 1965.

2. Carlos Lacerda, letter to Juracy Magalhães, Rio de Janeiro, July 18, 1965, in CCL. Juracy Magalhães, letter to Carlos Lacerda, Washington, D.C., July 27, 1965, in CCL.

3. *Jornal do Brasil*, September 11, 1965. *O Jornal*, editorials, September 14, 15, 1965.

4. *Jornal do Brasil*, September 12, 1965.

5. Ibid., September 18, 9, 10, 17, 1965.

6. *O Estado de S. Paulo*, September 12, 15, 1965. Carlos Castello Branco in *Jornal do Brasil*, September 16, 1965. Carlos Lacerda, letter to José de Magalhães Pinto, Rio de Janeiro, September 1, 1965, in CCL.

7. *Jornal do Brasil*, September 14, 15, 16, 1965. *O Estado de S. Paulo*, September 17, 16, 15, 1965. *Tribuna da Imprensa*, September 18–19, 1965.

8. *O Estado de S. Paulo*, September 12, January 7, 1965. Carlos Castello Branco, *Os Militares no Poder*, vol. 1, p. 316 (entry for September 15, 1965).

9. *O Estado de S. Paulo*, September 12, 16, 17, 1965. *Tribuna da Imprensa*, September 17, 1965.

10. Carlos Castello Branco, *Os Militares no Poder*, vol. 1, p. 321 (entry for September 24, 1965). *O Estado de S. Paulo*, September 23, 1965.

11. Humberto Castello Branco, handwritten notes for cable to Juracy Magalhães, File M (item 18), Castello Branco papers, CPDOC. Carlos Castello Branco, *Os Militares no Poder*, vol. 1, pp. 321–322 (entry for September 25, 1965).

4. "Brazil's Cleanest City" Becomes "The World's Cinema Capital" (September 1965)

1. Secretaria de Turismo advertisement in *Tribuna da Imprensa*, September 13, 1965. *O Globo*, September 7, 1965.

2. *Tribuna da Imprensa*, September 13, 1965. Carlos Lacerda, *Fala da Manhã que Nasce*, phonograph record (Rio de Janeiro: Som Indústria e Comércio S/A, 1965).

3. *O Estado de S. Paulo*, September 15, 29, 21, 1965. *Jornal do Brasil*, September 15, 1965.

4. Governor's office, Assessoria de Imprensa release of September 20, 1965 (in the Walter Cunto Collection). *O Estado de S. Paulo*, September 21, 1965.

5. Governor's office, Assessoria de Imprensa release of September 24, 1965 (in the Walter Cunto Collection). *Jornal do Brasil*, September 26, 1965. *O Estado de S. Paulo*, September 28, 25, 1965.

6. *O Estado de S. Paulo*, September 28, 1965. Governor's office, Assessoria de Imprensa releases of September 24, 26, 1965 (in the Walter Cunto Collection).

7. Carlos Lacerda, *Mensagem à Assembléia Legislativa: 5 Anos de Go-vêrno*, p. 54. *O Globo*, October 1, 1965. *O Estado de S. Paulo*, September 16, 21, 28, 19, 30, 1965. Governor's office, Assessoria de Imprensa releases of September 29, 30, 28, 1965 (in the Walter Cunto Collection). *Jornal do Brasil*, September 16, 26, 1965. *Tribuna da Imprensa*, September 20, 1965. "Urbani-zação do Rio de Janeiro e Viadutos da Ponte dos Marinheiros," *Revista de Engenharia do Estado da Guanabara* 30, nos. 1/2 (January–June 1963). Fer-nando Nascimento Silva, "Vias, Viadutos e Túneis," *Revista de Engenharia do Estado da Guanabara* 31, no. 1 (January–March 1965).

8. *O Estado de S. Paulo*, September 19, 21, 28, 29, 1965. *Jornal do Brasil*, September 14, 15, 17, 1965.

9. *O Globo*, August 6, 10, 1965. *O Estado de S. Paulo*, September 16, 21, 24, 28, 1965. *Jornal do Brasil*, September 15, 1965.

10. *Jornal do Brasil*, September 16, 1965. *O Jornal*, September 17, 1965. *O Estado de S. Paulo*, September 18, 19, 1965.

11. *O Estado de S. Paulo*, September 28, 29, 1965. *Jornal do Brasil*, Septem-ber 23, 24, 28, 1965.

5. Gubernatorial Candidates and the Press in Guanabara (September 1965)

1. *Última Hora* and *Diário de Notícias*, September 8, 1965. *Correio da Manhã*, September 7, 8, 1965.

2. *Tribuna da Imprensa*, September 14, 9, 1965. Aurélio Viana entry in *Dicionário Histórico-Biográfico Brasileiro, 1930–1983*. *Correio da Manhã*, September 14, 1965. *O Estado de S. Paulo*, September 21, 1965.

3. Raphael de Almeida Magalhães, interviews, Rio de Janeiro, August 8, 1977, August 9, 1989. *O Globo*, September 9, 1965.

4. *Tribuna da Imprensa*, August 10, 1965. Raphael de Almeida Magalhães, interviews, August 8, 1977, August 9, 1989. *O Globo*, August 27, 1965.

5. Raphael de Almeida Magalhães, interview, August 9, 1989. *Tribuna da Imprensa*, August 10, 1965. *O Globo*, August 27, 1965. *Diário de Notícias*, September 8, 11, 1965. Sandra Cavalcanti, interview, Rio de Janeiro, Au-gust 8, 1977.

6. Raphael de Almeida Magalhães, interview, August 9, 1989. *O Dia* entry in *Dicionário Histórico-Biográfico Brasileiro, 1930–1983*.

7. André de Séguin des Hons, "Os Diários do Rio de Janeiro, 1945–1982," p. 234. *Diário de Notícias*, editorials, September 12, 14, 1965.

8. *Jornal do Brasil*, editorials, September 10, 26, 1965.

9. *Tribuna da Imprensa*, September 13, 21, 29, October 2, 1, 1965.

10. *O Jornal*, editorials, September 9, 14, 28, 1965.

11. *O Globo*, editorial, September 9, 1965.

12. *Última Hora*, September 8, 9, 30, 1965.

13. André de Séguin des Hons, "Os Diários do Rio de Janeiro, 1945–1982," p. 234. *Correio da Manhã*, editorials, September 7, 9, 1965.

14. *Diário Carioca*, September 24, 1965.

6. Ponto Contraponto (September 1965)

1. Vera Lacerda Paiva, interview with DFR, Rio de Janeiro, September 1, 1985. Walter Ramos Poyares, Mario Lorenzo Fernandez, Ruth Alverga, and Antonio Dias Rebello Filho, interviews with DFR, Rio de Janeiro, July 30, August 9, August 15, August 24, 1985, respectively. Vera Lacerda Paiva and Lygia Paiva Derizans, interview with DFR, Rio de Janeiro, August 25, 1985. Regina Costard, interview with DFR, Rio de Janeiro, September 9, 1986. Gabriel Lacerda, interview, Rio de Janeiro, August 18, 1983.

2. Vera Lacerda Paiva and Lygia Paiva Derizans, interview with DFR, August 25, 1985.

3. Ibid.

4. Edgar Flexa Ribeiro, interview, Rio de Janeiro, August 19, 1989.

5. Isa Motta and Maurício de Lacerda Filho, "Ponto contraponto" columns in *Diário Carioca*, September 17, 20, 1965.

6. Ibid., September 20, 12, 10, July 7, 13, September 25, 26, 24, 1965.

7. Ibid., September 28, 26, 25, 21, 1965.

8. Ibid., September 20, 14, 12, 26, 1965.

9. *Diário Carioca*, October 2, 1965.

7. Negrão Forges Ahead (September 1965)

1. *O Estado de S. Paulo*, dateline Rio de Janeiro, September 17, 1965. *Tribuna da Imprensa*, September 17, 1965. Richard Bourne, *Political Leaders of Latin America*, p. 236.

2. Carlos Lacerda, *Depoimento*, p. 348.

3. *O Globo*, September 10, 11, 1965. David Nasser, "As Grandes Amizades (9): Meu Amigo Carlos Lacerda," *Manchete*, no. 802 (September 2, 1967).

4. *O Globo*, September 10, 14, 24, 1965. *Correio da Manhã*, September 11, 1965. *Diário Carioca*, September 28, 1965. *Jornal do Brasil*, September 19, 1965.

5. *Correio da Manhã*, September 21, 11, 1965. *Tribuna da Imprensa*, September 13, 1965. *O Globo*, September 14, 1965. *O Estado de S. Paulo*, September 29, 1965.

6. *O Globo*, September 11, 1965. *Jornal do Brasil*, September 15, 23, 10, 1965. *Correio da Manhã*, September 23, 1965. *Tribuna da Imprensa*, September 15, 17, 23, 1965. Danillo Nunes, letter to JWFD, Rio de Janeiro, September 29, 1992.

7. *Jornal do Brasil*, September 14, 1965. *O Jornal*, September 1, 1965. *Tribuna da Imprensa*, September 14, 1965. *Diário de Notícias*, September 11, 1965.

8. *Tribuna da Imprensa*, September 9, 1965. *O Globo*, September 10, 1965. Isa Motta and Maurício de Lacerda Filho in *Diário Carioca*, September 11, 1965.

9. *Tribuna da Imprensa*, September 14, 15, 25–26, 1965. *Correio da*

Manhã and *Jornal do Brasil,* September 15, 1965. *Diário Carioca,* September 14, 15, 1965. *O Globo,* September 4, 1965.

10. *Jornal do Brasil,* editorial, September 15, 1965. *Tribuna da Imprensa,* September 16, 1965.

11. Márcio Moreira Alves in *Correio da Manhã,* September 7, 1965.

12. *Diário Carioca,* September 14, 11, 1965. *Jornal do Brasil,* September 15, 1965. *O Globo,* September 17, 1965.

13. *O Globo,* editorials, September 14, 18, 24, 1965. *O Globo,* September 14, 25, 18, 1965. *Diário Carioca,* September 17, 1965. *Jornal do Brasil,* September 17, 30, 1965. *Tribuna da Imprensa,* September 22, 1965.

14. *Correio da Manhã,* September 29, 1965. *Diário Carioca,* September 21, 1965.

15. *O Globo,* September 11, 14, 1965. *Diário Carioca,* September 16, 17, August 28, September 12, 22, 10, 1965. *Correio da Manhã,* editorial, September 14, 1965. *O Jornal,* September 1, 1965. *Diário de Notícias,* September 10, 1965.

16. *O Globo,* September 20, 23, 1965. *Correio da Manhã,* September 21, 1965. *Diário Carioca,* September 21, 24, 1965. *Jornal do Brasil,* editorial, September 23, 1965.

17. Marcelo Garcia, interview, Rio de Janeiro, August 18, 1983. Antonio Dias Rebello Filho, *Carlos Lacerda, Meu Amigo,* p. 60. Carlos Osório da Silveira Neto, interview, Rio de Janeiro, August 7, 1989. Alfredo C. Machado, interview, Rio de Janeiro, August 8, 1989.

8. A Discouraged Lacerda Quarrels with Flexa (September 1965)

1. Raul Brunini, interview, Rio de Janeiro, August 12, 1983. Raphael de Almeida Magalhães, interview, Rio de Janeiro, August 9, 1989. Edgar Flexa Ribeiro, interview, Rio de Janeiro, August 19, 1989. Carlos Flexa Ribeiro, interview, Rio de Janeiro, July 5, 1983.

2. Carlos Lacerda, *Depoimento,* pp. 348, 347. Raphael de Almeida Magalhães, interview, August 9, 1989.

3. Carlos Flexa Ribeiro, interview, Rio de Janeiro, August 26, 1984. Danillo Nunes, interview, Rio de Janeiro, March 10, 1992.

4. Carlos Lacerda, *Depoimento,* p. 349.

5. *Diário Carioca,* August 26, 28, 30 (editorial), 1965. *Jornal do Brasil,* September 16, 1965. Luiz Ernesto Kawall, interview, São Paulo, July 31, 1983, and report, São Paulo, October 6, 1965, in CCL.

6. Raphael de Almeida Magalhães, interview, August 9, 1989. *Tribuna da Imprensa,* September 23, 1965.

7. Raphael de Almeida Magalhães, interview, August 9, 1989.

8. Ibid. *Diário Carioca,* October 8, 1965. Roberto de Abreu Sodré in *Jornal do Brasil,* October 6, 1965. Carlos Lacerda, *Depoimento,* pp. 348–349.

9. Edgar Flexa Ribeiro, interviews, Rio de Janeiro, July 8, 1983, August 19, 1989.

10. Cecil Borer, interview, Rio de Janeiro, October 7, 1966. Gustavo Borges, interview, Rio de Janeiro, August 14, 1983. Ferdinando de Carvalho, interviews, Rio de Janeiro, October 11, 1966, and Curitiba, November 10, 1967. Carlos Lacerda, interview, Rio de Janeiro, October 11, 1967. Carlos Lacerda in *O Estado de S. Paulo*, October 9, 1965.

11. *Jornal do Brasil*, September 26, and editorials, September 28, October 1, 1965.

12. *O Globo*, October 1, 6 (editorial), 1965. *Última Hora*, September 9, 30, 1965. *Correio da Manhã*, editorial, September 29, 1965.

13. Raphael de Almeida Magalhães, interview, Rio de Janeiro, August 8, 1977.

14. *O Estado de S. Paulo*, September 28, 1965.

9. Lacerda Collapses
(September 30, 1965)

1. *O Estado de S. Paulo*, September 29, 1965. *O Globo* and *Diário Carioca*, October 1, 1965.

2. Governor's office, Assessoria de Imprensa, release of September 30, 1965 (in the Walter Cunto Collection). *O Estado de S. Paulo* and *O Globo*, October 1, 1965.

3. *O Globo*, August 7, 1965.

4. Governor's office, Assessoria de Imprensa, release of September 30, 1965. *O Estado de S. Paulo* and *O Globo*, October 1, 1965.

5. Antonio Dias Rebello Filho, *Carlos Lacerda, Meu Amigo*, p. 210. Governor's office, Assessoria de Imprensa, releases of September 29, October 2, 1965 (in the Walter Cunto Collection). *O Globo*, October 1, 1965.

6. Governor's office, Assessoria de Imprensa, releases of October 1, 2, 1965 (in the Walter Cunto Collection). Carlos Lacerda, *Depoimento*, p. 350, and interviews, Tucson, Ariz., February 17, 18, 1976. Antonio Dias Rebello Filho, interview, Rio de Janeiro, August 7, 1983, and *Carlos Lacerda, Meu Amigo*, pp. 249–250. *O Estado de S. Paulo* and *Diário Carioca*, October 2, 1965. *O Globo* and *Jornal do Brasil*, October 1, 1965.

7. *O Estado de S. Paulo*, *O Globo*, and *Tribuna da Imprensa*, October 1, 1965.

8. *O Globo*, October 1, 1965.

9. *O Globo* and *O Estado de S. Paulo*, October 1, 1965.

10. *O Globo* and *O Estado de S. Paulo*, October 1, 1965.

11. *Jornal do Brasil*, October 1, 1965. *Diário Carioca*, October 2, 1965. Governor's office, Assessoria de Imprensa, release of October 1, 1965.

12. *O Estado de S. Paulo*, October 3, 1965.

13. Ibid., October 3, 5, 1965. Raul Brunini, interview, Rio de Janeiro, August 12, 1983. Rebello Filho, *Carlos Lacerda, Meu Amigo*, p. 208.

14. *Jornal do Brasil*, October 3, 5, 6, 1965. *O Globo*, October 4, 1965. *Diário Carioca*, October 6, 1965.

10. The Barracks React to Negrão's Victory
(October 5, 1965)

1. Cláudio Lacerda Paiva, interview, Rio de Janeiro, December 16, 1977. João Carlos Palhares dos Santos, interview, Rio de Janeiro, November 22, 1975.
2. *O Estado de S. Paulo*, October 5, 1965.
3. *Tribuna da Imprensa*, October 4, 1965. *O Estado de S. Paulo*, editorial, October 5, 1965.
4. *Tribuna da Imprensa*, October 6, 1965.
5. Raphael de Almeida Magalhães, interview, Rio de Janeiro, November 19, 1975. *Tribuna da Imprensa* (October 5, 1965) put the figure at 90 percent.
6. *Tribuna da Imprensa*, October 5, 1965. Carlos Castello Branco, *Os Militares no Poder*, vol. 1, p. 329 (entry for October 6, 1965).
7. Peri Constant Bevilacqua, interview, Rio de Janeiro, December 21, 1977. Álcio Barbosa da Costa e Silva, interview, Rio de Janeiro, July 15, 1977. Aliomar Baleeiro, "Recordações do Presidente H. Castelo Branco," p. 29, reproduced on p. 21 of Luiz Viana Filho, compiler, *Castello Branco: Testemunhos de uma época*. *Diário Carioca* and *Tribuna da Imprensa*, October 6, 1965. Luís Viana Filho, *O Governo Castelo Branco*, p. 349.
8. Guilherme da Silveira Filho, interview, Rio de Janeiro, August 30, 1984. Joaquim Guilherme da Silveira, interview, Rio de Janeiro, August 9, 1983.
9. Antônio Godinho, interview, São Paulo, November 7, 1975.
10. Carlos Lacerda, interviews, Tucson, Ariz., February 17, 18, 1976.
11. Antônio Godinho, interview, November 7, 1975.
12. *Tribuna da Imprensa*, October 6, 1965.
13. Antônio Godinho, interview, São Paulo, November 7, 1975. Raphael de Almeida Magalhães, interview, November 19, 1975.
14. Ibid.
15. Raphael de Almeida Magalhães, interview, November 19, 1975.
16. Ibid. Antônio Godinho, interview, November 7, 1975. Carlos Lacerda, interviews, February 17, 18, 1976. Carlos Lacerda, *Depoimento*, p. 350.
17. Carlos Lacerda, *Depoimento*, p. 350.
18. *Tribuna da Imprensa* and *O Estado de S. Paulo*, October 6, 1965. Antônio Godinho, interview, November 7, 1975. Álcio Barbosa da Costa e Silva, interview, July 15, 1977.
19. Mário David Andreazza, letter to Luís Viana Filho, n.p., n.d., (copy in files of JWFD), p. 5. Antônio Godinho, interview, November 7, 1975.
20. Mário David Andreazza, letter to Luís Viana Filho, p. 6.
21. Carlos Lacerda in *O Estado de S. Paulo*, October 9, 1965. Mário David Andreazza, letter to Luís Viana Filho, p. 7. Hélio Fernandes in *Tribuna da Imprensa*, October 7, 1965. Murilo Melo Filho, "E o Castelo (Quase) Caiu," *Manchete*, September 21, 1981.
22. Transcript of tape of speech of Artur da Costa e Silva at the First Infantry Regiment, Vila Militar, October 6, 1965 (tape made available by Álcio da Costa e Silva, July 1977).
23. *O Estado de S. Paulo*, October 7, 1965. Luís Viana Filho, *O Governo Castelo Branco*, pp. 337–338. *Jornal do Brasil*, editorial, October 7, 1965.

24. *O Globo*, editorial, October 7, 1965.
25. Carlos Castello Branco, *Os Militares no Poder*, vol. 1, p. 332 (entry for October 8, 1965). Raphael de Almeida Magalhães, interview, Rio de Janeiro, August 8, 1977. Antônio Godinho, interview, November 7, 1975.

11. Lacerda "Returns" His Candidacy and "Vomits" Castello (October 7–11, 1965)

1. Carlos Flexa Ribeiro, interviews, Rio de Janeiro, July 5, 1983, August 26, 1984. *O Estado de S. Paulo* showed, on October 12, the following "final results": Negrão 582,026; Flexa 442,363; Amaral Netto 40,403; Aurélio Viana 25,841; Hélio Damasceno 14,140.
2. Raphael de Almeida Magalhães, interview, Rio de Janeiro, August 9, 1989. Maria Cristina Lacerda Simões Lopes, interview, Petrópolis, August 13, 1983.
3. Carlos Lacerda, *Depoimento*, pp. 350–351.
4. *O Estado de S. Paulo*, October 8, 1965.
5. José de Magalhães Pinto, telegram to Carlos Lacerda, Belo Horizonte, October 7, 1965, in CCL. *O Estado de S. Paulo*, October 6, 1965.
6. Carlos Lacerda, letter to Ernâni Sátiro, Rio de Janeiro, October 7, 1965, in CCL.
7. *O Estado de S. Paulo*, *Diário Carioca*, and *O Globo*, October 8, 1965. *New York Times*, October 9, 1965.
8. *O Estado de S. Paulo*, October 9, 1965.
9. Ibid. *O Globo*, October 9, 1965.
10. *Jornal do Brasil*, editorial, October 9, 1965. *O Estado de S. Paulo*, editorial, October 10, 1965. *Brazil Herald*, October 13, 1965.
11. *Correio da Manhã* and *O Estado de S. Paulo*, October 10, 1965. *Correio da Manhã*, *Tribuna da Imprensa*, and *Última Hora*, October 12, 1965.

12. The UDN Favors a New Convention (October 21, 1965)

1. *O Estado de S. Paulo*, October 14, 1965. *Correio da Manhã*, October 16, 1965.
2. Justino Alves Bastos, quoted in *Correio da Manhã*, October 9, 1965. Carlos Castello Branco, *Os Militares no Poder*, vol. 1, p. 338 (entry for October 15, 1965).
3. *Correio da Manhã*, October 16, 19 (including editorial), 1965. *O Estado de S. Paulo*, October 22, 1965. *Jornal do Brasil*, October 9, 21, 1965. Carlos Castello Branco, *Os Militares no Poder*, vol. 1, p. 335 (entry for October 12, 1965).
4. *Jornal do Brasil*, October 12, 13, 1965. *O Estado de S. Paulo*, October 13, 14, 1965.
5. *Tribuna da Imprensa*, October 15, 11, 1965. *O Estado de S. Paulo*, October 14, 15, 1965. *Jornal do Brasil*, October 13, 14, 1965.

6. Raphael de Almeida Magalhães, interview, Rio de Janeiro, August 8, 1977.

7. *Diário Carioca,* October 13, 15, 1965. *Tribuna da Imprensa,* October 12, 13, 14, 15, 16–17, 18, 1965. *Brazil Herald,* October 12, 15, 1965. *Correio da Manhã,* October 16, 1965. *Jornal do Brasil,* October 19, 1965.

8. *Jornal do Brasil,* October 20, 21, 1965. *O Estado de S. Paulo,* October 20, 1965. "Conversa Juraci X Lacerda," *Tribuna da Imprensa,* October 20, 1965. *Correio da Manhã,* October 22, 1965. "Detalhes do encontro entre Juraci e Lacerda," *O Globo,* October 23, 1965.

9. *O Globo, O Estado de S. Paulo, Jornal do Brasil,* and *Correio da Manhã,* October 22, 1965.

10. *Jornal do Brasil,* October 21, 22, 1965. *O Globo, O Estado de S. Paulo,* and *Tribuna da Imprensa,* October 22, 1965.

11. *O Estado de S. Paulo,* October 22, 1965. *O Globo,* October 23, 1965.

13. Institutional Act Number Two (October 27, 1965)

1. *Jornal do Brasil,* October 20, 1965. Osvaldo Trigueiro do Vale, *O Supremo Tribunal Federal e a Instabilidade Político-Institucional* (Rio de Janeiro: Editora Civilização Brasileira, 1976), pp. 102–109.

2. Transcript of tape of speech of Artur da Costa e Silva, Itapeva, S.P., October 22, 1965 (transcript made available by Álcio da Costa e Silva, July 1977). *O Estado de S. Paulo,* October 23, 24, 26, 1965. *Jornal do Brasil,* October 23, 24, 1965.

3. Peri Constant Bevilacqua, interview, Rio de Janeiro, December 21, 1977. Trigueiro do Vale, *O Supremo Tribunal Federal,* pp. 112–113. *O Estado de S. Paulo,* October 24 (editorial), 26, 1965. *Correio da Manhã,* editorial, October 23, 1965.

4. *Jornal do Brasil,* October 21, 22, 24 ("Coluna do Castello"), 26, 27, 1965.

5. Juracy Magalhães, "Respostas do General Juracy Magalhães ao Professor John W. F. Dulles" (typewritten), Rio de Janeiro, December 3, 1974, p. 4. Paulo Bosísio, interview, São Paulo, November 8, 1975. Antônio Carlos Magalhães, interview, Rio de Janeiro, August 11, 1977. Vasco Leitão da Cunha, interview, Rio de Janeiro, November 23, 1974. Luís Viana Filho, *O Governo Castelo Branco,* pp. 352, 354. Paulo Guerra, interview, Brasília, November 11, 1975.

6. *O Estado de S. Paulo,* October 27, 1965. *Correio da Manhã,* October 27, 1965. Paulo Bosísio, interview, November 8, 1975.

7. Paulo Bosísio, interview, November 8, 1975. Luís Alberto Bahia, interview, Rio de Janeiro, December 8, 1975.

8. *Correio da Manhã,* October 27, 1965. *O Estado de S. Paulo,* editorials, October 26, 27, 1965.

9. Paulo Bosísio, interview, November 8, 1975. *Jornal do Brasil,* October 21, 27, 1965.

10. *Jornal do Brasil,* October 21, 26, 25, 1965.

11. Daniel Krieger, *Desde as Missões*, p. 199. Aliomar Baleeiro, "Recordações do Presidente H. Castelo Branco," p. 33, reproduced in Luiz Viana Filho, compiler, *Castello Branco: Testemunhos de uma época*, p. 24. *O Estado de S. Paulo*, October 27, 1965. *Jornal do Brasil*, October 28, 1965, including "Coluna do Castello." Artur da Costa e Silva, interview as recorded by Rádio Gazeta SP, Rio de Janeiro, October 28, 1965 (transcript of tape supplied by Álcio da Costa e Silva).

12. *O Globo* and *Jornal do Brasil*, October 28, 1965. Humberto de Alencar Castello Branco, *Discursos, 1965*, pp. 33–35.

13. "Coluna do Castello," *Jornal do Brasil*, October 28, 1965.

14. *Jornal do Brasil*, October 28, 1965. *O Estado de S. Paulo*, November 2, October 28, 1965. *O Globo*, October 28, 29, 1965.

15. *O Estado de S. Paulo*, October 28, 29, 1965. *Jornal do Brasil*, October 28, 29, 1965. *Correio da Manhã*, October 28, 30, 1965. *O Jornal*, October 31, 1965.

16. *O Globo*, October 29, 1965, including Eugênio Gudin, "Ato Institucional No. 2." *Jornal do Brasil*, November 7, 18, 1965.

17. *O Globo*, October 28, 1965. *O Estado de S. Paulo*, October 29, 1965.

18. *O Globo* and *O Estado de S. Paulo*, October 30, 1965. *Jornal do Brasil*, October 30, November 7, 1965. Carlos Lacerda, "Quem São os Militares," *Fatos & Fotos* 7, no. 345 (September 9, 1967), pp. 8–11; see p. 11.

19. *O Estado de S. Paulo*, October 29, 30, 1965. *Jornal do Brasil*, November 7, October 30, 1965.

14. Retiring from Public Office (November 4, 1965)

1. *Jornal do Brasil*, *O Estado de S. Paulo*, and *O Globo*, October 30, 1965.

2. Juracy Magalhães, interview, Rio de Janeiro, December 3, 1974, and "Respostas do General Juracy Magalhães ao Professor John W. F. Dulles," pp. 1–2. Afonso de Albuquerque Lima, interview, Rio de Janeiro, November 16, 1974.

3. Juracy Magalhães, interview, December 3, 1974. *O Estado de S. Paulo*, November 4, 1965. *Tenente:* military officer active in revolution in the 1920s and 1930.

4. Luiz Roberto Veiga de Brito, transcript of interview taped by the Sociedade dos Amigos de Carlos Lacerda, p. 28. Lamy Cunto, interview, Rio de Janeiro, August 26, 1994.

5. *O Estado de S. Paulo*, November 5, 1965.

6. Ibid., editorial.

15. Comments

1. Raphael de Almeida Magalhães, interview, Rio de Janeiro, November 19, 1975.

2. *Jornal do Brasil*, October 21, 1965.

IX. Background for the Frente Ampla Crusade (November 1965–October 1966)

1. Status of Lacerda Administration Projects (November 1965–April 1966)

1. *Jornal do Brasil*, December 1, 1965.

2. Ibid., November 7, 26, 28, December 1, 2, 4, 8, 1965. Afonso de Albuquerque Lima, interview, Rio de Janeiro, November 20, 1974. Carlos Castello Branco, *Os Militares no Poder*, vol. 1, pp. 374–375 (entries for December 1, 2, 1965). Heráclito Fontoura Sobral Pinto, interview, Rio de Janeiro, December 9, 1975.

3. Carlos Castello Branco, *Os Militares no Poder*, vol. 1, pp. 378–379 (entry for December 5, 1965).

4. *Jornal do Brasil*, November 30, December 3, 1965. Mauro Magalhães, *Carlos Lacerda*, pp. 22–23, 76–79, and interview, Rio de Janeiro, March 9, 1992. *Brazil Herald*, December 4, 1965. *Tribuna da Imprensa*, January 10, 11, February 17, 1966.

5. *Jornal do Brasil*, November 28, 1965. Carlos Lacerda, letter to Humberto Castello Branco, Rio de Janeiro, January 13, 1966, in File N4 (item 20), Castello Branco papers, CPDOC. Victor Vincent Valla, ed., *Educação e Favela: Política para as favelas do Rio de Janeiro, 1940–1985*, p. 91.

6. *Jornal do Brasil*, November 28, December 5, 31, 1965.

7. Euclides Quandt de Oliveira, interview, Brasília, October 21, 1975. *Jornal do Brasil*, December 21, 23, 24, 31, 1965. *Tribuna da Imprensa*, January 18, 1966.

8. *Jornal do Brasil*, October 23, November 28, December 11, 1965.

9. Ibid., October 20, 1965. *Água, afinal!* (phonograph record, Teleplan, 1966).

10. Luiz Roberto Veiga de Brito, transcript of interview taped by the Sociedade dos Amigos de Carlos Lacerda, pp. 20–21.

11. *Jornal do Brasil*, November 28, December 3, 4, 1965. Enaldo Cravo Peixoto, transcript of interview taped by the Sociedade dos Amigos de Carlos Lacerda, p. 20. *Água, afinal!*.

12. *Jornal do Brasil*, December 15, 1965. *Tribuna da Imprensa*, January 22–23, February 12–13, 1966. *Água, afinal!*.

13. *Jornal do Brasil*, December 24, 1965. *Tribuna da Imprensa*, January 3, 8–9, 1966.

14. *Tribuna da Imprensa*, January 3, 8–9, 1966.

15. *Água, afinal!*. *Jornal do Brasil*, January 14, 12, 16, 1966.

16. *Tribuna da Imprensa*, January 13, 14, 18, 21, 22–23, 24, April 5, 1966. *Água, afinal!*. Hélio Mamede, interview with DFR, Rio de Janeiro, August 9, 1985.

17. *Tribuna da Imprensa*, February 12–13, 1966. *Água, afinal!*.

18. Carlos Lacerda, "Rosas e Pedras do Meu Caminho," Chapter 12, *Manchete* 14, no. 793 (July 1, 1967), p. 104. *Tribuna da Imprensa*, March 19–20, 21, 22, 1966.

19. *Tribuna da Imprensa*, April 5, 1966.

20. Carlos Lacerda, *Depoimento*, pp. 232–233. *Tribuna da Imprensa*, March 18, 1966. *Jornal do Brasil*, December 23, 1965.

21. Gustavo Borges, letter to Diretor Geral do Departamento Federal de Segurança Pública, Rio de Janeiro, November 12, 1965, and attached copies of documents, October and November 1965, in CCL. *Jornal do Brasil*, December 3, 5, 25, 1965. *O Estado de S. Paulo*, May 28, 1966.

22. *Jornal do Brasil*, December 4, 1965.

23. Ibid., December 25, 1965.

2. Businessman Carlos Lacerda (October 1965–January 1966)

1. Antônio Carlos de Almeida Braga, interview, New York, September 2, 1988. Fernando Cícero da Franca Velloso, interviews, Rio de Janeiro, August 16, 1983, August 15, 1984. Tibiriçá Botelho Filho, interview, São Paulo, July 31, 1983.

2. Fernando Velloso, interviews, August 16, 1983, August 15, 1984. Epaminondas Moreira do Valle, interview with DFR, Rio de Janeiro, July 26, 1985. Antônio Carlos de Almeida Braga, interview, September 2, 1988.

3. José Maria Mayrink, "Lacerda é homem de emprêsa como corretor, editor, investidor e publicitário," *Jornal do Brasil*, November 6, 1965. Sérgio C. A. Lacerda, in "Lacerda/70 anos," *Jornal do Brasil*, April 30, 1984. For information about Lins Publicidade, see letters to Fernando Goldgaber from Jair Lins Netto (Rio de Janeiro, May 3, 1985) and Otto Lara Resende (Rio de Janeiro, April 10, 1985) and to JWFD from Joel Osório Alves (Brasília, April 9, 1985) and Oswaldo Alves (Nova Friburgo, R.J., February 2, 1985), and Oswaldo Alves, letter to Joel Osório Alves, Nova Friburgo [1985]. Information about Imobiliária Nova York was received from Mauro Magalhães, interview, Rio de Janeiro, March 9, 1992, and Sérgio C. A. Lacerda, Fernando Cícero da Franca Velloso, and João Hermene Guimarães dos Santos, letter to Sérgio Augusto Ribeiro of the Banco Central do Brasil, Rio de Janeiro, January 3, 1977 (in the files of Fernando Cícero da Franca Velloso), p. 1.

4. José Maria Mayrink, "Lacerda é homem de emprêsa," *Jornal do Brasil*, November 6, 1965.

5. Sebastião Lacerda, interview, Rio de Janeiro, March 5, 1992. Alfredo C. Machado, interview, Rio de Janeiro, July 7, 1983. Mayrink, "Lacerda é homem de emprêsa."

6. Maria Thereza Correia de Mello, interviews, Miami Beach, July 5–6, 1986. Maria Cristina Lacerda Simões Lopes, interview with DFR, Rio de Janeiro, August 26, 1986. Gabriel Lacerda, interview, Rio de Janeiro, August 16, 1983. Lygia Vaz Brito e Cunha and Rubens Vaz Júnior, interview, Rio de Janeiro, August 9, 1983.

7. Fernando Velloso, interview, August 16, 1983. Epaminondas Moreira do Valle, interview with DFR, July 26, 1985. Joaquim Marques, interview with DFR, Rio de Janeiro, August 7, 1985. Mario Lorenzo Fernandez, interview with DFR, Rio de Janeiro, August 9, 1985. Maria Thereza Correia de

Mello, interviews, July 5–6, 1986. César Seroa da Mota, transcript of interview taped by the Sociedade dos Amigos de Carlos Lacerda, p. 10.

8. Ruth Alverga, interview with DFR, Rio de Janeiro, March 20, 1983. Joaquim Marques, interview with DFR, August 7, 1985. Maria Thereza Correia de Mello, interviews, July 5–6, 1986.

9. Raul Brunini, interviews, Rio de Janeiro, August 12, 1983, August 1, 1989. Advertisements in *Jornal do Brasil*, December 16, 23, 1965.

10. *Brazil Herald*, November 10, 1965. Antonio Dias Rebello Filho, *Carlos Lacerda, Meu Amigo*, p. 211.

11. Luiz Ernesto Kawall, interview, São Paulo, July 25, 1983. Carlos Alberto Aulicino, interview, São Paulo, July 28, 1983. "As galinhas subversivas de Carlos Lacerda," *O Globo*, September 13, 1992.

12. *Jornal do Brasil*, December 2, 4, 14, 1965. *Tribuna da Imprensa*, January 11, 1966. Various letters from Carlos Lacerda, Rio de Janeiro, December 27, 28, 1965, in CCL; see letters to London banker Sir Geoffrey Wallinger and London's Lord Mayor Sir James Miller. William Shakespeare, *Júlio César*, tradução de Carlos Lacerda (Rio de Janeiro: Distribuidora Record, 1965).

13. Letter to Carlos Lacerda, signature unclear, Rio de Janeiro, January 14, 1966, in CCL. Carlos Lacerda, letter to Fernando Marques Reis, in *Tribuna da Imprensa*, January 20, 1966. Lacerda, writing in *Jornal da Tarde* on January 29, 1966, pointed to one of the translation mistakes.

14. *Tribuna da Imprensa*, January 11, 1966. Carlos Lacerda, letter to Humberto Castello Branco, Rio de Janeiro, January 13, 1966, in File N4 (item 20), Castello Branco papers, CPDOC.

15. Rebello Filho, *Carlos Lacerda, Meu Amigo*, p. 212. *Tribuna da Imprensa*, January 17, 1966.

3. The PAREDE (November 1965–July 1966)

1. Atos Complementares Nos. 4 and 6, of November 20, 1965, January 3, 1966, in Senado Federal, *Legislação Constitucional e Complementar* (Brasília: Senado Federal, 1972), pp. 143–149. *Jornal do Brasil*, November 27, December 8, 1965. Daniel Krieger, *Desde as Missões*, p. 204. Theódulo de Albuquerque, interview, Brasília, October 24, 1975.

2. *Jornal do Brasil*, December 8, November 28, 1965.

3. Roberto de Abreu Sodré, memorandum to JWFD, São Paulo, August 5, 1977, giving recollections of himself, Oscar Klabin Segall, Luís Francisco de Carvalho, Onadir Marcondes, and Ivo Ramos, p. 2. Roberto de Abreu Sodré, letter to Luís Viana Filho, São Paulo, September 28, 1971, pp. 17–18 (reproduced in Luiz Viana Filho, compiler, *Castello Branco: Testemunhos de uma época*, p. 97). *Jornal do Brasil*, December 7, 1965.

4. *O Globo*, November 5, 8, 1965. Juarez Távora, letter to Juracy Magalhães, n.d., in File N1, Part 1 (item 9), Castello Branco papers, CPDOC. Ademar de Barros entry in *Dicionário Histórico-Biográfico Brasileiro, 1930–1983*.

5. Carlos Flexa Ribeiro, interview, Rio de Janeiro, July 5, 1983.

6. Negrão de Lima entry in *Dicionário Histórico-Biográfico Brasileiro, 1930–1983. Tribuna da Imprensa,* January 18, 26, 27, March 11, 1966.

7. *Tribuna da Imprensa,* January 6, 20, 26, 27, 28, 29–30, 1966. Mauro Magalhães, *Carlos Lacerda,* pp. 305–312.

8. Abreu Sodré, letter to Viana Filho, September 28, 1971, pp. 16–17 (reproduced in Luiz Viana Filho, compiler, *Castello Branco: Testemunhos de uma época,* pp. 96–97).

9. Abreu Sodré, memorandum of August 5, 1977, to JWFD, p. 2. Abreu Sodré, letter to Viana Filho, September 28, 1971, pp. 16–18 (reproduced in Luiz Viana Filho, compiler, *Castello Branco: Testemunhos de uma época,* pp. 96–97). Lacerda has recalled (*Depoimento,* p. 262) that Abreu Sodré came to Rio to appeal that he continue in public life, prompting Lacerda to reply, "No, I consider this an error, for I was beaten in Guanabara."

10. *Tribuna da Imprensa,* February 5–6, 7, 8, 1966.

11. Ibid., February 7, 8, 1966.

12. Ibid., February 12, 13, 1966.

13. Carlos Castello Branco, *Os Militares no Poder,* vol. 1, pp. 423, 421 (entries for February 10, 8, 1966). *Jornal do Brasil,* January 7, 1966. Raphael de Almeida Magalhães, interview, Rio de Janeiro, August 8, 1977.

14. *Jornal do Brasil,* February 18, 1966. *Tribuna da Imprensa,* March 7, 1966. *Correio da Manhã,* March 8, 1966. Luís Viana Filho, *O Governo Castelo Branco,* p. 387.

15. *Boletim Cambial* poll, reported in *Jornal do Brasil,* March 24, 1966.

16. *Brazil Herald,* February 26, 1966. *Tribuna da Imprensa,* February 26–27, 1966. Anthony Vereker, typewritten report for JWFD, Rio de Janeiro, January 19, 1966.

17. *Tribuna da Imprensa,* March 2, February 26–27, 1966.

18. Ibid., March 3, 9, 10, 1966.

19. Ibid., March 12–13, 1966.

20. Ibid., March 12–13, 17, 21, 1966.

21. Ibid., March 16, 24, 1966. *Brazil Herald,* April 30, May 5, 1966. *O Estado de S. Paulo,* April 14, May 3, 4, 1966.

22. *O Estado de S. Paulo,* May 27, 25, 1966.

23. Ibid., June 22, 23, 25, 1966. Raphael de Almeida Magalhães, interview, August 8, 1977.

24. *Jornal do Brasil,* December 8, 1965. Raphael de Almeida Magalhães, interview, August 8, 1977. *O Estado de S. Paulo,* July 6, June 22, 1966.

25. *O Estado de S. Paulo,* July 12, 14, 15, August 9, 1966. Mauro Magalhães, *Carlos Lacerda,* pp. 310–313.

26. *O Estado de S. Paulo,* July 19, 29, 1966. Benedito Calasans entry in *Dicionário Histórico-Biográfico Brasileiro, 1930–1983.*

4. Traveling Columnist (March–June 1966)

1. *Tribuna da Imprensa,* March 16, 15, 1966. *O Estado de S. Paulo,* March 16, 17, 1966.

2. *O Estado de S. Paulo*, April 2, 3, 1966. Carlos Lacerda, "O encontro que não houve," *Jornal da Tarde*, March 29, 1966.

3. Letícia Lacerda, letter to Carlos Lacerda, Rio de Janeiro, March 30, 1966, in CCL.

4. *O Estado de S. Paulo*, April 19, 27, 1966. See Kanagawa Prefectural Government, Yokohama, Japan, "Itinerary for the visit of Mr. and Mrs. Carlos Lacerda to Kanagawa Prefecture," in CCL. Carlos Lacerda, "Entre o Japão e o Havaí," *Diário de Notícias*, May 10, 1966.

5. Sérgio and Sebastião Lacerda, letters and cable to Carlos Lacerda, Rio de Janeiro, June 1, 10, 6, 1966, in CCL.

6. *O Estado de S. Paulo*, June 17, 19, 1966. Decio de Almeida Prado, "Júlio César," *O Estado de S. Paulo*, June 1, 1966.

7. *Jornal da Tarde*, February 24, May 25, April 25, January 6, 1966.

8. Carlos Lacerda, "Revolução Morta, Viva a Revolução," *Diário de Notícias*, May 6, 8, 10, 11, 13, 14, 17, 18, 19, 1966 (see May 6, 17). Sérgio Lacerda, letter to Carlos Lacerda, May 8, 1966.

9. *Jornal da Tarde*, May 4, 17, June 3, 1966.

10. Ibid., May 5, April 12, 28, March 25, 1966.

11. Carlos Lacerda, "A Caminho da Monarquia," *Diário de Notícias*, April 12, 1966.

12. Carlos Lacerda, letter to Gildo Corrêa Ferraz, Rio de Janeiro, February 24, 1966, in File N5 (Anexo 12), Castello Branco papers, CPDOC. Roberto Marinho, letter to Humberto Castello Branco, May 24, 1966, in File M, Castello Branco papers, CPDOC.

13. *Jornal da Tarde*, March 4, April 20, May 25, June 14, 1966. *Diário de Notícias*, May 10, 1966. Carlos Lacerda, "Natureza, crise e rumos da Revolução Brasileira," *Jornal do Brasil* and *O Estado de S. Paulo*, April 3, 1966 (reprinted as a special supplement of *BC, Diário Econômico e Financeiro*, April 4, 1966).

14. Carlos Lacerda, "Adeus às armas," *Jornal da Tarde*, July 4, 1966.

5. Preparing an Alliance with Former Foes (August 1966)

1. Joaquim Guilherme da Silveira, interview, Rio de Janeiro, August 9, 1983. Carlos Lacerda, *Depoimento*, pp. 380–381.

2. Joaquim Guilherme da Silveira, interview, August 9, 1983.

3. Carlos Lacerda, *Crítica e Autocrítica* (Rio de Janeiro: Editôra Nova Fronteira, 1966), p. 78.

4. Ibid., p. 79. Hélio Fernandes, "A tão polêmica e famosa Frente Ampla," *Pasquim* 15, no. 779 (Rio de Janeiro, May 31–June 6, 1984), p. 7.

5. Hélio Fernandes, "A tão polêmica e famosa Frente Ampla." Sérgio Lacerda, interview, Rio de Janeiro, August 22, 1988.

6. *Jornal do Brasil*, August 19, 1966. Carlos Lacerda letter to *Jornal do Brasil*, in *Jornal do Brasil* and *O Estado de S. Paulo*, August 18, 1966.

7. Hélio Fernandes, "A tão polêmica e famosa Frente Ampla." Hélio

Fernandes, "Frente Ampla: Depoimento de um testemunho," *Tribuna da Imprensa*, September 23, 1966. Ênio Silveira, on jacket of Mauro Magalhães, *Carlos Lacerda.*

8. Renato Archer, interview, Rio de Janeiro, September 30, 1975. Renato Archer, quoted in "Lacerda/70 anos," *Jornal do Brasil*, April 30, 1984. Renato Archer, "Depoimento" (Rio de Janeiro: CPDOC, 1979), pp. 628–632.

9. Ibid. Aspásia Camargo, Lucia Hippolito, Maria Celina Soares D'Araújo, and Dora Rocha Flaksman, *Artes da Política: Diálogo com Amaral Peixoto*, p. 486. Hélio Fernandes, "A tão polêmica e famosa Frente Ampla."

10. Vera Lacerda Paiva and Lygia Paiva Derizans, interview with DFR, Rio de Janeiro, August 25, 1985. Sérgio Lacerda, interview, August 22, 1988. Renato Archer, quoted in "Lacerda/70 anos," *Jornal do Brasil*, April 30, 1984.

11. Carlos Lacerda, *Crítica e Autocrítica*, pp. 79–80. Hélio Fernandes, "Frente Ampla: Depoimento de um testemunho."

12. Ibid. Hélio Fernandes, "Jânio Quadros, mais do que nunca imaturo, instável e irresponsável," *Tribuna da Imprensa*, March 29, 1967.

13. *O Estado de S. Paulo*, September 2, 1966. Hélio Fernandes, "Jânio Quadros, mais do que nunca imaturo, instável e irresponsável." Carlos Lacerda, *Crítica e Autocrítica*, pp. 80–81.

14. *Jornal do Brasil*, September 1, 1966. Carlos Lacerda, "Lacerda: o que pensa e o que quer," *Visão*, September 2, 1966, pp. 12, 13.

15. Carlos Lacerda, "Lacerda: o que pensa e o que quer," pp. 9, 10.

16. Ibid., pp. 10, 11.

17. Ibid., p. 11.

18. *O Estado de S. Paulo*, September 2, 1966.

19. *Jornal do Brasil*, September 1, 3, 1966. Carlos Castello Branco, *Os Militares no Poder*, vol. 1, p. 557 (entry for September 1, 1966).

6. Reactions to the Frente Ampla Idea (August–September 1966)

1. Walter Cunto, transcript of interview taped by the Sociedade dos Amigos de Carlos Lacerda, p. 15. Carlos Lacerda, *Crítica e Autocrítica*, p. 81. Maria Thereza Correia de Mello, interviews, Miami Beach, July 5–6, 1986. Renato Archer, quoted in "Lacerda/70 anos," *Jornal do Brasil*, April 30, 1984.

2. Maria Thereza Correia de Mello, interviews, July 5–6, 1986. Carlos Lacerda, "A união de todos," *Tribuna da Imprensa*, October 3, 1966. Hélio Fernandes, "A tão polêmica e famosa Frente Ampla," *Pasquim* 15, no. 779 (Rio de Janeiro, May 31–June 6, 1984).

3. Antonio Dias Rebello Filho, *Carlos Lacerda, Meu Amigo*, pp. 213–214.

4. Walter Cunto, transcript of interview taped by the Sociedade dos Amigos de Carlos Lacerda, p. 15. Lamy Cunto, interview with DFR, Rio de Janeiro, January 4, 1988. Letícia Lacerda, interview with DFR, January 5, 1988. Lygia Gomide, interview, March 17, 1991.

5. *Tribuna da Imprensa*, September 1, 8, 1966. *O Globo*, September 4, 1966. *Jornal do Brasil*, September 6, 11, 1966.

6. *O Estado de S. Paulo*, September 11, 9, 1966. *Jornal do Brasil*, September 9, 10, 1966.

7. *O Estado de S. Paulo*, October 28, 1966. "Coisa da política," *Jornal do Brasil*, September 9, 1966. *O Globo*, October 7, 1966. *Última Hora*, September 9, 1966. *Diário de Notícias*, September 29, 1966.

8. Carlos Lacerda in *Jornal da Tarde*, September 6, 29, 1966. *Tribuna da Imprensa*, September 30, 1966.

9. *Correio da Manhã*, September 3, 4, 5, 6, 18, 19, 20, 28, 1966. *Jornal do Brasil*, September 24, 1966. *O Globo*, September 15, 17, 1966. *Brazil Herald*, April 4, 1963, September 16, 1966. Carlos Lacerda in *Jornal da Tarde*, September 28, 9, 20, 1966.

10. Carlos Lacerda in *Jornal da Tarde*, September 16, 1966. *Jornal do Brasil*, September 23, 1966. *O Globo*, September 15, 1966.

11. *Tribuna da Imprensa*, September 8, 13, 1966. Carlos Lacerda, *Crítica e Autocrítica*, p. 83.

12. Hélio Fernandes, "Frente Ampla: Depoimento de uma testemunha." William H. Gussman and United States Ambassador Henry A. Hoyt, interviews, Montevideo, November 13, 1967. Carlos Lacerda, *Crítica e Autocrítica*, p. 83. *Jornal do Brasil*, September 17, 1966.

13. Renato Archer, "Depoimento," pp. 635, 638, 641, 695–696. *Jornal do Brasil*, September 8, 20, 21, 10, 11, 1966. Carlos Lacerda, *Crítica e Autocrítica*, pp. 81–82.

14. *O Estado de S. Paulo*, September 17, 1966. *Jornal do Brasil*, September 8, 1966. Aspásia Camargo, Lucia Hippolito, Maria Celina Soares D'Araújo, and Dora Rocha Flaksman, *Artes da Política*, p. 486.

15. Raul Brunini, taped interview with Letícia Lacerda, Vera Lacerda Paiva, Cláudio Lacerda Paiva, Lamy Cunto, and DFR, Rio de Janeiro, March 9, 1989, p. 15 of transcript by DFR.

16. Nelson A. and Doris Pereira, interview, São Paulo, August 1, 1983. Antônio de Oliveira Godinho, interview, São Paulo, July 24, 1983.

17. *O Estado de S. Paulo*, September 15, 1966. Carlos Lacerda in *Fatos & Fotos*, reproduced in *Jornal do Brasil*, September 23, 1966.

18. Humberto de Alencar Castello Branco, *Discursos, 1966* (n.p.: Secretaria de Imprensa, n.d.), p. 235.

19. Ibid., p. 383. *O Globo*, September 27, 1966.

20. Lygia Vaz Brito e Cunha and Rubens Vaz Júnior, interview, Rio de Janeiro, August 9, 1983. Gustavo Borges, interview, Rio de Janeiro, August 14, 1983. *Jornal do Brasil*, September 22, 1966. Ferdinando de Carvalho, letter to Carlos Lacerda, Rio de Janeiro, September 25, 1966, in CCL.

21. Miguel Arraes, letter to "Prezado amigo," September 19, 1966, in CCL.

7. The Frente Ampla in Retreat
(Late September–Mid-October 1966)

1. *Jornal do Brasil*, September 29, 1966. *O Estado de S. Paulo*, September 22, 23, October 7, 1966. *Tribuna da Imprensa*, October 7, 1966.

2. *O Estado de S. Paulo,* September 22, 23, 1966. *Jornal do Brasil,* September 22, 1966.

3. *O Estado de S. Paulo,* September 27, October 6, 14, 22, 1966. *O Globo,* September 28, 1966. *Tribuna da Imprensa,* October 12, 1966.

4. *Tribuna da Imprensa,* October 7, 1966. *O Estado de S. Paulo,* October 7, 11, 1966.

5. *O Globo,* October 6, 1966. Carlos Lacerda, "A união de todos," *Tribuna da Imprensa,* October 3, 1966. Carlos Lacerda, "Bilhete a Costa e Silva," *Tribuna da Imprensa* and *O Estado de S. Paulo,* October 1, 1966. Carlos Lacerda, "O papel das Fôrças Armadas," *Jornal da Tarde,* September 30, 1966, and *Tribuna da Imprensa,* October 1–2, 1966.

6. Carlos Lacerda, "Como choram os pequeninos," *Tribuna da Imprensa,* October 11, 1966.

7. Carlos Castello Branco, *Os Militares no Poder,* vol. 1, pp. 578–579 (entries for October 11, 12, 13, 14, 1966). Ernâni Sátiro, interview, Rio de Janeiro, December 17, 1975. *Jornal do Brasil,* October 13, 1966.

8. *Jornal do Brasil,* October 13, 16, 17, 18, 20, 21, 1966. Carlos Castello Branco, *Os Militares no Poder,* vol. 1, pp. 580–581 (entries for October 14, 15, 16, 1966). *O Estado de S. Paulo,* October 20, 21, 1966.

9. Carlos Lacerda, "Carta a um amigo fardado," on pp. 41–60 of Carlos Lacerda, *Crítica e Autocrítica* (see p. 56).

10. Renato Archer, "Depoimento," pp. 535, 721, 556. José Cândido and Geli Moreira de Souza, interview with DFR, Rio de Janeiro, August 27, 1986.

11. Joaquim Guilherme da Silveira, interview, Rio de Janeiro, August 9, 1983.

12. Walter Cunto, transcript of interview taped by the Sociedade dos Amigos de Carlos Lacerda, p. 15. Carlos Lacerda, "Carta a um amigo fardado," *Tribuna da Imprensa,* October 21, 22–23, 1966 (see October 21).

13. Carlos Lacerda, "Carta a um amigo fardado," in Carlos Lacerda, *Crítica e Autocrítica,* see pp. 52, 56, 57, 59, 60, 61, 42, 43, 51.

14. Ibid., pp. 41, 60, 61.

15. Ibid., pp. 56–57, 59.

16. Ibid., pp. 42, 41.

17. Ibid., pp. 51, 50, 53.

18. Ibid., pp. 55, 44.

19. Ibid., pp. 46, 56.

8. Comments

1. Remarks of Humberto Castello Branco to Hal Hendrix, of the Scripps-Howard newspapers, on October 21, 1966, as given in U.S. Embassy, Rio de Janeiro, cable to Washington, D.C., October 21, 1966, National Security Files, Brazil, vol. 6, Box 3, Document 57, Lyndon Baines Johnson Library, Austin.

2. Humberto de Alencar Castello Branco, *Discursos, 1966,* p. 333.

3. Remarks of Humberto Castello Branco to Hal Hendrix, October 21, 1966.

4. William S. Gaud, memorandum, "Economic Assistance Program for Brazil," for President Lyndon B. Johnson, Office of the Administrator, AID, Washington, D.C., n.d., National Security Files, Brazil, Document 102a, Lyndon Baines Johnson Library, Austin.

5. Rachel de Queiroz, interview, Rio de Janeiro, August 5, 1983. Moacir Werneck de Castro, interview, Rio de Janeiro, December 2, 1967. Paulo Zingg, interview with DFR, São Paulo, March 9, 1983.

6. Gabriel Lacerda, interview, Rio de Janeiro, August 16, 1983. Maria Cristina Lacerda Simões Lopes, interview with DFR, Rio de Janeiro, January 4, 1988. Cristina Lacerda, "É preciso expor a mediocridade," *Jornal do Brasil,* October 26, 1986.

7. Sérgio Lacerda, quoted in "Lacerda/70 anos," *Jornal do Brasil,* April 30, 1984.

8. Renato Archer, quoted in "Lacerda/70 anos," *Jornal do Brasil,* April 30, 1984.

9. Fernando Pedreira, quoted in "Lacerda/70 anos," *Jornal do Brasil,* April 30, 1984.

X. The Frente Ampla (1966–1968)

1. The Frente Ampla Manifesto (October 27, 1966)

1. "Brunini vai ler na AL manifesto da Frente Ampla," newspaper clipping in File N6 (Anexo 64), Castello Branco papers, CPDOC. *Tribuna da Imprensa* and *Jornal do Brasil,* October 26, 1966.

2. *O Estado de S. Paulo,* October 21, 22, 27, 1966. *Jornal do Brasil,* October 23, 1966. *Tribuna da Imprensa,* October 26, 1966.

3. *O Estado de S. Paulo,* October 21, 1966. *O Globo* and *Jornal do Brasil,* October 26, 1966.

4. *O Globo* and *Tribuna da Imprensa,* October 26, 1966.

5. *O Estado de S. Paulo,* October 27, 1966.

6. Ibid., October 27, 28, 1966. Hélio Fernandes, "A tão polêmica e famosa Frente Ampla," *Pasquim* 15, no. 779 (Rio de Janeiro, May 31–June 6, 1984). *Última Hora,* October 28, 1966.

7. Carlos Lacerda, introduction to manifesto of the Frente Ampla, on p. 63 of Carlos Lacerda, *Crítica e Autocrítica. Última Hora, Brazil Herald, Jornal do Brasil, O Estado de S. Paulo, Tribuna da Imprensa,* and chiefly *O Globo,* October 28, 1966.

8. "A Frente Ampla," in Carlos Lacerda, *Crítica e Autocrítica,* pp. 63–75; see pp. 63–64.

9. Ibid., pp. 65–66, 69–70, 72.

10. Ibid., p. 67.

11. Ibid., pp. 67–68, 71.

12. Ibid., pp. 69, 71, 70.

13. Ibid., pp. 70–71.

14. Ibid., pp. 73, 74–75.

15. *Jornal do Brasil*, October 28, 1966. *O Estado de S. Paulo*, October 28, 29, 1966.

16. *O Estado de S. Paulo*, October 29, 1966.

17. *Jornal do Brasil* and *Tribuna da Imprensa*, October 28, 1966.

18. *Tribuna da Imprensa*, October 28, 29–30, 1966. *O Estado de S. Paulo*, October 19, 1966. *Correio da Manhã*, October 29, 1966.

19. *O Estado de S. Paulo*, editorial, October 28, 1966.

20. *O Globo*, editorial ("Messalinismo"), October 29, 1966.

21. *Jornal do Brasil*, editorial, October 28, 1966.

22. *Correio da Manhã*, editorial, October 30, 1966.

2. Congressional Elections and the *Cassação* of Hélio Fernandes (November 1966)

1. *O Estado de S. Paulo*, November 9, 1966. *Tribuna da Imprensa*, October 28, November 10, 1966. Carlos Lacerda in *Jornal da Tarde*, November 14, 1966.

2. Carlos Lacerda, "Voto para senador," *Tribuna da Imprensa*, November 9, 1966.

3. *O Estado de S. Paulo*, November 9, 1966. *Tribuna da Imprensa*, November 24, 1966.

4. *Jornal do Brasil*, October 28, 30, November 11, 1966. Hélio Fernandes, interview, Rio de Janeiro, July 6, 1977. *Tribuna da Imprensa*, November 10, 11, 1966. Hélio Fernandes, *Recordações de um Desterrado em Fernando de Noronha* (Rio de Janeiro: Editora Tribuna da Imprensa, 1967), p. 39.

5. *Tribuna da Imprensa*, November 11, 1966. *O Globo*, November 12, 1966.

6. *Tribuna da Imprensa*, November 11, 1966.

7. Ibid. See also reprint of the article in Hélio Fernandes, *Recordações de um Desterrado*, pp. 132–136.

8. *Tribuna da Imprensa*, November 16, 1966.

9. "Hélio Fernandes, 'Cassado por Subversão e Corrupção,'" *O Globo*, November 12, 1966. Hélio Fernandes, letter to Roberto Marinho, Rio de Janeiro, November 13, 1966, in *Tribuna da Imprensa*, November 16, 1966.

10. Ronald M. Schneider, *The Political System of Brazil: Emergence of a "Modernizing" Authoritarian Regime, 1964–1970* (New York and London: Columbia University Press, 1971), p. 191. Georges-André Fiechter, *Brazil since 1964: Modernization under a Military Regime* (New York and Toronto: John Wiley & Sons, 1975), p. 110. *Jornal do Brasil*, November 20, 1, 9, 1966.

11. *O Jornal*, November 20, 1966. *Jornal do Brasil*, November 18, 19, 1966.

12. Ronald M. Schneider, *The Political System of Brazil*, p. 190. *O Estado de S. Paulo*, November 17, 18, 19, 1966. *O Globo*, November 21, 1966. *Brazil Herald*, November 18, 1966.

13. Carlos Lacerda, "Os 10 Pecados da Revolução São 11" (interview given to Ubiratan de Lemos and Indalecio Wanderley), *O Cruzeiro*, December 10, 1966.

3. The "Declaration of Lisbon" (November 19, 1966)

1. Carlos Lacerda, "Os 10 Pecados da Revolução São 11," *O Cruzeiro*, December 10, 1966. Santana Mota, "O acôrdo visto em Lisboa," *O Estado de S. Paulo*, November 25, 1966.

2. Carlos Lacerda, *Depoimento*, p. 379. Carlos Lacerda, "Os 10 Pecados da Revolução São 11." "JK narra encontro com CL" (em carta dirigida a um seu ex-auxiliar, November 20, 1966), *Tribuna da Imprensa*, November 30, 1966. See also Carlos Heitor Cony, *JK: Memorial do Exílio*, pp. 119–120 for this account by Kubitschek (which was prepared for *Manchete* magazine).

3. "JK narra encontro com CL," *Tribuna da Imprensa*, November 30, 1966. Cony, *JK: Memorial do Exílio*, pp. 119–120.

4. Ibid.

5. Ibid.

6. Report to David Nasser from *Diário de Notícias* (of Lisbon) writer João Falcato, in *O Cruzeiro*, December 10, 1966.

7. Clipping from *Diário de Notícias* (of Lisbon), November 20, 1966, in File N6 (Anexo 74), Castello Branco papers, CPDOC. *Brazil Herald*, November 20, 1966.

8. "Há Quinze Anos o Inesperado Encontro JK-Lacerda," *Manchete*, February 6, 1982. Carlos Lacerda, *Depoimento*, pp. 379–380. "JK narra encontro com CL," *Tribuna da Imprensa*, November 30, 1966.

9. Carlos Lacerda, *Depoimento*, pp. 379–380. Juscelino Kubitschek, note to Adolpho Bloch, in Cony, *JK: Memorial do Exílio*, p. 120. Clipping from *Diário de Notícias* (of Lisbon), November 20, 1966, in File N6 (Anexo 75), Castello Branco papers, CPDOC.

10. Newspaper clipping in File N6 (Anexo 72), Castello Branco papers, CPDOC. *Última Hora*, November 21, 1966.

11. Juscelino Kubitschek, note to Adolpho Bloch, in Cony, *JK: Memorial do Exílio*, pp. 120–121. Newspaper clippings in File N6 (Anexos 75A and 76A), Castello Branco papers, CPDOC.

12. *Última Hora*, November 21, 22, 1966. *Correio da Manhã*, *Tribuna da Imprensa*, and *O Estado de S. Paulo*, November 22, 1966.

13. *O Estado de S. Paulo*, November 22, 1966. *Brazil Herald*, November 23, 1966.

14. *O Estado de S. Paulo*, November 22, 23, 1966. *Tribuna da Imprensa*, November 23, 1966.

15. Carlos Lacerda, *Depoimento*, pp. 382, 396. *O Estado de S. Paulo*, November 24, 1966.

4. Repercussions of the Pact of Lisbon (Late November 1966)

1. Carlos Lacerda, *Depoimento*, p. 381.

2. *O Globo*, November 22, 25, 1966. Carlos Castello Branco, *Os Militares no Poder*, vol. 1, p. 604 (entry for November 24, 1966).

3. *O Globo*, November 26, 1966. *O Estado de S. Paulo*, December 2, 1966.

4. Gustavo Borges, interview, Rio de Janeiro, August 14, 1983. Carlos Lacerda, *Depoimento*, p. 288. *O Globo*, November 22, 1966. *O Estado de S. Paulo*, December 2, 1966.

5. Carlos Lacerda, *Depoimento*, pp. 391–392. Carlos Lacerda, remarks following the death of Colonel Américo Fontenelle, in *O Estado de S. Paulo*, July 10, 1967. *Tribuna da Imprensa*, November 25, 1966.

6. *Jornal do Brasil* and *O Globo*, November 25, 1966.

7. "Pedroso responde a Lacerda," *Jornal do Brasil*, August 2, 1967. Oscar Pedroso Horta, "As Rosas e as Pedras do Caminho de Lacerda," *Manchete*, no. 799 (August 12, 1967), p. 35.

8. *Jornal do Brasil*, editorial, November 22, 1966. *Última Hora*, November 21, 1966. *Correio da Manhã*, editorial, November 20, 1966.

9. *O Estado de S. Paulo*, editorial, November 22, 1966.

10. Carlos Lacerda, *Depoimento*, p. 381. *O Globo*, November 21, 1966.

11. *O Estado de S. Paulo*, November 23, 1966. Rubens Vaz Júnior, interview, Rio de Janeiro, August 9, 1983. Rubens Florentino Vaz Júnior, letter to Roberto Marinho, Rio de Janeiro, November 22, 1966, and Lygia Figueiredo Vaz, Maria Cristina Figueiredo Vaz, Rubens Florentino Vaz Júnior, Ronaldo Figueiredo Vaz, and Rogério Figueiredo Vaz, letter to Roberto Marinho, November 22, 1966, both in *Tribuna da Imprensa*, November 23, 1966.

12. *O Estado de S. Paulo*, November 23, 1966.

13. Juracy Magalhães in *O Globo*, *Jornal do Brasil*, *O Estado de S. Paulo*, November 23, 1966. See Alberto Dines, Antônio Callado, Araújo Netto, Carlos Castello Branco, Cláudio Mello e Sousa, Eurilo Duarte, Pedro Gomes, and Wilson Figueiredo, *Os Idos de Março e a Queda em Abril*, p. 189.

14. "Juracy Desmascarado: Carta de Sérgio Lacerda desfaz intriga," *Tribuna da Imprensa*, November 24, 1966. "Filho de Lacerda contesta Juraci," *Jornal do Brasil*, November 24, 1966.

15. *O Globo*, November 25, 24, 22, 29, 1966.

16. Carlos Lacerda in *Tribuna da Imprensa*, December 2, 12, 1966. Carlos Lacerda in *Jornal da Tarde*, December 2, 14, 1966.

17. Carlos Lacerda in *Tribuna da Imprensa*, December 1, 2, 8, 1966. Carlos Lacerda in *Jornal da Tarde*, December 1, 9, 1966. *O Estado de S. Paulo*, January 22, 1967, December 16, 1966. *Tribuna da Imprensa*, December 16, 1966.

5. The Constitution, Press Law, and National Security Law (January–March 1967)

1. Humberto de Alencar Castello Branco, *Discursos, 1966*, pp. 334–335. Daniel Krieger, *Desde as Missões*, pp. 240–243. Jayme Portella de Mello, *A Revolução e o Governo Costa e Silva* (Rio de Janeiro: Guavira Editores Ltda., 1979), p. 388.

2. Daniel Krieger, *Desde as Missões*, p. 243. *Jornal do Brasil*, December 29, 1966. Humberto Castello Branco, longhand notes, File P1 (item 12), Castello Branco papers, CPDOC.

3. Daniel Krieger, *Desde as Missões,* pp. 244–246. Afonso Arinos de Melo Franco, *Planalto: Memórias,* p. 280. Carlos Castello Branco, "Coluna do Castello," *Jornal do Brasil,* January 4, 1967. Carlos Medeiros Silva, interview, Rio de Janeiro, July 22, 1977. *Jornal do Brasil,* January 3, 4, 17, 19, 20, 21, 1967. *O Jornal,* January 18, 1967. Luís Viana Filho, *O Governo Castelo Branco,* p. 461. 1967 Constitution of Brazil, Chapter VI, Section VI.

4. Carlos Lacerda, in *Tribuna da Imprensa,* January 6, 1967, December 9, 14, 1966, and in *Jornal da Tarde,* January 9, 1967, December 12, 1966. *O Estado de S. Paulo,* December 10, 1966. *Brazil Herald,* December 10, 1966. *Tribuna da Imprensa,* December 17–18, 1966.

5. *O Estado de S. Paulo,* December 10, 1966.

6. Carlos Medeiros Silva, interviews, Rio de Janeiro, November 12, 1975, August 9, 1977. Humberto de Alencar Castello Branco, *Discursos, 1966,* p. 335. *Jornal da Tarde,* December 23, 1966, January 4, 1967.

7. *O Globo,* January 5, 7, 1967. *Tribuna da Imprensa,* January 11, 1, 3, 1967. *O Estado de S. Paulo,* January 1, 7, 3, 1967.

8. *O Estado de S. Paulo,* January 22, 24, 1967. *Jornal da Tarde,* January 25, February 11, 1967.

9. *Correio da Manhã,* February 5, 1967. Carlos Medeiros Silva, interview, Rio de Janeiro, August 13, 1977. *Jornal da Tarde,* March 13, 15, 1967. *Jornal do Brasil,* March 17, 1967. *O Estado de S. Paulo,* March 14, 1967.

10. Carlos Medeiros Silva, interview, August 13, 1977. Carlos Lacerda in *Tribuna da Imprensa,* March 17, 1967.

11. *Jornal da Tarde,* March 13, 1967. *Tribuna da Imprensa,* March 16, 1967.

12. *O Estado de S. Paulo,* December 2, January 26, 14, 1967.

6. Politicians, Cool to the Frente, Await the New President (December 1966–March 1967)

1. *Tribuna da Imprensa,* December 8, 1966. *O Estado de S. Paulo,* December 13, 1966. *O Globo,* quoted in *Brazil Herald,* December 13, 1966. Brazilian Constitution of 1967, Article 149, Clause VII.

2. *O Estado de S. Paulo,* December 17, 1966. *Tribuna da Imprensa,* December 21, 1966.

3. Carlos Heitor Cony, *JK: Memorial do Exílio,* pp. 125–126. Carlos Lacerda, interview, Rio de Janeiro, October 11, 1967. *O Estado de S. Paulo,* December 24, 27, 1966.

4. *Jornal do Brasil,* January 18, 1967. *O Estado de S. Paulo,* December 27, 21, 1966.

5. *Jornal do Brasil,* January 19, 1967.

6. Carlos Lacerda, letter to Evon Z. Vogt, Rio de Janeiro, January 23, 1967, in CCL, gives information about Lacerda's visit to Harvard University and esteem for the *Harvard Crimson. O Estado de S. Paulo,* January 3, 12, 13, 1967. Juscelino Kubitschek de Oliveira, typewritten letter to Carlos Lacerda, New York, March 7, 1967, in CCL, and handwritten letter to Carlos Lacerda,

New York (shown as written in Lisbon), January 28, 1967 (copy furnished to JWFD by Maria Cristina Lacerda Simões Lopes).

7. *Jornal do Brasil*, January 27, 17, 1967. Carlos Lacerda in *Jornal da Tarde*, January 9, 31, 1967.

8. *Brazil Herald*, January 19, 1967. *O Estado de S. Paulo*, January 12, 22, 1967. *Tribuna da Imprensa*, January 23, 1967. *Jornal do Brasil*, January 27, 1967.

9. *Tribuna da Imprensa*, January 23, 1967. *O Estado de S. Paulo*, January 22, 24, 27, 1967. Juscelino Kubitschek de Oliveira, "Comentários de Juscelino Kubitschek de Oliveira sobre a Indicação do General Castelo Branco pelo PSD em Abril de 1964," typewritten manuscript, May 21, 1975, furnished to JWFD by Kubitschek.

10. Juscelino Kubitschek de Oliveira, letter to Carlos Lacerda, January 28, 1967.

11. *O Estado de S. Paulo*, February 1, 1967. *Tribuna da Imprensa*, February 14, 16, 18–19, 1967.

12. *O Estado de S. Paulo*, January 13, 23, 24, February 16, 17, 1967. *Jornal do Brasil*, February 26, March 3, 1967. Renato Archer, "Depoimento," pp. 298–306, 393, 642–644.

13. *O Estado de S. Paulo*, February 17, 23, 1967.

14. Ibid., February 18, 24, 25, 1967.

15. Juscelino Kubitschek de Oliveira, letter to Carlos Lacerda, New York, March 7, 1967. *O Estado de S. Paulo*, February 24, 1967. *Correio da Manhã*, February 11, 1967. *Tribuna da Imprensa*, February 27, 1967.

16. *Tribuna da Imprensa*, February 18–19, 1967. *O Estado de S. Paulo*, March 3, 1967.

17. Juscelino Kubitschek de Oliveira, letter to Carlos Lacerda, New York, March 7, 1967.

18. *O Estado de S. Paulo*, February 15, March 9, 10, 1967.

19. Flávio Galvão, "A Frente em São Paulo," *O Estado de S. Paulo*, March 22, 1967.

7. A Post for Lacerda in the New Administration? (April–July 1967)

1. Carlos Castello Branco, "Coluna do Castello," *Jornal do Brasil*, July 2, 1967. *Jornal do Brasil*, June 2, 1967.

2. Hélio Fernandes, "15 de março," *Tribuna da Imprensa*, March 15, 1967. *Jornal do Brasil*, March 17, June 7, 1967. Carlos Lacerda in *Tribuna da Imprensa*, March 17, 31, 1967. Article 173 of Brazilian Constitution of 1967. *O Estado de S. Paulo*, March 23, 24, 1967.

3. Carlos Castello Branco, "Coluna do Castello," *Jornal do Brasil*, June 18, 9, 1967.

4. Carlos Castello Branco, "Coluna do Castello," *Jornal do Brasil*, March 24, 1967. Carlos Lacerda, "Posição da Frente Ampla," *Tribuna da Imprensa*, March 23–24, 1967.

5. Carlos Lacerda in *Jornal da Tarde*, February 24, 1, 1967. *Jornal do Brasil*, March 23, 1967. *Tribuna da Imprensa*, April 7, 1967. Renato Archer, "Depoimento," pp. 556, 571–572. Carlos Lacerda, "Raízes e Perigo do Militarismo no Brasil," *bc/semanal*, no. 261 (April 10, 1967); see p. 22.

6. *Brazil Herald*, April 1, 1967. *Jornal do Brasil*, April 7, 1967. Carlos Lacerda, letter to Mrs. Selma W. Warner of the World Wide Lecture Bureau, Los Angeles, May 4, 1967, in CCL.

7. *O Estado de S. Paulo*, June 4, 8, 1967. Carlos Lacerda, letter to José de Magalhães Pinto, Rio de Janeiro, June 8, 1967 (and draft of the letter), in CCL.

8. Carlos Lacerda, "Rosas e Pedras do Meu Caminho," Chapter 12, *Manchete*, no. 793 (July 1, 1967), p. 108. *Tribuna da Imprensa*, June 13, 14, 1967.

9. *Tribuna da Imprensa*, June 15, 1967.

10. *Jornal do Brasil*, July 18, 22, 1967.

11. Ibid., March 24, April 7, 11, May 10, 11, 20, 1967. *Tribuna da Imprensa*, April 10, 1967. Mauro Magalhães, *Carlos Lacerda*, pp. 286–287.

12. *O Estado de S. Paulo*, June 22, 23, 1967. *Jornal do Brasil*, March 23, May 20, 1967. Carlos Castello Branco, "Coluna do Castello," *Jornal do Brasil*, April 5, 1967. *Tribuna da Imprensa*, April 13, 5, May 17, June 14, 1967. Carlos Lacerda, letter to Edward R. Fitzsimmons, Rio de Janeiro, June 23, 1967, in CCL. Carlos Lacerda, memorandum to Sebastião Lacerda, Rio de Janeiro, July 6, 1967, in CCL.

13. *O Estado de S. Paulo*, June 22, 28, July 7, 8, 11, 1967. *Tribuna da Imprensa*, June 14, 1967.

14. *O Estado de S. Paulo*, July 2, 1, 8, 1967. *Jornal do Brasil*, July 4, 5, 1967. See *O Estado de S. Paulo*, July 2, 4, 6, 1967, for interpretations of the Kubitschek-Quadros meeting.

8. "Rosas e Pedras do Meu Caminho" (April–July 1967)

1. Cláudio Lacerda, "Quem realmente conheceu este homem?" *Jornal da Tarde*, May 23, 1977. Cláudio Lacerda Paiva, letter to JWFD, October 1984.

2. "As amizades do homem que brigava," *O Estado de S. Paulo*, July 10, 1967.

3. Carlos Lacerda, "Rosas e Pedras do Meu Caminho," appearing weekly in *Manchete*, no. 782 (April 15, 1967) through no. 793 (July 1, 1967).

4. Ibid., Chapter 12 (*Manchete*, July 1, 1967), p. 110.

5. Carlos Lacerda, "Anúncio de favor," *Tribuna da Imprensa*, April 4, 1967, and *Jornal da Tarde*, April 5, 1967.

6. Carlos Lacerda, "Rosas e Pedras do Meu Caminho," Chapter 12, p. 107.

7. Ibid., Chapter 12, p. 110, and Chapter 11 (*Manchete*, June 24, 1967), p. 107.

8. Ibid., Chapter 7 (*Manchete*, May 27, 1967), pp. 38, 39.

9. Lourenço de Almeida Prado, letter to Carlos Lacerda, Mosteiro de São Bento, Rio de Janeiro, May 19, 1967, in CCL.

10. "Pedroso responde a Lacerda," *Jornal do Brasil*, August 2, 1967. Oscar

Pedroso Horta, "As Rosas e Pedras do Caminho de Lacerda," *Manchete*, no. 799 (August 12, 1967), pp. 32–35; see pp. 33, 35.

11. Carlos Lacerda, letter to Diretor da *Manchete*, Rio de Janeiro, August 2, 1967, in CCL.

9. Hélio Fernandes and Lacerda Anger Military Leaders (July–August 1967)

1. *O Estado de S. Paulo*, July 20, 1967.

2. Hélio Fernandes, "A morte do Sr. Humberto de Alencar Castello Branco," *Tribuna da Imprensa*, July 19, 1967.

3. *Jornal do Brasil*, July 20, 1967. Hélio Fernandes, "O meu artigo de ontem e algumas provocações encomendadas," *Tribuna da Imprensa*, July 20, 1967.

4. *O Estado de S. Paulo*, July 21, 22, 1967. Hélio Fernandes, *Recordações de um Desterrado*, p. 58.

5. *O Estado de S. Paulo*, July 21, 22, 1967. Carlos Castello Branco in *Jornal do Brasil*, July 22, 1967. Hélio Fernandes, *Recordações de um Desterrado*, pp. 64–65. Hélio Fernandes, letter to JWFD, Rio de Janeiro, October 28, 1987.

6. *Jornal do Brasil* and *O Estado de S. Paulo*, July 21, 22, 1967. Fernandes, *Recordações de um Desterrado*, pp. 68, 66. Jayme Portella de Mello, *A Revolução e o Governo Costa e Silva*, p. 470.

7. *Jornal do Brasil*, August 3, July 23, 1967. *O Estado de S. Paulo*, July 23, 1967.

8. *O Estado de S. Paulo*, July 26, 1967. *Tribuna da Imprensa*, July 29–30, 1967. *Jornal do Brasil*, July 29, 1967.

9. *O Estado de S. Paulo*, July 23, August 1, 1967. Carlos Lacerda, "Reparação, Conciliação, Redenção," *Tribuna da Imprensa*, July 31, 1967.

10. *O Estado de S. Paulo*, August 4, 8, 9, 10, 11, 1967. Fernandes, *Recordações de um Desterrado*, pp. 137–138. *Tribuna da Imprensa*, August 2, 5–6, 1967.

11. *O Estado de S. Paulo*, August 8, 1967. Fernandes, *Recordações de um Desterrado*, pp. 137, 140.

12. *Tribuna da Imprensa* and *O Estado de S. Paulo*, August 9, 1967.

13. *Tribuna da Imprensa*, August 9, 10, 1967.

14. *O Estado de S. Paulo*, August 13, 19, 1967. *Tribuna da Imprensa*, August 10, 9, 1967.

15. Fernandes, *Recordações de um Desterrado*, pp. 242, 235–236, 161; and pp. 163–167, giving letter of Fernandes to Jaime Costa e Silva, Fernando de Noronha, August 18, 1967. *Tribuna da Imprensa*, August 17, 19–20, 21, 1967. *O Estado de S. Paulo*, August 24, 1967.

16. A. C. Moniz de Aragão, "Afastai-vos das Forças Armadas!" *O Globo*, August 25, 1967.

17. *O Estado de S. Paulo*, August 26, 27, 1967. Lacerda's five articles, published in the *Tribuna da Imprensa*, August 25, 26, 28, 29, 31, 1967, are given on pp. 175–216 of Fernandes, *Recordações de um Desterrado*.

18. Carlos Lacerda, "Processo de Degradação Nacional," *Tribuna da Imprensa*, August 25, 1967. Carlos Lacerda, "Análise de uma Provocação," *Tribuna da Imprensa*, August 26, 1967. (See pp. 179, 178, 184, 187, 181, 182–183, 188 of Fernandes, *Recordações de um Desterrado*.)

19. *O Estado de S. Paulo*, August 30, 1967.

20. Jayme Portella de Mello, *A Revolução e o Governo Costa e Silva*, p. 550. *O Estado de S. Paulo*, August 30, 1967. A. C. Moniz de Aragão, "O Seu Destino É Decompor-se Vivo," *O Globo*, August 29, 1967.

21. A. C. Moniz de Aragão, "O Seu Destino É Decompor-se Vivo."

22. *O Estado de S. Paulo*, August 30, 31, 1967. Jayme Portella de Mello, *A Revolução e o Governo Costa e Silva*, p. 550. Carlos Lacerda, Frente Ampla, and Augusto César Muniz de Aragão entries in *Dicionário Histórico-Biográfico Brasileiro, 1930–1983*.

23. Hélio Fernandes, letter to General Moniz de Aragão, Pirassununga, August 30, 1967, in Fernandes, *Recordações de um Desterrado*, pp. 223–230.

24. Carlos Lacerda, "Quem São os Militares," *Fatos & Fotos*, September 9, 1967.

10. The Meeting with Goulart (September 24–25, 1967)

1. Carlos Lacerda, articles in the *Tribuna da Imprensa*, August 28, 29, 31, 1967, republished in Hélio Fernandes, *Recordações de um Desterrado*, pp. 188–216; see pp. 215, 203, 196, 192.

2. *O Estado de S. Paulo*, August 30, 1967. *O Globo*, September 1, 1967.

3. *O Globo*, September 2, 5, 1967. *Tribuna da Imprensa*, September 1, 1967.

4. *O Globo*, September 7, 8, 9, 4, 1967. Frente Ampla entry in *Dicionário Histórico-Biográfico Brasileiro, 1930–1983*.

5. *O Globo*, September 5 (editorial), 9, 8, 11, 12, 1967. *Tribuna da Imprensa*, September 9–10, 1967. *Jornal do Brasil*, October 27, 1967. Carlos Heitor Cony, *JK: Memorial do Exílio*, pp. 128–129.

6. Osvaldo Lima Filho, quoted by *O Globo*, September 26, 1967. *O Globo*, September 13, 1967. Frente Ampla entry in *Dicionário Histórico-Biográfico Brasileiro, 1930–1983*. *Tribuna da Imprensa*, September 15, 1967. Mauro Magalhães, *Carlos Lacerda*, p. 289. Renato Archer, "Depoimento," p. 712.

7. Carlos Lacerda, *Depoimento*, p. 383.

8. Edmundo Moniz, interview with DFR, Rio de Janeiro, February 6, 1983. *O Estado de S. Paulo*, August 5, 1967. *O Globo*, September 25, 1967. Carlos Lacerda, *Depoimento*, p. 383.

9. Joaquim Guilherme da Silveira, interview, Rio de Janeiro, August 9, 1983, and letter signed by Carlos Lacerda, Rio de Janeiro, September 22, 1967, disclosed during that interview. The letter was published in *Jornal do Brasil*, Section B, October 26, 1986, together with an article by Cristina Lacerda, "É preciso expor a mediocridade."

10. Renato Archer, "Depoimento," pp. 704–715, 638. "Lacerda e Jango no Uruguai: A Frente Ampla mais ampla," *Manchete*, no. 807 (October 7, 1967).

Carlos Lacerda, *Depoimento*, pp. 384–389. *O Globo* and *Última Hora*, September 26, 1967. *Jornal do Brasil*, September 26, October 3, 1967. Carlos Castello Branco, "Coluna do Castello," *Jornal do Brasil*, October 1, 3, 1967. João Goulart and Carlos Lacerda, Joint Declaration, Montevideo, September 25, 1967, in Carlos Lacerda, *Depoimento*, pp. 459–460. *Churrascaria:* restaurant serving barbecued beef.

11. Carlos Lacerda, *Depoimento*, p. 386. "Lacerda e Jango no Uruguai," *Manchete*, October 7, 1967. *Jornal do Brasil* and *O Globo*, September 26, 1967.

12. Carlos Lacerda, *Depoimento*, pp. 387, 389. *Jornal do Brasil* and *O Globo*, September 26, 1967.

13. *O Globo*, September 26, 1967.

14. "Lacerda e Jango no Uruguai," *Manchete*, October 7, 1967. *Jornal do Brasil*, September 26, 1967.

15. Carlos Lacerda, *Depoimento*, p. 388.

16. Carlos Lacerda, interview, Rio de Janeiro, October 11, 1967.

11. The Storm (September–October 1967)

1. Gustavo Borges, interview, Rio de Janeiro, August 14, 1983. Carlos Lacerda, interview, Rio de Janeiro, October 11, 1967.

2. Carlos Lacerda, speech to foreign correspondents, Rio de Janeiro, October 11, 1967 (notes taken by JWFD).

3. *O Globo*, editorial, September 27, 1967. Danton Jobim in *Última Hora*, September 27, 1967.

4. *Folha de S. Paulo*, editorial, September 26, 1967, and, on September 28, 29, transcriptions in it from *Diário Popular* and *O Jornal*. *O Estado de S. Paulo*, editorials, September 27, 26, 1967. *Correio da Manhã*, editorial, September 28, 1967.

5. *Jornal do Brasil*, editorial, September 27, 1967.

6. Carlos Lacerda, letter to Manoel Francisco do Nascimento Brito, Rio de Janeiro, September 27, 1967, in CCL. Nascimento Brito, letter to Carlos Lacerda, Rio de Janeiro, September 29, 1967, in CCL.

7. Roberto de Abreu Sodré, interview, São Paulo, August 3, 1983. *O Globo*, September 29, 30, 1967.

8. *O Globo*, September 27, 30, October 4, 1967. *Jornal do Brasil*, October 1, 4, 1967.

9. *Jornal do Brasil*, October 5, 1967. *O Globo*, September 28, October 7, 1967.

10. *Jornal do Brasil*, October 4, 1967. *O Globo*, October 10, 24, 1967.

11. *O Globo*, October 5, 1967. *Jornal do Brasil*, September 30, 1967.

12. *Jornal do Brasil*, October 1, 3, 1967.

13. Ibid., October 3, 4, 1967. *O Globo*, October 3, 4, 1967.

14. Carlos Castello Branco, "Coluna do Castello," *Jornal do Brasil*, October 3, 1967. *Jornal do Brasil*, October 5, 6, 1967. *Tribuna da Imprensa*, October 4, 1967.

15. *Jornal do Brasil*, October 7, 4, September 30, 1967. *Correio da Manhã*, October 7, 1967. *O Cruzeiro*, October 21, 1967, p. 117.

16. *Correio da Manhã*, editorial, October 6, 1967. *Jornal do Brasil*, editorial, October 3, 1967.

17. *Jornal do Brasil*, October 15, 1967.

18. Ibid., October 19, 1967.

12. Preparing to Go to the Streets
(October–December 1967)

1. *Jornal do Brasil*, October 1, 7, 1967. *O Globo*, October 13, 1967. *Tribuna da Imprensa*, October 17, 18, 1967.

2. Carlos Lacerda, letter to Júlio de Mesquita Filho, Rio de Janeiro, October 5, 1967, in CCL.

3. *Jornal do Brasil*, October 7, 11, 1967. *O Globo*, October 18, 1967. *Tribuna da Imprensa*, October 6, 18, 13, 14, 17, 1967. *O Estado de S. Paulo*, December 1, 1967.

4. *O Globo*, October 9, 1967. *Jornal do Brasil*, October 8, 11, 31, 1967.

5. *Tribuna da Imprensa*, September 30, 1967. *Jornal do Brasil*, October 6, 14, 24, 1967. *O Estado de S. Paulo*, December 5, 1967. *O Globo*, October 21, 1967.

6. *Jornal do Brasil*, October 24, 14, 1967. *O Globo*, October 21, 1967.

7. *Jornal do Brasil*, October 20, 14, 1967.

8. Ibid., October 25, 18, 13, 19, 26, 1967. *Janistas:* supporters of Jânio Quadros.

9. *Tribuna da Imprensa* and *Jornal do Brasil*, October 20, 1967. See Alcindo Guanabara, *A Presidência Campos Sales* (Brasília: Editora Universidade de Brasília, 1983). Carlos Lacerda, interview, Rio de Janeiro, October 11, 1967.

10. *Tribuna da Imprensa*, October 20, November 1, 1967. *Jornal da Tarde*, November 6, 1967. *Jornal do Brasil*, October 28, 1967.

11. Jânio Quadros and Afonso Arinos de Melo Franco, "O Porquê da Renúncia," and Carlos Castello Branco, "O Dia Seguinte," *Realidade*, November 1967. *O Estado de S. Paulo*, November 2, 4, 1967.

12. *O Estado de S. Paulo*, November 5, 7, 1967. "Há Quinze Anos o Inesperado Encontro JK-Lacerda," *Manchete*, February 6, 1982. *Tribuna da Imprensa*, November 9, 7, 1967.

13. *O Estado de S. Paulo*, November 18, 17, 28, 1967. *Tribuna da Imprensa*, November 28, 1967.

14. *Jornal do Brasil*, October 11, 31, 1967. Carlos Castello Branco in *Jornal do Brasil*, December 10, 1967. *O Estado de S. Paulo*, December 9, 1967.

15. *O Estado de S. Paulo*, December 16, 17, 1967.

16. Ibid., December 8, 15, 17, 1967. Carlos Castello Branco in *Jornal do Brasil*, December 17, 1967. *Correio da Manhã*, December 17, 1967.

17. *O Estado de S. Paulo*, December 20, 27, 1967. Carlos Lacerda, letter to Peri Bevilacqua, December 19, 1967, in CCL. *New York Times*, December 28, 1967. *Jornal do Brasil*, December 27, 1967.

18. *Jornal do Brasil*, December 27, 1967. Afonso Augusto de Albuquerque Lima, letter to Carlos Lacerda, Rio de Janeiro, December 27, 1967, in CCL.

19. *O Estado de S. Paulo*, November 23, 1967. Carlos Castello Branco in *Jornal do Brasil*, December 6, 9, 1967. *Jornal do Brasil*, December 8, 1967.

I 3. The Government, Nervous about Lacerda, Mobilizes Troops (January I 968)

1. *Jornal do Brasil*, January 4, 13, 14, 1968. *O Estado de S. Paulo*, January 14, 1968.

2. "Los Grupos Revolucionarios del Brasil," *Este & Oeste* (Caracas) 9, no. 142 (November 1970), p. 10. *Jornal do Brasil*, January 3, February 22, 23, 1968. *O Estado de S. Paulo*, January 12, 1968.

3. *O Estado de S. Paulo*, January 16, 18, 1968.

4. *Jornal do Brasil*, January 18, 19 (editorial), 1968.

5. Ibid., January 27, 24, 25, 23, 1968.

6. Carlos Castello Branco in *Jornal do Brasil*, January 26, 1968. *Jornal do Brasil*, January 19, 1968.

7. *Jornal do Brasil*, January 26, 1968. *O Estado de S. Paulo*, January 21, 30, 1968. *Jornal da Tarde*, editorial, January 26, 1968.

8. *O Estado de S. Paulo*, January 28, 26, 30, 1968. *Jornal do Brasil*, January 25, 1968. *Jornal da Tarde*, January 27, 1968. Mauro Magalhães, interview, Rio de Janeiro, March 9, 1992. Carlos Brickmann, "Lacerda, e a polícia atrás," *Jornal da Tarde*, July 4, 1972.

9. Mauro Magalhães, interview, March 9, 1992. Carlos Brickmann, "Lacerda, e a polícia atrás."

10. *O Estado de S. Paulo*, January 28, 1968. See John Kenneth Galbraith, *The Triumph* (Boston: Houghton Mifflin, 1968) and Galbraith, *O Triunfo* (Rio de Janeiro: Editora Nova Fronteira, 1968), translated by Lacerda with a commentary by Lacerda.

11. *O Estado de S. Paulo*, January 28, 1968.

12. *Jornal da Tarde*, January 29, 1968.

13. Carlos Castello Branco in *Jornal do Brasil*, February 29, 1968. Carlos Lacerda in *O Estado de S. Paulo*, March 16, 1968. *New York Times*, March 6, 1968. *Jornal do Brasil*, March 5, 6, 1968.

14. *Jornal do Brasil*, March 1, 5, 6 (editorial), 1968. *New York Times*, March 6, 1968. *O Estado de S. Paulo*, June 2, 1968.

15. *Jornal do Brasil*, March 13, 1968. *O Estado de S. Paulo*, March 13, 16, 1968.

16. *O Estado de S. Paulo*, March 5, 12, 13, 14, 16, 19, 1968. *Jornal do Brasil*, February 7, 9, 10, 11, 13, 14, 16, 20, March 6 (editorial), 8, 9, 1968. *O Globo*, March 5, 1968.

17. *Jornal do Brasil*, editorials, March 6, 8, 1968. *O Estado de S. Paulo*, March 14, 16, 1968.

18. *Jornal do Brasil* and *O Estado de S. Paulo*, March 9, 1968.

19. *Jornal do Brasil*, March 16, 1968.

14. The Frente, Finally, Participates in Street Rallies
(Late March 1968)

1. "Há 15 anos o inesperado encontro JK-Lacerda," *Manchete*, February 6, 1982. *Tribuna da Imprensa* and *Jornal da Tarde*, March 25, 1968. *O Estado de S. Paulo*, March 24, 1968. Cláudio Lacerda, *Carlos Lacerda: 10 Anos Depois*, p. 315.

2. *O Estado de S. Paulo*, March 24, 1968. *Jornal da Tarde*, March 25, 1968.

3. *Jornal da Tarde*, March 25, 1968. Cláudio Lacerda, "Lacerda: Uma Vida de Lutas" (*Fatos & Fotos*, nos. 1142–1161, 1983), Chapter 15 in no. 1156. "As Confissões de Lacerda (Último Capítulo)," *Jornal da Tarde*, June 15, 1977. Carlos Lacerda, *Depoimento*, p. 393.

4. *O Estado de S. Paulo*, March 26, 1968.

5. *Jornal da Tarde* and *O Estado de S. Paulo*, March 27, 28, 1968. Nelson Pereira, interview, São Paulo, August 4, 1983.

6. *O Estado de S. Paulo* and *Jornal da Tarde*, March 28, 29, 1968.

7. *O Estado de S. Paulo*, March 29, 30 (editorial), 1968. *Tribuna da Imprensa*, April 20–21, 1968. *O Globo*, March 29, 1968.

8. *O Estado de S. Paulo*, March 30, 1968.

9. Ibid., March 28, 1968. *Jornal da Tarde*, March 27, 1968. *Tribuna da Imprensa*, April 1, 1968.

15. The UNE Arouses the People and Repudiates the Frente
(March–April 1968)

1. *O Estado de S. Paulo*, March 29, 30, 1968. Zuenir Ventura, *1968: O Ano que não Terminou* (Rio de Janeiro: Editora Nova Fronteira, 1988), pp. 97–105. Daniel Aarão Reis Filho and Pedro de Moraes, *1968: A Paixão de uma Utopia* (Rio de Janeiro: Editora Espaço e Tempo, 1988), p. 14. Arthur José Poerner, *O Poder Jovem* (Rio de Janeiro: Editora Civilização Brasileira, 1968), pp. 363–366.

2. *Jornal do Brasil*, March 31, 1968. *O Estado de S. Paulo*, April 2, 1968.

3. *O Estado de S. Paulo*, April 2, 3 (editorial), 1968. *Jornal do Brasil*, April 2, 1968. Poerner, *O Poder Jovem*, p. 366.

4. Daniel Aarão Reis Filho and Pedro de Moraes, *1968: A Paixão de uma Utopia*, p. 14. Poerner, *O Poder Jovem*, p. 366. *O Estado de S. Paulo*, April 2, 1968.

5. See Ação Popular mimeographed releases: "Textos para Militantes" (1966), "Estratégia Revolucionária" (1966), "Ação Popular" (1966), "Resolução sôbre o Debate Teorético e Ideológico" (April 1967), and "Assuntos Gerais" (May 1967), in collection of JWFD, Austin.

6. *O Estado de S. Paulo*, April 3, 1968.

7. *Jornal do Brasil*, April 2, 3, 1968.

8. *O Estado de S. Paulo* and *Jornal do Brasil*, April 3, 1968. Jayme Portella de Mello, *A Revolução e o Governo Costa e Silva*, pp. 541–542.

9. *Jornal do Brasil*, April 4, 1968.

10. *O Estado de S. Paulo*, April 5, 1968.
11. *Jornal do Brasil*, April 3, 1968. Jayme Portella de Mello, *A Revolução e o Governo Costa e Silva*, p. 540.
12. *Jornal do Brasil*, editorial, April 4, 1968. *Folha de S. Paulo*, editorial, April 3, 1968.
13. *Jornal do Brasil*, April 5 (including editorial), 6, 1968. *Tribuna da Imprensa*, April 5, 1968. *O Estado de S. Paulo*, April 5, 6 (editorial), 1968. *Diário de Notícias*, April 5, 1968. *Última Hora*, April 4, 1968.
14. *O Estado de S. Paulo*, April 5, 6, 1968.
15. *Jornal do Brasil*, April 5, 1968.
16. Danton Jobim, "Agitador encanecido," *Última Hora*, April 4, 1968. *O Jornal*, editorials, April 2, 3, 4, 5, 1968. *O Globo*, April 4, 1968, and editorials, April 1, 2, 3, 5, 1968.
17. *Jornal do Brasil*, April 5, 6, 1968.

16. The Justice Minister Bans the Frente Ampla (April 5, 1968)

1. Jayme Portella de Mello, *A Revolução e o Governo Costa e Silva*, pp. 547, 545. *O Estado de S. Paulo*, April 7, 1968. *Jornal do Brasil*, April 4, 1968.
2. Jayme Portella de Mello, *A Revolução e o Governo Costa e Silva*, p. 544. Zuenir Ventura, *1968: O Ano que não Terminou*, p. 129.
3. *Jornal do Brasil* and *O Estado de S. Paulo*, April 6, 1968.
4. *Folha de S. Paulo*, editorial and article, April 7, 1968. *Jornal do Brasil*, editorial, April 7, 1968. *O Estado de S. Paulo*, editorial, April 7, 1968. *O Globo*, editorial, April 8, 1968.
5. Jayme Portella de Mello, *A Revolução e o Governo Costa e Silva*, pp. 545–546. *O Estado de S. Paulo*, April 7, 9, 1968.
6. *O Estado de S. Paulo*, April 9, 7, 1968. Clovis Stenzel entry in *Dicionário Histórico-Biográfico Brasileiro, 1930–1983*.
7. *O Estado de S. Paulo*, April 7, 9, 10, 11, 1968. *Jornal do Brasil*, April 9, 10, 11, 1968.
8. *Jornal do Brasil* and *O Estado de S. Paulo*, April 7, 1968.

17. Comments on the Frente Ampla

1. *Tribuna da Imprensa*, April 8, 1968.
2. Fernando Pedreira, "Ora, direis, a Frente Ampla," *O Estado de S. Paulo*, April 14, 1968.
3. Hélio Silva, *1945: Porque depuseram Vargas* (Rio de Janeiro: Editora Civilização Brasileira, 1976), pp. 65–75. Carolina Nabuco, *A Vida de Virgílio de Melo Franco* (Rio de Janeiro: Livraria José Olympio Editora, 1962), pp. 139–149.
4. *O Estado de S. Paulo*, December 10, 1966.
5. Ibid., August 12, 9, 1967. *Tribuna da Imprensa*, November 28, 1967.

6. Carolina Nabuco, *A Vida de Virgílio de Melo Franco*, p. 142. Cláudio Lacerda, *Carlos Lacerda: 10 Anos Depois*, p. 194.

7. Carlos Castello Branco, "Coluna do Castello," *Jornal do Brasil*, December 6, 1967.

8. Carlos Lacerda, *Depoimento*, p. 389.

9. *Tribuna da Imprensa*, December 21, 1966. Carlos Lacerda in Hélio Fernandes, *Recordações de um Desterrado*, p. 198. Cláudio Lacerda, *Carlos Lacerda: 10 Anos Depois*, p. 226. Manoel Francisco do Nascimento Brito, letter to Carlos Lacerda, Rio de Janeiro, September 29, 1967, in CCL.

10. Thomas E. Skidmore, *The Politics of Military Rule in Brazil, 1964–1985* (New York: Oxford University Press, 1988), p. 72.

11. Carlos Castello Branco, *Os Militares no Poder*, vol. 1, p. 557 (entry for September 1, 1966). Carlos Castello Branco, "Coluna do Castello," *Jornal do Brasil*, December 17, 1967.

XI. The Silencing of Lacerda as a Politician (1968)

1. Students Demonstrate while Lacerda Visits Europe (April–June 1968)

1. *O Estado de S. Paulo*, April 18, 1968.

2. Ibid., April 18, 17, 1968. *Tribuna da Imprensa*, April 17, 1968. Carlos Castello Branco, *Os Militares no Poder*, vol. 2, *O Ato 5* (Rio de Janeiro: Editora Nova Fronteira, 1977), p. 337 (entry for April 26, 1968). *Jornal do Brasil*, April 17, 18, 23, 1968.

3. *O Estado de S. Paulo*, April 23, 24, 1968. *Jornal do Brasil*, April 23, 1968. *Tribuna da Imprensa*, April 23, 24, 26, 1968.

4. *O Estado de S. Paulo*, May 10, 1968. *Tribuna da Imprensa*, April 16, 25, 1968.

5. Vladimir Palmeira, Luís Travassos, José Dirceu de Oliveira e Silva, and Antônio Ribas, interview in a São Paulo prison, November 21, 1968.

6. *Tribuna da Imprensa*, June 5, 1968.

7. *O Estado de S. Paulo*, May 3, 1968.

8. Ibid., May 19, 26, 23, 1968.

9. *Tribuna da Imprensa*, June 18, 20, 1968.

10. Ibid., June 21, 1968. *Jornal do Brasil*, June 22, 23, 1968.

11. *Tribuna da Imprensa*, June 19, 21, 1968. *Jornal do Brasil*, editorial, June 22, 1968.

12. *O Estado de S. Paulo*, June 27, 1968. *Tribuna da Imprensa*, June 24, 25, 26, 1968.

13. *Tribuna da Imprensa*, June 27, 28, 1968. *Jornal do Brasil*, June 26, 1968. *O Estado de S. Paulo*, June 27, 1968.

14. *Tribuna da Imprensa*, June 12, 14, 22–23, 24, 25, 1968.

15. Ibid., June 5, 14, 24, 1968. *O Estado de S. Paulo*, April 16, June 25, 26, 27, 1968. Zuenir Ventura, *1968: O Ano que não Terminou*, p. 227.

16. *O Estado de S. Paulo*, June 19, 21, 22, 25, 1968.

2. The Para-Sar Case (June–October 1968)

1. Para-Sar was the abbreviation for the 1ª Esquadrilha Aeroterrestre de Salvamento. "Caso Pára-Sar: o homem que evitou o banho de sangue" (by Luiz Carlos Sarmento and Gabriel de Barros Nogueira), *Fatos*, no. 15 (Rio de Janeiro, June 1, 1985), pp. 38–45; see pp. 38–39. Zuenir Ventura, *1968: O Ano que não Terminou*, pp. 209–219; see p. 213. Pery Cotta, "A 'Operação Mata-Estudante,'" *Correio da Manhã*, October 4, 1968. Jeferson de Andrade, *Um Jornal Assassinado: A Última Batalha do Correio da Manhã* (Rio de Janeiro: Livraria José Olympio Editora, 1991), pp. 174–179; see p. 175.

2. "Caso Pára-Sar," *Fatos*, June 1, 1985, pp. 40–42. Zuenir Ventura, *1968: O Ano que não Terminou*, pp. 214–217. Jeferson de Andrade, *Um Jornal Assassinado*, p. 178.

3. "Caso Pára-Sar," *Fatos*, June 1, 1985, p. 42. Jeferson de Andrade, *Um Jornal Assassinado*, p. 179. Zuenir Ventura, *1968: O Ano que não Terminou*, p. 211.

4. "Caso Pára-Sar," *Fatos*, June 1, 1985, pp. 44–45. Jeferson de Andrade, *Um Jornal Assassinado*, pp. 175–177. Zuenir Ventura, *1968: O Ano que não Terminou*, pp. 209, 213. João Paulo Burnier entry in *Dicionário Histórico-Biográfico Brasileiro, 1930–1983*. Cláudio Lacerda, *Carlos Lacerda: 10 Anos Depois*, p. 316.

5. Pery Cotta, "A 'Operação Mata-Estudante.'" Zuenir Ventura, *1968: O Ano que não Terminou*, pp. 209–210. Pery Cotta, interview, Rio de Janeiro, March 10, 1992.

6. *O Globo*, editorial, October 8, 1968. *Jornal do Brasil*, October 6, 8, 10, 15, 1968. Hermano Alves, "Mêdo e violência," *Correio da Manhã*, October 10, 1968. Carlos Castello Branco, *Os Militares no Poder*, vol. 2, p. 490 (entry for October 9, 1968).

7. Zuenir Ventura, *1968: O Ano que não Terminou*, p. 209.

3. Buildup for a Real Crisis (July–October 1968)

1. *Jornal do Brasil*, July 3, 1968. "Os Quadros do Pintor Carlos X," *Jornal da Tarde*, July 24, 1968. "O Amigo," *Fatos & Fotos*, June 6, 1977. *O Estado de S. Paulo*, July 25, 30, 31, August 1, 2, 1968. João Condé, interview, Rio de Janeiro, August 11, 1983, and interview with DFR, Rio de Janeiro, March 23, 1983. Edmundo Moniz, "O PARA-SAR e a cassação de mandatos," *Correio da Manhã*, December 3, 1968.

2. Hélio Fernandes, interview, Rio de Janeiro, August 1, 1984. *O Estado de S. Paulo*, July 6, 10, 18, August 9, 1968. *Jornal do Brasil*, July 9, 1968.

3. *O Estado de S. Paulo*, July 20, 1968.

4. *Jornal do Brasil*, July 23, 26, 27, 30, 1968.

5. *O Estado de S. Paulo*, July 30, August 27, 1968. *Jornal do Brasil*, August 3, 10, 13, 1968.

6. *Correio da Manhã*, September 17, 1968. *O Jornal*, September 12, 18, 20, 1968.

7. *Jornal do Brasil*, August 1, 7, 1968.

8. *O Estado de S. Paulo*, September 3, 1968. *O Jornal*, September 4, 1968.

9. *Jornal do Brasil*, July 18, 1968. *Correio da Manhã*, editorial and column by Hermano Alves, September 12, 1968.

10. *Jornal do Brasil*, July 3, August 1, 1968. *O Jornal*, September 20, 1968.

11. *Jornal do Brasil*, July 5, 1968. *Correio da Manhã*, September 19, 20, 1968. *O Jornal*, September 28, 1968. Vladimir Palmeira entry in *Dicionário Histórico-Biográfico Brasileiro, 1930–1983*.

12. Captions about student activities, July 10, 12, 1968, for photographs in the *Jornal do Brasil*. *O Estado de S. Paulo*, August 30, 31, 1968. *Correio da Manhã*, September 4, 1968.

13. Aurélio de Lyra Tavares, message to Artur da Costa e Silva (Ofício 01/68), in Daniel Krieger, *Desde as Missões*, pp. 328–329. Jayme Portella de Mello, *A Revolução e o Governo Costa e Silva*, p. 585.

14. *Correio da Manhã*, September 3, 5, 1968. Hermano Alves, "A verdadeira subversão," *Correio da Manhã*, September 5, 1968.

15. Carlos Castello Branco, *Os Militares no Poder*, vol. 2, *O Ato 5*, p. 458 (entry for September 5, 1968). *Correio da Manhã*, September 6, 1968.

16. Lyra Tavares message, in Krieger, *Desde as Missões*, pp. 328–329.

17. Jayme Portella de Mello, *A Revolução e o Governo Costa e Silva*, p. 586. *O Estado de S. Paulo*, October 10, 1968. Krieger, *Desde as Missões*, p. 329.

18. Daniel Krieger, letter to Costa e Silva, Brasília, October 10, 1968, and Costa e Silva, letter to Daniel Krieger, Laranjeiras Palace, Rio de Janeiro, n.d., both in Krieger, *Desde as Missões*, pp. 330–333. Jayme Portella de Mello, *A Revolução e o Governo Costa e Silva*, p. 586.

19. *Correio da Manhã*, September 12 (editorial), 13, 14, 1968.

20. *O Estado de S. Paulo*, September 10, 1968. *Correio da Manhã*, September 5, 18, 1968. Emílio Garrastazu Médici entry in *Dicionário Histórico-Biográfico Brasileiro, 1930–1983*.

21. *Correio da Manhã*, September 28, 1968. Hermano Alves, "Mêdo e violência," *Correio da Manhã*, October 10, 1968. *Jornal do Brasil*, October 10, 1968. Jayme Portella de Mello, *A Revolução e o Governo Costa e Silva*, p. 585.

22. *O Estado de S. Paulo*, October 4, 9, 1968. José Luís Sanfelice, *Movimento Estudantil: a UNE na resistência ao golpe de 64* (São Paulo: Cortez Editora/Autores Associados, 1986), pp. 147–148. Luís Raul Machado, "O grande fascenso do movimento estudantil em 1968," on pp. 55–64 of Editorial Livramento, *História da UNE*, vol. 1, *depoimentos de ex-dirigentes* (São Paulo: Editorial Livramento, 1980); see pp. 60–61. Zuenir Ventura, *1968: O Ano que não Terminou*, pp. 221–228. José Dirceu in *Gazeta do Povo* (Curitiba), April 3, 1994.

23. Sílvio Cardoso and Otávio Esteves, "A madrugada das algemas," *O Cruzeiro*, October 26, 1968. Zuenir Ventura, *1968: O Ano que não Terminou*, pp. 239–255; see pp. 239, 247–248. *O Estado de S. Paulo* and *Correio da Manhã*, October 13, 1968. Editorial Livramento, *História da UNE*, vol. 1, *depoimentos* of Luís Raul Machado (see pp. 62–64) and Jean Marc von der Weid (see pp. 82–86).

24. *Correio da Manhã,* editorial, October 13, 1968. *O Globo,* editorials, October 21, 15, 7, 8, 1968.

25. *Correio da Manhã,* October 13, 1968. Ninety-second Congress of the United States, First Session (May 4, 5, 11, 1971), *Hearings before the Subcommittee on Western Hemisphere Affairs* (Frank Church, chairman), p. 42. Zuenir Ventura, *1968: O Ano que não Terminou,* p. 228. Thomas E. Skidmore, *The Politics of Military Rule in Brazil, 1964–1985,* pp. 87–88.

4. Observing U.S. Politics, and Falling in Love (October–November 1968)

1. Carlos Lacerda, "Um Império Escolhe Seu Presidente," *Realidade* 3, no. 32 (November 1968), pp. 25–44; see pp. 27, 28, 31, 33, 35, 37. Alfredo C. Machado, interviews, Rio de Janeiro, July 7, 1983, August 8, 1989.

2. Carlos Lacerda, "Um Império Escolhe Seu Presidente," pp. 26, 37, 35.

3. Ibid., pp. 35, 38.

4. Ibid., pp. 25, 33, 31, 44.

5. Regina Costard, interview with DFR, Rio de Janeiro, September 9, 1986. Carlos Lacerda, "O Retrato de um Presidente," *Fatos & Fotos* 8, no. 408 (November 28, 1968), pp. 91–100; see pp. 91, 92, 99. Carlos Lacerda, "Um Império Escolhe Seu Presidente," p. 29.

6. Carlos Lacerda, "O Retrato de um Presidente," pp. 92, 95, 99, 96, 94.

5. Congress Supports the Immunity of Moreira Alves (December 12, 1968)

1. *Jornal do Brasil* ("Informe JB" columns), December 1, 10, 1968. Carlos Castello Branco in *Jornal do Brasil,* December 3, 1968.

2. *Jornal do Brasil* ("Informe JB" column), December 1, 1968. Carlos Lacerda, *Depoimento,* p. 392. Carlos Castello Branco in *Jornal do Brasil,* November 9, 1968. Márcio Moreira Alves, "Ditadura Nua e Crua," *Manchete Extra,* June 12, 1993.

3. Márcio Moreira Alves, "Ditadura Nua e Crua," writes that the only reference by the press to his speeches was a "minuscule mention in *Folha de S. Paulo.*" Daniel Krieger, letter to Costa e Silva, Brasília, October 10, 1968, in Krieger, *Desde as Missões,* pp. 330–331. *Jornal do Brasil,* November 1, 7, 1968. Zuenir Ventura, *1968: O Ano que não Terminou,* p. 261. *O Estado de S. Paulo,* November 27, 28, 1968.

4. Zuenir Ventura, *1968: O Ano que não Terminou,* pp. 260–261. *O Estado de S. Paulo,* November 28, 1968. Márcio Moreira Alves, "Ditadura Nua e Crua."

5. *O Estado de S. Paulo,* November 26, 27, 28, 29, 2, 13, October 15, 16, 1968. Krieger, *Desde as Missões,* pp. 334–335. Djalma Marinho entry in *Dicionário Histórico-Biográfico Brasileiro, 1930–1983. Jornal do Brasil,* editorial, December 3, 1968.

6. *O Estado de S. Paulo*, November 30, 1968. *Correio da Manhã*, December 1, 1968. *O Globo*, December 2, 1968. *Última Hora*, December 5, 1968. *Jornal do Brasil*, December 3, 4, 5, 6, 7, 8, 1968. Carlos Castello Branco in *Jornal do Brasil*, December 3, 5, 8, 1968. Carlos Castello Branco, *Os Militares no Poder*, vol. 2, *O Ato 5*, p. 549. Krieger, *Desde as Missões*, p. 336.

7. *Jornal do Brasil*, November 6 (editorial), 7, 8, 1968. *Correio da Manhã*, December 3, 8 (including editorial), 1968. *O Jornal*, December 3, 1968. *Última Hora*, December 6, 9, 1968. *O Estado de S. Paulo*, November 30, 1968.

8. *Jornal do Brasil*, December 10, 11, 1968. *O Globo*, December 10, 11, 1968. Zuenir Ventura, *1968: O Ano que não Terminou*, p. 261. Márcio Moreira Alves, "Ditadura Nua e Crua."

9. Carlos Castello Branco in *Jornal do Brasil*, December 11, 1968. *Jornal do Brasil*, December 12, 1968. Jayme Portella de Mello, *A Revolução e o Governo Costa e Silva*, p. 632.

10. Renato Archer, "Depoimento," pp. 579–582. Carlos Castello Branco in *Jornal do Brasil*, December 11, 1968.

11. *Jornal do Brasil*, December 10, 12, 1968. *Última Hora*, December 12, 1968. Jayme Portella de Mello, *A Revolução e o Governo Costa e Silva*, pp. 633–634.

12. *O Globo*, December 13, 1968. Márcio Moreira Alves, "Ditadura Nua e Crua." *Jornal do Brasil*, December 13, 1968. Zuenir Ventura, *1968: O Ano que não Terminou*, p. 264. Jayme Portella de Mello, *A Revolução e o Governo Costa e Silva*, p. 640. "Revolução, Ano Zero," *Veja*, no. 15 (December 18, 1968). Jarbas Passarinho, "Dezembro de 1968," *Folha de S. Paulo*, October 23, 1988.

13. *Última Hora*, *Correio da Manhã*, *O Estado de S. Paulo*, and *Jornal do Brasil*, editorials, December 13, 1968. Carlos Guilherme Mota and Maria Helena Capelato, *História da Folha de S. Paulo (1921–1981)* (São Paulo: IMPRES, 1980), pp. 200–201, 206, and caption for photograph of Cláudio Abramo. *Folha de S. Paulo*, editorials, November 1, December 1, 13, 1968. *O Globo*, December 12, 4, 1968, and editorials, December 9, 10, 2, 1968.

6. Institutional Act Number Five (December 13, 1968)

1. Jayme Portella de Mello, *A Revolução e o Governo Costa e Silva*, p. 639.
2. Ibid., pp. 641–643.
3. Ibid., pp. 646–648, 660.
4. Ibid., pp. 650–651. Emílio Garrastazu Médici entry in *Dicionário Histórico-Biográfico Brasileiro, 1930–1983*. Zuenir Ventura, *1968: O Ano que não Terminou*, pp. 272–273.
5. Jayme Portella de Mello, *A Revolução e o Governo Costa e Silva*, pp. 652–659. *O Globo*, December 14, 1968. Zuenir Ventura, *1968: O Ano que não Terminou*, pp. 274–284. Márcio Moreira Alves, "Ditadura Nua e Crua." *Folha de S. Paulo*, December 16, 1968. *Última Hora*, December 16, 17, 1968. *Jornal do Brasil*, December 17, 1968. *Correio da Manhã*, December 18, 1968.
6. *Jornal do Brasil*, December 14, 1968. Daniel Krieger, *Desde as Missões*,

p. 342. *Correio da Manhã, O Estado de S. Paulo,* and *Folha de S. Paulo,* December 17, 1968.

7. *Última Hora* and *Correio da Manhã,* December 13, 1968. "Revolução, Ano Zero," *Veja,* December 18, 1968, see p. 22. José Dirceu in *Gazeta do Povo* (Curitiba), April 3, 1994.

8. *O Estado de S. Paulo,* December 14, 1968. "Revolução, Ano Zero," *Veja,* December 18, 1968, see p. 25. "Instituições em frangalhos" (editorial), *O Estado de S. Paulo,* December 13, 1968.

9. *O Estado de S. Paulo,* December 14, 1968. *Folha de S. Paulo,* December 14, 1968 (including editorial). *Jornal do Brasil,* December 14, 1968. Carlos Castello Branco, introductory note in his *Os Militares no Poder,* vol. 3, *O Baile das Solteironas* (Rio de Janeiro: Editora Nova Fronteira, 1979). *New York Times,* December 16, 1968. Zuenir Ventura, *1968: O Ano que não Terminou,* pp. 288–289.

10. Carlos Castello Branco entry in *Dicionário Histórico-Biográfico Brasileiro, 1930–1983.* Maurício Caminha de Lacerda, "Por trás da notícia: O Muro," *O Jornal,* December 17, 1968. *New York Times,* December 18, 24, 1968. "Revolução, Ano Zero," *Veja,* December 18, 1968, see p. 25. *O Estado de S. Paulo* and *Folha de S. Paulo,* December 14, 15, 17, 1968. Hugo Gouthier, *Presença: Algumas Lembranças* (Rio de Janeiro: Editora Record, 1982), p. 206. Heráclito Fontoura Sobral Pinto entry in *Dicionário Histórico-Biográfico Brasileiro, 1930–1983.* Zuenir Ventura, *1968: O Ano que não Terminou,* pp. 295–306.

11. Daniel Krieger, *Desde as Missões,* p. 341. Jayme Portella de Mello, *A Revolução e o Governo Costa e Silva,* p. 660. Márcio Moreira Alves and Hermano Alves entries in *Dicionário Histórico-Biográfico Brasileiro, 1930–1983.* Zuenir Ventura, *1968: O Ano que não Terminou,* pp. 295–306.

12. Jayme Portella de Mello, *A Revolução e o Governo Costa e Silva,* p. 660. Carlos Heitor Cony, *JK: Memorial do Exílio,* p. 133. *O Estado de S. Paulo,* December 14, 1968.

13. Carlos Heitor Cony, *JK: Memorial do Exílio,* p. 133.

7. The Imprisonment of Lacerda (December 14, 1968)

1. Antonio Dias Rebello Filho, *Carlos Lacerda, Meu Amigo,* p. 224. Carlos Lacerda, *Depoimento,* p. 364.

2. Oscar Klabin Segall, interview, São Paulo, March 8, 1991.

3. Rebello Filho, *Carlos Lacerda, Meu Amigo,* p. 224.

4. Hélio Fernandes, letter in *O Estado de S. Paulo,* June 24, 1977 ("Jornalista rebate afirmações de Lacerda"); see Section 1 of letter.

5. Rebello Filho, *Carlos Lacerda, Meu Amigo,* p. 225. Carlos Lacerda, *Depoimento,* p. 365.

6. Jayme Portella de Mello, *A Revolução e o Governo Costa e Silva,* pp. 660–661.

7. Carlos Lacerda, *Depoimento,* p. 365. Rebello Filho, *Carlos Lacerda, Meu Amigo,* p. 225. Rebello Filho, interview with DFR, Rio de Janeiro, March 26, 1983. *Folha de S. Paulo,* December 15, 1968.

8. Rebello Filho, *Carlos Lacerda, Meu Amigo*, p. 226. Carlos Lacerda, *Depoimento*, pp. 365–366.

9. Ibid. *Jornal da Tarde*, December 16, 1968.

10. Carlos Lacerda, *Depoimento*, p. 366. Rebello Filho, *Carlos Lacerda, Meu Amigo*, p. 226. Jayme Portella de Mello, *A Revolução e o Governo Costa e Silva*, p. 661.

11. Jayme Portella de Mello, *A Revolução e o Governo Costa e Silva*, p. 661.

12. Hélio Fernandes, letter in *O Estado de S. Paulo*, June 24, 1977; see Sections 5, 6, and 7 of letter. Antonio Aragão, "Mário Lago," *Jornal do País*, May 16–22, 1985. "Em 68 a volta às prisões" (based on Mário Lago recollections), *O Estado de S. Paulo*, May 22, 1977. Carlos Lacerda, *Depoimento*, p. 367.

13. Hélio Fernandes, letter in *O Estado de S. Paulo*, June 24, 1977; see Section 8 of letter. Carlos Lacerda, *Depoimento*, pp. 367–369.

14. Pedro Ernesto Mariano de Azevedo, letter to JWFD, Rio de Janeiro, June 16, 1994. Carlos Osório da Silveira Neto, interview, Rio de Janeiro, August 7, 1989. Carlos Lacerda, *Depoimento*, p. 368. Hélio Fernandes, letter in *O Estado de S. Paulo*, June 24, 1977, Section 8 of letter.

15. Carlos Lacerda, *Depoimento*, pp. 367–372. Rebello Filho, *Carlos Lacerda, Meu Amigo*, pp. 227–228. Carlos Lacerda, *A Casa do Meu Avô*, 2d ed. (Rio de Janeiro: Editora Nova Fronteira, 1977), p. 167.

16. Hélio Fernandes, letter in *O Estado de S. Paulo*, June 24, 1977. Maria Cristina Lacerda Simões Lopes, interview with DFR, Rio de Janeiro, March 24, 1983. Carlos Lacerda, *Depoimento*, p. 373.

17. Carlos Lacerda, *Depoimento*, pp. 370–372. Mário Lago quoted in "Em 68 a volta às prisões," *O Estado de S. Paulo*, May 22, 1977.

18. Ibid. Hélio Fernandes, letter in *O Estado de S. Paulo*, June 24, 1977; see Section 9 of letter and paragraph following Section 10. Hélio Fernandes, interviews, Rio de Janeiro, July 6, 1977, August 1, 1984.

19. Carlos Lacerda, *Depoimento*, p. 373.

20. "Depoimento prestado pelo Sr. Carlos Lacerda a agentes do DOPS e dois coronéis do S.N.I. no dia 19-12-1968" (mimeographed copy), pp. 1–2.

21. Ibid., p. 3. Carlos Lacerda, *Depoimento*, p. 373.

22. Carlos Lacerda, *Depoimento*, pp. 374–375.

8. Lacerda, Freed, Loses His Political Rights (December 21 and 30, 1968)

1. Antonio Dias Rebello Filho, *Carlos Lacerda, Meu Amigo*, p. 233.

2. Lygia Vaz Brito e Cunha and Rubens Vaz Júnior, interview, Rio de Janeiro, August 9, 1983.

3. Ibid. Hugo Levy, interview, Rio de Janeiro, March 2, 1991.

4. Carlos Lacerda, letter to his wife and children, Military Police Barracks, Frei Caneca Street, Rio de Janeiro, December 20, 1968, in Carlos Lacerda, *Depoimento*, p. 454.

5. Carlos Lacerda, *Depoimento*, pp. 375–376. Maria Cristina Lacerda

Simões Lopes, handwritten notes for JWFD, Rio de Janeiro, August 1988. Hugo Levy, interview, March 2, 1991. Carlos Lacerda, *A Casa do Meu Avô*, pp. 167–168.

6. Maria Cristina Lacerda, letter to Artur da Costa e Silva, Rio de Janeiro, December 20, 1968, in Rebello Filho, *Carlos Lacerda, Meu Amigo*, pp. 235–236.

7. Antonio Dias Rebello Filho, letters to Artur da Costa e Silva and presidents of medical associations, Rio de Janeiro, December 20, 1968, on p. 455 of Carlos Lacerda, *Depoimento*, and editor's note on that page. Rebello Filho, *Carlos Lacerda, Meu Amigo*, pp. 233–234. *Jornal da Tarde*, December 21, 19, 1968.

8. Editor's note, p. 455 of Carlos Lacerda, *Depoimento*. Cláudio Lacerda, Chapter 17 ("A Última Prisão") of "Lacerda: Uma Vida de Lutas," *Fatos & Fotos*, nos. 1142–1161 (1983).

9. Jayme Portella de Mello, *A Revolução e o Governo Costa e Silva*, pp. 670–671. Artur da Costa e Silva, *Pronunciamentos do Presidente*, vol. 2 (n.p.: Presidência da República, Secretaria de Imprensa e Divulgação, n.d.), pp. 465–469.

10. Cláudio Lacerda, Chapter 17 of "Lacerda: Uma Vida de Lutas." Editor's note, p. 455, Carlos Lacerda, *Depoimento*. Jayme Portella de Mello, *A Revolução e o Governo Costa e Silva*, p. 679.

11. Carlos Lacerda, *Depoimento*, pp. 376–377.

12. Ibid., pp. 377–378. Jayme Portella de Mello, *A Revolução e o Governo Costa e Silva*, p. 679.

13. Carlos Lacerda, *Depoimento*, p. 378. Maria Cristina Lacerda Simões Lopes, handwritten notes for JWFD, August 1988.

14. Maria Cristina Lacerda Simões Lopes, handwritten notes for JWFD, August 1988. Rebello Filho, *Carlos Lacerda, Meu Amigo*, pp. 242–243.

15. Jayme Portella de Mello, *A Revolução e o Governo Costa e Silva*, pp. 686–689. Mauro Magalhães, *Carlos Lacerda*, p. 351. *O Globo*, December 31, 1968.

16. Gustavo Borges, letter in *Jornal do Brasil*, June 1, 1987. Cláudio Lacerda, Chapter 18 ("Profissão: Jornalista") of "Lacerda: Uma Vida de Lutas." Costa Cavalcanti entry in *Dicionário Histórico-Biográfico Brasileiro, 1930–1983*. Mauro Magalhães, interview, Rio de Janeiro, March 9, 1992. Carlos Lacerda, letters to Salvador Gonçalves Mandim, Rio de Janeiro, April 30, 1969, and to Mauro Magalhães, April 30, 1969, shown to JWFD during interviews with Mandim (Rio de Janeiro, August 16, 1984) and Mauro Magalhães (March 9, 1992).

17. Cláudio Lacerda, Chapter 17 of "Lacerda: Uma Vida de Lutas." *O Estado de S. Paulo*, January 25, 1969. *O Dia*, May 22, 1987.

9. Note about the Regime after 1968

1. Carlos Castello Branco, *Os Militares no Poder*, vol. 3, *O Baile das Solteironas*, introductory note. Thomas E. Skidmore, *The Politics of Military*

Rule in Brazil, 1964–1985, pp. 82–83. Ronald M. Schneider, *"Order and Progress": A Political History of Brazil* (Boulder, Colo.: Westview Press, 1991), pp. 260–261.

2. *Gazeta do Povo*, February 7, 1994. "O homem que disse não," *Veja*, February 16, 1994.

XII. Epilogue (1969–1977)

I. Africa and Portugal

1. *O Estado de S. Paulo*, May 8, 1969.
2. Ibid., July 18, 1969. Maria Thereza Correia de Mello, interviews, Miami Beach, July 5–6, 1986. Carlos Lacerda, in *Jornal da Tarde*, August 16, 1975, July 15, 1969, and in *O Estado de S. Paulo*, August 7, July 13, 1969.
3. Carlos Lacerda, in *O Estado de S. Paulo*, June 29, July 1, 2, 3, 20, August 3, 14, 1969, January 16, 17, 1970, and in *Jornal da Tarde*, June 30, July 2, 3, August 4, 14, September 11, 1969, January 6, 16, 1970. Carlos Lacerda, *O Cão Negro* (Rio de Janeiro: Editora Nova Fronteira, 1971), pp. 242–243. *O Estado de S. Paulo*, July 3, 1969. E. U. Essien-Udom, history of Nigeria's independence period in *Collier's Encyclopedia* (New York: Maxwell Macmillan International, 1992).
4. Carlos Lacerda in *O Estado de S. Paulo*, January 16, 1970, September 15, 1972, June 6, 1971, May 20, 1973.
5. Carlos Lacerda in *O Estado de S. Paulo*, September 17, 1972, September 25, 1969, May 20, 1973, April 26, 1974. Mário Soares, *Portugal's Struggle for Liberty* (London: George Allen & Unwin, 1975), pp. 271, 187.
6. Miguel Urbano Rodrigues in *O Estado de S. Paulo*, August 15, 1973. Marcelo Caetano, *Depoimento* (Rio de Janeiro: Distribuidora Record, 1974), pp. 189, 219, 220. Carlos Lacerda in *O Estado de S. Paulo*, June 6, 1971. H. V. Livermore and Douglas L. Wheeler, history of Portugal in *Collier's Encyclopedia*.
7. Carlos Lacerda in *O Estado de S. Paulo*, May 20, 1973.
8. Hugo Gil Ferreira and Michael W. Marshall, *Portugal's Revolution: Ten Years On* (Cambridge: Cambridge University Press, 1986), p. 14. Carlos Lacerda, in *Jornal do Brasil*, May 1, 1974, and in *O Estado de S. Paulo*, March 5, 12, April 5, 1974. Antônio de Spínola, *Portugal e o Futuro* (Rio de Janeiro: Editora Nova Fronteira, 1974); see, among others, pp. 57, 95.
9. Marcelo Caetano, *Depoimento*, p. 234. Ferreira and Marshall, *Portugal's Revolution*, pp. 30, 6. Carlos Lacerda, in *Jornal da Tarde*, April 26, 1974, in *Jornal do Brasil*, May 1, 1974, and in preface of Spínola, *Portugal e o Futuro*, p. 5.
10. Carlos Lacerda, in *Jornal da Tarde*, April 26, 1974, and in *Jornal do Brasil*, May 1, 1974.
11. Carlos Lacerda, in *O Estado de S. Paulo* and *Jornal da Tarde*, March 13, 1975, and in *O Estado de S. Paulo*, April 27, 1975.
12. Luís Forjaz Trigueiros, "Na Morte de Carlos Lacerda," pp. 43–49 of Luís

Forjaz Trigueiros, *Palavras na Academia Brasileira de Letras, 1975–1978* (Lisbon: n.p., 1981); see pp. 45–46. Luís Forjaz Trigueiros, interviews with DFR, Lisbon, June 21, 27, 1984, and letter to DFR, Lisbon, June 6, 1984.

13. Ferreira and Marshall, *Portugal's Revolution*, pp. 33, 40–41, 117, 185–188.

14. Carlos Lacerda in *O Estado de S. Paulo*, January 12, February 18, 1975.

15. Carlos Lacerda in *O Estado de S. Paulo*, February 18, 2, 25, 28, 1975.

16. Ferreira and Marshall, *Portugal's Revolution*, pp. 111, 191, 45–46. Carlos Lacerda, in *Jornal da Tarde*, March 17, May 10, 1975, and in *O Estado de S. Paulo*, April 27, 1975.

17. Carlos Lacerda, in *Jornal da Tarde*, March 13, 14, 15, 1975, and in *O Estado de S. Paulo*, March 13, 14, 15, April 6, 27, 1975. *O Estado de S. Paulo*, March 15, 1975. Lamy Cunto, interview, Rio de Janeiro, March 8, 1992, and interview with DFR, Rio de Janeiro, January 4, 1988. Maria Thereza Correia de Mello, interviews, July 5–6, 1986.

18. Carlos Lacerda, in *Jornal da Tarde*, March 17, May 10, 1975, and in *O Estado de S. Paulo*, April 6, 1975. Lamy Cunto, interview, March 8, 1992. Carlos Lacerda, *Depoimento*, p. 359.

19. Carlos Lacerda in *Jornal da Tarde*, May 10, August 16, 1975.

20. Ferreira and Marshall, *Portugal's Revolution*, pp. 46–50. Livermore and Wheeler, history of Portugal in *Collier's Encyclopedia*. Carlos Lacerda in *Jornal do Brasil*, August 4, 1975.

21. Carlos Lacerda in *O Estado de S. Paulo*, August 8, 1975.

22. *O Estado de S. Paulo*, October 24, 1975. Carlos Lacerda, talk to students of Brazilian history, University of Arizona, Tucson, February 18, 1976.

23. Ferreira and Marshall, *Portugal's Revolution*, pp. 50–63, 194–198, and interview of Costa Gomes on pp. 179–182. Livermore and Wheeler, history of Portugal in *Collier's Encyclopedia*.

2. Attacks on *Distensão* by a Productive Columnist

1. Carlos Lacerda in *O Estado de S. Paulo*, August 8, 1975. Roberto Campos, "Memórias" (typewritten pages received by JWFD, February 1991), p. 26 of chapter "O Grande Desencontro," about Lacerda.

2. Carlos Lacerda in *Jornal do Brasil*, June 30, 1975. Armando Daudt d'Oliveira, interview, Rio de Janeiro, August 14, 1983.

3. Carlos Lacerda in *Jornal do Brasil*, June 30, July 27, 1975.

4. *O Estado de S. Paulo*, May 16, July 1, 1975.

5. Oscar Macedo, "A Volta do Corvo: A nova cruzada de Carlos Lacerda," *Movimento*, August 25, 1975. Carlos Lacerda in *Jornal do Brasil*, July 7, 1975. *Movimento* entry in *Dicionário Histórico-Biográfico Brasileiro, 1930–1983*.

6. Oscar Macedo, "A Volta do Corvo." Armando Daudt d'Oliveira, interview, August 14, 1983. *Folha de S. Paulo*, August 17, 1975.

7. Antonio Carlos Villaça, transcript of interview taped by the Sociedade dos Amigos de Carlos Lacerda, pp. 3, 6. Júlio Tavares (Carlos Lacerda), "Anna Amélia Queiroz Carneiro de Mendonça," "Relendo Lobato, em todo um

pioneiro," "Guia da Oração sôbre a Acrópole," and translation of the Oração, *O Estado de S. Paulo*, May 2, November 7, August 19, 27, 1971. Carlos Lacerda, "O caminho do segundo centenário," *O Estado de S. Paulo*, January 4, 1975.

8. Carlos Lacerda in *O Estado de S. Paulo*, August 18, 20, September 3, October 1, 8, 22, November 5, 1972. Heliomar Empreendimentos Ltda., company files.

9. Carlos Lacerda in *Jornal do Brasil*, July 28, 1975.

10. Júlio Tavares (Carlos Lacerda), book review in *O Estado de S. Paulo*, July 26, 1970. Antonio Carlos Villaça, transcript of interview taped by the Sociedade dos Amigos de Carlos Lacerda. Antonio Carlos Villaça, interviews with DFR, Rio de Janeiro, August 17, 31, 1985. Regina Costard, interview with DFR, Rio de Janeiro, September 9, 1986. Vera Lacerda Paiva and Lygia Paiva Derizans, interview with DFR, Rio de Janeiro, August 25, 1985.

11. Interviews cited in note 10. Antonio Carlos Villaça, interview, Rio de Janeiro, March 16, 1991. Antonio Carlos Villaça, *O Livro de Antonio* (Rio de Janeiro: Livraria José Olympio Editora, 1974) pp. 37, 59–71, 93–105.

12. Carlos Lacerda, *O Cão Negro*. Carlos Lacerda, *Em Vez* (Rio de Janeiro: Editora Nova Fronteira, 1975). Antonio Carlos Villaça in *Jornal do Brasil*, September 3, 1975. Luís Martins in *O Estado de S. Paulo*, September 26, 1975. Mara Bentes in *Fatos & Fotos*, October 6, 1975. *Jornal da Tarde*, September 25, 1975.

13. Carlos Lacerda, *Em Vez*, pp. 57–82. Carlos Lacerda in *O Estado de S. Paulo*, September 2, 9, 16, 1973.

14. Carlos Lacerda, *Em Vez*, pp. 68–82. Carlos Lacerda in *O Estado de S. Paulo*, September, 9, 16, November 11, 1973.

15. Carlos Lacerda, in *O Estado de S. Paulo*, November 11, 1973, and in *Jornal do Brasil*, May 1, 1974.

3. Books

1. Sebastião Lacerda, interview, Rio de Janeiro, March 5, 1992. Carlos Lacerda in *Jornal da Tarde*, April 23, 1977 (also published in *O Estado de S. Paulo*, April 24, 1977). Pedro Paulo Sena Madureira, interview with DFR, Rio de Janeiro, September 2, 1985. Aurélio Buarque de Holanda Ferreira, *Novo Dicionário da Língua Portuguesa* (Rio de Janeiro: Editora Nova Fronteira, 1975), p. 1500. Vera Lacerda Paiva, interview, Rio de Janeiro, July 22, 1984.

2. Sebastião Lacerda, interview, March 5, 1992. Alfredo C. Machado, interview, Rio de Janeiro, July 7, 1983. Carlos Lacerda in *Jornal da Tarde*, March 30, 1977.

3. Sebastião Lacerda, interview, March 5, 1992. Carlos Lacerda in *Jornal da Tarde*, April 23, 1983.

4. Armando Bordallo, interview, São Paulo, July 24, 1983. Nelson Werneck Sodré, *História da Imprensa no Brasil* (Rio de Janeiro: Editôra Civilização Brasileira, 1966), p. 260. Barbara Weinstein, Appendix to Maria Helena

Capelato and Maria Lígia Prado, *O Bravo Matutino: Imprensa e ideologia: o jornal O Estado de S. Paulo* (São Paulo: Editora Alfa-Omega, 1980), p. 137. José Maria Homem de Montes, interview, São Paulo, July 26, 1983.

5. José Maria Homem de Montes, interview, July 26, 1983. Carlos Lacerda, Memorando No. 1/73 to Júlio de Mesquita Neto, Rio de Janeiro, July 26, 1973 (in collection of Luiz Ernesto Kawall), and letter to JWFD, Rio de Janeiro, July 26, 1973.

6. Carlos Lacerda, in *O Estado de S. Paulo*, January 4, 1975, and Carta-circular aos Mesquita, Rio de Janeiro, December 29, 1975 (in collection of Luiz Ernesto Kawall).

7. "O livro inacabado," *O Estado de S. Paulo*, May 22, 1977. Luiz Ernesto Kawall, interview, São Paulo, July 25, 1983, and interview with DFR, São Paulo, March 11, 1983. Luiz Ernesto Kawall, "O último encontro" (newspaper clipping in Kawall collection, apparently from *Folha de S. Paulo*, late May 1977). José Maria Homem de Montes, interview, July 26, 1983.

8. "A última obra: os Mesquita," *Jornal da Tarde*, May 23, 1977. Kawall, "O último encontro," and interview, July 25, 1983. Carlos Alberto Aulicino, interview, São Paulo, July 28, 1983. "O livro inacabado," *O Estado de S. Paulo*, May 22, 1977. Carlos Lacerda said in *Depoimento*, p. 87, "It is impossible to write the history of the Republic without writing the history of the Bucha." For information about the secret society, see entries under Bucha in the index of J. W. F. Dulles, *The São Paulo Law School* (Austin: University of Texas Press, 1986).

9. Kawall, "O último encontro." Carlos Alberto Aulicino, interview, July 28, 1983. Vera Lacerda Paiva, conversation with DFR, Rio de Janeiro, February 12, 1983. "O livro inacabado," *O Estado de S. Paulo*, May 22, 1977. Carlos Lacerda in *O Estado de S. Paulo*, January 4, 1975.

10. Carlos Lacerda, Carta-circular aos Mesquita, December 29, 1975.

11. Armando Bordallo, interview, July 24, 1983. Alfredo Mesquita, interview, São Paulo, July 24, 1983. Luiz Ernesto Kawall, interview, July 25, 1983. Carlos Alberto Aulicino, interview, July 28, 1983. José Maria Homem de Montes, interview, July 26, 1983.

12. "O livro inacabado," *O Estado de S. Paulo*, May 22, 1977. Carlos Lacerda, interview, Rio de Janeiro, September 23, 1975. Carlos Lacerda and Hélio Silva, letters in *Isto É*, September 1976.

13. Carlos Lacerda, letter in *O Estado de S. Paulo*, May 18, 1976. "Jornal dos Jornais" article of Alberto Dines, in *Folha de S. Paulo*, May 23, 1976.

14. Carlos Lacerda, in *O Estado de S. Paulo*, May 18, 1976, April 17, 1977, and in *Jornal da Tarde*, April 30, 1977. Ênio Matheus Guazzelli in *Diário Popular*, April 15, 1977. "Última briga foi contra estatização do livro," *Jornal do Brasil*, May 22, 1977.

15. Carlos Lacerda in *Jornal da Tarde*, April 23, 1977.

16. Carlos Lacerda in *Jornal da Tarde*, April 16, 1977 (also published in *O Estado de S. Paulo*, April 17, 1977).

17. Ênio Matheus Guazzelli, letter and statement in *Jornal da Tarde*, May 4, April 12, 1977, and statement in *Diário Popular*, April 15, 1977. Carlos

Lacerda in *Jornal da Tarde*, April 16, 30, 1977. Câmara Brasileira do Livro, letter and statement in *Jornal da Tarde*, April 28, March 30, 1977.

18. Carlos Lacerda, letter and article in *Jornal da Tarde*, April 23, March 30, 1977. "Última briga foi contra estatização do livro," *Jornal do Brasil*, May 22, 1977.

19. Carlos Lacerda in *Jornal da Tarde*, April 16, March 30, April 23, 1977. Carlos Lacerda, interview with Olimpia Ciabattari in *Última Hora*, April 2, 1977.

20. Carlos Lacerda in *Jornal da Tarde*, April 23, 1977. Ênio Matheus Guazzelli, letter in *Jornal da Tarde*, May 4, 1977.

21. Guazzelli, letter in *Jornal da Tarde*, May 4, 1977. Carlos Lacerda in *Jornal da Tarde*, May 7, April 30, 1977.

22. Carlos Lacerda, in *Jornal da Tarde*, April 30, March 30, 1977, interview with Olimpia Ciabattari in *Última Hora*, April 2, 1977, and article in *O Estado de S. Paulo*, May 22, 1977.

23. *Jornal da Tarde*, March 31, 1977. Carlos Lacerda, *A Casa do Meu Avô: Pensamentos, Palavras e Obras*.

24. Júlio Tavares (Carlos Lacerda), "Um menino e um velho," *O Estado de S. Paulo*, November 23, 1969. Carlos Lacerda, "O menino e o velho," pp. 269–273 of Carlos Lacerda, *O Cão Negro*. Lamy Cunto, interview with DFR, Rio de Janeiro, January 4, 1988. Sebastião Lacerda, interview, March 5, 1992. Carlos Lacerda in *O Estado de S. Paulo*, October 31, 1976. Carlos Lacerda, *A Casa do Meu Avô*, p. 17. Yedda Braga Miranda, interview with DFR, Rio de Janeiro, January 28, 1983. Regina Costard, interview with DFR, September 9, 1986.

25. Carlos Lacerda, interview in *O Estado de S. Paulo*, October 31, 1976. Sebastião Lacerda, interview with DFR, January 6, 1988. Carlos Lacerda, interview with Regina Penteado, in *Folha de S. Paulo*, April 7, 1977.

26. Pedro Paulo Sena Madureira, interview, São Paulo, March 7, 1991, and interview with DFR, Rio de Janeiro, September 2, 1985. Carlos Vogt, "Uma brincadeira de esconde-esconde com o passado," *Isto É*, May 11, 1977, reprinted on pp. 55–60 of Carlos Vogt, *Crítica Ligeira* (Campinas: Pontes Editores, 1989). Carlos Lacerda, interview with Olimpia Ciabattari, *Última Hora*, April 2, 1977. Maria Lúcia Pinho quoted on back cover of *A Casa do Meu Avô*. Josué Montello, "Uma casa e um menino," *Jornal do Brasil*, December 28, 1976. Paulo Rónai, "Mais que memórias," *O Estado de S. Paulo*, Suplemento Cultural, February 20, 1977. Aires da Mata Machado Filho in *O Estado de S. Paulo*, May 8, 1977. Luiz Carlos Lisboa in *Jornal da Tarde*, April 30, 1977.

27. Maria Helena Vieira da Silva, quoted in Paulo Rónai, "Mais que memórias," *O Estado de S. Paulo*, February 20, 1977. Carlos Lacerda, *A Casa do Meu Avô*, pp. 31–32, 35. Letícia Lacerda, interview with DFR, Rio de Janeiro, February 8, 1983. Cláudio Lacerda, "Quem realmente conheceu este homem?" *Jornal da Tarde*, May 23, 1977.

28. Carlos Lacerda, interview with Regina Penteado, *Folha de S. Paulo*, April 7, 1977.

4. Unsuccessful Businessman

1. Antônio Carlos de Almeida Braga, interview, New York, September 2, 1988.

2. Tibiriçá Botelho Filho, interview, São Paulo, July 31, 1983. Almeida Braga, interview, September 2, 1988. Fernando Cícero da Franca Velloso, interviews, Rio de Janeiro, August 16, 1983, August 15, 1984.

3. Epaminondas Moreira do Valle, interview with DFR, July 26, 1985.

4. Gabriel Lacerda, interview, Rio de Janeiro, August 16, 1983. Maria Thereza Correia de Mello, interviews, Miami Beach, July 5–6, 1986. Almeida Braga, interview, September 2, 1988.

5. Almeida Braga, interview, September 2, 1988. Brochure about EASE (Empresa de Administração, Serviços e Empreendimentos), in the collection of Wilson Lopes Machado. *O Estado de S. Paulo*, July 18, 1970. Tannay de Farias, interview, Rio de Janeiro, February 26, 1991. Marcos Tamoio entry in *Dicionário Histórico-Biográfico Brasileiro, 1930–1983*. Epaminondas Moreira do Valle, interview with DFR, July 26, 1985.

6. Brochure about EASE. Grupo Novo Rio, "Resumo histórico do Grupo Novo Rio (GNR)," typed in 1976 or 1977, in the collection of Fernando Cícero da Franca Velloso. Mario Lorenzo Fernandez, interview, Rio de Janeiro, August 23, 1988, and interview with DFR, Rio de Janeiro, August 9, 1985. Sérgio C. A. Lacerda, Fernando Cícero da Franca Velloso, and João Hermene Guimarães dos Santos, letter to the Banco Central do Brasil (Sérgio Augusto Ribeiro), Rio de Janeiro, January 3, 1977 (in the Fernando Velloso collection), pp. 1–2, 6–7. Herculano Borges da Fonseca, *As Instituições Financeiras do Brasil* (Rio de Janeiro: Crown, Editôres Internacionais, n.d.), p. 372. Almeida Braga, interview, September 2, 1988.

7. Brochure about EASE. Wilson Lopes Machado, "Algumas Lembranças de um Amigo," Curitiba, October 1988, p. 11, and interview, Rio de Janeiro, February 23, 1991. Carlos Lacerda, undated letter to Wilson Machado about Nova Miller, and clipping from *Folha de S. Paulo*, December 12, 1975, in the Wilson Lopes Machado collection.

8. Brochure about EASE. Sérgio Lacerda, interview, Rio de Janeiro, August 17, 1988. Fernando Velloso, interview, August 15, 1984. José Luiz Moreira de Souza, interview, Rio de Janeiro, August 15, 1983.

9. *O Estado de S. Paulo*, July 18, 1970. Brochure about EASE. José Alberto Gueiros and João Condé, interview with DFR, Rio de Janeiro, March 23, 1983. Armando Daudt d'Oliveira, interviews, Rio de Janeiro, August 10, 14, 1983. Regina Costard, interview with DFR, Rio de Janeiro, September 9, 1986. João Condé, interview, Rio de Janeiro, August 11, 1983. Maria Thereza Correia de Mello, interviews, July 5–6, 1986. Sérgio Lacerda, letter to Olga Lacerda, Rio de Janeiro, November 12, 1973 (in LFC). Fernando Tasso Fragoso Pires, *Antigas Fazendas de Café da Província Fluminense* (Rio de Janeiro: Editora Nova Fronteira, 1980), p. 63.

10. Sérgio Lacerda, interview, August 17, 1988. Letícia Abruzzini Lacerda, Sérgio C. A. Lacerda, Sebastião Lacerda, and Maria Cristina L. Simões Lopes,

Dois Processos—Uma Causa: O caso da DATAMEC e das empresas NOVO RIO (Rio de Janeiro: n.p., July 1983), pp. 9–10.

11. Sérgio Lacerda, Fernando Velloso, and João Hermene Guimarães dos Santos, letter to the Banco Central do Brasil, January 3, 1977, pp. 2–6. Grupo Novo Rio, "Resumo Histórico do Grupo Novo Rio (GNR)," p. 3.

12. Grupo Novo Rio, "Resumo histórico do Grupo Novo Rio (GNR)," p. 3. Sérgio Lacerda, Fernando Velloso, and Guimarães dos Santos, letter to the Banco Central do Brasil, January 3, 1977, pp. 7, 10. Letícia, Sérgio, and Sebastião Lacerda, and Maria Cristina L. Simões Lopes, *Dois Processos—Uma Causa*, pp. 10, 14–15. "Datamec volta para a família Lacerda," *Jornal do Brasil*, December 16, 1986.

13. Tibiriçá Botelho Filho, interview, July 31, 1983. Vera Lacerda Paiva, interview, Rio de Janeiro, July 22, 1984. Novo Rio—Crédito, Financiamento e Investimentos S. A., "Ata da Assembléia Geral Extraordinária realizada em 04 de novembro de 1975," in the Fernando Velloso collection. Sérgio Lacerda, interview, August 17, 1988. "Lacerda/70 anos," *Jornal do Brasil*, April 30, 1984. Fernando Velloso, interviews, August 16, 1983, August 15, 1984. Tannay de Farias, interview, Rio de Janeiro, February 26, 1991. Antonio Dias Rebello Filho, interview with DFR, Rio de Janeiro, March 26, 1983. Tannay de Farias, memorandum to Sebastião Lacerda, February 9, 1977 (in the Tannay de Farias papers). Pedro Paulo Sena Madureira, interview, São Paulo, March 7, 1991.

14. Fernando Velloso, interview, August 16, 1983. Carlos Lacerda, letter to Maria Thereza Correia de Mello, Madrid, November 29, 1976, in the collection of Maria Thereza Correia de Mello.

15. Grupo Novo Rio, "Resumo Histórico do Grupo Novo Rio (GNR)," p. 3. Letícia, Sérgio, and Sebastião Lacerda, and Maria Cristina L. Simões Lopes, *Dois Processos—Uma Causa*, p. 10. Sérgio Lacerda, Fernando Velloso, and Guimarães dos Santos, letter to the Banco Central do Brasil, January 3, 1977, pp. 10–13.

16. "Datamec volta para a família Lacerda," *Jornal do Brasil*, December 16, 1986. Letícia, Sérgio, and Sebastião Lacerda, and Maria Cristina L. Simões Lopes, *Dois Processos—Uma Causa*, p. 15.

17. Tannay de Farias, interview, February 26, 1991, and letter to Carlos Lacerda, Rio de Janeiro, March 17, 1977, including notations by Carlos Lacerda (in the Tannay de Farias papers).

5. Personal Relations (1973-1977)

1. Vera Lacerda Paiva and Lygia Paiva Derizans, interview, Rio de Janeiro, August 25, 1985.

2. Maria Cristina Lacerda Simões Lopes, Debate Sem Censura television interview, Rio de Janeiro, May 1988, p. 5 of transcript by DFR. Maria Cristina Simões Lopes, interview, Rio de Janeiro, March 5, 1991.

3. Carlos Lacerda, letter to Letícia Lacerda, Zurich, June 12, 1974. Carlos

Lacerda, letter to Maria Cristina Lacerda, Rio de Janeiro, October 1, 1973. (Both in LFC.)

4. Maria Cristina Lacerda Simões Lopes, interview with DFR, Rio de Janeiro, August 26, 1986. Sérgio Lacerda, interview, Rio de Janeiro, July 31, 1989.

5. Carlos Lacerda, "Morte Vizinha" (dedicated to João Condé), *Jornal do Brasil*, May 20, 1978.

6. Letícia Lacerda, interview with DFR, Rio de Janeiro, January 5, 1988. Carlos Lacerda, *Depoimento*, p. 94. Carlos Alberto Aulicino, interview, São Paulo, July 28, 1983. Maria Cristina Lacerda Simões Lopes, interview, Rio de Janeiro, August 8, 1983. Regina Costard, interview with DFR, Rio de Janeiro, September 9, 1986.

7. Adolpho Bloch, "Juscelino Kubitschek, Amigo Inesquecível," *Manchete* no. 1897 (August 27, 1988), pp. 20–21; see p. 21, column 2.

8. Maria Abreu Sodré, interview, São Paulo, July 21, 1983. Vera Lacerda Paiva, interview with DFR, Rio de Janeiro, February 13, 1983. Maria Cristina Lacerda Simões Lopes and Luiz Eduardo Simões Lopes, interview, Petrópolis, August 13, 1983.

9. Vera Lacerda Paiva, interview with DFR, Rio de Janeiro, February 13, 1983. Antonio Dias Rebello Filho, interview with DFR, Rio de Janeiro, March 26, 1983.

10. Carlos Lacerda, letter to JWFD, Rio de Janeiro, September 16, 1976. Sebastião Lacerda, interview with DFR, Rio de Janeiro, January 6, 1988. Regina Costard, interview with DFR, September 9, 1986. Alfredo C. Machado, interview, Rio de Janeiro, August 8, 1989. Antonio Carlos Villaça, interview with DFR, August 17, 1985, and p. 10 of transcript, interview taped by the Sociedade dos Amigos de Carlos Lacerda. Maria Fernanda Correia Dias, conversation with DFR, Rio de Janeiro, July 26, 1983. Virgil Lawlis, conversations with JWFD, Austin, November 1993.

11. Sandra Cavalcanti, interview, Rio de Janeiro, August 10, 1983. Tannay de Farias, interview, Rio de Janeiro, February 26, 1991. Pedro Paulo Sena Madureira, interview, São Paulo, March 7, 1991. João Condé, interview with DFR, Rio de Janeiro, March 23, 1983.

12. Tannay de Farias, interview, February 26, 1991. Maria Cristina Lacerda Simões Lopes, interview with DFR, Rio de Janeiro, January 4, 1988. Regina Costard said (interview with DFR, September 9, 1986) that "the great passion of Carlos was Cristina."

13. Alfredo C. Machado, interview, Rio de Janeiro, July 7, 1983. Afonso Arinos de Melo Franco, interview, Rio de Janeiro, July 29, 1984. Luís Forjaz Trigueiros, interview with DFR, Lisbon, June 21, 1984. Roberto Campos, "Memórias" (typewritten), p. 26 of chapter about Carlos Lacerda. Joel Silveira, interview, Rio de Janeiro, August 26, 1983, and "Carlos Lacerda, amigo bissexto," *O Liberal*, Belém, August 18, 1977. *Jornal do Brasil*, May 22, 1977, including Carlos Castello Branco column.

14. Joaquim Ponce Leal, interview, Rio de Janeiro, March 16, 1991. Regina Costard, interview with DFR, September 9, 1986. Also other interviews.

15. Vera Lacerda Paiva and Lygia Paiva Derizans, interview with DFR, Rio de Janeiro, January 6, 1988. Ruth Alverga, interview with DFR, Rio de Janeiro, July 29, 1985. Fernando Cícero da Franca Velloso, interview, Rio de Janeiro, August 15, 1984. Tannay de Farias, interview, February 26, 1991.

16. Luiz Roberto Veiga de Brito, interview with DFR, Rio de Janeiro, August 8, 1985, and p. 33 of transcript of interview taped by the Sociedade dos Amigos de Carlos Lacerda.

17. Maria Abreu Sodré, interview, São Paulo, July 21, 1983.

18. Regina Costard, interview with DFR, September 9, 1986.

19. Maria Fernanda Correia Dias, conversation with DFR, Rio de Janeiro, August 1985. Pedro Paulo Sena Madureira, interview, March 7, 1991, and interview with DFR, Rio de Janeiro, September 2, 1985. Luís Forjaz Trigueiros in *Fatos & Fotos*, no. 1012 (June 6, 1977); see p. 27.

20. Ruy Mesquita, Preface to Carlos Lacerda, *Depoimento*, pp. 11–18; see also frontispiece. Hélio Fernandes in *O Estado de S. Paulo*, June 24, August 6, 1977. Honório de Sylos and Juracy Magalhães in *O Estado de S. Paulo*, July 12, 20, 1977. Carlos Lacerda, *Depoimento*, pp. 403, 189, 99, 402, 408.

21. *Jornal da Tarde*, March 30, 31, 1977. Regina Penteado, "Lacerda: O Brasil já foi mais civilizado," *Folha de S. Paulo*, April 7, 1977.

22. *O Estado de S. Paulo*, May 22, 1977. Luiz Ernesto Kawall, interview, São Paulo, August 5, 1983. Carlos Alberto Aulicino, interview, July 28, 1983. Alfredo Mesquita, interview, São Paulo, July 24, 1983.

23. Luiz Ernesto Kawall, "O último encontro." Luiz Ernesto Kawall, "Diálogo com JQ em A Galeria" (typewritten), August 24, 1977 (in collection of Kawall).

24. Joel Silveira, interview, Rio de Janeiro, August 26, 1983. Alfredo C. Machado, interview, August 8, 1989. Maria Cristina Lacerda Simões Lopes, interview with DFR, Rio de Janeiro, January 4, 1988.

25. Leo Gilson Ribeiro, interview, São Paulo, March 8, 1991. Carlos Lacerda, interview with Leo Gilson Ribeiro, *Status*, no. 35 (June 1977), pp. 53–66; see pp. 64, 66, 59. Luiz Ernesto Kawall, "O último encontro."

6. What Killed Lacerda (May 1977)

1. João Condé, interview with DFR, Rio de Janeiro, March 23, 1983. *Jornal da Tarde*, May 23, 1977, including Cláudio Lacerda, "Quem realmente conheceu este homem?" Luís Forjaz Trigueiros in *Fatos & Fotos*, June 6, 1977, p. 27. Vera Lacerda Paiva, interviews with DFR, Rio de Janeiro, February 7, 1983, and December 29, 1987.

2. João Condé, interview with DFR, March 23, 1983. Tannay de Farias, interview, Rio de Janeiro, August 12, 1983, and cited in *Jornal da Tarde*, May 23, 1977. Pedro Paulo Sena Madureira, interview with DFR, Rio de Janeiro, September 2, 1985.

3. Emil Farhat, interview, São Paulo, August 2, 1983. Regina Costard, interview with DFR, September 9, 1986.

4. Antonio Dias Rebello Filho, *Carlos Lacerda, Meu Amigo*, pp. 257–258. *Jornal da Tarde*, May 23, 1977.

5. Ibid. Pedro Paulo Sena Madureira, interviews with DFR, Rio de Janeiro, August 27, September 2, 1985. Pedro Henrique de Paiva, interview with DFR, Rio de Janeiro, August 28, 1985. Roberto Edward Halbouti, interview, Rio de Janeiro, August 10, 1989. Rebello Filho, *Carlos Lacerda, Meu Amigo*, pp. 256, 257, 258–259.

6. Rebello Filho, *Carlos Lacerda, Meu Amigo*, p. 259. *Jornal da Tarde*, May 23, 1977. Pedro Paulo Sena Madureira, interview with DFR, September 2, 1985. Maria Cristina Lacerda Simões Lopes, interview, Rio de Janeiro, August 8, 1983.

7. Hugo Levy, interview with DFR, March 7, 1989. Sérgio Lacerda, interview, Rio de Janeiro, July 31, 1989. Vera and Odilon Lacerda Paiva, interview with DFR, Rio de Janeiro, February 7, 1983.

8. Maria Cristina Lacerda Simões Lopes, interview with DFR, January 4, 1988. Pedro Paulo Sena Madureira, interview with DFR, September 2, 1985.

9. Artis Quadros DaSilva, letter to JWFD, Brackenridge Hospital, Austin, July 29, 1987.

10. Virgil Lawlis, conversations with JWFD, Austin, late 1993, January 1994.

11. Rebello Filho, *Carlos Lacerda, Meu Amigo*, p. 259. Luís Forjaz Trigueiros and Maria Helena Trigueiros, interview with DFR, Lisbon, June 21, 27, 1984. Lamy Cunto and Letícia Lacerda, interview with DFR, Rio de Janeiro, January 5, 1988.

12. Vera Lacerda Paiva, interview with DFR, February 7, 1983. *Jornal da Tarde*, May 23, 1977. Lamy Cunto, interviews with DFR, Rio de Janeiro, January 4, 5, 1988. Regina Costard, interview with DFR, September 9, 1986.

13. Vera Lacerda Paiva and Lygia Paiva Derizans, interview with DFR, Rio de Janeiro, January 6, 1988. Maria Cristina Lacerda Simões Lopes, interview with DFR, January 4, 1988.

14. Rebello Filho, *Carlos Lacerda, Meu Amigo*, pp. 259–260. *Jornal da Tarde*, May 23, 1977. Pedro Henrique de Paiva, interview with DFR, August 28, 1985, and quoted in *O Estado de S. Paulo*, May 22, 1977.

15. *Jornal da Tarde*, May 23, 1977.

7. Post-Mortem

1. *O Estado de S. Paulo*, May 22, 1977.

2. *Jornal do Brasil*, May 22, 1977. *Jornal da Tarde*, May 24, 25, 26, 1977. Cláudio Lacerda in *Jornal do Brasil*, May 24, 1977. *O Estado de S. Paulo*, May 24, 28, 1977.

3. Antonio Carlos Villaça, interview with DFR, Rio de Janeiro, August 31, 1985. *Jornal do Brasil*, May 22, 24, 1977. *O Estado de S. Paulo*, May 22, 1977.

4. Sebastião Lacerda, interview, Rio de Janeiro, May 5, 1992. *Jornal do Brasil* and *O Estado de S. Paulo*, May 22, 1977.

5. Teotônio Vilela, speech, reported in *Diário do Congresso Nacional*, June 9, 1977, section 2, pp. 2609–2613; see p. 2609.

6. *Diário da Noite*, May 23, 1977. Roberto Marinho, "Carlos Lacerda," *O Globo*, May 22, 1977. *Jornal do Brasil*, editorial, May 22, 1977. Alberto Dines, "Jornal dos Jornais," *Folha de S. Paulo*, May 22, 1977. *O Estado de S. Paulo*, May 28, 1977.

8. Conclusion

1. Danton Jobim, Senate speech of June 8, 1977, reported in *Diário do Congresso Nacional*, June 9, 1977, section 2, pp. 2606–2608; see p. 2607. Célio Borja, speech of June 29, 1977, in the Chamber of Deputies, reported in *Diário do Congresso Nacional*, June 30, 1977, section 1, pp. 5670–5672; see p. 5671.

2. IBOPE-Opinião, Pesquisa de Opinião Pública, Rio de Janeiro: Para quem se lembra ou ouviu falar de Carlos Lacerda; e o(a) sr(a) tem simpatia ou antipatia por Carlos Lacerda? (Pesquisa que o Amaral Netto encomendou durante sua campanha, 1992, copy sent to JWFD by Wilson L. Machado, Rio de Janeiro, May 3, 1993.)

3. IBOPE poll taken among two thousand Brazilians nationwide, October 29–November 3, 1993, reported in *Brazil Watch*, November 8–22, 1993.

4. David Nasser, "Elogio ao Adversário," *O Cruzeiro*, September 17, 1960. Laerte Vieira, speech of June 29, 1977, reported in *Diário do Congresso Nacional*, June 30, 1977, section 1, pp. 5672–5674; see p. 5673. David Nasser in *O Cruzeiro*, October 30, 1965, p. 5.

5. Chagas Freitas entry in *Dicionário Histórico-Biográfico Brasileiro, 1930–1983*.

6. Afonso Arinos de Melo Franco, *A Escalada: Memórias* (Rio de Janeiro: Livraria José Olympio Editôra, 1965), pp. 366–367. Hugo Levy, interview with DFR, Rio de Janeiro, March 7, 1989. Nelson Pereira, interview, São Paulo, August 4, 1983.

7. José Honório Rodrigues, introduction to Carlos Lacerda, *Discursos Parlamentares* (Rio de Janeiro: Editora Nova Fronteira, 1982), p. 28.

8. Flávio Galvão, "A Frente em São Paulo," *O Estado de S. Paulo*, March 22, 1967.

9. Fernando Pedreira, quoted in "Um Terremoto," *Jornal do Brasil*, April 30, 1984.

Index